A Concise Dictionary of Minnesota Ojibwe

The University of Minnesota Press
gratefully acknowledges
the generous assistance provided
for publication of this book
by
the Mille Lacs Band of Ojibwe Indians
and
Grand Casino, Inc.

A Concise Dictionary of Minnesota Ojibwe

John D. Nichols and Earl Nyholm

Illustrations by Earl Nyholm

University of Minnesota Press
Minneapolis
London

Copyright 1995 by the Regents of the University of Minnesota

All rights reserved. No part of this publication may be reproduced, stored in a retrieval system, or transmitted, in any form or by any means, electronic, mechanical, photocopying, recording, or otherwise, without the prior written permission of the publisher.

Published by the University of Minnesota Press
111 Third Avenue South, Suite 290, Minneapolis, MN 55401-2520
http://www.upress.umn.edu
Printed in the United States of America on acid-free paper

Thirteenth printing, 2022

Library of Congress Cataloging-in-Publication Data

Nichols, John (John D.)
A concise dictionary of Minnesota Ojibwe / John D. Nichols and Earl Nyholm.
p. cm.
Includes index.
Rev., expanded ed. of: Ojibwewi-Ikidowinan. 1979.
ISBN 978-0-8166-2427-0 (acid-free paper).—ISBN 978-0-8166-2428-7 (pbk. : acid-free paper)
1. Ojibwa language—Dictionaries—English. 2. English language—Dictionaries—Ojibwa. I. Nyholm, Earl. II. Ojibwewi-Ikidowinan. III. Title.
PM853.N53 1995
497'.3—dc20 94-35219

The University of Minnesota is an
equal-opportunity educator and employer.

Contents

Preface vii

Key to Entries ix

Sounds and Orthography xxiii

Part I
Ojibwe-English 3

Part II
English-Ojibwe Index 133

Preface

This dictionary of Anishinaabemowin, the Ojibwe or Chippewa language, can be used by all interested in the linguistic and cultural heritage of the Anishinaabe. It is intended primarily for students of Ojibwe as a second language, and for speakers wishing models for spelling in a standardized orthography. Although, with just over seven thousand words, it contains but a small part of the language's total vocabulary, the words included have been selected to be representative of the everyday language of conversation and of narration. To these have been added a rich sample of traditional cultural vocabulary.

Anishinaabemowin is not spoken in a single standard form but varies from place to place in sounds, vocabulary, and grammar. The words in this dictionary represent the speech of several individuals belonging to the Mille Lacs Band of Ojibwe at Mille Lacs Lake, near Onamia, Minnesota. Other forms of the same words used there and elsewhere are equally valid. Teachers will want to supplement the words listed here with those prevalent in their home communities.

This book is an expansion and complete revision of *Ojibwewi-Ikidowinan: An Ojibwe Word Resource Book* published in 1979. We have long felt the need to revise that book and wish to thank Kent Smith, Director of Indian Studies at Bemidji State University, for his encouragement and support for the necessary editorial meetings. The Social Sciences and Humanities Research Council of Canada supported the data collection and analysis by John Nichols that underlies this book. The Mille Lacs Band of Ojibwe provided technical support for database processing and manuscript preparation. Richard Rhodes's superb *Eastern Ojibwa-Chippewa-Ottawa Dictionary* (1985), covering several of the more easterly dialects of Anishinaabemowin, introduced a number of new conventions for Ojibwe dictionaries, some of which we have adopted here.

The words are drawn largely from the stories and conversations of Maude Kegg (b. 1904) and the late Jim Littlewolf (b. 1895), among others. Many words were originally supplied by the late Selam Ross of Cass Lake for the first student word list prepared at Bemidji State University, or by Earl Nyholm. Others at Mille Lacs have supplied words or helped to determine meanings, among them Mildred Benjamin, James Clark, Jessie Clark, Lucy Clark, Loretta Kalk, Betty Kegg, Darrell Kegg, Donald Kegg, Ernest Kegg, Herman Kegg, Jesse Kegg, Matt Kegg, Batiste Sam, Frances Sam, and Frank Sam. The language lessons of Rose Barstow, Angeline Northbird, and Timothy Dunnigan (1977–80) of the University of Minnesota, Mildred Benjamin (1991) of Neyashing School at Mille Lacs, and Richard Gresczyk and James Clark (1992) of Minneapolis suggested many new words to include. The total database from which the words were selected has over 25,000 words. This will serve as the basis for a future reference dictionary. Nearly all of the words have been rechecked with Maude Kegg, to whom we owe the greatest debt.

John D. Nichols
Department of Native Studies/
Department of Linguistics
University of Manitoba
Winnipeg, Manitoba

Earl Nyholm
Department of Modern
Languages
Bemidji State University
Bemidji, Minnesota

Key to Entries

General Form of Entries

Each entry in the Ojibwe-English section begins with a **head word**, printed in boldface, and is sequenced according to the position of this head word in the Ojibwe alphabetical order:

a, aa, b, c, d, e, g, h, ', i, ii, j, k, m, n, o, oo, p, s, t, w, y, z

The head word is often only one of many inflected word forms sharing a common **word stem**. The word stem carries the basic meaning of a word. Inflections are prefixes, suffixes, or sound changes, applied to the core word stem, which express grammatical ideas such as 'plural' or 'first person'. The actual number of inflected word forms that share a stem can be large; for example, the stem *ganawaabam-* ('looks at someone') can occur in well over a thousand inflected forms, of which the following are only a few examples:

inganawaabamaa 'I look at someone'
giganawaabamaasiwaanaanig 'we don't look at them'
oganawaabamaawaan 'they look at someone'
inganawaabamigonaadog 'someone must be looking at us'
ganawaabamagiban 'had I looked at someone'
genawaabamajig 'the ones you look at'

The addition of prefixes called **preverbs** to indicate secondary ideas such as time and direction creates thousands more possible word forms for each word stem. A few examples related to the first of the examples above are as follows:

ingii-kanawaabamaa 'I looked at someone'
ingii-pi-ganawaabamaa 'I came here to look at someone'
inga-ganawaabamaa 'I will look at someone'
niwii-kanawaabamaa 'I want to look at someone'
inga-gagwe-ganawaabamaa 'I will try to look at someone'

Since the number of actual forms of a given word stem is too large for all of them to be in a dictionary, a single word form is selected as the head word to stand in for all of the inflected forms sharing the stem.

The head word is followed by a **class code**, printed in italics, identifying the kind of word the head word is, and a **gloss**, suggesting possible translations of the head word. The following illustrates a complete entry for a simple word:

HEAD WORD CLASS CODE GLOSS

biindig *pc* indoors, inside

Other kinds of information may be given in an entry. The following sample entry contains additional **forms** of the head word and a **reference** to an alternate form of the head word or to a similar word in another local variety of the language. These are printed in boldface. The **labels** that identify the forms and introduce a reference word are printed in italics, as are any other notes on the structure or use of the word:

HEAD WORD CLASS CODE GLOSS PLURAL FORM

babiigomakakii *na* toad; *pl* **babiigomakakiig**;

dim **babiigomakakiins**; *also* **obiigomakakii**

DIMINUTIVE FORM REFERENCE

Head words or reference words followed by an asterisk identify word forms not used at Mille Lacs by the contributors, but which are known to be used by others or in adjacent varieties of the language. For example, the equivalent of 'those' (when referring to animates) in Mille Lacs Ojibwe is *ingiw*, but two forms of the same word used in other varieties of Ojibwe are also given and marked with the asterisk as *igiw** and *agiw**.

Some entries present the **word stem** after the head word when the form of the stem cannot be determined by inspection of the head word. It appears in boldface and between slashes as a warning that it is not necessarily a complete word by itself without inflections:

HEAD WORD WORD STEM CLASS CODE GLOSS

bakite' /bakite'w-/ *vta* hit s.o., strike s.o.;

1sg **imbakite'waa**; *prt* **bekite'waad**

INDEPENDENT FORM PARTICIPLE FORM

In the English-Ojibwe Index, the words are grouped under English **keys**, sequenced in English alphabetical order. The keys are important words or phrases occurring in the gloss of one or more Anishinaabemowin words in the dictionary. The keys are printed in capitals flush to the left margin. Under each key appear one or more **secondary keys**, printed in small capitals and indented from the left margin. These are English words or phrases incorporating the key, but usually giving additional words to narrow down the range of meaning of the target word. Anishinaabemowin words whose gloss incorporates the meaning of the secondary key follow one by one, with a **gloss** for each (unless it is the same as an immediately preceding secondary key or the gloss for the previous word), a **word stem** or **plural ending** for some entries, then the **head word** in boldface, and a **class code** in italics:

KEY SECONDARY KEY

TEN

TEN: **midaaswi** *nm;* **midaaso-** *pv4;* they are ten **midaachinoon /midaachin-/** *vii*; **midaachiwag /midaachi-/** *vai;* ten (card) **midaasoobii'igan, -ag** *na*

TEN DAYS: **midaasogon** *pc;* be ten days **midaasogonagad** *vii*

TEN DOLLARS: **midaaswaabik** *pc*

PLURAL ENDING

Entries for the Different Word Classes

The major classes of words in Anishinaabemowin are verbs, nouns, pronouns, and particles. The verbs and nouns occur in a number of subclasses, each coded differently and using a particular set of inflections. Several kinds of pronouns exist, some with inflected forms. Particles are uninflected words and can be divided into many sub-classes depending on their structure and the way they are used in sentences. Major word-building prefixes called **preverbs** are given separate entries although the head of each entry is not a separate word by itself. The major forms of the inflec-

Table 1. Class Codes

Code	Word class	Description
na	animate noun	noun of the animate gender that is not obligatorily possessed
nad	dependent animate noun	noun of the animate gender that is obligatorily possessed
na-pt	animate participle	participle form of a verb functioning as a noun of the animate gender
ni	inanimate noun	noun of the inanimate gender that is not obligatorily possessed
nid	dependent inanimate noun	noun of the inanimate gender that is obligatorily possessed
ni-pt	inanimate participle	participle form of a verb functioning as a noun of the inanimate gender
nm	number	uninflectable number particle
pc	particle	uninflectable particle (adverb, conjunction, exclamation, etc.)
pf	prefix	personal prefix appearing on nouns and verbs
pn	prenoun	lexical prefix forming a particle from a noun stem
pr	pronoun	pronoun (demonstrative, dubitative, indefinite, interrogative, pausal, or personal)
pv1	preverb of class 1	tense, aspect, mood, or syntactic prefix appearing on verbs
pv2	preverb of class 2	directional prefix occurring on verbs
pv3	preverb of class 3	relative prefix occurring on verbs (and on some nouns and particles)
pv4	preverb of class 4	lexical prefix occurring on verbs, nouns, or particles
vai	animate intransitive verb	verb with an intransitive stem, an animate subject, and no object
vai2	class 2 animate intransitive verb	verb with a transitive stem (as for an inanimate object), an animate subject, and no object; inflected as intransitive
vai + o	animate intransitive verb with object	verb with an intransitive stem, an animate subject, and an object
vii	inanimate intransitive verb	verb with an intransitive stem, an inanimate subject, and no object
vta	transitive animate verb	verb with a transitive stem and an animate object

Table 1. Class Codes (cont.)

Code	Word class	Description
vti	transitive inanimate verb	verb with a transitive stem, and an inanimate object, and a characteristic set of inflections
vti2	class 2 transitive inanimate verb	verb with an inanimate object but with a different characteristic set of inflections
vti3	class 3 transitive inanimate verb	verb with an inanimate object but with a different characteristic set of inflections

tional personal prefixes are also given entries of their own. The class codes for words are interpreted in Table 1.

Entries for Nouns. The typical noun entry has the singular form of the noun as the head word. The class codes identify the **gender** of the noun: *na* for animate nouns and *ni* for **inanimate** nouns. Nouns in the animate gender include a number of non-living things (e.g., mitts, nets, and playing cards) as well as words identifying humans, animals, trees, and spirits. Other words referring to nouns agree with them in gender.

The full **plural** form of a noun, labelled *pl*, is given in noun entries in the Ojibwe-English section of the dictionary. A plural noun form contains the noun stem and a plural suffix, and reveals the gender: plurals ending in *g* are animate and those ending in *n* are inanimate. Although the stem of a noun is abstract and not necessarily identical to the singular form, it is convenient to view the plural form of most nouns as consisting of the singular form to which a plural ending is added. In the English-Ojibwe Index, the singular form of the noun is followed by this plural ending, cited with an initial hyphen.

In the Ojibwe-English section, certain other important inflected forms are provided to help students, although they are usually predictable from a comparison of the singular and plural forms, or from the abstract stem. The **locative** form, labelled *loc*, is an adverbial form of a noun stem indicating location 'in, at, to, from, etc.' or comparison. The locative forms of nouns naming living things and abstractions are omitted here; although possible, they are relatively uncommon. All the locative forms end in *-ng*. The **diminutive** form, labelled *dim*, indicates relative small size: 'a small one (small for the kind of thing named), a baby one'. The diminutive forms are omitted for nouns naming abstractions and for others where a diminutive seems to be uncommon. All of the productive diminutives cited end in a long nasalized vowel followed by *s*, indicated in the orthography with the long vowel followed by *ns*.

The following is a typical entry for a noun:

HEAD WORD CLASS CODE GLOSS PLURAL FORM

mookomaan *ni* knife; *pl* **mookomaanan**;

loc **mookomaaning**; *dim* **mookomaanens**

LOCATIVE FORM DIMINUTIVE FORM

The head word of a typical entry for a **dependent** noun, an obligatorily possessed noun always having a personal prefix before its stem, is a singular form with a first-person possessor shown by the personal prefix. The class codes also indicate gender: *nad* for animate dependent nouns and *nid* for inanimate dependent nouns. The underlying stem, to which other personal prefixes may be attached, is given between slashes and with preceding and trailing hyphens:

HEAD WORD WORD STEM CLASS CODE GLOSS

nininj /-ninjy-/ *nid* my hand, my finger;

pl **nininjiin**; *loc* **nininjiing**; *dim* **nininjiins**

PLURAL FORM LOCATIVE FORM DIMINUTIVE FORM

The stem of a noun is given for dependent nouns and for those nouns commonly occurring only in the plural form, which is then used as the head word of the entry. The stem in such entries is given with a trailing hyphen and between slashes, following the head word. The stem of other nouns may be determined from the singular form and the plural form.

Entries for Verbs. The form of the inflected word selected as the head word in entries for verbs varies according to the class of the verb. The classes are distinguished on the basis of the stem class, reflecting transitivity and gender, and the paradigm class of inflections used. Because of grammatical differences between Anishinaabemowin and English, it is convenient to use certain **gloss codes** in the glosses for special types of verb objects. Table 2 gives definitions of such codes.

Several additional inflected forms are supplied. Entries for the verbs most likely to have a first-person subject are supplied with an **independent**

Table 2. Gloss codes

Code	Expansion	Description
s.o.	someone	the object is animate, either human or non-human
s.t.	something	the object is inanimate
(s.t.)	(something)	optional second object of either gender

form (also called form A) word inflected for a first-person subject. Forms using the independent or A order (paradigm) of inflections occur primarily in main clauses. All verb entries also give a **participle** form inflected for a third-person subject. A participle is a nominalized verb form similar to the **conjunct** form (also called form B) of verbs appearing primarily in subordinate clauses. Both share the conjunct or B order (paradigm) of inflections to which participles may add noun-like plural or other inflections. The participles occur in a variety of grammatical constructions including relative clauses and who and what questions. The participle forms characteristically show the ablaut process called **initial change,** which alters the first syllable of the stem by a change in sounds, the insertion of a syllable, or the addition of a prefix. Initial change may also appear on certain other conjunct verb forms. The most common expressions of this process of initial change are presented in Table 3.

Entries for Animate Intransitive Verbs (*vai* and *vai2*). These are verbs that typically take an animate subject and make no inflectional reference to an object. The head word for an animate intransitive verb is a third-person singular subject form in the independent or A (main clause) order of inflections, meaning 'he, she, or it (something animate) is X, does X, is doing X'. If the stem differs from the head word, it is given between slashes and with a trailing hyphen. The class code and a gloss follow. The glosses are given as English infinitives but without the 'to'. The independent form, labelled *1sg*, is given for the verbs most likely to have a first-person singular subject. It means 'I am X, do X, am doing X'. The participle, labelled *prt*,

Table 3. Initial change

Initial change is a process that affects the first syllable of a preverb or verb stem in a conjunct verb or participle. In the regular process of initial change the first vowel of the preverb or stem is replaced as follows:

Unchanged	Changed
a	e
aa	ayaa
e	aye
i	e
ii	aa
o	we
oo	waa

Certain stems beginning in *dan*, *dazh*, *das*, *dash*, or *daa* do not undergo regular initial change but rather prefix *en*. The main other irregular form is the change of the direction prefix *bi-* 'here, hither' to *ba-*.

has a third-person singular subject and means 'one who is X, does X, is doing X'. The following is a typical entry for such a verb:

HEAD WORD CLASS CODE GLOSS

anokii *vai* work; *1sg* **indanokii**; *prt* **enokiid**

INDEPENDENT FORM PARTICIPLE FORM

For verbs most commonly used in a plural form, the head word is a third-person plural independent form and the gloss may include a plural pronoun. Many of these are **reciprocal** verbs, the reciprocal or mutual action of which is typically expressed by translations such as 'they see each other', and 'we run out together'. Other inflected forms in these entries are also plural: the independent form labelled *1pl* means 'we are X, do X, are doing X', and the participle means 'the ones who are X, do X, are doing X'. The word stem, stripped of all inflections, is presented with a trailing hyphen and between slashes following the plural head word. The following is a typical entry for such a verb:

HEAD WORD WORD STEM CLASS CODE GLOSS

ojiindiwag /ojiindi-/ *vai* they kiss each other;

1pl **indoojiindimin**; *prt* **wejiindijig**

INDEPENDENT FORM PARTICIPLE FORM

For some verbs commonly used in an impersonal form, the head word is such a form with the ending *-m*. The stem follows.

Entries for Animate Intransitive Verbs with Objects (*vai + o*). Although the animate intransitive (*vai*) verbs typically occur without objects, many of them may take objects and some often do. The later are labelled *vai + o* here. Their independent inflections may then be somewhat different from those used when no object is present. The gloss in the entry for one of these verbs includes the code (s.t.) to indicate an object may be present. The form of the entry follows that of the animate intransitive verbs, but two first-person singular subject independent forms are given, the first used without an object and the second with an inanimate object and meaning 'I do X to it, I am doing X to it'.

HEAD WORD CLASS CODE GLOSS INDEPENDENT FORMS

adaawe *vai + o* sell, sell (s.t.); *1sg* **indadaawe, indadaawen**;

prt **edaawed**

PARTICIPLE FORM

Entries for Inanimate Intransitive Verbs (*vii*). These verbs take an inanimate or impersonal subject, but no object. The head word is a singular subject independent order verb form, generally the same as the stem. The gloss, following the class code, omits the English subject pronoun 'it' when the subject is singular. Since the subject of such a verb is always inanimate and thus third person, there are no first-person forms. The singular participle form follows the gloss. Inanimate intransitive stems, especially those ending in a long vowel, may occur with an augment *-magad* with no apparent change in meaning. For the long vowel-final stems, the augmented singular subject independent form is given after the label *aug*, followed by the participle of the augment, labelled as *prt aug:*

HEAD WORD CLASS CODE GLOSS PARTICIPLE FORM

michaa *vii* be big; *prt* **mechaag**; *aug* **michaamagad**; *prt aug* **mechaamagak**

AUGMENTED FORM PARTICIPLE OF AUGMENTED FORM

Where the verb is most commonly used in the plural, the head word is given in the plural subject independent order form with the stem following. The other forms are also given with plural subjects:

HEAD WORD WORD STEM CLASS CODE GLOSS PARTICIPLE FORM

niizhinoon /niizhin-/ *vii* they are two; *prt* **naazhingin**

The stem is also given for verbs of this class that have a stem ending in a short vowel, but that generally add an augment *n* in the head word form:

HEAD WORD WORD STEM CLASS CODE GLOSS PARTICIPLE FORM

dagwaagin /dagwaagi-/ *vii* be fall, be autumn; *prt* **degwaagig**

Entries for Transitive Inanimate Verbs (*vti, vti2, vti3*). These verbs typically take an animate subject and an inanimate object. The head word is a second-person singular subject on inanimate singular object form in the **imperative** (command) order of inflections: '(you) do X to it!' The class code and gloss follow. The position of the inanimate object is shown in the gloss by the gloss code s.t., standing for 'something'. The first-person singular subject on inanimate singular object independent form, labelled *1sg*, means 'I do X to it, am doing X to it'. The participle form has a third-person singular subject and an inanimate singular object and means 'one who does X to it, is doing X to it':

HEAD WORD CLASS CODE GLOSS INDEPENDENT FORM

ganawaabandan *vti* look at s.t.; *1sg* **inganawaabandaan**;

prt **genawaabandang**

PARTICIPLE FORM

The underlying stem of each type of transitive inanimate verb can be found by stripping the inflectional ending from the head word. For the *vti*, the ending to remove is *an*; for the *vti2*, it is *oon*, and for most of the others it is *n*. Thus the stem of the preceding example is /ganawaaband-/ found by removing the ending *-an* from the head word.

Entries for Transitive Animate Verbs (*vta*). Transitive animate verbs take animate objects. The typical head word is a second-person singular subject on animate singular object form in the imperative (command) order of inflections: '(you) do X to her, him, or it (animate thing)'. Where this form is not identical to the stem, the word stem is given between slashes and with a trailing hyphen. Three special symbols using capital letters may appear in such word stems. They are explained in Table 4.

The class code and gloss follow. The position of the animate object in the gloss is marked by the gloss code s.o., standing for 'someone', meaning here 'him, her, or it (animate thing)'. This code indicates that the object is grammatically animate, not that it is necessarily human or a living being. Thus it stands for any animate noun object, including the non-living ones (e.g., mitts, nets, and playing cards), as well as humans and animals. The first-person singular subject on animate singular object independent form follows, labelled *1sg* and meaning 'I do X to her, him, or it (animate thing); I am doing X to her, him, or it (animate thing)'. All entries are given with a third-person subject on animate singular object participle meaning 'one who does X to him, her, or it (animate thing); one who is doing X to him, her, or it (animate thing)'.

HEAD WORD CLASS CODE GLOSS INDEPENDENT FORM

ganawaabam *vta* look at s.o.; *1sg* **inganawaabamaa**;

prt **genawaabamaad**

PARTICIPLE FORM

Some **double-object** verbs allow a second object of either gender in addition to the primary animate object (often the recipient or beneficiary). This second object is indicated in the glosses with (s.t.), here indicat-

Table 4. Special symbols in word stems

Symbol	Meaning
N	The stem shows an alternation between *n* in certain inflected forms and *zh* in others, e.g., */miiN-/* in *nimiinaa* 'I give it to someone' and *miizh* 'give it to someone!'
S	The stem shows an alternation between *s* in certain inflected forms and *sh* in others, e.g., /mawadiS-/ in *nimawadisaa* 'I visit someone' and *mawadishishin* 'visit me!'
nN	The stem shows an alternation between *n* in certain inflected forms and *nzh* in others, e.g., */wiinN-/* in *wiinaad* 'that he names him' and *wiinzh* 'name someone!'

ing a noun of either gender. No inflectional reference is made to this second object.

miizh /miiN-/ give (s.t.) to s.o.; *1sg* **nimiinaa**; *prt* **maanaad**

A few verbs of this class commonly do not occur in the imperative forms chosen as the head word. In these cases the head word is replaced by an underlying stem, indicated as such by a trailing hyphen.

Reduplication on Verb Stems. Verb stems may be extended by a process of reduplication in which a copy of all or part of the first syllable of the stem, sometimes altered, is added to the front of the stem. A reduplicated stem may carry meanings of extension, distribution, or repetition in time or space, or plurality, such as 'keep doing X', 'do X here and there', 'do X off and on', 'do X to or for each (of several)'. For example, the verb stem /niimi-/ 'dance' has a reduplicated form /naaniimi-/ as in *naaniimi* 'he/she keeps dancing, dances here and there, dances off and on'. On stative verbs it is commonly used by older speakers when the subject is plural: *ginwaa* 'it is long', *gagaanwaawan* 'they (inanimate) are long'. The most common regular strategies for reduplication are suggested in Table 5. However, there are many stems that use an irregular pattern of reduplication. It has not been possible to check all of the verbs in this dictionary with enough different speakers to establish all of the possible reduplicated forms of each stem. To help those looking up Ojibwe words here, some irregular reduplication strategies are shown in the Ojibwe-English section by cross-reference entries, with the head of the entry being the start of an irregular reduplicated stem followed by a reference to the unreduplicated form. For example, the entry indicating that stems beginning with *gagaanw-* (with the final *w* of such entries to be treated also as *o*, so also *gagaano-*) may be based on a stem beginning with *ginw-* (or *gino-*):

gagaanw= < ginw=

Table 5. Regular verb reduplication strategies

Reduplication is a process that prefixes a copy or partial copy of the first syllable of a word stem to that stem, generally adding meanings of extension, repetition, distribution, or plurality. While verb stems can be reduplicated with a regular reduplication strategy as suggested here, other stems require different strategies. Still others seem to allow the use of more than one strategy, with the resulting forms, perhaps, differing in meaning. In general, in the regular strategies, the length of the initial syllable is preserved and repeated in the prefixed element. Except for initial syllables with the vowel *e* the vowel of the prefixed element is *a*, or, if the vowel of the initial syllable is long, *aa*. Initial *o* is treated as if initial *wi-* or *wo-*, apparently in free variation. The cover symbol C stands for any initial consonant.

Unreduplicated initial sound	Reduplicated as
a=	aya=
aa=	aayaa=
e=	eye=
i=	ayi=
o=	wawo= or wawi=
Ca=	CaCa=
Caa=	CaaCaa=
Ce=	CeCe=
Ci=	CaCi=
Cii=	CaaCii=
Co=	CaCo=
Coo=	CaaCoo=

Some stems in initial *Cw-* retain the *w* in the prefixed element and others do not. Stems that prefix *en-* in initial change may add a prefix *in-* before undergoing regular reduplication. In irregular reduplication strategies, the vowel of the initial syllable of the stem, the vowel of the prefixed element, or both may change in ways other than those described above. The initial consonant may become fortis or appear as the second member of a consonant cluster when the prefixed element is added.

In a few cases full entries are given for stems that have reduplication, either regular or irregular. Several stems show a kind of frozen reduplication that is not the result of the productive application of a reduplication strategy. The common reduplicated forms of some of the particles are also given separate entries.

Entries for Pronouns (*pr*), Particles (*pc*), Numbers (*nm*), and Preverbs (*pv*). The entries for pronouns, particles, numbers, and preverbs contain the **head word** (not actually a full word in the case of preverbs), the **class code**, the **gloss**, and, in some entries, a note in italics providing some explanation of the classification or use of the word:

HEAD WORD CLASS CODE GLOSS GLOSS NOTE

niin *pr* I, me *first-person singular personal pronoun*

Entries for Prefixes (*pf*). The entries for personal prefixes begin with a prefix given with a trailing equal sign, indicating that the prefix is a word part, not a word. When written in a full word, the personal prefix (or other item so marked) is written without the equal sign and attached directly to the rest of the word in which it occurs.

Notes on Glosses

The glosses for verbs may include qualifying words, sometimes enclosed within parentheses, that indicate the nature or quality of the being or thing described. For example, the gloss for the head word *miskwaabikad* is 'be red (as something mineral)', showing that this verb is normally used only to describe things made of mineral substances such as metal, rock, or glass. Other classifying phrases may limit the usual application of a verb to something stick- or woodlike (sticks, trees, people, etc.), sheetlike (cloth, clothing, bark, paper, etc.), or stringlike (rope, lines, snakes, etc.), among others. There is usually a general verb for each meaning that is not limiting in this way, and this is the one preferred by younger apeakers. In translating from Ojibwe to English, such classifying phrases are not needed, but in translating from English to Ojibwe it is necessary to take these phrases into account to make sure the appropriate verb for the material described is used, unless the general form is preferred. In the traditional language, figurative use of such classifying verbs will also be found.

There are few single-word equivalents in English for Ojibwe verbs of motion. Most types of motion are represented in Ojibwe not by a general verb but by a word part, which combines with another word part or parts having directional or descriptive meaning. For example, there is no general word equivalent to English 'run' but rather a set of verb stems describing specific ways of running, all containing a common word part meaning 'run', as in *biijibatoo* 'run here', *gizhiikaabatoo* 'run fast', and *maajiibatoo* 'start off running'. The closest equivalents to English general motion verbs are forms with initial *bim(i)=* meaning 'along, by' as in *bimibatoo* 'run along, run by'.

Verb stems ending in *=bizo* (*vai*) or *=bide* (*vii*) are often translated here by phrases including English verbs such as 'drive, fly, operate, run, speed'. The basic meaning of such verb stems is that the action is one of rapid motion or operation, and the selection of the appropriate English equivalents requires the subject and situation to be taken into account. Similarly, verb stems ending in *=(i)se* (but not *=ose*) may be translated with a wide range of English words indicating smooth, rapid, and, often, uncontrolled or self-initiated movement or action such as 'fly, fall, happen, pass (as time)'. Again the subject and situation must be considered before the appropriate translation can be selected.

The glosses for transitive verbs may include indications of the means or instrument of execution of the action, or other qualifying words. For example, the gloss for the head word *bookoshkan* is 'break s.t. in two by foot or body', indicating the use of this verb is generally restricted to breaking done by the body (as in sitting on or bumping against something) or by the feet (as in kicking or stamping on something). Other common instrumental phrases are 'by hand' (which might also indicate some abstract means), 'with the hands' or 'by pulling', 'by heat', 'by hitting', 'by throwing or dropping' or 'in impact', and 'using something' (i.e., some tool). In translating from Ojibwe to English it may not be necessary to include such qualifying words, but in translating from English to Ojibwe it is necessary to look at the full gloss to make sure the correct verb for a given means or instrument is used.

Glosses containing the word 'certain' in phrases such as 'to a certain place', 'from a certain place', or 'a certain number' translate words or perverbs containing (or acting as if they contained) word parts called **relative roots**. Within a word these hold a place usually reserved for a part that specifies location, direction, manner, extent, shape, size, number, or some other adverbial idea. The relative roots classify the relative kind of specification required but leave its exact nature open. They just tell that some direction, way, extent, degree, amount, or number is to be specified. In sentences they are used to point to some word or phrase (or even a gesture) that specifies the adverbial idea more exactly. For example, the verb stem *izhaa* 'go to a certain place' contains the relative root *izh=* (sometimes turning up in other stems as *in=*), which points to some place or direction. In a statement this place or direction is specified with a separate word or phrase. The word *oodenaang* 'to town' serves as the specifier in this example: *Oodenaang ingii-izhaa* 'I went to town'. The relative root may also point to a question word asking for the exact specification, as in this example with *aandi* 'where?': *Aandi gaa-izhaayan?* "Where did you go?'

Sounds and Orthography

There is no standard orthography shared by all of the local varieties of Anishinaabemowin. Some speakers write in a kind of English folk phonetics. Many speakers in Northern Canada write with the special characters of the shorthand-based Northern Algonquian syllabary. The roman orthography used in the book is only one of many possible writing systems that have been recently developed for Anishinaabemowin. Devised by Charles Fiero, it has won wide acceptance among language teachers in the United States and Canada. The main principles underlying it are that the letters or combinations of letters, although drawn from the same alphabet used to write English, stand for Ojibwe sounds, not English sounds, and that only the basic sounds (phonemes) of the language are written, not the predictable phonetic variants of them.

As most speakers of Ojibwe familiar with this writing system are literate in English, they often adopt English capitalization and punctuation conventions. In this dictionary, however, capitalization is generally restricted to place-names and personal names. Writers of Ojibwe should feel free to follow English conventions of capitalization (and so capitalize names of nationalities, days of the week, months, spirits and deities, etc.) and punctuation if they find them helpful.

In the brief description of Ojibwe sounds and orthography given in this section, some English words containing equivalents for Ojibwe sounds are listed. These are only approximations as each language has its own system of sounds and pronunciations. The actual pronunciation of a speaker of Minnesota Ojibwe should be followed.

Ojibwe Alphabetical Order

In this dictionary Ojibwe words are alphabetized in the following order:

a, aa, b, c, d, e, g, h, ', i, ii, j, k, m, n, o, oo, p, s, t, w, y, z

Note that the double vowels are treated as standing for unit sounds and are alphabetized after the corresponding single vowels. The digraphs *ch, sh,* and *zh,* although standing for unit sounds, are alphabetized as sequences of two letters. The character ' stands for a glottal stop, which is a significant speech sound in Minnesota Ojibwe.

Vowels

Basic Vowels. There are three short vowels: a, i, and o.

Table 6. Short Vowels

	Short Vowels	
	Front	**Back**
High	i	o
Low	a	

The four long vowels take more time to say than the short vowels. Three of them are paired with corresponding short vowels and so are written double: *aa, ii, oo.* The fourth long vowel is not paired with any short vowel and so it is written without doubling: *e.*

Table 7. Long Vowels

	Long Vowels	
	Front	**Back**
High	ii	oo
Low	e	aa

Each basic vowel is given below along with a phonetic transcription, Ojibwe words containing it, and one or more English words containing roughly equivalent sounds. The letters standing for the sounds focused on are given in boldface in the examples.

	Phonetic	Ojibwe examples	English equivalents
a	[ə]~[ʌ]	***agim*** 'count someone!'	about
		namadabi 'sits down'	
		baashkizigan 'gun'	
aa	[a:]	***aagim*** 'snowshoe'	father
		maajaa 'goes away'	

e	[e:]~[ɛ:]	*emikwaan* 'spoon' *awenen* 'who' *anishinaabe* 'person, Indian, Ojibwe'	café
i	[I]	*inini* 'man' *mawi* 'cries'	pin
ii	[i:]	*niin* 'I' *googii* 'dives'	seen
o	[o]~[U]	*ozid* 'someone's foot' *anokii* 'works' *nibo* 'dies, is dead'	obey, book
oo	[o:]~[u:]	*oodena* 'town' *anookii* 'hires' *goon* 'snow' *bimibatoo* 'runs along'	boat, boot

Nasal Vowels. Nasal vowels are indicated by writing the appropriate basic vowel followed by *nh.* Before a *y* or a glottal stop ' the *h* may be omitted in writing. In some earlier versions of this orthography, they were written with a hook underneath or underlined. There are no direct English equivalents:

aanh	[ã:]	*banaj**aanh*** 'nestling'
enh	[ẽ:]~[ɛ̃:]	*nisay**enh*** 'my older brother'
iinh	[ĩ:]	*awes**iinh*** 'wild animal' *agaash**iinh**yi, agaash**iinh**yi* '(someone) is small'
oonh	[õ:]~[ũ:]	*giig**oonh*** 'fish'

Nasalized Vowels. Vowels are nasalized before *ns, nz,* and *nzh.* The *n* is then omitted in pronunciation. A few examples are:

*gaawiin ingikend**anz**iin* 'I don't know it'
*jiimaan**ens*** 'small boat'
*oshk**anz**hiin* 'someone's fingernail(s)'

Long vowels after a nasal consonant *m* or *n* are often nasalized, especially before *s, sh, z,* or *zh.* It is often difficult to decide whether to write these as nasalized vowels or not. For example, while we write the word for 'moose' without indicating the phonetic nasalization, many prefer to write it with an *n:*

mooz or ***moonz*** 'moose'

Consonants and Other Sounds

The non-nasal consonants occur in pairs with one member of the pair a strong or **fortis** consonant and the other member of the pair a weak or **lenis** consonant. The strong consonants do not occur at the beginning of words (unless a vowel is left off), may sound long or double, and are voiceless. The weak consonants can occur at the beginning of words and are often voiced, especially in the middle of words.

Table 8. Consonants and other sounds

		Labial	Aveolar	Palatal	Velar	Glottal
Stops and Affricates	Strong	p	t	ch	k	
	Weak	b	d	j	g	
Sibilants	Strong		s	sh		
	Weak		z	zh		
Nasals		m	n			
Other sounds		w		y		h, '

	Phonetic	Ojibwe examples	English equivalents
b	[b]~[p]	***b**akade* 'is hungry' *ni**bi*** 'water' *gigizhe**b*** 'in the morning'	**b**ig, sp**i**n
ch	[č:]	*mi**ch**aa* 'it is big' *miigwe**ch*** 'thanks'	sti**tch**
d	[d]~[t]	***d**ebwe* 'tells the truth' *bii**d**oon* 'bring it!' *waagaakwa**d*** 'ax'	**d**o, sto**p**
g	[g]~[k]	***g**iin* 'you' *waa**g**osh* 'fox' *ikwewa**g*** 'women'	**g**eese, s**k**i
h	[h]	***h**ay'*	**h**i
'	[ʔ]	*bakite'an* 'hit it!' *ode'* 'someone's heart'	

j	[j]~[č]	***j**iimaan* 'boat, canoe' *a**j**ina* 'a little while' *ingii**k**a**j*** 'I'm cold'	**j**ump
k	[k:]	*ma**k**izin* 'moccasin, shoe' *ami**k*** 'beaver'	pi**ck**
m	[m]	***m**iinan* 'blueberries' *ji**m**aan* 'boat, canoe' *mi**m**ijim* 'food'	**m**an
n	[n]	***n**aanan* 'five'	**n**ame
	[ŋ] before *g, k*	*ba**n**gii* 'a little bit'	hu**n**ger
p	[p:]	*o**p**in* 'potato' *imbaa**p*** 'I laugh'	ri**p**
s	[s:]	*a**s**in* 'stone, rock' *wiiyaa**s*** 'meat'	mi**s**s
sh	[š:]	*a**sh**igan* 'bass' *animo**sh*** 'dog'	bu**sh**
t	[t:]	*a**t**e* '(something) is there' *ani**t*** 'fish spear'	pi**t**
w	[w]	***w**aabang* 'tomorrow' *gii**w**e* 'goes home' *bizinda**w*** 'listen to someone!'	**w**ay
y	[y]	*wii**y**aw* 'someone's body' *inda**y*** 'my dog'	**y**ellow
z	[z]~[s]	***z**iibi* 'river' *o**z**id* 'someone's foot' *indaako**z*** 'I am sick'	**z**ebra
zh	[ž]~[š]	***zh**aabonigan* 'needle' *a**zh**igan* 'sock' *bii**zh*** 'bring someone!'	measure

Consonant Clusters

The following consonant clusters occur:

sk	[sk]	*mi**sk**ozi* 'is red'
shp	[šp]	***ish**piming* 'up above, in heaven'

sht	[št]	*nis**ht**igwaan* 'my head'
shk	[šk]	*is**hk**ode* 'fire'
		*gayaa**shk*** 'gull'
mb	[mb]	*wii**mb**aa* 'is hollow'
nd	[nd]	*aa**nd**i* 'where'
		*aani**nd*** 'some'
nj	[nj]	*bii**nj**ise* 'flies in'
		*nini**nj*** 'my hand'
ng	[ŋg]	*ba**ng**ii* 'a little bit'
		*waaba**ng*** 'tomorrow'

A single consonant (except *w, h,* and *y*) or a consonant cluster may be followed by *w* before a vowel. A few examples are ***bw**aan* 'Dakota', *op**w**aagan* 'pipe', ***gw**iiwizens* 'boy', *ami**kw**ag* 'beavers', *nis**w**i* 'three', *bagida'**w**aa* 'sets a net', *mis**kw**i* 'blood', and *bin**gw**i* 'sand, ashes'.

Part I

Ojibwe–English

A

abanzh *ni* lodge pole, rafter; *pl* **abanzhiin**; *loc* **abanzhiing**; *dim* **abanzhiins**
abashkwebiigininjiishin *vai* get a blister on one's hand; *1sg* **indabashkwebiigininjiishin**; *prt* **ebashkwebiigininjiishing**
abashkwebiigizi *vai* have a blister; *1sg* **indabashkwebiigiz**; *prt* **ebashkwebiigizid**
abashkwebiigizideshin *vai* get a blister on one's foot; *1sg* **indabashkwebiigizideshin**; *prt* **ebashkwebiigizideshing**
abaabas /abaabasw-/ *vta* cense s.o.; *1sg* **indabaabaswaa**; *prt* **ebaabaswaad**
abaabasan *vti* cense s.t.; *1sg* **indabaabasaan**; *prt* **ebaabasang**
abaabaso *vai* cense oneself; *1sg* **indabaabas**; *prt* **ebaabasod**
abaagamide *vii* be warm (as a liquid); *prt* **ebaagamideg**; *aug* **abaagamidemagad**; *prt aug* **ebaagamidemagak**
abaagamizan *vti* warm s.t. (as a liquid); *1sg* **indabaagamizaan**; *prt* **ebaagamizang**
abaasandeke *vai* bask in the sun; *1sg* **indabaasandeke**; *prt* **ebaasandeked**
abaaso *vai* warm up in the sun; *1sg* **indabaas**; *prt* **ebaasod**
abaate *vii* warm up (of the weather); *prt* **ebaateg**; *aug* **abaatemagad**; *prt aug* **ebaatemagak**
abaawiganezo *vai* warm one's back; *1sg* **indabaawiganez**; *prt* **ebaawiganezod**
abi *vai* be at home, be in a certain place, sit in a certain place; *1sg* **indab**; *prt* **ebid**
abininjiizo *vai* warm one's hands; *1sg* **indabininjiiz**; *prt* **ebininjiizod**
abinoojiinh *na* child; *pl* **abinoojiinyag**; *dim* **abinoojiiyens, abinoojiins**
abinoojiinh-biizikaagan *ni* item of children's clothing; *pl* **abinoojiinh-biizikaaganan**; *loc* **abinoojiinh-biizikaaganing**; *dim* **abinoojiinh-biizikaagaans**
abinoojiinyikaazo *vai* pretend to be a child; *1sg* **indabinoojiinyikaaz**; *prt* **ebinoojiinyikaazod**
abinoojiinyiwi *vai* be a child; *1sg* **indabinoojiinyiw**; *prt* **ebinoojiinyiwid**
abinoojiiyens *na* baby; *pl* **abinoojiiyensag**; *also* **abinoojiins**
abiwin *ni* room, living room; *pl* **abiwinan**; *loc* **abiwining**; *dim* **abiwinens**
abiz /abizw-/ *vta* warm s.o. at the fire; *1sg* **indabizwaa**; *prt* **ebizwaad**
abizamaw *vta* warm (s.t.) for s.o. at the fire; *1sg* **indabizamawaa**; *prt* **ebizamawaad**
abizan *vti* warm s.t. at the fire; *1sg* **indabizaan**; *prt* **ebizang**
abizidezo *vai* warm one's feet; *1sg* **indabizidez**; *prt* **ebizidezod**
abiichigaade *vii* be occupied; *prt* **ebiichigaadeg**; *aug* **abiichigaademagad**; *prt aug* **ebiichigaademagak**
abiitan *vti* live in s.t., occupy s.t.; *1sg* **indabiitaan**; *prt* **ebiitang**
abiitaw *vta* sit up with s.o. (e.g., the deceased at a wake); *1sg* **indabiitawaa**; *prt* **ebiitawaad**
abiiwigamig *ni* living room; *pl* **abiiwigamigoon**; *loc* **abiiwigamigong**; *dim* **abiiwigamigoons**
abwaadan *vti* roast s.t., cook s.t. over a fire; *1sg* **indabwaadaan**; *prt* **ebwaadang**
abwaajigan *na* bread cooked over an open fire; *pl* **abwaajiganag**; *loc* **abwaajiganing**; *dim* **abwaajigaans**
abwaajigan *ni* roasted meat, roasted fish; *pl* **abwaajiganan**; *dim* **abwaajigaans**
abwaajige *vai* roast things; *1sg* **indabwaajige**; *prt* **ebwaajiged**
abwaanaak *ni* drying rack for strips of meat over a fire; *pl* **abwaanaakoon**; *loc* **abwaanaakong**; *dim* **abwaanaakoons**
abwaazh /abwaaN-/ *vta* roast s.o., cook s.o. over a fire; *1sg* **indabwaanaa**; *prt* **ebwaanaad**
abwe *vai+o* roast (s.t.), cook (s.t.) over a fire; *1sg* **indabwe, indabwen**; *prt* **ebwed**
abweninjii *vai* have a sweaty hand; *1sg* **indabweninjii**; *prt* **ebweninjiid**
abwewas /abwewasw-/ *vta* cure s.o. over a fire; *1sg* **indabwewaswaa**; *prt* **ebwewaswaad**
abwewasan *vti* cure s.t. over a fire; *1sg* **indabwewasaan**; *prt* **ebwewasang**
abwewasigan *ni* fire-cured meat or fish; *pl* **abwewasiganan**; *loc* **abwewasiganing**; *dim* **abwewasigaans**
abwewasige *vai* cure things over a fire; *1sg* **indabwewasige**; *prt* **ebwewasiged**
abwewin *ni* frying pan; *pl* **abwewinan**; *loc* **abwewining**; *dim* **abwewinens**
abwezide *vai* have a sweaty foot; *1sg* **indabwezide**; *prt* **ebwezided**
abwezo *vai* sweat; *1sg* **indabwez**; *prt* **ebwezod**
abwi *ni* paddle; *pl* **abwiin**; *loc* **abwiing**; *dim* **abwiins**
achaab *ni* bowstring; *pl* **achaabiin**; *loc* **achaabiing**; *dim* **achaabiins**
achigaade *vii* be put in a certain place; *prt* **echigaadeg**; *aug* **achigaademagad**; *prt aug* **echigaademagak**
achigaazo *vai* be put in a certain place; *prt* **echigaazod**
achige *vai* put things in a certain place, place a bet; *1sg* **indachige**; *prt* **echiged**
adaam *vta* buy (s.t.) from s.o.; *1sg* **indadaamaa**; *prt* **edaamaad**
adaawam *vta* borrow (s.t.) from s.o., rent (s.t.) from s.o.; *1sg* **indadaawamaa**; *prt* **edaawamaad**
adaawange *vai+o* borrow (s.t.) from people, rent (s.t.) from people; *1sg* **indadaawange, indadaawangen**; *prt* **edaawanged**
adaawaagan *ni* fur for trade; *pl* **adaawaaganan**; *loc* **adaawaaganing**; *dim* **adaawaagaans**
adaawaage *vai+o* sell (s.t.); *1sg* **indadaawaage, indadaawaagen**; *prt* **edaawaaged**
adaawe *vai+o* buy (s.t.); *1sg* **indadaawe, indadaawen**; *prt* **edaawed**
adaawetamaw *vta* buy (s.t.) for s.o.; *1sg* **indadaawetamawaa**; *prt* **edaawetamawaad**
adaawetamaazo *vai* buy (s.t.) for oneself; *1sg* **indadaawetamaaz**; *prt* **edaawetamaazod**

adaawewigamig *ni* store; *pl* **adaawewigamigoon**; *loc* **adaawewigamigong**; *dim* **adaawewigamigoons**
adaawewinini *na* store clerk, trader; *pl* **adaawewininiwag**
adaawewininiikwe *na* store clerk (female), trader (female); *pl* **adaawewininiikweg**
adik *na* caribou, reindeer; *pl* **adikwag**; *dim* **adikoons**
adikameg *na* whitefish; *pl* **adikamegwag**; *dim* **adikamegoons**
adim *vta* catch up to s.o., overtake s.o.; *1sg* **indadimaa**; *prt* **edimaad**
adima' /adima'w-/ *vta* catch up to s.o. in a boat, overtake s.o. in a boat; *1sg* **indadima'waa**; *prt* **edima'waad**
adindan *vti* catch up to s.t., overtake s.t.; *1sg* **indadindaan**; *prt* **edindang**
adoopowin *ni* table; *pl* **adoopowinan**; *loc* **adoopowining**; *dim* **adoopowinens**
adoopowiniigin *ni* table cloth; *pl* **adoopowiniiginoon**; *loc* **adoopowiniiginong**; *dim* **adoopowiniiginoons**
agadendam *vai2* be ashamed, feel shy; *1sg* **indagadendam**; *prt* **egadendang**
agadendan *vti* be ashamed of s.t.; *1sg* **indagadendaan**; *prt* **egadendang**
agadendaagozi *vai* be ashamed, be embarrassed; *1sg* **indagadendaagoz**; *prt* **egadendaagozid**
agadendaagwad *vii* be shameful, be embarrassing; *prt* **egadendaagwak**
agadenim *vta* be ashamed of s.o., be embarrassed by s.o.; *1sg* **indagadenimaa**; *prt* **egadenimaad**
agaji *vai* be bashful, be shy; *1sg* **indagaj**; *prt* **egajid**
agaji' *vta* make s.o. ashamed, embarrass s.o.; *1sg* **indagaji'aa**; *prt* **egaji'aad**
agajishki *vai* be a shy person; *1sg* **indagajishk**; *prt* **egajishkid**
agajiitaw *vta* be shy in front of s.o., be ashamed before s.o.; *1sg* **indagajiitawaa**; *prt* **egajiitawaad**
agamiing *pc* on the shore, at the water, at the lake
agawaate'on *ni* umbrella; *pl* **agawaate'onan**; *loc* **agawaate'oning**; *dim* **agawaate'onens**
agawaatese *vai* cast a shadow flying; *prt* **egawaatesed**
agawaatese *vii* cast a shadow flying; *prt* **egawaateseg**; *aug* **agawaatesemagad**; *prt aug* **egawaatesemagak**
agawaateshin *vai* be in shade, be in shadow; *1sg* **indagawaateshin**; *prt* **egawaateshing**
agawaateshkan *vti* shade s.t., cast a shadow on s.t.; *1sg* **indagawaateshkaan**; *prt* **egawaateshkang**
agawaateshkaw *vta* shade s.o., cast a shadow on s.o.; *1sg* **indagawaateshkawaa**; *prt* **egawaateshkawaad**
agawaatesin *vii* be in shade, be in shadow; *prt* **egawaatesing**
agawaateyaa *vii* there is shadow, there is shade; *prt* **egawaateyaag**; *aug* **agawaateyaamagad**; *prt aug* **egawaateyaamagak**
agazom *vta* embarrass s.o. by speech; *1sg* **indagazomaa**; *prt* **egazomaad**
agaamakiing *pc* overseas, in Europe
agaamashkosiw *pc* on the other side of the meadow
agaamayi'ii *pc* on the other side of it, across it
agaamaakwaa *pc* on the other side of the clearing
agaami- *pn* on the other side of, across
agaamikana *pc* on the other side of the road or trail, across the road or trail
agaamindesi *pc* other side of the lodge
agaamindesing *pc* on the other side of the lodge
agaaming *pc* on the other side of the lake, across the lake
agaamishkode *pc* on the other side of the fire
agaasade' *vta* make s.o. narrow; *1sg* **indagaasade'aa**; *prt* **egaasade'aad**
agaasademon /agaasademo-/ *vii* be narrow (as a road or trail); *prt* **egaasademog**
agaasadengwe *vai* have a narrow face; *1sg* **indagaasadengwe**; *prt* **egaasadengwed**
agaasadetigweyaa *vii* be narrow (as a river); *prt* **egaasadetigweyaag**; *aug* **agaasadetigweyaamagad**; *prt aug* **egaasadetigweyaamagak**
agaasadetoon *vti2* make s.t. narrow; *1sg* **indagaasadetoon**; *prt* **egaasadetood**
agaasadeyaa *vii* be narrow; *prt* **egaasadeyaag**; *aug* **agaasadeyaamagad**; *prt aug* **egaasadeyaamagak**
agaasadeyaabikad *vii* be narrow (as something mineral); *prt* **egaasadeyaabikak**
agaasadeyaabikizi *vai* be narrow (as something mineral); *prt* **egaasadeyaabikizid**
agaasadeyaabiigad *vii* be narrow (as something string-like); *prt* **egaasadeyaabiigak**
agaasadeyaabiigizi *vai* be narrow (as something string-like); *prt* **egaasadeyaabiigizid**
agaasadeyiigad *vii* be narrow (as something sheet-like); *prt* **egaasadeyiigak**
agaasadeyiigizi *vai* be narrow (as something sheet-like); *prt* **egaasadeyiigizid**
agaasadeyoonagad *vii* be narrow (as a boat); *prt* **egaasadeyoonagak**
agaasadezi *vai* be narrow; *prt* **egaasadezid**
agaasadinaa *vii* there is a small hill; *prt* **egaasadinaag**; *aug* **agaasadinaamagad**; *prt aug* **egaasadinaamagak**
agaasate *vii* be small (as a room or house); *prt* **egaasateg**; *aug* **agaasatemagad**; *prt aug* **egaasatemagak**
agaasaa *vii* be small; *prt* **egaasaag**; *aug* **agaasaamagad**; *prt aug* **egaasaamagak**
agaasaabaminaagozi *vai* appear small, look small; *prt* **egaasaabaminaagozid**
agaasaabaminaagwad *vii* appear small, look small; *prt* **egaasaabaminaagwak**
agaasaabikad *vii* be small (as something mineral); *prt* **egaasaabikak**
agaasaabikizi *vai* be small (as something mineral); *prt* **egaasaabikizid**
agaasaabiigad *vii* be small (as something string-like), be fine (as something string-like); *prt* **egaasaabiigak**
agaasaabiigizi *vai* be small (as something string-like), be fine (as something string-like); *prt* **egaasaabiigizid**

agaasaakozi *vai* be small (as something stick- or wood-like); *prt* **egaasaakozid**
agaasaakwad *vii* be small (as something stick- or wood-like); *prt* **egaasaakwak**
agaasaatoon *vti2* make s.t. small; *1sg* **indagaasaatoon**; *prt* **egaasaatood**
agaasendan *vti* think little of s.t., consider s.t. insignificant; *1sg* **indagaasendaan**; *prt* **egaasendang**
agaasendaagozi *vai* be considered insignificant; *1sg* **indagaasendaagoz**; *prt* **egaasendaagozid**
agaasendaagwad *vii* be considered insignificant; *prt* **egaasendaagwak**
agaasenim *vta* think little of s.o., consider s.o. insignificant; *1sg* **indagaasenimaa**; *prt* **egaasenimaad**
agaashiinyi *vai* be small; *1sg* **indagaashiinh**; *prt* **egaashiinyid**
agaasi' *vta* make s.o. small; *1sg* **indagaasi'aa**; *prt* **egaasi'aad**
agaasiminagad *vii* be small (as something ball-like); *prt* **egaasiminagak**
agaasiminagizi *vai* be small (as something ball-like); *prt* **egaasiminagizid**
agaasiigad *vii* be small (as something sheet-like); *prt* **egaasiigak**
agaasiigizi *vai* be small (as something sheet-like); *prt* **egaasiigizid**
agaawaa *pc* hardly, barely
agaawaadan *vti* wish for s.t., desire s.t.; *1sg* **indagaawaadaan**; *prt* **egaawaadang**
agaawaazh /agaawaaN-/ *vta* wish for s.o., desire s.o.; *1sg* **indagaawaanaa**; *prt* **egaawaanaad**
agidajiw *pc* on top of a mountain; *also* **ogidajiw*, wagidajiw**
agidakamig *pc* on top of the ground; *also* **ogidakamig*, wagidakamig**
agidasin *pc* on top of a rock; *also* **ogidasin*, wagidasin**
agidaabik *pc* on something mineral (e.g., metal, glass, rock); *also* **ogidaabik*, wagidaabik**
agidaajiwan *pc* upstream; *also* **ogidaajiwan*, wagidaajiwan**
agidaaki *pc* on top of a hill; *also* **ogidaaki*, wagidaaki**
agidaakiiwe *vai* go uphill; *1sg* **indagidaakiiwe**; *prt* **egidaakiiwed**
agidaakiiwebatoo *vai* run uphill; *1sg* **indagidaakiiwebatoo**; *prt* **egidaakiiwebatood**
agidibiig *pc* on top of the water; *also* **ogidibiig*, wagidibiig**
agidigamig *pc* on top of the house; *also* **ogidigamig*, wagidigamig**
agidiskwam *pc* on top of the ice; *also* **ogidiskwam*, wagidiskwam**
agig *na* phlegm
agigokaa *vai* have a cold; *1sg* **indagigokaa**; *prt* **egigokaad**
agijayi'ii *pc* on top of it; *also* **ogijayi'ii*, wagijayi'ii**
agiji- *pn* on top of; *also* **ogiji-*, wagiji-**
agim *vta* count s.o.; *1sg* **indagimaa**; *prt* **egimaad**
agindamaw *vta* count (s.t.) for s.o., read (s.t.) for s.o.; *1sg* **indagindamawaa**; *prt* **egindamawaad**
agindamaage *vai* count (s.t.) for people, read (s.t.) for people; *1sg* **indagindamaage**; *prt* **egindamaaged**
agindan *vti* count s.t., read s.t.; *1sg* **indagindaan**; *prt* **egindang**
agindaaso *vai* count, read; *1sg* **indagindaas**; *prt* **egindaasod**
agindaasoowigamig *ni* library; *pl* **agindaasoowigamigoon**; *loc* **agindaasoowigamigong**; *dim* **agindaasoowigamigoons**
aginjigaade *vii* be counted, be read; *prt* **eginjigaadeg**; *aug* **aginjigaademagad**; *prt aug* **eginjigaademagak**
aginjigaazo *vai* be counted; *prt* **eginjigaazod**
aginzo *vai* be counted, belong to a group; *1sg* **indaginz**; *prt* **eginzod**
agiw* *pr* those *animate plural demonstrative*; *also* **ingiw, igiw***
agogwaadan *vti* sew s.t. on; *1sg* **indagogwaadaan**; *prt* **egogwaadang**
agogwaajigan *ni* appliqué piece, trim; *pl* **agogwaajiganan**; *loc* **agogwaajiganing**; *dim* **agogwaajigaans**
agogwaaso *vai* sew something on; *1sg* **indagogwaas**; *prt* **egogwaasod**
agogwaazh /agogwaaN-/ *vta* sew s.o. on; *1sg* **indagogwaanaa**; *prt* **egogwaanaad**
agokadoon *vti2* stick s.t. on; *1sg* **indagokadoon**; *prt* **egokadood**
agokazh /agokaN-/ *vta* stick s.o. on; *1sg* **indagokanaa**; *prt* **egokanaad**
agoke *vai* stick on, adhere; *1sg* **indagoke**; *prt* **egoked**
agoke *vii* stick on, adhere; *prt* **egokeg**; *aug* **agokemagad**; *prt aug* **egokemagak**
agokiwas /agokiwasw-/ *vta* glue s.o., paste something on s.o.; *1sg* **indagokiwaswaa**; *prt* **egokiwaswaad**
agokiwasan *vti* glue s.t., paste something on s.t.; *1sg* **indagokiwasaan**; *prt* **egokiwasang**
agokiwasigan *ni* glue, paste; *pl* **agokiwasiganan**; *loc* **agokiwasiganing**; *dim* **agokiwasigaans**
agokiwaso *vai* be glued, be pasted on; *1sg* **indagokiwas**; *prt* **egokiwasod**
agokiwate *vii* be glued, be pasted on; *prt* **egokiwateg**; *aug* **agokiwatemagad**; *prt aug* **egokiwatemagak**
agomo *vai* float, be suspended in water; *1sg* **indagom**; *prt* **egomod**
agon *vta* hold s.o. up against; *1sg* **indagonaa**; *prt* **egonaad**
agonan *vti* hold s.t. up against; *1sg* **indagonaan**; *prt* **egonang**
agonde *vii* float, be suspended in water; *prt* **egondeg**
agongos *na* chipmunk, Scandinavian; *pl* **agongosag**; *dim* **agongosens**
agongosimo *vai* speak a Scandinavian language; *1sg* **indagongosim**; *prt* **egongosimod**
agonjidoon *vti2* soak s.t., put s.t. in to soak; *1sg* **indagonjidoon**; *prt* **egonjidood**
agonjijigaade *vii* be put in to soak; *prt* **egonjijigaadeg**; *aug* **agonjijigaademagad**; *prt aug* **egonjijigaademagak**

agonjijigaazo *vai* be put in to soak; *prt* **egonjijigaazod**
agonjim *vta* soak s.o., put s.o. in to soak; *1sg* **indagonjimaa**; *prt* **egonjimaad**
agonjoonaagan *ni* net float; *pl* **agonjoonaaganan**; *loc* **agonjoonaaganing**; *dim* **agonjoonaagaans**
agoodakikwaan *ni* kettle hanger; *pl* **agoodakikwaanan**; *loc* **agoodakikwaaning**; *dim* **agoodakikwaanens**
agoodasabii *vai* hang up a net; *1sg* **indagoodasabii**; *prt* **egoodasabiid**
agoodaw *vta* hang (s.t.) for s.o., set a snare for s.o.; *1sg* **indagoodawaa**; *prt* **egoodawaad**
agoode *vii* hang; *prt* **egoodeg**; *aug* **agoodemagad**; *prt aug* **egoodemagak**
agoodoo *vai* set a snare; *1sg* **indagoodoo**; *prt* **egoodood**
agoodoon *vti2* hang s.t.; *1sg* **indagoodoon**; *prt* **egoodood**
agoodwaagan *ni* snare; *pl* **agoodwaaganan**; *loc* **agoodwaaganing**; *dim* **agoodwaagaans**
agoodwaaganeyaab *ni* snare wire; *pl* **agoodwaaganeyaabiin**; *loc* **agoodwaaganeyaabiing**; *dim* **agoodwaaganeyaabiins**
agoojiganaatig *ni* clothesline pole; *pl* **agoojiganaatigoon**; *loc* **agoojiganaatigong**; *dim* **agoojiganaatigoons**
agoojiganeyaab *ni* clothesline; *pl* **agoojiganeyaabiin**; *loc* **agoojiganeyaabiing**; *dim* **agoojiganeyaabiins**
agoojige *vai* hang things, hang up laundry; *1sg* **indagoojige**; *prt* **egoojiged**
agoojin *vai* hang, be in the sky (e.g., a star, the sun, or the moon); *1sg* **indagoojin**; *prt* **egoojing**
agoojiwanaanaak *ni* hanging rack for food drying; *pl* **agoojiwanaanaakoon**; *loc* **agoojiwanaanaakong**; *dim* **agoojiwanaanaakoons**
agoozh /agooN-/ *vta* hang s.o.; *1sg* **indagoonaa**; *prt* **egoonaad**
agoozi *vai* be perched up on something; *1sg* **indagooz**; *prt* **egoozid**
agwadaashi *na* sunfish; *pl* **agwadaashiwag**; *dim* **agwadaashiins**
agwajiing *pc* outside, outdoors
agwanem *vta* put s.o. in one's mouth, hold s.o. in one's mouth; *1sg* **indagwanemaa**; *prt* **egwanemaad**
agwanendan *vti* put s.t. in one's mouth, hold s.t. in one's mouth; *1sg* **indagwanendaan**; *prt* **egwanendang**
agwanenjige *vai* put things in one's mouth, hold things in one's mouth, chew tobacco; *1sg* **indagwanenjige**; *prt* **egwanenjiged**
agwanogaan *ni* canopy; *pl* **agwanogaanan**; *loc* **agwanogaaning**; *dim* **agwanogaanens**
agwapidoon *vti2* tie s.t. on something; *1sg* **indagwapidoon**; *prt* **egwapidood**
agwapijigaade *vii* be tied on, be hitched on; *prt* **egwapijigaadeg**; *aug* **agwapijigaademagad**; *prt aug* **egwapijigaademagak**
agwapijigaazo *vai* be tied on, be hitched on; *prt* **egwapijigaazod**
agwapizh /agwapiN-/ *vta* tie s.o. on something; *1sg* **indagwapinaa**; *prt* **egwapinaad**
agwazhe *vai* be covered with blankets; *1sg* **indagwazhe**; *prt* **egwazhed**
agwazhe' *vta* cover s.o. with blankets; *1sg* **indagwazhe'aa**; *prt* **egwazhe'aad**
agwazhe'on *ni* blanket, covering; *pl* **agwazhe'onan**; *loc* **agwazhe'oning**; *dim* **agwazhe'onens**
agwaabatoo *vai* run ashore; *1sg* **indagwaabatoo**; *prt* **egwaabatood**
agwaabidoon *vti2* pull s.t. ashore, pull s.t. from the water; *1sg* **indagwaabidoon**; *prt* **egwaabidood**
agwaabikide *vii* burn to the pan; *prt* **egwaabikideg**; *aug* **agwaabikidemagad**; *prt aug* **egwaabikidemagak**
agwaabikiz /agwaabikizw-/ *vta* burn s.o. to the pan; *1sg* **indagwaabikizwaa**; *prt* **egwaabikizwaad**
agwaabikizan *vti* burn s.t. to the pan; *1sg* **indagwaabikizaan**; *prt* **egwaabikizang**
agwaabikizo *vai* burn to the pan; *prt* **egwaabikizod**
agwaabizh /agwaabiN-/ *vta* pull s.o. ashore, pull s.o. from the water; *1sg* **indagwaabinaa**; *prt* **egwaabinaad**
agwaabiiga' /agwaabiiga'w-/ *vta* take s.o. off the water using something; *1sg* **indagwaabiiga'waa**; *prt* **egwaabiiga'waad**
agwaabiiga'amaw *vta* take (s.t.) off the water using something for s.o.; *1sg* **indagwaabiiga'amawaa**; *prt* **egwaabiiga'amawaad**
agwaabiiga'an *vti* take s.t. off the water using something; *1sg* **indagwaabiiga'aan**; *prt* **egwaabiiga'ang**
agwaabiigin *vta* take s.o. off the water, take s.o. off the fire; *1sg* **indagwaabiiginaa**; *prt* **egwaabiiginaad**
agwaabiiginan *vti* take s.t. off the water, take s.t. off the fire; *1sg* **indagwaabiiginaa**; *prt* **egwaabiiginaad**
agwaadaabaadan *vti* drag s.t. ashore; *1sg* **indagwaadaabaadaan**; *prt* **egwaadaabaadang**
agwaadaabaazh /agwaadaabaaN-/ *vta* drag s.o. ashore; *1sg* **indagwaadaabaanaa**; *prt* **egwaadaabaanaad**
agwaadaabii *vai* drag something ashore; *1sg* **indagwaadaabii**; *prt* **egwaadaabiid**
agwaagoshi *vai* be moldy; *prt* **egwaagoshid**
agwaagosin *vii* be moldy; *prt* **egwaagosing**
agwaagwaabikad *vii* be rusty; *prt* **egwaagwaabikak**
agwaagwaabikishin *vai* turn rusty; *prt* **egwaagwaabikishing**
agwaagwaabikisin *vii* turn rusty; *prt* **egwaagwaabikising**
agwaagwaabikizi *vai* be rusty; *prt* **egwaagwaabikizid**
agwaa'o *vai* land, come ashore in a boat; *1sg* **indagwaa'**; *prt* **egwaa'od**; *also* **agwaa'am**
agwaa'oodoon *vti2* take s.t. ashore by boat; *1sg* **indagwaa'oodoon**; *prt* **egwaa'oodood**

agwaakwa'an *vti* nail s.t. up against the wall, post s.t. up; *1sg* **indagwaakwa'aan**; *prt* **egwaakwa'ang**
agwaakwa'igan *ni* sign, notice, poster; *pl* **agwaakwa'iganan**; *loc* **agwaakwa'iganing**; *dim* **agwaakwa'igaans**
agwaanaaso *vai* unload a boat; *1sg* **indagwaanaas**; *prt* **egwaanaasod**
agwaashim *vta* take s.o. ashore, take s.o. off the fire; *1sg* **indagwaashimaa**; *prt* **egwaashimaad**
agwaasidoon *vti2* take s.t. ashore, take s.t. off the fire; *1sg* **indagwaasidoon**; *prt* **egwaasidood**
agwaasijigaade *vii* be taken ashore, be taken off the fire; *prt* **egwaasijigaadeg**; *aug* **agwaasijigaademagad**; *prt aug* **egwaasijigaademagak**
agwaasijigaazo *vai* be taken ashore, be taken off the fire; *prt* **egwaasijigaazod**
agwaataa *vai* go ashore, come ashore; *1sg* **indagwaataa**; *prt* **egwaataad**
agwaawebin *vta* throw s.o. out of the water; *1sg* **indagwaawebinaa**; *prt* **egwaawebinaad**
agwaawebinamaw *vta* throw (s.t.) out of the water for s.o.; *1sg* **indagwaawebinamawaa**; *prt* **egwaawebinamawaad**
agwaawebinan *vti* throw s.t. out of the water; *1sg* **indagwaawebinaan**; *prt* **egwaawebinang**
agwaayaadagaa *vai* swim ashore; *1sg* **indagwaayaadagaa**; *prt* **egwaayaadagaad**
agwaayaashi *vai* be blown ashore, sail ashore; *1sg* **indagwaayaash**; *prt* **egwaayaashid**
agwaayaasin *vii* be blown ashore; *prt* **egwaayaasing**
a'aw *pr* that *animate singular demonstrative*; *also* **aw, 'aw, 'a**
a'awedi *pr* that over there *animate singular demonstrative*; *also* **awedi**
ajidagoode *vii* hang upside down; *prt* **ejidagoodeg**; *aug* **ajidagoodemagad**; *prt aug* **ejidagoodemagak**
ajidagoodoon *vti2* hang s.t. upside down; *1sg* **indajidagoodoon**; *prt* **ejidagoodood**
ajidagoojin *vai* hang upside down; *prt* **ejidagoojing**
ajidagoozh /ajidagooN-/ *vta* hang s.o. upside down; *1sg* **indajidagoonaa**; *prt* **ejidagoonaad**
ajidamoo *na* red squirrel; *pl* **ajidamoog**; *dim* **ajidamoons**
ajidin *vta* hold s.o. upside down; *1sg* **indajidinaa**; *prt* **ejidinaad**
ajidinan *vti* hold s.t. upside down; *1sg* **indajidinaan**; *prt* **ejidinang**
ajijaak *na* sandhill crane; *pl* **ajijaakwag**; *dim* **ajijaakoons**
ajijibizo *vai* fall head first; *1sg* **indajijibiz**; *prt* **ejijibizod**
ajijiingwese *vai* fall on one's face; *1sg* **indajijiingwese**; *prt* **ejijiingwesed**
ajina *pc* a little while
akakanzhe *ni* charcoal, coals, coal; *loc* **akakanzheng**; *dim* **akakanzhens**
akakanzhebwe *vai+o* cook (s.t.) on the coals, grill (s.t.); *1sg* **indakakanzhebwe, indakakanzhebwen**; *prt* **ekakanzhebwed**
akakanzhekaa *vii* be coals, be hot ashes; *prt* **ekakanzhekaag**; *aug* **akakanzhekaamagad**; *prt aug* **ekakanzhekaamagak**
akakojiish *na* woodchuck; *pl* **akakojiishag**; *dim* **akakojiishens**
akamaw *vta* lie in wait for s.o.; *1sg* **indakamawaa**; *prt* **ekamawaad**
akandoo *vai* lie in wait for game, use a blind; *1sg* **indakandoo**; *prt* **ekandood**
akandoowin *ni* hunting blind; *pl* **akandoowinan**; *loc* **akandoowining**; *dim* **akandoowinens**
akawaabam *vta* wait in watch for s.o., expect s.o. to come; *1sg* **indakawaabamaa**; *prt* **ekawaabamaad**
akawaabandan *vti* wait in watch for s.t., expect s.t. to come; *1sg* **indakawaabandaan**; *prt* **ekawaabandang**
akawaabi *vai* wait in watch, expect; *1sg* **indakawaab**; *prt* **ekawaabid**
akawe *pc* first (in a time sequence), first of all; *also* **kawe**
akeyaa *pc* in the direction of; *also* **gakeyaa, nakakeyaa***
aki *ni* earth, land, ground, country; *pl* **akiin**; *loc* **akiing**; *dim* **akiins**
akik *na* kettle, pail, pot, pan; *pl* **akikoog**; *loc* **akikong**; *dim* **akikoons**
akikoons *na* outboard motor; *pl* **akikoonsag**; *loc* **akikoonsing**
akina *pc* all, every; *also* **kina, gakina**
akina gegoo *pr* everything; *also* **kina gegoo, gakina gegoo**
akiwenzii *na* old man; *pl* **akiwenziiyag**
akiwenziiyiwi *vai* be an old man; *1sg* **indakiwenziiyiw**; *prt* **ekiwenziiyiwid**
akii-mazina'igan *ni* map; *pl* **akii-mazina'iganan**; *loc* **akii-mazina'iganing**; *dim* **akii-mazina'igaans**
akiiwan *vii* be the earth; *prt* **ekiiwang**
akiiwe-wiigiwaam *ni* earth lodge; *pl* **akiiwe-wiigiwaaman**; *loc* **akiiwe-wiigiwaaming**; *dim* **akiiwe-wiigiwaamens**
akiiwigamig *ni* sod house, root house; *pl* **akiiwigamigoon**; *loc* **akiiwigamigong**; *dim* **akiiwigamigoons**
ako- *pv3* since, a certain length, as long as, as far as
akoo' *vta* make s.o. a certain length, make s.o. so long; *1sg* **indakoo'aa**; *prt* **ekoo'aad**
akootoon *vti2* make s.t. a certain length, make s.t. so long; *1sg* **indakootoon**; *prt* **ekootood**
akoozi *vai* be a certain length, be a certain height, be so long, be so tall; *1sg* **indakooz**; *prt* **ekoozid**
akwa'waa *vai* fish through the ice with spear; *1sg* **indakwa'waa**; *prt* **ekwa'waad**
akwa'wewigamig *ni* fish house for spearing; *pl* **akwa'wewigamigoon**; *loc* **akwa'wewigamigong**; *dim* **akwa'wewigamigoons**
akwanaamo *vai* be short of breath, take short breaths; *1sg* **indakwanaam**; *prt* **ekwanaamod**
akwaa *vii* be a certain length, be a certain height, be so long, be so tall; *prt* **ekwaag**; *aug* **akwaamagad**; *prt aug* **ekwaamagak**

akwaabikad *vii* be a certain length (as something mineral), be so long (as something mineral); *prt* **ekwaabikak**
akwaabikizi *vai* be a certain length (as something mineral), be so long (as something mineral); *prt* **ekwaabikizid**
akwaabiigad *vii* be a certain length (as something string-like), be so long (as something string-like); *prt* **ekwaabiigak**
akwaabiigizi *vai* be a certain length (as something string-like), be so long (as something string-like); *prt* **ekwaabiigizid**
akwaakozi *vai* be a certain height, be a certain length (as something stick- or wood-like); *1sg* **indakwaakoz**; *prt* **ekwaakozid**
akwaakwad *vii* be a certain height, be a certain length (as something stick- or wood-like); *prt* **ekwaakwak**
akwaakwaa *vii* woods go a certain distance; *prt* **ekwaakwaag**; *aug* **akwaakwaamagad**; *prt aug* **ekwaakwaamagak**
akwaandawaagan *ni* stairway, ladder, elevator; *pl* **akwaandawaaganan**; *loc* **akwaandawaaganing**; *dim* **akwaandawaagaans**
akwaandawe *vai* climb up, go upstairs; *1sg* **indakwaandawe**; *prt* **ekwaandawed**
akwaandawebatoo *vai* climb up fast; *1sg* **indakwaandawebatoo**; *prt* **ekwaandawebatood**
akwaandawebizo *vai* climb up fast (e.g., in an elevator); *1sg* **indakwaandawebiz**; *prt* **ekwaandawebizod**
akwaandawebizon *ni* elevator; *pl* **akwaandawebizonan**; *loc* **akwaandawebizoning**; *dim* **akwaandawebizonens**
akwegad *vii* be a certain length (as something sheet-like), be so long (as something sheet-like); *prt* **ekwegak**
akwegizi *vai* be a certain length (as something sheet-like), be so long (as something sheet-like); *prt* **ekwegizid**
akwiindimaa *vii* be deep to a certain extent; *prt* **ekwiindimaag**; *aug* **akwiindimaamagad**; *prt aug* **ekwiindimaamagak**
amadaji *vai* wake from being cold; *1sg* **indamadaj**; *prt* **emadajid**
amadin *vta* wake s.o.; *1sg* **indamadinaa**; *prt* **emadinaad**
amajim *vta* wake s.o. by vocal noise; *1sg* **indamajimaa**; *prt* **emajimaad**
amajine *vai* wake from pain; *1sg* **indamajine**; *prt* **emajined**
amajise *vai* come awake; *1sg* **indamajise**; *prt* **emajised**
amajwebin *vta* shake s.o. awake; *1sg* **indamajwebinaa**; *prt* **emajwebinaad**
amaniso *vai* be alarmed; *1sg* **indamanis**; *prt* **emanisod**
amanisodaw *vta* be alarmed by s.o.; *1sg* **indamanisodawaa**; *prt* **emanisodawaad**
amanj *pc* I don't know how, I wonder how *dubitative*; *also* **amanj iidog, namanj*, namanj iidog***
amanj apii *pc* I don't know when, I wonder when *dubitative*
amanj igo *pc* however *dubitative*
amanj igo apii *pc* whenever, anytime *dubitative*
ambe *pc* come on!, let's go!, attention!
amik *na* beaver; *pl* **amikwag**; *dim* **amikoons**
amikwayaan *na* beaver hide; *pl* **amikwayaanag**; *dim* **amikwayaanens**
amikwiish *ni* beaver lodge; *pl* **amikwiishan**; *loc* **amikwiishing**; *dim* **amikwiishens**
amo /amw-/ *vta* eat s.o.; *1sg* **indamwaa**; *prt* **emwaad**
ana'o *vai* choke on something stuck in one's throat; *1sg* **indana'**; *prt* **ena'od**
anama'e- *pv4* Christian; *also* **aname-**
anama'e-giizhigad *vii* be Sunday; *prt* **enama'e-giizhigak**; *also* **aname-giizhigad**
anama'e-mazina'igan *ni* prayer book; *pl* **anama'e-mazina'iganan**; *loc* **anama'e-mazina'iganing**; *dim* **anama'e-mazina'igaans**
anama'eminensag *na* rosary *plural*
anama'e-nagamon *ni* hymn; *pl* **anama'e-nagamonan**
anama'etaw *vta* pray for s.o.; *1sg* **indanama'etawaa**; *prt* **enama'etawaad**
anama'ewigamig *ni* church; *pl* **anama'ewigamigoon**; *loc* **anama'ewigamigong**; *dim* **anama'ewigamigoons**; *also* **anamewigamig**
anama'ewikwe *na* nun; *pl* **anama'ewikweg**; *dim* **anama'ewikwens**
anami'aa *vai* pray, be Christian; *1sg* **indanami'aa**; *prt* **enami'aad**
anamikaw *vta* greet s.o.; *1sg* **indanamikawaa**; *prt* **enamikawaad**
anamikaadiwag /anamikaadi-/ *vai* they greet each other; *1pl* **indanamikaadimin**; *prt* **enamikaadijig**
anamikaage *vai* greet people; *1sg* **indanamikaage**; *prt* **enamikaaged**
anang *na* star; *pl* **anangoog**; *loc* **anangong**; *dim* **anangoons**
anaakan *ni* woven mat, rug; *pl* **anaakanan**; *loc* **anaakaning**; *dim* **anaakanens**

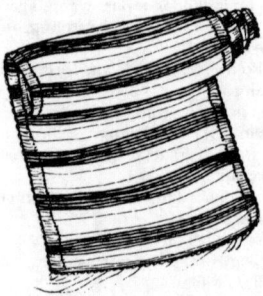

anaakan (mat)

anaakanashk *ni* reed, rush; *pl* **anaakanashkoon**; *loc* **anaakanashkong**; *dim* **anaakanashkoons**
anaamakamig *pc* under the ground

anaamaki *pc* underground
anaamayi'ii *pc* under it
anaamaagon *pc* under the snow; *also* **anaamaagonag**
anaamaatig *pc* under wood (e.g., a tree or stick)
anaamendan *vti* suspect s.t.; *1sg* **indanaamendaan**; *prt* **enaamendang**
anaamenim *vta* suspect s.o.; *1sg* **indanaamenimaa**; *prt* **enaamenimaad**
anaami- *pn* under
anaamibiig *pc* underwater
anaamim *vta* blame s.o. (in speech), accuse s.o.; *1sg* **indanaamimaa**; *prt* **enaamimaad**
anaamindiwag /anaamindi-/ *vai* they blame each other; *1pl* **indanaamindimin**; *prt* **enaamindijig**
anaamindizo *vai* blame oneself; *1sg* **indanaamindiz**; *prt* **enaamindizod**
anaaminge *vai* blame people; *1sg* **indanaaminge**; *prt* **enaaminged**
anaamisag *pc* under the floor, in the basement
anaamisagadaweshiinh *na* wren; *pl* **anaamisagadaweshiinyag**
anaamiskwam *pc* under the ice
anaamiindim *pc* in the depths of a body of water
anaamoonag *pc* under a boat
angobide *vii* wear out in operation; *prt* **engobideg**; *aug* **angobidemagad**; *prt aug* **engobidemagak**
angobizo *vai* wear out in operation; *prt* **engobizod**
ango' *vta* reduce s.o. to nothing; *1sg* **indango'aa**; *prt* **ango'aad**
angoshkan *vti* wear s.t. out with foot or body; *1sg* **indangoshkaan**; *prt* **engoshkang**
angoshkaw *vta* wear s.o. out with foot or body (e.g., pants); *1sg* **indangoshkawaa**; *prt* **engoshkawaad**
angotoon *vti2* reduce s.t. to nothing; *1sg* **indangotoon**; *prt* **engotood**
ani- *pv2* going away, going along, in progress, on the way, coming up to in time; *also* **ni-**
anijiiminan /anijiimin-/ *ni* peas *plural*
anijiiminaaboo *ni* pea soup; *loc* **anijiiminaaboong**
anikamaanan /anikamaan-/ *ni* suspenders *plural*
anima'adoo *vai* follow a trail away; *1sg* **indanima'adoo**; *prt* **enima'adood**
anima'adoon *vti2* follow s.t. away as a trail; *1sg* **indanima'adoon**; *prt* **enima'adood**
anima'amaazo *vai* go away singing; *1sg* **indanima'amaaz**; *prt* **enima'amaazod**
anima'azh /anima'aN-/ *vta* follow s.o.'s trail away; *1sg* **indanima'anaa**; *prt* **enima'anaad**
anima'oodoon *vti2* take s.t. away by boat; *1sg* **indanima'oodoon**; *prt* **enima'oodood**
anima'oozh /anima'ooN-/ *vta* take s.o. away by boat; *1sg* **indanima'oonaa**; *prt* **enima'oonaad**
animaabogo *vai* float away, drift away; *1sg* **indanimaabog**; *prt* **enimaabogod**
animaaboode *vii* float away, drift away; *prt* **enimaaboodeg**; *aug* **animaaboodemagad**; *prt aug* **enimaaboodemagak**
animaadagaa *vai* swim away; *1sg* **indanimaadagaa**; *prt* **enimaadagaad**
animaadagaako *vai* go away on the ice; *1sg* **indanimaadagaak**; *prt* **enimaadagaakod**
animaadagaazii *vai* wade away; *1sg* **indanimaadagaazii**; *prt* **enimaadagaaziid**
animaada'e *vai* skate away; *1sg* **indanimaada'e**; *prt* **enimaada'ed**
animaa'an *vii* drift away on the waves; *prt* **enimaa'ang**
animaa'ogo *vai* drift away on the waves; *1sg* **indanimaa'og**; *prt* **enimaa'ogod**
animaanakwad *vii* clouds go away; *prt* **enimaanakwak**
animaapi *vai* go away laughing; *1sg* **indanimaap**; *prt* **enimaapid**
animaashi *vai* be blown away, sail away; *1sg* **indanimaash**; *prt* **enimaashid**
animaasin *vii* be blown away, sail away; *prt* **enimaasing**
animaazakonenjige *vai* go away with a light; *1sg* **indanimaazakonenjige**; *prt* **enimaazakonenjiged**
animaazakonenjigebizo *vai* drive away with a light; *1sg* **indanimaazakonenjigebiz**; *prt* **enimaazakonenjigebizod**
animiba'idiwag /animiba'idi-/ *vai* they run away (in the other direction) together; *1pl* **indanimiba'idimin**; *prt* **enimiba'idijig**
animiba'igo *vai* drive away with horses; *1sg* **indanimiba'ig**; *prt* **enimiba'igod**
animibatoo *vai* run away; *1sg* **indanimibatoo**; *prt* **enimibatood**
animibatwaadan *vti* run away (in the other direction) with s.t.; *1sg* **indanimibatwaadaan**; *prt* **enimibatwaadang**
animibatwaazh /animibatwaaN-/ *vta* run away (in the other direction) with s.o.; *1sg* **indanimibatwaanaa**; *prt* **enimibatwaanaad**
animibide *vii* speed away, drive away, fly away; *prt* **enimibideg**; *aug* **animibidemagad**; *prt aug* **enimibidemagak**
animibizo *vai* speed away, drive away, fly away; *1sg* **indanimibiz**; *prt* **enimibizod**
animibizoni' *vta* drive away with s.o. (e.g., a car); *1sg* **indanimibizoni'aa**; *prt* **enimibizoni'aad**
animibizonitoon *vti2* drive away with s.t.; *1sg* **indanimibizonitoon**; *prt* **enimibizonitood**
animibiisaa *vii* rain goes away; *prt* **enimibiisaag**; *aug* **animibiisaamagad**; *prt aug* **enimibiisaamagak**
animidaabii *vai* drag away; *1sg* **indanimidaabii**; *prt* **enimidaabiid**
animidaabii'iwe *vai* drive away; *1sg* **indanimidaabii'iwe**; *prt* **enimidaabii'iwed**
animigidaazo *vai* go away mad; *1sg* **indanimigidaaz**; *prt* **enimigidaazod**
animijiwan *vii* flow away; *prt* **enimijiwang**
animikawe *vai* leave tracks going away; *1sg* **indanimikawe**; *prt* **enimikawed**
animikii *na* thunderbird, thunderer; *pl* **animikiig**; *dim* **animikiins**
animikiikaa *vii* there is thunder; *prt* **enimikiikaag**; *aug* **animikiikaamagad**; *prt aug* **enimikiikaamagak**
animikogaabawi *vai* stand with the back out; *1sg* **indanimikogaabaw**; *prt* **enimikogaabawid**
animikon *vta* turn s.o. face down, turn s.o. to face backwards; *1sg* **indanimikonaa**; *prt* **enimikonaad**

animikonan *vti* turn s.t. face down, turn s.t. to face backwards; *1sg* **indanimikonaan**; *prt* **enimikonang**
animikonigaade *vii* be turned face down, be turned to face backwards; *prt* **enimikonigaadeg**; *aug* **animikonigaademagad**; *prt aug* **enimikonigaademagak**
animikonigaazo *vai* be turned face down, be turned to face backwards; *prt* **enimikonigaazod**
animikose *vai* fall face down; *prt* **enimikosed**
animikose *vii* fall face down; *prt* **enimikoseg**; *aug* **animikosemagad**; *prt aug* **enimikosemagak**
animikoshim *vta* lay s.o. face down; *1sg* **indanimikoshimaa**; *prt* **enimikoshimaad**
animikoshin *vai* lie face down; *1sg* **indanimikoshin**; *prt* **enimikoshing**
animikosidoon *vti2* lay s.t. face down; *1sg* **indanimikosidoon**; *prt* **enimikosidood**
animikosin *vii* lie face down; *prt* **enimikosing**
animikwabi *vai* sit facing backwards; *1sg* **indanimikwab**; *prt* **enimikwabid**
animikwabiitaw *vta* sit with back to s.o.; *1sg* **indanimikwabiitawaa**; *prt* **enimikwabiitawaad**
animinizhimo *vai* run away scared; *1sg* **indaniminizhim**; *prt* **eniminizhimod**
animise *vai* fly away; *1sg* **indanimise**; *prt* **enimised**
animise *vii* fly away; *prt* **enimiseg**; *aug* **animisemagad**; *prt aug* **enimisemagak**
animishimo *vai* dance away; *1sg* **indanimishim**; *prt* **enimishimod**
animishkaa *vai* paddle away, go away in a canoe; *1sg* **indanimishkaa**; *prt* **enimishkaad**
animiwidoon *vti2* take s.t. away, carry s.t. away; *1sg* **indanimiwidoon**; *prt* **enimiwidood**
animiwizh /animiwiN-/ *vta* take s.o. away, carry s.o. away; *1sg* **indanimiwinaa**; *prt* **enimiwinaad**
animose *vai* walk away; *1sg* **indanimose**; *prt* **enimosed**
animosh *na* dog; *pl* **animoshag**; *dim* **animoons**; *also* **inday**
animoode *vai* crawl away; *1sg* **indanimoode**; *prt* **enimooded**
animoom *vta* carry s.o. away on one's back; *1sg* **indanimoomaa**; *prt* **enimoomaad**
animoomigo *vai* ride away on horseback; *1sg* **indanimoomig**; *prt* **enimoomigod**
animoondan *vti* carry s.t. away on one's back; *1sg* **indanimoondaan**; *prt* **enimoondang**
animoons *na* puppy; *pl* **animoonsag**
animwewebatoo *vai* run away making noise; *1sg* **indanimwewebatoo**; *prt* **enimwewebatood**
animwewebide *vii* speed away making noise, drive away making noise, fly away making noise; *prt* **enimwewebideg**; *aug* **animwewebidemagad**; *prt aug* **enimwewebidemagak**
animwewebizo *vai* speed away making noise, drive away making noise, fly away making noise; *1sg* **indanimwewebiz**; *prt* **enimwewebizod**
animwewetoo *vai* walk away making noise; *1sg* **indanimwewetoo**; *prt* **enimwewetood**
animwewidam *vai2* go away speaking; *1sg* **indanimwewidam**; *prt* **enimwewidang**
ani-naagozi *vai* go out of sight; *1sg* **indani-naagoz**; *prt* **eni-naagozid**
ani-naagwad *vii* go out of sight; *prt* **eni-naagwak**
aninaatig *na* maple; *pl* **aninaatigoog**; *loc* **aninaatigong**; *dim* **aninaatigoons**; *also* **ininaatig**
anishaa *pc* just for nothing, without purpose, just for fun, not really
anishinaabe *na* person, human (in contrast to non-human beings), Indian (in contrast to non-Indians), Ojibwe; *pl* **anishinaabeg**; *dim* **anishinaabens**
anishinaabe-bimaadizi *vai* live the Indian way; *1sg* **indanishinaabe-bimaadiz**; *prt* **enishinaabe-bimaadizid**
anishinaabe-gaagiigido *vai* speak in an Indian language (especially in Ojibwe); *1sg* **indanishinaabe-gaagiigid**; *prt* **enishinaabe-gaagiigidod**
anishinaabekaa *vii* there are many people, there are many Indians; *prt* **enishinaabekaag**
anishinaabekwe *na* Indian woman; *pl* **anishinaabekweg**; *dim* **anishinaabekwens**
anishinaabekwewi *vai* be an Indian woman; *1sg* **indanishinaabekwew**; *prt* **enishinaabekwewid**
anishinaabe-maawanjii'idiiwigamig *ni* Indian center; *pl* **anishinaabe-maawanjii'idiiwigamigoon**; *loc* **anishinaabe-maawanjii'idiiwigamigong**
anishinaabemo *vai* speak an Indian language (especially Ojibwe); *1sg* **indanishinaabem**; *prt* **enishinaabemod**
anishinaabemotaw *vta* speak an Indian language (Ojibwe) to s.o.; *1sg* **indanishinaabemotawaa**; *prt* **enishinaabemotawaad**
anishinaabemowin *ni* Indian language (especially Ojibwe); *pl* **anishinaabemowinan**
anishinaabewaki *ni* Indian country; *loc* **anishinaabewakiing**
anishinaabewi *vai* be human (in contrast to non-human beings), be Indian (in contrast to non-Indians), be Ojibwe; *1sg* **indanishinaabew**; *prt* **enishinaabewid**
anishinaabewibii'amaw *vta* write (s.t.) in Indian (Ojibwe) to s.o.; *1sg* **indanishinaabewibii'amawaa**; *prt* **enishinaabewibii'amawaad**
anishinaabewibii'an *vti* write s.t. in Indian (Ojibwe); *1sg* **indanishinaabewibii'aan**; *prt* **enishinaabewibii'ang**
anishinaabewibii'igan *ni* Indian (Ojibwe) writing, something written in Indian (Ojibwe); *pl* **anishinaabewibii'iganan**
anishinaabewibii'igaade *vii* be written in Indian (Ojibwe); *prt* **enishinaabewibii'igaadeg**; *aug* **anishinaabewibii'igaademagad**; *prt aug* **enishinaabewibii'igaademagak**
anishinaabewibii'ige *vai* write in Indian (Ojibwe); *1sg* **indanishinaabewibii'ige**; *prt* **enishinaabewibii'iged**
anishinaabewinikaadan *vti* call s.t. in Indian (Ojibwe); *1sg* **indanishinaabewinikaadaan**; *prt* **enishinaabewinikaadang**

anishinaabewinikaade *vii* be called in Indian (Ojibwe); *prt* **enishinaabewinikaadeg**; *aug* **anishinaabewinikaademagad**; *prt aug* **enishinaabewinikaademagak**
anishinaabewinikaazh /anishinaabewinikaaN-/ *vta* call s.o. in Indian (Ojibwe); *1sg* **indanishinaabewinikaanaa**; *prt* **enishinaabewinikaanaad**
anishinaabewinikaazo *vai* be called in Indian (Ojibwe); *1sg* **indanishinaabewinikaaz**; *prt* **enishinaabewinikaazod**
anishinaabewisidoon *vti2* write s.t. in Indian (Ojibwe) (e.g., a book); *1sg* **indanishinaabewisidoon**; *prt* **enishinaabewisidood**
anishinaabewisin *vii* be written in Indian (Ojibwe) (e.g., a book or document); *prt* **enishinaabewising**
anishinaabe-ziinzibaakwad *ni* maple sugar; *loc* **anishinaabe-ziinzibaakwadong**
anit *ni* fish spear; *pl* **anitiin**; *loc* **anitiing**; *dim* **anitiins**
aniw* *pr* those *inanimate plural demonstrative*, that, those *obviative demonstrative*; *also* **iniw**
aniib *na* elm; *pl* **aniibiig**; *loc* **aniibiing**; *dim* **aniibiins**
aniibiimin *ni* highbush cranberry; *pl* **aniibiiminan**; *dim* **aniibiiminens**
aniibiiminagaawanzh *na* highbush cranberry bush; *pl* **aniibiiminagaawanzhiig**; *loc* **aniibiiminagaawanzhiing**; *dim* **aniibiiminagaawanzhiins**
aniibiish *ni* leaf, tea; *pl* **aniibiishan**; *loc* **aniibiishing**; *dim* **aniibiishens**
aniibiishakik *na* teakettle; *pl* **aniibiishakikoog**; *loc* **aniibiishakikong**; *dim* **aniibiishakikoons**
aniibiishaaboo *ni* tea; *loc* **aniibiishaaboong**; *also* **aniibiish**
aniibiishaabooke *vai* make tea; *1sg* **indaniibiishaabooke**; *prt* **eniibiishaabooked**
aniibiishaabookewinini *na* Chinese, Oriental; *pl* **aniibiishaabookewininiwag**
aniibiishaabookewininiwi *vai* be Chinese, be Oriental; *1sg* **indaniibiishaabookewininiiw**; *prt* **eniibiishaabookewininiiwid**
aniibiishibag *ni* leaf; *pl* **aniibiishibagoon**; *loc* **aniibiishibagong**; *dim* **aniibiishibagoons**; *also* **aniibiish**
aniibiishikaa *vii* there are many leaves; *prt* **eniibiishikaag**; *aug* **aniibiishikaamagad**; *prt aug* **eniibiishikaamagak**
aniibiishike *vai* make tea; *1sg* **indaniibiishike**; *prt* **eniibiishiked**
anjiko *vai* be pregnant; *1sg* **indanjik**; *prt* **enjikod**
anokaadan *vti* work at s.t.; *1sg* **indanokaadaan**; *prt* **enokaadang**
anokaajigan *ni* manufacture, craft, something worked on, project; *pl* **anokaajiganan**; *loc* **anokaajiganing**; *dim* **anokaajigaans**
anokaazh /anokaaN-/ *vta* work at s.o.; *1sg* **indanokaanaa**; *prt* **enokaanaad**
anokii *vai* work; *1sg* **indanokii**; *prt* **enokiid**
anokii' *vta* make s.o. work; *1sg* **indanokii'aa**; *prt* **enokii'aad**
anokiikaazo *vai* pretend to work; *1sg* **indanokiikaaz**; *prt* **enokiikaazod**
anokiitaw *vta* work for s.o.; *1sg* **indanokiitawaa**; *prt* **enokiitawaad**
anokiitaage *vai* work for people; *1sg* **indanokiitaage**; *prt* **enokiitaaged**
anokiitaazo *vai* work for oneself; *1sg* **indanokiitaaz**; *prt* **enokiitaazod**
anokiiwigamig *ni* factory, workshop; *pl* **anokiiwigamigoon**; *loc* **anokiiwigamigong**
anokiiwikwe *na* worker (female); *pl* **anokiiwikweg**
anokiiwin *ni* work, job; *pl* **anokiiwinan**
anokiiwinini *na* worker; *pl* **anokiiwininiwag**
anooj *pc* various, all kinds
anooj gegoo *pr* a variety of things, various things; *also* **anooji-gegoo**
anookii *vai* hire, give an order, commission; *1sg* **indanookii**; *prt* **enookiid**
anoozh /anooN-/ *vta* hire s.o., give an order to s.o., commission s.o.; *1sg* **indanoonaa**; *prt* **enoonaad**
anwaataa *vai* finish (in work or an activity); *1sg* **indanwaataa**; *prt* **enwaataad**
anwaatin *vii* be calm weather; *prt* **enwaating**
anwebi *vai* rest; *1sg* **indanweb**; *prt* **enwebid**
anweshin *vai* rest lying down; *1sg* **indanweshin**; *prt* **enweshing**
anwi *ni* bullet, shotgun shell; *pl* **anwiin**; *loc* **anwiing**; *dim* **anwiins**
anwii-baashkizigan *ni* shotgun; *pl* **anwii-baashkiziganan**; *loc* **anwii-baashkiziganing**; *dim* **anwii-baashkizigaans**
anwiins *ni* twenty-two bullet; *pl* **anwiinsan**
apabiwin *ni* chair; *pl* **apabiwinan**; *loc* **apabiwining**; *dim* **apabiwinens**
apagajinaazhikamaw *vta* drive game for s.o.; *1sg* **indapagajinaazhikamawaa**; *prt* **epagajinaazhikamawaad**
apagajinaazhikaw *vta* drive s.o. as game; *1sg* **indapagajinaazhikawaa**; *prt* **epagajinaazhikawaad**
apagajinaazhikaage *vai* drive game; *1sg* **indapagajinaazhikaage**; *prt* **epagajinaazhikaaged**
apagidan *vti* throw s.t.; *1sg* **indapagidaan**; *prt* **epagidang**; *also* **apagidoon**
apagidaw *vta* throw (s.t.) at s.o.; *1sg* **indapagidawaa**; *prt* **epagidawaad**
apagidaadiwag /apagidaadi-/ *vai* they throw (s.t.) at each other; *1pl* **indapagidaadimin**; *prt* **epagidaadijig**
apagidoon *vti2* throw s.t.; *1sg* **indapagidoon**; *prt* **epagidood**; *also* **apagidan**
apagijige *vai* throw things; *1sg* **indapagijige**; *prt* **epagijiged**
apagijigewinini *na* pitcher (in baseball); *pl* **apagijigewininiwag**
apagizh /apagiN-/ *vta* throw s.o.; *1sg* **indapaginaa**; *prt* **epaginaad**
apagizo *vai* throw self down against something; *1sg* **indapagiz**; *prt* **epagizod**
apa' *vta* run with s.o. to a certain place; *1sg* **indapa'aa**; *prt* **epa'aad**
apa'idiwag /apa'idi-/ *vai* they run to a certain place together; *1pl* **indapa'idimin**; *prt* **epa'idijig**
apa'igo *vai* ride to a certain place with horses; *1sg* **indapa'ig**; *prt* **epa'igod**

apa'iwe *vai* run away from people to a certain place; *1sg* **indapa'iwe**; *prt* **epa'iwed**
apakwaan *ni* roofing; *pl* **apakwaanan**; *loc* **apakwaaning**; *dim* **apakwaanens**
apakwe *vai* put on a roof; *1sg* **indapakwe**; *prt* **epakwed**
apakweshkway *na* cattail mat, cattail; *pl* **apakweshkwayag**
apane *pc* always, all the time, continually
apangishin *vai* fall down against; *1sg* **indapangishin**; *prt* **epangishing**
apangisin *vii* fall down against; *prt* **epangising**
apanjige *vai* eat things with something else (e.g., butter with bread); *1sg* **indapanjige**; *prt* **epanjiged**
apatoo *vai* run to a certain place, run in a certain way; *1sg* **indapatoo**; *prt* **epatood**
apaabikinigan *ni* potholder; *pl* **apaabikiniganan**; *loc* **apaabikiniganing**; *dim* **apaabikinigaans**
apaabowe *vai+o* flavor (s.t.), season (s.t.); *1sg* **indapaabowe, indapaabowen**; *prt* **epaabowed**
apaakozigan *ni* kinnikinnick (tobacco and bark smoking mixture)
apaakozige *vai* make kinnikinnick; *1sg* **indapaakozige**; *prt* **epaakoziged**
apegish *pc* I wish that ...; *also* **ambegish*, ambesh***
apenimo *vai+o* rely on (s.t.), depend on (s.t.); *1sg* **indapenim, indapenimon**; *prt* **epenimod**
apenimonodan *vti* depend on s.t.; *1sg* **indapenimonodaan**; *prt* **epenimonodang**
apenimonodaw *vta* depend on s.o.; *1sg* **indapenimonodawaa**; *prt* **epenimonodawaad**; *also* **apenimodaw**
apibii'igan *ni* desk, writing surface; *pl* **apibii'iganan**; *loc* **apibii'iganing**; *dim* **apibii'igaans**
apibii'ige *vai* write on something; *1sg* **indapibii'ige**; *prt* **epibii'iged**
apiganegwaajigan *ni* moccasin cuff; *pl* **apiganegwaajiganan**; *loc* **apiganegwaajiganing**; *dim* **apiganegwaajigaans**; *also* **apigwanegwaason**
apigwayawegwaajigan *ni* collar; *pl* **apigwayawegwaajiganan**; *loc* **apigwayawegwaajiganing**; *dim* **apigwayawegwaajigaans**
apikan *ni* strap, harness; *pl* **apikanan**; *loc* **apikaning**; *dim* **apikaans**
apikaans *ni* fan belt; *pl* **apikaansan**
apikweshimo *vai* lie with head on something; *1sg* **indapikweshim**; *prt* **epikweshimod**
apikweshimon *ni* pillow; *pl* **apikweshimonan**; *loc* **apikweshimoning**; *dim* **apikweshimonens**
apikweshimoniigin *ni* pillowcase; *pl* **apikweshimoniiginoon**; *loc* **apikweshimoniiginong**; *dim* **apikweshimoniiginoons**
apishimo *vai* lie on something; *1sg* **indapishim**; *prt* **epishimod**
apishimon *ni* mattress, bed (made on the floor or ground); *pl* **apishimonan**; *loc* **apishimoning**; *dim* **apishimonens**
apishimonike *vai* make a bed (as in camp); *1sg* **indapishimonike**; *prt* **epishimoniked**
apishimoniigin *ni* sheet; *pl* **apishimoniiginoon**; *loc* **apishimoniiginong**; *dim* **apishimoniiginoons**
apishin *vai* lie as padding; *prt* **epishing**
apishkaamon *ni* mat on bottom of canoe; *pl* **apishkaamonan**; *loc* **apishkaamoning**; *dim* **apishkaamonens**
apisidaagan *na* floor piece of canoe; *pl* **apisidaaganag**; *loc* **apisidaaganing**; *dim* **apisidaagaans**
apisidoon *vti2* lay something on or under s.t. for protection; *1sg* **indapisidoon**; *prt* **episidood**
apisijigan *ni* protective mat, cushion; *pl* **apisijiganan**; *loc* **apisijiganing**; *dim* **apisijigaans**
apisin *vii* lie as padding; *prt* **epising**
apizideshinowin *ni* footstool; *pl* **apizideshinowinan**; *loc* **apizideshinowining**; *dim* **apizideshinowinens**
apizideyaakwa'igan *ni* cradle board footrest; *pl* **apizideyaakwa'iganan**
apii *pc* when, then, at the time
apiichaa *vii* be a certain distance; *prt* **epiichaag**; *aug* **apiichaamagad**; *prt aug* **epiichaamagak**
apiichi- *pv3* a certain extent, as much as
apiichibatoo *vai* run at a certain speed; *1sg* **indapiichibatoo**; *prt* **epiichibatood**
apiichibide *vii* drive at a certain speed, fly at a certain speed, run at a certain speed (e.g., a machine); *prt* **epiichibideg**; *aug* **apiichibidemagad**; *prt aug* **epiichibidemagak**
apiichibizo *vai* drive at a certain speed, fly at a certain speed, run at a certain speed (e.g., a machine); *1sg* **indapiichibiz**; *prt* **epiichibizod**
apiichigi *vai* grow up a certain extent, grow at a certain speed; *prt* **epiichigid**
apiichigidaazo *vai* be angry to a certain extent; *1sg* **indapiichigidaaz**; *prt* **epiichigidaazod**
apiichigin *vii* grow up a certain extent, grow at a certain speed; *prt* **epiichiging**
apiichi-giizhigad *vii* be so late in the day; *prt* **epiichi-giizhigak**
apiichishin *vai* lie to a certain depth; *prt* **epiichishing**
apiichisin *vii* lie to a certain depth; *prt* **epiichising**
apiichitaa *vai* be engaged in an activity to a certain extent, be so far along in an activity; *1sg* **indapiichitaa**; *prt* **epiichitaad**
apiingwe'igan *ni* moccasin vamp; *pl* **apiingwe'iganan**; *loc* **apiingwe'iganing**; *dim* **apiingwe'igaans**
apiitagim *vta* set a price of a certain height on s.o.; *1sg* **indapiitagimaa**; *prt* **epiitagimaad**
apiitagindan *vti* set a price of a certain height on s.t.; *1sg* **indapiitagindaan**; *prt* **epiitagindang**
apiitaginde *vii* have a price of a certain height; *prt* **epiitagindeg**; *aug* **apiitagindemagad**; *prt aug* **epiitagindemagak**
apiitaginzo *vai* have a price of a certain height; *prt* **epiitaginzod**
apiitaa *vii* be a certain height, be a certain thickness; *prt* **epiitaag**; *aug* **apiitaamagad**; *prt aug* **epiitaamagak**
apiitaanimad *vii* the wind has a certain speed; *prt* **epiitaanimak**

apiitendan *vti* be proud of s.t. to a certain extent, regard s.t. to a certain degree; *1sg* **indapiitendaan**; *prt* **epiitendang**
apiitendaagozi *vai* be valued to a certain extent, be at a certain rank; *1sg* **indapiitendaagoz**; *prt* **epiitendaagozid**
apiitendaagwad *vii* be valued to a certain extent, be at a certain rank; *prt* **epiitendaagwak**
apiitendi *vai* be absent a certain length of time, be gone a certain length of time; *1sg* **indapiitend**; *prt* **epiitendid**
apiitenim *vta* be proud of s.o. to a certain extent, feel about s.o. to a certain extent; *1sg* **indapiitenimaa**; *prt* **epiitenimaad**
apiitenimo *vai* be proud of oneself; *1sg* **indapiitenim**; *prt* **epiitenimod**
apiitinigozi *vai* weigh a certain amount, be so heavy; *1sg* **indapiitinigoz**; *prt* **epiitinigozid**
apiitinigwad *vii* weigh a certain amount, be so heavy; *prt* **epiitinigwak**
apiitizi *vai* be a certain age, have a certain thickness, have a certain extent; *1sg* **indapiitiz**; *prt* **epiitizid**
apiizikaa *vai* go a certain speed, go as fast as possible; *1sg* **indapiizikaa**; *prt* **epiizikaad**
asab *na* net; *pl* **asabiig**; *loc* **asabiing**; *dim* **asabiins**
asabaab *ni* thread; *pl* **asabaabiin**; *loc* **asabaabiing**; *dim* **asabaabiins**
asabaabiiwaatig *ni* spool (for thread); *pl* **asabaabiiwaatigoon**; *loc* **asabaabiiwaatigong**; *dim* **asabaabiiwaatigoons**
asabike *vai* make nets; *1sg* **indasabike**; *prt* **esabiked**
asabikeshiinh *na* spider; *pl* **asabikeshiinyag**
Asabikone-zaaga'iganiing *place* Nett Lake Reservation; *also* **Asabikonaye-zaaga'iganiing**
asanjigo *vai+o* cache (s.t.); *1sg* **indasanjig, indasanjigon**; *prt* **esanjigod**
asanjigoowigamig *ni* storage lodge; *pl* **asanjigoowigamigoon**; *loc* **asanjigoowigamigong**; *dim* **asanjigoowigamigoons**
asanjigoowin *ni* cache; *pl* **asanjigoowinan**; *loc* **asanjigoowining**; *dim* **asanjigoowinens**
asasawemin *ni* chokecherry; *pl* **asasaweminan**
asasaweminagaawanzh *na* chokecherry bush; *pl* **asasaweminagaawanzhiig**; *loc* **asasaweminagaawanzhiing**; *dim* **asasaweminagaawanzhiins**
asaawe *na* perch; *pl* **asaaweg**; *dim* **asaawens**
asekaan *na* tanned hide; *pl* **asekaanag**; *loc* **asekaaning**; *dim* **asekaanens**
asekaazh /asekaaN-/ *vta* tan s.o. (e.g., a hide); *1sg* **indasekaanaa**; *prt* **esekaanaad**
aseke *vai* tan hides; *1sg* **indaseke**; *prt* **eseked**
asekewin *ni* tanning
asemaa *na* tobacco; *loc* **asemaang**; *dim* **asemaans**
asemaawipwaagaans *na* cigarette; *pl* **asemaawipwaagaansag**; *also* **asemaa-opwaagaans**
asham *vta* feed (s.t.) to s.o.; *1sg* **indashamaa**; *prt* **eshamaad**
ashandiwin *ni* commodity food, rations; *pl* **ashandiwinan**
ashange *vai* feed people, serve food to people; *1sg* **indashange**; *prt* **eshanged**
ashangewigamig *ni* welfare office, commodity store; *pl* **ashangewigamigoon**; *loc* **ashangewigamigong**; *dim* **ashangewigamigoons**
ashangewikwe *na* social worker (female), welfare worker (female); *pl* **ashangewikweg**
ashangewinini *na* social worker, welfare worker; *pl* **ashangewininiwag**
ashaweshk *ni* sword; *pl* **ashaweshkoon**; *loc* **ashaweshkong**; *dim* **ashaweshkoons**
ashaageshiinh *na* crayfish, crab; *pl* **ashaageshiinyag**
ashi /aS-/ *vta* put s.o. in a certain place; *1sg* **indasaa**; *prt* **esaad**
ashi-aabita *nm* and a half
ashi-bezhig *nm* and one, eleven
ashi-bezhigo- *pv4* and one, eleven
ashi-bezhigo-diba'iganed *vii* be eleven o'clock; *prt* **eshi-bezhigo-diba'iganek**
ashidin *vta* hold s.o. against; *1sg* **indashidinaa**; *prt* **eshidinaad**
ashidinan *vti* hold s.t. against; *1sg* **indashidinaan**; *prt* **eshidinang**
ashigan *na* largemouth bass; *pl* **ashiganag**
ashi-ingodwaaso- *pv4* and six; *also* **ashi-ningodwaaso-***
ashi-ingodwaaswi *nm* and six, sixteen; *also* **ashi-ningodwaaswi***
ashi-ishwaaso- *pv4* and eight; *also* **ashi-nishwaaso***
ashi-ishwaaswi *nm* and eight, eighteen; *also* **ashi-nishwaaswi***
ashi-naanan *nm* and five, fifteen
ashi-naano- *pv4* and five
ashi-ningodwaaso-* *pv4* and six; *also* **ashi-ingodwaaso-**
ashi-ningodwaaswi* *nm* and six, sixteen; *also* **ashi-ingodwaaswi**
ashi-nishwaaso-* *pv4* and eight; *also* **ashi-ishwaaso-**
ashi-nishwaaswi* *nm* and eight, eighteen; *also* **ashi-ishwaaswi**
ashi-niso- *pv4* and three
ashi-niswi *nm* and three, thirteen
ashi-niiwin *nm* and four, fourteen
ashi-niiwo- *pv4* and four; *also* **ashi-niiyo-**
ashi-niiyo- *pv4* and four; *also* **ashi-niiwo-**
ashi-niizh *nm* and two, twelve
ashi-niizho- *pv4* and two
ashi-niizho-diba'iganed *vii* be twelve o'clock; *prt* **eshi-niizho-diba'iganek**
ashi-niizhwaaso- *pv4* and seven
ashi-niizhwaaswi *nm* and seven, seventeen
ashiwaa *vii* be dull; *prt* **eshiwaag**; *aug* **ashiwaamagad**; *prt aug* **eshiwaamagak**
ashi-zhaangaso- *pv4* and nine
ashi-zhaangaswi *nm* and nine, nineteen
ashki- *pv4* raw
ashkibagaa *vii* there are green leaves; *prt* **eshkibagaag**; *aug* **ashkibagaamagad**; *prt aug* **eshkibagaamagak**
ashkibagong inaande *vii* be leaf-green; *prt* **ashkibagong enaandeg**; *aug* **ashkibagong**

inaandemagad; *prt aug* **ashkibagong enaandemagak**
ashkibagong inaanzo *vai* be leaf-green; *prt* **ashkibagong enaanzod**
ashkide *vii* be incompletely cooked; *prt* **eshkideg**; *aug* **ashkidemagad**; *prt aug* **eshkidemagak**
ashkikomaan *ni* lead (metal); *loc* **ashkikomaaning**
ashkin *vii* be raw (as meat); *prt* **eshking**
ashkini *vai* be raw (as meat); *prt* **eshkinid**
ashkizo *vai* be incompletely cooked; *1sg* **indashkiz**; *prt* **eshkizod**
asho-wiidige *vai* be engaged; *1sg* **indasho-wiidige**; *prt* **esho-wiidiged**
asho-wiidigendiwag /asho-wiidigendi-/ *vai* they are engaged to each other; *1pl* **indasho-wiidigendimin**; *prt* **esho-wiidigendijig**
asigagim *vta* add s.o. together (e.g., money); *1sg* **indasigagimaa**; *prt* **esigagimaad**
asigagindan *vti* add s.t. together; *1sg* **indasigagindaan**; *prt* **esigagindang**
asigagindaaso *vai* add together, total up; *1sg* **indasigagindaas**; *prt* **esigagindaasod**
asigibii'igan *ni* number; *pl* **asigibii'iganan**; *loc* **asigibii'iganing**; *dim* **asigibii'igaans**
asigibii'ige *vai* write numbers; *1sg* **indasigibii'ige**; *prt* **esigibii'iged**
asigin *vta* gather s.o. up, collect s.o.; *1sg* **indasiginaa**; *prt* **esiginaad**
asiginan *vti* gather s.t. up, collect s.t.; *1sg* **indasiginaan**; *prt* **esiginang**
asiginaak *na* blackbird; *pl* **asiginaakwag**; *dim* **asiginaakoons**
asiginigaade *vii* be gathered up; *prt* **esiginigaadeg**; *aug* **asiginigaademagad**; *prt aug* **esiginigaademagak**
asiginigaazo *vai* be gathered up; *prt* **esiginigaazod**
asigizhooniyaawe *vai* collect money as a donation; *1sg* **indasigizhooniyaawe**; *prt* **esigizhooniyaawed**
asigobaan *ni* processed basswood bark fiber
asigobaani-mazinichigan *na* doll of processed basswood bark fiber; *pl* **asigobaani-mazinichiganag**; *dim* **asigobaani-mazinichigaans**
asin *na* stone, rock; *pl* **asiniig**; *loc* **asiniing**; *dim* **asiniins**
asinaab *na* net sinker; *pl* **asinaabiig**; *loc* **asinaabiing**; *dim* **asinaabiins**
asinii-bwaan *na* Assiniboin; *pl* **asinii-bwaanag**
asiniikaa *vii* there are many rocks, there are many stones; *prt* **esiniikaag**; *aug* **asiniikaamagad**; *prt aug* **esiniikaamagak**
asinii-miikana *ni* concrete road; *pl* **asinii-miikanan**; *loc* **asinii-miikanaang**; *dim* **asinii-miikanaans**
asinii-opwaagan *na* stone pipe; *loc* **asinii-opwaaganing**; *dim* **asinii-opwaagaans**
asiniiwan *vii* be of stone, be of rock; *prt* **esiniiwang**
ataw *vta* put (s.t.) in a certain place for s.o., play cards with s.o., bet with s.o.; *1sg* **indatawaa**; *prt* **etawaad**
ataadiwag /ataadi-/ *vai* they gamble with each other, they bet with each other; *1pl* **indataadimin**; *prt* **etaadijig**
ataadiwin *na* playing card; *pl* **ataadiwinag**; *loc* **ataadiwining**; *dim* **ataadiwinens**
ataage *vai* bet, gamble; *1sg* **indataage**; *prt* **etaaged**
ataagib *ni* algae; *loc* **ataagibiing**
ataaso *vai+o* store something, store (s.t.); *1sg* **indataas, indataason**; *prt* **etaasod**
ataasowin *ni* cupboard, closet; *pl* **ataasowinan**; *loc* **ataasowining**; *dim* **ataasowinens**
ataasoowigamig *ni* storage lodge, shed; *pl* **ataasoowigamigoon**; *loc* **ataasoowigamigong**; *dim* **ataasoowigamigoons**
ate *vii* be in a certain place; *prt* **eteg**; *aug* **atemagad**; *prt aug* **etemagak**
atis /atisw-/ *vta* dye s.o.; *1sg* **indatiswaa**; *prt* **etiswaad**; *also* **adis**
atisan *vti* dye s.t.; *1sg* **indatisaan**; *prt* **etisang**; *also* **adisan**
atisigan *ni* dye; *pl* **atisiganan**; *also* **adisigan**
atisige *vai* dye things; *1sg* **indatisige**; *prt* **etisiged**; *also* **adisige**
atiso *vai* be ripe; *prt* **etisod**; *also* **adiso**
atite *vii* be ripe; *prt* **etiteg**; *aug* **atitemagad**; *prt aug* **etitemagak**; *also* **adite**
atoobaan *ni* trough, tank; *pl* **atoobaanan**; *loc* **atoobaaning**
atoon *vti2* put s.t. in a certain place; *1sg* **indatoon**; *prt* **etood**
atoono *vai* make a canoe; *1sg* **indatoon**; *prt* **etoonod**
aw *pr* that *animate singular demonstrative*; *also* **a'aw, 'aw, 'a**
awakaan *na* domestic animal, slave; *pl* **awakaanag**
awakaanigamig *ni* barn; *pl* **awakaanigamigoon**; *loc* **awakaanigamigong**; *dim* **awakaanigamigoons**
awan *vii* be foggy, there is a fog; *prt* **ewang**
awanibiisaa *vii* be sprinkling rain, be misty; *prt* **ewanibiisaag**; *aug* **awanibiisaamagad**; *prt aug* **ewanibiisaamagak**
awanjish *pc* persistently, stubbornly, even though
awas *pc* go away!
awasagaam *pc* over across the water
awasajiw *pc* beyond the mountain, over across the mountain
awasayi'ii *pc* beyond it, over across it
awasaakwaa *pc* beyond the woods, over across the woods
awas-biboonong *pc* winter before last
awas-dagwaagong *pc* fall before last
awashime *pc* much more
awashtoyaa *na* blacksmith; *pl* **awashtoyaag**; *also* **awishtoyaa**
awasi- *pn* beyond, over across
awasishkode *pc* beyond the fire, over across the fire
awas-niibinong *pc* summer before last
awasonaago *pc* day before yesterday
awas-waabang *pc* day after tomorrow
awas-ziigwanong *pc* spring before last
awazo *vai* warm oneself by the fire; *1sg* **indawaz**; *prt* **ewazod**
awazowin *ni* heater; *pl* **awazowinan**; *loc* **awazowining**; *dim* **awazowinens**

awaazisii *na* bullhead; *pl* **awaazisiig**; *dim* **awaazisiins**; *also* **owaazisii, wawaazisii**
awedi *pr* that over there *animate singular demonstrative*; *also* **a'awedi**
awegonen *pr* what *inanimate interrogative; pl* **awegonenan**; *also* **wegonen**
awegwen *pr* I don't know who *animate dubitative*, I wonder who *animate dubitative; pl* **awegwenag**
awegwen igo *pr* whoever *animate dubitative*
awenen *pr* who *animate interrogative; pl* **awegnenag**
awenesh *pr* who, who then *animate interrogative*
awesiinh *na* wild animal; *pl* **awesiinyag**; *dim* **awesiins**
awi- *pv2* go over to; *after a personal prefix:* **a'o-**; *also* **'o-**
awibaa *vii* be calm, be windless; *prt* **ewibaag**; *aug* **awibaamagad**; *prt aug* **ewibaamagak**
awi' *vta* lend (s.t.) to s.o.; *1sg* **indawi'aa**; *prt* **ewi'aad**
awi'iwe *vai* lend (s.t.) to people, rent (s.t.) to people; *1sg* **indawi'iwe**; *prt* **ewi'iwed**
awiya *pr* somebody *animate indefinite*, anybody *animate indefinite*; *also* **awiiya**
aya'aa *pr* a being, someone, I don't remember who
ayaa *vai* be (in a certain place), *with a pv4* be in a certain state, *with a pv4* move a certain way; *1sg* **indayaa**; *prt* **eyaad**
ayaa *vii* be (in a certain place), *with a pv4* be in a certain state, *with a pv4* move a certain way; *prt* **eyaag**; *aug* **ayaamagad**; *prt aug* **eyaamagak**
ayaabe *na* buck; *pl* **ayaabeg**; *dim* **ayaabens**
ayaakw= < akw=
ayaan /ayaam-/ *vti3* have s.t., own s.t.; *1sg* **indayaan**; *prt* **eyaang**
ayaangodinong *pc* sometimes, occasionally; *also* **aangodinong**
ayaangwaamim *vta* warn s.o., caution s.o.; *1sg* **indayaangwaamimaa**; *prt* **eyaangwaamimaad**
ayaangwaamizi *vai* be careful, be cautious; *1sg* **indayaangwaamiz**; *prt* **eyaangwaamizid**
ayaanig= < inig=
ayaanigokw= < inigokw=
ayaapiich= < apiich=
ayaapiit= < apiit=
ayaapiiz= < apiiz=
ayaaw *vta* have s.o., own s.o.; *1sg* **indayaawaa**; *prt* **eyaawaad**
ayeko' *vta* make s.o. tired; *1sg* **indayeko'aa**; *prt* **eyeko'aad**
ayekozi *vai* be tired; *1sg* **indayekoz**; *prt* **eyekozid**
ayekwamanji'o *vai* feel tired; *1sg* **indayekwamanji'**; *prt* **eyekwamanji'od**
ayi'ii *pr* thing, something, I don't remember what
ayindan= < dan=
ayindap= < dap=
ayindas= < das=
ayindash= < dash=
ayindazh= < dazh=
ayindaa= < daa=
ayindood= < dood=
azaadi *na* poplar; *pl* **azaadiwag**; *loc* **azaadiing**; *dim* **azaadiins**
azhashki *ni* mud; *loc* **azhashkiing**
azhashkiikaa *vii* there is much mud; *prt* **ezhashkiikaag**; *aug* **azhashkiikaamagad**; *prt aug* **ezhashkiikaamagak**
azhashkiiwan *vii* be muddy; *prt* **ezhashkiiwang**
azhashkiiwizide *vai* have muddy feet; *1sg* **indazhashkiiwizide**; *prt* **ezhashkiiwizided**
azhe- *pv4* go back
azhebidoon *vti2* pull s.t. back; *1sg* **indazhebidoon**; *prt* **ezhebidood**
azhebizh /azhebiN-/ *vta* pull s.o. back; *1sg* **indazhebinaa**; *prt* **ezhebinaad**
azhebizo *vai* back up a vehicle; *1sg* **indazhebiz**; *prt* **ezhebizod**
azheboyaanaak *ni* oar; *pl* **azheboyaanaakoon**; *loc* **azheboyaanaakong**; *dim* **azheboyaanaakoons**
azheboye *vai* row (a boat); *1sg* **indazheboye**; *prt* **ezheboyed**
azhegaabawi *vai* stand back; *1sg* **indazhegaabaw**; *prt* **ezhegaabawid**
azhegiiwe *vai* go back, return; *1sg* **indazhegiiwe**; *prt* **ezhegiiwed**
azhe'o *vai* paddle backwards; *1sg* **indazhe'**; *prt* **ezhe'od**
azhen *vta* return s.o., take s.o. back, hand s.o. back; *1sg* **indazhenaa**; *prt* **ezhenaad**
azhenamaw *vta* return (s.t.) to s.o., take (s.t.) back to s.o.; *1sg* **indazhenamawaa**; *prt* **ezhenamawaad**
azhenamaage *vai* return (s.t.) to people; *1sg* **indazhenamaage**; *prt* **ezhenamaaged**
azhenan *vti* return s.t., take s.t. back, hand s.t. back; *1sg* **indazhenaan**; *prt* **ezhenang**
azheshkaa *vai* go backwards; *1sg* **indazheshkaa**; *prt* **ezheshkaad**
azhetaa *vai* go backwards, back up; *1sg* **indazhetaa**; *prt* **ezhetaad**
azhigan *ni* sock; *pl* **azhiganan**; *loc* **azhiganing**; *dim* **azhigaans**
azhigwa *pc* now, at this time, already, then; *also* **zhigwa, zhigo**
aabadad *vii* be useful, be used; *prt* **ayaabadak**
aabadizi *vai* be useful, be used; *1sg* **indaabadiz**; *prt* **ayaabadizid**
aaba' /aaba'w-/ *vta* undo s.o., untie s.o.; *1sg* **indaaba'waa**; *prt* **ayaaba'waad**
aaba'amaw *vta* undo (s.t.) for s.o., untie (s.t.) for s.o.; *1sg* **indaaba'amawaa**; *prt* **ayaaba'amawaad**
aaba'an *vti* undo s.t., untie s.t.; *1sg* **indaaba'aan**; *prt* **ayaaba'ang**
aaba'igaade *vii* be undone, be untied; *prt* **ayaaba'igaadeg**; *aug* **aaba'igaademagad**; *prt aug* **ayaaba'igaademagak**
aaba'igaazo *vai* be undone, be untied; *prt* **ayaaba'igaazod**
aaba'oodoo *vai* untie wild rice; *1sg* **indaaba'oodoo**; *prt* **ayaaba'oodood**
aaba'oodoon *vti2* untie s.t.; *1sg* **indaaba'oodoon**; *prt* **ayaaba'oodood**
aabajichigan *ni* tool; *pl* **aabajichiganan**; *loc* **aabajichiganing**; *dim* **aabajichigaans**
aabaji' *vta* use s.o.; *1sg* **indaabaji'aa**; *prt* **ayaabaji'aad**
aabajitoon *vti2* use s.t.; *1sg* **indaabajitoon**; *prt* **ayaabajitood**

aabanaabam *vta* turn and look back at s.o.; *1sg* **indaabanaabamaa**; *prt* **ayaabanaabamaad**
aabanaabandan *vti* turn and look back at s.t.; *1sg* **indaabanaabandaan**; *prt* **ayaabanaabandang**
aabanaabi *vai* turn and look back; *1sg* **indaabanaab**; *prt* **ayaabanaabid**
aabawaa *vii* be warm weather, be mild weather; *prt* **ayaabawaag**; *aug* **aabawaamagad**; *prt aug* **ayaabawaamagak**
aabaabika' /aabaabika'w-/ *vta* unlock s.o.; *1sg* **indaabaabika'waa**; *prt* **ayaabaabika'waad**
aabaabika'amaw *vta* unlock (s.t.) for s.o.; *1sg* **indaabaabika'amawaa**; *prt* **ayaabaabika'amawaad**
aabaabika'an *vti* unlock s.t.; *1sg* **indaabaabika'aan**; *prt* **ayaabaabika'ang**
aabaabika'igan *ni* key; *pl* **aabaabika'iganan**; *loc* **aabaabika'iganing**; *dim* **aabaabika'igaans**
aabaabika'igaade *vii* be unlocked; *prt* **ayaabaabika'igaadeg**; *aug* **aabaabika'igaademagad**; *prt aug* **ayaabaabika'igaademagak**
aabaabiigin *vta* unwind s.o. (as something string-like), unravel s.o. (as something string-like); *1sg* **indaabaabiiginaa**; *prt* **ayaabaabiiginaad**
aabaabiiginan *vti* unwind s.t. (as something string-like), unravel s.t. (as something string-like); *1sg* **indaabaabiiginaan**; *prt* **ayaabaabiiginang**
aabaakawad *vii* revive, clear off after a storm; *prt* **ayaabaakawak**
aabaakawi' *vta* revive s.o.; *1sg* **indaabaakawi'aa**; *prt* **ayaabaakawi'aad**
aabaakawizi *vai* revive, come to; *1sg* **indaabaakawiz**; *prt* **ayaabaakawizid**
aabibidoon *vti2* rip s.t. open; *1sg* **indaabibidoon**; *prt* **ayaabibidood**
aabibizh /aabibiN-/ *vta* rip s.o. open; *1sg* **indaabibinaa**; *prt* **ayaabibinaad**
aabidanokii *vai* work without stopping; *1sg* **indaabidanokii**; *prt* **ayaabidanokiid**
aabidaanagidoon *vai* talk without stopping; *1sg* **indaabidaanagidoon**; *prt* **ayaabidaanagidoong**
aabiding *pc* once, at one time
aabiji- *pv4* continually
aabijiibaa *vai* revive, come alive; *1sg* **indaabijiibaa**; *prt* **ayaabijiibaad**
aabiskon *vta* undo s.o. by hand; *1sg* **indaabiskonaa**; *prt* **ayaabiskonaad**
aabiskonan *vti* undo s.t. by hand; *1sg* **indaabiskonaan**; *prt* **ayaabiskonang**
aabiskose *vai* come undone, unravel; *prt* **ayaabiskosed**
aabiskose *vii* come undone, unravel; *prt* **ayaabiskoseg**; *aug* **aabiskosemagad**; *prt aug* **ayaabiskosemagak**
aabiskwegin *vta* unfold s.o. (as something sheet-like); *1sg* **indaabiskweginaa**; *prt* **ayaabiskweginaad**
aabiskweginan *vti* unfold s.t. (as something sheet-like); *1sg* **indaabiskweginaan**; *prt* **ayaabiskweginang**
aabita *pc* half
aabita- *pv4* half
aabita-niibino-giizis *na* July
aabitawayi'ii *pc* halfway along it
aabitawaabik *na* half-dollar
aabitawaabikizi *vai* be half (as something mineral, e.g., the moon); *prt* **ayaabitawaabikizid**
aabita-zhooniyaans *na* nickel (coin); *pl* **aabita-zhooniyaansag**
aabitaa-dibikad *vii* be midnight; *prt* **ayaabitaa-dibikak**
aabitoobadoon *vti2* fill s.t. half full (of liquid); *1sg* **indaabitoobadoon**; *prt* **ayaabitoobadood**
aabitoobazh /aabitoobaN-/ *vta* fill s.o. half full (of liquid); *1sg* **indaabitoobanaa**; *prt* **ayaabitoobanaad**
aabitoobii *vai* be half full (of liquid); *prt* **ayaabitoobiid**
aabitoobii *vii* be half full (of liquid); *prt* **ayaabitoobiig**; *aug* **aabitoobiimagad**; *prt aug* **ayaabitoobiimagak**
aabitoose *vii* be Wednesday; *prt* **ayaabitooseg**; *aug* **aabitoosemagad**; *prt aug* **ayaabitoosemagak**
aabitooshkin *pc* half a bag
aabitooshkinadoon *vti2* fill s.t. half full; *1sg* **indaabitooshkinadoon**; *prt* **ayaabitooshkinadood**
aabitooshkina' *vta* fill s.o. half full (of solids); *1sg* **indaabitooshkina'aa**; *prt* **ayaabitooshkina'aad**
aabitooshkine *vai* be half full (of solids); *prt* **ayaabitooshkined**
aabitooshkine *vii* be half full (of solids); *prt* **ayaabitooshkineg**; *aug* **aabitooshkinemagad**; *prt aug* **ayaabitooshkinemagak**
aaboodin *vta* turn s.o. inside out; *1sg* **indaaboodinaa**; *prt* **ayaaboodinaad**
aaboodinan *vti* turn s.t. inside out; *1sg* **indaaboodinaan**; *prt* **ayaaboodinang**
aaboozikan *vti* wear s.t. inside out; *1sg* **indaaboozikaan**; *prt* **ayaaboozikang**
aaboozikaw *vta* wear s.o. inside out; *1sg* **indaaboozikawaa**; *prt* **ayaaboozikawaad**
aaboozikaa *vai* turn inside out; *prt* **ayaaboozikaad**
aaboozikaa *vii* turn inside out; *prt* **ayaaboozikaag**; *aug* **aaboozikaamagad**; *prt aug* **ayaaboozikaamagak**
aadawa'am *vta* go with s.o. in a boat; *1sg* **indaadawa'amaa**; *prt* **ayaadawa'amaad**
aadizookaw *vta* tell a legend to s.o., tell a myth to s.o.; *1sg* **indaadizookawaa**; *prt* **ayaadizookawaad**
aadizookaan *na* traditional story, legend, myth, character of a legend or myth; *pl* **aadizookaanag**; *dim* **aadizookaanens**
aadizooke *vai* tell a traditional story, tell a legend, tell a myth; *1sg* **indaadizooke**; *prt* **ayaadizooked**
aadizookewinini *na* storyteller; *pl* **aadizookewininiwag**
aadodan *vti* tell a story of s.t.; *1sg* **indaadodaan**; *prt* **ayaadodang**
aagade *vai* burp; *1sg* **indaagade**; *prt* **ayaagaded**
aagask *na* prairie chicken; *pl* **aagaskwag**; *dim* **aagaskoons**
aagawe *vai* go out of sight (as around a corner); *1sg* **indaagawe**; *prt* **egaagawed**

aagim *na* snowshoe; *pl* **aagimag**; *loc* **aagiming**; *dim* **aagimens**
aagimaak *na* black ash (tree); *pl* **aagimaakwag**; *loc* **aagimaakong**; *dim* **aagimaakoons**
aagimose *vai* snowshoe; *1sg* **indaagimose**; *prt* **ayaagimosed**
aagonwetam *vai2* deny, contradict; *1sg* **indaagonwetam**; *prt* **ayaagonwetang**
aagonwetan *vti* deny s.t., contradict s.t., not believe s.t. said; *1sg* **indaagonwetaan**; *prt* **ayaagonwetang**
aagonwetaw *vta* deny what s.o. says, contradict s.o., not believe what s.o. says; *1sg* **indaagonwetawaa**; *prt* **ayaagonwetawaad**
aagonweyenim *vta* disbelieve s.o.; *1sg* **indaagonweyenimaa**; *prt* **ayaagonweyenimaad**
aajigade *na* coot, mud hen; *pl* **aajigadeg**; *dim* **aajigadens**
aajikode *vii* be notched; *prt* **ayaajikodeg**; *aug* **aajikodemagad**; *prt aug* **ayaajikodemagak**
aajim *vta* tell a story of s.o.; *1sg* **indaajimaa**; *prt* **ayaajimaad**
aajiningwa'on *ni* crutch; *pl* **aajiningwa'onan**; *loc* **aajiningwa'oning**; *dim* **aajiningwa'onens**
aajisag *pc* in the next room
aakoshkade *vai* have a stomachache; *1sg* **indaakoshkade**; *prt* **ayaakoshkaded**
aakoshkadekaw- *vta* give s.o. a stomachache; *in inverse forms: 1sg* **indaakoshkadekaagon**; *prt* **ayaakoshkadekaagod**
aakozi *vai+o* be sick, be sick (in s.t.), be ill; *1sg* **indaakoz, indaakozin**; *prt* **ayaakozid**
aakoziwin *ni* sickness, disease; *pl* **aakoziwinan**
aakoziwinikaa *vii* there is much sickness; *prt* **ayaakoziwinikaag**; *aug* **aakoziwinikaamagad**; *prt aug* **ayaakoziwinikaamagak**
aakoziikaazo *vai* pretend to be sick; *1sg* **indaakoziikaaz**; *prt* **ayaakoziikaazod**
aakoziishkaw- *vta* make s.o. sick (especially of a substance consumed); *in inverse forms: 1sg* **indaakoziishkaagon**; *prt* **ayaakoziishkaagod**
aakoziiwendaagozi *vai* be considered sickly; *prt* **ayaakoziiwendaagozid**
aakoziiwidaabaan *na* ambulance; *pl* **aakoziiwidaabaanag**; *loc* **aakoziiwidaabaaning**; *dim* **aakoziiwidaabaanens**
aakoziiwigamig *ni* hospital; *pl* **aakoziiwigamigoon**; *loc* **aakoziiwigamigong**; *dim* **aakoziiwigamigoons**
aakoziiwinaagozi *vai* look sick; *1sg* **indaakoziiwinaagoz**; *prt* **ayaakoziiwinaagozid**
aakwaadizi *vai* be fierce; *1sg* **indaakwaadiz**; *prt* **ayaakwaadizid**
aakwendam *vai2* have intense feelings or desires; *1sg* **indaakwendam**; *prt* **ayaakwendang**
aamiwag /aami-/ *vai* they spawn; *prt* **ayaamijig**
aamoo *na* bee, wasp; *pl* **aamoog**; *dim* **aamoons**
aamoo-wadiswan *ni* beehive, wasp nest; *pl* **aamoo-wadiswanan**; *loc* **aamoo-wadiswaning**
aamoo-ziinzibaakwad *ni* honey
aanakwad *ni* cloud; *pl* **aanakwadoon**; *loc* **aanakwadong**; *dim* **aanakwadoons**
aanapii *pc* when? *interrogative*; *also* **aanapiish, aaniin apii, aaniin iw apii**
aanapiish *pc* when? *interrogative*; *also* **aanapii, aaniin apii, aaniin iw apii**
aanawendan *vti* dislike s.t., reject s.t., find s.t. unsatisfactory; *1sg* **indaanawendaan**; *prt* **ayaanawendang**
aanawendaagozi *vai* be disliked, be rejected, be found unsatisfactory; *1sg* **indaanawendaagoz**; *prt* **ayaanawendaagozid**
aanawendaagwad *vii* be disliked, be rejected, be found unsatisfactory; *prt* **ayaanawendaagwak**
aanawenim *vta* dislike s.o., reject s.o., find s.o. unsatisfactory; *1sg* **indaanawenimaa**; *prt* **ayaanawenimaad**
aanawenjige *vai* dislike things, reject things, find things unsatisfactory; *1sg* **indaanawenjige**; *prt* **ayaanawenjiged**
aanawewizi *vai* be inadequate, be ineffective, do in vain; *1sg* **indaanawewiz**; *prt* **ayaanawewizid**
aanawi *pc* anyhow, although, despite, but
aandabi *vai* change seat; *1sg* **indaandab**; *prt* **ayaandabid**
aandagim *vta* count s.o. over; *1sg* **indaandagimaa**; *prt* **ayaandagimaad**
aandagindan *vti c* count s.t. over; *1sg* **indaandagindaan**; *prt* **ayaandaginang**
aandaginzo *vai* count over; *1sg* **indaandaginz**; *prt* **ayaandaginzod**
aandagoode *vai* change one's dress; *1sg* **indaandagoode**; *prt* **ayaandagoodeg**
aandakii *vai* live somewhere else, change countries; *1sg* **indaandakii**; *prt* **ayaandakiid**
aandaabikinigan *ni* gearshift; *pl* **aandaabikiniganan**; *loc* **aandaabikiniganing**; *dim* **aandaabikinigaans**
aandaabikinige *vai* shift gears; *1sg* **indaandaabikinige**; *prt* **ayaandaabikiniged**
aandaakonige *vai* change plans, change laws; *1sg* **indaandaakonige**; *prt* **ayaandaakoniged**
aandeg *na* crow; *pl* **aandegwag**; *dim* **aandegoons**
aandi *pc* where? *interrogative*; *also* **aandish, aaniindi**
aangodinong *pc* sometimes, occasionally; *also* **aaningodinong**
aanikanootan *vti* translate s.t., interpret s.t.; *1sg* **indaanikanootaan**; *prt* **ayaanikanootang**
aanikanootaw *vta* translate s.o., interpret s.o.; *1sg* **indaanikanootawaa**; *prt* **ayaanikanootawaad**
aanikanootaage *vai* translate for people, interpret for people; *1sg* **indaanikanootaage**; *prt* **ayaanikanootaaged**
aanikanootaagewinini *na* speaker (for others), interpreter, translator; *pl* **aanikanootaagewininiwag**
aanikanootaagozi *vai* be interpreted; *1sg* **indaanikanootaagoz**; *prt* **ayaanikanootaagozid**
aanikegamaa *vii* be a chain of lakes; *prt* **ayaanikegamaag**; *aug* **aanikegamaamagad**; *prt aug* **ayaanikegamaamagak**
aanike-ogimaa *na* someone next in succession to the leader (e.g., a vice president); *pl* **aanike-ogimaag**; *dim* **aanike-ogimaans**

aanikeshkaw *vta* stand in place of s.o., follow in s.o.'s steps, be next to s.o.; *1sg* **indaanikeshkawaa**; *prt* **ayaanikeshkawaad**
aanikeshkodaadiwag /aanikeshkodaadi-/ *vai* they are next to each other; *1pl* **indaanikeshkodaadimin**; *prt* **ayaanikeshkodaadijig**
aanikoobijigan *na* ancestor, great-grandparent, great-grandchild; *pl* **aanikoobijiganag**; *loc* **aanikoobijiganing**; *dim* **aanikoobijigaans**
aanikooshim *vta* lay s.o. joining something else; *1sg* **indaanikooshimaa**; *prt* **ayaanikooshimaad**
aanikooshin *vai* lie joining something else; *prt* **ayaanikooshing**
aanikoosidoon *vti2* lay s.t. joining something else; *1sg* **indaanikoosidoon**; *prt* **ayaanikoosidood**
aanikoosin *vii* lie joining something else; *prt* **ayaanikoosing**
aanimad *vii* wind blows wildly, be a disturbance, be danger; *prt* **ayaanimak**
aanimendam *vai2* suffer mentally, suffer emotionally; *1sg* **indaanimendam**; *prt* **ayaanimendang**
aanimi' *vta* abuse s.o., make s.o. suffer, cause s.o. trouble; *1sg* **indaanimi'aa**; *prt* **ayaanimi'aad**
aanimim *vta* reprimand s.o.; *1sg* **inaanimimaa**; *prt* **ayaanimimaad**
aanimitoon *vti2* abuse s.t.; *1sg* **indaanimitoon**; *prt* **ayaanimitood**
aanimizi *vai* be seriously ill, be very sick, suffer, be in distress; *1sg* **indaanimiz**; *prt* **ayaanimizid**
aanind *pc* some
aanish *pc* well, well then
aanishim *vta* discourage s.o.; *1sg* **indaanishimaa**; *prt* **ayaanishimaad**
aanizhiitam *vai2* change one's mind, quit working, decide against, give up; *1sg* **indaanizhiitam**; *prt* **ayaanizhiitang**
aaniin *pc* how?, why?, in what way? *interrogative*
aaniin *pc* hello!, greetings!
aaniin apii *pc* when? *interrogative*; *also* **aanapii, aanapiish, aaniin iw apii, aaniinwapii**
aaniin dash *pc* why? *interrogative*
aaniindi *pc* where? *interrogative*; *also* **aandi**
aaniin iwapii *pc* when? *interrogative*; *also* **aanapii, aanapiish, aaniin apii**
aaniin minik *pc* how many?, how much? *interrogative*
aaniin danaa *pc* well how?, well why?, why not?
aaniish *pc* how?, why?, in what way? *interrogative*, well now, you see
aaniish apii *pc* when? *interrogative*; *also* **anapii, aanin apii, aanapiish, aaniin iw apii**
aaniish naa *pc* well now, you see
aanji- *pv4* change
aanji-bimaadizi *vai* change one's life; *1sg* **indaanji-bimaadiz**; *prt* **ayaanji-bimaadizid**
aanjibii'an *vti* write s.t. over; *1sg* **indaanjibii'aan**; *prt* **ayaanjibii'ang**
aanji-gozi *vai* move to a new residence; *1sg* **indaanji-goz**; *prt* **ayaanji-gozid**
aanji' *vta* change s.o., make s.o. over; *1sg* **indaanji'aa**; *prt* **ayaanji'aad**
aanjitoon *vti2* change s.t., make s.t. over; *1sg* **indaanjitoon**; *prt* **ayaanjitood**
aano- *pv1* in vain, without result
aanzikan *vti* change s.t. with foot or body (e.g., clothes); *1sg* **indaanzikaan**; *prt* **ayaanzikang**
aanzikaw *vta* change s.o. with foot or body (e.g., clothes); *1sg* **indaanzikawaa**; *prt* **ayaanzikawaad**
aanzikonaye *vai* change one's clothes; *1sg* **indaanzikonaye**; *prt* **ayaanzikonayed**
aanzikonaye' *vta* change s.o.'s clothes; *1sg* **indaanzikonaye'aa**; *prt* **ayaanzikonaye'aad**
aanzinaago' *vta* change s.o.'s appearance, transform s.o.; *1sg* **indaanzinaago'aa**; *prt* **ayaanzinaago'aad**
aanzinaago'idizo *vai* change one's own appearance, transform oneself; *1sg* **indaanzinaago'idiz**; *prt* **ayaanzinaago'idizod**
aanzinaagotoon *vti2* change s.t.'s appearance, transform s.t.; *1sg* **indaanzinaagotoon**; *prt* **ayaanzinaagotood**
aanzinaagozi *vai* look changed; *1sg* **indaanzinaagoz**; *prt* **ayaanzinaagozid**
aanzinaagwad *vii* look changed; *prt* **ayaanzinaagwak**
aanziyaan *ni* man's apron (traditional dress), breech clout, diaper; *pl* **aanziyaanan**; *loc* **aanziyaaning**; *dim* **aanziyaanens**
aapidaanagidoon *vai* talk without stopping; *1sg* **indaapidaanagidoon**; *prt* **ayaapidaanagidoong**
aapideg *pc* without a doubt, certainly
aapidendi *vai* go and not return, be gone forever; *1sg* **indaapidend**; *prt* **ayaapidendid**
aapiji *pc* very, quite
aapijibatoo *vai* run away for good; *1sg* **indaapijibatoo**; *prt* **ayaapijibatood**
aapijinazh /aapijinaN-/ *vta* finally and completely kill s.o.; *1sg* **indaapijinanaa**; *prt* **ayaapijinanaad**
aapijinizhimo *vai* flee for good; *1sg* **indaapijinizhim**; *prt* **ayaapijinizhimod**
aapijishin *vai* have a bad fall, die from a fall; *1sg* **indaapijishin**; *prt* **ayaapijishing**
aapiji-wiidige *vai* be legally married; *1sg* **indaapiji-wiidige**; *prt* **ayaapiji-wiidiged**
aapiji-wiidige-mazina'igan *ni* marriage license; *pl* **aapiji-wiidige-mazina'iganan**
aas *ni* legging; *pl* **aasan**
aasamisag *ni* wall; *pl* **aasamisagoon**; *loc* **aasamisagong**
aasaakamig *ni* moss; *pl* **aasaakamigoon**
aasodoodooshimebizon *ni* brassiere; *pl* **aasodoodooshimebizonan**; *loc* **aasodoodooshimebizoning**; *dim* **aasodoodooshimebizonens**
aatayaa *pc man's expression of mild displeasure or disdain*; *also* **taayaa**
aate *vii* be extinguished; *prt* **ayaateg**; *aug* **aatemagad**; *prt aug* **ayaatemagak**
aatebidoon *vti2* turn s.t. out (e.g., stove or lamp); *1sg* **indaatebidoon**; *prt* **ayaatebidood**
aatebizh /aatebiN-/ *vta* put out a fire on s.o. with hands; *1sg* **indaatebinaa**; *prt* **ayaatebinaad**
aatebii *vai* sober up; *1sg* **indaatebii**; *prt* **ayaatebiid**
aate'an *vti* put s.t. out (e.g., fire or light), extinguish s.t.; *1sg* **indaate'aan**; *prt* **ayaate'ang**

aate'igan *ni* fire extinguisher; *pl* **aate'iganan**; *loc* **aate'iganing**; *dim* **aate'igaans**
aate'ishkodawewidaabaan *na* fire truck; *loc* **aate'ishkodawewidaabaaning**; *dim* **aate'ishkodawewidaabaanens**
aate'ishkodawewinini *na* fireman; *pl* **aate'ishkodawewininiwag**; *dim* **aate'ishkodawewininiins**
aatenaagozi *vai* appear to be extinguished (e.g., the moon or sun in an eclipse); *prt* **ayaatenaagozid**
aatewebinan *vti* put s.t. out quickly (e.g., fire or light); *1sg* **indaatewebinaan**; *prt* **ayaatewebinang**
aateyaabikishin *vai* be darkened (e.g. the moon or sun in an eclipse); *prt* **ayaateyaabikishing**
aatwaakogaabawi *vai* stand leaning against something; *1sg* **indaatwaakogaabaw**; *prt* **ayaatwaakogaabawid**
aatwaakoshim *vta* lean s.o. against (as something stick- or wood-like); *1sg* **indaatwaakoshimaa**; *prt* **ayaatwaakoshimaad**
aatwaakoshin *vai* lean against (as something stick- or wood-like); *1sg* **indaatwaakoshin**; *prt* **ayaatwaakoshing**
aatwaakosidoon *vti2* lean s.t. against (as something stick- or wood-like); *1sg* **indaatwaakosidoon**; *prt* **ayaatwaakosidood**
aatwaakosin *vii* lean against (as something stick- or wood-like); *prt* **ayaatwaakosing**
aatwaakowebin *vta* throw s.o. up against (as something stick- or wood-like); *1sg* **indaatwaakowebinaa**; *prt* **ayaatwaakowebinaad**
aatwaakowebinan *vti* throw s.t. up against (as something stick- or wood-like); *1sg* **indaatwaakowebinaan**; *prt* **ayaatwaakowebinang**
aawadaw *vta* haul (s.t.) for s.o.; *1sg* **indaawadawaa**; *prt* **ayaawadawaad**
aawadaaso *vai* haul something; *1sg* **indaawadaas**; *prt* **ayaawadaasod**
aawadaasoowidaabaan *na* truck; *pl* **aawadaasoowidaabaanag**; *loc* **aawadaasoowidaabaaning**; *dim* **aawadaasoowidaabaanens**
aawadoon *vti2* haul s.t.; *1sg* **indaawadoon**; *prt* **ayaawadood**
aawajimine *vai* haul wild rice; *1sg* **indaawajimine**; *prt* **ayaawajimined**
aawajinigaadan *vti* haul s.t. on one's shoulder; *1sg* **indaawajinigaadaan**; *prt* **ayaawajinigaadang**
aawajinigaazh /aawajinigaaN-/ *vta* haul s.o. on one's shoulder; *1sg* **indaawajinigaanaa**; *prt* **ayaawajinigaanaad**
aawajinige *vai* haul things on one's shoulder; *1sg* **indaawajinige**; *prt* **ayaawajiniged**
aawan *vii* be a certain thing; *prt* **ayaawang**
aawazh /aawaN-/ *vta* haul s.o.; *1sg* **indaawanaa**; *prt* **ayaawanaad**
aawazhiwe *vai* haul people; *1sg* **indaawazhiwe**; *prt* **ayaawazhiwed**
aawazhiwewidaabaan *na* van; *pl* **aawazhiwewidaabaanag**; *loc* **aawazhiwewidaabaaning**; *dim* **aawazhiwewidaabaanens**
aawekaazh /aawekaaN-/ *vta* recognize s.o.; *1sg* **indaawekaanaa**; *prt* **ayaawekaanaad**
aawenan *vti* recognize s.t. by sight, identify s.t. by sight; *1sg* **indaawenaan**; *prt* **ayaawenang**
aawenaw *vta* recognize s.o. by sight, identify s.o. by sight; *1sg* **indaawenawaa**; *prt* **ayaawenawaad**
aawendan *vti* recognize s.t., identify s.t.; *1sg* **indaawendaan**; *prt* **ayaawendang**
aawenim *vta* recognize s.o., identify s.o.; *1sg* **indaawenimaa**; *prt* **ayaawenimaad**
aawetan *vti* recognize s.t. by sound, identify s.t. by sound; *1sg* **indaawetaan**; *prt* **ayaawetang**
aawetaw *vta* recognize s.o. by sound, identify s.o. by sound; *1sg* **indaawetawaa**; *prt* **ayaawetawaad**
aawi *vai* be a certain thing or being; *1sg* **indaaw**; *prt* **ayaawid**
aayaapii *pc* every once in a while
aazhawagaazii *vai* wade across; *1sg* **indaazhawagaazii**; *prt* **ayaazhawagaaziid**
aazhawagaaziibatoo *vai* run across wading; *1sg* **indaazhawagaaziibatoo**; *prt* **ayaazhawagaaziibatood**
aazhawa'am *vai2* go across by boat; *1sg* **indaazhawa'am**; *prt* **ayaazhawa'ang**; *also* **aazhawa'o**
aazhawa'o *vai* go across by boat; *1sg* **indaazhawa'**; *prt* **ayaazhawa'od**; *also* **aazhawa'am**
aazhawa'oodoon *vti2* take s.t. across by boat, ferry s.t. across; *1sg* **indaazhawa'oodoon**; *prt* **ayaazhawa'oodood**
aazhawa'oozh /aazhawa'ooN-/ *vta* take s.o. across by boat, ferry s.o. across; *1sg* **indaazhawa'oonaa**; *prt* **ayaazhawa'oonaad**
aazhawayi'ii *pc* on the other side of it
aazhawaadagaa *vai* swim across; *1sg* **indaazhawaadagaa**; *prt* **ayaazhawaadagaad**
aazhawaakoshim *vta* lay s.o. across (as something stick- or wood-like); *1sg* **indaazhawaakoshimaa**; *prt* **ayaazhawaakoshimaad**
aazhawaakoshin *vai* lie across (as something stick- or wood-like); *1sg* **indaazhawaakoshin**; *prt* **ayaazhawaakoshing**
aazhawaakosidoon *vti2* lay s.t. across (as something stick- or wood-like); *1sg* **indaazhawaakosidoon**; *prt* **ayaazhawaakosidood**
aazhawaakosin *vii* lie across (as something stick- or wood-like); *prt* **ayaazhawaakosing**
aazhawaandawaagan *ni* foot bridge; *pl* **aazhawaandawaaganan**; *loc* **aazhawaandawaaganing**; *dim* **aazhawaandawaagaans**
aazhawaandawe *vai* climb across; *1sg* **indaazhawaandawe**; *prt* **ayaazhawaandawed**
aazhawibatoo *vai* run across; *1sg* **indaazhawibatoo**; *prt* **ayaazhawibatood**; *also* **aazhoobatoo**

aazhawigwaashkwani *vai* jump across; *1sg* **indaazhawigwaashkwan**; *prt* **ayaazhawigwaashkwanid**
aazhibik *ni* rock cliff; *pl* **aazhibikoon**; *loc* **aazhibikong**; *dim* **aazhibikoons**
aazhidem *vta* talk back to s.o., answer back to s.o.; *1sg* **indaazhidemaa**; *prt* **ayaazhidemaad**
aazhideyaatig *na* cross; *pl* **aazhideyaatigoog**; *loc* **aazhideyaatigong**; *dim* **aazhideyaatigoons**
aazhigidwebin *vta* throw s.o. over backwards; *1sg* **indaazhigidwebinaa**; *prt* **ayaazhigidwebinaad**
aazhigidwebinan *vti* throw s.t. over backwards; *1sg* **indaazhigidwebinaan**; *prt* **ayaazhigidwebinang**
aazhigijise *vai* turn over backwards, turn face up; *1sg* **indaazhigijise**; *prt* **ayaazhigijised**
aazhigijise *vii* turn over backwards, turn face up; *prt* **ayaazhigijiseg**; *aug* **aazhigijisemagad**; *prt aug* **ayaazhigijisemagak**
aazhigijishim *vta* lay s.o. over backwards, lay s.o. face up; *1sg* **indaazhigijishimaa**; *prt* **ayaazhigijishimaad**
aazhigijishin *vai* fall over backwards, lie face up; *1sg* **indaazhigijishin**; *prt* **ayaazhigijishing**
aazhigijisidoon *vti2* lay s.t. over backwards, lay s.t. face up; *1sg* **indaazhigijisidoon**; *prt* **ayaazhigijisidood**
aazhigijisin *vii* fall over backwards, lie face up; *prt* **ayaazhigijising**
aazhikwe *vai* scream; *1sg* **indaazhikwe**; *prt* **ayaazhikwed**
aazhogan *ni* bridge; *pl* **aazhoganan**; *loc* **aazhoganing**; *dim* **aazhogaans**
aazhoge *vai* go across water; *1sg* **indaazhoge**; *prt* **ayaazhoged**
aazhogeba'idiwag /aazhogeba'idi-/ *vai* they run across together; *1pl* **indaazhogeba'idimin**; *prt* **ayaazhogeba'idijig**
aazhogebizo *vai* drive across; *1sg* **indaazhogebiz**; *prt* **ayaazhogebizod**
aazhogedaabii'iwe *vai* drive across; *1sg* **indaazhogedaabii'iwe**; *prt* **ayaazhogedaabii'iwed**
aazhogewidoon *vti2* carry s.t. across, take s.t. across; *1sg* **indaazhogewidoon**; *prt* **ayaazhogewidood**
aazhogewizh /aazhogewiN-/ *vta* carry s.o. across, take s.o. across; *1sg* **indaazhogewinaa**; *prt* **ayaazhogewinaad**
aazhooba'idiwag /aazhooba'idi-/ *vai* they run across together; *1pl* **indaazhooba'idimin**; *prt* **ayaazhooba'idijig**
aazhoobatoo *vai* run across; *1sg* **indaazhoobatoo**; *prt* **ayaazhoobatood**; *also* **aazhawibatoo**
aazhoodamon /aazhoodamo-/ *vii* go across (as a road or trail); *prt* **ayaazhoodamog**
aazhoodaabii'iwe *vai* drive across; *1sg* **indaazhoodaabii'iwe**; *prt* **ayaazhoodaabii'iwed**
aazhoogaadebi *vai* sit with legs crossed; *1sg* **indaazhoogaadeb**; *prt* **ayaazhoogaadebid**
aazhookoodin *vta* infect s.o. with something; *1sg* **indaazhookoodinaa**; *prt* **ayaazhookoodinaad**
aazhooningwa'an *vti* wear s.t. across the shoulder; *1sg* **indaazhooningwa'aan**; *prt* **ayaazhooningwa'ang**
aazhooningwa'igan *na* bandolier bag; *pl* **aazhooningwa'iganag**; *dim* **aazhooningwa'igaans**; *also* **aazhooningwa'on**; *the usual Mille Lacs term is* **gashkibidaagan**
aazhooshkaa *vai* go across; *1sg* **indaazhooshkaa**; *prt* **ayaazhooshkaad**

B

ba- *pv2* toward the speaker, this way, here, hither *changed form of:* **bi-**
babagiwayaan *ni* shirt; *pl* **babagiwayaanan**; *loc* **babagiwayaaning**; *dim* **babagiwayaanens**; *also* **bagiwayaan**
babagiwayaanegamig *ni* tent; *pl* **babagiwayaanegamigoon**; *loc* **babagiwayaanegamigong**; *dim* **babagiwayaanegamigoons**; *also* **bagiwayaanegamig**
babagiwayaanegamigwegin *ni* canvas; *pl* **babagiwayaanegamigweginoon**
babagiwayaanekizin *ni* tennis shoe, canvas shoe; *pl* **babagiwayaanekizinan**; *loc* **babagiwayaanekizining**; *dim* **babagiwayaanekizinens**; *also* **bagiwayaanekizin**
babagiwayaaniigin *ni* cloth, cotton cloth; *pl* **babagiwayaaniiginoon**; *loc* **babagiwayaaniiginong**; *dim* **babagiwayaaniiginoons**; *also* **bagiwayaaniigin**
babaa- *pv2* going about
babaa-ayaa *vai* be around, wander about; *1sg* **imbabaa-ayaa**; *prt* **bebaa-ayaad**
babaabag= < bibag=
babaadagw= < badagw=
babaamadaawe *vai* go about trading, be a peddler; *1sg* **imbabaamadaawe**; *prt* **bebaamadaawed**
babaamadaawewinini *na* peddler; *pl* **babaamadaawewininiwag**; *also* **babaamadaawaagewinini**
babaamademo *vai* go about crying; *1sg* **imbabaamadem**; *prt* **bebaamademod**
babaamaadagaa *vai* swim about; *1sg* **imbabaamaadagaa**; *prt* **bebaamaadagaad**
babaamaadagaako *vai* go about on the ice; *1sg* **imbabaamaadagaak**; *prt* **bebaamaadagaakod**
babaamaadagaazii *vai* wade about; *1sg* **imbabaamaadagaazii**; *prt* **bebaamaadagaaziid**
babaamaada'e *vai* skate about; *1sg* **imbabaamaada'e**; *prt* **bebaamaada'ed**
babaamaadizi *vai* live about, travel about; *1sg* **imbabaamaadiz**; *prt* **bebaamaadizid**

babaamaadizii-makak *ni* suitcase; *pl* **babaamaadizii-makakoon**; *loc* **babaamaadizii-makakong**; *dim* **babaamaadizii-makakoons**
babaamaajimo *vai* spread the news about; *1sg* **imbabaamaajim**; *prt* **bebaamaajimod**
babaamaajimoo-mazina'igan *ni* newspaper; *pl* **babaamaajimoo-mazina'iganan**; *loc* **babaamaajimoo-mazina'iganing**; *dim* **babaamaajimoo-mazina'igaans**
babaamaanakwad *vii* clouds move about; *prt* **bebaamaanakwak**
babaamaashi *vai* be blown about, sail about; *1sg* **imbabaamaash**; *prt* **bebaamaashid**
babaamaasin *vii* be blown about, sail about; *prt* **bebaamaasing**
babaamendam *vai2* pay attention, worry; *1sg* **imbabaamendam**; *prt* **bebaamendang**
babaamendan *vti* pay attention to s.t., worry about s.t., bother s.t.; *1sg* **imbabaamendaan**; *prt* **bebaamendang**
babaamenim *vta* pay attention to s.o., worry about s.o., bother s.o.; *1sg* **imbabaamenimaa**; *prt* **bebaamenimaad**
babaamiba'idiwag /babaamiba'idi-/ *vai* they run about together; *1pl* **imbabaamiba'idimin**; *prt* **bebaamiba'idijig**
babaamibatoo *vai* run about; *1sg* **imbabaamibatoo**; *prt* **bebaamibatood**
babaamibide *vii* speed about, drive about, fly about; *prt* **bebaamibideg**; *aug* **babaamibidemagad**; *prt aug* **bebaamibidemagak**
babaamibizo *vai* speed about, drive about, fly about; *1sg* **imbabaamibiz**; *prt* **bebaamibizod**
babaamidaabii'iwe *vai* drive about; *1sg* **imbabaamidaabii'iwe**; *prt* **bebaamidaabii'iwed**
babaamigozi *vai* move one's residence about; *1sg* **imbabaamigoz**; *prt* **bebaamigozid**
babaaminizha' /babaaminizha'w-/ *vta* chase s.o. about; *1sg* **imbabaaminizha'waa**; *prt* **bebaaminizha'waad**
babaaminizha'an *vti* chase s.t. about; *1sg* **imbabaaminizha'aan**; *prt* **bebaaminizha'ang**
babaaminizha'ige *vai* chase things about; *1sg* **imbabaaminizha'ige**; *prt* **bebaaminizha'iged**
babaamise *vai* fly about; *1sg* **imbabaamise**; *prt* **bebaamised**
babaamise *vii* fly about; *prt* **bebaamiseg**; *aug* **babaamisemagad**; *prt aug* **bebaamisemagak**
babaamishimo *vai* dance about; *1sg* **imbabaamishim**; *prt* **bebaamishimod**
babaamishkaa *vai* paddle about, go about in a boat; *1sg* **imbabaamishkaa**; *prt* **bebaamishkaad**
babaamiwidoon *vti2* take s.t. about, carry s.t. about; *1sg* **imbabaamiwidoon**; *prt* **bebaamiwidood**
babaamiwizh /babaamiwiN-/ *vta* take s.o. about, carry s.o. about, guide s.o. about; *1sg* **imbabaamiwinaa**; *prt* **bebaamiwinaad**
babaamizi *vai* do business, go about on one's business; *1sg* **imbabaamiz**; *prt* **bebaamizid**
babaamose *vai* walk about; *1sg* **imbabaamose**; *prt* **bebaamosed**
babaamoode *vai* crawl about; *1sg* **imbabaamoode**; *prt* **bebaamooded**
babaamoomigo *vai* ride about on horseback; *1sg* **imbabaamoomig**; *prt* **bebaamoomigod**
babaazagw= < bazagw=
babig *na* flea; *pl* **babigwag**; *dim* **babigoons**
babimose *vai* walk about, take a stroll; *1sg* **imbabimose**; *prt* **bebimosed**
babiich= < bich=
babiichii *vai* put on one's shoes, put on one's moccasins; *1sg* **imbabiichii**; *prt* **bebiichiid**
babiigomakakii *na* toad; *pl* **babiigomakakiig**; *dim* **babiigomakakiins**
babiikw= < bikw=
babiinzikawaagan *ni* coat, jacket; *pl* **babiinzikawaaganan**; *loc* **babiinzikawaaganing**; *dim* **babiinzikawaagaans**
babiishag= < bishag=
babiiwaawan /babiiwaa-/ *vii* they are tiny; *prt* **bebiiwaagin**
babiiwiminagadoon /babiiwiminagad-/ *vii* they are tiny (as something ball-like); *prt* **bebiiwiminagakin**
babiiwiminagiziwag /babiiwiminagizi-/ *vai* they are tiny (as something ball-like); *prt* **bebiiwiminagizijig**
babiiwizhiinyiwag /babiiwizhiinyi-/ *vai* they are tiny *plural*; *1pl* **imbabiiwizhiinyimin**; *prt* **bebiiwizhiinyijig**
babiizigaakiz /babiizigaakizw-/ *vta* curl s.o.'s hair by heat; *1sg* **imbabiizigaakizwaa**; *prt* **bebiizigaakizwaad**
babiizigindibe *vai* have curly hair; *1sg* **imbabiizigindibe**; *prt* **bebiizigindibed**
babiizoge= < bizoge=
badagoshkan *vti* cover s.t. with body, lie protectively on s.t.; *1sg* **imbadagoshkaan**; *prt* **bedagoshkang**
badagoshkaw *vta* cover s.o. with body, lie protectively on s.o.; *1sg* **imbadagoshkawaa**; *prt* **bedagoshkawaad**
badagwana' /badagwana'w-/ *vta* cover s.o.; *1sg* **imbadagwana'waa**; *prt* **bedagwana'waad**
badagwana'an *vti* cover s.t.; *1sg* **imbadagwana'aan**; *prt* **bedagwana'ang**
badagwana'igaade *vii* be covered; *prt* **bedagwana'igaadeg**; *aug* **badagwana'igaademagad**; *prt aug* **bedagwana'igaademagak**
badagwana'igaazo *vai* be covered; *prt* **bedagwana'igaazod**
badagwana'ige *vai* cover things; *1sg* **imbadagwana'ige**; *prt* **bedagwana'iged**
badagwiingweshin *vai* lie with one's face covered; *1sg* **imbadagwiingweshin**; *prt* **bedagwiingweshing**
badaka' /badaka'w-/ *vta* stick something in s.o., prick s.o., use a fork on s.o.; *1sg* **imbadaka'waa**; *prt* **bedaka'waad**
badaka'an *vti* stick something in s.t., prick s.t., spear s.t., use a fork on s.t.; *1sg* **imbadaka'aan**; *prt* **bedaka'ang**

badaka'igan *ni* fork; *pl* **badaka'iganan**; *loc* **badaka'iganing**; *dim* **badaka'igaans**
badaka'ige *vai* stick something in things, prick things, spear; *1sg* **imbadaka'ige**; *prt* **bedaka'iged**
badakijin *vai* get pricked; *1sg* **imbadakijin**; *prt* **bedakijing**
badakibine'o *vai* stick a feather in one's hair or hat; *1sg* **imbadakibine'**; *prt* **bedakibine'od**
badakide *vii* stand up from a surface, be planted in; *prt* **bedakideg**; *aug* **badakidemagad**; *prt aug* **bedakidemagak**
badakidoon *vti2* stick s.t. in, plant s.t.; *1sg* **imbadakidoon**; *prt* **bedakidood**
badakise *vai* stick in a surface; *prt* **bedakised**
badakise *vii* stick in a surface; *prt* **bedakiseg**; *aug* **badakisemagad**; *prt aug* **bedakisemagak**
badakishim *vta* stick s.o. in, set s.o. in the ground; *1sg* **imbadakishimaa**; *prt* **bedakishimaad**
badakisidoon *vti2* stick s.t. in, set s.t. in the ground; *1sg* **imbadakisidoon**; *prt* **bedakisidood**
badakisijige *vai* stick things in, set things in the ground; *1sg* **imbadakisijige**; *prt* **bedakisijiged**
badakizh /badakiN-/ *vta* stick s.o. in, plant s.o. in; *1sg* **imbadakinaa**; *prt* **bedakinaad**
badakizo *vai* stand up from a surface, be planted in; *1sg* **imbadakiz**; *prt* **bedakizod**
bagakaabam *vta* see s.o. clearly; *1sg* **imbagakaabamaa**; *prt* **begakaabamaad**
bagakaabandan *vti* see s.t. clearly; *1sg* **imbagakaabandaan**; *prt* **begakaabandang**
bagakaabi *vai* see clearly; *1sg* **imbagakaab**; *prt* **begakaabid**
bagamaadagaa *vai* arrive swimming; *1sg* **imbagamaadagaa**; *prt* **begamaadagaad**
bagamaagan *ni* war club; *pl* **bagamaaganan**; *loc* **bagamaaganing**; *dim* **bagamaagaans**

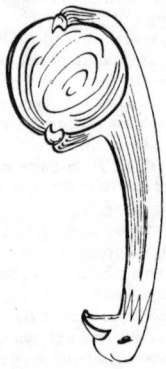

bagamaagan (war club)

bagamaajimo *vai* arrive with news; *1sg* **imbagamaajim**; *prt* **begamaajimod**
bagamaanimad *vii* wind comes in hard; *prt* **begamaanimak**
bagamaapi *vai* arrive laughing; *1sg* **imbagamaap**; *prt* **begamaapid**
bagamaashi *vai* be blown in, sail in; *1sg* **imbagamaash**; *prt* **begamaashid**
bagamaasin *vii* be blown in, sail in; *prt* **begamaasing**
bagami- *pv4* arriving
bagami-ayaa *vai* arrive; *1sg* **imbagami-ayaa**; *prt* **begami-ayaad**
bagami-ayaa *vii* arrive, come to be, come to pass; *prt* **begami-ayaag**; *aug* **bagami-ayaamagad**; *prt aug* **begami-ayaamagak**
bagamiba'idiwag /bagamiba'idi-/ *vai* they arrive on the run together; *1pl* **imbagamiba'idimin**; *prt* **begamiba'idijig**
bagamiba'iwe *vai* arrive fleeing from people; *1sg* **imbagamiba'iwe**; *prt* **begamiba'iwed**
bagamibatoo *vai* arrive on the run; *1sg* **imbagamibatoo**; *prt* **begamibatood**
bagamibide *vii* arrive speeding, arrive driving, arrive flying; *prt* **begamibideg**; *aug* **bagamibidemagad**; *prt aug* **begamibidemagak**
bagamibizo *vai* arrive speeding, arrive driving, arrive flying; *1sg* **imbagamibiz**; *prt* **begamibizod**
bagamibiisaa *vii* rain is on the way; *prt* **begamibiisaag**; *aug* **bagamibiisaamagad**; *prt aug* **begamibiisaamagak**
bagamidaabii'iwe *vai* arrive driving; *1sg* **imbagamidaabii'iwe**; *prt* **begamidaabii'iwed**
bagamigidaazo *vai* arrive mad; *1sg* **imbagamigidaaz**; *prt* **begamigidaazod**
bagamise *vai* arrive flying; *1sg* **imbagamise**; *prt* **begamised**
bagamise *vii* arrive flying; *prt* **begamiseg**; *aug* **bagamisemagad**; *prt aug* **begamisemagak**
bagamishkaa *vai* arrive paddling, arrive by boat; *1sg* **imbagamishkaa**; *prt* **begamishkaad**
bagamiwidoon *vti2* arrive carrying s.t.; *1sg* **imbagamiwidoon**; *prt* **begamiwidood**
bagamiwizh /bagamiwiN-/ *vta* arrive carrying s.o.; *1sg* **imbagamiwinaa**; *prt* **begamiwinaad**
bagamose *vai* arrive walking; *1sg* **imbagamose**; *prt* **begamosed**
bagamoode *vai* arrive crawling; *1sg* **imbagamoode**; *prt* **begamooded**
bagamoomigo *vai* arrive on horseback; *1sg* **imbagamoomig**; *prt* **begamoomigod**
bagandizi *vai* be lazy, be shiftless, be incompetent; *1sg* **imbagandiz**; *prt* **begandizid**
bagaan *na* nut, hazelnut, peanut; *pl* **bagaanag**; *loc* **bagaaning**; *dim* **bagaanens**
bagaani-bimide *ni* peanut butter; *also* **bagaanensi-bimide**
bagaaniminzh *na* hazelnut bush; *pl* **bagaaniminzhiig**; *loc* **bagaaniminzhiing**; *dim* **bagaaniminzhiins**
bagesaan *na* plum; *pl* **bagesaanag**; *loc* **bagesaaning**; *dim* **bagesaanens**
bagesaanaatig *na* plum tree; *pl* **bagesaanaatigoog**; *loc* **bagesaanaatigong**; *dim* **bagesaanaatigoons**
bagesaaniminagaawanzh *na* plum bush; *pl* **bagesaaniminagaawanzhiig**; *loc*

bagesaaniminagaawanzhiing; *dim* **bagesaaniminagaawanzhiins**
bagese *vai* play the dish game; *1sg* **imbagese**; *prt* **begesed**
bagida'waa *vai* fish with a net, set a net; *1sg* **imbagida'waa**; *prt* **begida'waad**
bagidam *vta* let s.o. drop from one's mouth; *1sg* **imbagidamaa**; *prt* **begidamaad**
bagidanaamo *vai* breathe, exhale; *1sg* **imbagidanaam**; *prt* **begidanaamod**
bagidandan *vti* let s.t. drop from one's mouth; *1sg* **imbagidandaan**; *prt* **begidandang**
bagidaabii *vai* fish with set lines; *1sg* **imbagidaabii**; *prt* **begidaabiid**
bagidendan *vti* release s.t. from one's mind; *1sg* **imbagidendaan**; *prt* **begidendang**
bagidenim *vta* release s.o. from one's mind, bury s.o., complete mourning for s.o.; *1sg* **imbagidenimaa**; *prt* **begidenimaad**
bagidenjigaazo *vai* be buried; *prt* **begidenjigaazod**
bagidenjige *vai* release things from one's mind, hold a funeral; *1sg* **imbagidenjige**; *prt* **begidenjiged**
bagidin *vta* set s.o. down, offer s.o., release s.o., let s.o. go, allow s.o.; *1sg* **imbagidinaa**; *prt* **begidinaad**
bagidinamaw *vta* set (s.t.) down for s.o., offer (s.t.) to s.o., release (s.t.) to s.o., allow (s.t.) to s.o.; *1sg* **imbagidinamawaa**; *prt* **begidinamawaad**
bagidinan *vti* set s.t. down, offer s.t., release s.t., let s.t. go, allow s.t.; *1sg* **imbagidinaan**; *prt* **begidinang**
bagidinigaade *vii* be set down, be offered, be released, be let go, be allowed; *prt* **begidinigaadeg**; *aug* **bagidinigaademagad**; *prt aug* **begidinigaademagak**
bagidinigaazo *vai* be set down, be offered, be released, be let go, be allowed; *prt* **begidinigaazod**
bagidinige *vai* set things down, offer things, release things, let things go, allow things, plant things in; *1sg* **imbagidinige**; *prt* **begidiniged**
bagidinise *vai* put wood on the fire; *1sg* **imbagidinise**; *prt* **begidinised**
bagidoom *vta* set s.o. down off one's back; *1sg* **imbagidoomaa**; *prt* **begidoomaad**
bagidoondan *vti* set s.t. down off one's back; *1sg* **imbagidoondaan**; *prt* **begidoondang**
bagijigan *ni* offering; *pl* **bagijiganan**; *dim* **bagijigaans**
bagijige *vai* make an offering; *1sg* **imbagijige**; *prt* **begijiged**
bagijiwane *vai* set down one's pack; *1sg* **imbagijiwane**; *prt* **begijiwaned**
bagijwebin *vta* release s.o. quickly, throw s.o. down quickly; *1sg* **imbagijwebinaa**; *prt* **begijwebinaad**
bagijwebinan *vti* release s.t. quickly, throw s.t. down quickly; *1sg* **imbagijwebinaan**; *prt* **begijwebinang**
bagiwayaan *ni* shirt, piece of cloth; *pl* **bagiwayaanan**; *loc* **bagiwayaaning**; *dim* **bagiwayaanens**; *also* **babagiwayaan**
bagiwayaanegamig *ni* tent; *pl* **bagiwayaanegamigoon**; *loc* **bagiwayaanegamigong**; *dim* **bagiwayaanegamigoons**; *also* **babagiwayaanegamig**
bagiwayaaneshkimod *ni* cloth bag; *pl* **bagiwayaaneshkimodan**; *loc* **bagiwayaaneshkimodaang**; *dim* **bagiwayaaneshkimodens**
bagiwayaanish *ni* cloth, rag; *pl* **bagiwayaanishan**; *loc* **bagiwayaanishing**; *dim* **bagiwayaanishens**; *also* **babagiwayaanish**
bagizo *vai* bathe, go swimming; *1sg* **imbagiz**; *prt* **begizod**
bagizowin *ni* bathtub; *pl* **bagizowinan**; *loc* **bagizowining**; *dim* **bagizowinens**
bagojiin *vta* gut s.o.; *1sg* **imbagojiinaa**; *prt* **begojiinaad**
bagone' /bagone'w-/ *vta* drill s.o., make a hole in s.o. using something; *1sg* **imbagone'waa**; *prt* **begone'waad**
bagone'an *vti* drill s.t., make a hole in s.t. using something; *1sg* **imbagone'aan**; *prt* **begone'ang**
bagone'igan *ni* drill; *pl* **bagone'iganan**; *loc* **bagone'iganing**; *dim* **bagone'igaans**
bagoneyaa *vii* have a hole; *prt* **begoneyaag**; *aug* **bagoneyaamagad**; *prt aug* **begoneyaamagak**
bagonezi *vai* have a hole; *prt* **begonezid**
bagosendam *vai2* wish, hope; *1sg* **imbagosendam**; *prt* **begosendang**
bagosendan *vti* wish for s.t., hope for s.t.; *1sg* **imbagosendaan**; *prt* **begosendang**
bagosenim *vta* wish of s.o., hope for s.o., have hope for s.o.; *1sg* **imbagosenimaa**; *prt* **begosenimaad**
bagoshkaa *vai* get a hole; *prt* **begoshkaad**
bagoshkaa *vii* get a hole; *prt* **begoshkaag**; *aug* **bagoshkaamagad**; *prt aug* **begoshkaamagak**
bagwa' /bagwa'w-/ *vta* patch s.o.; *1sg* **imbagwa'waa**; *prt* **begwa'waad**
bagwa'amaw *vta* patch (s.t.) for s.o.; *1sg* **imbagwa'amawaa**; *prt* **begwa'amawaad**
bagwa'an *vti* patch s.t.; *1sg* **imbagwa'aan**; *prt* **begwa'ang**
bagwa'igan *ni* patch; *pl* **bagwa'iganan**; *loc* **bagwa'iganing**; *dim* **bagwa'igaans**
bagwa'igaade *vii* be patched; *prt* **begwa'igaadeg**; *aug* **bagwa'igaademagad**; *prt aug* **begwa'igaademagak**
bagwa'igaazo *vai* be patched, wear patches; *prt* **begwa'igaazod**
bagwa'ige *vai* patch things; *1sg* **imbagwa'ige**; *prt* **begwa'iged**
bagwaj *pc* in the wilderness
bagwaji- *pv4* wild
bagwajipin *na* wild potato; *pl* **bagwajipiniig**; *loc* **bagwajipiniing**; *dim* **bagwajipiniins**; *also* **bagwaji-opin**
bagwana *pc* at random, anyhow
bagwanawizi *vai* be ignorant, be dumb; *1sg* **imbagwanawiz**; *prt* **begwanawizid**
bagwaakide *vii* have a hole burned in; *prt* **begwaakideg**; *aug* **bagwaakidemagad**; *prt aug* **begwaakidemagak**

bagwaakiz /bagwaakizw-/ *vta* burn a hole in s.o.; *1sg* **imbagwaakizwaa**; *prt* **begwaakizwaad**
bagwaakizan *vti* burn a hole in s.t.; *1sg* **imbagwaakizaan**; *prt* **begwaakizang**
bagwaakizo *vai* have a hole burned in; *prt* **begwaakizod**
bajiishka'ogaan *ni* tipi, lodge with pointed top; *pl* **bajiishka'ogaanan**; *loc* **bajiishka'ogaaning**; *dim* **bajiishka'ogaanens**

bajiishka'ogaan (tipi, lodge with pointed top)

bajiishkaa *vii* be pointed; *prt* **bejiishkaag**; *aug* **bajiishkaamagad**; *prt aug* **bejiishkaamagak**
bajiishkiga' /bajiishkiga'w-/ *vta* chop s.o. pointed; *1sg* **imbajiishkiga'waa**; *prt* **bejiishkiga'waad**
bajiishkiga'an *vti* chop s.t. pointed; *1sg* **imbajiishkiga'aan**; *prt* **bejiishkiga'ang**
bajiishkizi *vai* be pointed; *prt* **bejiishkizid**
bakade *vai* be hungry; *1sg* **imbakade**; *prt* **bekaded**
bakadekaazo *vai* pretend to be hungry; *1sg* **imbakadekaaz**; *prt* **bekadekaazod**
bakam *vta* bite s.o. through (e.g., something string-like); *1sg* **imbakamaa**; *prt* **bekamaad**
bakandan *vti* bite s.t. through (e.g., something string-like); *1sg* **imbakandaan**; *prt* **bekandang**
bakazhaawe *vai* clean a fish; *1sg* **imbakazhaawe**; *prt* **bekazhaawed**
bakaakadozo *vai* be thin (of a person), be skinny; *1sg* **imbakaakadoz**; *prt* **bekaakadozod**
bakaan *pc* different
bakaanad *vii* be different; *prt* **bekaanak**
bakaanige *vai* be secluded at first menses; *1sg* **imbakaanige**; *prt* **bekaaniged**
bakaanizi *vai* be different; *1sg* **imbakaaniz**; *prt* **bekaanizid**
bake *vai* go off to the side; *1sg* **imbake**; *prt* **beked**
bakebatoo *vai* run off to the side; *1sg* **imbakebatoo**; *prt* **bekebatood**
bakebide *vii* speed off to the side, drive off to the side; *prt* **bekebideg**; *aug* **bakebidemagad**; *prt aug* **bekebidemagak**
bakebizo *vai* speed off to the side, drive off to the side; *1sg* **imbakebiz**; *prt* **bekebizod**
bakegamaa *vii* lake goes off from another; *prt* **bekegamaag**; *aug* **bakegamaamagad**; *prt aug* **bekegamaamagak**
bakekazh /bakekaN-/ *vta* bypass s.o.; *1sg* **imbakekanaa**; *prt* **bekekanaad**
bakekazhiwe *vai* bypass people; *1sg* **imbakekazhiwe**; *prt* **bekekazhiwed**
bakemon /bakemo-/ *vii* go off to the side (as a road or trail); *prt* **bekemog**
baketigweyaa *vii* divide (as a river), branch (as a river); *prt* **beketigweyaag**; *aug* **baketigweyaamagad**; *prt aug* **beketigweyaamagak**
bakibidoon *vti2* snap s.t. off (e.g., something string-like), break s.t. off (e.g., something string-like); *1sg* **imbakibidoon**; *prt* **bekibidood**
bakibizh /bakibiN-/ *vta* snap s.o. off (e.g., something string-like), break s.o. off (e.g., something string-like); *1sg* **imbakibinaa**; *prt* **bekibinaad**
bakiboode *vii* break apart from rubbing (e.g., something string-like); *prt* **bekiboodeg**; *aug* **bakiboodemagad**; *prt aug* **bekiboodemagak**
bakiboozo *vai* break apart from rubbing (e.g., something string-like); *1sg* **imbakibooz**; *prt* **bekiboozod**
bakinaw *vta* win over s.o., beat s.o. in a contest; *1sg* **imbakinawaa**; *prt* **bekinawaad**
bakinaage *vai* win over people, beat people in a contest; *1sg* **imbakinaage**; *prt* **bekinaaged**
bakise *vai* part, break apart (e.g., something string-like); *prt* **bekised**
bakise *vii* part, break apart (e.g., something string-like); *prt* **bekiseg**; *aug* **bakisemagad**; *prt aug* **bekisemagak**
bakishkan *vti* snap s.t. off with foot or body (e.g., something string-like); *1sg* **imbakishkaan**; *prt* **bekishkang**
bakishkaw *vta* snap s.o. off with foot or body (e.g., something string-like); *1sg* **imbakishkawaa**; *prt* **bekishkawaad**
bakite' /bakite'w-/ *vta* hit s.o., strike s.o.; *1sg* **imbakite'waa**; *prt* **bekite'waad**
bakite'an *vti* hit s.t., strike s.t.; *1sg* **imbakite'aan**; *prt* **bekite'ang**
bakite'ibii'igan *ni* typewriter; *pl* **bakite'ibii'iganan**; *loc* **bakite'ibii'iganing**; *dim* **bakite'ibii'igaans**
bakite'igan *ni* hammer; *pl* **bakite'iganan**; *loc* **bakite'iganing**; *dim* **bakite'igaans**; *also* **bakite'igaans**
bakite'iganaak *ni* hammer handle; *pl* **bakite'iganaakoon**; *loc* **bakite'iganaakong**; *dim* **bakite'iganaakoons**
bakite'igaade *vii* be hit, be struck; *prt* **bekite'igaadeg**; *aug* **bakite'igaademagad**; *prt aug* **bekite'igaademagak**
bakite'igaans *ni* hand hammer; *pl* **bakite'igaansan**
bakite'igaazo *vai* be hit, be struck; *prt* **bekite'igaazod**
bakite'ige *vai* hit things, strike things; *1sg* **imbakite'ige**; *prt* **bekite'iged**
bakite'odiwag /bakite'odi-/ *vai* they hit each other, they strike each other; *1pl* **imbakite'odimin**; *prt* **bekite'odijig**
bakitejii'iganaak *ni* baseball bat; *pl* **bakitejii'iganaakoon**; *loc* **bakitejii'iganaakong**; *dim* **bakitejii'iganaakoons**

bakitejii'ige *vai* play baseball; *1sg* **imbakitejii'ige**; *prt* **bekitejii'iged**
bakitejii'igewinini *na* baseball player; *pl* **bakitejii'igewininiwag**
bakiteshin *vai* fall down hard; *1sg* **imbakiteshin**; *prt* **bekiteshing**
bakiteshka'ige *vai* thresh field crops; *1sg* **imbakiteshka'ige**; *prt* **bekiteshka'iged**
bakizh /bakizhw-/ *vta* snip s.o. off (e.g., something string-like); *1sg* **imbakizhwaa**; *prt* **bekizhwaad**
bakizhan *vti* snip s.t. off (e.g., something string-like); *1sg* **imbakizhaan**; *prt* **bekizhang**
bakobii *vai* go down into the water; *1sg* **imbakobii**; *prt* **bekobiid**
bakobiibatoo *vai* run into the water; *1sg* **imbakobiibatoo**; *prt* **bekobiibatood**
bakobiidaabaadan *vti* drag s.t. into the water; *1sg* **imbakobiidaabaadaan**; *prt* **bekobiidaabaadang**
bakobiidaabaazh /bakobiidaabaaN-/ *vta* drag s.o. into the water; *1sg* **imbakobiidaabaanaa**; *prt* **bekobiidaabaanaad**
bakobiigwaashkwani *vai* jump into the water; *1sg* **imbakobiigwaashkwan**; *prt* **bekobiigwaashkwanid**
bakobiise *vai* fall into the water; *1sg* **imbakobiise**; *prt* **bekobiised**
bakobiise *vii* fall into the water; *prt* **bekobiiseg**; *aug* **bakobiisemagad**; *prt aug* **bekobiisemagak**
bakobiiwebin *vta* throw s.o. into the water; *1sg* **imbakobiiwebinaa**; *prt* **bekobiiwebinaad**
bakobiiwebinan *vti* throw s.t. into the water; *1sg* **imbakobiiwebinaan**; *prt* **bekobiiwebinang**
bakobiiyaashi *vai* be blown into the water; *1sg* **imbakobiiyaash**; *prt* **bekobiiyaashid**
bakobiiyaasin *vii* be blown into the water; *prt* **bekobiiyaasing**
bakon *vta* skin s.o.; *1sg* **imbakonaa**; *prt* **bekonaad**
bakonige *vai* skin things; *1sg* **imbakonige**; *prt* **bekoniged**
bakwajibidoon *vti2* pull s.t. up, pluck s.t.; *1sg* **imbakwajibidoon**; *prt* **bekwajibidood**
bakwebidoon *vti2* tear a piece off of s.t.; *1sg* **imbakwebidoon**; *prt* **bekwebidood**
bakwebizh /bakwebiN-/ *vta* tear a piece off of s.o.; *1sg* **imbakwebinaa**; *prt* **bekwebinaad**
bakwega' /bakwega'w-/ *vta* chop a piece off s.o. (as something of wood); *1sg* **imbakwega'waa**; *prt* **bekwega'waad**
bakwega'an *vti* chop a piece off s.t. (as something of wood); *1sg* **imbakwega'aan**; *prt* **bekwega'ang**
bakwe' *vta* take a piece off s.o. using something; *1sg* **imbakwe'aa**; *prt* **bekwe'aad**
bakwe'an *vti* take a piece off s.t. using something; *1sg* **imbakwe'aan**; *prt* **bekwe'ang**
bakwem *vta* bite a piece off s.o.; *1sg* **imbakwemaa**; *prt* **bekwemaad**
bakwen *vta* take a piece off s.o. by hand; *1sg* **imbakwenaa**; *prt* **bekwenaad**
bakwenan *vti* take a piece off s.t. by hand; *1sg* **imbakwenaan**; *prt* **bekwenang**
bakwendan *vti* bite a piece off s.t.; *1sg* **imbakwendaan**; *prt* **bekwendang**
bakwene *vii* smoke, be smoky; *prt* **bekweneg**; *aug* **bakwenemagad**; *prt aug* **bekwenemagak**
bakwenibii *vai* choke while drinking; *1sg* **imbakwenibii**; *prt* **bekwenibiid**
bakwenige *vai* cut cards; *1sg* **imbakwenige**; *prt* **bekweniged**
bakwenishkaago *vai* choke on food; *1sg* **imbakwenishkaag**; *prt* **bekwenishkaagod**
bakweshkaa *vii* come off in pieces; *prt* **bekweshkaag**; *aug* **bakweshkaamagad**; *prt aug* **bekweshkaamagak**
bakwezh /bakwezhw-/ *vta* cut a piece off s.o.; *1sg* **imbakwezhwaa**; *prt* **bekwezhwaad**
bakwezhan *vti* cut a piece off s.t.; *1sg* **imbakwezhaan**; *prt* **bekwezhang**
bakwezhigan *na* bread, flour; *pl* **bakwezhiganag**; *loc* **bakwezhiganing**; *dim* **bakwezhigaans**
bakwezhiganaaboo *ni* gravy
bakwezhiganike *vai* make bread; *1sg* **imbakwezhiganike**; *prt* **bekwezhiganiked**
bakwezhiganikewigamig *ni* bakery; *pl* **bakwezhiganikewigamigoon**; *loc* **bakwezhiganikewigamigong**
bakwezhiganikewikwe *na* baker (female); *pl* **bakwezhiganikewikweg**
bakwezhiganikewinini *na* baker; *pl* **bakwezhiganikewininiwag**
bakwezhigani-makak *ni* flour box, bread box; *pl* **bakwezhigani-makakoon**; *loc* **bakwezhigani-makakong**; *dim* **bakwezhigani-makakoons**
bakwezhigaans *na* cookie, cracker, roll; *pl* **bakwezhigaansag**; *loc* **bakwezhigaansing**
bamendan *vti* care for s.t.; *1sg* **imbamendaan**; *prt* **bemendang**
bamenim *vta* care for s.o.; *1sg* **imbamenimaa**; *prt* **bemenimaad**
bami' *vta* support s.o., adopt s.o.; *1sg* **imbami'aa**; *prt* **bemi'aad**
bami'aagan *na* supported one, adopted one; *pl* **bami'aaganag**; *dim* **bami'aagaans**
bami'aagaans *na* pet; *pl* **bami'aagaansag**
bamoozhe *vai* take care of a child, baby-sit; *1sg* **imbamoozhe**; *prt* **bemoozhed**
bana' /bana'w-/ *vta* miss s.o. using something; *1sg* **imbana'waa**; *prt* **bena'waad**
bana'an *vti* miss s.t. using something; *1sg* **imbana'aan**; *prt* **bena'ang**
banajaanh *na* baby bird, nestling; *pl* **banajaanyag**
banaadad *vii* be spoiled, be damaged; *prt* **benaadak**
banaadendam *vai2* despair; *1sg* **imbanaadendam**; *prt* **benaadendang**
banaadendan *vti* despair of s.t., lose hope in s.t.; *1sg* **imbanaadendaan**; *prt* **benaadendang**
banaadenim *vta* despair of s.o., lose hope in s.o.; *1sg* **imbanaadenimaa**; *prt* **benaadenimaad**
banaadizi *vai* be spoiled, be damaged; *1sg* **imbanaadiz**; *prt* **benaadizid**
banaajibidoon *vti2* damage s.t. with hands; *1sg* **imbanaajibidoon**; *prt* **benaajibidood**
banaajibizh /banaajibiN-/ *vta* damage s.o. with hands; *1sg* **imbanaajibinaa**; *prt* **benaajibinaad**
banaaji' *vta* spoil s.o., damage s.o.; *1sg* **imbanaaji'aa**; *prt* **benaaji'aad**

banaajishin *vai* spoil; *1sg* **imbanaajishin**; *prt* **benaajishing**
banaajisin *vii* spoil; *prt* **benaajising**
banaajitoon *vti2* spoil s.t., damage s.t.; *1sg* **imbanaajitoon**; *prt* **benaajitood**
bande *vii* be singed; *prt* **bendeg**; *aug* **bandemagad**; *prt aug* **bendemagak**
bangan *vii* be peaceful, be quiet; *prt* **bengang**
bangate *vii* be a quiet house; *prt* **bengateg**; *aug* **bangatemagad**; *prt aug* **bengatemagak**
bangigaa *vii* drip down; *prt* **bengigaag**; *aug* **bangigaamagad**; *prt aug* **bengigaamagak**
bangishim *vta* drop s.o.; *1sg* **imbangishimaa**; *prt* **bengishimaad**
bangishimon /bangishimo-/ *vii* set as the sun; *conjunct* **bangishimog** in the west; *prt* **bengishimog**
bangishin *vai* fall; *1sg* **imbangishin**; *prt* **bengishing**
bangisidoon *vti2* drop s.t.; *1sg* **imbangisidoon**; *prt* **bengisidood**
bangisin *vii* fall; *prt* **bengising**
bangii *pc* a little, a little bit, few
bangiishenh *pc* a very little bit, just a little
bangiishenhwagad *vii* be a very little bit, be very few; *prt* **bengiishenhwagak**
bangiishenhwagizi *vai* be a very little bit, be very few; *prt* **bengiishenhwagizid**
bangiiwagad *vii* be a little bit, be few; *prt* **bengiiwagak**
bangiiwagizi *vai* be a little bit, be few; *prt* **bengiiwagizid**
banin *vta* let s.o. drop; *1sg* **imbaninaa**; *prt* **beninaad**
baninan *vti* let s.t. drop; *1sg* **imbaninaan**; *prt* **beninang**
banitan *vti* mishear s.t.; *1sg* **imbanitaan**; *prt* **benitang**
banitaw *vta* mishear s.o.; *1sg* **imbanitawaa**; *prt* **benitawaad**
banizi *vai* miss out; *1sg* **imbaniz**; *prt* **benizid**
banoomigo *vai* fall off a horse; *1sg* **imbanoomig**; *prt* **benoomigod**
banzan *vti* singe s.t.; *1sg* **imbanzaan**; *prt* **benzang**
banzo *vai* be singed; *1sg* **imbanz**; *prt* **benzod**
banzo /banzw-/ *vta* singe s.o.; *1sg* **imbanzwaa**; *prt* **benzwaad**
bapagone= < bagone=
bapagw= < bagw=
bapajiishk= < bajiishk=
bapak= < bak=
bapakine *na* grasshopper; *pl* **bapakineg**; *dim* **bapakinens**
bapakite= < bakite=
bapakwe= < bakwe=
bapakwaanaajiinh *na* bat; *pl* **bapakwaanaajiinyag**; *also* **apakwaanaajiinh**
bapan= < ban=
bapang= < bang=
bapas= < bas=
bapasangw= < basangw=
bapashanzhe= < bashanzhe=
bapashkw= < bashkw=
bapasidiye' /bapasidiye'w-/ *vta* spank s.o.; *1sg* **imbapasidiye'waa**; *prt* **bepasidiye'waad**
bapasikawe *vai* play shinny; *1sg* **imbapasikawe**; *prt* **bepasikawed**
bapasininjii'odizo *vai* clap one's hands; *1sg* **imbapasininjii'odiz**; *prt* **bepasininjii'odizod**
bapaw= < baw=
bapawaangeni *vai* shake one's wings; *1sg* **imbapawaangen**; *prt* **bepawaangenid**
bapazhib= < bazhib=
bapaadak= < badak=
bapaakwa'am *vai2* come out of the woods; *1sg* **imbapaakwa'am**; *prt* **bepaakwa'ang**
bapiimw= < bimw=
bapiin= < ban=
basadinaa *vii* be a valley; *prt* **besadinaag**; *aug* **basadinaamagad**; *prt aug* **besadinaamagak**
basangwaabapijigan *ni* blindfold; *pl* **basangwaabapijiganan**; *loc* **basangwaabapijiganing**; *dim* **basangwaabapijigaans**
basangwaabapizh /basangwaabapiN-/ *vta* blindfold s.o.; *1sg* **imbasangwaabapinaa**; *prt* **besangwaabapinaad**
basangwaabapizo *vai* be blindfolded; *1sg* **imbasangwaabapiz**; *prt* **besangwaabapizod**
basangwaabi *vai* shut one's eyes; *1sg* **imbasangwaab**; *prt* **besangwaabid**
bashanzhe' /bashanzhe'w-/ *vta* whip s.o.; *1sg* **imbashanzhe'waa**; *prt* **beshanzhe'waad**
bashanzhe'igan *ni* whip; *pl* **bashanzhe'iganan**; *loc* **bashanzhe'iganing**; *dim* **bashanzhe'igaans**
bashanzhe'ige *vai* whip; *1sg* **imbashanzhe'ige**; *prt* **beshanzhe'iged**
bashkobizh /bashkobiN-/ *vta* pluck s.o. (e.g., a bird); *1sg* **imbashkobinaa**; *prt* **beshkobinaad**
bashkwanige *vai* be toothless; *1sg* **imbashkwanige**; *prt* **beshkwaniged**
bashkwashkibidoon *vti2* pluck s.t. (as a plant), weed s.t.; *1sg* **imbashkwashkibidoon**; *prt* **beshkwashkibidood**
bashkwashkibijige *vai* weed things; *1sg* **imbashkwashkibijige**; *prt* **beshkwashkibijiged**
bashkwegin *ni* leather, hide; *pl* **bashkweginoon**; *loc* **bashkweginong**; *dim* **bashkweginoons**
bashkweginagooday *ni* buckskin dress; *pl* **bashkweginagoodayan**
bashkweginowayaan *ni* leather; *pl* **bashkweginowayaanan**
bashkweginwakizin *ni* hide moccasin; *pl* **bashkweginwakizinan**; *loc* **bashkweginwakizining**; *dim* **bashkweginwakizinens**; *also* **bashkwegino-makizin**
basidiye' /basidiye'w-/ *vta* slap s.o. on the rear; *1sg* **imbasidiye'waa**; *prt* **besidiye'waad**
basidiyeshkaw *vta* kick s.o. in the rear; *1sg* **imbasidiyeshkawaa**; *prt* **besidiyeshkawaad**
basikawaadan *vti* kick s.t.; *1sg* **imbasikawaadaan**; *prt* **besikawaadang**
basikawaazh /basikawaaN-/ *vta* kick s.o.; *1sg* **imbasikawaanaa**; *prt* **besikawaanaad**
basikwebizon *ni* headband; *pl* **basikwebizonan**; *loc* **basikwebizoning**; *dim* **basikwebizonens**
basindibe' /basindibe'w-/ *vta* slap s.o. on the head; *1sg* **imbasindibe'waa**; *prt* **besindibe'waad**

basiingwe' /basiingwe'w-/ *vta* slap s.o. on the face; *1sg* **imbasiingwe'waa**; *prt* **besiingwe'waad**
baswewe *vai* echo, resound; *1sg* **imbaswewe**; *prt* **beswewed**
baswewe *vii* echo, resound; *prt* **besweweg**; *aug* **baswewemagad**; *prt aug* **beswewemagak**
bawa'am *vai2* harvest wild rice, knock wild rice; *1sg* **imbawa'am**; *prt* **bewa'ang**
bawa'iganaak *na* rice knocker (stick for wild rice harvesting); *pl* **bawa'iganaakoog**; *loc* **bawa'iganaakong**; *dim* **bawa'iganaakoons**

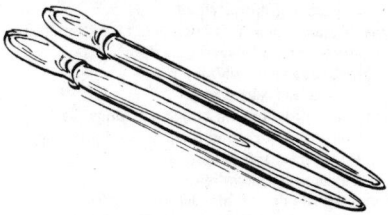

bawa'iganaakoog (rice knockers)

bawa'iminagaawanzh *na* pincherry bush; *pl* **bawa'iminagaawanzhiig**; *loc* **bawa'iminagaawanzhiing**; *dim* **bawa'iminagaawanzhiins**
bawa'iminaan *ni* pincherry; *pl* **bawa'iminaanan**
bawaadan *vti* dream of s.t.; *1sg* **imbawaadaan**; *prt* **bewaadang**
bawaagone' /bawaagone'w-/ *vta* brush snow off s.o. using something; *1sg* **imbawaagone'waa**; *prt* **bewaagone'waad**
bawaagone'an *vti* brush snow off s.t. using something; *1sg* **imbawaagone'aan**; *prt* **bewaagone'ang**
bawaagonen *vta* brush snow off s.o. by hand; *1sg* **imbawaagonenaa**; *prt* **bewaagonenaad**
bawaagonenan *vti* brush snow off s.t. by hand; *1sg* **imbawaagonenaan**; *prt* **bewaagonenang**
bawaajige *vai* have dreams; *1sg* **imbawaajige**; *prt* **bewaajiged**
bawaazh /bawaaN-/ *vta* dream of s.o.; *1sg* **imbawaanaa**; *prt* **bewaanaad**
bawega' /bawega'w-/ *vta* brush s.o. using something (as something sheet-like); *1sg* **imbawega'waa**; *prt* **bewega'waad**
bawega'an *vti* brush s.t. using something (as something sheet-like); *1sg* **imbawega'aan**; *prt* **bewega'ang**
bawegin *vta* shake s.o. out (as something sheet-like); *1sg* **imbaweginaa**; *prt* **beweginaad**
baweginan *vti* shake s.t. out (as something sheet-like); *1sg* **imbaweginaan**; *prt* **beweginang**
bawin *vta* shake s.o.; *1sg* **imbawinaa**; *prt* **bewinaad**
bawinan *vti* shake s.t.; *1sg* **imbawinaan**; *prt* **bewinang**
bazagokadoon *vti2* glue s.t.; *1sg* **imbazagokadoon**; *prt* **bezagokadood**
bazagokazh /bazagokaN-/ *vta* glue s.o.; *1sg* **imbazagokanaa**; *prt* **bezagokanaad**
bazagoke *vai* stick, adhere; *prt* **bezagoked**
bazagoke *vii* stick, adhere; *prt* **bezagokeg**; *aug* **bazagokemagad**; *prt aug* **bezagokemagak**
bazagozi *vai* be sticky; *1sg* **imbazagoz**; *prt* **bezagozid**
bazagwaa *vii* be sticky; *prt* **bezagwaag**; *aug* **bazagwaamagad**; *prt aug* **bezagwaamagak**
bazhiba' /bazhiba'w-/ *vta* stab s.o.; *1sg* **imbazhiba'waa**; *prt* **bezhiba'waad**
bazhiba'an *vti* stab s.t.; *1sg* **imbazhiba'aan**; *prt* **bezhiba'ang**
bazhiba'ige *vai* spear things; *1sg* **imbazhiba'ige**; *prt* **bezhiba'iged**
bazhidebii *vii* overflow (as a liquid); *prt* **bezhidebiig**; *aug* **bazhidebiimagad**; *prt aug* **bezhidebiimagak**
bazigonjise *vai* stand up suddenly; *1sg* **imbazigonjise**; *prt* **bezigonjised**
bazigwii *vai* stand up; *1sg* **imbazigwii**; *prt* **bezigwiid**
bazikwa'o *vai* take off into the air; *1sg* **imbazikwa'**; *prt* **bezikwa'od**
baa- *pv2* about a place (locally distributed)
baabii' *vta* keep waiting for s.o.; *1sg* **imbaabii'aa**; *prt* **bayaabii'aad**
baabii'o *vai* keep waiting; *1sg* **imbaabii'**; *prt* **bayaabii'od**
baabiitoon *vti2* keep waiting for s.t.; *1sg* **imbaabiitoon**; *prt* **bayaabiitood**
baaboonaw= < bwaanaw=
baaga'adowaan *ni* lacrosse stick; *pl* **baaga'adowaanan**
baaga'adowe *vai* play lacrosse; *1sg* **imbaaga'adowe**; *prt* **bayaaga'adowed**
baaga'akokwaan *ni* drumstick for hand drum; *pl* **baaga'akokwaanan**; *dim* **baaga'akokwaanens**
baaga'akokwe *vai* pound on drum; *1sg* **imbaaga'akokwe**; *prt* **bayaaga'akokwed**
baagijaane *vai* have a swollen nose; *1sg* **imbaagijaane**; *prt* **bayaagijaaned**
baagijigaade *vii* be struck by lightning; *prt* **bayaagijigaadeg**; *aug* **baagijigaademagad**; *prt aug* **bayaagijigaademagak**
baagijigaazo *vai* be struck by lightning; *prt* **bayaagijigaazod**
baaginiinjii *vai* have a swollen hand; *1sg* **imbaaginiinjii**; *prt* **bayaaginiinjiid**
baaginiishkwe *vai* have a swollen gland (lymph node); *1sg* **imbaaginiishkwe**; *prt* **bayaaginiishkwed**
baagishi *vai* be swollen; *1sg* **imbaagish**; *prt* **bayaagishid**
baagishkiinzhigwe *vai* have swollen eyes; *1sg* **imbaagishkiinzhigwe**; *prt* **bayaagishkiinzhigwed**
baagisin *vii* be swollen; *prt* **bayaagising**
baagizide *vai* have a swollen foot; *1sg* **imbaagizide**; *prt* **bayaagizided**
baagiingwe *vai* have a swollen face; *1sg* **imbaagiingwe**; *prt* **bayaagiingwed**
baagwaa *vii* be shallow; *prt* **bayaagwaag**; *aug* **baagwaamagad**; *prt aug* **bayaagwaamagak**

baaka'aakwenh *na* chicken; *pl* **baaka'aakwenyag**; *dim* **baaka'aakwens**
baaka'aakwenhwaaboo *ni* chicken soup; *loc* **baaka'aakwenhwaaboong**
baaka'aakwenhwigamig *ni* chicken coop; *pl* **baaka'aakwenhwigamigoon**; *loc* **baaka'aakwenhwigamigong**; *dim* **baaka'aakwenhwigamigoons**
baakaakonamaw *vta* open (s.t.) for s.o. (as something stick- or wood-like, e.g., a door); *1sg* **imbaakaakonamawaa**; *prt* **bayaakaakonamawaad**
baakaakonan *vti* open s.t. (as something stick- or wood-like, e.g., a door); *1sg* **imbaakaakonaan**; *prt* **bayaakaakonang**
baakaakonigaade *vii* be opened (as something stick- or wood-like, e.g., a door); *prt* **bayaakaakonigaadeg**; *aug* **baakaakonigaademagad**; *prt aug* **bayaakaakonigaademagak**
baakaakose *vii* fly open (as something stick- or wood-like, e.g., a door); *prt* **bayaakaakoseg**; *aug* **baakaakosemagad**; *prt aug* **bayaakaakosemagak**
baakaakosin *vii* be open (as something stick- or wood-like, e.g., a door); *prt* **bayaakaakosing**
baakaakowebinan *vti* fling s.t. open (as something stick- or wood-like, e.g., a door); *1sg* **imbaakaakowebinaan**; *prt* **bayaakaakowebinang**
baakaakozhigan *ni* can opener; *pl* **baakaakozhiganan**; *loc* **baakaakozhiganing**; *dim* **baakaakozhigaans**
baakibii'an *vii* ice clears off the lake; *prt* **bayaakibii'ang**
baakin *vta* uncover s.o., open s.o. up; *1sg* **imbaakinaa**; *prt* **bayaakinaad**
baakinamaw *vta* uncover (s.t.) for s.o.; *1sg* **imbaakinamawaa**; *prt* **bayaakinamawaad**
baakinan *vti* uncover s.t., open s.t. up; *1sg* **imbaakinaan**; *prt* **bayaakinang**
baakinige *vai* uncover things, open things up; *1sg* **imbaakinige**; *prt* **bayaakiniged**
baakise *vai* come uncovered, come open, fly open; *prt* **bayaakised**
baakise *vii* come uncovered, come open, fly open; *prt* **bayaakiseg**; *aug* **baakisemagad**; *prt aug* **bayaakisemagak**
baakishin *vai* lie uncovered, be open; *prt* **bayaakishing**
baakisin *vii* lie uncovered, be open; *prt* **bayaakising**
baakoshim *vta* leave s.o. uncovered; *1sg* **imbaakoshimaa**; *prt* **bayaakoshimaad**
baakosidoon *vti2* leave s.t. uncovered; *1sg* **imbaakosidoon**; *prt* **bayaakosidood**
baamaa *pc* later; *also* **baanimaa**
baamaapii *pc* later, after a while; *also* **baanimaa apii, baanimaapii**
baanimaa *pc* later, after a while; *also* **baamaa**
baanimaa apii *pc* later, after a while; *also* **baanimaapii, baamaapii**
baanizhan *vti* cut s.t. into strips; *1sg* **imbaanizhaan**; *prt* **bayaanizhang**
baanizhaawe *vai* cut meat into strips for preservation; *1sg* **imbaanizhaawe**; *prt* **bayaanizhaawed**
baapagishkaa *vai* tremble, shake; *1sg* **imbaapagishkaa**; *prt* **bayaapagishkaad**
baapagishkaa *vii* tremble, shake; *prt* **bayaapagishkaag**; *aug* **baapagishkaamagad**; *prt aug* **bayaapagishkaamagak**
baapaagaakwa' /baapaagaakwa'w-/ *vta* knock on s.o. (as something stick- or wood-like); *1sg* **imbaapaagaakwa'waa**; *prt* **bayaapaagaakwa'waad**
baapaagaakwa'an *vti* knock on s.t. (as something stick- or wood-like, e.g., a door); *1sg* **imbaapaagaakwa'aan**; *prt* **bayaapaagaakwa'ang**
baapaagaakwa'ige *vai* knock on things (as something stick- or wood-like, e.g., a door); *1sg* **imbaapaagaakwa'ige**; *prt* **bayaapaagaakwa'iged**
baapaagimaak *na* white ash (tree); *pl* **baapaagimaakwag**; *loc* **baapaagimaakong**; *dim* **baapaagimaakoons**
baapaagokozh /baapaagokoN-/ *vta* give s.o. a haircut; *1sg* **imbaapaagokonaa**; *prt* **bayaapaagokonaad**
baapaagokozhiwewigamig *ni* barber shop, hairdressing salon; *pl* **baapaagokozhiwewigamigoon**; *loc* **baapaagokozhiwewigamigong**
baapaagokozhiwewikwe *na* hairdresser (female); *pl* **baapaagokozhiwewikweg**
baapaagokozhiwewinini *na* barber, hairdresser (male); *pl* **baapaagokozhiwewininiwag**
baapaagokozo *vai* get a haircut; *1sg* **imbaapaagokoz**; *prt* **bayaapaagokozod**
baapaas= < baas=
baapaase *na* woodpecker; *pl* **baapaaseg**; *dim* **baapaasens**
baapaashk= < baashk=
baapaashkizige-giizhigad *vii* be the Fourth of July; *prt* **bayaapaashkizige-giizhigak**
baapaashkizige-giizis *na* July
baapaaw= < baw=
baapaawin *vta* hold and shake s.o. out; *1sg* **imbaapaawinaa**; *prt* **bayaapaawinaad**
baapaawinan *vti* hold and shake s.t. out; *1sg* **imbaapaawinaan**; *prt* **bayaapaawinang**
baapaazhid= < baazhid=
baapi *vai* laugh; *1sg* **imbaap**; *prt* **bayaapid**
baapi' *vta* laugh at s.o.; *1sg* **imbaapi'aa**; *prt* **bayaapi'aad**
baapinakamigad *vii* there are festivities; *prt* **bayaapinakamigak**
baapinakamigizi *vai* be excited; *1sg* **imbaapinakamigiz**; *prt* **bayaapinakamigizid**
baapiniziwaagan *pc* beware! (a warning based on a premonition)
baapinodaw *vta* mock s.o. disrespectfully, show disrespect for s.o.; *1sg* **imbaapinodawaa**; *prt* **bayaapinodawaad**

baapitoon *vti2* laugh at s.t.; *1sg* **imbaapitoon**; *prt* **bayaapitood**
baas /baasw-/ *vta* dry s.o.; *1sg* **imbaaswaa**; *prt* **bayaaswaad**
baasa' /baasa'w-/ *vta* crack s.o. using something, shatter s.o. using something; *1sg* **imbaasa'waa**; *prt* **bayaasa'waad**
baasa'an *vti* crack s.t. using something, shatter s.t. using something; *1sg* **imbaasa'aan**; *prt* **bayaasa'ang**
baasa'ige *vai* crack things using something, shatter things using something; *1sg* **imbaasa'ige**; *prt* **bayaasa'iged**
baasan *vti* dry s.t.; *1sg* **imbaasaan**; *prt* **bayaasang**
baasaabikiz /baasaabikizw-/ *vta* blast s.o.; *1sg* **imbaasaabikizwaa**; *prt* **bayaasaabikizwaad**
baasaabikizan *vti* blast s.t.; *1sg* **imbaasaabikizaan**; *prt* **bayaasaabikizang**
baasaabikizigan *ni* dynamite; *pl* **baasaabikiziganan**; *loc* **baasaabikiziganing**; *dim* **baasaabikizigaans**
baasaabikizige *vai* blast things; *1sg* **imbaasaabikizige**; *prt* **bayaasaabikiziged**
baashka' /baashka'w-/ *vta* burst s.o. using something; *1sg* **imbaashka'waa**; *prt* **bayaashka'waad**
baashka'an *vti* burst s.t. using something; *1sg* **imbaashka'aan**; *prt* **bayaashka'ang**
baashkakwa'am *vai2* make a thunderclap (of the thunderers); *prt* **bayaashkakwa'ang**
baashkaabigwanii *vii* blossom, bloom; *prt* **bayaashkaabigwaniig**; *aug* **baashkaabigwaniimagad**; *prt aug* **bayaashkaabigwaniimagak**
baashkaapi *vai* burst out laughing; *1sg* **imbaashkaap**; *prt* **bayaashkaapid**
baashkaawe'am *vai2* hatch; *prt* **bayaashkaawe'ang**; *also* **baashkaawe'o**
baashkaawe'o *vai* hatch; *prt* **bayaashkaawe'od**; *also* **baashkaawe'am**
baashkide *vii* explode, blow up; *prt* **bayaashkideg**; *aug* **baashkidemagad**; *prt aug* **bayaashkidemagak**
baashkijii' /baashkijii'w-/ *vta* burst s.o. open using something; *1sg* **imbaashkijii'waa**; *prt* **bayaashkijii'aad**
baashkijii'an *vti* burst s.t. open using something; *1sg* **imbaashkijii'aan**; *prt* **bayaashkijii'ang**
baashkijiisijige *vai* have a blowout; *prt* **bayaashkijiisijiged**
baashkiminasigan *ni* jam, preserves; *pl* **baashkiminasiganan**; *loc* **baashkiminasiganing**; *dim* **baashkiminasigaans**
baashkinede *vii* steam; *prt* **bayaashkinedeg**; *aug* **baashkinedemagad**; *prt aug* **bayaashkinedemagak**
baashkinezo *vai* steam; *prt* **bayaashkinezod**
baashkishim *vta* burst s.o. on impact; *1sg* **imbaashkishimaa**; *prt* **bayaashkishimaad**
baashkisidoon *vti2* burst s.t. on impact; *1sg* **imbaashkisidoon**; *prt* **bayaashkisidood**
baashkiz /baashkizw-/ *vta* shoot s.o.; *1sg* **imbaashkizwaa**; *prt* **bayaashkizwaad**
baashkizan *vti* shoot s.t.; *1sg* **imbaashkizaan**; *prt* **bayaashkizang**
baashkizigan *ni* gun; *pl* **baashkiziganan**; *loc* **baashkiziganing**; *dim* **baashkizigaans**
baashkizige *vai* shoot things, ejaculate; *1sg* **imbaashkizige**; *prt* **bayaashkiziged**
baashkizo *vai* explode, blow up; *prt* **bayaashkizod**
baashkizodizo *vai* shoot oneself; *1sg* **imbaashkizodiz**; *prt* **bayaashkizodizod**
baaside *vii* shatter from heat, crack from heat; *prt* **bayaasideg**; *aug* **baasidemagad**; *prt aug* **bayaasidemagak**
baasiga' /baasiga'w-/ *vta* chop s.o. into small pieces (as something of wood); *1sg* **imbaasiga'waa**; *prt* **bayaasiga'waad**
baasiga'an *vti* chop s.t. into small pieces (as something of wood); *1sg* **imbaasiga'aan**; *prt* **bayaasiga'ang**
baasigaade *vii* be dried; *prt* **bayaasigaadeg**; *aug* **baasigaademagad**; *prt aug* **bayaasigaademagak**
baasigaazo *vai* be dried; *prt* **bayaasigaazod**
baasikan *vti* shatter s.t. with foot or body; *1sg* **imbaasikaan**; *prt* **bayaasikang**
baasikaw *vta* shatter s.o. with foot or body; *1sg* **imbaasikawaa**; *prt* **bayaasikawaad**
baasikaa *vii* shatter (e.g., glass or china), crack (e.g., glass or china); *prt* **bayaasikaag**; *aug* **baasikaamagad**; *prt aug* **bayaasikaamagak**
baasindibeshin *vai* fall and crack one's head; *1sg* **imbaasindibeshin**; *prt* **bayaasindibeshing**
baasinigo *vai* be bloated; *1sg* **imbaasinig**; *prt* **bayaasinigod**
baasishim *vta* shatter s.o., crack s.o.; *1sg* **imbaasishimaa**; *prt* **bayaasishimaad**
baasishin *vai* shatter on impact, crack on impact; *prt* **bayaasishing**
baasisidoon *vti2* shatter s.t., crack s.t.; *1sg* **imbaasisidoon**; *prt* **bayaasisidood**
baasisin *vii* shatter on impact, crack on impact; *prt* **bayaasising**
baasiz /baasizw-/ *vta* shatter s.o. by heat, crack s.o. by heat; *1sg* **imbaasizwaa**; *prt* **bayaasizwaad**
baasizan *vti* shatter s.t. by heat, crack s.t. by heat; *1sg* **imbaasizaan**; *prt* **bayaasizang**
baasizo *vai* shatter from heat, crack from heat; *prt* **bayaasizod**
baaso *vai* be dry; *prt* **bayaasod**
baatayiinad *vii* be much, be many; *prt* **bayaatayiinak**
baatayiinatoon *vti2* have much of s.t., have many of s.t.; *1sg* **imbaatayiinatoon**; *prt* **bayaatayiinatood**
baatayiino *vai* be much, be many; *prt* **bayaatayiinod**; *also* **baatayiini**
baatayiino' *vta* have much of s.o., have many of s.o.; *1sg* **imbaatayiino'aa**; *prt* **bayaatayiino'aad**
baataam *vta* tell on s.o., testify against s.o.; *1sg* **imbaataamaa**; *prt* **bayaataamaad**

baataase *vai* get stuck; *1sg* **imbaataase**; *prt* **bayaataased**
baataase *vii* get stuck; *prt* **bayaataaseg**; *aug* **baataasemagad**; *prt aug* **bayaatesemagak**
baataashin *vai* be stuck; *1sg* **imbaataashin**; *prt* **bayaataashing**
baataasin *vii* be stuck; *prt* **bayaataasing**
baate *vii* be dry; *prt* **bayaateg**; *aug* **baatemagad**; *prt aug* **bayaatemagak**
baate- *pv4* dried
baazagobizh /baazagobiN-/ *vta* scratch s.o.; *1sg* **imbaazagobinaa**; *prt* **bayaazagobinaad**
baazhida' /baazhida'w-/ *vta* step over s.o.; *1sg* **imbaazhida'waa**; *prt* **bayaazhida'waad**
baazhida'an *vti* step over s.t.; *1sg* **imbaazhida'aan**; *prt* **bayaazhida'ang**
baazhidaandawe *vai* climb over; *1sg* **imbaazhidaandawe**; *prt* **bayaazhidaandawed**
baazhijigwaashkwani *vai* jump over; *1sg* **imbaazhijigwaashkwani**; *prt* **bayaazhijigwaashkwanid**
baazhijiwebin *vta* throw s.o. over; *1sg* **imbaazhijiwebinaa**; *prt* **bayaazhijiwebinaad**
baazhijiwebinan *vti* throw s.t. over; *1sg* **imbaazhijiwebinaan**; *prt* **bayaazhijiwebinang**
bebakaan= < bakaan=
bebakaan *pc* all different
bebangii *pc* a little bit each
bebangiiwag= < bangiiwag=
bebaamaadizid *na-pt* traveller, tourist; *pl* **bebaamaadizijig**
bebezhig *nm* one-by-one
bebezhigooganzhii *na* horse; *pl* **bebezhigooganzhiig**; *dim* **bebezhigooganzhiins**; *also* **mishtadim*, mashtadim***
bebinezid bakwezhigan *na* flour
bebiikominagak *ni-pt* pill; *pl* **bebiikominagakin**
bedose *vai* walk slowly; *1sg* **imbedose**; *prt* **bayedosed**
bedowe *vai* have a soft voice; *1sg* **imbedowe**; *prt* **bayedowed**
bejibatoo *vai* run slowly; *1sg* **imbejibatoo**; *prt* **bayejibatood**
bejibide *vii* move slowly, drive slowly; *prt* **bayejibideg**; *aug* **bejibidemagad**; *prt aug* **bayejibidemagak**
bejibizo *vai* move slowly, drive slowly; *1sg* **imbejibiz**; *prt* **bayejibizod**
bekaa *pc* wait!, slow down!, hold on!
bekaadizi *vai* be quiet, be easygoing; *1sg* **imbekaadiz**; *prt* **bayekaadizid**
bekish *pc* at the same time
bekwaawigang *na-pt* camel; *pl* **bekwaawigangig**
bemaadizid *na-pt* person; *pl* **bemaadizijig**
bemisemagak *ni-pt* airplane; *pl* **bemisemagakin**
bengozi *vai* be dry; *prt* **bayengozid**
bengwa' /bengwa'w-/ *vta* dry s.o. using something; *1sg* **imbengwa'waa**; *prt* **bayengwa'waad**
bengwa'an *vti* dry s.t. using something; *1sg* **imbengwa'aan**; *prt* **bayengwa'ang**
bengwan *vii* be dry; *prt* **bayengwang**
bepesh= < besh=
beshaa *vii* have a line, have a stripe; *prt* **bayeshaag**; *aug* **beshaamagad**; *prt aug* **bayeshaamagak**
beshibii' /beshibii'w-/ *vta* mark s.o. with a stripe; *1sg* **imbeshibii'waa**; *prt* **bayeshibii'waad**
beshibii'an *vti* mark s.t. with a stripe; *1sg* **imbeshibii'aan**; *prt* **bayeshibii'ang**
beshibii'ige *vai* mark things with a stripe; *1sg* **imbeshibii'ige**; *prt* **bayeshibii'iged**
beshizh /beshizhw-/ *vta* make a cut on s.o.; *1sg* **imbeshizhwaa**; *prt* **bayeshizhwaad**
beshizhan *vti* make a cut on s.t.; *1sg* **imbeshizhaan**; *prt* **bayeshizhang**
beshizi *vai* have a line, have a stripe; *1sg* **imbeshiz**; *prt* **bayeshizid**
besho *pc* near, close
beshonaagozi *vai* appear to be close; *prt* **bayeshonaagozid**
beshonaagwad *vii* appear to be close; *prt* **bayeshonaagwak**
beshowad *vii* be near, be close; *prt* **bayeshowak**
beshwaji' *vta* be close friends with s.o.; *1sg* **imbeshwaji'aa**; *prt* **bayeshwaji'aad**
beshwendan *vti* think s.t. to be close; *1sg* **imbeshwendaan**; *prt* **bayeshwendang**
beshwendaagozi *vai* be thought near; *prt* **bayeshwendaagozid**
beshwendaagwad *vii* be thought near; *prt* **bayeshwendaagwak**
bezhig *nm* one
bezhigo *vai* be alone, be the only one; *1sg* **imbezhig**; *prt* **bayezhigod**
bezhigo- *pv4* one
bezhigoobii'igan *na* ace (card); *pl* **bezhigoobii'iganag**
bezhigwan *vii* be one, be the only one, be the same; *prt* **bayezhigwang**
bezhigwanong *pc* one place, in one place
bezhigwaabik *pc* one dollar
bezhizhooniyaans *na* dime; *pl* **bezhizhooniyaansag**
bezikaa *vai* move slowly; *1sg* **imbezikaa**; *prt* **bayezikaad**
bezikaabatoo *vai* run slowly; *1sg* **imbezikaabatoo**; *prt* **bayezikaabatood**
bi- *pv2* toward the speaker, this way, here, hither
bibagaa *vii* be thin; *prt* **bebagaag**; *aug* **bibagaamagad**; *prt aug* **bebagaamagak**
bibagaabikaad *vii* be thin (as something mineral); *prt* **bebagaabikak**
bibagaabikizi *vai* be thin (as something mineral); *prt* **bebagaabikizid**
bibagaakwadin *vii* be frozen thin; *prt* **bebagaakwading**
bibagaakwaji *vai* be frozen thin; *prt* **bebagaakwajid**
bibagikodan *vti* slice s.t. thin; *1sg* **imbibagikodaan**; *prt* **bebagikodang**
bibagikozh /bibagikoN-/ *vta* slice s.o. thin; *1sg* **imbibagikonaa**; *prt* **bebagikonaad**
bibagishin *vai* lie in a thin layer; *prt* **bebagishing**
bibagisin *vii* lie in a thin layer; *prt* **bebagising**
bibagizi *vai* be thin; *prt* **bebagizid**
bibagiigad *vii* be thin (as something sheet-like); *prt* **bebagiigak**

bibagiigizi *vai* be thin (as something sheet-like); *prt* **bebagiigizid**
bibigwan *ni* flute; *pl* **bibigwanan**

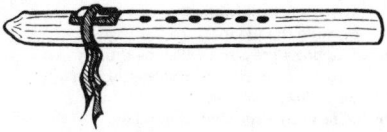

bibigwan (flute)

bibigwe *vai* play the flute; *1sg* **imbibigwe**; *prt* **bebigwed**
bibine-bakwezhigan *na* flour
bibine-ziinzibaakwad *ni* granulated sugar
biboon *vii* be winter; *prt* **beboong**
biboonagad *vii* be a winter, a year passes; *prt* **beboonagak**
biboonishi *vai* spend the winter somewhere; *1sg* **imbiboonish**; *prt* **beboonishid**
biboonodaabaan *na* sleigh; *pl* **biboonodaabaanag**; *loc* **biboonodaabaaning**; *dim* **biboonodaabaanens**
biboonodaabaanens *na* sled; *pl* **biboonodaabaanensag**
biboonong *pc* last winter
bichi- *pv4* by mistake, accidentally
bichinan *vti* shoot s.t. accidentally; *1sg* **imbichinaan**; *prt* **bechinang**
bichinaw *vta* shoot s.o. accidentally; *1sg* **imbichinawaa**; *prt* **bechinawaad**
bichinaadizo *vai* shoot oneself accidentally; *1sg* **imbichinaadiz**; *prt* **bechinaadizod**
bichinaage *vai* shoot things accidentally; *1sg* **imbichinaage**; *prt* **bechinaaged**
bigishkanad *vii* be rotten, fall to pieces; *prt* **begishkanak**
bigishkanani *vai* be rotten, fall to pieces; *prt* **begishkananid**
bigishkibidoon *vti2* tear s.t. to pieces; *1sg* **imbigishkibidoon**; *prt* **begishkibidood**
bigishkibizh /bigishkibiN-/ *vta* tear s.o. to pieces; *1sg* **imbigishkibinaa**; *prt* **begishkibinaad**
bigishkise *vai* go to pieces; *prt* **begishkiseg**
bigishkise *vii* go to pieces; *prt* **begishkiseg**; *aug* **bigishkisemagad**; *prt aug* **begishkisemagak**
bigishkizh /bigishkizhw-/ *vta* cut s.o. to pieces; *1sg* **imbigishkizhwaa**; *prt* **begishkizhwaad**
bigishkizhan *vti* cut s.t. to pieces; *1sg* **imbigishkizhaan**; *prt* **begishkizhang**
bigishki-zhooniyaans *na* loose change; *pl* **bigishki-zhooniyaans**
bigiw *ni* pitch, tar; *dim* **bigiins**
bigiwizigan *ni* maple taffy
bigiwizige *vai* make taffy; *1sg* **imbigiwizige**; *prt* **begiwiziged**
bigiikaadan *vti* apply pitch to s.t. (e.g., a canoe), putty s.t., tar s.t.; *1sg* **imbigiikaadaan**; *prt* **begiikaadang**
bigiike *vai* apply pitch, putty, tar; *1sg* **imbigiike**; *prt* **begiiked**
bigii-miikana *ni* asphalt road; *pl* **bigii-miikanan**; *loc* **bigii-miikanaang**
bigiins *na* chewing gum; *pl* **bigiinsag**
bi-izhaa *vai* come; *1sg* **imbi-izhaa**; *prt* **ba-izhaad**
bijiinag *pc* after a while, recently, just now
bijiinaago *pc* yesterday
bikonagizhii *vai* have a potbelly; *1sg* **imbikonagizhii**; *prt* **bekonagizhiid**
bikoojaan *ni* ball of twine or yarn; *pl* **bikoojaanan**; *loc* **bikoojaaning**; *dim* **bikoojaanens**
bikwadinaa *vii* be a knoll, be a small hill; *prt* **bekwadinaag**; *aug* **bikwadinaamagad**; *prt aug* **bekwadinaamagak**
bikwak *ni* arrow; *pl* **bikwakoon**; *loc* **bikwakong**; *dim* **bikwakoons**
bikwaakoganaan *ni* ankle joint; *pl* **bikwaakoganaanan**; *loc* **bikwaakoganaaning**; *dim* **bikwaakoganaanens**
bikwaakwad *ni* ball; *pl* **bikwaakwadoon**; *loc* **bikwaakwadong**; *dim* **bikwaakwadoons**
bikwaakwado-bagamaagan *ni* ball-headed club; *pl* **bikwaakwado-bagamaaganan**; *dim* **bikwaakwado-bagamaagaans**
bimademo *vai* cry walking along; *1sg* **imbimadem**; *prt* **bemademod**
bima'adoo *vai* follow a trail along; *1sg* **imbima'adoo**; *prt* **bema'adood**
bima'adoon *vti2* follow s.t. along as a trail; *1sg* **imbima'adoon**; *prt* **bema'adood**
bima'amaazo *vai* go along singing; *1sg* **imbima'amaaz**; *prt* **bema'amaazod**
bima'an *vti* skim s.t.; *1sg* **imbima'aan**; *prt* **bema'ang**
bima'azh /bima'aN-/ *vta* follow s.o.'s trail along; *1sg* **imbima'anaa**; *prt* **bema'anaad**
bima'ige *vai* skim things; *1sg* **imbima'ige**; *prt* **bema'iged**
bima'oodoo *vai* pole a boat along; *1sg* **imbima'oodoo**; *prt* **bema'oodood**
bima'oodoon *vti2* take s.t. along in a boat, pole s.t. along in a boat; *1sg* **imbima'oodoon**; *prt* **bema'oodood**
bima'ookii *vai* pole a boat along; *1sg* **imbima'ookii**; *prt* **bema'ookiid**
bima'oozh /bima'ooN-/ *vta* take s.o. along in a boat, pole s.o. along in a boat; *1sg* **imbima'oonaa**; *prt* **bema'oonaad**
bimakwazhiwe *vai* paddle along, swim along (as a fish); *1sg* **imbimakwazhiwe**; *prt* **bemakwazhiwed**
bimamon /bimamo-/ *vii* lead along (as a road or trail); *prt* **bemamog**; *aug* **bimamoomagad**; *prt aug* **bemamoomagak**
bimaabiigamon /bimaabiigamo-/ *vii* lead along (as something string-like); *prt* **bemaabiigamog**
bimaabiigin *vta* string s.o. along; *1sg* **imbimaabiiginaa**; *prt* **bemaabiiginaad**
bimaabiiginan *vti* string s.t. along; *1sg* **imbimaabiiginaan**; *prt* **bemaabiiginang**
bimaaboode *vii* drift along on current; *prt* **bemaaboodeg**; *aug* **bimaaboodemagad**; *prt aug* **bemaaboodemagak**
bimaaboono *vai* drift along on current; *prt* **bemaaboonod**

bimaadagaa *vai* swim along; *1sg* **imbimaadagaa**; *prt* **bemaadagaad**
bimaadagaako *vai* walk along on the ice; *1sg* **imbimaadagaak**; *prt* **bemaadagaakod**
bimaadagaazii *vai* wade along; *1sg* **imbimaadagaazii**; *prt* **bemaadagaaziid**
bimaada'e *vai* skate along; *1sg* **imbimaada'e**; *prt* **bemaada'ed**
bimaadizi *vai* live, be alive; *1sg* **imbimaadiz**; *prt* **bemaadizid**
bimaaji' *vta* save the life of s.o.; *1sg* **imbimaaji'aa**; *prt* **bemaaji'aad**
bimaakoshim *vta* put s.o. along (as something stick- or wood-like); *1sg* **imbimaakoshimaa**; *prt* **bemaakoshimaad**
bimaakoshin *vai* lie along (as something stick- or wood-like); *1sg* **imbimaakoshin**; *prt* **bemaakoshing**
bimaakosidoon *vti2* put s.t. along (as something stick- or wood-like); *1sg* **imbimaakosidoon**; *prt* **bemaakosidood**
bimaakosin *vii* lie along (as something stick- or wood-like); *prt* **bemaakosing**
bimaanakwad *vii* clouds go along; *prt* **bemaanakwak**
bimaandawe *vai* climb along; *1sg* **imbimaandawe**; *prt* **bemaandawed**
bimaashi *vai* be blown along, sail along; *1sg* **imbimaash**; *prt* **bemaashid**
bimaasin *vii* be blown along, sail along; *prt* **bemaasing**
bimaawadaaso *vai* travel along in a group (as a school of fish); *prt* **bemaawadaasod**
bimaazakonenjige *vai* go along with a light; *1sg* **imbimaazakonenjige**; *prt* **bemaazakonenjiged**
bimaazhagaame *vai* go along the edge, go along the shore; *1sg* **imbimaazhagaame**; *prt* **bemaazhagaamed**
bimi- *pv2* along, going along, going by, going past, on the way
bimi-ayaa *vai* go along, travel along; *1sg* **imbimi-ayaa**; *prt* **bemi-ayaad**
bimiba'idiwag /bimiba'idi-/ *vai* they run along together; *1pl* **imbimiba'idimin**; *prt* **bemiba'idijig**
bimiba'igo *vai* ride along drawn by horses; *1sg* **imbimiba'ig**; *prt* **bemiba'igod**
bimiba'iwe *vai* run along in flight from someone; *1sg* **imbimiba'iwe**; *prt* **bemiba'iwed**
bimibatoo *vai* run along; *1sg* **imbimibatoo**; *prt* **bemibatood**
bimibide *vii* speed along, drive along, fly along; *prt* **bemibideg**; *aug* **bimibidemagad**; *prt aug* **bemibidemagak**
bimibizo *vai* speed along, drive along, fly along; *1sg* **imbimibiz**; *prt* **bemibizod**
bimibizoni' *vta* drive s.o. along, take s.o. along for a ride; *1sg* **imbimibizoni'aa**; *prt* **bemibizoni'aad**
bimibizonitoon *vti2* drive s.t. along; *1sg* **imbimibizonitoon**; *prt* **bemibizonitood**
bimibiisaa *vii* rain goes along; *prt* **bemibiisaag**; *aug* **bimibiisaamagad**; *prt aug* **bemibiisaamagak**
bimidasaa *na* thwart; *pl* **bimidasaag**; *also* **bimidasaagan, -an**
bimidaabaadan *vti* drag s.t. along; *1sg* **imbimidaabaadaan**; *prt* **bemidaabaadang**
bimidaabaazh /bimidaabaaN-/ *vta* drag s.o. along; *1sg* **imbimidaabaanaa**; *prt* **bemidaabaanaad**
bimidaabiiba'igo *vai* drive along quickly in a wagon or sleigh; *1sg* **imbimidaabiiba'ig**; *prt* **bemidaabiiba'igod**
bimidaabii'iwe *vai* drive along; *1sg* **imbimidaabii'iwe**; *prt* **bemidaabii'iwed**
bimide *ni* grease, oil; *loc* **bimideng**
bimijiwan *vii* flow along; *prt* **bemijiwang**
bimikawaan *ni* footprint, track; *pl* **bimikawaanan**
bimikawe *vai* leave tracks going along; *1sg* **imbimikawe**; *prt* **bemikawed**
biminaazhikaage *vai* send people along, chase people along; *1sg* **imbiminaazhikaage**; *prt* **beminaazhikaaged**
biminizha' /biminizha'w-/ *vta* chase s.o. along; *1sg* **imbiminizha'waa**; *prt* **beminizha'waad**
biminizha'an *vti* chase s.t. along; *1sg* **imbiminizha'aan**; *prt* **beminizha'ang**
biminizha'ige *vai* chase things along; *1sg* **imbiminizha'ige**; *prt* **beminizha'iged**
biminizhikaw *vta* send s.o. along, chase s.o. along; *1sg* **imbiminizhikawaa**; *prt* **beminizhikawaad**
biminizhimo *vai* run along in flight; *1sg* **imbiminizhim**; *prt* **beminizhimod**
bimipon /bimipo-/ *vii* snow goes along; *prt* **bemipog**
bimise *vai* fly along; *1sg* **imbimise**; *prt* **bemised**
bimise *vii* fly along; *prt* **bemiseg**; *aug* **bimisemagad**; *prt aug* **bemisemagak**
bimishimo *vai* dance along; *1sg* **imbimishim**; *prt* **bemishimod**
bimishkaa *vai* paddle along, go along by boat; *1sg* **imbimishkaa**; *prt* **bemishkaad**
bimitigweyaa *vii* flow along (as a river); *prt* **bemitigweyaag**; *aug* **bimitigweyaamagad**; *prt aug* **bemitigweyaamagak**
bimiwanaan *ni* pack, backpack; *pl* **bimiwanaanan**; *loc* **bimiwanaaning**; *dim* **bimiwanaanens**
bimiwane *vai* carry a pack along; *1sg* **imbimiwane**; *prt* **bemiwaned**
bimiwidoon *vti2* carry s.t. along, take s.t. along; *1sg* **imbimiwidoon**; *prt* **bemiwidood**
bimiwijige *vai* carry things along, be pregnant; *1sg* **imbimiwijige**; *prt* **bemiwijiged**
bimiwizh /bimiwiN-/ *vta* carry s.o. along, take s.o. along; *1sg* **imbimiwinaa**; *prt* **bemiwinaad**
bimiwizhiwe *vai* take people along, drive people along (as in a bus); *1sg* **imbimiwizhiwe**; *prt* **bemiwizhiwed**
bimiwizhiwewidaabaan *na* taxi; *pl* **bimiwizhiwewidaabaanag**; *loc* **bimiwizhiwewidaabaaning**; *dim* **bimiwizhiwewidaabaanens**
bimiwizhiwewinini *na* taxi driver, chauffeur; *pl* **bimiwizhiwewininiwag**
bimo /bimw-/ *vta* shoot s.o. with an arrow or other missile; *1sg* **imbimwaa**; *prt* **bemwaad**
bimodan *vti* shoot s.t. with an arrow or other missile; *1sg* **imbimodaan**; *prt* **bemodang**

bimojigan *ni* slingshot; *pl* **bimojiganan**; *dim* **bimojigaans**
bimojige *vai* shoot things with an arrow or other missile; *1sg* **imbimojige**; *prt* **bemojiged**
bimose *vai* walk along; *1sg* **imbimose**; *prt* **bemosed**
bimoode *vai* crawl along; *1sg* **imbimoode**; *prt* **bemooded**
bimoom *vta* carry s.o. along on one's back; *1sg* **imbimoomaa**; *prt* **bemoomaad**
bimoomaawaso *vai* carry a baby along on one's back; *1sg* **imbimoomaawas**; *prt* **bemoomaawasod**
bimoomigo *vai* ride along on horseback; *1sg* **imbimoomig**; *prt* **bemoomigod**
bimoomigoo-apabiwin *ni* saddle; *pl* **bimoomigoo-apabiwinan**; *loc* **bimoomigoo-apabiwining**; *dim* **bimoomigoo-apabiwinens**
bimoondan *vti* carry s.t. along on one's back; *1sg* **imbimoondaan**; *prt* **bemoondang**
bimoonjigan *ni* dance bustle, pack frame; *pl* **bimoonjiganan**; *loc* **bimoonjiganing**; *dim* **bimoonjigaans**
bimwewebide *vii* be heard speeding along, be heard driving along; *prt* **bemwewebideg**; *aug* **bimwewebidemagad**; *prt aug* **bemwewebidemagak**
bimwewebizo *vai* be heard speeding along, be heard driving along; *1sg* **imbimwewebiz**; *prt* **bemwewebizod**
bimweweshin *vai* be heard walking along, be heard going along and falling; *1sg* **imbimweweshin**; *prt* **bemweweshing**
bina' /bina'w-/ *vta* take s.o. down; *1sg* **imbina'waa**; *prt* **bena'waad**
bina'an *vti* take s.t. down; *1sg* **imbina'aan**; *prt* **bena'ang**
bi-naagozi *vai* appear, come into view; *1sg* **imbi-naagoz**; *prt* **ba-naagozid**
bi-naagwad *vii* appear, come into view; *prt* **ba-naagwak**
binaakwaan *ni* comb; *pl* **binaakwaanan**; *loc* **binaakwaaning**; *dim* **binaakwaanens**
binaakwe' /binaakwe'w-/ *vta* comb s.o.; *1sg* **imbinaakwe'waa**; *prt* **benaakwe'waad**
binaakwe'igan *ni* rake; *pl* **binaakwe'iganan**; *loc* **binaakwe'iganing**; *dim* **binaakwe'igaans**
binaakwe'ige *vai* rake things; *1sg* **imbinaakwe'ige**; *prt* **benaakwe'iged**
binaakwe'o *vai* comb one's hair; *1sg* **imbinaakwe'**; *prt* **benaakwe'od**
binaakwii *vai* fall (as a leaf); *1sg* **imbinaakwii**; *prt* **benaakwiid**
binaakwii-giizis *na* October; *also* **binaakwe-giizis**
bine *na* partridge; *pl* **binewag**; *dim* **binens**
bineshiinh *na* bird; *pl* **bineshiinyag**; *dim* **bineshiins**
bineshiinhwayaan *na* bird skin; *pl* **bineshiinhwayaanag**; *loc* **bineshiinhwayaaning**; *dim* **bineshiinhwayaanens**
binesi *na* bird (of large species, e.g., hawk or eagle), thunderbird; *pl* **binesiwag**
bingoshens *na* gnat; *pl* **bingoshensag**
bingwi *ni* sand, ashes; *loc* **bingwiing**; *dim* **bingwiins**
bingwiikaa *vii* be much sand; *prt* **bengwiikaag**; *aug* **bingwiikaamagad**; *prt aug* **bengwiikaamagak**
bingwii-miikana *ni* gravel road; *pl* **bingwii-miikanan**; *loc* **bingwii-miikanaang**; *dim* **bingwii-miikanaans**
biniweba' /biniweba'w-/ *vta* knock s.o. down using something; *1sg* **imbiniweba'waa**; *prt* **beniweba'waad**
biniweba'an *vti* knock s.t. down using something; *1sg* **imbiniweba'aan**; *prt* **beniweba'ang**
binzini *vai* have something in one's eye; *1sg* **imbinzin**; *prt* **benzinid**
bipakoombens *ni* cucumber; *pl* **bipakoombensan**
bishagaakwa'ige *vai* peel timber using something; *1sg* **imbishagaakwa'ige**; *prt* **beshagaakwa'iged**
bishagaaso *vai* peel from sunburn; *1sg* **imbishagaas**; *prt* **beshagaasod**
bishagibidoon *vti2* peel s.t. with hands; *1sg* **imbishagibidoon**; *prt* **beshagibidood**
bishagibijige *vai* peel things with hands; *1sg* **imbishagibijige**; *prt* **beshagibijiged**
bishagibizh /bishagibiN-/ *vta* peel s.o. with hands; *1sg* **imbishagibinaa**; *prt* **beshagibinaad**
bishagigidigweshin *vai* skin one's knee; *1sg* **imbishagigidigweshin**; *prt* **beshagigidigweshing**
bishagikodan *vti* peel s.t. with a knife; *1sg* **imbishagikodaan**; *prt* **beshagikodang**
bishagikozh /bishagikoN-/ *vta* peel s.o. with a knife; *1sg* **imbishagikonaa**; *prt* **beshagikozhwaad**
bishagishkaa *vai* peel off; *prt* **beshagishkaad**
bishagishkaa *vii* peel off; *prt* **beshagishkaag**; *aug* **bishagishkaamagad**; *prt aug* **beshagishkaamagak**
bishagiishkate *vii* be dark indoors; *prt* **beshagiishkateg**; *aug* **bishagiishkatemagad**; *prt aug* **beshagiishkatemagak**
bishagiishkaa *vii* be dark; *prt* **beshagiishkaag**; *aug* **bishagiishkaamagad**; *prt aug* **beshagiishkaamagak**
bishagiishkaande *vii* be dark colored; *prt* **beshagiishkaandeg**; *aug* **bishagiishkaandemagad**; *prt aug* **beshagiishkaandemagak**
bishagiishkaanzo *vai* be dark colored; *prt* **beshagiishkaanzod**
bisha'igobii *vai* peel wigob (inner bark of basswood); *1sg* **imbisha'igobii**; *prt* **besha'igobiid**
bishkonan *vti* shoot at s.t. and miss; *1sg* **imbishkonaan**; *prt* **beshkonang**
bishkonaw *vta* shoot at s.o. and miss; *1sg* **imbishkonawaa**; *prt* **beshkonawaad**
bishkonaage *vai* shoot and miss; *1sg* **imbishkonaage**; *prt* **beshkonaaged**
bishkongwashi *vai* doze; *1sg* **imbishkongwash**; *prt* **beshkongwashid**
bisigadanaaboo *ni* dumpling soup; *loc* **bisigadanaaboong**
biskane *vii* catch fire, ignite; *prt* **beskaneg**; *aug* **biskanemagad**; *prt aug* **beskanemagak**

biskanebidoon *vti2* switch s.t. on; *1sg* **imbiskanebidoon**; *prt* **beskanebidood**
biskanesidoon *vti2* light s.t. by striking; *1sg* **imbiskanesidoon**; *prt* **beskanesidood**
biskaa *vii* be bent over, be folded; *prt* **beskaag**; *aug* **biskaamagad**; *prt aug* **beskaamagak**
biskaabii *vai* make a round trip in one day; *1sg* **imbiskaabii**; *prt* **beskaabiid**
biskaakonebijigan *ni* switch; *pl* **biskaakonebijiganan**; *loc* **biskaakonebijiganing**; *dim* **biskaakonebijigaans**
biskibidoon *vti2* bend s.t. over with hands, fold s.t. with hands; *1sg* **imbiskibidoon**; *prt* **beskibidood**
biskibizh /biskibiN-/ *vta* bend s.o. over with hands, fold s.o. with hands; *1sg* **imbiskibinaa**; *prt* **beskibinaad**
biskin *vta* bend s.o. over, fold s.o.; *1sg* **imbiskinaa**; *prt* **beskinaad**
biskinan *vti* bend s.t. over, fold s.t.; *1sg* **imbiskinaan**; *prt* **beskinang**
biskinigaade *vii* be bent over, be folded; *prt* **beskinigaadeg**; *aug* **biskinigaademagad**; *prt aug* **beskinigaademagak**
biskitenaagan *ni* sap bucket of folded birch bark; *pl* **biskitenaaganan**; *loc* **biskitenaaganing**; *dim* **biskitenaagaans**
biskiigin *vta* fold s.o. (as something sheet-like); *1sg* **imbiskiiginaa**; *prt* **beskiiginaad**
biskiiginan *vti* fold s.t. (as something sheet-like); *1sg* **imbiskiiginaan**; *prt* **beskiiginang**
bitaganaam *vta* accidentally hit s.o.; *1sg* **imbitaganaamaa**; *prt* **betaganaamaad**
bitaganaandan *vti* accidentally hit s.t.; *1sg* **imbitaganaandaan**; *prt* **betaganaandang**
bitaakondibeshin *vai* bump one's head; *1sg* **imbitaakondibeshin**; *prt* **betaakondibeshing**
bitaakoshin *vai* bump something, hit against something accidentally (as something stick- or wood-like); *1sg* **imbitaakoshin**; *prt* **betaakoshing**
bitaakoshkan *vti* bump into s.t.; *1sg* **imbitaakoshkaan**; *prt* **betaakoshkang**
bitaakoshkaw *vta* bump into s.o.; *1sg* **imbitaakoshkawaa**; *prt* **betaakoshkawaad**
bitaakoshkodaadiwag /bitaakoshkodaadi-/ *vai* they have a collision; *1pl* **imbitaakoshkodaadimin**; *prt* **betaakoshkodaadijig**
bitaakosin *vii* bump something, hit against something accidentally (as something stick- or wood-like); *prt* **betaakosing**
bitizh /bitizhw-/ *vta* cut s.o. accidentally; *1sg* **imbitizhwaa**; *prt* **betizhwaad**
bitizhan *vti* cut s.t. accidentally; *1sg* **imbitizhaan**; *prt* **betizhang**
bizaan *pc* quiet, still
bizaan-ayaa *vai* be quiet; *1sg* **imbizaan-ayaa**; *prt* **bezaan-ayaad**; *also* **bizaani-ayaa**
bizaanaakwadabi *vai* sit still; *1sg* **imbizaanaakwadab**; *prt* **bezaanaakwadabid**
bizaanigaabawi *vai* stand quietly; *1sg* **imbizaanigaabaw**; *prt* **bezaanigaabawid**
bizaanishin *vai* lie still; *1sg* **imbizaanishin**; *prt* **bezaanishing**
bizhiki *na* cow, bison, buffalo; *pl* **bizhikiwag**; *dim* **bizhikiins**
bizhikiwayaan *na* cowhide; *pl* **bizhikiwayaanag**; *dim* **bizhikiwayaanens**
bizhiki-wiiyaas *ni* beef; *also* **bizhikiwi-wiiyaas**
bizhikiins *na* calf; *pl* **bizhikiinsag**
bizhikiinsiwayaan *na* calfhide; *pl* **bizhikiinsiwayaanag**
bizhishigozi *vai* be empty; *prt* **bezhishigozid**
bizhishigwaa *vii* be empty; *prt* **bezhishigwaag**; *aug* **bizhishigwaamagad**; *prt aug* **bezhishigwaamagak**
bizhiw *na* lynx; *pl* **bizhiwag**; *dim* **bizhiwens**
bizhiwayaan *na* lynx hide; *pl* **bizhiwayaanag**; *loc* **bizhiwayaaning**; *dim* **bizhiwayaanens**
bizindam *vai2* listen; *1sg* **imbizindam**; *prt* **bezindang**
bizindamowin *ni* radio; *pl* **bizindamowinan**
bizindamoo-makak *ni* radio; *pl* **bizindamoo-makakoon**; *loc* **bizindamoo-makakong**; *dim* **bizindamoo-makakoons**
bizindan *vti* listen to s.t.; *1sg* **imbizindaan**; *prt* **bezindang**
bizindaw *vta* listen to s.o.; *1sg* **imbizindawaa**; *prt* **bezindawaad**
bizogeshin *vai* stumble; *1sg* **imbizogeshin**; *prt* **bezogeshing**
bizokan *vti* stumble on s.t.; *1sg* **imbizokaan**; *prt* **bezokang**
bizokaw *vta* stumble on s.o.; *1sg* **imbizokawaa**; *prt* **bezokawaad**
bizozideshin *vai* stub one's toe, trip; *1sg* **imbizozideshin**; *prt* **bezozideshing**
biibaagi *vai* call out, shout; *1sg* **imbiibaag**; *prt* **baabaagid**
biibaagim *vta* call out to s.o., shout at s.o.; *1sg* **imbiibaagimaa**; *prt* **baabaagimaad**
biibaagindan *vti* call out to s.t., shout at s.t.; *1sg* **imbiibaagindaan**; *prt* **baabaagindang**
biibii *na* baby; *pl* **biibiiyag**; *dim* **biibiiyens**
biichibabagiwayaane *vai* put on one's shirt; *1sg* **imbiichibabagiwayaane**; *prt* **baachibabagiwayaaned**
biichibabiinzikawaagane *vai* put on one's coat; *1sg* **imbiichibabiinzikawaagane**; *prt* **baachibabiinzikawaaganed**
biichigiboodiyegwaazone *vai* put on one's pants; *1sg* **imbiichigiboodiyegwaazone**; *prt* **baachigiboodiyegwaazoned**
biichiminjikaawane *vai* put on one's mittens; *1sg* **imbiichiminjikaawane**; *prt* **baachiminjikaawaned**
biichiwakwaane *vai* put on one's hat; *1sg* **imbiichiwakwaane**; *prt* **baachiwakwaaned**
biida'adoo *vai* follow a trail here; *1sg* **imbiida'adoo**; *prt* **baada'adood**
biida'adoon *vti2* follow s.t. as a trail here; *1sg* **imbiida'adoon**; *prt* **baada'adood**
biida'azh /biida'aN-/ *vta* follow s.o.'s trail here; *1sg* **imbiida'anaa**; *prt* **baada'anaad**
biida'oodoon *vti2* bring here in a boat; *1sg* **imbiida'oodoon**; *prt* **baada'oodood**

biida'oozh /biida'ooN-/ *vta* bring s.o. here in a boat; *1sg* **imbiida'oonaa**; *prt* **baada'oonaad**
biidakwazhiwe *vai* paddle here, swim here (as a fish); *1sg* **imbiidakwazhiwe**; *prt* **baadakwazhiwed**
biidaw *vta* bring (s.t.) for s.o.; *1sg* **imbiidawaa**; *prt* **baadawaad**; *also* **biidamaw**
biidaaban *vii* dawn comes, be daybreak; *prt* **baadaabang**
biidaadagaa *vai* swim here; *1sg* **imbiidaadagaa**; *prt* **baadaadagaad**
biidaadagaazii *vai* wade here; *1sg* **imbiidaadagaazii**; *prt* **baadaadagaaziid**
biidaada'e *vai* skate here; *1sg* **imbiidaada'e**; *prt* **baadaada'ed**
biidaajimo *vai* come telling news; *1sg* **imbiidaajim**; *prt* **baadaajimod**
biidaanakwad *vii* clouds approach; *prt* **baadaanakwak**
biidaandawe *vai* climb here; *1sg* **imbiidaandawe**; *prt* **baadaandawed**
biidaanimizi *vai* come in fear; *1sg* **imbiidaanimiz**; *prt* **baadaanimizid**
biidaapi *vai* come laughing; *1sg* **imbiidaap**; *prt* **baadaapid**
biidaasamabi *vai* sit facing this way; *1sg* **imbiidaasamab**; *prt* **baadaasamabid**
biidaasamishkaa *vai* paddle here, come in a boat; *1sg* **imbiidaasamishkaa**; *prt* **baadaasamishkaad**
biidaasamose *vai* walk here; *1sg* **imbiidaasamose**; *prt* **baadaasamosed**
biidaashi *vai* be blown here, sail here; *1sg* **imbiidaash**; *prt* **baadaashid**
biidaashkaa *vii* waves come in to shore; *prt* **baadaashkaag**; *aug* **biidaashkaamagad**; *prt aug* **baadaashkaamagak**
biidaasin *vii* be blown here, sail here; *prt* **baadaasing**
biidaazakonebizo *vai* drive here with a light; *1sg* **imbiidaazakonebiz**; *prt* **baadaazakonebizod**
biidaazakwanenjige *vai* come with a light; *1sg* **imbiidaazakwanenjige**; *prt* **baadaazakwanenjiged**
biidin *vta* hand s.o. over (here); *1sg* **imbiidinaa**; *prt* **baadinaad**
biidinamaw *vta* hand (s.t.) over (here) to s.o.; *1sg* **imbiidinamawaa**; *prt* **baadinamawaad**
biidinan *vti* hand s.t. over (here); *1sg* **imbiidinaan**; *prt* **baadinang**
biidoode *vai* crawl here; *1sg* **imbiidoode**; *prt* **baadooded**
biidoomigo *vai* ride here on horseback; *1sg* **imbiidoomig**; *prt* **baadoomigod**
biidoon *vti2* bring s.t.; *1sg* **imbiidoon**; *prt* **baadood**
biidwewebatoo *vai* be heard running here; *1sg* **imbiidwewebatoo**; *prt* **baadwewebatood**
biidwewebide *vii* be heard speeding here, be heard driving here; *prt* **baadwewebideg**; *aug* **biidwewebidemagad**; *prt aug* **baadwewebidemagak**
biidwewebizo *vai* be heard speeding here, be heard driving here; *1sg* **imbiidwewebiz**; *prt* **baadwewebizod**
biidwewekamigibatoo *vai* be heard running here on the ground; *1sg* **imbiidwewekamigibatoo**; *prt* **baadwewekamigibatood**
biidweweshin *vai* be heard walking here; *1sg* **imbiidweweshin**; *prt* **baadweweshing**
biidweweyaadagaa *vai* be heard swimming here; *1sg* **imbiidweweyaadagaa**; *prt* **baadweweyaadagaad**
biidwewidam *vai2* come making noise (e.g., thunder), come speaking; *1sg* **imbiidwewidam**; *prt* **baadwewidang**
biig *na* spade suite card; *pl* **biigwag**
biigobidoon *vti2* tear s.t., rip s.t.; *1sg* **imbiigobidoon**; *prt* **baagobidood**
biigobijigaade *vii* be torn, be ripped; *prt* **baagobijigaadeg**; *aug* **biigobijigaademagad**; *prt aug* **baagobijigaademagak**
biigobijigaazo *vai* be torn, be ripped; *prt* **baagobijigaazod**
biigobijige *vai* tear things, rip things; *1sg* **imbiigobijige**; *prt* **baagobijiged**
biigobizh /biigobiN-/ *vta* tear s.o., rip s.o.; *1sg* **imbiigobinaa**; *prt* **baagobinaad**
biigodaabaane *vai* have a broken-down car; *1sg* **imbiigodaabaane**; *prt* **baagodaabaaned**
biigode *vii* break by heat; *prt* **baagodeg**; *aug* **biigodemagad**; *prt aug* **baagodemagak**
biigojiishkaa *vai* burst open; *prt* **baagojiishkaad**
biigojiishkaa *vii* burst open; *prt* **baagojiishkaag**; *aug* **biigojiishkaamagad**; *prt aug* **baagojiishkaamagak**
biigon *vta* break s.o. by hand, dismantle s.o.; *1sg* **imbiigonaa**; *prt* **baagonaad**
biigonan *vti* break s.t. by hand, dismantle s.t.; *1sg* **imbiigonaan**; *prt* **baagonang**
biigoshim *vta* break s.o. by dropping, smash s.o.; *1sg* **imbiigoshimaa**; *prt* **baagoshimaad**
biigoshin *vai* break on impact; *1sg* **imbiigoshin**; *prt* **baagoshing**
biigoshkaa *vai* break, be broken, be broke (out of money); *prt* **baagoshkaad**
biigoshkaa *vii* break, be broken; *prt* **baagoshkaag**; *aug* **biigoshkaamagad**; *prt aug* **baagoshkaamagak**
biigosidoon *vti2* break s.t. by dropping, smash s.t.; *1sg* **imbiigosidoon**; *prt* **baagosidood**
biigosin *vii* break on impact; *prt* **baagosing**
biigozo *vai* break by heat; *prt* **baagozod**
biigwa' /biigwa'w-/ *vta* break s.o. using something; *1sg* **imbiigwa'waa**; *prt* **baagwa'waad**
biigwa'an *vti* break s.t. using something; *1sg* **imbiigwa'aan**; *prt* **baagwa'ang**
biigwakamigibidoon *vti2* break s.t. up (as ground), plow s.t.; *1sg* **imbiigwakamigibidoon**; *prt* **baagwakamigibidood**
biigwakamigibijigan *na* plow; *pl* **biigwakamigibijiganag**; *loc* **biigwakamigibijiganing**; *dim* **biigwakamigibijigaans**
biigwakamigibijige *vai* plow; *1sg* **imbiigwakamigibijige**; *prt* **baagwakamigibijiged**
biigwawe *vai* be bushy; *1sg* **imbiigwawe**; *prt* **baagwawed**

biigwaashi *vai* be blown apart; *prt* **baagwaashid**
biigwaasin *vii* be blown apart; *prt* **baagwaasing**
bii' *vta* wait for s.o.; *1sg* **imbii'aa**; *prt* **baa'aad**
bii'o *vai* wait; *1sg* **imbii'**; *prt* **baa'od**
biijiba'idiwag /biijiba'idi-/ *vai* they run here together; *1pl* **imbiijiba'idimin**; *prt* **baajiba'idijig**
biijibatoo *vai* run here; *1sg* **imbiijibatoo**; *prt* **baajibatood**
biijibide *vii* speed here, drive here, fly here; *prt* **baajibideg**; *aug* **biijibidemagad**; *prt aug* **baajibidemagak**
biijibizo *vai* speed here, drive here, fly here; *1sg* **imbiijibiz**; *prt* **baajibizod**
biijibii'amaw- *vta* write (s.t.) here to s.o. *in inverse forms: 1sg* **imbiijibii'amaag**; *prt* **baajibii'amaagod**
biijibii'ige *vai* write here, send a letter here; *prt* **baajibii'iged**
biijibiisaa *vii* rain comes; *prt* **baajibiisaag**; *aug* **biijibiisaamagad**; *prt aug* **baajibiisaamagak**
biijidaabaadan *vti* drag s.t. here; *1sg* **imbiijidaabaadaan**; *prt* **baajidaabaadang**
biijidaabaazh /biijidaabaaN-/ *vta* drag s.o. here; *1sg* **imbiijidaabaanaa**; *prt* **baajidaabaanaad**
biijidaabii *vai* drag here; *1sg* **imbiijidaabii**; *prt* **baajidaabiid**
biijidaabii'iwe *vai* drive here; *1sg* **imbiijidaabii'iwe**; *prt* **baajidaabii'iwed**
biijigaade *vii* be brought; *prt* **baajigaadeg**; *aug* **biijigaademagad**; *prt aug* **baajigaademagak**
biijigaazo *vai* be brought; *prt* **baajigaazod**
biijigidaazo *vai* come in anger; *1sg* **imbiijigidaaz**; *prt* **baajigidaazod**
biijigozi *vai* move one's residence here; *1sg* **imbiijigoz**; *prt* **baajigozid**
biijikawe *vai* come leaving tracks; *1sg* **imbiijikawe**; *prt* **baajikawed**
biijimaagozi *vai* give off a smell; *1sg* **imbiijimaagoz**; *prt* **baajimaagozid**
biijimaagwad *vii* give off a smell; *prt* **baajimaagwak**
biijimaam *vta* smell s.o.; *1sg* **imbiijimaamaa**; *prt* **baajimaamaad**
biijimaandan *vti* smell s.t.; *1sg* **imbiijimaandaan**; *prt* **baajimaandang**
biijimaaso *vai* give off a smell in cooking or burning; *prt* **baajimaasod**
biijimaate *vii* give off a smell in cooking or burning; *prt* **baajimaateg**; *aug* **biijimaatemagad**; *prt aug* **baajimaatemagak**
biijise *vai* fly here; *1sg* **imbiijise**; *prt* **baajised**
biijise *vii* fly here; *prt* **baajiseg**; *aug* **biijisemagad**; *prt aug* **baajisemagak**
biijwebin *vta* throw s.o. here; *1sg* **imbiijwebinaa**; *prt* **baajwebinaad**
biijwebinamaw *vta* throw (s.t.) here to s.o.; *1sg* **imbiijwebinamawaa**; *prt* **baajwebinamawaad**
biijwebinan *vti* throw s.t. here; *1sg* **imbiijwebinaan**; *prt* **baajwebinang**
biimashkwemaginigan *ni* bark torch; *pl* **biimashkwemaginiganan**; *loc* **biimashkwemaginiganing**; *dim* **biimashkwemaginigaans**
biimaakwad *ni* vine; *pl* **biimaakwadoon**; *loc* **biimaakwadong**; *dim* **biimaakwadoons**
biimidoon *vai* have a twisted mouth (as from a stroke); *1sg* **imbiimidoon**; *prt* **baamidoong**
biiminakwaan *ni* rope; *pl* **biiminakwaanan**; *loc* **biiminakwaaning**; *dim* **biiminakwaanens**
biiminakwaanens *ni* string; *pl* **biiminakwaanensan**; *loc* **biiminakwaanensing**
biiminakwe *vai* make rope, make string; *1sg* **imbiiminakwe**; *prt* **baaminakwed**
biiminigan *ni* brace and bit; *pl* **biiminiganan**
biimiskodisii *na* snail; *pl* **biimiskodisiig**
biimiskon *vta* turn s.o., twist s.o.; *1sg* **imbiimiskonaa**; *prt* **baamiskonaad**
biimiskonan *vti* turn s.t., twist s.t.; *1sg* **imbiimiskonaan**; *prt* **baamiskonang**
biimiskonigan *ni* screw; *pl* **biimiskoniganan**; *dim* **biimiskonigaans**
biimiskonikeshin *vai* fall and twist one's arm; *1sg* **imbiimiskonikeshin**; *prt* **baamiskonikeshing**
biimiskwa'an *vti* screw s.t.; *1sg* **imbiimiskwa'aan**; *prt* **baamiskwa'ang**
biimiskwa'igan *ni* screwdriver, wrench; *pl* **biimiskwa'iganan**; *loc* **biimiskwa'iganing**; *dim* **biimiskwa'igaans**
biimiskwa'igaans *ni* screw; *pl* **biimiskwa'igaansan**; *loc* **biimiskwa'igaansing**
biinad *vii* be clean; *prt* **baanak**
biina' /biina'w-/ *vta* put s.o. in; *1sg* **imbiina'waa**; *prt* **baana'waad**
biina'an *vti* put s.t. in; *1sg* **imbiina'aan**; *prt* **baana'ang**
biina'igaade *vii* be put in; *prt* **baana'igaadeg**; *aug* **biina'igaademagad**; *prt aug* **baana'igaademagak**
biina'igaazo *vai* be put in; *prt* **baana'igaazod**
biinaagamin /biinaagami-/ *vii* be clean (as a liquid); *prt* **baanaagamig**
biinda'am *vai2* be caught in a net; *1sg* **imbiinda'am**; *prt* **baanda'ang**
biindashkwaadan *vti* stuff s.t.; *1sg* **imbiindashkwaadaan**; *prt* **baandashkwaadang**
biindashkwaazh /biindashkwaaN-/ *vta* stuff s.o.; *1sg* **imbiindashkwaanaa**; *prt* **baandashkwaanaad**
biindaabikibijigan *ni* gearshift; *pl* **biindaabikibijiganan**
biindaabikibijige *vai* shift gears; *1sg* **imbiindaabikibijige**; *prt* **baandaabikibijiged**
biindaabikibizh /biindaabikibiN-/ *vta* shift s.o. (e.g., a car); *1sg* **imbiindaabikibinaa**; *prt* **baandaabikibinaad**
biindaakoojige *vai* make an offering of tobacco; *1sg* **imbiindaakoojige**; *prt* **baandaakoojiged**
biindaakoozh /biindaakooN-/ *vta* make an offering of tobacco to s.o.; *1sg* **imbiindaakoonaa**; *prt* **baandaakoonaad**
biindaakwaan *na* snuff; *loc* **biindaakwaaning**
biindaakwe *vai* chew snuff or tobacco; *1sg* **imbiindaakwe**; *prt* **baandaakwed**
biinde *vii* be in; *prt* **baandeg**; *aug* **biindemagad**; *prt aug* **baandemagak**
biindig *pc* inside

biindigadoon *vti2* bring s.t. inside, take s.t. inside; *1sg* **imbiindigadoon**; *prt* **baandigadood**
biindigaw *vta* enter into where s.o. is, come into where s.o. is; *1sg* **imbiindigawaa**; *prt* **baandigawaad**
biindigazh /biindigaN-/ *vta* bring s.o. inside, take s.o. inside; *1sg* **imbiindiganaa**; *prt* **baandiganaad**
biindige *vai* enter, go inside, come inside; *1sg* **imbiindige**; *prt* **baandiged**
biindigeba'idiwag /biindigeba'idi-/ *vai* they run inside together; *1pl* **imbiindigeba'idimin**; *prt* **baandigeba'idijig**
biindigeba'iwe *vai* run inside from people; *1sg* **imbiindigeba'iwe**; *prt* **baandigeba'iwed**
biindigebatoo *vai* run inside; *1sg* **imbiindigebatoo**; *prt* **baandigebatood**
biindigebatwaadan *vti* run inside with s.t.; *1sg* **imbiindigebatwaadaan**; *prt* **baandigebatwaadang**
biindigebatwaazh /biindigebatwaaN-/ *vta* run inside with s.o.; *1sg* **imbiindigebatwaanaa**; *prt* **baandigebatwaanaad**
biindigebide *vii* speed inside, drive inside, fly inside; *prt* **baandigebideg**; *aug* **biindigebidemagad**; *prt aug* **baandigebidemagak**
biindigebizo *vai* speed inside, drive inside, fly inside; *1sg* **imbiindigebiz**; *prt* **baandigebizod**
biindigenaazha' /biindigenaazha'w-/ *vta* tell s.o. to go inside; *1sg* **imbiindigenaazha'waa**; *prt* **baandigenaazha'waad**
biindigenaazhikaw *vta* chase s.o. inside; *1sg* **imbiindigenaazhikawaa**; *prt* **baandigenaazhikawaad**
biindigenise *vai* bring firewood inside; *1sg* **imbiindigenise**; *prt* **baandigenised**
biindigenizhikaw *vta* chase s.o. inside; *1sg* **imbiindigenizhikawaa**; *prt* **baandigenizhikawaad**
biindigeshimo *vai* dance inside (as in a Grand Entry); *1sg* **imbiindigeshim**; *prt* **baandigeshimod**
biindigewebin *vta* throw s.o. inside; *1sg* **imbiindigewebinaa**; *prt* **baandigewebinaad**
biindigewebinan *vti* throw s.t. inside; *1sg* **imbiindigewebinaan**; *prt* **baandigewebinang**
biindigewebinige *vai* throw things inside; *1sg* **imbiindigewebinige**; *prt* **baandigewebiniged**
biindigeyaashi *vai* be blown inside; *prt* **baandigeyaashid**
biindigeyaasin *vii* be blown inside; *prt* **baandigeyaasing**
biindoode *vii* crawl in; *prt* **baandooded**
biingeji *vai* feel cold; *1sg* **imbiingeji**; *prt* **baangejid**
biingeyendam *vai2* have something on one's mind, worry; *1sg* **imbiingeyendam**; *prt* **baangeyendang**
biinichigaade *vii* be cleaned; *prt* **baanichigaadeg**; *aug* **biinichigaademagad**; *prt aug* **baanichigaademagak**
biinichigaazo *vai* be cleaned; *prt* **baanichigaazod**
biinichige *vai* clean things; *1sg* **imbiinichige**; *prt* **baanichiged**
biinichigewikwe *na* cleaner (female), janitor (female); *pl* **biinichigewikweg**
biinichigewinini *na* cleaner, janitor; *pl* **biinichigewininiwag**
biini' *vta* clean s.o.; *1sg* **imbiini'aa**; *prt* **baani'aad**
biinininjii *vai* have a clean hand; *1sg* **imbiinininjii**; *prt* **baaninininjiid**
biinish *pc* until, up to
biinitaw *vta* clean (s.t.) for s.o.; *1sg* **imbiinitawaa**; *prt* **baanitawaad**
biinitoon *vti2* clean s.t.; *1sg* **imbiinitoon**; *prt* **baanitood**
biinizi *vai* be clean; *1sg* **imbiiniz**; *prt* **baanizid**
biinizikaa *pc* spontaneously, for no purpose at all
biinjayi'ii *pc* inside it
biinjibide *vii* speed in, drive in, fly in, fall in; *prt* **baanjibideg**; *aug* **biinjibidemagad**; *prt aug* **baanjibidemagak**
biinjibizo *vai* speed in, drive in, fly in, fall in; *1sg* **imbiinjibiz**; *prt* **baanjibizod**
biinjiboonaagan *na* fish trap; *pl* **biinjiboonaaganag**; *loc* **biinjiboonaaganing**; *dim* **biinjiboonaagaans**
biinjidawaa *vii* be an outlet; *prt* **baanjidawaag**
biinjidoon *pc* inside the mouth
biinjijaanzh *pc* inside the nose
biinjijiwan *vii* flow in; *prt* **baanjijiwang**
biinjikomaan *ni* knife sheath; *pl* **biinjikomaanan**; *loc* **biinjikomaaning**; *dim* **biinjikomaanens**
biinjina *pc* inside the body
biinjise *vai* fly in, fall in; *1sg* **imbiinjise**; *prt* **baanjised**
biinjise *vii* fly in, fall in; *prt* **baanjiseg**; *aug* **biinjisemagad**; *prt aug* **baanjisemagak**
biinjitawag *pc* inside an ear
biinjwebin *vta* throw s.o. in; *1sg* **imbiinjwebinaa**; *prt* **baanjwebinaad**
biinjwebinan *vti* throw s.t. in; *1sg* **imbiinjwebinaan**; *prt* **baanjwebinang**
biinjwebinige *vai* throw things in, vote; *1sg* **imbiinjwebinige**; *prt* **baanjwebiniged**
biinjwebinigetamaw *vta* vote for s.o.; *1sg* **imbiinjwebinigetamawaa**; *prt* **baanjwebinigetamawaad**
biinjwebinigewi-giizhigad *vii* be election day; *prt* **baanjwebinigewi-giizhigak**
biinzibii *vai* burp grease; *1sg* **imbiinzibii**; *prt* **baanzibiid**
biinzo *vai* be in; *1sg* **imbiinz**; *prt* **baanzod**
biipiinjigana'onag *na* dew-claw game *plural*
biisa' /biisa'w-/ *vta* chop s.o. fine; *1sg* **imbiisa'waa**; *prt* **baasa'waad**
biisa'an *vti* chop s.t. fine; *1sg* **imbiisa'aan**; *prt* **baasa'ang**
biisaa *vii* be fine, be in particles; *prt* **baasaag**; *aug* **biisaamagad**; *prt aug* **baasaamagak**
biisibidoon *vti2* crumble s.t., pull s.t. into particles; *1sg* **imbiisibidoon**; *prt* **baasibidood**
biisibizh /biisibiN-/ *vta* crumble s.o., pull s.o. into particles; *1sg* **imbiisibinaa**; *prt* **baasibinaad**
biisiboodoon *vti2* grind s.t. up; *1sg* **imbiisiboodoon**; *prt* **baasiboodood**
biisiboojigan *na* cornmeal; *loc* **biisiboojiganing**
biisiboojigan *ni* grinder, mill; *pl* **biisiboojiganan**; *loc* **biisiboojiganing**; *dim* **biisiboojigaans**

biisiboozh /biisibooN-/ *vta* grind s.o. up; *1sg* **imbiisiboonaa**; *prt* **baasiboonaad**
biisiga'isaan *ni* kindling wood; *pl* **biisiga'isaanan**; *loc* **biisiga'isaaning**; *dim* **biisiga'isaanens**
biisiga'ise *vai* make kindling; *1sg* **imbiisiga'ise**; *prt* **baasiga'ised**
biisitaagan *ni* bubble; *pl* **biisitaaganan**; *loc* **biisitaaganing**; *dim* **biisitaagaans**
biisizi *vai* be fine, be in particles; *prt* **baasizid**
biitagoode *vai* put on one's dress; *1sg* **imbiitagoode**; *prt* **baatagoodeg**
biitawagoodaan *ni* slip; *pl* **biitawagoodaanan**; *loc* **biitawagoodaaning**; *dim* **biitawagoodaanens**
biitazhigane *vai* put on one's socks; *1sg* **imbiitazhigane**; *prt* **baatazhiganed**
biite *ni* foam
biitewan *vii* be foamy; *prt* **baatewang**
biitewaaboo *ni* beer; *loc* **biitewaaboong**
biitoo- *pv4* as a layer
biitoo-babagiwayaan *ni* undershirt; *pl* **biitoo-babagiwayaanan**; *loc* **biitoo-babagiwayaaning**; *dim* **biitoo-babagiwayaanens**
biitoo-giboodiyegwaazon *na* underpants; *pl* **biitoo-giboodiyegwaazonag**; *loc* **biitoo-giboodiyegwaazoning**; *dim* **biitoo-giboodiyegwaazonens**
biitookizinaan *ni* overshoe; *pl* **biitookizinaanan**; *loc* **biitookizinaaning**; *dim* **biitookizinaanens**; *also* **biitookizin**
biitookizine *vai* wear overshoes; *1sg* **imbiitookizine**; *prt* **baatookizined**
biitookonaye *vai* wear layers (as underwear); *1sg* **imbiitookonaye**; *prt* **baatookonayed**
biitoon *vti2* wait for s.t.; *1sg* **imbiitoon**; *prt* **baatood**
biitooshin *vai* lie in a layer; *prt* **baatooshing**
biitooshkigan *ni* men's underwear; *pl* **biitooshkiganan**; *loc* **biitooshkiganing**; *dim* **biitooshkigaans**
biitoosijigan *na* pie; *pl* **biitoosijiganag**; *loc* **biitoosijiganing**; *dim* **biitoosijigaans**
biitoosijigani-bakwezhigan *na* pie; *pl* **biitoosijigani-bakwezhiganag**; *loc* **biitoosijigani-bakwezhiganing**; *dim* **biitoosijigani-bakwezhigaans**
biitoosin *vii* lie in a layer; *prt* **baatoosing**
biiwan *vii* be a blizzard; *prt* **baawang**
biiwaabik *ni* (piece of) metal, iron; *pl* **biiwaabikoon**; *loc* **biiwaabikong**; *dim* **biiwaabikoons**
biiwaabiko-adaawewigamig *ni* hardware store; *pl* **biiwaabiko-adaawewigamigoon**; *loc* **biiwaabiko-adaawewigamigong**; *also* **biiwaabikwadaawewigamig**
biiwaabiko-jiimaan *ni* aluminum canoe; *pl* **biiwaabiko-jiimaanan**; *loc* **biiwaabiko-jiimaaning**; *dim* **biiwaabiko-jiimaanens**
biiwaabikokaan *ni* mine; *pl* **biiwaabikokaanan**; *loc* **biiwaabikokaaning**; *dim* **biiwaabikokaanens**
biiwaabikokewinini *na* miner; *pl* **biiwaabikokewininiwag**
biiwaabikoons *ni* can, wire; *pl* **biiwaabikoonsan**; *loc* **biiwaabikoonsing**
biiwaanag *na* flint; *pl* **biiwaanagoog**; *loc* **biiwaanagong**; *dim* **biiwaanagoons**
biiwega'igan *ni* chip; *pl* **biiwega'iganan**; *loc* **biiwega'iganing**; *dim* **biiwega'igaans**
biiwide *na* stranger, visitor; *pl* **biiwideg**
biiwise *vai* scatter, disperse; *prt* **baawised**
biiwise *vii* scatter, disperse; *prt* **baawiseg**; *aug* **biiwisemagad**; *prt aug* **baawisemagak**
biiwiwebin *vta* scatter s.o.; *1sg* **imbiiwiwebinaa**; *prt* **baawiwebinaad**
biiwiwebinan *vti* scatter s.t.; *1sg* **imbiiwiwebinaan**; *prt* **baawiwebinang**
biizh /biiN-/ *vta* bring s.o.; *1sg* **imbiinaa**; *prt* **baanaad**
biizikan *vti* wear s.t., have s.t. on (e.g., clothes), put s.t. on (e.g., clothes); *1sg* **imbiizikaan**; *prt* **baazikang**
biizikaw *vta* wear s.o., have s.o. on (e.g., clothes), put s.o. on (e.g., clothes); *1sg* **imbiizikawaa**; *prt* **baazikawaad**
biizikiigan *ni* item of clothing; *pl* **biizikiiganan**; *loc* **biizikiiganing**; *dim* **biizikiigaans**
biizikonaye *vai* dress, be dressed, put on one's clothes; *1sg* **imbiizikonaye**; *prt* **baazikonayed**
biizikonaye' *vta* dress s.o.; *1sg* **imbiizikonaye'aa**; *prt* **baazikonaye'aad**
booch *pc* it is necessary, it is certain
boodawaade *vii* there is a fire made in a fireplace; *prt* **bwaadawaadeg**; *aug* **boodawaademagad**; *prt aug* **bwaadawaademagak**
boodawaan *ni* fireplace; *pl* **boodawaanan**; *loc* **boodawaaning**; *dim* **boodawaanens**
boodawe *vai* build a fire; *1sg* **imboodawe**; *prt* **bwaadawed**
boodawewinini *na* maintenance engineer, school custodian; *pl* **boodawewininiwag**; *dim* **boodawewinininiins**
boodaadan *vti* blow on s.t.; *1sg* **imboodaadaan**; *prt* **bwaadaadang**
boodaajige *vai* blow on things; *1sg* **imboodaajige**; *prt* **bwaadaajiged**
boodaajii' /boodaajii'w-/ *vta* inflate s.o.; *1sg* **imboodaajii'waa**; *prt* **bwaadaajii'waad**
boodaajii'an *vti* inflate s.t.; *1sg* **imboodaajii'aan**; *prt* **bwaadaajii'ang**
boodaajii'igan *ni* tire pump, air pump; *pl* **boodaajii'iganan**; *loc* **boodaajii'iganing**; *dim* **boodaajii'igaans**
boodaajii'ige *vai* inflate things; *1sg* **imboodaajii'ige**; *prt* **bwaadaajii'iged**
boodaakwe *vai+o* put (s.t.) in the kettle; *1sg* **imboodaakwe, imboodaakwen**; *prt* **bwaadaakwed**
boodaazh /boodaaN-/ *vta* blow on s.o.; *1sg* **imboodaanaa**; *prt* **bwaadaanaad**
boodewaadamii *na* Potawatomi; *pl* **boodewaadamiig**; *dim* **boodewaadamiins**
boodoonh *na* tadpole; *pl* **boodoonyag**
boogidi *vai* fart; *1sg* **imboogid**; *prt* **bwaagidid**
bookadinigan *na* doughnut; *pl* **bookadiniganag**; *loc* **bookadiniganing**; *dim* **bookadinigaans**; *also* **bwaakadinigaazod**
bookobidoon *vti2* pull s.t. in two, break s.t. in two with hands; *1sg* **imbookobidoon**; *prt* **bwaakobidood**

bookobizh /bookobiN-/ *vta* pull s.o. in two, break s.o. in two with hands; *1sg* **imbookobinaa**; *prt* **bwaakobinaad**
bookoganaam *vta* break s.o. in two by hitting; *1sg* **imbookoganaamaa**; *prt* **bwaakoganaamaad**
bookoganaandan *vti* break s.t. in two by hitting; *1sg* **imbookoganaandaan**; *prt* **bwaakoganaandang**
bookogaade *vai* break one's leg, have a broken leg; *1sg* **imbookogaade**; *prt* **bwaakogaaded**
bookogaadeshin *vai* fall and break one's leg; *1sg* **imbookogaadeshin**; *prt* **bwaakogaadeshing**
bookogwebizh /bookogwebiN-/ *vta* wring s.o.'s neck; *1sg* **imbookogwebinaa**; *prt* **bwaakogwebinaad**
bookojaane *vai* have a broken nose; *1sg* **imbookojaane**; *prt* **bwaakojaaned**
bookonike *vai* break one's arm, have a broken arm; *1sg* **imbookonike**; *prt* **bwaakoniked**
bookonikeshin *vai* fall and break one's arm; *1sg* **imbookonikeshin**; *prt* **bwaakonikeshing**
bookoshkan *vti* break s.t. in two by foot or body; *1sg* **imbookoshkaan**; *prt* **bwaakoshkang**
bookoshkaw *vta* break s.o. in two by foot or body; *1sg* **imbookoshkawaa**; *prt* **bwaakoshkawaad**
bookoshkaa *vai* break in two, be broken in two; *1sg* **imbookoshkaa**; *prt* **bwaakoshkaad**
bookoshkaa *vii* break in two, be broken in two; *prt* **bwaakoshkaag**; *aug* **bookoshkaamagad**; *prt aug* **bwaakoshkaamagak**
bookwaabik *ni* piece of metal; *pl* **bookwaabikoon**; *loc* **bookwaabikong**; *dim* **bookwaabikoons**
bookwaawiganeshin *vai* fall and break one's back; *1sg* **imbookwaawiganeshin**; *prt* **bwaakwaawiganeshing**
boonakadoon *vti2* anchor s.t.; *1sg* **imboonakadoon**; *prt* **bwaanakadood**
boonakajigan *ni* anchor; *pl* **boonakajiganan**; *loc* **boonakajiganing**; *dim* **boonakajigaans**
boonam *vai2* lay an egg; *prt* **bwaanang**
boonaanimad *vii* wind lets up, wind dies down; *prt* **bwaanaanimak**
boonendam *vai2* give up, not think about, ignore; *1sg* **imboonendam**; *prt* **bwaanendang**
boonendan *vti* forget s.t., ignore s.t.; *1sg* **imboonendaan**; *prt* **bwaanendang**
boonenim *vta* forget s.o., ignore s.o.; *1sg* **imboonenimaa**; *prt* **bwaanenimaad**
boonichigaade *vii* be left alone; *prt* **bwaanichigaadeg**; *aug* **boonichigaademagad**; *prt aug* **bwaanichigaademagak**
boonichigaazo *vai* be left alone; *prt* **bwaanichigaazod**
booni' *vta* leave s.o. alone, quit s.o.; *1sg* **imbooni'aa**; *prt* **bwaani'aad**
boonim *vta* stop talking to s.o., avoid talking to s.o.; *1sg* **imboonimaa**; *prt* **bwaanimaad**
boonitoon *vti2* leave s.t. alone, quit s.t.; *1sg* **imboonitoon**; *prt* **bwaanitood**
boonii *vai* alight, land (from flight); *1sg* **imboonii**; *prt* **bwaaniid**
boopoogid= < boogid=
booshke *pc* it's up to you, it's your decision; *also* **booshke giniin**
bootaagan *na* mortar for wild rice; *pl* **bootaaganag**; *loc* **bootaaganing**; *dim* **bootaagaans**
bootaaganaak *ni* pestle; *pl* **bootaaganaakoon**; *loc* **bootaaganaakong**; *dim* **bootaaganaakoons**
bootaagaadan *vti* stamp s.t. in a mortar; *1sg* **imbootaagaadaan**; *prt* **bwaataagaadang**
bootaage *vai* stamp things in a mortar (e.g., wild rice); *1sg* **imbootaage**; *prt* **bwaataaged**
boozhoo *pc* hello!, greetings!
boozi *vai* get in a vehicle or boat, board, embark, get aboard; *1sg* **imbooz**; *prt* **bwaazid**
boozigwaashkwani *vai* jump in a vehicle or boat, jump aboard; *1sg* **imboozigwaashkwan**; *prt* **bwaazigwaashkwanid**
boozi' *vta* give a ride to s.o.; *1sg* **imboozi'aa**; *prt* **bwaazi'aad**
boozikinaagan *ni* bowl; *pl* **boozikinaaganan**; *loc* **boozikinaaganing**; *dim* **boozikinaagaans**
boozinaazha' /boozinaazha'w-/ *vta* tell s.o. to get in (a vehicle or boat), tell s.o. to go aboard; *1sg* **imboozinaazha'waa**; *prt* **bwaazinaazha'waad**
boozinodaw *vta* catch a ride with s.o.; *1sg* **imboozinodawaa**; *prt* **bwaazinodawaad**
boozitaw *vta* load (s.t.) with cargo for s.o.; *1sg* **imboozitawaa**; *prt* **bwaazitawaad**
boozitaaso *vai* load cargo; *1sg* **imboozitaas**; *prt* **bwaazitaasod**
boozitoon *vti2* load s.t. as cargo; *1sg* **imboozitoon**; *prt* **bwaazitood**
bwaa- *pv1* not able to, not before
bwaakadinigaazod *na-pt* doughnut; *pl* **bwaakadinigaazojig**; *also* **bookadinigan**
bwaan *na* Dakota (Sioux); *pl* **bwaanag**; *dim* **bwaanens**
bwaanawichige *vai* be unable (to do something); *1sg* **imbwaanawichige**; *prt* **bwayaanawichiged**
bwaanawi' *vta* be unable to do something to s.o., be unable to manage s.o.; *1sg* **imbwaanawi'aa**; *prt* **bwayaanawi'aad**
bwaanawi'o *vai* be unable to do something, be stuck; *1sg* **imbwaanawi'**; *prt* **bwayaanawi'od**
bwaanawitoon *vti2* be unable to do s.t., be unable to manage s.t.; *1sg* **imbwaanawitoon**; *prt* **bwayaanawitood**
bwaanikwe *na* Dakota woman; *pl* **bwaanikweg**; *dim* **bwaanikwens**
bwaanimo *vai* speak Dakota; *1sg* **imbwaanim**; *prt* **bwayaanimod**
bwaanimotaw *vta* speak Dakota to s.o.; *1sg* **imbwaanimotawaa**; *prt* **bwayaanimotawaad**
bwaanzhii-nagamo *vai* sing war songs; *1sg* **imbwaanzhii-nagam**; *prt* **bwayaanzhii-nagamod**
bwaanzhii-niimi *vai* dance a war dance; *1sg* **imbwaanzhii-niim**; *prt* **bwayaanzhii-niimid**
bwaanzhii-niimi'idiwag /bwaanzhii-niimi'idi-/ *vai* they dance a war dance; *1pl* **imbwaanzhii-niimi'idimin**; *prt* **bwayaanzhii-niimi'idijig**
bwaanzhii-niimi'idiwin *ni* war dance; *pl* **bwaanzhii-niimi'idiwinan**
bwaanzhiiwi'o *vai* wear a dance outfit; *1sg* **imbwaanzhiiwi'**; *prt* **bwayaanzhiiwi'od**

bwaanzhiiwi'on *ni* dance outfit; *pl* **bwaanzhiiwi'onan**; *loc* **bwaanzhiiwi'oning**; *dim* **bwaanzhiiwi'onens**
bwaawane *vai* hardly be able to carry a pack; *1sg* **imbwaawane**; *prt* **bwayaawaned**

D

da- *pv1 future verb prefix in independent verbs with no personal prefix*
dabasagoode *vii* hang low; *prt* **debasagoodeg**; *aug* **dabasagoodemagad**; *prt aug* **debasagoodemagak**
dabasagoodoon *vti2* hang s.t. low; *1sg* **indabasagoodoon**; *prt* **debasagoodood**
dabasagoojin *vai* hang low; *prt* **debasagoojing**
dabasagoozh /dabasagooN-/ *vta* hang s.o. low; *1sg* **indabasagoonaa**; *prt* **debasagoonaad**
dabasakamigaa *vii* be low ground; *prt* **debasakamigaag**; *aug* **dabasakamigaamagad**; *prt aug* **debasakamigaamagak**
dabasaa *vii* be low; *prt* **debasaag**; *aug* **dabasaamagad**; *prt aug* **debasaamagak**
dabasendan *vti* hold s.t. in low regard; *1sg* **indabasendaan**; *prt* **debasendang**
dabasendaagozi *vai* be held in low regard; *1sg* **indabasendaagoz**; *prt* **debasendaagozid**
dabasendaagwad *vii* be held in low regard; *prt* **debasendaagwak**
dabasenim *vta* hold s.o. in low regard; *1sg* **indabasenimaa**; *prt* **debasenimaad**
dabazhish *pc* low
dabazi *vai* dodge; *1sg* **indabaz**; *prt* **debazid**; *also* **dabazii***
dabinoo'igan *ni* shelter; *pl* **dabinoo'iganan**; *loc* **dabinoo'iganing**; *dim* **dabinoo'igaans**
dadaabas= < dabas=
dadaakw= < dakw=
dadaakwanagweyaa *vii* have short sleeves; *prt* **dedaakwanagweyaag**; *aug* **dadaakwanagweyaamagad**; *prt aug* **dedaakwanagweyaamagak**
dadaakwaanikwe *vai* have short hair; *1sg* **indadaakwaanikwe**; *prt* **dedaakwaanikwed**
dadaatabanaamo *vai* have fast respiration; *1sg* **indadaatabanaam**; *prt* **dedaatabanaamod**
dadaatabaanagidoon *vai* talk quickly; *1sg* **indadaatabaanagidoon**; *prt* **dedaatabaanagidoong**
dadaatabii *vai* be quick; *1sg* **indadaatabii**; *prt* **dedaatabiid**
dadibaajimo *vai* tell stories, report, narrate; *1sg* **indadibaajim**; *prt* **dedibaajimod**
dadibaajimotaw *vta* tell stories to s.o., narrate to s.o.; *1sg* **indadibaajimotawaa**; *prt* **dedibaajimotawaad**
dadibaajimoowinini *na* storyteller; *pl* **dadibaajimoowininiwag**
daga *pc* please!, come on!
dago- *pv4* in a place with
dagode *vii* be cooked with something else; *prt* **degodeg**; *aug* **dagodemagad**; *prt aug* **degodemagak**
dagon /dago-/ *vii* be in a certain place, be situated in a certain place; *prt* **endagog**
dagon *vta* add s.o. in, mix s.o. in; *1sg* **indagonaa**; *prt* **degonaad**
dagonan *vti* add s.t. in, mix s.t. in; *1sg* **indagonaan**; *prt* **degonang**
dagonigaade *vii* be added in, be mixed in; *prt* **degonigaadeg**; *aug* **dagonigaademagad**; *prt aug* **degonigaademagak**
dagonigaazo *vai* be added in, be mixed in; *prt* **degonigaazod**
dagonige *vai* mix things in; *1sg* **indagonige**; *prt* **degoniged**
dagoshim *vta* arrive with s.o., get s.o. to destination; *1sg* **indagoshimaa**; *prt* **degoshimaad**
dagoshin *vai* arrive; *1sg* **indagoshin**; *prt* **degoshing**
dagoshinoomagad *vii* arrive; *prt* **degoshinoomagak**
dagoz /dagozw-/ *vta* cook s.o. with something else; *1sg* **indagozwaa**; *prt* **degozwaad**
dagozan *vti* cook s.t. with something else; *1sg* **indagozaan**; *prt* **degozang**
dagozo *vai* be cooked with something else; *1sg* **indagoz**; *prt* **degozod**
dagwagim *vta* count s.o. in; *1sg* **indagwagimaa**; *prt* **degwagimaad**
dagwagindan *vti* count s.t. in; *1sg* **indagwagindaan**; *prt* **degwagindang**
dagwaginde *vii* be included, be counted in; *prt* **degwagindeg**; *aug* **dagwagindemagad**; *prt aug* **degwagindemagak**
dagwaginzo *vai* be included, be counted in; *1sg* **indagwaginz**; *prt* **degwaginzod**
dagwaagin /dagwaagi-/ *vii* be fall, be autumn; *prt* **degwaagig**
dagwaagishi *vai* spend the fall somewhere; *1sg* **indagwaagish**; *prt* **degwaagishid**
dagwaagong *pc* last fall, last autumn
dakaji *vai* get a chill, have a cold; *1sg* **indakaj**; *prt* **dekajid**
dakamanji'o *vai* be chilled, feel cold; *1sg* **indakamanji'**; *prt* **dekamanji'od**
dakate *vii* be cold (as a house or room); *prt* **dekateg**; *aug* **dakatemagad**; *prt aug* **dekatemagak**
dakaa *vii* be cool (of a thing); *prt* **dekaag**; *aug* **dakaamagad**; *prt aug* **dekaamagak**
dakaagamin /dakaagami-/ *vii* be cold (as a liquid); *prt* **dekaagamig**
dakaagamisin *vii* cool off (as a liquid); *prt* **dekaagamising**
dakaanimad *vii* be a cold wind; *prt* **dekaanimak**
dakaashi *vai* be cooled by the wind; *prt* **dekaashid**
dakaasin *vii* be cooled by the wind; *prt* **dekaasing**
dakaayaa *vii* be cool (weather); *prt* **dekaayaag**; *aug* **dakaayaamagad**; *prt aug* **dekaayaamagak**; *also* **daki-ayaa**
dakib *ni* cold water

dakibiisaa *vii* be cold rain; *prt* **dekibiisaag**; *aug* **dakibiisaamagad**; *prt aug* **dekibiisaamagak**
dakininjii *vai* have a cold hand; *1sg* **indakininjii**; *prt* **dekininjiid**
dakise *vai* cool; *prt* **dekised**
dakise *vii* cool; *prt* **dekiseg**; *aug* **dakisemagad**; *prt aug* **dekisemagak**
dakishim *vta* set s.o. to cool; *1sg* **indakishimaa**; *prt* **dekishimaad**
dakishin *vai* cool off; *prt* **dekishing**
dakisidoon *vti2* set s.t. to cool; *1sg* **indakisidoon**; *prt* **dekisidood**
dakisijigan *ni* refrigerator, freezer; *pl* **dakisijiganan**; *loc* **dakisijiganing**; *dim* **dakisijigaans**
dakisin *vii* cool off; *prt* **dekising**
dakizi *vai* be cool (of a thing); *prt* **dekizid**
dakobide *vii* be tied, be bound; *prt* **dekobideg**; *aug* **dakobidemagad**; *prt aug* **dekobidemagak**
dakobidoo *vai* tie wild rice; *1sg* **indakobidoo**; *prt* **dekobidood**
dakobidoon *vti2* tie s.t., bind s.t.; *1sg* **indakobidoon**; *prt* **dekobidood**
dakobijigan *ni* tied wild rice
dakobijige *vai* tie things, bind things; *1sg* **indakobijige**; *prt* **dekobijiged**
dakobinaawaso *vai* have a baby in a cradle board; *1sg* **indakobinaawaso**; *prt* **dekobinaawasod**
dakobinaawaswaan *na* baby in a cradle board; *pl* **dakobinaawaswaanag**; *dim* **dakobinaawaswaanens**
dakobizh /dakobiN-/ *vta* tie s.o., bind s.o.; *1sg* **indakobinaa**; *prt* **dekobinaad**
dakobizo *vai* be tied, be bound, be in a cradle board; *1sg* **indakobiz**; *prt* **dekobizod**
dakokaadan *vti* step on s.t.; *1sg* **indakokaadaan**; *prt* **dekokaadang**
dakokaazh /dakokaaN-/ *vta* step on s.o.; *1sg* **indakokaanaa**; *prt* **dekokaanaad**
dakokii *vai* step; *1sg* **indakokii**; *prt* **dekokiid**
dakon *vta* hold s.o., take hold of s.o., arrest s.o.; *1sg* **indakonaa**; *prt* **dekonaad**
dakonamaw *vta* hold (s.t.) for s.o.; *1sg* **indakonamawaa**; *prt* **dekonamawaad**
dakonan *vti* hold s.t., take hold of s.t.; *1sg* **indakonaan**; *prt* **dekonang**
dakoniwe *vai* arrest people; *1sg* **indakoniwe**; *prt* **dekoniwed**
dakoniwewidaabaan *na* police car; *pl* **dakoniwewidaabaanag**; *loc* **dakoniwewidaabaaning**; *dim* **dakoniwewidaabaanens**
dakoniwewigamig *ni* police station; *pl* **dakoniwewigamigoon**; *loc* **dakoniwewigamigong**
dakoniwewinini *na* sheriff, policeman; *pl* **dakoniwewininiwag**
dakoonagad *vii* be short (as a boat); *prt* **dekoonagak**
dakoozi *vai* be short; *1sg* **indakooz**; *prt* **dekoozid**
dakwam *vta* bite s.o.; *1sg* **indakwamaa**; *prt* **dekwamaad**
dakwandan *vti* bite s.t.; *1sg* **indakwandaan**; *prt* **dekwandang**
dakwange *vai* bite people; *1sg* **indakwange**; *prt* **dekwanged**
dakwanjigan *ni* pliers; *pl* **dakwanjiganan**; *loc* **dakwanjiganing**; *dim* **dakwanjigaans**
dakwanjige *vai* bite things; *1sg* **indakwanjige**; *prt* **dekwanjiged**
dakwaa *vii* be short; *prt* **dekwaag**; *aug* **dakwaamagad**; *prt aug* **dekwaamagak**
dakwaabikad *vii* be short (as something mineral); *prt* **dekwaabikak**
dakwaabikizi *vai* be short (as something mineral); *prt* **dekwaabikizid**
dakwaabiigad *vii* be short (as something string-like); *prt* **dekwaabiigak**
dakwaabiigizh /dakwaabiigizhw-/ *vta* cut s.o. short (as something string-like); *1sg* **indakwaabiigizhwaa**; *prt* **dekwaabiigizhwaad**
dakwaabiigizhan *vti* cut s.t. short (as something string-like); *1sg* **indakwaabiigizhaan**; *prt* **dekwaabiigizhang**
dakwaabiigizi *vai* be short (as something string-like); *prt* **dekwaabiigizid**
dakwaakozi *vai* be short (as something stick- or wood-like); *prt* **dekwaakozid**
dakwaakwad *vii* be short (as something stick- or wood-like); *prt* **dekwaakwak**
dakwegad *vii* be short (as something sheet-like); *prt* **dekwegak**
dakwegizi *vai* be short (as something sheet-like); *prt* **dekwegizid**
danakamigad *vii* take place in a certain place, happen in a certain place; *prt* **endanakamigak**
danakamigizi *vai* have an event in a certain place, play in a certain place; *1sg* **indanakamigiz**; *prt* **endanakamigizid**
danakii *vai* live in a certain place; *1sg* **indanakii**; *prt* **endanakiid**
dananjige *vai* eat in a certain place; *1sg* **indananjige**; *prt* **endananjiged**
dananokii *vai* work in a certain place; *1sg* **indananokii**; *prt* **endanokiid**
danaadodan *vti* tell of s.t. in a certain place; *1sg* **indanaadodaan**; *prt* **endanaadodang**
danaajim *vta* tell of s.o. in a certain place; *1sg* **indanaajimaa**; *prt* **endanaajimaad**
danendan *vti* think s.t. to be in a certain place, expect s.t. to be in a certain place; *1sg* **indanendaan**; *prt* **endanendang**
danenim *vta* think s.o. to be in a certain place, expect s.o. to be in a certain place; *1sg* **indanenimaa**; *prt* **endanenimaad**
danens *na* club suite card; *pl* **danensag**
dangishkan *vti* kick s.t.; *1sg* **indangishkaan**; *prt* **dengishkang**
dangishkaw *vta* kick s.o.; *1sg* **indangishkawaa**; *prt* **dengishkawaad**
dangishkaage *vai* kick people; *1sg* **indangishkaage**; *prt* **dengishkaaged**
dangishkige *vai* kick things; *1sg* **indangishkige**; *prt* **dengishkiged**
dani *vai* be rich; *1sg* **indan**; *prt* **denid**
danitan *vti* hear s.t. in a certain place; *1sg* **indanitaan**; *prt* **endanitang**
danitaw *vta* hear s.o. in a certain place; *1sg* **indanitawaa**; *prt* **endanitawaad**
danitaagozi *vai* be heard in a certain place; *1sg* **indanitaagoz**; *prt* **endanitaagozid**

danitaagwad *vii* be heard in a certain place; *prt* **endanitaagwak**
daniwin *ni* wealth, riches, property, belongings; *pl* **daniwinan**; *loc* **daniwining**; *dim* **daniwinens**
danwewe *vii* there is noise in a certain place; *prt* **endanweweg**; *aug* **danwewemagad**; *prt aug* **endanwewemagak**
danwewidam *vai2* be heard speaking in a certain place; *1sg* **indanwewidam**; *prt* **endanwewidang**
dapaabam *vta* peek through an opening at s.o., look through a window at s.o.; *1sg* **indapaabamaa**; *prt* **depaabamaad**
dapaabandan *vti* peek through an opening at s.t., look through a window at s.t.; *1sg* **indapaabandaan**; *prt* **depaabandang**
dapaabi *vai* peek through an opening, look through a window; *1sg* **indapaab**; *prt* **depaabid**
dapine *vai* suffer in a certain place, die in a certain place; *1sg* **indapine**; *prt* **endapined**
dash *pc* and; *also* **idash, -sh**
dashiwag /dashi-/ *vai* they are a certain number, they are so many; *1pl* **indashimin**; *prt* **endashijig**
dasing *pc* a certain number of times, so many times
dasinoon /dasin-/ *vii* they are a certain number, they are so many; *prt* **endasingin**
daso- *pv3* a certain number, so many, every
daso-anama'e-giizhik *pc* a certain number of weeks, so many weeks
daso-anama'e-giizhikwagad *vii* be a certain number of weeks, be so many weeks; *prt* **endaso-anama'e-giizhikwagad**; *also* **daswanama'e-giizhikwagad**
daso-biboon *pc* a certain number of years, so many years
daso-biboonagad *vii* be a certain number of years, be so many years; *prt* **endaso-biboonagak**
daso-biboonagizi *vai* be a certain number of years old, be so many years old; *1sg* **indaso-biboonagiz**; *prt* **endaso-biboonagizid**
daso-diba'igan *pc* a certain number of hours, so many hours, a certain number of miles, so many miles
daso-diba'iganed *vii* be a certain hour, be a certain time in hours; *prt* **endaso-diba'iganek**
daso-diba'igaans *pc* a certain number of minutes, a certain number of acres, so many minutes, so many acres
daso-diba'iminaan *pc* a certain number of bushels, so many bushels
daso-dibaabiishkoojigan *pc* a certain number of pounds, so many pounds
daso-dibik *pc* a certain number of nights, so many nights
daso-gikinoonowin *pc* a certain number of years, so many years
daso-giizhigad *vii* be a certain date; *prt* **endaso-giizhigak**
daso-giizhik *pc* a certain number of days, so many days
daso-giizis *pc* a certain number of months, so many months
dasogon *pc* a certain number of days, so many days
dasogonagad *vii* be a certain number of days, be so many days; *prt* **endasogonagak**
dasogonagizi *vai* be a certain day of the month, be a certain number of days old; *prt* **endasogonagizid**
dasogonendi *vai* be gone a certain number of days, be absent a certain number of days; *1sg* **indasogonend**; *prt* **endasogonendid**
dasonaagaans *pc* a certain number of cupfuls, so many cupfuls
dasoninj *pc* a certain number of inches, so many inches
dasosagoons *nm* a certain number of thousands, so many thousand
dasozid *pc* a certain number of feet, so many feet
dasoonaagan *ni* trap; *pl* **dasoonaaganan**; *loc* **dasoonaaganing**; *dim* **dasoonaagaans**
dasooshkin *pc* certain number of bags, so many bags
dasoozh /dasooN-/ *vta* trap s.o.; *1sg* **indasoonaa**; *prt* **desoonaad**
dasoozo *vai* be trapped, be pinned down; *1sg* **indasooz**; *prt* **desoozod**
daswaabik *pc* a certain number of dollars, so many dollars
daswewaan *pc* a certain number of sets, so many sets, a certain number of pairs, so many pairs
daswi *nm* a certain number, so many
datak= < dak=
datakw= < dakw=
datang= < dang=
datap= < dap=
dawaa *vii* be space, be room; *prt* **dewaamagak**; *aug* **dawaamagad**; *prt aug* **dewaamagak**
dawibidoon *vti2* pull s.t. apart to form a gap; *1sg* **indawibidoon**; *prt* **dewibidood**
dawibijige *vai* pull things apart to form a gap; *1sg* **indawibijige**; *prt* **dewibijiged**
dawibizh /dawibiN-/ *vta* pull s.o. apart to form a gap; *1sg* **indawibinaa**; *prt* **dewibinaad**
dazhi- *pv3* in a certain place, of a certain place, there
dazhim *vta* talk about s.o., gossip about s.o.; *1sg* **indazhimaa**; *prt* **endazhimaad**
dazhindan *vti* talk about s.t., gossip about s.t.; *1sg* **indazhindaan**; *prt* **endazhindang**
dazhinge *vai* talk about people, gossip; *1sg* **indazhinge**; *prt* **endazhinged**
dazhishimo *vai* dance in a certain place; *1sg* **indazhishim**; *prt* **endazhishimod**
dazhishin *vai* lie in a certain place, be buried in a certain place; *1sg* **indazhishin**; *prt* **endazhishing**
dazhisin *vii* lie in a certain place; *prt* **endazhising**
dazhitaa *vai* spend time in a certain place, play in a certain place; *1sg* **indazhitaa**; *prt* **endazhitaad**
dazhiikan *vti* work on s.t., be involved with s.t.; *1sg* **indazhiikaan**; *prt* **endazhiikang**
dazhiikaw *vta* work on s.o., be involved with s.o.; *1sg* **indazhiikawaa**; *prt* **endazhiikawaad**
dazhiike *vai* stay in a certain place, spend time in a certain place; *1sg* **indazhiike**; *prt* **endazhiiked**

dazhiikigaade *vii* be worked on; *prt* **endazhiikigaadeg**; *aug* **dazhiikigaademagad**; *prt aug* **endazhiikigaademagak**
daa *vai* live in a certain place; *1sg* **indaa**; *prt* **endaad**
daa- *pv1* would *modal*, could *modal*, should *modal*, can *modal*, might *modal*
daadwaa= < dwaa=
daangam *vta* taste a sample of s.o.; *1sg* **indaangamaa**; *prt* **dayaangamaad**
daangandan *vti* taste a sample of s.t.; *1sg* **indaangandaan**; *prt* **dayaangandang**
daangigwanenan *vti* sign s.t.; *1sg* **indaangigwanenaan**; *prt* **dayaangigwanenang**
daangigwanenige *vai* sign things; *1sg* **indaangigwanenige**; *prt* **dayaangigwaneniged**
daangin *vta* touch s.o. with hand; *1sg* **indaanginaa**; *prt* **dayaanginaad**
daanginan *vti* touch s.t. with hand; *1sg* **indaanginaan**; *prt* **dayaanginang**
daangishim *vta* put s.o. touching; *1sg* **indaangishimaa**; *prt* **dayaangishimaad**
daangishin *vai* lie touching; *1sg* **indaangishin**; *prt* **dayaangishing**
daangisidoon *vti2* put s.t. touching; *1sg* **indaangisidoon**; *prt* **dayaangisidood**
daangisin *vii* lie touching; *prt* **dayaangising**
daashkaa *vii* be split, be torn apart; *prt* **dayaashkaag**; *aug* **daashkaamagad**; *prt aug* **dayaashkaamagak**
daashkibidoon *vti2* split s.t. lengthwise with hands, tear s.t. apart; *1sg* **indaashkibidoon**; *prt* **dayaashkibidood**
daashkibizh /daashkibiN-/ *vta* split s.o. lengthwise with hands, tear s.o. apart; *1sg* **indaashkibinaa**; *prt* **dayaashkibinaad**
daashkiboodoon *vti2* saw s.t. apart lengthwise; *1sg* **indaashkiboodoon**; *prt* **dayaashkiboodood**
daashkiboojigan *na* saw mill, ripsaw; *pl* **daashkiboojiganag**; *loc* **daashkiboojiganing**; *dim* **daashkiboojigaans**
daashkiboojige *vai* saw things apart lengthwise; *1sg* **indaashkiboojige**; *prt* **dayaashkiboojiged**
daashkiboozh /daashkibooN-/ *vta* saw s.o. apart lengthwise; *1sg* **indaashkiboonaa**; *prt* **dayaashkiboonaad**
daashkiga' /daashkiga'w-/ *vta* split s.o. by chopping (as something of wood); *1sg* **indaashkiga'waa**; *prt* **dayaashkiga'waad**
daashkiga'an *vti* split s.t. by chopping (as something of wood); *1sg* **indaashkiga'aan**; *prt* **dayaashkiga'ang**
daashkiga'ige *vai* split wood; *1sg* **indaashkiga'ige**; *prt* **dayaashkiga'iged**
daashkiga'ise *vai* split firewood; *1sg* **indaashkiga'ise**; *prt* **dayaashkiga'ised**
daashkigishkaa *vai* split (as something of wood); *prt* **dayaashkigishkaad**
daashkigishkaa *vii* split (as something of wood); *prt* **dayaashkigishkaag**; *aug* **daashkigishkaamagad**; *prt aug* **dayaashkigishkaamagak**
daashkikaa *vii* split apart, crack apart; *prt* **dayaashkikaag**; *aug* **daashkikaamagad**; *prt aug* **dayaashkikaamagak**
daashkikwadin *vii* there is a crack in the ice; *prt* **dayaashkikwading**
daashkizh /daashkizhw-/ *vta* split s.o. by cutting; *1sg* **indaashkizhwaa**; *prt* **dayaashkizhwaad**
daashkizhan *vti* split s.t. by cutting; *1sg* **indaashkizhaan**; *prt* **dayaashkizhang**
daataagwa'igan *ni* rolled oats, oatmeal; *pl* **daataagwa'iganan**; *loc* **daataagwa'iganing**; *dim* **daataagwa'igaans**
daataang= < daang=
daataaw= < daaw=
daawani *vai* open one's mouth; *1sg* **indaawan**; *prt* **dayaawanid**
de- *pv4* sufficient, suitable, enough
deba'ookii *vai* have enough to give away; *1sg* **indeba'ookii**; *prt* **dayeba'ookiid**
deba'oozh /deba'ooN-/ *vta* have enough to give to or feed s.o.; *1sg* **indeba'oonaa**; *prt* **dayeba'oonaad**
debakii'ige *vai* determine the depth; *1sg* **indebakii'ige**; *prt* **dayebakii'iged**
debashkine *vai* fit, adequately hold; *prt* **dayebashkined**
debashkine *vii* fit, adequately hold; *prt* **dayebashkineg**; *aug* **debashkinemagad**; *prt aug* **dayebashkinemagak**
debaabam *vta* have s.o. in sight, see s.o. at a distance; *1sg* **indebaabamaa**; *prt* **dayebaabamaad**
debaabaminaagozi *vai* be in sight, be visible at a distance; *1sg* **indebaabaminaagoz**; *prt* **dayebaabaminaagozid**
debaabaminaagwad *vii* be in sight, be visible at a distance; *prt* **dayebaabaminaagwak**
debaabandan *vti* have s.t. in sight, see s.t. at a distance; *1sg* **indebaabandaan**; *prt* **dayebaabandang**
debibidaw *vta* grab (s.t.) for s.o., catch (s.t.) for s.o., get hold of (s.t.) for s.o.; *1sg* **indebibidawaa**; *prt* **dayebibidawaad**
debibidoon *vti2* grab s.t., catch s.t., get hold of s.t.; *1sg* **indebibidoon**; *prt* **dayebibidood**
debibizh /debibiN-/ *vta* grab s.o., catch s.o., get hold of s.o.; *1sg* **indebibinaa**; *prt* **dayebibinaad**
debibii *vii* fit (as something liquid), adequately hold (something liquid); *prt* **dayebibiig**; *aug* **debibiimagad**; *prt aug* **dayebibiimagak**
debi' *vta* satisfy s.o., benefit s.o., give s.o. something appropriate; *1sg* **indebi'aa**; *prt* **dayebi'aad**
debinaak *pc* badly, carelessly, any old way
debisachige *vai* have enough of things; *1sg* **indebisachige**; *prt* **dayebisachiged**
debisa' *vta* have enough of s.o.; *1sg* **indebisa'aa**; *prt* **dayebisa'aad**
debisatoon *vti2* have enough of s.t.; *1sg* **indebisatoon**; *prt* **dayebisatood**
debise *vai* be enough, be sufficient; *prt* **dayebised**
debise *vii* be enough, be sufficient; *prt* **dayebiseg**; *aug* **debisemagad**; *prt aug* **dayebisemagak**
debisewendam *vai2* feel satisfied, think there is enough; *1sg* **indebisewendam**; *prt* **dayebisewendang**
debishkan *vti* fit s.t. with foot or body; *1sg* **indebishkaan**; *prt* **dayebishkang**

debishkaw *vta* fit s.o. with foot or body; *1sg* **indebishkawaa**; *prt* **dayebishkawaad**
debisinii *vai* eat enough, be full (after eating); *1sg* **indebisinii**; *prt* **dayebisiniid**
debizi *vai* be satisfied, be lucky, have enough; *1sg* **indebiz**; *prt* **dayebizid**
debwe *vai* tell the truth; *1sg* **indebwe**; *prt* **dayebwed**
debwetam *vai2* believe, agree; *1sg* **indebwetam**; *prt* **dayebwetang**
debwetan *vti* believe s.t.; *1sg* **indebwetaan**; *prt* **dayebwetang**
debwetaw *vta* believe s.o., agree with s.o., obey s.o.; *1sg* **indebwetawaa**; *prt* **dayebwetawaad**
debwetaagozi *vai* be believable, be believed; *1sg* **indebwetaagoz**; *prt* **dayebwetaagozid**
debwetaagwad *vii* be believable, be believed; *prt* **dayebwetaagwak**
debwewidam *vai2* be heard speaking at a distance; *1sg* **indebwewidam**; *prt* **dayebwewidang**
debweyendam *vai2* believe; *1sg* **indebweyendam**; *prt* **dayebweyendang**
debweyendan *vti* believe in s.t.; *1sg* **indebweyendaan**; *prt* **dayebweyendang**
debweyenim *vta* believe in s.o.; *1sg* **indebweyenimaa**; *prt* **dayebweyenimaad**
dekaag *ni-pt* ice cream
de-miijin *vti3* eat enough of s.t.; *1sg* **inde-miijin**; *prt* **daye-miijid**
desabi *vai* sit astride; *1sg* **indesab**; *prt* **dayesabid**
desa'an *vti* prop s.t. up to be a level surface; *1sg* **indesa'aan**; *prt* **dayesa'ang**
desa'on *ni* platform, bench, bed (in wigwam); *pl* **desa'onan**; *loc* **desa'oning**; *dim* **desa'onens**
desaa *vii* be a level surface; *prt* **dayesaag**; *aug* **desaamagad**; *prt aug* **dayesaamagak**
desaabaan *ni* shelf; *pl* **desaabaanan**; *loc* **desaabaaning**; *dim* **desaabaanens**
desinaagan *ni* dinner plate; *pl* **desinaaganan**; *loc* **desinaaganing**; *dim* **desinaagaans**
desinaagaans *ni* saucer; *pl* **desinaagaansan**; *loc* **desinaagaansing**
deteba'agonjichigan *ni* bobber, float; *pl* **deteba'agonjichiganan**; *loc* **deteba'agonjichiganing**; *dim* **deteba'agonjichigaans**
detibised *na-pt* wheel; *pl* **detibisejig**
detiwe *pc man's exclamation at making a small mistake*
dewaabide *vai* have a toothache; *1sg* **indewaabide**; *prt* **dayewaabided**
dewaawigan *vai* have a backache; *1sg* **indewaawigan**; *prt* **dayewaawigang**
dewe'igan *na* drum; *pl* **dewe'iganag**; *loc* **dewe'iganing**; *dim* **dewe'igaans**
dewe'iganaak *na* drumstick; *pl* **dewe'iganaakoon**; *loc* **dewe'iganaakong**; *dim* **dewe'iganaakoons**; *also* **dewe'iganaatig**
dewigaade *vai* have an ache in one's leg; *1sg* **indewigaade**; *prt* **dayewigaaded**
dewikwe *vai* have a headache; *1sg* **indewikwe**; *prt* **dayewikwed**
dewikwe-mashkikiins *ni* aspirin; *pl* **dewikwe-mashkikiinsan**; *loc* **dewikwe-mashkikiinsing**
dewikwese *vai* get a sudden headache; *1sg* **indewikwese**; *prt* **dayewikwesed**
dewinike *vai* have an ache in one's arm; *1sg* **indewinike**; *prt* **dayewiniked**
dewininjii *vai* have an ache in one's hand; *1sg* **indewininjii**; *prt* **dayewininjiid**
dewipikwan *vai* have a backache; *1sg* **indewipikwan**; *prt* **dayewipikwang**
dewizi *vai* ache; *1sg* **indewiz**; *prt* **dayewizid**
dewizide *vai* have an ache in one's foot; *1sg* **indewizide**; *prt* **dayewizided**
di- *vai* be in a certain condition, have a certain thing the matter with one *used primarily in the conjunct*; *prt* **endid**
diba' /diba'w-/ *vta* pay for s.o., bail s.o. out; *1sg* **indiba'waa**; *prt* **deba'waad**
diba'akii *vai* survey land; *1sg* **indiba'akii**; *prt* **deba'akiid**
diba'akiiwinini *na* surveyor; *pl* **diba'akiiwininiwag**
diba'amaw *vta* pay s.o. for (s.t.), pay (s.t.) to s.o.; *1sg* **indiba'amawaa**; *prt* **deba'amawaad**
diba'amaadiwag /diba'amaadi-/ *vai* they pay each other for (s.t.); *1pl* **indiba'amaadimin**; *prt* **deba'amaadijig**
diba'amaage *vai* pay people for (s.t.); *1sg* **indiba'amaage**; *prt* **deba'amaaged**
diba'an *vti* pay for s.t.; *1sg* **indiba'aan**; *prt* **deba'ang**
diba'aatigwaan *ni* yardstick, measuring stick for timber; *pl* **diba'aatigwaanan**
diba'aatigwe *vai* scale timber; *1sg* **indiba'aatigwe**; *prt* **deba'aatigwed**
diba'ige *vai* pay things, measure things; *1sg* **indiba'ige**; *prt* **deba'iged**
diba'igese *vii* pay off, pay for itself; *prt* **deba'igeseg**; *aug* **diba'igesemagad**; *prt aug* **deba'igesemagak**
diba'igiiziswaan *na* clock; *pl* **diba'igiiziswaanag**; *loc* **diba'igiiziswaaning**; *dim* **diba'igiiziswaanens**
diba'igiiziswaanens *na* watch; *pl* **diba'igiiziswaanensag**; *loc* **diba'igiiziswaanensing**

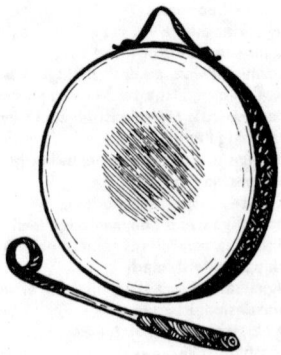

dewe'igan (drum), dewe'iganaak (drumstick)

dibaabam *vta* inspect s.o., look s.o. over, check up on s.o.; *1sg* **indibaabamaa**; *prt* **debaabamaad**
dibaabandan *vti* inspect s.t., look s.t. over; *1sg* **indibaabandaan**; *prt* **debaabandang**
dibaabiigin *vta* measure s.o. (as with something string-like); *1sg* **indibaabiiginaa**; *prt* **debaabiiginaad**
dibaabiiginan *vti* measure s.t. (as with something string-like); *1sg* **indibaabiiginaan**; *prt* **debaabiiginang**
dibaabiishkoodoon *vti2* weigh s.t.; *1sg* **indibaabiishkoodoon**; *prt* **debaabiishkoodood**
dibaabiishkoojigan *ni* scale; *pl* **dibaabiishkoojiganan**; *loc* **dibaabiishkoojiganing**; *dim* **dibaabiishkoojigaans**
dibaabiishkoojige *vai* weigh things; *1sg* **indibaabiishkoojige**; *prt* **debaabiishkoojiged**
dibaabiishkoozh /dibaabiishkooN-/ *vta* weigh s.o.; *1sg* **indibaabiishkoonaa**; *prt* **debaabiishkoonaad**
dibaadodan *vti* tell of s.t.; *1sg* **indibaadodaan**; *prt* **debaadodang**
dibaajim *vta* tell of s.o.; *1sg* **indibaajimaa**; *prt* **debaajimaad**
dibaajimo *vai* tell, narrate; *1sg* **indibaajim**; *prt* **debaajimod**
dibaajimotaw *vta* tell (s.t.) to s.o., narrate (s.t.) to s.o.; *1sg* **indibaajimotawaa**; *prt* **debaajimotawaad**
dibaajimowin *ni* story, narrative; *pl* **dibaajimowinan**; *dim* **dibaajimowinens**
dibaakon *vta* judge s.o.; *1sg* **indibaakonaa**; *prt* **debaakonaad**
dibaakonan *vti* judge s.t.; *1sg* **indibaakonaan**; *prt* **debaakonang**
dibaakonigaade *vai* be a court matter; *1sg* **indibaakonigaade**; *prt* **debaakonigaaded**
dibaakonigaazo *vai* be judged, be sentenced; *prt* **debaakonigaazod**
dibaakonige *vai* judge things, be in politics; *1sg* **indibaakonige**; *prt* **debaakoniged**
dibaakonigewigamig *ni* courthouse; *pl* **dibaakonigewigamigoon**; *loc* **dibaakonigewigamigong**
dibaakonigewinini *na* judge, lawyer; *pl* **dibaakonigewininiwag**
dibendan *vti* control s.t., be the master of s.t., own s.t., earn s.t.; *1sg* **indibendaan**; *prt* **debendang**
dibendaagozi *vai* be controlled, be owned, belong, be a member; *1sg* **indibendaagoz**; *prt* **debendaagozid**
dibendaagwad *vii* be controlled, be owned, belong; *prt* **debendaagwak**
dibendaaso *vai* own for oneself; *1sg* **indibendaas**; *prt* **debendaasod**
dibenim *vta* control s.o., own s.o., be the master of s.o.; *1sg* **indibenimaa**; *prt* **debenimaad**
dibenindizo *vai* be independent, be one's own master; *1sg* **indibenindiz**; *prt* **debenindizod**
dibenjigaade *vii* be owned; *prt* **debenjigaadeg**; *aug* **dibenjigaademagad**; *prt aug* **debenjigaademagak**
dibenjigaazo *vai* be owned, be an initiated member; *prt* **debenjigaazod**
dibi *pc* I don't know where, I wonder where *dubitative*
dibi go *pc* wherever, anywhere *dubitative*
dibi' *vta* keep up even with s.o.; *1sg* **indibi'aa**; *prt* **debi'aad**
dibikad *vii* be night; *prt* **debikak**
dibikate *vii* be dark (as in a room or house); *prt* **debikateg**; *aug* **dibikatemagad**; *prt aug* **debikatemagak**
dibikaabaminaagwad *vii* be twilight; *prt* **debikaabaminaagwak**
dibik-giizis *na* moon; *pl* **dibik-giizisoog**; *also* **dibiki-giizis**
dibiki-ayaa *vai* be dark; *prt* **debiki-ayaad**
dibikong *pc* last night
dibinawe *pc* by oneself, inherently
dibishkaa *vai* have a birthday; *1sg* **indibishkaa**; *prt* **debishkaad**
dibishkoo *pc* just like, even, equal, direct
dibishkookamig *pc* right across, opposite
dididibide *vii* roll; *prt* **dedibibideg**; *aug* **dididibidemagad**; *prt aug* **dedibibidemagak**
dididibizo *vai* roll; *1sg* **indididibiz**; *prt* **dedibibizod**
dididibin *vta* roll s.o.; *1sg* **indididibinaa**; *prt* **dedibinaad**
dididibinan *vti* roll s.t.; *1sg* **indididibinaan**; *prt* **dedibinang**
dididibininjiibizon *na* ring; *pl* **dididibininjiibizonag**; *loc* **dididibininjiibizoning**; *dim* **dididibininjiibizonens**
dididibise-apabiwin *ni* rocking chair; *pl* **dididibise-apabiwinan**; *loc* **dididibise-apabiwining**; *dim* **dididibise-apabiwinens**
digow *na* wave; *pl* **digowag**; *also* **digo**
dikinaagan *ni* cradle board; *pl* **dikinaaganan**; *loc* **dikinaaganing**; *dim* **dikinaagaans**
dikineyaab *ni* cradle board wrapper; *pl* **dikineyaabiin**; *loc* **dikineyaabiing**; *dim* **dikineyaabiins**
dimii *vii* be deep (of a body of water); *prt* **demiig**; *aug* **dimiimagad**; *prt aug* **demiimagak**
dino *pr* sort *inanimate*, kind *inanimate*; *also* **dinowa**
dino *pr* sort *animate*, kind *animate*; *also* **dinowa**
ditibibide *vii* roll along; *prt* **detibibideg**; *aug* **ditibibidemagad**; *prt aug* **detibibidemagak**
ditibidaabaan *na* wagon, truck; *pl* **ditibidaabaanag**; *loc* **ditibidaabaaning**; *dim* **ditibidaabaanens**
ditibise *vai* roll, go around (e.g., a wheel); *prt* **detibised**
ditibise *vii* roll, go around; *prt* **detibiseg**; *aug* **ditibisemagad**; *prt aug* **detibisemagak**
ditibiwebishkigan *na* bicycle; *pl* **ditibiwebishkiganag**; *loc* **ditibiwebishkiganing**; *dim* **ditibiwebishkiganens**
ditibiwebishkige *vai* pedal, roll things along by kicking; *1sg* **inditibiwebishkige**; *prt* **detibiwebishkiged**
diindiisi *na* blue jay; *pl* **diindiisiwag**; *dim* **diindiisiins**
diitiba'an *vti* knock s.t. down off using something; *1sg* **indiitiba'aan**; *prt* **daatiba'ang**

diitiba' /diitiba'w-/ *vta* knock s.o. down off using something; *1sg* **indiitiba'waa**; *prt* **daatiba'waad**
diitibibidoon *vti2* knock s.t. down off something with hands; *1sg* **indiitibibidoon**; *prt* **daatibibidood**
diitibibizh /diitibibiN-/ *vta* knock s.o. down off something with hands; *1sg* **indiitibibinaa**; *prt* **daatibibinaad**
diitibishkan *vti* bump s.t. down off, knock s.t. down off something with foot or body; *1sg* **indiitibishkaan**; *prt* **daatibishkang**
diitibishkaw *vta* bump s.o. down off, knock s.o. down off something with foot or body; *1sg* **indiitibishkawaa**; *prt* **daatibishkawaad**
doodam *vai2* do something; *1sg* **indoodam**; *prt* **endoodang**
doodan *vti* do something to s.t.; *1sg* **indoodaan**; *prt* **endoodang**
doodaw *vta* do something to s.o.; *1sg* **indoodawaa**; *prt* **endoodawaad**
doodaadiwag /doodaadi-/ *vai* they do something to each other; *1pl* **indoodaadimin**; *prt* **endoodaadijig**
doodaadizo *vai* do something to oneself; *1sg* **indoodaadiz**; *prt* **endoodaadizod**
doodaazo *vai* do something to oneself; *1sg* **indoodaaz**; *prt* **endoodaazod**
doodooshaaboo *ni* milk; *loc* **doodooshaaboong**
doodooshaaboo-bimide *ni* butter; *loc* **doodooshaaboo-bimideng**
doonoo *na* bull; *pl* **doonoog**
dooskaabi *vai* open one's eyes; *1sg* **indooskaab**; *prt* **dwaaskaabid**
dootooban *vii* be springy ground; *prt* **dwaatoobang**
dwaa'ibaan *ni* hole made in the ice for water; *pl* **dwaa'ibaanan**; *loc* **dwaa'ibaaning**; *also* **dwaa'igan**
dwaa'ibii *vai* make a water hole in the ice; *1sg* **indwaa'ibii**; *prt* **dwayaa'ibiid**; *also* **dwaa'ige**
dwaa'ige *vai* make a hole in the ice; *1sg* **indwaa'ige**; *prt* **dwayaa'iged**
dwaashin *vai* fall through the ice; *1sg* **indwaashin**; *prt* **dwayaashing**

E

edawayi'ii *pc* on both sides of it
edawi-zaka'o *vai* use crutches; *1sg* **indedawi-zaka'**; *prt* **ayedawi-zaka'od**
edawi-zaka'on *ni* crutch; *pl* **edawi-zaka'onan**; *dim* **edawi-zaka'onens**
eko- *pv3* since, a certain length, as long as (in time): *changed form of* **ako-**
eko-nising *pc* the third
eko-niizhing *pc* the second
emikwaan *ni* spoon, ladle; *pl* **emikwaanan**; *loc* **emikwaaning**; *dim* **emikwaanens**
emikwaanens *ni* spoon, teaspoon; *pl* **emikwaanensan**; *loc* **emikwaanensing**
enange *pc* sure! you bet!
enda- *pv4* just, real, very *nonitially:* **wenda-**
endaso- *pv3* so many, every: *changed form of:* **daso-**
endaso-dibik *pc* every night
endaso-gigizheb *pc* every morning
endaso-giizhik *pc* every day
endaso-giizis *pc* every month
endazhi- *pv3* in a certain place: *changed form of* **dazhi-**
endazhi-ataading *ni-pt* casino
endazhi-booniimagak *ni-pt* airport; *pl* **endazhi-booniimagakin**
endaad *vai* his/her home: *changed form of:* **daa**
endogwen *pc* I don't know, I am not sure
en' *pc* yes
eni- *pv2* going away from the speaker, coming up to in time *changed form of ani-*
enigok *pc* with effort, harder
enigoons *na* ant; *pl* **enigoonsag**; *also* **enig**
eniwek *pc* somewhat, a little bit, just so, middling
enyan' *pc* yes; *also* **en', eya'**
es *na* clam, shell; *pl* **esag**
eshkam *pc* gradually, more and more, less and less
eshkan *na* horn (of an animal); *pl* **eshkanag**
eshkan *ni* ice chisel; *pl* **eshkanan**
eshkandaming *ni-pt* watermelon; *pl* **eshkandamingin**
eshkwaa *pc* while
eshpabid *na-pt* leader, chairman; *pl* **eshpabijig**
esiban *na* raccoon; *pl* **esibanag**; *dim* **esibanens**
eta *pc* only
eya' *pc* yes
eyishwaaswi *nm* eight each; *also* **nenishwaaswi***
eyiidawayi'ii *pc* on both sides of it
eyiidawininj *pc* at both hands
eyiizh *pc* both
ezhi- *pv3* in a certain way, to a certain place, thus, so, there *changed form of* **izhi-**
ezhininjiishin *vai* leave a handprint; *1sg* **indezhininjiishin**; *prt* **ayezhininjiishing**
ezhishin *vai* leave a mark; *1sg* **indezhishin**; *prt* **ayezhishing**
ezhisin *vii* leave a mark; *prt* **ezhising**
ezigaa *na* wood tick; *pl* **ezigaag**; *dim* **ezigaans**

G

ga- *pv1 future tense prefix after a personal prefix*; *also* **gad-**
gabaa *vai* get off a vehicle or boat, disembark; *1sg* **ingabaa**; *prt* **gebaad**
gabaa' *vta* get s.o. off a vehicle or boat, disembark s.o.; *1sg* **ingabaa'aa**; *prt* **gebaa'aad**

gabaanaazha' /gabaanaazha'w-/ *vta* tell s.o. to get off, tell s.o. to disembark; *1sg* **ingabaanaazha'waa**; *prt* **gebaanaazha'waad**
gabaashim *vta* cook s.o. by boiling; *1sg* **ingabaashimaa**; *prt* **gebaashimaad**
gabaatoon *vti2* cook s.t. by boiling; *1sg* **ingabaatoon**; *prt* **gebaatood**
gabe- *pv4* whole extent of, throughout
gabe-ayi'ii *pc* throughout it, a long time; *also* **gabeyi'ii**
gabe-dibik *pc* all night
gabe-dibikwe *vai* spend the whole night; *1sg* **ingabe-dibikwe**; *prt* **gebe-dibikwed**
gabe-gikendaasoowigamig *ni* college, university; *pl* **gabe-gikendaasoowigamigoon**; *loc* **gabe-gikendaasoowigamigong**
gabe-giizhik *pc* all day
gabekana *pc* at the end of the road or trail
gabenaw *vta* win from s.o. in a game, beat s.o. in a game; *1sg* **ingabenawaa**; *prt* **gebenawaad**
gabenaage *vai* score in a game, win; *1sg* **ingabenaage**; *prt* **gebenaaged**
gabe-onaagosh *pc* all evening
gabeshi *vai* camp, set up camp; *1sg* **ingabesh**; *prt* **gebeshid**
gabeshiwin *ni* campsite; *pl* **gabeshiwinan**; *loc* **gabeshiwining**; *dim* **gabeshiwinens**
gabeshkan *vti* go to the end of s.t.; *1sg* **ingabeshkaan**; *prt* **gebeshkang**
gabeshkaa *vai* go to the end; *1sg* **ingabeshkaa**; *prt* **gebeshkaad**
gabikan *vti* pass s.t. by; *1sg* **ingabikaan**; *prt* **gebikang**
gabikaw *vta* pass s.o. by; *1sg* **ingabikawaa**; *prt* **gebikawaad**
gad- *pv1 future tense prefix after a personal prefix, optional form before vowels*
gaganoonidiwag /gaganoonidi-/ *vai* they talk to each other, they converse with each other; *1pl* **ingaganoonidimin**; *prt* **geganoonidijig**
gaganoozh /gaganooN-/ *vta* talk to s.o., converse with s.o.; *1sg* **ingaganoonaa**; *prt* **geganoonaad**
gagaanonagweyaa *vii* have long sleeves; *prt* **gegaanonagweyaag**; *aug* **gagaanonagweyaamagad**; *prt aug* **gegaanonagweyaamagak**
gagaanw= < ginw=
gagaanwaanikwe *vai* have long hair; *1sg* **ingagaanwaanikwe**; *prt* **gegaanwaanikwed**
gagaanwaawan /gagaanwaa-/ *vii* be long *plural*; *prt* **gegaanwaagin**; *aug* **gagaanwaamagadoon**; *prt aug* **gegaanwaamagakin**
gagaanzitaw *vta* act contrary to s.o.'s instructions; *1sg* **ingagaanzitawaa**; *prt* **gegaanzitawaad**
gagaanzom *vta* persuade s.o., urge s.o., convince s.o.; *1sg* **ingagaanzomaa**; *prt* **gegaanzomaad**
gagaapag= < gipag=
gagiib= < gib=
gagiibanagaskwe *vai* stutter; *1sg* **ingagiibanagaskwe**; *prt* **gegiibanagaskwed**
gagiibaadad *vii* be foolish; *prt* **gegiibaadak**
gagiibaadaatese *vii* be a comedy, be a funny movie; *prt* **gegiibaadaateseg**; *aug* **gagiibaadaatesemagad**; *prt aug* **gegiibaadaatesemagak**
gagiibaadizi *vai* be foolish; *1sg* **ingagiibaadiz**; *prt* **gegiibaadizid**
gagiibaajichige *vai* do foolish things; *1sg* **ingagiibaajichige**; *prt* **gegiibaajichiged**
gagiibijaane *vai* have a stuffed-up nose; *1sg* **ingagiibijaane**; *prt* **gegiibijaaned**
gagiibishe *vai* be deaf; *1sg* **ingagiibishe**; *prt* **gegiibished**
gagiibiingwe *vai* be blind; *1sg* **ingagiibiingwe**; *prt* **gegiibiingwed**
gagiibw= < gibw=
gagiichii *vai* take off one's shoes, take off one's moccasins; *1sg* **ingagiichii**; *prt* **gegiichiid**
gagiidag= < gidag=
gagiidisk= < gidisk=
gagiigin *vta* select from s.o., pick from s.o.; *1sg* **ingagiinaa**; *prt* **gegiiginaad**
gagiiginan *vti* select from s.t., pick from s.t.; *1sg* **ingagiiginaan**; *prt* **gegiiginang**
gagiij= < gij=
gagiik= < gik=
gagiikim *vta* preach to s.o.; *1sg* **ingagiikimaa**; *prt* **gegiikimaad**
gagiikimaawasowin *ni* education by preaching and exhortation
gagiikwe *vai* preach; *1sg* **ingagiikwe**; *prt* **gegiikwed**
gagiikwe-mazina'igan *ni* bible; *pl* **gagiikwe-mazina'iganan**; *loc* **gagiikwe-mazina'iganing**; *dim* **gagiikwe-mazina'igaans**
gagiikwewinini *na* preacher, minister; *pl* **gagiikwewininiwag**
gagiimood= < gimood=
gagiinawishki *vai* be a habitual liar; *1sg* **ingagiinawishk**; *prt* **gegiinawishkid**
gagiipidoon *vai* have chapped lips; *1sg* **ingagiipidoon**; *prt* **gegiipidoong**
gagiipizi *vai* be chapped; *1sg* **ingagiipiz**; *prt* **gegiipizid**
gagiipiingwe *vai* have a chapped face; *1sg* **ingagiipiingwe**; *prt* **gegiipiingwed**
gagiizh= < gizh=
gagiizhibaa= < gizhibaa=
gagiizhiib= < gizhiib=
gagwaadagitoo *vai* suffer; *1sg* **ingagwaadagitoo**; *prt* **gegwaadagitood**
gagwaanisagad *vii* be terrible; *prt* **gegwaanisagak**
gagwaanisagakamig *pc* terrible, awful
gagwaanisagendam *vai2* consider things to be terrible, suffer in one's mind; *1sg* **ingagwaanisagendam**; *prt* **gegwaanisagendang**
gagwaanisagendan *vti* consider s.t. terrible, consider s.t. disgusting; *1sg* **ingagwaanisagendaan**; *prt* **gegwaanisagendang**
gagwaanisagendaagozi *vai* be considered terrible, be considered disgusting; *1sg* **ingagwaanisagendaagoz**; *prt* **gegwaanisagendaagozid**
gagwaanisagendaagwad *vii* be considered terrible, be considered disgusting; *prt* **gegwaanisagendaagwak**
gagwaanisagenim *vta* consider s.o. to be terrible, consider s.o. disgusting; *1sg*

ingagwaanisagenimaa; *prt* **gegwaanisagenimaad**
gagwaanisagizi *vai* be mean, be terrible; *1sg* **ingagwaanisagiz**; *prt* **gegwaanisagizid**
gagwaayakw= < gwayakw=
gagwaazigw= < gozigw=
gagwe- *pv4* try
gagwedaganaam *vta* box s.o.; *1sg* **ingagwedaganaamaa**; *prt* **gegwedaganaamaad**
gagwedaganaandiwag /gagwedaganaandi-/ *vai* they box each other; *1pl* **ingagwedaganaandimin**; *prt* **gegwedaganaandijig**
gagwedaganewinini *na* boxer; *pl* **gagwedaganewininiwag**
gagweda'aakwe *vai* practice shooting; *1sg* **ingagweda'aakwe**; *prt* **gegweda'aakwed**
gagwedin *vta* test s.o. by touch; *1sg* **ingagwedinaa**; *prt* **gegwedinaad**
gagwedinan *vti* test s.t. by touch; *1sg* **ingagwedinaan**; *prt* **gegwedinang**
gagwedoomigo *vai* practice riding on horseback; *1sg* **ingagwedoomig**; *prt* **gegwedoomigod**
gagwedwe *vai* ask questions, inquire; *1sg* **ingagwedwe**; *prt* **gegwedwed**
gagwejichige *vai* try things; *1sg* **ingagwejichige**; *prt* **gegwejichiged**
gagweji' *vta* try to get s.o. to...; *1sg* **ingagweji'aa**; *prt* **gegweji'aad**
gagwejikada' /gagwejikada'w-/ *vta* race s.o. in boats; *1sg* **ingagwejikada'waa**; *prt* **gegwejikada'waad**
gagwejikada'odiwag /gagwejikada'odi-/ *vai* they race each other in boats; *1pl* **ingagwejikada'odimin**; *prt* **gegwejikada'odijig**
gagwejikanidiwag /gagwejikanidi-/ *vai* they race each other; *1pl* **ingagwejikanidimin**; *prt* **gegwejikanidijig**
gagwejikazh /gagwejikaN-/ *vta* race s.o.; *1sg* **ingagwejikanaa**; *prt* **gegwejikanaad**
gagwejikazhiwe *vai* race people; *1sg* **ingagwejikazhiwe**; *prt* **gegwejikazhiwed**
gagwejikazhiwewidaabaan *na* race car; *pl* **gagwejikazhiwewidaabaanag**
gagwejim *vta* ask s.o. questions; *1sg* **ingagwejimaa**; *prt* **gegwejimaad**
gagwejindiwag /gagwejindi-/ *vai* they ask each other questions; *1pl* **ingagwejindimin**; *prt* **gegwejindijig**
gagwejitoon *vti2* try s.t., test s.t.; *1sg* **ingagwejitoon**; *prt* **gegwejitood**
gagwejii *vai* test one's strength; *1sg* **ingagwejii**; *prt* **gegwejiid**
gagwejiiwaanidiwag /gagwejiiwaanidi-/ *vai* they wrestle each other; *1pl* **ingagwejiiwaanidimin**; *prt* **gegwejiiwaanidijig**
gagwejiiwaazh /gagwejiiwaaN-/ *vta* wrestle s.o.; *1sg* **ingagwejiiwaanaa**; *prt* **gegwejiiwaanaad**
gagwejiiwaazoowinini *na* wrestler; *pl* **gagwejiiwaazoowininiwag**
gagwezikan *vti* test s.t. with foot or body; *1sg* **ingagwezikaan**; *prt* **gegwezikang**
gagwezikaw *vta* test s.o. with foot or body; *1sg* **ingagwezikawaa**; *prt* **gegwezikawaad**
gakakaa *vii* be square; *prt* **gekakaag**; *aug* **gakakaamagad**; *prt aug* **gekakaamagak**
gakakaabikad *vii* be square (as something mineral); *prt* **gekakaabikak**
gakakaabikizi *vai* be square (as something mineral); *prt* **gekakaabikizid**
gakakaakozi *vai* be square (as something stick- or wood-like); *prt* **gekakaakozid**
gakakaakwad *vii* be square (as something stick- or wood-like); *prt* **gekakaakwak**
gakaki' *vta* make s.o. square; *1sg* **ingakaki'aa**; *prt* **gekaki'aad**
gakakishin *vai* have a square pattern; *prt* **gekakishing**
gakakisin *vii* have a square pattern; *prt* **gekakising**
gakakitoon *vti2* make s.t. square; *1sg* **ingakakitoon**; *prt* **gekakitood**
gakakizi *vai* be square; *prt* **gekakizid**
gakakiigad *vii* be square (as something sheet-like); *prt* **gekakiigak**
gakakiigizi *vai* be square (as something sheet-like); *prt* **gekakiigizid**
Gakaabikaang *place* Minneapolis
gakaaga'ogaan *ni* house-like lodge; *pl* **gakaaga'ogaanan**; *loc* **gakaaga'ogaaning**; *dim* **gakaaga'ogaanens**
gakaamikijiwan *vii* be a waterfall; *prt* **gekaamikijiwang**
gakeyaa *pc* in the direction of; *also* **akeyaa, keyaa, nakakeyaa***
gakijiwan *vii* be a waterfall; *prt* **gekijiwang**
gakina *pc* all; *also* **akina, kina**
gakina awiya *pr* everybody; *also* **akina awiya, kina awiya**
gakina gegoo *pr* everything; *also* **akina gegoo, kina gegoo**
gakiiwe *vai* go over a point, portage; *1sg* **ingakiiwe**; *prt* **gekiiwed**
gakiiwenige *vai* carry things over a portage; *1sg* **ingakiiwenige**; *prt* **gekiiweniged**
ganabaj *pc* perhaps, maybe
ganage *pc* in the least, by any means
ganakin *vta* take a handful of s.o.; *1sg* **inganakinaa**; *prt* **genakinaad**
ganakinan *vti* take a handful of s.t.; *1sg* **inganakinaan**; *prt* **genakinang**
ganawaabam *vta* look at s.o., watch s.o.; *1sg* **inganawaabamaa**; *prt* **genawaabamaad**
ganawaabandan *vti* look at s.t., watch s.t.; *1sg* **inganawaabandaan**; *prt* **genawaabandang**
ganawaabandiwag /ganawaabandi-/ *vai* they look at each other, they watch each other; *1pl* **inganawaabandimin**; *prt* **genawaabandijig**
ganawaabanjigaade *vii* be looked at, be watched; *prt* **genawaabanjigaadeg**; *aug* **ganawaabanjigaademagad**; *prt aug* **genawaabanjigaademagak**
ganawaabanjigaazo *vai* be looked at, be watched, be on parole; *prt* **genawaabanjigaazod**
ganawaabanjige *vai* look at things, watch things; *1sg* **inganawaabanjige**; *prt* **genawaabanjiged**
ganawaabi *vai* look, watch; *1sg* **inganawaab**; *prt* **genawaabid**
ganawendamaw *vta* take care of (s.t.) for s.o.; *1sg* **inganawendamawaa**; *prt* **genawendamawaad**

ganawendan *vti* take care of s.t.; *1sg* **inganawendaan**; *prt* **genawendang**
ganawendaagwad *vii* be taken care of; *prt* **genawendaagwak**
ganawendaawaso *vai* take care of a child; *1sg* **inganawendaawas**; *prt* **genawendaawasod**
ganawenim *vta* take care of s.o.; *1sg* **inganawenimaa**; *prt* **genawenimaad**
ganawenindiwag /ganawenindi-/ *vai* they take care of each other; *1pl* **inganawenindimin**; *prt* **genawenindijig**
ganawenjigaade *vii* be taken care of; *prt* **genawenjigaadeg**; *aug* **ganawenjigaademagad**; *prt aug* **genawenjigaademagak**
ganawenjigaazo *vai* be taken care of, be on parole; *prt* **genawenjigaazod**
ganawenjige *vai* take care of things; *1sg* **inganawenjige**; *prt* **genawenjiged**
ganoodan *vti* speak to s.t.; *1sg* **inganoodaan**; *prt* **genoodang**
ganoonidiwag /ganoonidi-/ *vai* they speak to each other; *1pl* **inganoonidimin**; *prt* **genoonidijig**
ganoozh /ganooN-/ *vta* address s.o., speak to s.o., call s.o. on the phone; *1sg* **inganoonaa**; *prt* **genoonaad**
gashkadin *vii* freeze over, be frozen over; *prt* **geshkading**
gashkadino-giizis *na* November
gashka'oode *vii* be knotted, be tangled; *prt* **geshka'oodeg**; *aug* **gashka'oodemagad**; *prt aug* **geshka'oodemagak**
gashka'oodoon *vti2* tie s.t. with a knot; *1sg* **ingashka'oodoon**; *prt* **geshka'oodood**
gashka'oojigan *ni* knot; *pl* **gashka'oojiganan**; *dim* **gashka'oojigaans**
gashka'oozh /gashka'ooN-/ *vta* tie s.o. with a knot; *1sg* **ingashka'oonaa**; *prt* **geshka'oonaad**
gashka'oozo *vai* be knotted, be tangled; *prt* **geshka'oozod**
gashkanokii *vai* be able to work; *1sg* **ingashkanokii**; *prt* **geshkanokiid**
gashkapidoon *vti2* tie s.t. shut, tie s.t. in a bundle; *1sg* **ingashkapidoon**; *prt* **geshkapidood**
gashkapizh /gashkapiN-/ *vta* tie s.o. shut, tie s.o. in a bundle; *1sg* **ingashkapinaa**; *prt* **geshkapinaad**
gashkawan *vii* be a dense fog; *prt* **geshkawang**
gashkaabika' /gashkaabika'w-/ *vta* lock s.o.; *1sg* **ingashkaabika'waa**; *prt* **geshkaabika'waad**
gashkaabika'an *vti* lock s.t.; *1sg* **ingashkaabika'aan**; *prt* **geshkaabika'ang**
gashkaabika'igan *ni* lock; *pl* **gashkaabika'iganan**; *loc* **gashkaabika'iganing**; *dim* **gashkaabika'igaans**
gashkaabika'igaade *vii* be locked; *prt* **geshkaabika'igaadeg**; *aug* **gashkaabika'igaademagad**; *prt aug* **geshkaabika'igaademagak**
gashkaabika'igaazo *vai* be locked; *prt* **geshkaabika'igaazod**
gashkaabika'ige *vai* lock things; *1sg* **ingashkaabika'ige**; *prt* **geshkaabika'iged**
gashkaakonan *vti* bar s.t. (as something stick- or wood-like), lock s.t. (as or as with something stick- or wood-like; *1sg* **ingashkaakonaan**; *prt* **geshkaakonang**
gashkaakwa'amaw *vta* lock (s.t.) for s.o. (as or as with something stick- or wood-like); *1sg* **ingashkaakwa'amawaa**; *prt* **geshkaakwa'amawaad**
gashkaaso *vai* be sunburned; *1sg* **ingashkaas**; *prt* **geshkaasod**
gashkendam *vai2* be lonely, be sad; *1sg* **ingashkendam**; *prt* **geshkendang**
gashkibidaagan *na* bag with closeable top, tobacco bag, pipe bag, bandolier bag; *pl* **gashkibidaaganag**; *loc* **gashkibidaaganing**; *dim* **gashkibidaagaans**

gashkibidaagan (bandolier bag;); see also aazhooningwa'igan

gashkibide *vii* be wrapped and tied in a bundle; *prt* **geshkibideg**; *aug* **gashkibidemagad**; *prt aug* **geshkibidemagak**
gashkibidoon *vti2* wrap and tie s.t. in a bundle; *1sg* **ingashkibidoon**; *prt* **geshkibidood**
gashkibijigan *ni* bundle, package, packet; *pl* **gashkibijiganan**; *loc* **gashkibijiganing**; *dim* **gashkibijigaans**
gashkibijigaade *vii* be wrapped and tied in a bundle; *prt* **geshkibijigaadeg**; *aug* **gashkibijigaademagad**; *prt aug* **geshkibijigaademagak**
gashkibijigaazo *vai* be wrapped and tied in a bundle; *prt* **geshkibijigaazod**
gashkibijige *vai* wrap and tie things in a bundle; *1sg* **ingashkibijige**; *prt* **geshkibijiged**
gashkibizh /gashkibiN-/ *vta* wrap and tie s.o. in a bundle; *1sg* **ingashkibinaa**; *prt* **geshkibinaad**
gashkichige *vai* acquire, earn, be able (to do something); *1sg* **ingashkichige**; *prt* **geshkichiged**
gashkidaasebizo *vai* wear leg garters; *1sg* **ingashkidaasebiz**; *prt* **geshkidaasebizod**
gashkidaasebizon *ni* leg garter; *pl* **gashkidaasebizonan**; *loc*

gashkidaasebizoning; *dim* **gashkidaasebizonens**
gashkigwaadan *vti* sew s.t.; *1sg* **ingashkigwaadaan**; *prt* **geshkigwaadang**
gashkigwaade *vii* be sewn; *prt* **geshkigwaadeg**; *aug* **gashkigwaademagad**; *prt aug* **geshkigwaademagak**
gashkigwaaso *vai* sew; *1sg* **ingashkigwaas**; *prt* **geshkigwaasod**
gashkigwaason *na* sewing machine; *pl* **gashkigwaasonag**; *loc* **gashkigwaasoning**; *dim* **gashkigwaasonens**
gashkigwaasoneyaab *ni* sewing thread; *pl* **gashkigwaasoneyaabiin**; *loc* **gashkigwaasoneyaabiing**; *dim* **gashkigwaasoneyaabiins**
gashkigwaazh /gashkigwaaN-/ *vta* sew s.o. (e.g., a pair of pants); *1sg* **ingashkigwaanaa**; *prt* **geshkigwaanaad**
gashkigwaazo *vai* be sewn; *prt* **geshkigwaazod**
gashki' *vta* prevail over s.o., manage s.o., earn s.o. (e.g., money); *1sg* **ingashki'aa**; *prt* **geshki'aad**
gashki'ewizi *vai* accomplish, succeed, have power; *1sg* **ingashki'ewiz**; *prt* **geshki'ewizid**
gashki'o *vai* be able, get free; *1sg* **ingashki'**; *prt* **geshki'od**
gashkitaw *vta* be able to get (s.t.) for s.o., be able to manage (s.t.) for s.o.; *1sg* **ingashkitawaa**; *prt* **geshkitawaad**
gashkitoon *vti2* be able to do s.t., succeed at s.t., manage s.t.; *1sg* **ingashkitoon**; *prt* **geshkitood**
gashkiwidoon *vti2* be able to take s.t., be able to carry s.t.; *1sg* **ingashkiwidoon**; *prt* **geshkiwidood**
gashkiwizh /gashkiwiN-/ *vta* be able to take s.o., be able to carry s.o.; *1sg* **ingashkiwinaa**; *prt* **geshkiwinaad**
gashkii-dibikad *vii* be very dark at night; *prt* **geshkii-dibikak**
gashkii-dibik-ayaa *vii* be dark as night; *prt* **geshkii-dibik-ayaag**; *aug* **gashkii-dibik-ayaamagad**; *prt aug* **geshkii-dibik-ayaamagak**
gawa' /gawa'w-/ *vta* fell s.o., chop s.o. down; *1sg* **ingawa'waa**; *prt* **gewa'waad**
gawa'an *vti* fell s.t., chop s.t. down; *1sg* **ingawa'aan**; *prt* **gewa'ang**
gawa'igaade *vii* be chopped down; *prt* **gewa'igaadeg**; *aug* **gawa'igaademagad**; *prt aug* **gewa'igaademagak**
gawa'igaazo *vai* be chopped down; *prt* **gewa'igaazod**
gawaji *vai* freeze to death; *1sg* **ingawaj**; *prt* **gewajid**
gawanaandam *vai2* starve; *1sg* **ingawanaandam**; *prt* **gewanaandang**
gawanokii *vai* collapse from overwork; *1sg* **ingawanokii**; *prt* **gewanokiid**
gawaabaagwe *vai* suffer from thirst; *1sg* **ingawaabaagwe**; *prt* **gewaabaagwed**
gawaakose *vai* fall over (as something stick- or wood-like); *prt* **gewaakosed**
gawaakose *vii* fall over (as something stick- or wood-like); *prt* **gewaakoseg**; *aug* **gawaakosemagad**; *prt aug* **gewaakosemagak**
gawaashi *vai* be blown over; *prt* **gewaashid**
gawaasin *vii* be blown over; *prt* **gewaasing**
gawin *vta* upset s.o. by hand, tip s.o. over by hand; *1sg* **ingawinaa**; *prt* **gewinaad**
gawinan *vti* upset s.t. by hand, tip s.t. over by hand; *1sg* **ingawinaan**; *prt* **gewinang**
gawingwashi *vai* fall asleep; *1sg* **ingawingwash**; *prt* **gewingwashid**
gawise *vai* fall over; *prt* **gewised**
gawise *vii* fall over; *prt* **gewiseg**; *aug* **gawisemagad**; *prt aug* **gewisemagak**
gawishimo *vai* lie down, go to bed; *1sg* **ingawishim**; *prt* **gewishimod**
gawiwebin *vta* throw s.o. down, knock s.o. down, pull s.o. down with hands; *1sg* **ingawiwebinaa**; *prt* **gewiwebinaad**
gawiwebinan *vti* throw s.t. down, knock s.t. down, pull s.t. down with hands; *1sg* **ingawiwebinaan**; *prt* **gewiwebinang**
gayat *pc* formerly, previously, some time ago
gayaashk *na* seagull; *pl* **gayaashkwag**; *dim* **gayaashkoons**
gaye *pc* as for, also, too, and; *also* **ge**
gaa- *pv1 past tense prefix under initial change*
gaadaw *vta* hide (s.t.) from s.o.; *1sg* **ingaadawaa**; *prt* **gayaadawaad**
gaadoon *vti2* hide s.t.; *1sg* **ingaadoon**; *prt* **gayaadood**
gaag *na* porcupine; *pl* **gaagwag**; *dim* **gaagoons**
gaagaagiw *na* raven; *pl* **gaagaagiwag**; *dim* **gaagaagiins**; *also* **gaagaagi***
gaagige- *pv4* forever
gaagiidaawigan *vai* have a sore back; *1sg* **ingaagiidaawigan**; *prt* **gayaagiidaawigang**
gaagiidizi *vai* be sore; *1sg* **ingaagiidiz**; *prt* **gayaagiidizid**
gaagiigido *vai* talk, speak; *1sg* **ingaagiigid**; *prt* **gayaagiigidod**
gaagiigidoo-bineshiinh *na* parrot; *pl* **gaagiigidoo-bineshiinyag**
gaagiigidoo-makakoons *ni* telephone, phonograph, record player; *pl* **gaagiigidoo-makakoonsan**; *loc* **gaagiigidoo-makakoonsing**
gaagiigidoowinini *na* councillor; *pl* **gaagiigidoowininiwag**
gaagiijidooskwan *vai* have a sore elbow; *1sg* **ingaagiijidooskwan**; *prt* **gayaagiijidooskwang**
gaagiijigaade *vai* have a sore leg; *1sg* **ingaagiijigaade**; *prt* **gayaagiijigaaded**
gaagiijinike *vai* have a sore arm; *1sg* **ingaagiijinike**; *prt* **gayaagiijiniked**
gaagiijininjii *vai* have a sore hand, have a sore finger; *1sg* **ingaagiijininjii**; *prt* **gayaagiijininjiid**
gaagiijizide *vai* have a sore foot; *1sg* **ingaagiijizide**; *prt* **gayaagiijizided**
gaagiizom *vta* appease s.o., apologize to s.o.; *1sg* **ingaagiizomaa**; *prt* **gayaagiizomaad**
gaajigaade *vii* be hidden; *prt* **gayaajigaadeg**; *aug* **gaajigaademagad**; *prt aug* **gayaajigaademagak**
gaajigaazo *vai* be hidden; *prt* **gayaajigaazod**

gaajige *vai* hide things; *1sg* **ingaajige**; *prt* **gayaajiged**
gaakaabishiinh *na* screech owl; *pl* **gaakaabishiinyag**
gaakaand= < gaand=
gaakaanj= < gaanj=
gaakaanz= < gaanz=
gaakaasii= < gaasii=
gaakaask= < gaask=
gaa mashi *pc* not yet; *also* **gaawiin mashi**
Gaa-miskwaawaakokaag *place* Cass Lake
gaanda'igwaason *ni* thimble; *pl* **gaanda'igwaasonan**; *loc* **gaanda'igwaasoning**; *dim* **gaanda'igwaasonens**
gaandakii'an *vti* pole s.t.; *1sg* **ingaandakii'aan**; *prt* **gayaandakii'ang**
gaandakii'iganaak *ni* push pole; *pl* **gaandakii'iganaakoon**; *loc* **gaandakii'iganaakong**; *dim* **gaandakii'iganaakoons**; *also* **gaandakii'iganaatig**
gaandakii'ige *vai* pole a boat; *1sg* **ingaandakii'ige**; *prt* **gayaandakii'iged**
gaandakii'o *vai* pole a boat; *1sg* **ingaandakii'**; *prt* **gayaandakii'od**
gaandin *vta* push s.o.; *1sg* **ingaandinaa**; *prt* **gayaandinaad**
gaandinamaw *vta* push (s.t.) for s.o.; *1sg* **ingaandinamawaa**; *prt* **gayaandinamawaad**
gaandinan *vti* push s.t.; *1sg* **ingaandinaan**; *prt* **gayaandinang**
gaandinige *vai* push things; *1sg* **ingaandinige**; *prt* **gayaandiniged**
gaanjida' /gaanjida'w-/ *vta* push s.o. with a stick; *1sg* **ingaanjida'waa**; *prt* **gayaanjida'waad**
gaanjida'an *vti* push s.t. with a stick; *1sg* **ingaanjida'aan**; *prt* **gayaanjida'ang**
gaanjida'ige *vai* push things with a stick; *1sg* **ingaanjida'ige**; *prt* **gayaanjida'iged**
gaanjweba' /gaanjweba'w-/ *vta* shove s.o. using something; *1sg* **ingaanjweba'waa**; *prt* **gayaanjweba'waad**
gaanjweba'an *vti* shove s.t. using something; *1sg* **ingaanjweba'aan**; *prt* **gayaanjweba'ang**
gaanjweba'ige *vai* shove things using something, pole logs; *1sg* **ingaanjweba'ige**; *prt* **gayaanjweba'iged**
gaanjwebin *vta* shove s.o.; *1sg* **ingaanjwebinaa**; *prt* **gayaanjwebinaad**
gaanjwebinan *vti* shove s.t.; *1sg* **ingaanjwebinaan**; *prt* **gayaanjwebinang**
gaanjwebishkan *vti* shove s.t. with foot or body; *1sg* **ingaanjwebishkaan**; *prt* **gayaanjwebishkang**
gaanjwebishkaw *vta* shove s.o. with foot or body; *1sg* **ingaanjwebishkawaa**; *prt* **gayaanjwebishkawaad**
gaanoo *na* diamond suite card; *pl* **gaanoog**
gaanzikan *vti* push s.t. with foot or body; *1sg* **ingaanzikaan**; *prt* **gayaanzikang**
gaanzikaw *vta* push s.o. with foot or body; *1sg* **ingaanzikawaa**; *prt* **gayaanzikawaad**
gaapam *vta* crunch s.o. in mouth; *1sg* **ingaapamaa**; *prt* **gayaapamaad**
gaapan *vii* be brittle; *prt* **gayaapang**; *also* **gaapaa**
gaapandan *vti* crunch s.t. in mouth; *1sg* **ingaapandaan**; *prt* **gayaapandang**
gaapanjige *vai* crunch things in mouth; *1sg* **ingaapanjige**; *prt* **gayaapanjiged**
gaapizan *vti* parch s.t.; *1sg* **ingaapizaan**; *prt* **gayaapizang**
gaapizi *vai* be brittle; *prt* **gayaapizid**
gaapizigan *ni* popped wild rice; *pl* **gaapiziganan**; *loc* **gaapiziganing**; *dim* **gaapizigaans**
gaapizige *vai* parch things; *1sg* **ingaapizige**; *prt* **gayaapiziged**
gaapii *ni* coffee
gaashkakokwe'igan *ni* paddle for stirring boiling maple sap; *pl* **gaashkakokwe'iganan**; *dim* **gaashkakokwe'igaans**
gaashkibaajigan *ni* razor; *pl* **gaashkibaajiganan**; *loc* **gaashkibaajiganing**; *dim* **gaashkibaajigaans**
gaashkibaazh /gaashkibaaN-/ *vta* shave s.o.; *1sg* **ingaashkibaanaa**; *prt* **gayaashkibaanaad**
gaashkibaazo *vai* shave; *1sg* **ingaashkibaaz**; *prt* **gayaashkibaazod**
gaasiibii'an *vti* erase s.t.; *1sg* **ingaasiibii'aan**; *prt* **gayaasiibii'ang**
gaasiibii'igan *na* eraser; *pl* **gaasiibii'iganag**; *loc* **gaasiibii'iganing**; *dim* **gaasiibii'igaans**
gaasiibii'ige *vai* erase things; *1sg* **ingaasiibii'ige**; *prt* **gayaasiibii'iged**
gaasiidoone'o *vai* wipe one's mouth; *1sg* **ingaasiidoone'**; *prt* **gayaasiidoone'od**
gaasii' /gaasii'w-/ *vta* wipe s.o. using something; *1sg* **ingaasii'waa**; *prt* **gayaasii'waad**
gaasii'an *vti* wipe s.t. using something; *1sg* **ingaasii'aan**; *prt* **gayaasii'ang**
gaasii'ige *vai* wipe things using something; *1sg* **ingaasii'ige**; *prt* **gayaasii'iged**
gaasiinaagane *vai* wipe dishes; *1sg* **ingaasiinaagane**; *prt* **gayaasiinaaganed**
gaasiininjii *vai* wipe one's hands; *1sg* **ingaasiininjii**; *prt* **gayaasiininjiid**
gaaskanazo *vai* whisper; *1sg* **ingaaskanaz**; *prt* **gayaaskanazod**
gaaskanazootaw *vta* whisper to s.o.; *1sg* **ingaaskanazootawaa**; *prt* **gayaaskanazootawaad**
gaaskanaamo *vai* wheeze; *1sg* **ingaaskanaam**; *prt* **gayaaskanaamod**
gaaskaaska' /gaaskaaska'w-/ *vta* scrape s.o. using something; *1sg* **ingaaskaaska'waa**; *prt* **gayaaskaaska'waad**
gaaskaaska'an *vti* scrape s.t. using something; *1sg* **ingaaskaaska'aan**; *prt* **gayaaskaaska'ang**
gaaskide *vii* be dried out, be shrivelled; *prt* **gayaaskideg**; *aug* **gaaskidemagad**; *prt aug* **gayaaskidemagak**
gaaskiz /gaaskizw-/ *vta* dry s.o. by smoking; *1sg* **ingaaskizwaa**; *prt* **gayaaskizwaad**
gaaskizan *vti* dry s.t. by smoking; *1sg* **ingaaskizaan**; *prt* **gayaaskizang**

gaaskizo *vai* be dried out, be shrivelled; *1sg* **ingaaskiz**; *prt* **gayaaskizod**
gaawam *vta* be jealous of s.o.; *1sg* **ingaawamaa**; *prt* **gayaawamaad**
gaawaa *vii* be rough; *prt* **gayaawaag**; *aug* **gaawaamagad**; *prt aug* **gayaawaamagak**
Gaa-waabaabiganikaag *place* White Earth Reservation
gaawaabikad *vii* be rough (as something mineral); *prt* **gayaawaabikak**
gaawaabikizi *vai* be rough (as something mineral); *prt* **gayaawaabikizid**
gaawaandag *na* white spruce; *pl* **gaawaandagoog**; *loc* **gaawaandagong**; *dim* **gaawaandagoons**
gaawe *vai* be jealous; *1sg* **ingaawe**; *prt* **gayaawed**
gaawegad *vii* be rough (as something sheet-like); *prt* **gayaawegak**
gaawegizi *vai* be rough (as something sheet-like); *prt* **gayaawegizid**
gaawendam *vai2* be jealous; *1sg* **ingaawendam**; *prt* **gayaawendang**
gaawesa *pc* can't do it!, no way!, not at all
gaawizi *vai* be rough; *prt* **gayaawizid**
gaa wiikaa *pc* never; *also* **gaawiin wiikaa**
gaawiin *pc* no, not *negative*
gaawiin awiya *pr* nobody; *also* **gaawiin awiiya**
gaawiin ganage *pc* not in the least
gaawiin gegoo *pr* nothing
gaawiin geyaabi *pc* no more, no longer
gaawiin mashi *pc* not yet; *also* **gaa mashi**
gaawiin memwech *pc* it's not necessary, you don't have to
gaawiin wiikaa *pc* never; *also* **gaa wiikaa**
gaa-wiisagang *ni-pt* pepper
Gaa-zagaskwaajimekaag *place* Leech Lake Reservation
gaazh /gaaN-/ *vta* hide s.o.; *1sg* **ingaanaa**; *prt* **gayaanaad**
gaazhagens *na* cat; *pl* **gaazhagensag**
gaazo *vai* hide self; *1sg* **ingaaz**; *prt* **gayaazod**
gaazootaw *vta* hide from s.o.; *1sg* **ingaazootawaa**; *prt* **gayaazootawaad**
ge *pc* as for, also, too; *also* **gaye**
ge- *pv1 future tense prefix under initial change*
gebaakwa'ond *na-pt* prisoner; *pl* **gebaakwa'onjig**
gegapii *pc* after a while, eventually, finally
gegaa *pc* nearly, almost
geget *pc* sure, indeed, certainly, really
gego *pc* don't
gego bina *pc* just don't
gego ganage *pc* don't in any way
gego wiikaa *pc* don't ever
gegoo *pr* something *inanimate definite*, anything *inanimate indefinite*
gekek *na* hawk; *pl* **gekekwag**; *dim* **gekekoons**
gekinoo'amawind *na-pt* student; *pl* **gekinoo'amawinjig**
gekinoo'amaaged *na-pt* teacher; *pl* **gekinoo'amaagejig**
gemaa *pc* or, or maybe; *also* **gemaa gaye**
genwaabiigigwed *na-pt* giraffe; *pl* **genwaabiigigwejig**
genwaakwak apabiwin *ni* couch; *pl* **genwaakwakin apabiwinan**; *loc* **genwaakwak apabiwining**; *dim* **genwaakwak apabiwinens**
geshawishim *vta* put s.o. loosely; *1sg* **ingeshawishimaa**; *prt* **gayeshawishimaad**
geshawishkan *vti* fit s.t. loosely; *1sg* **ingeshawishkaan**; *prt* **gayeshawishkang**
geshawishkaw *vta* fit s.o. loosely; *1sg* **ingeshawishkawaa**; *prt* **gayeshawishkawaad**
geshawisidoon *vti2* put s.t. loosely; *1sg* **ingeshawisidoon**; *prt* **gayeshawisidood**
gete- *pv4* old, old-time
gete-aya'aa *na* someone old; *pl* **gete-aya'aag**
gete-ayi'ii *ni* something old; *pl* **gete-ayi'iin**
geyaabi *pc* still, yet
gezika *pc* suddenly
gezikwendam *vai2* vaguely remember; *1sg* **ingezikwendam**; *prt* **gayezikwendang**
gezikwendan *vti* vaguely remember s.t.; *1sg* **ingezikwendaan**; *prt* **gayezikwendang**
gezikwenim *vta* vaguely remember s.o.; *1sg* **ingezikwenimaa**; *prt* **gayezikwenimaad**
gi= *pre second person prefix before consonants in nouns and verbs*
gibadoonh *na* button; *pl* **gibadoonyag**; *loc* **gibadoons**; *also* **gibodoonh**
gibagoojigan *ni* cloth partition; *pl* **gibagoojiganan**; *loc* **gibagoojiganing**; *dim* **gibagoojigaans**
giba' /giba'w-/ *vta* stop s.o. up, plug s.o.; *1sg* **ingiba'waa**; *prt* **geba'waad**
giba'an *vti* stop s.t. up, plug s.t.; *1sg* **ingiba'aan**; *prt* **geba'ang**
giba'igaade *vii* be stopped up, be plugged; *prt* **geba'igaadeg**; *aug* **giba'igaademagad**; *prt aug* **geba'igaademagak**
giba'igaazo *vai* be stopped up, be plugged; *prt* **geba'igaazod**
giba'ige *vai* stop things up, plug things; *1sg* **ingiba'ige**; *prt* **geba'iged**
gibaabowe' /gibaabowe'w-/ *vta* put a lid on s.o.; *1sg* **ingibaabowe'waa**; *prt* **gebaabowe'waad**
gibaabowe'an *vti* put a lid on s.t.; *1sg* **ingibaabowe'aan**; *prt* **gebaabowe'ang**
gibaabowe'igan *ni* pot lid; *pl* **gibaabowe'iganan**; *loc* **gibaabowe'iganing**; *dim* **gibaabowe'igaans**
gibaabowe'ige *vai* put a lid on things; *1sg* **ingibaabowe'ige**; *prt* **gebaabowe'iged**
gibaakobidoon *vti2* can s.t., pull s.t. shut (as something stick- or wood-like); *1sg* **ingibaakobidoon**; *prt* **gebaakobidood**
gibaakobijigan *ni* canned goods; *pl* **gibaakobijiganan**
gibaakowebinan *vti* slam s.t. shut (as something stick- or wood-like, e.g., a door); *1sg* **ingibaakowebinaan**; *prt* **gebaakowebinang**
gibaakwadin *vii* be frozen shut; *prt* **gebaakwading**
gibaakwa' /gibaakwa'w-/ *vta* shut s.o. (as or as with something stick- or wood-like), dam s.o., obstruct s.o., jail s.o.; *1sg* **ingibaakwa'waa**; *prt* **gebaakwa'waad**
gibaakwa'an *vti* shut s.t. (as or as with something stick- or wood-like), dam s.t., obstruct s.t.; *1sg* **ingibaakwa'aan**; *prt* **gebaakwa'ang**
gibaakwa'igan *ni* dam, stopper, plug; *pl* **gibaakwa'iganan**; *loc* **gibaakwa'iganing**; *dim* **gibaakwa'igaans**
gibaakwa'igaade *vii* be shut (as or as with something stick- or wood-like); *prt*

gebaakwa'igaadeg; *aug* **gibaakwa'igaademagad**; *prt aug* **gebaakwa'igaademagak**
gibaakwa'igaazo *vai* be imprisoned; *prt* **gebaakwa'igaazod**
gibaakwa'ige *vai* dam things, plug things; *1sg* **ingibaakwa'ige**; *prt* **gebaakwa'iged**
gibaakwa'odiiwigamig *ni* jail, prison; *pl* **gibaakwa'odiiwigamigoon**; *loc* **gibaakwa'odiiwigamigong**; *dim* **gibaakwa'odiiwigamigoons**
gibaakwaji *vai* be frozen shut; *prt* **gebaakwajid**
gibichiitaa *vai* take a break; *1sg* **ingibichiitaa**; *prt* **gebichiitaad**
gibide'ebizon *ni* vest; *pl* **gibide'ebizonan**; *loc* **gibide'ebizoning**; *dim* **gibide'ebizonens**

gibide'ebizon (vest)

gibijaane *vai* have a stuffed-up nose; *1sg* **ingibijaane**; *prt* **gebijaaned**; *also* **gagiibijaane**
gibinewen *vta* choke s.o.; *1sg* **ingibinewenaa**; *prt* **gebinewenaad**
gibishaganzhii *vai* be constipated; *1sg* **ingibishaganzhii**; *prt* **gebishaganzhiid**
gibishe *vai* be deaf (in one ear); *1sg* **ingibishe**; *prt* **gebished**
gibishkan *vti* block s.t. with foot or body; *1sg* **ingibishkaan**; *prt* **gebishkang**
gibishkaw *vta* block s.o. with foot or body; *1sg* **ingibishkawaa**; *prt* **gebishkawaad**
gibishkwaande'on *ni* lodge door cover; *pl* **gibishkwaande'on**
gibiskwe *vai* be hoarse; *1sg* **ingibiskwe**; *prt* **gebiskwed**
gibitan *vai* have a nosebleed; *1sg* **ingibitan**; *prt* **gebitang**; *also* **gibitane***
gibitaneganaam *vta* bloody s.o.'s nose; *1sg* **ingibitaneganaamaa**; *prt* **gebitaneganaamaad**
gibitaneshin *vai* bloody one's nose falling; *1sg* **ingibitaneshin**; *prt* **gebitaneshing**
gibiiga'igan *ni* curtain, drapes; *pl* **gibiiga'iganan**; *loc* **gibiiga'iganing**; *dim* **gibiiga'igaans**
gibiiga'iganiigin *ni* window shade; *pl* **gibiiga'iganiiginoon**; *loc* **gibiiga'iganiiginong**; *dim* **gibiiga'iganiiginoons**
gibiiga'igaade *vii* be curtained; *prt* **gebiiga'igaadeg**; *aug* **gibiiga'igaademagad**; *prt aug* **gebiiga'igaademagak**
gibokiwas /gibokiwasw-/ *vta* glue s.o. shut; *1sg* **ingibokiwaswaa**; *prt* **gebokiwaswaad**
gibokiwasan *vti* glue s.t. shut; *1sg* **ingibokiwasaan**; *prt* **gebokiwasang**
gibokiwasigaade *vii* be glued shut; *prt* **gebokiwasigaadeg**; *aug* **gibokiwasigaademagad**; *prt aug* **gebokiwasigaademagak**
gibokiwasigaazo *vai* be glued shut; *prt* **gebokiwasigaazod**
giboz /gibozw-/ *vta* bake s.o., roast s.o. in the oven; *1sg* **ingibozwaa**; *prt* **gebozwaad**
gibozan *vti* bake s.t., roast s.t. in the oven; *1sg* **ingibozaan**; *prt* **gebozang**
giboziganaabik *ni* roasting pan; *pl* **giboziganaabikoon**; *loc* **giboziganaabikong**; *dim* **giboziganaabikoons**
gibozige *vai* roast things in the oven, bake things; *1sg* **ingibozige**; *prt* **geboziged**
giboobijiganeyaab *ni* drawstring; *pl* **giboobijiganeyaabiin**; *loc* **giboobijiganeyaabiing**; *dim* **giboobijiganeyaabiins**
giboobinidizo *vai* zip oneself up; *1sg* **ingiboobinidiz**; *prt* **geboobinidizod**
giboodiyegwaazon *na* pants; *pl* **giboodiyegwaazonag**; *loc* **giboodiyegwaazoning**; *dim* **giboodiyegwaazonens**
giboodiyegwaazoniigin *ni* denim; *pl* **giboodiyegwaazoniiginoon**
giboogwaadan *vti* sew s.t. shut; *1sg* **ingiboogwaadaan**; *prt* **geboogwaadang**
giboogwaazh /giboogwaaN-/ *vta* sew s.o. shut; *1sg* **ingiboogwaanaa**; *prt* **geboogwaanaad**
gibwanaabaawe *vai* drown; *1sg* **ingibwanaabaawe**; *prt* **gebwanaabaawed**
gibwanaamode *vii* be full of smoke; *prt* **gebwanaamodeg**; *aug* **gibwanaamodemagad**; *prt aug* **gebwanaamodemagak**
gibwanaamoz /gibwanaamozw-/ *vta* smoke s.o. out; *1sg* **ingibwanaamozwaa**; *prt* **gebwanaamozwaad**
gibwanaamozo *vai* suffocate from smoke; *1sg* **ingibwanaamoz**; *prt* **gebwanaamozod**
gichi- *pv4* big, great, very; *also* **chi-**
gichi-aniibiish *ni* cabbage; *pl* **gichi-aniibiishan**; *loc* **gichi-aniibiishing**; *dim* **gichi-aniibiishens**
gichi-aya'aa *na* adult, elder; *pl* **gichi-aya'aag**
gichi-aya'aawi *vai* be an adult, be an elder; *1sg* **ingichi-aya'aaw**; *prt* **gechi-aya'aawid**
gichi-aya'aawinaagozi *vai* look old; *1sg* **ingichi-aya'aawinaagoz**; *prt* **gechi-aya'aawinaagozid**
gichi-dibaakonigewinini *na* judge; *pl* **gichi-dibaakonigewininiwag**
gichigami *ni* sea, one of the Great Lakes, Lake Superior; *pl* **gichigamiin**; *loc* **gichigamiing**; *dim* **gichigamiins**
gichigamiiwashk *ni* reed; *pl* **gichigamiiwashkoon**; *loc* **gichigamiiwashkong**; *dim* **gichigamiiwashkoons**

gichi-gigizheb *pc* early in the morning
gichi-gizhizo *vai* have pneumonia; *1sg* **ingichi-gizhiz**; *prt* **gechi-gizhizod**
gichi-izhiwebad *vii* be stormy; *prt* **gechi-izhiwebak**
gichi-manidoo *na* Great Spirit, God; *pl* **gichi-manidoog**
gichi-manidoo-giizis *na* January; *also* **manidoo-giizis**
gichi-miikana *ni* highway; *pl* **gichi-miikanan**; *loc* **gichi-miikanaang**
gichi-mookomaan *na* white person, American; *pl* **gichi-mookomaanag**; *dim* **gichi-mookomaanens**
gichi-mookomaan *ni* large knife, butcher knife; *pl* **gichi-mookomaanan**; *loc* **gichi-mookomaaning**; *dim* **gichi-mookomaanens**
Gichi-mookomaan-aki *ni* United States; *loc* **Gichi-mookomaan-akiing**
gichi-mookomaanikwe *na* white woman; *pl* **gichi-mookomaanikweg**; *dim* **gichi-mookomaanikwens**
gichi-mookomaanimo *vai* speak English; *1sg* **ingichi-mookomaanim**; *prt* **gechi-mookomaanimod**
gichinik *ni* right hand *usually possessed*; *loc* **gichinikaang**
gichi-noodin *vii* be very windy, be a storm; *prt* **gechi-nooding**
gichi-ogimaa *na* highest leader, king; *pl* **gichi-ogimaag**; *dim* **gichi-ogimaans**
gichi-ogimaawi *vai* be the highest leader, be a king; *1sg* **ingichi-ogimaaw**; *prt* **gechi-ogimaawid**
gichi-ogin *na* tomato; *pl* **gichi-oginiig**; *loc* **gichi-oginiing**; *dim* **gichi-oginiins**
gichi-onaagan *ni* large pan, dish pan; *loc* **gichi-onaaganing**
Gichi-onigamiing *place* Grand Portage Reservation
gichi-oodena *ni* city; *pl* **gichi-oodenawan**; *loc* **gichi-oodenaang**
gichi-ziibi *ni* big river, Mississippi River; *pl* **gichi-ziibiwan**; *loc* **gichi-ziibiing**
gid= *pre second person prefix before vowels in verbs and non-dependent nouns*
gidagagwadaashi *na* crappie; *pl* **gidagagwadaashiwag**; *dim* **gidagagwadaashiins**
gidagaa *vii* be variegated, be spotted; *prt* **gedagaag**; *aug* **gidagaamagad**; *prt aug* **gedagaamagak**
gidagaa-bizhiw *na* bobcat; *pl* **gidagaa-bizhiwag**; *dim* **gidagaa-bizhiwens**
gidagaakoons *na* fawn; *pl* **gidagaakoonsag**
gidagizi *vai* be variegated, be spotted; *prt* **gedagizid**
gidagiigad *vii* be variegated (as something sheet-like), be spotted (as something sheet-like); *prt* **gedagiigak**
gidagiigin *ni* calico, cotton cloth; *pl* **gidagiiginoon**
gidagiigizi *vai* be variegated (as something sheet-like), be spotted (as something sheet-like); *prt* **gedagiigizid**
gida' /gida'w-/ *vta* remove s.o. using something; *1sg* **ingida'waa**; *prt* **geda'waad**
gida'an *vti* remove s.t. using something; *1sg* **ingida'aan**; *prt* **geda'ang**
gidamo /gidamw-/ *vta* eat up s.o.; *1sg* **ingidamwaa**; *prt* **gedamwaad**
gidasan *vti* parch s.t. (e.g., wild rice); *1sg* **ingidasaan**; *prt* **gedasang**
gidasige *vai* parch things (e.g., wild rice); *1sg* **ingidasige**; *prt* **gedasiged**
gidaan /gidaam-/ *vti3* eat up s.t.; *1sg* **ingidaan**; *prt* **gedaang**
gidaanawe *vai* eat everything up; *1sg* **ingidaanawe**; *prt* **gedaanawed**
gidimaagenim *vta* pity s.o.; *1sg* **ingidimaagenimaa**; *prt* **gedimaagenimaad**
gidimaaginaagozi *vai* look poor; *1sg* **ingidimaaginaagoz**; *prt* **gedimaaginaagozid**
gidimaaginaagwad *vii* look poor; *prt* **gedimaaginaagwak**
gidimaagizi *vai* be poor; *1sg* **ingidimaagiz**; *prt* **gedimaagizid**
gidiskaabiigishkaa *vii* come unconnected (as something string-like), come loose (as something string-like); *prt* **gediskaabiigishkaag**; *aug* **gidiskaabiigishkaamagad**; *prt aug* **gediskaabiigishkaamagak**
gidiskibidoon *vti2* pull s.t. free, disconnect s.t. with hands; *1sg* **ingidiskibidoon**; *prt* **gediskibidood**
gidiskibizh /gidiskibiN-/ *vta* pull s.o. free, disconnect s.o. with hands; *1sg* **ingidiskibinaa**; *prt* **gediskibinaad**
gidiskin *vta* free s.o., take s.o. off, disconnect s.o.; *1sg* **ingidiskinaa**; *prt* **gediskinaad**
gidiskinan *vti* free s.t., take s.t. off, disconnect s.t.; *1sg* **ingidiskinaan**; *prt* **gediskinang**
gidiskise *vai* come apart, come off; *prt* **gediskised**
gidiskise *vii* come apart, come off; *prt* **gediskiseg**; *aug* **gidiskisemagad**; *prt aug* **gediskisemagak**
gidoonagise *vai* fall out of a boat; *1sg* **ingidoonagise**; *prt* **gedoonagised**
gigazhigane *vai* wear socks; *1sg* **ingigazhigane**; *prt* **gegazhiganed**
gigaatigwaan *ni* sliver (in one's body); *pl* **gigaatigwaanan**; *loc* **gigaatigwaaning**; *dim* **gigaatigwaanens**
gigaatigwe *vai* have a sliver; *1sg* **ingigaatigwe**; *prt* **gegaatigwed**
gigibabagiwayaane *vai* wear a shirt; *1sg* **ingigibabagiwayaane**; *prt* **gegibabagiwayaaned**
gigibabiinzikawaagane *vai* wear a coat; *1sg* **ingigibabiinzikawaagane**; *prt* **gegibabiinzikawaaganed**
gigigiboodiyegwaazone *vai* wear pants; *1sg* **ingigigiboodiyegwaazone**; *prt* **gegigiboodiyegwaazoned**
gigiminjikaawane *vai* wear mittens; *1sg* **ingigiminjikaawane**; *prt* **gegiminjikaawaned**
gigishkan *vti* bear s.t. on one's body, have s.t. on one's body; *1sg* **ingigishkaan**; *prt* **gegishkang**
gigishkaw *vta* bear s.o. on one's body, be pregnant with s.o.; *1sg* **ingigishkawaa**; *prt* **gegishkawaad**
gigishkawaawaso *vai* be pregnant; *1sg* **ingigishkawaawas**; *prt* **gegishkawaawasod**

gigishkaajige *vai* be pregnant; *1sg* **ingigishkaajige**; *prt* **gegishkaajiged**
gigizheb *pc* in the morning
gigizhebaa-miijin *vti3* eat s.t. for breakfast; *1sg* **ingigizhebaa-miijin**; *prt* **gegizhebaa-miijid**
gigizhebaawagad *vii* be morning; *prt* **gegizhebaawagak**
gigizhebaa-wiisini *vai* eat breakfast; *1sg* **ingigizhebaa-wiisin**; *prt* **gegizhebaa-wiisinid**
gigizhebaa-wiisiniwin *ni* breakfast
gijibidoon *vti* remove s.t. with hands, pull s.t. off; *1sg* **ingijibidoon**; *prt* **gejibidood**
gijibizh /gijibiN-/ *vta* remove s.o. with hands, pull s.o. off; *1sg* **ingijibinaa**; *prt* **gejibinaad**
gijigijigaaneshiinh *na* chickadee; *pl* **gijigijigaaneshiinyag**
gijigwaadan *vti* remove s.t. with something sharp; *1sg* **ingijigwaadaan**; *prt* **gejigwaadang**
gijigwaazh /gijigwaaN-/ *vta* remove s.o. with something sharp; *1sg* **ingijigwaanaa**; *prt* **gejigwaanaad**
gijikonayezigan *na* hominy; *pl* **gijikonayeziganag**
gijinagizhiin *vta* disembowel s.o., gut s.o.; *1sg* **ingijinagizhiinaa**; *prt* **gejinagizhiinaad**
gijipizon *ni* belt; *pl* **gijipizonan**; *loc* **gijipizoning**; *dim* **gijipizonens**
gijipizonaabik *ni* belt buckle; *pl* **gijipizonaabikoon**; *loc* **gijipizonaabikong**; *dim* **gijipizonaabikoons**
gijipizonens *ni* fan belt; *loc* **gijipizonensing**
gikaa *vai* be elderly; *1sg* **ingikaa**; *prt* **gekaad**
gikendan *vti* know s.t.; *1sg* **ingikendaan**; *prt* **gekendang**
gikendaagozi *vai* be known; *1sg* **ingikendaagoz**; *prt* **gekendaagozid**
gikendaagwad *vii* be known; *prt* **gekendaagwak**
gikendaaso *vai* be smart, be educated; *1sg* **ingikendaas**; *prt* **gekendaasod**
gikenim *vta* know s.o.; *1sg* **ingikenimaa**; *prt* **gekenimaad**
gikenjige *vai* know things; *1sg* **ingikenjige**; *prt* **gekenjiged**
gikinawaabam *vta* learn by observation of s.o.; *1sg* **ingikinawaabamaa**; *prt* **gekinawaabamaad**
gikinawaabi *vai* learn by observation; *1sg* **ingikinawaab**; *prt* **gekinawaabid**
gikinawaajichige *vai* mark things; *1sg* **ingikinawaajichige**; *prt* **gekinawaajichiged**
gikinawaaji' *vta* mark s.o.; *1sg* **ingikinawaaji'aa**; *prt* **gekinawaaji'aad**
gikinawaajitoon *vti2* mark s.t.; *1sg* **ingikinawaajitoon**; *prt* **gekinawaajitood**
gikinjigwen *vta* embrace s.o., hug s.o.; *1sg* **ingikinjigwenaa**; *prt* **gekinjigwenaad**
gikinjigwenidiwag /gikinjigwenidi-/ *vai* they hug each other; *1pl* **ingikinjigwenidimin**; *prt* **gekinjigwenidijig**
gikinoo'amaw *vta* teach (s.t.) to s.o.; *1sg* **ingikinoo'amawaa**; *prt* **gekinoo'amawaad**
gikinoo'amaadizo *vai* teach oneself; *1sg* **ingikinoo'amaadiz**; *prt* **gekinoo'amaadizod**
gikinoo'amaadii-mazina'igan *ni* schoolbook; *loc* **gikinoo'amaadii-mazina'iganing**; *dim* **gikinoo'amaadii-mazina'igaans**
gikinoo'amaadiiwigamig *ni* school; *pl* **gikinoo'amaadiiwigamigoon**; *loc* **gikinoo'amaadiiwigamigong**; *dim* **gikinoo'amaadiiwigamigoons**
gikinoo'amaagan *na* student; *pl* **gikinoo'amaaganag**; *dim* **gikinoo'amaagaans**
gikinoo'amaage *vai* teach; *1sg* **ingikinoo'amaage**; *prt* **gekinoo'amaaged**
gikinoo'amaagewikwe *na* teacher (female); *pl* **gikinoo'amaagewikweg**
gikinoo'amaagewinini *na* teacher; *pl* **gikinoo'amaagewininiwag**
gikinoo'amaagozi *vai* be taught, go to school; *1sg* **ingikinoo'amaagoz**; *prt* **gekinoo'amaagozid**
gikinoonowagad *vii* a year passes; *prt* **gekinoonowagak**
gikinoonowin *ni* year
gikinootaw *vta* say something after s.o., follow s.o.'s instructions; *1sg* **ingikinootawaa**; *prt* **gekinootawaad**
gikiwe'on *ni* flag; *pl* **gikiwe'onan**; *loc* **gikiwe'oning**; *dim* **gikiwe'onens**
gimiwan *vii* rain; *prt* **gemiwang**
gimiwanoowayaan *ni* raincoat; *pl* **gimiwanoowayaanan**; *loc* **gimiwanoowayaaning**; *dim* **gimiwanoowayaanens**
gimoodi *vai+o* steal (s.t.); *1sg* **ingimood, ingimoodin**; *prt* **gemoodid**
gimoodim *vta* steal from s.o.; *1sg* **ingimoodimaa**; *prt* **gemoodimaad**
gimoodindiwag /gimoodindi-/ *vai* they steal from each other; *1pl* **ingimoodindimin**; *prt* **gemoodindijig**
gimoodishki *vai* be a thief; *1sg* **ingimoodishk**; *prt* **gemoodishkid**
gimoodishkiiwinini *na* thief, robber; *pl* **gimoodishkiiwininiwag**; *dim* **gimoodishkiiwininiins**
ginagaapi *vai* laugh, giggle; *1sg* **inginagaap**; *prt* **genagaapid**
ginagijiin *vta* tickle s.o. (at the mid-section); *1sg* **inginagijiinaa**; *prt* **genagijiinaad**
gina'amaw *vta* forbid s.o. to, warn s.o. against (s.t.); *1sg* **ingina'amawaa**; *prt* **gena'amawaad**
gina'amaadim /gina'amaadi-/ *vai* there is a prohibition, it is forbidden; *prt* **gena'amaading**
ginebig *na* snake; *pl* **ginebigoog**; *dim* **ginebigoons**
ginebigwayaan *na* snakeskin; *pl* **ginebigwayaanag**; *loc* **ginebigwayaaning**; *dim* **ginebigwayaanens**
ginigawin *vta* mix s.o.; *1sg* **inginigawinaa**; *prt* **genigawinaad**
ginigawinan *vti* mix s.t.; *1sg* **inginigawinaan**; *prt* **genigawinang**
ginigawinigaade *vii* be mixed; *prt* **genigawinigaadeg**; *aug* **ginigawinigaademagad**; *prt aug* **genigawinigaademagak**
ginigawinigaazo *vai* be mixed; *prt* **genigawinigaazod**
ginigawinige *vai* mix things; *1sg* **inginigawinige**; *prt* **genigawiniged**
ginigawisin *vii* be mixed; *prt* **genigawising**

ginigawiwebin *vta* mix s.o. by shaking; *1sg* **inginigawiwebinaa**; *prt* **genigawiwebinaad**
ginigawiwebinan *vti* mix s.t. by shaking; *1sg* **inginigawiwebinaan**; *prt* **genigawiwebinang**
giniw *na* golden eagle; *pl* **giniwag**; *dim* **giniwens**
ginjiba' *vta* flee from s.o., run away from s.o.; *1sg* **inginjiba'aa**; *prt* **genjiba'aad**
ginjiba'iwe *vai* flee from people, run away from people; *1sg* **inginjiba'iwe**; *prt* **genjiba'iwed**
ginjida' /ginjida'w-/ *vta* tap s.o. in, pound s.o. in; *1sg* **inginjida'waa**; *prt* **genjida'waad**
ginjida'an *vti* tap s.t. in, pound s.t. in; *1sg* **inginjida'aan**; *prt* **genjida'ang**
ginoodaawangaa *vii* be a long stretch of sand beach; *prt* **genoodaawangaag**; *aug* **ginoodaawangaamagad**; *prt aug* **genoodaawangaamagak**
ginoo' *vta* make s.o. long; *1sg* **inginoo'aa**; *prt* **genoo'aad**
ginoonagad *vii* be a long boat; *prt* **genoonagak**
ginoondawaan *ni* long lodge; *pl* **ginoondawaanan**; *loc* **ginoondawaaning**; *dim* **ginoondawaanens**
ginoozhe *na* northern pike; *pl* **ginoozheg**; *dim* **ginoozhens**
ginoozi *vai* be tall, be long; *1sg* **inginooz**; *prt* **genoozid**
ginwaa *vii* be long; *prt* **genwaag**; *aug* **ginwaamagad**; *prt aug* **genwaamagak**
ginwaabikad *vii* be long (as something mineral); *prt* **genwaabikak**
ginwaabikizi *vai* be long (as something mineral); *prt* **genwaabikizid**
ginwaabiigad *vii* be long (as something string-like); *prt* **genwaabiigak**
ginwaabiigizh /ginwaabiigizhw-/ *vta* cut s.o. long (as something string-like); *1sg* **inginwaabiigizhwaa**; *prt* **genwaabiigizhwaad**
ginwaabiigizhan *vti* cut s.t. long (as something string-like); *1sg* **inginwaabiigizhaan**; *prt* **genwaabiigizhang**
ginwaabiigizi *vai* be long (as something string-like); *prt* **genwaabiigizid**
ginwaako-apabiwin *ni* couch; *pl* **ginwaako-apabiwinan**; *loc* **ginwaako-apabiwining**; *dim* **ginwaako-apabiwinens**
ginwaakozi *vai* be tall (of a person), be long (as something wood or stick-like); *1sg* **inginwaakoz**; *prt* **genwaakozid**
ginwaakwad *vii* be long (as something stick- or wood-like); *prt* **genwaakwak**
ginwaatoon *vti2* make s.t. long; *1sg* **inginwaatoon**; *prt* **genwaatood**
ginwegad *vii* be long (as something sheet-like); *prt* **genwegak**
ginwegi' *vta* make s.o. long (as something sheet-like); *1sg* **inginwegi'aa**; *prt* **genwegi'aad**
ginwegitoon *vti2* make s.t. long (as something sheet-like); *1sg* **inginwegitoon**; *prt* **genwegitood**
ginwegizi *vai* be long (as something sheet-like); *prt* **genwegizid**
ginwenzh *pc* for a long time
ginzhizhawizi *vai* be a hard worker; *1sg* **inginzhizhawiz**; *prt* **genzhizhawizid**
gipagawe *vai* have thick fur; *prt* **gepagawed**
gipagaa *vii* be thick; *prt* **gepagaag**; *aug* **gipagaamagad**; *prt aug* **gepagaamagak**
gipagaabikad *vii* be thick (as something mineral); *prt* **gepagaabikak**
gipagaabikizi *vai* be thick (as something mineral); *prt* **gepagaabikizid**
gipagaabiigad *vii* be thick (as something string-like); *prt* **gepagaabiigak**
gipagaabiigizi *vai* be thick (as something string-like); *prt* **gepagaabiigizid**
gipagaakwadin *vii* be frozen thick; *prt* **gepagaakwading**
gipagaakwaji *vai* be frozen thick; *prt* **gepagaakwajid**
gipagikodan *vti* slice s.t. thick; *1sg* **ingipagikodaan**; *prt* **gepagikodang**
gipagikozh /gipagikoN-/ *vta* slice s.o. thick; *1sg* **ingipagikonaa**; *prt* **gepagikonaad**
gipagishin *vai* lie in a thick layer; *prt* **gepagishing**
gipagisin *vii* lie in a thick layer; *prt* **gepagising**
gipagizi *vai* be thick; *prt* **gepagizid**
gipagiigad *vii* be thick (as something sheet-like); *prt* **gepagiigak**
gipagiigizi *vai* be thick (as something sheet-like); *prt* **gepagiigizid**
gishkishenh *na* female dog; *pl* **gishkishenyag**
gisinaa *vii* be cold (weather); *prt* **gesinaag**; *aug* **gisinaamagad**; *prt aug* **gesinaamagak**
gitigaadan *vti* plant s.t.; *1sg* **ingitigaadaan**; *prt* **getigaadang**
gitigaade *vii* be planted; *prt* **getigaadeg**; *aug* **gitigaademagad**; *prt aug* **getigaademagak**
gitigaan *ni* garden, field, farm; *pl* **gitigaanan**; *loc* **gitigaaning**; *dim* **gitigaanens**
gitigaanens *ni* vegetable; *pl* **gitigaanensan**
gitigaazh /gitigaaN-/ *vta* plant s.o.; *1sg* **ingitigaanaa**; *prt* **getigaanaad**
gitigaazo *vai* be planted; *prt* **getigaazod**
gitige *vai* garden, farm, plant; *1sg* **ingitige**; *prt* **getiged**
gitigewinini *na* farmer; *pl* **gitigewininiwag**
gitimi *vai* be lazy; *1sg* **ingitim**; *prt* **getimid**
gitimishki *vai* be habitually lazy, be a lazybones; *1sg* **ingitimishk**; *prt* **getimishkid**
gitizi *vai* be older; *prt* **getizid**
gizhaabikiz /gizhaabikizw-/ *vta* heat s.o. (as something mineral); *1sg* **ingizhaabikizwaa**; *prt* **gezhaabikizwaad**
gizhaabikizan *vti* heat s.t. (as something mineral); *1sg* **ingizhaabikizaan**; *prt* **gezhaabikizang**
gizhaabikizigan *ni* stove; *pl* **gizhaabikiziganan**; *loc* **gizhaabikiziganing**; *dim* **gizhaabikizigaans**
gizhaabikizige *vai* heat things (as something mineral); *1sg* **ingizhaabikizige**; *prt* **gezhaabikiziged**
gizhaadan *vti* guard s.t., watch over s.t.; *1sg* **ingizhaadaan**; *prt* **gezhaadang**
gizhaadige *vai* guard things, watch over things; *1sg* **ingizhaadige**; *prt* **gezhaadiged**
gizhaadigewinini *na* game warden; *pl* **gizhaadigewininiwag**
gizhaagamide *vii* be hot (as a liquid); *prt* **gezhaagamideg**; *aug* **gizhaagamidemagad**; *prt aug* **gezhaagamidemagak**

gizhaagamizan *vti* heat s.t. (as a liquid); *1sg* **ingizhaagamizaan**; *prt* **gezhaagamizang**
gizhaagamizige *vai* heat things (as a liquid); *1sg* **ingizhaagamizige**; *prt* **gezhaagamiziged**
gizhaanimad *vii* be a hot wind; *prt* **gezhaanimak**
gizhaate *vii* be hot (weather); *prt* **gezhaateg**; *aug* **gizhaatemagad**; *prt aug* **gezhaatemagak**
gizhaawaso *vai* protect one's young; *1sg* **ingizhaawas**; *prt* **gezhaawasod**
gizhaawenim *vta* be jealous of s.o.; *1sg* **ingizhaawenimaa**; *prt* **gezhaawenimaad**
gizhaawenjige *vai* be jealous of things; *1sg* **ingizhaawenjige**; *prt* **gezhaawenjiged**
gizhaazh /gizhaaN-/ *vta* guard s.o., watch over s.o.; *1sg* **ingizhaanaa**; *prt* **gezhaanaad**
gizhe-manidoo *na* God (especially in Christian usage)
gizhewaadizi *vai* be kind, be generous; *1sg* **ingizhewaadiz**; *prt* **gezhewaadizid**
gizhibaabide *vii* spin, whirl, revolve; *prt* **gezhibaabideg**; *aug* **gizhibaabidemagad**; *prt aug* **gezhibaabidemagak**
gizhibaabise *vai* spin, whirl, revolve; *prt* **gezhibaabised**
gizhibaabise *vii* spin, whirl, revolve; *prt* **gezhibaabiseg**; *aug* **gizhibaabisemagad**; *prt aug* **gezhibaabisemagak**
gizhibaabizo *vai* spin, whirl, revolve; *prt* **gezhibaabizod**
gizhibaayaanimad *vii* be a whirlwind; *prt* **gezhibaayaanimak**
gizhibaayaasijigan *ni* rotary fan; *pl* **gizhibaayaasijiganan**; *loc* **gizhibaayaasijiganing**; *dim* **gizhibaayaasijigaans**
gizhide *vii* be hot; *prt* **gezhideg**; *aug* **gizhidemagad**; *prt aug* **gezhidemagak**
gizhizo *vai* be hot, have a fever; *1sg* **ingizhiz**; *prt* **gezhizod**
gizhiibatoo *vai* run fast; *1sg* **ingizhiibatoo**; *prt* **gezhiibatood**
gizhiibazhe *vai* have itchy skin; *1sg* **ingizhiibazhe**; *prt* **gezhiibazhed**
gizhiibide *vii* move fast, speed fast, fly fast; *prt* **gezhiibideg**; *aug* **gizhiibidemagad**; *prt aug* **gezhiibidemagak**
gizhiibizi *vai* itch; *1sg* **ingizhiibiz**; *prt* **gezhiibizid**
gizhiibizo *vai* move fast, speed fast, drive fast, fly fast; *1sg* **ingizhiibiz**; *prt* **gezhiibizod**
gizhiidaabii'iwe *vai* drive fast; *1sg* **ingizhiidaabii'iwe**; *prt* **gezhiidaabii'iwed**
gizhiigaa *vii* drip fast, leak fast; *prt* **gezhiigaag**; *aug* **gizhiigaamagad**; *prt aug* **gezhiigaamagak**
gizhiigi *vai* grow fast; *1sg* **ingizhiig**; *prt* **gezhiigid**
gizhiigin *vii* grow fast; *prt* **gezhiiging**
gizhiijiwan *vii* flow fast; *prt* **gezhiijiwang**
gizhiikaa *vai* go fast; *1sg* **ingizhiikaa**; *prt* **gezhiikaad**
gizhiikaabatoo *vai* run fast; *1sg* **ingizhiikaabatoo**; *prt* **gezhiikaabatood**
gizhiikaakwazhiwe *vai* paddle fast; *1sg* **ingizhiikaakwazhiwe**; *prt* **gezhiikaakwazhiwed**
gizhiise *vai* fly fast; *1sg* **ingizhiise**; *prt* **gezhiised**
gizhiise *vii* fly fast; *prt* **gezhiiseg**; *aug* **gizhiisemagad**; *prt aug* **gezhiisemagak**
gizhiiwe *vai* speak loud; *1sg* **ingizhiiwe**; *prt* **gezhiiwed**
gizhiiyaanimad *vii* wind blows fast; *prt* **gezhiiyaanimak**
gizizan *vti* heat s.t.; *1sg* **ingizizaan**; *prt* **gezizang**
giziibiiga' /giziibiiga'w-/ *vta* wash s.o. using something; *1sg* **ingiziibiiga'waa**; *prt* **geziibiiga'waad**
giziibiiga'an *vti* wash s.t. (clothes); *1sg* **ingiziibiiga'aan**; *prt* **geziibiiga'ang**
giziibiiga'igan *ni* soap; *pl* **giziibiiga'iganan**; *loc* **giziibiiga'iganing**; *dim* **giziibiiga'igaans**
giziibiiga'ige *vai* wash things, wash clothes; *1sg* **ingiziibiiga'ige**; *prt* **geziibiiga'iged**
giziibiiga'ige-makak *ni* washtub, washing machine; *pl* **giziibiiga'ige-makakoon**; *loc* **giziibiiga'ige-makakong**; *dim* **giziibiiga'ige-makakoons**
giziibiiga'igewigamig *ni* laundromat; *pl* **giziibiiga'igewigamigoon**; *loc* **giziibiiga'igewigamigong**; *dim* **giziibiiga'igewigamigoons**
giziibiigazhe *vai* take a bath, wash up; *1sg* **ingiziibiigazhe**; *prt* **geziibiigazhed**
giziibiigazhewaaboo *ni* rubbing alcohol
giziibiigin *vta* wash s.o. by hand; *1sg* **ingiziibiiginaa**; *prt* **geziibiiginaad**
giziibiiginakokwe *vai* wash pail, wash kettle; *1sg* **ingiziibiiginakokwe**; *prt* **geziibiiginakokwed**
giziibiiginan *vti* wash s.t. by hand; *1sg* **ingiziibiiginaan**; *prt* **geziibiiginang**
giziibiiginaagane *vai* wash dishes; *1sg* **ingiziibiiginaagane**; *prt* **geziibiiginaaganed**
giziibiiginaaganewaaboo *ni* liquid detergent
giziibiigindibe *vai* wash one's hair; *1sg* **ingiziibiigindibe**; *prt* **geziibiigindibed**
giziibiigindiben *vta* wash s.o.'s hair; *1sg* **ingiziibiigindibenaa**; *prt* **geziibiigindibenaad**
giziibiiginigaade *vii* be washed; *prt* **geziibiiginigaadeg**; *aug* **giziibiiginigaademagad**; *prt aug* **geziibiiginigaademagak**
giziibiigininjii *vai* wash one's hands; *1sg* **ingiziibiigininjii**; *prt* **geziibiigininjiid**
giziibiigisaginige *vai* wash floors; *1sg* **ingiziibiigisaginige**; *prt* **geziibiigisaginiged**
giziibiigisaginige-giizhigad *vii* be Saturday; *prt* **geziibiigisaginige-giizhigak**
giziibiigii *vai* wash; *1sg* **ingiziibiigii**; *prt* **geziibiigiid**
giziibiigiingwe *vai* wash one's face; *1sg* **ingiziibiigiingwe**; *prt* **geziibiigiingwed**
giziibiigiingwewinaagan *ni* wash basin; *loc* **giziibiigiingwewinaaganing**; *dim* **giziibiigiingwewinaagaans**
giziibwewe *vai* squeak, creak; *prt* **geziibwewed**
giziibwewe *vii* squeak, creak; *prt* **geziibweweg**; *aug* **giziibwewemagad**; *prt aug* **geziibwewemagak**
giziibweweshkaa *vai* squeak in motion, creak; *prt* **geziibweweshkaad**
giziibweweshkaa *vii* squeak in motion, creak; *prt* **geziibweweshkaag**; *aug*

giziibweweshkaamagad; *prt aug* **geziibweweshkaamagak**
giziibweweyaashi *vai* creak in the wind; *prt* **geziibweweyaashid**
giziibweweyaasin *vii* creak in the wind; *prt* **geziibweweyaasing**
giziidoone'on *ni* napkin; *pl* **giziidoone'onan**; *loc* **giziidoone'oning**; *dim* **giziidoone'onens**
giziin *vta* wipe s.o. by hand; *1sg* **ingiziinaa**; *prt* **geziinaad**
giziinan *vti* wipe s.t. by hand; *1sg* **ingiziinaan**; *prt* **geziinang**
giziindime'o *vai* wipe oneself after defecating; *1sg* **ingiziindime'**; *prt* **geziindime'od**
giziindime'on *ni* toilet tissue; *pl* **giziindime'onan**; *loc* **giziindime'oning**; *dim* **giziindime'onens**
giziingwe'o *vai* wipe one's face with something; *1sg* **ingiziingwe'**; *prt* **geziingwe'od**
giziingwe'on *ni* towel; *pl* **giziingwe'onan**; *loc* **giziingwe'oning**; *dim* **giziingwe'onens**
giziininjii'on *ni* napkin; *pl* **giziininjii'onan**; *loc* **giziininjii'oning**; *dim* **giziininjii'onens**
giziiyaabide'o *vai* brush one's teeth; *1sg* **ingiziiyaabide'**; *prt* **geziiyaabide'od**
giziiyaabide'odizo *vai* brush one's teeth; *1sg* **ingiziiyaabide'odiz**; *prt* **geziiyaabide'odizod**
giziiyaabide'on *ni* toothbrush; *pl* **giziiyaabide'onan**; *loc* **giziiyaabide'oning**; *dim* **giziiyaabide'onens**
giziiyaabika'igan *ni* dish towel; *pl* **giziiyaabika'iganan**; *loc* **giziiyaabika'iganing**; *dim* **giziiyaabika'igaans**
gii- *pv1 past verb prefix*
giichibabagiwayaane *vai* take off one's shirt; *1sg* **ingiichibabagiwayaane**; *prt* **gaachibabagiwayaaned**
giichibabiinzikawaagane *vai* take off one's coat; *1sg* **ingiichibabiinzikawaagane**; *prt* **gaachibabiinzikawaaganed**
giichigiboodiyegwaazone *vai* take off one's pants; *1sg* **ingiichigiboodiyegwaazone**; *prt* **gaachigiboodiyegwaazoned**
giichigobidoon *vti2* pull s.t. off; *1sg* **ingiichigobidoon**; *prt* **gaachigobidood**
giichigobizh /giichigobiN-/ *vta* pull s.t. off; *1sg* **ingiichigobinaa**; *prt* **gaachigobinaad**
giichigon *vta* take s.o. off, extricate s.o.; *1sg* **ingiichigonaa**; *prt* **gaachigonaad**
giichigonan *vti* take s.t. off, extricate s.t.; *1sg* **ingiichigonaan**; *prt* **gaachigonang**
giichigwam *vta* pull s.o. off with teeth; *1sg* **ingiichigwamaa**; *prt* **gaachigwamaad**
giichigwandan *vti* pull s.t. off with teeth; *1sg* **ingiichigwandaan**; *prt* **gaachigwandang**
giichiminjikaawane *vai* take off one's mittens; *1sg* **ingiichiminjikaawane**; *prt* **gaachiminjikaawaned**
giichiwakwaane *vai* take off one's hat; *1sg* **ingiichiwakwaane**; *prt* **gaachiwakwaaned**
giige *vai* heal up; *1sg* **ingiige**; *prt* **gaaged**
giigido *vai* speak; *1sg* **ingiigid**; *prt* **gaagidod**
giigidowin *ni* speech, telephone; *pl* **giigidowinan**; *loc* **giigidowining**; *dim* **giigidowinens**
giigidoo-biiwaabikoons *ni* telephone, telephone wire; *pl* **giigidoo-biiwaabikoonsan**; *loc* **giigidoo-biiwaabikoonsing**
giigidoowinini *na* councillor, representative; *pl* **giigidoowininiwag**
giigoonh *na* fish; *pl* **giigoonyag**
giigoonhwaaboo *ni* fish soup; *loc* **giigoonhwaaboong**
giigoonyike *vai* fish; *1sg* **ingiigoonyike**; *prt* **gaagoonyiked**
giigoonyikewinini *na* fisherman; *pl* **giigoonyikewininiwag**
giigoozens *na* minnow; *pl* **giigoozensag**
gii' *vta* get away from s.o., escape from s.o.; *1sg* **ingii'aa**; *prt* **gaa'aad**
gii'igoshimo *vai* fast for a vision; *1sg* **ingii'igoshim**; *prt* **gaa'igoshimod**
gii'iwe *vai* escape from people; *1sg* **ingii'iwe**; *prt* **gaa'iwed**
giikaji *vai* feel cold; *1sg* **ingiikaj**; *prt* **gaakajid**
giikanaamode *vii* be smoky inside; *prt* **gaakanaamodeg**; *aug* **giikanaamodemagad**; *prt aug* **gaakanaamodemagak**
giikanaamozigan *na* bacon
giikaam *vta* argue with s.o., quarrel with s.o.; *1sg* **ingiikaamaa**; *prt* **gaakaamaad**
giikaandiwag /giikaandi-/ *vai* they argue with each other, they quarrel with each other; *1pl* **ingiikaandimin**; *prt* **gaakaandijig**
giikimanizi *vai* feel numb, tingle; *1sg* **ingiikimaniz**; *prt* **gaakimanizid**
giikiibingwashi *vai* be sleepy; *1sg* **ingiikiibingwash**; *prt* **gaakiibingwashid**
giimaabam *vta* peek at s.o., spy on s.o.; *1sg* **ingiimaabamaa**; *prt* **gaamaabamaad**
giimaabi *vai* peek, spy; *1sg* **ingiimaab**; *prt* **gaamaabid**
giimaadoode *vai* creep away; *1sg* **ingiimaadoode**; *prt* **gaamaadooded**
giimitaw *vta* eavesdrop on s.o.; *1sg* **ingiimitawaa**; *prt* **gaamitawaad**
giimii *vai* flee, escape; *1sg* **ingiimii**; *prt* **gaamiid**
giimoodad *vii* be secret; *prt* **gaamoodak**
giimoodanjige *vai* eat things secretly; *1sg* **ingiimoodanjige**; *prt* **gaamoodanjiged**
giimoodaapi *vai* laugh secretly; *1sg* **ingiimoodaap**; *prt* **gaamoodaapid**
giimooj *pc* secretly
giimoozaabi *vai* peek; *1sg* **ingiimoozaab**; *prt* **gaamoozaabid**
giimoozikaw *vta* sneak up on s.o.; *1sg* **ingiimoozikawaa**; *prt* **gaamoozikawaad**
giin *pr* you *second person singular personal pronoun*
giinawaa *pr* you *second person plural personal pronoun*
giinawind *pr* we *first person inclusive personal pronoun*, us *first person inclusive personal pronoun*
giinaa *vii* be sharp; *prt* **gaanaag**; *aug* **giinaamagad**; *prt aug* **gaanaamagak**
giineta *pr* only you *second person singular personal pronoun*
giinetawaa *pr* only you *second personal plural personal pronoun*
giinetawind *pr* only us *first person inclusive personal pronoun*

giiniboodoon *vti2* file s.t. sharp; *1sg* **ingiiniboodoon**; *prt* **gaaniboodood**
giiniboozh /giinibooN-/ *vta* file s.o. sharp; *1sg* **ingiiniboonaa**; *prt* **gaaniboonaad**
giinitam *pr* your turn *second person singular personal pronoun*
giinitamawaa *pr* your turn *second person plural personal pronoun*
giinitamawind *pr* our turn *first person inclusive personal pronoun*
giinizi *vai* be sharp; *prt* **gaanizid**
giishkada'igan *ni* cleaver, chopping tool; *pl* **giishkada'iganan**; *loc* **giishkada'iganing**; *dim* **giishkada'igaans**
giishkadinaa *vii* be a cliff, be a steep bank; *prt* **gaashkadinaag**; *aug* **giishkadinaamagad**; *prt aug* **gaashkadinaamagak**
giishka' /giishka'w-/ *vta* chop s.o. off; *1sg* **ingiishka'waa**; *prt* **gaashka'waad**
giishka'an *vti* chop s.t. off; *1sg* **ingiishka'aan**; *prt* **gaashka'ang**
giishka'aakwe *vai* cut timber; *1sg* **ingiishka'aakwe**; *prt* **gaashka'aakwed**
giishka'aakwewigamig *ni* lumber camp; *pl* **giishka'aakwewigamigoon**; *loc* **giishka'aakwewigamigong**; *dim* **giishka'aakwewigamigoons**
giishka'aakwewinini *na* lumberjack, logger; *pl* **giishka'aakwewininiwag**
giishkam *vta* bite through s.o. cleanly; *1sg* **ingiishkamaa**; *prt* **gaashkamaad**
giishkanakad *ni* stump; *pl* **giishkanakadoon**; *loc* **giishkanakadong**; *dim* **giishkanakadoons**
giishkandan *vti* bite through s.t. cleanly; *1sg* **ingiishkandaan**; *prt* **gaashkandang**
giishkashkimod *ni* cedar bark bag; *pl* **giishkashkimodan**; *loc* **giishkashkimodaang**; *dim* **giishkashkimodens**
giishkaabaagwe *vai* be thirsty; *1sg* **ingiishkaabaagwe**; *prt* **gaashkaabaagwed**
giishkaabikaa *vii* be a steep rock face; *prt* **gaashkaabikaag**; *aug* **giishkaabikaamagad**; *prt aug* **gaashkaabikaamagak**
giishkaamikaa *vii* there is a drop-off; *prt* **gaashkaamikaag**; *aug* **giishkaamikaamagad**; *prt aug* **gaashkaamikaamagak**
giishkaazhibikaa *vii* there is a rock cliff; *prt* **gaashkaazhibikaag**; *aug* **giishkaazhibikaamagad**; *prt aug* **gaashkaazhibikaamagak**
giishkibidoon *vti2* tear s.t. off; *1sg* **ingiishkibidoon**; *prt* **gaashkibidood**
giishkibijigaade *vii* be torn off; *prt* **gaashkibijigaadeg**; *aug* **giishkibijigaademagad**; *prt aug* **gaashkibijigaademagak**
giishkibijigaazo *vai* be torn off; *prt* **gaashkibijigaazod**
giishkibijige *vai* tear things off; *1sg* **ingiishkibijige**; *prt* **gaashkibijiged**
giishkibizh /giishkibiN-/ *vta* tear s.o. off; *1sg* **ingiishkibinaa**; *prt* **gaashkibinaad**
giishkiboodoon *vti2* saw s.t. off; *1sg* **ingiishkiboodoon**; *prt* **gaashkiboodood**
giishkiboojigan *ni* crosscut saw; *pl* **giishkiboojiganan**; *loc* **giishkiboojiganing**; *dim* **giishkiboojigaans**
giishkiboojige *vai* saw things off; *1sg* **ingiishkiboojige**; *prt* **gaashkiboojiged**
giishkiboozh /giishkibooN-/ *vta* saw s.o. off; *1sg* **ingiishkiboonaa**; *prt* **gaashkiboonaad**
giishkiga' /giishkiga'w-/ *vta* chop s.o. off; *1sg* **ingiishkiga'waa**; *prt* **gaashkiga'waad**
giishkiga'an *vti* chop s.t. off; *1sg* **ingiishkiga'aan**; *prt* **gaashkiga'ang**
giishkiganzhiikonidizo *vai* cut one's own nails; *1sg* **ingiishkiganzhiikonidiz**; *prt* **gaashkiganzhiikonidizod**
giishkijiin *vta* hug s.o., embrace s.o.; *1sg* **ingiishkijiinaa**; *prt* **gaashkijiinaad**
giishkijiinidiwag /giishkijiinidi-/ *vai* they hug each other, they embrace each other; *1pl* **ingiishkijiinidimin**; *prt* **gaashkijiinidijig**
giishkijiiwagooday *ni* skirt; *pl* **giishkijiiwagoodayan**; *dim* **giishkijiiwagoodayens**
giishkikaa *vai* tear, rip; *prt* **gaashkikaad**
giishkikaa *vii* tear, rip; *prt* **gaashkikaag**; *aug* **giishkikaamagad**; *prt aug* **gaashkikaamagak**
giishkikozhiwe *vai* cut hair; *1sg* **ingiishkikozhiwe**; *prt* **gaashkikozhiwed**
giishkikozhiwewikwe *na* barber (female); *pl* **giishkikozhiwewikweg**
giishkikozhiwewinini *na* barber; *pl* **giishkikozhiwewininiwag**
giishkishin *vai* get cut falling; *1sg* **ingiishkishin**; *prt* **gaashkishing**
giishkizh /giishkizhw-/ *vta* cut s.o. off, cut through s.o.; *1sg* **ingiishkizhwaa**; *prt* **gaashkizhwaad**
giishkizhan *vti* cut s.t. off, cut through s.o.; *1sg* **ingiishkizhaan**; *prt* **gaashkizhang**
giishkizhigan *ni* scythe; *pl* **giishkizhiganan**; *loc* **giishkizhiganing**; *dim* **giishkizhigaans**
giishkizhige *vai* cut things off, cut things; *1sg* **ingiishkizhige**; *prt* **gaashkizhiged**
giishkizhodizo *vai* cut oneself; *1sg* **ingiishkizhodiz**; *prt* **gaashkizhodizod**
giishkowe *vai* stop crying, stop making vocal noise; *1sg* **ingiishkowe**; *prt* **gaashkowed**
giishpin *pc* if
giitagoode *vai* take off one's dress; *1sg* **ingiitagoode**; *prt* **gaatagooded**
giitazhigane *vai* take off one's socks; *1sg* **ingiitazhigane**; *prt* **gaatazhiganed**
giiwanaadingwaam *vai* have a bad dream, have a nightmare; *1sg* **ingiiwanaadingwaam**; *prt* **gaawanaadingwaang**
giiwanaadizi *vai* be crazy, be insane; *1sg* **ingiiwanaadiz**; *prt* **gaawanaadizid**
giiwanaadiziiwigamig *ni* mental hospital; *pl* **giiwanaadiziiwigamigoon**; *loc* **giiwanaadiziiwigamigong**
giiwanim *vta* lie to s.o., deceive s.o. in speech; *1sg* **ingiiwanimaa**; *prt* **gaawanimaad**
giiwanimo *vai* lie, be deceptive in speech; *1sg* **ingiiwanim**; *prt* **gaawanimod**
giiwashkwe *vai* be dizzy; *1sg* **ingiiwashkwe**; *prt* **gaawashkwed**

giiwashkwebazh /giiwashkwebaN-/ *vta* make s.o. drunk; *1sg* **ingiiwashkwebanaa**; *prt* **gaawashkwebanaad**
giiwashkwebii *vai* be drunk; *1sg* **ingiiwashkwebii**; *prt* **gaawashkwebiid**
giiwashkweganaam *vta* knock s.o. senseless; *1sg* **ingiiwashkweganaamaa**; *prt* **gaawashkweganaamaad**
giiwashkwe'ogo *vai* be seasick; *1sg* **ingiiwashkwe'og**; *prt* **gaawashkwe'ogod**
giiwashkweshin *vai* be knocked senseless in impact; *1sg* **ingiiwashkweshin**; *prt* **gaawashkweshing**
giiwashkweshkaw- *vta* make s.o. dizzy (especially of a substance) *in inverse forms: 1sg* **ingiiwashkweshkaagon**; *prt* **gaawashkweshkaagod**
giiwashkweyaabandam *vai2* be dizzy, feel unsteady; *1sg* **ingiiwashkweyaabandam**; *prt* **gaawashkweyaabandang**
giiwashkweyendam *vai2* be confused; *1sg* **ingiiwashkweyendam**; *prt* **gaawashkweyendang**
giiwe *vai* go home, return; *1sg* **ingiiwe**; *prt* **gaawed**
giiwebatoo *vai* run back, run home; *1sg* **ingiiwebatoo**; *prt* **gaawebatood**
giiwe-biboon *vii* be after mid-winter, be late winter; *prt* **gaawe-biboong**
giiwedaabii'iwe *vai* drive home; *1sg* **ingiiwedaabii'iwe**; *prt* **gaawedaabii'iwed**
giiwedin *ni* north wind, north; *loc* **giiwedinong**
giiwegidaazo *vai* go home mad; *1sg* **ingiiwegidaaz**; *prt* **gaawegidaazod**
giiwe'o *vai* go home by boat; *1sg* **ingiiwe'**; *prt* **gaawe'od**
giiwekii *vai* return to one's own country; *1sg* **ingiiwekii**; *prt* **gaawekiid**
giiwenamaw *vta* give presents to s.o. in exchange; *1sg* **ingiiwenamawaa**; *prt* **gaawenamawaad**
giiwenaazha' /giiwenaazha'w-/ *vta* tell s.o. to go home; *1sg* **ingiiwenaazha'waa**; *prt* **gaawenaazha'waad**
giiwenh *pc* so the story goes, so it is said
giiwenige *vai* give presents to relatives of someone deceased in completion of mourning on anniversary of the death; *1sg* **ingiiwenige**; *prt* **gaaweniged**
giiwe-niibin *vii* be after mid-summer, late summer; *prt* **gaawe-niibing**
giiwewidaw *vta* take (s.t.) home for s.o., carry (s.t.) home for s.o.; *1sg* **ingiiwewidawaa**; *prt* **gaawewidawaad**
giiwewidoon *vti2* take s.t. home, carry s.t. home; *1sg* **ingiiwewidoon**; *prt* **gaawewidood**
giiwewizh /giiwewiN-/ *vta* take s.o. home, carry s.o. home; *1sg* **ingiiwewinaa**; *prt* **gaawewinaad**
giiweyendam *vai2* think about returning, think about going home again; *1sg* **ingiiweyendam**; *prt* **gaaweyendang**
giiwitaa-ayi'ii *pc* all around it; *also* **giiwitaayi'ii**
giiwitaabatoo *vai* run around something; *1sg* **ingiiwitaabatoo**; *prt* **gaawitaabatood**
giiwitaabatwaadan *vti* run around s.t.; *1sg* **ingiiwitaabatwaadaan**; *prt* **gaawitaabatwaadang**
giiwitaashim *vta* lay s.o. down around; *1sg* **ingiiwitaashimaa**; *prt* **gaawitaashimaad**
giiwitaashkan *vti* walk around s.t.; *1sg* **ingiiwitaashkaan**; *prt* **gaawitaashkang**
giiwitaashkaw *vta* walk around s.o.; *1sg* **ingiiwitaashkawaa**; *prt* **gaawitaashkawaad**
giiwitaashkaa *vai* go around, encircle; *1sg* **ingiiwitaashkaa**; *prt* **gaawitaashkaad**
giiwitaashkode *pc* around the fire
giiwitaasidoon *vti2* lay s.t. down around; *1sg* **ingiiwitaasidoon**; *prt* **gaawitaasidood**
giiwitaawose *vai* walk around something; *1sg* **ingiiwitaawose**; *prt* **gaawitaawosed**; *also* **giiwitaa'ose**
giiwitaayaazhagaame *vai* walk around the edge, walk around a lake; *1sg* **ingiiwitaayaazhagaame**; *prt* **gaawitaayaazhagaamed**
giiwizi *vai* be orphaned; *1sg* **ingiiwiz**; *prt* **gaawizid**
giiwose *vai* hunt; *1sg* **ingiiwose**; *prt* **gaawosed**; *also* **giiyose**
giiwosewasim *na* hunting dog; *pl* **giiwosewasimoog**; *also* **giiyosewasim**
giiwosewinini *na* hunter; *pl* **giiwosewininiwag**; *also* **giiyosewinini**
giiwoon *na* heart suite card; *pl* **giiwoonag**; *also* **giiyoon**
giizhakidoon *vti2* finish setting s.t. up; *1sg* **ingiizhakidoon**; *prt* **gaazhakidood**
giizhakizh /giizhakiN-/ *vta* finish setting s.o. up; *1sg* **ingiizhakinaa**; *prt* **gezhakinaad**
giizhaa *pc* beforehand, in advance
giizhaajimo *vai* tell all; *1sg* **ingiizhaajim**; *prt* **gaazhaajimod**
giizhaande *vii* be fully ripe; *prt* **gaazhaandeg**; *aug* **giizhaandemagad**; *prt aug* **gaazhaandemagak**
giizhaanzo *vai* be fully ripe; *prt* **gaazhaanzod**
giizhendam *vai2* have one's mind made up; resolve; *1sg* **ingiizhendam**; *prt* **gaazhendang**
giizhi- *pv4* finish, complete
giizhichigaade *vii* be finished; *prt* **gaazhichigaadeg**; *aug* **giizhichigaademagad**; *prt aug* **gaazhichigaademagak**
giizhichigaazo *vai* be finished; *prt* **gaazhichigaazod**
giizhide *vii* be done cooking; *prt* **gaazhideg**; *aug* **giizhidemagad**; *prt aug* **gaazhidemagak**
giizhig *ni* sky, heaven, day; *loc* **giizhigong**
giizhigad *vii* be day; *prt* **gaazhigak**
giizhigamide *vii* finish boiling; *prt* **gaazhigamideg**; *aug* **giizhigamidemagad**; *prt aug* **gaazhigamidemagak**
giizhigamizige *vai* finish boiling things; *1sg* **ingiizhigamizige**; *prt* **gaazhigamiziged**
giizhigaate *vii* there is moonlight; *prt* **gaazhigaateg**; *aug* **giizhigaatemagad**; *prt aug* **gaazhigaatemagak**
giizhige *vai* finish building a dwelling; *1sg* **ingiizhige**; *prt* **gaazhiged**
giizhigi *vai* be ripe, be full grown; *1sg* **ingiizhig**; *prt* **gaazhigid**
giizhigin *vii* be ripe, be full grown; *prt* **gaazhiging**
giizhi' *vta* finish s.o., finish making s.o.; *1sg* **ingiizhi'aa**; *prt* **gaazhi'aad**

giizhik *na* white cedar; *pl* **giizhikag**; *loc* **giizhiking**; *dim* **giizhikens**
giizhikaandag *na* cedar bough; *pl* **giizhikaandagoog**; *loc* **giizhikaandagong**; *dim* **giizhikaandagoons**
giizhitoon *vti2* finish s.t., finish making s.t.; *1sg* **ingiizhitoon**; *prt* **gaazhitood**
giizhiikan *vti* finish with s.t.; *1sg* **ingiizhiikaan**; *prt* **gaazhiikang**
giizhiikaw *vta* finish with s.o.; *1sg* **ingiizhiikawaa**; *prt* **gaazhiikawaad**
giizhiitaa *vai* finish a task, finish work; *1sg* **ingiizhiitaa**; *prt* **gaazhiitaad**
giizhoo'o *vai* dress warmly; *1sg* **ingiizhoo'**; *prt* **gaazhoo'od**
giizhoopizo *vai* be wrapped up warm; *1sg* **ingiizhoopiz**; *prt* **gaazhoopizod**
giizhoopizon *na* scarf; *pl* **giizhoopizonag**; *loc* **giizhoopizoning**; *dim* **giizhoopizonens**
giizhooshin *vai* lie in warmth; *1sg* **ingiizhooshin**; *prt* **gaazhooshing**
giizhootawage'o *vai* wear earmuffs; *1sg* **ingiizhootawage'**; *prt* **gaazhootawage'od**
giizhootawage'on *na* earmuff; *pl* **giizhootawage'onag**; *dim* **giizhootawage'onens**
giizhoote *vii* be hot inside; *prt* **gaazhooteg**; *aug* **giizhootemagad**; *prt aug* **gaazhootemagak**
giizikan *vti* take s.t. off the body (e.g., clothes); *1sg* **ingiizikaan**; *prt* **gaazikang**
giizikaw *vta* take s.o. off the body (e.g., clothes); *1sg* **ingiizikawaa**; *prt* **gaazikawaad**
giizikonaye *vai* undress, take off one's clothes; *1sg* **ingiizikonaye**; *prt* **gaazikonayed**
giizikonaye' *vta* undress s.o.; *1sg* **ingiizikonaye'aa**; *prt* **gaazikonaye'aad**
giizis *na* sun, moon, month; *pl* **giizisoog**; *loc* **giizisong**; *dim* **giizisoons**
giizisoo-mazina'igan *ni* calendar; *pl* **giizisoo-mazina'iganan**; *loc* **giizisoo-mazina'iganing**; *dim* **giizisoo-mazina'igaans**
giiziz /giizizw-/ *vta* finish cooking s.o.; *1sg* **ingiizizwaa**; *prt* **gaazizwaad**
giizizamaw *vta* cook (s.t.) for s.o.; *1sg* **ingiizizamawaa**; *prt* **gaazizamawaad**
giizizan *vti* finish cooking s.t.; *1sg* **ingiizizaan**; *prt* **gaazizang**
giizizekwe *vai* cook; *1sg* **ingiizizekwe**; *prt* **gaazizekwed**
giizizo *vai* be done cooking; *prt* **gaazizod**; *also* **giizhizo**
go *pc emphatic word*; *also* **igo**
goda *pc emphatic word*
godam *vta* take a taste of s.t.; *1sg* **ingodamaa**; *prt* **gwedamaad**
godandan *vti* take a taste of s.o.; *1sg* **ingodandaan**; *prt* **gwedandang**
godigoshin *vai* fall and be injured; *1sg* **ingodigoshin**; *prt* **gwedigoshing**
godin *vta* test s.o. with hand; *1sg* **ingodinaa**; *prt* **gwedinaad**
godinan *vti* test s.t. with hand; *1sg* **ingodinaan**; *prt* **gwedinang**
godotaagan *ni* bell; *pl* **godotaaganan**; *loc* **gototaaganing**; *dim* **gototaagaans**
goji- *pv4* try, attempt
gojichige *vai* try things; *1sg* **ingojichige**; *prt* **gwejichiged**
goji'ewizi *vai* try, make an effort; *1sg* **ingoji'ewiz**; *prt* **gweji'ewizid**
gojimaam *vta* take a smell of s.o.; *1sg* **ingojimaamaa**; *prt* **gwejimaamaad**
gojimaandan *vti* take a smell of s.t.; *1sg* **ingojimaandaan**; *prt* **gwejimaandang**
goji-nagamo *vai* practice singing; *1sg* **ingoji-nagam**; *prt* **gweji-nagamod**
gojipidan *vti* take a taste of s.t., check s.t. by tasting; *1sg* **ingojipidaan**; *prt* **gwejipidang**
gojipijige *vai* taste things; *1sg* **ingojipijige**; *prt* **gwejipijiged**
gojipozh /gojipw-/ *vta* take a taste of s.o., check s.o. by tasting; *1sg* **ingojipwaa**; *prt* **gwejipwaad**
gomaa *pc* some amount, to a middling degree
gomaapii *pc* for some time, some distance
gondan *vti* swallow s.t.; *1sg* **ingondaan**; *prt* **gwendang**
gondaabiigin *vta* put s.o. in water, dip s.o.; *1sg* **ingondaabiiginaa**; *prt* **gwendaabiiginaad**
gondaabiiginan *vti* put s.t. in water, dip s.t.; *1sg* **ingondaabiiginaan**; *prt* **gwendaabiiginang**
gonzaabii *vii* sink in water; *prt* **gwenzaabiig**; *aug* **gonzaabiimagad**; *prt aug* **gwenzaabiimagak**
gonzaabiishkoojigan *ni* sinker (fishing tackle); *pl* **gonzaabiishkoojiganan**; *loc* **gonzaabiishkoojiganing**; *dim* **gonzaabiishkoojigaans**
gonzhi /gonN-/ *vta* swallow s.o.; *1sg* **ingonaa**; *prt* **gwenaad**
gopibatoo *vai* run inland; *1sg* **ingopibatoo**; *prt* **gwepibatood**
gopimine *vai* take wild rice inland; *1sg* **ingopimine**; *prt* **gwepimined**
gopiwidoon *vti2* take s.t. inland, carry s.t. inland; *1sg* **ingopiwidoon**; *prt* **gwepiwidood**
gopiwizh /gopiwiN-/ *vta* take s.o. inland, carry s.o. inland; *1sg* **ingopiwinaa**; *prt* **gwepiwinaad**
gopii *vai* go away from the water, go inland; *1sg* **ingopii**; *prt* **gwepiid**
gosha *pc emphatic particle*
goshi /goS-/ *vta* fear s.o.; *1sg* **ingosaa**; *prt* **gwesaad**
goshko' *vta* surprise s.o.; *1sg* **ingoshko'aa**; *prt* **gweshko'aad**
goshkokaa *vai* be surprised, be startled; *1sg* **ingoshkokaa**; *prt* **gweshkokaad**
goshkom *vta* surprise s.o. verbally; *1sg* **ingoshkomaa**; *prt* **gweshkomaad**
goshkozi *vai* wake up, be awake; *1sg* **ingoshkoz**; *prt* **gweshkozid**
goshkwaawaadabi *vai* sit quietly, remain tranquilly in place; *1sg* **ingoshkwaawaadab**; *prt* **gweshkwaawaadabid**
goshkwaawaadizi *vai* be still, be quiet; *1sg* **ingoshkwaawaadiz**; *prt* **gweshkwaawaadizid**
gotan *vti* be afraid of s.t., fear s.t.; *1sg* **ingotaan**; *prt* **gwetang**
gotaaji *vai* be afraid, have fear; *1sg* **ingotaaj**; *prt* **gwetaajid**
gotaajishki *vai* be timid; *1sg* **ingotaajishk**; *prt* **gwetaajishkid**

gotaamigozi *vai* be a good worker, be a good provider; *1sg* **ingotaamigoz**; *prt* **gwetaamigozid**
gotigobide *vii* roll over, go out of place; *prt* **gwetigobideg**; *aug* **gotigobidemagad**; *prt aug* **gwetigobidemagak**
gotigobidoon *vti2* roll s.t. over, tip s.t.; *1sg* **ingotigobidoon**; *prt* **gwetigobidood**
gotigobizh /gotigobiN-/ *vta* roll s.o. over, tip s.o.; *1sg* **ingotigobinaa**; *prt* **gwetigobinaad**
gotigobizo *vai* roll over, go out of place; *1sg* **ingotigobiz**; *prt* **gwetigobizod**
gozi *vai* move one's residence; *1sg* **ingoz**; *prt* **gwezid**
gozigwan *vii* be heavy; *prt* **gwezigwang**
gozigwani *vai* be heavy; *1sg* **ingozigwan**; *prt* **gwezigwanid**
gozigwaakomin *na* Juneberry; *pl* **gozigwaakominag**
gozigwaakominagaawanzh *na* Juneberry bush; *pl* **gozigwaakominagaawanzhiig**; *loc* **gozigwaakominagaawanzhiing**; *dim* **gozigwaakominagaawanzhiins**
gozikan *vti* test s.t. with foot or body, try on s.t. (e.g., clothes); *1sg* **ingozikaan**; *prt* **gwezikang**
gozikaw *vta* test s.o. with foot or body, try on s.o. (e.g., clothes); *1sg* **ingozikawaa**; *prt* **gwezikawaad**
googa'am *vai2* jump out of the water as a fish; *prt* **gwaaga'ang**
googii *vai* dive; *1sg* **ingoogii**; *prt* **gwaagiid**
gookooko'oo *na* owl; *pl* **gookooko'oog**; *dim* **gookooko'oons**
gookoosh *na* pig, pork; *pl* **gookooshag**; *dim* **gookooshens**
gookooshi-bimide *ni* lard
gookooshi-wiiyaas *ni* pork; *loc* **gookooshi-wiiyaasing**
goon *na* snow; *loc* **gooning**; *dim* **goonens**
goonikaa *vii* be much snow; *prt* **gwaanikaag**; *aug* **goonikaamagad**; *prt aug* **gwaanikaamagak**
goopadendan *vti* consider s.t. worthless; *1sg* **ingoopadendaan**; *prt* **gwaapadendang**
goopadenim *vta* consider s.o. worthless; *1sg* **ingoopadenimaa**; *prt* **gwaapadenimaad**
goopadizi *vai* be worthless, be useless; *1sg* **ingoopadiz**; *prt* **gwaapadizid**
goopaji' *vta* mistreat s.o., ruin s.o.; *1sg* **ingoopaji'aa**; *prt* **gwaapaji'aad**
goopajitoon *vti2* mistreat s.t., ruin s.t.; *1sg* **ingoopajitoon**; *prt* **gwaapajitood**
gwanabishkan *vti* tip s.t. with foot or body; *1sg* **ingwanabishkaan**; *prt* **gwenabishkang**
gwanabishkaa *vai* capsize, tip; *1sg* **ingwanabishkaa**; *prt* **gwenabishkaad**
gwayak *pc* straight, right, correct
gwayakobidoon *vti2* pull s.t. straight, tear s.t. straight; *1sg* **ingwayakobidoon**; *prt* **gweyakobidood**
gwayako-bimaadizi *vai* live a proper life; *1sg* **ingwayako-bimaadiz**; *prt* **gweyako-bimaadizid**
gwayakobizh /gwayakobiN-/ *vta* pull s.o. straight, tear s.o. straight; *1sg* **ingwayakobinaa**; *prt* **gweyakobidood**
gwayakobii'an *vti* write s.t. correctly; *1sg* **ingwayakobii'aan**; *prt* **gweyakobii'ang**
gwayakobii'ige *vai* write correctly; *1sg* **ingwayakobii'ige**; *prt* **gweyakobii'iged**
gwayakoboodoon *vti2* saw s.t. straight; *1sg* **ingwayakoboodoon**; *prt* **gweyakoboodood**
gwayakoboozh /gwayakobooN-/ *vta* saw s.o. straight; *1sg* **ingwayakoboonaa**; *prt* **gweyakoboonaad**
gwayakochige *vai* make things right, do things right; *1sg* **ingwayakochige**; *prt* **gweyakochiged**
gwayakogaabawi *vai* stand straight, have good posture; *1sg* **ingwayakogaabaw**; *prt* **gweyakogaabawid**
gwayakogi *vai* grow straight; *1sg* **ingwayakog**; *prt* **gweyakogid**
gwayakogin *vii* grow straight; *prt* **gweyakoging**
gwayakokweni *vai* hold one's head straight; *1sg* **ingwayakokwen**; *prt* **gweyakokwenid**
gwayakoshim *vta* lay s.o. straight; *1sg* **ingwayakoshimaa**; *prt* **gweyakoshimaad**
gwayakoshin *vai* lie straight, lie correctly; *1sg* **ingwayakoshin**; *prt* **gweyakoshing**
gwayakoshkaa *vai* go straight, go the right way; *1sg* **ingwayakoshkaa**; *prt* **gweyakoshkaad**
gwayakosidoon *vti2* lay s.t. straight; *1sg* **ingwayakosidoon**; *prt* **gweyakosidood**
gwayakosin *vii* lie straight, lie correctly; *prt* **gweyakosing**
gwayakotam *vai2* hear the right thing, find out the truth; *1sg* **ingwayakotam**; *prt* **gweyakotang**
gwayakowe *vai* speak correctly; *1sg* **ingwayakowe**; *prt* **gweyakowed**
gwayakozh /gwayakozhw-/ *vta* cut s.o. straight; *1sg* **ingwayakozhwaa**; *prt* **gweyakozhwaad**
gwayakozhan *vti* cut s.t. straight; *1sg* **ingwayakozhaan**; *prt* **gweyakozhang**
gwayako-zhooniyaa *na* cash, ready money
gwayakozi *vai* be straight; *prt* **gweyakozid**
gwayakwakamigaa *vii* be level ground; *prt* **gweyakwakamigaag**; *aug* **gwayakwakamigaamagad**; *prt aug* **gweyakwakamigaamagak**
gwayakwaa *vii* be straight, be correct; *prt* **gweyakwaag**; *aug* **gwayakwaamagad**; *prt aug* **gweyakwaamagak**
gwayakwaabidoo'an *vti* thread s.t. correctly, bead s.t. correctly (on a loom); *1sg* **ingwayakwaabidoo'aan**; *prt* **gweyakwaabidoo'ang**
gwayakwaabidoo'ige *vai* bead things correctly (on a loom); *1sg* **ingwayakwaabidoo'ige**; *prt* **gweyakwaabidoo'iged**
gwayakwaabikad *vii* be straight (as something mineral); *prt* **gweyakwaabikak**
gwayakwaabikizi *vai* be straight (as something mineral); *prt* **gweyakwaabikizid**
gwayakwaabiigad *vii* be straight (as something string-like); *prt* **gweyakwaabiigak**
gwayakwaabiigizi *vai* be straight (as something string-like); *prt* **gweyakwaabiigizid**
gwayakwaakozi *vai* be straight (as something stick- or wood-like); *prt* **gweyakwaakozid**
gwayakwaakwad *vii* be straight (as something stick- or wood-like); *prt* **gweyakwaakwak**

gwayakwendam *vai2* think correctly, be certain; *1sg* **ingwayakwendam**; *prt* **gweyakwendang**
gwayakwendan *vti* consider s.t. right; *1sg* **ingwayakwendaan**; *prt* **gweyakwendang**
gwayakwendaagozi *vai* be considered right; *1sg* **ingwayakwendaagoz**; *prt* **gweyakwendaagozid**
gwayakwendaagwad *vii* be considered right; *prt* **gweyakwendaagwak**
gwaaba' *vta* scoop s.o. up; *1sg* **ingwaaba'aa**; *prt* **gwayaaba'aad**
gwaaba'amaw *vta* scoop (s.t.) up for s.o., get water for s.o.; *1sg* **ingwaaba'amawaa**; *prt* **gwayaaba'amawaad**
gwaaba'an *vti* scoop s.t. up; *1sg* **ingwaaba'aan**; *prt* **gwayaaba'ang**
gwaaba'ibii *vai* draw water, scoop up water; *1sg* **ingwaaba'ibii**; *prt* **gwayaaba'ibiid**
gwaaba'igan *ni* dipper; *pl* **gwaaba'iganan**; *loc* **gwaaba'iganing**; *dim* **gwaaba'igaans**
gwaaba'ige *vai* scoop up things, dip up things; *1sg* **ingwaaba'ige**; *prt* **gwayaaba'iged**
gwaaba'waawangwaan *ni* shovel (for dirt); *pl* **gwaaba'waawangwaanan**; *loc* **gwaaba'waawangwaaning**; *dim* **gwaaba'waawangwaanens**
gwaashkwani *vai* jump; *1sg* **ingwaashkwan**; *prt* **gwayaashkwanid**
gwaashkwaashkw= < gwaashkw=
gwaashkwesin *vii* bounce; *prt* **gwayaashkwesing**
gwaashkwezi *vai* be eager, be ambitious, be energetic; *1sg* **ingwaashkwez**; *prt* **gwayaashkwezid**
gwech *pc* enough, sufficient
gwekabi *vai* turn around while sitting; *1sg* **ingwekab**; *prt* **gwayekabid**
gwekaanimad *vii* wind shifts; *prt* **gwayekaanimak**
gwekendam *vai* change one's mind; *1sg* **ingwekendam**; *prt* **gwayekendang**
gwekibagizo *vai* turn quickly, right self; *1sg* **ingwekibagiz**; *prt* **gwayekibagizod**
gwekibatoo *vai* turn running; *1sg* **ingwekibatoo**; *prt* **gwayekibatood**
gwekibidoon *vti2* turn s.t. with hands; *1sg* **ingwekibidoon**; *prt* **gwayekibidood**
gwekibizh /gwekibiN-/ *vta* turn s.o. with hands; *1sg* **ingwekibinaa**; *prt* **gwayekibinaad**
gwekibizo *vai* turn driving; *1sg* **ingwekibiz**; *prt* **gwayekibizod**
gwekigaabawi *vai* turn while standing; *1sg* **ingwekigaabaw**; *prt* **gwayekigaabawid**
gwekikweni *vai* turn one's head around; *1sg* **ingwekikwen**; *prt* **gwayekikwenid**
gwekin *vta* turn s.o. by hand; *1sg* **ingwekinaa**; *prt* **gwayekinaad**
gwekinan *vti* turn s.t. by hand; *1sg* **ingwekinaan**; *prt* **gwekinang**
gwekinige *vai* turn things by hand; *1sg* **ingwekinige**; *prt* **gwayekiniged**
gwekishim *vta* put s.o. turned; *1sg* **ingwekishimaa**; *prt* **gwayekishimaad**
gwekishin *vai* turn lying in place; *1sg* **ingwekishin**; *prt* **gwayekishing**
gwekisidoon *vti2* put s.t. turned; *1sg* **ingwekisidoon**; *prt* **gwayekisidood**
gwekisin *vii* turn lying in place; *prt* **gwayekising**
gwekitaa *vai* turn (one's body); *1sg* **ingwekitaa**; *prt* **gwayekitaad**
gwekiwebinigan *na* pancake; *pl* **gwekiwebiniganag**; *loc* **gwekiwebiniganing**; *dim* **gwekiwebinigaans**
gwekiigin *vta* turn s.o. over (as something sheet-like); *1sg* **ingwekiiginaa**; *prt* **gwayekiiginaad**
gwekiiginan *vti* turn s.t. over (as something sheet-like); *1sg* **ingwekiiginaan**; *prt* **gwekiiginang**
gwekwek= < gwek=
gwendaaseg *ni-pt* liniment; *pl* **gwendaasegin**
gwiikwiin= < gwiin=
gwiinawaabam *vta* fail to see s.o.; *1sg* **ingwiinawaabamaa**; *prt* **gwaanawaabamaad**
gwiinawaabandan *vti* fail to see s.t.; *1sg* **ingwiinawaabandaan**; *prt* **gwaanawaabandang**
gwiinawendan *vti* miss s.t. absent; *1sg* **ingwiinawendaan**; *prt* **gwaanawendang**
gwiinawenim *vta* miss s.o. absent; *1sg* **ingwiinawenimaa**; *prt* **gwaanawenimaad**
gwiinawi- *pv4* not knowing, not able
gwiinawi-doodam *vai2* not know what to do; *1sg* **ingwiinawi-doodam**; *prt* **gwaanawi-doodang**
gwiinawi-inendam *vai2* not know what to think; *1sg* **ingwiinawi-inendam**; *prt* **gwaanawi-inendang**
gwiingwa'aage *na* wolverine; *pl* **gwiingwa'aageg**; *dim* **gwiingwa'aagens**
gwiinobii *vai* be unable to find a drink; *1sg* **ingwiinobii**; *prt* **gwaanobiid**
gwiishkoshi *vai* whistle; *1sg* **ingwiishkosh**; *prt* **gwaashkoshid**
gwiishkoshim *vta* whistle to s.o.; *1sg* **ingwiishkoshimaa**; *prt* **gwaashkoshimaad**
gwiishkoshwewegamide *vii* whistle from boiling; *prt* **gwaashkoshwewegamideg**; *aug* **gwiishkoshwewegamidemagad**; *prt aug* **gwaashkoshwewegamidemagak**
gwiishkoshwewegamizo *vai* whistle from boiling; *prt* **gwaashkoshwewegamizod**
gwiiwizens *na* boy; *pl* **gwiiwizensag**
gwiiwizensiwi *vai* be a boy; *1sg* **ingwiiwizensiw**; *prt* **gwaawizensiwid**

H

hay' *pc expression of displeasure at accident or mistake*

I

idan *vti* say so to s.t., speak to s.t.; *1sg* **indidaan**; *prt* **edang**
idash *pc* and, but; *also* **dash, -sh**
idiwag /idi-/ *vai* they say to each other, they speak to each other in a certain way; *1pl* **indidimin**; *prt* **edijig**
igaye *pc* and, as for; *also* **gaye, ge**
igiw* *pr* those *animate plural demonstrative*; *also* **ingiw, ingi, agiw***
igiwedig* *pr* those over there *animate plural demonstrative*; *also* **ingiwedig**
igo *pc emphatic word*; *also* **go**
i'imaa *pc* there; *also* **imaa**
i'iw *pr* that *inanimate singular demonstrative*; *also* **iw, 'iw, i'i, 'i**
i'iwedi *pr* that over there *inanimate singular demonstrative*; *also* **iwedi, 'iwedi**
ikido *vai* say, speak so; *1sg* **indikid**; *prt* **ekidod**
ikidowin *ni* word; *pl* **ikidowinan**; *dim* **ikidowinens**
iko *pc* used to, formerly, it was the custom to...; *also* **ko**
ikogaabawi *vai* stand out of the way; *1sg* **indikogaabaw**; *prt* **ekogaabawid**
ikon *vta* set s.o. out of the way; *1sg* **indikonaa**; *prt* **ekonaad**
ikonan *vti* set s.t. out of the way; *1sg* **indikonaan**; *prt* **ekonang**
ikonaazhikaw *vta* chase s.o. out of the way; *1sg* **indikonaazhikawaa**; *prt* **ekonaazhikawaad**
ikonigaade *vii* be set out of the way; *prt* **ekonigaadeg**; *aug* **ikonigaademagad**; *prt aug* **ekonigaademagak**
ikonigaazo *vai* be set out of the way, be evicted; *prt* **ekonigaazod**
ikoshim *vta* put s.o. out of the way; *1sg* **indikoshimaa**; *prt* **ekoshimaad**
ikoshin *vai* lie out of the way; *1sg* **indikoshin**; *prt* **ekoshing**
ikosidoon *vti2* put s.t. out of the way; *1sg* **indikosidoon**; *prt* **ekosidood**
ikosin *vii* lie out of the way; *prt* **ekosing**
ikoweba' /ikoweba'w-/ *vta* shove s.o. out of the way with something; *1sg* **indikoweba'waa**; *prt* **ekoweba'waad**
ikoweba'an *vti* shove s.t. out of the way with something; *1sg* **indikoweba'aan**; *prt* **ekoweba'ang**
ikowebin *vta* toss s.o. aside, shove aside s.o.; *1sg* **indikowebinaa**; *prt* **ekowebinaad**
ikowebinan *vti* toss s.t. aside, shove aside s.t.; *1sg* **indikowebinaan**; *prt* **ekowebinang**
ikowebishkan *vti* kick s.t. out of the way; *1sg* **indikowebishkaan**; *prt* **ekowebishkang**
ikowebishkaw *vta* kick s.o. out of the way; *1sg* **indikowebishkawaa**; *prt* **ekowebishkawaad**
ikwa *na* louse; *pl* **ikwag**
ikwabi *vai* sit aside, move out of the way sitting; *1sg* **indikwab**; *prt* **ekwabid**
ikwanagweni *vai* roll up one's sleeve; *1sg* **indikwanagwen**; *prt* **ekwanagwenid**
ikwanaamo *vai* draw breath in; *1sg* **indikwanaam**; *prt* **ekwanaamod**
ikwe *na* woman, queen (card); *pl* **ikwewag**; *dim* **ikwens**
ikwe-biizikiigan *ni* item of women's clothing; *loc* **ikwe-biizikiiganing**; *dim* **ikwe-biizikiigaans**
ikwe-niimi *vai* dance the women's dance; *1sg* **indikwe-niim**; *prt* **ekwe-niimid**
ikwe-niimi'idiwag /ikwe-niimi'idi-/ *vai* they dance the women's dance; *1pl* **indikwe-niimi'idimin**; *prt* **ekwe-niimi'idijig**
ikwe-niimi'idiwin *ni* women's dance; *pl* **ikwe-niimi'idiwinan**
ikwewi *vai* be a woman; *1sg* **indikwew**; *prt* **ekwewid**
ikwezens *na* girl; *pl* **ikwezensag**
ikwezensiwi *vai* be a girl; *1sg* **indikwezensiw**; *prt* **ekwezensiwid**
im= *pre first person prefix before b-*; *also* **nim=, m=**
imaa *pc* there; *also* **maa, i'imaa**
imbaabaa /-baabaay-/ *nad* my father; *pl* **imbaabaayag**
imbaabaayinaan *nad* our father = grandfather; *also* **imbaabaanaan, baabaanaan**
imbwaam /-bwaam-/ *nid* my thigh (back of thigh), my hindquarter; *pl* **imbwaaman**; *loc* **imbwaaming**; *dim* **imbwaamens**
in= *pre first person prefix before d-, j-, g-, z, zh-*; *also* **nin=, n=**
ina *pc yes-no question word*; *also* **na**
inabi *vai* sit a certain way; *1sg* **indinab**; *prt* **enabid**
inademo *vai* cry a certain way, go to a certain place crying; *1sg* **indinadem**; *prt* **enademod**
inagim *vta* set a certain price on s.o.; *1sg* **indinagimaa**; *prt* **enagimaad**
inagindamaw *vta* set a certain price on (s.t.) for s.o.; *1sg* **indinagindamawaa**; *prt* **enagindamawaad**
inagindan *vti* set a certain price on s.t.; *1sg* **indinagindaan**; *prt* **enagindang**
inaginde *vii* have a certain cost, have a certain price; *prt* **enagindeg**; *aug* **inagindemagad**; *prt aug* **enagindemagak**
inaginzo *vai* have a certain cost, have a certain price, be a certain date of the month; *prt* **enaginzod**
inagoode *vii* hang a certain way; *prt* **enagoodeg**; *aug* **inagoodemagad**; *prt aug* **enagoodemagak**
inagoodoon *vti2* hang s.t. a certain way; *1sg* **indinagoodoon**; *prt* **enagoodood**
inagoojin *vai* hang a certain way; *1sg* **indinagoojin**; *prt* **enagoojing**
inagoozh /inagooN-/ *vta* hang s.o. a certain way; *1sg* **indinagoonaa**; *prt* **enagoonaad**
ina'adoon *vti2* follow s.t. as a trail to a certain place; *1sg* **indina'adoon**; *prt* **ena'adood**
ina'am *vai2* sing a certain way; *1sg* **indina'am**; *prt* **ena'ang**
ina'azh /ina'aN-/ *vta* follow s.o.'s trail to a certain place; *1sg* **indina'anaa**; *prt* **ena'anaad**
ina'e *vai* shoot in a certain way or place; *1sg* **indina'e**; *prt* **ena'ed**
ina'o *vai* paddle to a certain place; *1sg* **indina'**; *prt* **ena'od**

ina'oodoo *vai* pole a boat to a certain place; *1sg* **indina'oodoo**; *prt* **ena'oodood**
ina'oodoon *vti2* take s.t. to a certain place by boat; *1sg* **indina'oodoon**; *prt* **ena'oodood**
ina'oozh /ina'ooN-/ *vta* take s.o. to a certain place by boat; *1sg* **indina'oonaa**; *prt* **ena'oonaad**
inakamigad *vii* be a certain event, happen a certain way; *prt* **enakamigak**
inakamigizi *vai* do a certain thing, have certain things happen to one; *1sg* **indinakamigiz**; *prt* **enakamigizid**
inakwazhiwe *vai* paddle a certain way, paddle to a certain place, swim to a certain place (as a fish); *1sg* **indinakwazhiwe**; *prt* **enakwazhiwed**
inamanji'o *vai* feel a certain way; *1sg* **indinamanji'**; *prt* **enamanji'od**
inamon /inamo-/ *vii* lead to a certain place (as a road or trail); *prt* **enamog**
inanjige *vai* eat a certain way, have a certain diet; *1sg* **indinanjige**; *prt* **enanjiged**
inanokii *vai* work a certain way, have a certain job; *1sg* **indinanokii**; *prt* **enanokiid**
inanokiitaw *vta* do a certain job for s.o.; *1sg* **indinanokiitawaa**; *prt* **enanokiitawaad**
inanoozh /inanooN-/ *vta* hire s.o. to do a certain job, hire s.o. to go to a certain place; *1sg* **indinanoonaa**; *prt* **enanoonaad**
inapizowin *ni* kitchen apron; *pl* **inapizowinan**; *loc* **inapizowining**; *dim* **inapizowinens**
inashke *pc* look!, behold!; *also* **nashke**
inawem *vta* be related to s.o.; *1sg* **indinawemaa**; *prt* **enawemaad**
inawendiwag /inawendi-/ *vai* they are related to each other; *1pl* **indinawendimin**; *prt* **enawendijig**
inaa *pc emphatic particle*; *also* **naa**
inaabadad *vii* be useful in a certain way, be employed in a certain way; *prt* **enaabadak**
inaabadizi *vai* be useful in a certain way, be employed in a certain way; *1sg* **indinaabadiz**; *prt* **enaabadizid**
inaabajichige *vai* use things a certain way; *1sg* **indinaabajichige**; *prt* **enaabajichiged**
inaabaji' *vta* use s.o. a certain way; *1sg* **indinaabaji'aa**; *prt* **enaabaji'aad**
inaabajitoon *vti2* use s.t. a certain way; *1sg* **indinaabajitoon**; *prt* **enaabajitood**
inaabam *vta* see s.o. a certain way as in a dream; *1sg* **indinaabamaa**; *prt* **enaabamaad**
inaabaminaagozi *vai* appear a certain way (especially as in a dream); *prt* **enaabaminaagozid**
inaabaminaagwad *vii* appear a certain way (especially as in a dream); *prt* **enaabaminaagwak**
inaabandam *vai2* dream a certain way; *1sg* **indinaabandam**; *prt* **enaabandang**
inaabandan *vti* see s.t. a certain way as in a dream; *1sg* **indinaabandaan**; *prt* **enaabandang**
inaabasige *vai* send smoke to a certain place; *1sg* **indinaabasige**; *prt* **enaabasiged**
inaabate *vii* go a certain direction (as smoke); *prt* **enaabateg**; *aug* **inaabatemagad**; *prt aug* **enaabatemagak**
inaabi *vai* peek, look to a certain place; *1sg* **indinaab**; *prt* **enaabid**
inaabikad *vii* be a certain way (as something mineral); *prt* **enaabikak**
inaabikizi *vai* be a certain way (as something mineral); *prt* **enaabikizid**
inaabiwin *ni* lightning
inaabiigad *vii* be a certain way (as something string-like); *prt* **enaabiigak**
inaabiigin *vta* string s.o. a certain way; *1sg* **inaabiiginaa**; *prt* **enaabiiginaad**
inaabiiginan *vti* string s.t. a certain way; *1sg* **indinaabiiginaan**; *prt* **enaabiiginang**
inaabiigizi *vai* be a certain way (as something string-like); *prt* **enaabiigizid**
inaadagaa *vai* swim to a certain place; *1sg* **indinaadagaa**; *prt* **enaadagaad**
inaadagaako *vai* go to a certain place on the ice; *1sg* **indinaadagaak**; *prt* **enaadagaakod**
inaadagaazii *vai* wade to a certain place; *1sg* **indinaadagaazii**; *prt* **enaadagaaziid**
inaada'e *vai* skate to a certain place; *1sg* **indinaada'e**; *prt* **enaada'ed**
inaadizi *vai* have a certain character, have a certain way of life; *1sg* **indinaadiz**; *prt* **enaadizid**
inaadiziwin *ni* way of life; *pl* **inaadiziwinan**
inaadodan *vti* tell a certain way about s.t., narrate a certain way about s.t.; *1sg* **indinaadodaan**; *prt* **enaadodang**
inaagamin /inaagami-/ *vii* be a certain way (as a liquid); *prt* **enaagamig**
inaagin *vta* bend s.o. a certain way; *1sg* **indinaaginaa**; *prt* **enaaginaad**
inaaginan *vti* bend s.t. a certain way; *1sg* **indinaaginaan**; *prt* **enaaginang**
inaaginigaade *vii* be bent a certain way; *prt* **enaaginigaadeg**; *aug* **inaaginigaademagad**; *prt aug* **enaaginigaademagak**
inaaginigaazo *vai* be bent a certain way; *prt* **enaaginigaazod**
inaajim *vta* tell of s.o. a certain way, narrate of s.o. a certain way; *1sg* **indinaajimaa**; *prt* **enaajimaad**
inaajimo *vai* tell a certain way, narrate a certain way; *1sg* **indinaajim**; *prt* **enaajimod**
inaajimotaw *vta* tell s.o. of (s.t.) a certain way, narrate (s.t.) to s.o. a certain way; *1sg* **indinaajimotawaa**; *prt* **enaajimotawaad**
inaakide *vii* burn a certain way; *prt* **enaakideg**; *aug* **inaakidemagad**; *prt aug* **enaakidemagak**
inaakiz /inaakizw-/ *vta* burn s.o. a certain way; *1sg* **indinaakizwaa**; *prt* **enaakizwaad**
inaakizan *vti* burn s.t. a certain way; *1sg* **indinaakizaan**; *prt* **enaakizang**
inaakizo *vai* burn a certain way; *prt* **enaakizod**
inaakon *vta* decide about s.o. a certain way, judge s.o. a certain way, sentence s.o. a certain way; *1sg* **indinaakonaa**; *prt* **enaakonaad**
inaakonan *vti* decide a certain way about s.t., judge s.t. a certain way; *1sg* **indinaakonaan**; *prt* **enaakonang**
inaakonigaade *vii* be decided in a certain way, be decreed a certain way; *prt* **enaakonigaadeg**; *aug* **inaakonigaademagad**
inaakonigaazo *vai* be judged a certain way, be sentenced a certain way; *prt* **enaakonigaazod**

inaakonige *vai* make a certain judgement, decide things a certain way, agree on something; *1sg* **indinaakonige**; *prt* **enaakoniged**
inaakonigewin *ni* law; *pl* **inaakonigewinan**
inaakozi *vai* be a certain way (as something stick- or wood-like); *prt* **enaakozid**
inaakwad *vii* be a certain way (as something stick- or wood-like); *prt* **enaakwak**
inaandawe *vai* climb to a certain place; *1sg* **indinaandawe**; *prt* **enaandawed**
inaande *vii* be colored a certain way; *prt* **enaandeg**; *aug* **inaandemagad**; *prt aug* **enaandemagak**
inaanzo *vai* be colored a certain way; *prt* **enaanzod**
inaapine *vai* be sick in a certain way; *1sg* **indinaapine**; *prt* **enaapined**
inaasamabi *vai* sit facing in a certain way; *1sg* **indinaasamab**; *prt* **enaasamabid**
inaasamigaabawi *vai* stand facing a certain way; *1sg* **indinaasamigaabaw**; *prt* **enaasamigaabawid**
inaasamishin *vai* lie facing a certain way; *1sg* **indinaasamishin**; *prt* **enaasamishing**
inaashi *vai* be blown a certain way, sail to a certain place; *1sg* **indinaash**; *prt* **enaashid**
inaasin *vii* be blown a certain way, sail to a certain place; *prt* **enaasing**
inaatese *vii* be a certain kind of movie; *prt* **enaateseg**; *aug* **inaatesemagad**; *prt aug* **enaatesemagak**
inaawadaaso *vai* haul something to a certain place; *1sg* **indinaawadaas**; *prt* **enaawadaasod**
inaawadoon *vti2* haul s.t. to a certain place; *1sg* **indinaawadoon**; *prt* **enaawadood**
inaawanidiwag /inaawanidi-/ *vai* they travel in a group to a certain place; *1pl* **indinaawanidimin**; *prt* **enaawanidijig**
inaawazh /inaawaN-/ *vta* haul s.o. to a certain place; *1sg* **indinaawanaa**; *prt* **enaawanaad**
inaazakonenjige *vai* go to a certain place with light; *1sg* **indinaazakonenjige**; *prt* **enaazakonenjiged**
inaazhagaame *vai* walk along shore to a certain place; *1sg* **indinaazhagaame**; *prt* **enaazhagaamed**
ind= *pre first person prefix before vowels in verbs and non-dependent nouns*; *also* **nind=, nd=**
indawaaj *pc* therefore, consequently, rather, preferably
indawemaa /-dawemaaw-/ *nad* my sibling of the opposite sex (brother or sister), my parallel cousin of the opposite sex; *pl* **indawemaag**
inday /-day-/ *nad* my dog, my horse; *pl* **indayag**; *dim* **indayens**
indaamikan /-daamikan-/ *nid* my chin, my jaw; *pl* **indaamikanan**; *loc* **indaamikanaang**
indaan /-daan-/ *nad* my daughter; *pl* **indaanag**; *also* **indaanis**
indaangoshenh /-daangosheny-/ *nad* my (female's) female cross-cousin (mother's brother's daughter or father's sister's daughter); *pl* **indaangoshenyag**
indaangwe /-daangwew-/ *nad* my (female's) sister-in-law, my (female's) female friend; *pl* **indaangweg**
indaanis /-daanis-/ *nad* my daughter; *pl* **indaanisag**; *loc* **indaanisens**; *also* **indaan**
indede /-dedey-/ *nad* my father; *pl* **indedeyag**
indedeyinaan *nad* our father = grandfather
inde' /-de'-/ *nid* my heart; *pl* **inde'an**; *loc* **inde'ing**
indenaniw /-denaniw-/ *nid* my tongue; *pl* **indenaniwan**; *loc* **indenaniwaang**
indengway /-dengway-/ *nid* my face; *pl* **indengwayan**; *loc* **indengwaang**
indenigom /-denigom-/ *nad* my nostril; *pl* **indenigomag**; *loc* **indenigomaang**
indigo *pc* just like, as if; *also* **nindigo***
indindawaa /-dindawaa-/ *nad* my fellow parent-in-law; *pl* **indindawaag**
indinimaangan /-dinimaangan-/ *nid* my shoulder; *pl* **indinimaanganan**; *loc* **indinimaanganaang**
indiniigan /-diniigan-/ *nad* my shoulder blade; *pl* **indiniiganag**; *loc* **indiniiganaang**
indis /-disy-/ *nid* my navel, my umbilical cord; *loc* **indisiing**; *dim* **indisiins**
indiskweyaab *nid* my vein; *pl* **indiskweyaabiin**
indiy /-diy-/ *nid* my rump, my rear end; *loc* **indiyaang**; *also* **indiyaash**
indoodem /-doodem-/ *nad* my totem, my clan; *pl* **indoodemag**
indoodikosiw /-doodikosiw-/ *na* my kidney; *pl* **indoodikosiwag**
indoodooshim /-doodooshim-/ *nad* my breast; *pl* **indoodooshimag**; *loc* **indoodooshimaang**
indoon /-doon-/ *nid* my mouth; *pl* **indoonan**; *loc* **indooning**
indoondan /-doondan-/ *nid* my heel; *pl* **indoondanan**; *loc* **indoondanaang**
indooskwan /-dooskwan-/ *nid* my elbow; *pl* **indooskwanan**; *loc* **indooskwanaang**
indoozhim /-doozhim-/ *nad* my parallel nephew (male's brother's son or female's sister's son); *pl* **indoozhimag**
indoozhimikwem /-doozhimikwem-/ *nad* my stepdaughter; *pl* **indoozhimikwemag**
indoozhimis /-doozhimis-/ *nad* my parallel niece (male's brother's daughter or female's sister's daughter); *pl* **indoozhimisag**
ine *pc exclamation of denial*
inendam *vai2* think a certain way, feel a certain way, decide, be of a certain mind, agree; *1sg* **indinendam**; *prt* **enendang**
inendan *vti* think a certain way of s.t.; *1sg* **indinendaan**; *prt* **enendang**
inendaagozi *vai* be thought of a certain way, seem to be a certain way, have a certain destiny; *1sg* **indinendaagoz**; *prt* **enendaagozid**
inendaagwad *vii* be thought of a certain way, seem to be a certain way; *prt* **enendaagwak**
inendi *vai* be gone a certain length of time, be absent a certain length of time; *1sg* **indinend**; *prt* **enendid**
inenim *vta* think of s.o. a certain way; *1sg* **indinenimaa**; *prt* **enenimaad**
inga *nad* my mother *archaic; obviative* **ogiin**
inge *pc woman's expression of mild displeasure or disdain*

ingidig /-gidigw-/ *nad* my knee; *pl* **ingidigwag**; *loc* **ingidigwaang**
ingitiziim /-gitiziim-/ *nad* my parent; *pl* **ingitiziimag**
ingiw *pr* those *animate plural demonstrative*; *also* **ingi, igiw*, igi*, agiw***
ingiwedig *pr* those over there *animate plural demonstrative*; *also* **igiwedig***
ingo- /ningo-/ *pv4* one; *also* **ningo-***
ingo-anama'e-giizhik *pc* one week; *also* **ningo-anama'e-giizhik***
ingo-biboon *pc* one year; *also* **ningo-biboon***
ingo-biboonagad /ningo-biboonagad-/ *vii* be one year; *prt* **nengo-biboonagak**; *also* **ningo-biboonagad***
ingo-biboonagizi /ningo-biboonagizi-/ *vai* be one year old; *1sg* **niningo-biboonagiz**; *prt* **nengo-biboonagizid**; *also* **ningo-biboonagizi***
ingo-diba'igan *pc* one hour, one mile; *also* **ningo-diba'igan***
ingo-diba'iganed /ningo-diba'iganed-/ *vii* be one o'clock; *prt* **nengo-diba'iganek**; *also* **ningo-diba'iganed***
ingo-diba'igaans *pc* one minute, one acre; *also* **ningo-diba'igaans***
ingo-dibik *pc* one night; *also* **ningo-dibik***
ingoding *pc* sometime, at one time; *also* **ningoding***
ingodobaneninj *pc* one handful; *also* **ningodobaneninj***
ingodoninj *pc* one inch; *also* **ningodoninj***
ingodosagoons *nm* one thousand; *also* **ningodosagoons***
ingodozid *pc* one foot; *also* **ningodozid***
ingodooshkin *pc* one bag; *also* **ningodooshkin***
ingodwaaching *pc* six times; *also* **ningodwaaching***
ingodwaachinoon /ningodwaachin-/ *vii* they are six; *prt* **nengodwaaching**; *also* **ningodwaachinoon***
ingodwaachiwag /ningodwaachi-/ *vai* they are six; *1pl* **niningodwaachimin**; *prt* **nengodwaachijig**; *also* **ningodwaachiwag***
ingodwaak *nm* one hundred; *also* **ningodwaak***
ingodwaasimidana *nm* sixty; *also* **ningodwaasimidana***
ingodwaaso- /ningodwaaso-/ *pv4* six; *also* **ningodwaaso***
ingodwaaso-anama'e-giizhigad /ningodwaaso-anama'e-giizhigad-/ *vii* be six weeks; *prt* **nengodwaaso-anama'e-giizhigak**; *also* **ningodwaaso-anama'e-giizhigad***
ingodwaaso-anama'e-giizhik *pc* six weeks; *also* **ningodwaaso-anama'e-giizhik***
ingodwaaso-biboon *pc* six years; *also* **ningodwaaso-biboon***
ingodwaaso-biboonagad /ningodwaaso-biboonagad-/ *vii* be six years; *prt* **nengodwaaso-biboonagak**; *also* **ningodwaaso-biboonagad***
ingodwaaso-biboonagizi /ningodwaaso-biboonagizi-/ *vai* be six years old; *1sg* **niningodwaaso-biboonagiz**; *prt* **nengodwaaso-biboonagizid**; *also* **ningodwaaso-biboonagaizi***
ingodwaaso-diba'igan *pc* six hours, six miles; *also* **ningodwaaso-diba'igan***
ingodwaaso-diba'iganed /ningodwaaso-diba'iganed-/ *vii* be six o'clock; *prt* **nengodwaaso-diba'iganek**; *also* **ningodwaaso-diba'iganed***
ingodwaaso-diba'igaans *pc* six minutes, six acres; *also* **ningodwaaso-diba'igaans***
ingodwaaso-dibik *pc* six nights; *also* **ningodwaaso-dibik***
ingodwaaso-giizhik *pc* six days; *also* **ningodwaaso-giizhik***
ingodwaaso-giizis *pc* six months; *also* **ningodwaaso-giizis***
ingodwaasogon *pc* six days; *also* **ningodwaasogon***
ingodwaasogonagad /ningodwaasogonagad-/ *vii* be six days; *prt* **nengodwaasogonagak**; *also* **ningodwaasogonagad***
ingodwaasogonagizi /ningodwaasogonagizi-/ *vai* be the sixth day of the month, be six days old; *prt* **nengodwaasogonagizid**; *also* **ningodwaasogonagizi***
ingodwaasoninj *pc* six inches; *also* **ningodwaasoninj***
ingodwaasosagoons /ningodwaasosagoons-/ *nm* six thousand; *also* **ningodwaasosagoons***
ingodwaasoobii'igan *na* six (card); *pl* **ingodwaasoobii'iganag**; *also* **ningodwaasoobii'igan***
ingodwaasooshkin *pc* six bags; *also* **ningodwaasooshkin***
ingodwaaswaabik *pc* six dollars; *also* **ningodwaaswaabik***
ingodwaaswaak *nm* six hundred; *also* **ningodwaaswaak***
ingodwaaswi *nm* six; *also* **ningodwaaswi***
ingodwaaswewaan *pc* six sets, six pairs; *also* **ningodwaaswewaan***
ingo-giizhik *pc* one day; *also* **ningo-giizhik***
ingo-giizis *pc* one month; *also* **ningo-giizis***
ingoji *pc* somewhere, approximately, nearly; *also* **ningoji***
ingondashkway /-gondashkway-/ *nid* my throat; *pl* **ingondashkway**; *loc* **ingondashkwaang**
ingos /-gos-/ *nad* my son; *pl* **ingosag**; *also* **ingwis***
ingozis /-gozis-/ *nad* my son; *pl* **ingozisag**; *also* **ingwizis***
ingoodaas /-goodaas-/ *nid* my dress; *pl* **ingoodaasan**
ingwana *pc* it was just so, it turns out that, so it was that; *also* **nangwana, ngwana**
inigaa' *vta* be mean to s.o., injure s.o.; *1sg* **indinigaa'aa**; *prt* **enigaa'aad**
inigaazi *vai* be poor, be pitiable, mourn; *1sg* **indinigaaz**; *prt* **enigaazid**
inigini *vai* be a certain size, be so big; *1sg* **indinigin**; *prt* **eniginid**
inigokwadeyaa *vii* be a certain width, be so wide; *prt* **enigokwadeyaag**; *aug* **inigokwadeyaamagad**; *prt aug* **enigokwadeyaamagak**
inigokwadeyaabikad *vii* be a certain width (as something mineral), be so wide (as something mineral); *prt* **enigokwadeyaabikak**

inigokwadeyaabikizi *vai* be a certain width (as something mineral), be so wide (as something mineral); *prt* **enigokwadeyaabikizid**
inigokwadeyaabiigad *vii* be a certain width (as something string-like), be so wide (as something string-like); *prt* **enigokwadeyaabiigak**
inigokwadeyaabiigizi *vai* be a certain width (as something string-like), be so wide (as something string-like); *prt* **enigokwadeyaabiigizid**
inigokwadeyaakozi *vai* be a certain width (as something stick- or wood-like), be so wide (as something stick- or wood-like); *prt* **enigokwadeyaakozid**
inigokwadeyaakwad *vii* be a certain width (as something stick- or wood-like), be so wide (as something stick- or wood-like); *prt* **enigokwadeyaakwak**
inigokwadeyiigad *vii* be a certain width (as something sheet-like), be so wide (as something sheet-like); *prt* **enigokwadeyiigak**
inigokwadeyiigizi *vai* be a certain width (as something sheet-like), be so wide (as something sheet-like); *prt* **enigokwadeyiigizid**
inigokwadezi *vai* be a certain width, be so wide; *prt* **enigokwadezid**
inigokwaa *vii* be a certain size, be so big; *prt* **enigokwaag**; *aug* **inigokwaamagad**; *prt aug* **enigokwaamagak**
inigokwaabikad *vii* be a certain size (as something mineral), be so big (as something mineral); *prt* **enigokwaabikak**
inigokwaabikizi *vai* be a certain size (as something mineral), be so big (as something mineral); *prt* **enigokwaabikizid**
inigokwaabiigad *vii* be a certain size (as something string-like), be so big (as something string-like); *prt* **enigokwaabiigak**
inigokwaabiigizi *vai* be a certain size (as something string-like), be so big (as something string-like); *prt* **enigokwaabiigizid**
inigokwaakozi *vai* be a certain size (as something stick- or wood-like), be so big (as something stick- or wood-like); *prt* **enigokwaakozid**
inigokwaakwad *vii* be a certain size (as something stick- or wood-like), be so big (as something stick- or wood-like); *prt* **enigokwaakwak**
inigokwegad *vii* be a certain size (as something sheet-like), be so big (as something sheet-like); *prt* **enigokwegak**
inigokwegizi *vai* be a certain size (as something sheet-like), be so big (as something sheet-like); *prt* **enigokwegizid**
inikodan *vti* slice s.t. a certain way; *1sg* **indinikodaan**; *prt* **enikodang**
inikonaye *vai* dress a certain way; *1sg* **indinikonaye**; *prt* **enikonayed**
inikozh /inikoN-/ *vta* slice s.o. a certain way; *1sg* **indinikonaa**; *prt* **enikonaad**
inikwe' /inikwe'w-/ *vta* steer s.o. a certain way; *1sg* **indinikwe'waa**; *prt* **enikwe'waad**
inikwe'an *vti* steer s.t. a certain way; *1sg* **indinikwe'aan**; *prt* **enikwe'ang**
inikweni *vai* put one's head a certain way; *1sg* **indinikwen**; *prt* **enikwenid**
inikweshin *vai* lie with one's head a certain way; *1sg* **indinikweshin**; *prt* **enikweshing**
inikwetaw *vta* nod one's head to s.o. a certain way; *1sg* **indinikwetawaa**; *prt* **enikwetawaad**
inin *vta* hold s.o. a certain way, handle s.o. a certain way; *1sg* **indininaa**; *prt* **eninaad**
ininamaw *vta* hand (s.t.) to s.o. a certain way; *1sg* **indininamawaa**; *prt* **eninamawaad**
ininan *vti* hold s.t. a certain way, handle s.t. a certain way; *1sg* **indininaan**; *prt* **eninang**
ininaatig *na* maple; *pl* **ininaatigoog**; *loc* **ininaatigong**; *also* **aninaatig**
inini *na* man; *pl* **ininiwag**; *dim* **ininiins**
ininigaade *vii* be held a certain way, be handled a certain way; *prt* **eninigaadeg**; *aug* **ininigaademagad**; *prt aug* **eninigaademagak**
ininigaazo *vai* be held a certain way, be handled a certain way; *prt* **eninigaazod**
ininishib *na* mallard; *pl* **ininishibag**; *dim* **ininishibens**
ininii-biizikiigan *ni* item of men's clothing; *pl* **ininii-biizikiiganan**; *loc* **ininii-biizikiiganing**; *dim* **ininii-biizikiigaans**
ininiiwi *vai* be a man; *1sg* **indinininiiw**; *prt* **eninininiiwid**
initam *vai2* hear a certain noise, understand a certain way; *1sg* **indinitam**; *prt* **enitang**
initan *vti* hear s.t. a certain way, understand s.t. a certain way; *1sg* **indinitaan**; *prt* **enitang**
initaw *vta* hear s.o. a certain way, understand s.o. a certain way; *1sg* **indinitawaa**; *prt* **enitawaad**
initaagozi *vai* be heard a certain way, be understood a certain way; *prt* **enitaagozid**
initaagwad *vii* be heard a certain way, be understood a certain way; *prt* **enitaagwak**
iniw *pr* those *inanimate plural demonstrative*, that *obviative*, those *obviative*; *also* **niw, ini, ni, aniw***
iniwedin *pr* those over there *inanimate plural*, that over there *obiative*, those over there *obviative*; *also* **niwedin**
iniz /inizw-/ *vta* cook s.o. a certain way; *1sg* **indinizwaa**; *prt* **enizwaad**
inizan *vti* cook s.t. a certain way; *1sg* **indinizaan**; *prt* **enizang**
inizekwe *vai* cook (something) a certain way; *1sg* **indinizekwe**; *prt* **enizekwed**
inizh /inizhw-/ *vta* cut s.o. a certain way; *1sg* **indinizhwaa**; *prt* **enizhwaad**
inizhan *vti* cut s.t. a certain way; *1sg* **indinizhaan**; *prt* **enizhang**
injaanzh /-jaanzh-/ *nid* my nose; *pl* **injaanzhan**; *loc* **injaanzhing**
injichaag /-jichaagw-/ *nad* my soul, my spirit; *pl* **injichaagwag**; *loc* **injichaagong**
injiid /-jiidy-/ *nid* my rectum; *pl* **injiidiin**; *loc* **injiidiing**; *also* **injiidiish**
injiingwan /-jiingwan-/ *nad* my lap, my thigh (front of thigh); *pl* **injiingwanag**; *loc* **injiingwanaang**
injiitad /-jiitad-/ *nid* my sinew; *pl* **injiitadan**; *loc* **injiitadaang**
inose *vai* walk to a certain place, walk a certain way; *1sg* **indinose**; *prt* **enosed**
inoode *vai* crawl to a certain place, crawl a certain way; *1sg* **indinoode**; *prt* **enooded**

inoom *vta* carry s.o. to a certain place on one's back; *1sg* **indinoomaa**; *prt* **enoomaad**
inoomaawaso *vai* carry a baby to a certain place on one's back; *1sg* **indinoomaawas**; *prt* **enoomaawasod**
inoomigo *vai* ride to a certain place on horseback; *1sg* **indinoomig**; *prt* **enoomigod**
inoondan *vti* carry s.t. to a certain place on one's back; *1sg* **indinoondaan**; *prt* **enoondang**
inootaw *vta* quote s.o. a certain way; *1sg* **indinootawaa**; *prt* **enootawaad**
inootaage *vai* report what people say, quote people; *1sg* **indinootaage**; *prt* **enootaaged**
inwe *vai* make a characteristic call (neigh, etc.), speak a certain language; *1sg* **indinwe**; *prt* **enwed**
inwewe *vii* make a certain noise; *prt* **enweweg**; *aug* **inwewemagad**; *prt aug* **enwewemagak**
inwewidam *vai* be heard speaking going to a certain place; *1sg* **indinwewidam**; *prt* **enwewidang**
inwewin *ni* language; *pl* **inwewinan**
inzhaga'ay /-zhaga'ay-/ *nid* my skin; *loc* **inzhaga'aang**
inzhigwan /zhigwan-/ *nid* my tail (of a fish)
inzhishenh /-zhisheny-/ *nad* my cross-uncle (mother's brother); *pl* **inzhishenyag**
inzhiigan /-zhiigan-/ *nid* the small of my back; *loc* **inzhiiganaang**
inzid /-zid-/ *nid* my foot; *pl* **inzidan**; *loc* **inzidaang**; *dim* **inzidens**
inzigos /-zigos-/ *nad* my cross-aunt (father's sister); *pl* **inzigosag**
inzigozis /-zigozis-/ *nad* my mother-in-law; *pl* **inzigozisag**
inzinis /-zinis-/ *nad* my father-in-law; *pl* **inzinisag**
inzow /-zow-/ *nid* my tail (of an animal); *pl* **inzowan**; *loc* **inzowaang**
ipide *vii* speed to a certain place, drive to a certain place, fly to a certain place; *prt* **epideg**; *aug* **ipidemagad**; *prt aug* **epidemagak**
ipizo *vai* drive to a certain place, speed to a certain place, fly to a certain place; *1sg* **indipiz**; *prt* **epizod**
ipizoni' *vta* drive s.o. to a certain place; *1sg* **indipizoni'aa**; *prt* **epizoni'aad**
ipizonitoon *vti2* drive s.t. to a certain place; *1sg* **indipizonitoon**; *prt* **epizonitood**
ipogozi *vai* have a certain taste; *prt* **epogozid**
ipogwad *vii* have a certain taste; *prt* **epogwak**
isa *pc emphatic word*; *also* **sa**
ise *pc* for shame!
ishkendam *vai2* be disturbed, be upset; *1sg* **indishkendam**; *prt* **eshkendang**
ishkode *ni* fire; *pl* **ishkoden**; *loc* **ishkodeng**; *dim* **ishkodens**
ishkode-bingwi *ni* ashes
ishkode-jiimaan *ni* steamboat, ship; *pl* **ishkode-jiimaanan**; *loc* **ishkode-jiimaaning**; *dim* **ishkode-jiimaanens**
ishkodekaan *ni* lighter; *pl* **ishkodekaanan**; *loc* **ishkodekaaning**; *dim* **ishkodekaanens**
ishkodeke *vai* make a fire; *1sg* **indishkodeke**; *prt* **eshkodeked**
ishkode-makakoons *ni* battery; *pl* **ishkode-makakoonsan**; *loc* **ishkode-makakoonsing**
ishkodens *ni* match; *pl* **ishkodensan**; *loc* **ishkodensing**
ishkodewan *vii* be on fire; *prt* **eshkodewang**
ishkodewaaboo *ni* liquor; *loc* **ishkodewaaboong**
ishkodewidaabaan *na* train; *pl* **ishkodewidaabaanag**; *loc* **ishkodewidaabaaning**; *dim* **ishkodewidaabaanens**; *also* **mashkodewidaabaan***
ishkodewidaabaanikana *ni* train track; *pl* **ishkodewidaabaanikanan**; *loc* **ishkodewidaabaanikanaang**
ishkon *vta* reserve s.o., save s.o. back; *1sg* **indishkonaa**; *prt* **eshkonaad**
ishkonamaw *vta* reserve (s.t.) for s.o., save (s.t.) back for s.o.; *1sg* **indishkonamawaa**; *prt* **eshkonamawaad**
ishkonan *vti* reserve s.t., save s.t. back; *1sg* **indishkonaan**; *prt* **eshkonang**
ishkonigan *ni* reservation; *pl* **ishkoniganan**; *loc* **ishkoniganing**; *dim* **ishkonigaans**
ishkonigaade *vii* be reserved, be saved back; *prt* **eshkonigaadeg**; *aug* **ishkonigaademagad**; *prt aug* **eshkonigaademagak**
ishkonigaazo *vai* be reserved, be saved back; *prt* **eshkonigaazod**
ishkwam *vta* leave s.o. behind uneaten; *1sg* **indishkwamaa**; *prt* **eshkwamaad**
ishkwandan *vti* leave s.t. behind uneaten; *1sg* **indishkwandaan**; *prt* **eshkwandang**
ishkwanjigan *ni* leftover food; *pl* **ishkwanjiganan**; *loc* **ishkwanjiganing**; *dim* **ishkwanjigaans**
ishkwanjige *vai* leave leftovers; *1sg* **indishkwanjige**; *prt* **eshkwanjiged**
ishkwaa- *pv4* after
ishkwaa-anama'e-giizhigad *vii* be Monday; *prt* **eshkwaa-anama'e-giizhigak**; *also* **ishkwaa-aname-giizhigad**
ishkwaabiisaa *vii* stop raining; *prt* **eshkwaabiisaag**; *aug* **ishkwaabiisaamagad**; *prt aug* **eshkwaabiisaamagak**
ishkwaagamizige *vai* finish boiling sap; *1sg* **indishkwaagamizige**; *prt* **eshkwaagamiziged**
ishkwaagaa *vii* be the last run of sap; *prt* **eshkwaagaag**; *aug* **ishkwaagaamagad**; *prt aug* **eshkwaagaamagak**
ishkwaaj *pc* last, finally
ishkwaakajanokii-giizhigad *vii* be Saturday; *prt* **eshkwaajanokii-giizhigak**
ishkwaakamigad *vii* be over (of an event); *prt* **eshkwaakamigak**
ishkwaanaamo *vai* stop breathing; *1sg* **indishkwaanaam**; *prt* **eshkwaanaamod**
ishkwaa-naawakwe *vii* be afternoon; *prt* **eshkwaa-naawakweg**; *aug* **ishkwaa-naawakwemagad**; *prt aug* **eshkwaa-naawakwemagak**
ishkwaandem *ni* door; *pl* **ishkwaandeman**; *loc* **ishkwaandeming**; *dim* **ishkwaandemens**
ishkwaapon /ishkwaapo-/ *vii* stop snowing; *prt* **eshkwaapog**
ishkwaase *vii* come to an end; *prt* **eshkwaaseg**; *aug* **ishkwaasemagad**; *prt aug* **eshkwaasemagak**

ishkwaataa *vai* be at the end of an activity, stop an activity; *1sg* **indishkwaataa**; *prt* **eshkwaataad**
ishkwaayaanimad *vii* wind dies down; *prt* **eskwaayaanimak**
ishkwe-ayi'ii *pc* at the end of it; *also* **iskweya'ii**
ishkwebi *vai* sit at the end; *1sg* **indishkweb**; *prt* **eshkwebid**
ishkwegaabawi *vai* stand at the end; *1sg* **indishkwegaabaw**; *prt* **eshkwegaabawid**
ishkwege *vai* live at the end of town, live in the last house; *1sg* **indishkwege**; *prt* **eshkweged**
ishkwegoode *vii* hang at the end; *prt* **eshkwegoodeg**; *aug* **ishkwegoodemagad**; *prt aug* **eshkwegoodemagak**
ishkwegoodoon *vti2* hang s.t. at the end; *1sg* **indishkwegoodoon**; *prt* **eshkwegoodood**
ishkwegoojin *vai* hang at the end; *prt* **eshkwegoojing**
ishkwegoozh /ishkwegooN-/ *vta* hang s.o. at the end; *1sg* **indishkwegoonaa**; *prt* **eshkwegoonaad**
ishkwejaagan *na* last born child, youngest child; *pl* **ishkwejaaganag**
ishkwenikaazo *vai* have a last name; *1sg* **indishkwenikaaz**; *prt* **eshkwenikaazod**
ishkwenikaazowin *ni* last name; *pl* **ishkwenikaazowinan**
ishkweninj *ni* little finger; *pl* **ishkweninjiin**
ishkwesa'igan *na* toy top; *pl* **ishkwesa'iganag**; *loc* **ishkwesa'iganing**; *dim* **ishkwesa'igaans**
ishkweshin *vai* lie at the end; *1sg* **indishkweshin**; *prt* **eshkweshing**
ishkwesin *vii* lie at the end; *prt* **eshkwesing**
ishkweyaang *pc* behind, in the back, back (in time)
ishkwii *vai* stay behind; *1sg* **indishkwii**; *prt* **eshkwiid**
ishpadinaa *vii* be a hill, be a high place; *prt* **eshpadinaag**; *aug* **ishpadinaamagad**; *prt aug* **eshpadinaamagak**
ishpagindan *vti* charge a high price for s.t.; *1sg* **indishpagindaan**; *prt* **eshpagindang**
ishpagindaaso *vai* charge a high price; *1sg* **indishpagindaas**; *prt* **eshpagindaasod**
ishpaginde *vii* be high-priced; *prt* **eshpagindeg**; *aug* **ishpagindemagad**; *prt aug* **eshpagindemagak**
ishpaginzo *vai* be high-priced, be high in status or office; *1sg* **indishpaginz**; *prt* **eshpaginzod**
ishpagoode *vii* hang up high; *prt* **eshpagoodeg**; *aug* **ishpagoodemagad**; *prt aug* **eshpagoodemagak**
ishpagoodoon *vti2* hang s.t. up high; *1sg* **indishpagoodoon**; *prt* **eshpagoodood**
ishpagoojin *vai* hang up high, be high (e.g., the sun); *1sg* **indishpagoojin**; *prt* **eshpagoojing**
ishpagoozh /ishpagooN-/ *vta* hang s.o. up high; *1sg* **indishpagoonaa**; *prt* **eshpagoonaad**
ishpayi'ii *pc* above it, over it
ishpaa *vii* be high up; *prt* **eshpaag**; *aug* **ishpaamagad**; *prt aug* **eshpaamagak**
ishpaagonagaa *vii* be deep snow; *prt* **eshpaagonagaag**; *aug* **ishpaagonagaamagad**; *prt aug* **eshpaagonagaamagak**
ishpaatoon *vti2* make s.t. high; *1sg* **indishpaatoon**; *prt* **eshpaatood**
ishpenim *vta* think highly of s.o.; *1sg* **indishpenimaa**; *prt* **eshpenimaad**
ishpenimo *vai* be proud, have high aspirations; *1sg* **indishpenim**; *prt* **eshpenimod**
ishpi- *pv4* high, advanced into a time
ishpi-dibik *pc* late at night
ishpi-dibikad *vii* be late at night; *prt* **eshpi-dibikak**
ishpi-giizhigad *vii* be late morning or early afternoon; *prt* **eshpi-giizhigak**
ishpiming *pc* in the sky, above, in heaven
ishpimisag *ni* the floor above; *pl* **ishpimisagoon**; *loc* **ishpimisagong**
ishpimisagokaade *vii* have an upper story; *prt* **eshpimisagokaadeg**; *aug* **ishpimisagokaademagad**; *prt aug* **eshpimisagokaademagak**
ishpishin *vai* lie high up; *1sg* **indishpishin**; *prt* **eshpishing**
ishpisin *vii* lie high up; *prt* **eshpising**
ishwaaching *pc* eight times; *also* **nishwaaching***
ishwaachinoon /ishwaachin-/ *vii* they are eight; *prt* **eshwaachingin**; *also* **nishwaachinoon***
ishwaachiwag /ishwaachi-/ *vai* they are eight; *1pl* **indishwaachimin**; *prt* **eshwaachijig**; *also* **nishwaachiwag***
ishwaasimidana *nm* eighty; *also* **nishwaasimidana***
ishwaaso- *pv4* eight; *also* **nishwaaso-***
ishwaaso-anama'e-giizhigad *vii* be eight weeks; *also* **nishwaaso-anama'e-giizhigad***
ishwaaso-anama'e-giizhik *pc* eight weeks; *also* **nishwaaso-anama'e-giizhik***
ishwaaso-biboon *pc* eight years; *also* **nishwaaso-biboon***
ishwaaso-biboonagad *vii* be eight years; *prt* **eshwaaso-biboonagak**; *also* **nishwaaso-biboonagad***
ishwaaso-biboonagizi *vai* be eight years old; *1sg* **indishwaaso-biboonagiz**; *prt* **eshwaaso-biboonagizid**; *also* **nishwaaso-biboonagizi***
ishwaaso-diba'igan *pc* eight miles, eight hours; *also* **nishwaaso-diba'igan***
ishwaaso-diba'iganed *vii* be eight o'clock; *prt* **eshwaaso-diba'iganek**; *also* **nishwaaso-diba'iganed***
ishwaaso-diba'igaans *pc* eight minutes, eight acres; *also* **nishwaaso-diba'igaans***
ishwaaso-dibik *pc* eight nights; *also* **nishwaaso-dibik***
ishwaaso-giizhik *pc* eight days; *also* **nishwaaso-giizhik***
ishwaaso-giizis *pc* eight months; *also* **nishwaaso-giizis***
ishwaasogon *pc* eight days; *also* **nishwaasogon***
ishwaasogonagad *vii* be eight days; *prt* **eshwaasogonagak**; *also* **nishwaasogonagad***
ishwaasogonagizi *vai* be the eighth day of the month, be eight days old; *prt* **eshwaasogonagizid**; *also* **nishwaasogonagizi***
ishwaasoninj *pc* eight inches; *also* **nishwaasoninj***
ishwaasosagoons *nm* eight thousand; *also* **nishwaasosagoons***
ishwaasozid *pc* eight feet; *also* **nishwaasozid***

ishwaasoobii'igan *na* eight (card); *pl* **ishwaasoobii'iganag**; *also* **nishwaasoobii'igan***
ishwaasooshkin *pc* eight bags; *also* **nishwaasooshkin***
ishwaaswaabik *pc* eight dollars; *also* **nishwaaswaabik***
ishwaaswaak *nm* eight hundred; *also* **nishwaaswaak***
ishwaaswewaan *pc* eight sets, eight pairs; *also* **nishwaaswewaan***
ishwaaswi *nm* eight; *also* **nishwaaswi***
iska'ibii *vai* bail; *1sg* **indiska'ibii**; *prt* **eska'ibiid**
iskandan *vti* drain s.t. dry; *1sg* **indiskandaan**; *prt* **eskandang**
iskate *vii* go down (of a body of water), dry up (of a body of water); *prt* **eskateg**; *aug* **iskatemagad**; *prt aug* **eskatemagak**
iskaakizige *vai* run out of fuel; *1sg* **indiskaakizige**; *prt* **eskaakiziged**
iskigamide *vii* boil down; *prt* **eskigamideg**; *aug* **iskigamidemagad**; *prt aug* **eskigamidemagak**
iskigamizan *vti* boil s.t. down; *1sg* **indiskigamizaan**; *prt* **eskigamizang**
iskigamizigan *ni* sugar camp, sugar bush; *pl* **iskigamiziganan**; *loc* **iskigamiziganing**; *dim* **iskigamizigaans**
iskigamiziganaak *ni* frame for holding sap-boiling kettles; *pl* **iskigamiziganaakoon**; *loc* **iskigamiziganaakong**; *dim* **iskigamiziganaakoons**
iskigamiziganaatig *ni* sap-boiling pole; *pl* **iskigamiziganaatigoon**; *loc* **iskigamiziganaatigong**; *dim* **iskigamiziganaatigoons**
iskigamizige *vai* boil things down (e.g., maple sap); *1sg* **indiskigamizige**; *prt* **eskigamiziged**
iskigamizige-giizis *na* April
iskigamizigewigamig *ni* sap-boiling lodge; *pl* **iskigamizigewigamigoon**; *loc* **iskigamizigewigamigong**; *dim* **iskigamizigewigamigoons**
iskigamizo *vai* boil down; *prt* **eskigamizod**
iw *pr* that *inanimate singular demonstrative*; *also* **i'iw, i'i, 'i**
iw apii *pr* at that time; *also* **i'iw apii**
iwedi *pr* that over there *inanimate singular demonstrative*; *also* **i'iwedi**
iwidi *pc* over there
izhaa *vai* go to a certain place; *1sg* **indizhaa**; *prt* **ezhaad**
izhaamagad *vii* go to a certain place; *prt* **ezhaamagak**
izhi /iN-/ *vta* say to s.o., speak so to s.o.; *1sg* **indinaa**; *prt* **enaad**
izhi- *pv3* in a certain way, to a certain place, thus, so, there
izhi-ayaa *vai* be a certain way; *1sg* **indizhi-ayaa**; *prt* **ezhi-ayaad**
izhibii'an *vti* write s.t. a certain way; *1sg* **indizhibii'aan**; *prt* **ezhibii'ang**
izhibii'igaade *vii* be written a certain way; *prt* **ezhibii'igaadeg**; *aug* **izhibii'igaademagad**; *prt aug* **ezhibii'igaademagak**
izhibii'ige *vai* write things a certain way; *1sg* **indizhibii'ige**; *prt* **ezhibii'iged**
izhichigaade *vii* be made a certain way; *prt* **ezhichigaadeg**; *aug* **izhichigaademagad**; *prt aug* **ezhichigaademagak**
izhichigaazo *vai* be made a certain way; *prt* **ezhichigaazod**
izhichige *vai* do things a certain way; *1sg* **indizhichige**; *prt* **ezhichiged**
izhichigewin *ni* way of doing, deed; *pl* **izhichigewinan**; *dim* **izhichigewinens**
izhidaabaadan *vti* drag s.t. to a certain place; *1sg* **indizhidaabaadaan**; *prt* **ezhidaabaadang**
izhidaabaazh /izhidaabaaN-/ *vta* drag s.o. to a certain place; *1sg* **indizhidaabaanaa**; *prt* **ezhidaabaanaad**
izhidaabii'iwe *vai* drive to a certain place; *1sg* **indizhidaabii'iwe**; *prt* **ezhidaabii'iwed**
izhidoonem *vta* point s.o. out with lips; *1sg* **indizhidoonemaa**; *prt* **ezhidoonemaad**
izhidooneni *vai* point a certain way with lips; *1sg* **indizhidoonen**; *prt* **ezhidoonenid**
izhidoonetaw *vta* point (s.t.) out to s.o. with lips; *1sg* **indizhidoonetawaa**; *prt* **ezhidoonetawaad**
izhi-giizhigad *vii* be a certain day of the week; *prt* **ezhi-giizhigak**
izhigiizhwe *vai* talk a certain way; *1sg* **indizhigiizhwe**; *prt* **ezhigiizhwed**
izhi' *vta* cause s.o. to do something, make s.o. do something; *1sg* **indizhi'aa**; *prt* **ezhi'aad**
izhi'o *vai* dress a certain way; *1sg* **indizhi'**; *prt* **ezhi'od**
izhijiwan *vii* flow a certain way, flow to a certain place; *prt* **ezhijiwang**
izhikawe *vai* leave tracks going to a certain place; *1sg* **indizhikawe**; *prt* **ezhikawed**
izhimaagozi *vai* smell a certain way; *1sg* **indizhimaagoz**; *prt* **ezhimaagozid**
izhimaagwad *vii* smell a certain way; *prt* **ezhimaagwak**
izhimaam *vta* have s.o. smell a certain way to one; *1sg* **indizhimaamaa**; *prt* **ezhimaamaad**
izhimaandan *vti* have s.t. smell a certain way to one; *1sg* **indizhimaandaan**; *prt* **ezhimaandang**
izhimaaso *vai* smell a certain way cooking or burning; *prt* **ezhimaasod**
izhimaate *vii* smell a certain way cooking or burning; *prt* **ezhimaateg**; *aug* **izhimaatemagad**; *prt aug* **ezhimaatemagak**
izhinan *vti* see s.t. a certain way, perceive s.t. a certain way; *1sg* **indizhinaan**; *prt* **ezhinang**
izhinaw *vta* see s.o. a certain way, perceive s.o. a certain way; *1sg* **indizhinawaa**; *prt* **ezhinawaad**
izhinaago' *vta* make s.o. look a certain way; *1sg* **indizhinaago'aa**; *prt* **ezhinaago'aad**
izhinaago'idizo *vai* transform oneself in appearance; *1sg* **indizhinaago'idiz**; *prt* **ezhinaago'idizod**
izhinaagotoon *vti2* make s.t. look a certain way; *1sg* **indizhinaagotoon**; *prt* **ezhinaagotood**
izhinaagozi *vai* have a certain appearance, have a certain look; *1sg* **indizhinaagoz**; *prt* **ezhinaagozid**
izhinaagwad *vii* have a certain appearance, have a certain look; *prt* **ezhinaagwak**

izhinaazhikaw *vta* send s.o. to a certain place, chase s.o. to a certain place; *1sg* **indizhinaazhikawaa**; *prt* **ezhinaazhikawaad**
izhinikaadan *vti* name s.t. a certain way; *1sg* **indizihinikaadaan**; *prt* **ezhinikaadang**
izhinikaade *vii* be named a certain way; *prt* **ezhinikaadeg**; *aug* **izhinikaademagad**; *prt aug* **ezhinikaademagak**
izhinikaazh /izhinikaaN-/ *vta* name s.o. a certain way; *1sg* **indizhinikaanaa**; *prt* **ezhinikaanaad**
izhinikaazo *vai* be named a certain way; *1sg* **indizhinikaaz**; *prt* **ezhinikaazod**
izhinikeni *vai* move one's arm a certain way; *1sg* **indizhiniken**; *prt* **ezhinikenid**
izhininjiini *vai* move one's hand a certain way; *1sg* **indizhininjiin**; *prt* **ezhininjiinid**
izhinizha' /izhinizha'w-/ *vta* send s.o. to a certain place; *1sg* **indizhinizha'waa**; *prt* **ezhinizha'waad**
izhinizha'amaw *vta* send (s.t.) to s.o. to a certain place; *1sg* **indizhinizha'amawaa**; *prt* **ezhinizha'amawaad**
izhinizha'an *vti* send s.t. to a certain place; *1sg* **indizhinizha'aan**; *prt* **ezhinizha'ang**
izhinizha'igaade *vii* be sent to a certain place; *prt* **ezhinizha'igaadeg**; *aug* **izhinizha'igaademagad**; *prt aug* **ezhinizha'igaademagak**
izhinizha'igaazo *vai* be sent to a certain place; *prt* **ezhinizha'igaazod**
izhinizhikaw *vta* chase s.o. to a certain place; *1sg* **indizhinizhikawaa**; *prt* **ezhinizhikawaad**
izhinizhimo *vai* run to a certain place in flight; *1sg* **indizhinizhim**; *prt* **ezhinizhimod**
izhinoo' *vta* point to s.o. a certain way; *1sg* **indizhinoo'aa**; *prt* **ezhinoo'aad**
izhinoo'amaw *vta* point to (s.t.) for s.o.; *1sg* **indizhinoo'amawaa**; *prt* **ezhinoo'amawaad**
izhinoo'an *vti* point to s.t. a certain way; *1sg* **indizhinoo'aan**; *prt* **ezhinoo'ang**
izhinoo'iganinj *ni* index finger; *pl* **izhinoo'iganinjiin**
izhise *vai* fly to a certain place; *1sg* **indizhise**; *prt* **ezhised**
izhise *vii* fly to a certain place, pass (as time); *prt* **ezhiseg**; *aug* **izhisemagad**; *prt aug* **ezhisemagak**
izhishim *vta* lay s.o. a certain way, put s.o. a certain way; *1sg* **indizhishimaa**; *prt* **ezhishimaad**
izhishin *vai* lie a certain way; *1sg* **indizhishin**; *prt* **ezhishing**
izhisidoon *vti2* lay s.t. a certain way, set s.t. a certain way; *1sg* **indizhisidoon**; *prt* **ezhisidood**
izhisin *vii* lie a certain way, be written a certain way, be printed a certain way; *prt* **ezhising**
izhitigweyaa *vii* flow to a certain place (as a river); *prt* **ezhitigweyaag**; *aug* **izhitigweyaamagad**; *prt aug* **ezhitigweyaamagak**
izhitoon *vti2* cause s.t. to, make s.t. a certain way; *1sg* **indizhitoon**; *prt* **ezhitood**
izhitwaa *vai* have a certain custom, practice a certain religion; *1sg* **indizhitwaa**; *prt* **ezhitwaad**
izhiwebad *vii* happen a certain way, be a certain event, be a certain weather condition; *prt* **ezhiwebak**
izhiwebizi *vai* behave a certain way, have certain things happen to one, fare a certain way; *1sg* **indizhiwebiz**; *prt* **ezhiwebizid**
izhiwidaw *vta* take (s.t.) to s.o. at a certain place; *1sg* **indizhiwidawaa**; *prt* **ezhiwidawaad**
izhiwidoon *vti2* take s.t. to a certain place, carry s.t. to a certain place; *1sg* **indizhiwidoon**; *prt* **ezhiwidood**
izhiwijigaade *vii* be carried to a certain place, be taken to a certain place; *prt* **ezhiwijigaadeg**; *aug* **izhiwijigaademagad**; *prt aug* **ezhiwijigaademagak**
izhiwijigaazo *vai* be carried to a certain place, be taken to a certain place; *prt* **ezhiwijigaazod**
izhiwizh /izhiwiN-/ *vta* take s.o. to a certain place, carry s.o. to a certain place; *1sg* **indizhiwinaa**; *prt* **ezhiwinaad**
izhi-wiindan *vti* call s.t. a certain way, name s.t. a certain way; *1sg* **indizhi-wiindaan**; *prt* **ezhi-wiindang**
izhi-wiinde *vii* be called a certain way, be named a certain way; *prt* **ezhi-wiindeg**; *aug* **izhi-wiindemagad**; *prt aug* **ezhi-wiindemagak**
izhi-wiinzh /izhi-wiinN-/ *vta* call s.o. a certain way, name s.o. a certain way; *1sg* **indizhi-wiinaa**; *prt* **ezhi-wiinaad**
izhi-wiinzo *vai* be called a certain way, be named a certain way; *1sg* **indizhi-wiinz**; *prt* **ezhi-wiinzod**
izhizideni *vai* move one's foot a certain way; *1sg* **indizhiziden**; *prt* **ezhizidenid**
izhiigad *vii* be a certain way (as something sheet-like); *prt* **ezhiigak**
izhiigizi *vai* be a certain way (as something sheet-like); *prt* **ezhiigizid**
iidog *pc* maybe, must be

J

jachakan= < jakan=
jakanaamo *vai* have chest pains while breathing; *1sg* **injakanaam**; *prt* **jekanaamod**
jakiiwii *vai* strain self in lifting; *1sg* **injakiiwii**; *prt* **jekiiwiid**
jaachaag= < jaag=
jaachaamo *vai* sneeze; *1sg* **injaachaam**; *prt* **jayaachaamod**
jaagadaawaage *vai+o* sell out (of s.t.); *1sg* **injaagadaawaage, injaagadaawaagen**; *prt* **jayaagadaawaaged**
jaaga'e *vai* use up all of the ammunition; *1sg* **injaaga'e**; *prt* **jayaaga'ed**
jaagaabaji' *vta* use s.o. up; *1sg* **injaagaabaji'aa**; *prt* **jayaagaabaji'aad**
jaagaabajitoon *vti2* use s.t. up; *1sg* **injaagaabajitoon**; *prt* **jayaagaabajitood**
jaagaakide *vii* burn up; *prt* **jayaagaakideg**; *aug* **jaagaakidemagad**; *prt aug* **jayaagaakidemagak**

jaagaakiz /jaagaakizw-/ *vta* burn s.o. up; *1sg* **injaagaakizwaa**; *prt* **jayaagaakizwaad**
jaagaakizan *vti* burn s.t. up; *1sg* **injaagaakizaan**; *prt* **jayaagaakizang**
jaagaakizo *vai* burn up; *prt* **jayaagaakizod**
jaagide *vii* burn up; *prt* **jayaagideg**; *aug* **jaagidemagad**; *prt aug* **jayaagidemagak**
jaagin *vta* be out of s.o.; *1sg* **injaaginaa**; *prt* **jayaaginaad**
jaaginan *vti* be out of s.t.; *1sg* **injaaginaan**; *prt* **jayaaginang**
jaaginazh /jaaginaN-/ *vta* kill s.o. off; *1sg* **injaaginanaa**; *prt* **jayaaginanaad**
jaaginigaade *vii* be used up; *prt* **jayaaginigaadeg**; *aug* **jaaginigaademagad**; *prt aug* **jayaaginigaademagak**
jaaginige *vai* use things up, take everything, spend everything; *1sg* **injaaginige**; *prt* **jayaaginiged**
jaagise *vai+o* run out, become exhausted; *1sg* **injaagise, injaagisen**; *prt* **jayaagised**
jaagise *vii* run out; *prt* **jayaagiseg**; *aug* **jaagisemagad**; *prt aug* **jayaagisemagak**
jaagiz /jaagizw-/ *vta* burn s.o. up; *1sg* **injaagizwaa**; *prt* **jayaagizwaad**
jaagizan *vti* burn s.t. up; *1sg* **injaagizaan**; *prt* **jayaagizang**
jaagizhooniyaaweshin *vai* use up all of the money; *1sg* **injaagizhooniyaaweshin**; *prt* **jayaagizhooniyaaweshing**
jaagizige *vai* use up all of the ammunition; *1sg* **injaagizige**; *prt* **jayaagiziged**
jaagizo *vai* burn up; *1sg* **injaagiz**; *prt* **jayaagizod**
jaagizodizo *vai* burn oneself; *1sg* **injaagizodiz**; *prt* **jayaagizodizod**
jaangate *vii* be a corner of a room; *prt* **jayaangateg**; *aug* **jaangatemagad**; *prt aug* **jayaangatemagak**
jaangidiyeshin *vai* lie with one's rear end sticking out; *1sg* **injaangidiyeshin**; *prt* **jayaangidiyeshing**
jejiibajikii *na* elephant; *pl* **jejiibajikiig**; *dim* **jejiibajikiins**
jekaagaminan *vti* dip s.t. in; *1sg* **injekaagaminaan**; *prt* **jayekaagaminang**
jekaakwa'am *vai2* go into the woods; *1sg* **injekaakwa'am**; *prt* **jayekaakwa'ang**
jeko-mazina'igan *ni* check; *pl* **jeko-mazina'iganan**; *loc* **jeko-mazina'iganing**; *dim* **jeko-mazina'igaans**
ji- *pv1* that, so that, in order to; *future and modal prefix in unchanged conjunct*
jibwaa- *pv1* before; *also* **ji-bwaa-**
jiibadabi *vai* sit stiffly; *1sg* **injiibadab**; *prt* **jaabadabid**
jiibadaakogaabawi *vai* stand stiffly; *1sg* **injiibadaakogaabaw**; *prt* **jaabadaakogaabawid**
jiibadaakogaade *vai* have a stiff leg; *1sg* **injiibadaakogaade**; *prt* **jaabadaakogaaded**
jiibadaakonike *vai* have a stiff arm; *1sg* **injiibadaakonike**; *prt* **jaabadaakoniked**
jiibajigaade *vai* have a stiff leg; *1sg* **injiibajigaade**; *prt* **jaabajigaaded**
jiibajigwayawe *vai* have a stiff neck; *1sg* **injiibajigwayawe**; *prt* **jaabajigwayawed**
jiibajinike *vai* have a stiff arm; *1sg* **injiibajinike**; *prt* **jaabajiniked**
jiibay *na* ghost, spirit; *pl* **jiibayag**
jiibayag niimi'idiwag /niimi'idi-/ *vai* they are the northern lights; *prt* **jiibayag naami'idijig**
jiibayaki *ni* graveyard, cemetery; *pl* **jiibayakiin**; *loc* **jiibayakiing**; *dim* **jiibayakiins**
jiibayaatig *na* grave marker; *pl* **jiibayaatigoog**; *loc* **jiibayaatigong**; *dim* **jiibayaatigoons**
jiibaakwaadan *vti* cook s.t.; *1sg* **injiibaakwaadaan**; *prt* **jaabaakwaadang**
jiibaakwaazh /jiibaakwaaN-/ *vta* cook s.o.; *1sg* **injiibaakwaanaa**; *prt* **jaabaakwaanaad**
jiibaakwe *vai* cook; *1sg* **injiibaakwe**; *prt* **jaabaakwed**
jiibaakwe-gizhaabikizigan *ni* cook stove; *pl* **jiibaakwe-gizhaabikiziganan**; *loc* **jiibaakwe-gizhaabikiziganing**; *dim* **jiibaakwe-gizhaabikizigaans**
jiibaakwewakik *na* cooking pot, pan; *pl* **jiibaakwewakikoog**; *loc* **jiibaakwewakikong**; *dim* **jiibaakwewakikoons**
jiibaakwewigamig *ni* kitchen, cook shack; *pl* **jiibaakwewigamigoon**; *loc* **jiibaakwewigamigong**; *dim* **jiibaakwewigamigoons**
jiibaakwewikwe *na* cook (female); *pl* **jiibaakwewikweg**
jiibaakwewinini *na* cook (male); *pl* **jiibaakwewininiwag**
jiibegamig *ni* grave house, casket; *pl* **jiibegamigoon**; *loc* **jiibegamigong**; *dim* **jiibegamigoons**
jiibenaake *vai* have a feast honoring the dead; *1sg* **injiibenaake**; *prt* **jaabenaaked**
jiibiingweni *vai* wink; *1sg* **injiibiingwen**; *prt* **jaabiingwenid**
jiibiingwetaw *vta* wink at s.o.; *1sg* **injiibiingwetawaa**; *prt* **jaabiingwetawaad**
jiichiibishkaa *vai* quiver; *1sg* **injiichiibishkaa**; *prt* **jaachiibishkaad**
jiichiibizideni *vai* tap one's foot; *1sg* **injiichiibiziden**; *prt* **jaachiibizidenid**
jiichiibiingwetaw *vta* wink at s.o.; *1sg* **injiichiibiingwetawaa**; *prt* **jaachiibiingwetawaad**
jiichiigaawiganebizh /jiichiigaawiganebiN-/ *vta* scratch s.o.'s back; *1sg* **injiichiigaawiganebinaa**; *prt* **jaachiigaawiganebinaad**
jiichiigibidoon *vti2* scratch s.t. (leaving a visible mark); *1sg* **injiichiigibidoon**; *prt* **jaachiigibidood**
jiichiigibizh /jiichiigibiN-/ *vta* scratch s.o. (leaving a visible mark); *1sg* **injiichiigibinaa**; *prt* **jaachiigibinaad**
jiichiigii *vai* scratch (leaving a visible mark); *1sg* **injiichiigii**; *prt* **jaachiigiid**
jiichiigom *na* wart; *pl* **jiichiigomag**
jiichiigwam *vta* chew on s.o.; *1sg* **injiichiigwamaa**; *prt* **jaachiigwamaad**
jiichiigwandan *vti* chew on s.t.; *1sg* **injiichiigwandaan**; *prt* **jaachiigwandang**
jiichiigwanjige *vai* chew on things; *1sg* **injiichiigwanjige**; *prt* **jaachiigwanjiged**
jiichiishkinzhe'igan *ni* fire poker; *pl* **jiichiishkinzhe'iganan**; *loc*

jiichiishkinzhe'iganing; *dim* **jiichiishkinzhe'igaans**
jiichiishkinzhe'ige *vai* stir the fire; *1sg* **injiichiishkinzhe'ige**; *prt* **jaachiishkinzhe'iged**
jiigada'igan *ni* broom; *pl* **jiigada'iganan**; *loc* **jiigada'iganing**; *dim* **jiigada'igaans**
jiiga'azh /jiiga'aN-/ *vta* scale s.o.; *1sg* **injiiga'anaa**; *prt* **jaaga'anaad**
jiiga'e *vai* scale fish; *1sg* **injiiga'e**; *prt* **jaaga'ed**
jiigashkosiw *pc* by a meadow
jiigayi'ii *pc* by it, along it
jiigaakwaa *pc* near the woods
jiigaatig *pc* by a tree, by a wall
jiigew *pc* along the shore
jiigewe *vai* go along the shore, go along the edge; *1sg* **injiigewe**; *prt* **jaagewed**
jiigewebatoo *vai* run along the shore; *1sg* **injiigewebatoo**; *prt* **jaagewebatood**
jiigewebizo *vai* drive along the shore, speed along the shore; *1sg* **injiigewebiz**; *prt* **jaagewebizod**
jiigewedaabii'iwe *vai* drive along the shore; *1sg* **injiigewedaabii'iwe**; *prt* **jaagewedaabii'iwed**
jiigewe'am *vai2* paddle along the shore; *1sg* **injiigewe'am**; *prt* **jaagewe'ang**
jiigewe'o *vai* paddle along the shore; *1sg* **injiigewe'**; *prt* **jaagewe'od**
jiigewekwazhiwe *vai* paddle along the shore; *1sg* **injiigewekwazhiwe**; *prt* **jaagewekwazhiwed**
jiigeweyaazhagaame *vai* walk along the shore; *1sg* **injiigeweyaazhagaame**; *prt* **jaageweyaazhagaamed**
jiigeweyaazhagaamebatoo *vai* run along the shore; *1sg* **injiigeweyaazhagaamebatoo**; *prt* **jaageweyaazhagaamebatood**
jiigi- *pn* near, by
jiigibiig *pc* along the shore, by the water
jiigigamig *pc* by a house
jiigikana *pc* by a road or trail
jiigishkode *pc* by a fire
jiigishkwaand *pc* by a door
jiimaan *ni* canoe, boat; *pl* **jiimaanan**; *loc* **jiimaaning**; *dim* **jiimaanens**
jiimaanike *vai* make a canoe, make a boat; *1sg* **injiimaanike**; *prt* **jaamaaniked**
jiime *vai* go by canoe, paddle; *1sg* **injiime**; *prt* **jaamed**
jiingwe *vii* rumble; *prt* **jaangweg**; *aug* **jiingwemagad**; *prt aug* **jaangwemagak**
jiis *ni* rutabaga; *pl* **jiisan**; *loc* **jiising**; *dim* **jiisens**
jiisakaan *ni* shaking tent; *pl* **jiisakaanan**; *loc* **jiisakaaning**; *dim* **jiisakaanens**
jiisakii *vai* practice divination in a shaking tent; *1sg* **injiisakii**; *prt* **jaasakiid**
jiisakiiwinini *na* seer who uses a shaking tent; *pl* **jiisakiiwininiwag**
jiishada'igan *ni* broom; *pl* **jiishada'iganan**; *loc* **jiishada'iganing**; *dim* **jiishada'igaans**
jiishada'ige *vai* sweep; *1sg* **injiishada'ige**; *prt* **jaashada'iged**
jiishakamiga'igan *ni* rake; *pl* **jiishakamiga'iganan**; *loc* **jiishakamiga'iganing**; *dim* **jiishakamiga'igaans**
jiishaakwa' /jiishaakwa'w-/ *vta* scrape s.o. to remove hair (e.g., a hide); *1sg* **injiishaakwa'waa**; *prt* **jaashaakwa'aad**
jiishaakwa'igan *ni* hide scraper; *pl* **jiishaakwa'iganan**
jiishaakwa'ige *vai* scrape hides; *1sg* **injiishaakwa'ige**; *prt* **jaashaakwa'iged**
jiisibizh /jiisibiN-/ *vta* pinch s.o.; *1sg* **injiisibinaa**; *prt* **jaasibinaad**
jiiskinikebizo *vai* wear a bracelet, wear arm garters; *1sg* **injiiskinikebiz**; *prt* **jaaskinikebizod**
jiiskinikebizon *ni* arm garter, bracelet; *pl* **jiiskinikebizonan**; *loc* **jiiskinikebizoning**; *dim* **jiiskinikebizonens**

M

madaabii *vai* go to the shore; *1sg* **nimadaabii**; *prt* **medaabiid**
madaabiibatoo *vai* run to the shore; *1sg* **nimadaabiibatoo**; *prt* **medaabiibatood**
madaabiiwidoon *vti2* take s.t. to the shore, carry s.t. to the shore; *1sg* **nimadaabiiwidoon**; *prt* **medaabiiwidood**
madaabiiwizh /madaabiiwiN-/ *vta* take s.o. to the shore, carry s.o. to the shore; *1sg* **nimadaabiiwinaa**; *prt* **medaabiiwinaad**
madaagamin /madaagami-/ *vii* be turbulent water; *prt* **medaagamig**
madoodiswan *ni* sweat lodge; *pl* **madoodiswanan**; *loc* **madoodiswaning**
madoodoo *vai* take a sweat bath; *1sg* **nimadoodoo**; *prt* **medoodood**
madoodoowasin *na* rock for sweat lodge; *pl* **madoodoowasiniig**; *loc* **madoodoowasiniing**
madoodoowinini *na* Finn; *pl* **madoodoowininiwag**
madwe- *pv4* being heard, making noise
madwebiisaa *vii* rain is heard; *prt* **medwebiisaag**; *aug* **madwebiisaamagad**; *prt aug* **medwebiisaamagak**
madwegamide *vii* make noise boiling; *prt* **medwegamideg**; *aug* **madwegamidemagad**; *prt aug* **medwegamidemagak**
madwegamijii *vai* one's stomach growls; *1sg* **nimadwegamijii**; *prt* **medwegamijiid**
madwegamizo *vai* make noise boiling; *prt* **medwegamizod**
madwe' /madwe'w-/ *vta* drum on s.o.; *1sg* **nimadwe'**; *prt* **medwe'waad**
madwe'an *vti* drum on s.t.; *1sg* **nimadwe'aan**; *prt* **medwe'ang**
madwejiwan *vii* be heard flowing (e.g., a rapids); *prt* **medwejiwang**
madwekwadin *vii* be heard cracking (as ice); *prt* **medwekwading**
madwengwaam *vai* make noise in one's sleep, snore; *1sg* **nimadwengwaam**; *prt* **medwengwaang**
madwenjige *vai* be heard eating; *1sg* **nimadwenjige**; *prt* **medwenjiged**

madwesagishin *vai* be heard falling on the floor, be heard walking on the floor; *1sg* **nimadwesagishin**; *prt* **medwesagishing**
madweshin *vai* ring, make noise hitting; *1sg* **nimadweshin**; *prt* **medweshing**
madwesidoon *vti2* ring s.t., make noise hitting s.t.; *1sg* **nimadwesidoon**; *prt* **medwesidood**
madwesijige *vai* ring things, make noise hitting things; *1sg* **nimadwesijige**; *prt* **medwesijiged**
madwesin *vii* ring, make noise hitting; *prt* **medwesing**
madwetaa *vai* be heard in an activity; *1sg* **nimadwetaa**; *prt* **medwetaad**
madwewe *vii* make noise; *prt* **medweweg**; *aug* **madwewemagad**; *prt aug* **medwewemagak**
madwewechigan *ni* musical instrument, piano, organ; *pl* **madwewechiganan**; *loc* **madwewechiganing**; *dim* **madwewechigaans**
madwewechige *vai* make sounds on things, play music; *1sg* **nimadwewechige**; *prt* **medwewechiged**
madwewetaw *vta* play music for s.o.; *1sg* **nimadwewetawaa**; *prt* **medwewetawaad**; *also* **madwewetamaw**
madwewetoon *vti2* make sounds on s.t., make noise on s.t.; *1sg* **nimadwewetoon**; *prt* **medwewetood**
madweyaabiigibijigan *ni* guitar; *pl* **madweyaabiigibijiganan**; *loc* **madweyaabiigibijiganing**; *dim* **madweyaabiigibijigaans**
madweyaabiigibijige *vai* play a guitar; *1sg* **nimadweyaabiigibijige**; *prt* **medweyaabiigibijiged**
madwezige *vai* be heard shooting; *1sg* **nimadwezige**; *prt* **medweziged**
ma'iingan *na* wolf; *pl* **ma'iinganag**; *dim* **ma'iingaans**
ma'iinganasim *na* German shepherd; *pl* **ma'iinganasimoog**; *dim* **ma'iinganasimoons**
ma'iinganiwayaan *na* wolf hide; *pl* **ma'iinganiwayaanag**; *loc* **ma'iinganiwayaaning**; *dim* **ma'iinganiwayaanens**
maji- *pv4* bad
majigiizhwe *vai* swear; *1sg* **nimajigiizhwe**; *prt* **mejigiizhwed**
majigoode *ni* dress; *pl* **majigoodeyan**
maji-izhiwebizi *vai* misbehave, lead an evil life; *1sg* **nimaji-izhiwebiz**; *prt* **meji-izhiwebizid**
maji-manidoo *na* evil manitou, devil; *pl* **maji-manidoog**; *dim* **maji-manidoons**
maji-manidoowaadizi *vai* be evil, be possessed by an evil spirit; *1sg* **nimaji-manidoowaadiz**; *prt* **meji-manidoowaadizid**
maji-mashkiki *ni* poison; *pl* **maji-mashkikiwan**; *loc* **maji-mashkikiing**; *dim* **maji-mashkikiins**
makade *ni* black gunpowder; *loc* **makadeng**
makade- *pv4* black
makade-aniibiish *ni* black tea; *loc* **makade-aniibiishing**
makade-bigiw *na* tar, asphalt
makadeke *vai* undergo puberty fast; *1sg* **nimakadeke**; *prt* **mekadeked**
makade-mashkikiwaaboo *ni* coffee; *loc* **makade-mashkikiwaaboong**
makadeshib *na* black duck; *pl* **makadeshibag**; *dim* **makadeshibens**
makadewaa *vii* be black, be dark; *prt* **mekadewaag**; *aug* **makadewaamagad**; *prt aug* **mekadewaamagak**
makadewaabikad *vii* be black (as something mineral); *prt* **mekadewaabikak**
makadewaabikizi *vai* be black (as something mineral), be in eclipse; *prt* **mekadewaabikizid**
makadewaabiigad *vii* be black (as something string-like); *prt* **mekadewaabiigak**
makadewaabiigizi *vai* be black (as something string-like); *prt* **mekadewaabiigizid**
makadewaagamin /makadewaagami-/ *vii* be black (as a liquid), be dark (as a liquid); *prt* **mekadewaagamig**
makade-waagosh *na* fox (in black phase); *pl* **makade-waagoshag**; *dim* **makade-waagoshens**
makadewaakozi *vai* be black (as something stick- or wood-like); *prt* **mekadewaakozid**
makadewaakwad *vii* be black (as something stick- or wood-like); *prt* **mekadewaakwak**
makadewaande *vii* be colored black; *prt* **mekadewaandeg**; *aug* **makadewaandemagad**; *prt aug* **mekadewaandemagak**
makadewaanzo *vai* be colored black; *prt* **mekadewaanzod**
makadewegad *vii* be black (as something sheet-like); *prt* **mekadewegak**
makadewegizi *vai* be black (as something sheet-like); *prt* **mekadewegizid**
makadewi'o *vai* wear black; *1sg* **nimakadewi'**; *prt* **mekadewi'od**
makadewindibe *vai* have black hair; *1sg* **nimakadewindibe**; *prt* **mekadewindibed**
makadewizi *vai* be black, be dark; *prt* **mekadewizid**
makade-wiiyaas *na* Black person, person of African descent; *pl* **makade-wiiyaasag**
makade-wiiyaasikwe *na* Black woman, woman of African descent; *pl* **makade-wiiyaasikweg**
makadeyaanakwad *vii* there are dark clouds; *prt* **mekadeyaanakwak**
makak *ni* box, birch bark basket; *pl* **makakoon**; *loc* **makakong**; *dim* **makakoons**

makak (birch bark basket)

makakoke *vai* make a box, make a birch bark basket; *1sg* **nimakakoke**; *prt* **mekakoked**
makakosag *ni* tub, barrel; *pl* **makakosagoon**; *loc* **makakosagong**; *dim* **makakosagoons**
makam *vta* take (s.t.) from s.o. forcibly, rob s.o. of (s.t.); *1sg* **nimakamaa**; *prt* **mekamaad**
makandwe *vai* rob people, take captives; *1sg* **nimakandwe**; *prt* **mekandwed**
makizin *ni* moccasin, shoe; *pl* **makizinan**; *loc* **makizining**; *dim* **makizinens**

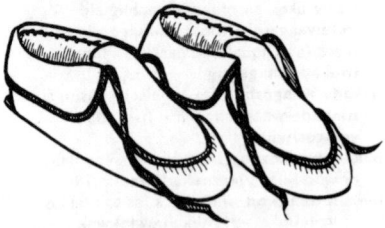

makizinan (moccasins); see also bashkweginwakizinan, bashkwegino-makizinan

makizinataadiwag /makizinataadi-/ *vai* they play the moccasin game with each other; *1pl* **nimakizinataadimin**; *prt* **mekizinataadijig**
makizinataage *vai* play the moccasin game; *1sg* **nimakizinataage**; *prt* **mekizinataaged**
makizinataage-nagamon *ni* moccasin game song; *pl* **makizinataage-nagamonan**
makizinataagewin *ni* moccasin game
makizineyaab *ni* shoelace; *pl* **makizineyaabiin**; *loc* **makizineyaabiing**; *dim* **makizineyaabiins**
makizinike *vai* make moccasins, make shoes; *1sg* **nimakizinike**; *prt* **mekiziniked**
makominagaawanzh *na* mountain ash; *pl* **makominagaawanzhiig**; *loc* **makominagaawanzhiing**; *dim* **makominagaawanzhiins**
makoons *na* bear cub; *pl* **makoonsag**
makwa *na* bear; *pl* **makwag**; *dim* **makoons**
makwasaagim *na* bear paw snowshoe; *pl* **makwasaagimag**; *loc* **makwasaagiming**; *dim* **makwasaagimens**
mamadweyaashkaa *vii* roar (as waves); *prt* **memadweyaashkaag**; *aug* **mamadweyaashkaamagad**; *prt aug* **memadweyaashkaamagak**
mamagoniishkwe *vai* have the mumps; *1sg* **nimamagoniishkwe**; *prt* **memagoniishkwed**
mamakiziwin *ni* smallpox
mamakii' *vta* allot s.o. land; *1sg* **nimamakii'aa**; *prt* **memakii'aad**
mamakii'idim /mamakii'idi-/ *vai* there is an allotment of land; *prt* **memakii'iding**
mamaw *vta* take (s.t.) from s.o., pick (s.t.) up from s.o.; *1sg* **nimamawaa**; *prt* **memawaad**
mamaach= < mich=
mamaachaawan /mamaachaa-/ *vii* they are big; *prt* **memaachaagin**; *aug* **mamaachaamagadoon**; *prt aug* **memaachaamagakin**
mamaadwe *vai* groan; *1sg* **nimamaadwe**; *prt* **memaadwed**
mamaajide'eshkaa *vai* have a heart attack; *1sg* **nimamaajide'eshkaa**; *prt* **memaajide'eshkaad**
mamaajise *vai* move; *1sg* **nimamaajise**; *prt* **memaajised**
mamaajise *vii* move; *prt* **memaajiseg**; *aug* **mamaajisemagad**; *prt aug* **memaajisemagak**
mamaajii *vai* move, be in motion; *1sg* **nimamaajii**; *prt* **memaajiid**
mamaakadew= < makadew=
mamaandaagochige *vai* perform tricks; *1sg* **nimamaandaagochige**; *prt* **memaandaagochiged**
mamaandaagochigewin *ni* circus, carnival; *pl* **mamaandaagochigewinan**
mamaandid= < mindid=
mamaandidowag /mamaandido-/ *vai* they are big; *prt* **memaandidojig**
mamaang= < mang=
mamaangade= < mangade=
mamaangadepon /mamaangadepo-/ *vii* snow in large flakes; *prt* **memaangadepog**
mamaangaashkaa *vii* be big waves; *prt* **memaangaashkaag**; *aug* **mamaangaashkaamagad**; *prt aug* **memaangaashkaamagak**
mamaashkaw= < mashkaw=
mamaayag= < mayag=
mamaazhi' *vta* prevail over s.o., conquer s.o.; *1sg* **nimamaazhi'aa**; *prt* **memaazhi'aad**
mamaazhitoon *vti2* prevail over s.t., conquer s.t.; *1sg* **nimamaazhitoon**; *prt* **memaazhitood**
mamaazhii *vai* make things badly, do a poor job; *1sg* **nimamaazhii**; *prt* **memaazhiid**
mamaazikaa *vai* move, agitate; *1sg* **nimamaazikaa**; *prt* **memaazikaad**
mami /mam-/ *vta* take s.o., pick s.o. up; *1sg* **nimamaa**; *prt* **memaad**
mamigaade *vii* be taken, be picked up; *prt* **memigaadeg**; *aug* **mamigaademagad**; *prt aug* **memigaademagak**
mamigaazo *vai* be taken, be picked up; *prt* **memigaazod**
mamige *vai* take things, pick up things; *1sg* **nimamige**; *prt* **memiged**
maminaadendam *vai2* have proud thoughts, have an arrogant attitude; *1sg* **nimaminaadendam**; *prt* **meminaadendang**
maminaadizi *vai* be arrogant; *1sg* **nimaminaadiz**; *prt* **meminaadizid**
mamizh /mamizhw-/ *vta* cut s.o. out; *1sg* **nimamizhwaa**; *prt* **memizhwaad**
mamizhan *vti* cut s.t. out; *1sg* **nimamizhaan**; *prt* **memizhang**
mamiidaawendam *vai2* be disturbed in one's mind, be troubled in one's mind; *1sg* **nimamiidaawendam**; *prt* **memiidaawendang**
mamiikw= < mikw=
mamiisaw= < misaw=
mamiiziwe= < miziwe=

mamoon *vti2* take s.t., pick s.t. up; *1sg* **nimamoon**; *prt* **memood**
manashkikiiwe *vai* gather medicine; *1sg* **nimanashkikiiwe**; *prt* **menashkikiiwed**
manaaji' *vta* spare s.o., go easy on s.o.; *1sg* **nimanaaji'aa**; *prt* **menaaji'aad**
manaajitoon *vti2* spare s.t., go easy on s.t.; *1sg* **nimanaajitoon**; *prt* **menaajitood**
mandaamin *na* corn, kernel of corn; *pl* **mandaaminag**; *loc* **mandaamining**; *dim* **mandaaminens**
mandaaminashk *ni* cornstalk; *pl* **mandaaminashkoon**; *loc* **mandaaminashkong**; *dim* **mandaaminashkoons**
mandaaminaaboo *ni* corn soup; *loc* **mandaaminaaboong**
mandaaminaak *ni* ear of corn; *pl* **mandaaminaakoon**; *loc* **mandaaminaakong**; *dim* **mandaaminaakoons**
mandaamini-gitigaan *ni* cornfield; *pl* **mandaamini-gitigaanan**; *loc* **mandaamini-gitigaaning**; *dim* **mandaamini-gitigaanens**
mandaaminiwazh *ni* gunnysack; *pl* **mandaaminiwazhan**; *loc* **mandaaminiwazhing**; *dim* **mandaaminiwazhens**
manepwaa *vai* be short of tobacco, need to smoke; *1sg* **nimanepwaa**; *prt* **menepwaad**
manezi *vai-o* be in need of (s.t.), be short of (s.t.); *1sg* **nimanez, nimanezin**; *prt* **menezid**
mangade' *vta* make s.o. wide, widen s.o.; *1sg* **nimangade'aa**; *prt* **mengade'aad**
mangademon /mangademo-/ *vii* be wide (as a road or trail); *prt* **mengademog**; *also* **mangadademon**
mangadengwe *vai* have a broad face; *1sg* **nimangadengwe**; *prt* **mengadengwed**
mangadetoon *vti2* make s.t. wide, widen s.t.; *1sg* **nimangadetoon**; *prt* **mengadetood**
mangadeyaa *vii* be wide; *prt* **mengadeyaag**; *aug* **mangadeyaamagad**; *prt aug* **mengadeyaamagak**
mangadeyoonagad *vii* be wide (as a boat); *prt* **mengadeyoonagak**
mangadezi *vai* be wide; *prt* **mengadezid**
mangadinaa *vii* there is a big hill; *prt* **mengadinaag**; *aug* **mangadinaamagad**; *prt aug* **mengadinaamagak**
mangate *vii* be roomy; *prt* **mengateg**; *aug* **mangatemagad**; *prt aug* **mengatemagak**
mangaanibaadan *vti* shovel s.t.; *1sg* **nimangaanibaadaan**; *prt* **mengaanibaadang**
mangaanibaajigan *ni* shovel; *pl* **mangaanibaajiganan**; *loc* **mangaanibaajiganing**; *dim* **mangaanibaajigaans**
mangaanibaajige *vai* shovel things (e.g., snow); *1sg* **nimangaanibaajige**; *prt* **mengaanibaajiged**
mangaanibaazh /mangaanibaaN-/ *vta* shovel s.o. (e.g., snow); *1sg* **nimangaanibaanaa**; *prt* **mengaanibaanaad**
mangaanibii *vai* shovel; *1sg* **nimangaanibii**; *prt* **mengaanibiid**
mangide'e *vai* be courageous; *1sg* **nimangide'e**; *prt* **mengide'ed**
mangi' *vta* make s.o. big; *1sg* **nimangi'aa**; *prt* **mengi'aad**
mangindibe *vai* have a big head; *1sg* **nimangindibe**; *prt* **mengindibed**
mangininjii *vai* have a big hand; *1sg* **nimangininjii**; *prt* **mengininjiid**
mangishkiinzhigwe *vai* have a big eye; *1sg* **nimangishkiinzhigwe**; *prt* **mengishkiinzhigwed**
mangitigweyaa *vii* be wide (as a river); *prt* **mengitigweyaag**; *aug* **mangitigweyaamagad**; *prt aug* **mengitigweyaamagak**
mangiwane *vai* carry a big pack; *1sg* **nimangiwane**; *prt* **mengiwaned**
mangizide *vai* have a big foot; *1sg* **nimangizide**; *prt* **mengizided**
manidoo *na* god, spirit, manitou; *pl* **manidoog**; *dim* **manidoons**
manidoo-biiwaabik *ni* steel, magnet; *loc* **manidoo-biiwaabikong**; *dim* **manidoo-biiwaabikoons**
manidoo-giizis *na* January; *also* **gichi-manidoo-giiizis**
manidoo-giizisoons *na* December
manidookaazo *vai* take on spiritual power by one's own authority; *1sg* **nimanidookaaz**; *prt* **menidookaazod**
manidooke *vai* have spiritual power, conduct a ceremony; *1sg* **nimanidooke**; *prt* **menidooked**
manidoominens *na* bead; *pl* **manidoominensag**; *loc* **manidoominensing**
manidoominensikaan *na* item of bead work; *pl* **manidoominensikaanag**; *loc* **manidoominensikaaning**; *dim* **manidoominensikaanens**
manidoo-nagamon *ni* spiritual song; *pl* **manidoo-nagamonan**; *loc* **manidoo-nagamoning**; *dim* **manidoo-nagamonens**
manidoons *na* bug, insect; *pl* **manidoonsag**
manidoonsikaa *vii* there are many bugs; *prt* **menidoonsikaag**; *aug* **manidoonsikaamagad**; *prt aug* **menidoonsikaamagak**
manidoo-waabooz *na* cottontail rabbit; *pl* **manidoo-waaboozoog**; *dim* **manidoo-waaboozoons**
manidoowaadizi *vai* have a spiritual nature; *1sg* **nimanidoowaadiz**; *prt* **menidoowaadizid**
manidoowi *vai* be a spirit, be a manitou; *1sg* **nimanidoow**; *prt* **menidoowid**
manisaw *vta* cut (s.t.) as firewood for s.o.; *1sg* **nimanisawaa**; *prt* **menisawaad**
manisaadan *vti* cut s.t. as firewood; *1sg* **nimanisaadaan**; *prt* **menisaadang**
manise *vai* cut firewood; *1sg* **nimanise**; *prt* **menised**
maniwiigwaase *vai* gather birch bark; *1sg* **nimaniwiigwaase**; *prt* **meniwiigwaased**
manoomin *ni* wild rice; *loc* **manoomining**; *dim* **manoominens**; *also* **anishinaabe-manoomin**
manoominaganzh *ni* wild rice stalk; *pl* **manoominaganzhiin**
manoominaaboo *ni* wild rice broth; *loc* **manoominaaboong**

manoominikaa *vii* there is much wild rice; *prt* **menoominikaag**; *aug* **manoominikaamagad**; *prt aug* **menoominikaamagak**
manoominike *vai* harvest wild rice, make rice; *1sg* **nimanoominike**; *prt* **menoominiked**
manoominike-giizis *na* the month of ricing: September, August
manoominike-mazina'igaans *ni* ricing license; *pl* **manoominike-mazina'igaansan**
manoominikeshiinh *na* rice bird; *pl* **manoominikeshiinyag**
manoomini-mashkimod *ni* rice bag; *pl* **manoomini-mashkimodan**; *loc* **manoomini-mashkimodaang**
manoominiwazh *ni* rice bag; *pl* **manoominiwazhan**; *loc* **manoominiwazhing**
mashkawadin *vii* freeze, be frozen; *prt* **meshkawading**
mashkawaji *vai* freeze, be frozen, be frostbitten; *1sg* **nimashkawaj**; *prt* **meshkawajid**
mashkawaji-bimide *ni* tallow; *loc* **mashkawaji-bimideng**
mashkawajininjiiwaji *vai* have a hand stiff from cold; *1sg* **nimashkawajininjiiwaj**; *prt* **meshkawajininjiiwajid**
mashkawapide *vii* be tied tight; *prt* **meshkawapideg**; *aug* **mashkawapidemagad**; *prt aug* **meshkawapidemagak**
mashkawapidoon *vti2* tie s.t. tight; *1sg* **nimashkawapidoon**; *prt* **meshkawapidood**
mashkawapizh /mashkawapiN-/ *vta* tie s.o. tight; *1sg* **nimashkawapinaa**; *prt* **meshkawapinaad**
mashkawapizo *vai* be tied tight; *1sg* **nimashkawapiz**; *prt* **meshkawapizod**
mashkawaa *vii* be strong, be hard, be dense; *prt* **meshkawaag**; *aug* **mashkawaamagad**; *prt aug* **meshkawaamagak**
mashkawaagamin /mashkawaagami-/ *vii* be strong (as a liquid); *prt* **meshkawaagamig**
mashkawaakwadin *vii* be frozen stiff; *prt* **meshkawaakwading**
mashkawaakwaji *vai* be frozen stiff, be frostbitten; *1sg* **nimashkawaakwaj**; *prt* **meshkawaakwajid**
mashkawaakwajidoon *vti2* freeze s.t. stiff; *1sg* **nimashkawaakwajidoon**; *prt* **meshkawaakwajidood**
mashkawaakwajim *vta* freeze s.o. stiff; *1sg* **nimashkawaakwajimaa**; *prt* **meshkawaakwajimaad**
mashkawaakwajininjiiwaji *vai* have a frozen hand; *1sg* **nimashkawaakwajininjiiwaj**; *prt* **meshkawaakwajininjiiwajid**
mashkawimaaso *vai* smell strong burning or cooking; *prt* **meshkawimaasod**
mashkawimaate *vii* smell strong burning or cooking; *prt* **meshkawimaateg**; *aug* **mashkawimaatemagad**; *prt aug* **meshkawimaatemagak**
mashkawizi *vai* be strong, be dense, be hard; *prt* **meshkawizid**
mashkawizii *vai* be strong (of a person), have inner strength; *1sg* **nimashkawizii**; *prt* **meshkawiziid**
mashkawiziiwin *ni* power; muscle; *pl* **mashkawiziiwinan**; *loc* **mashkawiziiwining**; *dim* **mashkawiziiwinens**
mashkiki *ni* medicine; *pl* **mashkikiwan**; *loc* **mashkikiing**; *dim* **mashkikiins**
mashkikiwaaboo *ni* liquid medicine; *pl* **mashkikiwaaboon**; *loc* **mashkikiwaaboong**
mashkikii-adaawewigamig *ni* pharmacy, drugstore; *pl* **mashkikii-adaawewigamigoon**; *loc* **mashkikii-adaawewigamigong**; *dim* **mashkikii-adaawewigamigoons**; *also* **mashkikiiwi-adaawewigamig**
mashkikii-adaawewinini *na* pharmacist, druggist; *pl* **mashkikii-adaawewininiwag**; *also* **mashkikiiwi-adaawewinini**
mashkikiikaazh /mashkikiikaaN-/ *vta* doctor s.o.; *1sg* **nimashkikiikaanaa**; *prt* **meshkikiikaanaad**
mashkikiike *vai* make medicine; *1sg* **nimashkikiike**; *prt* **meshkikiiked**
mashkikiins *ni* pill; *pl* **mashkikiinsan**
mashkikiiwikwe *na* nurse (female); *pl* **mashkikiiwikweg**; *dim* **mashkikiiwikwens**
mashkikiiwinini *na* doctor; *pl* **mashkikiiwininiwag**; *dim* **mashkikiiwinininiins**
mashkikiiwinininiikwe *na* doctor (female); *pl* **mashkikiiwinininiikweg**
mashkimod *ni* bag, sack; *pl* **mashkimodan**; *loc* **mashkimodaang**; *dim* **mashkimodens, mashkimodaans**
mashkimodegwaajigan *ni* pocket; *pl* **mashkimodegwaajiganan**; *loc* **mashkimodegwaajiganing**; *dim* **mashkimodegwaajigaans**
mashkimodens *ni* envelope; *pl* **mashkimodensan**; *loc* **mashkimodensing**
mashkiigimin *na* lowbush cranberry; *pl* **mashkiigiminag**; *loc* **mashkiigimining**; *dim* **mashkiigiminens**
mashkiigiminagaawanzh *ni* lowbush cranberry bush; *pl* **mashkiigiminagaawanzhiin**; *loc* **mashkiigiminagaawanzhiing**; *dim* **mashkiigiminagaawanzhiins**
mashkiigwaatig *na* tamarack; *pl* **mashkiigwaatigoog**; *loc* **mashkiigwaatigong**; *dim* **mashkiigwaatigoons**
mashkode *ni* prairie, plain; *pl* **mashkoden**; *loc* **mashkodeng**; *dim* **mashkodens**
mashkode-bizhiki *na* bison, buffalo; *pl* **mashkode-bizhikiwag**; *dim* **mashkode-bizhikiins**
mashkodesimin *na* bean; *pl* **mashkodesiminag**; *loc* **mashkodesimining**; *dim* **mashkodesiminens**; *also* **mashkodiisimin**
mashkodesiminaaboo *ni* bean soup; *loc* **mashkodesiminaaboong**
mashkosiw *ni* grass, hay; *pl* **mashkosiwan**; *loc* **mashkosiing**; *dim* **mashkosiins**
mashkosiigaan *ni* lodge of grass; *pl* **mashkosiigaanan**; *loc* **mashkosiigaaning**; *dim* **mashkosiigaanens**
mawadish /mawadiS-/ *vta* visit s.o.; *1sg* **nimawadisaa**; *prt* **mewadisaad**
mawadishiwe *vai* visit people; *1sg* **nimawadishiwe**; *prt* **mewadishiwed**

mawadisidiwag /mawadisidi-/ *vai* they visit each other; *1pl* **nimawadisidimin**; *prt* **mewadisidijig**
mawi *vai* cry, weep; *1sg* **nimaw**; *prt* **mewid**
mawim *vta* cry for s.o.; *1sg* **nimawimaa**; *prt* **mewimaad**
mawinazh /mawinaN-/ *vta* run at s.o., attack s.o.; *1sg* **nimawinanaa**; *prt* **mewinanaad**
mawindan *vti* cry for s.t.; *1sg* **nimawindaan**; *prt* **mewindang**
mawinzo *vai* pick berries; *1sg* **nimawinz**; *prt* **mewinzod**
mawishki *vai* be a crybaby; *1sg* **nimawishk**; *prt* **mewishkid**
mawiikaazo *vai* pretend to cry; *1sg* **nimawiikaaz**; *prt* **mewiikaazod**
mawiinsiwi *vai* cry a little; *1sg* **nimawiinsiw**; *prt* **mewiinsiwid**
mayagendam *vai2* feel strange; *1sg* **nimayagendam**; *prt* **meyagendang**
mayagendaagwad *vii* be considered strange; *prt* **meyagendaagwak**
mayagenim *vta* consider s.o. strange; *1sg* **nimayagenimaa**; *prt* **meyagenimaad**
mayagi- *pv4* strange, foreign, exotic
mayagi-anishinaabe *na* non-local Indian; *pl* **mayagi-anishinaabeg**; *dim* **mayagi-anishinaabens**
mayagi-bine *na* pheasant; *pl* **mayagi-binewag**; *dim* **mayagi-binens**
mayaginaagozi *vai* look strange, look foreign; *1sg* **nimayaginaagoz**; *prt* **meyaginaagozid**
mayaginaagwad *vii* look strange, look foreign; *prt* **meyaginaagwak**
mayagitaagozi *vai* sound strange, sound foreign; *prt* **meyagitaagozid**
mayagitaagwad *vii* sound strange, sound foreign; *prt* **meyagitaagwak**
mayagizi *vai* be strange, be foreign; *1sg* **nimayagiz**; *prt* **meyagizid**
mayagwe *vai* speak a strange language; *1sg* **nimayagwe**; *prt* **meyagwed**
mayagwewinini *na* foreigner, speaker of a strange language; *pl* **mayagwewininiwag**
mayaajiibizod *na-pt* engine; *pl* **maayaajiibizojig**
mazaanag /mazaan-/ *na* chaff from wild rice *plural*; *loc* **mazaaning**; *dim* **mazaanens**
mazaanaatig *na* thistle; *pl* **mazaanaatigoog**; *loc* **mazaanaatigong**; *dim* **mazaanaatigoons**
mazhi /maN-/ *vta* have sexual intercourse with s.o.; *1sg* **nimanaa**; *prt* **menaad**
mazhiwe *vai* have sexual intercourse; *1sg* **nimazhiwe**; *prt* **mezhiwed**
mazhii'igan *ni* cut-over clearing; *pl* **mazhii'iganan**; *loc* **mazhii'iganing**; *dim* **mazhii'igaans**
mazhii'ige *vai* clear land; *1sg* **nimazhii'ige**; *prt* **mezhii'iged**
mazina'amaw *vta* owe (s.t.) to s.o., get credit from s.o.; *1sg* **nimazina'amawaa**; *prt* **mezina'amawaad**
mazina'igan *ni* book, paper, letter, document; *pl* **mazina'iganan**; *loc* **mazina'iganing**; *dim* **mazina'igaans**
mazina'igani-makak *ni* cardboard box; *pl* **mazina'igani-makakoon**; *loc* **mazina'igani-makakong**; *dim* **mazina'igani-makakoons**
mazina'igani-mashkimodens *ni* paper bag; *pl* **mazina'igani-mashkimodensan**; *loc* **mazina'igani-mashkimodensing**
mazina'iganiiwidaabaan *na* mail truck; *pl* **mazina'iganiiwidaabaanag**; *loc* **mazina'iganiiwidaabaaning**; *dim* **mazina'iganiiwidaabaanens**
mazina'iganiiwigamig *ni* post office; *pl* **mazina'iganiiwigamigoon**; *loc* **mazina'iganiiwigamigong**; *dim* **mazina'iganiiwigamigoons**
mazina'iganiiwinini *na* postman; *pl* **mazina'iganiiwininiwag**
mazina'igaans *ni* ticket, license; *pl* **mazina'igaansan**; *loc* **mazina'igaansing**
mazina'ige *vai* owe, go into debt, get credit; *1sg* **nimazina'ige**; *prt* **mezina'iged**
mazinashkibijigan *na* doll of hay or grass; *pl* **mazinashkibijiganag**; *loc* **mazinashkibijiganing**; *dim* **mazinashkibijigaans**
mazinaabidoo'an *vti* bead s.t. on a loom; *1sg* **nimazinaabidoo'aan**; *prt* **mezinaabidoo'ang**
mazinaabidoo'iganaatig *ni* bead loom; *pl* **mazinaabidoo'iganaatigoon**; *loc* **mazinaabidoo'iganaatigong**; *dim* **mazinaabidoo'iganaatigoons**
mazinaabidoo'ige *vai* bead things on a loom; *1sg* **nimazinaabidoo'ige**; *prt* **mezinaabidoo'iged**
mazinaabikiwebinigan *ni* typewriter, computer; *pl* **mazinaabikiwebiniganan**; *loc* **mazinaabikiwebiniganing**; *dim* **mazinaabikiwebinigaans**
mazinaabikiwebinige *vai* type; *1sg* **nimazinaabikiwebinige**; *prt* **mezinaabikiwebiniged**
mazinaadin *vta* make an image of s.o.; *1sg* **nimazinaadinaa**; *prt* **mezinaadinaad**
mazinaakide *vii* be pictured, be photographed; *prt* **mezinaakideg**; *aug* **mazinaakidemagad**; *prt aug* **mezinaakidemagak**
mazinaakiz /mazinaakizw-/ *vta* take pictures of s.o., photograph s.o.; *1sg* **nimazinaakizwaa**; *prt* **mezinaakizwaad**
mazinaakizan *vti* take pictures of s.t., photograph s.t.; *1sg* **nimazinaakizaan**; *prt* **mezinaakizang**
mazinaakizigan *ni* camera; *pl* **mazinaakiziganan**; *loc* **mazinaakiziganing**; *dim* **mazinaakizigaans**
mazinaakizige *vai* take pictures, photograph things; *1sg* **nimazinaakizige**; *prt* **mezinaakiziged**
mazinaakizo *vai* be pictured, be photographed; *1sg* **nimazinaakiz**; *prt* **mezinaakizod**
mazinaakizon *ni* picture, photograph; *pl* **mazinaakizonan**; *loc* **mazinaakizoning**; *dim* **mazinaakizonens**
mazinaatese *vii* be a movie; *prt* **mezinaateseg**; *aug* **mazinaatesemagad**; *prt aug* **mezinaatesemagak**
mazinaatesewigamig *ni* movie theater; *pl* **mazinaatesewigamigoon**; *loc* **mazinaatesewigamigong**; *dim* **mazinaatesewigamigoons**; *also* **mazinaatesijigewigamig**

mazinaatesijigan *ni* television set; *pl* **mazinaatesijiganan**; *loc* **mazinaatesijiganing**; *dim* **mazinaatesijigaans**
mazinaatewebinigan *ni* movie projector; *pl* **mazinaatewebiniganan**; *loc* **mazinaatewebiniganing**; *dim* **mazinaatewebinigaans**
mazinibaganjigan *ni* dental pictograph on birch bark; *pl* **mazinibaganjiganan**; *loc* **mazinibaganjiganing**; *dim* **mazinibaganjigaans**
mazinibaganjige *vai* make a dental pictograph on birch bark; *1sg* **nimazinibaganijge**; *prt* **mezinibaganjiged**
mazinibii' /mazinibii'w-/ *vta* draw s.o.; *1sg* **nimazinibii'waa**; *prt* **mezinibii'waad**
mazinibii'an *vti* draw s.t.; *1sg* **nimazinibii'aan**; *prt* **mezinibii'ang**
mazinibii'igan *ni* drawing, design; *pl* **mazinibii'iganan**; *loc* **mazinibii'iganing**; *dim* **mazinibii'igaans**
mazinibii'ige *vai* draw things; *1sg* **nimazinibii'ige**; *prt* **mezinibii'iged**
mazinibii'igewinini *na* artist; *pl* **mazinibii'igewininiwag**
mazinichigan *na* doll, image, statue; *pl* **mazinichiganag**; *loc* **mazinichiganing**; *dim* **mazinichigaans**
mazinigwaadan *vti* embroider s.t., bead s.t.; *1sg* **nimazinigwaadaan**; *prt* **mezinigwaadang**
mazinigwaaso *vai* embroider, bead; *1sg* **nimazinigwaas**; *prt* **mezinigwaasod**
mazinigwaazh /mazinigwaaN-/ *vta* embroider s.o., bead on s.o.; *1sg* **nimazinigwaanaa**; *prt* **mezinigwaanaad**
mazinishin *vai* be imprinted, have a design; *prt* **mezinishing**
mazinisin *vii* be imprinted, have a design; *prt* **mezinising**
maadaginzo *vai* start a month, be the first day (of a month); *prt* **mayaadaginzod**
maada'adoo *vai* go off following a trail; *1sg* **nimaada'adoo**; *prt* **mayaada'adood**
maada'azh /maada'aN-/ *vta* go off following s.o.'s trail; *1sg* **nimaada'anaa**; *prt* **mayaada'anaad**
maada'ookii *vai* share, distribute; *1sg* **nimaada'ookii**; *prt* **mayaada'ookiid**
maada'oonidiwag /maada'oonidi-/ *vai* they distribute (s.t.) to each other, they share (s.t.); *1pl* **nimaada'oonidimin**; *prt* **mayaada'oonidijig**
maada'oozh /maada'ooN-/ *vta* distribute (s.t.) to s.o., share (s.t.) out to s.o.; *1sg* **nimaada'oonaa**; *prt* **mayaada'oonaad**
maadakamigad *vii* start (as an event); *prt* **mayaadakamigak**
maadakamigizi *vai* start (in some event); *1sg* **nimaadakamigiz**; *prt* **mayaadakamigizid**
maadanjige *vai* start eating; *1sg* **nimaadanjige**; *prt* **mayaadanjiged**
maadanokaadan *vti* start to work on s.t.; *1sg* **nimaadanokaadaan**; *prt* **mayaadanokaadang**
maadanokaazh /maadanokaaN-/ *vta* start to work on s.o.; *1sg* **nimaadanokaanaa**; *prt* **mayaadanokaanaad**
maadanoki *vai* start to work; *1sg* **nimaadanokii**; *prt* **mayaadanokiid**
maadaaboode *vii* drift off on the current; *prt* **mayaadaaboodeg**; *aug* **maadaaboodemagad**; *prt aug* **mayaadaaboodemagak**
maadaaboono *vai* drift off on the current; *prt* **mayaadaaboonod**
maadaadizi *vai* start a journey; *1sg* **nimaadaadiz**; *prt* **mayaadaadizid**
maadaa'an *vii* drift off on the waves; *prt* **mayaadaa'ang**
maadaa'ogo *vai* drift off on the waves; *prt* **mayaadaa'ogod**
maadaajim *vta* start to tell of s.o.; *1sg* **nimaadaajimaa**; *prt* **mayaadaajimaad**
maadaajimo *vai* start to tell; *1sg* **nimaadaajim**; *prt* **mayaadaajimod**
maadaajimotaw *vta* start to tell (s.t.) to s.o.; *1sg* **nimaadaajimotawaa**; *prt* **mayaadaajimotawaad**
maadaanimad *vii* wind picks up; *prt* **mayaadaanimak**
maadaawanidiwag /maadaawanidi-/ *vai* they start off in a group; *1pl* **nimaadaawanidimin**; *prt* **mayaadaawanidijig**
maadodan *vti* start to tell of s.t.; *1sg* **nimaadodaan**; *prt* **mayaadodang**
maadoode *vai* crawl off; *1sg* **nimaadoode**; *prt* **mayaadooded**
maadoom *vta* carry s.o. off on one's back; *1sg* **nimaadoomaa**; *prt* **mayaadoomaad**
maadoondan *vti* carry s.t. off on one's back; *1sg* **nimaadoondaan**; *prt* **mayaadoondang**
maadwewebizoni' *vta* start s.o. (e.g., a car); *1sg* **nimaadwewebizoni'aa**; *prt* **mayaadwewebizoni'aad**
maagizhaa *pc* maybe, perhaps; *also* **maazhaa**
maagobidoon *vti2* squeeze s.t.; *1sg* **nimaagobidoon**; *prt* **mayaagobidood**
maagobizh /maagobiN-/ *vta* squeeze s.o.; *1sg* **nimaagobinaa**; *prt* **mayaagobinaad**
maagon *vta* press on s.o.; *1sg* **nimaaagonaa**; *prt* **mayaagonaad**
maagonan *vti* press on s.t.; *1sg* **nimaagonaan**; *prt* **mayaagonang**
maa'ishkam *vai2* shop; *1sg* **nimaa'ishkam**; *prt* **mayaa'ishkang**
maajaa *vai* leave, depart, start off; *1sg* **nimaajaa**; *prt* **mayaajaad**; *also* **ani-maajaa**
maajaa' *vta* hold a funeral for s.o.; *1sg* **nimaajaa'aa**; *prt* **mayaajaa'aad**
maajaa'iwe *vai* hold a funeral, speak at a funeral; *1sg* **nimaajaa'iwe**; *prt* **mayaajaa'iwed**
maajibiisaa *vii* start to rain; *prt* **mayaajibiisaag**; *aug* **maajibiisaamagad**; *prt aug* **mayaajibiisaamagak**
maajidaabiiba'igo *vai* drive off in a wagon; *1sg* **nimaajidaabiiba'ig**; *prt* **mayaajidaabiiba'igod**
maajidaabii'iwe *vai* drive off; *1sg* **nimaajidaabii'iwe**; *prt* **mayaajidaabii'iwed**
maajigaa *vii* start to leak, start to drip, start to run with sap; *prt* **mayaajigaag**; *aug* **maajigaamagad**; *prt aug* **mayaajigaamagak**
maaji' *vta* start to make s.o.; *1sg* **nimaaji'aa**; *prt* **mayaaji'aad**

maajijiwan *vii* start to flow, be a whirlpool; *prt* **mayaajijiwang**
maajinaazha' /maajinaazha'w-/ *vta* send s.o. off; *1sg* **nimaajinaazha'waa**; *prt* **mayaajinaazha'waad**
maajinizha' /maajinizha'w-/ *vta* send s.o. off; *1sg* **nimaajinizha'waa**; *prt* **mayaajinizha'waad**
maajinizha'amaw *vta* send (s.t.) off to s.o.; *1sg* **nimaajinizha'amawaa**; *prt* **mayaajinizha'amawaad**
maajinizha'an *vti* send s.t. off; *1sg* **nimaajinizha'aan**; *prt* **mayaajinizha'ang**
maajinizhikaw *vta* chase s.o. off; *1sg* **nimaajinizhikawaa**; *prt* **maayaajinizhikawaad**
maajipon /maajipo-/ *vii* start to snow; *prt* **mayaajipog**
maajise *vai* begin, start, move off; *1sg* **nimaajise**; *prt* **mayaajised**
maajise *vii* begin, start, move off; *prt* **mayaajiseg**; *aug* **maajisemagad**; *prt aug* **mayaajisemagak**
maajitaa *vai* start an activity; *1sg* **nimaajitaa**; *prt* **mayaajitaad**
maajitoon *vti2* start to make s.t.; *1sg* **nimaajitoon**; *prt* **mayaajitood**
maajii- *pv4* start, begin, start off
maajiiba'idiwag /maajiiba'idi-/ *vai* they run off together; *1pl* **nimaajiiba'idimin**; *prt* **mayaajiiba'idijig**
maajiiba'igo *vai* drive off drawn by horses; *1sg* **nimaajiiba'ig**; *prt* **mayaajiiba'igod**
maajiiba'iwe *vai* start to flee; *1sg* **nimaajiiba'iwe**; *prt* **mayaajiiba'iwed**
maajiibatoo *vai* start to run, run off; *1sg* **nimaajiibatoo**; *prt* **mayaajiibatood**
maajiibide *vii* drive off, speed off, start to run (as a machine); *prt* **mayaajiibideg**; *aug* **maajiibidemagad**; *prt aug* **mayaajiibidemagak**
maajiibizo *vai* drive off, speed off, start to run (as a machine); *1sg* **nimaajiibiz**; *prt* **mayaajiibizod**
maajiibii'amaw *vta* write a letter to s.o.; *1sg* **nimaajiibii'amawaa**; *prt* **mayaajiibii'amawaad**
maajiibii'igan *ni* letter; *pl* **maajiibii'iganan**; *loc* **maajiibii'iganing**; *dim* **maajiibii'igaans**
maajiibii'ige *vai* write a letter; *1sg* **nimaajiibii'ige**; *prt* **mayaajiibii'iged**
maajiibii'ige-mashkimodens *ni* envelope; *pl* **maajiibii'ige-mashkimodensan**; *loc* **maajiibii'ige-mashkimodensing**
maajiidaw *vta* take (s.t.) along for s.o.; *1sg* **nimaajiidawaa**; *prt* **mayaajiidawaad**
maajiidoon *vti2* take s.t. away, take s.t. along; *1sg* **nimaajiidoon**; *prt* **mayaajiidood**
maajiigi *vai* grow up, start to grow; *1sg* **nimaajiig**; *prt* **mayaajiigid**
maajiigidaazo *vai* go off mad; *1sg* **nimaajiigidaaz**; *prt* **mayaajiigidaazod**
maajiigin *vii* grow up, start to grow; *prt* **mayaajiiging**
maajii'am *vai2* start to sing; *1sg* **nimaajii'am**; *prt* **mayaajii'ang**
maajiijigaade *vii* be taken along; *prt* **mayaajiijigaadeg**; *aug* **maajiijigaademagad**; *prt aug* **mayaajiijigaademagak**
maajiijigaazo *vai* be taken along; *prt* **mayaajiijigaazod**
maajiikan *vti* start to work on s.t.; *1sg* **nimaajiikaan**; *prt* **mayaajiikang**
maajiikaw *vta* start to work on s.o.; *1sg* **nimaajiikawaa**; *prt* **mayaajiikawaad**
maajiikwazhiwe *vai* paddle off, swim off (as a fish); *1sg* **nimaajiikwazhiwe**; *prt* **mayaajiikwazhiwed**
maajiishkaa *vii* start to move; *prt* **mayaajiishkaag**; *aug* **maajiishkaamagad**; *prt aug* **mayaajiishkaamagak**
maajiishkaa' *vta* start s.o. (e.g., a car, a clock); *1sg* **nimaajiishkaa'aa**; *prt* **mayaajiishkaa'aad**
maajiiyaadagaako *vai* start off on the ice; *1sg* **nimaajiiyaadagaak**; *prt* **mayaajiiyaadagaakod**
maajiizh /maajiiN-/ *vta* take s.o. away, take s.o. along; *1sg* **nimaajiinaa**; *prt* **mayaajiinaad**
maajiizhiwe *vai* take people away; *1sg* **nimaajiizhiwe**; *prt* **mayaajiizhiwed**
maakigaade *vai* have a lame leg; *1sg* **nimaakigaade**; *prt* **mayaakigaaded**
maakinaw *vta* shoot and wound s.o.; *1sg* **nimaakinawaa**; *prt* **mayaakinawaad**
maakizi *vai* be lame; *1sg* **nimaakiz**; *prt* **mayaakizid**
maamakaadakamig *pc* amazing!, astonishing!
maamakaadendam *vai2* be amazed, be astonished; *1sg* **nimaamakaadendam**; *prt* **mayaamakaadendang**
maamakaadendan *vti* be amazed at s.t., be astonished at s.t., wonder at s.t.; *1sg* **nimaamakaadendaan**; *prt* **mayaamakaadendang**
maamakaadendaagwad *vii* be considered amazing, be considered astonishing; *prt* **mayaamakaadendaagwak**
maamakaadenim *vta* be amazed at s.o., be astonished at s.o., wonder at s.o.; *1sg* **nimaamakaadenimaa**; *prt* **mayaamakaadenimaad**
maamakaadizi *vai* be amazing, astonish; *1sg* **nimaamakaadiz**; *prt* **mayaamakaadizid**
maamakaaj *pc* amazing, astonishing
maamakaajichige *vai* do amazing things; *1sg* **nimaamakaajichige**; *prt* **mayaamakaajichiged**
maamakaazitaw *vta* be amazed at what s.o. says; *1sg* **nimaamakaazitawaa**; *prt* **mayaamakaazitawaad**
maamawi *pc* together
maamawoo- *pv4* together
maamigin *vta* pick s.o. up, gather s.o.; *1sg* **nimaamiginaa**; *prt* **mayaamiginaad**
maamiginan *vti* pick s.t. up, gather s.t.; *1sg* **nimaamiginaan**; *prt* **mayaamiginang**
maaminonendam *vai2* think, consider, ponder; *1sg* **nimaaminonendam**; *prt* **mayaaminonendang**
maaminonendan *vti* think on s.t., consider s.t., realize of s.t. that; *1sg* **nimaaminonendaan**; *prt* **mayaaminonendang**
maaminonenim *vta* think on s.o., consider s.o., realize of s.o. that; *1sg* **nimaaminonenimaa**; *prt* **mayaaminonenimaad**

maanabi *vai* sit uncomfortably; *1sg* **nimaanab**; *prt* **mayaanabid**
maanadamon /maanadamo-/ *vii* be bad (as a road or trail); *prt* **mayaanadamog**
maanadikoshens *na* goat; *pl* **maanadikoshensag**
maana'e *vai* take a bad shot; *1sg* **nimaana'e**; *prt* **mayaana'ed**
maanamanji'o *vai* feel bad, be in poor health; *1sg* **nimaanamanji'**; *prt* **mayaanamanji'od**
maanameg *na* catfish; *pl* **maanamegwag**; *dim* **maanamegoons**
maananoons *na* hop hornbeam, ironwood; *pl* **maananoonsag**; *loc* **maananoonsing**
maanashigan *na* sheepshead (fish); *pl* **maanashiganag**; *dim* **maanashigaans**
maanazaadi *na* balsam poplar, Balm of Gilead tree; *pl* **maanazaadiwag**; *loc* **maanazaadiing**; *dim* **maanazaadiins**
maanaadad *vii* be ugly; *prt* **mayaanaadak**
maanaadizi *vai* be ugly, be homely; *1sg* **nimaanaadiz**; *prt* **mayaanaadizid**
maanaagamin /maanaagami-/ *vii* taste bad (as a liquid); *prt* **mayaanaagamig**
maanaaji' *vta* make s.o. wrong, make s.o. odd; *1sg* **nimaanaaji'aa**; *prt* **mayaanaaji'aad**
maanaajitoon *vti2* make s.t. wrong, make s.t. odd; *1sg* **nimaanaajitoon**; *prt* **mayaanaajitood**
maanendam *vai2* feel bad, feel depressed; *1sg* **nimaanendam**; *prt* **mayaanendang**; *also* **maazhendam**
maanendan *vti* feel bad about s.t., consider s.t. disagreeable; *1sg* **nimaanendaan**; *prt* **mayaanendang**
maanendaagozi *vai* be considered bad-off, be considered disagreeable; *1sg* **nimaanendaagoz**; *prt* **mayaanendaagozid**
maanendaagwad *vii* be considered bad, be considered disagreeable; *prt* **mayaanendaagwak**
maanenim *vta* consider s.o. bad-off, consider s.o. disagreeable; *1sg* **nimaanenimaa**; *prt* **mayaanenimaad**
maang *na* loon; *pl* **maangwag**; *dim* **maangoons**
maanikaw- *vta* disagree with s.o. (of something consumed) *in inverse forms: 1sg* **nimaanikaagon**; *prt* **mayaanikaagod**
maanishtaanish *na* sheep; *pl* **maanishtaanishag**; *dim* **maanishtaanishens**; *also* **maanitaanish**
maanishtaanishiwayaan *ni* sheepskin
maanitan *vti* hear s.t. sounding bad; *1sg* **nimaanitaan**; *prt* **mayaanitang**
maanitaw *vta* hear s.o. sounding bad; *1sg* **nimaanitawaa**; *prt* **mayaanitawaad**
maanose *vai* walk with discomfort; *1sg* **nimaanose**; *prt* **mayaanosed**
maanowe *vai* be hoarse, have a bad voice; *1sg* **nimaanowe**; *prt* **mayaanowed**
maanoo *pc* never mind, let it be, don't bother, don't care
maashkinoozhe *na* muskellunge; *pl* **maashkinoozheg**; *dim* **maashkinoozhens**
maawandoobiwag /maawandoobi-/ *vai* they sit together; *1pl* **nimaawandoobimin**; *prt* **mayaawandoobijig**
maawandoogindan *vti* total up s.t. (as an account); *1sg* **nimaawandoogindaan**; *prt* **mayaawandoogindang**
maawandoogindaaso *vai* total up (as an account); *1sg* **nimaawandoogindaas**; *prt* **mayaawandoogindaasod**
maawandoogwaadan *vti* sew s.t. together (e.g., pieces for a quilt); *1sg* **nimaawandoogwaadaan**; *prt* **mayaawandoogwaadang**
maawandoogwaaso *vai* sew together; *1sg* **nimaawandoogwaas**; *prt* **mayaawandoogwaasod**
maawandoogwaason *ni* quilt; *pl* **maawandoogwaasonan**; *loc* **maawandoogwaasoning**; *dim* **maawandoogwaasonens**
maawandoogwaazh /maawandoogwaaN-/ *vta* sew s.o. together; *1sg* **nimaawandoogwaanaa**; *prt* **mayaawandoogwaanaad**
maawandoonan *vti* bring s.t. together; *1sg* **nimaawandoonaan**; *prt* **mayaawandoonang**
maawanji' *vta* collect s.o.; *1sg* **nimaawanji'aa**; *prt* **mayaawanji'aad**
maawanji'idiwag /maawanji'idi-/ *vai* they come together, they meet with each other, they have a meeting; *1pl* **nimaawanji'idimin**; *prt* **mayaawanji'idijig**
maawanjitoon *vti2* collect s.t.; *1sg* **nimaawanjitoon**; *prt* **mayaawanjitood**
maazhaa *pc* maybe, perhaps; *also* **maagizhaa**
maazhendam *vai2* feel out of sorts; *1sg* **nimaazhendam**; *prt* **mayaazhendang**
maazhi- *pv4* bad, ill-formed
maazhi-ayaa *vai* be bad-off, be in poor health; *1sg* **nimaazhi-ayaa**; *prt* **mayaazhi-ayaad**
maazhibide *vii* run poorly (e.g., a machine), operate poorly; *prt* **mayaazhibideg**; *aug* **maazhibidemagad**; *prt aug* **mayaazhibidemagak**
maazhi-bimaadizi *vai* behave badly, lead a bad life; *1sg* **nimaazhi-bimaadiz**; *prt* **mayaazhi-bimaadizid**
maazhibizo *vai* run poorly (e.g., a car), operate poorly; *prt* **mayaazhibizod**
maazhide'e *vai* have heartburn; *1sg* **nimaazhide'e**; *prt* **mayaazhide'ed**
maazhi-giizhigad *vii* be a bad day; *prt* **mayaazhi-giizhigak**
maazhigiizhwe *vai* have difficulty speaking, have abnormal speech; *1sg* **nimaazhigiizhwe**; *prt* **mayaazhigiizhwed**
maazhigondaagan *vai* have difficulty with one's voice; *1sg* **nimaazhigondaagan**; *prt* **mayaazhigondaagang**
maazhi-izhiwebizi *vai* behave badly; *1sg* **nimaazhi-izhiwebiz**; *prt* **mayaazhi-izhiwebizid**
maazhimaagozi *vai* smell bad; *1sg* **nimaazhimaagoz**; *prt* **mayaazhimaagozid**
maazhimaagwad *vii* smell bad; *prt* **mayaazhimaagwak**
maazhimaagwanaamo *vai* have bad breath; *1sg* **nimaazhimaagwanaam**; *prt* **mayaazhimaagwanaamod**

maazhimaaso *vai* smell bad burning or cooking; *prt* **mayaazhimaasod**
maazhimaate *vii* smell bad burning or cooking; *prt* **mayaazhimaateg**
maazhingwaam *vai* sleep uncomfortably; *1sg* **nimaazhingwaam**; *prt* **mayaazhingwaang**
maazhinikaade *vii* have an ugly name; *prt* **mayaazhinikaadeg**; *aug* **maazhinikaademagad**; *prt aug* **mayaazhinikaademagak**
maazhinikaazo *vai* have an ugly name; *1sg* **nimaazhinikaaz**; *prt* **mayaazhinikaazod**
maazhipogozi *vai* taste bad; *prt* **mayaazhipogozid**
maazhipogwad *vii* taste bad; *prt* **mayaazhipogwak**
maazhise *vai* have things go wrong, have bad luck; *1sg* **nimaazhise**; *prt* **mayaazhised**
maazhishin *vai* lie uncomfortably; *1sg* **nimaazhishin**; *prt* **mayaazhishing**
megade *vai* burp; *1sg* **nimegade**; *prt* **mayegaded**
megwaa *pc* while, during
megwe- *pn* among, in the midst of
megwe-aya'ii *pc* in among it; *also* **megweya'ii**
megwejiishkiwag *pc* in the mud
megwekob *pc* in the brush
megwaayaak *pc* in the woods
mekadewikonayed *na-pt* priest; *pl* **mekadewikonayejig**
mekadewikonayewikwe *na* nun; *pl* **mekadewikonayewikweg**; *dim* **mekadewikonayewikwens**; *also* **mekadewikonayekwe**
mekadewikonayewinini *na* priest; *pl* **mekadewikonayewininiwag**
memaangishens *na* mule; *pl* **memaangishensag**
meme *na* red-headed woodpecker; *pl* **memeg**; *dim* **memens**
memegwesi *na* hairy-faced bank-dwelling dwarf spirit; *pl* **memegwesiwag**; *dim* **memegwesiins**
memengwaa *na* butterfly; *pl* **memengwaag**; *dim* **memengwaans**
memeshkwad *pc* in turns, alternately
memidaaswi *nm* ten each
memindage *pc* of course, especially, above all
memookiwidoo *na* pocket gopher; *pl* **memookiwidoog**; *dim* **memookiwidoons**
memwech *pc* just that, exactly, it is so
menwaagamig *ni-pt* soft drink; *pl* **menwaagamigin**
meshkwad *pc* in turn, in exchange
meshkwadoon *vta* trade s.o., exchange s.o.; *1sg* **nimeshkwadoonaa**; *prt* **mayeshkwadoonaad**
meshkwadoonamaw *vta* trade (s.t.) with s.o.; *1sg* **nimeshkwadoonamawaa**; *prt* **mayeshkwadoonamawaad**
meshkwadoonamaage *vai* trade things with people; *1sg* **nimeshkwadoonamaage**; *prt* **mayeshkwadoonamaaged**
meshkwadoonan *vti* trade s.t., exchange s.t.; *1sg* **nimeshkwadoonaan**; *prt* **mayeshkwadoonang**
meshkwadoonige *vai* trade for things, exchange things; *1sg* **nimeshkwadoonige**; *prt* **mayeshkwadooniged**
meskwanagekozid *na-pt* cinnamon; *pl* **meskwanagekozijig**
meskwaazhigwaneshi *na* redhorse (fish); *pl* **meskwaazhigwaneshiwag**; *dim* **meskwaazhigwaneshiins**
meta *pc* it is only that; *also* **mii eta**
mewinzha *pc* a long time ago, long ago
michayi'ii *pc* on a bare surface
michaa *vii* be big; *prt* **mechaag**; *aug* **michaamagad**; *prt aug* **mechaamagak**
michaabaminaagwad *vii* appear big; *prt* **mechaabaminaagwak**
michaabikad *vii* be big (as something mineral); *prt* **mechaabikak**
michaabikizi *vai* be big (as something mineral), be full (as something mineral, e.g., the moon); *prt* **mechaabikizid**
michaakozi *vai* be big (as something stick- or wood-like); *prt* **mechaakozid**
michaakwad *vii* be big (as something stick- or wood-like); *prt* **mechaakwak**
michaatoon *vti2* make s.t. big; *1sg* **nimichaatoon**; *prt* **mechaatood**
michi- *pv4* by hand, without anything special, barely
michininjiikanjige *vai* eat with one's fingers; *1sg* **nimichininjiikanjige**; *prt* **mechininjiikanjiged**
michisag *ni* floor; *pl* **michisagoon**; *loc* **michisagong**
michishin *vai* lie uncovered; *prt* **mechishing**
michisin *vii* lie uncovered; *prt* **mechising**
michiigad *vii* be big (as something sheet-like); *prt* **mechiigak**
michiigizi *vai* be big (as something sheet-like); *prt* **mechiigizid**
midaaching *pc* ten times
midaachinoon /midaachin-/ *vii* they are ten; *prt* **medaaching**
midaachiwag /midaachi-/ *vai* they are ten; *1pl* **nimidaachimin**; *prt* **medaachijig**
midaaso- *pv4* ten
midaaso-anama'e-giizhigad *pc* ten weeks
midaaso-anama'e-giizhik *pc* ten weeks
midaaso-biboon *pc* ten years
midaaso-biboonagad *vii* be ten years; *prt* **medaaso-biboonagak**
midaaso-biboonagizi *vai* be ten years old; *1sg* **nimidaaso-biboonagiz**; *prt* **medaaso-biboonagizid**
midaaso-diba'igan *pc* ten miles, ten hours
midaaso-diba'iganed *vii* be ten o'clock; *prt* **medaaso-diba'iganek**
midaaso-diba'igaans *pc* ten minutes
midaaso-dibik *pc* ten nights
midaaso-giizhik *pc* ten days
midaaso-giizis *pc* ten months
midaasogon *pc* ten days
midaasogonagad *vii* be ten days; *prt* **medaasogonagak**
midaasogonagizi *vai* be the tenth day of the month, be ten days old; *prt* **medaasogonagizid**
midaasoninj *pc* ten inches
midaasozid *pc* ten feet
midaasosagoons *nm* ten thousand

midaasoobii'igan *na* ten (card); *pl* **midaasoobii'iganag**
midaasooshkin *pc* ten bags
midaaswaabik *pc* ten dollars
midaaswaak *nm* thousand
midaaswewaan *pc* ten sets, ten pairs
midaaswi *nm* ten
midaaswi ashi-bezhig *nm* eleven
midaaswi ashi-ingodwaaswi *nm* sixteen; *also* **midaaswi ashi-ningodwaaswi***
midaaswi ashi-ishwaaswi *nm* eighteen; *also* **midaaswi ashi-nishwaaswi***
midaaswi ashi-naanan *nm* fifteen
midaaswi ashi-ningodwaaswi* *nm* sixteen; *also* **midaaswi ashi-ingodwaaswi**
midaaswi ashi-nishwaaswi* *nn* eighteen; *also* **midaaswi ashi-ishwaaswi**
midaaswi ashi-niswi *nm* thirteen
midaaswi ashi-niiwin *nm* fourteen
midaaswi ashi-niizh *nm* twelve
midaaswi ashi-niizhwaaswi *nm* seventeen
midaaswi ashi-zhaangaswi *nm* nineteen
midechininj *ni* thumb; *pl* **midechininjiin**
midechizid *ni* big toe; *pl* **midechizidan**
midewayaan *na* Mide medicine bag; *pl* **midewayaanag**; *loc* **midewayaaning**; *dim* **midewayaanens**
midewi *vai* join the Midewiwin, participate in the Midewiwin; *1sg* **nimidew**; *prt* **medewid**
midewigaan *ni* Mide lodge; *pl* **midewigaanan**; *loc* **midewigaaning**; *dim* **midewigaanens**
midewigaanaak *ni* Mide lodge frame; *pl* **midewigaanaakoon**; *loc* **midewigaamaakong**
midewiwin *ni* Midewiwin, Medicine Dance, Grand Medicine Society
migi *vai* bark; *1sg* **nimig**; *prt* **megid**
migidan *vti* bark at s.t.; *1sg* **nimigidaan**; *prt* **megidang**
migiskan *ni* fish hook; *pl* **migiskanan**; *loc* **migiskaning**; *dim* **migiskaans**
migiskanaak *ni* fishing pole; *pl* **migiskanaakoon**; *loc* **migiskanaakong**; *dim* **migiskanaakoons**; *also* **migiskanaatig**
migiskaneyaab *ni* hook and line; *pl* **migiskaneyaabiin**; *loc* **migiskaneyaabiing**; *dim* **migiskaneyaabiins**
migizh /migiN-/ *vta* bark at s.o.; *1sg* **nimiginaa**; *prt* **meginaad**
migizi *na* bald eagle; *pl* **migiziwag**; *dim* **migiziins**
migoshkaadendam *vai2* be annoyed; *1sg* **nimigoshkaadendam**; *prt* **megoshkaadendang**
migoshkaaji' *vta* annoy s.o., bother s.o.; *1sg* **nimigoshkaaji'aa**; *prt* **megoshkaaji'aad**
migoos *ni* awl; *pl* **migoosan**; *loc* **migoosing**; *dim* **migoosens**

migoos (awl)

mikamaw *vta* find (s.t.) for s.o., find (s.t.) of s.o.'s; *1sg* **nimikamawaa**; *prt* **mekamawaad**
mikan *vti* find s.t.; *1sg* **nimikaan**; *prt* **mekang**
mikaw *vta* find s.o.; *1sg* **nimikawaa**; *prt* **mekawaad**
mikawi *vai* come to, regain consciousness; *1sg* **nimikaw**; *prt* **mekawid**
mikaage *vai* find people; *1sg* **nimikaage**; *prt* **mekaaged**
mikigaade *vii* be found; *prt* **mekigaadeg**; *aug* **mikigaademagad**; *prt aug* **mekigaademagak**
mikigaazo *vai* be found; *prt* **mekigaazod**
mikige *vai* find things; *1sg* **nimikige**; *prt* **mekiged**
mikinaak *na* snapping turtle; *pl* **mikinaakwag**; *dim* **mikinaakoons**
mikobidaw *vta* find (s.t.) for s.o. with hands; *1sg* **nimikobidawaa**; *prt* **mekobidawaad**
mikobidoon *vti2* find s.t. with hands; *1sg* **nimikobidoon**; *prt* **mekobidood**
mikobijige *vai* find things with hands; *1sg* **nimikobijige**; *prt* **mekobijiged**
mikobizh /mikobiN-/ *vta* find s.o. with hands; *1sg* **nimikobinaa**; *prt* **mekobinaad**
mikom *vta* mention s.o. come to one's mind; *1sg* **nimikomaa**; *prt* **mekomaad**
mikond *na* binding stick; *pl* **mikondiig**; *loc* **mikondiing**; *dim* **mikondiins**; *also* **mikwand**
mikondan *vti* mention s.t. come to one's mind; *1sg* **nimikondaan**; *prt* **mekondang**
mikoojiin *vta* feel s.o., feel for s.o.; *1sg* **nimikoojiinaa**; *prt* **mekoojiinaad**
mikoojiinan *vti* feel s.t., feel for s.t.; *1sg* **nimikoojiinaan**; *prt* **mekoojiinang**
mikwam *na* ice; *pl* **mikwamiig**; *loc* **mikwamiing**; *dim* **mikwamiins**
mikwamiikaa *vii* there is much ice; *prt* **mekwamiikaag**; *aug* **mikwamiikaamagad**; *prt aug* **mekwamiikaamagak**
mikwamii-makak *ni* ice box, refrigerator; *pl* **mikwamii-makakoon**; *loc* **mikwamii-makakong**; *dim* **mikwamii-makakoons**
mikwamiiwadamon /mikwamiiwadamo-/ *vii* be icy (as a road or trail); *prt* **mekwamiiwadamog**
mikwamiiwinaagaans *ni* drinking glass; *pl* **mikwamiiwinaagaansan**; *loc* **mikwamiiwinaagaansing**
mikwendam *vai2* recollect, remember, have things come to one's mind; *1sg* **nimikwendam**; *prt* **mekwendang**
mikwendan *vti* recollect s.t., remember s.t., come to think of s.t.; *1sg* **nimikwendaan**; *prt* **mekwendang**
mikwendaagozi *vai* be remembered, be recollected, come to mind; *1sg* **nimikwendaagoz**; *prt* **mekwendaagozid**
mikwendaagwad *vii* be remembered, be recollected, come to mind; *prt* **mekwendaagwak**
mikwenim *vta* recollect s.o., remember s.o., come to think of s.o.; *1sg* **nimikwenimaa**; *prt* **mekwenimaad**
mimigosaga'igan *ni* scrub brush; *pl* **mimigosaga'iganan**; *loc* **mimigosaga'iganing**; *dim* **mimigosaga'igaans**

mimigoshkam *vai2* thresh something, jig something (e.g., wild rice); *1sg* **nimimigoshkam**; *prt* **memigoshkang**
mimigoshkamwaagan *ni* barrel or tub used in threshing wild rice; *pl* **mimigoshkamwaaganan**; *loc* **mimigoshkamwaaganing**
mimigoshkan *vti* thresh s.t. (e.g., wild rice), jig s.t. (e.g., wild rice); *1sg* **nimimigoshkaan**; *prt* **memigoshkang**
mimigwaabika'igan *ni* pot scrubber; *pl* **mimigwaabika'iganan**; *loc* **mimigwaabika'iganing**; *dim* **mimigwaabika'igaans**
mimigwaakosijigan *ni* washboard; *pl* **mimigwaakosijiganan**; *loc* **mimigwaakosijiganing**; *dim* **mimigwaakosijigaans**
mina' *vta* give s.o. a drink, give s.o. (s.t.) to drink; *1sg* **nimina'aa**; *prt* **mena'aad**
minawaanigozi *vai* be happy, be joyous, have a good time; *1sg* **niminawaanigoz**; *prt* **menawaanigozid**
minawaanigwad *vii* be happy, be exciting; *prt* **menawaanigwak**
mindawe *vai* be dissatisfied (with what has been given), pout; *1sg* **nimindawe**; *prt* **mendawed**
mindaweganzhii *vai* have white spots on fingernails; *1sg* **nimindaweganzhii**; *prt* **mendaweganzhiid**
mindido *vai* be big; *1sg* **nimindid**; *prt* **mendidod**
mindido' *vta* make s.o. big; *1sg* **nimindido'aa**; *prt* **mendido'aad**
mindimooyenh *na* old woman, old lady; *pl* **mindimooyenyag**; *dim* **mindimooyens**
mindimooyenyiwi *vai* be an old woman, be an old lady; *1sg* **nimindimooyenyiw**; *prt* **mendimooyenyiwid**
mindookad *vii* there is dew; *prt* **mendookak**
mini /miny-/ *ni* pus
minik *pc* a certain amount, a certain number, so much, so many
minikwaajigan *ni* drinking vessel; *pl* **minikwaajiganan**; *loc* **minikwaajiganing**; *dim* **minikwaajigaans**
minikwe *vai+o* drink (s.t.); *1sg* **niminikwe, niminikwen**; *prt* **menikwed**
minikwewigamig *ni* tavern, bar; *pl* **minikwewigamigoon**; *loc* **minikwewigamigong**; *dim* **minikwewigamigoons**
minis *ni* island; *pl* **minisan**; *loc* **minising**; *dim* **minisens**
minisaabik *ni* rocky island; *pl* **minisaabikoon**; *loc* **minisaabikong**; *dim* **minisaabikoons**
miniiwaabide *vai* have an abscessed tooth; *1sg* **niminiiwaabide**; *prt* **meniiwaabided**
miniiwitawage *vai* have an infected ear; *1sg* **niminiiwitawage**; *prt* **meniiwitawaged**
minjikanaakobijigan *ni* fence; *pl* **minjikanaakobijiganan**; *loc* **minjikanaakobijiganing**; *dim* **minjikanaakobijigaans**
minjikaawan *na* mitten; *pl* **minjikaawanag**; *loc* **minjikaawaning**
minjimaakwii *vai* cling (as to something stick- or wood-like), hold on (as to something stick- or wood-like); *1sg* **niminjimaakwii**; *prt* **menjimaakwiid**
minjimendan *vti* keep s.t. in one's mind, remember s.t.; *1sg* **niminjimendaan**; *prt* **menjimendang**
minjimenim *vta* keep s.o. in one's mind, remember s.o.; *1sg* **niminjimenimaa**; *prt* **menjimenimaad**
minjimin *vta* hold s.o. in place, steady s.o.; *1sg* **niminjiminaa**; *prt* **menjiminaad**
minjiminamaw *vta* hold (s.t.). in place for s.o., steady (s.t.) for s.o.; *1sg* **niminjiminamawaa**; *prt* **menjiminamawaad**
minjiminan *vti* hold s.t. in place, steady s.t.; *1sg* **niminjiminaan**; *prt* **menjiminang**
minjiminigan *ni* handle; *pl* **minjiminiganan**; *loc* **minjiminiganing**; *dim* **minjiminigaans**
minjimishkan *vti* hold s.t. in place with foot or body, steady s.t. with foot or body; *1sg* **niminjimishkaan**; *prt* **menjimishkang**
minjimishkaw *vta* hold s.o. in place with foot or body, steady s.o. with foot or body; *1sg* **niminjimishkawaa**; *prt* **menjimishkawaad**
minjimishkoode *vii* be held in place with weight; *prt* **menjimishkoodeg**; *aug* **minjimishkoodemagad**; *prt aug* **menjimishkoodemagak**
minjimishkoodoon *vti2* hold s.t. in place with weight; *1sg* **niminjimishkoodoon**; *prt* **menjimishkoodood**
minjimishkoozh /minjimishkooN-/ *vta* hold s.o. in place with weight; *1sg* **niminjimishkoonaa**; *prt* **menjimishkoonaad**
minjimishkoozo *vai* be held in place with weight; *1sg* **niminjimishkooz**; *prt* **menjimishkoozod**
minjimii *vai* cling, hold on; *1sg* **niminjimii**; *prt* **menjimiid**
minjinawezi *vai* have regrets, be disappointed; *1sg* **niminjinawez**; *prt* **menjinawezid**
mino- *pv4* good, nice, well
mino-ayaa *vai* be good, be fine, be well; *1sg* **nimino-ayaa**; *prt* **meno-ayaad**
minobide *vii* run well (e.g., a machine); *prt* **menobideg**; *aug* **minobidemagad**; *prt aug* **menobidemagak**
mino-bimaadizi *vai* live well, have good health, lead a good life; *1sg* **nimino-bimaadiz**; *prt* **meno-bimaadizid**
minobizo *vai* run well (e.g., a car); *prt* **menobizod**
minobii *vai* drink and be merry; *1sg* **niminobii**; *prt* **menobiid**
minochige *vai* do things well, do good things; *1sg* **niminochige**; *prt* **menochiged**
minode *vii* be well cooked; *prt* **menodeg**; *aug* **minodemagad**; *prt aug* **menodemagak**
minode'e *vai* be kind; *1sg* **niminode'e**; *prt* **menode'ed**
mino-doodaw *vta* treat s.o. well; *1sg* **nimino-doodawaa**; *prt* **meno-doodawaad**
minogi *vai* grow well; *1sg* **niminog**; *prt* **menogid**
minogin *vii* grow well; *prt* **menoging**
mino-giizhigad *vii* be a nice day; *prt* **meno-giizhigak**

mino-giizhiganishi *vai* have good travelling weather; *1sg* **nimino-giizhiganish**; *prt* **meno-giizhiganishid**
minogondaagan *vai* have a good voice; *1sg* **niminogondaagan**; *prt* **menogondaagang**
mino'o *vai* dress well; *1sg* **nimino'**; *prt* **meno'od**
mino-izhiwebizi *vai* behave well, lead a good life; *1sg* **nimino-izhiwebiz**; *prt* **meno-izhiwebizid**
minokan *vti* fit s.t. well; *1sg* **niminokaan**; *prt* **menokang**
minokaw *vta* fit s.o. well (e.g., pants), agree with s.o. (especially of something consumed); *in inverse forms: 1sg* **niminokaagon**; *prt* **menokaagod**
minomaagochigan *ni* perfume; *pl* **minomaagochiganan**; *loc* **minomaagochiganing**; *dim* **minomaagochigaans**
minomaagochige *vai* use perfume; *1sg* **niminomaagochige**; *prt* **menomaagochiged**
minomaagozi *vai* have a good smell; *1sg* **niminomaagoz**; *prt* **menomaagozid**
minomaagwad *vii* have a good smell; *prt* **menomaagwak**
minomaam *vta* like the smell of s.o.; *1sg* **niminomaamaa**; *prt* **menomaamaad**
minomaandan *vti* like the smell of s.t.; *1sg* **niminomaandaan**; *prt* **menomaandang**
minomaaso *vai* smell good burning or cooking; *prt* **menomaasod**
minomaate *vii* smell good burning or cooking; *prt* **menomaateg**; *aug* **minomaatemagad**; *prt aug* **menomaatemagak**
minopidan *vti* find a good taste in s.t.; *1sg* **niminopidaan**; *prt* **menopidang**
minopijige *vai* like the taste of things; *1sg* **niminopijige**; *prt* **menopijiged**
minopogozi *vai* taste good; *prt* **menopogozid**
minopogwad *vii* taste good; *prt* **menopogwak**
minopozh /minopw-/ *vta* find a good taste in s.o.; *1sg* **niminopwaa**; *prt* **menopwaad**
minose *vai* have things go well for one, get along well, have good luck; *1sg* **niminose**; *prt* **menosed**
minose *vii* go well; *prt* **menoseg**; *aug* **minosemagad**; *prt aug* **menosemagak**
minoshim *vta* put s.o. in the right position; *1sg* **niminoshimaa**; *prt* **menoshimaad**
minoshin *vai* lie comfortably, lie in a good position; *1sg* **niminoshin**; *prt* **menoshing**
minosidoon *vti2* put s.t. in the right position; *1sg* **niminosidoon**; *prt* **menosidood**
minosin *vii* lie in a good position, lie well in place; *prt* **menosing**
minotam *vai2* like hearing something, like the sound; *1sg* **niminotam**; *prt* **menotang**
minotan *vti* like hearing s.t., hear s.t. sounding good; *1sg* **niminotaan**; *prt* **menotang**
minotaw *vta* like hearing s.o., hear s.o. sounding good; *1sg* **niminotawaa**; *prt* **menotawaad**
minotaagozi *vai* sound good; *1sg* **niminotaagoz**; *prt* **menotaagozid**
minotaagwad *vii* sound good; *prt* **menotaagwak**
minowe *vai* have a good voice, speak well; *1sg* **niminowe**; *prt* **menowed**
minoz /minozw-/ *vta* cook s.o. well; *1sg* **niminozwaa**; *prt* **menozwaad**
minozan *vti* cook s.t. well; *1sg* **niminozaan**; *prt* **menozang**
minozekwe *vai* cook well; *1sg* **niminozekwe**; *prt* **menozekwed**
minozo *vai* be well cooked; *prt* **menozod**
minwabi *vai* sit comfortably; *1sg* **niminwab**; *prt* **menwabid**
minwamanji'o *vai* feel good, be in good health; *1sg* **niminwamanji'**; *prt* **menwamanji'od**
minwanjige *vai* eat well; *1sg* **niminwanjige**; *prt* **menwanjiged**
minwashkine *vai* fit well, be well filled; *prt* **menwashkined**
minwashkine *vii* fit well, be well filled; *prt* **menwashkineg**; *aug* **minwashkinemagad**; *prt aug* **menwashkinemagak**
minwaabadad *vii* be very useful, be of good use; *prt* **menwaabadak**
minwaabadizi *vai* be very useful, be of good use; *1sg* **niminwaabadiz**; *prt* **menwaabadizid**
minwaabaji' *vta* get good use of s.o.; *1sg* **niminwaabaji'aa**; *prt* **menwaabaji'aad**
minwaabajitoon *vti2* get good use of s.t.; *1sg* **niminwaabajitoon**; *prt* **menwaabajitood**
minwaabam *vta* like the look of s.o.; *1sg* **niminwaabamaa**; *prt* **menwaabamaad**
minwaabamewizi *vai* be admired, be respected; *1sg* **niminwaabamewiz**; *prt* **menwaabamewizid**
minwaabaminaagozi *vai* look good; *1sg* **niminwaabaminaagoz**; *prt* **menwaabaminaagozid**
minwaabaminaagwad *vii* look good; *prt* **menwaabaminaagwak**
minwaabandan *vti* like the look of s.t.; *1sg* **niminwaabandaan**; *prt* **menwaabandang**
minwaabewizi *vai* have a good body; *1sg* **niminwaabewiz**; *prt* **menwaabewizid**
minwaabi *vai* have good eyesight, see well; *1sg* **niminwaab**; *prt* **menwaabid**
minwaabikad *vii* be good (as something mineral); *prt* **menwaabikak**
minwaabikizi *vai* be good (as something mineral); *prt* **menwaabikizid**
minwaadizi *vai* lead a good life; *1sg* **niminwaadiz**; *prt* **menwaadizid**
minwaadodan *vti* tell good news of s.t.; *1sg* **niminwaadodaan**; *prt* **menwaadodang**
minwaagamin /minwaagami-/ *vii* taste good (as a liquid); *prt* **menwaagamig**
minwaajim *vta* tell good news of s.o.; *1sg* **niminwaajimaa**; *prt* **menwaajimaad**
minwaajimo *vai* tell good news, tell a good story; *1sg* **niminwaajim**; *prt* **menwaajimod**
minwaakozi *vai* be good (as something stick- or wood-like); *prt* **menwaakozid**
minwaakwad *vii* be good (as something stick- or wood-like); *prt* **menwaakwak**
minwaande *vii* be a good color; *prt* **menwaandeg**; *aug* **minwaandemagad**; *prt aug* **menwaandemagak**
minwaanimad *vii* there is a good breeze, there is a favorable wind; *prt* **menwaanimak**

minwaanzo *vai* be a good color; *1sg* **niminwaanz**; *prt* **menwaanzod**
minwaatese *vii* be a good movie; *prt* **menwaateseg**; *aug* **minwaatesemagad**; *prt aug* **menwaatesemagak**
minwegad *vii* be good (as something sheet-like); *prt* **menwegak**
minwegizi *vai* be good (as something sheet-like); *prt* **menwegizid**
minwendam *vai2* be happy, be glad; *1sg* **niminwendam**; *prt* **menwendang**
minwendan *vti* like s.t.; *1sg* **niminwendaan**; *prt* **menwendang**
minwendaagozi *vai* be likeable, be agreeable, be fun; *prt* **menwendaagozid**
minwendaagwad *vii* be likeable, be fun; *prt* **menwendaagwak**
minwenim *vta* like s.o.; *1sg* **niminwenimaa**; *prt* **menwenimaad**
misajidamoo *na* grey squirrel; *pl* **misajidamoog**; *dim* **misajidamoons**
misakakojiish *na* badger; *pl* **misakakojiishag**; *dim* **misakakojiishens**
misan /miS-/ *ni* firewood *plural of:* **mishi**; *loc* **mising**
misawendam *vai2* desire, want; *1sg* **nimisawendam**; *prt* **mesawendang**
misawendan *vti* desire s.t., want s.t.; *1sg* **nimisawendaan**; *prt* **mesawendang**
misawenim *vta* desire s.o., want s.o.; *1sg* **nimisawenimaa**; *prt* **mesawenimaad**
misawenjige *vai* desire things, want things; *1sg* **nimisawenjige**; *prt* **mesawenjiged**
misaabe *na* giant; *pl* **misaabeg**; *dim* **misaabens**
misaabooz *na* jack rabbit; *pl* **misaaboozoog**; *dim* **misaaboozoons**
mishi /miS-/ *ni* piece of firewood; *pl* **misan**; *loc* **mising**
mishibizhii *na* lion, panther, underwater panther; *pl* **mishibizhiig**; *dim* **mishibizhiins**
mishiikenh *na* snapping turtle; *pl* **mishiikenyag**
mishiimin *na* apple; *pl* **mishiiminag**; *loc* **mishiimining**; *dim* **mishiiminens**
mishiiminaaboo *ni* apple juice; *loc* **mishiiminaaboong**
mishiiminaatig *na* apple tree; *pl* **mishiiminaatigoog**; *loc* **mishiiminaatigong**; *dim* **mishiiminaatigoons**
mishiiwaatig *ni* dry wood; *pl* **mishiiwaatigoon**; *loc* **mishiiwaatigong**; *dim* **mishiiwaatigoons**
Misi-zaaga'iganiing *place* Mille Lacs Reservation
misko- *pv4* red
miskobagaa *vii* there are red leaves on the trees; *prt* **meskobagaag**; *aug* **miskobagaamagad**; *prt aug* **meskobagaamagak**
miskobagizi *vai* have red leaves; *prt* **meskobagizid**
misko-bineshiinh *na* cardinal; *pl* **misko-bineshiinyag**; *dim* **misko-bineshiins**
miskodoonechigan *ni* lipstick; *pl* **miskodoonechiganan**; *loc* **miskodoonechiganing**; *dim* **miskodoonechigaans**
miskogaadeyaab *ni* yarn; *pl* **miskogaadeyaabiin**
misko'o *vai* wear red; *1sg* **nimisko'**; *prt* **mesko'od**
miskojaane *vai* have a red nose; *1sg* **nimiskojaane**; *prt* **meskojaaned**
misko-jiis *ni* beet; *pl* **misko-jiisan**; *loc* **misko-jiising**; *dim* **misko-jiisens**
miskomin *na* raspberry; *pl* **miskominag**; *loc* **miskomining**; *dim* **miskominens**
miskondibe *vai* be red-headed; *1sg* **nimiskondibe**; *prt* **meskondibed**
miskozi *vai* be red; *prt* **meskozid**
miskwakone *vii* blaze up; *prt* **meskwakoneg**; *aug* **miskwakonemagad**; *prt aug* **meskwakonemagak**
miskwanowe *vai* have a red cheek; *1sg* **nimiskwanowe**; *prt* **meskwanowed**
miskwanowechigan *ni* rouge; *pl* **miskwanowechiganan**; *loc* **miskwanowechiganing**; *dim* **miskwanowechigaans**
miskwanowechige *vai* use rouge; *1sg* **nimiskwanowechige**; *prt* **meskwanowechiged**
miskwazhe *vai* have measles; *1sg* **nimiskwazhe**; *prt* **meskwazhed**
miskwaa *vii* be red; *prt* **meskwaag**; *aug* **miskwaamagad**; *prt aug* **meskwaamagak**
miskwaabik *ni* (piece of) copper; *loc* **miskwaabikong**; *dim* **miskwaabikoons**
miskwaabikad *vii* be red (as something mineral); *prt* **meskwaabikak**
miskwaabikide *vii* be red-hot (as something mineral); *prt* **meskwaabikideg**; *aug* **miskwaabikidemagad**; *prt aug* **meskwaabikidemagak**
miskwaabikizi *vai* be red (as something mineral); *prt* **meskwaabikizid**
miskwaabikizo *vai* be red-hot (as something mineral); *prt* **meskwaabikizod**
miskwaabikoons *na* cent, penny; *pl* **miskwaabikoonsag**; *loc* **miskwaabikoonsing**
miskwaabiigad *vii* be red (as something string-like); *prt* **meskwaabiigak**
miskwaabiigizi *vai* be red (as something string-like); *prt* **meskwaabiigizid**
miskwaabiimizh *na* red osier (locally known as dogwood); *pl* **miskwaabiimizhiig**; *loc* **miskwaabiimizhiing**; *dim* **miskwaabiimizhiins**
miskwaadesi *na* painted turtle; *pl* **miskwaadesiwag**; *dim* **miskwaadesiins**
Miskwaagamiiwi-zaaga'iganiing *place* Red Lake Reservation
miskwaakonaye *vai* dress in red; *1sg* **nimiskwaakonaye**; *prt* **meskwaakonayed**
miskwaakozi *vai* be red (as something stick- or wood-like); *prt* **meskwaakozid**
miskwaakwad *vii* be red (as something stick- or wood-like); *prt* **meskwaakwak**
miskwaanakwad *vii* be red clouds; *prt* **meskwaanakwak**
miskwaande *vii* be colored red; *prt* **meskwaandeg**; *aug* **miskwaandemagad**; *prt aug* **meskwaandemagak**
miskwaanzigan *ni* roach headdress; *pl* **miskwaanziganan**; *loc* **miskwaanziganing**; *dim* **miskwaanzigaans**

miskwaanzo *vai* be colored red; *prt* **meskwaanzod**
miskwaawaak *na* red cedar; *pl* **miskwaawaakoog**; *loc* **miskwaawaakong**; *dim* **miskwaawaakoons**
miskwegad *vii* be red (as something sheet-like); *prt* **meskwegak**
miskwegizi *vai* be red (as something sheet-like); *prt* **meskwegizid**
miskwi *ni* blood; *loc* **miskwiing**
miskwiingwese *vai* blush; *1sg* **nimiskwiingwese**; *prt* **meskwiingwesed**
miskwiiwi *vai* bleed, be bloody; *1sg* **nimiskwiiw**; *prt* **meskwiiwid**
miskwiiwijaane *vai* have a bloody nose; *1sg* **nimiskwiiwijaane**; *prt* **meskwiiwijaaned**
mitabi *vai* sit on the bare ground; *1sg* **nimitab**; *prt* **metabid**
mitagwazhe *vai* be naked; *1sg* **nimitagwazhe**; *prt* **metagwazhed**
mitakamig *pc* on bare ground
mitaakondibe *vai* be bare-headed; *1sg* **nimitaakondibe**; *prt* **metaakondibed**
mitaawangaa *vii* be a sandy beach; *prt* **metaawangaag**; *aug* **mitaawangaamagad**; *prt aug* **metaawangaamagak**
mitig *na* tree; *pl* **mitigoog**; *loc* **mitigong**; *dim* **mitigoons**
mitig *ni* stick, piece of wood; *pl* **mitigoon**; *loc* **mitigong**; *dim* **mitigoons**
mitigo-jiimaan *ni* wooden boat, wooden canoe; *pl* **mitigo-jiimaanan**; *loc* **mitigo-jiimaaning**; *dim* **mitigo-jiimaanens**
mitigokaa *vii* there are many trees; *prt* **metigokaag**; *aug* **mitigokaamagad**; *prt aug* **metigokaamagak**
mitigo-makak *ni* wooden box, crate; *pl* **mitigo-makakoon**; *loc* **mitigo-makakong**; *dim* **mitigo-makakoons**
mitigomin *ni* acorn; *pl* **mitigominan**; *loc* **mitigomining**; *dim* **mitigominens**
mitigomizh *na* oak; *pl* **mitigomizhiig**; *loc* **mitigomizhiing**; *dim* **mitigomizhiins**
mitigonaagan *ni* wooden dish; *pl* **mitigonaaganan**; *loc* **mitigonaaganing**; *dim* **mitigonaagaans**
mitigo-waakaa'igan *ni* log cabin; *pl* **mitigo-waakaa'iganan**; *loc* **mitigo-waakaa'iganing**; *dim* **mitigo-waakaa'igaans**
mitigoons *ni* stick; *pl* **mitigoonsan**; *loc* **mitigoonsing**
mitigwakik *na* Mide drum; *pl* **mitigwakikoog**; *loc* **mitigwakikong**; *dim* **mitigwakikoons**
mitigwaab *na* bow; *pl* **mitigwaabiig**; *loc* **mitigwaabiing**; *dim* **mitigwaabiins**
mitigwaabaak *na* hickory; *pl* **mitigwaabaakoog**; *loc* **mitigwaabaakong**; *dim* **mitigwaabaakoons**
mitigwemikwaan *ni* wooden spoon, wooden ladle; *pl* **mitigwemikwaanan**; *dim* **mitigwemikwaanens**
mitose *vai* go on foot; *1sg* **nimitose**; *prt* **metosed**
mizay *na* ling, eelpout, burbot, mariah, lawyer (fish); *pl* **mizayag**
mizhagaa *vai* come ashore in canoe; *1sg* **nimizhagaa**; *prt* **mezhagaad**
mizhakiise *vai* hit the bottom; *1sg* **nimizhakiise**; *prt* **mezhakiised**
mizhakiise *vii* hit the bottom; *prt* **mezhakiiseg**; *aug* **mizhakiisemagad**; *prt aug* **mezhakiisemagak**
mizhakwad *vii* be clear sky, be good weather; *prt* **mezhakwak**
mizhaakigwe *vai* get a cold; *1sg* **nimizhaakigwe**; *prt* **mezhaakigwed**
mizhisha *pc* in plain view
mizho /mizhw-/ *vta* hit s.o. (in shooting); *1sg* **nimizhwaa**; *prt* **mezhwaad**
mizhodam *vai2* win, hit the target; *1sg* **nimizhodam**; *prt* **mezhodang**
mizhodan *vti* hit s.t. (in shooting); *1sg* **nimizhodaan**; *prt* **mezhodang**
mizise *na* turkey; *pl* **miziseg**; *dim* **mizisens**
miziwe *pc* all over, everywhere
miziwebii'an *vti* write s.t. all over; *1sg* **nimiziwebii'aan**; *prt* **meziwebii'ang**
miziwebii'igaade *vii* be written on all over; *prt* **meziwebii'igaadeg**; *aug* **miziwebii'igaademagad**; *prt aug* **meziwebii'igaademagak**
miziwebii'ige *vai* write all over; *1sg* **nimiziwebii'ige**; *prt* **meziwebii'iged**
miziwe' *vta* make s.o. of a whole piece; *1sg* **nimiziwe'aa**; *prt* **meziwe'aad**
miziwekamig *pc* all over the world
miziweshkaa *vii* be everywhere, go everywhere, spread all over; *prt* **meziweshkaag**; *aug* **miziweshkaamagad**; *prt aug* **meziweshkaamagak**
miziwetoon *vti2* make s.t. of a whole piece; *1sg* **nimiziwetoon**; *prt* **meziwetood**
miziweyaa *vii* be whole, be intact; *prt* **meziweyaag**; *aug* **miziweyaamagad**; *prt aug* **meziweyaamagak**
miziweyaabikizi *vai* be full (as something mineral, e.g., the moon); *prt* **meziweyaabikizid**
miziwezi *vai* be whole, be intact; *1sg* **nimiziwez**; *prt* **meziwezid**
mizizaak *na* horsefly; *pl* **mizizaakwag**; *dim* **mizizaakoons**

mitigwemikwaan (wooden spoon, wooden ladle)

mizizi *vai* start to get sick, catch a disease; *1sg* **nimiziz**; *prt* **mezizid**
mii *pc* it is thus that, it is that *existential particle*
mii dash *pc* and then; *also* **miish**
miigaadiwag /miigaadi-/ *vai* they fight each other; *1pl* **nimiigaadimin**; *prt* **maagaadijig**
miigaadiwin *ni* battle, war; *pl* **miigaadiwinan**
miigaazh /miigaaN-/ *vta* fight s.o.; *1sg* **nimiigaanaa**; *prt* **maagaanaad**
miigaazo *vai* fight; *1sg* **nimiigaaz**; *prt* **maagaazod**
miigis *na* Mide shell, pearl; *pl* **miigisag**; *loc* **miigising**; *dim* **miigisens**
miigiwe *vai+o* give away (s.t.); *1sg* **nimiigiwe, nimiigiwen**; *prt* **maagiwed**
miigwan *na* feather; *pl* **miigwanag**; *loc* **miigwaning**; *dim* **miigwaans**
miigwani-wiiwakwaan *ni* feather headdress, feather bonnet; *pl* **miigwani-wiiwakwaanan**; *loc* **miigwani-wiiwakwaaning**; *dim* **miigwani-wiiwakwaanens**
miigwech *pc* thanks!
miigwechiwendam *vai2* be thankful; *1sg* **nimiigwechiwendam**; *prt* **maagwechiwendang**
miigwechiwendan *vti* be thankful for s.t.; *1sg* **nimiigwechiwendaan**; *prt* **maagwechiwendang**
miigwechiwenim *vta* be thankful for s.o.; *1sg* **nimiigwechiwenimaa**; *prt* **maagwechiwenimaad**
miigwechiwi-giizhigad *vii* be Thanksgiving Day; *prt* **maagwechiwi-giizhigak**
miigwechiwi' *vta* thank s.o.; *1sg* **nimiigwechiwi'aa**; *prt* **maagwechiwi'aad**
miijim *ni* food; *pl* **miijiman**
miijimadaawe *vai* buy food; *1sg* **nimiijimadaawe**; *prt* **maajimadaawed**
miijimikanjigan *ni* bait; *pl* **miijimikanjiganan**; *loc* **miijimikanjiganing**; *dim* **miijimikanjigaans**
miijimikanjige *vai* bait things; *1sg* **nimiijimikanjige**; *prt* **maajimikanjiged**
miijin *vti3* eat s.t.; *1sg* **nimiijin**; *prt* **maajid**
miikana *ni* road, trail; *pl* **miikanan**; *loc* **miikanaang**; *dim* **miikanens, miikaans**
miikanaake *vai* make a road or trail; *1sg* **nimiikanaake**; *prt* **maakanaaked**
miikanaakewinini *na* road worker; *pl* **miikanaakewininiwag**
miikanaawan *vii* be a road, be a trail; *prt* **maakanaawang**
miikawaadad *vii* be handsome, be beautiful; *prt* **maakawaadak**
miikawaadizi *vai* be handsome, be beautiful; *1sg* **nimiikawaadiz**; *prt* **mekawaadizid**
miikindizi *vai* tease; *1sg* **nimiikindiz**; *prt* **maakindizid**
miikinji' *vta* tease s.o., harass s.o.; *1sg* **nimiikinji'aa**; *prt* **maakinji'aad**
miikonan *vti* shoot and hit s.t.; *1sg* **nimiikonaan**; *prt* **maakonang**
miikonaw *vta* shoot and hit s.o.; *1sg* **nimiikonawaa**; *prt* **maakonawaad**
miikwa' /miikwa'w-/ *vta* hit s.o. dead center with something; *1sg* **nimiikwa'waa**; *prt* **maakwa'waad**
miikwa'an *vti* hit s.t. dead center with something; *1sg* **nimiikwa'aan**; *prt* **maakwa'ang**
miinagaawanzh *na* blueberry plant; *pl* **miinagaawanzhiig**; *loc* **miinagaawanzhiing**; *dim* **miinagaawanzhiins**
miinan /miin-/ *ni* blueberries *plural; loc* **miining**; *dim* **miinensan**
mii nange *pc* yes, for sure, certainly
miinawaa *pc* and, also, again
miinens *na* hawthorn fruit; *pl* **miinensag**
miinensagaawanzh *na* hawthorn tree; *pl* **miinensagaawanzhiig**; *loc* **miinensagaawanzhiing**; *dim* **miinensagaawanzhiins**
miini-baashkiminasigan *ni* blueberry sauce
miinidiwag /miinidi-/ *vai* they give (s.t.) to each other, they have a give-away; *1pl* **nimiinidimin**; *prt* **maanidijig**
miini-giizis *na* August, July; *also* **miinike-giizis**
miinikaan *ni* seed; *pl* **miinikaanan**; *loc* **miinikaaning**; *dim* **miinikaanens**
miish *pc* it is thus that, and then
miishaabiwinaan *ni* eyelash; *pl* **miishaabiwinaanan**
miishidaamikan *vai* have a beard; *1sg* **nimiishidaamikan**; *prt* **maashidaamikang**
miishidoon *vai* have a moustache; *1sg* **nimiishidoon**; *prt* **maashidoong**
miishiigin *ni* velvet; *pl* **miishiiginoon**; *loc* **miishiiginong**; *dim* **miishiiginoons**
miishiijiimin *na* peach; *pl* **miishiijiiminag**; *loc* **miishiijiimining**; *dim* **miishiijiiminens**
miizh /miiN-/ *vta* give (s.t.) to s.o.; *1sg* **nimiinaa**; *prt* **maanaad**
miizii *vai* defecate; *1sg* **nimiizii**; *prt* **maaziid**
miiziwigamig *ni* toilet, bathroom; *pl* **miiziiwigamigoon**; *loc* **miiziiwigamigong**; *dim* **miiziiwigamigoons**
moshwe *na* shawl; *pl* **moshweg**; *loc* **moshweng**; *dim* **moshwens**
moshwens *ni* handkerchief; *pl* **moshwensan**; *loc* **moshwensing**
moo *ni* feces, excrement; *pl* **moowan**
moo' *vta* make s.o. cry; *1sg* **nimoo'aa**; *prt* **mwaa'aad**
mooka'am *vai2* be sunrise, rise (as the sun); *1sg* **nimooka'am**; *prt* **mwaaka'ang**
mookawaakii *vai* cry to go along; *1sg* **nimookawaakii**; *prt* **mwaakawaakiid**
mookibii *vai* emerge from the water; *prt* **mwaakibiid**
mookijiwanibiig *ni* spring (water source); *loc* **mookijiwanibiigong**; *dim* **mookijiwanibiigoons**
mookii *vai* emerge from surface; *1sg* **nimookii**; *prt* **mwaakiid**
mookiitaw *vta* attack s.o. from hiding; *1sg* **nimookiitawaa**; *prt* **mwaakiitawaad**
mookodaaso *vai* carve, whittle; *1sg* **nimookodaas**; *prt* **mwaakodaasod**
mookodaasowinini *na* carpenter, carver; *pl* **mookodaasowininiwag**
mookojigan *ni* drawknife, plane (tool); *pl* **mookojiganan**; *loc* **mookojiganing**; *dim* **mookojigaans**

mookomaan *ni* knife; *pl* **mookomaanan**; *loc* **mookomaaning**; *dim* **mookomaanens**
moona' /moona'w-/ *vta* dig up s.o.; *1sg* **nimoona'waa**; *prt* **mwaana'waad**
moona'an *vti* dig up s.t.; *1sg* **nimoona'aan**; *prt* **mwaana'ang**
moona'ige *vai* dig up things; *1sg* **nimoona'ige**; *prt* **mwaana'iged**
moonenim *vta* suspect s.o.; *1sg* **nimoonenimaa**; *prt* **mwaanenimaad**
moonikaan *ni* cellar; *pl* **moonikaanan**; *loc* **moonikaaning**; *dim* **moonikaanens**
mooningwane *na* yellow-shafted flicker; *pl* **mooningwaneg**; *dim* **mooningwanens**
moose *na* worm; *pl* **mooseg**; *dim* **moosens**
moosewiingwe *vai* have acne on one's face; *1sg* **nimoosewiingwe**; *prt* **mwaasewiingwed**
mooshka'an *vii* be flooded, there is a flood; *prt* **mwaashka'ang**
mooshka'osi *na* American bittern (locally called shypoke); *pl* **mooshka'osiwag**; *dim* **mooshka'osiins**
mooshkamo *vai* come up to the surface of the water; *1sg* **nimooshkam**; *prt* **mwaashkamod**
mooshkinadoon *vti2* fill s.t. (with solids); *1sg* **nimooshkinadoon**; *prt* **mwaashkinadood**
mooshkina' *vta* fill s.o. (with solids); *1sg* **nimooshkina'aa**; *prt* **mwaashkina'aad**
mooshkine *vai* be full (of solids); *1sg* **nimooshkine**; *prt* **mwaashkined**
mooshkine *vii* be full (of solids); *prt* **mwaashkineg**; *aug* **mooshkinemagad**; *prt aug* **mwaashkinemagak**
mooshkinebadoon *vti2* fill s.t. (with a liquid); *1sg* **nimooshkinebadoon**; *prt* **mwaashkinebadood**
mooshkinebazh /mooshkinebaN-/ *vta* fill s.o. (with a liquid); *1sg* **nimooshkinebanaa**; *prt* **mwaashkinebanaad**
mooshkinebii *vii* be full (of a liquid); *prt* **mwaashkinebiig**; *aug* **mooshkinebiimagad**; *prt aug* **mwaashkinebiimagak**
mooshkinebii'ige *vai* fill out a form; *1sg* **nimooshkinebii'ige**; *prt* **mwaashkinebii'iged**
mooshkineyaabate *vii* be filled with smoke; *prt* **mwaashkineyaabateg**; *aug* **mooshkineyaabatemagad**; *prt aug* **mwaashkineyaabatemagak**
mooz *na* moose; *pl* **moozoog**; *dim* **moozoons**
moozhag *pc* always, often, all the time
moozhaabe *na* unmarried man; *pl* **moozhaabeg**
moozhi' *vta* feel s.o. in or on one's body; *1sg* **nimoozhi'aa**; *prt* **mwaazhi'aad**
moozhikwe *na* unmarried woman; *pl* **moozhikweg**
moozhitoon *vti2* feel s.t. in or on one's body; *1sg* **nimoozhitoon**; *prt* **mwaazhitood**
moozhwaagan *ni* scissors; *pl* **moozhwaaganan**; *loc* **moozhwaaganing**; *dim* **moozhwaagaans**

N

n= *pre first person prefix before long vowels in dependent noun stems*
na *pc yes-no question word*
nabagaa *vii* be flat; *prt* **nebagaag**; *aug* **nabagaamagad**; *prt aug* **nebagaamagak**
nabagidaabaan *na* toboggan; *pl* **nabagidaabaanag**; *loc* **nabagidaabaaning**; *dim* **nabagidaabaanens**
nabagijaane *vai* have a flat nose; *1sg* **ninabagijaane**; *prt* **nebagijaaned**
nabagijiishin *vai* have a flat tire; *prt* **nebagijiishing**
nabagisag *na* board; *pl* **nabagisagoog**; *loc* **nabagisagong**; *dim* **nabagisagoons**
nabagizi *vai* be flat; *prt* **nebagizid**
nabon *vta* fold s.o. over; *1sg* **ninabonaa**; *prt* **nebonaad**
nabonan *vti* fold s.t. over; *1sg* **ninabonaan**; *prt* **nebonang**
naboob *ni* soup; *pl* **naboobiin**; *loc* **naboobiing**; *dim* **naboobiins**
naboobiike *vai* make soup; *1sg* **ninaboobiike**; *prt* **neboobiiked**
nagadamaw *vta* leave (s.t.) behind for s.o.; *1sg* **ninagadamawaa**; *prt* **negadamawaad**
nagadan *vti* abandon s.t., leave s.t. behind; *1sg* **ninagadaan**; *prt* **negadang**
nagadendan *vti* be used to s.t., be familiar with s.t.; *1sg* **ninagadendaan**; *prt* **negadendang**
nagadenim *vta* be used to s.o., be familiar with s.o., be acquainted with s.o.; *1sg* **ninagadenimaa**; *prt* **negadenimaad**
nagadenindiwag /nagadenindi-/ *vai* they are acquainted with each other, they are friends with each other; *1pl* **ninagadenindimin**; *prt* **negadenindijig**
nagaji' *vta* be used to making s.o., know how to handle s.o.; *1sg* **ninagaji'aa**; *prt* **negaji'aad**
nagajitoon *vti2* be used to making s.t., know how to handle s.t.; *1sg* **ninagajitoon**; *prt* **negajitood**
nagamo *vai* sing; *1sg* **ninagam**; *prt* **negamod**
nagamon *ni* song; *pl* **nagamonan**; *dim* **nagamonens**
nagamotaw *vta* sing for s.o.; *1sg* **ninagamotawaa**; *prt* **negamotawaad**
nagamowin *ni* singing, song
nagamoo-makak *ni* phonograph, record player; *pl* **nagamoo-makakoon**; *loc* **nagamoo-makakong**; *dim* **nagamoo-makakoons**
nagazh /nagaN-/ *vta* abandon s.o., leave s.o. behind; *1sg* **ninaganaa**; *prt* **neganaad**
nagazhiwe *vai* abandon people; *1sg* **ninagazhiwe**; *prt* **negazhiwed**
Nagaajiwanaang *place* Fond du Lac Reservation
nagaashkaa *vai* halt, stop moving; *1sg* **ninagaashkaa**; *prt* **negaashkaad**
nagaashkaa *vii* halt, stop moving; *prt* **negaashkaag**; *aug* **nagaashkaamagad**; *prt aug* **negaashkaamagak**

nagaashkaa' *vta* make s.o. stop (e.g., a car); *1sg* **ninagaashkaa'aa**; *prt* **negaashkaa'aad**
nagaashkaatoon *vti2* make s.t. stop; *1sg* **ninagaashkaatoon**; *prt* **negaashkaatood**
nagaawebishkigan *ni* brakes; *pl* **nagaawebishkiganan**; *loc* **nagaawebishkiganing**
nagaawebishkige *vai* apply the brakes; *1sg* **ninagaawebishkige**; *prt* **negaawebishkiged**
nagishkan *vti* meet s.t. (while going somewhere); *1sg* **ninagishkaan**; *prt* **negishkang**
nagishkaw *vta* meet s.o. (while going somewhere); *1sg* **ninagishkawaa**; *prt* **negishkawaad**
nagishkodaadiwag /nagishkodaadi-/ *vai* they meet each other; *1pl* **ninagishkodaadimin**; *prt* **negishkodaadijig**
nagwaagan *ni* snare; *pl* **nagwaaganan**; *loc* **nagwaaganing**; *dim* **nagwaagaans**
nagwaaganeyaab *ni* snare wire; *pl* **nagwaaganeyaabiin**; *loc* **nagwaaganeyaabiing**; *dim* **nagwaaganeyaabiins**
nagwaazh /nagwaaN-/ *vta* snare s.o.; *1sg* **ninagwaanaa**; *prt* **negwaanaad**
nagweyaab *ni* rainbow; *pl* **nagweyaabiin**; *loc* **nagweyaabiing**; *dim* **nagweyaabiins**
na'aanganikwe *na* daughter-in-law; *pl* **na'aanganikweg**
na'aangish *na* son-in-law; *pl* **na'aangishiig**
na'egaaj *pc* not too hard!, go easy!
na'enimo *vai* store things away; *1sg* **nina'enim**; *prt* **ne'enimod**
na'idaa *pc* right at the time, just then
na'isijige *vai* put things in order; *1sg* **nina'isijige**; *prt* **ne'isijiged**
nakodan *vti* answer s.t.; *1sg* **ninakodaan**; *prt* **nekodang**
nakom *vta* answer s.o., reply to s.o.; *1sg* **ninakomaa**; *prt* **nekomaad**
nakondiwag /nakondi-/ *vai* they answer each other, they reply to each other; *1pl* **ninakondìmin**; *prt* **nekondijig**
nakwebidoon *vti2* catch s.t. with hands; *1sg* **ninakwebidoon**; *prt* **nekwebidood**
nakwebijige *vai* catch things with hands; *1sg* **ninakwebijige**; *prt* **nekwebijiged**
nakwebijigewinini *na* catcher (in baseball); *pl* **nakwebijigewininiwag**; *dim* **nakwebijigewininiins**
nakwebizh /nakwebiN-/ *vta* catch s.o. with hands; *1sg* **ninakwebinaa**; *prt* **nekwebinaad**
nakwebii'amaw *vta* write (s.t.) back to s.o.; *1sg* **ninakwebii'amawaa**; *prt* **nekwebii'amawaad**
nakwebii'amaadiwag /nakwebii'amaadi-/ *vai* they write back to each other; *1pl* **ninakwebii'amaadimin**; *prt* **nekwebii'amaadijig**
nakweshkaw *vta* meet s.o.; *1sg* **ninakweshkawaa**; *prt* **nekweshkawaad**
nakweshkodaadiwag /nakweshkodaadi-/ *vai* they meet each other; *1pl* **ninakweshkodaadimin**; *prt* **nekweshkodaadijig**
nakwetam *vai2* answer; *1sg* **ninakwetam**; *prt* **nekwetang**
nakwetan *vti* answer s.t.; *1sg* **ninakwetaan**; *prt* **nekwetang**
nakwetaw *vta* answer s.o.; *1sg* **ninakwetawaa**; *prt* **nekwetawaad**
namadabi *vai* sit, sit down; *1sg* **ninamadab**; *prt* **nemadabid**
namanjinik *ni* left hand *usually possessed*; *pl* **namanjinikan**; *loc* **namanjinikaang**
namanjii *vai* be left-handed; *1sg* **ninamanjii**; *prt* **nemanjiid**
name *na* sturgeon; *pl* **namewag**; *dim* **namens**
namebin *na* sucker (fish); *pl* **namebinag**; *dim* **namebinens**
namebini-giizis *na* February
name' *vta* find signs of s.o.'s presence; *1sg* **niname'aa**; *prt* **neme'aad**
nameshin *vai* leave signs of one's presence; *1sg* **ninameshin**; *prt* **nemeshing**
namesin *vii* leave signs of its presence; *prt* **nemesing**
nametoo *vai* leave signs of one's presence; *1sg* **ninametoo**; *prt* **nemetood**
nanagin *vta* hold s.o. back, prevent s.o. (from doing something); *1sg* **ninanaginaa**; *prt* **nenaginaad**
nanaabag= < nabag=
nanaa'ichige *vai* fix things, repair things; *1sg* **ninanaa'ichige**; *prt* **nenaa'ichiged**
nanaa'idaabaane *vai* repair a car; *1sg* **ninanaa'idaabaane**; *prt* **nenaa'idaabaaned**
nanaa'idaabaanewinini *na* automobile mechanic; *pl* **nanaa'idaabaanewininiwag**
nanaa'idaabaanikewinini *na* automobile mechanic; *pl* **nanaa'idaabaanikewininiwag**
nanaa'in *vta* put s.o. in order, put s.o. away, fix s.o.; *1sg* **ninanaa'inaa**; *prt* **nenaa'inaad**
nanaa'inan *vti* put s.t. in order, put s.t. away, fix s.t.; *1sg* **ninanaa'inaan**; *prt* **nenaa'inang**
nanaa'itaw *vta* fix (s.t.) for s.o., repair (s.t.) for s.o.; *1sg* **ninanaa'itawaa**; *prt* **nenaa'itawaad**; *also* **nanaa'itamaw**
nanaa'itoon *vti2* fix s.t., repair s.t.; *1sg* **ninanaa'itoon**; *prt* **nenaa'itood**
nanaa'ii *vai* be dressed up; *1sg* **ninanaa'ii**; *prt* **nenaa'iid**
nanaamad= < namad=
nanaandaw= < nandaw=
nanaandawi' *vta* heal s.o., doctor s.o.; *1sg* **ninanaandawi'aa**; *prt* **nenaandawi'aad**
nanaandawi'iwe *vai* heal people, doctor people; *1sg* **ninanaandawi'iwe**; *prt* **nenaandawi'iwed**
nanaando= < nando=
nanaawad= < nawad=
nanda- *pv4* seek, look for
nanda-anokii *vai* look for work; *1sg* **ninanda-anokii**; *prt* **nenda-anokiid**
nanda-gikendan *vti* seek to know s.t., seek to learn s.t.; *1sg* **ninanda-gikendaan**; *prt* **nenda-gikendang**
nanda-gikenim *vta* seek to know s.o.; *1sg* **ninanda-gikenimaa**; *prt* **nenda-gikenimaad**

nanda-mikwendan *vti* try to think of s.t., try to remember s.t.; *1sg* **ninanda-mikwendaan**; *prt* **nenda-mikwendang**
nanda-mikwenim *vta* try to think of s.o., try to remember s.o.; *1sg* **ninanda-mikwenimaa**; *prt* **nenda-mikwenimaad**
nandawaabam *vta* look for s.o., search for s.o.; *1sg* **ninandawaabamaa**; *prt* **nendawaabamaad**
nandawaabandan *vti* look for s.t., search for s.t.; *1sg* **ninandawaabandaan**; *prt* **nendawaabandang**
nandawaabanjige *vai* look for things, search for things; *1sg* **ninandawaabanjige**; *prt* **nendawaabanjiged**
nandawaaboozwe *vai* hunt for rabbits; *1sg* **ninandawaaboozwe**; *prt* **nendawaaboozwed**
nandawaatoo *vai* scout; *1sg* **ninandawaatoo**; *prt* **nendawaatood**
nandawendam *vai2* want, desire; *1sg* **ninandawendam**; *prt* **nendawendang**
nandawendan *vti* want s.t., desire s.t.; *1sg* **ninandawendaan**; *prt* **nendawendang**
nandawendaagozi *vai* be suitable, be desirable; *prt* **nendawendaagozid**
nandawendaagwad *vii* be suitable, be desirable; *prt* **nendawendaagwak**
nandawenim *vta* want s.o. (to do...), desire s.o.; *1sg* **ninandawenimaa**; *prt* **nendawenimaad**
nandawenjige *vai* get food by hunting or fishing; *1sg* **ninandawenjige**; *prt* **nendawenjiged**
nandawishibe *vai* hunt ducks; *1sg* **ninandawishibe**; *prt* **nendawishibed**
nandawisimwe *vai* look for horses; *1sg* **ninandawisimwe**; *prt* **nendawisimwed**
nandobani *vai* go to war *archaic*; *1sg* **ninandoban**; *prt* **nendobanid**
nandodamaw *vta* ask s.o. for (s.t.), beg s.o. for (s.t.); *1sg* **ninandodamawaa**; *prt* **nendodamawaad**
nandodamaage *vai* ask people for (s.t.), beg people for (s.t.); *1sg* **ninandodamaage**; *prt* **nendodamaaged**
nandodan *vti* ask for s.t.; *1sg* **ninandodaan**; *prt* **nendodang**
nandokawechige *vai* look for tracks; *1sg* **ninandokawechige**; *prt* **nendokawechiged**
nandokawe' *vta* look for s.o.'s tracks, be on s.o.'s trail; *1sg* **ninandokawe'aa**; *prt* **nendokawe'aad**
nandom *vta* call s.o., summon s.o.; *1sg* **ninandomaa**; *prt* **nendomaad**
nandomaam *vta* smell for s.o., sniff s.o.; *1sg* **ninandomaamaa**; *prt* **nendomaamaad**
nandomaandan *vti* smell for s.t., sniff s.t.; *1sg* **ninandomaandaan**; *prt* **nendomaandang**
nandone' /nandone'w-/ *vta* look for s.o.; *1sg* **ninandone'waa**; *prt* **nendone'waad**
nandone'an *vti* look for s.t.; *1sg* **ninandone'aan**; *prt* **nendone'ang**
nandone'igaade *vii* be looked for; *prt* **nendone'igaadeg**; *aug* **nandone'igaademagad**; *prt aug* **nendone'igaademagak**
nandone'igaazo *vai* be looked for; *prt* **nendone'igaazod**
nandone'ige *vai* look for things; *1sg* **ninandone'ige**; *prt* **nendone'iged**
nandotam *vai2* listen for something; *1sg* **ninandotam**; *prt* **nendotang**
nandotan *vti* listen for s.t.; *1sg* **ninandotaan**; *prt* **nendotang**
nandotaw *vta* listen for s.o.; *1sg* **ninandotawaa**; *prt* **nendotawaad**
nandoobii *vai* look for a drink; *1sg* **ninandoobii**; *prt* **nendoobiid**
nandoojiin *vta* feel for s.o., grope for s.o.; *1sg* **ninandoojiinaa**; *prt* **nendoojiinaad**
nandoojiinan *vti* feel for s.t., grope for s.t.; *1sg* **ninandoojiinaan**; *prt* **nendoojiinang**
nandoojiinige *vai* feel for things, grope for things; *1sg* **ninandoojiinige**; *prt* **nendoojiiniged**
nandookome *vai* look for lice; *1sg* **ninandookome**; *prt* **nendookomed**
nandookomeshiinh *na* monkey; *pl* **nandookomeshiinyag**
nandwaanikaadan *vti* dig for s.t.; *1sg* **ninandwaanikaadaan**; *prt* **nendwaanikaadang**
nandwaanikaazh /nandwaanikaaN-/ *vta* dig for s.o.; *1sg* **ninandwaanikaanaa**; *prt* **nendwaanikaanaad**
nandwewem *vta* go and ask for s.o.; *1sg* **ninandwewemaa**; *prt* **nendwewemaad**
nandwewendamaw *vta* go and ask s.o. (for s.t.); *1sg* **ninandwewendamawaa**; *prt* **nendwewendamawaad**
nandwewendan *vti* go and ask for s.t.; *1sg* **ninandwewendaan**; *prt* **nendwewendang**
nandwewezige *vai* signal by shooting; *1sg* **ninandwewezige**; *prt* **nendwewezigeg**
nangwana *pc* it turns out that, it happens to be; *also* **ngwana, ingwana**
naniibikim *vta* scold s.o.; *1sg* **ninaniibikimaa**; *prt* **neniibikimaad**
naniisido= < nisido=
naniizaanad *vii* be dangerous; *prt* **neniizaanak**
naniizaanendan *vti* consider s.t. dangerous; *1sg* **ninaniizaanendaan**; *prt* **neniizaanendang**
naniizaanendaagwad *vii* be considered dangerous; *prt* **neniizaanendaagwak**
naniizaanenim *vta* consider s.o. dangerous, think s.o. to be in danger; *1sg* **ninaniizaanenimaa**; *prt* **neniizaanenimaad**
naniizaanizi *vai* be dangerous; *1sg* **ninaniizaaniz**; *prt* **neniizaanizid**
napaazikan *vti* wear s.t. the wrong way; *1sg* **ninapaazikaan**; *prt* **nepaazikang**
napaazikaw *vta* wear s.o. the wrong way; *1sg* **ninapaazikawaa**; *prt* **nepaazikawaad**
napodin *na* dumpling; *pl* **napodinag**; *loc* **napodining**; *dim* **napodinens**
napodinike *vai* make dumplings; *1sg* **ninapodinike**; *prt* **nepodiniked**
nasanaamo *vai* exhale, recover one's breath; *1sg* **ninasanaam**; *prt* **nesanaamod**
nase'an *vti* stir s.t. to form sugar; *1sg* **ninase'aan**; *prt* **nese'ang**
nase'igan *ni* granulated maple sugar
nase'ige *vai* stir to form sugar; *1sg* **ninase'ige**; *prt* **nese'iged**

naseyaawangwaan *ni* sugaring trough; *pl* **naseyaawangwaanan**; *loc* **naseyaawangwaaning**; *dim* **naseyaawangwaanens**

naseyaawangwaan (sugaring trough)

naseyaawangwe *vai* granulate sugar; *1sg* **ninaseyaawangwe**; *prt* **neseyaawangwed**
nashke *pc* look!, behold!; *also* **inashke**
nawadam *vta* take hold of s.o. in mouth, take a bite of s.o.; *1sg* **ninawadamaa**; *prt* **newadamaad**
nawadandan *vti* take hold of s.t. in mouth, take a bite of s.t.; *1sg* **ninawadandaan**; *prt* **newadandang**
nawadanjige *vai* take hold of things in mouth, take a bite of things; *1sg* **ninawadanjige**; *prt* **newadanjiged**
nawadide *vii* catch fire; *prt* **newadideg**; *aug* **nawadidemagad**; *prt aug* **newadidemagak**
nawadin *vta* grab s.o., seize s.o.; *1sg* **ninawadinaa**; *prt* **newadinaad**
nawadinamaw *vta* grab (s.t.) of s.o.'s, seize (s.t.) of s.o.'s; *1sg* **ninawadinamawaa**; *prt* **newadinamawaad**
nawadinan *vti* grab s.t., seize s.t.; *1sg* **ninawadinaan**; *prt* **newadinang**
nawadiniwe *vai* grab people, seize people, take captives; *1sg* **ninawadiniwe**; *prt* **newadiniwed**
nawadizo *vai* catch fire; *prt* **newadizod**
nawaj *pc* more
nawajii *vai* take a lunch break; *1sg* **ninawajii**; *prt* **newajiid**
nawapo *vai* take a lunch along; *1sg* **ninawap**; *prt* **newapod**
nawapwaan *ni* lunch taken along; *pl* **nawapwaanan**; *dim* **nawapwaanens**
nawapwaanike *vai* make a lunch to take along; *1sg* **ninawapwaanike**; *prt* **newapwaaniked**
nayaag *pc* ahead of time
nayenzh *pc* both
nazhikewaakwadabi *vai* sit alone; *1sg* **ninazhikewaakwadab**; *prt* **nezhikewaakwadabid**
nazhikewige *vai* live alone; *1sg* **ninazhikewige**; *prt* **nezhikewiged**
nazhikewizi *vai* be alone; *1sg* **ninazhikewiz**; *prt* **nezhikewizid**
nazikwe' /nazikwe'w-/ *vta* comb s.o.'s hair; *1sg* **ninazikwe'waa**; *prt* **nezikwe'waad**
nazikwe'o *vai* comb one's hair; *1sg* **ninazikwe'**; *prt* **nezikwe'od**
naa *pc emphatic particle*
naaba'anidizo *vai* step in the same tracks; *1sg* **ninaaba'anidizo**; *prt* **nayaaba'anidizod**
naabe- *pv4* male
naabese *na* male bird, rooster; *pl* **naabeseg**; *dim* **naabesens**
naabesim *na* male dog, stallion; *pl* **naabesimoog**; *dim* **naabesimoons**
naabidoo' /naabidoo'w-/ *vta* thread s.o., string s.o. (e.g., beads); *1sg* **ninaabidoo'waa**; *prt* **nayaabidoo'waad**
naabidoo'an *vti* thread s.t., string s.t.; *1sg* **ninaabidoo'aan**; *prt* **nayaabidoo'ang**
naabidoo'igan *ni* beading needle; *pl* **naabidoo'iganan**; *loc* **naabidoo'iganing**; *dim* **naabidoo'igaans**
naabidoo'ige *vai* thread things, string things; *1sg* **ninaabidoo'ige**; *prt* **nayaabidoo'iged**
naabikan *vti* wear s.t. around one's neck; *1sg* **ninaabikaan**; *prt* **nayaabikang**
naabikaw *vta* wear s.o. around one's neck; *1sg* **ninaabikawaa**; *prt* **nayaabikawaad**
naabikawaagan *na* necktie, necklace; *pl* **naabikawaaganag**; *loc* **naabikawaaganing**; *dim* **naabikawaagaans**
naabikwaan *ni* ship, vessel; *pl* **naabikwaanan**; *loc* **naabikwaaning**; *dim* **naabikwaanens**
naabinootaw *vta* repeat what s.o. says, mock s.o.; *1sg* **ninaabinootawaa**; *prt* **nayaabinootawaad**
naabinootaage *vai* repeat what people say, mock people; *1sg* **ninaabinootaage**; *prt* **nayaabinootaaged**
naabinootaage-makak *ni* tape recorder; *pl* **naabinootaage-makakoon**; *loc* **naabinootaage-makakong**; *dim* **naabinootaage-makakoons**
naabishebizon *ni* earring; *pl* **naabishebizonan**; *loc* **naabishebizoning**; *dim* **naabishebizonens**
naabishkaw *vta* take s.o.'s place; *1sg* **ninaabishkawaa**; *prt* **nayaabishkawaad**
naabishkaage *vai* take someone's place; *1sg* **ninaabishkaage**; *prt* **nayaabishkaaged**
naabizhigan *ni* pattern (in sewing); *pl* **naabizhiganan**; *loc* **naabizhiganing**; *dim* **naabizhigaans**
naadagoodoo *vai* check one's snares; *1sg* **ninaadagoodoo**; *prt* **nayaadagoodood**
naada' /naada'w-/ *vta* go get s.o. by boat; *1sg* **ninaada'waa**; *prt* **nayaada'waad**
naada'an *vti* go get s.t. by boat; *1sg* **ninaada'aan**; *prt* **nayaada'ang**
naada'oodoon *vti2* go to get s.t. by boat; *1sg* **ninaada'oodoon**; *prt* **nayaada'oodood**
naada'oozh /naada'ooN-/ *vta* go to get s.o. by boat; *1sg* **ninaada'oonaa**; *prt* **nayaada'oonaad**
naadamaw *vta* help s.o.; *1sg* **ninaadamawaa**; *prt* **nayaadamawaad**
naadamaadiwag /naadamaadi-/ *vai* they help each other; *1pl* **ninaadamaadimin**; *prt* **nayaadamaadijig**

naadamaage *vai* help people; *1sg* **ninaadamaage**; *prt* **nayaadamaaged**
naadasabii *vai* go get a net, pick up a net; *1sg* **ninaadasabii**; *prt* **nayaadasabiid**
naadashkosiwe *vai* go after hay; *1sg* **ninaadashkosiwe**; *prt* **nayaadashkosiwed**
naadasoonaagane *vai* check one's traps, go get one's traps; *1sg* **ninaadasoonaagane**; *prt* **nayaadasoonaaganed**
naadaw *vta* go get (s.t.) for s.o., fetch (s.t.) for s.o.; *1sg* **ninaadawaa**; *prt* **nayaadawaad**
naadazina'igane *vai* go get mail; *1sg* **ninaadazina'igane**; *prt* **nayaadazina'iganed**
naadazina'ige *vai* go collect a debt; *1sg* **ninaadazina'ige**; *prt* **nayaadazina'iged**
naadin *vti3* go get s.t., fetch s.t., go after s.t.; *1sg* **ninaadin**; *prt* **nayaadid**
naadinise *vai* go get firewood; *1sg* **ninaadinise**; *prt* **nayaadinised**; *also* **naajinise**
naadoobii *vai* go get water or other liquid, gather sap; *1sg* **ninaadoobii**; *prt* **nayaadoobiid**
naagadawaabam *vta* observe s.o.; *1sg* **ninaagadawaabamaa**; *prt* **nayaagadawaabamaad**
naagadawaabandan *vti* observe s.t.; *1sg* **ninaagadawaabandaan**; *prt* **nayaagadawaabandang**
naagadawendam *vai2* think; *1sg* **ninaagadawendam**; *prt* **nayaagadawendang**
naagadawendan *vti* think about s.t.; *1sg* **ninaagadawendaan**; *prt* **nayaagadawendang**
naagadawenim *vta* think about s.o.; *1sg* **ninaagadawenimaa**; *prt* **nayaagadawenimaad**
naagaj *pc* later, after a while
naago' *vta* make s.o. show, reveal s.o.; *1sg* **ninaago'aa**; *prt* **nayaago'aad**
naagotoon *vti2* make s.t. show, reveal s.t.; *1sg* **ninaagotoon**; *prt* **nayaagotood**
naagozi *vai* be visible; *1sg* **ninaagoz**; *prt* **nayaagozid**
naagwad *vii* be visible; *prt* **nayaagwak**
naajibatwaadan *vti* run to get s.t.; *1sg* **ninaajibatwaadaan**; *prt* **nayaajibatwaadang**
naajibatwaazh /naajibatwaaN-/ *vta* run to get s.o.; *1sg* **ninaajibatwaanaa**; *prt* **nayaajibatwaanaad**
naajigaade *vii* be fetched, be picked up; *prt* **nayaajigaadeg**; *aug* **naajigaademagad**; *prt aug* **nayaajigaademagak**
naajigaazo *vai* be fetched, be picked up; *prt* **nayaajigaazod**
naajimiijime *vai* go get food; *1sg* **ninaajimiijime**; *prt* **nayaajimiijimed**
naajinizha'an *vti* go after s.t., send for s.t.; *1sg* **ninaajinizha'aan**; *prt* **nayaajinizha'ang**
naajinizha' /naajinizha'w-/ *vta* go after s.o., send for s.o.; *1sg* **ninaajinizha'waa**; *prt* **nayaajinizha'waad**
naajinizha'amaw *vta* order (s.t.) for s.o.; *1sg* **ninaajinizha'amawaa**; *prt* **nayaajinizha'amawaad**
naajinizha'ige *vai* order things; *1sg* **ninaajinizha'ige**; *prt* **nayaajinizha'iged**
naajiwanii'ige *vai* go after traps; *1sg* **ninaajiwanii'ige**; *prt* **nayaajiwanii'iged**
naan *nad* grandma (vocative of **nimaamaanaan** grandmother)
naanabem *pc* too late, it should have been done
naanan *nm* five
naananinoon /naananin-/ *vii* they are five; *prt* **nayaananingin**
naananiwag /naanani-/ *vai* they are five; *1pl* **ninaananimin**; *prt* **nayaananijig**
naanaabishebizo *vai* wear earrings; *1sg* **ninaanaabishebiz**; *prt* **nayaanaabishebizod**
naanaagadawaabam *vta* watch s.o. carefully, observe s.o.; *1sg* **ninaanaagadawaabamaa**; *prt* **nayaanaagadawaabamaad**
naanaagadawaabandan *vti* watch s.t. carefully, observe s.t.; *1sg* **ninaanaagadawaabandaan**; *prt* **nayaanaagadawaabandang**
naanaagadawendam *vai2* consider, think; *1sg* **ninaanaagadawendam**; *prt* **nayaanaagadawendang**
naanaagadawendan *vti* consider s.t., think about s.t.; *1sg* **ninaanaagadawendaan**; *prt* **nayaanaagadawendang**
naanaagadawenim *vta* consider s.o., think about s.o.; *1sg* **ninaanaagadawenimaa**; *prt* **nayaanaagadawenimaad**
naangan *vii* be light in weight; *prt* **nayaangang**
naangendan *vti* consider s.t. light in weight; *1sg* **ninaangendaan**; *prt* **nayaangendang**
naangenim *vta* consider s.o. light in weight; *1sg* **ninaangenimaa**; *prt* **nayaangenimaad**
naangide'e *vai* be carefree; *1sg* **ninaangide'e**; *prt* **nayaangide'ed**
naangiwane *vai* carry a light pack; *1sg* **ninaangiwane**; *prt* **nayaangiwaned**
naangizi *vai* be light in weight; *1sg* **ninaangiz**; *prt* **nayaangizid**
naanibaayawe *vai* yawn; *1sg* **ninaanibaayawe**; *prt* **nayaanibaayawed**
naanimidana *nm* fifty
naaning *pc* five times
naaningim *pc* often
naaningodinong* *pc* now and then, every once in a while, sometimes; *also* **naangodinong***
naano- *pv4* five
naano-anama'e-giizhigad *vii* be five weeks; *prt* **nayaano-anama'e-giizhigak**
naano-anama'e-giizhik *pc* five weeks
naano-biboon *pc* five years
naano-biboonagad *vii* be five years; *prt* **nayaano-biboonagak**
naano-biboonagizi *vai* be five years old; *1sg* **ninaano-biboonagiz**; *prt* **nayaano-biboonagizid**
naano-diba'igan *pc* five miles, five hours
naano-diba'iganed *vii* be five o'clock; *prt* **nayaano-diba'iganek**
naano-diba'igaans *pc* five minutes, five acres
naano-dibik *pc* five nights
naano-giizhigad *vii* be Friday; *prt* **nayaano-giizhigak**
naano-giizhik *pc* five days
naano-giizis *pc* five months
naanogon *pc* five days
naanogonagad *vii* be five days; *prt* **nayaanogonagak**

naanogonagizi *vai* be the fifth day of the month, be five days old; *prt* **nayaanogonagizid**
naanoninj *pc* five inches
naanosagoons *nm* five thousand
naanozid *pc* five feet
naanoobii'igan *na* five (card); *pl* **naanoobii'iganag**
naanoomaya *pc* a little while ago
naanooshkin *pc* five bags
naanwaabik *pc* five dollars
naanwaak *nm* five hundred
naanwewaan *pc* five sets, five pairs
naasanaa *pc* look out!, come on!
naasaab *pc* like, the same
naasaabibii'an *vti* copy s.t. in writing; *1sg* **ninaasaabibii'aan**; *prt* **nayaasaabibii'ang**
naasaabibii'ige *vai* copy things in writing; *1sg* **ninaasaabibii'ige**; *prt* **nayaasaabibii'iged**
naawagaam *pc* in the middle of the lake
naawakwe *vii* be noon; *prt* **nayaawakweg**; *aug* **naawakwemagad**; *prt aug* **nayaawakwemagak**
naawakwe-miijin *vti3* eat s.t. for dinner (noon meal), eat s.t. for lunch (noon meal); *1sg* **ninaawakwe-miijin**; *prt* **nayaawakwe-miijid**
naawakwe-wiisini *vai* eat dinner (noon meal), eat lunch (noon meal); *1sg* **ninaawakwe-wiisin**; *prt* **nayaawakwe-wiisinid**
naawashkosiw *pc* in the middle of a meadow
naawayi'ii *pc* in the middle of it
naawaakigan *pc* in the middle of the chest
naawaakwaa *pc* in the middle of the woods
naawaawigan *pc* in the middle of the back
naawi- *pn* in the middle of
naawigatig *pc* in the middle of the forehead
naawij *pc* out in the lake
naawikana *pc* in the middle of the road or trail
naawinaagozi *vai* be barely visible, be a distant sight; *1sg* **ninaawinaagoz**; *prt* **nayaawinaagozid**
naawinaagwad *vii* be barely visible, be a distant sight; *prt* **nayaawinaagwak**
naawininj *ni* middle finger; *pl* **naawininjiin**
naawisag *pc* in the middle of the floor
naawoonag *pc* in the middle of a boat
naayanh *pc* correct?, right?
naazh /naaN-/ *vta* go get s.o., fetch s.o., go after s.o.; *1sg* **ninaanaa**; *prt* **nayaanaad**
naazhaabii'igan *ni* violin, fiddle; *pl* **naazhaabii'iganan**; *loc* **naazhaabii'iganing**; *dim* **naazhaabii'igaans**
naazhiiga'igan *ni* hide stretcher; *pl* **naazhiiga'iganan**; *loc* **naazhiiga'iganing**; *dim* **naazhiiga'igaans**
naazhiiga'ige *vai* stretch a hide; *1sg* **ninaazhiiga'ige**; *prt* **nayaazhiiga'iged**
naazikan *vti* go to s.t., approach s.t.; *1sg* **ninaazikaan**; *prt* **nayaazikang**
naazikaw *vta* go to s.o., approach s.o.; *1sg* **ninaazikawaa**; *prt* **nayaazikawaad**
naazikaage *vai* go to people, approach people; *1sg* **ninaazikaage**; *prt* **nayaazikaaged**
negwaabam *vta* look malevolently out of corner of one's eye at s.o.; *1sg* **ninegwaabamaa**; *prt* **nayegwaabamaad**
negwaakwaan *ni* tap, spile (for sugaring); *pl* **negwaakwaanan**; *loc* **negwaakwaaning**; *dim* **negwaakwaanens**
nemaab *ni* marble, pool ball; *pl* **nemaabiin**
nemaabii *vai* play pool; *1sg* **ninemaabii**; *prt* **nayemaabiid**
nemaabiiwigamig *ni* pool hall; *pl* **nemaabiiwigamigoon**; *loc* **nemaabiiwigamigong**; *dim* **nemaabiiwigamigoons**
nenaandawi'iwed *na-pt* traditional healer; *pl* **nenaandawi'iwejig**
nenaapaajinikesi *na* mole; *pl* **nenaapaajinikesiwag**; *dim* **nenaapaajinikesiins**
nendodamaageshkid *na-pt* beggar; *pl* **nendodamaageshkijig**
neningo= < ingo=
neningodwaaso= < ingodwaaso=
neningodwaaswi *nm* six each
neniswi *nm* three each
neniibowa *pc* a whole lot
neniiwin *nm* four each
neniizh *nm* two each
neniizhwaaswi *nm* seven each
nenookaasi *na* hummingbird; *pl* **nenookaasiwag**; *dim* **nenookaasiins**
nesezo *vai* pant; *1sg* **ninesez**; *prt* **nayesezod**
neshangaa *vii* be limber, be slack; *prt* **nayeshangaag**; *aug* **neshangaamagad**; *prt aug* **nayeshangaamagak**
neshangaabiigad *vii* be slack (as something string-like); *prt* **nayeshangaabiigak**
neshangaabiigizi *vai* be slack (as something string-like); *prt* **nayeshangaabiigizid**
neshangishin *vai* be relaxed, lie limp; *1sg* **nineshangishin**; *prt* **nayeshangishing**
neshangisin *vii* lie limp, lie slack; *prt* **nayeshangising**
neshangizi *vai* be limber, be slack; *1sg* **nineshangiz**; *prt* **nayeshangizid**
newe *na* bull snake; *pl* **neweg**; *dim* **newens**
neyaab *pc* back to previous place or condition, as before
neyaashi *ni* point of land, peninsula; *pl* **neyaashiwan**; *loc* **neyaashiing**; *dim* **neyaashiins**
neyaashiiwan *vii* there is a peninsula, there is a point of land; *prt* **nayeyaashiiwang**
ni= *pre first person prefix*; *also* **ni=, in=, im=, n=, nin=*, nim=***
ni- *pv2* going away, coming up to in time; *also* **ani-**
nibaa *vai* sleep; *1sg* **ninibaa**; *prt* **nebaad**
nibaagan *ni* bed; *pl* **nibaaganan**; *loc* **nibaaganing**; *dim* **nibaagaans**
nibaaganaatig *ni* bed frame; *pl* **nibaaganaatigoon**; *loc* **nibaaganaatigong**; *dim* **nibaaganaatigoons**
nibe' *vta* make s.o. sleep, put s.o. to bed; *1sg* **ninibe'aa**; *prt* **nebe'aad**
nibekaazo *vai* pretend to sleep; *1sg* **ninibekaaz**; *prt* **nebekaazod**
nibendaw *vta* stay overnight with s.o.; *1sg* **ninibendawaa**; *prt* **nebendawaad**
nibendaage *vai* stay overnight with people; *1sg* **ninibendaage**; *prt* **nebendaaged**

nibeshkaw- *vta* make s.o. sleep *in inverse forms: 1sg* **ninibeshkaagon**; *prt* **nebeshkaagod**
nibewigamig *ni* bedroom; *pl* **nibewigamigoon**; *loc* **nibewigamigong**; *dim* **nibewigamigoons**
nibi *ni* water; *loc* **nibiing**
nibinaadi *vai* get water; *1sg* **ninibinaad**; *prt* **nebinaadid**
nibiikaa *vii* be much water; *prt* **nebiikaag**; *aug* **nibiikaamagad**; *prt aug* **nebiikaamagak**
nibiiwadamon /nibiiwadamo-/ *vii* be wet (as a road or trail); *prt* **nebiiwadamog**
nibiiwakamigaa *vii* be wet ground; *prt* **nebiiwakamigaag**; *aug* **nibiiwakamigaamagad**; *prt aug* **nebiiwakamigaamagak**
nibiiwakik *na* water pail; *pl* **nibiiwakikoog**; *loc* **nibiiwakikong**; *dim* **nibiiwakikoons**
nibiiwan *vii* be wet, be watery; *prt* **nebiiwang**
nibiiwi *vai* be wet; *1sg* **ninibiiw**; *prt* **nebiiwid**
nibo *vai* die, be dead; *1sg* **ninib**; *prt* **nebod**
nibooke *vai* have a death in one's family; *1sg* **ninibooke**; *prt* **nebooked**
niboowi *vai* be paralyzed; *1sg* **niniboow**; *prt* **neboowid**
niboowidaabaan *na* hearse; *pl* **niboowidaabaanag**; *loc* **niboowidaabaaning**; *dim* **niboowidaabaanens**
niboowigamig *ni* mortuary; *pl* **niboowigamigoon**; *loc* **niboowigamigong**
niboowigaade *vai* have a numb leg; *1sg* **niniboowigaade**; *prt* **neboowigaaded**
niboowinike *vai* have a numb arm; *1sg* **niniboowinike**; *prt* **neboowiniked**
niboowininjii *vai* have a numb hand; *1sg* **niniboowininjii**; *prt* **neboowininjiid**
niboowise *vai* have a stroke, become paralyzed, fall ill from bad medicine; *1sg* **niniboowise**; *prt* **neboowised**
niboowizide *vai* have a numb foot; *1sg* **niniboowizide**; *prt* **neboowizided**
nibwaakaa *vai* be wise, be intelligent; *1sg* **ninibwaakaa**; *prt* **nebwaakaad**
nichiiwad *vii* there is a severe storm, there is a catastrophe; *prt* **nechiiwak**
nigig *na* otter; *pl* **nigigwag**; *dim* **nigigoons**
nigigwayaan *na* otter hide; *pl* **nigigwayaanag**
nika *na* Canada goose; *pl* **nikag**; *dim* **nikens**
nikakwan /-kakwan-/ *nid* my shin; *pl* **nikakwanan**; *loc* **nikakwanaang**
nikan /-kan-/ *nid* my bone; *pl* **nikanan**; *loc* **nikaning**
nikanendi *vai* be gone overnight; *1sg* **ninikanend**; *prt* **nekanendid**
nikatig /-katigw-/ *nid* my forehead; *pl* **nikatigoon**; *loc* **nikatigwaang**
nikaad /-kaad-/ *nid* my leg; *pl* **nikaadan**; *loc* **nikaading**
nikaakigan /-kaakigan-/ *nid* my chest; *pl* **nikaakiganan**; *loc* **nikaakiganaang**
nikibii *vai* be flooded; *prt* **nekibiid**
nikibii *vii* be flooded; *prt* **nekibiig**; *aug* **nikibiimagad**; *prt aug* **nekibiimagak**
nikidin /-kidin-/ *nad* my vulva
nikon /-kon-/ *nid* my liver; *pl* **nikonan**; *loc* **nikoning**
nikonaas /-konaas-/ *nid* my blanket; *pl* **nikonaasan**
nikoonzh /-koonzh-/ *nid* my bill, my beak; *loc* **nikoonzhing**
nikwegan /-kwegan-/ *nid* the back of my neck; *pl* **nikweganan**; *loc* **nikweganaang**
nimaamaa /-maamaay-/ *nad* my mother; *pl* **nimaamaayag**
nimaamaa /-maamaay-/ *nad* my eyebrow hair; *pl* **nimaamaayag**
niminaawe'o *vai* paddle out from shore; *1sg* **niniminaawe'**; *prt* **neminaawe'od**
niminaaweyaadagaako *vai* go out from shore on the ice; *1sg* **niniminaaweyaadagaak**; *prt* **neminaaweyaadagaakod**
niminaaweyaandawaagan *ni* dock; *pl* **niminaaweyaandawaaganan**; *loc* **niminaaweyaandawaaganing**; *dim* **niminaaweyaandawaagaans**
nimisad /-misad-/ *nid* my stomach; *pl* **nimisadan**; *loc* **nimisadaang**
nimisenh /-miseny-/ *nad* my older sister, my older female parallel cousin; *pl* **nimisenyag**
nimishoo *nad* grandpa *vocative of* **nimishoomis**
nimishoome /-mishoomey-/ *nad* my parallel uncle (father's brother); *pl* **nimishoomeyag**
nimishoomis /-mishoomis-/ *nad* my grandfather; *pl* **nimishoomisag**
nimiishigwaan /-miishigwaan-/ *nid* my pubic hair; *pl* **nimiishigwaanan**
ninaga'ayag /-naga'ay-/ *nad* my scales *plural*
ninagaskway /-nagaskway-/ *nid* my palate; *loc* **ninagaskwaang**
ninagaakininj /-nagaakininjy-/ *nid* my palm; *pl* **ninagaakininjiin**; *loc* **ninagaakininjiing**
ninagaakizid /-nagaakizid-/ *nid* my sole; *pl* **ninagaakizidan**; *loc* **ninagaakizidaang**
ninagizh /-nagizhy-/ *nid* my intestine; *pl* **ninagizhiin**; *loc* **ninagizhiing**
ninagway /-nagway-/ *nid* my sleeve; *pl* **ninagwayan**; *loc* **ninagwaang**; *dim* **ninagwens**
ninashkid /-nashkidy-/ *nid* my tail (of a bird); *pl* **ninashkidiin**; *loc* **ninashkidiing**
ninasid /-nasid-/ *nid* my hoof; *loc* **ninasidaang**
ninaabem /-naabem-/ *nad* my husband; *pl* **ninaabemag**
ninaan /-naan-/ *nad* my calf; *pl* **ninaanag**; *loc* **ninaaning**
nindigo *pc* as if, just like; *also* **indigo**
ningaabii'an *ni* west; *loc* **ningaabii'anong**
ningaasimoo-jiimaan *ni* sailboat; *pl* **ningaasimoo-jiimaanan**; *loc* **ningaasimoo-jiimaaning**; *dim* **ningaasimoo-jiimaanens**
ningaasimoono *vai* sail (in a boat); *1sg* **niningaasimoon**; *prt* **nengaasimoonod**
ningaasimoonowin *ni* sail; *loc* **ningaasimoonowining**; *dim* **ningaasimoonowinens**
ningaasimoowinini *na* sailor; *pl* **ningaasimoowininiwag**
ningide *vii* melt, thaw; *prt* **nengideg**; *aug* **ningidemagad**; *prt aug* **nengidemagak**
ningiz /ningizw-/ *vta* melt s.o.; *1sg* **niningizwaa**; *prt* **nengizwaad**
ningizan *vti* melt s.t.; *1sg* **niningizaan**; *prt* **nengizang**
ningizo *vai* melt, thaw; *prt* **nengizod**

ningiigwadin *vii* be frosted; *prt* **nengiigwading**
ningiigwaji *vai* be frosted; *prt* **nengiigwajid**
ningo-* *pv4* one; *also* **ingo-**
ningo-anama'e-giizhik* *pc* one week; *also* **ingo-anama'e-giizhik**
ningo-biboon* *pc* one year; *also* **ingo-biboon**
ningo-biboonagad* *vii* be one year; *prt* **nengo-biboonagak**; *also* **ingo-biboonagad**
ningo-diba'igan* *pc* one hour, one mile; *also* **ingo-diba'igan**
ningo-diba'iganed* *vii* be one o'clock; *prt* **nengo-diba'iganek**; *also* **ingo-diba'iganed**
ningo-diba'igaans* *pc* one minute, one acre; *also* **ingo-diba'igaans**
ningo-dibik* *pc* one night; *also* **ingo-dibik**
ningoding* *pc* sometime, at one time; *also* **ingoding**
ningodoninj* *pc* one inch; *also* **ingodoninj**
ningodozid* *pc* one foot; *also* **ingodozid**
ningodooshkin* *pc* one bag; *also* **ingodooshkin**
ningodwaaching* *pc* six times; *also* **ingodwaaching**
ningodwaachinoon* /ningodwaachin-/ *vii* they are six; *prt* **nengodwaachingin**; *also* **ingodwaachinoon**
ningodwaachiwag* /ningodwaachi-/ *vai* they are six; *1pl* **niningodwaachimin**; *prt* **nengodwaachijig**; *also* **ingodwaachiwag**
ningodwaak* *nm* one hundred; *also* **ingodwaak**
ningodwaasimidana* *nm* sixty; *also* **ingodwaasimidana**
ningodwaaso-* *pv4* six; *also* **ingodwaaso-**
ningodwaaso-anama'e-giizhik* *pc* six weeks; *also* **ingodwaaso-anama'e-giizhik**
ningodwaasosagoons* *nm* six thousand; *also* **ingodwaasosagoons**
ningodwaasoobii'igan* *na* six (card); *pl* **ningodwaasoobii'iganag**
ningodwaasooshkin* *pc* six bags; *also* **ingodwaasooshkin**
ningodwaaswaabik* *pc* six dollars; *also* **ingodwaaswaabik**
ningodwaaswaak* *nm* six hundred; *also* **ingodwaaswaak**
ningodwaaswewaan* *pc* six sets, six pairs; *also* **ingodwaaswewaan**
ningodwaaswi* *nm* six; *also* **ingodwaaswi**
ningodwewaan* *pc* one pair, one set; *also* **ingodwewaan**
ningo-giizhik* *pc* one day; *also* **ingo-giizhik**
ningo-giizis* *pc* one month; *also* **ingo-giizis**
ningoji* *pc* somewhere; *also* **ingoji**
ningwa' /ningwa'w-/ *vta* bury s.o.; *1sg* **niningwa'waa**; *prt* **nengwa'waad**
ningwa'abwaan *na* bread baked under the ashes; *pl* **ningwa`abwaanag**
ningwa'abwe *vai+o* cook (s.t.) under the ashes; *1sg* **niningwa'abwe, niningwa'abwen**; *prt* **nengwa'abwed**
ningwa'an *vti* bury s.t.; *1sg* **niningwa'aan**; *prt* **nengwa'ang**
ningwa'igaazo *vai* be buried; *prt* **nengwa'igaazod**
ningwaja' /ningwaja'w-/ *vta* hoe s.o.; *1sg* **niningwaja'waa**; *prt* **nengwaja'waad**
ningwaja'an *vti* hoe s.t.; *1sg* **niningwaja'aan**; *prt* **nengwaja'ang**
ningwaja'ige *vai* hoe; *1sg* **niningwaja'ige**; *prt* **nengwaja'iged**
ningwakamigin *vta* put s.o. under the ground; *1sg* **niningwakamiginaa**; *prt* **nengwakamiginaad**
ningwaanakwad *vii* be cloudy; *prt* **nengwaanakwak**
ninik /-nik-/ *nid* my arm; *pl* **ninikan**; *loc* **ninikaang**
ninING /-ningwy-/ *nid* my armpit; *pl* **niningwiin**; *loc* **niningwiing**
niningwan *nad* my son-in-law; *pl* **niningwanag**
niningwanis /-ningwanis-/ *nad* my cross-nephew (male's sister's son or female's brother's son); *pl* **niningwanisag**
niningwiigan /-ningwiigan-/ *nid* my wing; *pl* **niningwiiganan**; *loc* **niningwiiganaang**
nininj /-ninjy-/ *nid* my hand, my finger; *pl* **nininjiin**; *loc* **nininjiing**; *dim* **nininjiins**
nininjiins /-ninjiins-/ *nid* my finger; *pl* **nininjiinsan**; *loc* **nininjiinsing**
ninishiwag /-nishiw-/ *nad* my testicles *plural*; *loc* **ninishiwaang**
niniigi'igoog /-niigi'igw-/ *nad* my parents *plural*
niniijaanis /-niijaanis-/ *nad* my child; *pl* **niniijaanisag**; *dim* **niniijaanisens**
niniishk /-niishkw-/ *nad* my gland (lymph node); *pl* **niniishkwag**
ninoshenh /-nosheny-/ *nad* my parallel aunt (mother's sister); *pl* **ninoshenyag**
ninow /-now-/ *nid* my cheek; *pl* **ninowan**; *loc* **ninowaang**
ninoogan /-noogan-/ *nid* my hip; *pl* **ninooganan**; *loc* **ninooganaang**
nipan /-pan-/ *nid* my lung; *pl* **nipanan**; *loc* **nipaning**
nipigemag /-pigemagw-/ *nid* my rib; *pl* **nipigemagoon**; *loc* **nipigemagong**
nipikwan /-pikwan-/ *nid* my back; *pl* **nipikwanan**; *loc* **nipikwanaang**
nisawa'ogaan *ni* lodge with peaked roof; *pl* **nisawa'ogaanan**; *loc* **nisawa'ogaaning**; *dim* **nisawa'ogaanens**
nisawayi'ii *pc* in between it
nisayenh /-sayeny-/ *nad* my older brother, my older male parallel cousin; *pl* **nisayenyag**
nisaabaawe *vai* get wet; *1sg* **ninisaabaawe**; *prt* **nesaabaawed**
nisaabaawe *vii* get wet; *prt* **nesaabaaweg**; *aug* **nisaabaawemagad**; *prt aug* **nesaabaawemagak**
nishi /niS-/ *vta* kill s.o.; *1sg* **ninisaa**; *prt* **nesaad**
nishimis /-shimis-/ *nad* my cross-niece (female's brother's daughter or male's sister's daughter); *pl* **nishimisag**
nishiwe *vai* kill people; *1sg* **ninishiwe**; *prt* **neshiwed**
nishiime /-shiimey-/ *nad* my younger sibling, my younger brother, my younger sister, my younger parallel cousin; *pl* **nishiimeyag**
nishkanzh /-shkanzhy-/ *nad* my nail (fingernail, toenail), my claw; *pl* **nishkanzhiig**; *loc* **nishkanzhiing**
nishkatay /-shkatay-/ *nid* my skin
nishkaadizi *vai* be angry, be mad; *1sg* **ninishkaadiz**; *prt* **neshkaadizid**

nishkaajitaa *vai* behave angrily, act up in anger; *1sg* **ninishkaajitaa**; *prt* **neshkaajitaad**
nishkendam *vai2* feel angry, feel mad; *1sg* **ninishkendam**; *prt* **neshkendang**
nishkenim *vta* be angry at s.o., be mad at s.o.; *1sg* **ninishkenimaa**; *prt* **neshkenimaad**
nishki' *vta* anger s.o., make s.o. mad; *1sg* **ninishki'aa**; *prt* **neshki'aad**
nishki'idiwag /nishki'idi-/ *vai* they anger each other, they make each other mad; *1pl* **ninishki'idimin**; *prt* **neshki'idijig**
nishkim *vta* anger s.o. by speech, speak and make s.o. mad; *1sg* **ninishkimaa**; *prt* **neshkimaad**
nishkitaa *vai* anger people, make people mad; *1sg* **ninishkitaa**; *prt* **neshkitaad**
nishkiinzhig /-shkiinzhigw-/ *nid* my eye; *pl* **nishkiinzhigoon**; *loc* **nishkiinzhigong**
nishkoonzh *nid* my snout
nishtigwaan /-shtigwaan-/ *nid* my head; *pl* **nishtigwaanan**; *loc* **nishtigwaaning**
nishtigwaanigegan /-shtigwaanigegan-/ *nid* my skull; *pl* **nishtigwaanigeganan**
nishwanaajichige *vai* waste things, spoil things, destroy things; *1sg* **ninishwanaajichige**; *prt* **neshwanaajichiged**
nishwanaaji' *vta* waste s.o., spoil s.o., destroy s.o.; *1sg* **ninishwanaaji'aa**; *prt* **neshwanaaji'aad**
nishwanaajitoon *vti2* waste s.t., spoil s.t., destroy s.t.; *1sg* **ninishwanaajitoon**; *prt* **neshwanaajitood**
nishwaaching* *pc* eight times; *also* **ishwaaching**
nishwaachinoon* /nishwaachin-/ *vii* they are eight; *prt* **neshwaachingin**; *also* **ishwaachinoon**
nishwaachiwag* /nishwaachi-/ *vai* they are eight; *1pl* **ninishwaachimin**; *prt* **neshwaachijig**; *also* **ishwaachiwag**
nishwaasimidana* *nm* eighty; *also* **ishwaasimidana**
nishwaaso-* *pv4* eight; *also* **ishwaaso-**
nishwaaso-anama'e-giizhik* *pc* eight weeks; *also* **ishwaaso-anama'e-giizhik**
nishwaaso-biboon* *pc* eight years; *also* **ishwaaso-biboon**
nishwaaso-biboonagad* *vii* be eight years; *prt* **neshwaaso-biboonagak**; *also* **ishwaaso-biboonagad**
nishwaaso-biboonagizi* *vai* be eight years old; *1sg* **ninishwaaso-biboonagiz**; *prt* **neshwaaso-biboonagizid**; *also* **ishwaaso-biboonagizi**
nishwaaso-diba'igan* *pc* eight miles, eight hours; *also* **ishwaaso-diba'igan**
nishwaaso-diba'iganed* *vii* be eight o'clock; *prt* **neshwaaso-diba'iganek**; *also* **ishwaaso-diba'iganed**
nishwaaso-diba'igaans* *pc* eight minutes, eight acres; *also* **ishwaaso-diba'igaans**
nishwaaso-dibik* *pc* eight nights; *also* **ishwaaso-dibik**
nishwaaso-giizhik* *pc* eight days; *also* **ishwaaso-giizhik**
nishwaaso-giizis* *pc* eight months; *also* **ishwaaso-giizis**
nishwaasogon* *pc* eight days; *also* **ishwaasogon**
nishwaasogonagad* *vii* be eight days; *prt* **neshwaasogonagak**; *also* **ishwaasogonagad**
nishwaasogonagizi* *vai* be the eighth day of the month, be eight days old; *prt* **neshwaasogonagizid**; *also* **ishwaasogonagizi**
nishwaasoninj* *pc* eight inches; *also* **ishwaasoninj**
nishwaasosagoons* *nm* eight thousand; *also* **ishwaasosagoons**
nishwaasozid* *pc* eight feet; *also* **ishwaasozid**
nishwaasoobii'igan* *na* eight (card); *pl* **nishwaasoobii'iganag**; *also* **ishwaasoobii'igan**
nishwaasooshkin *pc* eight bags; *also* **ishwaasooshkin**
nishwaaswaabik* *pc* eight dollars; *also* **ishwaaswaabik**
nishwaaswaak* *nm* eight hundred; *also* **ishwaaswaak**
nishwaaswewaan* *pc* eight sets, eight pairs; *also* **ishwaaswewaan**
nishwaaswi* *nm* eight; *also* **ishwaaswi**
nisidawinan *vti* recognize s.t. by sight; *1sg* **ninisidawinaan**; *prt* **nesidawinang**
nisidawinaw *vta* recognize s.o. by sight; *1sg* **ninisidawinawaa**; *prt* **nesidawinawaad**
nisidawinaadiwag /nisidawinaadi-/ *vai* they recognize each other; *1pl* **ninisidawinaadimin**; *prt* **nesidawinaadijig**
nisidiwag /nisidi-/ *vai* they kill each other; *1pl* **ninisidimin**; *prt* **nesidijig**
nisidizo *vai* kill oneself, commit suicide; *1sg* **ninisidiz**; *prt* **nesidizod**
nisidomaam *vta* recognize s.o. by smell; *1sg* **ninisidomaamaa**; *prt* **nesidomaamaad**
nisidomaandan *vti* recognize s.t. by smell; *1sg* **ninisidomaandaan**; *prt* **nesidomaandang**
nisidotam *vai2* understand; *1sg* **ninisidotam**; *prt* **nesidotang**
nisidotan *vti* understand s.t., recognize s.t. by sound; *1sg* **ninisidotaan**; *prt* **nesidotang**
nisidotaw *vta* understand s.o., recognize s.o. by sound; *1sg* **ninisidotawaa**; *prt* **nesidotawaad**
nisidotaadiwag /nisidotaadi-/ *vai* they understand each other; *1pl* **ninisidotaadimin**; *prt* **nesidotaadijig**
nisidotaagozi *vai* be understood; *prt* **nesidotaagozid**
nisidotaagwad *vii* be understood; *prt* **nesidotaagwak**
nisimidana *nm* thirty
nisinoon /nisin-/ *vii* they are three; *prt* **nesingin**
nising *pc* three times, thrice
nisiwag /nisi-/ *vai* they are three; *1pl* **ninisimin**; *prt* **nesijig**
niso- *pv4* three
niso-anama'e-giizhigad *vii* be three weeks; *prt* **neso-anama'e-giizhigak**
niso-anama'e-giizhik *pc* three weeks
niso-biboon *pc* three years
niso-biboonagad *vii* be three years; *prt* **neso-biboonagak**
niso-biboonagizi *vai* be three years old; *1sg* **niniso-biboonagiz**; *prt* **neso-biboonagizid**
niso-diba'igan *pc* three hours, three miles
niso-diba'iganed *vii* be three o'clock; *prt* **neso-diba'iganek**

niso-diba'igaans *pc* three minutes, three acres
niso-dibik *pc* three nights
niso-giizhik *pc* three days
niso-giizis *pc* three months
nisogon *pc* three days
nisogonagad *vii* be three days; *prt* **nesogonagak**
nisogonagizi *vai* be the third day of the month, be three days old; *prt* **nesogonagizid**
nisoninj *pc* three inches
nisosagoons *nm* three thousand
nisozid *pc* three feet
nisoobii'igan *na* three (card), trey; *pl* **nisoobii'iganag**
nisooshkin *pc* three bags
niswaabik *pc* three dollars
niswaak *nm* three hundred
niswaakodaabaan *ni* travois; *pl* **niswaakodaabaanan**
niswewaan *pc* three sets, three pairs
niswi *nm* three
nitam *pc* first
nitamaw *vta* kill (s.t.) for s.o.; *1sg* **ninitamawaa**; *prt* **netamawaad**
nitamaage *vai* kill (s.t.) for people; *1sg* **ninitamaage**; *prt* **netamaaged**
nitamaazo *vai* kill (s.t.) for oneself; *1sg* **ninitamaaz**; *prt* **netamaazod**
nitamige *vai* live in the first house; *1sg* **ninitamige**; *prt* **netamiged**
nitamoozhaan *na* eldest child, first-born; *pl* **nitamoozhaanag**; *dim* **nitamoozhaanens**
nitawag /-tawag-/ *nid* my ear; *pl* **nitawagan**; *loc* **nitawagaang**
nitaa- *pv4* know how to do something, being good at, being skilled at, frequently do
nitaage *vai* kill game, mourn; *1sg* **ninitaage**; *prt* **netaaged**
nitaawe *vai* be skilled in speaking or singing; *1sg* **ninitaawe**; *prt* **netaawed**
nitaawichige *vai* be skilled at things, know how to make things; *1sg* **ninitaawichige**; *prt* **netaawichiged**
nitaawigi *vai* grow up; *1sg* **ninitaawig**; *prt* **netaawigid**
nitaawigi' *vta* grow s.o., raise s.o. (e.g., a child); *1sg* **ninitaawigi'aa**; *prt* **netaawigi'aad**
nitaawigin *vii* grow up; *prt* **netaawiging**
nitaawigitoon *vti2* grow s.t., raise s.t. (e.g., a crop); *1sg* **ninitaawigitoon**; *prt* **netaawigitood**
nitaawi' *vta* know how to make s.o.; *1sg* **ninitaawi'aa**; *prt* **netaawi'aad**
nitaawitoon *vti2* know how to make s.t.; *1sg* **ninitaawitoon**; *prt* **netaawitood**
nitoon *vti2* kill s.t.; *1sg* **ninitoon**; *prt* **netood**
niwiidigemaagan /-wiidigemaagan-/ *na* my spouse, my wife, my husband, my companion; *pl* **niwiidigemaaganag**
niwiiw /-wiiw-/ *nad* my wife; *pl* **niwiiwag**
niibawi *vai* stand; *1sg* **niniibaw**; *prt* **naabawid**
niibawi' *vta* make s.o. stand up; *1sg* **niniibawi'aa**; *prt* **naabawi'aad**
niibawitoon *vti2* make s.t. stand up; *1sg* **niniibawitoon**; *prt* **naabawitood**
niibaa- *pv4* at night
niibaa-anama'e-giizhigad *vii* be Christmas; *prt* **naabaa-anama'e-giizhigak**
niibaabizo *vai* drive at night; *1sg* **niniibaabiz**; *prt* **naabaabizod**
niibaa-dibik *pc* late at night
niibaashkaa *vai* travel at night; *1sg* **niniibaashkaa**; *prt* **naabaashkaad**
niibid /-iibid-/ *nid* my tooth; *pl* **niibidan**; *loc* **niibidaang**
niibidebiwag /niibidebi-/ *vai* they sit side by side in a row; *1pl* **niniibidebimin**; *prt* **naabidebijig**
niibideshinoog /niibideshin-/ *vai* they lie side-by-side in a row; *1pl* **niniibideshinimin**; *prt* **naabideshingig**
niibidesinoon /niibidesin-/ *vii* they lie side by side in a row; *prt* **naabidesingin**
niibidoon *vti2* weave s.t.; *1sg* **niniibidoon**; *prt* **naabidood**
niibin *vii* be summer; *prt* **naabing**
niibinaakwaaninj *ni* finger; *pl* **niibinaakwaanininjiin**; *loc* **niibinakwaaninjiing**; *dim* **niibinaakwaaninjiins**
niibinaakwaanizidaan *ni* toe; *pl* **niibinaakwaanizidaanan**; *loc* **niibinaakwaanizidaaning**; *dim* **niibinaakwaanizidaanens**
niibinishi *vai* spend the summer somewhere; *1sg* **niniibinish**; *prt* **naabinishid**
niibinishiiwigamig *ni* cottage, resort; *pl* **niibinishiiwigamigoon**; *loc* **niibinishiiwigamigong**; *dim* **niibinishiiwigamigoons**
niibinong *pc* last summer
niibowa *pc* many, much; *also* **niibiwa***
niibowagadoon /niibowagad-/ *vii* they are many, there is much of it; *prt* **naabowagakin**
niibowagiziwag /niibowagizi-/ *vai* they are many, there is much of it; *prt* **naabowagizijig**
niigaan *pc* ahead, leading, at the front
niigaanabi *vai* sit in front; *1sg* **niniigaanab**; *prt* **naagaanabid**
niigaanagoode *vii* hang in front; *prt* **naagaanagoodeg**; *aug* **niigaanagoodemagad**; *prt aug* **naagaanagoodemagak**
niigaanagoozh /niigaanagooN-/ *vta* hang s.o. in front; *1sg* **niniigaanagoonaa**; *prt* **naagaanagoonaad**
niigaanagoodoon *vti2* hang s.t. in front; *1sg* **niniigaanagoodoon**; *prt* **naagaanagoodood**
niigaanagoojin *vai* hang in front; *prt* **naagaanagoojing**
niigaanigaabawi *vai* stand in front; *1sg* **niniigaanigaabaw**; *prt* **naagaanigaabawid**
niigaaniwizh /nigaaniwiN-/ *vta* lead s.o.; *1sg* **niniigaaniwinaa**; *prt* **naagaaniwinaad**
niigaanii *vai* go ahead, lead; *1sg* **niniigaanii**; *prt* **naagaaniid**
niigi *vai* be born, increase in number; *1sg* **niniig**; *prt* **naagid**
niigi' *vta* bear s.o., make s.o. grow, make s.o. increase in number; *1sg* **niniigi'aa**; *prt* **naagi'aad**
niigitoon *vti2* make s.t. grow, make s.t. increase in number; *1sg* **niniigitoon**; *prt* **naagitood**

niigode *vii* break by heat; *prt* **naagodeg**; *aug* **niigodemagad**; *prt aug* **naagodemagak**
niigoshin *vai* break on impact; *prt* **naagoshing**
niigoshkan *vti* break s.t. with foot or body; *1sg* **niniigoshkaan**; *prt* **naagoshkang**
niigoshkaa *vii* be broken; *prt* **naagoshkaag**; *aug* **niigoshkaamagad**; *prt aug* **naagoshkaamagak**
niigosidoon *vti2* break s.t. by dropping; *1sg* **niniigosidoon**; *prt* **naagosidood**
niigosin *vii* break on impact; *prt* **naagosing**
niigozo *vai* break by heat; *prt* **naagozod**
niiji- *pn* my fellow
niijikiwenh /-iijikiweny-/ *nad* my (male's) brother, my (male's) male friend; *pl* **niijikiwenyag**
niijikwe /-iijikwew-/ *nad* my (female's) female friend; *pl* **niijikweg**
niijii *nad* my friend *vocative form, usually male to male*
niijiinini *nad* my fellow man
niikaan /-iikaan-/ *nad* my (male's) male friend *ritual use*, my (male's) brother *ritual use*; *pl* **niikaanag**
niikaanis /-iikaanis-/ *nad* my (male's) brother *ritual use*, my (male's) male friend *ritual use*; *pl* **niikaanisag**
niikimo *vai* growl (of a dog); *1sg* **niniikim**; *prt* **naakimod**
niima' /niima'w-/ *vta* pick s.o. up using something, carry s.o. using something; *1sg* **niniima'waa**; *prt* **naama'waad**
niima'an *vti* pick s.t. up using something, carry s.t. using something; *1sg* **niniima'aan**; *prt* **naama'ang**
niimam *vta* pick s.o. up in mouth, carry s.o. in mouth; *1sg* **niniimamaa**; *prt* **naamamaad**
niimandan *vti* pick s.t. up in mouth, carry s.t. in mouth; *1sg* **niniimandaan**; *prt* **naamandang**
niimaakwa' /niimaakwa'w-/ *vta* pick s.o. up (as or as with something stick- or wood-like); *1sg* **niniimaakwa'waa**; *prt* **naamaakwa'waad**
niimaakwa'an *vti* pick s.t. up (as or as with something stick- or wood-like); *1sg* **niniimaakwa'aan**; *prt* **naamaakwa'ang**
niimi *vai* dance; *1sg* **niniim**; *prt* **naamid**
niimibaashkizigane *vai* take along a gun; *1sg* **niniimibaashkizigane**; *prt* **naamibaashkiziganed**
niimidana *nm* forty
niimi'idii-nagamon *ni* dance song; *pl* **niimi'idii-nagamonan**
niimi' *vta* make s.o. dance; *1sg* **niniimi'aa**; *prt* **naami'aad**
niimi'idiwag /niimi'idi-/ *vai* they dance; *1pl* **niniimi'idimin**; *prt* **naami'idijig**
niimi'idiiwigamig *ni* dance hall; *pl* **niimi'idiiwigamigoon**; *loc* **niimi'idiiwigamigong**; *dim* **niimi'idiiwigamigoons**
niimi'iwe *vai* give a dance; *1sg* **niniimi'iwe**; *prt* **naami'iwed**
niimikaw *vta* dance for s.o.; *1sg* **niniimikawaa**; *prt* **naamikawaad**
niimikaage *vai* dance for people (for a purpose); *1sg* **niniimikaage**; *prt* **naamikaaged**
niin *pr* I, me *first person singular personal pronoun*
niinag /-iinag-/ *nid* my penis; *loc* **niinagaang**
niinamad *vii* be weak; *prt* **naanamak**
niinaminaagozi *vai* look weak; *1sg* **niniinaminaagoz**; *prt* **naanaminaagozid**
niinaminaagwad *vii* look weak; *prt* **naanaminaagwak**
niinamizi *vai* be weak, be frail; *1sg* **niniinamiz**; *prt* **naanamizid**
niinawind *pr* we *first person exclusive plural pronoun*, us *first person exclusive plural pronoun*
niindaa' *vta* send (s.t.) to s.o.; *1sg* **niniindaa'aa**; *prt* **naandaa'aad**
niindaa'iwe *vai* send (s.t.) to people; *1sg* **niniindaa'iwe**; *prt* **naandaa'iwed**
niineta *pr* only me *first person singular personal pronoun*
niinetawind *pr* only us *first person exclusive plural personal pronoun*
niingidawadamon /niingidawadamo-/ *vii* fork (as a road or trail); *prt* **naangidawadamog**
niingidawitigweyaa *vii* fork (as a river); *prt* **naangidawitigweyaag**; *aug* **niingidawitigweyaamagad**; *prt aug* **naangidawitigweyaamagak**
niinim /-iinimw-/ *nad* my sibling-in-law of the opposite sex, my (female's) brother-in-law, my (male's) sister-in-law; *pl* **niinimoog**
niinimoshenh /-iinimosheny-/ *nad* my sweetheart, my cross-cousin of the opposite sex; *pl* **niinimoshenyag**
niinindib /-iinindib-/ *nid* my brain; *loc* **niinindibaang**
niinitam *pr* my turn *first person singular personal pronoun*
niinitamawind *pr* our turn *first person exclusive plural personal pronoun*
niinizis /-iinisiz-/ *nid* my (strand of) hair; *pl* **niinizisan**; *loc* **niinizising**
niinzob /-iinzoby-/ *nid* my gallbladder; *pl* **niinzobiin**; *loc* **niinzobiing**
niisayi'ii *pc* down from it
niisaajiwan *pc* downstream
niisaakiiwe *vai* go downhill; *1sg* **niniisaakiiwe**; *prt* **naasaakiiwed**
niisaakiiwebatoo *vai* run downhill; *1sg* **niniisaakiiwebatoo**; *prt* **naasaakiiwebatood**
niisaandawe *vai* climb down, go downstairs; *1sg* **niniisaandawe**; *prt* **naasaandawed**
niisaandawebatoo *vai* run down; *1sg* **niniisaandawebatoo**; *prt* **naasaandawebatood**
niisaandawebizo *vai* climb down fast; *1sg* **niniisaandawebiz**; *prt* **naasaandawebizod**
niisaanendam *vai* feel depressed; *1sg* **niniisaanendam**; *prt* **naasaanendang**
niishtana *nm* twenty
niishtana-ashi-niizh *ni* twenty-two (gun)
niisibidoon *vti2* pull s.t. down, tear s.t. down; *1sg* **niniisibidoon**; *prt* **naasibidood**
niisibizh /niisibiN-/ *vta* pull s.o. down, tear s.o. down; *1sg* **niniisibinaa**; *prt* **naasibinaad**
niisiiwe-minjikaawan *na* glove; *pl* **niisiiwe-minjikaawanag**
niisiiwezh /niisiiwezhw-/ *vta* cut fringe in s.o.; *1sg* **niniisiiwezhwaa**; *prt* **naasiiwezhwaad**

niisiiwezhan *vti* cut fringe in s.t.; *1sg* **niniisiiwezhaan**; *prt* **naasiiwezhang**
niisiiwezhigan *ni* fringe; *pl* **niisiiwezhiganan**; *loc* **niisiiwezhiganing**; *dim* **niisiiwezhigaans**
niisiiwezhigaade *vii* be fringed; *prt* **naasiiwezhigaadeg**; *aug* **niisiiwezhigaademagad**; *prt aug* **naasiiwezhigaademagak**
niisiiwezhigaazo *vai* be fringed; *prt* **naasiiwezhigaazod**
niiskaadad *vii* be bad weather; *prt* **naaskaadak**
niiskindibe *vai* have messy hair; *1sg* **niniiskindibe**; *prt* **naaskindibed**
niitaa /-iitaaw-/ *nad* my (male's) brother-in-law; *pl* **niitaag**
niitaawis /-iitaawis-/ *nad* my (male's) male cross-cousin (male's father's sister's son or male's mother's brother's son); *pl* **niitaawisag**
niiwana' /niiwana'w-/ *vta* slaughter s.o., beat s.o. to death; *1sg* **niniiwana'waa**; *prt* **naawana'waad**
niiwanishin *vai* die in an accident; *1sg* **niniiwanishin**; *prt* **naawanishing**
niiwaabik *pc* four dollars
niiwaak *nm* four hundred
niiwewaan *pc* four sets, four pairs
niiwezh /niiweN-/ *vta* defeat s.o. in a contest or game, beat s.o.; *1sg* **niniiwenaa**; *prt* **naawenaad**
niiwezhiwe *vai* defeat people in a contest or game; *1sg* **niniiwezhiwe**; *prt* **naawezhiwed**
niiwin *nm* four
niiwing *pc* four times
niiwinoon /niiwin-/ *vii* they are four; *prt* **naawingin**
niiwiwag /niiwi-/ *vai* they are four; *1pl* **niniiwimin**; *prt* **naawijig**
niiwo- *pv4* four; *also* **niiyo-**
niiwo-anama'e-giizhigad *vii* be four weeks; *prt* **naawo-anama'e-giizhigak**; *also* **niiyo-anama'e-giizhigad**
niiwo-anama'e-giizhik *pc* four weeks; *also* **niiyo-anama'e-giizhik**
niiwo-biboon *pc* four years; *also* **niiyo-biboon**
niiwo-biboonagad *vii* be four years; *prt* **naawo-biboonagak**; *also* **niiyo-biboonagad**
niiwo-biboonagizi *vai* be four years old; *1sg* **niniiwo-biboonagiz**; *prt* **naawo-biboonagizid**; *also* **niiyo-biboonagizi**
niiwo-diba'igan *pc* four hours, four miles; *also* **niiyo-diba'igan**
niiwo-diba'igaans *pc* four minutes, four acres; *also* **niiyo-diba'igaans**
niiwo-dibik *pc* four nights; *also* **niiyo-dibik**
niiwo-giizhigad *vii* be Thursday; *prt* **naawo-giizhigak**; *also* **niiyo-giizhigad**
niiwo-giizhik *pc* four days; *also* **niiyo-giizhik**
niiwo-giizis *pc* four months; *also* **niiyo-giizis**
niiwogon *pc* four days; *also* **niiyogon**
niiwogonagad *vii* be four days; *prt* **naawogonagak**; *also* **niiyogonagad**
niiwogonagizi *vai* be the fourth day of the month, be four days old; *prt* **naawogonagizid**; *also* **niiyogonagizi**
niiwoninj *pc* four inches; *also* **niiyoninj**
niiwosagoons *nm* four thousand; *also* **niiyosagoons**
niiwozid *pc* four feet; *also* **niiyozid**
niiwoobii'igan *na* four (card); *pl* **niiwoobii'iganag**; *also* **niiyoobii'igan**
niiwooshkin *pc* four bags; *also* **niiyooshkin**
niiyaw /-iiyaw-/ *nid* my body; *pl* **niiyawan**; *loc* **niiyawing**
niiyawen'enh /-iiyawen'eny-/ *nad* my namesake (reciprocal relationship between name-giving sponsor and child); *pl* **niiyawen'enyag**
niiyaas /-iiyaas-/ *nid* my flesh, my meat (of the body); *loc* **niiyaasing**
niiyo- *pv4* four; *also* **niiwo-**
niiyo-anama'e-giizhigad *vii* be four weeks; *prt* **naayo-anama'e-giizhigak**; *also* **niiwo-anama'e-giizhigad**
niiyo-anama'e-giizhik *pc* four weeks; *also* **niiwo-anama'e-giizhik**
niiyo-biboon *pc* four years; *also* **niiwo-biboon**
niiyo-biboonagad *vii* be four years; *prt* **naayo-biboonagak**; *also* **niiwo-biboonagad**
niiyo-biboonagizi *vai* be four years old; *1sg* **niniiyo-biboonagiz**; *prt* **naayo-biboonagizid**; *also* **niiwo-biboonagizi**
niiyo-diba'igan *pc* four hours, four miles; *also* **niiwo-diba'igan**
niiyo-diba'iganed *vii* be four o'clock; *prt* **naayo-diba'iganek**; *also* **niiwo-diba'iganed**
niiyo-diba'igaans *pc* four minutes, four acres; *also* **niiwo-diba'igaans**
niiyo-dibik *pc* four nights; *also* **niiwo-dibik**
niiyo-giizhigad *vii* be Thursday; *prt* **naayo-giizhigak**; *also* **niiwo-giizhigad**
niiyo-giizhik *pc* four days; *also* **niiwo-giizhik**
niiyo-giizis *pc* four months; *also* **niiwo-giizis**
niiyogon *pc* four days; *also* **niiwogon**
niiyogonagad *vii* be four days; *prt* **naayogonagak**; *also* **niiwogonagad**
niiyogonagizi *vai* be the fourth day of the month, be four days old; *prt* **naayogonagizid**; *also* **niiwogonagizi**
niiyoninj *pc* four inches; *also* **niiwoninj**
niiyosagoons *nm* four thousand; *also* **niiwosagoons**
niiyoobii'igan *na* four (card); *pl* **niiyoobii'iganag**; *also* **niiwoobii'igan**
niizh *nm* two
niizhing *pc* two times, twice
niizhinoon /niizhin-/ *vii* they are two; *prt* **naazhingin**
niizhiwag /niizhi-/ *vai* they are two; *1pl* **niniizhimin**; *prt* **naazhijig**
niizho- *pv4* two
niizho-anama'e-giizhigad *pc* be two weeks
niizho-anama'e-giizhik *pc* two weeks
niizho-biboon *pc* two years
niizho-biboonagad *vii* be two years; *prt* **naazho-biboonagak**
niizho-biboonagizi *vai* be two years old; *1sg* **niniizho-biboonagiz**; *prt* **naazho-biboonagizid**
niizho-diba'igan *pc* two hours, two miles
niizho-diba'iganed *vii* be two o'clock; *prt* **naazho-diba'iganek**

niizho-diba'igaans *pc* two minutes, two acres
niizho-dibik *pc* two nights
niizho-giizhigad *vii* be Tuesday; *prt* **naazho-giizhigak**
niizho-giizhik *pc* two days
niizho-giizis *pc* two months
niizhogon *pc* two days
niizhogonagad *vii* be two days; *prt* **naazhogonagak**
niizhogonagizi *vai* be the second day of the month, be two days old; *prt* **naazhogonagizid**
niizhoninj *pc* two inches
niizhosagoons *nm* two thousand
niizhozid *pc* two feet
niizhoobii'igan *na* deuce, two (card); *pl* **niizhoobii'iganag**
niizhoodenh *na* twin; *pl* **niizhoodenyag**
niizhooshkin *pc* two bags
niizhwaabik *pc* two dollars
niizhwaaching *pc* seven times
niizhwaachinoon /niizhwaachin-/ *vii* they are seven; *prt* **naazhwaachingin**
niizhwaachiwag /niizhwaachi-/ *vai* they are seven; *1pl* **niniizhwaachimin**; *prt* **naazhwaachijig**
niizhwaak *nm* two hundred
niizhwaasimidana *nm* seventy
niizhwaaso- *pv4* seven
niizhwaaso-anama'e-giizhigad *pc* be seven weeks
niizhwaaso-anama'e-giizhik *pc* seven weeks
niizhwaaso-biboon *pc* seven years
niizhwaaso-biboonagad *vii* be seven years; *prt* **naazhwaaso-biboonagak**
niizhwaaso-biboonagizi *vai* be seven years old; *1sg* **niniizhwaaso-biboonagiz**; *prt* **naazhwaaso-biboonagizid**
niizhwaaso-diba'igan *pc* seven hours, seven miles
niizhwaaso-diba'iganed *vii* be seven o'clock; *prt* **naazhwaaso-diba'iganek**
niizhwaaso-diba'igaans *pc* seven minutes, seven acres
niizhwaaso-dibik *pc* seven nights
niizhwaaso-giizhik *pc* seven days
niizhwaaso-giizis *pc* seven months
niizhwaasogon *pc* seven days
niizhwaasogonagad *vii* be seven days; *prt* **naazhwaasogonagak**
niizhwaasogonagizi *vai* be the seventh day of the month, be seven days old; *prt* **naazhwaasogonagizid**
niizhwaasoninj *pc* seven inches
niizhwaasosagoons *nm* seven thousand
niizhwaasozid *pc* seven feet
niizhwaasoobii'igan *na* seven (card); *pl* **niizhwaasoobii'iganag**
niizhwaasooshkin *pc* seven bags
niizhwaaswaabik *pc* seven dollars
niizhwaaswaak *nm* seven hundred
niizhwaaswewaan *pc* seven sets, seven pairs
niizhwaaswi *nm* seven
niizhwewaan *pc* two sets, two pairs
noodamikwe *vai* hunt beaver, trap beaver; *1sg* **ninoodamikwe**; *prt* **nwaadamikwed**
noodendam *vai2* flirt; *1sg* **ninoodendam**; *prt* **nwaadendang**
noodin *vii* be windy, there is a wind; *prt* **nwaading**
noogibatoo *vai* stop running; *1sg* **ninoogibatoo**; *prt* **nwaagibatood**
noogibide *vii* stop speeding, stop driving; *prt* **nwaagibideg**; *aug* **noogibidemagad**; *prt aug* **nwaagibidemagak**
noogibizo *vai* stop speeding, stop driving; *1sg* **ninoogibiz**; *prt* **nwaagibizod**
noogigaabawi *vai* stop and stand in place; *1sg* **ninoogigaabaw**; *prt* **nwaagigaabawid**
noogin *vta* stop s.o. by hand; *1sg* **ninooginaa**; *prt* **nwaaginaad**
nooginan *vti* stop s.t. by hand; *1sg* **ninooginaan**; *prt* **nwaaginang**
noogise *vai* come to a stop; *1sg* **ninoogise**; *prt* **nwaagised**
noogishkaa *vai* stop (moving); *1sg* **ninoogishkaa**; *prt* **nwaagishkaad**
noogishkaa *vii* stop (moving); *prt* **nwaagishkaag**; *aug* **noogishkaamagad**; *prt aug* **nwaagishkaamagak**
noogishkaawigamig *ni* hotel; *pl* **noogishkaawigamigoon**; *loc* **noogishkaawigamigong**; *dim* **noogishkaawigamigoons**
noojigiigoonyiwe *vai* go fishing; *1sg* **ninoojigiigoonyiwe**; *prt* **nwaajigiigoonyiwed**
nooji' *vta* seek s.o., go after s.o., hunt for s.o.; *1sg* **ninooji'aa**; *prt* **nwaaji'aad**
nooji'iwe *vai* seek people, hunt for people; *1sg* **ninooji'iwe**; *prt* **nwaaji'iwed**
noojimo *vai* recover from an illness; *1sg* **ninoojim**; *prt* **nwaajimod**
noojitoon *vti2* seek s.t., go after s.t., hunt for s.t.; *1sg* **ninoojitoon**; *prt* **nwaajitood**
noojiikwewe *vai* actively seek the company of women; *1sg* **ninoojiikwewe**; *prt* **nwaajiikwewed**
nookaa *vii* be soft, be tender; *prt* **nwaakaag**; *aug* **nookaamagad**; *prt aug* **nwaakaamagak**
nookaabaawe *vai* be softened in water; *prt* **nwaakaabaawed**
nookaabaawe *vii* be softened in water; *prt* **nwaakaabaaweg**; *aug* **nookaabaawemagad**; *prt aug* **nwaakaabaawemagak**
nookaadad *vii* be mild; *prt* **nwaakaadak**
nookaadizi *vai* be meek, be mild; *1sg* **ninookaadiz**; *prt* **nwaakaadizid**
nookide *vii* be cooked tender; *prt* **nwaakideg**; *aug* **nookidemagad**; *prt aug* **nwaakidemagak**
nookiz /nookizw-/ *vta* cook s.o. tender; *1sg* **ninookizwaa**; *prt* **nwaakizwaad**
nookizan *vti* cook s.t. tender; *1sg* **ninookizaan**; *prt* **nwaakizang**
nookizi *vai* be soft, be tender; *prt* **nwaakizid**
nookizo *vai* be cooked tender; *prt* **nwaakizod**
nookiigad *vii* be soft (as something sheet-like); *prt* **nwaakiigak**
nookiigizi *vai* be soft (as something sheet-like); *prt* **nwaakiigizid**
nookomis /-ookomis-/ *nad* my grandmother; *pl* **nookomisag**
nookoo *nad* grandma *vocative form of* **nookomis** my grandmother
nookwezan *vti* burn s.t. as medicine; *1sg* **ninookwezaan**; *prt* **nwaakwezang**

nookwezigan *ni* medicine for burning; *pl* **nookwezigan**
nookwezige *vai* burn things as medicine; *1sg* **ninookwezige**; *prt* **nwaakweziged**
noomag *pc* for a spell, a short while
noomaya *pc* recently
noomininjii *vai* put lotion on one's hand; *1sg* **ninoomininjii**; *prt* **nwaamininjiid**
noomininjiiwin *ni* hand lotion; *pl* **noomininjiiwinan**
noonaawaso *vai* nurse a child; *1sg* **ninoonaawas**; *prt* **nwaanaawasod**
noondam *vai2* hear; *1sg* **ninoondam**; *prt* **nwaandang**
noondan *vti* hear s.t.; *1sg* **ninoondaan**; *prt* **nwaandang**
noondaw *vta* hear s.o.; *1sg* **ninoondawaa**; *prt* **nwaandawaad**
noondaagochigan *ni* musical instrument (especially a wind instrument), whistle, horn, harmonica; *pl* **noondaagochiganan**; *loc* **noondaagochiganing**; *dim* **noondaagochigaans**

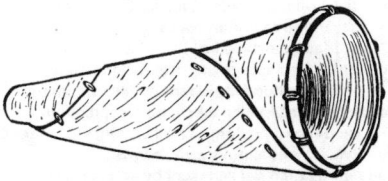

noondaagochigan (horn)

noondaagochige *vai* play a wind instrument; *1sg* **ninoondaagochige**; *prt* **nwaandaagochiged**
noondaagotoon *vti2* play s.t. as a wind instrument; *1sg* **ninoondaagotoon**; *prt* **nwaandaagotood**
noondaagozi *vai* can be heard, make noise, make a characteristic call (e.g., neigh, moo); *1sg* **ninoondaagoz**; *prt* **nwaandaagozid**
noondaagwad *vii* be heard, make noise; *prt* **nwaandaagwak**
noonde- *pv4* need to, before the usual time
noondesachige *vai* run short of things; *1sg* **ninoondesachige**; *prt* **nwaandesachiged**
noondesa' *vta* run short of s.o.; *1sg* **ninoondesa'aa**; *prt* **nwaandesa'aad**
noondesatoon *vti2* run short of s.t.; *1sg* **ninoondesatoon**; *prt* **nwaandesatood**
noondese *vai* run short; *1sg* **ninoondese**; *prt* **nwaandesed**
noondeshin *vai* be fatigued, be exhausted; *1sg* **ninoondeshin**; *prt* **nwaandeshing**
noongom *pc* now, today, nowadays
nooni *vai* suckle (of child or offspring); *1sg* **ninoon**; *prt* **nwaanid**
nooni' *vta* breast feed s.o.; *1sg* **ninooni'aa**; *prt* **nwaani'aad**
noopiming *pc* inland, in the woods, in the bush
noopinadoon *vti2* go after s.t., follow s.t.; *1sg* **ninoopinadoon**; *prt* **nwaapinadood**
noopinazh /noopinaN-/ *vta* go after s.o., follow s.o.; *1sg* **ninoopinanaa**; *prt* **nwaapinanaad**
noos /-oos-/ *nad* my father *old-fashioned*; *pl* **noosag**
nooshkaachigaade *vii* be winnowed; *prt* **nwaashkaachigaadeg**; *aug* **nooshkaachigaademagad**; *prt aug* **nwaashkaachigaademagak**
nooshkaachige *vai* winnow things (e.g., wild rice); *1sg* **ninooshkaachige**; *prt* **nwaashkaachiged**
nooshkaachinaagan *ni* winnowing tray; *pl* **nooshkaachinaaganan**; *loc* **nooshkaachinaaganing**; *dim* **nooshkaachinaagaans**

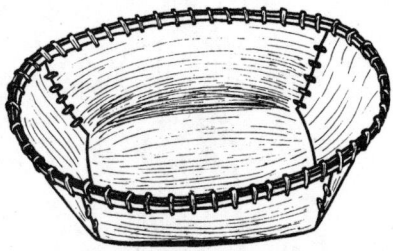

nooshkaachinaagan (winnowing tray)

nooshkaatoon *vti2* winnow s.t. (e.g., wild rice); *1sg* **ninooshkaatoon**; *prt* **nwaashkaatood**
nooskwaada' /nooskwaada'w-/ *vta* lick s.o.; *1sg* **ninooskwaada'waa**; *prt* **nwaaskwaada'waad**
nooskwaada'an *vti* lick s.t.; *1sg* **ninooskwaada'aan**; *prt* **nwaaskwaada'ang**
noozh /nooN-/ *vta* nurse s.o. (e.g., a baby); *1sg* **ninoonaa**; *prt* **nwaanaad**
noozhishenh /-oozhisheny-/ *nad* my grandchild; *pl* **noozhishenyag**
noozis *nad* grandchild *vocative form of* **noozhishenh** my grandchild

O

---

o= *pre third person prefix before consonants in verbs and nouns*
o- *pv2* go over to; *also* **a'o-, awi-**
obikwaaj *nid* bulb; *pl* **obikwaajiin**; *loc* **obikwaajiing**; *dim* **obikwaajiins**
obiigomakakii *na* toad; *pl* **obiigomakakiig**; *dim* **obiigomakakiins**
obiimiskodisii *na* snail; *pl* **obiimiskodisiig**; *dim* **obiimiskodisiins**
oboodashkwaanishiinh *na* dragonfly; *pl* **oboodashkwaanishiinyag**

od= *pre third person prefix before vowels in verbs and non-dependent nouns*
odakiimi *vai* have land; *1sg* **indoodakiim**; *prt* **wedakiimid**
odamino *vai* play; *1pl* **indoodamin**; *prt* **wedaminod**
odaminoowigamig *ni* recreation building; *pl* **odaminoowigamigoon**; *loc* **odaminoowigamigong**; *dim* **odaminoowigamigoons**
odaminwaagan *na* doll; *pl* **odaminwaaganag**; *loc* **odaminwaaganing**; *dim* **odaminwaagaans**

odaminwaagan (doll)

odaminwaagan *ni* toy, plaything; *pl* **odaminwaaganan**; *loc* **odaminwaaganing**; *dim* **odaminwaagaans**
odaminwaage *vai+o* use (s.t.) as a toy; *1sg* **indoodaminwaage, indoodaminwaagen**; *prt* **wedaminwaaged**
odasiniinsimi *vai* have gallstones; *1sg* **indoodasiniinsimi**; *prt* **wedasiniinsimid**
odatagaagomin *na* blackberry; *pl* **odatagaagominag**; *dim* **odatagaagominens**
odatagaagominagaawanzh *na* blackberry bush; *pl* **odatagaagominagaawanzhiig**; *loc* **odatagaagominagaawanzhiing**; *dim* **odatagaagominagaawanzhiins**
odayi *vai* have a dog, have a horse; *1sg* **indooday**; *prt* **wedayid**
odaabaadan *vti* drag s.t.; *1sg* **indoodaabaadaan**; *prt* **wedaabaadang**
odaabaan *na* car, wagon, sled, sleigh; *pl* **odaabaanag**; *loc* **odaabaaning**; *dim* **odaabaanens**
odaabaanikewigamig *ni* repair garage; *pl* **odaabaanikewigamigoon**; *loc* **odaabaanikewigamigong**; *dim* **odaabaanikewigamigoons**
odaabaanikewinini *na* mechanic; *pl* **odaabaanikewininiwag**
odaabaazh /odaabaaN-/ *vta* drag s.o.; *1sg* **indoodaabaanaa**; *prt* **wedaabaanaad**
odaabii *vai* drag (something); *1sg* **indoodaabii**; *prt* **wedaabiid**
odaabii' *vta* drive s.o. (e.g., a draft animal or a car); *1sg* **indoodaabii'aa**; *prt* **wedaabii'aad**
odaabii'aagan *na* draft animal; *pl* **odaabii'aaganag**; *dim* **odaabii'aagaans**
odaabii'iwe *vai* drive; *1sg* **indoodaabii'iwe**; *prt* **wedaabii'iwed**
odaabii'iwe-mazina'igaans *ni* driver's license; *pl* **odaabii'iwe-mazina'igaansan**
odaabii'iwewinini *na* driver; *pl* **odaabii'iwewininiwag**; *dim* **odaabii'iwewininiins**
odaake *vai* steer, direct affairs; *1sg* **indoodaake**; *prt* **wedaaked**
odaakewigimaa *na* director, governor; *pl* **odaakewigimaag**; *dim* **odaakewigimaans**; *also* **odaake-ogimaa**
odaani *vai* have a daughter; *1sg* **indoodaan**; *prt* **wedaanid**
odaanisi *vai* have a daughter; *1sg* **indoodaanis**; *prt* **wedaanisid**
odaapin *vta* accept s.o., take s.o. offered, pick s.o. up; *1sg* **indoodaapinaa**; *prt* **wedaapinaad**
odaapinamaw *vta* accept (s.t.) from s.o., take (s.t.) offered by s.o., pick (s.t.) up from s.o.; *1sg* **indoodaapinamawaa**; *prt* **wedaapinamawaad**
odaapinan *vti* accept s.t., take s.t. offered, pick s.t. up; *1sg* **indoodaapinaan**; *prt* **wedaapinang**
odaapinigaade *vii* be taken, be accepted; *prt* **wedaapinigaadeg**; *aug* **odaapinigaademagad**; *prt aug* **wedaapinigaademagak**
odaapinigaazo *vai* be taken, be accepted; *prt* **wedaapinigaazod**
odaapinige *vai* accept things, take things offered, pick up things; *1sg* **indoodaapinige**; *prt* **wedaapiniged**
odaapishkaa *vii* shrink; *prt* **wedaapishkaag**; *aug* **odaapishkaamagad**; *prt aug* **wedaapishkaamagak**
odaapishkaa *vai* shrink; *prt* **wedaapishkaad**
odaawaa *na* Odawa (Ottawa); *pl* **odaawaag**; *dim* **odaawaans**
odaawaamo *vai* speak Odawa (Ottawa); *1sg* **indoodaawaam**; *prt* **wedaawaamod**
ode'imin *ni* strawberry; *pl* **ode'iminan**; *dim* **ode'iminens**
ode'imini-giizis *na* June
odish /odiS-/ *vta* come up to s.o., visit s.o., reach s.o.; *1sg* **indoodisaa**; *prt* **wedisaad**
odishiwe *vai* visit people; *1sg* **indoodishiwe**; *prt* **wedishiwed**
oditan *vti* come up to s.t., reach s.t.; *1sg* **indooditaan**; *prt* **weditang**
odoodemi *vai* have a totem (clan); *1sg* **indoodoodem**; *prt* **wedoodemid**
odoodemindiwag /odoodemindi-/ *vai* they have a mutual totem (clan); *1pl* **indoodoodemindimin**; *prt* **wedoodemindijig**
odoondanegwaajigan *ni* tab at heel of moccasin; *pl* **odoondanegwaajiganan**; *dim* **odoondanegwaajigaans**
odoonibii *na* tullibee; *pl* **odoonibiig**; *dim* **odoonibiins**; *also* **odoonibiins, -ag**

ogaa *na* pickerel, walleye; *pl* **ogaawag**; *dim* **ogaans**
ogichidaa *na* warrior, ceremonial headman; *pl* **ogichidaag**
ogichidaakwe *na* ceremonial headwoman, wife of ceremonial headman; *pl* **ogichidaakweg**
ogidajiw* *pc* on top of a mountain; *also* **agidajiw, wagidajiw**
ogidakamig* *pc* on top of the ground; *also* **agidakamig, wagidakamig**
ogidasin* *pc* on top of a rock; *also* **agidasin, wagidasin**
ogidaabik* *pc* on something mineral (e.g., metal, glass, rock); *also* **agidaabik, wagidaabik**
ogidaajiwan* *pc* upstream; *also* **agidaajiwan, wagidaajiwan**
ogidaaki* *pc* on top of a hill; *also* **agidaaki, wagidaaki**
ogidibiig* *pc* on top of the water; *also* **agidibiig, wagidibiig**
ogidigamig* *pc* on top of the house; *also* **agidigamig, wagidigamig**
ogidiskwam* *pc* on top of the ice; *also* **agidiskwam, wagidiskwam**
ogijayi'ii* *pc* on top of it; *also* **agijayi'ii, wagijayi'ii**
ogiji-* *pn* on top of; *also* **agiji-, wagiji-**
ogimaa *na* chief, boss, leader; *pl* **ogimaag**; *dim* **ogimaans**
ogimaa *na* king (card); *pl* **ogimaag**
ogimaakandan *vti* rule s.t., govern s.t.; *1sg* **indoogimaakandaan**; *prt* **wegimaakandang**
ogimaakandaw *vta* rule s.o., govern s.o.; *1sg* **indoogimaakandawaa**; *prt* **wegimaakandawaad**
ogimaakaw *vta* make s.o. chief, make s.o. leader; *1sg* **indoogimaakawaa**; *prt* **wegimaakawaad**
ogimaakwe *na* wife of chief or leader, woman leader, queen; *pl* **ogimaakweg**; *dim* **ogimaakwens**
ogimaakwens *na* princess; *pl* **ogimaakwensag**
ogimaawi *vai* be a leader, be a chief; *1sg* **indoogimaaw**; *prt* **wegimaawid**
ogimaawigamig *ni* head office, administration office; *pl* **ogimaawigamigoon**; *loc* **ogimaawigamigong**; *dim* **ogimaawigamigoons**
ogimaawiwin *ni* government, authority, leadership; *pl* **ogimaawiwinan**
ogin *na* rose hip, tomato; *pl* **oginiig**; *loc* **oginiing**; *dim* **oginiins**
oginii-dagonigan *ni* catsup
oginii-waabigwan *ni* rose; *pl* **oginii-waabigwaniin**; *loc* **oginii-waabigwaniing**; *dim* **oginii-waabigwaniins**
ogiishkimanisii *na* kingfisher; *pl* **ogiishkimanisiig**; *dim* **ogiishkimanisiins**
ogow* *pr* these *animate plural demonstrative; also* **ogo*, ongow, ongo**
ogowedig* *pr* these over here *animate plural demonstrative*; *also* **ongowedig**
o'o *pr* this *inanimate singular demonstrative*; *also* **o'ow, 'ow, 'o, o'o**
o'omaa *pc* here; *also* **omaa**
o'owedi *pr* this over here *inanimate singular demonstrative; also* **owedi**
ojaanimendam *vai2* be anxious, be impatient; *1sg* **indoojaanimendam**; *prt* **wejaanimendang**
ojaanimi- *pv4* busy, noisy
ojaanimi' *vta* make s.o. hurry, rush s.o.; *1sg* **indoojaanimi'aa**; *prt* **wejaanimi'aad**
ojaanimim *vta* hurry s.o. by speech; *1sg* **indoojaanimimaa**; *prt* **wejaanimimaad**
ojaanimitaa *vai* be busy (in some work or activity); *1sg* **indoojaanimitaa**; *prt* **wejaanimitaad**
ojaanimitoon *vti2* be eager to do s.t.; *1sg* **indoojaanimitoon**; *prt* **wejaanimitood**
ojaanimizekwe *vai* cook in a hurry; *1sg* **indoojaanimizekwe**; *prt* **wejaanimizekwed**
ojaanimizi *vai* be busy; *1sg* **indoojaanimiz**; *prt* **wejaanimizid**
ojibwe *na* Ojibwe; *pl* **ojibweg**; *dim* **ojibwens**
ojibwekwe *na* Ojibwe woman; *pl* **ojibwekweg**; *dim* **ojibwekwens**
ojibwemo *vai* speak Ojibwe; *1sg* **indoojibwem**; *prt* **wejibwemod**
ojibwemotaw *vta* speak Ojibwe to s.o.; *1sg* **indoojibwemotawaa**; *prt* **wejibwemotawaad**
ojibwemowin *ni* Ojibwe language; *pl* **ojibwemowin**
ojibwewanishinaabe *na* Ojibwe; *pl* **ojibwewanishinaabeg**; *dim* **ojibwewanishinaabens**; *also* **ojibwe-anishinaabe**
ojibwewi *vai* be Ojibwe; *1sg* **indoojibwew**; *prt* **wejibwewid**
ojibwewibii'an *vti* write s.t. in Ojibwe; *1sg* **indoojibwewibii'aan**; *prt* **wejibwewibii'ang**
ojibwewibii'igaade *vii* be written in Ojibwe; *prt* **wejibwewibii'igaadeg**; *aug* **ojibwewibii'igaademagad**; *prt aug* **wejibwewibii'igaademagak**
ojibwewibii'ige *vai* write things in Ojibwe; *1sg* **indoojibwewibii'ige**; *prt* **wejibwewibii'iged**
ojibwewisidoon *vti2* put s.t. into Ojibwe; *1sg* **indoojibwewisidoon**; *prt* **wejibwewisidood**
ojibwewisin *vii* be written in Ojibwe (e.g., a book); *prt* **wejibwewising**
ojichaagobiishin *vii* reflect in water; *prt* **wejichaagobiishing**
ojichaagobiisin *vii* reflect in water; *prt* **wejichaagobiising**
ojijise *vii* come (as time), pass (as time); *prt* **wejijiseg**; *aug* **ojijisemagad**; *prt aug* **wejijisemagak**
ojijiingwanabi *vai* kneel; *1sg* **indoojijiingwanab**; *prt* **wejijiingwanabid**
ojiibik *ni* root; *pl* **ojiibikan**; *loc* **ojiibikaang**; *dim* **ojiibikens**
ojiibikaawan *vii* have roots; *prt* **wejiibikaawang**
ojiibikaawi *vai* have roots; *prt* **wejiibikaawid**
ojiig *na* fisher; *pl* **ojiigag**; *dim* **ojiigens**
ojiigiwayaan *na* fisher hide; *pl* **ojiigiwayaanag**; *loc* **ojiigiwayaaning**; *dim* **ojiigiwayaanens**
ojiim *vta* kiss s.o.; *1sg* **indoojiimaa**; *prt* **wejiimaad**
ojiindiwag /ojiindi-/ *vai* they kiss each other; *1pl* **indoojiindimin**; *prt* **wejiindijig**
ojiishigi *vai* have a scar; *1sg* **indoojiishig**; *prt* **wejiishigid**
ojiishinike *vai* have scar on one's arm; *1sg* **indoojiishinike**; *prt* **wejiishiniked**

ojiishininjii *vai* have scar on one's hand; *1sg* **indoojiishininjii**; *prt* **wejiishininjiid**
ojiishiingwe *vai* have scar on one's face; *1sg* **indoojiishiingwe**; *prt* **wejiishiingwed**
okanakosimaan *ni* squash; *pl* **okanakosimaanan**; *loc* **okanakosimaaning**; *dim* **okanakosimaanens**
okanaapine *vai* have arthritis, have rheumatism; *1sg* **indookanaapine**; *prt* **wekanaapined**
okawi' *vta* find s.o.'s tracks; *1sg* **indookawi'aa**; *prt* **wekawi'aad**
okawitoon *vti2* find the tracks of s.t.; *1sg* **indookawitoon**; *prt* **wekawitood**
okaadakik *na* legged kettle, treaty kettle; *pl* **okaadakikoog**; *loc* **okaadakikong**; *dim* **okaadakikoons**
okaadaak *ni* carrot; *pl* **okaadaakoon**; *loc* **okaadaakong**; *dim* **okaadaakoons**
okaaden *vta* braid s.o., braid s.o.'s hair; *1sg* **indookaadenaa**; *prt* **wekaadenaad**
okaadenan *vti* braid s.t.; *1sg* **indookaadenaan**; *prt* **wekaadenang**
okaadenigan *ni* braided rug, braid; *pl* **okaadeniganan**; *loc* **okaadeniganing**; *dim* **okaadenigaans**
okaadenigaade *vii* be braided; *prt* **wekaadenigaadeg**; *aug* **okaadenigaademagad**; *prt aug* **wekaadenigaademagak**
okaadenige *vai* braid things, have braids; *1sg* **indookaadenige**; *prt* **wekaadeniged**
okeyaw *na* fish decoy; *pl* **okeyawag**
okij *ni* pipestem; *pl* **okijiin**; *loc* **okijiing**; *dim* **okijiins**
okijaabik *ni* stovepipe, tailpipe; *pl* **okijaabikoon**; *loc* **okijaabikong**; *dim* **okijaabikoons**
okikaandag *na* jack pine; *pl* **okikaandagoog**; *loc* **okikaandagong**; *dim* **okikaandagoons**; *also* **wakikaandag**
okoshim *vta* pile s.o., stack s.o.; *1sg* **indookoshimaa**; *prt* **wekoshimaad**
okoshin *vai* lie in a pile; *prt* **wekoshing**
okosidoon *vti2* pile s.t., stack s.t.; *1sg* **indookosidoon**; *prt* **wekosidood**
okosimaan *ni* pumpkin, squash; *pl* **okosimaanan**; *loc* **okosimaaning**; *dim* **okosimaanens**
okosin *vii* lie in a pile; *prt* **wekosing**
okwapide *vii* be tied in a bunch; *prt* **wekwapideg**; *aug* **okwapidemagad**; *prt aug* **wekwapidemagak**
okwapidoon *vti2* tie s.t. in a bunch; *1sg* **indookwapidoon**; *prt* **wekwapidood**
okwapizh /okwapiN-/ *vta* tie s.o. in a bunch; *1sg* **indookwapinaa**; *prt* **wekwapinaad**
okwapizo *vai* be tied in a bunch; *prt* **wekwapizod**
okwaakoshim *vta* stack s.o. (as something stick- or wood-like); *1sg* **indookwaakoshimaa**; *prt* **wekwaakoshimaad**
okwaakosidoon *vti2* stack s.t. (as something stick- or wood-like); *1sg* **indookwaakosidoon**; *prt* **wekwaakosidood**
omakakii *na* frog; *pl* **omakakiig**; *dim* **omakakiins**
omakakiiwinini *na* Finn; *pl* **omakakiiwininiwag**
omanoominii *na* Menominee; *pl* **omanoominiig**
omashkiigoo *na* Cree; *pl* **omashkiigoog**
omashkiigoomo *vai* speak Cree; *1sg* **indoomashkiigoom**; *prt* **wemashkiigoomod**
omashkooz *na* elk; *pl* **omashkoozoog**; *dim* **omashkoozoons**
omaa *pc* here; *also* **o'omaa**
omaamaayi *vai* have a mother; *1sg* **indoomaamaay**; *prt* **wemaamaayid**
ombaabate *vii* go upwards as smoke; *prt* **wembaabateg**
ombaabiigin *vta* hoist s.o., lift s.o. (as with something string-like); *1sg* **indoombaabiiginaa**; *prt* **wembaabiiginaad**
ombaabiiginan *vti* hoist s.t., lift s.t. (as with something string-like); *1sg* **indoombaabiiginaan**; *prt* **wembaabiiginang**
ombaakwa' /ombaakwa'w-/ *vta* raise s.o. (as or as with something stick- or wood-like); *1sg* **indoombaakwa'waa**; *prt* **wembaakwa'waad**
ombaakwa'an *vti* raise s.t. (as or as with something stick- or wood-like); *1sg* **indoombaakwa'aan**; *prt* **wembaakwa'ang**
ombaashi *vai* be blown upwards; *1sg* **indoombaash**; *prt* **wembaashid**
ombaasin *vii* be blown upwards; *prt* **wembaasing**
ombendam *vai2* be excited, be hopeful; *1sg* **indoombendam**; *prt* **wembendang**
ombibide *vii* fly upwards, speed upwards; *prt* **wembibideg**; *aug* **ombibidemagad**; *prt aug* **wembibidemagak**
ombibizo *vai* fly upwards, speed upwards; *1sg* **indoombibiz**; *prt* **wembibizod**
ombigamizan *vti* boil s.t. to sugar; *1sg* **indoombigamizaan**; *prt* **wembigamizang**
ombigamiziganan *ni* boiling sugar; *pl* **ombigamiziganan**; *loc* **ombigamiziganing**
ombigamizige *vai* boil to sugar, sugar off; *1sg* **indoombigamizige**; *prt* **wembigamiziged**
ombigwaashkwani *vai* jump upwards; *1sg* **indoombigwaashkwan**; *prt* **wembigwaashkwanid**
ombi' *vta* excite s.o., stir s.o. up; *1sg* **indoombi'aa**; *prt* **wembi'aad**
ombijiishkaa *vai* have a swollen stomach; *1sg* **indoombijiishkaa**; *prt* **wembijiishkaad**
ombin *vta* lift s.o.; *1sg* **indoombinaa**; *prt* **wembinaad**
ombinamaw *vta* lift (s.t.) for s.o.; *1sg* **indoombinamawaa**; *prt* **wembinamawaad**
ombinan *vti* lift s.t.; *1sg* **indoombinaan**; *prt* **wembinang**
ombinikeni *vai* lift one's arm; *1sg* **indoombiniken**; *prt* **wembinikenid**
ombishkaa *vai* go upwards; *1sg* **indoombishkaa**; *prt* **wembishkaad**
ombishkaa *vii* go upwards; *prt* **wembishkaag**; *aug* **ombishkaamagad**; *prt aug* **wembishkaamagak**
ombisijigaans *ni* baking powder; *pl* **ombisijigaansan**; *loc* **ombisijigaansing**
ombiwane *vai* lift a pack to one's back; *1sg* **indoombiwane**; *prt* **wembiwaned**
ombiwebin *vta* throw s.o. upwards; *1sg* **indoombiwebinaa**; *prt* **wembiwebinaad**
ombiwebinan *vti* throw s.t. upwards; *1sg* **indoombiwebinaan**; *prt* **wembiwebinang**

ombiwidoon *vti2* lift and carry s.t.; *1sg* **indoombiwidoon**; *prt* **wembiwidood**
ombiwizh /ombiwiN-/ *vta* lift and carry s.o.; *1sg* **indoombiwinaa**; *prt* **wembiwinaad**
ombizigan *ni* baking soda; *loc* **ombiziganing**
ombiigizi *vai* be loud, be noisy; *1sg* **indoombiigiz**; *prt* **wembiigizid**
ombiigwewe *vai* be loud (in operation); *prt* **wembiigwewed**
ombiigwewe *vii* be loud (in operation); *prt* **wembiigweweg**; *aug* **ombiigwewemagad**; *prt aug* **wembiigwewemagak**
omboom *vta* lift s.o. on one's back; *prt* **wemboomaad**
omboondan *vti* lift s.t. on one's back; *1sg* **indoomboondaan**; *prt* **wemboondang**
ombwewebinige *vai* throw things around, make a mess; *1sg* **indoombwewebinige**; *prt* **wembwewebiniged**
omigii *vai* have sores, have scabs; *1sg* **indoomigii**; *prt* **wemigiid**
omigiingwe *vai* have scabs on one's face; *1sg* **indoomigiingwe**; *prt* **wemigiingwed**
omiimii *na* dove, pigeon; *pl* **omiimiig**; *dim* **omiimiins**
omiimiisi *na* mayfly; *pl* **omiimiisiwag**
omooday *ni* bottle; *pl* **omoodayan**; *loc* **omoodaang**
omoodayaabik *ni* (piece of) glass, broken glass (as from a bottle); *pl* **omoodayaabikoon**; *loc* **omoodayaabikong**; *dim* **omoodayaabikoons**
onabi *vai* take a seat; *1sg* **indoonab**; *prt* **wenabid**
onabi' *vta* seat s.o.; *1sg* **indoonabi'aa**; *prt* **wenabi'aad**
onabi'iwe *vai* seat people; *1sg* **indoonabi'iwe**; *prt* **wenabi'iwed**
onadin *vta* mold s.o., knead s.o., sculpt s.o.; *1sg* **indoonadinaa**; *prt* **wenadinaad**
onadinan *vti* mold s.t., knead s.t., sculpt s.t.; *1sg* **indoonadinaan**; *prt* **wenadinang**
onadinige *vai* knead things, mold things; *1sg* **indoonadinige**; *prt* **wenadiniged**
onagim *vta* decide on s.o., appoint s.o., set a price on s.o.; *1sg* **indoonagimaa**; *prt* **wenagimaad**
onagindan *vti* set a price on s.t.; *1sg* **indoonagindaan**; *prt* **wenagindang**
onagindaaso *vai* set a price; *1sg* **indoonagindaas**; *prt* **wenagindaasod**
onagizh *ni* sausage; *pl* **onagizhiin**; *loc* **onagizhiing**; *dim* **onagizhiins**; *also* **onagizhiins**
onagizhiinsan /onagizhiins-/ *ni* macaroni *plural*
onagoode *vii* hang in place; *prt* **wenagoodeg**; *aug* **onagoodemagad**; *prt aug* **wenagoodemagak**
onagoodoon *vti2* hang s.t. in place; *1sg* **indoonagoodoon**; *prt* **wenagoodood**
onagoojin *vai* hang in place; *prt* **wenagoojing**
onagoozh /onagooN-/ *vta* hang s.o. in place; *1sg* **indoonagoonaa**; *prt* **wenagoonaad**
onakidoon *vti2* set s.t. up; *1sg* **indoonakidoon**; *prt* **wenakidood**
onakizh /onakiN-/ *vta* set s.o. up; *1sg* **indoonakinaa**; *prt* **wenakinaad**
onapide *vii* be tied in place; *prt* **wenapideg**; *aug* **onapidemagad**; *prt aug* **wenapidemagak**
onapidoon *vti2* tie s.t. in place; *1sg* **indoonapidoon**; *prt* **wenapidood**
onapijige *vai* harness up; *1sg* **indoonapijige**; *prt* **wenapijiged**
onapizh /onapiN-/ *vta* tie s.o. in place, harness s.o.; *1sg* **indoonapinaa**; *prt* **wenapinaad**
onapizo *vai* be harnessed; *prt* **wenapizod**
onashkinade *vii* be loaded; *prt* **wenashkinadeg**; *aug* **onashkinademagad**; *prt aug* **wenashkinademagak**
onashkinadoon *vti2* load s.t. (e.g., a gun); *1sg* **indoonashkinadoon**; *prt* **wenashkinadood**
onashkina' *vta* load s.o. (e.g., a pipe); *1sg* **indoonashkina'aa**; *prt* **wenashkina'aad**
onaabam *vta* choose s.o., pick s.o.; *1sg* **indoonaabamaa**; *prt* **wenaabamaad**
onaabanad *vii* there is a crust on the snow; *prt* **wenaabanak**
onaabandan *vti* choose s.t., pick s.t.; *1sg* **indoonaabandaan**; *prt* **wenaabandang**
onaabani-giizis *na* March
onaabanjigaade *vii* be chosen, be picked; *prt* **wenaabanjigaadeg**; *aug* **onaabanjigaademagad**; *prt aug* **wenaabanjigaademagak**
onaabanjigaazo *vai* be chosen, be picked; *prt* **wenaabanjigaazod**
onaabanjige *vai* choose things, pick things; *1sg* **indoonaabanjige**; *prt* **wenaabanjiged**
onaabemi *vai* have a husband; *1sg* **indoonaabem**; *prt* **wenaabemid**
onaagan *ni* dish, plate; *pl* **onaaganan**; *loc* **onaaganing**; *dim* **onaagaans**

onaagan (dish) or boozikinaagan (bowl)

onaagaans *ni* cup, small plate; *pl* **onaagaansan**; *loc* **onaagaansing**
onaagin *vta* bend s.o. into form; *1sg* **indoonaaginaa**; *prt* **wenaaginaad**
onaaginan *vti* bend s.t. into form; *1sg* **indoonaaginaan**; *prt* **wenaaginang**
onaagoshi-miijin *vti3* eat s.t. for supper; *1sg* **indoonaagoshi-miijin**; *prt* **wenaagoshi-miijid**
onaagoshin /onaagoshi-/ *vii* be evening; *prt* **wenaagoshig**
onaagoshi-wiisini *vai* eat supper; *1sg* **indoonaagoshi-wiisin**; *prt* **wenaagoshi-wiisinid**

onaakon *vta* decide on s.o., judge s.o.; *1sg* **indoonaakonaa**; *prt* **wenaakonaad**
onaakonan *vti* decide on s.t., plan s.t.; *1sg* **indoonaakonaan**; *prt* **wenaakonang**
onaakonige *vai* plan things, decide things, judge things, be in court; *1sg* **indoonaakonige**; *prt* **wenaakoniged**
onaakosidoon *vti2* set s.t. up as a frame; *1sg* **indoonaakosidoon**; *prt* **wenaakosidood**
ondadamon /ondadamo-/ *vii* lead from a certain place (as a road or trail); *prt* **wendadamog**
ondademo *vai* cry for a certain reason, come from a certain place crying; *1sg* **indoondadem**; *prt* **wendademod**
onda'ibaan *ni* water well, water source; *pl* **onda'ibaanan**; *loc* **onda'ibaaning**; *dim* **onda'ibaanens**
onda'ibii *vai* get water from a certain place; *1sg* **indoonda'ibii**; *prt* **wenda'ibiid**
ondakwazhiwe *vai* paddle from a certain place, swim from a certain place (as a fish); *1sg* **indoondakwazhiwe**; *prt* **wendakwazhiwed**
ondamanokii *vai* be kept busy in work; *1sg* **indoondamanokii**; *prt* **wendamanokiid**
ondamendam *vai2* be preoccupied, be worried; *1sg* **indoondamendam**; *prt* **wendamendang**
ondamendan *vti* worry about s.t., be preoccupied with s.t.; *1sg* **indoondamendaan**; *prt* **wendamendang**
ondamenim *vta* worry about s.o., be preoccupied with s.o.; *1sg* **indoondamenimaa**; *prt* **wendamenimaad**
ondami' *vta* hinder s.o., get in s.o.'s way; *1sg* **indoondami'aa**; *prt* **wendami'aad**
ondamitaa *vai* be kept busy in an activity; *1sg* **indoondamitaa**; *prt* **wendamitaad**
ondamizi *vai* be busy; *1sg* **indoondamiz**; *prt* **wendamizid**
ondaabate *vii* come from a certain place (as smoke); *prt* **wendaabateg**; *aug* **ondaabatemagad**; *prt aug* **wendaabatemagak**
ondaadad *vii* come from a certain place, originate in a certain place; *prt* **wendaadak**
ondaadagaa *vai* swim from a certain place; *1sg* **indoondaadagaa**; *prt* **wendaadagaad**
ondaadagaazii *vai* wade from a certain place; *1sg* **indoondaadagaazii**; *prt* **wendaadagaaziid**
ondaada'e *vai* skate from a certain place; *1sg* **indoondaada'e**; *prt* **wendaada'ed**
ondaadizi *vai* be born, come from a certain place; *1sg* **indoondaadiz**; *prt* **wendaadizid**
ondaadiziike *vai* give birth; *1sg* **indoondaadiziike**; *prt* **wendaadiziiked**
ondaanimad *vii* come as wind from a certain direction; *prt* **wendaanimak**
ondaas *pc* on this side, come here!
ondaasagaam *pc* on this side of the water
ondaasayi'ii *pc* on this side of it
ondaashaan *pc* come here! (especially said to children)
ondaashi *vai* be blown from a certain place, sail from a certain place; *1sg* **indoondaash**; *prt* **wendaashid**
ondaasikana *pc* on this side of the road, on this side of the trail
ondaasin *vii* be blown from a certain place, sail from a certain place; *prt* **wendaasing**
ondaasishkode *pc* on this side of the fire
onde *vii* boil; *prt* **wendeg**; *aug* **ondemagad**; *prt aug* **wendemagak**
ondendam *vai2* strongly desire; *1sg* **indoondendam**; *prt* **wendendang**
ondendi *vai* be gone from a certain place, be absent from a certain place; *1sg* **indoondend**; *prt* **wendendid**
ondenim *vta* envy s.o.; *1sg* **indoondenimaa**; *prt* **wendenimaad**
ondin *vii* wind comes from a certain direction; *prt* **wending**
ondin *vta* get s.o. from a certain place, obtain s.o. from a certain place; *1sg* **indoondinaa**; *prt* **wendinaad**
ondinamaw *vta* get (s.t.) for s.o. from a certain place, obtain (s.t.) for s.o. from a certain place; *1sg* **indoondinamawaa**; *prt* **wendinamawaad**
ondinamaazo *vai* get (s.t.) for oneself from a certain place; *1sg* **indoondinamaaz**; *prt* **wendinamaazod**
ondinan *vti* get s.t. from a certain place, obtain s.t. from a certain place; *1sg* **indoondinaan**; *prt* **wendinang**
ondinigaade *vii* be obtained from a certain place; *prt* **wendinigaadeg**; *aug* **ondinigaademagad**; *prt aug* **wendinigaademagak**
ondinigaazo *vai* be obtained from a certain place; *prt* **wendinigaazod**
ondinige *vai* get things from a certain place, obtain things from a certain place; *1sg* **indoondinige**; *prt* **wendiniged**
ondizi *vai* make a living a certain way, earn from a certain place, inherit from a certain source; *1sg* **indoondiz**; *prt* **wendizid**
ondose *vai* walk from a certain place; *1sg* **indoondose**; *prt* **wendosed**
ondoode *vai* crawl from a certain place; *1sg* **indoondoode**; *prt* **wendooded**
ondoom *vta* carry s.o. on back from a certain place; *1sg* **indoondoomaa**; *prt* **wendoomaad**
ondoomigo *vai* ride from a certain place on horseback; *1sg* **indoondoomig**; *prt* **wendoomigod**
ondoondan *vti* carry s.t. on back from a certain place; *1sg* **indoondoondaan**; *prt* **wendoondang**
onendam *vai2* decide what to do, figure something out; *1sg* **indoonendam**; *prt* **wenendang**
ongow *pr* these *animate plural demonstrative*; *also* **ongo, ogow*, ogo***
ongowedig *pr* these over here *animate plural demonstrative*; *also* **ogowedig***
Onigamiinsing *place* Duluth
onikodan *vti* cut s.t. to shape; *1sg* **indoonikodaan**; *prt* **wenikodang**
onikozh /onikoN-/ *vta* cut s.o. to shape; *1sg* **indoonikonaa**; *prt* **wenikonaad**
onin *vta* put s.o. in order, assemble s.o., deal s.o. (e.g., cards); *1sg* **indooninaa**; *prt* **weninaad**
oninan *vti* put s.t. in order, assemble s.t.; *1sg* **indooninaan**; *prt* **weninang**

oninasabii *vai* prepare a net for setting; *1sg* **indooninasabii**; *prt* **weninasabiid**
oninige *vai* put things in order, assemble things, deal cards; *1sg* **indooninige**; *prt* **weniniged**
oninjii-baashkizigan *ni* handgun; *pl* **oninjii-baashkiziganan**; *loc* **oninjii-baashkiziganing**; *dim* **oninjii-baashkizigaans**
onishkaa *vai* get up (from a prone position); *1sg* **indoonishkaa**; *prt* **wenishkaad**
onizhishi *vai* be nice, be pretty; *1sg* **indoonizhish**; *prt* **wenizhishid**
onizhishi' *vta* make s.o. nice, make s.o. well; *1sg* **indoonizhishi'aa**; *prt* **wenizhishi'aad**
onizhishin *vii* be nice, be pretty; *prt* **wenizhishing**
onizhishitoon *vti2* make s.t. nice, make s.t. well; *1sg* **indoonizhishitoon**; *prt* **wenizhishitood**
oniijaanisensi *vai* have a small child; *1sg* **indooniijaanisens**; *prt* **weniijaanisensid**
oniijaanisi *vai* have a child; *1sg* **indooniijaanis**; *prt* **weniijaanisid**
oniijaaniw *na* doe; *pl* **oniijaaniwag**; *dim* **oniijaaniins**
onji- *pv3* from a certain place, for a certain reason, because
onjibatoo *vai* run from a certain place; *1sg* **indoonjibatoo**; *prt* **wenjibatood**
onjibaa *vai* come from a certain place; *1sg* **indoonjibaa**; *prt* **wenjibaad**
onjibide *vii* speed from a certain place, drive from a certain place, fall from a certain place; *prt* **wenjibideg**; *aug* **onjibidemagad**; *prt aug* **wenjibidemagak**
onjibizo *vai* speed from a certain place, drive from a certain place, fall from a certain place; *1sg* **indoonjibiz**; *prt* **wenjibizod**
onjida *pc* on purpose
onjidaabii'iwe *vai* drive from a certain place; *1sg* **indoonjidaabii'iwe**; *prt* **wenjidaabii'iwed**
onjigaa *vii* leak, drip, run with sap; *prt* **wenjigaag**; *aug* **onjigaamagad**; *prt aug* **wenjigaamagak**
onjijiwan *vii* flow from a certain place; *prt* **wenjijiwang**
onjinawe' *vta* anger s.o. for a certain reason, make s.o. mad for a certain reason; *1sg* **indoonjinawe'aa**; *prt* **wenjinawe'aad**
onjinazh /onjinaN-/ *vta* kill s.o. for a certain reason; *1sg* **indoonjinanaa**; *prt* **wenjinanaad**
onjinizhimo *vai* run from a certain place in flight; *1sg* **indoonjinizhim**; *prt* **wenjinizhimod**
onjise *vai* fly from a certain place; *1sg* **indoonjise**; *prt* **wenjised**
onjise *vii* fly from a certain place; *prt* **wenjiseg**; *aug* **onjisemagad**; *prt aug* **wenjisemagak**
onjishkawa'o *vai* paddle against the wind; *1sg* **indoonjishkawa'**; *prt* **wenjishkawa'od**; *also* **onjishkawa'am**
onjishkawishkaa *vai* go against the wind; *1sg* **indoonjishkawishkaa**; *prt* **wenjishkawishkaad**
onjiwidoon *vti2* take s.t. from a certain place, carry s.t. from a certain place; *1sg* **indoonjiwidoon**; *prt* **wenjiwidood**
onjiwizh /onjiwiN-/ *vta* take s.o. from a certain place, carry s.o. from a certain place; *1sg* **indoonjiwinaa**; *prt* **wenjiwinaad**
onjii *vai* come from a certain place; *1sg* **indoonjii**; *prt* **wenjiid**
onow *pr* these *inanimate plural demonstrative*, this, these *animate obviative demonstrative*; *also* **ono**
onowedin *pr* these over here *inanimate plural demonstrative*, this/these over here *obviative demonstrative*
onwaachige *vai* foretell the future; *1sg* **indoonwaachige**; *prt* **wenwaachiged**
onwaawe *vai* hiccough; *1sg* **indoonwaawe**; *prt* **wenwaawed**
onzan *vti* boil s.t.; *1sg* **indoonzaan**; *prt* **wenzang**
onzaabi *vai* look out from a certain place; *1sg* **indoonzaab**; *prt* **wenzaabid**
onzaam *pc* too much, excessively, extremely
onzaamashkinadoon *vti2* overfill s.t. with solids; *1sg* **indoonzaamashkinadoon**; *prt* **wenzaamashkinadood**
onzaamashkina' *vta* overfill s.o. with solids; *1sg* **indoonzaamashkina'aa**; *prt* **wenzaamashkina'aad**
onzaamaakide *vii* be burnt crisp; *prt* **wenzaamaakideg**; *aug* **onzaamaakidemagad**; *prt aug* **wenzaamaakidemagak**
onzaamaakizo *vai* be burnt crisp; *prt* **wenzaamaakizod**
onzaamendam *vai2* give too much consideration; *1sg* **indoonzaamendam**; *prt* **wenzaamendang**
onzaamenimo *vai* be elated, be overexcited; *1sg* **indoonzaamenim**; *prt* **wenzaamenimod**
onzaamibadoon *vti2* overfill s.t. (with a liquid); *1sg* **indoonzaamibadoon**; *prt* **wenzaamibadood**
onzaamibazh /onzaamibaN-/ *vta* give s.o. too much to drink; *1sg* **indoonzaamibanaa**; *prt* **wenzaamibanaad**
onzaamibii *vai* drink too much; *1sg* **indoonzaamibii**; *prt* **wenzaamibiid**
onzaamichige *vai* overdo things; *1sg* **indoonzaamichige**; *prt* **wenzaamichiged**
onzaamide *vii* be overcooked; *prt* **wenzaamideg**; *aug* **onzaamidemagad**; *prt aug* **wenzaamidemagak**
onzaamidoon *vai* talk too much; *1sg* **indoonzaamidoon**; *prt* **wenzaamidoong**
onzaamine *vai* be very sick; *1sg* **indoonzaamine**; *prt* **wenzaamined**
onzaamingwaam *vai* oversleep; *1sg* **indoonzaamingwaam**; *prt* **wenzaamingwaang**
onzaamiwane *vai* pack too much of a load; *1sg* **indoonzaamiwane**; *prt* **wenzaamiwaned**
onzaamiz /onzaamizw-/ *vta* overcook s.o., overheat s.o.; *1sg* **indoonzaamizwaa**; *prt* **wenzaamizwaad**
onzaamizan *vti* overcook s.t., overheat s.t.; *1sg* **indoonzaamizaan**; *prt* **wenzaamizang**
onzaamizo *vai* be overcooked; *prt* **wenzaamizod**
onzaamiinad *vii* be too much, be too many; *prt* **wenzaamiinak**
onzaamiino *vai* be too much, be too many; *prt* **wenzaamiinod**
onzo *vai* boil; *prt* **wenzod**

onzo /onzw-/ *vta* boil s.o.; *1sg* **indoonzwaa**; *prt* **wenzwaad**
opichi *na* robin; *pl* **opichiwag**; *dim* **opichiins**
opime-ayi'ii *pc* on the side of it; *also* **opimeya'ii**
opimekana *pc* along the side of the road, along the side of the trail
opimese *vai* fall on the side; *prt* **wepimesed**
opimeshim *vai* lay s.o. on side; *1sg* **indoopimeshimaa**; *prt* **wepimeshimaad**
opimeshin *vai* lie on one's side; *1sg* **indoopimeshin**; *prt* **wepimeshing**
opimesidoon *vti2* lay s.t. on side; *1sg* **indoopimesidoon**; *prt* **wepimesidood**
opimesin *vii* lie on side; *prt* **wepimesing**
opin *na* potato; *pl* **opiniig**; *dim* **opiniins**
opwaagan *na* pipe (for smoking); *pl* **opwaaganag**; *loc* **opwaaganing**; *dim* **opwaagaans**

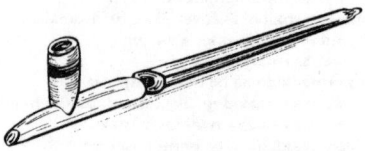

opwaagan (pipe), okij (pipe stem)

opwaaganasin *na* pipestone; *pl* **opwaaganasiniig**
opwaagaans *na* cigarette; *pl* **opwaagaansag**; *loc* **opwaagaansing**
oshaakaw *vta* scare s.o. away (e.g., game); *1sg* **indooshaakawaa**; *prt* **weshaakawaad**
oshedinaa *vii* there is a ridge; *prt* **weshedinaag**; *aug* **oshedinaamagad**; *prt aug* **weshedinaamagak**
oshkagoojin *vai* be new (of a moon); *prt* **weshkagoojing**; *also* **oshki-agoojin**
oshkanzhiikaajigan *ni* horseshoe; *pl* **oshkanzhiikaajiganan**; *loc* **oshkanzhiikaajiganing**; *dim* **oshkanzhiikaajigaans**
oshkaya'aawi *vai* be young; *1sg* **indooshkaya'aaw**; *prt* **wedooshkaya'aawid**; *also* **oshki-aya'aawi**
oshkaya'aa *na* someone new, someone young; *pl* **oshkaya'aag**; *dim* **oshkaya'aans**; *also* **oshki-aya'aa**
oshkayi'ii *ni* something new, something young; *pl* **oshkayi'iin**; *dim* **oshkayi'iins**; *also* **oshki-ayi'ii**
oshkayi'iiwan *vii* be young, be new; *prt* **weshkayi'iiwang**
oshkaabewis *na* ceremonial attendant, ceremonial messenger; *pl* **oshkaabewisag**; *dim* **oshkaabewisens**
oshki- *pv4* new, young, for the first time
oshki-bimaadizi *vai* be young; *1sg* **indooshki-bimaadiz**; *prt* **weshki-bimaadizid**
oshki-dibikad *vii* be early in the night; *prt* **weshki-dibikak**
oshki'o *vai* wear new clothes; *1sg* **indooshki'**; *prt* **weshki'od**
oshki-inini *na* young man; *pl* **oshki-ininiwag**
oshkikonaye *vai* dress in a new outfit; *1sg* **indooshkikonaye**; *prt* **weshkikonayed**
oshkinawe *na* young man, adolescent boy; *pl* **oshkinaweg**; *dim* **oshkinawens**
oshkinawewi *vai* be a young man, be an adolescent boy; *1sg* **indooshkinawew**; *prt* **weshkinawewid**
oshkiniigi *vai* be young, be an adolescent; *1sg* **indooshkiniig**; *prt* **weshkiniigid**
oshkiniigikwe *na* young woman, adolescent girl; *pl* **oshkiniigikweg**; *dim* **oshkiniigikwens**
oshkiniigikwewi *vai* be a young woman, be an adolescent girl; *1sg* **indooshkiniigikwew**; *prt* **weshkiniigikwewid**
oshkiinaagozi *vai* look young, look new; *1sg* **indooshkiinaagoz**; *prt* **weshkiinaagozid**
oshkiinaagwad *vii* look new; *prt* **weshkiinaagwak**
oshkiinzhigokaajiganan *ni* eyeglasses *plural*; *loc* **oshkiinzhigokaajiganing**; *dim* **oshkiinzhigokaajigaansan**; *also* **oshkiinzhikokaanan**
oshkiinzhigokewinini *na* optometrist; *pl* **oshkiinzhigokewininiwag**
oshtigwaanens *ni* postage stamp; *pl* **oshtigwaanensan**; *loc* **oshtigwaanensing**
oshtigwaanzhaabonigan *ni* common pin; *pl* **oshtigwaanzhaaboniganan**
osidaawendam *vai2* be sad, be dejected, be sorrowful; *1sg* **indoosidaawendam**; *prt* **wesidaawendang**
owa *pc exclamation of agreeable surprise*
owedi *pr* this over here *inanimate singular demonstrative; also* **o'owedi**
owidi *pc* over here; *also* **o'owidi**
owiiyawen'enyi *vai* be a namesake; *1sg* **indoowiiyawen'enh**; *prt* **wewiiyawen'enyid**
ozagaskwaajime *na* leech, bloodsucker; *pl* **ozagaskwaajimeg**; *dim* **ozagaskwaajimens**; *also* **zagaskwaajime**
ozaawaa *vii* be brown, be yellow; *prt* **wezaawaag**; *aug* **ozaawaamagad**; *prt aug* **wezaawaamagak**
ozaawaabik *ni* (piece of) brass; *pl* **ozaawaabikoon**; *loc* **ozaawaabikong**
ozaawaabikad *vii* be brown (as something mineral), be yellow (as something mineral), be brass; *prt* **wezaawaabikak**
ozaawaabikizi *vai* be brown (as something mineral), be yellow (as something mineral), be brass; *prt* **wezaawaabikizid**
ozaawaabikoons *na* cent, penny; *pl* **ozaawaabikoonsag**; *loc* **ozaawaabikoonsing**
ozaawaabiigad *vii* be brown (as something string-like), be yellow (as something string-like); *prt* **wezaawaabiigak**
ozaawaabiigizi *vai* be brown (as something string-like), be yellow (as something string-like); *prt* **wezaawaabiigizid**
ozaawaakizan *vti* brown s.t. by fire, toast s.t. brown; *1sg* **indoozaawaakizaan**; *prt* **wezaawaakizang**
ozaawaakozi *vai* be brown (as something stick- or wood-like), be yellow (as something stick- or wood-like); *prt* **wezaawaakozid**
ozaawaakwad *vii* be brown (as something stick- or wood-like), be yellow (as something stick- or wood-like); *prt* **wezaawaakwak**

ozaawaande *vii* be colored brown, be colored yellow; *prt* **wezaawaandeg**; *aug* **ozaawaandemagad**; *prt aug* **wezaawaandemagak**
ozaawaanzo *vai* be colored brown, be colored yellow; *prt* **wezaawaanzod**
ozaawaa-zhooniyaa *ni* gold; *loc* **ozaawaa-zhooniyaang**; *dim* **ozaawaa-zhooniyaans**; *also* **ozhaawaa-zhooniyaa**
ozaawaa-zhooniyaawaande *vii* be colored gold; *prt* **wezaawaa-zhooniyaawaandeg**; *aug* **ozaawaa-zhooniyaawaandemagad**; *prt aug* **wezaawaa-zhooniyaawaandemagak**; *also* **ozhaawaa-zhooniyaawaande**
ozaawaa-zhooniyaawaanzo *vai* be colored gold; *prt* **wezaawaa-zhooniyaawaanzod**; *also* **ozhaawaa-zhooniyaanzo**
ozaawegad *vii* be brown (as something sheet-like), be yellow (as something sheet-like); *prt* **wezaawegak**
ozaawegizi *vai* be brown (as something sheet-like), be yellow (as something sheet-like); *prt* **wezaawegizid**
ozaawi- *pv4* brown, yellow
ozaawi-bimide *ni* butter; *loc* **ozaawi-bimideng**
ozaawi'o *vai* wear brown, wear yellow; *1sg* **indoozaawi'**; *prt* **wezaawi'od**
ozaawikaadaak *ni* carrot; *pl* **ozaawikaadaakoon**; *loc* **ozaawikaadaakong**; *dim* **ozaawikaadaakoons**
ozaawikosimaan *ni* pumpkin; *pl* **ozaawikosimaanan**; *loc* **ozaawikosimaaning**; *dim* **ozaawikosimaanens**
ozaawindibe *vai* be blond, have brown hair; *1sg* **indoozaawindibe**; *prt* **wezaawindibed**
ozaawizi *vai* be brown, be yellow; *prt* **wezaawizid**
ozhaashadamon /ozhaashadamo-/ *vii* be slippery (as a road or trail); *prt* **wezhaashadamog**
ozhaashaa *vii* be slippery, be slick; *prt* **wezhaashaag**; *aug* **ozhaashaamagad**; *prt aug* **wezhaashaamagak**
ozhaashaabikad *vii* be slippery (as something mineral); *prt* **wezhaashaabikak**
ozhaashaabikizi *vai* be slippery (as something mineral); *prt* **wezhaashaabikizid**
ozhaashaakozi *vai* be slippery (as something stick- or wood-like); *prt* **wezhaashaakozid**
ozhaashaakwad *vii* be slippery (as something stick- or wood-like); *prt* **wezhaashaakwak**
ozhaashigob *na* slippery elm; *pl* **ozhaashigobiig**; *loc* **ozhaashigobiing**; *dim* **ozhaashigobiins**
ozhaashikoshin *vai* slip and fall on the ice; *1sg* **indoozhaashikoshin**; *prt* **wezhaashikoshing**
ozhaashikwadamon /ozhaashikwadamo-/ *vii* be slippery with ice (as a road or trail); *prt* **wezhaashikwadamog**
ozhaashikwaa *vii* there is slippery ice; *prt* **wezhaashikwaag**; *aug* **ozhaashikwaamagad**; *prt aug* **wezhaashikwaamagak**
ozhaashishin *vai* slip and fall; *1sg* **indoozhaashishin**; *prt* **wezhaashishing**
ozhaashizi *vai* be slippery, be slick; *prt* **wezhaashizid**
ozhaawashko- *pv4* blue, green
ozhaawashko-aniibiish *ni* green tea; *loc* **ozhaawashko-aniibiishing**
ozhaawashko-bineshiinh *na* bluebird; *pl* **ozhaawashko-bineshiinyag**
ozhaawashko'o *vai* wear blue, wear green; *1sg* **indoozhaawashko'**; *prt* **wezhaawashko'od**
ozhaawashko-manoomin *ni* green wild rice; *loc* **ozhaawashko-manoomining**
ozhaawashkozi *vai* be blue, be green; *prt* **wezhaawashkozid**
ozhaawashkwaa *vii* be blue, be green; *prt* **wezhaawashkwaag**; *aug* **ozhaawashkwaamagad**; *prt aug* **wezhaawashkwaamagak**
ozhaawashkwaabi *vai* have a black eye; *1sg* **indoozhaawashkwaab**; *prt* **wezhaawashkwaabid**
ozhaawashkwaabikad *vii* be blue (as something mineral), be green (as something mineral); *prt* **wezhaawashkwaabikak**
ozhaawashkwaabikizi *vai* be blue (as something mineral), be green (as something mineral); *prt* **wezhaawashkwaabikizid**
ozhaawashkwaabiigad *vii* be blue (as something string-like), be green (as something string-like); *prt* **wezhaawashkwaabiigak**
ozhaawashkwaabiigizi *vai* be blue (as something string-like), be green (as something string-like); *prt* **wezhaawashkwaabiigizid**
ozhaawashkwaakozi *vai* be blue (as something stick- or wood-like), be green (as something stick- or wood-like); *prt* **wezhaawashkwaakozid**
ozhaawashkwaakwad *vii* be blue (as something stick- or wood-like), be green (as something stick- or wood-like); *prt* **wezhaawashkwaakwak**
ozhaawashkwaanagiingwe *vai* have a bruised face; *1sg* **indoozhaawashkwaanagiingwe**; *prt* **wezhaawashkwaanagiingwed**
ozhaawashkwegad *vii* be blue (as something sheet-like), be green (as something sheet-like); *prt* **wezhaawashkwegak**
ozhaawashkwegizi *vai* be blue (as something sheet-like), be green (as something sheet-like); *prt* **wezhaawashkwegizid**
ozhibii' /ozhibii'w-/ *vta* write s.o. down; *1sg* **indoozhibii'waa**; *prt* **wezhibii'waad**
ozhibii'amaw *vta* write (s.t.) for s.o.; *1sg* **indoozhibii'amawaa**; *prt* **wezhibii'amawaad**
ozhibii'an *vti* write s.t., write s.t. down; *1sg* **indoozhibii'aan**; *prt* **wezhibii'ang**
ozhibii'igan *ni* letter of the alphabet, something written; *pl* **ozhibii'iganan**; *loc* **ozhibii'iganing**; *dim* **ozhibii'igaans**
ozhibii'iganaaboo *ni* ink; *loc* **ozhibii'iganaaboong**
ozhibii'iganaak *ni* pen, pencil; *pl* **ozhibii'iganaakoon**; *loc* **ozhibii'iganaakong**; *dim* **ozhibii'iganaakoons**
ozhibii'igaade *vii* be written; *prt* **wezhibii'igaadeg**; *aug* **ozhibii'igaademagad**; *prt aug* **wezhibii'igaademagak**
ozhibii'ige *vai* write; *1sg* **indoozhibii'ige**; *prt* **wezhibii'iged**

ozhibii'ige-adoopowin *ni* desk; *pl* **ozhibii'ige-adoopowinan**; *loc* **ozhibii'ige-adoopowining**; *dim* **ozhibii'ige-adoopowinens**
ozhibii'igewigamig *ni* office; *pl* **ozhibii'igewigamigoon**; *loc* **ozhibii'igewigamigong**; *dim* **ozhibii'igewigamigoons**
ozhibii'igewikwe *na* secretary (female), clerk (female); *pl* **ozhibii'igewikweg**
ozhibii'igewinini *na* secretary (male), clerk (male); *pl* **ozhibii'igewininiwag**
ozhichigaade *vii* be made, be built; *prt* **wezhichigaadeg**; *aug* **ozhichigaademagad**; *prt aug* **wezhichigaademagak**
ozhichigaazo *vai* be made, be built; *prt* **wezhichigaazod**
ozhichige *vai* make things; *1sg* **indoozhichige**; *prt* **wezhichiged**
ozhiga'ige *vai* tap trees; *1sg* **indoozhiga'ige**; *prt* **wezhiga'iged**
ozhigaw *vta* build a house for s.o.; *1sg* **indoozhigawaa**; *prt* **wezhigawaad**
ozhige *vai* build a lodge; *1sg* **indoozhige**; *prt* **wezhiged**
ozhi' *vta* make s.o., build s.o., form s.o.; *1sg* **indoozhi'aa**; *prt* **wezhi'aad**
ozhim *vta* escape from s.o.; *1sg* **indoozhimaa**; *prt* **wezhimaad**
ozhimo *vai* flee; *1sg* **indoozhim**; *prt* **wezhimod**
ozhitamaw *vta* make (s.t.) for s.o., build (s.t.) for s.o.; *1sg* **indoozhitamawaa**; *prt* **wezhitamawaad**
ozhitaw *vta* make (s.t.) for s.o., build (s.t.) for s.o.; *1sg* **indoozhitawaa**; *prt* **wezhitawaad**
ozhitoon *vti2* make s.t., build s.t., form s.t.; *1sg* **indoozhitoon**; *prt* **wezhitood**
ozhiwanikaadan *vti* make a pack of s.t.; *1sg* **indoozhiwanikaadaan**; *prt* **wezhiwanikaadang**
ozhiwanike *vai* pack up; *1sg* **indoozhiwanike**; *prt* **wezhiwaniked**
ozhiitaa *vai* get ready, prepare; *1sg* **indoozhiitaa**; *prt* **wezhiitaad**
ozhooniyaami *vai* have money; *1sg* **indoozhooniyaam**; *prt* **wezhooniyaamid**
ozide-miikana *ni* footpath; *pl* **ozide-miikanan**; *loc* **ozide-miikanaang**; *dim* **ozide-miikanens, ozide-miikanaans**
ozisijige *vai* make a bed; *1sg* **indoozisijige**; *prt* **wezisijiged**; *also* **ozhisijige**
ozisinaagane *vai* set the table; *1sg* **indoozisinaagane**; *prt* **wezisinaaganed**
oziigaa *vii* be wrinkled; *prt* **weziigaag**; *aug* **oziigaamagad**; *prt aug* **weziigaamagak**
oziigishkaa *vai* wrinkle up; *prt* **weziigishkaad**
oziigishkaa *vii* wrinkle up; *prt* **weziigishkaag**; *aug* **oziigishkaamagad**; *prt aug* **weziigishkaamagak**
oziigizi *vai* be wrinkled; *1sg* **indooziigiz**; *prt* **weziigizid**
oziigiingwe *vai* have a wrinkled face; *1sg* **indooziigiingwe**; *prt* **weziigiingwed**
oziisigobimizh *na* willow; *pl* **oziisigobimizhiig**; *loc* **oziisigobimizhiing**; *dim* **oziisigobimizhiins**
oziisigobimizhii-makak *ni* willow basket; *pl* **oziisigobimizhii-makakoon**; *loc* **oziisigobimizhii-makakong**; *dim* **oziisigobimizhii-makakoons**
ozosodam *vai2* cough; *1sg* **indoozosodam**; *prt* **wezosodang**
ozosodamoo-mashkiki *ni* cough medicine
ozosodamwaapine *vai* have a respiratory illness, have tuberculosis; *1sg* **indoozosodamwaapine**; *prt* **wezosodamwaapined**
ozosodamwaapinewin *ni* tuberculosis
oo *pc* oh!
oodena *ni* town; *pl* **oodenawan**; *loc* **oodenaang**; *dim* **oodenawens, oodenaans**
oojii *na* fly (insect); *pl* **oojiig**; *dim* **oojiins**; *also* **oojiins**
ookwe *na* maggot; *pl* **ookweg**; *dim* **ookwens**
ookwemin *ni* black cherry; *pl* **ookweminan**; *dim* **ookweminens**
ookweminagaawanzh *na* black cherry bush; *pl* **ookweminagaawanzhiig**; *loc* **ookweminagaawanzhiing**; *dim* **ookweminagaawanzhiins**
oonh *pc* oh!, so...

P

pane *pc* always, continuously; *also* **apane**

S

sa *pc emphatic*; *also* **isa**
-sh *pc* and, and then; *also* **dash, idash**
shi *pc* plus *used in counting*; *also* **ashi**

T

taayaa *pc man's expression of mild displeasure or disdain*; *also* **aatayaa**

W

w= *pre third person prefix before an initial* ii *of a dependent noun stem*
wabaashiiwan *vii* there is a narrows; *prt* **webaashiiwang**
wabigamaa *vii* there is a channel between lakes, there is a narrows; *prt* **webigamaag**; *aug* **wabigamaamagad**; *prt aug* **webigamaamagak**
wadab *na* spruce root; *pl* **wadabiig**; *loc* **wadabiing**; *dim* **wadabiins**
wadabii-makak *ni* basket of spruce root; *pl* **wadabii-makakoon**; *loc* **wadabii-makakong**; *dim* **wadabii-makakoons**
wadikwan *ni* branch; *pl* **wadikwanan**; *loc* **wadikwaning**; *dim* **wadikwaans**
wadiswan *ni* bird nest; *pl* **wadiswanan**; *loc* **wadiswaning**; *dim* **wadiswaans**
wado *na* blood clot; *pl* **wadowag**
wadoop *ni* alder; *pl* **wadoopiin**; *loc* **wadoopiing**; *dim* **wadoopiins**
wagidajiw *pc* on top of a mountain; *also* **ogidajiw*, agidajiw**
wagidakamig *pc* on top of the ground; *also* **ogidakamig*, agidakamig**
wagidasin *pc* on top of a rock; *also* **ogidasin*, agidasin**
wagidaabik *pc* on something mineral (e.g., metal, glass, rock); *also* **ogidaabik*, agidaabik**
wagidaajiwan *pc* upstream; *also* **ogidaajiwan*, agidaajiwan**
wagidaaki *pc* on top of a hill; *also* **ogidaaki*, agidaaki**
wagidibiig *pc* on top of the water; *also* **ogidibiig*, agidibiig**
wagidigamig *pc* on top of the house; *also* **ogidigamig*, agidigamig**
wagidiskwam *pc* on top of the ice; *also* **ogidiskwam*, agidiskwam**
wagijayi'ii *pc* on top of it; *also* **ogijayi'ii*, agijayi'ii**
wagiji- *pn* on top of; *also* **ogiji-*, agiji-**
wa'aw *pr* this *animate singular demonstrative*
wa'awedi *pr* this over here *animate singular demonstrative*
wajepii *vai* be fast; *1sg* **niwajepii**; *prt* **wejepiid**
wajiw *ni* mountain; *pl* **wajiwan**; *loc* **wajiwing**; *dim* **wajiwens**
wakewaji *vai* can't take the cold, get chilled easily; *1sg* **niwakewaj**; *prt* **wekewajid**
wanagek *na* bark (of a tree); *pl* **wanagekwag**; *loc* **wanagekong**; *dim* **wanagekoons**
wanagekogamig *ni* bark lodge; *pl* **wanagekogamigoon**; *loc* **wanagekogamigong**; *dim* **wanagekogamigoons**
wanagim *vta* miscount s.o.; *1sg* **niwanagimaa**; *prt* **wenagimaad**
wanagindan *vti* miscount s.t., misread s.t.; *1sg* **niwanagindaan**; *prt* **wenagindang**
wanagindaaso *vai* miscount, misread; *1sg* **niwanagindaas**; *prt* **wenagindaasod**
wanakong *pc* on the tip, on the treetop
wanaabidoo'an *vti* make a mistake beading s.t. on a loom; *1sg* **niwanaabidoo'aan**; *prt* **wenaabidoo'ang**
wanaabidoo'ige *vai* make a mistake beading things on a loom; *1sg* **niwanaabidoo'ige**; *prt* **wenaabidoo'iged**
wanaanimizi *vai* have stage fright, be confused; *1sg* **niwanaanimiz**; *prt* **wenaanimizid**
wanendam *vai2* forget; *1sg* **niwanendam**; *prt* **wenendang**
wanendamaa *vai* faint; *1sg* **niwanendamaa**; *prt* **wenendamaad**
wanendan *vti* forget s.t.; *1sg* **niwanendaan**; *prt* **wenendang**
wanenim *vta* forget s.o.; *1sg* **niwanenimaa**; *prt* **wenenimaad**
wani- *pv4* in error, by mistake
wanibatoo *vai* run the wrong way; *1sg* **niwanibatoo**; *prt* **wenibatood**
wanibizo *vai* get lost driving; *1sg* **niwanibiz**; *prt* **wenibizod**
wanibii'an *vti* make a mistake writing s.t.; *1sg* **niwanibii'aan**; *prt* **wenibii'ang**
wanibii'ige *vai* make a mistake writing; *1sg* **niwanibii'ige**; *prt* **wenibii'iged**
wanichige *vai* make a mistake; *1sg* **niwanichige**; *prt* **wenichiged**
wanigiizhwe *vai* make a mistake speaking, mispronounce; *1sg* **niwanigiizhwe**; *prt* **wenigiizhwed**
wanigwaadan *vti* make a mistake sewing on s.t.; *1sg* **niwanigwaadaan**; *prt* **wenigwaadang**
wanigwaaso *vai* make a mistake sewing; *1sg* **niwanigwaas**; *prt* **wenigwaasod**
wanigwaazh /wanigwaaN-/ *vta* make a mistake sewing on s.o.; *1sg* **niwanigwaanaa**; *prt* **wenigwaanaad**
wani' *vta* lose s.o.; *1sg* **niwani'aa**; *prt* **weni'aad**
wanim *vta* mislead s.o. by speech, confuse s.o. by speech; *1sg* **niwanimaa**; *prt* **wenimaad**
wanin *vta* take s.o. who/that is the wrong one, touch s.o. who/that is the wrong one; *1sg* **niwaninaa**; *prt* **weninaad**
waninan *vti* take s.t. that is the wrong one, touch s.t. that is the wrong one; *1sg* **niwaninaan**; *prt* **weninang**
waninawe'an *vti* stir s.t.; *1sg* **niwaninawe'aan**; *prt* **weninawe'ang**
waninawe'igan *ni* eggbeater, mixer; *pl* **waninawe'iganan**; *loc* **waninawe'iganing**; *dim* **waninawe'igaans**
wanishim *vta* misplace s.o.; *1sg* **niwanishimaa**; *prt* **wenishimaad**
wanishin *vai* be lost, get lost; *1sg* **niwanishin**; *prt* **wenishing**
wanishkwe' *vta* distract s.o., interrupt s.o.; *1sg* **niwanishkwe'aa**; *prt* **wenishkwe'aad**
wanishkwem *vta* disturb s.o. by speech, interrupt s.o. by speech; *1sg* **niwanishkwemaa**; *prt* **wenishkwemaad**
wanishkweyendam *vai* be distracted; *1sg* **niwanishkweyendam**; *prt* **wenishkweyendang**
wanisidoon *vti2* misplace s.t.; *1sg* **niwanisidoon**; *prt* **wenisidood**
wanisin *vii* be lost, get lost; *prt* **wenising**

wanitam *vai2* misunderstand something heard; *1sg* **niwanitam**; *prt* **wenitang**
wanitaw *vta* misunderstand (what) s.o. (says); *1sg* **niwanitawaa**; *prt* **wenitawaad**
wanitoon *vti2* lose s.t.; *1sg* **niwanitoon**; *prt* **wenitood**
wanii'amaw *vta* trap for s.o.; *1sg* **niwanii'amawaa**; *prt* **wenii'amawaad**
wanii'igan *ni* trap; *pl* **wanii'iganan**; *loc* **wanii'iganing**; *dim* **wanii'igaans**
wanii'ige *vai* trap; *1sg* **niwanii'ige**; *prt* **wenii'iged**
wanii'igewinini *na* trapper; *pl* **wanii'igewininiwag**
waniike *vai+o* forget (s.t.); *1sg* **niwaniike, niwaniiken**; *prt* **weniiked**
wapaa' *vta* disturb s.o.'s sleep; *1sg* **niwapaa'aa**; *prt* **wepaa'aad**
washkibagizo *vai* turn in place; *1sg* **niwashkibagiz**; *prt* **weshkibagizod**
washkigaabawi *vai* turn while standing; *1sg* **niwashkigaabaw**; *prt* **weshkigaabawid**
washki-giiwe *vai* turn and go back; *1sg* **niwashki-giiwe**; *prt* **weshki-giiwed**
washkitigweyaa *vii* flow around a bend (as a river); *prt* **weshkitigweyaag**; *aug* **washkitigweyaamagad**; *prt aug* **weshkitigweyaamagak**
wawaase= < waase
wawaasese *vii* there is lightning; *prt* **wewaaseseg**; *aug* **wawaasesemagad**; *prt aug* **wewaasesemagak**
wawenabi *vai* sit down, be seated; *1sg* **niwawenab**; *prt* **wewenabid**
wawezhichigaade *vii* be decorated, be made pretty; *prt* **wewezhichigaadeg**; *aug* **wawezhichigaademagad**; *prt aug* **wewezhichigaademagak**
wawezhichigaazo *vai* be decorated; *prt* **wewezhichigaazod**
wawezhichige *vai* decorate things; *1sg* **niwawezhichige**; *prt* **wewezhichiged**
wawezhi' *vta* decorate s.o., dress s.o. up, make s.o. up; *1sg* **niwawezhi'aa**; *prt* **wewezhi'aad**
wawezhi'o *vai* dress up, make up oneself; *1sg* **niwawezhi'**; *prt* **wewezhi'od**
wawezhitoon *vti2* decorate s.t.; *1sg* **niwawezhitoon**; *prt* **wewezhitood**
wawiyadendaagozi *vai* be considered cute, be considered funny (comical); *1sg* **niwawiyadendaagoz**; *prt* **wewiyadendaagozid**
wawiyadendaagwad *vii* be cute; *prt* **wewiyadendaagwak**
wawiyadenim *vta* think s.o. cute, think s.o. comical; *1sg* **niwawiyadenimaa**; *prt* **wewiyadenimaad**
wawiyazh *pc* funny, comical
wawiyazhinaagozi *vai* look cute, look funny (comical); *1sg* **niwawiyazhinaagoz**; *prt* **wewiyazhinaagozid**
wawiyazhinaagwad *vii* look cute, look funny (comical); *prt* **wewiyazhinaagwak**
wawiyazhitaagozi *vai* sound cute, sound funny (comical); *1sg* **niwawiyazhitaagoz**; *prt* **wewiyazhitaagozid**
wawiyazhitaagwad *vii* sound cute, sound funny (comical); *prt* **wewiyazhitaagwak**
wawiinge *pc* well, properly, carefully, completely
wawiingechige *vai* do exactly, do skilfully; *1sg* **niwawiingechige**; *prt* **wewiingechiged**
wawiinge' *vta* make s.o. skilfully; *1sg* **niwawiinge'aa**; *prt* **wewiinge'aad**
wawiingetoon *vti2* make s.t. skilfully; *1sg* **niwawiingetoon**; *prt* **wewiingetood**
wawiingezi *vai* be skilful; *1sg* **niwawiingez**; *prt* **wewiingezid**
way *pc exclamation*
wayaabishkiiwed *na-pt* white person; *pl* **wayaabishkiiwejig**
wayekwaase *vii* come to an end; *prt* **weyekwaaseg**; *aug* **wayekwaasemagad**; *prt aug* **weyekwaasemagak**
wayeshkad *pc* at first, in the beginning
wayezhim *vta* cheat s.o., deceive s.o.; *1sg* **niwayezhimaa**; *prt* **weyezhimaad**
wayezhinge *vai* cheat people, deceive people; *1sg* **niwayezhinge**; *prt* **weyezhinged**
wayiiba *pc* soon, early, in a little while; *also* **wiiba***
wazhashk *na* muskrat; *pl* **wazhashkwag**; *dim* **wazhashkoons**
wazhashkwayaan *na* muskrat hide; *pl* **wazhashkwayaanag**; *loc* **wazhashkwayaaning**; *dim* **wazhashkwayaanens**
wazhashkwedo *na* fungus; *pl* **wazhashkwedowag**; *dim* **wazhaskwedoons**
wazhashkwedoons *na* mushroom; *pl* **wazhashkwedoonsag**
wazhashkwiish *ni* muskrat lodge; *pl* **wazhashkwiishan**; *loc* **wazhashkwiishing**
waa *pc exclamation*
waa- *pv1* will, want to *changed form of future/desiderative verb prefix*
waabam *vta* see s.o.; *1sg* **niwaabamaa**; *prt* **wayaabamaad**
waabamoojichaagwaan *ni* mirror; *pl* **waabamoojichaagwaanan**; *loc* **waabamoojichaagwaaning**; *dim* **waabamoojichaagwaanens**
waaban *vii* be dawn, be tomorrow; *prt* **wayaabang**
waabananokii *vai* work until dawn; *1sg* **niwaabananokii**; *prt* **wayaabananokiid**
waabanda' *vta* show (s.t.) to s.o.; *1sg* **niwaabanda'aa**; *prt* **wayaabanda'aad**
waabanda'iwe *vai* show (s.t.) to people; *1sg* **niwaabanda'iwe**; *prt* **wayaabanda'iwed**
waabanda'iwewin *ni* show, exhibition; *pl* **waabanda'iwewinan**; *loc* **waabanda'iwewining**
waabandan *vti* see s.t.; *1sg* **niwaabandaan**; *prt* **wayaabandang**
waabandiwag /waabandi-/ *vai* they see each other; *1pl* **niwaabandimin**; *prt* **wayaabandijig**
waabandizo *vai* see oneself; *1sg* **niwaabandiz**; *prt* **wayaabandizod**
waabandizowin *ni* mirror; *pl* **waabandizowinan**; *loc* **waabandizowining**; *dim* **waabandizowinens**

waabang *vii* tomorrow *conjunct form of verb* **waaban**
waabange *vai* observe people, be a spectator, be a witness; *1sg* **niwaabange**; *prt* **wayaabanged**
waabani-noodin *ni* east wind
waabanjigaade *vii* be seen; *prt* **wayaabanjigaadeg**; *aug* **waabanjigaademagad**; *prt aug* **wayaabanjigaademagak**
waabanjigaazo *vai* be seen; *prt* **wayaabanjigaazod**
waabanong *pc* in the east, to the east
waabashkiki *ni* swamp; *pl* **waabashkikiin**; *loc* **waabashkikiing**; *dim* **waabashkikiins**
waabashkikiiwan *vii* be swampy; *prt* **wayaabashkikiiwang**
waabaabigan *na* white clay
waabaaso *vai* fade from light; *prt* **wayaabaasod**
waabaate *vii* fade from light; *prt* **wayaabaateg**; *aug* **waabaatemagad**; *prt aug* **wayaabaatemagak**
waabi *vai* have vision, see; *1sg* **niwaab**; *prt* **wayaabid**
waabide *vii* be faded, be bleached; *prt* **wayaabideg**; *aug* **waabidemagad**; *prt aug* **wayaabidemagak**
waabigan *na* clay; *loc* **waabiganing**
waabiganikaade *vii* be made of clay, be made of concrete; *prt* **wayaabiganikaadeg**; *aug* **waabiganikaademagad**; *prt aug* **wayaabiganikaademagak**
waabigwan *ni* flower; *pl* **waabigwaniin**; *loc* **waabigwaniing**; *dim* **waabigwaniins**
waabigwanii-giizis *na* May
waabijiiyaa *vii* be grey; *prt* **wayaabijiiyaag**; *aug* **waabijiiyaamagad**; *prt aug* **wayaabijiiyaamagak**
waabijiizi *vai* be grey; *prt* **wayaabijiizid**
waabikwe *vai* have grey hair; *1sg* **niwaabikwe**; *prt* **wayaabikwed**
waabi-makade *ni* smokeless gunpowder
waabi-manoomin *ni* white rice; *loc* **waabi-manoomining**
waabishkawedoon *vai* have white whiskers; *1sg* **niwaabishkawedoon**; *prt* **wayaabishkawedoong**
waabishkaa *vii* be white; *prt* **wayaabishkaag**; *aug* **waabishkaamagad**; *prt aug* **wayaabishkaamagak**
waabishkaabikad *vii* be white (as something mineral); *prt* **wayaabishkaabikak**
waabishkaabikizi *vai* be white (as something mineral); *prt* **wayaabishkaabikizid**
waabishkaabiigad *vii* be white (as something string-like); *prt* **wayaabishkaabiigak**
waabishkaabiigizi *vai* be white (as something string-like); *prt* **wayaabishkaabiigizid**
waabishkaakozi *vai* be white (as something stick- or wood-like); *prt* **wayaabishkaakozid**
waabishkaakwad *vii* be white (as something stick- or wood-like); *prt* **wayaabishkaakwak**
waabishkaanakwad *vii* there are white clouds; *prt* **wayaabishkaanakwak**
waabishkaande *vii* be colored white; *prt* **wayaabishkaandeg**; *aug* **waabishkaandemagad**; *prt aug* **wayaabishkaandemagak**
waabishkaanzo *vai* be colored white; *prt* **wayaabishkaanzod**
waabishki- *pv4* white
waabishki'o *vai* wear white; *1sg* **niwaabishki'**; *prt* **wayaabishki'od**
waabishkindibe *vai* have white hair; *1sg* **niwaabishkindibe**; *prt* **wayaabishkindibed**
waabishkizi *vai* be white; *prt* **wayaabishkizid**
waabishkiigad *vii* be white (as something sheet-like); *prt* **wayaabishkiigak**
waabishkiigin *ni* sheet, white cloth; *pl* **waabishkiiginoon**; *loc* **waabishkiiginong**; *dim* **waabishkiiginoons**
waabishkiigizi *vai* be white (as something sheet-like); *prt* **wayaabishkiigizid**
waabishkiingwechigan *ni* face powder; *loc* **waabishkiingwechiganing**; *dim* **waabishkiingwechigaans**
waabishkiingwechige *vai* use face powder; *1sg* **niwaabishkiingwechige**; *prt* **wayaabishkiingwechiged**
waabishkiiwe *vai* be a white person; *1sg* **niwaabishkiiwe**; *prt* **wayaabishkiiwed**
waabizhagindibe *vai* be bald; *1sg* **niwaabizhagindibe**; *prt* **wayaabizhagindibed**
waabizheshi *na* marten; *pl* **waabizheshiwag**; *dim* **waabizheshiins**
waabizheshiwayaan *na* marten hide; *pl* **waabizheshiwayaanag**; *loc* **waabizheshiwayaaning**; *dim* **waabizheshiwayaanens**
waabizii *na* swan; *pl* **waabiziig**; *dim* **waabiziins**
waabizo *vai* be faded, be bleached; *prt* **wayaabizod**
waabiingwe *vai* be pale faced; *1sg* **niwaabiingwe**; *prt* **wayaabiingwed**
waaboozwayaan *na* rabbit skin; *pl* **waaboozwayaanag**; *dim* **waaboozwayaanens**
waabooyaan *ni* blanket; *pl* **waabooyaanan**; *loc* **waabooyaaning**; *dim* **waabooyaanens**; *also* **waabowayaan**
waabooz *na* snowshoe hare, rabbit; *pl* **waaboozoog**; *dim* **waaboozoons**
waaboozwaaboo *ni* rabbit soup; *loc* **waaboozwaaboong**
waagaa *vii* be bent; *prt* **wayaagaag**; *aug* **waagaamagad**; *prt aug* **wayaagaamagak**
waagaabikad *vii* be bent (as something mineral); *prt* **wayaagaabikak**
waagaabikizi *vai* be bent (as something mineral); *prt* **wayaagaabikizid**
waagaakozi *vai* be bent (as something stick- or wood-like); *prt* **wayaagaakozid**
waagaakwad *ni* ax; *pl* **waagaakwadoon**; *loc* **waagaakwadong**; *dim* **waagaakwadoons**
waagaakwad *vii* be bent (as something stick- or wood-like); *prt* **wayaagaakwak**
waagaakwadoons *ni* hatchet; *pl* **waagaakwadoonsan**; *loc* **waagaakwadoonsing**

waagaakwadwaatig *ni* ax handle; *pl* **waagaakwadwaatigoon**; *loc* **waagaakwadwaatigong**; *dim* **waagaakwadwaatigoons**
waagibidoon *vti2* bend s.t. with hands; *1sg* **niwaagibidoon**; *prt* **wayaagibidood**
waagibizh /waagibiN-/ *vta* bend s.o. with hands; *1sg* **niwaagibinaa**; *prt* **wayaagibinaad**
waagikomaan *ni* crooked knife; *pl* **waagikomaanan**; *dim* **waagikomaanens**

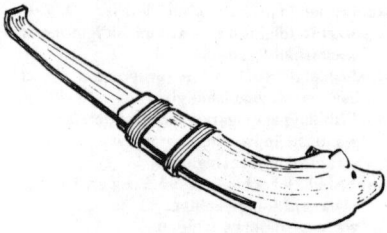

waagikomaan (crooked knife)

waagin *vta* bend s.o. with hand; *1sg* **niwaaginaa**; *prt* **wayaaginaad**
waaginan *vti* bend s.t. with hand; *1sg* **niwaaginaan**; *prt* **wayaaginang**
waaginaa *na* canoe rib; *pl* **waaginaag**; *loc* **waaginaang**; *dim* **waaginaans**
waaginogaan *ni* domed lodge, wigwam; *pl* **waaginogaanan**; *loc* **waaginogaaning**; *dim* **waaginogaanens**

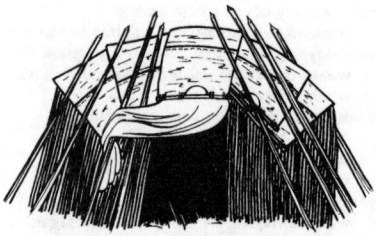

waaginogaan (domed lodge, wigwam)

waagizi *vai* be bent; *prt* **wayaagizid**
waagosh *na* fox; *pl* **waagoshag**; *dim* **waagoshens**
waagoshiwayaan *na* fox hide; *pl* **waagoshiwayaanag**; *dim* **waagoshiwayaanens**
waak *ni* fish egg; *pl* **waakwan**
waakaa'igan *ni* house, building; *pl* **waakaa'iganan**; *loc* **waakaa'iganing**; *dim* **waakaa'igaans**
waakaa'ige *vai* build a house; *1sg* **niwaakaa'ige**; *prt* **wayaakaa'iged**
waakaa'igewinini *na* carpenter; *pl* **waakaa'igewininiwag**
waangawi' *vta* tame s.o.; *1sg* **niwaangawi'aa**; *prt* **wayaangawi'aad**
waangawizi *vai* be tame; *1sg* **niwaangawiz**; *prt* **wayaangawizid**
waangoom *vta* adopt s.o.; *1sg* **niwaangoomaa**; *prt* **wayaangoomaad**
waanikaan *ni* excavated hole; *pl* **waanikaanan**; *loc* **waanikaaning**; *dim* **waanikaanens**
waanike *vai* dig a hole; *1sg* **niwaanike**; *prt* **wayaaniked**
waanzh *ni* den, cave, burrow; *pl* **waanzhan**; *loc* **waanzhing**; *dim* **waanzhens**
waanzhibiiyaa *vii* be a pond, be a pothole of water, be a puddle; *prt* **wayaanzhibiiyaag**; *aug* **waanzhibiiyaamagad**; *prt aug* **wayaanzhibiiyaamagak**
waasa *pc* far, distant
waasamowin *ni* lightning, electricity
waasamoo- *pv4* powered, electric
waasamoo-anokiiwinini *na* electrician; *pl* **waasamoo-anokiiwininiwag**
waasamoo-bimide *ni* gasoline; *loc* **waasamoo-bimideng**
waasamoo-jiimaan *ni* motor launch; *pl* **waasamoo-jiimaanan**; *loc* **waasamoo-jiimaaning**; *dim* **waasamoo-jiimaanens**
waasamoo-waazakonenjigan *ni* electric lamp; *pl* **waasamoo-waazakonenjiganan**; *loc* **waasamoo-waazakonenjiganing**; *dim* **waasamoo-waazakonenjigaans**
waasamoowidaabaan *na* car; *pl* **waasamoowidaabaanag**; *loc* **waasamoowidaabaaning**; *dim* **waasamoowidaabaanens**
waasawad *vii* be far; *prt* **wayaasawak**
waasaabikide *vii* shine (as something mineral), reflect (as something mineral); *prt* **wayaasaabikideg**; *aug* **waasaabikidemagad**; *prt aug* **wayaasaabikidemagak**
waasaabikizo *vai* shine (as something mineral), reflect (as something mineral); *prt* **wayaasaabikizod**
waasechigan *ni* window; *pl* **waasechiganan**; *loc* **waasechiganing**; *dim* **waasechigaans**
waasechiganaabik *ni* window glass, window pane; *pl* **waasechiganaabikoon**; *loc* **waasechiganaabikong**; *dim* **waasechiganaabikoons**
waasese *vii* there is a flash of lightning; *prt* **wayaaseseg**; *aug* **waasesemagad**; *prt aug* **wayaasesemagak**
waasete *vii* be bright inside; *prt* **wayaaseteg**; *aug* **waasetemagad**; *prt aug* **wayaasetemagak**
waaseyaa *vii* be bright, be sunny; *prt* **wayaaseyaag**; *aug* **waaseyaamagad**; *prt aug* **wayaaseyaamagak**
waaseyaaban *vii* be light at dawn; *prt* **wayaaseyaabang**
waaseyaanakwad *vii* clouds can be seen through; *prt* **wayaaseyaanakwak**
waaseyiigad *vii* be bright (as something sheet-like), be shiny (as something sheet-like); *prt* **wayaaseyiigak**

waaseyiigizi *vai* be bright (as something sheet-like), be shiny (as something sheet-like); *prt* **wayaaseyiigizid**
waashkobaagamig *ni-pt* soft drink; *pl* **waashkobaagamigin**
waashkobizid bakwezhigan *na-pt* sweet roll, pastry, cake; *pl* **waashkobizijig bakwezhiganag**
Waashtanong *place* Washington, D.C.
waasiko' *vta* make s.o. shiny; *1sg* **niwaasiko'aa**; *prt* **wayaasiko'aad**
waasikotoon *vti2* make s.t. shiny; *1sg* **niwaasikotoon**; *prt* **wayaasikotood**
waasikwa' *vta* polish s.o., shine s.o.; *1sg* **niwaasikwa'waa**; *prt* **wayaasikwa'waad**
waasikwa'an *vti* polish s.t., shine s.t.; *1sg* **niwaasikwa'aan**; *prt* **wayaasikwa'ang**
waaswaa *vai* shine for game or fish, jacklight; *1sg* **niwaaswaa**; *prt* **wayaaswaad**
waaswaagan *ni* torch; *pl* **waaswaaganan**; *loc* **waaswaaganing**; *dim* **waaswaagaans**
waatebagaa *vii* there are bright leaves; *prt* **wayaatebagaag**; *aug* **waatebagaamagad**; *prt aug* **wayaatebagaamagak**
waatebagaa-giizis *na* October, September; *also* **waatebago-giizis**
waawan *ni* egg; *pl* **waawanoon**; *loc* **waawanong**; *dim* **waawanoons**
waawaabiganoojiinh *na* mouse; *pl* **waawaabiganoojiinyag**; *dim* **waawaabiganoojiins**
waawaashkeshi *na* deer; *pl* **waawaashkeshiwag**; *dim* **waawaashkeshiins**
waawaashkeshiwayaan *na* deer hide; *pl* **waawaashkeshiwayaanag**; *loc* **waawaashkeshiwayaaning**; *dim* **waawaashkeshiwayaanens**
waawaashkeshiwi-wiiyaas *ni* deer meat
waawaatesi *na* firefly; *pl* **waawaatesiwag**; *dim* **waawaatesiins**; *also* **wewaatesi**
waawiyebii'igan *ni* compass (drawing instrument); *pl* **waawiyebii'iganan**; *loc* **waawiyebii'iganing**; *dim* **waawiyebii'igaans**
waawiyebii'ige *vai* draw a circle; *1sg* **niwaawiyebii'ige**; *prt* **wayaawiyebii'iged**
waawiye' *vta* make s.o. round; *1sg* **niwaawiye'aa**; *prt* **wayaawiye'aad**
waawiyeminagad *vii* be round (as something ball-like); *prt* **wayaawiyeminagak**
waawiyeminagizi *vai* be round (as something ball-like); *prt* **wayaawiyeminagizid**
waawiyetoon *vti2* make s.t. round; *1sg* **niwaawiyetoon**; *prt* **wayaawiyetood**
waawiyeyaa *vii* be round, be circular; *prt* **wayaawiyeyaag**; *aug* **waawiyeyaamagad**; *prt aug* **wayaawiyeyaamagak**
waawiyeyaabikad *vii* be round (as something mineral); *prt* **wayaawiyeyaabikak**
waawiyeyaabikizi *vai* be round (as something mineral); *prt* **wayaawiyeyaabikizid**
waawiyeyaakozi *vai* be round (as something stick- or wood-like); *prt* **wayaawiyeyaakozid**
waawiyeyaakwad *vii* be round (as something stick- or wood-like); *prt* **wayaawiyeyaakwak**
waawiyezi *vai* be round, be circular; *1sg* **niwaawiyez**; *prt* **wayaawiyezid**
waawiindamaw *vta* explain (s.t.) to s.o., tell about (s.t.) to s.o., promise (s.t.) to s.o.; *1sg* **niwaawiindamawaa**; *prt* **wayaawiindamawaad**
waawiindamaage *vai* explain (s.t.) to people, promise (s.t.) to people; *1sg* **niwaawiindamaage**; *prt* **wayaawiindamaaged**
waawiinjigaade *vii* be explained, be talked about all the time; *prt* **wayaawiinjigaadeg**; *aug* **waawiinjigaademagad**; *prt aug* **wayaawiinjigaademagak**
waawiinjigaazo *vai* be talked about all the time; *prt* **wayaawiinjigaazod**
waawiinzh /waawiinN-/ *vta* mention s.o., name s.o.; *1sg* **ninwaawiinaa**; *prt* **wayaawiinaad**
waawoono *vai* howl (e.g., a dog); *prt* **wayaawoonod**
waazakone *vii* glow, give off light; *prt* **wayaazakoneg**; *aug* **waazakonemagad**; *prt aug* **wayaazakonemagak**
waazakonebidoon *vti2* turn s.t. on for a light; *1sg* **niwaazakonebidoon**; *prt* **wayaazakonebidood**
waazakonenjigan *ni* lamp; *pl* **waazakonenjiganan**; *loc* **waazakonenjiganing**; *dim* **waazakonenjigaans**
waazakonenjiganaaboo *ni* kerosene; *loc* **waazakonenjiganaaboong**
waazakonenjiganaaboowadaawewigamig *ni* gas station; *also* **waazakonenjiganaaboo-adaawewigamig**
waazakonenjiganaaboowakik *na* gas tank, gas can; *pl* **waazakonenjiganaaboowakikoog**; *loc* **waazakonenjiganaaboowakikong**; *dim* **waazakonenjiganaaboowakikoons**
waazakonenjiganaatig *ni* light pole; *pl* **waazakonenjiganaatigoon**; *loc* **waazakonenjiganaatigong**; *dim* **waazakonenjiganaatigoons**
weba' /weba'w-/ *vta* shove s.o. away using something; *1sg* **niweba'waa**; *prt* **wayeba'waad**
weba'an *vti* shove s.t. away using something; *1sg* **niweba'aan**; *prt* **wayeba'ang**
webaashi *vai* be blown away; *1sg* **niwebaash**; *prt* **wayebaashid**
webaasin *vii* be blown away; *prt* **wayebaasing**
webin *vta* throw s.o. away; *1sg* **niwebinaa**; *prt* **wayebinaad**
webinan *vti* throw s.t. away; *1sg* **niwebinaan**; *prt* **wayebinang**
webinidiwag /webinidi-/ *vai* they separate from each other, they divorce each other; *1pl* **niwebinidimin**; *prt* **wayebinidijig**
webinigan *na* someone abandoned; *pl* **webiniganag**; *dim* **webinigaans**
webinigaade *vii* be thrown away; *prt* **wayebinigaadeg**; *aug* **webinigaademagad**; *prt aug* **wayebinigaademagak**
webinigaazo *vai* be thrown away; *prt* **wayebinigaazod**
webinige *vai* throw things away; *1sg* **niwebinige**; *prt* **wayebiniged**

wegimaawabid *na-pt* councillor, government official; *pl* **wegimaawabijig**
wegodogwen *pr* I don't know what *inanimate dubitative*, I wonder what *inanimate dubitative; plural* **wegodogwenan**
wegodogwen igo *pr* whatever it might be *inanimate dubitative*
wegonen *pr* what *inanimate interrogative; plural* **wegonenan**; *also* **awegonen**
wegonesh *pr* what, and what *inanimate interrogative*
wegwaagi *pc* behold!
wemitigoozhi *na* Frenchman; *pl* **wemitigoozhiwag**; *dim* **wemitigoozhiins**
wemitigoozhiimo *vai* speak French; *1sg* **niwemitigoozhiim**; *prt* **wayemitigoozhiimod**
Wenabozho *na* name of **aadizookaan** character viewed as culture hero and trickster; *also* **Nenabozho***
wenda- *pv4* really, completely, just so
wendad *vii* be easy, be cheap; *prt* **wayendak**
wendaginde *vii* be cheap; *prt* **wayendagindeg**; *aug* **wendagindemagad**; *prt aug* **wayendagindemagak**
wendaginzo *vai* be cheap; *prt* **wayendaginzod**
wendaabang *vii* east, where the dawn comes from *conjunct of:* **ondaaban**
wendizi *vai* be easy, be cheap; *prt* **wayendizid**
weniban *pc* disappeared!, gone!
wenipanad *vii* be easy, be cheap; *prt* **wayenipanak**
wenipanendan *vti* consider s.t. easy; *1sg* **niwenipanendaan**; *prt* **wayenipanendang**
wenipanizi *vai* be easy; *prt* **wayenipanizid**
wenipazh *pc* at hand, easily
wenipazhi' *vta* get s.o. easily; *1sg* **niwenipazhi'aa**; *prt* **wayenipazhi'aad**
wenipazhitoon *vti2* get s.t. easily; *1sg* **niwenipazhitoon**; *prt* **wayenipazhitood**
wenji- *pv3* from a certain place, for a certain reason, because *changed from of* **onji-**
wese'an *vii* be a tornado; *prt* **wayese'ang**
wetotwaag *ni-pt* jello
wewayiiba *pc* every little while; *also* **wewiiba***
wewaagijiizid *ni-pt* banana; *pl* **wewaagijiizijig**
wewebanaabii *vai* fish with a hook and line; *1sg* **niwewebanaabii**; *prt* **wayewebanaabiid**
wewebaanoweni *vai* wag one's tail; *prt* **wayewebaanowenid**
wewebikweni *vai* nod one's head; *1sg* **niwewebikwen**; *prt* **wayewebikwenid**
wewebikwetaw *vta* shake one's head at s.o.; *1sg* **niwewebikwetawaa**; *prt* **wayewebikwetawaad**
wewebizo *vai* swing; *1sg* **niwewebiz**; *prt* **wayewebizod**
wewebizon *ni* swing; *pl* **wewebizonan**; *loc* **wewebizoning**; *dim* **wewebizonens**
wewebizoo-apabiwin *ni* rocking chair; *pl* **wewebizoo-apabiwinan**; *loc* **wewebizoo-apabiwining**; *dim* **wewebizoo-apabiwinens**
weweni *pc* properly, correctly, carefully
wewese' /wewese'w-/ *vta* fan s.o.; *1sg* **niwewese'waa**; *prt* **wayewese'waad**
wewese'idizo *vai* fan oneself; *1sg* **niwewese'idiz**; *prt* **wayewese'idizod**
wewese'igan *ni* hand fan; *pl* **wewese'iganan**; *loc* **wewese'iganing**; *dim* **wewese'igaans**
wewese'ige *vai* fan things; *1sg* **niwewese'ige**; *prt* **wayewese'iged**
wewiib *pc* in a hurry, quickly, hurry
wewiibendam *vai* be eager, want to hurry; *1sg* **niwewiibendam**; *prt* **wayewiibendang**
wewiibi' *vta* hurry s.o., hurry making s.o.; *1sg* **niwewiibi'aa**; *prt* **wayewiibi'aad**
wewiibim *vta* tell s.o. to hurry; *1sg* **niwewiibimaa**; *prt* **wayewiibimaad**
wewiibingwaange *na* teal; *pl* **wewiibingwaangeg**; *dim* **wewiibingwaangens**
wewiibishkaa *vai* hurry; *1sg* **niwewiibishkaa**; *prt* **wayewiibishkaad**
wewiibitaa *vai* hurry (in some work or activity); *1sg* **niwewiibitaa**; *prt* **wayewiibitaad**
wewiibitoon *vti* hurry s.t., hurry making s.t.; *1sg* **niwewiibitoon**; *prt* **wayewiibitood**
wewiibizi *vai* be in a hurry; *1sg* **niwewiibiz**; *prt* **wayewiibizid**
wezaawiminagazid *na-pt* orange (fruit); *pl* **wezaawiminagizijig**
wii- *pv1* want to, will *future/desiderative verb prefix*
wiibidaakaajiganan *ni* false teeth *plural*; *also* **wiibidaakaanan**
wiibidaa-mashkikiiwinini *na* dentist; *pl* **wiibidaa-mashkikiiwininiwag**
wiibwaa *vii* become narrow, constrict; *prt* **waabwaag**; *aug* **wiibwaamagad**; *prt aug* **waabwaamagak**
wiidabim *vta* sit with s.o.; *1sg* **niwiidabimaa**; *prt* **waadabimaad**
wiidagwazhem *vta* share a cover with s.o.; *1sg* **niwiidagwazhemaa**; *prt* **waadagwazhemaad**
wiidanokiim *vta* work with s.o.; *1sg* **niwiidanokiimaa**; *prt* **waadanokiimaad**
wiidige *vai* marry, be married; *1sg* **niwiidige**; *prt* **waadiged**
wiidigem *vta* marry s.o., be married to s.o.; *1sg* **niwiidigemaa**; *prt* **waadigemaad**
wiidigendiwag /wiidigendi-/ *vai* they marry each other, they are married to each other; *1pl* **niwiidigendimin**; *prt* **waadigendijig**
wiidosem *vta* walk with s.o.; *1sg* **niwiidosemaa**; *prt* **waadosemaad**
wiidookaw *vta* help s.o.; *1sg* **niwiidookawaa**; *prt* **waadookawaad**
wiidookaage *vai* help people; *1sg* **niwiidookaage**; *prt* **waadookaaged**
wiidookaazo *vai* help; *1sg* **niwiidookaaz**; *prt* **waadookaazod**
wiidookodaadiwag /wiidookodaadi-/ *vai* they help each other; *1pl* **niwiidookodaadimin**; *prt* **waadookodaadijig**
wiidoopam *vta* eat with s.o.; *1sg* **niwiidoopamaa**; *prt* **waadoopamaad**
wiidoopange *vai* eat with people; *1sg* **niwiidoopange**; *prt* **waadoopanged**
wiigiwaam *ni* wigwam, lodge; *pl* **wiigiwaaman**; *loc* **wiigiwaaming**; *dim* **wiigiwaamens**
wiigiwaamaak *ni* wigwam frame; *pl* **wiigiwaamaakoon**; *loc* **wiigiwaamaakong**; *dim* **wiigiwaamaakoons**

wiigiwaamaatig *ni* wigwam pole; *pl* **wiigiwaamaatigoon**; *loc* **wiigiwaamaatigong**; *dim* **wiigiwaamaatigoons**
wiigiwaamige *vai* live in a wigwam; *1sg* **niwiigiwaamige**; *prt* **waagiwaamiged**
wiigiwaamike *vai* make a wigwam; *1sg* **niwiigiwaamike**; *prt* **waagiwaamiked**
wiigob *na* basswood tree; *pl* **wiigobiig**
wiigob *ni* inner bark of basswood; *pl* **wiigobiin**; *loc* **wiigobiing**; *dim* **wiigobiins**
wiigobaatig *na* basswood tree; *pl* **wiigobaatigoog**; *loc* **wiigobaatigong**; *dim* **wiigobaatigoons**
wiigobimizh *na* basswood tree; *pl* **wiigobimizhiig**; *dim* **wiigobimizhiins**
wiigwaas *na* birch tree; *pl* **wiigwaasag**; *loc* **wiigwaasing**; *dim* **wiigwaasens**
wiigwaas *ni* birch bark; *pl* **wiigwaasan**; *loc* **wiigwaasing**; *dim* **wiigwaasens**
wiigwaasabakway *ni* birch bark covering, roll of birch bark roofing; *pl* **wiigwaasabakwayan**
wiigwaasabakwaan *na* birch bark roof; *pl* **wiigwaasabakwaanag**; *loc* **wiigwaasabakwaaning**
wiigwaasigamig *ni* birch bark lodge; *pl* **wiigwaasigamigoon**; *loc* **wiigwaasigamigong**; *dim* **wiigwaasigamigoons**
wiigwaasi-jiimaan *ni* birch bark canoe; *pl* **wiigwaasi-jiimaanan**; *loc* **wiigwaasi-jiimaaning**; *dim* **wiigwaasi-jiimanens**
wiigwaasikaa *vii* there are many birches; *prt* **waagwaasikaag**; *aug* **wiigwaasikaamagad**; *prt aug* **waagwaasikaamagak**
wiigwaasike *vai* remove birch bark from the tree; *1sg* **niwiigwaasike**; *prt* **waagwaasiked**
wiigwaasi-makak *ni* birch bark box, birch bark basket; *pl* **wiigwaasi-makakoon**; *loc* **wiigwaasi-makakong**; *dim* **wiigwaasi-makakoons**
wiigwaasi-mitig *na* birch (tree); *pl* **wiigwaasi-mitigoog**; *loc* **wiigwaasi-mitigong**; *dim* **wiigwaasi-mitigoons**; *also* **wiigwaasaatig**
wiigwaasinaagan *ni* birch bark dish; *pl* **wiigwaasinaaganan**; *loc* **wiigwaasinaaganing**; *dim* **wiigwaasinaagaans**
wiij'anokiim *vta* work with s.o.; *1sg* **niwiij'anokiimaa**; *prt* **waaj'anokiimaad**; *also* **wiiji-anokiim**
wiij'ayaaw *vta* be with s.o., stay with s.o.; *1sg* **niwiij'ayaawaa**; *prt* **waaj'ayaawaad**; *also* **wiiji-ayaaw**
wiiji- *pv4* with, in company with
wiijigamigishkaw *vta* be a neighbor to s.o.; *1sg* **niwiijigamigishkawaa**; *prt* **waajigamigishkawaad**
wiijigim *vta* be the same age as s.o.; *1sg* **niwiijigimaa**; *prt* **waajigimaad**
wiijigindiwag /wiijigindi-/ *vai* they are the same age; *1pl* **niwiijigindimin**; *prt* **waajigindijig**
wiiji' *vta* play with s.o.; *1sg* **niwiiji'aa**; *prt* **waaji'aad**
wiijishimotaw *vta* dance with s.o.; *1sg* **niwiijishimotawaa**; *prt* **waajishimotawaad**
wiijii'iwe *vai* go with people, accompany people; *1sg* **niwiijii'iwe**; *prt* **waajii'iwed**
wiijiindiwag /wiijiindi-/ *vai* they go with each other, they accompany each other; *1pl* **niwiijiindimin**; *prt* **waajiindijig**
wiijiiw *vta* go with s.o., accompany s.o.; *1sg* **niwiijiiwaa**; *prt* **waajiiwaad**
wiijiiwaagan *na* companion, partner; *pl* **wiijiiwaaganag**
wiikaa *pc* late, seldom, ever
wiikenh *na* sweet flag; *pl* **wiikenyag**
wiikobidaw *vta* pull (s.t.) for s.o.; *1sg* **niwiikobidawaa**; *prt* **waakobidawaad**
wiikobidoon *vti2* pull s.t.; *1sg* **niwiikobidoon**; *prt* **waakobidood**
wiikobijigan *ni* dresser, chest of drawers; *pl* **wiikobijiganan**; *loc* **wiikobijiganing**; *dim* **wiikobijigaans**
wiikobijigaade *vii* be pulled; *prt* **waakobijigaadeg**; *aug* **wiikobijigaademagad**; *prt aug* **waakobijigaademagak**
wiikobijigaazo *vai* be pulled; *prt* **waakobijigaazod**
wiikobijige *vai* pull things; *1sg* **niwiikobijige**; *prt* **waakobijiged**
wiikobizh /wiikobiN-/ *vta* pull s.o.; *1sg* **niwiikobinaa**; *prt* **waakobinaad**
wiikom *vta* invite s.o. to a feast (especially as part of a religious ceremony); *1sg* **niwiikomaa**; *prt* **waakomaad**
wiikondiwag /wiikondi-/ *vai* they have a feast; *1pl* **niwiikondimin**; *prt* **waakondijig**
wiikonge *vai* give a feast, invite people to a feast (especially as part of a religious ceremony); *1sg* **niwiikonge**; *prt* **waakonged**
wiikwa'ibaan *ni* pump; *pl* **wiikwa'ibaanan**; *loc* **wiikwa'ibaaning**; *dim* **wiikwa'ibaanens**
wiikwa'ibii *vai* pump water; *1sg* **niwiikwa'ibii**; *prt* **waakwa'ibiid**
wiikwaji'o *vai* try to get free; *1sg* **niwiikwaji'**; *prt* **waakwaji'od**
wiikwajitoon *vti2* try to do s.t., try to get free of s.t.; *1sg* **niwiikwajitoon**; *prt* **waakwajitood**
wiikwam *vta* suck on s.o., draw on s.o. with mouth (e.g., a pipe); *1sg* **niwiikwamaa**; *prt* **waakwamaad**
wiikwamo *vai* suck; *1sg* **niwiikwam**; *prt* **waakwamod**
wiikwandan *vti* suck on s.t., draw on s.t. with mouth; *1sg* **niwiikwandaan**; *prt* **waakwandang**
wiikwanjige *vai* suck on things, draw on things with mouth; *1sg* **niwiikwanjige**; *prt* **waakwanjiged**
wiikwaabiigin *vta* pull s.o. (as with something string-like); *1sg* **niwiikwaabiiginaa**; *prt* **waakwaabiiginaad**
wiikwaabiiginan *vti* pull s.t. (as with something string-like); *1sg* **niwiikwaabiiginaan**; *prt* **waakwaabiiginang**
wiikwegamaa *vii* be a bay; *prt* **waakwegamaag**; *aug* **wiikwegamaamagad**; *prt aug* **waakwegamaamagak**
wiimaashkaa *vai* detour; *1sg* **niwiimaashkaa**; *prt* **waamaashkaad**
wiimbaa *vii* be hollow; *prt* **waambaag**; *aug* **wiimbaamagad**; *prt aug* **waambaamagak**
wiimbizi *vai* be hollow; *1sg* **niwiimbiz**; *prt* **waambizid**
wiimbwewe *vii* give a hollow sound; *prt* **waambweweg**; *aug* **wiimbwewemagad**; *prt aug* **waambwewemagak**

wiin *pc contrastive particle*
wiin *pr* he *third person singular personal pronoun*, she *third person singular personal pronoun*
wiinad *vii* be dirty; *prt* **waanak**
wiinawaa *pr* they *third person plural personal pronoun*
wiinaagamin /wiinaagami-/ *vii* be dirty (as a liquid); *prt* **waanaagamig**
wiinaajimo *vai* tell a dirty story; *1sg* **niwiinaajim**; *prt* **waanaajimod**
wiindamaw *vta* tell s.o. about (s.t.); *1sg* **niwiindamawaa**; *prt* **waandamawaad**
wiindamaage *vai* tell about (s.t.) to people, announce (s.t.) to people; *1sg* **niwiindamaage**; *prt* **waandamaaged**
wiindan *vti* name s.t., mention the name of s.t.; *1sg* **niwiindaan**; *prt* **waandang**
wiinde *vii* have a name; *prt* **waandeg**; *aug* **wiindemagad**; *prt aug* **waandemagak**
wiindigoo *na* windigo: winter cannibal monster; *pl* **wiindigoog**; *dim* **wiindigoons**
wiindigoo-bineshiinh *na* kingbird; *pl* **wiindigoo-bineshiinyag**
wiindigoowi *vai* be a windigo; *1sg* **niwiindigoow**; *prt* **waandigoowid**
wiineta *pr* only him *third person singular personal pronoun*, only her *third person singular personal pronoun*
wiinetawaa *pr* only them *third person plural personal pronoun*
wiingashk *ni* sweet grass; *pl* **wiingashkoon**; *loc* **wiingashkong**; *dim* **wiingashkoons**
wiinibiigoo *na* Winnebago; *pl* **wiinibiigoog**; *dim* **wiinibiigoons**
wiinichige *vai* dirty things; *1sg* **niwiinichige**; *prt* **waanichiged**
wiinigiizhwe *vai* speak nastily; *1sg* **niwiinigiizhwe**; *prt* **waanigiizhwed**
wiini' *vta* make s.o. dirty; *1sg* **niwiini'aa**; *prt* **waani'aad**
wiinijiishkiwagaa *vii* there is a muddy patch; *prt* **waanijiishkiwagaag**; *aug* **wiinijiishkiwagaamagad**; *prt aug* **waanijiishkiwagaamagak**
wiinin *ni* fat; *loc* **wiininong**
wiininjii *vai* have a dirty hand; *1sg* **niwiininjii**; *prt* **waaninjiid**
wiinino *vai* be fat; *1sg* **niwiinin**; *prt* **waaninod**
wiinishagaandibaan *ni* dandruff
wiinishagaandibe *vai* have a dirty scalp; *1sg* **niwiinishagaandibe**; *prt* **waanishagaandibed**
wiinitam *pr* his turn *third person singular personal pronoun*, her turn *third person singular personal pronoun*
wiinitamawaa *pr* their turn *third person plural personal pronoun*
wiinitoon *vti2* dirty s.t.; *1sg* **niwiinitoon**; *prt* **waanitood**
wiinizi *vai* be dirty; *1sg* **niwiiniz**; *prt* **waanizid**
wiinizik *na* yellow birch; *pl* **wiinizikoog**; *dim* **wiinizikoons**
wiinizisimaani-zagaakwa'igan *ni* hairpin; *pl* **wiinizisimaani-zagaakwa'iganan**; *dim* **wiinizisimaani-zagaakwa'igaans**
wiinzh /wiinN-/ *vta* name s.o., mention the name of s.o., give s.o. a name; *1sg* **niwiinaa**; *prt* **waanaad**
wiinzo *vai* have a name; *1sg* **niwiinz**; *prt* **waanzod**
wiipem *vta* sleep with s.o.; *1sg* **niwiipemaa**; *prt* **waapemaad**
wiipendan *vti* sleep with s.t.; *1sg* **niwiipendaan**; *prt* **waapendang**
wiipemaawaso *vai* sleep with children protectively; *1sg* **niwiipemaawas**; *prt* **waapemaawasod**
wiipendiwag /wiipendi-/ *vai* they sleep with each other; *1pl* **niwiipendimin**; *prt* **waapendijig**
wiisagan *vii* be bitter; *prt* **waasagang**; *also* **wiisagaa**
wiisagaagamin /wiisagaagami-/ *vii* be bitter (as a liquid); *prt* **waasagaagamig**
wiisagendam *vai* suffer pain; *1sg* **niwiisagendam**; *prt* **waasagendang**
wiisagigonewe *vai* have a sore throat; *1sg* **niwiisagigonewe**; *prt* **waasagigonewed**
wiisagi-jiisens *ni* radish; *pl* **wiisagi-jiisensan**; *loc* **wiisagi-jiisensing**
wiisagine *vai* be in pain; *1sg* **niwiisagine**; *prt* **waasagined**
wiisagipogozi *vai* taste bitter; *prt* **waasagipogozid**
wiisagipogwad *vii* taste bitter; *prt* **waasagipogwak**
wiisagishin *vai* get hurt; *1sg* **niwiisagishin**; *prt* **waasagishing**
wiisagishkaw *vta* hurt s.o. with foot or body; *1sg* **niwiisagishkawaa**; *prt* **waasagishkawaad**
wiisagizi *vai* be bitter; *prt* **waasagizid**
wiisaakodewikwe *na* woman of mixed ancestry, Metis woman; *pl* **wiisaakodewikweg**
wiisaakodewinini *na* person of mixed ancestry, Metis; *pl* **wiisaakodewininiwag**
wiishkoban *vii* be sweet; *prt* **waashkobang**
wiishkobaaboo *ni* maple sap; *loc* **wiishkobaaboong**
wiishkobaagamin /wiishkobaagami-/ *vii* be sweet (as a liquid); *prt* **waashkobaagamig**
wiishkobi- *pv4* sweet
wiishkobi-bakwezhigan *na* sweet roll, pastry, cake; *pl* **wiishkobi-bakwezhiganag**; *loc* **wiishkobi-bakwezhiganing**; *dim* **wiishkobi-bakwezhigaans**
wiishkobi-jiis *ni* sugar beet; *pl* **wiishkobi-jiisan**
wiishkobipogozi *vai* taste sweet; *prt* **waashkobipogozid**
wiishkobipogwad *vii* taste sweet; *prt* **waashkobipogwak**
wiishkobizi *vai* be sweet; *prt* **waashkobizid**
wiisini *vai* eat; *1sg* **niwiisin**; *prt* **waasinid**
wiisiniwin *ni* food; *pl* **wiisiniwinan**; *loc* **wiisiniwining**
wiisinii-adaawewigamig *ni* grocery store; *pl* **wiisinii-adaawewigamigoon**; *loc* **wiisinii-adaawewigamigong**; *dim* **wiisinii-adaawewigamigoons**
wiisiniiwigamig *ni* restaurant, cafe; *pl* **wiisiniiwigamigoon**; *loc* **wiisiniiwigamigong**; *dim* **wiisiniiwigamigoons**
wiisookaw *vta* associate with s.o.; *1sg* **niwiisookawaa**; *prt* **waasookawaad**

wiiwakwaan *ni* hat; *pl* **wiiwakwaanan**; *loc* **wiiwakwaaning**; *dim* **wiiwakwaanens**
wiiwegin *vta* wrap s.o. (as or as with something sheet-like); *1sg* **niwiiweginaa**; *prt* **waaweginaad**
wiiweginan *vti* wrap s.t. (as or as with something sheet-like); *1sg* **niwiiweginaan**; *prt* **waaweginang**
wiiweginigan *ni* wrapped package; *pl* **wiiweginiganan**; *loc* **wiiweginiganing**; *dim* **wiiweginigaans**
wiiyagasenh *ni* dust, dirt; *pl* **wiiyagasenyan**
wiiyaas *ni* meat; *loc* **wiiyaasing**; *dim* **wiiyaasens**
wiiyaas-adaawewigamig *ni* meat market; *pl* **wiiyaas-adaawewigamigoon**; *loc* **wiiyaas-adaawewigamigong**
wiiyaasaaboo *ni* broth; *loc* **wiiyaasaaboong**
wiiyaasi-dakoniwewinini *na* game warden, conservation officer; *pl* **wiiyaasi-dakoniwewininiwag**
wiiyaasi-naboob *ni* stew; *loc* **wiiyaasi-naboobiing**
wiizhaam *vta* ask s.o. along, urge s.o. to come; *1sg* **niwiizhaamaa**; *prt* **waazhaamaad**

Z

zaga' /zaga'w-/ *vta* fasten s.o. together; *1sg* **inzaga'waa**; *prt* **zega'waad**
zaga'an *vti* fasten s.t. together; *1sg* **inzaga'aan**; *prt* **zega'ang**
zaga'igan *ni* nail; *pl* **zaga'iganan**; *loc* **zaga'iganing**; *dim* **zaga'igaans**
zagakim *vta* tell s.o. to settle down; *1sg* **inzagakimaa**; *prt* **zegakimaad**
zagakin *vta* put s.o. away, tidy s.o.; *1sg* **inzagakinaa**; *prt* **zegakinaad**
zagakinan *vti* put s.t. away, tidy s.t.; *1sg* **inzagakinaan**; *prt* **zegakinang**
zagakinigaade *vii* be put away, be tidied; *prt* **zegakinigaadeg**; *aug* **zagakinigaademagad**; *prt aug* **zegakinigaademagak**
zagakinigaazo *vai* be put away, be tidied; *prt* **zegakinigaazod**
zagakinige *vai* put things away, tidy things; *1sg* **inzagakinige**; *prt* **zegakiniged**
zagakishim *vta* put s.o. in order; *1sg* **inzagakishimaa**; *prt* **zegakishimaad**
zagakisidoon *vti2* put s.t. in order; *1sg* **inzagakisidoon**; *prt* **zegakisidood**
zagakisijige *vti* put things in order; *1sg* **inzagakisijige**; *prt* **zegakisijiged**
zagapide *vii* be tied on, be towed; *prt* **zegapideg**; *aug* **zagapidemagad**; *prt aug* **zegapidemagak**
zagapidoon *vti2* tie s.t. on, tow s.t.; *1sg* **inzagapidoon**; *prt* **zegapidood**
zagapijigan *ni* trailer; *pl* **zagapijiganan**; *loc* **zagapijiganing**; *dim* **zagapijigaans**
zagapizh /zagapiN-/ *vta* tie s.o. on, tow s.o.; *1sg* **inzagapinaa**; *prt* **zegapinaad**
zagapizo *vai* be tied on, be towed; *1sg* **inzagapiz**; *prt* **zegapizod**
zagaswaa *vai* smoke (tobacco); *1sg* **inzagaswaa**; *prt* **zegaswaad**
zagaswaadan *vti* smoke s.t. (e.g., kinnickinnick); *1sg* **inzagaswaadaan**; *prt* **zegaswaadang**
zagaswaazh /zagaswaaN-/ *vta* smoke s.o. (e.g., tobacco); *1sg* **inzagaswaanaa**; *prt* **zegaswaanaad**
zagaswe' *vta* give a smoke to s.o., share a smoke with s.o. (especially a pipe in a ceremony); *1sg* **inzagaswe'aa**; *prt* **zegaswe'aad**
zagaswe'idiwag /zagaswe'idi-/ *vai* they have a council meeting; *1pl* **inzagaswe'idimin**; *prt* **zegaswe'idijig**
zagaswe'idiiwinini *na* councillor; *pl* **zagaswe'idiiwininiwag**
zagaswe'iwe *vai* give a ceremony, convene a council; *1sg* **inzagaswe'iwe**; *prt* **zegaswe'iwed**
zagataagan *na* tinder, punk; *pl* **zagataaganag**; *loc* **zagataaganing**
zagaakwa' /zagaakwa'w-/ *vta* fasten s.o., pin s.o., button s.o. up; *1sg* **inzagaakwa'waa**; *prt* **zegaakwa'waad**
zagaakwa'an *vti* fasten s.t., pin s.t.; *1sg* **inzagaakwa'aan**; *prt* **zegaakwa'ang**
zagaakwa'igan *ni* pin, safety pin; *pl* **zagaakwa'iganan**; *loc* **zagaakwa'iganing**; *dim* **zagaakwa'igaans**
zagaakwa'igaade *vii* be fastened, be pinned; *prt* **zegaakwa'igaadeg**; *aug* **zagaakwa'igaademagad**; *prt aug* **zegaakwa'igaademagak**
zagaakwa'igaazo *vai* be fastened, be pinned; *prt* **zegaakwa'igaazod**
zagaakwa'ige *vai* fasten things, pin things; *1sg* **inzagaakwa'ige**; *prt* **zegaakwa'iged**
zagaakwa'odizo *vai* button up oneself; *1sg* **inzagaakwa'odiz**; *prt* **zegaakwa'odizod**
zagaakwa'on *na* brooch, pin; *pl* **zagaakwa'onag**; *loc* **zagaakwa'oning**; *dim* **zagaakwa'onens**
zagaakwajin *vai* get snagged on a limb; *1sg* **inzagaakwajin**; *prt* **zegaakwajing**
zagaakwaa *vii* be dense woods; *prt* **zegaakwaag**; *aug* **zagaakwaamagad**; *prt aug* **zegaakwaamagak**
zagidoonebijigan *ni* bridle, bit; *pl* **zagidoonebijiganan**; *loc* **zagidoonebijiganing**; *dim* **zagidoonebijigaans**
zagime *na* mosquito; *pl* **zagimeg**; *dim* **zagimens**
zagimekaa *vii* there are many mosquitoes; *prt* **zegimekaag**; *aug* **zagimekaamagad**; *prt aug* **zegimekaamagak**
zagimewayaan *na* mosquito net; *pl* **zagimewayaanag**; *loc* **zagimewayaaning**; *dim* **zagimewayaanens**
zaginiinjiin *vta* shake hands with s.o.; *1sg* **inzaginiinjiinaa**; *prt* **zeginiinjiinaad**
zaginiinjiinidiwag /zaginiinjiinidi-/ *vai* they shake hands with each other; *1pl* **inzaginiinjiinidimin**; *prt* **zeginiinjiinidijig**
zaka' /zaka'w-/ *vta* set s.o. on fire, light s.o. (e.g., a pipe); *1sg* **inzaka'waa**; *prt* **zeka'waad**

zaka'amaw *vta* set (s.t.) on fire for s.o., light (s.t.) for s.o.; *1sg* **inzaka'amawaa**; *prt* **zeka'amawaad**
zaka'an *vti* set s.t. on fire, light s.t.; *1sg* **inzaka'aan**; *prt* **zeka'ang**
zaka'igan *ni* lighter; *pl* **zaka'iganan**; *loc* **zaka'iganing**; *dim* **zaka'igaans**
zaka'ipwaagane *vai* light a pipe; *1sg* **inzaka'ipwaagane**; *prt* **zeka'ipwaaganed**
zaka'o *vai* use a cane; *1sg* **inzaka'**; *prt* **zeka'od**
zaka'on *ni* cane; *pl* **zaka'onan**; *loc* **zaka'oning**; *dim* **zaka'onens**
zakaasigan *ni* flashlight; *pl* **zakaasiganan**; *loc* **zakaasiganing**; *dim* **zakaasigaans**
zakide *vii* burn; *prt* **zekideg**; *aug* **zakidemagad**; *prt aug* **zekidemagak**
zakiz /zakizw-/ *vta* burn s.o., light s.o.; *1sg* **inzakizwaa**; *prt* **zekizwaad**
zakizan *vti* burn s.t., light s.t.; *1sg* **inzakizaan**; *prt* **zekizang**
zakizige *vai* burn things, light things; *1sg* **inzakizige**; *prt* **zekiziged**
zakizo *vai* burn, have a fire at one's place; *1sg* **inzakiz**; *prt* **zekizod**
zanagad *vii* be difficult, be hard (to manage); *prt* **zenagak**
zanagendam *vai2* consider things hard, consider things difficult; *1sg* **inzanagendam**; *prt* **zenagendang**
zanagendan *vti* consider s.t. hard, consider s.t. difficult; *1sg* **inzanagendaan**; *prt* **zenagendang**
zanagenim *vta* consider s.o. hard, consider s.o. difficult; *1sg* **inzanagenimaa**; *prt* **zenagenimaad**
zanagi' *vta* make it difficult for s.o.; *1sg* **inzanagi'aa**; *prt* **zenagi'aad**
zanagizi *vai* be difficult; *1sg* **inzanagiz**; *prt* **zenagizid**
zasag= < zag=
zasak= < zak=
zasakwaa *vii* there is a heavy frost; *prt* **zesakwaag**
zasaswe < zaswe=
zasiko= < ziko=
zasiiko= < ziko=
zaswebidoon *vti2* scatter s.t. with hands; *1sg* **inzaswebidoon**; *prt* **zeswebidood**
zaswebizh /zaswebiN-/ *vta* scatter s.o. with hands; *1sg* **inzaswebinaa**; *prt* **zeswebinaad**
zaswebiiga'andaw *vta* splash s.o.; *1sg* **inzaswebiiga'andawaa**; *prt* **zeswebiiga'andawaad**
zaswe'an *vti* scatter s.t. using something; *1sg* **inzaswe'aan**; *prt* **zeswe'ang**
zasweshkan *vti* scatter s.t. with foot or body; *1sg* **inzasweshkaan**; *prt* **zesweshkang**
zasweshkaw *vta* scatter s.o. with foot or body; *1sg* **inzasweshkawaa**; *prt* **zesweshkawaad**
zazagaa *vii* there is dense underbrush; *prt* **zezagaag**; *aug* **zazagaamagad**; *prt aug* **zezagaamagak**
zazaagizi *vai* be stingy; *1sg* **inzazaagiz**; *prt* **zezaagizid**
zazaanag= < zanag=
zazegaa *pc* dressed up, decorated
zazegaa'o *vai* dress up; *1sg* **inzazegaa'**; *prt* **zezegaa'od**
zazegaa-ikwe *na* dressed-up woman; *pl* **zazegaa-ikwewag**; *dim* **zazegaa-ikwens**
zazegaa-inini *na* dressed-up man; *pl* **zazegaa-ininiwag**; *dim* **zazegaa-ininiins**
zaziikizi *vai* be the eldest (of siblings); *1sg* **inzaziikiz**; *prt* **zeziikizid**
zaaga'am *vai2* go out, exit, go to the toilet; *1sg* **inzaaga'am**; *prt* **zayaaga'ang**
zaaga'amoowigamig *ni* toilet, outhouse, privy; *pl* **zaaga'amoowigamigoon**; *loc* **zaaga'amoowigamigong**; *dim* **zaaga'amoowigamigoons**
zaaga'igan *ni* lake; *pl* **zaaga'iganiin**; *loc* **zaaga'iganiing**; *dim* **zaaga'igaans**
zaagajiwe *vai* come out over a hill; *1sg* **inzaagajiwe**; *prt* **zayaagajiwed**
zaagakii *vai* sprout; *prt* **zayaagakiid**
zaagakii *vii* sprout; *prt* **zayaagakiig**; *aug* **zaagakiimagad**; *prt aug* **zayaagakiimagak**
zaagaakoshin *vai* lie sticking out (as something stick- or wood-like); *1sg* **inzaagaakoshin**; *prt* **zayaagaakoshing**
zaagaakosin *vii* lie sticking out (as something stick- or wood-like); *prt* **zayaagaakosing**
zaagewe *vai* come suddenly into view as from around a corner; *1sg* **inzaagewe**; *prt* **zayaagewed**
zaagewebatoo *vai* run suddenly into view; *1sg* **inzaagewebatoo**; *prt* **zayaagewebatood**
zaagewebide *vii* speed suddenly into view, drive suddenly into view; *prt* **zayaagewebideg**; *aug* **zaagewebidemagad**; *prt aug* **zayaagewebidemagak**
zaagewebizo *vai* speed suddenly into view, drive suddenly into view; *1sg* **inzaagewebiz**; *prt* **zayaagewebizod**
zaagewe'o *vai* paddle suddenly into view; *1sg* **inzaagewe'**; *prt* **zayaagewe'od**
zaagewekwazhiwe *vai* paddle suddenly into view, swim as a fish suddenly into view; *1sg* **inzaagewekwazhiwe**; *prt* **zayaagewekwazhiwed**
zaagibagaa *vii* leaves bud; *prt* **zayaagibagaag**; *aug* **zaagibagaamagad**; *prt aug* **zayaagibagaamagak**
zaagibagaa-giizis *na* May
zaagichigaade *vii* be loved, be treasured, be held stingily; *prt* **zayaagichigaadeg**; *aug* **zaagichigaademagad**; *prt aug* **zayaagichigaademagak**
zaagichigaazo *vai* be loved, be treasured, be held stingily; *prt* **zayaagichigaazod**
zaagidawaa *vii* flow into a lake, be an inlet; *prt* **zayaagidawaag**; *aug* **zaagidawaamagad**; *prt aug* **zayaagidawaamagak**
zaagidaawanidiwag /zaagidaawanidi-/ *vai* they go out in a group; *1pl* **inzaagidaawanidimin**; *prt* **zayaagidaawanidijig**
zaagidenaniweni *vai* stick out one's tongue; *1sg* **inzaagidenaniwen**; *prt* **zayaagidenaniwenid**
zaagidenaniwetaw *vta* stick out one's tongue at s.o.; *1sg* **inzaagidenaniwetawaa**; *prt* **zayaagidenaniwetawaad**

zaagidin *vta* put s.o. out, evict s.o.; *1sg* **inzaagidinaa**; *prt* **zayaagidinaad**
zaagidinan *vti* put s.t. out; *1sg* **inzaagidinaan**; *prt* **zayaagidinang**
zaagidinidiwag /zaagidinidi-/ *vai* they are let out together (as from school or a meeting); *prt* **zayaagidinidijig**
zaagidoode *vai* crawl out; *1sg* **inzaagidoode**; *prt* **zayaagidooded**
zaagigi *vai* sprout, grow out; *prt* **zayaagigid**
zaagigin *vii* sprout, grow out; *prt* **zayaagiging**
zaagi' *vta* love s.o., treasure s.o.; *1sg* **inzaagi'aa**; *prt* **zayaagi'aad**
zaagi'idiwag /zaagi'idi-/ *vai* they love each other; *1pl* **inzaagi'idimin**; *prt* **zayaagi'idijig**
zaagijinaazha' /zaagijinaazha'w-/ *vta* tell s.o. to go outside; *1sg* **inzaagijinaazha'waa**; *prt* **zayaagijinaazha'waad**
zaagijinizhikaw *vta* chase s.o. outside; *1sg* **inzaagijinizhikawaa**; *prt* **zayaagijinizhikawaad**
zaagijiwan *vii* flow out; *prt* **zayaagijiwang**
zaagijiwebin *vta* throw s.o. outside; *1sg* **inzaagijiwebinaa**; *prt* **zayaagijiwebinaad**
zaagijiwebinan *vti* throw s.t. outside; *1sg* **inzaagijiwebinaan**; *prt* **zayaagijiwebinang**
zaagijiwebinigaade *vii* be thrown outside; *prt* **zayaagijiwebinigaadeg**; *aug* **zaagijiwebinigaademagad**; *prt aug* **zayaagijiwebinigaademagak**
zaagijiwebinige *vai* throw things outside; *1sg* **inzaagijiwebinige**; *prt* **zayaagijiwebiniged**
zaagikweni *vai* stick out one's head; *1sg* **inzaagikwen**; *prt* **zayaagikwenid**
zaagitoon *vti2* love s.t., treasure s.t.; *1sg* **inzaagitoon**; *prt* **zayaagitood**
zaagiziba' *vta* run out with s.o.; *1sg* **inzaagiziba'aa**; *prt* **zayaagiziba'aad**
zaagiziba'idiwag /zaagiziba'idi-/ *vai* they run out together; *1pl* **inzaagiziba'idimin**; *prt* **zayaagiziba'idijig**
zaagizibatoo *vai* run out; *1sg* **inzaagizibatoo**; *prt* **zayaagizibatood**
zaagizibatwaadan *vti* run out with s.t.; *1sg* **inzaagizibatwaadaan**; *prt* **zayaagizibatwaadang**
zaagizibatwaazh /zaagizibatwaaN-/ *vta* run out with s.o.; *1sg* **inzaagizibatwaanaa**; *prt* **zayaagizibatwaanaad**
zaagizi' *vta* take s.o. out, make s.o. go out; *1sg* **inzaagizi'aa**; *prt* **zayaagizi'aad**
zaagizitaw *vta* take (s.t.) out for s.o.; *1sg* **inzaagizitawaa**; *prt* **zayaagizitawaad**
zaagizitoon *vti2* take s.t. out; *1sg* **inzaagizitoon**; *prt* **zayaagizitood**
zaagiing *pc* at the inlet
zaasakokwaadan *vti* fry s.t.; *1sg* **inzaasakokwaadaan**; *prt* **zayaasakokwaadang**
zaasakokwaade *vii* be fried; *prt* **zayaasakokwaadeg**; *aug* **zaasakokwaademagad**; *prt aug* **zayaasakokwaademagak**
zaasakokwaan *na* fry bread; *pl* **zaasakokwaanag**; *loc* **zaasakokwaaning**; *dim* **zaasakokwaanens**
zaasakokwaazh /zaasakokwaaN-/ *vta* fry s.o.; *1sg* **inzaasakokwaanaa**; *prt* **zayaasakokwaanaad**
zaasakokwaazo *vai* be fried; *prt* **zayaasakokwaazod**
zaasakokwe *vai* fry; *1sg* **inzaasakokwe**; *prt* **zayaasakokwed**
zaasaag= < zaag=
zaasaakwe *vai* give war whoops, whoop; *1sg* **inzaasaakwe**; *prt* **zayaasaakwed**
zaasigan *na* cracklings; *pl* **zaasiganag**
zaasijiwan *vii* flow with a ripple; *prt* **zayaasijiwang**
zaasoong= < zoong=
zaatemaagozi *vai* smell rancid; *prt* **zayaatemaagozid**
zaatemaagwad *vii* smell rancid; *prt* **zayaatemaagwak**
zaatepogozi *vai* taste rancid; *prt* **zayaatepogozid**
zaatepogwad *vii* taste rancid; *prt* **zayaatepogwak**
zaateshin *vai* turn rancid; *prt* **zayaateshing**
zaatesin *vii* turn rancid; *prt* **zayaatesing**
zegaabandam *vai2* have a scary dream; *1sg* **inzegaabandam**; *prt* **zayegaabandang**
zegaanakwad *vii* there are storm clouds; *prt* **zayegaanakwak**
zegaatese *vii* be a scary movie; *prt* **zayegaateseg**; *aug* **zegaatesemagad**; *prt aug* **zayegaatesemagak**
zegendam *vai2* be nervous, be fearful; *1sg* **inzegendam**; *prt* **zayegendang**
zegendaagozi *vai* be considered scary, be considered dangerous; *1sg* **inzegendaagoz**; *prt* **zayegendaagozid**
zegendaagwad *vii* be considered scary, be considered dangerous; *prt* **zayegendaagwak**
zegibanwaanishiinh *na* cedar waxwing; *pl* **zegibanwaanishiinyag**
zegigaadeshin *vai* sprain one's leg; *1sg* **inzegigaadeshin**; *prt* **zayegigaadeshing**
zegi' *vta* scare s.o., frighten s.o.; *1sg* **inzegi'aa**; *prt* **zayegi'aad**
zegim *vta* intimidate s.o. by speech; *1sg* **inzegimaa**; *prt* **zayegimaad**
zeginaagozi *vai* look scary; *1sg* **inzeginaagoz**; *prt* **zayeginaagozid**
zeginaagwad *vii* look scary; *prt* **zayeginaagwak**
zegingwashi *vai* have a nightmare; *1sg* **inzegingwash**; *prt* **zayegingwashid**
zeginikeshin *vai* sprain one's arm; *1sg* **inzeginikeshin**; *prt* **zayeginikeshing**
zegizi *vai* be scared, be afraid; *1sg* **inzegiz**; *prt* **zayegizid**
zegizideshin *vai* sprain one's foot; *1sg* **inzegizideshin**; *prt* **zayegizideshing**
zegwewe *vii* rumble; *prt* **zayegweweg**; *aug* **zegwewemagad**; *prt aug* **zayegwewemagak**
zenibaanh *na* ribbon, silk; *pl* **zenibaanyag**; *loc* **zenibaanying**; *dim* **zenibaans**
zenibaawegin *ni* silk, satin; *pl* **zenibaaweginoon**; *loc* **zenibaaweginong**; *dim* **zenibaaweginoons**
zesab *na* nettle; *pl* **zesabiig**; *loc* **zesabiing**
zeseg= < zeg=
zesegwaabide'o *vai* pick one's teeth; *1sg* **inzesegwaabide'**; *prt* **zayesegwaabide'od**

zesegwaabide'on *ni* toothpick; *pl* **zesegwaabide'onan**; *loc* **zesegwaabide'oning**; *dim* **zesegwaabide'onens**
zhagashkaandawe *na* flying squirrel; *pl* **zhagashkaandaweg**; *dim* **zhagashkaandawens**
zhagashkitaa *vai* bend down; *1sg* **inzhagashkitaa**; *prt* **zhegashkitaad**
zhakamo *vai* put (something) in one's mouth; *1sg* **inzhakam**; *prt* **zhekamod**
zhakamodaw *vta* spoon feed s.o.; *1sg* **inzhakamodawaa**; *prt* **zhekamodawaad**
zhakaa *vii* be damp; *prt* **zhekaag**; *aug* **zhakaamagad**; *prt aug* **zhekaamagak**
zhakaagonagaa *vii* there is soft snow; *prt* **zhekaagonagaag**; *aug* **zhakaagonagaamagad**; *prt aug* **zhekaagonagaamagak**
zhakipon /zhakipo-/ *vii* there is heavy wet snow falling; *prt* **zhekipog**
zhakizi *vai* be damp; *prt* **zhekizid**
zhakiigad *vii* be damp (as something sheet-like); *prt* **zhekiigak**
zhakiigizi *vai* be damp (as something sheet-like); *prt* **zhekiigizid**
zhashagi *na* blue heron; *pl* **zhashagiwag**; *dim* **zhashagiins**
zhashingade= < zhingade=
zhawendaagozi *vai* be blessed, be pitied, be fortunate; *1sg* **inzhawendaagoz**; *prt* **zhewendaagozid**
zhawenim *vta* bless s.o., pity s.o.; *1sg* **inzhawenimaa**; *prt* **zhewenimaad**
zhawenjige *vai* be merciful, be kind-hearted, have pity; *1sg* **inzhawenjige**; *prt* **zhewenjiged**
zhawimin *ni* grape; *pl* **zhawiminan**; *also* **zhoomin**
zhayiigwa *pc* now, already *old-fashioned*
zhazhiibitam *vai2* be stubborn, be disobedient; *1sg* **inzhazhiibitam**; *prt* **zhezhiibitang**
zhaabobatoo *vai* run through; *1sg* **inzhaabobatoo**; *prt* **zhayaabobatood**
zhaabobii *vii* be saturated; *prt* **zhayaabobiig**; *aug* **zhaabobiimagad**; *prt aug* **zhayaabobiimagak**
zhaabobiiginan *vti* strain s.t.; *1sg* **inzhaabobiiginaan**; *prt* **zhayaabobiiginang**
zhaabobiiginigan *ni* strainer; *pl* **zhaabobiiginiganan**; *loc* **zhaabobiiginiganing**; *dim* **zhaabobiiginigaans**
zhaabokaawizi *vai* have diarrhea; *1sg* **inzhaabokaawiz**; *prt* **zhayaabokaawizid**
zhaabon *vta* put s.o. through; *1sg* **inzhaabonaa**; *prt* **zhayaabonaad**
zhaabonan *vti* put s.t. through; *1sg* **inzhaabonaan**; *prt* **zhayaabonang**
zhaabonigan *ni* needle; *pl* **zhaaboniganan**; *loc* **zhaaboniganing**; *dim* **zhaabonigaans**
zhaabose *vii* go through, pass through; *prt* **zhayaaboseg**; *aug* **zhaabosemagad**; *prt aug* **zhayaabosemagak**
zhaaboshkaachigan *ni* sifter; *pl* **zhaaboshkaachiganan**; *loc* **zhaaboshkaachiganing**; *dim* **zhaaboshkaachigaans**
zhaaboshkaachige *vai* sift things; *1sg* **inzhaaboshkaachige**; *prt* **zhayaaboshkaachiged**
zhaaboshkaas /zhaaboshkaasw-/ *vta* sift s.o.; *1sg* **inzhaaboshkaaswaa**; *prt* **zhayaaboshkaaswaad**
zhaaboshkaatoon *vti2* sift s.t.; *1sg* **inzhaaboshkaatoon**; *prt* **zhayaaboshkaatood**
zhaabowe *vai* sing an accompaniment (of women); *1sg* **inzhaabowe**; *prt* **zhayaabowed**
zhaabozigan *ni* laxative; *pl* **zhaaboziganan**; *loc* **zhaaboziganing**
zhaaboomin *na* gooseberry; *pl* **zhaaboominag**; *dim* **zhaaboominens**
zhaaboominagaawanzh *na* gooseberry bush; *pl* **zhaaboominagaawanzhiig**; *loc* **zhaaboominagaawanzhiing**; *dim* **zhaaboominagaawanzhiins**
zhaaboondawaan *ni* long lodge with doors at both ends; *pl* **zhaaboondawaanan**; *loc* **zhaaboondawaaning**; *dim* **zhaaboondawaanens**
zhaabwayi'ii *pc* through it
zhaabwaabam *vta* see through s.o.; *1sg* **inzhaabwaabamaa**; *prt* **zhayaabwaabamaad**
zhaabwaabandan *vti* see through s.t.; *1sg* **inzhaabwaabandaan**; *prt* **zhayaabwaabandang**
zhaabwaakizigan *ni* x-ray plate; *pl* **zhaabwaakiziganan**
zhaabwaakizo *vai* get an x-ray; *1sg* **inzhaabwaakiz**; *prt* **zhayaabwaakizod**
zhaabwii *vai* go through, pass through, survive; *1sg* **inzhaabwii**; *prt* **zhayaabwiid**
zhaaganaash *na* Englishman; *pl* **zhaaganaashag**; *also* **zhaaganaashi**
zhaaganaashiimo *vai* speak English; *1sg* **inzhaaganaashiim**; *prt* **zhayaaganaashiimod**
zhaaganaashiimotaw *vta* speak English to s.o.; *1sg* **inzhaaganaashiimotawaa**; *prt* **zhayaaganaashiimotawaad**
Zhaaganaashiiwaki *ni* Canada; *loc* **Zhaaganaashiiwakiing**
zhaaganaashiiwibii'amaw *vta* write in English to s.o.; *1sg* **inzhaaganaashiiwibii'amawaa**; *prt* **zhayaaganaashiiwibii'amawaad**
zhaaganaashiiwibii'an *vti* write s.t. in English; *1sg* **inzhaaganaashiiwibii'aan**; *prt* **zhayaaganaashiiwibii'ang**
zhaaganaashiiwibii'ige *vai* write in English; *1sg* **inzhaaganaashiiwibii'ige**; *prt* **zhayaaganaashiiwibii'iged**
zhaagode'e *vai* be cowardly; *1sg* **inzhaagode'e**; *prt* **zhayaagode'ed**
zhaagoodenim *vta* think s.o. is inadequate; *1sg* **inzhaagoodenimaa**; *prt* **zhayaagoodenimaad**
zhaagooji' *vta* defeat s.o., overcome s.o.; *1sg* **inzhaagooji'aa**; *prt* **zhayaagooji'aad**
zhaagooji'iwe *vai* defeat people, overcome people; *1sg* **inzhaagooji'iwe**; *prt* **zhayaagooji'iwed**
zhaagoojitoon *vti2* defeat s.t., overcome s.t.; *1sg* **inzhaagoojitoon**; *prt* **zhayaagoojitood**
zhaagoozom *vta* defeat s.o. in speech, overcome s.o. with speech; *1sg* **inzhaagoozomaa**; *prt* **zhayaagoozomaad**
zhaagwaadad *vii* be weak in power, be ineffective; *prt* **zhayaagwaadak**

zhaagwaadizi *vai* be weak in power, be ineffective; *1sg* **inzhaagwaadiz**; *prt* **zhayaagwaadizid**
zhaagwaagamin /zhaagwaagami-/ *vii* be weak (as a liquid); *prt* **zhayaagwaagamig**
zhaagwendan *vti* consider s.t. weak; *1sg* **inzhaagwendaan**; *prt* **zhayaagwendang**
zhaagwenim *vta* consider s.o. weak, have doubts about s.o.; *1sg* **inzhaagwenimaa**; *prt* **zhayaagwenimaad**
zhaagwenimo *vai* lack self-confidence, be introverted; *1sg* **inzhaagwenim**; *prt* **zhayaagwenimod**
zhaagwiiwii *vai* be weak in muscular strength; *1sg* **inzhaagwiiwii**; *prt* **zhayaagwiiwiid**
zhaangaching *pc* nine times
zhaangachinoon /zhaangachin-/ *vii* they are nine; *prt* **zhayaangachingin**
zhaangachiwag /zhaangachi-/ *vai* they are nine; *1pl* **inzhaangachimin**; *prt* **zhayaangachijig**
zhaangasimidana *nm* ninety
zhaangaso- *pv4* nine
zhaangaso-anama'e-giizhik *pc* nine weeks
zhaangaso-biboon *pc* nine years
zhaangaso-biboonagad *vii* be nine years; *prt* **zhayaangaso-biboonagak**
zhaangaso-biboonagizi *vai* be nine years old; *1sg* **inzhaangaso-biboonagiz**; *prt* **zhayaangaso-biboonagizid**
zhaangaso-diba'igan *pc* nine hours, nine miles
zhaangaso-diba'iganed *vii* be nine o'clock; *prt* **zhayaangaso-diba'iganek**
zhaangaso-diba'igaans *pc* nine minutes, nine acres
zhaangaso-giizhik *pc* nine days
zhaangaso-giizis *pc* nine months
zhaangasogon *pc* nine days
zhaangasogonagad *vii* be nine days; *prt* **zhayaangasogonagak**
zhaangasogonagizi *vai* be the ninth day of the month, be nine days old; *prt* **zhayaangasogonagizid**
zhaangasoninj *pc* nine inches
zhaangasosagoons *nm* nine thousand
zhaangasozid *pc* nine feet
zhaangasoobii'igan *na* nine (card); *pl* **zhaangasoobii'iganag**
zhaangasooshkin *pc* nine bags
zhaangaswaabik *pc* nine dollars
zhaangaswaak *nm* nine hundred
zhaangaswewaan *pc* nine sets, nine pairs
zhaangaswi *nm* nine
zhaangweshi *na* mink; *pl* **zhaangweshiwag**; *dim* **zhaangweshiins**
zhaangweshiwayaan *na* mink hide; *pl* **zhaangweshiwayaanag**; *dim* **zhaangweshiwayaanens**
zhaashaabw= < zhaabw=
zhaashaaginizide *vai* be barefoot; *1sg* **inzhaashaaginizide**; *prt* **zhayaashaaginizided**
zhaashaagw= < zhaagw=
zhaashaagwam *vta* chew s.o.; *1sg* **inzhaashaagwamaa**; *prt* **zhayaashaagwamaad**
zhaashaagwamikiwe *vai* chew gum; *1sg* **inzhaashaagwamikiwe**; *prt* **zhayaashaagwamikiwed**
zhaashaagwandan *vti* chew s.t.; *1sg* **inzhaashaagwandaan**; *prt* **zhayaashaagwandang**
zhaashaagwanjige *vai* chew things; *1sg* **inzhaashaagwanjige**; *prt* **zhayaashaagwanjiged**
zhaashaawanibiisens *na* purple martin; *pl* **zhaashaawanibiisensag**
zhaashiing= < zhiing=
zhaawan *pc* south
zhaawani-noodin *ni* south wind
zhaawanong *pc* in the south, to the south
zhaawaabookaadeg bipakoombens *ni* pickle; *pl* **zhaawaabookaadegin bipakoombensan**
zhebaa *pc* this morning (just past)
zhede *na* pelican; *pl* **zhedeg**; *dim* **zhedens**
zhegon *vta* stick s.o. in a tight place; *1sg* **inzhegonaa**; *prt* **zhayegonaad**
zhegonan *vti* stick s.t. in a tight place; *1sg* **inzhegonaan**; *prt* **zhayegonang**
zhegoshim *vta* put s.o. in a tight place; *1sg* **inzhegoshimaa**; *prt* **zhayegoshimaad**
zhegoshin *vai* lie in a tight place; *1sg* **inzhegoshin**; *prt* **zhayegoshing**
zhegosidoon *vti2* put s.t. in a tight place; *1sg* **inzhegosidoon**; *prt* **zhayegosidood**
zhegosin *vii* lie in a tight place; *prt* **zhayegosing**
zhegoode *vai* crawl in a tight place; *1sg* **inzhegoode**; *prt* **zhayegoodeg**
zhezhaangaswi *nm* nine each
zhigagowe *vai* vomit; *1sg* **inzhigagowe**; *prt* **zhegagowed**
zhigajibii' *vta* be tired of waiting for s.o.; *1sg* **inzhigajibii'aa**; *prt* **zhegajibii'aad**
zhigajibii'o *vai* be tired of waiting; *1sg* **inzhigajibii'**; *prt* **zhegajibii'od**
zhigajibiitoon *vti2* be tired of waiting for s.t.; *1sg* **inzhigajibiitoon**; *prt* **zhegajibiitood**
zhigajii *vai* be tired, be impatient; *1sg* **inzhigajii**; *prt* **zhegajiid**
zhigaag *na* skunk; *pl* **zhigaagwag**; *dim* **zhigaagoons**
zhigaagawanzh *na* onion; *pl* **zhigaagawanzhiig**; *loc* **zhigaagawanzhiing**; *dim* **zhigaagawanzhiins**
zhigidan *vti* urinate on s.t.; *1sg* **inzhigidaan**; *prt* **zhegidang**
zhigingwaam *vai* wet the bed; *1sg* **inzhigingwaam**; *prt* **zhegingwaang**
zhiginidizo *vai* urinate on oneself; *1sg* **inzhiginidiz**; *prt* **zheginidizod**
zhigizh /zhigiN-/ *vta* urinate on s.o.; *1sg* **inzhiginaa**; *prt* **zheginaad**
zhigwa *pc* now, at this time; *also* **azhigwa, zhigo**
zhigwameg *na* dogfish; *pl* **zhigwamegwag**; *dim* **zhigwamegoons**
zhigwaajiganaak *ni* tool for extracting marrow from bones; *pl* **zhigwaajiganaakoon**
zhigwaajige *vai* extract marrow from bones; *1sg* **inzhigwaajige**; *prt* **zhegwaajiged**
zhigweyaabam *vta* aim at s.o.; *1sg* **inzhigweyaabamaa**; *prt* **zhegweyaabamaad**
zhigweyaabandan *vti* aim at s.t.; *1sg* **inzhigweyaabandaan**; *prt* **zhegweyaabandang**

zhigweyaabi *vai* aim sights; *1sg* **inzhigweyaab**; *prt* **zhegweyaabid**
zhimaagan *ni* spear, lance; *pl* **zhimaaganan**; *loc* **zhimaaganing**; *dim* **zhimaagaans**
zhimaaganish *na* soldier, jack (card); *pl* **zhimaaganishag**; *dim* **zhimaaganishens**
zhimaaganishii-aakoziiwigamig *ni* veteran's hospital; *pl* **zhimaaganishii-aakoziiwigamigoon**; *loc* **zhimaaganishii-aakoziiwigamigong**; *dim* **zhimaaganishii-aakoziiwigamigoons**
zhimaaganishii-ogimaa *na* military officer; *pl* **zhimaaganishii-ogimaag**
zhimaaganishiiwigamig *ni* veteran's home; *pl* **zhimaaganishiiwigamigoon**; *loc* **zhimaaganishiiwigamigong**
zhinawa'oojigan *ni* small round bell, sleigh bell, dance bell; *pl* **zhinawa'oojiganan**; *loc* **zhinawa'oojiganing**; *dim* **zhinawa'oojigaans**
zhingaden *vta* spread s.o. out; *1sg* **inzhingadenaa**; *prt* **zhengadenaad**
zhingadenan *vti* spread s.t. out; *1sg* **inzhingadenaan**; *prt* **zhengadenang**
zhingadeshim *vta* lay s.o. spread out; *1sg* **inzhingadeshimaa**; *prt* **zhengadeshimaad**
zhingadeshin *vai* lie spread out; *1sg* **inzhingadeshin**; *prt* **zhengadeshing**
zhingadesidoon *vti2* lay s.t. spread out; *1sg* **inzhingadesidoon**; *prt* **zhengadesidood**
zhingadesin *vii* lie spread out; *prt* **zhengadesing**
zhingibis *na* grebe *locally called* hell diver; boil, carbuncle; *pl* **zhingibisag**; *dim* **zhingibisens**
zhingishin *vai* lie down; *1sg* **inzhingishin**; *prt* **zhengishing**
zhingob *na* balsam fir; *pl* **zhingobiig**; *loc* **zhingobiing**; *dim* **zhingobiins**
zhingobaaboo *ni* beer; *loc* **zhingobaaboong**
zhingobaandag *na* fir bough; *pl* **zhingobaandagoog**; *loc* **zhingobaandagong**; *dim* **zhingobaandagoons**
zhingos *na* weasel; *pl* **zhingosag**; *dim* **zhingosens**
zhingosiwayaan *na* weasel skin; *pl* **zhingosiwayaanag**; *loc* **zhingosiwayaaning**; *dim* **zhingosiwayaanens**
zhingwaak *na* white pine; *pl* **zhingwaakwag**; *loc* **zhingwaakong**; *dim* **zhingwaakoons**
zhingwaakwaandag *na* pine bough; *pl* **zhingwaakwaandagoog**; *loc* **zhingwaakwaandagong**; *dim* **zhingwaakwaandagoons**
zhinoodaagan *ni* net cord; *pl* **zhinoodaaganan**; *dim* **zhinoodaagaans**
zhishigagowe *vai* keep vomiting; *1sg* **inzhishigagowe**; *prt* **zheshigagowed**
zhishigobidoon *vti2* crush s.t. with hands; *1sg* **inzhishigobidoon**; *prt* **zheshigobidood**
zhishigobizh /zhishigobiN-/ *vta* crush s.o. with hands; *1sg* **inzhishigobinaa**; *prt* **zheshigobinaad**
zhishigoshkan *vti* crush s.t. by foot or body; *1sg* **inzhishigoshkaan**; *prt* **zheshigoshkang**
zhishigoshkaw *vta* crush s.o. by foot or body; *1sg* **inzhishigoshkawaa**; *prt* **zheshigoshkawaad**
zhishigwam *vta* gnaw s.o., chew s.o. to bits; *1sg* **inzhishigwamaa**; *prt* **zheshigwamaad**
zhishigwandan *vti* gnaw s.t., chew s.t. to bits; *1sg* **inzhishigwandaan**; *prt* **zheshigwandang**
zhishwajayi'ii *pc* alongside it
zhishwajigamig *pc* alongside the house
zhishwajikana *pc* alongside the road
zhizhoobii' /zhizhoobii'w-/ *vta* paint s.o.; *1sg* **inzhizhoobii'waa**; *prt* **zhezhoobii'waad**
zhizhoobii'amaw *vta* paint (s.t.) for s.o.; *1sg* **inzhizhoobii'amawaa**; *prt* **zhezhoobii'amawaad**
zhizhoobii'an *vti* paint s.t.; *1sg* **inzhizhoobii'aan**; *prt* **zhezhoobii'ang**
zhizhoobii'igan *ni* paint; *pl* **zhizhoobii'iganan**; *loc* **zhizhoobii'iganing**
zhizhoobii'iganaatig *ni* paint brush; *pl* **zhizhoobii'iganaatigoon**; *loc* **zhizhoobii'iganaatigong**; *dim* **zhizhoobii'iganaatigoons**
zhizhoobii'ige *vai* paint things; *1sg* **inzhizhoobii'ige**; *prt* **zhezhoobii'iged**
zhizhoobii'igewinini *na* painter; *pl* **zhizhoobii'igewininiwag**
zhizhoo' /zhizhoo'w-/ *vta* spread s.o. using something; *1sg* **inzhizhoo'waa**; *prt* **zhezhoo'waad**
zhizhoo'an *vti* spread s.t. using something; *1sg* **inzhizhoo'aan**; *prt* **zhezhoo'ang**
zhizhoo'ige *vai* spread things using something; *1sg* **inzhizhoo'ige**; *prt* **zhezhoo'iged**
zhiibawaaseyaa *vii* be transparent; *prt* **zhaabawaaseyaag**; *aug* **zhiibawaaseyaamagad**; *prt aug* **zhaabawaaseyaamagak**
zhiibawaasezi *vai* be transparent; *1sg* **inzhiibawaasez**; *prt* **zhaabawaasezid**
zhiibaakwa' /zhiibaakwa'w-/ *vta* stretch s.o. on a hide stretcher; *1sg* **inzhiibaakwa'waa**; *prt* **zhaabaakwa'waad**
zhiibaakwa'ataan *ni* flat hide stretcher (especially for muskrats); *pl* **zhiibaakwa'ataanan**; *loc* **zhiibaakwa'ataaning**; *dim* **zhiibaakwa'ataanens**
zhiibaangwashi *vai* take a quick nap; *1sg* **inzhiibaangwash**; *prt* **zhaabaangwashid**
zhiibaayaabanjigan *ni* telescope, binoculars; *pl* **zhiibaayaabanjiganan**; *loc* **zhiibaayaabanjiganing**; *dim* **zhiibaayaabanjigaans**
zhiibaayaakizo *vai* get x-rayed; *1sg* **inzhiibaayaakiz**; *prt* **zhaabaayaakizod**
zhiibii *vai* stretch one's body; *1sg* **inzhiibii**; *prt* **zhaabiid**
zhiibiiga' /zhiibiiga'w-/ *vta* stretch s.o. using something (as something sheet-like); *1sg* **inzhiibiiga'waa**; *prt* **zhaabiiga'waad**
zhiibiiga'an *vti* stretch s.t. using something (as something sheet-like); *1sg* **inzhiibiiga'aan**; *prt* **zhaabiiga'ang**
zhiibiigibidoon *vti2* stretch s.t. by pulling (as something sheet-like); *1sg* **inzhiibiigibidoon**; *prt* **zhaabiigibidood**
zhiibiigibizh /zhiibiigibiN-/ *vta* stretch s.o. by pulling (as something sheet-like); *1sg* **inzhiibiigibinaa**; *prt* **zhaabiigibinaad**
zhiibiigishkaa *vii* stretch (as something sheet-like); *prt* **zhaabiigishkaag**; *aug*

zhiibiigishkaamagad; *prt aug* **zhaabiigishkaamagak**
zhiigaa *na* widow, widower; *pl* **zhiigaag**
zhiigaawi *vai* be a widow, be a widower; *1sg* **inzhiigaaw**; *prt* **zhaagaawid**
zhiigon *vta* empty s.o.; *1sg* **inzhiigonaa**; *prt* **zhaagonaad**
zhiigonan *vti* empty s.t.; *1sg* **inzhiigonaan**; *prt* **zhaagonang**
zhiigonigaade *vii* be emptied; *prt* **zhaagonigaadeg**; *aug* **zhiigonigaademagad**; *prt aug* **zhaagonigaademagak**
zhiigonigaazo *vai* be emptied; *prt* **zhaagonigaazod**
zhiigonige *vai* empty things; *1sg* **inzhiigonige**; *prt* **zhaagoniged**
zhiigoshkigani-adaawewigamig *ni* secondhand clothing store; *pl* **zhiigoshkigani-adaawewigamigoon**; *loc* **zhiigoshkigani-adaawewigamigong**
zhiigozhigan *ni* carcass; *pl* **zhiigozhiganan**; *loc* **zhiigozhiganing**; *dim* **zhiigozhigaans**
zhiigoojiinan *vti* deflate s.t.; *1sg* **inzhiigoojiinaan**; *prt* **zhaagoojiinang**
zhiigwanaabik *na* grindstone; *pl* **zhiigwanaabikoog**; *loc* **zhiigwanaabikong**; *dim* **zhiigwanaabikoons**
zhiingendan *vti* dislike s.t., disapprove of s.t., hate s.t.; *1sg* **inzhiingendaan**; *prt* **zhaangendang**
zhiingendaagozi *vai* be disliked, be disapproved of, be hated; *1sg* **inzhiingendaagoz**; *prt* **zhaangendaagozid**
zhiingendaagwad *vii* be disliked, be disapproved of, be hated; *prt* **zhaangendaagwak**
zhiingenim *vta* dislike s.o., disapprove of s.o., hate s.o.; *1sg* **inzhiingenimaa**; *prt* **zhaangenimaad**
zhiingenindiwag /zhiingenindi-/ *vai* they dislike each other, they disapprove of each other, they hate each other; *1pl* **inzhiingenindimin**; *prt* **zhaangeninindijig**
zhiishiib= < zhiib=
zhiishiib *na* duck; *pl* **zhiishiibag**; *dim* **zhiishiibens**
zhiishiibanwii-baashkizigan *ni* shotgun; *pl* **zhiishiibanwii-baashkiziganan**; *loc* **zhiishiibanwii-baashkiziganing**; *dim* **zhiishiibanwii-baashkizigaans**
zhiishiibikojigan *na* duck decoy; *pl* **zhiishiibikojigan**; *loc* **zhiishiibikojiganing**; *dim* **zhiishiibikojigaans**
zhiishiig= < zhig=
zhiishiigi *vai* urinate; *1sg* **inzhiishiig**; *prt* **zhaashiigid**
zhiishiigwan *na* rattle; *pl* **zhiishiigwanag**; *loc* **zhiishiigwaning**; *dim* **zhiishiigwaans**
zhiishiigwaans *na* sugar cone; *pl* **zhiishiigwaansag**; *loc* **zhiishiigwaansing**
zhiishiigwe *na* rattlesnake; *pl* **zhiishiigweg**; *dim* **zhiishiigwens**
zhiiwan *vii* be sour; *prt* **zhaawang**
zhiiwaaboo *ni* vinegar; *loc* **zhiiwaaboong**
zhiiwaabookaade *vii* be pickled; *prt* **zhaawaabookaadeg**; *aug* **zhiiwaabookaademagad**; *prt aug* **zhaawaabookaademagak**
zhiiwaagamide *vii* thicken into syrup; *prt* **zhaawaagamideg**; *aug* **zhiiwaagamidemagad**; *prt aug* **zhaawaagamidemagak**
zhiiwaagamin /zhiiwaagami-/ *vii* be sour (as a liquid); *prt* **zhaawaagamig**
zhiiwaagamizigan *ni* syrup; *loc* **zhiiwaagamiziganing**
zhiiwaagamiziganike *vai* make syrup; *1sg* **inzhiiwaagamiziganike**; *prt* **zhaawaagamiziganiked**
zhiiwaagamizige *vai* make syrup; *1sg* **inzhiiwaagamizige**; *prt* **zhaawaagamiziged**
zhiiwibag *ni* rhubarb; *pl* **zhiiwibagoon**; *loc* **zhiiwibagong**; *dim* **zhiiwibagoons**
zhiiwi-bipakoombens *ni* pickle; *pl* **zhiiwi-bipakoombensan**
zhiiwisijigan *na* sourdough; *pl* **zhiiwisijiganag**; *loc* **zhiiwisijiganing**
zhiiwitaagan *ni* salt; *loc* **zhiiwitaaganing**
zhiiwitaagana' /zhiiwitaagana'w-/ *vta* salt s.o.; *1sg* **inzhiiwitaagana'waa**; *prt* **zhaawitaagana'waad**
zhiiwitaagana'an *vti* salt s.t.; *1sg* **inzhiiwitaagana'aan**; *prt* **zhaawitaagana'ang**
zhiiwitaagana'ige *vai* salt things; *1sg* **inzhiiwitaagana'ige**; *prt* **zhaawitaagana'iged**
zhiiwitaaganaagamin /zhiiwitaaganaagami-/ *vii* be salty (as a liquid); *prt* **zhaawitaaganaagamig**
zhiiwitaaganipogozi *vai* taste salty; *prt* **zhaawitaaganipogozid**
zhiiwitaaganipogwad *vii* taste salty; *prt* **zhaawitaaganipogwak**
zhiiwitaagani-gookoosh *na* salt pork
zhiiwizi *vai* be sour; *prt* **zhaawizid**
zhoobi' *vta* attract s.o., please s.o.; *1sg* **inzhoobi'aa**; *prt* **zhwaabi'aad**
zhoobizi *vai* be tempted; *1sg* **inzhoobiz**; *prt* **zhwaabizid**
zhoominaaboo *ni* wine; *loc* **zhoominaaboong**; *also* **zhawiminaaboo**
zhoominens *ni* raisin; *pl* **zhoominensan**

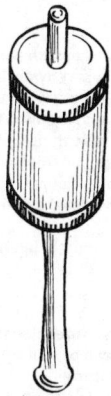

zhiishiigwan (rattle)

zhoomiingweni *vai* smile; *1sg* **inzhoomiingwen**; *prt* **zhwaamiingwenid**
zhoomiingwetaw *vta* smile at s.o.; *1sg* **inzhoomiingwetawaa**; *prt* **zhwaamiingwetawaad**
zhooniyaa *na* money; *loc* **zhooniyaang**; *dim* **zhooniyaans**
zhooniyaake *vai* make money, earn money; *1sg* **inzhooniyaake**; *prt* **zhwaaniyaaked**
zhooniyaa-mashkimod *ni* purse, handbag; *pl* **zhooniyaa-mashkimodan**; *loc* **zhooniyaa-mashkimodaang**; *dim* **zhooniyaa-mashkimodens**; *also* **zhooniyaa-mashkimodens**
zhooniyaans *na* coin, dime; *pl* **zhooniyaansag**; *loc* **zhooniyaansing**
zhooniyaawaabik *na* coin; *pl* **zhooniyaawaabikoog**; *loc* **zhooniyaawaabikong**; *dim* **zhooniyaawaabikoons**
zhooniyaawaabik *ni* silver; *pl* **zhooniyaawaabikoon**; *dim* **zhooniyaawaabikoons**
zhooniyaawigamig *ni* bank; *pl* **zhooniyaawigamigoon**; *loc* **zhooniyaawigamigong**
zhooshkodaabaan *na* toboggan; *pl* **zhooshkodaabaanag**; *loc* **zhooshkodaabaaning**; *dim* **zhooshkodaanaanens**

zhooshkodaabaan (toboggan)

zhooshkon *vta* slide s.o. with hand; *1sg* **inzhooshkonaa**; *prt* **zhwaashkonaad**
zhooshkonan *vti* slide s.t. with hand; *1sg* **inzhooshkonaan**; *prt* **zhwaashkonang**
zhooshkonige *vai* slide things, play checkers; *1sg* **inzhooshkonige**; *prt* **zhwaashkoniged**
zhooshkoshimaan *na* ski; *pl* **zhooshkoshimaanag**; *also* **zhooshkoshime-aagim**
zhooshkozi *vai* be smooth, be slick; *prt* **zhwaashkozid**
zhooshkwabi *vai* slide over sitting; *1sg* **inzhooshkwab**; *prt* **zhwaashkwabid**
zhooshkwadamon /zhooshkwadamo-/ *vii* be slippery (as a road or trail); *prt* **zhwaashkwadamog**
zhooshkwajiwe *vai* go sliding; *1sg* **inzhooshkwajiwe**; *prt* **zhwaashkwajiwed**
zhooshkwaa *vii* be smooth, be slick; *prt* **zhwaashkwaag**; *aug* **zhooshkwaamagad**; *prt aug* **zhwaashkwaamagak**
zhooshkwaabikad *vii* be smooth (as something mineral), be rustless; *prt* **zhwaashkwaabikak**
zhooshkwaabikizi *vai* be smooth (as something mineral), be rustless; *prt* **zhwaashkwaabikizid**
zhooshkwaada'aagan *ni* skate; *pl* **zhooshkwaada'aaganan**; *loc* **zhooshkwaada'aaganing**; *dim* **zhooshkwaada'aagaans**
zhooshkwaada'e *vai* skate; *1sg* **inzhooshkwaada'e**; *prt* **zhwaashkwaada'ed**
zhooshkwaada'ewigamig *ni* arena, rink; *pl* **zhooshkwaada'ewigamigoon**; *loc* **zhooshkwaada'ewigamigong**; *dim* **zhooshkwaada'ewigamigoons**
zhooshkwaagim *na* ski; *pl* **zhooshkwaagimag**; *loc* **zhooshkwaagiming**; *dim* **zhooshkwaagimens**
zhooshkwaagime *vai* ski; *1sg* **inzhooshkwaagime**; *prt* **zhwaashkwaagimed**
zhooshkwaakozi *vai* be smooth (as something stick- or wood-like); *prt* **zhwaashkwaakozid**
zhooshkwaakwad *vii* be smooth (as something stick- or wood-like); *prt* **zhwaashkwaakwak**
zhooshkwegad *vii* be smooth (as something sheet-like); *prt* **zhwaashkwegak**
zhooshkwega' /zhooshkwega'w-/ *vta* iron s.o. (e.g., pants); *1sg* **inzhooshkwega'waa**; *prt* **zhwaashkwega'waad**
zhooshkwega'an *vti* iron s.t.; *1sg* **inzhooshkwega'aan**; *prt* **zhwaashkwega'ang**
zhooshkwega'igan *ni* clothes iron; *pl* **zhooshkwega'iganan**; *loc* **zhooshkwega'iganing**; *dim* **zhooshkwega'igaans**
zhooshkwega'ige *vai* iron clothes; *1sg* **inzhooshkwega'ige**; *prt* **zhwaashkwega'iged**
zhooshkwegizi *vai* be smooth (as something sheet-like); *prt* **zhwaashkwegizid**
ziko *vai* spit; *1sg* **inzik**; *prt* **zekod**
zikowin *ni* saliva, spit
zikwaadan *vti* spit on s.t.; *1sg* **inzikwaadaan**; *prt* **zekwaadang**
zikwaajige *vai* spit on things; *1sg* **inzikwaajige**; *prt* **zekwaajiged**
zikwaazh /zikwaaN-/ *vta* spit on s.o.; *1sg* **inzikwaanaa**; *prt* **zekwaanaad**
zinigobidoon *vti2* massage s.t. with something; *1sg* **inzinigobidoon**; *prt* **zenigobidood**
zinigobizh /zinigobiN-/ *vta* massage s.o. with something; *1sg* **inzinigobinaa**; *prt* **zenigobinaad**
zinigon *vta* rub s.o. with something; *1sg* **inzinigonaa**; *prt* **zenigonaad**
zinigonan *vti* rub s.t. with something; *1sg* **inzinigonaan**; *prt* **zenigonang**
zisiboodoon *vti2* file s.t., grind s.t. down; *1sg* **inzisiboodoon**; *prt* **zesiboodood**
zisiboojigan *ni* file, rasp; *pl* **zisiboojiganan**; *loc* **zisiboojiganing**; *dim* **zisiboojigaans**
zisiboojige *vai* file things; *1sg* **inzisiboojige**; *prt* **zesiboojiged**
zisiboozh /zisibooN-/ *vta* file s.o., grind s.o. down; *1sg* **inzisiboonaa**; *prt* **zesiboonaad**

ziibaaska'igan *ni* jingle (on dress); *pl* **ziibaaska'iganan**; *loc* **ziibaaska'iganing**; *dim* **ziibaaska'igaans**
ziibaaska'iganagooday *ni* jingle dress; *pl* **ziibaaska'iganagoodayan**

ziibaaska'iganagooday (jingle dress)

ziibaaskobijige *vai* set a net under the ice; *1sg* **inziibaaskobijige**; *prt* **zaabaaskobijiged**
ziibi *ni* river; *pl* **ziibiwan**; *loc* **ziibiing**; *dim* **ziibiins**
ziibiins *ni* creek; *pl* **ziibiinsan**; *loc* **ziibiinsing**
ziiga'andan *vti* water s.t., pour liquid on s.t.; *1sg* **inziiga'andaan**; *prt* **zaaga'andang**
ziiga'andaw *vta* pour liquid on s.o., baptize s.o.; *1sg* **inziiga'andawaa**; *prt* **zaaga'andawaad**
ziiga'igan *ni* sugar cake, sugar cone; *pl* **ziiga'iganan**; *loc* **ziiga'iganing**; *dim* **ziiga'igaans**
ziiga'iganike *vai* make a sugar cone; *1sg* **inziiga'iganike**; *prt* **zaaga'iganiked**
ziiga'ige *vai* cast sugar cones; *1sg* **inziiga'ige**; *prt* **zaaga'iged**
ziigana' /ziigana'w-/ *vta* spoon feed s.o. a liquid; *1sg* **inziigana'waa**; *prt* **zaagana'waad**
ziigashkinadoon *vti2* fill s.t. to overflowing with solids; *1sg* **inziigashkinadoon**; *prt* **zaagashkinadood**
ziigashkina' *vta* fill s.o. to overflowing with solids; *1sg* **inziigashkina'aa**; *prt* **zaagashkina'aad**
ziigibadoon *vti2* fill s.t. to overflowing with a liquid; *1sg* **inziigibadoon**; *prt* **zaagibadood**
ziigigamide *vii* boil over; *prt* **zaagigamideg**; *aug* **ziigigamidemagad**; *prt aug* **zaagigamidemagak**
ziigigamizo *vai* boil over; *prt* **zaagigamizod**
ziiginan *vti* pour s.t., spill s.t.; *1sg* **inziiginaan**; *prt* **zaaginang**
ziiginige *vai* pour things, spill things; *1sg* **inziiginige**; *prt* **zaaginiged**
ziiginigewigamig *ni* tavern, bar; *pl* **ziiginigewigamigoon**; *loc* **ziiginigewigamigong**; *dim* **ziiginigewigamigoons**
ziiginigewikwe *na* barmaid; *pl* **ziiginigewikweg**
ziiginigewinini *na* bartender; *pl* **ziiginigewininiwag**
ziiginishaan *ni* ear drops
ziiginiingwaan *ni* eye drops
ziigise *vii* pour out, spill out; *prt* **zaagiseg**; *aug* **ziigisemagad**; *prt aug* **zaagisemagak**
ziigwan *vii* be spring; *prt* **zaagwang**
ziigwanishi *vai* spend the spring somewhere; *1sg* **inziigwanish**; *prt* **zaagwanishid**
ziigwanong *pc* last spring
ziigwebinan *vti* spill s.t.; *1sg* **inziigwebinaan**; *prt* **zaagwebinang**
ziigwebinigan *ni* dump, trash; *pl* **ziigwebiniganan**; *loc* **ziigwebiniganing**; *dim* **ziigwebinigaans**
ziigwebinigewakik *na* slop pail; *pl* **ziigwebinigewakikoog**; *loc* **ziigwebinigewakikong**; *dim* **ziigwebinigewakikoons**
ziikaa *na* car *old fashioned*; *pl* **ziikaag**; *loc* **ziikaang**; *dim* **ziikaans**
ziikaapidan *vti* drink s.t. quickly; *1sg* **inziikaapidaan**; *prt* **zaakaapidang**
ziikoobiiginan *vti* strain s.t.; *1sg* **inziikoobiiginaan**; *prt* **zaakoobiiginang**
ziinaakwa'igan *ni* clothes wringer, clothespin; *pl* **ziinaakwa'iganan**; *loc* **ziinaakwa'iganing**; *dim* **ziinaakwa'igaans**
ziindaakoshin *vai* be wedged in tightly (as something stick- or wood-like); *1sg* **inziindaakoshin**; *prt* **zaandaakoshing**
ziindaakosin *vii* be wedged in tightly (as something stick- or wood-like); *prt* **zaandaakosing**
ziinibidoon *vti2* squeeze s.t., wring s.t.; *1sg* **inziinibidoon**; *prt* **zaanibidood**
ziinibizh /ziinibiN-/ *vta* squeeze s.o., wring s.o.; *1sg* **inziinibinaa**; *prt* **zaanibinaad**
ziinikiigomaan *na* snot
ziinikiigome *vai* blow one's nose; *1sg* **inziinikiigome**; *prt* **zaanikiigomed**
ziinin *vta* milk s.o.; *1sg* **inziininaa**; *prt* **zaaninaad**
ziininiwe *vai* milk cows; *1sg* **inziininiwe**; *prt* **zaaniniwed**
ziinzibaakwad *ni* maple sugar, sugar; *loc* **ziinzibaakwadong**; *dim* **ziinzibaakwadoons**
ziinzibaakwado-makak *ni* birch bark basket for maple sugar; *pl* **ziinzibaakwado-makakoon**
ziinzibaakwad-onaagaans *ni* sugar bowl; *pl* **ziinzibaakwad-onaagaansan**; *loc* **ziinzibaakwad-onaagaansing**
ziinzibaakwadowaapine *vai* have diabetes; *1sg* **inziinzibaakwadowaapine**; *prt* **zaanzibaakwadowaapined**; *also* **ziinzibaakwadwaapine**
ziinzibaakwadoons *ni* candy; *pl* **ziinzibaakwadoonsan**; *loc* **ziinzibaakwadoonsing**
ziinzibaakwadwaaboo *ni* maple sap; *loc* **ziinzibaakwadwaaboong**
ziinzoopizon *ni* bandage; *pl* **ziinzoopizonan**; *loc* **ziinzoopizoning**; *dim* **ziinzoopizonens**
zoobam *vta* suck out of s.o.; *1sg* **inzoobamaa**; *prt* **zwaabamaad**
zoobandan *vti* suck out of s.t.; *1sg* **inzoobandaan**; *prt* **zwaabandang**
zoogipon /zoogipo-/ *vii* snow; *prt* **zwaagipog**

zoongan *vii* be solid, be strong; *prt* **zwaangang**
zoongide'e *vai* be brave; *1sg* **inzoongide'e**; *prt* **zwaangide'ed**
zoongigane *vai* have strong bones; *1sg* **inzoongigane**; *prt* **zwaangiganed**
zoongi' *vta* make s.o. strong, make s.o. solid; *1sg* **inzoongi'aa**; *prt* **zwaangi'aad**
zoongingwashi *vai* sleep deeply
zoonginike *vai* have a strong arm; *1sg* **inzoonginike**; *prt* **zwaanginiked**
zoongininjii *vai* have a strong hand; *1sg* **inzoongininjii**; *prt* **zwaanginiinjiid**
zoongishin *vai* lie firmly fixed in place; *1sg* **inzoongishin**; *prt* **zwaangishing**
zoongisin *vii* lie firmly fixed in place; *prt* **zwaangising**
zoongitoon *vti2* make s.t. strong, make s.t. solid; *1sg* **inzoongitoon**; *prt* **zwaangitood**
zoongizi *vai* be solid, be strong; *1sg* **inzoongiz**; *prt* **zwaangizid**

Part II

English–Ojibwe Index

A

ABANDON
ABANDON: abandon s.o. **nagazh /nagaN-/** *vta;* abandon s.t. **nagadan** *vti;* abandon people **nagazhiwe** *vai*
ABLE
ABLE: be able **gashki'o** *vai;* be able (to do something) **gashkichige** *vai*
ABLE TO CARRY: be able to carry s.o. **gashkiwizh /gashkiwiN-/** *vta;* be able to carry s.t. **gashkiwidoon** *vti2*
ABLE TO DO: be able to do s.t. **gashkitoon** *vti2*
ABLE TO GET: be able to get (s.t.) for s.o. **gashkitaw** *vta*
ABLE TO MANAGE: be able to manage (s.t.) for s.o. **gashkitaw** *vta*
ABLE TO TAKE: be able to take s.o. **gashkiwizh /gashkiwiN-/** *vta;* be able to take s.t. **gashkiwidoon** *vti2*
ABLE TO WORK: be able to work **gashkanokii** *vai*
NOT ABLE: not able to **bwaa-** *pv1*
ABOARD
GET ABOARD: **boozi** *vai*
JUMP ABOARD: **boozigwaashkwani** *vai*
TELL TO GO ABOARD: tell s.o. to go aboard **boozinaazha' /boozinaazha'w-/** *vta*
ABOUT
ABOUT: going about **babaa-** *pv2*
BLOWN ABOUT: be blown about **babaamaashi** *vai;* **babaamaasin** *vii*
CARRY ABOUT: carry s.o. about **babaamiwizh /babaamiwiN-/** *vta;* carry s.t. about **babaamiwidoon** *vti2*
CHASE ABOUT: chase s.o. about **babaaminizha' /babaaminizha'w-/** *vta;* chase s.t. about **babaaminizha'an** *vti;* chase things about **babaaminizha'ige** *vai*
CLOUDS MOVE ABOUT: **babaamaanakwad** *vii*
CRAWL ABOUT: **babaamoode** *vai*
DANCE ABOUT: **babaamishimo** *vai*
DRIVE ABOUT: **babaamibide, babaamibidemagad** *vii;* **babaamibizo** *vai;* **babaamidaabii'iwe** *vai*
FLY ABOUT: **babaamibide, babaamibidemagad** *vii;* **babaamibizo** *vai;* **babaamise** *vai;* **babaamise, babaamisemagad** *vii*
GO ABOUT CRYING: **babaamademo** *vai*
GO ABOUT IN A BOAT: **babaamishkaa** *vai*
GO ABOUT ON BUSINESS: go about on one's business **babaamizi** *vai*
GO ABOUT ON THE ICE: **babaamaadagaako** *vai*
GO ABOUT TRADING: **babaamadaawe** *vai*
GOING ABOUT: **babaa-** *pv2*
GUIDE ABOUT: guide s.o. about **babaamiwizh /babaamiwiN-/** *vta*
LIVE ABOUT: **babaamaadizi** *vai*
MOVE RESIDENCE ABOUT: move one's residence about **babaamigozi** *vai*
PADDLE ABOUT: **babaamishkaa** *vai*
RIDE ABOUT ON HORSEBACK: **babaamoomigo** *vai*
RUN ABOUT: **babaamibatoo** *vai;* they run about together **babaamiba'idiwag /babaamiba'idi-/** *vai*
SAIL ABOUT: **babaamaashi** *vai;* **babaamaasin** *vii*
SKATE ABOUT: **babaamaada'e** *vai*
SPEED ABOUT: **babaamibide, babaamibidemagad** *vii;* **babaamibizo** *vai*
SPREAD THE NEWS ABOUT: **babaamaajimo** *vai*
SWIM ABOUT: **babaamaadagaa** *vai*
TAKE ABOUT: take s.o. about **babaamiwizh /babaamiwiN-/** *vta;* take s.t. about **babaamiwidoon** *vti2*
TRAVEL ABOUT: **babaamaadizi** *vai*
WADE ABOUT: **babaamaadagaazii** *vai*
WALK ABOUT: **babaamose** *vai;* **babimose** *vai*
WANDER ABOUT: **babaa-ayaa** *vai*
ABOVE
ABOVE: **ishpiming** *pc;* above it **ishpayi'ii** *pc*
ABOVE ALL
ABOVE ALL: **memindage** *pc*
ABSCESSED
ABSCESSED TOOTH: have an abscessed tooth **miniiwaabide** *vai*
ABSENT
ABSENT A CERTAIN LENGTH OF TIME: be absent a certain length of time **apiitendi** *vai;* **inendi** *vai*
ABSENT A CERTAIN NUMBER OF DAYS: be absent a certain number of days **dasogonendi** *vai*
ABSENT FROM A CERTAIN PLACE: be absent from a certain place **ondendi** *vai*
ABUSE
ABUSE: abuse s.o. **aanimi'** *vta;* abuse s.t. **aanimitoon** *vti2*
ACCEPT
ACCEPT: accept s.o. **odaapin** *vta;* accept s.t. **odaapinan** *vti;* accept (s.t.) from s.o. **odaapinamaw** *vta;* accept things **odaapinige** *vai*
ACCEPTED
ACCEPTED: be accepted **odaapinigaade, odaapinigaademagad** *vii;* **odaapinigaazo** *vai*
ACCIDENT
DIE IN AN ACCIDENT: **niiwanishin** *vai*
ACCIDENTALLY
ACCIDENTALLY: **bichi-** *pv4*
ACCIDENTALLY HIT: accidentally hit s.o. **bitaganaam** *vta;* accidentally hit s.t. **bitaganaandan** *vti*
CUT ACCIDENTALLY: cut s.o. accidentally **bitizh /bitizhw-/** *vta;* cut s.t. accidentally **bitizhan** *vti*

HIT AGAINST ACCIDENTALLY: hit against something accidentally (as something stick- or wood-like) **bitaakoshin** *vai;* **bitaakosin** *vii*
SHOOT ACCIDENTALLY: shoot s.o. accidentally **bichinaw** *vta;* shoot s.t. accidentally **bichinan** *vti;* shoot things accidentally **bichinaage** *vai;* shoot oneself accidentally **bichinaadizo** *vai*

ACCOMPANY
ACCOMPANY: accompany s.o. **wiijiiw** *vta;* accompany people **wiijii'iwe** *vai;* they accompany each other **wiijiindiwag /wiijiindi-/** *vai*

ACCOMPLISH
ACCOMPLISH: **gashki'ewizi** *vai*

ACCUSE
ACCUSE: accuse s.o. **anaamim** *vta*

ACE
ACE: ace (card) **bezhigoobii'igan, -ag** *na*

ACHE
ACHE: **dewizi** *vai*
ACHE IN ARM: have an ache in one's arm **dewinike** *vai*
ACHE IN BACK: have a backache **dewaawigan** *vai;* **dewipikwan** *vai*
ACHE IN FOOT: have an ache in one's foot **dewizide** *vai*
ACHE IN HAND: have an ache in one's hand **dewininjii** *vai*
ACHE IN LEG: have an ache in one's leg **dewigaade** *vai*
TOOTHACHE: have a toothache **dewaabide** *vai*

ACNE
ACNE ON FACE: have acne on one's face **moosewiingwe** *vai*

ACORN
ACORN: **mitigomin, -an** *ni*

ACQUAINTED
ACQUAINTED: be acquainted with s.o. **nagadenim** *vta;* they are acquainted with each other **nagadenindiwag /nagadenindi-/** *vai*

ACQUIRE
ACQUIRE: **gashkichige** *vai*

ACRE
CERTAIN NUMBER OF ACRES: a certain number of acres **daso-diba'igaans** *pc*

ACROSS
ACROSS: **agaami-** *pn;* across it **agaamayi'ii** *pc*
ACROSS THE LAKE: **agaaming** *pc*
ACROSS THE ROAD: across the road or trail **agaamikana** *pc*
CARRY ACROSS: carry s.o. across **aazhogewizh /aazhogewiN-/** *vta;* carry s.t. across **aazhogewidoon** *vti2*
CLIMB ACROSS: **aazhawaandawe** *vai*
DRIVE ACROSS: **aazhogebizo** *vai;* **aazhogedaabii'iwe** *vai;* **aazhoodaabii'iwe** *vai*
FERRY ACROSS: ferry s.o. across **aazhawa'oozh /aazhawa'ooN-/** *vta;* ferry s.t. across **aazhawa'oodoon** *vti2*
GO ACROSS: **aazhooshkaa** *vai*
GO ACROSS BY BOAT: **aazhawa'am** *vai2, also* **aazhawa'o**
GO ACROSS WATER: **aazhoge** *vai*
JUMP ACROSS: **aazhawigwaashkwani** *vai*
LAY ACROSS: lay s.o. across (as something stick- or wood-like) **aazhawaakoshim** *vta;* lay s.t. across (as something stick- or wood-like) **aazhawaakosidoon** *vti2*
LIE ACROSS: lie across (as something stick- or wood-like) **aazhawaakoshin** *vai;* **aazhawaakosin** *vii*
OVER ACROSS: **awasi-** *pn;* over across it **awasayi'ii** *pc*
OVER ACROSS THE FIRE: **awasishkode** *pc*
OVER ACROSS THE MOUNTAIN: **awasajiw** *pc*
OVER ACROSS THE WATER: **awasagaam** *pc*
OVER ACROSS THE WOODS: **awasaakwaa** *pc*
RIGHT ACROSS: **dibishkookamig** *pc*
ROAD GOES ACROSS: go across (as a road or trail) **aazhoodamon /aazhoodamo-/** *vii*
RUN ACROSS: **aazhoobatoo** *vai, also* **aazhawibatoo**; they run across together **aazhogeba'idiwag /aazhogeba'idi-/** *vai;* **aazhooba'idiwag /aazhooba'idi-/** *vai*
RUN ACROSS WADING: **aazhawagaaziibatoo** *vai*
SWIM ACROSS: **aazhawaadagaa** *vai*
TAKE ACROSS: take s.o. across **aazhogewizh /aazhogewiN-/** *vta;* take s.t. across **aazhogewidoon** *vti2*
TAKE ACROSS BY BOAT: take s.o. across by boat **aazhawa'oozh /aazhawa'ooN-/** *vta;* take s.t. across by boat **aazhawa'oodoon** *vti2*
TRAIL GOES ACROSS: go across (as a road or trail) **aazhoodamon /aazhoodamo-/** *vii*
WADE ACROSS: **aazhawagaazii** *vai*

ADD
ADD IN: add s.o. in **dagon** *vta;* add s.t. in **dagonan** *vti*
ADD TOGETHER: **asigagindaaso** *vai;* add s.o. together (e.g., money) **asigagim** *vta;* add s.t. together **asigagindan** *vti*

ADDED
ADDED IN: be added in **dagonigaade, dagonigaademagad** *vii;* **dagonigaazo** *vai*

ADDRESS
ADDRESS: address s.o. **ganoozh /ganooN-/** *vta*

ADHERE
ADHERE: **agoke** *vai;* **agoke, agokemagad** *vii;* **bazagoke** *vai;* **bazagoke, bazagokemagad** *vii*

ADMIRED
ADMIRED: be admired **minwaabamewizi** *vai*

ADOLESCENT
ADOLESCENT: be an adolescent **oshkiniigi** *vai*
ADOLESCENT BOY: **oshkinawe, -g** *na;* be an adolescent boy **oshkinawewi** *vai*
ADOLESCENT GIRL: **oshkiniigikwe, -g** *na;* be an adolescent girl **oshkiniigikwewi** *vai*
ADOPT
ADOPT: adopt s.o. **bami'** *vta;* **waangoom** *vta*
ADOPTED
ADOPTED ONE: **bami'aagan, -ag** *na*
ADULT
ADULT: **gichi-aya'aa, -g** *na;* be an adult **gichi-aya'aawi** *vai*
ADVANCE
IN ADVANCE: **giizhaa** *pc*
ADVANCED
ADVANCED INTO A TIME: **ishpi-** *pv4*
AFRAID
AFRAID: be afraid **gotaaji** *vai;* **zegizi** *vai;* be afraid of s.t. **gotan** *vti*
AFRICAN
AFRICAN: person of African descent **makade-wiiyaas, -ag** *na*
AFRICAN WOMAN: woman of African descent **makade-wiiyaasikwe, -g** *na*
AFTER
AFTER: **ishkwaa-** *pv4*
AFTER A WHILE
AFTER A WHILE: **baanimaa** *pc, also* **baamaa; baanimaa apii** *pc, also* **baanimaapii, baamaapii; bijiinag** *pc;* **gegapii** *pc;* **naagaj** *pc*
AFTERNOON
AFTERNOON: be afternoon **ishkwaa-naawakwe, ishkwaa-naawakwemagad** *vii*
LATE MORNING OR EARLY AFTERNOON: be late morning or early afternoon **ishpi-giizhigad** *vii*
AGAIN
AGAIN: **miinawaa** *pc*
AGAINST THE WIND
GO AGAINST THE WIND: **onjishkawishkaa** *vai*
PADDLE AGAINST THE WIND: **onjishkawa'o** *vai, also* **onjishkawa'am**
AGE
CERTAIN AGE: be a certain age **apiitizi** *vai*
SAME AGE: they are the same age **wiijigindiwag /wiijigindi-/** *vai;* be the same age as s.o. **wiijigim** *vta*
AGITATE
AGITATE: **mamaazikaa** *vai*
AGO
A LITTLE WHILE AGO: **naanoomaya** *pc*
LONG AGO: **mewinzha** *pc*
AGREE
AGREE: **debwetam** *vai2;* **inendam** *vai2;* agree on something **inaakonige** *vai;* agree with s.o. **debwetaw** *vta;* agree with s.o. *especially of something consumed; inverse forms of:* **minokaw-** *vta*
AGREEABLE
AGREEABLE: be agreeable **minwendaagozi** *vai*
AHEAD
AHEAD: **niigaan** *pc*
GO AHEAD: **niigaanii** *vai*
AHEAD OF TIME
AHEAD OF TIME: **nayaag** *pc*
AIM
AIM: aim at s.o. **zhigweyaabam** *vta;* aim at s.t. **zhigweyaabandan** *vti*
AIM SIGHTS: **zhigweyaabi** *vai*
AIR PUMP
AIR PUMP: **boodaajii'igan, -an** *ni*
AIRPLANE
AIRPLANE: **bemisemagak, -in** *ni-pt*
AIRPORT
AIRPORT: **endazhi-booniimagak, -in** *ni-pt*
ALARMED
ALARMED: be alarmed **amaniso** *vai;* be alarmed by s.o. **amanisodaw** *vta*
ALCOHOL
RUBBING ALCOHOL: **giziibiigazhewaaboo** *ni*
ALDER
ALDER: **wadoop, -iin** *ni*
ALGAE
ALGAE: **ataagib** *ni*
ALIGHT
ALIGHT: **boonii** *vai*
ALIVE
ALIVE: be alive **bimaadizi** *vai*
COME ALIVE: **aabijiibaa** *vai*
ALL
ALL: **akina** *pc, also* **kina, gakina**
ALL DAY: **gabe-giizhik** *pc*
ALL EVENING: **gabe-onaagosh** *pc*
ALL KINDS: **anooj** *pc*
ALL NIGHT: **gabe-dibik** *pc*
ALL OVER: **miziwe** *pc*
ALL THE TIME: **apane** *pc*
ALLOT
ALLOT LAND: allot s.o. land **mamakii'** *vta*
ALLOTMENT
ALLOTMENT OF LAND: there is an allotment of land **mamakii'idim /mamakii'idi-/** *vai*
ALLOW
ALLOW: allow s.o. **bagidin** *vta;* allow s.t. **bagidinan** *vti;* allow (s.t.) to s.o. **bagidinamaw** *vta;* allow things **bagidinige** *vai*
ALLOWED
ALLOWED: be allowed **bagidinigaade, bagidinigaademagad** *vii;* **bagidinigaazo** *vai*
ALMOST
ALMOST: **gegaa** *pc*
ALONE
ALONE: be alone **bezhigo** *vai;* **nazhikewizi** *vai*
LIVE ALONE: **nazhikewige** *vai*

SIT ALONE: **nazhikewaakwadabi** *vai*

ALONG

ALONG: **bimi-** *pv2;* along it **jiigayi'ii** *pc*

ALONG THE SHORE: **jiigew** *pc;* **jiigibiig** *pc*

BLOWN ALONG: be blown along **bimaashi** *vai;* **bimaasin** *vii*

CARRY A BABY ALONG ON BACK: carry a baby along on one's back **bimoomaawaso** *vai*

CARRY A PACK ALONG: **bimiwane** *vai*

CARRY ALONG: carry s.o. along **bimiwizh /bimiwiN-/** *vta;* carry s.t. along **bimiwidoon** *vti2;* carry things along **bimiwijige** *vai*

CARRY ALONG ON BACK: carry s.o. along on one's back **bimoom** *vta;* carry s.t. along on one's back **bimoondan** *vti*

CHASE ALONG: chase s.o. along **biminizha' /biminizha'w-/** *vta;* **biminizhikaw** *vta;* chase s.t. along **biminizha'an** *vti;* chase things along **biminizha'ige** *vai;* chase people along **biminaazhikaage** *vai*

CLIMB ALONG: **bimaandawe** *vai*

CLOUDS GO ALONG: **bimaanakwad** *vii*

CRAWL ALONG: **bimoode** *vai*

CRY WALKING ALONG: **bimademo** *vai*

DANCE ALONG: **bimishimo** *vai*

DRAG ALONG: drag s.o. along **bimidaabaazh /bimidaabaaN-/** *vta;* drag s.t. along **bimidaabaadan** *vti*

DRIFT ALONG ON CURRENT: **bimaaboode, bimaaboodemagad** *vii;* **bimaaboono** *vai*

DRIVE ALONG: **bimibide, bimibidemagad** *vii;* **bimibizo** *vai;* **bimidaabii'iwe** *vai;* drive s.o. along **bimibizoni'** *vta;* drive s.t. along **bimibizonitoon** *vti2;* drive people along (as in a bus) **bimiwizhiwe** *vai*

DRIVE ALONG IN A WAGON OR SLEIGH: drive along quickly in a wagon or sleigh **bimidaabiiba'igo** *vai*

FLOW ALONG: **bimijiwan** *vii*

FLY ALONG: **bimibide, bimibidemagad** *vii;* **bimibizo** *vai;* **bimise** *vai;* **bimise, bimisemagad** *vii*

FOLLOW A TRAIL ALONG: **bima'adoo** *vai;* follow s.o.'s trail along **bima'azh /bima'aN-/** *vta;* follow s.t. along as a trail **bima'adoon** *vti2*

GO ALONG: **bimi-ayaa** *vai*

GO ALONG BY BOAT: **bimishkaa** *vai*

GO ALONG SINGING: **bima'amaazo** *vai*

GO ALONG THE EDGE: **bimaazhagaame** *vai*

GO ALONG THE SHORE: **bimaazhagaame** *vai*

GO ALONG WITH A LIGHT: **bimaazakonenjige** *vai*

GOING ALONG: **ani-** *pv2, also* **ni-; bimi-** *pv2*

HEARD DRIVING ALONG: be heard driving along **bimwewebide, bimwewebidemagad** *vii;* **bimwewebizo** *vai*

HEARD SPEEDING ALONG: be heard speeding along **bimwewebide, bimwewebidemagad** *vii;* **bimwewebizo** *vai*

HEARD WALKING ALONG: be heard walking along **bimweweshin** *vai*

LEAD ALONG: lead along (as something string-like) **bimaabiigamon /bimaabiigamo-/** *vii*

LEAVE TRACKS GOING ALONG: **bimikawe** *vai*

LIE ALONG: lie along (as something stick- or wood-like) **bimaakoshin** *vai;* **bimaakosin** *vii*

PADDLE ALONG: **bimakwazhiwe** *vai;* **bimishkaa** *vai*

POLE A BOAT ALONG: **bima'oodoo** *vai;* **bima'ookii** *vai*

PUT ALONG: put s.o. along (as something stick- or wood-like) **bimaakoshim** *vta;* put s.t. along (as something stick- or wood-like) **bimaakosidoon** *vti2*

RAIN GOES ALONG: **bimibiisaa, bimibiisaamagad** *vii*

RIDE ALONG DRAWN BY HORSES: **bimiba'igo** *vai*

RIDE ALONG ON HORSEBACK: **bimoomigo** *vai*

RIVER FLOWS ALONG: flow along (as a river) **bimitigweyaa, bimitigweyaamagad** *vii*

ROAD LEADS ALONG: lead along (as a road or trail) **bimamon /bimamo-/, bimamoomagad** *vii*

RUN ALONG: **bimibatoo** *vai;* they run along together **bimiba'idiwag /bimiba'idi-/** *vai*

RUN ALONG IN FLIGHT: **biminizhimo** *vai;* run along in flight from someone **bimiba'iwe** *vai*

SAIL ALONG: **bimaashi** *vai;* **bimaasin** *vii*

SEND ALONG: send s.o. along **biminizhikaw** *vta;* send people along **biminaazhikaage** *vai*

SKATE ALONG: **bimaada'e** *vai*

SNOW GOES ALONG: **bimipon /bimipo-/** *vii*

SPEED ALONG: **bimibide, bimibidemagad** *vii;* **bimibizo** *vai*

STRING ALONG: string s.o. along **bimaabiigin** *vta;* string s.t. along **bimaabiiginan** *vti*

SWIM ALONG: **bimaadagaa** *vai;* swim along (as a fish) **bimakwazhiwe** *vai*

TAKE ALONG: take s.o. along **bimiwizh /bimiwiN-/** *vta;* take s.t. along **bimiwidoon** *vti2;* take people along **bimiwizhiwe** *vai*

TAKE ALONG FOR A RIDE: take s.o. along for a ride **bimibizoni'** *vta*

TAKE ALONG IN A BOAT: take s.o. along in a boat **bima'oozh /bima'ooN-/** *vta;* take s.t. along in a boat **bima'oodoon** *vti2*

TRAIL LEADS ALONG: lead along (as a road or trail) **bimamon /bimamo-/, bimamoomagad** *vii*

TRAVEL ALONG: **bimi-ayaa** *vai;* travel along in a group (as a school of fish) **bimaawadaaso** *vai*

WADE ALONG: **bimaadagaazii** *vai*
WALK ALONG: **bimose** *vai*
WALK ALONG ON THE ICE: **bimaadagaako** *vai*

ALONGSIDE
ALONGSIDE: alongside it **zhishwajayi'ii** *pc*
ALONGSIDE THE HOUSE: **zhishwajigamig** *pc*
ALONGSIDE THE ROAD: **zhishwajikana** *pc*

ALPHABET
LETTER OF THE ALPHABET: **ozhibii'igan, -an** *ni*

ALREADY
ALREADY: **azhigwa** *pc, also* **zhigwa, zhigo**; already *old-fashioned* **zhayiigwa** *pc*

ALSO
ALSO: **gaye** *pc, also* **ge**; **miinawaa** *pc*

ALTERNATELY
ALTERNATELY: **memeshkwad** *pc*

ALTHOUGH
ALTHOUGH: **aanawi** *pc*

ALWAYS
ALWAYS: **apane** *pc;* **moozhag** *pc*

AMAZED
AMAZED: be amazed **maamakaadendam** *vai2;* be amazed at s.o. **maamakaadenim** *vta;* be amazed at s.t. **maamakaadendan** *vti;* be amazed at what s.o. says **maamakaazitaw** *vta*

AMAZING
AMAZING: **maamakaaj** *pc;* amazing! **maamakaadakamig** *pc;* be amazing **maamakaadizi** *vai*
CONSIDERED AMAZING: be considered amazing **maamakaadendaagwad** *vii*
DO AMAZING THINGS: **maamakaajichige** *vai*

AMBITIOUS
AMBITIOUS: be ambitious **gwaashkwezi** *vai*

AMBULANCE
AMBULANCE: **aakoziiwidaabaan, -ag** *na*

AMERICAN
AMERICAN: **gichi-mookomaan, -ag** *na*

AMERICAN BITTERN
AMERICAN BITTERN: American bittern (locally called shypoke) **mooshka'osi, -wag** *na*

AMMUNITION
USE UP AMMUNITION: use up all of the ammunition **jaaga'e** *vai;* **jaagizige** *vai*

AMONG
AMONG: **megwe-** *pn*
IN AMONG: in among it **megwe-aya'ii** *pc, also* **megweya'ii**

AMOUNT
CERTAIN AMOUNT: a certain amount **minik** *pc*
SOME AMOUNT: **gomaa** *pc*

ANCESTOR
ANCESTOR: **aanikoobijigan, -ag** *na*

ANCHOR
ANCHOR: **boonakajigan, -an** *ni;* anchor s.t. **boonakadoon** *vti2*

AND
AND: **dash** *pc, also* **idash, -sh**; **gaye** *pc, also* **ge**; **miinawaa** *pc*
AND THEN: **mii dash** *pc, also* **miish**

ANGER
ANGER: anger s.o. **nishki'** *vta;* anger people **nishkitaa** *vai;* they anger each other **nishki'idiwag /nishki'idi-/** *vai*
ACT UP IN ANGER: **nishkaajitaa** *vai*
ANGER FOR A CERTAIN REASON: anger s.o. for a certain reason **onjinawe'** *vta*
COME IN ANGER: **biijigidaazo** *vai*

ANGRILY
BEHAVE ANGRILY: **nishkaajitaa** *vai*

ANGRY
ANGRY: be angry **nishkaadizi** *vai;* be angry at s.o. **nishkenim** *vta*
ANGRY TO A CERTAIN EXTENT: be angry to a certain extent **apiichigidaazo** *vai*
FEEL ANGRY: **nishkendam** *vai2*

ANIMAL
DOMESTIC ANIMAL: **awakaan, -ag** *na*
DRAFT ANIMAL: **odaabii'aagan, -ag** *na*
WILD ANIMAL: **awesiinh, -yag** *na*

ANKLE JOINT
ANKLE JOINT: **bikwaakoganaan, -an** *ni*

ANNOUNCE
ANNOUNCE: announce (s.t.) to people **wiindamaage** *vai*

ANNOY
ANNOY: annoy s.o. **migoshkaaji'** *vta*

ANNOYED
ANNOYED: be annoyed **migoshkaadendam** *vai2*

ANSWER
ANSWER: **nakwetam** *vai2;* answer s.o. **nakom** *vta;* **nakwetaw** *vta;* answer s.t. **nakodan** *vti;* **nakwetan** *vti;* they answer each other **nakondiwag /nakondi-/** *vai*
ANSWER BACK: answer back to s.o. **aazhidem** *vta*

ANT
ANT: **enigoons, -ag** *na, also* **enig**

ANXIOUS
ANXIOUS: be anxious **ojaanimendam** *vai2*

ANYBODY
ANYBODY: anybody *animate indefinite* **awiya, -g** *pr, also* **awiiya**

ANYHOW
ANYHOW: **aanawi** *pc;* **bagwana** *pc*

ANYTHING
ANYTHING: anything *inanimate indefinite* **gegoo** *pr*

ANYTIME
ANYTIME: anytime *dubitative* **amanj igo apii** *pc*

ANYWHERE
ANYWHERE: anywhere *dubitative* **dibi go** *pc*

APART
COME APART: **gidiskise** *vai;* **gidiskise, gidiskisemagad** *vii*

APOLOGIZE
APOLOGIZE: apologize to s.o. **gaagiizom** *vta*
APPEAR
APPEAR: **bi-naagozi** *vai;* **bi-naagwad** *vii*
APPEAR A CERTAIN WAY: appear a certain way (especially as in a dream) **inaabaminaagozi** *vai;* **inaabaminaagwad** *vii*
APPEARANCE
CHANGE APPEARANCE: change s.o.'s appearance **aanzinaago'** *vta;* change s.t.'s appearance **aanzinaagotoon** *vti2;* change one's own appearance **aanzinaago'idizo** *vai*
HAVE A CERTAIN APPEARANCE: **izhinaagozi** *vai;* **izhinaagwad** *vii*
APPEASE
APPEASE: appease s.o. **gaagiizom** *vta*
APPLE
APPLE: **mishiimin, -ag** *na*
APPLE JUICE
APPLE JUICE: **mishiiminaaboo** *ni*
APPLE TREE
APPLE TREE: **mishiiminaatig, -oog** *na*
APPLIQUE
APPLIQUE: appliqué piece **agogwaajigan, -an** *ni*
APPOINT
APPOINT: appoint s.o. **onagim** *vta*
APPROACH
APPROACH: approach s.o. **naazikaw** *vta;* approach s.t. **naazikan** *vti;* approach people **naazikaage** *vai*
APPROXIMATELY
APPROXIMATELY: **ingoji** *pc, also* **ningoji***
APRIL
APRIL: **iskigamizige-giizis** *na*
APRON
KITCHEN APRON: **inapizowin, -an** *ni*
MAN'S APRON: man's apron (traditional dress) **aanziyaan, -an** *ni*
ARENA
ARENA: **zhooshkwaada'ewigamig, -oon** *ni*
ARGUE
ARGUE: argue with s.o. **giikaam** *vta;* they argue with each other **giikaandiwag /giikaandi-/** *vai*
ARM
ARM: my arm **ninik, -an /-nik-/** *nid*
ACHE IN ARM: have an ache in one's arm **dewinike** *vai*
BREAK ARM: break one's arm **bookonike** *vai*
BROKEN ARM: have a broken arm **bookonike** *vai*
FALL AND BREAK ARM: fall and break one's arm **bookonikeshin** *vai*
FALL AND TWIST ARM: fall and twist one's arm **biimiskonikeshin** *vai*
HAVE SCAR ON ARM: have scar on one's arm **ojiishinike** *vai*
LIFT ARM: lift one's arm **ombinikeni** *vai*
MOVE ARM A CERTAIN WAY: move one's arm a certain way **izhinikeni** *vai*
NUMB ARM: have a numb arm **niboowinike** *vai*
SORE ARM: have a sore arm **gaagiijinike** *vai*
SPRAIN ARM: sprain one's arm **zeginikeshin** *vai*
STIFF ARM: have a stiff arm **jiibadaakonike** *vai;* **jiibajinike** *vai*
STRONG ARM: have a strong arm **zoonginike** *vai*
ARM GARTER
ARM GARTER: **jiiskinikebizon, -an** *ni*
WEAR ARM GARTERS: **jiiskinikebizo** *vai*
ARMPIT
ARMPIT: my armpit **nining, -wiin /-ningwy-/** *nid*
AROUND
ALL AROUND: all around it **giiwitaa-ayi'ii** *pc, also* **giiwitaayi'ii**
AROUND THE FIRE: **giiwitaashkode** *pc*
GO AROUND: **giiwitaashkaa** *vai*
LAY DOWN AROUND: lay s.o. down around **giiwitaashim** *vta;* lay s.t. down around **giiwitaasidoon** *vti2*
RUN AROUND: run around s.t. **giiwitaabatwaadan** *vti;* run around something **giiwitaabatoo** *vai*
WALK AROUND: walk around s.o. **giiwitaashkaw** *vta;* walk around s.t. **giiwitaashkan** *vti;* walk around something **giiwitaawose** *vai, also* **giiwitaa'ose**
WALK AROUND THE EDGE: **giiwitaayaazhagaame** *vai*
ARREST
ARREST: arrest s.o. **dakon** *vta;* arrest people **dakoniwe** *vai*
ARRIVE
ARRIVE: **dagoshin** *vai;* **dagoshinoomagad** *vii;* **bagami-ayaa** *vai;* **bagami-ayaa, bagami-ayaamagad** *vii;* arrive with s.o. **dagoshim** *vta;* arriving **bagami-** *pv4*
ARRIVE BY BOAT: **bagamishkaa** *vai*
ARRIVE CARRYING: arrive carrying s.o. **bagamiwizh /bagamiwiN-/** *vta;* arrive carrying s.t. **bagamiwidoon** *vti2*
ARRIVE CRAWLING: **bagamoode** *vai*
ARRIVE DRIVING: **bagamibide, bagamibidemagad** *vii;* **bagamibizo** *vai;* **bagamidaabii'iwe** *vai*
ARRIVE FLEEING: arrive fleeing from people **bagamiba'iwe** *vai*
ARRIVE FLYING: **bagamibide, bagamibidemagad** *vii;* **bagamibizo** *vai;* **bagamise** *vai;* **bagamise, bagamisemagad** *vii*
ARRIVE LAUGHING: **bagamaapi** *vai*
ARRIVE MAD: **bagamigidaazo** *vai*
ARRIVE ON HORSEBACK: **bagamoomigo** *vai*
ARRIVE ON THE RUN: **bagamibatoo** *vai;* they arrive on the run together **bagamiba'idiwag /bagamiba'idi-/** *vai*
ARRIVE PADDLING: **bagamishkaa** *vai*
ARRIVE SPEEDING: **bagamibide, bagamibidemagad** *vii;* **bagamibizo** *vai*

ARRIVE SWIMMING: **bagamaadagaa** *vai*
ARRIVE WALKING: **bagamose** *vai*
ARRIVE WITH NEWS: **bagamaajimo** *vai*

ARROGANT
ARROGANT: be arrogant **maminaadizi** *vai*
ARROGANT ATTITUDE: have an arrogant attitude **maminaadendam** *vai2*

ARROW
ARROW: **bikwak, -oon** *ni*
SHOOT WITH AN ARROW: shoot s.o. with an arrow or other missile **bimo /bimw-/** *vta;* shoot s.t. with an arrow or other missile **bimodan** *vti;* shoot things with an arrow or other missile **bimojige** *vai*

ARTHRITIS
ARTHRITIS: have arthritis **okanaapine** *vai*

ARTIST
ARTIST: **mazinibii'igewinini, -wag** *na*

AS FOR
AS FOR: **gaye** *pc, also* **ge**

AS IF
AS IF: **indigo** *pc, also* **nindigo***

ASH
BLACK ASH: black ash (tree) **aagimaak, -wag** *na*
WHITE ASH: white ash (tree) **baapaagimaak, -wag** *na*

ASHAMED
ASHAMED: be ashamed **agadendam** *vai2;* **agadendaagozi** *vai;* be ashamed before s.o. **agajiitaw** *vta;* be ashamed of s.o. **agadenim** *vta;* be ashamed of s.t. **agadendan** *vti*
MAKE ASHAMED: make s.o. ashamed **agaji'** *vta*

ASHES
ASHES: **bingwi** *ni;* **ishkode-bingwi** *ni*
HOT ASHES: be hot ashes **akakanzhekaa, akakanzhekaamagad** *vii*

ASHORE
BLOWN ASHORE: be blown ashore **agwaayaashi** *vai;* **agwaayaasin** *vii*
COME ASHORE: **agwaataa** *vai;* come ashore in a boat **agwaa'o** *vai, also* **agwaa'am**; come ashore in canoe **mizhagaa** *vai*
DRAG ASHORE: drag s.o. ashore **agwaadaabaazh /agwaadaabaaN-/** *vta;* drag s.t. ashore **agwaadaabaadan** *vti;* drag something ashore **agwaadaabii** *vai*
GO ASHORE: **agwaataa** *vai*
PULL ASHORE: pull s.o. ashore **agwaabizh /agwaabiN-/** *vta;* pull s.t. ashore **agwaabidoon** *vti2*
RUN ASHORE: **agwaabatoo** *vai*
SAIL ASHORE: **agwaayaashi** *vai*
SWIM ASHORE: **agwaayaadagaa** *vai*
TAKE ASHORE BY BOAT: take s.t. ashore by boat **agwaa'oodoon** *vti2*
TAKEN ASHORE: be taken ashore **agwaasijigaade, agwaasijigaademagad** *vii;* **agwaasijigaazo** *vai*

ASK
ASK: ask for s.t. **nandodan** *vti;* ask s.o. for (s.t.) **nandodamaw** *vta;* ask people for (s.t.) **nandodamaage** *vai*
ASK ALONG: ask s.o. along **wiizhaam** *vta*
ASK QUESTIONS: **gagwedwe** *vai;* ask s.o. questions **gagwejim** *vta;* they ask each other questions **gagwejindiwag /gagwejindi-/** *vai*
GO AND ASK: go and ask for s.o. **nandwewem** *vta;* go and ask for s.t. **nandwewendan** *vti;* go and ask s.o. (for s.t.) **nandwewendamaw** *vta*

ASLEEP
FALL ASLEEP: **gawingwashi** *vai*

ASPHALT
ASPHALT: **makade-bigiw** *na*

ASPHALT ROAD
ASPHALT ROAD: **bigii-miikana, -n** *ni*

ASPIRIN
ASPIRIN: **dewikwe-mashkikiins, -an** *ni*

ASSEMBLE
ASSEMBLE: assemble s.o. **onin** *vta;* assemble s.t. **oninan** *vti;* assemble things **oninige** *vai*

ASSINIBOIN
ASSINIBOIN: **asinii-bwaan, -ag** *na*

ASSOCIATE
ASSOCIATE: associate with s.o. **wiisookaw** *vta*

ASTONISH
ASTONISH: **maamakaadizi** *vai*

ASTONISHED
ASTONISHED: be astonished **maamakaadendam** *vai2;* be astonished at s.o. **maamakaadenim** *vta;* be astonished at s.t. **maamakaadendan** *vti*

ASTONISHING
ASTONISHING: **maamakaaj** *pc;* astonishing! **maamakaadakamig** *pc*
CONSIDERED ASTONISHING: be considered astonishing **maamakaadendaagwad** *vii*

ASTRIDE
SIT ASTRIDE: **desabi** *vai*

AT HAND
AT HAND: **wenipazh** *pc*

AT RANDOM
AT RANDOM: **bagwana** *pc*

ATTACK
ATTACK: attack s.o. **mawinazh /mawinaN-/** *vta;* attack s.o. from hiding **mookiitaw** *vta*

ATTEMPT
ATTEMPT: **goji-** *pv4*

ATTENDANT
CEREMONIAL ATTENDANT: **oshkaabewis, -ag** *na*

ATTENTION
ATTENTION: attention! **ambe** *pc*

ATTRACT
ATTRACT: attract s.o. **zhoobi'** *vta*

AUGUST
AUGUST: **manoominike-giizis** *na;* **miini-giizis** *na, also* **miinike-giizis**
AUNT
AUNT: my cross aunt (father's sister) **inzigos, -ag /-zigos-/** *nad;* my parallel aunt (mother's sister) **ninoshenh, -yag /-nosheny-/** *nad*
AUTHORITY
AUTHORITY: **ogimaawiwin, -an** *ni*
AUTOMOBILE MECHANIC
AUTOMOBILE MECHANIC: **nanaa'idaabaanewinini, -wag** *na;* **nanaa'idaabaanikewinini, -wag** *na*
AUTUMN
AUTUMN: be autumn **dagwaagin /dagwaagi-/** *vii*
LAST AUTUMN: **dagwaagong** *pc*
AVOID
AVOID TALKING: avoid talking to s.o. **boonim** *vta*
AWAKE
AWAKE: be awake **goshkozi** *vai*
COME AWAKE: **amajise** *vai*
SHAKE AWAKE: shake s.o. awake **amajwebin** *vta*
AWAY
BLOWN AWAY: be blown away **animaashi** *vai;* **animaasin** *vii*
CARRY AWAY: carry s.o. away **animiwizh /animiwiN-/** *vta;* carry s.t. away **animiwidoon** *vti2*
CARRY AWAY ON BACK: carry s.o. away on one's back **animoom** *vta;* carry s.t. away on one's back **animoondan** *vti*
CLOUDS GO AWAY: **animaanakwad** *vii*
CRAWL AWAY: **animoode** *vai*
DANCE AWAY: **animishimo** *vai*
DRAG AWAY: **animidaabii** *vai*
DRIFT AWAY: **animaabogo** *vai;* **animaaboode, animaaboodemagad** *vii*
DRIFT AWAY ON THE WAVES: **animaa'an** *vii;* **animaa'ogo** *vai*
DRIVE AWAY: **animibide, animibidemagad** *vii;* **animibizo** *vai;* **animidaabii'iwe** *vai;* drive away with horses **animiba'igo** *vai;* drive away with s.o. (e.g., a car) **animibizoni'** *vta;* drive away with s.t. **animibizonitoon** *vti2*
DRIVE AWAY MAKING NOISE: **animwewebide, animwewebidemagad** *vii;* **animwewebizo** *vai*
DRIVE AWAY WITH A LIGHT: **animaazakonenjigebizo** *vai*
FLOAT AWAY: **animaabogo** *vai;* **animaaboode, animaaboodemagad** *vii*
FLOW AWAY: **animijiwan** *vii*
FLY AWAY: **animibide, animibidemagad** *vii;* **animibizo** *vai;* **animise** *vai;* **animise, animisemagad** *vii*
FLY AWAY MAKING NOISE: **animwewebide, animwewebidemagad** *vii;* **animwewebizo** *vai*
FOLLOW A TRAIL AWAY: **anima'adoo** *vai;* follow s.o.'s trail away **anima'azh /anima'aN-/** *vta;* follow s.t. away as a trail **anima'adoon** *vti2*
GO AWAY: go away! **awas** *pc*
GO AWAY IN A CANOE: **animishkaa** *vai*
GO AWAY LAUGHING: **animaapi** *vai*
GO AWAY MAD: **animigidaazo** *vai*
GO AWAY ON THE ICE: **animaadagaako** *vai*
GO AWAY SINGING: **anima'amaazo** *vai*
GO AWAY SPEAKING: **animwewidam** *vai2*
GO AWAY WITH A LIGHT: **animaazakonenjige** *vai*
GOING AWAY: **ani-** *pv2, also* **ni-**
LEAVE TRACKS GOING AWAY: **animikawe** *vai*
PADDLE AWAY: **animishkaa** *vai*
RAIN GOES AWAY: **animibiisaa, animibiisaamagad** *vii*
RIDE AWAY ON HORSEBACK: **animoomigo** *vai*
RUN AWAY: **animibatoo** *vai;* run away (in the other direction) with s.o. **animibatwaazh /animibatwaaN-/** *vta;* run away (in the other direction) with s.t. **animibatwaadan** *vti;* they run away (in the other direction) together **animiba'idiwag /animiba'idi-/** *vai*
RUN AWAY MAKING NOISE: **animwewebatoo** *vai*
RUN AWAY SCARED: **animinizhimo** *vai*
SAIL AWAY: **animaashi** *vai;* **animaasin** *vii*
SKATE AWAY: **animaada'e** *vai*
SPEED AWAY: **animibide, animibidemagad** *vii;* **animibizo** *vai*
SPEED AWAY MAKING NOISE: **animwewebide, animwewebidemagad** *vii;* **animwewebizo** *vai*
SWIM AWAY: **animaadagaa** *vai*
TAKE AWAY: take s.o. away **animiwizh /animiwiN-/** *vta;* take s.t. away **animiwidoon** *vti2*
TAKE AWAY BY BOAT: take s.o. away by boat **anima'oozh /anima'ooN-/** *vta;* take s.t. away by boat **anima'oodoon** *vti2*
WADE AWAY: **animaadagaazii** *vai*
WALK AWAY: **animose** *vai*
WALK AWAY MAKING NOISE: **animwewetoo** *vai*
AWFUL
AWFUL: **gagwaanisagakamig** *pc*
AWL
AWL: **migoos, -an** *ni*
AX
AX: **waagaakwad, -oon** *ni*
AX HANDLE
AX HANDLE: **waagaakwadwaatig, -oon** *ni*

B

BABY
BABY: **abinoojiiyens, -ag** *na, also* **abinoojiins; biibii, -yag** *na*
BABY IN A CRADLE BOARD: **dakobinaawaswaan, -ag** *na*
CARRY A BABY ALONG ON BACK: carry a baby along on one's back **bimoomaawaso** *vai*
CARRY A BABY TO A CERTAIN PLACE ON BACK: carry a baby to a certain place on one's back **inoomaawaso** *vai*
HAVE A BABY IN A CRADLE BOARD: **dakobinaawaso** *vai*

BABY-SIT
BABY-SIT: **bamoozhe** *vai*

BACK
BACK: my back **nipikwan, -an /-pikwan-/** *nid*
FALL AND BREAK BACK: fall and break one's back **bookwaawiganeshin** *vai*
MIDDLE OF THE BACK: in the middle of the back **naawaawigan** *pc*
SCRATCH BACK: scratch s.o.'s back **jiichiigaawiganebizh /jiichiigaawiganebiN-/** *vta*
SMALL OF BACK: the small of my back **inzhiigan /-zhiigan-/** *nid*
SORE BACK: have a sore back **gaagiidaawigan** *vai*
WARM BACK: warm one's back **abaawiganezo** *vai*

BACK
BACK: back (in time) **ishkweyaang** *pc;* back to previous place or condition **neyaab** *pc*
BACK UP: **azhetaa** *vai*
GO BACK: **azhe-** *pv4;* **azhegiiwe** *vai*
HAND BACK: hand s.o. back **azhen** *vta;* hand s.t. back **azhenan** *vti*
IN THE BACK: **ishkweyaang** *pc*
PULL BACK: pull s.o. back **azhebizh /azhebiN-/** *vta;* pull s.t. back **azhebidoon** *vti2*
TAKE BACK: take s.o. back **azhen** *vta;* take s.t. back **azhenan** *vti;* take (s.t.) back to s.o. **azhenamaw** *vta*
TURN AND LOOK BACK: **aabanaabi** *vai;* turn and look back at s.o. **aabanaabam** *vta;* turn and look back at s.t. **aabanaabandan** *vti*

BACK UP
BACK UP A VEHICLE: **azhebizo** *vai*

BACKACHE
BACKACHE: have a backache **dewaawigan** *vai;* **dewipikwan** *vai*

BACKPACK
BACKPACK: **bimiwanaan, -an** *ni*

BACKWARDS
FALL OVER BACKWARDS: **aazhigijishin** *vai;* **aazhigijisin** *vii*
GO BACKWARDS: **azheshkaa** *vai;* **azhetaa** *vai*
LAY OVER BACKWARDS: lay s.o. over backwards **aazhigijishim** *vta;* lay s.t. over backwards **aazhigijisidoon** *vti2*
PADDLE BACKWARDS: **azhe'o** *vai*
SIT FACING BACKWARDS: **animikwabi** *vai*
THROW OVER BACKWARDS: throw s.o. over backwards **aazhigidwebin** *vta;* throw s.t. over backwards **aazhigidwebinan** *vti*
TURN OVER BACKWARDS: **aazhigijise** *vai;* **aazhigijise, aazhigijisemagad** *vii*
TURN TO FACE BACKWARDS: turn s.o. to face backwards **animikon** *vta;* turn s.t. to face backwards **animikonan** *vti*
TURNED TO FACE BACKWARDS: be turned to face backwards **animikonigaade, animikonigaademagad** *vii;* **animikonigaazo** *vai*

BACON
BACON: **giikanaamozigan** *na*

BAD
BAD: **maji-** *pv4;* **maazhi-** *pv4*
BAD BREATH: have bad breath **maazhimaagwanaamo** *vai*
BAD DAY: be a bad day **maazhi-giizhigad** *vii*
BAD DREAM: have a bad dream **giiwanaadingwaam** *vai*
BAD LUCK: have bad luck **maazhise** *vai*
BAD ROAD: be bad (as a road or trail) **maanadamon /maanadamo-/** *vii*
BAD TRAIL: be bad (as a road or trail) **maanadamon /maanadamo-/** *vii*
BAD VOICE: have a bad voice **maanowe** *vai*
BAD WEATHER: be bad weather **niiskaadad** *vii*
CONSIDERED BAD: be considered bad **maanendaagwad** *vii*
FEEL BAD: **maanamanji'o** *vai;* **maanendam** *vai2, also* **maazhendam**; feel bad about s.t. **maanendan** *vti*
HAVE A BAD FALL: **aapijishin** *vai*
LEAD A BAD LIFE: **maazhi-bimaadizi** *vai*
SMELL BAD: **maazhimaagozi** *vai;* **maazhimaagwad** *vii*
SMELL BAD BURNING OR COOKING: **maazhimaaso** *vai;* **maazhimaate** *vii*
SOUND BAD: hear s.o. sounding bad **maanitaw** *vta;* hear s.t. sounding bad **maanitan** *vti*
TASTE BAD: **maazhipogozi** *vai;* **maazhipogwad** *vii;* taste bad (as a liquid) **maanaagamin /maanaagami-/** *vii*

BAD OFF
BAD OFF: be bad off **maazhi-ayaa** *vai*
CONSIDER BAD OFF: consider s.o. bad off **maanenim** *vta*
CONSIDERED BAD OFF: be considered bad off **maanendaagozi** *vai*

BADGER
BADGER: **misakakojiish, -ag** *na*

BADLY
BADLY: **debinaak** *pc*

BEHAVE BADLY: **maazhi-bimaadizi** *vai;* **maazhi-izhiwebizi** *vai*

BAG

BAG: **mashkimod, -an** *ni*

BAG WITH CLOSEABLE TOP: **gashkibidaagan, -ag** *na*

CEDAR BARK BAG: **giishkashkimod, -an** *ni*

CERTAIN NUMBER OF BAGS: **dasooshkin** *pc*

CLOTH BAG: **bagiwayaaneshkimod, -an** *ni*

HALF A BAG: **aabitooshkin** *pc*

MEDICINE BAG: Mide medicine bag **midewayaan, -ag** *na*

PAPER BAG: **mazina'igani-mashkimodens, -an** *ni*

RICE BAG: **manoomini-mashkimod, -an** *ni;* **manoominiwazh, -an** *ni*

BAIL

BAIL: **iska'ibii** *vai*

BAIL OUT: bail s.o. out **diba' /diba'w-/** *vta*

BAIT

BAIT: **miijimikanjigan, -an** *ni;* bait things **miijimikanjige** *vai*

BAKE

BAKE: bake s.o. **giboz /gibozw-/** *vta;* bake s.t. **gibozan** *vti;* bake things **gibozige** *vai*

BAKER

BAKER: **bakwezhiganikewinini, -wag** *na;* baker (female) **bakwezhiganikewikwe, -g** *na*

BAKERY

BAKERY: **bakwezhiganikewigamig, -oon** *ni*

BAKING POWDER

BAKING POWDER: **ombisijigaans, -an** *ni*

BAKING SODA

BAKING SODA: **ombizigan** *ni*

BALD

BALD: be bald **waabizhagindibe** *vai*

BALD EAGLE

BALD EAGLE: **migizi, -wag** *na*

BALL

BALL: **bikwaakwad, -oon** *ni*

BALL OF TWINE OR YARN: **bikoojaan, -an** *ni*

POOL BALL: **nemaab, -iin** *ni*

BALM OF GILEAD

BALM OF GILEAD TREE: **maanazaadi, -wag** *na*

BALSAM FIR

BALSAM FIR: **zhingob, -iig** *na*

BALSAM POPLAR

BALSAM POPLAR: **maanazaadi, -wag** *na*

BANANA

BANANA: **wewaagijiizid** *ni-pt*

BANDAGE

BANDAGE: **ziinzoopizon, -an** *ni*

BANDOLIER BAG

BANDOLIER BAG: **gashkibidaagan, -ag** *na, also* **aazhoningwa'igan**

BANK

BANK: **zhooniyaawigamig, -oon** *ni*

BANK

STEEP BANK: be a steep bank **giishkadinaa, giishkadinaamagad** *vii*

BAPTIZE

BAPTIZE: baptize s.o. **ziiga'andaw** *vta*

BAR

BAR: **minikwewigamig, -oon** *ni;* **ziiginigewigamig, -oon** *ni*

BAR

BAR: bar s.t. (as something stick- or wood-like) **gashkaakonan** *vti*

BARBER

BARBER: **baapaagokozhiwewinini, -wag** *na;* **giishkikozhiwewinini, -wag** *na*

BARBER SHOP

BARBER SHOP: **baapaagokozhiwewigamig, -oon** *ni*

BARE

ON A BARE SURFACE: **michayi'ii** *pc*

BARE GROUND

ON BARE GROUND: **mitakamig** *pc*

SIT ON THE BARE GROUND: **mitabi** *vai*

BARE-HEADED

BARE-HEADED: be bare-headed **mitaakondibe** *vai*

BAREFOOT

BAREFOOT: be barefoot **zhaashaaginizide** *vai*

BARELY

BARELY: **agaawaa** *pc;* **michi-** *pv4*

BARK

BARK: **migi** *vai;* bark at s.o. **migizh /migiN-/** *vta;* bark at s.t. **migidan** *vti*

BARK

BARK: bark (of a tree) **wanagek, -wag** *na*

INNER BARK OF BASSWOOD: **wiigob, -iin** *ni*

BARK LODGE

BARK LODGE: **wanagekogamig, -oon** *ni*

BARK TORCH

BARK TORCH: **biimashkwemaginigan, -an** *ni*

BARMAID

BARMAID: **ziiginigewikwe, -g** *na*

BARN

BARN: **awakaanigamig, -oon** *ni*

BARREL

BARREL: **makakosag, -oon** *ni*

BARTENDER

BARTENDER: **ziiginigewinini, -wag** *na*

BASEBALL

PLAY BASEBALL: **bakitejii'ige** *vai*

BASEBALL BAT

BASEBALL BAT: **bakitejii'iganaak, -oon** *ni*

BASEBALL PLAYER

BASEBALL PLAYER: **bakitejii'igewinini, -wag** *na*

BASEMENT

IN THE BASEMENT: **anaamisag** *pc*

BASHFUL

BASHFUL: be bashful **agaji** *vai*

BASK
BASK: bask in the sun **abaasandeke** *vai*
BASKET
BASKET OF SPRUCE ROOT: **wadabii-makak, -oon** *ni*
BIRCH BARK BASKET: **makak, -oon** *ni;* **wiigwasi-makak, -oon** *ni;* birch bark basket for maple sugar **ziinzibaakwado-makak, -oon** *ni*
WILLOW BASKET: **oziisigobimizhii-makak, -oon** *ni*
BASS
LARGEMOUTH BASS: **ashigan, -ag** *na*
BASSWOOD
BASSWOOD: basswood tree **wiigob, -iig** *na;* **wiigobaatig, -oog** *na;* **wiigobimizh, -iig** *na*
INNER BARK OF BASSWOOD: **wiigob, -iin** *ni*
BASSWOOD BARK FIBER
BASSWOOD BARK FIBER: processed basswood bark fiber **asigobaan** *ni*
BAT
BASEBALL BAT: **bakitejii'iganaak, -oon** *ni*
BAT
BAT: **bapakwaanaajiinh, -yag** *na, also* **apakwaanaajiinh**
BATH
TAKE A BATH: **giziibiigazhe** *vai*
BATHE
BATHE: **bagizo** *vai*
BATHROOM
BATHROOM: **miiziiwigamig, -oon** *ni*
BATHTUB
BATHTUB: **bagizowin, -an** *ni*
BATTERY
BATTERY: **ishkode-makakoons, -an** *ni*
BATTLE
BATTLE: **miigaadiwin, -an** *ni*
BAY
BAY: be a bay **wiikwegamaa, wiikwegamaamagad** *vii*
BE
BE: be (in a certain place) **ayaa** *vai;* **ayaa, ayaamagad** *vii;* be a certain thing **aawan** *vii;* be a certain thing or being **aawi** *vai*
BE A CERTAIN WAY: **izhi-ayaa** *vai;* be a certain way (as a liquid) **inaagamin /inaagami-/** *vii;* be a certain way (as something mineral) **inaabikad** *vii;* **inaabikizi** *vai;* be a certain way (as something sheet-like) **izhiigad** *vii;* **izhiigizi** *vai;* be a certain way (as something stick- or wood-like) **inaakozi** *vai;* **inaakwad** *vii;* be a certain way (as something string-like) **inaabiigad** *vii;* **inaabiigizi** *vai*
BE IN: **biinde, biindemagad** *vii;* **biinzo** vai
BE IN A CERTAIN PLACE: **abi** *vai;* **ate, atemagad** *vii;* **dagon /dago-/** *vii;* be (in a certain place) **ayaa** *vai;* **ayaa, ayaamagad** *vii*
BE IN A CERTAIN STATE: *with a pv4* be in a certain state **ayaa, ayaamagad** *vii;* **ayaa** *vai*
BE IN THE SKY: be in the sky (e.g., a star, the sun, or the moon) **agoojin** *vai*
BE WITH: be with s.o. **wiij'ayaaw** *vta, also* **wiiji-ayaaw**
COME TO BE: **bagami-ayaa, bagami-ayaamagad** *vii*
SEEM TO BE A CERTAIN WAY: **inendaagwad** *vii*
THINK TO BE IN A CERTAIN PLACE: think s.o. to be in a certain place **danenim** *vta;* think s.t. to be in a certain place **danendan** *vti*
BEACH
LONG STRETCH OF SAND BEACH: be a long stretch of sand beach **ginoodaawangaa, ginoodaawangaamagad** *vii*
SANDY BEACH: be a sandy beach **mitaawangaa, mitaawangaamagad** *vii*
BEAD
BEAD: **manidoominens, -ag** *na;* **mazinigwaaso** *vai;* bead on s.o. **mazinigwaazh /mazinigwaaN-/** *vta;* bead s.t. **mazinigwaadan** *vti*
BEAD CORRECTLY: bead s.t. correctly (on a loom) **gwayakwaabidoo'an** *vti;* bead things correctly (on a loom) **gwayakwaabidoo'ige** *vai*
BEAD ON A LOOM: bead s.t. on a loom **mazinaabidoo'an** *vti;* bead things on a loom **mazinaabidoo'ige** *vai*
MAKE A MISTAKE BEADING: make a mistake beading s.t. on a loom **wanaabidoo'an** *vti;* make a mistake beading things on a loom **wanaabidoo'ige** *vai*
BEAD LOOM
BEAD LOOM: **mazinaabidoo'iganaatig, -oon** *ni*
BEAD WORK
BEAD WORK: item of bead work **manidoominensikaan, -ag** *na*
BEADING NEEDLE
BEADING NEEDLE: **naabidoo'igan, -an** *ni*
BEAK
BEAK: my beak **nikoonzh /-koonzh-/** *nid*
BEAN
BEAN: **mashkodesimin, -ag** *na, also* **mashkodiisimin**
BEAN SOUP
BEAN SOUP: **mashkodesiminaaboo** *ni*
BEAR
BEAR: bear s.o. (e.g., a child) **niigi'** *vta*
BEAR ON BODY: bear s.o. on one's body **gigishkaw** *vta;* bear s.t. on one's body **gigishkan** *vti*
BEAR
BEAR: **makwa, -g** *na*
BEAR CUB: **makoons, -ag** *na*
BEAR PAW SNOWSHOE
BEAR PAW SNOWSHOE: **makwasaagim, -ag** *na*

BEARD
BEARD: have a beard **miishidaamikan** *vai*
BEAT
BEAT: beat s.o. **niiwezh /niiweN-/** *vta*
BEAT IN A CONTEST: beat s.o. in a contest **bakinaw** *vta;* beat people in a contest **bakinaage** *vai*
BEAT IN A GAME: beat s.o. in a game **gabenaw** *vta*
BEAT TO DEATH: beat s.o. to death **niiwana' /niiwana'w-/** *vta*
BEAUTIFUL
BEAUTIFUL: be beautiful **miikawaadad** *vii;* **miikawaadizi** *vai*
BEAVER
BEAVER: **amik, -wag** *na*
HUNT BEAVER: **noodamikwe** *vai*
BEAVER HIDE
BEAVER HIDE: **amikwayaan, -ag** *na*
BEAVER LODGE
BEAVER LODGE: **amikwiish, -an** *ni*
BECAUSE
BECAUSE: **onji-** *pv3*
BED
BED: **nibaagan, -an** *ni;* bed (in wigwam) **desa'on, -an** *ni;* bed (made on the floor or ground) **apishimon, -an** *ni*
GO TO BED: **gawishimo** *vai*
MAKE A BED: **ozisijige** *vai, also* **ozhisijige**; make a bed (as in camp) **apishimonike** *vai*
PUT TO BED: put s.o. to bed **nibe'** *vta*
WET THE BED: **zhigingwaam** *vai*
BED FRAME
BED FRAME: **nibaaganaatig, -oon** *ni*
BEDROOM
BEDROOM: **nibewigamig, -oon** *ni*
BEE
BEE: **aamoo, -g** *na*
BEEHIVE
BEEHIVE: **aamoo-wadiswan, -an** *ni*
BEEF
BEEF: **bizhiki-wiiyaas** *ni, also* **bizhikiwi-wiiyaas**
BEER
BEER: **biitewaaboo** *ni;* **zhingobaaboo** *ni*
BEET
BEET: **misko-jiis, -an** *ni*
SUGAR BEET: **wiishkobi-jiis, -an** *ni*
BEFORE
BEFORE: **jibwaa-** *pv1, also* **ji-bwaa-**
AS BEFORE: **neyaab** *pc*
BEFORE THE USUAL TIME: **noonde-** *pv4*
BEFOREHAND
BEFOREHAND: **giizhaa** *pc*
BEG
BEG: beg s.o. for (s.t.) **nandodamaw** *vta;* beg people for (s.t.) **nandodamaage** *vai*
BEGGAR
BEGGAR: **nendodamaageshkid** *na-pt*
BEGIN
BEGIN: **maajii-** *pv4;* **maajise** *vai;* **maajise, maajisemagad** *vii*
BEGINNING
IN THE BEGINNING: **wayeshkad** *pc*
BEHAVE
BEHAVE A CERTAIN WAY: **izhiwebizi** *vai*
BEHAVE ANGRILY: **nishkaajitaa** *vai*
BEHAVE BADLY: **maazhi-bimaadizi** *vai;* **maazhi-izhiwebizi** *vai*
BEHAVE WELL: **mino-izhiwebizi** *vai*
BEHIND
BEHIND: **ishkweyaang** *pc*
BEHOLD
BEHOLD: behold! **inashke** *pc, also* **nashke**; **wegwaagi** *pc*
BEING
BEING: a being **aya'aa, -g** *pr*
BELIEVABLE
BELIEVABLE: be believable **debwetaagozi** *vai;* **debwetaagwad** *vii*
BELIEVE
BELIEVE: **debwetam** *vai2;* **debweyendam** *vai2;* believe s.o. **debwetaw** *vta;* believe s.t. **debwetan** *vti*
BELIEVE IN: believe in s.o. **debweyenim** *vta;* believe in s.t. **debweyendan** *vti*
NOT BELIEVE: not believe s.t. said **aagonwetan** *vti;* not believe what s.o. says **aagonwetaw** *vta*
BELIEVED
BELIEVED: be believed **debwetaagozi** *vai;* **debwetaagwad** *vii*
BELL
BELL: **godotaagan, -an** *ni*
SMALL ROUND BELL: **zhinawa'oojigan, -an** *ni*
BELONG
BELONG: **dibendaagozi** *vai;* **dibendaagwad** *vii*
BELONG TO A GROUP: **aginzo** *vai*
BELONGING
BELONGINGS: **daniwin, -an** *ni*
BELT
BELT: **gijipizon, -an** *ni*
BELT BUCKLE
BELT BUCKLE: **gijipizonaabik, -oon** *ni*
BENCH
BENCH: **desa'on, -an** *ni*
BEND
BEND A CERTAIN WAY: bend s.o. a certain way **inaagin** *vta;* bend s.t. a certain way **inaaginan** *vti*
BEND DOWN: **zhagashkitaa** *vai*
BEND INTO FORM: bend s.o. into form **onaagin** *vta;* bend s.t. into form **onaaginan** *vti*
BEND OVER: bend s.o. over **biskin** *vta;* bend s.t. over **biskinan** *vti*
BEND OVER WITH HANDS: bend s.o. over with hands **biskibizh /biskibiN-/** *vta;* bend s.t. over with hands **biskibidoon** *vti2*
BEND WITH HAND: bend s.o. with hand **waagin** *vta;* bend s.t. with hand **waaginan** *vti*

BEND WITH HANDS: bend s.o. with hands **waagibizh /waagibiN-/** *vta;* bend s.t. with hands **waagibidoon** *vti2*

BENEFIT

BENEFIT: benefit s.o. **debi'** *vta*

BENT

BENT: be bent **waagaa, waagaamagad** *vii;* **waagizi** *vai;* be bent (as something mineral) **waagaabikad** *vii;* **waagaabikizi** *vai;* be bent (as something stick- or wood-like) **waagaakozi** *vai;* **waagaakwad** *vii*

BENT A CERTAIN WAY: be bent a certain way **inaaginigaade, inaaginigaademagad** *vii;* **inaaginigaazo** *vai*

BENT OVER: be bent over **biskaa, biskaamagad** *vii;* **biskinigaade, biskinigaademagad** *vii*

BERRY

PICK BERRIES: **mawinzo** *vai*

BET

BET: **ataage** *vai;* they bet with each other **ataadiwag /ataadi-/** *vai*

PLACE A BET: **achige** *vai*

BETWEEN

IN BETWEEN: in between it **nisawayi'ii** *pc*

BEWARE

BEWARE: beware! (a warning based on a premonition) **baapiniziwaagan** *pc*

BEYOND

BEYOND: **awasi-** *pn;* beyond it **awasayi'ii** *pc*

BEYOND THE FIRE: **awasishkode** *pc*

BEYOND THE MOUNTAIN: **awasajiw** *pc*

BEYOND THE WOODS: **awasaakwaa** *pc*

BIBLE

BIBLE: **gagiikwe-mazina'igan, -an** *ni*

BICYCLE

BICYCLE: **ditibiwebishkigan, -ag** *na*

BIG

BIG: **gichi-** *pv4, also* **chi-**; be big **michaa, michaamagad** *vii;* **mindido** *vai;* they are big **mamaachaawan /mamaachaa-/, mamaachaamagadoon** *vii;* **mamaandidowag /mamaandido-/** *vai;* be big (as something mineral) **michaabikad** *vii;* **michaabikizi** *vai;* be big (as something sheet-like) **michiigad** *vii;* **michiigizi** *vai;* be big (as something stick- or wood-like) **michaakozi** *vai;* **michaakwad** *vii*

APPEAR BIG: **michaabaminaagwad** *vii*

BIG EYE: have a big eye **mangishkiinzhigwe** *vai*

BIG FOOT: have a big foot **mangizide** *vai*

BIG HAND: have a big hand **mangininjii** *vai*

BIG HEAD: have a big head **mangindibe** *vai*

BIG HILL: there is a big hill **mangadinaa, mangadinaamagad** *vii*

MAKE BIG: make s.o. big **mangi'** *vta;* **mindido'** *vta;* make s.t. big **michaatoon** *vti2*

SO BIG: be so big **inigini** *vai;* **inigokwaa, inigokwaamagad** *vii;* be so big (as something mineral) **inigokwaabikad** *vii;* **inigokwaabikizi** *vai;* be so big (as something sheet-like) **inigokwegad** *vii;* **inigokwegizi** *vai;* be so big (as something stick- or wood-like) **inigokwaakozi** *vai;* **inigokwaakwad** *vii;* be so big (as something string-like) **inigokwaabiigad** *vii;* **inigokwaabiigizi** *vai*

BILL

BILL: my bill **nikoonzh /-koonzh-/** *nid*

BIND

BIND: bind s.o. **dakobizh /dakobiN-/** *vta;* bind s.t. **dakobidoon** *vti2;* bind things **dakobijige** *vai*

BINDING

BINDING STICK: **mikond, -ag** *na, also* **mikwand**

BINOCULARS

BINOCULARS: **zhiibaayaabanjigan, -an** *ni*

BIRCH

BIRCH: birch (tree) **wiigwaasi-mitig, -oog** *na, also* **wiigwaasaatig; wiigwaas, -ag** *na*

MANY BIRCHES: there are many birches **wiigwaasikaa, wiigwaasikaamagad** *vii*

YELLOW BIRCH: **wiinizik, -oog** *na*

BIRCH BARK

BIRCH BARK: **wiigwaas, -an** *ni*

GATHER BIRCH BARK: **maniwiigwaase** *vai*

REMOVE BIRCH BARK: remove birch bark from the tree **wiigwaasike** *vai*

BIRCH BARK BASKET

BIRCH BARK BASKET: **makak, -oon** *ni;* **wiigwaasi-makak, -oon** *ni;* birch bark basket for maple sugar **ziinzibaakwado-makak, -oon** *ni*

MAKE A BIRCH BARK BASKET: **makakoke** *vai*

BIRCH BARK BOX

BIRCH BARK BOX: **wiigwaasi-makak, -oon** *ni*

BIRCH BARK CANOE

BIRCH BARK CANOE: **wiigwaasi-jiimaan, -an** *ni*

BIRCH BARK COVERING

BIRCH BARK COVERING: **wiigwaasabakway, -an** *ni*

BIRCH BARK DISH

BIRCH BARK DISH: **wiigwaasinaagan, -an** *ni*

BIRCH BARK LODGE

BIRCH BARK LODGE: **wiigwaasigamig, -oon** *ni*

BIRCH BARK ROOF

BIRCH BARK ROOF: **wiigwaasabakwaan, -ag** *na*

BIRCH BARK ROOFING

ROLL OF BIRCH BARK ROOFING: **wiigwaasabakway, -an** *ni*

BIRD

BIRD: **bineshiinh, -yag** *na;* bird (of large species, e.g., hawk or eagle) **binesi, -wag** *na*

BABY BIRD: **banajaanh, -yag** *na*

MALE BIRD: **naabese, -g** *na*

BIRD SKIN
BIRD SKIN: **bineshiinhwayaan, -ag** *na*
BIRTH
GIVE BIRTH: **ondaadiziike** *vai*
BIRTHDAY
HAVE A BIRTHDAY: **dibishkaa** *vai*
BISON
BISON: **bizhiki, -wag** *na;* **mashkode-bizhiki, -wag** *na*
BIT
BIT: **zagidoonebijigan, -an** *ni*
BITE
BITE: bite s.o. **dakwam** *vta;* bite s.t. **dakwandan** *vti;* bite things **dakwanjige** *vai;* bite people **dakwange** *vai*
BITE A PIECE OFF: bite a piece off s.o. **bakwem** *vta;* bite a piece off s.t. **bakwendan** *vti*
BITE THROUGH: bite s.o. through (e.g., something string-like) **bakam** *vta;* bite s.t. through (e.g., something string-like) **bakandan** *vti;* bite through s.o. cleanly **giishkam** *vta;* bite through s.t. cleanly **giishkandan** *vti*
TAKE A BITE: take a bite of s.o. **nawadam** *vta;* take a bite of s.t. **nawadandan** *vti;* take a bite of things **nawadanjige** *vai*
BITTER
BITTER: be bitter **wiisagan** *vii, also* **wiisagaa; wiisagizi** *vai;* be bitter (as a liquid) **wiisagaagamin /wiisagaagami-/** *vii*
TASTE BITTER: **wiisagipogozi** *vai;* **wiisagipogwad** *vii*
BITTERN
AMERICAN BITTERN: **mooshka'osi, -wag** *na*
BLACK
BLACK: **makade-** *pv4;* be black **makadewaa, makadewaamagad** *vii;* **makadewizi** *vai;* be black (as a liquid) **makadewaagamin /makadewaagami-/** *vii;* be black (as something mineral) **makadewaabikad** *vii;* **makadewaabikizi** *vai;* be black (as something sheet-like) **makadewegad** *vii;* **makadewegizi** *vai;* be black (as something stick- or wood-like) **makadewaakozi** *vai;* **makadewaakwad** *vii;* be black (as something string-like) **makadewaabiigad** *vii;* **makadewaabiigizi** *vai*
BLACK HAIR: have black hair **makadewindibe** *vai*
COLORED BLACK: be colored black **makadewaande, makadewaandemagad** *vii;* **makadewaanzo** *vai*
HAVE A BLACK EYE: **ozhaawashkwaabi** *vai*
WEAR BLACK: **makadewi'o** *vai*
BLACK ASH
BLACK ASH: black ash (tree) **aagimaak, -wag** *na*
BLACK CHERRY
BLACK CHERRY: **ookwemin, -an** *ni*
BLACK CHERRY BUSH
BLACK CHERRY BUSH: **ookweminagaawanzh, -iig** *na*
BLACK DUCK
BLACK DUCK: **makadeshib, -ag** *na*
BLACK
BLACK PERSON: **makade-wiiyaas, -ag** *na*
BLACK WOMAN: **makade-wiiyaasikwe, -g** *na*
BLACKBERRY
BLACKBERRY: **odatagaagomin, -ag** *na*
BLACKBERRY BUSH
BLACKBERRY BUSH: **odatagaagominagaawanzh, -iig** *na*
BLACKBIRD
BLACKBIRD: **asiginaak, -wag** *na*
BLACKSMITH
BLACKSMITH: **awashtoyaa, -g** *na, also* **awishtoyaa**
BLAME
BLAME: blame s.o. (in speech) **anaamim** *vta;* blame people **anaaminge** *vai;* they blame each other **anaamindiwag /anaamindi-/** *vai;* blame oneself **anaamindizo** *vai*
BLANKET
BLANKET: **waabooyaan, -an** *ni, also* **waabowayaan; agwazhe'on, -an** *ni;* my blanket **nikonaas, -an /-konaas-/** *nid*
COVER WITH BLANKETS: cover s.o. with blankets **agwazhe'** *vta*
COVERED WITH BLANKETS: be covered with blankets **agwazhe** *vai*
BLAST
BLAST: blast s.o. **baasaabikiz /baasaabikizw-/** *vta;* blast s.t. **baasaabikizan** *vti;* blast things **baasaabikizige** *vai*
BLAZE
BLAZE UP: **miskwakone, miskwakonemagad** *vii*
BLEACHED
BLEACHED: be bleached **waabide, waabidemagad** *vii;* **waabizo** *vai*
BLEED
BLEED: **miskwiiwi** *vai*
BLESS
BLESS: bless s.o. **zhawenim** *vta*
BLESSED
BLESSED: be blessed **zhawendaagozi** *vai*
BLIND
HUNTING BLIND: **akandoowin, -an** *ni*
USE A BLIND: **akandoo** *vai*
BLIND
BLIND: be blind **gagiibiingwe** *vai*
BLINDFOLD
BLINDFOLD: **basangwaabapijigan, -an** *ni;* blindfold s.o. **basangwaabapizh /basangwaabapiN-/** *vta*
BLINDFOLDED
BLINDFOLDED: be blindfolded **basangwaabapizo** *vai*

BLISTER
BLISTER: have a blister **abashkwebiigizi** *vai*
BLISTER ON FOOT: get a blister on one's foot **abashkwebiigizideshin** *vai*
BLISTER ON HAND: get a blister on one's hand **abashkwebiigininjiishin** *vai*
BLIZZARD
BLIZZARD: be a blizzard **biiwan** *vii*
BLOATED
BLOATED: be bloated **baasinigo** *vai*
BLOCK
BLOCK WITH FOOT OR BODY: block s.o. with foot or body **gibishkaw** *vta;* block s.t. with foot or body **gibishkan** *vti*
BLOND
BLOND: be blond **ozaawindibe** *vai*
BLOOD
BLOOD: **miskwi** *ni*
BLOOD CLOT
BLOOD CLOT: **wado, -wag** *na*
BLOODSUCKER
BLOODSUCKER: **ozagaskwaajime, -g** *na, also* **zagaskwaajime**
BLOODY
BLOODY: be bloody **miskwiiwi** *vai*
BLOODY NOSE: bloody s.o.'s nose **gibitaneganaam** *vta;* have a bloody nose **miskwiiwijaane** *vai*
BLOODY NOSE FALLING: bloody one's nose falling **gibitaneshin** *vai*
BLOOM
BLOOM: **baashkaabigwanii, baashkaabigwaniimagad** *vii*
BLOSSOM
BLOSSOM: **baashkaabigwanii, baashkaabigwaniimagad** *vii*
BLOW
BLOW: blow on s.o. **boodaazh /boodaaN-/** *vta;* blow on s.t. **boodaadan** *vti;* blow on things **boodaajige** *vai*
BLOW NOSE: blow one's nose **ziinikiigome** *vai*
BLOW UP: **baashkide, baashkidemagad** *vii;* **baashkizo** *vai*
BLOWN
BLOWN A CERTAIN WAY: be blown a certain way **inaashi** *vai;* **inaasin** *vii*
BLOWN ABOUT: be blown about **babaamaashi** *vai;* **babaamaasin** *vii*
BLOWN ALONG: be blown along **bimaashi** *vai;* **bimaasin** *vii*
BLOWN APART: be blown apart **biigwaashi** *vai;* **biigwaasin** *vii*
BLOWN ASHORE: be blown ashore **agwaayaashi** *vai;* **agwaayaasin** *vii*
BLOWN AWAY: be blown away **animaashi** *vai;* **animaasin** *vii;* **webaashi** *vai;* **webaasin** *vii*
BLOWN FROM A CERTAIN PLACE: be blown from a certain place **ondaashi** *vai;* be blown from a certain place **ondaasin** *vii*
BLOWN HERE: be blown here **biidaashi** *vai;* **biidaasin** *vii*
BLOWN IN: be blown in **bagamaashi** *vai;* **bagamaasin** *vii*
BLOWN INSIDE: be blown inside **biindigeyaashi** *vai;* **biindigeyaasin** *vii*
BLOWN INTO THE WATER: be blown into the water **bakobiiyaashi** *vai;* **bakobiiyaasin** *vii*
BLOWN OVER: be blown over **gawaashi** *vai;* **gawaasin** *vii*
BLOWN UPWARDS: be blown upwards **ombaashi** *vai;* **ombaasin** *vii*
BLOWOUT
BLOWOUT: have a blowout **baashkijiisijige** *vai*
BLUE
BLUE: **ozhaawashko-** *pv4;* be blue **ozhaawashkozi** *vai;* **ozhaawashkwaa, ozhaawashkwaamagad** *vii;* be blue (as something mineral) **ozhaawashkwaabikad** *vii;* **ozhaawashkwaabikizi** *vai;* be blue (as something sheet-like) **ozhaawashkwegad** *vii;* **ozhaawashkwegizi** *vai;* be blue (as something stick- or wood-like) **ozhaawashkwaakozi** *vai;* **ozhaawashkwaakwad** *vii;* be blue (as something string-like) **ozhaawashkwaabiigad** *vii;* **ozhaawashkwaabiigizi** *vai*
WEAR BLUE: **ozhaawashko'o** *vai*
BLUE HERON
BLUE HERON: **zhashagi, -wag** *na*
BLUE JAY
BLUE JAY: **diindiisi, -wag** *na*
BLUEBERRY
BLUEBERRY: blueberries *plural* **miinan /miin-/** *ni*
BLUEBERRY PLANT
BLUEBERRY PLANT: **miinagaawanzh, -iig** *na*
BLUEBERRY SAUCE
BLUEBERRY SAUCE: **miini-baashkiminasigan** *ni*
BLUEBIRD
BLUEBIRD: **ozhaawashko-bineshiinh, -yag** *na*
BLUSH
BLUSH: **miskwiingwese** *vai*
BOARD
BOARD: **nabagisag, -oog** *na*
BOARD
BOARD: **boozi** *vai*
BOAT
BOAT: **jiimaan, -an** *ni*
ARRIVE BY BOAT: **bagamishkaa** *vai*
COME IN A BOAT: **biidaasamishkaa** *vai*
GO ABOUT IN A BOAT: **babaamishkaa** *vai*
GO HOME BY BOAT: **giiwe'o** *vai*
LONG BOAT: be a long boat **ginoonagad** *vii*
MAKE A BOAT: **jiimaanike** *vai*
MIDDLE OF A BOAT: in the middle of a boat **naawoonag** *pc*
NARROW BOAT: be narrow (as a boat) **agaasadeyoonagad** *vii*

POLE A BOAT: **gaandakii'ige** *vai;* **gaandakii'o** *vai*
POLE A BOAT ALONG: **bima'ookii** *vai*
SHORT BOAT: be short (as a boat) **dakoonagad** *vii*
UNDER A BOAT: **anaamoonag** *pc*
WIDE BOAT: be wide (as a boat) **mangadeyoonagad** *vii*
WOODEN BOAT: **mitigo-jiimaan, -an** *ni*

BOBBER
BOBBER: **deteba'agonjichigan, -an** *ni*

BOBCAT
BOBCAT: **gidagaa-bizhiw, -ag** *na*

BODY
BODY: my body **niiyaw, -an /-iiyaw-/** *nid*
GOOD BODY: have a good body **minwaabewizi** *vai*
INSIDE BODY: inside the body **biinjina** *pc*

BOIL
BOIL: **onde, ondemagad** *vii;* **onzo** *vai;* boil s.o. **onzo /onzw-/** *vta;* boil s.t. **onzan** *vti*
BOIL DOWN: **iskigamide, iskigamidemagad** *vii;* **iskigamizo** *vai;* boil s.t. down **iskigamizan** *vti;* boil things down (e.g., maple sap) **iskigamizige** *vai*
BOIL OVER: **ziigigamide, ziigigamidemagad** *vii;* **ziigigamizo** *vai*
BOIL TO SUGAR: **ombigamizige** *vai;* boil s.t. to sugar **ombigamizan** *vti*
COOK BY BOILING: cook s.o. by boiling **gabaashim** *vta;* cook s.t. by boiling **gabaatoon** *vti2*
FINISH BOILING: **giizhigamide, giizhigamidemagad** *vii;* finish boiling things **giizhigamizige** *vai*
FINISH BOILING SAP: **ishkwaagamizige** *vai*
MAKE NOISE BOILING: **madwegamide, madwegamidemagad** *vii;* **madwegamizo** *vai*
WHISTLE FROM BOILING: **gwiishkoshwewegamide, gwiishkoshwewegamidemagad** *vii;* **gwiishkoshwewegamizo** *vai*

BONE
BONE: my bone **nikan, -an /-kan-/** *nid*
STRONG BONES: have strong bones **zoongigane** *vai*

BOOK
BOOK: **mazina'igan, -an** *ni*
PRAYER BOOK: **anama'e-mazina'igan, -an** *ni*
SCHOOLBOOK: **gikinoo'amaadii-mazina'igan** *ni*

BORN
BORN: be born **niigi** *vai;* **ondaadizi** *vai*

BORROW
BORROW: borrow (s.t.) from people **adaawange** *vai+o;* borrow (s.t.) from s.o. **adaawam** *vta*

BOSS
BOSS: **ogimaa, -g** *na*

BOTH
BOTH: **eyiizh** *pc;* **nayenzh** *pc*
AT BOTH HANDS: **eyiidawininj** *pc*
ON BOTH SIDES: on both sides of it **edawayi'ii** *pc*

BOTHER
BOTHER: bother s.o. **babaamenim** *vta;* **migoshkaaji'** *vta;* bother s.t. **babaamendan** *vti*

BOTTLE
BOTTLE: **omooday, -an** *ni*

BOUGH
CEDAR BOUGH: **giizhikaandag, -oog** *na*
FIR BOUGH: **zhingobaandag, -oog** *na*
PINE BOUGH: **zhingwaakwaandag, -oog** *na*

BOUNCE
BOUNCE: **gwaashkwesin** *vii*

BOUND
BOUND: be bound **dakobide, dakobidemagad** *vii;* **dakobizo** *vai*

BOW
BOW: **mitigwaab, -iig** *na*

BOWL
BOWL: **boozikinaagan, -an** *ni*

BOWSTRING
BOWSTRING: **achaab, -iin** *ni*

BOX
BOX: **makak, -oon** *ni*
BIRCH BARK BOX: **wiigwaasi-makak, -oon** *ni*
CARDBOARD BOX: **mazina'igani-makak, -oon** *ni*
MAKE A BOX: **makakoke** *vai*
WOODEN BOX: **mitigo-makak, -oon** *ni*

BOX
BOX: box s.o. **gagwedaganaam** *vta;* they box each other **gagwedaganaandiwag /gagwedaganaandi-/** *vai*

BOXER
BOXER: **gagwedaganewinini, -wag** *na*

BOY
BOY: **gwiiwizens, -ag** *na;* be a boy **gwiiwizensiwi** *vai*
ADOLESCENT BOY: **oshkinawe, -g** *na;* be an adolescent boy **oshkinawewi** *vai*

BRACE AND BIT
BRACE AND BIT: **biiminigan, -an** *ni*

BRACELET
BRACELET: **jiiskinikebizon, -an** *ni*
WEAR A BRACELET: **jiiskinikebizo** *vai*

BRAID
BRAID: **okaadenigan, -an** *ni;* braid s.o.'s hair **okaaden** *vta;* braid s.t. **okaadenan** *vti;* braid things **okaadenige** *vai*
HAVE BRAIDS: **okaadenige** *vai*

BRAIDED
BRAIDED: be braided **okaadenigaade, okaadenigaademagad** *vii*

BRAIDED RUG
BRAIDED RUG: **okaadenigan, -an** *ni*

BRAIN
BRAIN: my brain **niinindib /-iinindib-/** *nid*

BRAKES
BRAKES: **nagaawebishkigan, -an** *ni*

APPLY THE BRAKES: **nagaawebishkige** *vai*

BRANCH

BRANCH: **wadikwan, -an** *ni*

RIVER BRANCHES: branch (as a river) **baketigweyaa, baketigweyaamagad** *vii*

BRASS

BRASS: (piece of) brass **ozaawaabik, -oon** *ni;* be brass **ozaawaabikad** *vii;* **ozaawaabikizi** *vai*

BRASSIERE

BRASSIERE: **aasodoodooshimebizon, -an** *ni*

BRAVE

BRAVE: be brave **zoongide'e** *vai*

BREAD

BREAD: **bakwezhigan, -ag** *na;* bread cooked over an open fire **abwaajigan, -ag** *na*

BREAD BAKED UNDER THE ASHES: **ningwa'abwaan, -ag** *na*

FRY BREAD: **zaasakokwaan, -ag** *na*

MAKE BREAD: **bakwezhiganike** *vai*

BREAD BOX

BREAD BOX: **bakwezhigani-makak, -oon** *ni*

BREAK

BREAK: **biigoshkaa** *vai;* **biigoshkaa, biigoshkaamagad** *vii*

BREAK APART: break apart (e.g., something string-like) **bakise** *vai;* **bakise, bakisemagad** *vii*

BREAK APART FROM RUBBING: break apart from rubbing (e.g., something string-like) **bakiboode, bakiboodemagad** *vii;* **bakiboozo** *vai*

BREAK ARM: break one's arm **bookonike** *vai*

BREAK BY DROPPING: break s.o. by dropping **biigoshim** *vta;* break s.t. by dropping **biigosidoon** *vti2;* **niigosidoon** *vti2*

BREAK BY HAND: break s.o. by hand **biigon** *vta;* break s.t. by hand **biigonan** *vti*

BREAK BY HEAT: **biigode, biigodemagad** *vii;* **biigozo** *vai;* **niigode, niigodemagad** *vii;* **niigozo** *vai*

BREAK IN TWO: **bookoshkaa** *vai;* **bookoshkaa, bookoshkaamagad** *vii*

BREAK IN TWO BY FOOT OR BODY: break s.o. in two by foot or body **bookoshkaw** *vta;* break s.t. in two by foot or body **bookoshkan** *vti*

BREAK IN TWO BY HITTING: break s.o. in two by hitting **bookoganaam** *vta;* break s.t. in two by hitting **bookoganaandan** *vti*

BREAK IN TWO WITH HANDS: break s.o. in two with hands **bookobizh /bookobiN-/** *vta;* break s.t. in two with hands **bookobidoon** *vti2*

BREAK LEG: break one's leg **bookogaade** *vai*

BREAK OFF: break s.o. off (e.g., something string-like) **bakibizh /bakibiN-/** *vta;* break s.t. off (e.g., something string-like) **bakibidoon** *vti2*

BREAK ON IMPACT: **biigoshin** *vai;* **biigosin** *vii;* **niigoshin** *vai;* **niigosin** *vii*

BREAK UP: break s.t. up (as ground) **biigwakamigibidoon** *vti2*

BREAK USING SOMETHING: break s.o. using something **biigwa' /biigwa'w-/** *vta;* break s.t. using something **biigwa'an** *vti*

FALL AND BREAK ARM: fall and break one's arm **bookonikeshin** *vai*

FALL AND BREAK BACK: fall and break one's back **bookwaawiganeshin** *vai*

FALL AND BREAK LEG: fall and break one's leg **bookogaadeshin** *vai*

BREAK

TAKE A BREAK: **gibichiitaa** *vai*

BREAKFAST

BREAKFAST: **gigizhebaa-wiisiniwin** *ni*

EAT BREAKFAST: **gigizhebaa-wiisini** *vai;* eat s.t. for breakfast **gigizhebaa-miijin** *vti3*

BREAST

BREAST: my breast **indoodooshim, -ag /-doodooshim-/** *nad*

BREAST FEED

BREAST FEED: breast feed s.o. **nooni'** *vta*

BREATH

BAD BREATH: have bad breath **maazhimaagwanaamo** *vai*

DRAW BREATH IN: **ikwanaamo** *vai*

RECOVER ONE'S BREATH: **nasanaamo** *vai*

SHORT OF BREATH: be short of breath **akwanaamo** *vai*

TAKE SHORT BREATHS: **akwanaamo** *vai*

BREATHE

BREATHE: **bagidanaamo** *vai*

STOP BREATHING: **ishkwaanaamo** *vai*

BREECH CLOUT

BREECH CLOUT: **aanziyaan, -an** *ni*

BREEZE

GOOD BREEZE: there is a good breeze **minwaanimad** *vii*

BRIDGE

BRIDGE: **aazhogan, -an** *ni;* foot bridge **aazhawaandawaagan, -an** *ni*

BRIDLE

BRIDLE: **zagidoonebijigan, -an** *ni*

BRIGHT

BRIGHT: be bright **waaseyaa, waaseyaamagad** *vii;* be bright (as something sheet-like) **waaseyiigad** *vii;* **waaseyiigizi** *vai*

BRIGHT INSIDE: be bright inside **waasete, waasetemagad** *vii*

BRIGHT LEAVES: there are bright leaves **waatebagaa, waatebagaamagad** *vii*

BRING

BRING: bring s.o. **biizh /biiN-/** *vta;* bring s.t. **biidoon** *vti2;* bring (s.t.) for s.o. **biidaw** *vta, also* **biidamaw**

BRING FIREWOOD INSIDE: **biindigenise** *vai*

BRING HERE IN A BOAT: **biida'oodoon** *vti2;* bring s.o. here in a boat **biida'oozh /biida'ooN-/** *vta*

BRING INSIDE: bring s.o. inside **biindigazh /biindigaN-/** *vta;* bring s.t. inside **biindigadoon** *vti2*

BRING TOGETHER: bring s.t. together **maawandoonan** *vti*

BRITTLE

BRITTLE: be brittle **gaapan** *vii, also* **gaapaa**; **gaapizi** *vai*

BROKE

BROKE: be broke (out of money) **biigoshkaa** *vai*

BROKEN

BROKEN: be broken **biigoshkaa** *vai;* **biigoshkaa, biigoshkaamagad** *vii;* **niigoshkaa, niigoshkaamagad** *vii*

BROKEN ARM: have a broken arm **bookonike** *vai*

BROKEN IN TWO: be broken in two **bookoshkaa** *vai;* **bookoshkaa, bookoshkaamagad** *vii*

BROKEN LEG: have a broken leg **bookogaade** *vai*

HAVE A BROKEN NOSE: **bookojaane** *vai*

BROKEN GLASS

BROKEN GLASS: broken glass (as from a bottle) **omoodayaabik, -oon** *ni*

BROOCH

BROOCH: **zagaakwa'on, -ag** *na*

BROOM

BROOM: **jiigada'igan, -an** *ni;* **jiishada'igan, -an** *ni*

BROTH

BROTH: **wiiyaasaaboo** *ni*

WILD RICE BROTH: **manoominaaboo** *ni*

BROTHER

BROTHER: my (male's) brother **niijikiwenh, -yag /-iijikiweny-/** *nad;* my (male's) brother *ritual use* **niikaan, -ag /-iikaan-/** *nad;* **niikaanis, -ag /-iikaanis-/** *nad;* my sibling of the opposite sex (brother or sister) **indawemaa, -g /-dawemaaw-/** *nad*

OLDER BROTHER: my older brother **nisayenh, -yag /-sayeny-/** *nad*

YOUNGER BROTHER: my younger brother **nishiime, -yag /-shiimey-/** *nad*

BROTHER-IN-LAW

BROTHER-IN-LAW: my (female's) brother-in-law **niinim, -oog /-iinimw-/** *nad;* my (male's) brother-in-law **niitaa, -g /-iitaaw-/** *nad*

BROUGHT

BROUGHT: be brought **biijigaade, biijigaademagad** *vii;* **biijigaazo** *vai*

BROWN

BROWN: **ozaawi-** *pv4;* be brown **ozaawaa, ozaawaamagad** *vii;* **ozaawizi** *vai;* be brown (as something mineral) **ozaawaabikad** *vii;* **ozaawaabikizi** *vai;* be brown (as something sheet-like) **ozaawegad** *vii;* **ozaawegizi** *vai;* be brown (as something stick- or wood-like) **ozaawaakozi** *vai;* **ozaawaakwad** *vii;* be brown (as something string-like) **ozaawaabiigad** *vii;* **ozaawaabiigizi** *vai*

BROWN BY FIRE: brown s.t. by fire **ozaawaakizan** *vti*

COLORED BROWN: be colored brown **ozaawaande, ozaawaandemagad** *vii;* **ozaawaanzo** *vai*

HAVE BROWN HAIR: **ozaawindibe** *vai*

TOAST BROWN: toast s.t. brown **ozaawaakizan** *vti*

WEAR BROWN: **ozaawi'o** *vai*

BRUISED

BRUISED FACE: have a bruised face **ozhaawashkwaanagiingwe** *vai*

BRUSH

BRUSH: brush s.o. using something (as something sheet-like) **bawega' /bawega'w-/** *vta;* brush s.t. using something (as something sheet-like) **bawega'an** *vti*

BRUSH SNOW: brush snow off s.o. by hand **bawaagonen** *vta;* brush snow off s.o. using something **bawaagone' /bawaagone'w-/** *vta;* brush snow off s.t. by hand **bawaagonenan** *vti;* brush snow off s.t. using something **bawaagone'an** *vti*

BRUSH TEETH: brush one's teeth **giziiyaabide'o** *vai;* **giziiyaabide'odizo** *vai*

PAINT BRUSH: **zhizhoobii'iganaatig, -oon** *ni*

SCRUB BRUSH: **mimigosaga'igan, -an** *ni*

BRUSH

IN THE BRUSH: **megwekob** *pc*

BUBBLE

BUBBLE: **biisitaagan, -an** *ni*

BUCK

BUCK: **ayaabe, -g** *na*

BUCKLE

BELT BUCKLE: **gijipizonaabik, -oon** *ni*

BUCKSKIN DRESS

BUCKSKIN DRESS: **bashkweginagooday, -an** *ni*

BUD

LEAVES BUD: **zaagibagaa, zaagibagaamagad** *vii*

BUFFALO

BUFFALO: **bizhiki, -wag** *na;* **mashkode-bizhiki, -wag** *na*

BUG

BUG: **manidoons, -ag** *na*

MANY BUGS: there are many bugs **manidoonsikaa, manidoonsikaamagad** *vii*

BUILD

BUILD: build s.o. **ozhi'** *vta;* build s.t. **ozhitoon** *vti2;* build (s.t.) for s.o. **ozhitamaw** *vta;* **ozhitaw** *vta*

BUILD A HOUSE: **waakaa'ige** *vai;* build a house for s.o. **ozhigaw** *vta*

BUILD A LODGE: **ozhige** *vai*

FINISH BUILDING A DWELLING: **giizhige** *vai*

BUILDING

BUILDING: **waakaa'igan, -an** *ni*

BUILT

BUILT: be built **ozhichigaade, ozhichigaademagad** *vii;* **ozhichigaazo** *vai*

BULB
BULB: **obikwaaj, -iin** *nid*
BULL
BULL: **doonoo, -g** *na*
BULL SNAKE
BULL SNAKE: **newe, -g** *na*
BULLET
BULLET: **anwi, -in** *ni*
TWENTY-TWO BULLET: **anwiins, -an** *ni*
BULLHEAD
BULLHEAD: **awaazisii, -g** *na, also* **owaazisii, wawaazisii**
BUMP
BUMP: bump into s.o. **bitaakoshkaw** *vta;* bump into s.t. **bitaakoshkan** *vti;* bump something **bitaakoshin** *vai;* **bitaakosin** *vii*
BUMP DOWN OFF: bump s.o. down off **diitibishkaw** *vta;* bump s.t. down off **diitibishkan** *vti*
BUMP HEAD: bump one's head **bitaakondibeshin** *vai*
BUNCH
TIE IN A BUNCH: tie s.o. in a bunch **okwapizh /okwapiN-/** *vta;* tie s.t. in a bunch **okwapidoon** *vti2*
TIED IN A BUNCH: be tied in a bunch **okwapide, okwapidemagad** *vii;* **okwapizo** *vai*
BUNDLE
BUNDLE: **gashkibijigan, -an** *ni*
TIE IN A BUNDLE: tie s.o. in a bundle **gashkapizh /gashkapiN-/** *vta;* tie s.t. in a bundle **gashkapidoon** *vti2*
WRAP AND TIE IN A BUNDLE: wrap and tie s.o. in a bundle **gashkibizh /gashkibiN-/** *vta;* wrap and tie s.t. in a bundle **gashkibidoon** *vti2;* wrap and tie things in bundle **gashkibijige** *vai*
WRAPPED AND TIED IN A BUNDLE: be wrapped and tied in a bundle **gashkibide, gashkibidemagad** *vii;* **gashkibijigaade, gashkibijigaademagad** *vii;* **gashkibijigaazo** *vai*
BURBOT
BURBOT: **mizay, -ag** *na*
BURIED
BURIED: be buried (of a person) **bagidenjigaazo** *vai;* **ningwa'igaazo** *vai*
BURIED IN A CERTAIN PLACE: be buried in a certain place **dazhishin** *vai*
BURN
BURN: **zakide, zakidemagad** *vii;* **zakizo** *vai;* burn s.o. **zakiz /zakizw-/** *vta;* burn s.t. **zakizan** *vti;* burn things **zakizige** *vai;* burn oneself **jaagizodizo** *vai*
BURN A CERTAIN WAY: **inaakide, inaakidemagad** *vii;* **inaakizo** *vai;* burn s.o. a certain way **inaakiz /inaakizw-/** *vta;* burn s.t. a certain way **inaakizan** *vti*
BURN A HOLE: burn a hole in s.o. **bagwaakiz /bagwaakizw-/** *vta;* burn a hole in s.t. **bagwaakizan** *vti*
BURN AS MEDICINE: burn s.t. as medicine **nookwezan** *vti;* burn things as medicine **nookwezige** *vai*
BURN TO THE PAN: **agwaabikide, agwaabikidemagad** *vii;* **agwaabikizo** *vai;* burn s.o. to the pan **agwaabikiz /agwaabikizw-/** *vta;* burn s.t. to the pan **agwaabikizan** *vti*
BURN UP: **jaagaakide, jaagaakidemagad** *vii;* **jaagaakizo** *vai;* **jaagide, jaagidemagad** *vii;* **jaagizo** *vai;* burn s.o. up **jaagaakiz /jaagaakizw-/** *vta;* **jaagiz /jaagizw-/** *vta;* burn s.t. up **jaagaakizan** *vti;* **jaagizan** *vti*
BURNED
HAVE A HOLE BURNED IN: **bagwaakide, bagwaakidemagad** *vii;* **bagwaakizo** *vai*
BURP
BURP: **aagade** *vai;* **megade** *vai*
BURP GREASE: **biinzibii** *vai*
BURROW
BURROW: **waanzh, -an** *ni*
BURST
BURST: burst s.o. using something **baashka' /baashka'w-/** *vta;* burst s.t. using something **baashka'an** *vti*
BURST ON IMPACT: burst s.o. on impact **baashkishim** *vta;* burst s.t. on impact **baashkisidoon** *vti2*
BURST OPEN: **biigojiishkaa** *vai;* **biigojiishkaa, biigojiishkaamagad** *vii*
BURST OPEN USING SOMETHING: burst s.o. open using something **baashkijii' /baashkijii'w-/** *vta;* burst s.t. open using something **baashkijii'an** *vti*
BURST OUT LAUGHING: **baashkaapi** *vai*
BURY
BURY: bury s.o. (e.g., a person) **bagidenim** *vta;* bury s.o. **ningwa' /ningwa'w-/** *vta;* bury s.t. **ningwa'an** *vti*
BUSH
IN THE BUSH: **noopiming** *pc*
BUSHEL
CERTAIN NUMBER OF BUSHELS: a certain number of bushels **dasodiba'iminaan** *pc*
BUSHY
BUSHY: be bushy **biigwawe** *vai*
BUSINESS
DO BUSINESS: **babaamizi** *vai*
GO ABOUT ON BUSINESS: go about on one's business **babaamizi** *vai*
BUSTLE
DANCE BUSTLE: **bimoonjigan, -an** *ni*
BUSY
BUSY: **ojaanimi-** *pv4;* be busy **ojaanimizi** *vai;* **ondamizi** *vai;* be busy (in some work or activity) **ojaanimitaa** *vai*
KEPT BUSY IN AN ACTIVITY: be kept busy in an activity **ondamitaa** *vai*
KEPT BUSY IN WORK: be kept busy in work **ondamanokii** *vai*
BUT
BUT: **aanawi** *pc*

BUTTER
BUTTER: **doodooshaaboo-bimide** *ni;* **ozaawi-bimide** *ni*
BUTTERFLY
BUTTERFLY: **memengwaa, -g** *na*
BUTTON
BUTTON: **gibadoonh, -yag** *na, also* **gibodoonh**
BUTTON UP: button s.o. up **zagaakwa' /zagaakwa'w-/** *vta;* button up oneself **zagaakwa'odizo** *vai*
BUY
BUY: buy (s.t.) **adaawe** *vai+o;* buy (s.t.) for oneself **adaawetamaazo** *vai;* buy (s.t.) for s.o. **adaawetamaw** *vta;* buy (s.t.) from s.o. **adaam** *vta*
BUY FOOD: **miijimadaawe** *vai*
BY
BY: **jiigi-** *pn;* by it **jiigayi'ii** *pc*
BY A DOOR: **jiigishkwaand** *pc*
BY A FIRE: **jiigishkode** *pc*
BY A HOUSE: **jiigigamig** *pc*
BY A MEADOW: **jiigashkosiw** *pc*
BY A ROAD: by a road or trail **jiigikana** *pc*
BY A TRAIL: by a road or trail **jiigikana** *pc*
BY A TREE: **jiigaatig** *pc*
BY A WALL: **jiigaatig** *pc*
GOING BY: **bimi-** *pv2*
BY ONESELF
BY ONESELF: **dibinawe** *pc*
BYPASS
BYPASS: bypass s.o. **bakekazh /bakekaN-/** *vta;* bypass people **bakekazhiwe** *vai*

C

CABBAGE
CABBAGE: **gichi-aniibiish, -an** *ni*
CABIN
LOG CABIN: **mitigo-waakaa'igan, -an** *ni*
CACHE
CACHE: **asanjigoowin, -an** *ni;* cache (s.t.) **asanjigo** *vai+o*
CAFE
CAFE: **wiisiniiwigamig, -oon** *ni*
CAKE
CAKE: **waashkobizid bakwezhigan, -ag** *na-pt;* **wiishkobi-bakwezhigan, -ag** *na*
CALENDAR
CALENDAR: **giizisoo-mazina'igan, -an** *ni*
CALF
CALF: **bizhikiins, -ag** *na*
CALF
CALF: my calf **ninaan, -ag /-naan-/** *nad*
CALFHIDE
CALFHIDE: **bizhikiinsiwayaan, -ag** *na*
CALICO
CALICO: **gidagiigin, -oon** *ni*
CALL
CALL: call s.o. **nandom** *vta*
CALL A CERTAIN WAY: call s.o. a certain way **izhi-wiinzh /izhi-wiinN-/** *vta;* call s.t. a certain way **izhi-wiindan** *vti*
CALL IN INDIAN: call s.o. in Indian (Ojibwe) **anishinaabewinikaazh /anishinaabewinikaaN-/** *vta;* call s.t. in Indian (Ojibwe) **anishinaabewinikaadan** *vti*
CALL IN OJIBWE: call s.o. in Indian (Ojibwe) **anishinaabewinikaazh /anishinaabewinikaaN-/** *vta;* call s.t. in Indian (Ojibwe) **anishinaabewinikaadan** *vti*
CALL ON THE PHONE: call s.o. on the phone **ganoozh /ganooN-/** *vta*
CALL OUT: **biibaagi** *vai;* call out to s.o. **biibaagim** *vta;* call out to s.t. **biibaagindan** *vti*
MAKE A CHARACTERISTIC CALL: make a characteristic call (e.g., neigh, moo) **noondaagozi** *vai;* make a characteristic call (neigh, etc.) **inwe** *vai*
CALLED
CALLED A CERTAIN WAY: be called a certain way **izhi-wiinde, izhi-wiindemagad** *vii;* **izhi-wiinzo** *vai*
CALLED IN INDIAN: be called in Indian (Ojibwe) **anishinaabewinikaade, anishinaabewinikaademagad** *vii;* **anishinaabewinikaazo** *vai*
CALLED IN OJIBWE: be called in Indian (Ojibwe) **anishinaabewinikaade, anishinaabewinikaademagad** *vii;* **anishinaabewinikaazo** *vai*
CALM
CALM: be calm **awibaa, awibaamagad** *vii*
CALM WEATHER: be calm weather **anwaatin** *vii*
CAMEL
CAMEL: **bekwaawigang** *na-pt*
CAMERA
CAMERA: **mazinaakizigan, -an** *ni*
CAMP
CAMP: **gabeshi** *vai*
CAMPSITE
CAMPSITE: **gabeshiwin, -an** *ni*
CAN
CAN: *modal* **daa-** *pv1*
CAN
CAN: **biiwaabikoons, -an** *ni;* can s.t. **gibaakobidoon** *vti2*
CAN OPENER
CAN OPENER: **baakaakozhigan, -an** *ni*
CAN'T DO IT
CAN'T DO IT: can't do it! **gaawesa** *pc*
CANADA
CANADA: **Zhaaganaashiiwaki** *ni*
CANADA GOOSE
CANADA GOOSE: **nika, -g** *na*

CANDY
CANDY: **ziinzibaakwadoons, -an** *ni*
CANE
CANE: **zaka'on, -an** *ni*
USE A CANE: **zaka'o** *vai*
CANNED GOODS
CANNED GOODS: **gibaakobijigan, -an** *ni*
CANNIBAL
WINTER CANNIBAL MONSTER: windigo: winter cannibal monster **wiindigoo, -g** *na*
CANOE
CANOE: **jiimaan, -an** *ni*
ALUMINUM CANOE: **biiwaabiko-jiimaan, -an** *ni*
BIRCH BARK CANOE: **wiigwaasi-jiimaan, -an** *ni*
GO BY CANOE: **jiime** *vai*
MAKE A CANOE: **atoono** *vai;* **jiimaanike** *vai*
WOODEN CANOE: **mitigo-jiimaan, -an** *ni*
CANOE RIB
CANOE RIB: **waaginaa, -g** *na*
CANOPY
CANOPY: **agwanogaan, -an** *ni*
CANVAS
CANVAS: **babagiwayaanegamigwegin, -oon** *ni*
CANVAS SHOE
CANVAS SHOE: **babagiwayaanekizin, -an** *ni, also* **bagiwayaanekizin**
CAPSIZE
CAPSIZE: **gwanabishkaa** *vai*
CAPTIVE
TAKE CAPTIVES: **makandwe** *vai;* **nawadiniwe** *vai*
CAR
CAR: **odaabaan, -ag** *na;* **waasamoowidaabaan, -ag** *na;* car *old fashioned* **ziikaa, -g** *na*
HAVE A BROKEN-DOWN CAR: **biigodaabaane** *vai*
POLICE CAR: **dakoniwewidaabaan, -ag** *na*
RACE CAR: **gagwejikazhiwewidaabaan, -ag** *na*
REPAIR A CAR: **nanaa'idaabaane** *vai*
CARCASS
CARCASS: **zhiigozhigan, -an** *ni*
CARD
CARD: playing card **ataadiwin, -ag** *na*
CLUB SUITE CARD: **danens, -ag** *na*
CUT CARDS: **bakwenige** *vai*
DIAMOND SUITE CARD: **gaanoo, -g** *na*
HEART SUITE CARD: **giiwoon, -ag** *na, also* **giiyoon**
SPADE SUITE CARD: **biig, -wag** *na*
CARDBOARD BOX
CARDBOARD BOX: **mazina'igani-makak, -oon** *ni*
CARDINAL
CARDINAL: **misko-bineshiinh, -yag** *na*
CARE
CARE: care for s.o. **bamenim** *vta;* care for s.t. **bamendan** *vti*
CAREFREE
CAREFREE: be carefree **naangide'e** *vai*
CAREFUL
CAREFUL: be careful **ayaangwaamizi** *vai*
CAREFULLY
CAREFULLY: **wawiinge** *pc;* **weweni** *pc*
CARELESSLY
CARELESSLY: **debinaak** *pc*
CARGO
LOAD CARGO: **boozitaaso** *vai;* load s.t. as cargo **boozitoon** *vti2;* load (s.t.) with cargo for s.o. **boozitaw** *vta*
CARIBOU
CARIBOU: **adik, -wag** *na*
CARNIVAL
CARNIVAL: **mamaandaagochigewin, -an** *ni*
CARPENTER
CARPENTER: **mookodaasowinini, -wag** *na;* **waakaa'igewinini, -wag** *na*
CARRIED
CARRIED TO A CERTAIN PLACE: be carried to a certain place **izhiwijigaade, izhiwijigaademagad** *vii;* **izhiwijigaazo** *vai*
CARROT
CARROT: **okaadaak, -oon** *ni;* **ozaawikaadaak, -oon** *ni*
CARRY
ABLE TO CARRY: be able to carry s.o. **gashkiwizh /gashkiwiN-/** *vta;* be able to carry s.t. **gashkiwidoon** *vti2*
ARRIVE CARRYING: arrive carrying s.o. **bagamiwizh /bagamiwiN-/** *vta;* arrive carrying s.t. **bagamiwidoon** *vti2*
CARRY A BABY ALONG ON BACK: carry a baby along on one's back **bimoomaawaso** *vai*
CARRY A BABY TO A CERTAIN PLACE ON BACK: carry a baby to a certain place on one's back **inoomaawaso** *vai*
CARRY A BIG PACK: **mangiwane** *vai*
CARRY A PACK ALONG: **bimiwane** *vai*
CARRY ABOUT: carry s.o. about **babaamiwizh /babaamiwiN-/** *vta;* carry s.t. about **babaamiwidoon** *vti2*
CARRY ACROSS: carry s.o. across **aazhogewizh /aazhogewiN-/** *vta;* carry s.t. across **aazhogewidoon** *vti2*
CARRY ALONG: carry s.o. along **bimiwizh /bimiwiN-/** *vta;* carry s.t. along **bimiwidoon** *vti2;* carry things along **bimiwijige** *vai*
CARRY ALONG ON BACK: carry s.o. along on one's back **bimoom** *vta;* carry s.t. along on one's back **bimoondan** *vti*
CARRY AWAY: carry s.o. away **animiwizh /animiwiN-/** *vta;* carry s.t. away **animiwidoon** *vti2*
CARRY AWAY ON BACK: carry s.o. away on one's back **animoom** *vta;* carry s.t. away on one's back **animoondan** *vti*
CARRY FROM A CERTAIN PLACE: carry s.o. from a certain place **onjiwizh**

/onjiwiN-/ *vta;* carry s.t. from a certain place **onjiwidoon** *vti2*
CARRY HOME: carry s.o. home **giiwewizh /giiwewiN-/** *vta;* carry s.t. home **giiwewidoon** *vti2;* carry (s.t.) home for s.o. **giiwewidaw** *vta*
CARRY IN MOUTH: carry s.o. in mouth **niimam** *vta;* carry s.t. in mouth **niimandan** *vti*
CARRY INLAND: carry s.o. inland **gopiwizh /gopiwiN-/** *vta;* carry s.t. inland **gopiwidoon** *vti2*
CARRY OFF ON BACK: carry s.o. off on one's back **maadoom** *vta;* carry s.t. off on one's back **maadoondan** *vti*
CARRY ON BACK FROM A CERTAIN PLACE: carry s.o. on back from a certain place **ondoom** *vta;* carry s.t. on back from a certain place **ondoondan** *vti*
CARRY OVER A PORTAGE: carry things over a portage **gakiiwenige** *vai*
CARRY TO A CERTAIN PLACE: carry s.o. to a certain place **izhiwizh /izhiwiN-/** *vta;* carry s.t. to a certain place **izhiwidoon** *vti2*
CARRY TO A CERTAIN PLACE ON BACK: carry s.o. to a certain place on one's back **inoom** *vta;* carry s.t. to a certain place on one's back **inoondan** *vti*
CARRY TO THE SHORE: carry s.o. to the shore **madaabiiwizh /madaabiiwiN-/** *vta;* carry s.t. to the shore **madaabiiwidoon** *vti2*
CARRY USING SOMETHING: carry s.o. using something **niima' /niima'w-/** *vta;* carry s.t. using something **niima'an** *vti*
HARDLY BE ABLE TO CARRY THE PACK: hardly be able to carry a pack **bwaawane** *vai*
LIFT AND CARRY: lift and carry s.o. **ombiwizh /ombiwiN-/** *vta;* lift and carry s.t. **ombiwidoon** *vti2*

CARVE
CARVE: **mookodaaso** *vai*

CARVER
CARVER: **mookodaasowinini, -wag** *na*

CASH
CASH: **gwayako-zhooniyaa** *na*

CASINO
CASINO: **endazhi-ataading** *ni-pt*

CASKET
CASKET: **jiibegamig, -oon** *ni*

CASS LAKE
CASS LAKE: **Gaa-miskwaawaakokaag** *place*

CAST
CAST SUGAR CONES: **ziiga'ige** *vai*

CAT
CAT: **gaazhagens, -ag** *na*

CATASTROPHE
CATASTROPHE: there is a catastrophe **nichiiwad** *vii*

CATCH
CATCH: catch s.o. **debibizh /debibiN-/** *vta;* catch s.t. **debibidoon** *vti2;* catch (s.t.) for s.o. **debibidaw** *vta*
CATCH A DISEASE: **mizizi** *vai*
CATCH A RIDE: catch a ride with s.o. **boozinodaw** *vta*
CATCH WITH HANDS: catch s.o. with hands **nakwebizh /nakwebiN-/** *vta;* catch s.t. with hands **nakwebidoon** *vti2;* catch things with hands **nakwebijige** *vai*

CATCH FIRE
CATCH FIRE: **biskane, biskanemagad** *vii;* **nawadide, nawadidemagad** *vii;* **nawadizo** *vai*

CATCH UP
CATCH UP: catch up to s.o. **adim** *vta;* catch up to s.t. **adindan** *vti*
CATCH UP IN A BOAT: catch up to s.o. in a boat **adima' /adima'w-/** *vta*

CATCHER
CATCHER: catcher (in baseball) **nakwebijigewinini, -wag** *na*

CATFISH
CATFISH: **maanameg, -wag** *na*

CATSUP
CATSUP: **oginii-dagonigan** *ni*

CATTAIL
CATTAIL: **apakweshkway, -ag** *na*
CATTAIL MAT: **apakweshkway, -ag** *na*

CAUGHT
CAUGHT IN A NET: be caught in a net **biinda'am** *vai2*

CAUSE
CAUSE: cause s.o. to do something **izhi'** *vta;* cause s.t. to **izhitoon** *vti2*

CAUTION
CAUTION: caution s.o. **ayaangwaamim** *vta*

CAUTIOUS
CAUTIOUS: be cautious **ayaangwaamizi** *vai*

CAVE
CAVE: **waanzh, -an** *ni*

CEDAR
RED CEDAR: **miskwaawaak, -oog** *na*
WHITE CEDAR: **giizhik, -ag** *na*

CEDAR BARK BAG
CEDAR BARK BAG: **giishkashkimod, -an** *ni*

CEDAR BOUGH
CEDAR BOUGH: **giizhikaandag, -oog** *na*

CEDAR WAXWING
CEDAR WAXWING: **zegibanwaanishiinh, -yag** *na*

CELLAR
CELLAR: **moonikaan, -an** *ni*

CEMETERY
CEMETERY: **jiibayaki, -in** *ni*

CENSE
CENSE: cense s.o. **abaabas /abaabasw-/** *vta;* cense s.t. **abaabasan** *vti;* cense oneself **abaabaso** *vai;*

CENT
CENT: **miskwaabikoons, -ag** *na;* **ozaawaabikoons, -ag** *na*

CEREMONY
CONDUCT A CEREMONY: **manidooke** *vai*
GIVE A CEREMONY: **zagaswe'iwe** *vai*

CERTAIN
CERTAIN: be certain **gwayakwendam** *vai2;* it is certain **booch** *pc*
CERTAIN EVENT: be a certain event **inakamigad** *vii*
CERTAINLY
CERTAINLY: **geget** *pc;* **mii nange** *pc*
CHAFF
CHAFF: chaff from wild rice *plural* **mazaanag /mazaan-/** *na*
CHAIN
CHAIN OF LAKES: be a chain of lakes **aanikegamaa, aanikegamaamagad** *vii*
CHAIR
CHAIR: **apabiwin, -an** *ni*
ROCKING CHAIR: **didibise-apabiwin, -an** *ni;* **wewebizoo-apabiwin, -an** *ni*
CHAIRMAN
CHAIRMAN: **eshpabid** *na-pt*
CHANGE
CHANGE: **aanji-** *pv4;* change s.o. **aanji'** *vta;* change s.o. with foot or body (e.g., clothes) **aanzikaw** *vta;* change s.t. **aanjitoon** *vti2;* change s.t. with foot or body (e.g., clothes) **aanzikan** *vti*
CHANGE APPEARANCE: change one's own appearance **aanzinaago'idizo** *vai;* change s.o.'s appearance **aanzinaago'** *vta;* change s.t.'s appearance **aanzinaagotoon** *vti2*
CHANGE CLOTHES: change one's clothes **aanzikonaye** *vai;* change s.o. with foot or body (e.g., clothes) **aanzikaw** *vta;* change s.o.'s clothes **aanzikonaye'** *vta;* change s.t. with foot or body (e.g., clothes) **aanzikan** *vti*
CHANGE COUNTRIES: **aandakii** *vai*
CHANGE DRESS: change one's dress **aandagoode** *vai*
CHANGE LAWS: **aandaakonige** *vai*
CHANGE LIFE: change one's life **aanji-bimaadizi** *vai*
CHANGE MIND: change one's mind **aanizhiitam** *vai2;* **gwekendam** *vai*
CHANGE PLANS: **aandaakonige** *vai*
CHANGE SEAT: **aandabi** *vai*
CHANGE
LOOSE CHANGE: **bigishki-zhooniyaans, -ag** *na*
CHANGED
LOOK CHANGED: **aanzinaagozi** *vai;* **aanzinaagwad** *vii*
CHANNEL
CHANNEL: there is a channel between lakes **wabigamaa, wabigamaamagad** *vii*
CHAPPED
CHAPPED: be chapped **gagiipizi** *vai*
CHAPPED FACE: have a chapped face **gagiipiingwe** *vai*
CHAPPED LIPS: have chapped lips **gagiipidoon** *vai*
CHARACTER
CERTAIN CHARACTER: have a certain character **inaadizi** *vai*
CHARCOAL
CHARCOAL: **akakanzhe** *ni*
CHARGE
CHARGE A HIGH PRICE: **ishpagindaaso** *vai;* charge a high price for s.t. **ishpagindan** *vti*
CHASE
CHASE ABOUT: chase s.o. about **babaaminizha' /babaaminizha'w-/** *vta;* chase s.t. about **babaaminizha'an** *vti;* chase things about **babaaminizha'ige** *vai*
CHASE ALONG: chase s.o. along **biminizha' /biminizha'w-/** *vta;* **biminizhikaw** *vta;* chase s.t. along **biminizha'an** *vti;* chase things along **biminizha'ige** *vai;* chase people along **biminaazhikaage** *vai*
CHASE INSIDE: chase s.o. inside **biindigenaazhikaw** *vta;* **biindigenizhikaw** *vta*
CHASE OFF: chase s.o. off **maajinizhikaw** *vta*
CHASE OUT OF THE WAY: chase s.o. out of the way **ikonaazhikaw** *vta*
CHASE OUTSIDE: chase s.o. outside **zaagijinizhikaw** *vta*
CHASE TO A CERTAIN PLACE: chase s.o. to a certain place **izhinaazhikaw** *vta;* **izhinizhikaw** *vta*
CHAUFFEUR
CHAUFFEUR: **bimiwizhiwewinini, -wag** *na*
CHEAP
CHEAP: be cheap **wendad** *vii;* **wendaginde, wendagindemagad** *vii;* **wendaginzo** *vai;* **wendizi** *vai;* **wenipanad** *vii*
CHEAT
CHEAT: cheat s.o. **wayezhim** *vta;* cheat people **wayezhinge** *vai*
CHECK
CHECK BY TASTING: check s.o. by tasting **gojipozh /gojipw-/** *vta;* check s.t. by tasting **gojipidan** *vti*
CHECK SNARES: check one's snares **naadagoodoo** *vai*
CHECK TRAPS: check one's traps **naadasoonaagane** *vai*
CHECK UP: check up on s.o. **dibaabam** *vta*
CHECK
CHECK: **jeko-mazina'igan, -an** *ni*
CHECKERS
PLAY CHECKERS: **zhooshkonige** *vai*
CHEEK
CHEEK: my cheek **ninow, -an /-now-/** *nid*
RED CHEEK: have a red cheek **miskwanowe** *vai*
CHERRY
BLACK CHERRY: **ookwemin, -an** *ni*
CHEST
CHEST: my chest **nikaakigan, -an /-kaakigan-/** *nid*
CHEST PAINS: have chest pains while breathing **jakanaamo** *vai*
MIDDLE OF THE CHEST: in the middle of the chest **naawaakigan** *pc*

CHEST OF DRAWERS
CHEST OF DRAWERS: **wiikobijigan, -an** *ni*
CHEW
CHEW: chew s.o. **zhaashaagwam** *vta;* chew s.t. **zhaashaagwandan** *vti;* chew things **zhaashaagwanjige** *vai*
CHEW GUM: **zhaashaagwamikiwe** *vai*
CHEW ON: chew on s.o. **jiichiigwam** *vta;* chew on s.t. **jiichiigwandan** *vti;* chew on things **jiichiigwanjige** *vai*
CHEW SNUFF OR TOBACCO: **biindaakwe** *vai*
CHEW TO BITS: chew s.o. to bits **zhishigwam** *vta;* chew s.t. to bits **zhishigwandan** *vti*
CHEW TOBACCO: **agwanenjige** *vai*
CHEWING GUM
CHEWING GUM: **bigiins, -ag** *na*
CHICKADEE
CHICKADEE: **gijigijigaaneshiinh, -yag** *na*
CHICKEN
CHICKEN: **baaka'aakwenh, -yag** *na*
CHICKEN COOP
CHICKEN COOP: **baaka'aakwenhwigamig, -oon** *ni*
CHICKEN SOUP
CHICKEN SOUP: **baaka'aakwenhwaaboo** *ni*
CHIEF
CHIEF: **ogimaa, -g** *na;* be a chief **ogimaawi** *vai*
MAKE CHIEF: make s.o. chief **ogimaakaw** *vta*
WIFE OF CHIEF OR LEADER: **ogimaakwe, -g** *na*
CHILD
CHILD: **abinoojiinh, -yag** *na;* be a child **abinoojiinyiwi** *vai;* my child **niniijaanis, -ag /-niijaanis-/** *nad*
ELDEST CHILD: **nitamoozhaan, -ag** *na*
HAVE A CHILD: **oniijaanisi** *vai;* have a small child **oniijaanisensi** *vai*
PRETEND TO BE A CHILD: **abinoojiinyikaazo** *vai*
TAKE CARE OF A CHILD: **bamoozhe** *vai;* **ganawendaawaso** *vai*
YOUNGEST CHILD: **ishkwejaagan, -ag** *na*
CHILL
GET A CHILL: **dakaji** *vai*
CHILLED
CHILLED: be chilled **dakamanji'o** *vai*
GET CHILLED EASILY: **wakewaji** *vai*
CHIN
CHIN: my chin **indaamikan, -an /-daamikan-/** *nid*
CHINESE
CHINESE: **aniibiishaabookewinini, -wag** *na;* be Chinese **aniibiishaabookewininiiwi** *vai*
CHIP
CHIP: **biiwega'igan, -an** *ni*
CHIPMUNK
CHIPMUNK: **agongos, -ag** *na*
CHISEL
ICE CHISEL: **eshkan, -an** *ni*
CHOKE
CHOKE: choke on food **bakwenishkaago** *vai;* choke on something stuck in one's throat **ana'o** *vai;* choke s.o. **gibinewen** *vta*
CHOKE WHILE DRINKING: **bakwenibii** *vai*
CHOKECHERRY
CHOKECHERRY: **asasawemin, -an** *ni*
CHOKECHERRY BUSH
CHOKECHERRY BUSH: **asasaweminagaawanzh, -iig** *na*
CHOOSE
CHOOSE: choose s.o. **onaabam** *vta;* choose s.t. **onaabandan** *vti;* choose things **onaabanjige** *vai*
CHOP
CHOP A PIECE OFF: chop a piece off s.o. (as something of wood) **bakwega' /bakwega'w-/** *vta;* chop a piece off s.t. (as something of wood) **bakwega'an** *vti*
CHOP DOWN: chop s.o. down **gawa' /gawa'w-/** *vta;* chop s.t. down **gawa'an** *vti*
CHOP FINE: chop s.o. fine **biisa' /biisa'w-/** *vta;* chop s.t. fine **biisa'an** *vti*
CHOP INTO SMALL PIECES: chop s.o. into small pieces (as something of wood) **baasiga' /baasiga'w-/** *vta;* chop s.t. into small pieces (as something of wood) **baasiga'an** *vti*
CHOP OFF: chop s.o. off **giishka' /giishka'w-/** *vta;* chop s.t. off **giishka'an** *vti*
CHOP OFF WITH AX: chop s.o. off with ax **giishkiga' /giishkiga'w-/** *vta;* chop s.t. off with ax **giishkiga'an** *vti*
CHOP POINTED: chop s.o. pointed **bajiishkiga' /bajiishkiga'w-/** *vta;* chop s.t. pointed **bajiishkiga'an** *vti*
CHOPPED
CHOPPED DOWN: be chopped down **gawa'igaade, gawa'igaademagad** *vii;* **gawa'igaazo** *vai*
CHOSE
CHOSE: be chosen **onaabanjigaade, onaabanjigaademagad** *vii*
CHOSEN
CHOSEN: be chosen **onaabanjigaazo** *vai*
CHRISTIAN
CHRISTIAN: **anama'e-** *pv4, also* **aname-**; be Christian **anami'aa** *vai*
CHRISTMAS
CHRISTMAS: be Christmas **niibaa-anama'e-giizhigad** *vii*
CHURCH
CHURCH: **anama'ewigamig, -oon** *ni, also* **anamewigamig**
CIGARETTE
CIGARETTE: **asemaawipwaagaans, -ag** *na, also* **asemaa-opwaagaans**; **opwaagaans, -ag** *na*
CINNAMON
CINNAMON: **meskwanagekozid** *na-pt*

CIRCLE
DRAW A CIRCLE: **waawiyebii'ige** *vai*
CIRCULAR
CIRCULAR: be circular **waawiyeyaa, waawiyeyaamagad** *vii;* **waawiyezi** *vai*
CIRCUS
CIRCUS: **mamaandaagochigewin, -an** *ni*
CITY
CITY: **gichi-oodena, -wan** *ni*
CLAM
CLAM: **es, -ag** *na*
CLAN
CLAN: my clan **indoodem, -ag /-doodem-/** *nad*
CLAP
CLAP HANDS: clap one's hands **bapasininjii'odizo** *vai*
CLAW
CLAW: my claw **nishkanzh, -iig /-shkanzhy-/** *nad*
CLAY
CLAY: **waabigan** *na*
MADE OF CLAY: be made of clay **waabiganikaade, waabiganikaademagad** *vii*
WHITE CLAY: **waabaabigan** *na*
CLEAN
CLEAN: be clean **biinad** *vii;* **biinizi** *vai;* be clean (as a liquid) **biinaagamin /biinaagami-/** *vii;* clean s.o. **biini'** *vta;* clean s.t. **biinitoon** *vti2;* clean (s.t.) for s.o. **biinitaw** *vta;* clean things **biinichige** *vai*
CLEAN A FISH: **bakazhaawe** *vai*
CLEAN HAND: have a clean hand **biinininjii** *vai*
CLEANED
CLEANED: be cleaned **biinichigaade, biinichigaademagad** *vii;* **biinichigaazo** *vai*
CLEANER
CLEANER: **biinichigewinini, -wag** *na;* cleaner (female) **biinichigewikwe, -g** *na*
CLEAR
CLEAR LAND: **mazhii'ige** *vai*
CLEAR OFF: clear off after a storm **aabaakawad** *vii;* ice clears off the lake **baakibii'an** *vii*
CLEAR SKY: be clear sky **mizhakwad** *vii*
CLEARING
CUT-OVER CLEARING: **mazhii'igan, -an** *ni*
ON THE OTHER SIDE OF THE CLEARING: **agaamaakwaa** *pc*
CLEARLY
SEE CLEARLY: **bagakaabi** *vai;* see s.o. clearly **bagakaabam** *vta;* see s.t. clearly **bagakaabandan** *vti*
CLEAVER
CLEAVER: **giishkada'igan, -an** *ni*
CLERK
CLERK: clerk (female) **ozhibii'igewikwe, -g** *na;* clerk (male) **ozhibii'igewinini, -wag** *na*
CLIFF
CLIFF: be a cliff **giishkadinaa, giishkadinaamagad** *vii*
ROCK CLIFF: **aazhibik, -oon** *ni;* there is a rock cliff **giishkaazhibikaa, giishkaazhibikaamagad** *vii*
CLIMB
CLIMB ACROSS: **aazhawaandawe** *vai*
CLIMB ALONG: **bimaandawe** *vai*
CLIMB DOWN: **niisaandawe** *vai;* climb down fast **niisaandawebizo** *vai*
CLIMB HERE: **biidaandawe** *vai*
CLIMB OVER: **baazhidaandawe** *vai*
CLIMB TO CERTAIN PLACE: climb to a certain place **inaandawe** *vai*
CLIMB UP: **akwaandawe** *vai*
CLIMB UP FAST: **akwaandawebatoo** *vai;* climb up fast (e.g., in an elevator) **akwaandawebizo** *vai*
CLING
CLING: **minjimii** *vai;* cling (as to something stick- or wood-like) **minjimaakwii** *vai*
CLOCK
CLOCK: **diba'igiiziswaan, -ag** *na*
CLOSE
CLOSE: **besho** *pc;* be close **beshowad** *vii*
APPEAR TO BE CLOSE: **beshonaagozi** *vai;* **beshonaagwad** *vii*
THINK TO BE CLOSE: think s.t. to be close **beshwendan** *vti*
CLOSET
CLOSET: **ataasowin, -an** *ni*
CLOT
BLOOD CLOT: **wado, -wag** *na*
CLOTH
CLOTH: **babagiwayaaniigin, -oon** *ni, also* **bagiwayaaniigin**
CLOTH BAG: **bagiwayaaneshkimod, -an** *ni*
COTTON CLOTH: **gidagiigin, -oon** *ni*
WHITE CLOTH: **waabishkiigin, -oon** *ni*
CLOTHES
CLOTHES: item of clothing **biizikiigan, -an** *ni*
CHANGE CLOTHES: change one's clothes **aanzikonaye** *vai;* change s.o. with foot or body (e.g., clothes) **aanzikaw** *vta;* change s.o.'s clothes **aanzikonaye'** *vta;* change s.t. with foot or body (e.g., clothes) **aanzikan** *vti*
PUT ON CLOTHES: put on one's clothes **biizikonaye** *vai*
TAKE OFF CLOTHES: take off one's clothes **giizikonaye** *vai;* take s.o. off the body (e.g., clothes) **giizikaw** *vta;* take s.t. off the body (e.g., clothes) **giizikan** *vti*
WASH CLOTHES: **giziibiiga'ige** *vai*
WEAR NEW CLOTHES: **oshki'o** *vai*
CLOTHES IRON
CLOTHES IRON: **zhooshkwega'igan, -an** *ni*
CLOTHES WRINGER
CLOTHES WRINGER: **ziinaakwa'igan, -an** *ni*
CLOTHESLINE
CLOTHESLINE: **agoojiganeyaab, -iin** *ni*
CLOTHESLINE POLE: **agoojiganaatig, -oon** *ni*

CLOTHESPIN
CLOTHESPIN: **ziinaakwa'igan, -an** *ni*
CLOTHING
CHILDREN'S CLOTHING: item of children's clothing **abinoojiinh-biizikaagan, -an** *ni*
ITEM OF CLOTHING: **biizikiigan, -an** *ni*
MEN'S CLOTHING: item of men's clothing **ininii-biizikiigan** *ni*
WOMEN'S CLOTHING: item of women's clothing **ikwe-biizikiigan** *ni*
CLOUD
CLOUD: **aanakwad, -oon** *ni*
CLOUDS APPROACH: **biidaanakwad** *vii*
CLOUDS GO ALONG: **bimaanakwad** *vii*
CLOUDS GO AWAY: **animaanakwad** *vii*
CLOUDS MOVE ABOUT: **babaamaanakwad** *vii*
CLOUDS SEEN THROUGH: clouds can be seen through **waaseyaanakwad** *vii*
DARK CLOUDS: there are dark clouds **makadeyaanakwad** *vii*
RED CLOUDS: be red clouds **miskwaanakwad** *vii*
STORM CLOUDS: there are storm clouds **zegaanakwad** *vii*
WHITE CLOUDS: there are white clouds **waabishkaanakwad** *vii*
CLOUDY
CLOUDY: be cloudy **ningwaanakwad** *vii*
CLUB
CLUB SUITE CARD: **danens, -ag** *na*
CLUB
BALL-HEADED CLUB: ball-headed club **bikwaakwado-bagamaagan, -an** *ni*
WAR CLUB: war club **bagamaagan, -an** *ni*
COAL
COAL: **akakanzhe** *ni*
COALS
COALS: **akakanzhe** *ni;* be coals **akakanzhekaa, akakanzhekaamagad** *vii*
COAT
COAT: **babiinzikawaagan, -an** *ni*
PUT ON COAT: put on one's coat **biichibabiinzikawaagane** *vai*
TAKE OFF COAT: take off one's coat **giichibabiinzikawaagane** *vai*
WEAR A COAT: **gigibabiinzikawaagane** *vai*
COFFEE
COFFEE: **makade-mashkikiwaaboo** *ni;* **gaapii** *ni*
COIN
COIN: **zhooniyaans, -ag** *na;* **zhooniyaawaabik, -oog** *na*
COLD
COLD: be cold (as a liquid) **dakaagamin /dakaagami-/** *vii*
CAN'T TAKE THE COLD: **wakewaji** *vai*
COLD HAND: have a cold hand **dakininjii** *vai*
COLD HOUSE: be cold (as a house or room) **dakate, dakatemagad** *vii*
COLD RAIN: be cold rain **dakibiisaa, dakibiisaamagad** *vii*
COLD ROOM: be cold (as a house or room) **dakate, dakatemagad** *vii*
COLD WATER: **dakib** *ni*
COLD WEATHER: be cold (weather) **gisinaa, gisinaamagad** *vii*
COLD WIND: be a cold wind **dakaanimad** *vii*
FEEL COLD: **biingeji** *vai;* **dakamanji'o** *vai;* **giikaji** *vai*
HAVE A COLD: **dakaji** *vai*
WAKE FROM BEING COLD: **amadaji** *vai*
COLD
GET A COLD: **mizhaakigwe** *vai*
HAVE A COLD: **agigokaa** *vai*
COLLAPSE
COLLAPSE FROM OVERWORK: **gawanokii** *vai*
COLLAR
COLLAR: **apigwayawegwaajigan, -an** *ni*
COLLECT
COLLECT: collect s.o. **asigin** *vta;* **maawanji'** *vta;* collect s.t. **asiginan** *vti;* **maawanjitoon** *vti2*
COLLECT MONEY AS A DONATION: **asigizhooniyaawe** *vai*
COLLEGE
COLLEGE: **gabe-gikendaasoowigamig, -oon** *ni*
COLLISION
COLLISION: they have a collision **bitaakoshkodaadiwag /bitaakoshkodaadi-/** *vai*
COLOR
GOOD COLOR: be a good color **minwaande, minwaandemagad** *vii;* **minwaanzo** *vai*
COLORED
COLORED A CERTAIN WAY: be colored a certain way **inaande, inaandemagad** *vii;* **inaanzo** *vai*
COMB
COMB: **binaakwaan, -an** *ni;* comb one's hair **binaakwe'o** *vai;* **nazikwe'o** *vai;* comb s.o. **binaakwe' /binaakwe'w-/** *vta;* **nazikwe' /nazikwe'w-/** *vta*
COME
COME: **bi-izhaa** *vai;* come (as time) **ojijise, ojijisemagad** *vii*
COME AS WIND FROM A CERTAIN PLACE: come as wind from a certain direction **ondaanimad** *vii*
COME ASHORE: **agwaataa** *vai;* come ashore in a boat **agwaa'o** *vai, also* **agwaa'am**; come ashore in canoe **mizhagaa** *vai*
COME FROM A CERTAIN PLACE: **ondaadad** *vii;* **ondaadizi** *vai;* **onjibaa** *vai;* **onjii** *vai;* come from a certain place (as smoke) **ondaabate, ondaabatemagad** *vii*
COME FROM A CERTAIN PLACE CRYING: **ondademo** *vai*
COME HERE: come here! **ondaas** *pc;* **ondaashaan** *pc*
COME IN: come into where s.o. is **biindigaw** *vta*
COME IN A BOAT: **biidaasamishkaa** *vai*
COME IN ANGER: **biijigidaazo** *vai*

COME IN FEAR: **biidaanimizi** *vai*
COME INSIDE: **biindige** *vai*
COME INTO VIEW: **bi-naagozi** *vai;* **bi-naagwad** *vii*
COME LAUGHING: **biidaapi** *vai*
COME LEAVING TRACKS: **biijikawe** *vai*
COME MAKING NOISE: come making noise (e.g., thunder) **biidwewidam** *vai2*
COME OUT OF THE WOODS: **bapaakwa'am** *vai2*
COME OUT OVER A HILL: **zaagajiwe** *vai*
COME SPEAKING: **biidwewidam** *vai2*
COME SUDDENLY INTO VIEW: come suddenly into view as from around a corner **zaagewe** *vai*
COME TELLING NEWS: **biidaajimo** *vai*
COME TO AN END: **ishkwaase, ishkwaasemagad** *vii*
COME TO BE: **bagami-ayaa, bagami-ayaamagad** *vii*
COME TO PASS: **bagami-ayaa, bagami-ayaamagad** *vii*
COME UP: come up to the surface of the water **mooshkamo** *vai*
COME UP TO: come up to s.o. **odish /odiS-/** *vta;* come up to s.t. **oditan** *vti*
COME WITH A LIGHT: **biidaazakwanenjige** *vai*
RAIN COMES: **biijibiisaa, biijibiisaamagad** *vii*

COME ON
COME ON: come on! **ambe** *pc;* **daga** *pc;* **naasanaa** *pc*

COME TO
COME TO: **aabaakawizi** *vai;* **mikawi** *vai*

COMEDY
COMEDY: be a comedy **gagiibaadaatese, gagiibaadaatesemagad** *vii*

COMFORTABLY
LIE COMFORTABLY: **minoshin** *vai*
SIT COMFORTABLY: **minwabi** *vai*

COMICAL
COMICAL: **wawiyazh** *pc*
THINK COMICAL: think s.o. comical **wawiyadenim** *vta*

COMING UP TO
COMING UP TO IN TIME: **ani-** *pv2, also* **ni-**

COMMISSION
COMMISSION: **anookii** *vai;* commission s.o. **anoozh /anooN-/** *vta*

COMMODITY FOOD
COMMODITY FOOD: **ashandiwin, -an** *ni*

COMMODITY STORE
COMMODITY STORE: **ashangewigamig, -oon** *ni*

COMMON PIN
COMMON PIN: **oshtigwaanzhaabonigan, -an** *ni*

COMPANION
COMPANION: **wiijiiwaagan, -ag** *na;* my companion **niwiidigemaagan, -ag /-wiidigemaagan-/** *na*

COMPANY
IN COMPANY WITH: **wiiji-** *pv4*

COMPASS
COMPASS: compass (drawing instrument) **waawiyebii'igan, -an** *ni*

COMPLETE
COMPLETE: **giizhi-** *pv4*

COMPLETELY
COMPLETELY: **wawiinge** *pc;* **wenda-** *pv4*

COMPUTER
COMPUTER: **mazinaabikiwebinigan, -an** *ni*

CONCRETE
MADE OF CONCRETE: be made of concrete **waabiganikaade, waabiganikaademagad** *vii*

CONCRETE ROAD
CONCRETE ROAD: **asinii-miikana, -n** *ni*

CONFUSE
CONFUSE: confuse s.o. by speech **wanim** *vta*

CONFUSED
CONFUSED: be confused **giiwashkweyendam** *vai2;* **wanaanimizi** *vai*

CONQUER
CONQUER: conquer s.o. **mamaazhi'** *vta;* conquer s.t. **mamaazhitoon** *vti2*

CONSCIOUSNESS
REGAIN CONSCIOUSNESS: **mikawi** *vai*

CONSEQUENTLY
CONSEQUENTLY: **indawaaj** *pc*

CONSERVATION OFFICER
CONSERVATION OFFICER: **wiiyaasi-dakoniwewinini, -wag** *na*

CONSIDER
CONSIDER: **maaminonendam** *vai2;* **naanaagadawendam** *vai2;* consider s.o. **maaminonenim** *vta;* **naanaagadawenim** *vta;* consider s.t. **maaminonendan** *vti;* **naanaagadawendan** *vti*

CONSIDERATION
GIVE TOO MUCH CONSIDERATION: **onzaamendam** *vai2*

CONSTIPATED
CONSTIPATED: be constipated **gibishaganzhii** *vai*

CONSTRICT
CONSTRICT: **wiibwaa, wiibwaamagad** *vii*

CONTEST
BEAT IN A CONTEST: beat s.o. in a contest **bakinaw** *vta;* beat people in a contest **bakinaage** *vai*

CONTINUALLY
CONTINUALLY: **apane** *pc;* **aabiji-** *pv4*

CONTRADICT
CONTRADICT: **aagonwetam** *vai2;* contradict s.o. **aagonwetaw** *vta;* contradict s.t. **aagonwetan** *vti*

CONTRARY
ACT CONTRARY TO INSTRUCTIONS: act contrary to s.o.'s instructions **gagaanzitaw** *vta*

CONTROL
CONTROL: control s.o. **dibenim** *vta;* control s.t. **dibendan** *vti*

CONTROLLED
CONTROLLED: be controlled **dibendaagozi** *vai;* **dibendaagwad** *vii*
CONVENE
CONVENE A COUNCIL: **zagaswe'iwe** *vai*
CONVERSE
CONVERSE: converse with s.o. **gaganoozh /gaganooN-/** *vta;* they converse with each other **gaganoonidiwag /gaganoonidi-/** *vai*
CONVINCE
CONVINCE: convince s.o. **gagaanzom** *vta*
COOK
COOK: cook (female) **jiibaakwewikwe, -g** *na;* cook (male) **jiibaakwewinini, -wag** *na;* **giizizekwe** *vai;* **jiibaakwe** *vai;* cook s.o. **jiibaakwaazh /jiibaakwaaN-/** *vta;* cook s.t. **jiibaakwaadan** *vti;* cook (s.t.) for s.o. **giizizamaw** *vta*
COOK A CERTAIN WAY: cook (something) a certain way **inizekwe** *vai;* cook s.o. a certain way **iniz /inizw-/** *vta;* cook s.t. a certain way **inizan** *vti*
COOK BY BOILING: cook s.o. by boiling **gabaashim** *vta;* cook s.t. by boiling **gabaatoon** *vti2*
COOK IN A HURRY: **ojaanimizekwe** *vai*
COOK ON THE COALS: cook (s.t.) on the coals **akakanzhebwe** *vai+o*
COOK OVER A FIRE: cook (s.t.) over a fire **abwe** *vai+o;* cook s.o. over a fire **abwaazh /abwaaN-/** *vta;* cook s.t. over a fire **abwaadan** *vti*
COOK TENDER: cook s.o. tender **nookiz /nookizw-/** *vta;* cook s.t. tender **nookizan** *vti*
COOK UNDER THE ASHES: cook (s.t.) under the ashes **ningwa'abwe** *vai+o*
COOK WELL: **minozekwe** *vai;* cook s.o. well **minoz /minozw-/** *vta;* cook s.t. well **minozan** *vti*
COOK WITH: cook s.o. with something else **dagoz /dagozw-/** *vta;* cook s.t. with something else **dagozan** *vti*
DONE COOKING: be done cooking **giizhide, giizhidemagad** *vii;* **giizizo** *vai, also* **giizhizo**
FINISH COOKING: finish cooking s.o. **giiziz /giizizw-/** *vta;* finish cooking s.t. **giizizan** *vti*
COOK SHACK
COOK SHACK: **jiibaakwewigamig, -oon** *ni*
COOKED
COOKED TENDER: be cooked tender **nookide, nookidemagad** *vii;* **nookizo** *vai*
COOKED WITH: be cooked with something else **dagode, dagodemagad** *vii;* **dagozo** *vai*
INCOMPLETELY COOKED: be incompletely cooked **ashkide, ashkidemagad** *vii;* **ashkizo** *vai*
WELL COOKED: be well cooked **minode, minodemagad** *vii;* **minozo** *vai*
COOKIE
COOKIE: **bakwezhigaans, -ag** *na*
COOKING POT
COOKING POT: **jiibaakwewakik, -oog** *na*
COOL
COOL: **dakise** *vai;* **dakise, dakisemagad** *vii;* be cool (of a thing) **dakaa, dakaamagad** *vii;* **dakizi** *vai*
COOL OFF: **dakishin** *vai;* **dakisin** *vii;* cool off (as a liquid) **dakaagamisin** *vii*
COOL WEATHER: be cool (weather) **dakaayaa, dakaayaamagad** *vii, also* **dakiayaa**
SET TO COOL: set s.o. to cool **dakishim** *vta;* set s.t. to cool **dakisidoon** *vti2*
COOLED
COOLED BY THE WIND: be cooled by the wind **dakaashi** *vai;* **dakaasin** *vii*
COOP
CHICKEN COOP: **baaka'aakwenhwigamig, -oon** *ni*
COOT
COOT: **aajigade, -g** *na*
COPPER
COPPER: (piece of) copper **miskwaabik** *ni*
COPY
COPY IN WRITING: copy s.t. in writing **naasaabibii'an** *vti;* copy things in writing **naasaabibii'ige** *vai*
CORN
CORN: **mandaamin, -ag** *na*
EAR OF CORN: **mandaaminaak, -oon** *ni*
KERNEL OF CORN: **mandaamin, -ag** *na*
CORNFIELD
CORNFIELD: **mandaamini-gitigaan, -an** *ni*
CORNMEAL
CORNMEAL: **biisiboojigan** *na*
CORN SOUP
CORN SOUP: **mandaaminaaboo** *ni*
CORNER
CORNER OF A ROOM: be a corner of a room **jaangate, jaangatemagad** *vii*
CORNSTALK
CORNSTALK: **mandaaminashk, -oon** *ni*
CORRECT
CORRECT: **gwayak** *pc;* correct? **naayanh** *pc*
CORRECTLY
CORRECTLY: **weweni** *pc*
BEAD CORRECTLY: bead s.t. correctly (on a loom) **gwayakwaabidoo'an** *vti;* bead things correctly (on a loom) **gwayakwaabidoo'ige** *vai*
LIE CORRECTLY: **gwayakoshin** *vai;* **gwayakosin** *vii*
SPEAK CORRECTLY: **gwayakowe** *vai*
THINK CORRECTLY: **gwayakwendam** *vai2*
THREAD CORRECTLY: thread s.t. correctly **gwayakwaabidoo'an** *vti*
WRITE CORRECTLY: **gwayakobii'ige** *vai;* write s.t. correctly **gwayakobii'an** *vti*
COST
HAVE A CERTAIN COST: **inaginde, inagindemagad** *vii;* **inaginzo** *vai*

COTTAGE
COTTAGE: **niibinishiiwigamig, -oon** *ni*
COTTON
COTTON CLOTH: **babagiwayaaniigin, -oon** *ni, also* **bagiwayaaniigin; gidagiigin, -oon** *ni*
COTTONTAIL RABBIT
COTTONTAIL RABBIT: **manidoo-waabooz, -oog** *na*
COUCH
COUCH: **genwaakwak apabiwin** *ni;* **ginwaako-apabiwin, -an** *ni*
COUGH
COUGH: **ozosodam** *vai2*
COUGH MEDICINE
COUGH MEDICINE: **ozosodamoo-mashkiki** *ni*
COULD
COULD: could *modal* **daa-** *pv1*
COUNCIL
CONVENE A COUNCIL: **zagaswe'iwe** *vai*
COUNCIL MEETING: they have a council meeting **zagaswe'idiwag /zagaswe'idi-/** *vai*
COUNCILLOR
COUNCILLOR: **gaagiigidoowinini, -wag** *na;* **giigidoowinini, -wag** *na;* **wegimaawabid** *na-pt;* **zagaswe'idiiwinini, -wag** *na*
COUNT
COUNT: **agindaaso** *vai;* count s.o. **agim** *vta;* count s.t. **agindan** *vti;* count (s.t.) for s.o. **agindamaw** *vta;* count (s.t.) for people **agindamaage** *vai*
COUNT IN: count s.o. in **dagwagim** *vta;* count s.t. in **dagwagindan** *vti*
COUNT OVER: **aandaginzo** *vai;* count s.o. over **aandagim** *vta;* count s.t. over **aandagindan** *vti*
COUNTED
COUNTED: be counted **aginjigaade, aginjigaademagad** *vii;* **aginjigaazo** *vai;* **aginzo** *vai*
COUNTED IN: be counted in **dagwaginde, dagwagindemagad** *vii;* **dagwaginzo** *vai*
COUNTRY
COUNTRY: **aki, -in** *ni*
CHANGE COUNTRIES: **aandakii** *vai*
RETURN TO OWN COUNTRY: return to one's own country **giiwekii** *vai*
COURAGEOUS
COURAGEOUS: be courageous **mangide'e** *vai*
COURT
IN COURT: be in court **onaakonige** *vai*
COURT MATTER
COURT MATTER: be a court matter **dibaakonigaade** *vai*
COURTHOUSE
COURTHOUSE: **dibaakonigewigamig, -oon** *ni*
COUSIN
CROSS-COUSIN: my (female's) female cross-cousin (mother's brother's daughter or father's sister's daughter) **indaangoshenh, -yag /-daangosheny-/** *nad;* my (male's) male cross-cousin (male's father's sister's son or male's mother's brother's son) **niitaawis, -ag /-iitaawis-/** *nad;* my cross-cousin of the opposite sex **niinimoshenh, -yag /-iinimosheny-/** *nad*
PARALLEL COUSIN: my older male parallel cousin **nisayenh, -yag /-sayeny-/** *nad;* my older female parallel cousin **nimisenh, -yag /-miseny-/** *nad;* my parallel cousin of the opposite sex **indawemaa, -g /-dawemaaw-/** *nad;* my younger parallel cousin **nishiime, -yag /-shiimey-/** *nad*
COVER
COVER: cover s.o. **badagwana' /badagwana'w-/** *vta;* cover s.t. **badagwana'an** *vti;* cover things **badagwana'ige** *vai*
COVER WITH BLANKETS: cover s.o. with blankets **agwazhe'** *vta*
COVER WITH BODY: cover s.o. with body **badagoshkaw** *vta;* cover s.t. with body **badagoshkan** *vti*
SHARE COVER WITH: share a cover with s.o. **wiidagwazhem** *vta*
COVERED
COVERED: be covered **badagwana'igaade, badagwana'igaademagad** *vii;* **badagwana'igaazo** *vai*
COVERED WITH BLANKETS: be covered with blankets **agwazhe** *vai*
LIE WITH FACE COVERED: lie with one's face covered **badagwiingweshin** *vai*
COVERING
COVERING: **agwazhe'on, -an** *ni*
COW
COW: **bizhiki, -wag** *na*
COWARDLY
COWARDLY: be cowardly **zhaagode'e** *vai*
COWHIDE
COWHIDE: **bizhikiwayaan, -ag** *na*
CRAB
CRAB: **ashaageshiinh, -yag** *na*
CRACK
CRACK: crack (e.g., glass or china) **baasikaa, baasikaamagad** *vii;* crack on impact **baasishin** *vai;* **baasisin** *vii;* crack s.o. **baasishim** *vta;* crack s.t. **baasisidoon** *vti2*
CRACK APART: **daashkikaa, daashkikaamagad** *vii*
CRACK BY HEAT: crack s.o. by heat **baasiz /baasizw-/** *vta;* crack s.t. by heat **baasizan** *vti*
CRACK FROM HEAT: **baaside, baasidemagad** *vii;* **baasizo** *vai*
CRACK IN THE ICE: there is a crack in the ice **daashkikwadin** *vii*
CRACK USING SOMETHING: crack s.o. using something **baasa' /baasa'w-/** *vta;* crack s.t. using something **baasa'an** *vti;* crack things using something **baasa'ige** *vai*
FALL AND CRACK HEAD: fall and crack one's head **baasindibeshin** *vai*

HEARD CRACKING: be heard cracking (as ice) **madwekwadin** *vii*

CRACKER

CRACKER: **bakwezhigaans, -ag** *na*

CRACKLINGS

CRACKLINGS: **zaasigan, -ag** *na*

CRADLE BOARD

CRADLE BOARD: **dikinaagan, -an** *ni*

BABY IN A CRADLE BOARD: **dakobinaawaswaan, -ag** *na*

HAVE A BABY IN A CRADLE BOARD: **dakobinaawaso** *vai*

IN CRADLE BOARD: be in a cradle board **dakobizo** *vai*

CRADLE BOARD FOOTREST

CRADLE BOARD FOOTREST: **apizideyaakwa'igan, -an** *ni*

CRADLE BOARD WRAPPER

CRADLE BOARD WRAPPER: **dikineyaab, -iin** *ni*

CRAFT

CRAFT: **anokaajigan, -an** *ni*

CRANBERRY

HIGHBUSH CRANBERRY: **aniibiimin, -an** *ni*

LOWBUSH CRANBERRY: **mashkiigimin, -ag** *na*

CRANBERRY BUSH

HIGHBUSH CRANBERRY BUSH: **aniibiiminagaawanzh, -iig** *na*

LOWBUSH CRANBERRY BUSH: **mashkiigiminagaawanzh, -iin** *ni*

CRANE

SANDHILL CRANE: **ajijaak, -wag** *na*

CRAPPIE

CRAPPIE: **gidagagwadaashi, -wag** *na*

CRATE

CRATE: **mitigo-makak, -oon** *ni*

CRAWL

ARRIVE CRAWLING: **bagamoode** *vai*

CRAWL A CERTAIN WAY: **inoode** *vai*

CRAWL ABOUT: **babaamoode** *vai*

CRAWL ALONG: **bimoode** *vai*

CRAWL AWAY: **animoode** *vai*

CRAWL FROM A CERTAIN PLACE: **ondoode** *vai*

CRAWL HERE: **biidoode** *vai*

CRAWL IN: **biindoode** *vii*

CRAWL IN A TIGHT PLACE: **zhegoode** *vai*

CRAWL OFF: **maadoode** *vai*

CRAWL OUT: **zaagidoode** *vai*

CRAWL TO A CERTAIN PLACE: **inoode** *vai*

CRAYFISH

CRAYFISH: **ashaageshiinh, -yag** *na*

CRAZY

CRAZY: be crazy **giiwanaadizi** *vai*

CREAK

CREAK: **giziibwewe** *vai;* **giziibwewe, giziibwewemagad** *vii;* **giziibweweshkaa** *vai;* **giziibweweshkaa, giziibweweshkaamagad** *vii*

CREAK IN THE WIND: **giziibweweyaashi** *vai;* **giziibweweyaasin** *vii*

CREDIT

GET CREDIT: **mazina'ige** *vai;* get credit from s.o. **mazina'amaw** *vta*

CREE

CREE: **omashkiigoo, -g** *na*

SPEAK CREE: **omashkiigoomo** *vai*

CREEK

CREEK: **ziibiins, -an** *ni*

CREEP

CREEP AWAY: **giimaadoode** *vai*

CRISP

BURNT CRISP: be burnt crisp **onzaamaakide, onzaamaakidemagad** *vii;* **onzaamaakizo** *vai*

CROOKED KNIFE

CROOKED KNIFE: **waagikomaan, -an** *ni*

CROSS

CROSS: **aazhideyaatig, -oog** *na*

CROSSCUT SAW

CROSSCUT SAW: **giishkiboojigan, -an** *ni*

CROSSED

SIT WITH LEGS CROSSED: **aazhoogaadebi** *vai*

CROW

CROW: **aandeg, -wag** *na*

CRUMBLE

CRUMBLE: crumble s.o. **biisibizh /biisibiN-/** *vta;* crumble s.t. **biisibidoon** *vti2*

CRUNCH

CRUNCH IN MOUTH: crunch s.o. in mouth **gaapam** *vta;* crunch s.t. in mouth **gaapandan** *vti;* crunch things in mouth **gaapanjige** *vai*

CRUSH

CRUSH BY FOOT OR BODY: crush s.o. by foot or body **zhishigoshkaw** *vta;* crush s.t. by foot or body **zhishigoshkan** *vti*

CRUSH WITH HANDS: crush s.o. with hands **zhishigobizh /zhishigobiN-/** *vta;* crush s.t. with hands **zhishigobidoon** *vti2*

CRUST

CRUST ON THE SNOW: there is a crust on the snow **onaabanad** *vii*

CRUTCH

CRUTCH: **aajiningwa'on, -an** *ni;* **edawi-zaka'on, -an** *ni*

USE CRUTCHES: **edawi-zaka'o** *vai*

CRY

CRY: **mawi** *vai;* cry for s.o. **mawim** *vta;* cry for s.t. **mawindan** *vti*

COME FROM A CERTAIN PLACE CRYING: **ondademo** *vai*

CRY A CERTAIN WAY: **inademo** *vai*

CRY A LITTLE: **mawiinsiwi** *vai*

CRY FOR A CERTAIN REASON: **ondademo** *vai*

CRY TO GO ALONG: **mookawaakii** *vai*

CRY WALKING ALONG: **bimademo** *vai*

GO ABOUT CRYING: **babaamademo** *vai*

GO TO A CERTAIN PLACE CRYING: **inademo** *vai*

MAKE CRY: make s.o. cry **moo'** *vta*
PRETEND TO CRY: **mawiikaazo** *vai*
STOP CRYING: **giishkowe** *vai*

CRYBABY
CRYBABY: be a crybaby **mawishki** *vai*

CUB
BEAR CUB: **makoons, -ag** *na*

CUCUMBER
CUCUMBER: **bipakoombens, -an** *ni*

CUFF
MOCCASIN CUFF: **apiganegwaajigan, -an** *ni, also* **apigwanegwaason, -an**

CULTURE HERO
CULTURE HERO: name of **aadizookaan** character viewed as culture hero and trickster **Wenabozho** *na, also* **Nenabozho***

CUP
CUP: **onaagaans, -an** *ni*

CUPBOARD
CUPBOARD: **ataasowin, -an** *ni*

CUPFUL
CERTAIN NUMBER OF CUPFULS: a certain number of cupfuls **dasonaagaans** *pc*

CURE
CURE OVER A FIRE: cure s.o. over a fire **abwewas /abwewasw-/** *vta;* cure s.t. over a fire **abwewasan** *vti;* cure things over a fire **abwewasige** *vai*

CURL
CURL HAIR BY HEAT: curl s.o.'s hair by heat **babiizigaakiz /babiizigaakizw-/** *vta*

CURLY
CURLY HAIR: have curly hair **babiizigindibe** *vai*

CURRENT
DRIFT ALONG ON CURRENT: **bimaaboode, bimaaboodemagad** *vii;* **bimaaboono** *vai*
DRIFT OFF ON THE CURRENT: **maadaaboode, maadaaboodemagad** *vii;* **maadaaboono** *vai*

CURTAIN
CURTAIN: **gibiiga'igan, -an** *ni*

CURTAINED
CURTAINED: be curtained **gibiiga'igaade, gibiiga'igaademagad** *vii*

CUSHION
CUSHION: **apisijigan, -an** *ni*

CUSTOM
HAVE A CERTAIN CUSTOM: **izhitwaa** *vai*
IT WAS THE CUSTOM TO: it was the custom to... **iko** *pc, also* **ko**

CUT
CUT: cut things **giishkizhige** *vai;* cut oneself **giishkizhodizo** *vai*
CUT A CERTAIN WAY: cut s.o. a certain way **inizh /inizhw-/** *vta;* cut s.t. a certain way **inizhan** *vti*
CUT A PIECE OFF: cut a piece off s.o. **bakwezh /bakwezhw-/** *vta;* cut a piece off s.t. **bakwezhan** *vti*
CUT ACCIDENTALLY: cut s.o. accidentally **bitizh /bitizhw-/** *vta;* cut s.t. accidentally **bitizhan** *vti*
CUT CARDS: **bakwenige** *vai*
CUT FIREWOOD: **manise** *vai;* cut s.t. as firewood **manisaadan** *vti;* cut (s.t.) as firewood for s.o. **manisaw** *vta*
CUT FRINGE: cut fringe in s.o. **niisiiwezh /niisiiwezhw-/** *vta;* cut fringe in s.t. **niisiiwezhan** *vti*
CUT HAIR: **giishkikozhiwe** *vai*
CUT INTO STRIPS: cut s.t. into strips **baanizhan** *vti*
CUT LONG: cut s.o. long (as something string-like) **ginwaabiigizh /ginwaabiigizhw-/** *vta;* cut s.t. long (as something string-like) **ginwaabiigizhan** *vti*
CUT MEAT INTO STRIPS: cut meat into strips for preservation **baanizhaawe** *vai*
CUT NAILS: cut one's own nails **giishkiganzhiikonidizo** *vai*
CUT OFF: cut s.o. off **giishkizh /giishkizhw-/** *vta;* cut s.t. off **giishkizhan** *vti;* cut things off **giishkizhige** *vai*
CUT OUT: cut s.o. out **mamizh /mamizhw-/** *vta;* cut s.t. out **mamizhan** *vti*
CUT SHORT: cut s.o. short (as something string-like) **dakwaabiigizh /dakwaabiigizhw-/** *vta;* cut s.t. short (as something string-like) **dakwaabiigizhan** *vti*
CUT STRAIGHT: cut s.o. straight **gwayakozh /gwayakozhw-/** *vta;* cut s.t. straight **gwayakozhan** *vti*
CUT THROUGH: cut through s.o. **giishkizh /giishkizhw-/** *vta;* **giishkizhan** *vti*
CUT TIMBER: **giishka'aakwe** *vai*
CUT TO PIECES: cut s.o. to pieces **bigishkizh /bigishkizhw-/** *vta;* cut s.t. to pieces **bigishkizhan** *vti*
CUT TO SHAPE: cut s.o. to shape **onikozh /onikoN-/** *vta;* cut s.t. to shape **onikodan** *vti*
GET CUT FALLING: **giishkishin** *vai*
MAKE A CUT: make a cut on s.o. **beshizh /beshizhw-/** *vta;* make a cut on s.t. **beshizhan** *vti*

CUTE
CUTE: be cute **wawiyadendaagwad** *vii*
CONSIDERED CUTE: be considered cute **wawiyadendaagozi** *vai*
LOOK CUTE: **wawiyazhinaagozi** *vai;* **wawiyazhinaagwad** *vii*
SOUND CUTE: **wawiyazhitaagozi** *vai;* **wawiyazhitaagwad** *vii*
THINK CUTE: think s.o. cute **wawiyadenim** *vta*

D

DAKOTA
DAKOTA: Dakota (Sioux) **bwaan, -ag** *na*
DAKOTA WOMAN: **bwaanikwe, -g** *na*
SPEAK DAKOTA: **bwaanimo** *vai;* speak Dakota to s.o. **bwaanimotaw** *vta*

DAM
DAM: **gibaakwa'igan, -an** *ni;* dam s.o. **gibaakwa' /gibaakwa'w-/** *vta;* dam s.t. **gibaakwa'an** *vti;* dam things **gibaakwa'ige** *vai*

DAMAGE
DAMAGE: damage s.o. **banaaji'** *vta;* damage s.t. **banaajitoon** *vti2*
DAMAGE WITH HANDS: damage s.o. with hands **banaajibizh /banaajibiN-/** *vta;* damage s.t. with hands **banaajibidoon** *vti2*

DAMAGED
DAMAGED: be damaged **banaadad** *vii;* **banaadizi** *vai*

DAMMED
DAMMED: be shut (as or as with something stick- or wood-like) **gibaakwa'igaade, gibaakwa'igaademagad** *vii*

DAMP
DAMP: be damp **zhakaa, zhakaamagad** *vii;* **zhakizi** *vai;* be damp (as something sheet-like) **zhakiigad** *vii;* **zhakiigizi** *vai*

DANCE
DANCE: **niimi** *vai;* dance a war dance **bwaanzhii-niimi** *vai;* dance for s.o. **niimikaw** *vta;* they dance **niimi'idiwag /niimi'idi-/** *vai;* they dance a war dance **bwaanzhii-niimi'idiwag /bwaanzhii-niimi'idi-/** *vai;* war dance **bwaanzhii-niimi'idiwin, -an** *ni;* dance for people (for a purpose) **niimikaage** *vai*
DANCE ABOUT: **babaamishimo** *vai*
DANCE ALONG: **bimishimo** *vai*
DANCE AWAY: **animishimo** *vai*
DANCE IN A CERTAIN PLACE: **dazhishimo** *vai*
DANCE INSIDE: dance inside (as in a Grand Entry) **biindigeshimo** *vai*
DANCE THE WOMEN'S DANCE: **ikwe-niimi** *vai;* they dance the women's dance **ikwe-niimi'idiwag /ikwe-niimi'idi-/** *vai*
DANCE WITH: dance with s.o. **wiijishimotaw** *vta*
GIVE A DANCE: **niimi'iwe** *vai*
MAKE DANCE: make s.o. dance **niimi'** *vta*
WOMEN'S DANCE: **ikwe-niimi'idiwin, -an** *ni*

DANCE BELL
DANCE BELL: **zhinawa'oojigan, -an** *ni*

DANCE BUSTLE
DANCE BUSTLE: **bimoonjigan, -an** *ni*

DANCE HALL
DANCE HALL: **niimi'idiiwigamig, -oon** *ni*

DANCE OUTFIT
DANCE OUTFIT: **bwaanzhiiwi'on, -an** *ni*
WEAR A DANCE OUTFIT: **bwaanzhiiwi'o** *vai*

DANCE SONG
DANCE SONG: **niimi'idii-nagamon, -an** *ni*

DANDRUFF
DANDRUFF: **wiinishagaandibaan** *ni*

DANGER
DANGER: be danger **aanimad** *vii*
THINK TO BE IN DANGER: think s.o. to be in danger **naniizaanenim** *vta*

DANGEROUS
DANGEROUS: be dangerous **naniizaanad** *vii;* **naniizaanizi** *vai*
CONSIDER DANGEROUS: consider s.o. dangerous **naniizaanenim** *vta;* consider s.t. dangerous **naniizaanendan** *vti*
CONSIDERED DANGEROUS: be considered dangerous **naniizaanendaagwad** *vii;* **zegendaagozi** *vai;* **zegendaagwad** *vii*

DARK
DARK: be dark **bishagiishkaa, bishagiishkaamagad** *vii;* **dibiki-ayaa** *vai;* **makadewaa, makadewaamagad** *vii;* **makadewizi** *vai;* be dark (as a liquid) **makadewaagamin /makadewaagami-/** *vii*
DARK AS NIGHT: be dark as night **gashkii-dibik-ayaa, gashkii-dibik-ayaamagad** *vii*
DARK AT NIGHT: be very dark at night **gashkii-dibikad** *vii*
DARK COLORED: be dark colored **bishagiishkaande, bishagiishkaandemagad** *vii;* **bishagiishkaanzo** *vai*
DARK HOUSE: be dark (as in a room or house) **dibikate, dibikatemagad** *vii*
DARK INDOORS: be dark indoors **bishagiishkate, bishagiishkatemagad** *vii*
DARK ROOM: be dark (as in a room or house) **dibikate, dibikatemagad** *vii*

DARKENED
DARKENED: be darkened (e.g. the moon or sun in an eclipse) **aateyaabikishin** *vai*

DATE
CERTAIN DATE: be a certain date **daso-giizhigad** *vii*
CERTAIN DATE OF THE MONTH: be a certain date of the month **inaginzo** *vai*

DAUGHTER
DAUGHTER: my daughter **indaanis, -ag /-daanis-/** *nad, also* **indaan**
HAVE A DAUGHTER: **odaani** *vai;* **odaanisi** *vai*

DAUGHTER-IN-LAW
DAUGHTER-IN-LAW: **na'aanganikwe, -g** *na*

DAWN
DAWN: be dawn **waaban** *vii*
DAWN COMES: **biidaaban** *vii*
LIGHT AT DAWN: be light at dawn **waaseyaaban** *vii*

WORK UNTIL DAWN: **waabananokii** *vai*

DAY

DAY: **giizhig** *ni;* be day **giizhigad** *vii*

ABSENT A CERTAIN NUMBER OF DAYS: be absent a certain number of days **dasogonendi** *vai*

ALL DAY: **gabe-giizhik** *pc*

BAD DAY: be a bad day **maazhi-giizhigad** *vii*

CERTAIN DAY OF THE MONTH: be a certain day of the month **dasogonagizi** *vai*

CERTAIN DAY OF THE WEEK: be a certain day of the week **izhi-giizhigad** *vii*

CERTAIN NUMBER OF DAYS: a certain number of days **daso-giizhik** *pc;* **dasogon** *pc;* be a certain number of days **dasogonagad** *vii*

CERTAIN NUMBER OF DAYS OLD: be a certain number of days old **dasogonagizi** *vai*

DAY AFTER TOMORROW: **awas-waabang** *pc*

DAY BEFORE YESTERDAY: **awasonaago** *pc*

EVERY DAY: **endaso-giizhik** *pc*

GONE A CERTAIN NUMBER OF DAYS: be gone a certain number of days **dasogonendi** *vai*

NICE DAY: be a nice day **mino-giizhigad** *vii*

SO LATE IN THE DAY: be so late in the day **apiichi-giizhigad** *vii*

THE FIRST DAY: be the first day (of a month) **maadaginzo** *vai*

DAYBREAK

DAYBREAK: be daybreak **biidaaban** *vii*

DEAD

DEAD: be dead **nibo** *vai*

HAVE A FEAST HONORING THE DEAD: **jiibenaake** *vai*

DEAF

DEAF: be deaf **gagiibishe** *vai;* be deaf (in one ear) **gibishe** *vai*

DEAL

DEAL: deal cards **oninige** *vai;* deal s.o. (e.g., cards) **onin** *vta*

DEATH

BEAT TO DEATH: beat s.o. to death **niiwana' /niiwana'w-/** *vta*

HAVE A DEATH IN FAMILY: have a death in one's family **nibooke** *vai*

DEBT

GO COLLECT A DEBT: **naadazina'ige** *vai*

GO INTO DEBT: **mazina'ige** *vai*

DECEIVE

DECEIVE: deceive s.o. **wayezhim** *vta;* deceive s.o. in speech **giiwanim** *vta;* deceive people **wayezhinge** *vai*

DECEMBER

DECEMBER: **manidoo-giizisoons** *na*

DECEPTIVE

DECEPTIVE: be deceptive in speech **giiwanimo** *vai*

DECIDE

DECIDE: **inendam** *vai2;* decide what to do **onendam** *vai2*

DECIDE A CERTAIN WAY: decide a certain way about s.t. **inaakonan** *vti;* decide about s.o. a certain way **inaakon** *vta;* decide things a certain way **inaakonige** *vai*

DECIDE AGAINST: **aanizhiitam** *vai2*

DECIDE ON: decide on s.o. **onagim** *vta;* **onaakon** *vta;* decide on s.t. **onaakonan** *vti*

DECIDED

DECIDED IN A CERTAIN WAY: be decided in a certain way **inaakonigaade, inaakonigaademagad** *vii*

DECISION

IT'S YOUR DECISION: **booshke** *pc, also* **booshke giniin**

DECORATE

DECORATE: decorate s.o. **wawezhi'** *vta;* decorate s.t. **wawezhitoon** *vti2;* decorate things **wawezhichige** *vai*

DECORATED

DECORATED: **zazegaa** *pc;* be decorated **wawezhichigaade, wawezhichigaademagad** *vii;* **wawezhichigaazo** *vai*

DECOY

DUCK DECOY: **zhiishiibikojigan, -ag** *na*

FISH DECOY: **okeyaw, -ag** *na*

DECREED

DECREED A CERTAIN WAY: be decreed a certain way **inaakonigaade, inaakonigaademagad** *vii*

DEED

DEED: **izhichigewin, -an** *ni*

DEEP

DEEP: be deep (of a body of water) **dimii, dimiimagad** *vii*

DEEP SNOW: be deep snow **ishpaagonagaa, ishpaagonagaamagad** *vii*

DEEP TO A CERTAIN EXTENT: be deep to a certain extent **akwiindimaa, akwiindimaamagad** *vii*

DEER

DEER: **waawaashkeshi, -wag** *na*

DEER HIDE

DEER HIDE: **waawaashkeshiwayaan, -ag** *na*

DEER MEAT

DEER MEAT: **waawaashkeshiwi-wiiyaas** *ni*

DEFEAT

DEFEAT: defeat s.o. **zhaagooji'** *vta;* defeat s.o. in speech **zhaagoozom** *vta;* defeat s.t. **zhaagoojitoon** *vti2;* defeat people **zhaagooji'iwe** *vai*

DEFEAT IN A CONTEST OR GAME: defeat s.o. in a contest or game **niiwezh /niiweN-/** *vta;* defeat people in a contest or game **niiwezhiwe** *vai*

DEFECATE

DEFECATE: **miizii** *vai*

DEFLATE

DEFLATE: deflate s.t. **zhiigoojiinan** *vti*

DEJECTED
DEJECTED: be dejected **osidaawendam** *vai2*
DEN
DEN: **waanzh, -an** *ni*
DENIAL
DENIAL: exclamation of denial **ine** *pc*
DENIM
DENIM: **giboodiyegwaazoniigin, -oon** *ni*
DENSE
DENSE: be dense **mashkawaa, mashkawaamagad** *vii;* **mashkawizi** *vai*
DENTAL PICTOGRAPH
DENTAL PICTOGRAPH: dental pictograph on birch bark **mazinibaganjigan, -an** *ni*
MAKE A DENTAL PICTOGRAPH: make a dental pictograph on birch bark **mazinibaganjige** *vai*
DENTIST
DENTIST: **wiibidaa-mashkikiiwinini, -wag** *na*
DENY
DENY: **aagonwetam** *vai2;* deny s.t. **aagonwetan** *vti;* deny what s.o. says **aagonwetaw** *vta*
DEPART
DEPART: **maajaa** *vai, also* **ani-maajaa**
DEPEND
DEPEND ON: depend on (s.t.) **apenimo** *vai+o;* depend on s.o. **apenimonodaw** *vta, also* **apenimodaw**; depend on s.t. **apenimonodan** *vti*
DEPRESSED
FEEL DEPRESSED: **maanendam** *vai2, also* **maazhendam**; **niisaanendam** *vai*
DEPTH
DETERMINE THE DEPTH: **debakii'ige** *vai*
LIE TO A CERTAIN DEPTH: **apiichishin** *vai;* **apiichisin** *vii*
DEPTHS
IN THE DEPTHS OF A BODY OF WATER: **anaamiindim** *pc*
DESIGN
DESIGN: **mazinibii'igan, -an** *ni*
HAVE A DESIGN: **mazinishin** *vai;* **mazinisin** *vii*
DESIRABLE
DESIRABLE: be desirable **nandawendaagozi** *vai;* **nandawendaagwad** *vii*
DESIRE
DESIRE: **misawendam** *vai2;* **nandawendam** *vai2;* desire s.o. **agaawaazh /agaawaaN-/** *vta;* **misawenim** *vta;* **nandawenim** *vta;* desire s.t. **agaawaadan** *vti;* **misawendan** *vti;* **nandawendan** *vti;* desire things **misawenjige** *vai*
STRONGLY DESIRE: **ondendam** *vai2*
DESIRES
HAVE INTENSE FEELINGS OR DESIRES: **aakwendam** *vai2*
DESK
DESK: **apibii'igan, -an** *ni;* **ozhibii'ige-adoopowin, -an** *ni*
DESPAIR
DESPAIR: **banaadendam** *vai2;* despair of s.o. **banaadenim** *vta;* despair of s.t. **banaadendan** *vti*
DESPITE
DESPITE: **aanawi** *pc*
DESTINY
HAVE A CERTAIN DESTINY: **inendaagozi** *vai*
DESTROY
DESTROY: destroy s.t. **nishwanaajitoon** *vti2;* destroy s.o. **nishwanaaji'** *vta;* destroy things **nishwanaajichige** *vai*
DETERGENT
LIQUID DETERGENT: **giziibiiginaaganewaaboo** *ni*
DETOUR
DETOUR: **wiimaashkaa** *vai*
DEUCE
DEUCE: **niizhoobii'igan, -ag** *na*
DEVIL
DEVIL: **maji-manidoo, -g** *na*
DEW
DEW: there is dew **mindookad** *vii*
DEW-CLAW GAME
DEW-CLAW GAME: dew-claw game *plural* **biipiinjigana'onag** *na*
DIABETES
HAVE DIABETES: **ziinzibaakwadowaapine** *vai, also* **ziinzibaakwadwaapine**
DIAMOND
DIAMOND SUITE CARD: **gaanoo, -g** *na*
DIAPER
DIAPER: **aanziyaan, -an** *ni*
DIARRHEA
HAVE DIARRHEA: **zhaabokaawizi** *vai*
DIE
DIE: **nibo** *vai*
DIE FROM A FALL: **aapijishin** *vai*
DIE IN A CERTAIN PLACE: **dapine** *vai*
DIE IN AN ACCIDENT: **niiwanishin** *vai*
DIFFERENT
DIFFERENT: **bakaan** *pc;* be different **bakaanad** *vii;* **bakaanizi** *vai*
ALL DIFFERENT: **bebakaan** *pc*
DIFFICULT
DIFFICULT: be difficult **zanagad** *vii;* **zanagizi** *vai*
CONSIDER DIFFICULT: consider s.o. difficult **zanagenim** *vta;* consider s.t. difficult **zanagendan** *vti;* consider things difficult **zanagendam** *vai2*
MAKE IT DIFFICULT: make it difficult for s.o. **zanagi'** *vta*
DIG
DIG: dig for s.o. **nandwaanikaazh /nandwaanikaaN-/** *vta;* dig for s.t. **nandwaanikaadan** *vti*
DIG A HOLE: **waanike** *vai*
DIG UP: dig up s.o. **moona' /moona'w-/** *vta;* dig up s.t. **moona'an** *vti;* dig up things **moona'ige** *vai*

DIME
DIME: **bezhizhooniyaans, -ag** *na;* **zhooniyaans, -ag** *na*
DINNER
EAT DINNER: eat dinner (noon meal) **naawakwe-wiisini** *vai;* eat s.t. for dinner (noon meal) **naawakwe-miijin** *vti3*
DINNER PLATE
DINNER PLATE: **desinaagan, -an** *ni*
DIP
DIP: dip s.o. **gondaabiigin** *vta;* dip s.t **gondaabiiginan** *vti*
DIP IN: dip s.t. in **jekaagaminan** *vti*
DIP UP: dip up things **gwaaba'ige** *vai*
DIPPER
DIPPER: **gwaaba'igan, -an** *ni*
DIRECT
DIRECT: **dibishkoo** *pc*
DIRECTION
IN THE DIRECTION OF: **gakeyaa** *pc, also* **akeyaa, keyaa, nakakeyaa***
DIRECTOR
DIRECTOR: **odaakewigimaa, -g** *na, also* **odaake-ogimaa**
DIRT
DIRT: **wiiyagasenh** *ni*
DIRTY
DIRTY: be dirty **wiinad** *vii;* **wiinizi** *vai;* be dirty (as a liquid) **wiinaagamin /wiinaagami-/** *vii*
DIRTY HAND: have a dirty hand **wiinininjii** *vai*
DIRTY SCALP: have a dirty scalp **wiinishagaandibe** *vai*
MAKE DIRTY: make s.o. dirty **wiini'** *vta;* make s.t. dirty **wiinitoon** *vti2;* make things dirty **wiinichige** *vai*
TELL A DIRTY STORY: **wiinaajimo** *vai*
DISAGREE
DISAGREE: disagree with s.o. (of something consumed) *inverse forms of:* **maanikaw-** *vta*
DISAGREEABLE
CONSIDER DISAGREEABLE: consider s.o. disagreeable **maanenim** *vta;* consider s.t. disagreeable **maanendan** *vti*
CONSIDERED DISAGREEABLE: be considered disagreeable **maanendaagozi** *vai;* **maanendaagwad** *vii*
DISAPPEARED
DISAPPEARED: disappeared! **weniban** *pc*
DISAPPOINTED
DISAPPOINTED: be disappointed **minjinawezi** *vai*
DISAPPROVE
DISAPPROVE: disapprove of s.o. **zhiingenim** *vta;* disapprove of s.t. **zhiingendan** *vti;* they disapprove of each other **zhiingenindiwag /zhiingenindi-/** *vai*
DISAPPROVED
DISAPPROVED OF: be disapproved of **zhiingendaagozi** *vai;* **zhiingendaagwad** *vii*
DISBELIEVE
DISBELIEVE: disbelieve s.o. **aagonweyenim** *vta*
DISCOMFORT
WALK WITH DISCOMFORT: **maanose** *vai*
DISCONNECT
DISCONNECT: disconnect s.o. **gidiskin** *vta;* disconnect s.t. **gidiskinan** *vti*
DISCONNECT WITH HANDS: disconnect s.o. with hands **gidiskibizh /gidiskibiN-/** *vta;* disconnect s.t. with hands **gidiskibidoon** *vti2*
DISCOURAGE
DISCOURAGE: discourage s.o. **aanishim** *vta*
DISEASE
DISEASE: **aakoziwin, -an** *ni*
CATCH A DISEASE: **mizizi** *vai*
DISEMBARK
DISEMBARK: **gabaa** *vai;* disembark s.o. **gabaa'** *vta*
TELL TO DISEMBARK: tell s.o. to disembark **gabaanaazha' /gabaanaazha'w-/** *vta*
DISEMBOWEL
DISEMBOWEL: disembowel s.o. **gijinagizhiin** *vta*
DISGUSTING
CONSIDER DISGUSTING: consider s.o. disgusting **gagwaanisagenim** *vta;* consider s.t. disgusting **gagwaanisagendan** *vti*
CONSIDERED DISGUSTING: be considered disgusting **gagwaanisagendaagozi** *vai;* **gagwaanisagendaagwad** *vii*
DISH
DISH: **onaagan, -an** *ni*
BIRCH BARK DISH: **wiigwaasinaagan, -an** *ni*
WASH DISHES: **giziibiiginaagane** *vai*
WIPE DISHES: **gaasiinaagane** *vai*
WOODEN DISH: **mitigonaagan, -an** *ni*
DISH GAME
PLAY THE DISH GAME: **bagese** *vai*
DISH PAN
DISH PAN: **gichi-onaagan** *ni*
DISH TOWEL
DISH TOWEL: **giziiyaabika'igan, -an** *ni*
DISLIKE
DISLIKE: dislike s.o. **aanawenim** *vta;* **zhiingenim** *vta;* dislike s.t. **aanawendan** *vti;* **zhiingendan** *vti;* they dislike each other **zhiingenindiwag /zhiingenindi-/** *vai;* dislike things **aanawenjige** *vai*
DISLIKED
DISLIKED: be disliked **aanawendaagozi** *vai;* **aanawendaagwad** *vii;* **zhiingendaagozi** *vai;* **zhiingendaagwad** *vii*
DISMANTLE
DISMANTLE: dismantle s.o. **biigon** *vta;* dismantle s.t. **biigonan** *vti*
DISOBEDIENT
DISOBEDIENT: be disobedient **zhazhiibitam** *vai2*

DISPERSE
DISPERSE: **biiwise** *vai;* **biiwise, biiwisemagad** *vii*
DISRESPECT
SHOW DISRESPECT: show disrespect for s.o. **baapinodaw** *vta*
DISSATISFIED
DISSATISFIED: be dissatisfied (with what has been given) **mindawe** *vai*
DISTANCE
CERTAIN DISTANCE: be a certain distance **apiichaa, apiichaamagad** *vii*
HEARD SPEAKING AT A DISTANCE: be heard speaking at a distance **debwewidam** *vai2*
SOME DISTANCE: **gomaapii** *pc*
DISTANT
DISTANT: **waasa** *pc*
DISTANT SIGHT: be a distant sight **naawinaagozi** *vai;* **naawinaagwad** *vii*
DISTRACT
DISTRACT: distract s.o. **wanishkwe'** *vta*
DISTRACTED
DISTRACTED: be distracted **wanishkweyendam** *vai*
DISTRESS
IN DISTRESS: be in distress **aanimizi** *vai*
DISTRIBUTE
DISTRIBUTE: **maada'ookii** *vai;* distribute (s.t.) to s.o. **maada'oozh /maada'ooN-/** *vta;* they distribute (s.t.) to each other **maada'oonidiwag /maada'oonidi-/** *vai*
DISTURB
DISTURB BY SPEECH: disturb s.o. by speech **wanishkwem** *vta*
DISTURB SLEEP: disturb s.o.'s sleep **wapaa'** *vta*
DISTURBANCE
DISTURBANCE: be a disturbance **aanimad** *vii*
DISTURBED
DISTURBED: be disturbed **ishkendam** *vai2;* be disturbed in one's mind **mamiidaawendam** *vai2*
DIVE
DIVE: **googii** *vai*
DIVIDE
RIVER DIVIDES: divide (as a river) **baketigweyaa, baketigweyaamagad** *vii*
DIVORCE
DIVORCE: they divorce each other **webinidiwag /webinidi-/** *vai*
DIZZY
DIZZY: be dizzy **giiwashkwe** *vai;* **giiwashkweyaabandam** *vai2*
MAKE DIZZY: make s.o. dizzy (especially of a substance) *inverse forms of:* **giiwashkweshkaw-** *vta*
DO
DO: do something **doodam** *vai2;* do something to s.o. **doodaw** *vta;* do something to s.t. **doodan** *vti;* they do something to each other **doodaadiwag /doodaadi-/** *vai;* do something to oneself **doodaadizo** *vai;* **doodaazo** *vai*
DO A CERTAIN THING: **inakamigizi** *vai*
DO A CERTAIN WAY: do things a certain way **izhichige** *vai*
DO AMAZING THINGS: **maamakaajichige** *vai*
DO EXACTLY: **wawiingechige** *vai*
DO GOOD: do good things **minochige** *vai*
DO IN VAIN: **aanawewizi** *vai*
DO RIGHT: do things right **gwayakochige** *vai*
DO SKILFULLY: **wawiingechige** *vai*
DO WELL: do things well **minochige** *vai*
FREQUENTLY DO: **nitaa-** *pv4*
MAKE DO: make s.o. do something **izhi'** *vta*
NOT KNOW WHAT TO DO: **gwiinawi-doodam** *vai2*
TRY TO DO: try to do s.t. **wiikwajitoon** *vti2*
UNABLE TO DO: be unable to do something **bwaanawi'o** *vai;* be unable to do s.t. **bwaanawitoon** *vti2;* be unable to do something to s.o. **bwaanawi'** *vta*
DOCK
DOCK: **niminaaweyaandawaagan, -an** *ni*
DOCTOR
DOCTOR: **mashkikiiwinini, -wag** *na;* doctor (female) **mashkikiiwininiikwe, -g** *na;* doctor s.o. **mashkikiikaazh /mashkikiikaaN-/** *vta;* **nanaandawi'** *vta;* doctor people **nanaandawi'iwe** *vai*
DOCUMENT
DOCUMENT: **mazina'igan, -an** *ni*
DODGE
DODGE: **dabazi** *vai, also* **dabazii***
DOE
DOE: **oniijaaniw, -ag** *na*
DOG
DOG: **animosh, -ag** *na;* my dog **inday, -ag /-day-/** *nad*
FEMALE DOG: **gishkishenh, -yag** *na*
HAVE A DOG: **odayi** *vai*
HUNTING DOG: **giiwosewasim, -oog** *na, also* **giiyosewasim**
MALE DOG: **naabesim, -oog** *na*
DOGFISH
DOGFISH: **zhigwameg, -wag** *na*
DOGWOOD
DOGWOOD: red osier (locally known as dogwood) **miskwaabiimizh, -iig** *na*
DOING
WAY OF DOING: **izhichigewin, -an** *ni*
DOLL
DOLL: **mazinichigan, -ag** *na;* **odaminwaagan, -ag** *na*
DOLL OF HAY OR GRASS: **mazinashkibijigan, -ag** *na*
DOLL OF PROCESSED BASSWOOD BARK FIBER: **asigobaani-mazinichigan, -ag** *na*
DOLLAR
CERTAIN NUMBER OF DOLLARS: a certain number of dollars **daswaabik** *pc*

EIGHT DOLLARS: **ishwaaswaabik** *pc, also* **nishwaaswaabik***
FIVE DOLLARS: **naanwaabik** *pc*
FOUR DOLLARS: **niiwaabik** *pc*
NINE DOLLARS: **zhaangaswaabik** *pc*
ONE DOLLAR: **bezhigwaabik** *pc*
SEVEN DOLLARS: **niizhwaaswaabik** *pc*
SIX DOLLARS: **ingodwaaswaabik** *pc, also* **ningodwaaswaabik***
TEN DOLLARS: **midaaswaabik** *pc*
THREE DOLLARS: **niswaabik** *pc*
TWO DOLLARS: **niizhwaabik** *pc*

DOMESTIC ANIMAL
DOMESTIC ANIMAL: **awakaan, -ag** *na*

DON'T
DON'T: **gego** *pc*
DON'T BOTHER: **maanoo** *pc*
DON'T CARE: **maanoo** *pc*
DON'T EVER: **gego wiikaa** *pc*
DON'T IN ANY WAY: **gego ganage** *pc*
I DON'T KNOW WHAT: I don't know what *inanimate dubitative* **wegodogwen, -an** *pr*
JUST DON'T: **gego bina** *pc*
YOU DON'T HAVE TO: **gaawiin memwech** *pc*

DONATION
COLLECT MONEY AS A DONATION: **asigizhooniyaawe** *vai*

DOOR
DOOR: **ishkwaandem, -an** *ni*
BY A DOOR: **jiigishkwaand** *pc*
LODGE DOOR COVER: **gibishkwaande'on, -an** *ni*

DOUBTS
HAVE DOUBTS: have doubts about s.o. **zhaagwenim** *vta*

DOUGHNUT
DOUGHNUT: **bookadinigan, -ag** *na, also* **bwaakadinigaazod**

DOVE
DOVE: **omiimii, -g** *na*

DOWN
DOWN: down from it **niisayi'ii** *pc*
CLIMB DOWN: **niisaandawe** *vai;* climb down fast **niisaandawebizo** *vai*
KNOCK DOWN OFF WITH HANDS: knock s.o. down off something with hands **diitibibizh /diitibibiN-/** *vta;* knock s.t. down off something with hands **diitibibidoon** *vti2*
PULL DOWN: pull s.o. down **niisibizh /niisibiN-/** *vta;* pull s.t. down **niisibidoon** *vti2*
RUN DOWN: **niisaandawebatoo** *vai*
TEAR DOWN: tear s.o. down **niisibizh /niisibiN-/** *vta;* tear s.t. down **niisibidoon** *vti2*

DOWNHILL
GO DOWNHILL: **niisaakiiwe** *vai*
RUN DOWNHILL: **niisaakiiwebatoo** *vai*

DOWNSTAIRS
GO DOWNSTAIRS: **niisaandawe** *vai*

DOWNSTREAM
DOWNSTREAM: **niisaajiwan** *pc*

DOZE
DOZE: **bishkongwashi** *vai*

DRAFT ANIMAL
DRAFT ANIMAL: **odaabii'aagan, -ag** *na*

DRAG
DRAG: drag (something) **odaabii** *vai;* drag s.o. **odaabaazh /odaabaaN-/** *vta;* drag s.t. **odaabaadan** *vti*
DRAG ALONG: drag s.o. along **bimidaabaazh /bimidaabaaN-/** *vta;* drag s.t. along **bimidaabaadan** *vti*
DRAG ASHORE: drag s.o. ashore **agwaadaabaazh /agwaadaabaaN-/** *vta;* drag s.t. ashore **agwaadaabaadan** *vti;* drag something ashore **agwaadaabii** *vai*
DRAG AWAY: **animidaabii** *vai*
DRAG HERE: **biijidaabii** *vai;* drag s.o. here **biijidaabaazh /biijidaabaaN-/** *vta;* drag s.t. here **biijidaabaadan** *vti*
DRAG INTO THE WATER: drag s.o. into the water **bakobiidaabaazh /bakobiidaabaaN-/** *vta;* drag s.t. into the water **bakobiidaabaadan** *vti*
DRAG TO A CERTAIN PLACE: drag s.o. to a certain place **izhidaabaazh /izhidaabaaN-/** *vta;* drag s.t. to a certain place **izhidaabaadan** *vti*

DRAGONFLY
DRAGONFLY: **oboodashkwaanishiinh, -yag** *na*

DRAIN
DRAIN DRY: drain s.t. dry **iskandan** *vti*

DRAPES
DRAPES: **gibiiga'igan, -an** *ni*

DRAW
DRAW WITH MOUTH: draw on s.o. with mouth (e.g., a pipe) **wiikwam** *vta;* draw on s.t. with mouth **wiikwandan** *vti;* draw on things with mouth **wiikwanjige** *vai*

DRAW WATER
DRAW WATER: **gwaaba'ibii** *vai*

DRAW
DRAW: draw s.o. **mazinibii' /mazinibii'w-/** *vta;* draw s.t. **mazinibii'an** *vti;* draw things **mazinibii'ige** *vai*
DRAW A CIRCLE: **waawiyebii'ige** *vai*

DRAWING
DRAWING: **mazinibii'igan, -an** *ni*

DRAWKNIFE
DRAWKNIFE: **mookojigan, -an** *ni*

DRAWSTRING
DRAWSTRING: **giboobijiganeyaab, -iin** *ni*

DREAM
DREAM: dream of s.o. **bawaazh /bawaaN-/** *vta;* dream of s.t. **bawaadan** *vti;* have dreams **bawaajige** *vai*
BAD DREAM: have a bad dream **giiwanaadingwaam** *vai*
DREAM A CERTAIN WAY: **inaabandam** *vai2*

SCARY DREAM: have a scary dream **zegaabandam** *vai2*
SEE A CERTAIN WAY AS IN A DREAM: see s.o. a certain way as in a dream **inaabam** *vta;* see s.t. a certain way as in a dream **inaabandan** *vti*

DRESS
DRESS: **majigoode, -yan** *ni;* my dress **ingoodaas, -an /-goodaas-/** *nid*
BUCKSKIN DRESS: buckskin dress **bashkweginagooday, -an** *ni*
CHANGE DRESS: change one's dress **aandagoode** *vai*
JINGLE DRESS: **ziibaaska'iganagooday, -an** *ni*
PUT ON DRESS: put on one's dress **biitagoode** *vai*
TAKE OFF DRESS: take off one's dress **giitagoode** *vai*

DRESS
DRESS: **biizikonaye** *vai;* dress s.o. **biizikonaye'** *vta*
DRESS A CERTAIN WAY: **inikonaye** *vai;* **izhi'o** *vai*
DRESS IN A NEW OUTFIT: **oshkikonaye** *vai*
DRESS IN RED: **miskwaakonaye** *vai*
DRESS UP: **wawezhi'o** *vai;* **zazegaa'o** *vai;* dress s.o. up **wawezhi'** *vta*
DRESS WARMLY: **giizhoo'o** *vai*
DRESS WELL: **mino'o** *vai*

DRESSED
DRESSED: be dressed **biizikonaye** *vai*
DRESSED UP: **zazegaa** *pc;* be dressed up **nanaa'ii** *vai*

DRESSED-UP
DRESSED-UP MAN: **zazegaa-inini, -wag** *na*
DRESSED-UP WOMAN: **zazegaa-ikwe, -wag** *na*

DRESSER
DRESSER: **wiikobijigan, -an** *ni*

DRIED
DRIED: **baate-** *pv4;* be dried **baasigaade, baasigaademagad** *vii;* **baasigaazo** *vai*
DRIED OUT: be dried out **gaaskide, gaaskidemagad** *vii;* **gaaskizo** *vai*

DRIFT
DRIFT ALONG ON CURRENT: **bimaaboode, bimaaboodemagad** *vii;* **bimaaboono** *vai*
DRIFT AWAY: **animaabogo** *vai;* **animaaboode, animaaboodemagad** *vii*
DRIFT AWAY ON THE WAVES: **animaa'an** *vii;* **animaa'ogo** *vai*
DRIFT OFF ON THE CURRENT: **maadaaboode, maadaaboodemagad** *vii;* **maadaaboono** *vai*
DRIFT OFF ON THE WAVES: **maadaa'an** *vii;* **maadaa'ogo** *vai*

DRILL
DRILL: **bagone'igan, -an** *ni;* drill s.o. **bagone' /bagone'w-/** *vta;* drill s.t. **bagone'an** *vti*

DRINK
DRINK: drink (s.t.) **minikwe** *vai+o*
CHOKE WHILE DRINKING: **bakwenibii** *vai*
DRINK AND BE MERRY: **minobii** *vai*
DRINK QUICKLY: drink s.t. quickly **ziikaapidan** *vti*
DRINK TOO MUCH: **onzaamibii** *vai*
GIVE A DRINK: give s.o. a drink **mina'** *vta*
GIVE TOO MUCH TO DRINK: give s.o. too much to drink **onzaamibazh /onzaamibaN-/** *vta*
LOOK FOR A DRINK: **nandoobii** *vai*
UNABLE TO FIND A DRINK: be unable to find a drink **gwiinobii** *vai*

DRINKING GLASS
DRINKING GLASS: **mikwamiiwinaagaans, -an** *ni*

DRINKING VESSEL
DRINKING VESSEL: **minikwaajigan, -an** *ni*

DRIP
DRIP: **onjigaa, onjigaamagad** *vii*
DRIP DOWN: **bangigaa, bangigaamagad** *vii*
DRIP FAST: **gizhiigaa, gizhiigaamagad** *vii*
START TO DRIP: **maajigaa, maajigaamagad** *vii*

DRIVE
DRIVE: **odaabii'iwe** *vai;* drive s.o. (e.g., a draft animal or a car) **odaabii'** *vta*
ARRIVE DRIVING: **bagamibide, bagamibidemagad** *vii;* **bagamibizo** *vai;* **bagamidaabii'iwe** *vai*
DRIVE ABOUT: **babaamibide, babaamibidemagad** *vii;* **babaamibizo** *vai;* **babaamidaabii'iwe** *vai*
DRIVE ACROSS: **aazhogebizo** *vai;* **aazhogedaabii'iwe** *vai;* **aazhoodaabii'iwe** *vai*
DRIVE ALONG: **bimibide, bimibidemagad** *vii;* **bimibizo** *vai;* **bimidaabii'iwe** *vai;* drive s.o. along **bimibizoni'** *vta;* drive s.t. along **bimibizonitoon** *vti2;* drive people along (as in a bus) **bimiwizhiwe** *vai*
DRIVE ALONG IN A WAGON OR SLEIGH: drive along quickly in a wagon or sleigh **bimidaabiiba'igo** *vai*
DRIVE ALONG THE SHORE: **jiigewebizo** *vai;* **jiigewedaabii'iwe** *vai*
DRIVE AT A CERTAIN SPEED: **apiichibide, apiichibidemagad** *vii;* **apiichibizo** *vai*
DRIVE AT NIGHT: **niibaabizo** *vai*
DRIVE AWAY: **animibide, animibidemagad** *vii;* **animibizo** *vai;* **animidaabii'iwe** *vai;* drive away with horses **animiba'igo** *vai;* drive away with s.o. (e.g., a car) **animibizoni'** *vta;* drive away with s.t. **animibizonitoon** *vti2*
DRIVE AWAY MAKING NOISE: **animwewebide, animwewebidemagad** *vii;* **animwewebizo** *vai*
DRIVE AWAY WITH A LIGHT: **animaazakonenjigebizo** *vai*
DRIVE FAST: **gizhiibizo** *vai;* **gizhiidaabii'iwe** *vai*

DRIVE FROM A CERTAIN PLACE: **onjibide, onjibidemagad** *vii;* **onjibizo** *vai;* **onjidaabii'iwe** *vai*
DRIVE HERE: **biijibide, biijibidemagad** *vii;* **biijibizo** *vai;* **biijidaabii'iwe** *vai*
DRIVE HERE WITH A LIGHT: **biidaazakonebizo** *vai*
DRIVE HOME: **giiwedaabii'iwe** *vai*
DRIVE IN: drive in **biinjibide, biinjibidemagad** *vii;* **biinjibizo** *vai*
DRIVE INSIDE: **biindigebide, biindigebidemagad** *vii;* **biindigebizo** *vai*
DRIVE OFF: **maajidaabii'iwe** *vai;* **maajiibide, maajiibidemagad** *vii;* **maajiibizo** *vai;* drive off in a wagon **maajidaabiiba'igo** *vai*
DRIVE OFF DRAWN BY HORSES: **maajiiba'igo** *vai*
DRIVE OFF TO THE SIDE: **bakebide, bakebidemagad** *vii;* **bakebizo** *vai*
DRIVE SLOWLY: **bejibide, bejibidemagad** *vii;* **bejibizo** *vai*
DRIVE SUDDENLY INTO VIEW: **zaagewebide, zaagewebidemagad** *vii;* **zaagewebizo** *vai*
DRIVE TO A CERTAIN PLACE: **ipide, ipidemagad** *vii;* **ipizo** *vai;* **izhidaabii'iwe** *vai;* drive s.o. to a certain place **ipizoni'** *vta;* drive s.t. to a certain place **ipizonitoon** *vti2*
GET LOST DRIVING: **wanibizo** *vai*
HEARD DRIVING ALONG: be heard driving along **bimwewebide, bimwewebidemagad** *vii;* **bimwewebizo** *vai*
HEARD DRIVING HERE: be heard driving here **biidwewebide, biidwewebidemagad** *vii;* **biidwewebizo** *vai*
STOP DRIVING: **noogibide, noogibidemagad** *vii;* **noogibizo** *vai*
TURN DRIVING: **gwekibizo** *vai*

DRIVE GAME
DRIVE GAME: **apagajinaazhikaage** *vai;* drive game for s.o. **apagajinaazhikamaw** *vta;* drive s.o. as game **apagajinaazhikaw** *vta*

DRIVER
DRIVER: **odaabii'iwewinini, -wag** *na*
TAXI DRIVER: **bimiwizhiwewinini, -wag** *na*

DRIVER'S LICENSE
DRIVER'S LICENSE: **odaabii'iwe-mazina'igaans, -an** *ni*

DROP
DROP: drop s.o. **bangishim** *vta;* drop s.t. **bangisidoon** *vti2*
LET DROP: let s.o. drop **banin** *vta;* let s.t. drop **baninan** *vti*
LET DROP FROM MOUTH: let s.o. drop from one's mouth **bagidam** *vta;* let s.t. drop from one's mouth **bagidandan** *vti*

DROP-OFF
DROP-OFF: there is a drop-off **giishkaamikaa, giishkaamikaamagad** *vii*

DROWN
DROWN: **gibwanaabaawe** *vai*

DRUGGIST
DRUGGIST: **mashkikii-adaawewinini, -wag** *na, also* **mashkikiiwi-adaawewinini**

DRUGSTORE
DRUGSTORE: **mashkikii-adaawewigamig, -oon** *ni, also* **mashkikiiwi-adaawewigamig**

DRUM
DRUM: **dewe'igan, -ag** *na;* drum on s.o. **madwe' /madwe'w-/** *vta;* drum on s.t. **madwe'an** *vti*
MIDE DRUM: **mitigwakik, -oog** *na*
POUND ON DRUM: **baaga'akokwe** *vai*

DRUMSTICK
DRUMSTICK: **dewe'iganaak, -oon** *na, also* **dewe'iganaatig**; drumstick for hand drum **baaga'akokwaan, -an** *ni*

DRUNK
DRUNK: be drunk **giiwashkwebii** *vai*
MAKE DRUNK: make s.o. drunk **giiwashkwebazh /giiwashkwebaN-/** *vta*

DRY
DRY: be dry **baaso** *vai;* **baate, baatemagad** *vii;* **bengozi** *vai;* **bengwan** *vii;* dry s.o. **baas /baasw-/** *vta;* dry s.o. using something **bengwa' /bengwa'w-/** *vta;* dry s.t. **baasan** *vti;* dry s.t. using something **bengwa'an** *vti*
DRAIN DRY: drain s.t. dry **iskandan** *vti*
DRY BY SMOKING: dry s.o. by smoking **gaaskiz /gaaskizw-/** *vta;* dry s.t. by smoking **gaaskizan** *vti*
DRY UP: dry up (of a body of water) **iskate, iskatemagad** *vii*

DRY WOOD
DRY WOOD: **mishiiwaatig, -oon** *ni*

DRYING RACK
DRYING RACK: drying rack for strips of meat over a fire **abwaanaak, -oon** *ni*

DUCK
DUCK: **zhiishiib, -ag** *na*
HUNT DUCKS: **nandawishibe** *vai*

DUCK DECOY
DUCK DECOY: **zhiishiibikojigan, -ag** *na*

DULL
DULL: be dull **ashiwaa, ashiwaamagad** *vii*

DULUTH
DULUTH: **Onigamiinsing** *place*

DUMB
DUMB: be dumb **bagwanawizi** *vai*

DUMP
DUMP: **ziigwebinigan, -an** *ni*

DUMPLING
DUMPLING: **napodin, -ag** *na*
MAKE DUMPLINGS: **napodinike** *vai*

DUMPLING SOUP
DUMPLING SOUP: **bisigadanaaboo** *ni*

DURING
DURING: **megwaa** *pc*

DUST
DUST: **wiiyagasenh** *ni*

DWARF
HAIRY-FACED BANK-DWELLING DWARF SPIRIT: **memegwesi, -wag** *na*
DYE
DYE: **atisigan, -an** *ni, also* **adisigan**; dye s.o. **atis /atisw-/** *vta, also* **adis**; dye s.t. **atisan** *vti, also* **adisan**; dye things **atisige** *vai, also* **adisige**
DYNAMITE
DYNAMITE: **baasaabikizigan, -an** *ni*

E

EAGER
EAGER: be eager **gwaashkwezi** *vai;* **wewiibendam** *vai;* be eager to do s.t. **ojaanimitoon** *vti2*
EAGLE
BALD EAGLE: **migizi, -wag** *na*
GOLDEN EAGLE: **giniw, -ag** *na*
EAR
EAR: my ear **nitawag, -an /-tawag-/** *nid*
INFECTED EAR: have an infected ear **miniiwitawage** *vai*
INSIDE EAR: inside an ear **biinjitawag** *pc*
EAR DROPS
EAR DROPS: **ziiginishaan, -an** *ni*
EAR OF CORN
EAR OF CORN: **mandaaminaak, -oon** *ni*
EARLY
EARLY: **wayiiba** *pc, also* **wiiba**
EARLY IN THE MORNING: **gichi-gigizheb** *pc*
EARLY IN THE NIGHT: be early in the night **oshki-dibikad** *vii*
EARMUFF
EARMUFF: **giizhootawage'on, -ag** *na*
WEAR EARMUFFS: **giizhootawage'o** *vai*
EARN
EARN: **gashkichige** *vai;* earn s.o. (e.g., money) **gashki'** *vta;* earn s.t. **dibendan** *vti*
EARN FROM A CERTAIN PLACE: **ondizi** *vai*
EARN MONEY: **zhooniyaake** *vai*
EARRING
EARRING: **naabishebizon, -an** *ni*
WEAR EARRINGS: **naanaabishebizo** *vai*
EARTH
EARTH: **aki, -in** *ni*; be the earth **akiiwan** *vii*
EARTH LODGE
EARTH LODGE: **akiiwe-wiigiwaam, -an** *ni*
EASILY
EASILY: **wenipazh** *pc*
GET EASILY: get s.o. easily **wenipazhi'** *vta;* get s.t. easily **wenipazhitoon** *vti2*

EAST
EAST: east: where the dawn comes from *conjunct of* **ondaaban: wendaabang** *vii*
IN THE EAST: **waabanong** *pc*
TO THE EAST: **waabanong** *pc*
EAST WIND
EAST WIND: **waabani-noodin** *ni*
EASY
EASY: be easy **wendad** *vii;* **wendizi** *vai;* **wenipanad** *vii;* **wenipanizi** *vai*
CONSIDER EASY: consider s.t. easy **wenipanendan** *vti*
EASY GOING: be easygoing **bekaadizi** *vai*
GO EASY: go easy on s.o. **manaaji'** *vta;* go easy on s.t. **manaajitoon** *vti2;* go easy! **na'egaaj** *pc*
EAT
EAT: **wiisini** *vai;* eat s.o. **amo /amw-/** *vta;* eat s.t. **miijin** *vti3*
EAT A CERTAIN WAY: **inanjige** *vai*
EAT BREAKFAST: **gigizhebaa-wiisini** *vai;* eat s.t. for breakfast **gigizhebaa-miijin** *vti3*
EAT DINNER: eat dinner (noon meal) **naawakwe-wiisini** *vai;* eat s.t. for dinner (noon meal) **naawakwe-miijin** *vti3*
EAT ENOUGH: **debisinii** *vai;* eat enough of s.t. **de-miijin** *vti3*
EAT IN A CERTAIN PLACE: **dananjige** *vai*
EAT LUNCH: eat lunch (noon meal) **naawakwe-wiisini** *vai;* eat s.t. for lunch (noon meal) **naawakwe-miijin** *vti3*
EAT SECRETLY: eat things secretly **giimoodanjige** *vai*
EAT SUPPER: **onaagoshi-wiisini** *vai;* eat s.t. for supper **onaagoshi-miijin** *vti3*
EAT UP: eat everything up **gidaanawe** *vai;* eat up s.t. **gidaan /gidaam-/** *vti3;* eat up s.o. **gidamo /gidamw-/** *vta*
EAT WELL: **minwanjige** *vai*
EAT WITH: eat with s.o. **wiidoopam** *vta;* eat with people **wiidoopange** *vai*
EAT WITH FINGERS: eat with one's fingers **michininjiikanjige** *vai*
EAT WITH SOMETHING ELSE: eat things with something else (e.g., butter with bread) **apanjige** *vai*
HEARD EATING: be heard eating **madwenjige** *vai*
LEAVE BEHIND UNEATEN: leave s.o. behind uneaten **ishkwam** *vta;* leave s.t. behind uneaten **ishkwandan** *vti*
START EATING: **maadanjige** *vai*
EAVESDROP
EAVESDROP: eavesdrop on s.o. **giimitaw** *vta*
ECHO
ECHO: **baswewe** *vai;* **baswewe, baswewemagad** *vii*
ECLIPSE
IN ECLIPSE: be in eclipse **makadewaabikizi** *vai*
EDGE
WALK AROUND THE EDGE: **giiwitaayaazhagaame** *vai*

EDUCATED
EDUCATED: be educated **gikendaaso** *vai*
EDUCATION
EDUCATION BY PREACHING AND EXHORTATION: **gagiikimaawasowin** *ni*
EELPOUT
EELPOUT: **mizay, -ag** *na*
EFFORT
MAKE AN EFFORT: **goji'ewizi** *vai*
WITH EFFORT: **enigok** *pc*
EGG
EGG: **waawan, -oon** *ni*
FISH EGG: **waak, -wan** *ni*
LAY AN EGG: **boonam** *vai2*
EGGBEATER
EGGBEATER: **waninawe'igan, -an** *ni*
EIGHT
EIGHT: **ishwaaswi** *nm, also* **nishwaaswi***; **ishwaaso-** *pv4, also* **nishwaaso-***; eight (card) **ishwaasoobii'igan, -ag** *na, also* **nishwaasoobii'igan***; they are eight **ishwaachinoon /ishwaachin-/** *vii, also* **nishwaachinoon***; **ishwaachiwag /ishwaachi-/** *vai, also* **nishwaachiwag***
AND EIGHT: **ashi-ishwaaso-** *pv4, also* **ashi-nishwaaso-***; **ashi-ishwaaswi** *nm, also* **ashi-nishwaaswi***
EIGHT ACRES: **ishwaaso-diba'igaans** *pc, also* **nishwaaso-diba'igaans***
EIGHT DAYS: **ishwaaso-giizhik** *pc, also* **nishwaaso-giizhik***; **ishwaasogon** *pc, also* **nishwaasogon***; be eight days **ishwaasogonagad** *vii, also* **nishwaasogonagad***
EIGHT DAYS OLD: be eight days old **ishwaasogonagizi** *vai, also* **nishwaasogonagizi***
EIGHT DOLLARS: **ishwaaswaabik** *pc, also* **nishwaaswaabik***
EIGHT EACH: **eyishwaaswi** *nm, also* **nenishwaaswi***
EIGHT FEET: **ishwaasozid** *pc, also* **nishwaasozid***
EIGHT HOURS: **ishwaaso-diba'igan** *pc, also* **nishwaaso-diba'igan***
EIGHT HUNDRED: **ishwaaswaak** *nm, also* **nishwaaswaak***
EIGHT INCHES: **ishwaasoninj** *pc, also* **nishwaasoninj***
EIGHT MILES: **ishwaaso-diba'igan** *pc, also* **nishwaaso-diba'igan***
EIGHT MINUTES: **ishwaaso-diba'igaans** *pc, also* **nishwaaso-diba'igaans***
EIGHT MONTHS: **ishwaaso-giizis** *pc, also* **nishwaaso-giizis***
EIGHT NIGHTS: **ishwaaso-dibik** *pc, also* **nishwaaso-dibik***
EIGHT O'CLOCK: be eight o'clock **ishwaaso-diba'iganed** *vii, also* **nishwaaso-diba'iganed***
EIGHT PAIRS: **ishwaaswewaan** *pc, also* **nishwaaswewaan***
EIGHT SETS: **ishwaaswewaan** *pc, also* **nishwaaswewaan***
EIGHT THOUSAND: **ishwaasosagoons** *nm, also* **nishwaasosagoons***
EIGHT TIMES: **ishwaaching** *pc, also* **nishwaaching***
EIGHT WEEKS: **ishwaaso-anama'e-giizhik** *pc, also* **nishwaaso-anama'e-giizhik***; be eight weeks **ishwaaso-anama'e-giizhigad** *vii, also* **nishwaaso-anama'e-giizhigad***
EIGHT YEARS: **ishwaaso-biboon** *pc, also* **nishwaaso-biboon***; be eight years **ishwaaso-biboonagad** *vii, also* **nishwaaso-biboonagad***
EIGHT YEARS OLD: be eight years old **ishwaaso-biboonagizi** *vai, also* **nishwaaso-biboonagizi***
EIGHTEEN
EIGHTEEN: **ashi-ishwaaswi** *nm, also* **ashi-nishwaaswi***; **midaaswi ashi-ishwaaswi** *nm, also* **midaaswi ashi-nishwaaswi***
EIGHTH
THE EIGHTH DAY OF THE MONTH: be the eighth day of the month **ishwaasogonagizi** *vai, also* **nishwaasogonagizi***
EIGHTY
EIGHTY: **ishwaasimidana** *nm, also* **nishwaasimidana***
EJACULATE
EJACULATE: **baashkizige** *vai*
ELATED
ELATED: be elated **onzaamenimo** *vai*
ELBOW
ELBOW: my elbow **indooskwan, -an /-dooskwan-/** *nid*
SORE ELBOW: have a sore elbow **gaagiijidooskwan** *vai*
ELDER
ELDER: **gichi-aya'aa, -g** *na*
ELDERLY
ELDERLY: be elderly **gikaa** *vai*
ELDEST
ELDEST CHILD: **nitamoozhaan, -ag** *na*
THE ELDEST: be the eldest (of siblings) **zaziikizi** *vai*
ELECTION DAY
ELECTION DAY: be election day **biinjwebinigewi-giizhigad** *vii*
ELECTRIC
ELECTRIC: **waasamoo-** *pv4*
ELECTRIC LAMP
ELECTRIC LAMP: **waasamoo-waazakonenjigan, -an** *ni*
ELECTRICIAN
ELECTRICIAN: **waasamoo-anokiiwinini, -wag** *na*
ELECTRICITY
ELECTRICITY: **waasamowin** *ni*
ELEPHANT
ELEPHANT: **jejiibajikii, -g** *na*
ELEVATOR
ELEVATOR: **akwaandawaagan, -an** *ni;* **akwaandawebizon, -an** *ni*

ELEVEN
ELEVEN: **ashi-bezhig** *nm;* **midaaswi ashi-bezhig** *nm;* **ashi-bezhigo-** *pv4*
ELK
ELK: **omashkooz, -oog** *na*
ELM
ELM: **aniib, -iig** *na*
SLIPPERY ELM: **ozhaashigob, -iig** *na*
EMBARK
EMBARK: **boozi** *vai*
EMBARRASS
EMBARRASS: embarrass s.o. **agaji'** *vta*
EMBARRASS BY SPEECH: embarrass s.o. by speech **agazom** *vta*
EMBARRASSED
EMBARRASSED: be embarrassed **agadendaagozi** *vai;* be embarrassed by s.o. **agadenim** *vta*
EMBARRASSING
EMBARRASSING: be embarrassing **agadendaagwad** *vii*
EMBRACE
EMBRACE: embrace s.o. **gikinjigwen** *vta;* **giishkijiin** *vta;* they embrace each other **giishkijiinidiwag /giishkijiinidi-/** *vai*
EMBROIDER
EMBROIDER: **mazinigwaaso** *vai;* embroider s.o. **mazinigwaazh /mazinigwaaN-/** *vta;* embroider s.t. **mazinigwaadan** *vti*
EMERGE
EMERGE FROM SURFACE: **mookii** *vai*
EMERGE FROM THE WATER: **mookibii** *vai*
EMPLOYED
EMPLOYED IN A CERTAIN WAY: be employed in a certain way **inaabadad** *vii;* **inaabadizi** *vai*
EMPTIED
EMPTIED: be emptied **zhiigonigaade, zhiigonigaademagad** *vii;* **zhiigonigaazo** *vai*
EMPTY
EMPTY: be empty **bizhishigozi** *vai;* **bizhishigwaa, bizhishigwaamagad** *vii;* empty s.o. **zhiigon** *vta;* empty s.t. **zhiigonan** *vti;* empty things **zhiigonige** *vai*
ENCIRCLE
ENCIRCLE: **giiwitaashkaa** *vai*
END
AT THE END: at the end of it **ishkwe-ayi'ii** *pc, also* **iskweya'ii**
AT THE END OF AN ACTIVITY: be at the end of an activity **ishkwaataa** *vai*
AT THE END OF THE ROAD: at the end of the road or trail **gabekana** *pc*
AT THE END OF THE TRAIL: at the end of the road or trail **gabekana** *pc*
COME TO AN END: **ishkwaase, ishkwaasemagad** *vii;* **wayekwaase, wayekwaasemagad** *vii*
GO TO THE END: **gabeshkaa** *vai;* go to the end of s.t. **gabeshkan** *vti*
HANG AT THE END: **ishkwegoode, ishkwegoodemagad** *vii;* **ishkwegoojin** *vai;* hang s.o. at the end **ishkwegoozh /ishkwegooN-/** *vta;* hang s.t. at the end **ishkwegoodoon** *vti2*
LIE AT THE END: **ishkweshin** *vai;* **ishkwesin** *vii*
LIVE ON THE END OF TOWN: live at the end of town **ishkwege** *vai*
SIT AT THE END: **ishkwebi** *vai*
STAND AT THE END: **ishkwegaabawi** *vai*
ENERGETIC
ENERGETIC: be energetic **gwaashkwezi** *vai*
ENGAGED
ENGAGED IN AN ACTIVITY TO A CERTAIN EXTENT: be engaged in an activity to a certain extent **apiichitaa** *vai*
ENGAGED
ENGAGED: be engaged **asho-wiidige** *vai;* they are engaged to each other **asho-wiidigendiwag /asho-wiidigendi-/** *vai*
ENGINE
ENGINE: **mayaajiibizod** *na-pt*
ENGLISH
SPEAK ENGLISH: **gichi-mookomaanimo** *vai;* **zhaaganaashiimo** *vai;* speak English to s.o. **zhaaganaashiimotaw** *vta*
WRITE IN ENGLISH: **zhaaganaashiiwibii'ige** *vai;* write in English to s.o. **zhaaganaashiiwibii'amaw** *vta;* write s.t. in English **zhaaganaashiiwibii'an** *vti*
ENGLISHMAN
ENGLISHMAN: **zhaaganaash, -ag** *na, also* **zhaaganaashi, -wag**
ENOUGH
ENOUGH: **de-** *pv4;* **gwech** *pc;* be enough **debise** *vai;* **debise, debisemagad** *vii*
EAT ENOUGH: **debisinii** *vai;* eat enough of s.t. **de-miijin** *vti3*
HAVE ENOUGH: **debizi** *vai;* have enough of s.o. **debisa'** *vta;* have enough of s.t. **debisatoon** *vti2;* have enough of things **debisachige** *vai*
HAVE ENOUGH TO GIVE: have enough to give away **deba'ookii** *vai;* have enough to give to or feed s.o. **deba'oozh /deba'ooN-/** *vta*
THINK THERE IS ENOUGH: **debisewendam** *vai2*
ENTER
ENTER: **biindige** *vai;* enter into where s.o. is **biindigaw** *vta*
ENVELOPE
ENVELOPE: **mashkimodens, -an** *ni;* **maajiibii'ige-mashkimodens, -an** *ni*
ENVY
ENVY: envy s.o. **ondenim** *vta*
EQUAL
EQUAL: **dibishkoo** *pc*
ERASE
ERASE: erase s.t. **gaasiibii'an** *vti;* erase things **gaasiibii'ige** *vai*

ERASER
ERASER: **gaasiibii'igan, -ag** *na*
ERROR
IN ERROR: **wani-** *pv4*
ESCAPE
ESCAPE: **giimii** *vai;* escape from s.o. **gii'** *vta;* **ozhim** *vta;* escape from people **gii'iwe** *vai*
ESPECIALLY
ESPECIALLY: **memindage** *pc*
EUROPE
IN EUROPE: **agaamakiing** *pc*
EVEN
EVEN: **dibishkoo** *pc*
KEEP UP EVEN: keep up even with s.o. **dibi'** *vta*
EVEN THOUGH
EVEN THOUGH: **awanjish** *pc*
EVENING
EVENING: be evening **onaagoshin /onaagoshi-/** *vii*
ALL EVENING: **gabe-onaagosh** *pc*
EVENT
CERTAIN EVENT: be a certain event **inakamigad** *vii;* **izhiwebad** *vii*
HAVE AN EVENT IN A CERTAIN PLACE: **danakamigizi** *vai*
EVENTUALLY
EVENTUALLY: **gegapii** *pc*
EVER
EVER: **wiikaa** *pc*
DON'T EVER: **gego wiikaa** *pc*
EVERY
EVERY: **akina** *pc, also* **kina, gakina; daso-** *pv3*
EVERY DAY: **endaso-giizhik** *pc*
EVERY MONTH: **endaso-giizis** *pc*
EVERY MORNING: **endaso-gigizheb** *pc*
EVERY NIGHT: **endaso-dibik** *pc*
EVERY ONCE IN A WHILE: **aayaapii** *pc*
EVERYTHING
EVERYTHING: **akina gegoo** *pr, also* **kina gegoo, gakina gegoo**
EVERYWHERE
EVERYWHERE: **miziwe** *pc;* be everywhere **miziweshkaa, miziweshkaamagad** *vii*
GO EVERYWHERE: **miziweshkaa, miziweshkaamagad** *vii*
EVICT
EVICT: evict s.o. **zaagidin** *vta*
EVICTED
EVICTED: be evicted **ikonigaazo** *vai*
EVIL
EVIL: be evil **maji-manidoowaadizi** *vai*
EVIL MANITOU: **maji-manidoo, -g** *na*
LEAD AN EVIL LIFE: **maji-izhiwebizi** *vai*
EXACTLY
EXACTLY: **memwech** *pc*
DO EXACTLY: **wawiingechige** *vai*
EXCESSIVELY
EXCESSIVELY: **onzaam** *pc*

EXCHANGE
EXCHANGE: exchange s.o. **meshkwadoon** *vta;* exchange s.t. **meshkwadoonan** *vti;* exchange things **meshkwadoonige** *vai*
IN EXCHANGE: **meshkwad** *pc*
EXCITE
EXCITE: excite s.o. **ombi'** *vta*
EXCITED
EXCITED: be excited **baapinakamigizi** *vai;* **ombendam** *vai2*
EXCITING
EXCITING: be exciting **minawaanigwad** *vii*
EXCREMENT
EXCREMENT: **moo, -wan** *ni*
EXHALE
EXHALE: **bagidanaamo** *vai;* **nasanaamo** *vai*
EXHAUSTED
EXHAUSTED: be exhausted **noondeshin** *vai*
EXHIBITION
EXHIBITION: **waabanda'iwewin, -an** *ni*
EXHORTATION
EDUCATION BY PREACHING AND EXHORTATION: **gagiikimaawasowin** *ni*
EXIT
EXIT: **zaaga'am** *vai2*
EXOTIC
EXOTIC: **mayagi-** *pv4*
EXPECT
EXPECT: **akawaabi** *vai;* expect s.o. to come **akawaabam** *vta;* expect s.t. to come **akawaabandan** *vti*
EXPECT TO BE IN A CERTAIN PLACE: expect s.o. to be in a certain place **danenim** *vta;* expect s.t. to be in a certain place **danendan** *vti*
EXPLAIN
EXPLAIN: explain (s.t.) to s.o. **waawiindamaw** *vta;* explain (s.t.) to people **waawiindamaage** *vai*
EXPLAINED
EXPLAINED: be explained **waawiinjigaade, waawiinjigaademagad** *vii*
EXPLODE
EXPLODE: **baashkide, baashkidemagad** *vii;* **baashkizo** *vai*
EXTENT
CERTAIN EXTENT: a certain extent **apiichi-** *pv3*
WHOLE EXTENT OF: **gabe-** *pv4*
EXTINGUISH
EXTINGUISH: extinguish s.t. **aate'an** *vti*
EXTINGUISHED
EXTINGUISHED: be extinguished **aate, aatemagad** *vii*
APPEAR TO BE EXTINGUISHED: appear to be extinguished (e.g., the moon or sun in an eclipse) **aatenaagozi** *vai*
EXTREMELY
EXTREMELY: **onzaam** *pc*
EXTRICATE
EXTRICATE: extricate s.o. **giichigon** *vta;* extricate s.t. **giichigonan** *vti*

EYE
EYE: my eye **nishkiinzhig, -oon /-shkiinzhigw-/** *nid*
BIG EYE: have a big eye **mangishkiinzhigwe** *vai*
HAVE A BLACK EYE: **ozhaawashkwaabi** *vai*
HAVE SOMETHING IN EYE: have something in one's eye **binzini** *vai*
OPEN EYES: open one's eyes **dooskaabi** *vai*
SHUT EYES: shut one's eyes **basangwaabi** *vai*
SWOLLEN EYES: have swollen eyes **baagishkiinzhigwe** *vai*

EYE DROPS
EYE DROPS: **ziiginiingwaan** *ni*

EYEGLASSES
EYEGLASSES: eyeglasses *plural* **oshkiinzhigokaajiganan** *ni, also* **oshkiinzhikokaanan**

EYEBROW
EYEBROW HAIR: my eyebrow hair **nimaamaa, -yag /-maamaay-/** *nad*

EYELASH
EYELASH: **miishaabiwinaan, -an** *ni*

EYESIGHT
GOOD EYESIGHT: have good eyesight **minwaabi** *vai*

F

FACE
FACE: my face **indengway, -an /-dengway-/** *nid*
ACNE ON FACE: have acne on one's face **moosewiingwe** *vai*
BROAD FACE: have a broad face **mangadengwe** *vai*
BRUISED FACE: have a bruised face **ozhaawashkwaanagiingwe** *vai*
CHAPPED FACE: have a chapped face **gagiipiingwe** *vai*
FALL ON FACE: fall on one's face **ajijiingwese** *vai*
HAVE SCAR ON FACE: have scar on one's face **ojiishiingwe** *vai*
LIE WITH FACE COVERED: lie with one's face covered **badagwiingweshin** *vai*
NARROW FACE: have a narrow face **agaasadengwe** *vai*
SCABS ON FACE: have scabs on one's face **omigiingwe** *vai*
SLAP ON FACE: slap s.o. on the face **basiingwe' /basiingwe'w-/** *vta*
SWOLLEN FACE: have a swollen face **baagiingwe** *vai*
WASH FACE: wash one's face **giziibiigiingwe** *vai*
WIPE FACE: wipe one's face with something **giziingwe'o** *vai*
WRINKLED FACE: have a wrinkled face **oziigiingwe** *vai*

FACE POWDER
FACE POWDER: **waabishkiingwechigan** *ni*
USE FACE POWDER: **waabishkiingwechige** *vai*

FACE DOWN
FALL FACE DOWN: **animikose** *vai;* **animikose, animikosemagad** *vii*
LAY FACE DOWN: lay s.o. face down **animikoshim** *vta;* lay s.t. face down **animikosidoon** *vti2*
LIE FACE DOWN: **animikoshin** *vai;* **animikosin** *vii*
TURN FACE DOWN: turn s.o. face down **animikon** *vta;* turn s.t. face down **animikonan** *vti*
TURNED FACE DOWN: be turned face down **animikonigaade, animikonigaademagad** *vii;* **animikonigaazo** *vai*

FACE UP
LAY FACE UP: lay s.o. face up **aazhigijishim** *vta;* lay s.t. face up **aazhigijisidoon** *vti2*
LIE FACE UP: **aazhigijishin** *vai;* **aazhigijisin** *vii*
TURN FACE UP: **aazhigijise** *vai;* **aazhigijise, aazhigijisemagad** *vii*

FACTORY
FACTORY: **anokiiwigamig, -oon** *ni*

FADE
FADE: fade from light **waabaaso** *vai;* **waabaate, waabaatemagad** *vii*

FADED
FADED: be faded **waabide, waabidemagad** *vii;* **waabizo** *vai*

FAIL
FAIL TO SEE: fail to see s.o. **gwiinawaabam** *vta;* fail to see s.t. **gwiinawaabandan** *vti*

FAINT
FAINT: **wanendamaa** *vai*

FALL
FALL: **bangishin** *vai;* **bangisin** *vii;* fall (as a leaf) **binaakwii** *vai*
DIE FROM A FALL: **aapijishin** *vai*
FALL AND BREAK ARM: fall and break one's arm **bookonikeshin** *vai*
FALL AND BREAK BACK: fall and break one's back **bookwaawiganeshin** *vai*
FALL AND BREAK LEG: fall and break one's leg **bookogaadeshin** *vai*
FALL AND CRACK HEAD: fall and crack one's head **baasindibeshin** *vai*
FALL AND TWIST ARM: fall and twist one's arm **biimiskonikeshin** *vai*
FALL DOWN AGAINST: **apangishin** *vai;* **apangisin** *vii*
FALL DOWN HARD: **bakiteshin** *vai*
FALL FACE DOWN: **animikose** *vai;* **animikose, animikosemagad** *vii*

FALL FROM A CERTAIN PLACE: **onjibide, onjibidemagad** *vii;* **onjibizo** *vai*
FALL HEAD FIRST: **ajijibizo** *vai*
FALL IN: **biinjibide, biinjibidemagad** *vii;* **biinjibizo** *vai;* **biinjise** *vai;* **biinjise, biinjisemagad** *vii*
FALL INTO THE WATER: **bakobiise** *vai;* **bakobiise, bakobiisemagad** *vii*
FALL OFF A HORSE: **banoomigo** *vai*
FALL ON FACE: fall on one's face **ajijiingwese** *vai*
FALL ON THE SIDE: **opimese** *vai*
FALL OUT OF A BOAT: **gidoonagise** *vai*
FALL OVER: **gawise** *vai;* **gawise, gawisemagad** *vii;* fall over (as something stick- or wood-like) **gawaakose** *vai;* **gawaakose, gawaakosemagad** *vii*
FALL OVER BACKWARDS: **aazhigijishin** *vai;* **aazhigijisin** *vii*
FALL THROUGH THE ICE: **dwaashin** *vai*
HAVE A BAD FALL: **aapijishin** *vai*
HEARD FALLING: be heard falling on the floor **madwesagishin** *vai;* be heard going along and falling **bimweweshin** *vai*
SLIP AND FALL: **ozhaashishin** *vai*
SLIP AND FALL ON THE ICE: **ozhaashikoshin** *vai*

FALL
FALL: be fall **dagwaagin /dagwaagi-/** *vii*
FALL BEFORE LAST: **awas-dagwaagong** *pc*
LAST FALL: **dagwaagong** *pc*
SPEND THE FALL: spend the fall somewhere **dagwaagishi** *vai*

FALSE TEETH
FALSE TEETH: false teeth *plural* **wiibidaakaajiganan** *ni, also* **wiibidaakaanan**

FAMILIAR
FAMILIAR: be familiar with s.o. **nagadenim** *vta;* be familiar with s.t. **nagadendan** *vti*

FAN
FAN: fan s.o. **wewese' /wewese'w-/** *vta;* fan things **wewese'ige** *vai;* fan oneself **wewese'idizo** *vai*
HAND FAN: **wewese'igan, -an** *ni*
ROTARY FAN: **gizhibaayaasijigan, -an** *ni*

FAN BELT
FAN BELT: **apikaans, -an** *ni;* **gijipizonens** *ni*

FAR
FAR: **waasa** *pc;* be far **waasawad** *vii*
AS FAR AS: **ako-** *pv3*
SO FAR ALONG IN AN ACTIVITY: be so far along in an activity **apiichitaa** *vai*

FARE
FARE A CERTAIN WAY: **izhiwebizi** *vai*

FARM
FARM: **gitigaan, -an** *ni;* **gitige** *vai*

FARMER
FARMER: **gitigewinini, -wag** *na*

FART
FART: **boogidi** *vai*

FAST
FAST: be fast **wajepii** *vai*
CLIMB UP FAST: **akwaandawebatoo** *vai*
DRIP FAST: **gizhiigaa, gizhiigaamagad** *vii*
DRIVE FAST: **gizhiibizo** *vai;* **gizhiidaabii'iwe** *vai*
FLOW FAST: **gizhiijiwan** *vii*
FLY FAST: **gizhiibide, gizhiibidemagad** *vii;* **gizhiibizo** *vai;* **gizhiise** *vai;* **gizhiise, gizhiisemagad** *vii*
GO AS FAST AS POSSIBLE: **apiizikaa** *vai*
GO FAST: **gizhiikaa** *vai*
GROW FAST: **gizhiigi** *vai;* **gizhiigin** *vii*
LEAK FAST: **gizhiigaa, gizhiigaamagad** *vii*
MOVE FAST: **gizhiibide, gizhiibidemagad** *vii;* **gizhiibizo** *vai*
PADDLE FAST: **gizhiikaakwazhiwe** *vai*
RUN FAST: **gizhiibatoo** *vai;* **gizhiikaabatoo** *vai*
SPEED FAST: **gizhiibide, gizhiibidemagad** *vii;* **gizhiibizo** *vai*
WIND BLOWS FAST: **gizhiiyaanimad** *vii*

FAST
FAST FOR A VISION: **gii'igoshimo** *vai*
UNDERGO A PUBERTY FAST: **makadeke** *vai*

FASTEN
FASTEN: fasten s.o. **zagaakwa' /zagaakwa'w-/** *vta;* fasten s.t. **zagaakwa'an** *vti;* fasten things **zagaakwa'ige** *vai*
FASTEN TOGETHER: fasten s.o. together **zaga' /zaga'w-/** *vta;* fasten s.t. together **zaga'an** *vti*

FASTENED
FASTENED: be fastened **zagaakwa'igaade, zagaakwa'igaademagad** *vii;* **zagaakwa'igaazo** *vai*

FAT
FAT: **wiinin** *ni;* be fat **wiinino** *vai*

FATHER
FATHER: my father **imbaabaa, -yag /-baabaay-/** *nad;* **indede, -yag /-dedey-/** *nad;* my father *old-fashioned* **noos, -ag /-oos-/** *nad*

FATHER-IN-LAW
FATHER-IN-LAW: my father-in-law **inzinis, -ag /-zinis-/** *nad*

FATIGUED
FATIGUED: be fatigued **noondeshin** *vai*

FAWN
FAWN: **gidagaakoons, -ag** *na*

FEAR
FEAR: fear s.o. **goshi /goS-/** *vta;* fear s.t. **gotan** *vti*
COME IN FEAR: **biidaanimizi** *vai*
HAVE FEAR: **gotaaji** *vai*

FEARFUL
FEARFUL: be fearful **zegendam** *vai2*

FEAST
GIVE A FEAST: **wiikonge** *vai*
HAVE A FEAST: they have a feast **wiikondiwag /wiikondi-/** *vai*
HAVE A FEAST HONORING THE DEAD: **jiibenaake** *vai*

INVITE TO A FEAST: invite s.o. to a feast (especially as part of a religious ceremony) **wiikom** *vta;* invite people to a feast (especially as part of a religious ceremony) **wiikonge** *vai*

FEATHER

FEATHER: **miigwan, -ag** *na*

STICK IN A FEATHER: stick a feather in one's hair or hat **badakibine'o** *vai*

FEATHER HEADDRESS

FEATHER HEADDRESS: **miigwani-wiiwakwaan, -an** *ni*

FEBRUARY

FEBRUARY: **namebini-giizis** *na*

FECES

FECES: **moo, -wan** *ni*

FEED

FEED: feed (s.t.) to s.o. **asham** *vta;* feed people **ashange** *vai*

FEEL

FEEL: feel s.o. **mikoojiin** *vta;* feel s.o. in or on one's body **moozhi'** *vta;* feel s.t. **mikoojiinan** *vti;* feel s.t. in or on one's body **moozhitoon** *vti2*

FEEL A CERTAIN WAY: **inamanji'o** *vai;* **inendam** *vai2*

FEEL ABOUT TO A CERTAIN EXTENT: feel about s.o. to a certain extent **apiitenim** *vta*

FEEL BAD: **maanamanji'o** *vai;* **maanendam** *vai2, also* **maazhendam**; feel bad about s.t. **maanendan** *vti*

FEEL COLD: **biingeji** *vai;* **dakamanji'o** *vai;* **giikaji** *vai*

FEEL DEPRESSED: **maanendam** *vai2, also* **maazhendam**

FEEL FOR: feel for s.o. **mikoojiin** *vta;* **nandoojiin** *vta;* feel for s.t. **mikoojiinan** *vti;* **nandoojiinan** *vti;* feel for things **nandoojiinige** *vai*

FEEL GOOD: **minwamanji'o** *vai*

FEEL NUMB: **giikimanizi** *vai*

FEEL OUT OF SORTS: **maazhendam** *vai2*

FEEL SATISFIED: **debisewendam** *vai2*

FEEL STRANGE: **mayagendam** *vai2*

FEEL TIRED: **ayekwamanji'o** *vai*

FEELINGS

HAVE INTENSE FEELINGS OR DESIRES: **aakwendam** *vai2*

FELL

FELL: fell s.o. **gawa' /gawa'w-/** *vta;* fell s.t. **gawa'an** *vti*

FELLOW

FELLOW: my fellow **niiji-** *pn*

FELLOW MAN: my fellow man **niijiinini** *nad*

FENCE

FENCE: **minjikanaakobijigan, -an** *ni*

FERRY

FERRY ACROSS: ferry s.o. across **aazhawa'oozh /aazhawa'ooN-/** *vta;* ferry s.t. across **aazhawa'oodoon** *vti2*

FESTIVITIES

FESTIVITIES: there are festivities **baapinakamigad** *vii*

FETCH

FETCH: fetch s.o. **naazh /naaN-/** *vta;* fetch s.t. **naadin** *vti3;* fetch (s.t.) for s.o. **naadaw** *vta*

FETCHED

FETCHED: be fetched **naajigaade, naajigaademagad** *vii;* **naajigaazo** *vai*

FEVER

HAVE A FEVER: **gizhizo** *vai*

FEW

FEW: **bangii** *pc;* be few **bangiiwagad** *vii;* **bangiiwagizi** *vai*

VERY FEW: be very few **bangiishenhwagad** *vii;* **bangiishenhwagizi** *vai*

FIDDLE

FIDDLE: **naazhaabii'igan, -an** *ni*

FIELD

FIELD: **gitigaan, -an** *ni*

CORNFIELD: **mandaamini-gitigaan, -an** *ni*

FIERCE

FIERCE: be fierce **aakwaadizi** *vai*

FIFTEEN

FIFTEEN: **ashi-naanan** *nm;* **midaaswi ashi-naanan** *nm*

FIFTH

THE FIFTH DAY OF THE MONTH: be the fifth day of the month **naanogonagizi** *vai*

FIFTY

FIFTY: **naanimidana** *nm*

FIGHT

FIGHT: **miigaazo** *vai;* fight s.o. **miigaazh /miigaaN-/** *vta;* they fight each other **miigaadiwag /miigaadi-/** *vai*

FIGURE

FIGURE OUT: figure something out **onendam** *vai2*

FILE

FILE: **zisiboojigan, -an** *ni;* file s.o. **zisiboozh /zisibooN-/** *vta;* file s.t. **zisiboodoon** *vti2;* file things **zisiboojige** *vai*

FILE SHARP: file s.o. sharp **giiniboozh /giinibooN-/** *vta;* file s.t. sharp **giiniboodoon** *vti2*

FILL

FILL: fill s.o. (with a liquid) **mooshkinebazh /mooshkinebaN-/** *vta;* fill s.o. (with solids) **mooshkina'** *vta;* fill s.t. (with a liquid) **mooshkinebadoon** *vti2;* fill s.t. (with solids) **mooshkinadoon** *vti2*

FILL HALF FULL: fill s.o. half full (of liquid) **aabitoobazh /aabitoobaN-/** *vta;* fill s.o. half full (of solids) **aabitooshkina'** *vta;* fill s.t. half full **aabitooshkinadoon** *vti2;* fill s.t. half full (of liquid) **aabitoobadoon** *vti2*

FILL TO OVERFLOWING: fill s.o. to overflowing with solids **ziigashkina'** *vta;* fill s.t. to overflowing with a liquid **ziigibadoon** *vti2;* fill s.t. to overflowing with solids **ziigashkinadoon** *vti2*

FILL OUT
FILL OUT A FORM: **mooshkinebii'ige** *vai*
FILLED
FILLED WITH SMOKE: be filled with smoke **mooshkineyaabate, mooshkineyaabatemagad** *vii*
WELL FILLED: be well filled **minwashkine** *vai;* **minwashkine, minwashkinemagad** *vii*
FINALLY
FINALLY: **gegapii** *pc;* **ishkwaaj** *pc*
FIND
FIND: find s.o. **mikaw** *vta;* find s.t. **mikan** *vti;* find (s.t.) for s.o. **mikamaw** *vta;* find things **mikige** *vai;* find people **mikaage** *vai*
FIND TRACKS: find s.o.'s tracks **okawi'** *vta;* find the tracks of s.t. **okawitoon** *vti2*
FIND WITH HANDS: find s.o. with hands **mikobizh /mikobiN-/** *vta;* find s.t. with hands **mikobidoon** *vti2;* find (s.t.) for s.o. with hands **mikobidaw** *vta;* find things with hands **mikobijige** *vai*
FINE
FINE: be fine **biisaa, biisaamagad** *vii;* **biisizi** *vai;* be fine (as something string-like) **agaasaabiigad** *vii;* **agaasaabiigizi** *vai*
CHOP FINE: chop s.o. fine **biisa' /biisa'w-/** *vta;* chop s.t. fine **biisa'an** *vti*
FINE
FINE: be fine **mino-ayaa** *vai*
FINGER
FINGER: **niibinaakwaanininj, -iin** *ni;* my finger **nininj, -iin /-ninjy-/** *nid;* **nininjiins, -an /-ninjiins-/** *nid*
EAT WITH FINGERS: eat with one's fingers **michininjiikanjige** *vai*
INDEX FINGER: **izhinoo'iganinj, -iin** *ni*
LITTLE FINGER: **ishkweninj, -iin** *ni*
MIDDLE FINGER: **naawininj, -iin** *ni*
SORE FINGER: have a sore finger **gaagiijininjii** *vai*
FINGERNAIL
FINGERNAIL: my nail (fingernail, toenail) **nishkanzh, -iig /-shkanzhy-/** *nad*
WHITE SPOTS ON FINGERNAILS: have white spots on fingernails **mindaweganzhii** *vai*
FINISH
FINISH: **giizhi-** *pv4;* finish (in work or an activity) **anwaataa** *vai;* finish a task **giizhiitaa** *vai;* finish s.o. **giizhi'** *vta;* finish s.t. **giizhitoon** *vti2;* finish with s.o. **giizhiikaw** *vta;* finish with s.t. **giizhiikan** *vti*
FINISH A TASK: **giizhiitaa** *vai*
FINISH BOILING: **giizhigamide, giizhigamidemagad** *vii;* finish boiling things **giizhigamizige** *vai*
FINISH BOILING SAP: **ishkwaagamizige** *vai*
FINISH BUILDING A DWELLING: **giizhige** *vai*
FINISH COOKING: finish cooking s.o. **giiziz /giizizw-/** *vta;* finish cooking s.t. **giizizan** *vti*
FINISH MAKING: finish making s.o. **giizhi'** *vta;* finish making s.t. **giizhitoon** *vti2*
FINISH WORK: **giizhiitaa** *vai*
FINISHED
FINISHED: be finished **giizhichigaade, giizhichigaademagad** *vii;* **giizhichigaazo** *vai*
FINN
FINN: **madoodoowinini, -wag** *na;* **omakakiiwinini, -wag** *na*
FIR
BALSAM FIR: **zhingob, -iig** *na*
FIR BOUGH
FIR BOUGH: **zhingobaandag, -oog** *na*
FIRE
FIRE: **ishkode, -n** *ni;* there is a fire made in a fireplace **boodawaade, boodawaademagad** *vii*
AROUND THE FIRE: **giiwitaashkode** *pc*
BEYOND THE FIRE: **awasishkode** *pc*
BUILD A FIRE: **boodawe** *vai*
BY A FIRE: **jiigishkode** *pc*
CATCH FIRE: **nawadide, nawadidemagad** *vii;* **nawadizo** *vai*
HAVE A FIRE: have a fire at one's place **zakizo** *vai*
MAKE A FIRE: **ishkodeke** *vai*
ON FIRE: be on fire **ishkodewan** *vii*
ON THE OTHER SIDE OF THE FIRE: **agaamishkode** *pc*
ON THIS SIDE OF THE FIRE: **ondaasishkode** *pc*
OVER ACROSS THE FIRE: **awasishkode** *pc*
PUT WOOD ON THE FIRE: **bagidinise** *vai*
SET ON FIRE: set s.o. on fire **zaka' /zaka'w-/** *vta;* set s.t. on fire **zaka'an** *vti;* set (s.t.) on fire for s.o. **zaka'amaw** *vta*
STIR THE FIRE: **jiichiishkinzhe'ige** *vai*
TAKEN OFF THE FIRE: be taken off the fire **agwaasijigaade, agwaasijigaademagad** *vii;* **agwaasijigaazo** *vai*
WARM BY THE FIRE: warm oneself by the fire **awazo** *vai*
FIRE EXTINGUISHER
FIRE EXTINGUISHER: **aate'igan, -an** *ni*
FIRE POKER
FIRE POKER: **jiichiishkinzhe'igan, -an** *ni*
FIRE TRUCK
FIRE TRUCK: **aate'ishkodawewidaabaan** *na*
FIREFLY
FIREFLY: **waawaatesi, -wag** *na, also* **wewaatesi**
FIREMAN
FIREMAN: **aate'ishkodawewinini, -wag** *na*
FIREPLACE
FIREPLACE: **boodawaan, -an** *ni*
FIREWOOD
FIREWOOD: piece of firewood **mishi /miS-/** *ni*

BRING FIREWOOD INSIDE: **biindigenise** *vai*
CUT FIREWOOD: **manise** *vai;* cut s.t. as firewood **manisaadan** *vti;* cut (s.t.) as firewood for s.o. **manisaw** *vta*
GO GET FIREWOOD: **naadinise** *vai, also* **naajinise**
SPLIT FIREWOOD: **daashkiga'ise** *vai*

FIRST
FIRST: **nitam** *pc;* first (in a time sequence) **akawe** *pc, also* **kawe**
AT FIRST: **wayeshkad** *pc*
FIRST OF ALL: **akawe** *pc, also* **kawe**
LIVE IN THE FIRST HOUSE: **nitamige** *vai*
THE FIRST DAY: be the first day (of a month) **maadaginzo** *vai*

FIRST PERSON
FIRST PERSON: *first person prefix* **ni=** *pre; also* **n=, in=, ind=, im=, nin=*, nim=*, nind=***
FIRST PERSON EXCLUSIVE PLURAL: we *first person exclusive plural personal pronoun* **niinawind** *pr;* only us *first person exclusive plural personal pronoun* **niinetawind** *pr;* our turn *first person exclusive plural personal pronoun* **niinitamawind** *pr*
FIRST PERSON INCLUSIVE PLURAL: we *first person inclusive personal pronoun* **giinawind** *pr;* only us *first person inclusive personal pronoun* **giinetawind** *pr;* our turn *first person inclusive personal pronoun* **giinitamawind** *pr*
FIRST PERSON SINGULAR: I *first person singular personal pronoun* **niin** *pr;* my turn *first person singular personal pronoun* **niinitam** *pr;* only me *first person singular personal pronoun* **niineta** *pr*

FIRST TIME
FOR THE FIRST TIME: **oshki-** *pv4*

FIRST-BORN
FIRST-BORN: **nitamoozhaan, -ag** *na*

FISH
FISH: **giigoonh, -yag** *na;* **giigoonyike** *vai*
CLEAN A FISH: **bakazhaawe** *vai*
FIRE-CURED MEAT OR FISH: **abwewasigan, -an** *ni*
FISH THROUGH THE ICE WITH SPEAR: **akwa'waa** *vai*
FISH WITH A HOOK AND LINE: **wewebanaabii** *vai*
FISH WITH A NET: **bagida'waa** *vai*
FISH WITH SET LINES: **bagidaabii** *vai*
GO FISHING: **noojigiigoonyiwe** *vai*
SCALE FISH: **jiiga'e** *vai*

FISH DECOY
FISH DECOY: **okeyaw, -ag** *na*

FISH EGG
FISH EGG: **waak, -wan** *ni*

FISH HOOK
FISH HOOK: **migiskan, -an** *ni*

FISH HOUSE
FISH HOUSE FOR SPEARING: **akwa'wewigamig, -oon** *ni*

FISH SOUP
FISH SOUP: **giigoonhwaaboo** *ni*

FISH SPEAR
FISH SPEAR: **anit, -iin** *ni*

FISH TRAP
FISH TRAP: **biinjiboonaagan, -ag** *na*

FISHER
FISHER: **ojiig, -ag** *na*

FISHER HIDE
FISHER HIDE: **ojiigiwayaan, -ag** *na*

FISHERMAN
FISHERMAN: **giigoonyikewinini, -wag** *na*

FISHING POLE
FISHING POLE: **migiskanaak, -oon** *ni, also* **migiskanaatig**

FIT
FIT: **debashkine** *vai;* **debashkine, debashkinemagad** *vii;* fit (as something liquid) **debibii, debibiimagad** *vii*
FIT LOOSELY: fit s.o. loosely **geshawishkaw** *vta;* fit s.t. loosely **geshawishkan** *vti*
FIT WELL: **minwashkine** *vai;* **minwashkine, minwashkinemagad** *vii;* fit s.o. well (e.g., pants) **minokaw** *vta;* fit s.t. well **minokan** *vti*
FIT WITH FOOT OR BODY: fit s.o. with foot or body **debishkaw** *vta;* fit s.t. with foot or body **debishkan** *vti*

FIVE
FIVE: **naanan** *nm;* **naano-** *pv4;* they are five **naananinoon /naananin-/** *vii;* **naananiwag /naanani-/** *vai;* five (card) **naanoobii'igan, -ag** *na*
AND FIVE: **ashi-naanan** *nm;* **ashi-naano-** *pv4*
FIVE ACRES: **naano-diba'igaans** *pc*
FIVE DAYS: **naano-giizhik** *pc;* **naanogon** *pc;* be five days **naanogonagad** *vii*
FIVE DAYS OLD: be five days old **naanogonagizi** *vai*
FIVE DOLLARS: **naanwaabik** *pc*
FIVE FEET: **naanozid** *pc*
FIVE HOURS: **naano-diba'igan** *pc*
FIVE HUNDRED: **naanwaak** *nm*
FIVE INCHES: **naanoninj** *pc*
FIVE MILES: **naano-diba'igan** *pc*
FIVE MINUTES: **naano-diba'igaans** *pc*
FIVE MONTHS: **naano-giizis** *pc*
FIVE NIGHTS: **naano-dibik** *pc*
FIVE O'CLOCK: be five o'clock **naano-diba'iganed** *vii*
FIVE PAIRS: **naanwewaan** *pc*
FIVE SETS: **naanwewaan** *pc*
FIVE THOUSAND: **naanosagoons** *nm*
FIVE TIMES: **naaning** *pc*
FIVE WEEKS: **naano-anama'e-giizhik** *pc;* be five weeks **naano-anama'e-giizhigad** *vii*
FIVE YEARS: **naano-biboon** *pc;* be five years **naano-biboonagad** *vii*
FIVE YEARS OLD: be five years old **naano-biboonagizi** *vai*

FIX
FIX: fix s.o. **nanaa'in** *vta;* fix s.t. **nanaa'inan** *vti;* **nanaa'itoon** *vti2;* fix (s.t.) for s.o. **nanaa'itaw** *vta, also* **nanaa'itamaw**; fix things **nanaa'ichige** *vai*

FLAG
FLAG: **gikiwe'on, -an** *ni*
FLASHLIGHT
FLASHLIGHT: **zakaasigan, -an** *ni*
FLAT
FLAT: be flat **nabagaa, nabagaamagad** *vii;* **nabagizi** *vai*
FLAT NOSE: have a flat nose **nabagijaane** *vai*
FLAT TIRE: have a flat tire **nabagijiishin** *vai*
FLAVOR
FLAVOR: flavor (s.t.) **apaabowe** *vai+o*
FLEA
FLEA: **babig, -wag** *na*
FLEE
FLEE: **giimii** *vai;* **ozhimo** *vai;* flee from s.o. **ginjiba'** *vta;* flee from people **ginjiba'iwe** *vai*
ARRIVE FLEEING: arrive fleeing from people **bagamiba'iwe** *vai*
FLEE FOR GOOD: **aapijinizhimo** *vai*
START TO FLEE: **maajiiba'iwe** *vai*
FLESH
FLESH: my flesh **niiyaas /-iiyaas-/** *nid*
FLIGHT
RUN ALONG IN FLIGHT: **biminizhimo** *vai;* run along in flight from someone **bimiba'iwe** *vai*
RUN FROM CERTAIN PLACE IN FLIGHT: run from a certain place in flight **onjinizhimo** *vai*
RUN TO A CERTAIN PLACE IN FLIGHT: **izhinizhimo** *vai*
FLING
FLING OPEN: fling s.t. open (as something stick- or wood-like, e.g., a door) **baakaakowebinan** *vti*
FLINT
FLINT: **biiwaanag, -oog** *na*
FLIRT
FLIRT: **noodendam** *vai2*
FLOAT
FLOAT: **agomo** *vai;* **agonde** *vii*
FLOAT AWAY: **animaabogo** *vai;* **animaaboode, animaaboodemagad** *vii*
FLOAT
FLOAT: **deteba'agonjichigan, -an** *ni;* net float **agonjoonaagan, -an** *ni*
FLOOD
FLOOD: there is a flood **mooshka'an** *vii*
FLOODED
FLOODED: be flooded **mooshka'an** *vii;* **nikibii** *vai;* **nikibii, nikibiimagad** *vii*
FLOOR
FLOOR: **michisag, -oon** *ni*
FLOOR ABOVE: the floor above **ishpimisag, -oon** *ni*
FLOOR PIECE OF CANOE: **apisidaagan, -ag** *na*
IN THE MIDDLE OF THE FLOOR: **naawisag** *pc*
UNDER THE FLOOR: **anaamisag** *pc*
WASH FLOORS: **giziibiigisaginige** *vai*
FLOUR
FLOUR: **bakwezhigan, -ag** *na;* **bebinezid bakwezhigan** *na;* **bibine-bakwezhigan** *na*
FLOUR BOX
FLOUR BOX: **bakwezhigani-makak, -oon** *ni*
FLOW
FLOW A CERTAIN WAY: **izhijiwan** *vii*
FLOW ALONG: **bimijiwan** *vii*
FLOW AWAY: **animijiwan** *vii*
FLOW FAST: **gizhiijiwan** *vii*
FLOW FROM A CERTAIN PLACE: **onjijiwan** *vii*
FLOW IN: **biinjijiwan** *vii*
FLOW INTO A LAKE: **zaagidawaa, zaagidawaamagad** *vii*
FLOW OUT: **zaagijiwan** *vii*
FLOW TO A CERTAIN PLACE: **izhijiwan** *vii*
FLOW WITH A RIPPLE: **zaasijiwan** *vii*
HEARD FLOWING: be heard flowing (e.g., a rapids) **madwejiwan** *vii*
RIVER FLOWS ALONG: flow along (as a river) **bimitigweyaa, bimitigweyaamagad** *vii*
RIVER FLOWS AROUND A BEND: flow around a bend (as a river) **washkitigweyaa, washkitigweyaamagad** *vii*
RIVER FLOWS TO A CERTAIN PLACE: flow to a certain place (as a river) **izhitigweyaa, izhitigweyaamagad** *vii*
START TO FLOW: **maajijiwan** *vii*
FLOWER
FLOWER: **waabigwan, -iin** *ni*
FLUTE
FLUTE: **bibigwan, -an** *ni*
PLAY THE FLUTE: **bibigwe** *vai*
FLY
ARRIVE FLYING: **bagamibide, bagamibidemagad** *vii;* **bagamibizo** *vai;* **bagamise** *vai;* **bagamise, bagamisemagad** *vii*
FLY ABOUT: **babaamibide, babaamibidemagad** *vii;* **babaamibizo** *vai;* **babaamise** *vai;* **babaamise, babaamisemagad** *vii*
FLY ALONG: **bimibide, bimibidemagad** *vii;* **bimibizo** *vai;* **bimise** *vai;* **bimise, bimisemagad** *vii*
FLY AT A CERTAIN SPEED: **apiichibide, apiichibidemagad** *vii;* **apiichibizo** *vai*
FLY AWAY: **animibide, animibidemagad** *vii;* **animibizo** *vai;* **animise** *vai;* **animise, animisemagad** *vii*
FLY AWAY MAKING NOISE: **animwewebide, animwewebidemagad** *vii;* **animwewebizo** *vai*
FLY FAST: **gizhiibide, gizhiibidemagad** *vii;* **gizhiibizo** *vai;* **gizhiise** *vai;* **gizhiise, gizhiisemagad** *vii*
FLY FROM A CERTAIN PLACE: **onjise** *vai;* **onjise, onjisemagad** *vii*

FLY HERE: **biijibide, biijibidemagad** *vii;* **biijibizo** *vai;* **biijise** *vai;* **biijise, biijisemagad** *vii*
FLY IN: **biinjibide, biinjibidemagad** *vii;* **biinjibizo** *vai;* **biinjise** *vai;* **biinjise, biinjisemagad** *vii*
FLY INSIDE: **biindigebide, biindigebidemagad** *vii;* **biindigebizo** *vai*
FLY OPEN: fly open (as something stick- or wood-like, e.g., a door) **baakaakose, baakaakosemagad** *vii*
FLY TO A CERTAIN PLACE: **ipide, ipidemagad** *vii;* **ipizo** *vai;* **izhise** *vai;* **izhise, izhisemagad** *vii*
FLY UPWARDS: **ombibide, ombibidemagad** *vii;* **ombibizo** *vai*

FLY
FLY: fly (insect) **oojii, -g** *na, also* **oojiins**

FLYING SQUIRREL
FLYING SQUIRREL: **zhagashkaandawe, -g** *na*

FOAM
FOAM: **biite** *ni*

FOAMY
FOAMY: be foamy **biitewan** *vii*

FOG
FOG: there is a fog **awan** *vii*
DENSE FOG: be a dense fog **gashkawan** *vii*

FOGGY
FOGGY: be foggy **awan** *vii*

FOLD
FOLD: fold s.o. **biskin** *vta;* fold s.o. (as something sheet-like) **biskiigin** *vta;* fold s.t. **biskinan** *vti;* fold s.t. (as something sheet-like) **biskiiginan** *vti*
FOLD OVER: fold s.o. over **nabon** *vta;* fold s.t. over **nabonan** *vti*
FOLD WITH HANDS: fold s.o. with hands **biskibizh /biskibiN-/** *vta;* fold s.t. with hands **biskibidoon** *vti2*

FOLDED
FOLDED: be folded **biskaa, biskaamagad** *vii;* **biskinigaade, biskinigaademagad** *vii*

FOLLOW
FOLLOW: follow in s.o.'s steps **aanikeshkaw** *vta;* follow s.o. **noopinazh /noopinaN-/** *vta;* follow s.t. **noopinadoon** *vti2*
FOLLOW A TRAIL: go off following a trail **maada'adoo** *vai;* go off following s.o.'s trail **maada'azh /maada'aN-/** *vta*
FOLLOW A TRAIL ALONG: **bima'adoo** *vai;* follow s.o.'s trail along **bima'azh /bima'aN-/** *vta;* follow s.t. along as a trail **bima'adoon** *vti2*
FOLLOW A TRAIL AWAY: **anima'adoo** *vai;* follow s.o.'s trail away **anima'azh /anima'aN-/** *vta;* follow s.t. away as a trail **anima'adoon** *vti2*
FOLLOW A TRAIL HERE: **biida'adoo** *vai;* follow s.o.'s trail here **biida'azh /biida'aN-/** *vta;* follow s.t. as a trail here **biida'adoon** *vti2*
FOLLOW A TRAIL TO A CERTAIN PLACE: follow s.o.'s trail to a certain place **ina'azh /ina'aN-/** *vta;* follow s.t. as a trail to a certain place **ina'adoon** *vti2*

FOND DU LAC
FOND DU LAC: Fond du Lac Reservation **Nagaajiwanaang** *place*

FOOD
FOOD: **miijim, -an** *ni;* **wiisiniwin** *ni*
BUY FOOD: **miijimadaawe** *vai*
GET FOOD: get food by hunting or fishing **nandawenjige** *vai*
GO GET FOOD: **naajimiijime** *vai*
SERVE FOOD: serve food to people **ashange** *vai*

FOOLISH
FOOLISH: be foolish **gagiibaadad** *vii;* **gagiibaadizi** *vai*
DO FOOLISH THINGS: **gagiibaajichige** *vai*

FOOT
FOOT: my foot **inzid, -an /-zid-/** *nid*
ACHE IN FOOT: have an ache in one's foot **dewizide** *vai*
BIG FOOT: have a big foot **mangizide** *vai*
BLISTER ON FOOT: get a blister on one's foot **abashkwebiigizideshin** *vai*
CERTAIN NUMBER OF FEET: a certain number of feet **dasozid** *pc*
MOVE FOOT A CERTAIN WAY: move one's foot a certain way **izhizideni** *vai*
MUDDY FEET: have muddy feet **azhashkiiwizide** *vai*
NUMB FOOT: have a numb foot **niboowizide** *vai*
SORE FOOT: have a sore foot **gaagiijizide** *vai*
SPRAIN FOOT: sprain one's foot **zegizideshin** *vai*
SWEATY FOOT: have a sweaty foot **abwezide** *vai*
SWOLLEN FOOT: have a swollen foot **baagizide** *vai*
TAP FOOT: tap one's foot **jiichiibizideni** *vai*
WARM FEET: warm one's feet **abizidezo** *vai*

FOOTBRIDGE
FOOTBRIDGE: foot bridge **aazhawaandawaagan, -an** *ni*

FOOTPATH
FOOTPATH: **ozide-miikana, -n** *ni*

FOOTPRINT
FOOTPRINT: **bimikawaan, -an** *ni*

FOOTREST
CRADLE BOARD FOOTREST: **apizideyaakwa'igan, -an** *ni*

FOOTSTOOL
FOOTSTOOL: **apizideshinowin, -an** *ni*

FORBID
FORBID: forbid s.o. to **gina'amaw** *vta*

FORBIDDEN
FORBIDDEN: it is forbidden **gina'amaadim** *vai*

FOREHEAD
FOREHEAD: my forehead **nikatig, -oon /-katigw-/** *nid*
MIDDLE OF THE FOREHEAD: in the middle of the forehead **naawigatig** *pc*

FOREIGN
FOREIGN: **mayagi-** *pv4;* be foreign **mayagizi** *vai*
LOOK FOREIGN: **mayaginaagozi** *vai;* **mayaginaagwad** *vii*
SOUND FOREIGN: **mayagitaagozi** *vai;* **mayagitaagwad** *vii*
FOREIGNER
FOREIGNER: **mayagwewinini, -wag** *na*
FORETELL
FORETELL THE FUTURE: **onwaachige** *vai*
FOREVER
FOREVER: **gaagige-** *pv4*
FORGET
FORGET: **wanendam** *vai2;* forget (s.t.) **waniike** *vai+o;* forget s.o. **boonenim** *vta;* **wanenim** *vta;* forget s.t. **boonendan** *vti;* **wanendan** *vti*
FORK
FORK: **badaka'igan, -an** *ni*
USE A FORK ON: use a fork on s.o. **badaka' /badaka'w-/** *vta;* use a fork on s.t. **badaka'an** *vti*
FORK
RIVER FORKS: fork (as a river) **niingidawitigweyaa, niingidawitigweyaamagad** *vii*
ROAD FORKS: fork (as a road or trail) **niingidawadamon /niingidawadamo-/** *vii*
TRAIL FORKS: fork (as a road or trail) **niingidawadamon /niingidawadamo-/** *vii*
FORM
FORM: form s.o. **ozhi'** *vta;* form s.t. **ozhitoon** *vti2*
FORMERLY
FORMERLY: **gayat** *pc;* **iko** *pc, also* **ko**
FORTUNATE
FORTUNATE: be fortunate **zhawendaagozi** *vai*
FORTY
FORTY: **niimidana** *nm*
FOUND
FOUND: be found **mikigaade, mikigaademagad** *vii;* **mikigaazo** *vai*
FOUR
FOUR: **niiwin** *nm;* **niiwo-** *pv4, also* **niiyo-**; they are four **niiwinoon /niiwin-/** *vii;* **niiwiwag /niiwi-/** *vai;* four (card) **niiwoobii'igan, -ag** *na, also* **niiyoobii'igan**
AND FOUR: **ashi-niiwin** *nm;* **ashi-niiwo-** *pv4, also* **ashi-niiyo-**; **ashi-niiyo-** *pv4, also* **ashi-niiwo-**
FOUR ACRES: **niiwo-diba'igaans** *pc, also* **niiyo-diba'igaans**
FOUR DAYS: **niiwo-giizhik** *pc, also* **niiyo-giizhik**; **niiwogon** *pc, also* **niiyogon**; be four days **niiwogonagad** *vii, also* **niiyogonagad**
FOUR DAYS OLD: be four days old **niiwogonagizi** *vai, also* **niiyogonagizi**
FOUR DOLLARS: **niiwaabik** *pc*
FOUR EACH: **neniiwin** *nm*
FOUR FEET: **niiwozid** *pc, also* **niiyozid**
FOUR HOURS: **niiwo-diba'igan** *pc, also* **niiyo-diba'igan**
FOUR HUNDRED: **niiwaak** *nm*
FOUR INCHES: **niiwoninj** *pc, also* **niiyoninj**
FOUR MILES: **niiwo-diba'igan** *pc, also* **niiyo-diba'igan**
FOUR MINUTES: **niiwo-diba'igaans** *pc, also* **niiyo-diba'igaans**
FOUR MONTHS: **niiwo-giizis** *pc, also* **niiyo-giizis**
FOUR NIGHTS: **niiwo-dibik** *pc, also* **niiyo-dibik**
FOUR PAIRS: **niiwewaan** *pc*
FOUR SETS: **niiwewaan** *pc*
FOUR THOUSAND: **niiwosagoons** *nm, also* **niiyosagoons**
FOUR TIMES: **niiwing** *pc*
FOUR WEEKS: **niiwo-anama'e-giizhik** *pc, also* **niiyo-anama'e-giizhik**; **niiwo-anama'e-giizhik** *pc, also* **niiyo-anama'e-giizhik**; be four weeks **niiwo-anama'e-giizhigad** *vii, also* **niiyo-anama'e-giizhigad**
FOUR YEARS: **niiwo-biboon** *pc, also* **niiyo-biboon**; be four years **niiwo-biboonagad** *vii*
FOUR YEARS OLD: be four years old **niiwo-biboonagizi** *vai, also* **niiyo-biboonagizi**
FOURTEEN
FOURTEEN: **ashi-niiwin** *nm;* **midaaswi ashi-niiwin** *nm*
FOURTH
THE FOURTH DAY OF THE MONTH: be the fourth day of the month **niiwogonagizi** *vai, also* **niiyogonagizi**
FOURTH OF JULY
FOURTH OF JULY: be the Fourth of July **baapaashkizige-giizhigad** *vii*
FOX
FOX: **waagosh, -ag** *na*
FOX HIDE
FOX HIDE: **waagoshiwayaan, -ag** *na*
FRAIL
FRAIL: be frail **niinamizi** *vai*
FRAME
SAP-BOILING FRAME: frame for holding sap-boiling kettles **iskigamiziganaak, -oon** *ni*
SET UP AS A FRAME: set s.t. up as a frame **onaakosidoon** *vti2*
FREE
FREE: free s.o. **gidiskin** *vta;* free s.t. **gidiskinan** *vti*
GET FREE: **gashki'o** *vai*
PULL FREE: pull s.o. free **gidiskibizh /gidiskibiN-/** *vta;* pull s.t. free **gidiskibidoon** *vti2*
TRY TO GET FREE: **wiikwaji'o** *vai;* try to get free of s.t. **wiikwajitoon** *vti2*
FREEZE
FREEZE: **mashkawadin** *vii;* **mashkawaji** *vai*
FREEZE OVER: **gashkadin** *vii*
FREEZE STIFF: freeze s.o. stiff **mashkawaakwajim** *vta;* freeze s.t. stiff **mashkawaakwajidoon** *vti2*

FREEZE TO DEATH: **gawaji** *vai*

FREEZER

FREEZER: **dakisijigan, -an** *ni*

FRENCH

SPEAK FRENCH: **wemitigoozhiimo** *vai*

FRENCHMAN

FRENCHMAN: **wemitigoozhi, -wag** *na*

FRIDAY

FRIDAY: be Friday **naano-giizhigad** *vii*

FRIED

FRIED: be fried **zaasakokwaade, zaasakokwaademagad** *vii;* **zaasakokwaazo** *vai*

FRIEND

FRIEND: my (female's) female friend **niijikwe, -g /-iijikwew-/** *nad;* my (female's) female friend **indaangwe, -g /-daangwew-/** *nad;* my (male's) male friend **niijikiwenh, -yag /-iijikiweny-/** *nad;* my (male's) male friend *ritual use* **niikaan, -ag /-iikaan-/** *nad;* **niikaanis, -ag /-iikaanis-/** *nad;* my friend (vocative form, usually male to male) **niijii** *nad*

CLOSE FRIENDS: be close friends with s.o. **beshwaji'** *vta*

FRIENDS: they are friends with each other **nagadenindiwag /nagadenindi-/** *vai*

FRIGHTEN

FRIGHTEN: frighten s.o. **zegi'** *vta*

FRINGE

FRINGE: **niisiiwezhigan, -an** *ni*

CUT FRINGE: cut fringe in s.o. **niisiiwezh /niisiiwezhw-/** *vta;* cut fringe in s.t. **niisiiwezhan** *vti*

FRINGED

FRINGED: be fringed **niisiiwezhigaade, niisiiwezhigaademagad** *vii;* **niisiiwezhigaazo** *vai*

FROG

FROG: **omakakii, -g** *na*

FROM

ABSENT FROM A CERTAIN PLACE: be absent from a certain place **ondendi** *vai*

BLOWN FROM A CERTAIN PLACE: be blown from a certain place **ondaashi** *vai;* be blown from a certain place **ondaasin** *vii*

CARRY FROM A CERTAIN PLACE: carry s.o. from a certain place **onjiwizh /onjiwiN-/** *vta;* carry s.t. from a certain place **onjiwidoon** *vti2*

CARRY ON BACK FROM A CERTAIN PLACE: carry s.o. on back from a certain place **ondoom** *vta;* carry s.t. on back from a certain place **ondoondan** *vti*

COME AS WIND FROM A CERTAIN PLACE: come as wind from a certain direction **ondaanimad** *vii*

COME FROM A CERTAIN PLACE: **ondaadad** *vii;* **ondaadizi** *vai;* **onjibaa** *vai;* **onjii** *vai;* come from a certain place (as smoke) **ondaabate, ondaabatemagad** *vii*

COME FROM A CERTAIN PLACE CRYING: **ondademo** *vai*

CRAWL FROM A CERTAIN PLACE: **ondoode** *vai*

DRIVE FROM A CERTAIN PLACE: **onjibide, onjibidemagad** *vii;* **onjibizo** *vai;* **onjidaabii'iwe** *vai*

EARN FROM A CERTAIN PLACE: **ondizi** *vai*

FALL FROM A CERTAIN PLACE: **onjibide, onjibidemagad** *vii;* **onjibizo** *vai*

FLOW FROM A CERTAIN PLACE: **onjijiwan** *vii*

FLY FROM A CERTAIN PLACE: **onjise** *vai;* **onjise, onjisemagad** *vii*

FROM A CERTAIN PLACE: **onji-** *pv3*

GET FROM A CERTAIN PLACE: get (s.t.) for oneself from a certain place **ondinamaazo** *vai;* get s.o. from a certain place **ondin** *vta;* get s.t. from a certain place **ondinan** *vti;* get (s.t.) for s.o. from a certain place **ondinamaw** *vta;* get things from a certain place **ondinige** *vai*

GET WATER FROM A CERTAIN PLACE: **onda'ibii** *vai*

GONE FROM A CERTAIN PLACE: be gone from a certain place **ondendi** *vai*

INHERIT FROM A CERTAIN SOURCE: **ondizi** *vai*

LOOK OUT FROM A CERTAIN PLACE: **onzaabi** *vai*

OBTAIN FROM A CERTAIN PLACE: obtain s.o. from a certain place **ondin** *vta;* obtain s.t. from a certain place **ondinan** *vti;* obtain (s.t.) for s.o. from a certain place **ondinamaw** *vta;* obtain things from a certain place **ondinige** *vai*

OBTAINED FROM A CERTAIN PLACE: be obtained from a certain place **ondinigaade, ondinigaademagad** *vii;* **ondinigaazo** *vai*

PADDLE FROM A CERTAIN PLACE: **ondakwazhiwe** *vai*

RIDE FROM A CERTAIN PLACE ON HORSEBACK: **ondoomigo** *vai*

ROAD LEADS FROM A CERTAIN PLACE: lead from a certain place (as a road or trail) **ondadamon /ondadamo-/** *vii*

RUN FROM CERTAIN PLACE IN FLIGHT: run from a certain place in flight **onjinizhimo** *vai*

RUN FROM A CERTAIN PLACE: **onjibatoo** *vai*

SAIL FROM A CERTAIN PLACE: **ondaashi** *vai;* **ondaasin** *vii*

SKATE FROM A CERTAIN PLACE: **ondaada'e** *vai*

SPEED FROM A CERTAIN PLACE: **onjibide, onjibidemagad** *vii;* **onjibizo** *vai*

SWIM FROM A CERTAIN PLACE: **ondaadagaa** *vai;* swim from a certain place (as a fish) **ondakwazhiwe** *vai*

TAKE FROM A CERTAIN PLACE: take s.o. from a certain place **onjiwizh /onjiwiN-/** *vta;* take s.t. from a certain place **onjiwidoon** *vti2*

TRAIL LEADS FROM A CERTAIN PLACE: lead from a certain place (as a road or trail) **ondadamon /ondadamo-/** *vii*
WADE FROM A CERTAIN PLACE: **ondaadagaazii** *vai*
WALK FROM A CERTAIN PLACE: **ondose** *vai*

FRONT
AT THE FRONT: **niigaan** *pc*
HANG IN FRONT: **niigaanagoode, niigaanagoodemagad** *vii;* **niigaanagoojin** *vai;* hang s.o. in front **niigaanagoozh /niigaanagooN-/** *vta;* hang s.t. in front **niigaanagoodoon** *vti2*
SIT IN FRONT: **niigaanabi** *vai*
STAND IN FRONT: **niigaanigaabawi** *vai*

FROST
HEAVY FROST: there is a heavy frost **zasakwaa** *vii*

FROSTBITTEN
FROSTBITTEN: be frostbitten **mashkawaji** *vai;* **mashkawaakwaji** *vai*

FROSTED
FROSTED: be frosted **ningiigwadin** *vii;* **ningiigwaji** *vai*

FROZEN
FROZEN: be frozen **mashkawadin** *vii;* **mashkawaji** *vai*
FROZEN HAND: have a frozen hand **mashkawaakwajininjiiwaji** *vai*
FROZEN OVER: be frozen over **gashkadin** *vii*
FROZEN SHUT: be frozen shut **gibaakwadin** *vii;* **gibaakwaji** *vai*
FROZEN STIFF: be frozen stiff **mashkawaakwadin** *vii;* **mashkawaakwaji** *vai*
FROZEN THICK: be frozen thick **gipagaakwadin** *vii;* **gipagaakwaji** *vai*
FROZEN THIN: be frozen thin **bibagaakwadin** *vii;* **bibagaakwaji** *vai*

FRY
FRY: **zaasakokwe** *vai;* fry s.o. **zaasakokwaazh /zaasakokwaaN-/** *vta;* fry s.t. **zaasakokwaadan** *vti*

FRY BREAD
FRY BREAD: **zaasakokwaan, -ag** *na*

FRYING PAN
FRYING PAN: **abwewin, -an** *ni*

FUEL
RUN OUT OF FUEL: **iskaakizige** *vai*

FULL
FULL: be full (after eating) **debisinii** *vai;* be full (of a liquid) **mooshkinebii, mooshkinebiimagad** *vii;* be full (of solids) **mooshkine** *vai;* **mooshkine, mooshkinemagad** *vii*
FULL MOON: be full (as something mineral, e.g., the moon) **miziweyaabikizi** *vai*
FULL OF SMOKE: be full of smoke **gibwanaamode, gibwanaamodemagad** *vii*

FULLY
FULLY RIPE: be fully ripe **giizhaande, giizhaandemagad** *vii;* **giizhaanzo** *vai*

FUN
FUN: be fun **minwendaagozi** *vai;* **minwendaagwad** *vii*
JUST FOR FUN: **anishaa** *pc*

FUNERAL
HOLD A FUNERAL: **bagidenjige** *vai;* **maajaa'iwe** *vai;* hold a funeral for s.o. **maajaa'** *vta*
SPEAK AT A FUNERAL: **maajaa'iwe** *vai*

FUNGUS
FUNGUS: **wazhashkwedo, -wag** *na*

FUNNY
FUNNY: **wawiyazh** *pc*
CONSIDERED FUNNY: be considered funny (comical) **wawiyadendaagozi** *vai*
FUNNY MOVIE: be a funny movie **gagiibaadaatese, gagiibaadaatesemagad** *vii*
LOOK FUNNY: look funny (comical) **wawiyazhinaagozi** *vai;* **wawiyazhinaagwad** *vii*
SOUND FUNNY: sound funny (comical) **wawiyazhitaagozi** *vai;* **wawiyazhitaagwad** *vii*

FUR
FUR FOR TRADE: **adaawaagan, -an** *ni*
THICK FUR: have thick fur **gipagawe** *vai*

FUTURE
FORETELL THE FUTURE: **onwaachige** *vai*

FUTURE TENSE
FUTURE TENSE: *future tense prefix after a personal prefix* **ga-** *pv1; future tense prefix optional form after a personal prefix and before a vowel* **gad-**; *future tense prefix in independent order with no personal prefix* **da-** *pv1*; *future tense prefix in unchanged conjunct order* **ji-** *pv1*
FUTURE/DESIDERATIVE TENSE: want to **wii-** *pv1*

G

GALLBLADDER
GALLBLADDER: my gall bladder **niinzob, -iin /-iinzoby-/** *nid*

GALLSTONE
HAVE GALLSTONES: **odasiniinsimi** *vai*

GAMBLE
GAMBLE: **ataage** *vai;* they gamble with each other **ataadiwag /ataadi-/** *vai*

GAME WARDEN
GAME WARDEN: **gizhaadigewinini, -wag** *na;* **wiiyaasi-dakoniwewinini, -wag** *na*

GAP
PULL APART TO FORM A GAP: pull s.o. apart to form a gap **dawibizh /dawibiN-/** *vta;* pull s.t. apart to form a gap **dawibidoon** *vti2;* pull things apart to form a gap **dawibijige** *vai*

GARDEN
GARDEN: **gitigaan, -an** *ni;* **gitige** *vai*

GARTER
ARM GARTER: **jiiskinikebizon, -an** *ni*
LEG GARTER: **gashkidaasebizon, -an** *ni*

GAS CAN
GAS CAN: **waazakonenjiganaaboowakik, -oog** *na*

GAS STATION
GAS STATION: **waazakonenjiganaaboowadaawewigamig, -oon** *ni, also* **waazakonenjiganaaboo-adaawewigamig**

GAS TANK
GAS TANK: **waazakonenjiganaaboowakik, -oog** *na*

GASOLINE
GASOLINE: **waasamoo-bimide** *ni;* **waazakonenjiganaaboo** *ni*

GATHER
GATHER: gather s.o. **maamigin** *vta;* gather s.t. **maamiginan** *vti*
GATHER SAP: **naadoobii** *vai*
GATHER UP: gather s.o. up **asigin** *vta;* gather s.t. up **asiginan** *vti*

GATHERED
GATHERED UP: be gathered up **asiginigaade, asiginigaademagad** *vii;* **asiginigaazo** *vai*

GEAR
GEARSHIFT: **aandaabikinigan, -an** *ni*
SHIFT GEARS: **aandaabikinige** *vai;* **biindaabikibijige** *vai*

GEARSHIFT
GEARSHIFT: **biindaabikibijigan, -an** *ni*

GENEROUS
GENEROUS: be generous **gizhewaadizi** *vai*

GERMAN SHEPHERD
GERMAN SHEPHERD: **ma'iinganasim, -oog** *na*

GET
GET EASILY: get s.o. easily **wenipazhi'** *vta;* get s.t. easily **wenipazhitoon** *vti2*
GET FROM A CERTAIN PLACE: get s.o. from a certain place **ondin** *vta;* get s.t. from a certain place **ondinan** *vti;* get (s.t.) for s.o. from a certain place **ondinamaw** *vta;* get things from a certain place **ondinige** *vai;* get (s.t.) for oneself from a certain place **ondinamaazo** *vai*
GET WATER: **nibinaadi** *vai;* get water for s.o. **gwaaba'amaw** *vta*
GO GET: go get s.o. **naazh /naaN-/** *vta;* go get s.t. **naadin** *vti3;* go get (s.t.) for s.o. **naadaw** *vta*
GO GET A NET: **naadasabii** *vai*
GO GET BY BOAT: go get s.o. by boat **naada' /naada'w-/** *vta;* go get s.t. by boat **naada'an** *vti*
GO GET FIREWOOD: **naadinise** *vai, also* **naajinise**
GO GET FOOD: **naajimiijime** *vai*
GO GET MAIL: **naadazina'igane** *vai*
GO GET TRAPS: go get one's traps **naadasoonaagane** *vai*
GO GET WATER: go get water or other liquid **naadoobii** *vai*
GO TO GET: go to get s.o. by boat **naada'oozh /naada'ooN-/** *vta;* go to get s.t. by boat **naada'oodoon** *vti2*
RUN TO GET: run to get s.o. **naajibatwaazh /naajibatwaaN-/** *vta;* run to get s.t. **naajibatwaadan** *vti*

GET AWAY
GET AWAY: get away from s.o. **gii'** *vta*

GET IN
GET IN: get in a vehicle or boat **boozi** *vai*
TELL TO GET IN: tell s.o. to get in (a vehicle or boat) **boozinaazha' /boozinaazha'w-/** *vta*

GET OFF
GET OFF: get off a vehicle or boat **gabaa** *vai;* get s.o. off a vehicle or boat **gabaa'** *vta*
TELL TO GET OFF: tell s.o. to get off **gabaanaazha' /gabaanaazha'w-/** *vta*

GET UP
GET UP: get up (from a prone position) **onishkaa** *vai*

GHOST
GHOST: **jiibay, -ag** *na*

GIANT
GIANT: **misaabe, -g** *na*

GIGGLE
GIGGLE: **ginagaapi** *vai*

GIRAFFE
GIRAFFE: **genwaabiigigwed** *na-pt*

GIRL
GIRL: **ikwezens, -ag** *na;* be a girl **ikwezensiwi** *vai*
ADOLESCENT GIRL: **oshkiniigikwe, -g** *na;* be an adolescent girl **oshkiniigikwewi** *vai*

GIVE
GIVE: give (s.t.) to s.o. **miizh /miiN-/** *vta;* they give (s.t.) to each other **miinidiwag /miinidi-/** *vai*
GIVE AWAY: give away (s.t.) **miigiwe** *vai+o*
GIVE PRESENTS: give presents to relatives of someone deceased in completion of mourning on anniversary of the death **giiwenige** *vai*
GIVE PRESENTS IN EXCHANGE: give presents to s.o. in exchange **giiwenamaw** *vta*
GIVE SOMETHING APPROPRIATE: give s.o. something appropriate **debi'** *vta*
HAVE ENOUGH TO GIVE: have enough to give away **deba'ookii** *vai;* have enough to give to or feed s.o. **deba'oozh /deba'ooN-/** *vta*

GIVE UP
GIVE UP: **aanizhiitam** *vai2;* **boonendam** *vai2*
GIVEAWAY
GIVEAWAY: they have a giveaway **miinidiwag /miinidi-/** *vai*
GLAD
GLAD: be glad **minwendam** *vai2*
GLAND
GLAND: my gland (lymph node) **niniishk, -wag /-niishkw-/** *nad*
SWOLLEN GLAND: have a swollen gland (lymph node) **baaginiishkwe** *vai*
GLASS
GLASS: (piece of) glass **omoodayaabik, -oon** *ni*
BROKEN GLASS: (piece of) glass **omoodayaabik, -oon** *ni*
DRINKING GLASS: **mikwamiiwinaagaans, -an** *ni*
WINDOW GLASS: **waasechiganaabik, -oon** *ni*
GLASSES
EYEGLASSES: eyeglasses *plural* **oshkiinzhigokaajiganan** *ni, also* **oshkiinzhikokaanan**
GLOVE
GLOVE: **niisiiwe-minjikaawan, -ag** *na*
GLOW
GLOW: **waazakone, waazakonemagad** *vii*
GLUE
GLUE: **agokiwasigan, -an** *ni;* glue s.o. **agokiwas /agokiwasw-/** *vta;* **bazagokazh /bazagokaN-/** *vta;* glue s.t. **agokiwasan** *vti;* **bazagokadoon** *vti2*
GLUE SHUT: glue s.o. shut **gibokiwas** *vta;* glue s.t. shut **gibokiwasan** *vti*
GLUED
GLUED: be glued **agokiwaso** *vai;* **agokiwate, agokiwatemagad** *vii*
GLUED SHUT: be glued shut **gibokiwasigaade, gibokiwasigaademagad** *vii;* **gibokiwasigaazo** *vai*
GNAT
GNAT: **bingoshens, -ag** *na*
GNAW
GNAW: gnaw s.o. **zhishigwam** *vta;* gnaw s.t. **zhishigwandan** *vti*
GO
GO: go to a certain place **izhaa** *vai;* **izhaamagad** *vii*
GO A CERTAIN DIRECTION: go a certain direction (as smoke) **inaabate, inaabatemagad** *vii*
GO A CERTAIN SPEED: **apiizikaa** *vai*
GO ACROSS: **aazhooshkaa** *vai*
GO ACROSS BY BOAT: **aazhawa'am** *vai2, also* **aazhawa'o**
GO ACROSS WATER: **aazhoge** *vai*
GO AFTER: go after s.o. **naajinizha' /naajinizha'w-/** *vta;* **naazh /naaN-/** *vta;* **nooji'** *vta;* **noopinazh /noopinaN-/** *vta;* go after s.t. **naadin** *vti3;* **naajinizha'an** *vti;* **noojitoon** *vti2;* **noopinadoon** *vti2*
GO AFTER HAY: **naadashkosiwe** *vai*
GO AFTER TRAPS: **naajiwanii'ige** *vai*
GO AGAINST THE WIND: **onjishkawishkaa** *vai*
GO AHEAD: **niigaanii** *vai*
GO ALONG: **bimi-ayaa** *vai*
GO ALONG THE EDGE: **jiigewe** *vai*
GO ALONG THE SHORE: **bimaazhagaame** *vai;* **jiigewe** *vai*
GO AND ASK: go and ask for s.o. **nandwewem** *vta;* go and ask for s.t. **nandwewendan** *vti;* go and ask s.o. (for s.t.) **nandwewendamaw** *vta*
GO AND NOT RETURN: **aapidendi** *vai*
GO AROUND: **ditibise, ditibisemagad** *vii;* **giiwitaashkaa** *vai;* go around (e.g., a wheel) **ditibise** *vai*
GO AS FAST AS POSSIBLE: **apiizikaa** *vai*
GO ASHORE: **agwaataa** *vai*
GO AWAY: go away! **awas** *pc*
GO AWAY FROM THE WATER: **gopii** *vai*
GO AWAY IN A CANOE: **animishkaa** *vai*
GO BACK: **azhe-** *pv4;* **azhegiiwe** *vai*
GO BACKWARDS: **azheshkaa** *vai;* **azhetaa** *vai*
GO BY CANOE: **jiime** *vai*
GO DOWN: go down (of a body of water) **iskate, iskatemagad** *vii*
GO DOWN INTO THE WATER: **bakobii** *vai*
GO DOWNHILL: **niisaakiiwe** *vai*
GO DOWNSTAIRS: **niisaandawe** *vai*
GO EASY: go easy on s.o. **manaaji'** *vta;* go easy on s.t. **manaajitoon** *vti2*
GO EVERYWHERE: **miziweshkaa, miziweshkaamagad** *vii*
GO FAST: **gizhiikaa** *vai*
GO GET: go get s.o. **naazh /naaN-/** *vta;* go get s.t. **naadin** *vti3;* go get (s.t.) for s.o. **naadaw** *vta*
GO GET A NET: **naadasabii** *vai*
GO GET BY BOAT: go get s.o. by boat **naada' /naada'w-/** *vta;* go get s.t. by boat **naada'an** *vti*
GO GET FIREWOOD: **naadinise** *vai, also* **naajinise**
GO GET FOOD: **naajimiijime** *vai*
GO GET MAIL: **naadazina'igane** *vai*
GO GET TRAPS: go get one's traps **naadasoonaagane** *vai*
GO GET WATER: go get water or other liquid **naadoobii** *vai*
GO HOME: **giiwe** *vai*
GO HOME BY BOAT: **giiwe'o** *vai*
GO HOME MAD: **giiwegidaazo** *vai*
GO INLAND: **gopii** *vai*
GO INSIDE: **biindige** *vai*
GO INTO THE WOODS: **jekaakwa'am** *vai2*
GO OFF MAD: **maajiigidaazo** *vai*
GO OFF TO THE SIDE: **bake** *vai*
GO ON FOOT: **mitose** *vai*
GO OUT: **zaaga'am** *vai2*

GO OUT OF PLACE: **gotigobide, gotigobidemagad** *vii;* **gotigobizo** *vai*
GO OUT OF SIGHT: **ani-naagozi** *vai;* **ani-naagwad** *vii;* go out of sight (as around a corner) **aagawe** *vai*
GO OVER A POINT: **gakiiwe** *vai*
GO OVER TO: go over to; *after a personal prefix:* **a'o- awi-** *pv2, also* **'o-**
GO STRAIGHT: **gwayakoshkaa** *vai*
GO THE RIGHT WAY: **gwayakoshkaa** *vai*
GO THROUGH: **zhaabose, zhaabosemagad** *vii;* **zhaabwii** *vai*
GO TO: go to s.o. **naazikaw** *vta;* go to s.t. **naazikan** *vti;* go to people **naazikaage** *vai*
GO TO A CERTAIN PLACE: **izhaa** *vai;* **izhaamagad** *vii*
GO TO BED: **gawishimo** *vai*
GO TO GET: go to get s.o. by boat **naada'oozh /naada'ooN-/** *vta;* go to get s.t. by boat **naada'oodoon** *vti2*
GO TO SCHOOL: **gikinoo'amaagozi** *vai*
GO TO THE END: **gabeshkaa** *vai;* go to the end of s.t. **gabeshkan** *vti*
GO TO THE SHORE: **madaabii** *vai*
GO TO THE TOILET: **zaaga'am** *vai2*
GO TO WAR: go to war *archaic* **nandobani** *vai*
GO UPHILL: **agidaakiiwe** *vai*
GO UPSTAIRS: **akwaandawe** *vai*
GO UPWARDS: **ombishkaa** *vai;* **ombishkaa, ombishkaamagad** *vii*
GO UPWARDS AS SMOKE: **ombaabate** *vii*
GO WELL: **minose, minosemagad** *vii;* have things go well for one **minose** *vai*
GO WITH: go with s.o. **wiijiiw** *vta;* go with people **wiijii'iwe** *vai;* they go with each other **wiijiindiwag /wiijiindi-/** *vai*
GO WITH IN A BOAT: go with s.o. in a boat **aadawa'am** *vta*
GO WRONG: have things go wrong **maazhise** *vai*

GOAT

GOAT: **maanadikoshens, -ag** *na*

GOD

GOD: **gichi-manidoo, -g** *na;* **manidoo, -g** *na;* God (especially in Christian usage) **gizhe-manidoo** *na*

GOLD

GOLD: **ozaawaa-zhooniyaa** *ni, also* **ozhaawaa-zhooniyaa**
COLORED GOLD: be colored gold **ozaawaa-zhooniyaawaande, ozaawaa-zhooniyaawaandemagad** *vii, also* **ozhaawaa-zhooniyaawaande; ozaawaa-zhooniyaawaanzo** *vai, also* **ozhaawaa-zhooniyaanzo**

GOLDEN EAGLE

GOLDEN EAGLE: **giniw, -ag** *na*

GONE

GONE: gone! **weniban** *pc*
GONE A CERTAIN LENGTH OF TIME: be gone a certain length of time **apiitendi** *vai;* **inendi** *vai*
GONE A CERTAIN NUMBER OF DAYS: be gone a certain number of days **dasogonendi** *vai*
GONE FOREVER: be gone forever **aapidendi** *vai*
GONE FROM A CERTAIN PLACE: be gone from a certain place **ondendi** *vai*
GONE OVERNIGHT: be gone overnight **nikanendi** *vai*

GOOD

GOOD: **mino-** *pv4;* be good **mino-ayaa** *vai;* be good (as something mineral) **minwaabikad** *vii;* **minwaabikizi** *vai;* be good (as something sheet-like) **minwegad** *vii;* **minwegizi** *vai;* be good (as something stick- or wood-like) **minwaakozi** *vai;* **minwaakwad** *vii*
DO GOOD: do good things **minochige** *vai*
FEEL GOOD: **minwamanji'o** *vai*
FIND A GOOD TASTE: find a good taste in s.o. **minopozh /minopw-/** *vta;* find a good taste in s.t. **minopidan** *vti*
GET GOOD USE: get good use of s.o. **minwaabaji'** *vta;* get good use of s.t. **minwaabajitoon** *vti2*
GOOD AT: being good at **nitaa-** *pv4*
GOOD BODY: have a good body **minwaabewizi** *vai*
GOOD BREEZE: there is a good breeze **minwaanimad** *vii*
GOOD COLOR: be a good color **minwaande, minwaandemagad** *vii;* **minwaanzo** *vai*
GOOD EYESIGHT: have good eyesight **minwaabi** *vai*
GOOD HEALTH: have good health **mino-bimaadizi** *vai*
GOOD LUCK: have good luck **minose** *vai*
GOOD MOVIE: be a good movie **minwaatese, minwaatesemagad** *vii*
GOOD PROVIDER: be a good provider **gotaamigozi** *vai*
GOOD SMELL: have a good smell **minomaagozi** *vai;* **minomaagwad** *vii*
GOOD USE: be of good use **minwaabadad** *vii;* **minwaabadizi** *vai*
GOOD VOICE: have a good voice **minogondaagan** *vai;* **minowe** *vai*
GOOD WEATHER: be good weather **mizhakwad** *vii*
GOOD WORKER: be a good worker **gotaamigozi** *vai*
HAVE A GOOD TIME: **minawaanigozi** *vai*
IN GOOD HEALTH: be in good health **minwamanji'o** *vai*
LEAD A GOOD LIFE: **mino-izhiwebizi** *vai;* **minwaadizi** *vai*
LIE IN A GOOD POSITION: **minosin** *vii*
LOOK GOOD: **minwaabaminaagozi** *vai;* **minwaabaminaagwad** *vii*
SMELL GOOD: have a good smell **minomaagozi** *vai;* **minomaagwad** *vii*
SMELL GOOD BURNING OR COOKING: **minomaaso** *vai;* **minomaate, minomaatemagad** *vii*

SOUND GOOD: **minotaagozi** *vai;* **minotaagwad** *vii*
SOUNDING GOOD: hear s.o. sounding good **minotaw** *vta;* hear s.t. sounding good **minotan** *vti*
TASTE GOOD: **minopogozi** *vai;* **minopogwad** *vii;* taste good (as a liquid) **minwaagamin /minwaagami-/** *vii*
TELL A GOOD STORY: **minwaajimo** *vai*
TELL GOOD NEWS: **minwaajimo** *vai;* tell good news of s.o. **minwaajim** *vta;* tell good news of s.t. **minwaadodan** *vti*

GOOSE
CANADA GOOSE: **nika, -g** *na*

GOOSEBERRY
GOOSEBERRY: **zhaaboomin, -ag** *na*

GOOSEBERRY BUSH
GOOSEBERRY BUSH: **zhaaboominagaawanzh, -iig** *na*

GOPHER
POCKET GOPHER: **memookiwidoo, -g** *na*

GOSSIP
GOSSIP: **dazhinge** *vai;* gossip about s.o. **dazhim** *vta;* gossip about s.t. **dazhindan** *vti*

GOVERN
GOVERN: govern s.o. **ogimaakandaw** *vta;* govern s.t. **ogimaakandan** *vti*

GOVERNMENT
GOVERNMENT: **ogimaawiwin, -an** *ni*

GOVERNOR
GOVERNOR: **odaakewigimaa, -g** *na, also* **odaake-ogimaa**

GRAB
GRAB: grab s.o. **debibizh /debibiN-/** *vta;* **nawadin** *vta;* grab s.t. **debibidoon** *vti2;* **nawadinan** *vti;* grab (s.t.) for s.o. **debibidaw** *vta;* grab (s.t.) of s.o.'s **nawadinamaw** *vta;* grab people **nawadiniwe** *vai*

GRADUALLY
GRADUALLY: **eshkam** *pc*

GRAND MEDICINE SOCIETY
GRAND MEDICINE SOCIETY: **midewiwin** *ni*

GRAND PORTAGE
GRAND PORTAGE: Grand Portage Reservation **gichi-onigamiing** *place*

GRANDCHILD
GRANDCHILD: grandchild *vocative form of* **noozhishenh** my grandchild **noozis** *nad;* my grandchild **noozhishenh, -yag /-oozhisheny-/** *nad*

GRANDFATHER
GRANDFATHER: my grandfather **nimishoomis, -ag /-mishoomis-/** *nad*

GRANDMA
GRANDMA: grandma! **naan** *nad (vocative);* **nookoo** *nad (vocative)*

GRANDMOTHER
GRANDMOTHER: my grandmother **nookomis, -ag /-ookomis-/** *nad*

GRANDPA
GRANDPA: grandpa! **nimishoo** *nad (vocative)*

GRANULATE
GRANULATE SUGAR: **naseyaawangwe** *vai*

GRANULATED SUGAR
GRANULATED SUGAR: **bibine-ziinzibaakwad** *ni*

GRAPE
GRAPE: **zhawimin, -an** *ni, also* **zhoomin**

GRASS
GRASS: **mashkosiw, -an** *ni*

GRASSHOPPER
GRASSHOPPER: **bapakine, -g** *na*

GRAVE HOUSE
GRAVE HOUSE: **jiibegamig, -oon** *ni*

GRAVE MARKER
GRAVE MARKER: **jiibayaatig, -oog** *na*

GRAVEL ROAD
GRAVEL ROAD: **bingwii-miikana, -n** *ni*

GRAVEYARD
GRAVEYARD: **jiibayaki, -in** *ni*

GRAVY
GRAVY: **bakwezhiganaaboo** *ni*

GREASE
GREASE: **bimide** *ni*
BURP GREASE: **biinzibii** *vai*

GREAT
GREAT: **gichi-** *pv4, also* **chi-**

GREAT SPIRIT
GREAT SPIRIT: **gichi-manidoo, -g** *na*

GREAT-GRANDCHILD
GREAT-GRANDCHILD: **aanikoobijigan, -ag** *na*

GREAT-GRANDPARENT
GREAT-GRANDPARENT: **aanikoobijigan, -ag** *na*

GREBE
GREBE: **zhingibis, -ag** *na*

GREEN
GREEN: **ozhaawashko-** *pv4;* be green **ozhaawashkozi** *vai;* **ozhaawashkwaa, ozhaawashkwaamagad** *vii;* be green (as something mineral) **ozhaawashkwaabikad** *vii;* **ozhaawashkwaabikizi** *vai;* be green (as something sheet-like) **ozhaawashkwegad** *vii;* **ozhaawashkwegizi** *vai;* be green (as something stick- or wood-like) **ozhaawashkwaakozi** *vai;* **ozhaawashkwaakwad** *vii;* be green (as something string-like) **ozhaawashkwaabiigad** *vii;* **ozhaawashkwaabiigizi** *vai;* be leaf-green **ashkibagong inaande, ashkibagong inaandemagad** *vii;* **ashkibagong inaanzo** *vai*
GREEN LEAVES: there are green leaves **ashkibagaa, ashkibagaamagad** *vii*
WEAR GREEN: **ozhaawashko'o** *vai*

GREEN TEA
GREEN TEA: **ozhaawashko-aniibiish** *ni*

GREET
GREET: greet s.o. **anamikaw** *vta;* greet people **anamikaage** *vai;* they greet each other **anamikaadiwag /anamikaadi-/** *vai*
GREETINGS
GREETINGS: greetings! **aaniin** *pc;* **boozhoo** *pc*
GREY
GREY: be grey **waabijiiyaa, waabijiiyaamagad** *vii;* **waabijiizi** *vai*
GREY HAIR: have grey hair **waabikwe** *vai*
GREY SQUIRREL
GREY SQUIRREL: **misajidamoo, -g** *na*
GRILL
GRILL: grill (s.t.) **akakanzhebwe** *vai+o*
GRIND
GRIND DOWN: grind s.o. down **zisiboozh /zisibooN-/** *vta;* grind s.t. down **zisiboodoon** *vti2*
GRIND UP: grind s.o. up **biisiboozh /biisibooN-/** *vta;* grind s.t. up **biisiboodoon** *vti2*
GRINDER
GRINDER: **biisiboojigan, -an** *ni*
GRINDSTONE
GRINDSTONE: **zhiigwanaabik, -oog** *na*
GROAN
GROAN: **mamaadwe** *vai*
GROCERY STORE
GROCERY STORE: grocery store **wiisinii-adaawewigamig, -oon** *ni*
GROPE
GROPE: grope for s.o. **nandoojiin** *vta;* grope for s.t. **nandoojiinan** *vti;* grope for things **nandoojiinige** *vai*
GROUND
GROUND: **aki, -in** *ni*
LEVEL GROUND: be level ground **gwayakwakamigaa, gwayakwakamigaamagad** *vii*
LOW GROUND: be low ground **dabasakamigaa, dabasakamigaamagad** *vii*
ON TOP OF THE GROUND: **agidakamig** *pc, also* **ogidakamig*, wagidakamig**
PUT UNDER THE GROUND: put s.o. under the ground **ningwakamigin** *vta*
SPRINGY GROUND: be springy ground **dootooban** *vii*
UNDER THE GROUND: **anaamakamig** *pc*
WET GROUND: be wet ground **nibiiwakamigaa, nibiiwakamigaamagad** *vii*
GROW
GROW: grow s.o. **nitaawigi'** *vta;* grow s.t. **nitaawigitoon** *vti2;* make s.o. grow **niigi'** *vta;* make s.t. grow **niigitoon** *vti2*
GROW AT A CERTAIN SPEED: **apiichigi** *vai;* **apiichigin** *vii*
GROW FAST: **gizhiigi** *vai;* **gizhiigin** *vii*
GROW OUT: **zaagigi** *vai;* **zaagigin** *vii*
GROW STRAIGHT: **gwayakogi** *vai;* **gwayakogin** *vii*
GROW UP: **maajiigi** *vai;* **maajiigin** *vii;* **nitaawigi** *vai;* **nitaawigin** *vii*
GROW UP A CERTAIN EXTENT: **apiichigi** *vai;* **apiichigin** *vii*
GROW WELL: **minogi** *vai;* **minogin** *vii*
START TO GROW: **maajiigi** *vai;* **maajiigin** *vii*
GROWL
GROWL: growl (of a dog) **niikimo** *vai*
STOMACH GROWLS: one's stomach growls **madwegamijii** *vai*
GUARD
GUARD: guard s.o. **gizhaazh /gizhaaN-/** *vta;* guard s.t. **gizhaadan** *vti;* guard things **gizhaadige** *vai*
GUIDE
GUIDE ABOUT: guide s.o. about **babaamiwizh /babaamiwiN-/** *vta*
GUITAR
GUITAR: **madweyaabiigibijigan, -an** *ni*
PLAY A GUITAR: **madweyaabiigibijige** *vai*
GUM
CHEW GUM: **zhaashaagwamikiwe** *vai*
CHEWING GUM: **bigiins, -ag** *na*
GUN
GUN: **baashkizigan, -an** *ni*
HANDGUN: **oninjii-baashkizigan, -an** *ni*
TAKE ALONG A GUN: **niimibaashkizigane** *vai*
GUNNYSACK
GUNNYSACK: **mandaaminiwazh, -an** *ni*
GUNPOWDER
BLACK GUNPOWDER: **makade** *ni*
SMOKELESS GUNPOWDER: **waabi-makade** *ni*
GUT
GUT: gut s.o. **bagojiin** *vta;* **gijinagizhiin** *vta*

H

HAIR
HAIR: my (strand of) hair **niinizis, -an /-iinisiz-/** *nid*
BLACK HAIR: have black hair **makadewindibe** *vai*
CURL HAIR BY HEAT: curl s.o.'s hair by heat **babiizigaakiz /babiizigaakizw-/** *vta*
CURLY HAIR: have curly hair **babiizigindibe** *vai*
CUT HAIR: **giishkikozhiwe** *vai*
GREY HAIR: have grey hair **waabikwe** *vai*
HAVE BROWN HAIR: **ozaawindibe** *vai*
LONG HAIR: have long hair **gagaanwaanikwe** *vai*
MESSY HAIR: have messy hair **niiskindibe** *vai*

PUBIC HAIR: my pubic hair **nimiishigwaan, -an /-miishigwaan-/** *nid*
SHORT HAIR: have short hair **dadaakwaanikwe** *vai*
WASH HAIR: wash one's hair **giziibiigindibe** *vai*
WHITE HAIR: have white hair **waabishkindibe** *vai*

HAIRPIN
HAIRPIN: **wiinizisimaani-zagaakwa'igan, -an** *ni*

HAIRCUT
GET A HAIRCUT: **baapaagokozo** *vai*
GIVE A HAIRCUT: give s.o. a haircut **baapaagokozh /baapaagokoN-/** *vta*

HAIRDRESSER
HAIRDRESSER: hairdresser (female) **baapaagokozhiwewikwe, -g** *na;* hairdresser (male) **baapaagokozhiwewinini, -wag** *na*

HAIRDRESSING SALON
HAIRDRESSING SALON: **baapaagokozhiwewigamig, -oon** *ni*

HALF
HALF: **aabita** *pc;* **aabita-** *pv4*
AND A HALF: **ashi-aabita** *nm*
HALF A BAG: **aabitooshkin** *pc*
HALF MOON: be half (as something mineral, e.g., the moon) **aabitawaabikizi** *vai*

HALF FULL
HALF FULL: be half full (of liquid) **aabitoobii** *vai;* **aabitoobii, aabitoobiimagad** *vii;* be half full (of solids) **aabitooshkine** *vai;* **aabitooshkine, aabitooshkinemagad** *vii*
FILL HALF FULL: fill s.o. half full (of liquid) **aabitoobazh /aabitoobaN-/** *vta;* fill s.o. half full (of solids) **aabitooshkina'** *vta;* fill s.t. half full **aabitooshkinadoon** *vti2;* fill s.t. half full (of liquid) **aabitoobadoon** *vti2*

HALF-DOLLAR
HALF-DOLLAR: **aabitawaabik** *na*

HALFWAY
HALFWAY: halfway along it **aabitawayi'ii** *pc*

HALT
HALT: **nagaashkaa** *vai;* **nagaashkaa, nagaashkaamagad** *vii*

HAMMER
HAMMER: **bakite'igan, -an** *ni, also* **bakite'igaans**
HAND HAMMER: **bakite'igaans, -an** *ni*

HAMMER HANDLE
HAMMER HANDLE: **bakite'iganaak, -oon** *ni*

HAND
HAND A CERTAIN WAY: hand (s.t.) to s.o. a certain way **ininamaw** *vta*
HAND BACK: hand s.o. back **azhen** *vta;* hand s.t. back **azhenan** *vti*
HAND OVER: hand s.o. over (here) **biidin** *vta;* hand s.t. over (here) **biidinan** *vti;* hand (s.t.) over (here) to s.o. **biidinamaw** *vta*

HAND
HAND: my hand **nininj, -iin /-ninjy-/** *nid*
ACHE IN HAND: have an ache in one's hand **dewininjii** *vai*
AT BOTH HANDS: **eyiidawininj** *pc*
BIG HAND: have a big hand **mangininjii** *vai*
BLISTER ON HAND: get a blister on one's hand **abashkwebiigininjiishin** *vai*
BY HAND: **michi-** *pv4*
CLAP HANDS: clap one's hands **bapasininjii'odizo** *vai*
CLEAN HAND: have a clean hand **biinininjii** *vai*
COLD HAND: have a cold hand **dakininjii** *vai*
DIRTY HAND: have a dirty hand **wiinininjii** *vai*
FROZEN HAND: have a frozen hand **mashkawaakwajininjiiwaji** *vai*
HAVE SCAR ON HAND: have scar on one's hand **ojiishininjii** *vai*
LEFT HAND: left hand *usually possessed* **namanjinik, -an** *ni*
MOVE HAND A CERTAIN WAY: move one's hand a certain way **izhininjiini** *vai*
NUMB HAND: have a numb hand **niboowininjii** *vai*
PUT LOTION ON HAND: put lotion one's hand **noomininjii** *vai*
RIGHT HAND: right hand *usually possessed* **gichinik** *ni*
SHAKE HANDS: shake hands with s.o. **zagininjiin** *vta;* they shake hands with each other **zagininjiinidiwag /zagininjiinidi-/** *vai*
SORE HAND: have a sore hand **gaagiijininjii** *vai*
STIFF HAND: have a hand stiff from cold **mashkawajininjiiwaji** *vai*
STRONG HAND: have a strong hand **zoongininjii** *vai*
SWEATY HAND: have a sweaty hand **abweninjii** *vai*
SWOLLEN HAND: have a swollen hand **baaginiinjii** *vai*
WARM HANDS: warm one's hands **abininjiizo** *vai*
WASH HANDS: wash one's hands **giziibiigininjii** *vai*
WIPE HANDS: wipe one's hands **gaasiininjii** *vai*

HAND LOTION
HAND LOTION: **noomininjiiwin, -an** *ni*

HANDBAG
HANDBAG: **zhooniyaa-mashkimod, -an** *ni, also* **zhooniyaa-mashkimodens**

HANDFUL
ONE HANDFUL: **ingodobaneninj** *pc, also* **ningodobaneninj***
TAKE A HANDFUL: take a handful of s.o. **ganakin** *vta;* take a handful of s.t. **ganakinan** *vti*

HANDGUN
HANDGUN: **oninjii-baashkizigan, -an** *ni*

HANDKERCHIEF
HANDKERCHIEF: **moshwens, -an** *ni*
HANDLE
HANDLE: **minjiminigan, -an** *ni*
HANDLE A CERTAIN WAY: handle s.o. a certain way **inin** *vta;* handle s.t. a certain way **ininan** *vti*
HANDLED
HANDLED A CERTAIN WAY: be handled a certain way **ininigaade, ininigaademagad** *vii;* **ininigaazo** *vai*
HANDPRINT
LEAVE HANDPRINT: leave a handprint **ezhininjiishin** *vai*
HANDSOME
HANDSOME: be handsome **miikawaadad** *vii;* **miikawaadizi** *vai*
HANG
HANG: **agoode, agoodemagad** *vii;* **agoojin** *vai;* hang s.o. **agoozh /agooN-/** *vta;* hang s.t. **agoodoon** *vti2;* hang (s.t.) for s.o. **agoodaw** *vta;* hang things **agoojige** *vai*
HANG A CERTAIN WAY: **inagoode, inagoodemagad** *vii;* **inagoojin** *vai;* hang s.o. a certain way **inagoozh /inagooN-/** *vta;* hang s.t. a certain way **inagoodoon** *vti2*
HANG AT THE END: **ishkwegoode, ishkwegoodemagad** *vii;* **ishkwegoojin** *vai;* hang s.o. at the end **ishkwegoozh /ishkwegooN-/** *vta;* hang s.t. at the end **ishkwegoodoon** *vti2*
HANG IN FRONT: **niigaanagoode, niigaanagoodemagad** *vii;* **niigaanagoojin** *vai;* hang s.o. in front **niigaanagoozh /niigaanagooN-/** *vta;* hang s.t. in front **niigaanagoodoon** *vti2*
HANG IN PLACE: **onagoode, onagoodemagad** *vii;* **onagoojin** *vai;* hang s.o. in place **onagoozh /onagooN-/** *vta;* hang s.t. in place **onagoodoon** *vti2*
HANG LOW: **dabasagoode, dabasagoodemagad** *vii;* **dabasagoojin** *vai;* hang s.o. low **dabasagoozh /dabasagooN-/** *vta;* hang s.t. low **dabasagoodoon** *vti2*
HANG UP A NET: **agoodasabii** *vai*
HANG UP HIGH: **ishpagoode, ishpagoodemagad** *vii;* **ishpagoojin** *vai;* hang s.o. up high **ishpagoozh /ishpagooN-/** *vta;* hang s.t. up high **ishpagoodoon** *vti2*
HANG UP LAUNDRY: **agoojige** *vai*
HANG UPSIDE DOWN: **ajidagoode, ajidagoodemagad** *vii;* **ajidagoojin** *vai;* hang s.o. upside down **ajidagoozh /ajidagooN-/** *vta;* hang s.t. upside down **ajidagoodoon** *vti2*
HANGER
KETTLE HANGER: **agoodakikwaan, -an** *ni*
HAPPEN
HAPPEN A CERTAIN WAY: **inakamigad** *vii;* **izhiwebad** *vii*
HAPPEN IN A CERTAIN PLACE: **danakamigad** *vii*
HAPPENS TO BE: it happens to be **nangwana** *pc, also* **ngwana, ingwana**
HAVE CERTAIN THINGS HAPPEN: have certain things happen to one **inakamigizi** *vai;* **izhiwebizi** *vai*
HAPPY
HAPPY: be happy **minawaanigozi** *vai;* **minawaanigwad** *vii;* **minwendam** *vai2*
HARASS
HARASS: harass s.o. **miikinji'** *vta*
HARD
CONSIDER HARD: consider s.o. hard **zanagenim** *vta;* consider s.t. hard **zanagendan** *vti;* consider things hard **zanagendam** *vai2*
HARD TO MANAGE: be hard (to manage) **zanagad** *vii*
HARD WORKER
HARD WORKER: be a hard worker **ginzhizhawizi** *vai*
HARD
HARD: be hard **mashkawaa, mashkawaamagad** *vii;* **mashkawizi** *vai*
HARDER
HARDER: **enigok** *pc*
HARDLY
HARDLY: **agaawaa** *pc*
HARDWARE STORE
HARDWARE STORE: **biiwaabikoadaawewigamig, -oon** *ni, also* **biiwaabikwadaawewigamig**
HARE
SNOWSHOE HARE: snowshoe hare **waabooz, -oog** *na*
HARMONICA
HARMONICA: **noondaagochigan, -an** *ni*
HARNESS
HARNESS: **apikan, -an** *ni;* harness s.o. **onapizh /onapiN-/** *vta;* harness up **onapijige** *vai*
HARNESSED
HARNESSED: be harnessed **onapizo** *vai*
HARVEST
HARVEST WILD RICE: **bawa'am** *vai2;* **manoominike** *vai*
HAT
HAT: **wiiwakwaan, -an** *ni*
PUT ON HAT: put on one's hat **biichiwakwaane** *vai*
TAKE OFF HAT: take off one's hat **giichiwakwaane** *vai*
HATCH
HATCH: **baashkaawe'am** *vai2, also* **baashkaawe'o**
HATCHET
HATCHET: **waagaakwadoons, -an** *ni*
HATE
HATE: hate s.o. **zhiingenim** *vta;* hate s.t. **zhiingendan** *vti;* they hate each other **zhiingenindiwag /zhiingenindi-/** *vai*

HATED
HATED: be hated **zhiingendaagozi** *vai;* **zhiingendaagwad** *vii*
HAUL
HAUL: haul s.o. **aawazh /aawaN-/** *vta;* haul s.t. **aawadoon** *vti2;* haul something **aawadaaso** *vai;* haul (s.t.) for s.o. **aawadaw** *vta;* haul people **aawazhiwe** *vai*
HAUL ON SHOULDER: haul s.o. on one's shoulder **aawajinigaazh /aawajinigaaN-/** *vta;* haul s.t. on one's shoulder **aawajinigaadan** *vti;* haul things on one's shoulder **aawajinige** *vai*
HAUL TO A CERTAIN PLACE: haul s.o. to a certain place **inaawazh /inaawaN-/** *vta;* haul s.t. to a certain place **inaawadoon** *vti2;* haul something to a certain place **inaawadaaso** *vai*
HAUL WILD RICE: **aawajimine** *vai*
HAVE
HAVE: have s.o. **ayaaw** *vta;* have s.t. **ayaan /ayaam-/** *vti3*
HAVE ON
HAVE ON: have s.o. on (e.g., clothes) **biizikaw** *vta;* have s.t. on (e.g., clothes) **biizikan** *vti*
HAWK
HAWK: **gekek, -wag** *na*
HAWTHORN
HAWTHORN: hawthorn tree **miinensagaawanzh, -iig** *na*
HAWTHORN FRUIT
HAWTHORN FRUIT: **miinens, -ag** *na*
HAY
HAY: **mashkosiw, -an** *ni*
GO AFTER HAY: **naadashkosiwe** *vai*
HAZELNUT
HAZELNUT: **bagaan, -ag** *na*
HAZELNUT BUSH
HAZELNUT BUSH: **bagaaniminzh, -iig** *na*
HE
HE: he *third person singular personal pronoun* **wiin** *pr*
HEAD
HEAD: my head **nishtigwaan, -an /-shtigwaan-/** *nid*
BIG HEAD: have a big head **mangindibe** *vai*
BUMP HEAD: bump one's head **bitaakondibeshin** *vai*
FALL AND CRACK HEAD: fall and crack one's head **baasindibeshin** *vai*
HOLD HEAD STRAIGHT: hold one's head straight **gwayakokweni** *vai*
LIE WITH HEAD A CERTAIN WAY: lie with one's head a certain way **inikweshin** *vai*
LIE WITH HEAD ON: lie with head on something **apikweshimo** *vai*
NOD HEAD: nod one's head **wewebikweni** *vai*
NOD HEAD A CERTAIN WAY: nod one's head to s.o. a certain way **inikwetaw** *vta*
PUT HEAD A CERTAIN WAY: put one's head a certain way **inikweni** *vai*
SHAKE HEAD: shake head at s.o. **wewebikwetaw** *vta*
SLAP ON HEAD: slap s.o. on the head **basindibe' /basindibe'w-/** *vta*
STICK OUT HEAD: stick out one's head **zaagikweni** *vai*
TURN HEAD AROUND: turn one's head around **gwekikweni** *vai*
HEAD OFFICE
HEAD OFFICE: **ogimaawigamig, -oon** *ni*
HEADACHE
HEADACHE: have a headache **dewikwe** *vai*
GET A SUDDEN HEADACHE: **dewikwese** *vai*
HEADBAND
HEADBAND: **basikwebizon, -an** *ni*
HEADDRESS
FEATHER HEADDRESS: feather bonnet **miigwani-wiiwakwaan, -an** *ni*
HEADMAN
CEREMONIAL HEADMAN: **ogichidaa, -g** *na*
HEADWOMAN
CEREMONIAL HEADWOMAN: **ogichidaakwe, -g** *na*
HEAL
HEAL: heal s.o. **nanaandawi'** *vta;* heal people **nanaandawi'iwe** *vai*
HEAL UP: **giige** *vai*
HEALER
TRADITIONAL HEALER: **nenaandawi'iwed** *na-pt*
HEAR
HEAR: **noondam** *vai2;* hear s.o. **noondaw** *vta;* hear s.t. **noondan** *vti*
HEAR A CERTAIN NOISE: **initam** *vai2*
HEAR A CERTAIN WAY: hear s.o. a certain way **initaw** *vta;* hear s.t. a certain way **initan** *vti*
HEAR IN A CERTAIN PLACE: hear s.o. in a certain place **danitaw** *vta;* hear s.t. in a certain place **danitan** *vti*
HEAR RIGHT: hear the right thing **gwayakotam** *vai2*
LIKE HEARING: like hearing s.o. **minotaw** *vta;* like hearing s.t. **minotan** *vti;* like hearing something **minotam** *vai2*
HEARD
HEARD: be heard **noondaagwad** *vii;* can be heard **noondaagozi** *vai*
BEING HEARD: **madwe-** *pv4*
HEARD A CERTAIN WAY: be heard a certain way **initaagozi** *vai;* **initaagwad** *vii*
HEARD DRIVING ALONG: be heard driving along **bimwewebide, bimwewebidemagad** *vii;* **bimwewebizo** *vai*
HEARD DRIVING HERE: be heard driving here **biidwewebide, biidwewebidemagad** *vii;* **biidwewebizo** *vai*
HEARD FALLING: be heard going along and falling **bimweweshin** *vai*

HEARD IN A CERTAIN PLACE: be heard in a certain place **danitaagozi** *vai;* **danitaagwad** *vii*
HEARD IN AN ACTIVITY: be heard in an activity **madwetaa** *vai*
HEARD RUNNING HERE: be heard running here **biidwewebatoo** *vai*
HEARD RUNNING HERE ON THE GROUND: be heard running here on the ground **biidwewekamigibatoo** *vai*
HEARD SPEEDING ALONG: be heard speeding along **bimwewebide, bimwewebidemagad** *vii;* **bimwewebizo** *vai*
HEARD SPEEDING HERE: be heard speeding here **biidwewebide, biidwewebidemagad** *vii;* **biidwewebizo** *vai*
HEARD SWIMMING HERE: be heard swimming here **biidweweyaadagaa** *vai*
HEARD WALKING ALONG: be heard walking along **bimweweshin** *vai*
HEARD WALKING HERE: be heard walking here **biidweweshin** *vai*

HEARSE
HEARSE: **niboowidaabaan, -ag** *na*

HEART
HEART: my heart **inde', -an /-de'-/** *nid*

HEART ATTACK
HAVE A HEART ATTACK: **mamaajide'eshkaa** *vai*

HEART
HEART SUITE CARD: **giiwoon, -ag** *na, also* **giiyoon**

HEARTBURN
HAVE HEARTBURN: **maazhide'e** *vai*

HEAT
HEAT: heat s.o. (as something mineral) **gizhaabikiz /gizhaabikizw-/** *vta;* heat s.t. **gizizan** *vti;* heat s.t. (as a liquid) **gizhaagamizan** *vti;* heat s.t. (as something mineral) **gizhaabikizan** *vti;* heat things (as a liquid) **gizhaagamizige** *vai;* heat things (as something mineral) **gizhaabikizige** *vai*

HEATER
HEATER: **awazowin, -an** *ni*

HEAVEN
HEAVEN: **giizhig** *ni*
IN HEAVEN: **ishpiming** *pc*

HEAVY
HEAVY: be heavy **gozigwan** *vii;* **gozigwani** *vai*
SO HEAVY: be so heavy **apiitinigozi** *vai;* **apiitinigwad** *vii*

HEEL
HEEL: my heel **indoondan, -an /-doondan-/** *nid*

HEIGHT
CERTAIN HEIGHT: be a certain height **akoozi** *vai;* **akwaa, akwaamagad** *vii;* **akwaakozi** *vai;* **akwaakwad** *vii;* **apiitaa, apiitaamagad** *vii*

HELD
HELD A CERTAIN WAY: be held a certain way **ininigaade, ininigaademagad** *vii;* **ininigaazo** *vai*
HELD IN PLACE: be held in place with weight **minjimishkoode, minjimishkoodemagad** *vii;* **minjimishkoozo** *vai*

HELL DIVER
HELL DIVER: **zhingibis, -ag** *na*

HELLO
HELLO: hello! **aaniin** *pc;* **boozhoo** *pc*

HELP
HELP: **wiidookaazo** *vai;* help s.o. **naadamaw** *vta;* **wiidookaw** *vta;* help people **naadamaage** *vai;* **wiidookaage** *vai;* they help each other **naadamaadiwag /naadamaadi-/** *vai;* **wiidookodaadiwag /wiidookodaadi-/** *vai*

HERE
HERE: **bi-** *pv2;* **omaa** *pc, also* **o'omaa**
BLOWN HERE: be blown here **biidaashi** *vai;* **biidaasin** *vii*
BRING HERE IN A BOAT: **biida'oodoon** *vti2;* bring s.o. here in a boat **biida'oozh /biida'ooN-/** *vta*
CLIMB HERE: **biidaandawe** *vai*
CRAWL HERE: **biidoode** *vai*
DRAG HERE: **biijidaabii** *vai;* drag s.o. here **biijidaabaazh /biijidaabaaN-/** *vta;* drag s.t. here **biijidaabaadan** *vti*
DRIVE HERE: **biijibide, biijibidemagad** *vii;* **biijibizo** *vai;* **biijidaabii'iwe** *vai*
DRIVE HERE WITH A LIGHT: **biidaazakonebizo** *vai*
FLY HERE: **biijibide, biijibidemagad** *vii;* **biijibizo** *vai;* **biijise** *vai;* **biijise, biijisemagad** *vii*
FOLLOW A TRAIL HERE: **biida'adoo** *vai;* follow s.o.'s trail here **biida'azh /biida'aN-/** *vta;* follow s.t. as a trail here **biida'adoon** *vti2*
HEARD DRIVING HERE: be heard driving here **biidwewebide, biidwewebidemagad** *vii;* **biidwewebizo** *vai*
HEARD RUNNING HERE: be heard running here **biidwewebatoo** *vai*
HEARD RUNNING HERE ON THE GROUND: be heard running here on the ground **biidwewekamigibatoo** *vai*
HEARD SPEEDING HERE: be heard speeding here **biidwewebide, biidwewebidemagad** *vii;* **biidwewebizo** *vai*
HEARD SWIMMING HERE: be heard swimming here **biidweweyaadagaa** *vai*
HEARD WALKING HERE: be heard walking here **biidweweshin** *vai*
MOVE RESIDENCE HERE: move one's residence here **biijigozi** *vai*
OVER HERE: **owidi** *pc, also* **o'owidi**
PADDLE HERE: **biidakwazhiwe** *vai;* **biidaasamishkaa** *vai*

RIDE HERE ON HORSEBACK: **biidoomigo** *vai*
RUN HERE: **biijibatoo** *vai;* they run here together **biijiba'idiwag /biijiba'idi-/** *vai*
SAIL HERE: **biidaashi** *vai;* **biidaasin** *vii*
SEND A LETTER HERE: **biijibii'ige** *vai*
SKATE HERE: **biidaada'e** *vai*
SPEED HERE: **biijibide, biijibidemagad** *vii;* **biijibizo** *vai*
SWIM HERE: **biidaadagaa** *vai;* swim here (as a fish) **biidakwazhiwe** *vai*
THROW HERE: throw s.o. here **biijwebin** *vta;* throw s.t. here **biijwebinan** *vti;* throw (s.t.) here to s.o. **biijwebinamaw** *vta*
WADE HERE: **biidaadagaazii** *vai*
WALK HERE: **biidaasamose** *vai*
WRITE HERE: **biijibii'ige** *vai;* write (s.t.) here to s.o. *inverse forms of:* **biijibii'amaw-** *vta*

HERON
BLUE HERON: **zhashagi, -wag** *na*

HICCOUGH
HICCOUGH: **onwaawe** *vai*

HICKORY
HICKORY: **mitigwaabaak, -oog** *na*

HIDDEN
HIDDEN: be hidden **gaajigaade, gaajigaademagad** *vii;* **gaajigaazo** *vai*

HIDE
HIDE: hide from s.o. **gaazootaw** *vta;* hide s.o. **gaazh /gaaN-/** *vta;* hide s.t. **gaadoon** *vti2;* hide self **gaazo** *vai;* hide (s.t.) from s.o. **gaadaw** *vta;* hide things **gaajige** *vai*

HIDE
HIDE: **bashkwegin, -oon** *ni*
BEAVER HIDE: **amikwayaan, -ag** *na*
CALFHIDE: **bizhikiinsiwayaan, -ag** *na*
DEER HIDE: **waawaashkeshiwayaan, -ag** *na*
FISHER HIDE: **ojiigiwayaan, -ag** *na*
FOX HIDE: **waagoshiwayaan, -ag** *na*
LYNX HIDE: **bizhiwayaan, -ag** *na*
MARTEN HIDE: **waabizheshiwayaan, -ag** *na*
MINK HIDE: **zhaangweshiwayaan, -ag** *na*
MUSKRAT HIDE: **wazhashkwayaan, -ag** *na*
OTTER HIDE: **nigigwayaan, -ag** *na*
STRETCH A HIDE: **naazhiiga'ige** *vai*
TANNED HIDE: **asekaan, -ag** *na*
WOLF HIDE: **ma'iinganiwayaan, -ag** *na*

HIDE SCRAPER
HIDE SCRAPER: **jiishaakwa'igan, -an** *ni*

HIDE STRETCHER
HIDE STRETCHER: **naazhiiga'igan, -an** *ni*
FLAT HIDE STRETCHER: flat hide stretcher (especially for muskrats) **zhiibaakwa'ataan, -an** *ni*

HIGH
HIGH: **ishpi-** *pv4;* be high (e.g., the sun) **ishpagoojin** *vai*
CHARGE A HIGH PRICE: **ishpagindaaso** *vai;* charge a high price for s.t. **ishpagindan** *vti*
HANG UP HIGH: **ishpagoode, ishpagoodemagad** *vii;* **ishpagoojin** *vai;* hang s.o. up high **ishpagoozh /ishpagooN-/** *vta;* hang s.t. up high **ishpagoodoon** *vti2*
HIGH IN STATUS OR OFFICE: be high in status or office **ishpaginzo** *vai*
HIGH PLACE: be a high place **ishpadinaa, ishpadinaamagad** *vii*
HIGH UP: be high up **ishpaa, ishpaamagad** *vii*
LIE HIGH UP: **ishpishin** *vai;* **ishpisin** *vii*
MAKE HIGH: make s.t. high **ishpaatoon** *vti2*

HIGH-PRICED
HIGH-PRICED: be high-priced **ishpaginde, ishpagindemagad** *vii;* **ishpaginzo** *vai*

HIGHLY
THINK HIGHLY: think highly of s.o. **ishpenim** *vta*

HIGHWAY
HIGHWAY: **gichi-miikana, -n** *ni*

HILL
HILL: be a hill **ishpadinaa, ishpadinaamagad** *vii*
BIG HILL: there is a big hill **mangadinaa, mangadinaamagad** *vii*
COME OUT OVER A HILL: **zaagajiwe** *vai*
ON TOP OF A HILL: **agidaaki** *pc, also* **ogidaaki*, wagidaaki**
SMALL HILL: be a small hill **bikwadinaa, bikwadinaamagad** *vii;* there is a small hill **agaasadinaa, agaasadinaamagad** *vii*

HINDER
HINDER: hinder s.o. **ondami'** *vta*

HINDQUARTER
HINDQUARTER: my hindquarter **imbwaam, -an /-bwaam-/** *nid*

HIP
HIP: my hip **ninoogan, -an /-noogan-/** *nid*

HIRE
HIRE: **anookii** *vai;* hire s.o. **anoozh /anooN-/** *vta*
HIRE TO DO A CERTAIN JOB: hire s.o. to do a certain job **inanoozh /inanooN-/** *vta*
HIRE TO GO TO A CERTAIN PLACE: hire s.o. to go to a certain place **inanoozh /inanooN-/** *vta*

HIT
HIT: be hit **bakite'igaade, bakite'igaademagad** *vii;* **bakite'igaazo** *vai;* hit s.o. **bakite' /bakite'w-/** *vta;* hit s.o. (in shooting) **mizho /mizhw-/** *vta;* hit s.t. **bakite'an** *vti;* hit s.t. (in shooting) **mizhodan** *vti;* hit things **bakite'ige** *vai;* they hit each other **bakite'odiwag /bakite'odi-/** *vai*
ACCIDENTALLY HIT: accidentally hit s.o. **bitaganaam** *vta;* accidentally hit s.t. **bitaganaandan** *vti*
HIT AGAINST ACCIDENTALLY: hit against something accidentally (as something stick- or wood-like) **bitaakoshin** *vai;* **bitaakosin** *vii*
HIT DEAD CENTER: hit s.o. dead center with something **miikwa' /miikwa'w-/** *vta;* hit s.t. dead center with something **miikwa'an** *vti*

HIT THE BOTTOM: **mizhakiise** *vai;* **mizhakiise, mizhakiisemagad** *vii*
HIT THE TARGET: **mizhodam** *vai2*
MAKE NOISE HITTING: **madweshin** *vai;* **madwesin** *vii;* make noise hitting s.t. **madwesidoon** *vti2;* make noise hitting things **madwesijige** *vai*
SHOOT AND HIT: shoot and hit s.o. **miikonaw** *vta;* shoot and hit s.t. **miikonan** *vti*

HITCHED
HITCHED ON: be hitched on **agwapijigaade, agwapijigaademagad** *vii;* **agwapijigaazo** *vai*

HITHER
HITHER: **bi-** *pv2*

HIVE
BEEHIVE: **aamoo-wadiswan, -an** *ni*

HOARSE
HOARSE: be hoarse **gibiskwe** *vai;* **maanowe** *vai*

HOE
HOE: **ningwaja'ige** *vai;* hoe s.o. **ningwaja' /ningwaja'w-/** *vta;* hoe s.t. **ningwaja'an** *vti*

HOIST
HOIST: hoist s.o. **ombaabiigin** *vta;* hoist s.t. **ombaabiiginan** *vti*

HOLD
HOLD: hold s.o. **dakon** *vta;* hold s.t. **dakonan** *vti;* hold (s.t.) for s.o. **dakonamaw** *vta*
ADEQUATELY HOLD: **debashkine** *vai;* **debashkine, debashkinemagad** *vii;* adequately hold (something liquid) **debibii, debibiimagad** *vii*
GET HOLD: get hold of s.o. **debibizh /debibiN-/** *vta;* get hold of s.t. **debibidoon** *vti2;* get hold of (s.t.) for s.o. **debibidaw** *vta*
HOLD A CERTAIN WAY: hold s.o. a certain way **inin** *vta;* hold s.t. a certain way **ininan** *vti*
HOLD AGAINST: hold s.o. against **ashidin** *vta;* hold s.t. against **ashidinan** *vti*
HOLD BACK: hold s.o. back **nanagin** *vta*
HOLD IN MOUTH: hold s.o. in one's mouth **agwanem** *vta;* hold s.t. in one's mouth **agwanendan** *vti;* hold things in one's mouth **agwanenjige** *vai*
HOLD IN PLACE: hold s.o. in place **minjimin** *vta;* hold s.o. in place with foot or body **minjimishkaw** *vta;* hold s.o. in place with weight **minjimishkoozh /minjimishkooN-/** *vta;* hold s.t. in place **minjiminan** *vti;* hold s.t. in place with foot or body **minjimishkan** *vti;* hold s.t. in place with weight **minjimishkoodoon** *vti2;* hold (s.t.). in place for s.o. **minjiminamaw** *vta*
HOLD ON: **minjimii** *vai;* hold on (as to something stick- or wood-like) **minjimaakwii** *vai*
HOLD UP AGAINST: hold s.o. up against **agon** *vta;* hold s.t. up against **agonan** *vti*
HOLD UPSIDE DOWN: hold s.o. upside down **ajidin** *vta;* hold s.t. upside down **ajidinan** *vti*
TAKE HOLD: take hold of s.o. **dakon** *vta;* take hold of s.t. **dakonan** *vti*

HOLD ON
HOLD ON: hold on! **bekaa** *pc*

HOLE
BURN A HOLE: burn a hole in s.o. **bagwaakiz /bagwaakizw-/** *vta;* burn a hole in s.t. **bagwaakizan** *vti*
DIG A HOLE: **waanike** *vai*
EXCAVATED HOLE: **waanikaan, -an** *ni*
GET A HOLE: **bagoshkaa** *vai;* **bagoshkaa, bagoshkaamagad** *vii*
HAVE A HOLE: **bagoneyaa, bagoneyaamagad** *vii;* **bagonezi** *vai*
HAVE A HOLE BURNED IN: **bagwaakide, bagwaakidemagad** *vii;* **bagwaakizo** *vai*
HOLE MADE IN THE ICE FOR WATER: **dwaa'ibaan, -an** *ni, also* **dwaa'igan**
MAKE A HOLE IN THE ICE: **dwaa'ige** *vai*
MAKE A HOLE USING SOMETHING: make a hole in s.o. using something **bagone' /bagone'w-/** *vta;* make a hole in s.t. using something **bagone'an** *vti*
MAKE A WATER HOLE IN THE ICE: **dwaa'ibii** *vai, also* **dwaa'ige**

HOLLOW
HOLLOW: be hollow **wiimbaa, wiimbaamagad** *vii;* **wiimbizi** *vai*
GIVE A HOLLOW SOUND: **wiimbwewe, wiimbwewemagad** *vii*

HOME
HOME: his/her home: **endaad** *changed form of:* **daa** *vai*
BE AT HOME: **abi** *vai*
CARRY HOME: carry s.o. home **giiwewizh /giiwewiN-/** *vta;* carry s.t. home **giiwewidoon** *vti2;* carry (s.t.) home for s.o. **giiwewidaw** *vta*
DRIVE HOME: **giiwedaabii'iwe** *vai*
GO HOME: **giiwe** *vai*
GO HOME BY BOAT: **giiwe'o** *vai*
GO HOME MAD: **giiwegidaazo** *vai*
RUN HOME: **giiwebatoo** *vai*
TAKE HOME: take s.o. home **giiwewizh /giiwewiN-/** *vta;* take s.t. home **giiwewidoon** *vti2;* take (s.t.) home for s.o. **giiwewidaw** *vta*
TELL TO GO HOME: tell s.o. to go home **giiwenaazha' /giiwenaazha'w-/** *vta*

HOMELY
HOMELY: be homely **maanaadizi** *vai*

HOMINY
HOMINY: **gijikonayezigan, -ag** *na*

HONEY
HONEY: **aamoo-ziinzibaakwad** *ni*

HOOF
HOOF: my hoof **ninasid /-nasid-/** *nid*

HOOK
FISH HOOK: **migiskan, -an** *ni*
FISH WITH A HOOK AND LINE: **wewebanaabii** *vai*

HOOK AND LINE: **migiskaneyaab, -iin** *ni*

HOP HORNBEAM

HOP HORNBEAM: **maananoons, -ag** *na*

HOPE

HOPE: **bagosendam** *vai2;* hope for s.o., have hope for s.o. **bagosenim** *vta;* hope for s.t. **bagosendan** *vti*

LOSE HOPE: lose hope in s.o. **banaadenim** *vta;* lose hope in s.t. **banaadendan** *vti*

HOPEFUL

HOPEFUL: be hopeful **ombendam** *vai2*

HORN

HORN: **noondaagochigan, -an** *ni*

HORN

HORN: horn (of an animal) **eshkan, -ag** *na*

HORSE

HORSE: **bebezhigooganzhii, -g** *na, also* **mishtadim*, mashtadim***; my horse **inday, -ag /-day-/** *nad*

FALL OFF A HORSE: **banoomigo** *vai*

HAVE A HORSE: **odayi** *vai*

LOOK FOR HORSES: **nandawisimwe** *vai*

RIDE TO A CERTAIN PLACE WITH HORSES: **apa'igo** *vai*

HORSEBACK

ARRIVE ON HORSEBACK: **bagamoomigo** *vai*

RIDE ABOUT ON HORSEBACK: **babaamoomigo** *vai*

RIDE ALONG ON HORSEBACK: **bimoomigo** *vai*

RIDE AWAY ON HORSEBACK: **animoomigo** *vai*

RIDE FROM A CERTAIN PLACE ON HORSEBACK: **ondoomigo** *vai*

RIDE HERE ON HORSEBACK: **biidoomigo** *vai*

RIDE TO A CERTAIN PLACE ON HORSEBACK: ride to a certain place on horseback **inoomigo** *vai*

HORSEFLY

HORSEFLY: **mizizaak, -wag** *na*

HORSESHOE

HORSESHOE: **oshkanzhiikaajigan, -an** *ni*

HOSPITAL

HOSPITAL: **aakoziiwigamig, -oon** *ni*

MENTAL HOSPITAL: **giiwanaadiziiwigamig, -oon** *ni*

VETERAN'S HOSPITAL: **zhimaaganishii-aakoziiwigamig, -oon** *ni*

HOT

HOT: be hot **gizhide, gizhidemagad** *vii;* **gizhizo** *vai;* be hot (as a liquid) **gizhaagamide, gizhaagamidemagad** *vii*

HOT INSIDE: be hot inside **giizhoote, giizhootemagad** *vii*

HOT WEATHER: be hot (weather) **gizhaate, gizhaatemagad** *vii*

HOT WIND: be a hot wind **gizhaanimad** *vii*

HOTEL

HOTEL: **noogishkaawigamig, -oon** *ni*

HOUR

CERTAIN HOUR: be a certain hour **daso-diba'iganed** *vii*

CERTAIN NUMBER OF HOURS: a certain number of hours **daso-diba'igan** *pc*

CERTAIN TIME IN HOURS: be a certain time in hours **daso-diba'iganed** *vii*

HOUSE

HOUSE: **waakaa'igan, -an** ni

ALONGSIDE THE HOUSE: **zhishwajigamig** *pc*

BUILD A HOUSE: **waakaa'ige** *vai;* build a house for s.o. **ozhigaw** *vta*

BY A HOUSE: **jiigigamig** *pc*

COLD HOUSE: be cold (as a house or room) **dakate, dakatemagad** *vii*

DARK HOUSE: be dark (as in a room or house) **dibikate, dibikatemagad** *vii*

ON TOP OF THE HOUSE: **agidigamig** *pc, also* **ogidigamig*, wagidigamig**

QUIET HOUSE: be a quiet house **bangate, bangatemagad** *vii*

SMALL HOUSE: be small (as a room or house) **agaasate, agaasatemagad** *vii*

HOW

HOW: how? **aaniin** *pc;* **aaniish** *pc*

HOW MANY: how many? **aaniin minik** *pc*

HOW MUCH: how much? *interrogative* **aaniin minik** *pc*

I DON'T KNOW HOW: **amanj** *dubitative pc, also* **amanj iidog, namanj*, namanj iidog***

I WONDER HOW: I wonder how *dubitative* **amanj** *pc, also* **amanj iidog, namanj*, namanj iidog***

HOWEVER

HOWEVER: however *dubitative* **amanj igo** *pc*

HOWL

HOWL: howl **waawoono** *vai*

HUG

HUG: hug s.o. **gikinjigwen** *vta;* **giishkijiin** *vta;* they hug each other **gikinjigwenidiwag /gikinjigwenidi-/** *vai;* **giishkijiinidiwag /giishkijiinidi-/** *vai*

HUMAN

HUMAN: human (in contrast to non-human beings) **anishinaabe, -g** *na;* be human (in contrast to non-human beings) **anishinaabewi** *vai*

HUMMINGBIRD

HUMMINGBIRD: **nenookaasi, -wag** *na*

HUNDRED

CERTAIN NUMBER OF HUNDREDS: **daswaak** *nm*

EIGHT HUNDRED: **ishwaaswaak** *nm, also* **nishwaaswaak***

FIVE HUNDRED: **naanwaak** *nm*

FOUR HUNDRED: **niiwaak** *nm*

NINE HUNDRED: **zhaangaswaak** *nm*

ONE HUNDRED: **ingodwaak** *nm, also* **ningodwaak***

SEVEN HUNDRED: **niizhwaaswaak** *nm*

SIX HUNDRED: **ingodwaaswaak** *nm, also* **ningodwaaswaak***

THREE HUNDRED: **niswaak** *nm*

TWO HUNDRED: **niizhwaak** *nm*

HUNGRY

HUNGRY: be hungry **bakade** *vai*

PRETEND TO BE HUNGRY: **bakadekaazo** *vai*

HUNT

HUNT: **giiwose** *vai, also* **giiyose**; get food by hunting or fishing **nandawenjige** *vai;* hunt for s.o. **nooji'** *vta;* hunt for s.t. **noojitoon** *vti2;* hunt for people **nooji'iwe** *vai*

HUNT BEAVER: **noodamikwe** *vai*

HUNT DUCKS: **nandawishibe** *vai*

HUNT FOR RABBITS: **nandawaaboozwe** *vai*

HUNTER

HUNTER: **giiwosewinini, -wag** *na, also* **giiyosewinini**

HUNTING BLIND

HUNTING BLIND: **akandoowin, -an** *ni*

HUNTING DOG

HUNTING DOG: **giiwosewasim, -oog** *na, also* **giiyosewasim**

HURRY

HURRY: **wewiib** *pc;* **wewiibishkaa** *vai;* hurry (in some work or activity) **wewiibitaa** *vai;* hurry s.o. **wewiibi'** *vta;* hurry s.t. **wewiibitoon** *vti*

COOK IN A HURRY: **ojaanimizekwe** *vai*

HURRY BY SPEECH: hurry s.o. by speech **ojaanimim** *vta*

HURRY MAKING: hurry making s.o. **wewiibi'** *vta;* hurry making s.t. **wewiibitoon** *vti*

IN A HURRY: **wewiib** *pc;* be in a hurry **wewiibizi** *vai*

MAKE HURRY: make s.o. hurry **ojaanimi'** *vta*

TELL TO HURRY: tell s.o. to hurry **wewiibim** *vta*

WANT TO HURRY: **wewiibendam** *vai*

HURT

GET HURT: **wiisagishin** *vai*

HURT WITH FOOT OR BODY: hurt s.o. with foot or body **wiisagishkaw** *vta*

HUSBAND

HUSBAND: my husband **ninaabem, -ag /-naabem-/** *nad;* **niwiidigemaagan, -ag /-wiidigemaagan-/** *na*

HAVE A HUSBAND: **onaabemi** *vai*

HYMN

HYMN: **anama'e-nagamon, -an** *ni*

I

I

I: I *first person singular personal pronoun* **niin** *pr*

I DON'T KNOW

I DON'T KNOW HOW: *dubitative* **amanj** *pc, also* **amanj iidog, namanj*, namanj iidog***

I DON'T KNOW WHEN: *dubitative* **amanj apii** *pc*

I DON'T KNOW WHERE: *dubitative* **dibi** *pc*

I DON'T KNOW WHO: I don't know who *animate dubitative* **awegwen, -ag** *pr*

I DON'T REMEMBER

I DON'T REMEMBER WHAT: **ayi'ii, -n** *pr*

I DON'T REMEMBER WHO: **aya'aa, -g** *pr*

ICE

ICE: **mikwam, -iig** *na*

CRACK IN THE ICE: there is a crack in the ice **daashkikwadin** *vii*

FALL THROUGH THE ICE: **dwaashin** *vai*

FISH THROUGH THE ICE WITH SPEAR: **akwa'waa** *vai*

GO ABOUT ON THE ICE: **babaamaadagaako** *vai*

GO AWAY ON THE ICE: **animaadagaako** *vai*

GO OUT FROM SHORE ON THE ICE: **niminaaweyaadagaako** *vai*

GO TO A CERTAIN PLACE ON THE ICE: **inaadagaako** *vai*

HOLE MADE IN THE ICE FOR WATER: **dwaa'ibaan, -an** *ni, also* **dwaa'igan**

MAKE A HOLE IN THE ICE: **dwaa'ige** *vai*

MAKE A WATER HOLE IN THE ICE: **dwaa'ibii** *vai, also* **dwaa'ige**

MUCH ICE: there is much ice **mikwamiikaa, mikwamiikaamagad** *vii*

ON TOP OF THE ICE: **agidiskwam** *pc, also* **ogidiskwam*, wagidiskwam**

SLIP AND FALL ON THE ICE: **ozhaashikoshin** *vai*

SLIPPERY ICE: there is slippery ice **ozhaashikwaa, ozhaashikwaamagad** *vii*

START OFF ON THE ICE: **maajiiyaadagaako** *vai*

UNDER THE ICE: **anaamiskwam** *pc*

WALK ALONG ON THE ICE: **bimaadagaako** *vai*

ICE BOX

ICE BOX: **mikwamii-makak, -oon** *ni*

ICE CHISEL

ICE CHISEL: **eshkan, -an** *ni*

ICE CREAM

ICE CREAM: **dekaag** *ni-pt*

ICY

ICY ROAD: be icy (as a road or trail) **mikwamiiwadamon /mikwamiiwadamo-/** *vii*

ICY TRAIL: be icy (as a road or trail) **mikwamiiwadamon /mikwamiiwadamo-/** *vii*

IDENTIFY

IDENTIFY: identify s.o. **aawenim** *vta;* identify s.t. **aawendan** *vti*

IDENTIFY BY SIGHT: identify s.o. by sight **aawenaw** *vta;* identify s.t. by sight **aawenan** *vti*

IDENTIFY BY SOUND: identify s.o. by sound **aawetaw** *vta;* identify s.t. by sound **aawetan** *vti*

IF

IF: **giishpin** *pc*

IGNITE

IGNITE: **biskane, biskanemagad** *vii*

IGNORANT

IGNORANT: be ignorant **bagwanawizi** *vai*

IGNORE

IGNORE: **boonendam** *vai2;* ignore s.o. **boonenim** *vta;* ignore s.t. **boonendan** *vti*

ILL

ILL: be ill **aakozi** *vai+o*

FALL ILL FROM BAD MEDICINE: **niboowise** *vai*

SERIOUSLY ILL: be seriously ill **aanimizi** *vai*

ILL-FORMED

ILL-FORMED: **maazhi-** *pv4*

ILLNESS

HAVE A RESPIRATORY ILLNESS: **ozosodamwaapine** *vai*

IMAGE

IMAGE: **mazinichigan, -ag** *na*

MAKE AN IMAGE: make an image of s.o. **mazinaadin** *vta*

IMPATIENT

IMPATIENT: be impatient **ojaanimendam** *vai2;* **zhigajii** *vai*

IMPRINTED

IMPRINTED: be imprinted **mazinishin** *vai;* **mazinisin** *vii*

IMPRISONED

IMPRISONED: be imprisoned **gibaakwa'igaazo** *vai*

IN

IN: be in **biinde, biindemagad** *vii;* **biinzo** *vai*

CRAWL IN: **biindoode** *vii*

DRIVE IN: speed in **biinjibide, biinjibidemagad** *vii;* **biinjibizo** *vai*

FALL IN: **biinjibide, biinjibidemagad** *vii;* **biinjibizo** *vai;* **biinjise** *vai;* **biinjise, biinjisemagad** *vii*

FLOW IN: **biinjijiwan** *vii*

FLY IN: **biinjibide, biinjibidemagad** *vii;* **biinjibizo** *vai;* **biinjise** *vai;* **biinjise, biinjisemagad** *vii*

IN A CERTAIN PLACE: **dazhi-** *pv3;* be in a certain place **dagon /dago-/** *vii*

IN A PLACE WITH: **dago-** *pv4*

IN AMONG: in among it **megwe-aya'ii** *pc, also* **megweya'ii**

IN THE BRUSH: **megwekob** *pc*

IN THE MIDST: in the midst of **megwe-** *pn*

IN THE MUD: **megwejiishkiwag** *pc*

IN THE WOODS: **megwaayaak** *pc*

SPEED IN: drive in **biinjibide, biinjibidemagad** *vii;* **biinjibizo** *vai*

THROW IN: throw s.o. in **biinjwebin** *vta;* throw s.t. in **biinjwebinan** *vti;* throw things in **biinjwebinige** *vai*

IN ORDER TO

IN ORDER TO: **ji-** *pv1*

IN TURN

IN TURN: **meshkwad** *pc*

IN TURNS

IN TURNS: **memeshkwad** *pc*

IN VAIN

IN VAIN: **aano-** *pv1*

DO IN VAIN: **aanawewizi** *vai*

INADEQUATE

INADEQUATE: be inadequate **aanawewizi** *vai*

THINK INADEQUATE: think s.o. is inadequate **zhaagoodenim** *vta*

INCH

CERTAIN NUMBER OF INCHES: a certain number of inches **dasoninj** *pc*

INCLUDED

INCLUDED: be included **dagwaginde, dagwagindemagad** *vii;* **dagwaginzo** *vai*

INCOMPETENT

INCOMPETENT: be incompetent **bagandizi** *vai*

INCREASE

INCREASE IN NUMBER: **niigi** *vai;* make s.o. increase in number **niigi'** *vta;* make s.t. increase in number **niigitoon** *vti2*

INDEED

INDEED: **geget** *pc*

INDEPENDENT

INDEPENDENT: be independent **dibenindizo** *vai*

INDEX FINGER

INDEX FINGER: **izhinoo'iganinj, -iin** *ni*

INDIAN

INDIAN: Indian (in contrast to non-Indians) **anishinaabe, -g** *na;* be Indian (in contrast to non-Indians) **anishinaabewi** *vai*

CALL IN INDIAN: call s.o. in Indian (Ojibwe) **anishinaabewinikaazh /anishinaabewinikaaN-/** *vta;* call s.t. in Indian (Ojibwe) **anishinaabewinikaadan** *vti*

CALLED IN INDIAN: be called in Indian (Ojibwe) **anishinaabewinikaade, anishinaabewinikaademagad** *vii;* **anishinaabewinikaazo** *vai*

INDIAN WRITING: Indian (Ojibwe) writing **anishinaabewibii'igan, -an** *ni*

MANY INDIANS: there are many Indians **anishinaabekaa** *vii*

NON-LOCAL INDIAN: **mayagi-anishinaabe, -g** *na*

SOMETHING WRITTEN IN INDIAN: something written in Indian (Ojibwe) **anishinaabewibii'igan, -an** *ni*

SPEAK IN AN INDIAN LANGUAGE: speak in an Indian language (especially in Ojibwe) **anishinaabe-gaagiigido** *vai*

WRITE IN INDIAN: write in Indian (Ojibwe) **anishinaabewibii'ige** *vai;* write s.t. in Indian (Ojibwe) **anishinaabewibii'an** *vti;* write s.t. in Indian (Ojibwe) (e.g., a book) **anishinaabewisidoon** *vti2;* write (s.t.) in

Indian (Ojibwe) to s.o. **anishinaabewibii'amaw** *vta*
WRITTEN IN INDIAN: be written in Indian (Ojibwe) **anishinaabewibii'igaade, anishinaabewibii'igaademagad** *vii;* be written in Indian (Ojibwe) (e.g., a book or document) **anishinaabewisin** *vii*

INDIAN CENTER
INDIAN CENTER: **anishinaabemaawanjii'idiiwigamig, -oon** *ni*

INDIAN COUNTRY
INDIAN COUNTRY: **anishinaabewaki** *ni*

INDIAN LANGUAGE
INDIAN LANGUAGE: Indian language (especially Ojibwe) **anishinaabemowin, -an** *ni*
SPEAK AN INDIAN LANGUAGE: speak an Indian language (especially Ojibwe) to s.o. **anishinaabemotaw** *vta;* speak an Indian language (especially Ojibwe) **anishinaabemo** *vai*

INDIAN WOMAN
INDIAN WOMAN: **anishinaabekwe, -g** *na;* be an Indian woman **anishinaabekwewi** *vai*

INEFFECTIVE
INEFFECTIVE: be ineffective **aanawewizi** *vai;* **zhaagwaadad** *vii;* **zhaagwaadizi** *vai*

INFECT
INFECT: infect s.o. with something **aazhookoodin** *vta*

INFECTED
INFECTED EAR: have an infected ear **miniiwitawage** *vai*

INFLATE
INFLATE: inflate s.o. **boodaajii' /boodaajii'w-/** *vta;* inflate s.t. **boodaajii'an** *vti;* inflate things **boodaajii'ige** *vai*

INHERENTLY
INHERENTLY: **dibinawe** *pc*

INHERIT
INHERIT FROM A CERTAIN SOURCE: **ondizi** *vai*

INJURE
INJURE: injure s.o. **inigaa'** *vta*

INJURED
INJURED: fall and be injured **godigoshin** *vai*

INK
INK: **ozhibii'iganaaboo** *ni*

INLAND
INLAND: **noopiming** *pc*
CARRY INLAND: carry s.o. inland **gopiwizh /gopiwiN-/** *vta;* carry s.t. inland **gopiwidoon** *vti2*
GO INLAND: **gopii** *vai*
RUN INLAND: **gopibatoo** *vai*
TAKE INLAND: take s.o. inland **gopiwizh /gopiwiN-/** *vta;* take s.t. inland **gopiwidoon** *vti2*

INLET
INLET: at the inlet **zaagiing** *pc;* be an inlet **zaagidawaa, zaagidawaamagad** *vii*

INQUIRE
INQUIRE: **gagwedwe** *vai*

INSANE
INSANE: be insane **giiwanaadizi** *vai*

INSECT
INSECT: **manidoons, -ag** *na*

INSIDE
INSIDE: **biindig** *pc;* inside it **biinjayi'ii** *pc*
BLOWN INSIDE: be blown inside **biindigeyaashi** *vai;* **biindigeyaasin** *vii*
BRING FIREWOOD INSIDE: **biindigenise** *vai*
BRING INSIDE: bring s.o. inside **biindigazh /biindigaN-/** *vta;* bring s.t. inside **biindigadoon** *vti2*
CHASE INSIDE: chase s.o. inside **biindigenaazhikaw** *vta;* **biindigenizhikaw** *vta*
COME INSIDE: **biindige** *vai*
DANCE INSIDE: dance inside (as in a Grand Entry) **biindigeshimo** *vai*
DRIVE INSIDE: **biindigebide, biindigebidemagad** *vii;* **biindigebizo** *vai*
FLY INSIDE: **biindigebide, biindigebidemagad** *vii;* **biindigebizo** *vai*
GO INSIDE: **biindige** *vai*
INSIDE BODY: inside the body **biinjina** *pc*
INSIDE EAR: inside an ear **biinjitawag** *pc*
INSIDE MOUTH: inside the mouth **biinjidoon** *pc*
INSIDE NOSE: inside the nose **biinjijaanzh** *pc*
RUN INSIDE: **biindigebatoo** *vai;* they run inside together **biindigeba'idiwag /biindigeba'idi-/** *vai;* run inside with s.o. **biindigebatwaazh /biindigebatwaaN-/** *vta;* run inside with s.t. **biindigebatwaadan** *vti;* run inside from people **biindigeba'iwe** *vai*
SPEED INSIDE: **biindigebide, biindigebidemagad** *vii;* **biindigebizo** *vai*
TAKE INSIDE: take s.o. inside **biindigazh /biindigaN-/** *vta;* take s.t. inside **biindigadoon** *vti2*
TELL TO GO INSIDE: tell s.o. to go inside **biindigenaazha' /biindigenaazha'w-/** *vta*
THROW INSIDE: throw s.o. inside **biindigewebin** *vta;* throw s.t. inside **biindigewebinan** *vti;* throw things inside **biindigewebinige** *vai*

INSIDE OUT
TURN INSIDE OUT: **aaboozikaa** *vai;* **aaboozikaa, aaboozikaamagad** *vii;* turn s.o. inside out **aaboodin** *vta;* turn s.t. inside out **aaboodinan** *vti*
WEAR INSIDE OUT: wear s.o. inside out **aaboozikaw** *vta;* wear s.t. inside out **aaboozikan** *vti*

INSIGNIFICANT
CONSIDER INSIGNIFICANT: consider s.o. insignificant **agaasenim** *vta;* consider s.t. insignificant **agaasendan** *vti*
CONSIDERED INSIGNIFICANT: be considered insignificant **agaasendaagozi** *vai;* **agaasendaagwad** *vii*

INSPECT
INSPECT: inspect s.o. **dibaabam** *vta;* inspect s.t. **dibaabandan** *vti*
INSTRUMENT
MUSICAL INSTRUMENT: **madwewechigan, -an** *ni;* musical instrument (especially a wind instrument) **noondaagochigan, -an** *ni*
INTACT
INTACT: be intact **miziweyaa, miziweyaamagad** *vii;* **miziwezi** *vai*
INTELLIGENT
INTELLIGENT: be intelligent **nibwaakaa** *vai*
INTENSE
HAVE INTENSE FEELINGS OR DESIRES: **aakwendam** *vai2*
INTERCOURSE
HAVE SEXUAL INTERCOURSE: **mazhiwe** *vai;* have sexual intercourse with s.o. **mazhi /maN-/** *vta*
INTERPRET
INTERPRET: interpret s.o. **aanikanootaw** *vta;* interpret s.t. **aanikanootan** *vti;* interpret for people **aanikanootaage** *vai*
INTERPRETED
INTERPRETED: be interpreted **aanikanootaagozi** *vai*
INTERPRETER
INTERPRETER: **aanikanootaagewinini, -wag** *na*
INTERRUPT
INTERRUPT: interrupt s.o. **wanishkwe'** *vta*
INTERRUPT BY SPEECH: interrupt s.o. by speech **wanishkwem** *vta*
INTESTINE
INTESTINE: my intestine **ninagizh, -iin /-nagizhy-/** *nid*
INTIMIDATE
INTIMIDATE: intimidate s.o. by speech **zegim** *vta*
INTROVERTED
INTROVERTED: be introverted **zhaagwenimo** *vai*
INVITE
INVITE TO A FEAST: invite s.o. to a feast (especially as part of a religious ceremony) **wiikom** *vta;* invite people to a feast (especially as part of a religious ceremony) **wiikonge** *vai*
INVOLVED
INVOLVED: be involved with s.o. **dazhiikaw** *vta;* be involved with s.t. **dazhiikan** *vti*
IRON
IRON: **biiwaabik, -oon** *ni;* clothes iron **zhooshkwega'igan, -an** *ni;* iron s.o. (e.g., pants) **zhooshkwega' /zhooshkwega'w-/** *vta;* iron s.t. **zhooshkwega'an** *vti*
IRON CLOTHES: **zhooshkwega'ige** *vai*
IRONWOOD
IRONWOOD: **maananoons, -ag** *na*
ISLAND
ISLAND: **minis, -an** *ni*
ROCKY ISLAND: **minisaabik, -oon** *ni*

IT IS SO
IT IS SO: **memwech** *pc*
IT IS THUS THAT
IT IS THUS THAT: **miish** *pc;* **mii** *pc*
ITCH
ITCH: **gizhiibizi** *vai*
ITCHY
ITCHY SKIN: have itchy skin **gizhiibazhe** *vai*

J

JACK
JACK: jack (card) **zhimaaganish, -ag** *na*
JACK PINE
JACK PINE: **okikaandag, -oog** *na, also* **wakikaandag**
JACK RABBIT
JACK RABBIT: **misaabooz, -oog** *na*
JACKET
JACKET: **babiinzikawaagan, -an** *ni*
JACKLIGHT
JACKLIGHT: **waaswaa** *vai*
JAIL
JAIL: **gibaakwa'odiiwigamig, -oon** *ni;* jail s.o. **gibaakwa' /gibaakwa'w-/** *vta*
JAM
JAM: **baashkiminasigan, -an** *ni*
JANITOR
JANITOR: **biinichigewinini, -wag** *na;* janitor (female) **biinichigewikwe, -g** *na*
JANUARY
JANUARY: **gichi-manidoo-giizis** *na, also* **manidoo-giizis**
JAW
JAW: my jaw **indaamikan, -an /-daamikan-/** *nid*
JAY
BLUE JAY: **diindiisi, -wag** *na*
JEALOUS
JEALOUS: be jealous **gaawe** *vai;* **gaawendam** *vai2;* be jealous of s.o. **gaawam** *vta;* **gizhaawenim** *vta;* be jealous of things **gizhaawenjige** *vai*
JELLO
JELLO: **wetotwaag** *ni-pt*
JIG
JIG: jig s.t. (e.g., wild rice) **mimigoshkan** *vti;* jig something (e.g., wild rice) **mimigoshkam** *vai2*
JINGLE
JINGLE: jingle (on dress) **ziibaaska'igan, -an** *ni*
JINGLE DRESS
JINGLE DRESS: jingle dress **ziibaaska'iganagooday, -an** *ni*

JOB
JOB: **anokiiwin, -an** *ni*
DO A CERTAIN JOB: do a certain job for s.o. **inanokiitaw** *vta*
HAVE A CERTAIN JOB: **inanokii** *vai*
HIRE TO DO A CERTAIN JOB: hire s.o. to do a certain job **inanoozh /inanooN-/** *vta*

JOINING
LAY JOINING: lay s.o. joining something else **aanikooshim** *vta;* lay s.t. joining something else **aanikoosidoon** *vti2*
LIE JOINING: lie joining something else **aanikooshin** *vai;* **aanikoosin** *vii*

JOURNEY
START A JOURNEY: **maadaadizi** *vai*

JOYOUS
JOYOUS: be joyous **minawaanigozi** *vai*

JUDGE
JUDGE: **dibaakonigewinini, -wag** *na;* **gichi-dibaakonigewinini, -wag** *na;* judge s.o. **dibaakon** *vta;* **onaakon** *vta;* judge s.t. **dibaakonan** *vti;* judge things **dibaakonige** *vai;* **onaakonige** *vai*
JUDGE A CERTAIN WAY: judge s.o. a certain way **inaakon** *vta;* judge s.t. a certain way **inaakonan** *vti*

JUDGED
JUDGED: be judged **dibaakonigaazo** *vai*
JUDGED A CERTAIN WAY: be judged a certain way **inaakonigaazo** *vai*

JUDGEMENT
MAKE A CERTAIN JUDGEMENT: **inaakonige** *vai*

JUICE
APPLE JUICE: **mishiiminaaboo** *ni*

JULY
JULY: **aabita-niibino-giizis** *na;* **baapaashkizige-giizis** *na;* **miini-giizis** *na, also* **miinike-giizis**

JUMP
JUMP: **gwaashkwani** *vai*
JUMP ABOARD: **boozigwaashkwani** *vai*
JUMP ACROSS: **aazhawigwaashkwani** *vai*
JUMP IN A VEHICLE OR BOAT: **boozigwaashkwani** *vai*
JUMP INTO THE WATER: **bakobiigwaashkwani** *vai*
JUMP OUT OF THE WATER: jump out of the water as a fish **googa'am** *vai2*
JUMP OVER: **baazhijigwaashkwani** *vai*
JUMP UPWARDS: **ombigwaashkwani** *vai*

JUNE
JUNE: **ode'imini-giizis** *na*

JUNEBERRY
JUNEBERRY: **gozigwaakomin, -ag** *na*

JUNEBERRY BUSH
JUNEBERRY BUSH: **gozigwaakominagaawanzh, -iig** *na*

JUST
JUST: **enda-** *pv4*
JUST DON'T: **gego bina** *pc*
JUST FOR FUN: **anishaa** *pc*
JUST FOR NOTHING: **anishaa** *pc*
JUST LIKE: **indigo** *pc, also* **nindigo***
JUST NOW: **bijiinag** *pc*
JUST SO: **eniwek** *pc;* **wenda-** *pv4*
JUST THAT: **memwech** *pc*
JUST THEN: **na'idaa** *pc*

K

KEROSENE
KEROSENE: **waazakonenjiganaaboo** *ni*

KETTLE
KETTLE: **akik, -oog** *na*
LEGGED KETTLE: **okaadakik, -oog** *na*
PUT IN THE KETTLE: put (s.t.) in the kettle **boodaakwe** *vai+o*
WASH KETTLE: **giziibiiginakokwe** *vai*

KETTLE HANGER
KETTLE HANGER: **agoodakikwaan, -an** *ni*

KEY
KEY: **aabaabika'igan, -an** *ni*

KICK
KICK: kick s.o. **basikawaazh /basikawaaN-/** *vta;* **dangishkaw** *vta;* kick s.t. **basikawaadan** *vti;* **dangishkan** *vti;* kick things **dangishkige** *vai;* kick people **dangishkaage** *vai*
KICK IN REAR: kick s.o. in the rear **basidiyeshkaw** *vta*
KICK OUT OF THE WAY: kick s.o. out of the way **ikowebishkaw** *vta;* kick s.t. out of the way **ikowebishkan** *vti*

KIDNEY
KIDNEY: my kidney **indoodikosiw, -ag /-doodikosiw-/** *na*

KILL
KILL: kill game **nitaage** *vai;* kill s.o. **nishi /niS-/** *vta;* kill s.t. **nitoon** *vti2;* kill oneself **nisidizo** *vai;* kill (s.t.) for s.o. **nitamaw** *vta;* kill (s.t.) of people or for people **nitamaage** *vai;* kill (s.t.) for oneself **nitamaazo** *vai;* kill people **nishiwe** *vai;* they kill each other **nisidiwag /nisidi-/** *vai*
FINALLY AND COMPLETELY KILL: finally and completely kill s.o. **aapijinazh /aapijinaN-/** *vta*
KILL FOR A CERTAIN REASON: kill s.o. for a certain reason **onjinazh /onjinaN-/** *vta*
KILL OFF: kill s.o. off **jaaginazh /jaaginaN-/** *vta*

KIND
KIND: be kind **gizhewaadizi** *vai;* **minode'e** *vai*

KIND
KIND: kind *animate* **dino, -wag** *pr, also* **dinowa**; kind *inanimate* **dino, -wan** *pr, also* **dinowa**

ALL KINDS: **anooj** *pc*

KIND-HEARTED

KIND-HEARTED: be kind-hearted **zhawenjige** *vai*

KINDLING

KINDLING WOOD: **biisiga'isaan, -an** *ni*

MAKE KINDLING: **biisiga'ise** *vai*

KING

KING: **gichi-ogimaa, -g** *na;* be a king **gichi-ogimaawi** *vai;* king (card) **ogimaa, -g** *na*

KINGBIRD

KINGBIRD: **wiindigoo-bineshiinh, -yag** *na*

KINGFISHER

KINGFISHER: **ogiishkimanisii, -g** *na*

KINNIKINNICK

KINNIKINNICK: kinnikinnick (tobacco and bark smoking mixture) **apaakozigan** *ni*

MAKE KINNIKINNICK: **apaakozige** *vai*

KISS

KISS: kiss s.o. **ojiim** *vta;* they kiss each other **ojiindiwag /ojiindi-/** *vai*

KITCHEN

KITCHEN: **jiibaakwewigamig, -oon** *ni*

KITCHEN APRON

KITCHEN APRON: **inapizowin, -an** *ni*

KNEAD

KNEAD: knead s.o. **onadin** *vta;* knead s.t. **onadinan** *vti;* knead things **onadinige** *vai*

KNEE

KNEE: my knee **ingidig, -wag /-gidigw-/** *nad*

SKIN KNEE: skin one's knee **bishagigidigweshin** *vai*

KNEEL

KNEEL: **ojijiingwanabi** *vai*

KNIFE

KNIFE: **mookomaan, -an** *ni*

BUTCHER KNIFE: **gichi-mookomaan, -an** *ni*

CROOKED KNIFE: **waagikomaan, -an** *ni*

LARGE KNIFE: **gichi-mookomaan, -an** *ni*

KNIFE SHEATH

KNIFE SHEATH: **biinjikomaan, -an** *ni*

KNOCK

KNOCK: knock on s.o. (as something stick- or wood-like) **baapaagaakwa' /baapaagaakwa'w-/** *vta;* knock on s.t. (as something stick- or wood-like, e.g., a door) **baapaagaakwa'an** *vti;* knock on things (as something stick- or wood-like, e.g., a door) **baapaagaakwa'ige** *vai*

KNOCK DOWN: knock s.o. down **gawiwebin** *vta;* knock s.t. down **gawiwebinan** *vti*

KNOCK DOWN OFF: knock s.o. down off something with foot or body **diitibishkaw** *vta;* knock s.t. down off something with foot or body **diitibishkan** *vti*

KNOCK DOWN OFF USING SOMETHING: knock s.o. down off using something **diitiba' /diitiba'w-/** *vta;* knock s.t. down off using something **diitiba'an** *vti*

KNOCK DOWN OFF WITH HANDS: knock s.o. down off something with hands **diitibibizh /diitibibiN-/** *vta;* knock s.t. down off something with hands **diitibibidoon** *vti2*

KNOCK DOWN USING SOMETHING: knock s.o. down using something **biniweba' /biniweba'w-/** *vta;* knock s.t. down using something **biniweba'an** *vti*

KNOCK SENSELESS: knock s.o. senseless **giiwashkweganaam** *vta*

KNOCK WILD RICE: **bawa'am** *vai2*

KNOCKER

RICE KNOCKER: rice knocker (stick for wild rice harvesting) **bawa'iganaak, -oog** *na*

KNOLL

KNOLL: be a knoll **bikwadinaa, bikwadinaamagad** *vii*

KNOT

KNOT: **gashka'oojigan, -an** *ni*

TIE WITH A KNOT: tie s.o. with a knot **gashka'oozh /gashka'ooN-/** *vta;* tie s.t. with a knot **gashka'oodoon** *vti2*

KNOTTED

KNOTTED: be knotted **gashka'oode, gashka'oodemagad** *vii;* **gashka'oozo** *vai*

KNOW

KNOW: know s.o. **gikenim** *vta;* know s.t. **gikendan** *vti;* know things **gikenjige** *vai*

KNOW HOW: know how to do something **nitaa-** *pv4;* know how to handle s.o. **nagaji'** *vta;* know how to handle s.t. **nagajitoon** *vti2*

KNOW HOW TO MAKE: know how to make s.o. **nitaawi'** *vta;* know how to make s.t. **nitaawitoon** *vti2;* know how to make things **nitaawichige** *vai*

SEEK TO KNOW: seek to know s.o. **nanda-gikenim** *vta;* seek to know s.t. **nanda-gikendan** *vti*

KNOWN

KNOWN: be known **gikendaagozi** *vai;* **gikendaagwad** *vii*

L

LACROSSE

PLAY LACROSSE: **baaga'adowe** *vai*

LACROSSE STICK

LACROSSE STICK: **baaga'adowaan, -an** *ni*

LADDER

LADDER: **akwaandawaagan, -an** *ni*

LADLE

LADLE: spoon **emikwaan, -an** *ni*

WOODEN LADLE: **mitigwemikwaan, -an** *ni*

LAKE

LAKE: **zaaga'igan, -iin** *ni*

ACROSS THE LAKE: **agaaming** *pc*

AT THE LAKE: **agamiing** *pc*

CHAIN OF LAKES: be a chain of lakes **aanikegamaa, aanikegamaamagad** *vii*
FLOW INTO A LAKE: **zaagidawaa, zaagidawaamagad** *vii*
GREAT LAKE: one of the Great Lakes **gichigami, -in** *ni*
IN THE MIDDLE OF THE LAKE: **naawagaam** *pc*
LAKE GOES OFF FROM ANOTHER: **bakegamaa, bakegamaamagad** *vii*
ON THE OTHER SIDE OF THE LAKE: **agaaming** *pc*
OUT IN THE LAKE: **naawij** *pc*
WALK AROUND A LAKE: **giiwitaayaazhagaame** *vai*

LAKE SUPERIOR
LAKE SUPERIOR: **gichigami** *ni usually in locative* **gichigamiing**

LAME
LAME: be lame **maakizi** *vai*
LAME LEG: have a lame leg **maakigaade** *vai*

LAMP
LAMP: **waazakonenjigan, -an** *ni*
ELECTRIC LAMP: **waasamoo-waazakonenjigan, -an** *ni*

LANCE
LANCE: **zhimaagan, -an** *ni*

LAND
LAND: **aki, -in** *ni*
ALLOT LAND: allot s.o. land **mamakii'** *vta*
ALLOTMENT OF LAND: there is an allotment of land **mamakii'idim /mamakii'idi-/** *vai*
CLEAR LAND: **mazhii'ige** *vai*
HAVE LAND: **odakiimi** *vai*
SURVEY LAND: **diba'akii** *vai*

LAND
LAND: **agwaa'o** *vai, also* **agwaa'am**; land (from flight) **boonii** *vai*

LANGUAGE
LANGUAGE: **inwewin, -an** *ni*
OJIBWE LANGUAGE: **ojibwemowin** *ni;* Indian language (especially Ojibwe) **anishinaabemowin, -an** *ni*

LAP
LAP: my lap **injiingwan, -ag /-jiingwan-/** *nad*

LARD
LARD: **gookooshi-bimide** *ni*

LAST
LAST: **ishkwaaj** *pc*
LAST AUTUMN: **dagwaagong** *pc*
LAST BORN CHILD: **ishkwejaagan, -ag** *na*
LAST FALL: **dagwaagong** *pc*
LAST NIGHT: **dibikong** *pc*
LAST SPRING: **ziigwanong** *pc*
LAST SUMMER: **niibinong** *pc*
LAST WINTER: **biboonong** *pc*

LAST NAME
LAST NAME: **ishkwenikaazowin, -an** *ni*
HAVE A LAST NAME: **ishkwenikaazo** *vai*

LATE
LATE: **wiikaa** *pc*
LATE AT NIGHT: **ishpi-dibik** *pc;* **niibaa-dibik** *pc;* be late at night **ishpi-dibikad** *vii*
LATE SUMMER: **giiwe-niibin** *vii*
LATE WINTER: be late winter **giiwe-biboon** *vii*
SO LATE IN THE DAY: be so late in the day **apiichi-giizhigad** *vii*
TOO LATE: **naanabem** *pc*

LATER
LATER: **baanimaa** *pc, also* **baamaa**; **baanimaa apii** *pc, also* **baanimaapii, baamaapii; naagaj** *pc*

LAUGH
LAUGH: **baapi** *vai;* **ginagaapi** *vai;* laugh at s.o. **baapi'** *vta;* laugh at s.t. **baapitoon** *vti2*
ARRIVE LAUGHING: **bagamaapi** *vai*
BURST OUT LAUGHING: **baashkaapi** *vai*
COME LAUGHING: **biidaapi** *vai*
GO AWAY LAUGHING: **animaapi** *vai*
LAUGH SECRETLY: **giimoodaapi** *vai*

LAUNCH
MOTOR LAUNCH: **waasamoo-jiimaan, -an** *ni*

LAUNDROMAT
LAUNDROMAT: **giziibiiga'igewigamig, -oon** *ni*

LAUNDRY
HANG UP LAUNDRY: **agoojige** *vai*

LAW
LAW: **inaakonigewin, -an** *ni*
CHANGE LAWS: **aandaakonige** *vai*

LAWYER
LAWYER: **dibaakonigewinini, -wag** *na*

LAWYER
LAWYER: lawyer (fish) **mizay, -ag** *na*

LAXATIVE
LAXATIVE: **zhaabozigan, -an** *ni*

LAY
LAY A CERTAIN WAY: lay s.o. a certain way **izhishim** *vta;* lay s.t. a certain way **izhisidoon** *vti2*
LAY ACROSS: lay s.o. across (as something stick- or wood-like) **aazhawaakoshim** *vta;* lay s.t. across (as something stick- or wood-like) **aazhawaakosidoon** *vti2*
LAY AN EGG: **boonam** *vai2*
LAY DOWN AROUND: lay s.o. down around **giiwitaashim** *vta;* lay s.t. down around **giiwitaasidoon** *vti2*
LAY FACE DOWN: lay s.o. face down **animikoshim** *vta;* lay s.t. face down **animikosidoon** *vti2*
LAY FACE UP: lay s.o. face up **aazhigijishim** *vta;* lay s.t. face up **aazhigijisidoon** *vti2*
LAY JOINING: lay s.o. joining something else **aanikooshim** *vta;* lay s.t. joining something else **aanikoosidoon** *vti2*
LAY ON SIDE: lay s.o. on side **opimeshim** *vai;* lay s.t. on side **opimesidoon** *vti2*
LAY OVER BACKWARDS: lay s.o. over backwards **aazhigijishim** *vta;* lay s.t. over backwards **aazhigijisidoon** *vti2*

LAY SOMETHING FOR PROTECTION: lay something on or under s.t. for protection **apisidoon** *vti2*
LAY SPREAD OUT: lay s.o. spread out **zhingadeshim** *vta;* lay s.t. spread out **zhingadesidoon** *vti2*
LAY STRAIGHT: lay s.o. straight **gwayakoshim** *vta;* lay s.t. straight **gwayakosidoon** *vti2*

LAYER
AS A LAYER: **biitoo-** *pv4*
LIE IN A LAYER: **biitooshin** *vai;* **biitoosin** *vii*
LIE IN A THICK LAYER: **gipagishin** *vai;* **gipagisin** *vii*
LIE IN A THIN LAYER: **bibagishin** *vai;* **bibagisin** *vii*
WEAR LAYERS: wear layers (as underwear) **biitookonaye** *vai*

LAZY
LAZY: be habitually lazy **gitimishki** *vai;* be lazy **bagandizi** *vai;* **gitimi** *vai*

LAZYBONES
LAZYBONES: be a lazybones **gitimishki** *vai*

LEAD
LEAD: **niigaanii** *vai;* lead s.o. **niigaaniwizh /nigaaniwiN-/** *vta*
LEAD ALONG: lead along (as something string-like) **bimaabiigamon /bimaabiigamo-/** *vii*
ROAD LEADS ALONG: lead along (as a road or trail) **bimamon /bimamo-/, bimamoomagad** *vii*
ROAD LEADS FROM A CERTAIN PLACE: lead from a certain place (as a road or trail) **ondadamon /ondadamo-/** *vii*
ROAD LEADS TO A CERTAIN PLACE: lead to a certain place (as a road or trail) **inamon /inamo-/** *vii*
TRAIL LEADS ALONG: lead along (as a road or trail) **bimamon /bimamo-/, bimamoomagad** *vii*
TRAIL LEADS FROM A CERTAIN PLACE: lead from a certain place (as a road or trail) **ondadamon /ondadamo-/** *vii*
TRAIL LEADS TO A CERTAIN PLACE: lead to a certain place (as a road or trail) **inamon /inamo-/** *vii*

LEAD
LEAD: lead (metal) **ashkikomaan** *ni*

LEADER
LEADER: **eshpabid** *na-pt;* **ogimaa, -g** *na;* be a leader **ogimaawi** *vai*
HIGHEST LEADER: **gichi-ogimaa, -g** *na;* be the highest leader **gichi-ogimaawi** *vai*
MAKE LEADER: make s.o. leader **ogimaakaw** *vta*
WIFE OF CHIEF OR LEADER: **ogimaakwe, -g** *na*
WOMAN LEADER: **ogimaakwe, -g** *na*

LEADERSHIP
LEADERSHIP: **ogimaawiwin, -an** *ni*

LEADING
LEADING: **niigaan** *pc*

LEAF
LEAF: **aniibiish, -an** *ni;* **aniibiishibag, -oon** *ni*
BRIGHT LEAVES: there are bright leaves **waatebagaa, waatebagaamagad** *vii*
GREEN LEAVES: there are green leaves **ashkibagaa, ashkibagaamagad** *vii*
LEAVES BUD: **zaagibagaa, zaagibagaamagad** *vii*
MANY LEAVES: there are many leaves **aniibiishikaa, aniibiishikaamagad** *vii*
RED LEAVES: have red leaves **miskobagizi** *vai;* there are red leaves on the trees **miskobagaa, miskobagaamagad** *vii*

LEAF-GREEN
LEAF-GREEN: be leaf-green **ashkibagong inaande, ashkibagong inaandemagad** *vii;* **ashkibagong inaanzo** *vai*

LEAK
LEAK: **onjigaa, onjigaamagad** *vii*
LEAK FAST: **gizhiigaa, gizhiigaamagad** *vii*
START TO LEAK: **maajigaa, maajigaamagad** *vii*

LEAN
LEAN AGAINST: lean against (as something stick- or wood-like) **aatwaakoshin** *vai;* **aatwaakosin** *vii;* lean s.o. against (as something stick- or wood-like) **aatwaakoshim** *vta;* lean s.t. against (as something stick- or wood-like) **aatwaakosidoon** *vti2*
STAND LEANING AGAINST: stand leaning against something **aatwaakogaabawi** *vai*

LEARN
LEARN BY OBSERVATION: **gikinawaabi** *vai;* learn by observation of s.o. **gikinawaabam** *vta*
SEEK TO LEARN: seek to learn s.t. **nandagikendan** *vti*

LEAST
IN THE LEAST: **ganage** *pc*

LEATHER
LEATHER: **bashkwegin, -oon** *ni;* **bashkweginowayaan, -an** *ni*

LEAVE
LEAVE: **maajaa** *vai, also* **ani-maajaa**
LEAVE ALONE: leave s.o. alone **booni'** *vta;* leave s.t. alone **boonitoon** *vti2*
LEAVE BEHIND: leave s.o. behind **nagazh /nagaN-/** *vta;* leave s.t. behind **nagadan** *vti;* leave (s.t.) behind for s.o. **nagadamaw** *vta;* abandon people **nagazhiwe** *vai*
LEAVE BEHIND UNEATEN: leave s.o. behind uneaten **ishkwam** *vta;* leave s.t. behind uneaten **ishkwandan** *vti*

LEECH
LEECH: **ozagaskwaajime, -g** *na, also* **zagaskwaajime**

LEECH LAKE
LEECH LAKE: Leech Lake Reservation **Gaazagaskwaajimekaag** *place*

LEFT
LEFT HAND: left hand *usually possessed* **namanjinik, -an** *ni*

LEFT ALONE
LEFT ALONE: be left alone **boonichigaade, boonichigaademagad** *vii;* **boonichigaazo** *vai*
LEFT-HANDED
LEFT-HANDED: be left-handed **namanjii** *vai*
LEFTOVERS
LEFTOVERS: leftover food **ishkwanjigan, -an** *ni*
LEAVE LEFTOVERS: **ishkwanjige** *vai*
LEG
LEG: my leg **nikaad, -an /-kaad-/** *nid*
ACHE IN LEG: have an ache in one's leg **dewigaade** *vai*
BREAK LEG: break one's leg **bookogaade** *vai*
BROKEN LEG: have a broken leg **bookogaade** *vai*
FALL AND BREAK LEG: fall and break one's leg **bookogaadeshin** *vai*
LAME LEG: have a lame leg **maakigaade** *vai*
NUMB LEG: have a numb leg **niboowigaade** *vai*
SIT WITH LEGS CROSSED: **aazhoogaadebi** *vai*
SORE LEG: have a sore leg **gaagiijigaade** *vai*
SPRAIN LEG: sprain one's leg **zegigaadeshin** *vai*
STIFF LEG: have a stiff leg **jiibadaakogaade** *vai;* **jiibajigaade** *vai*
LEG GARTER
LEG GARTER: **gashkidaasebizon, -an** *ni*
WEAR LEG GARTERS: **gashkidaasebizo** *vai*
LEGEND
LEGEND: **aadizookaan, -ag** *na*
CHARACTER OF A LEGEND OR MYTH: **aadizookaan, -ag** *na*
TELL A LEGEND: **aadizooke** *vai;* tell a legend to s.o. **aadizookaw** *vta*
LEGGING
LEGGING: **aas, -an** *ni*
LEND
LEND: lend (s.t.) to s.o. **awi'** *vta;* lend (s.t.) to people **awi'iwe** *vai*
LENGTH
CERTAIN LENGTH: **ako-** *pv3;* be a certain length **akoozi** *vai;* **akwaa, akwaamagad** *vii;* be a certain length (as something mineral) **akwaabikad** *vii;* **akwaabikizi** *vai;* be a certain length (as something sheet-like) **akwegad** *vii;* **akwegizi** *vai;* be a certain length (as something stick- or wood-like) **akwaakozi** *vai;* **akwaakwad** *vii;* be a certain length (as something string-like) **akwaabiigad** *vii;* **akwaabiigizi** *vai*
MAKE A CERTAIN LENGTH: make s.o. a certain length **akoo'** *vta;* make s.t. a certain length **akootoon** *vti2*
LESS AND LESS
LESS AND LESS: **eshkam** *pc*
LET GO
LET GO: be let go **bagidinigaade, bagidinigaademagad** *vii;* **bagidinigaazo** *vai;* let s.o. go **bagidin** *vta;* let s.t. go **bagidinan** *vti;* let things go **bagidinige** *vai*
LET IT BE
LET IT BE: **maanoo** *pc*
LET OUT
LET OUT: they are let out together (as from school or a meeting) **zaagidinidiwag /zaagidinidi-/** *vai*
LET'S GO
LET'S GO: let's go! **ambe** *pc*
LETTER
LETTER: **mazina'igan, -an** *ni;* **maajiibii'igan, -an** *ni*
LETTER OF THE ALPHABET: **ozhibii'igan, -an** *ni*
SEND A LETTER HERE: **biijibii'ige** *vai*
WRITE A LETTER: **maajiibii'ige** *vai;* write a letter to s.o. **maajiibii'amaw** *vta*
LEVEL
LEVEL GROUND: be level ground **gwayakwakamigaa, gwayakwakamigaamagad** *vii*
LEVEL SURFACE: be a level surface **desaa, desaamagad** *vii*
LIAR
LIAR: be a habitual liar **gagiinawishki** *vai*
LIBRARY
LIBRARY: **agindaasoowigamig, -oon** *ni*
LICE
LOOK FOR LICE: **nandookome** *vai*
LICENSE
LICENSE: **mazina'igaans, -an** *ni*
DRIVER'S LICENSE: **odaabii'iwe-mazina'igaans, -an** *ni*
MARRIAGE LICENSE: **aapiji-wiidige-mazina'igan, -an** *ni*
RICING LICENSE: **manoominike-mazina'igaans, -an** *ni*
LICK
LICK: lick s.o. **nooskwaada' /nooskwaada'w-/** *vta;* lick s.t. **nooskwaada'an** *vti*
LID
POT LID: **gibaabowe'igan, -an** *ni*
PUT A LID ON: put a lid on s.o. **gibaabowe' /gibaabowe'w-/** *vta;* put a lid on s.t. **gibaabowe'an** *vti;* put a lid on things **gibaabowe'ige** *vai*
LIE
LIE A CERTAIN WAY: **izhishin** *vai;* **izhisin** *vii*
LIE ACROSS: lie across (as something stick- or wood-like) **aazhawaakoshin** *vai;* **aazhawaakosin** *vii*
LIE ALONG: lie along (as something stick- or wood-like) **bimaakoshin** *vai;* **bimaakosin** *vii*
LIE AS PADDING: **apishin** *vai;* **apisin** *vii*
LIE AT THE END: **ishkweshin** *vai;* **ishkwesin** *vii*
LIE COMFORTABLY: **minoshin** *vai*
LIE CORRECTLY: **gwayakoshin** *vai;* **gwayakosin** *vii*

LIE DOWN: **gawishimo** *vai;* **zhingishin** *vai*
LIE FACE DOWN: **animikoshin** *vai;* **animikosin** *vii*
LIE FACE UP: **aazhigijishin** *vai;* **aazhigijisin** *vii*
LIE FACING A CERTAIN WAY: **inaasamishin** *vai*
LIE FIRMLY FIXED: lie firmly fixed in place **zoongishin** *vai;* **zoongisin** *vii*
LIE HIGH UP: **ishpishin** *vai;* **ishpisin** *vii*
LIE IN A CERTAIN PLACE: **dazhishin** *vai;* **dazhisin** *vii*
LIE IN A GOOD POSITION: **minoshin** *vai;* **minosin** *vii*
LIE IN A LAYER: **biitooshin** *vai;* **biitoosin** *vii*
LIE IN A PILE: **okoshin** *vai;* **okosin** *vii*
LIE IN A THICK LAYER: **gipagishin** *vai;* **gipagisin** *vii*
LIE IN A THIN LAYER: **bibagishin** *vai;* **bibagisin** *vii*
LIE IN A TIGHT PLACE: **zhegoshin** *vai;* **zhegosin** *vii*
LIE IN WAIT: lie in wait for game **akandoo** *vai;* lie in wait for s.o. **akamaw** *vta*
LIE IN WARMTH: **giizhooshin** *vai*
LIE JOINING: lie joining something else **aanikooshin** *vai;* **aanikoosin** *vii*
LIE LIMP: **neshangishin** *vai;* **neshangisin** *vii*
LIE ON: lie on something **apishimo** *vai*
LIE ON SIDE: **opimesin** *vii;* lie on one's side **opimeshin** *vai*
LIE OUT OF THE WAY: **ikoshin** *vai;* **ikosin** *vii*
LIE PROTECTIVELY ON: lie protectively on s.o. **badagoshkaw** *vta;* lie protectively on s.t. **badagoshkan** *vti*
LIE SIDE BY SIDE IN A ROW: they lie side by side in a row **niibidesinoon /niibidesin-/** *vii;* they lie side by side in a row **niibideshinoog /niibideshin-/** *vai*
LIE SLACK: **neshangisin** *vii*
LIE SPREAD OUT: **zhingadeshin** *vai;* **zhingadesin** *vii*
LIE STICKING OUT: lie sticking out (as something stick- or wood-like) **zaagaakoshin** *vai;* **zaagaakosin** *vii*
LIE STILL: **bizaanishin** *vai*
LIE STRAIGHT: **gwayakoshin** *vai;* **gwayakosin** *vii*
LIE TO A CERTAIN DEPTH: **apiichishin** *vai;* **apiichisin** *vii*
LIE TOUCHING: **daangishin** *vai;* **daangisin** *vii*
LIE UNCOMFORTABLY: **maazhishin** *vai*
LIE UNCOVERED: **baakishin** *vai;* **baakisin** *vii;* **michishin** *vai;* **michisin** *vii*
LIE WELL IN PLACE: **minosin** *vii*
LIE WITH FACE COVERED: lie with one's face covered **badagwiingweshin** *vai*
LIE WITH HEAD A CERTAIN WAY: lie with one's head a certain way **inikweshin** *vai*
LIE WITH HEAD ON: lie with head on something **apikweshimo** *vai*
LIE WITH REAR END STICKING OUT: lie with one's rear end sticking out **jaangidiyeshin** *vai*
TURN LYING IN PLACE: **gwekishin** *vai;* **gwekisin** *vii*

LIE

LIE: **giiwanimo** *vai;* lie to s.o. **giiwanim** *vta*

LIFE

CHANGE LIFE: change one's life **aanji-bimaadizi** *vai*
LEAD A BAD LIFE: **maazhi-bimaadizi** *vai*
LEAD A GOOD LIFE: **mino-bimaadizi** *vai;* **mino-izhiwebizi** *vai;* **minwaadizi** *vai*
LEAD AN EVIL LIFE: **maji-izhiwebizi** *vai*
LIVE A PROPER LIFE: **gwayako-bimaadizi** *vai*
SAVE LIFE: save the life of s.o. **bimaaji'** *vta*

LIFT

LIFT: lift s.o. **ombin** *vta;* lift s.o. (as with something string-like) **ombaabiigin** *vta;* lift s.t. **ombinan** *vti;* lift s.t. (as with something string-like) **ombaabiiginan** *vti;* lift (s.t.) for s.o. **ombinamaw** *vta*
LIFT A PACK: lift a pack to one's back **ombiwane** *vai*
LIFT AND CARRY: lift and carry s.o. **ombiwizh /ombiwiN-/** *vta;* lift and carry s.t. **ombiwidoon** *vti2*
LIFT ARM: lift one's arm **ombinikeni** *vai*
LIFT ON BACK: lift s.o. on one's back **omboom** *vta;* lift s.t. on one's back **omboondan** *vti*
STRAIN IN LIFTING: strain self in lifting **jakiiwii** *vai*

LIGHT

LIGHT: light s.o. **zakiz /zakizw-/** *vta;* light s.o. (e.g., a pipe) **zaka' /zaka'w-/** *vta;* light s.t. **zaka'an** *vti;* **zakizan** *vti;* light (s.t.) for s.o. **zaka'amaw** *vta;* light things **zakizige** *vai*
COME WITH A LIGHT: **biidaazakwanenjige** *vai*
DRIVE AWAY WITH A LIGHT: **animaazakonenjigebizo** *vai*
DRIVE HERE WITH A LIGHT: **biidaazakonebizo** *vai*
GIVE OFF LIGHT: **waazakone, waazakonemagad** *vii*
GO ALONG WITH A LIGHT: **bimaazakonenjige** *vai*
GO AWAY WITH A LIGHT: **animaazakonenjige** *vai*
GO TO A CERTAIN PLACE WITH LIGHT: **inaazakonenjige** *vai*
LIGHT A PIPE: **zaka'ipwaagane** *vai*
LIGHT AT DAWN: be light at dawn **waaseyaaban** *vii*
LIGHT BY STRIKING: light s.t. by striking **biskanesidoon** *vti2*
TURN ON A LIGHT: turn s.t. on for a light **waazakonebidoon** *vti2*

LIGHT

LIGHT: be light in weight **naangan** *vii;* **naangizi** *vai*

CARRY A LIGHT PACK: **naangiwane** *vai*
CONSIDER LIGHT: consider s.o. light in weight **naangenim** *vta;* consider s.t. light in weight **naangendan** *vti*

LIGHT POLE
LIGHT POLE: **waazakonenjiganaatig, -oon** *ni*

LIGHTER
LIGHTER: **ishkodekaan, -an** *ni;* **zaka'igan, -an** *ni*

LIGHTNING
LIGHTNING: **inaabiwin** *ni;* **waasamowin** *ni;* there is a flash of lightning **waasese, waasesemagad** *vii;* there is lightning **wawaasese, wawaasesemagad** *vii*
STRUCK BY LIGHTNING: be struck by lightning **baagijigaade, baagijigaademagad** *vii;* **baagijigaazo** *vai*

LIKE
LIKE: like s.o. **minwenim** *vta;* like s.t. **minwendan** *vti*

LIKE
LIKE: **naasaab** *pc*
JUST LIKE: **dibishkoo** *pc;* **indigo** *pc, also* **nindigo***

LIKEABLE
LIKEABLE: be likeable **minwendaagozi** *vai;* **minwendaagwad** *vii*

LIMBER
LIMBER: be limber **neshangaa, neshangaamagad** *vii;* **neshangizi** *vai*

LIMP
LIE LIMP: **neshangishin** *vai;* **neshangisin** *vii*

LINE
FISH WITH A HOOK AND LINE: **wewebanaabii** *vai*
HAVE A LINE: **beshaa, beshaamagad** *vii;* **beshizi** *vai*
HOOK AND LINE: **migiskaneyaab, -iin** *ni*

LING
LING: **mizay, -ag** *na*

LINIMENT
LINIMENT: **gwendaaseg** *ni-pt*

LION
LION: **mishibizhii, -g** *na*

LIP
CHAPPED LIPS: have chapped lips **gagiipidoon** *vai*

LIPSTICK
LIPSTICK: **miskodoonechigan, -an** *ni*

LIQUOR
LIQUOR: **ishkodewaaboo** *ni*

LISTEN
LISTEN: **bizindam** *vai2;* listen to s.o. **bizindaw** *vta;* listen to s.t. **bizindan** *vti*
LISTEN FOR: listen for s.o. **nandotaw** *vta;* listen for s.t. **nandotan** *vti;* listen for something **nandotam** *vai2*

LITTLE
A LITTLE: **bangii** *pc*
JUST A LITTLE: **bangiishenh** *pc*
THINK LITTLE OF: think little of s.o. **agaasenim** *vta;* think little of s.t. **agaasendan** *vti*

LITTLE BIT
LITTLE BIT: be a little bit **bangiiwagad** *vii;* **bangiiwagizi** *vai*
A LITTLE BIT: **bangii** *pc;* **eniwek** *pc*
A LITTLE BIT EACH: **bebangii** *pc*
A VERY LITTLE BIT: **bangiishenh** *pc*
VERY LITTLE BIT: be a very little bit **bangiishenhwagad** *vii;* **bangiishenhwagizi** *vai*

LITTLE FINGER
LITTLE FINGER: **ishkweninj, -iin** *ni*

LITTLE WHILE
A LITTLE WHILE: **ajina** *pc*
A LITTLE WHILE AGO: **naanoomaya** *pc*
IN A LITTLE WHILE: **wayiiba** *pc*

LIVE
LIVE: **bimaadizi** *vai*
LIVE A PROPER LIFE: **gwayako-bimaadizi** *vai*
LIVE ABOUT: **babaamaadizi** *vai*
LIVE ALONE: **nazhikewige** *vai*
LIVE IN: live in s.t. **abiitan** *vti*
LIVE IN A CERTAIN PLACE: **danakii** *vai;* **daa** *vai*
LIVE IN A WIGWAM: **wiigiwaamige** *vai*
LIVE IN THE FIRST HOUSE: **nitamige** *vai*
LIVE IN THE LAST HOUSE: **ishkwege** *vai*
LIVE ON THE END OF TOWN: live at the end of town **ishkwege** *vai*
LIVE SOMEWHERE ELSE: **aandakii** *vai*
LIVE THE INDIAN WAY: **anishinaabe-bimaadizi** *vai*
LIVE WELL: **mino-bimaadizi** *vai*

LIVER
LIVER: my liver **nikon, -an /-kon-/** *nid*

LIVING
MAKE A LIVING A CERTAIN WAY: **ondizi** *vai*

LIVING ROOM
LIVING ROOM: **abiwin, -an** *ni;* **abiiwigamig, -oon** *ni*

LOAD
LOAD: load s.o. (e.g., a pipe) **onashkina'** *vta;* load s.t. (e.g., a gun) **onashkinadoon** *vti2*
LOAD CARGO: **boozitaaso** *vai;* load s.t. as cargo **boozitoon** *vti2;* load (s.t.) with cargo for s.o. **boozitaw** *vta*
PACK TOO MUCH OF A LOAD: **onzaamiwane** *vai*

LOADED
LOADED: be loaded **onashkinade, onashkinademagad** *vii*

LOCK
LOCK: **gashkaabika'igan, -an** *ni;* lock s.o. **gashkaabika' /gashkaabika'w-/** *vta;* lock s.t. **gashkaabika'an** *vti;* lock s.t. (as or as with something stick- or wood-like **gashkaakonan** *vti;* lock (s.t.) for s.o. (as or as with something stick- or wood-like) **gashkaakwa'amaw** *vta;* lock things **gashkaabika'ige** *vai*

LOCKED
LOCKED: be locked **gashkaabika'igaade, gashkaabika'igaademagad** *vii;* **gashkaabika'igaazo** *vai*
LODGE
LODGE: **wiigiwaam, -an** *ni*
BARK LODGE: **wanagekogamig, -oon** *ni*
BEAVER LODGE: **amikwiish, -an** *ni*
BIRCH BARK LODGE: **wiigwaasigamig, -oon** *ni*
BUILD A LODGE: **ozhige** *vai*
DOMED LODGE: **waaginogaan, -an** *ni*
EARTH LODGE: **akiiwe-wiigiwaam, -an** *ni*
HOUSE-LIKE LODGE: **gakaaga'ogaan, -an** *ni*
LODGE OF GRASS: **mashkosiigaan, -an** *ni*
LODGE WITH PEAKED ROOF: **nisawa'ogaan, -an** *ni*
LODGE WITH POINTED TOP: **bajiishka'ogaan, -an** *ni*
LONG LODGE: **ginoondawaan, -an** *ni;* long lodge with doors at both ends **zhaaboondawaan, -an** *ni*
MIDE LODGE: **midewigaan, -an** *ni*
OTHER SIDE OF THE LODGE: **agaamindesi** *pc;* on the other side of the lodge **agaamindesing** *pc*
SAP-BOILING LODGE: **iskigamizigewigamig, -oon** *ni*
STORAGE LODGE: **asanjigoowigamig, -oon** *ni*
SWEAT LODGE: **madoodiswan, -an** *ni*
LODGE POLE
LODGE POLE: **abanzh, -iin** *ni*
LOG CABIN
LOG CABIN: **mitigo-waakaa'igan, -an** *ni*
LOGGER
LOGGER: **giishka'aakwewinini, -wag** *na*
LONELY
LONELY: be lonely **gashkendam** *vai2*
LONG
LONG: be long **ginoozi** *vai;* **ginwaa, ginwaamagad** *vii;* they are long *plural* **gagaanwaawan /gagaanwaa-/, gagaanwaamagadoon** *vii;* be long (as something mineral) **ginwaabikad** *vii;* **ginwaabikizi** *vai;* be long (as something sheet-like) **ginwegad** *vii;* **ginwegizi** *vai;* be long (as something stick- or wood-like) **ginwaakozi** *vai;* **ginwaakwad** *vii;* be long (as something string-like) **ginwaabiigad** *vii;* **ginwaabiigizi** *vai*
AS LONG AS: **ako-** *pv3*
CUT LONG: cut s.o. long (as something string-like) **ginwaabiigizh /ginwaabiigizhw-/** *vta;* cut s.t. long (as something string-like) **ginwaabiigizhan** *vti*
HAVE LONG SLEEVES: **gagaanonagweyaa, gagaanonagweyaamagad** *vii*
LONG BOAT: be a long boat **ginoonagad** *vii*
LONG HAIR: have long hair **gagaanwaanikwe** *vai*
MAKE LONG: make s.o. long **ginoo'** *vta;* make s.t. long **ginwaatoon** *vti2;* make s.o. long (as something sheet-like) **ginwegi'** *vta;* make s.t. long (as something sheet-like) **ginwegitoon** *vti2*
MAKE SO LONG: make s.o. so long **akoo'** *vta;* make s.t. so long **akootoon** *vti2*
SO LONG: be so long **akoozi** *vai;* **akwaa, akwaamagad** *vii;* be so long (as something mineral) **akwaabikad** *vii;* **akwaabikizi** *vai;* be so long (as something sheet-like) **akwegad** *vii;* **akwegizi** *vai;* be so long (as something string-like) **akwaabiigad** *vii;* **akwaabiigizi** *vai*
LONG TIME
A LONG TIME: **gabe-ayi'ii** *pc, also* **gabeyi'ii**
A LONG TIME AGO: **mewinzha** *pc*
FOR A LONG TIME: **ginwenzh** *pc*
LOOK
HAVE A CERTAIN LOOK: **izhinaagozi** *vai;* **izhinaagwad** *vii*
LOOK GOOD: **minwaabaminaagozi** *vai;* **minwaabaminaagwad** *vii*
LOOK NEW: **oshkiinaagozi** *vai;* **oshkiinaagwad** *vii*
LOOK OLD: **gichi-aya'aawinaagozi** *vai*
LOOK POOR: **gidimaaginaagozi** *vai;* **gidimaaginaagwad** *vii*
LOOK SICK: **aakoziiwinaagozi** *vai*
LOOK WEAK: **niinaminaagozi** *vai;* **niinaminaagwad** *vii*
LOOK YOUNG: **oshkiinaagozi** *vai*
MAKE LOOK A CERTAIN WAY: make s.o. look a certain way **izhinaago'** *vta;* make s.t. look a certain way **izhinaagotoon** *vti2*
LOOK
LOOK: **ganawaabi** *vai;* look! **inashke** *pc, also* **nashke**
LIKE THE LOOK: like the look of s.o. **minwaabam** *vta;* like the look of s.t. **minwaabandan** *vti*
LOOK AT: look at s.o. **ganawaabam** *vta;* look at s.t. **ganawaabandan** *vti;* look at things **ganawaabanjige** *vai;* they look at each other **ganawaabandiwag /ganawaabandi-/** *vai*
LOOK MALEVOLENTLY: look malevolently out of corner of one's eye at s.o. **negwaabam** *vta*
LOOK OUT FROM A CERTAIN PLACE: **onzaabi** *vai*
LOOK OVER: look s.o. over **dibaabam** *vta;* look s.t. over **dibaabandan** *vti*
LOOK THROUGH A WINDOW: **dapaabi** *vai;* look through a window at s.o. **dapaabam** *vta;* look through a window at s.t. **dapaabandan** *vti*
LOOK TO A CERTAIN PLACE: **inaabi** *vai*
TURN AND LOOK BACK: **aabanaabi** *vai;* turn and look back at s.o. **aabanaabam** *vta;* turn and look back at s.t. **aabanaabandan** *vti*
LOOK FOR
LOOK FOR: **nanda-** *pv4;* look for s.o. **nandawaabam** *vta;* **nandone' /nandone'w-/** *vta;* look for s.t.

nandawaabandan *vti;* **nandone'an** *vti;* look for things **nandawaabanjige** *vai;* **nandone'ige** *vai*
LOOK FOR A DRINK: **nandoobii** *vai*
LOOK FOR HORSES: **nandawisimwe** *vai*
LOOK FOR LICE: **nandookome** *vai*
LOOK FOR TRACKS: **nandokawechige** *vai;* look for s.o.'s tracks **nandokawe'** *vta*
LOOK FOR WORK: **nanda-anokii** *vai*

LOOK OUT
LOOK OUT: look out! **naasanaa** *pc*

LOOKED
LOOKED AT: be looked at **ganawaabanjigaade, ganawaabanjigaademagad** *vii;* **ganawaabanjigaazo** *vai*

LOOKED FOR
LOOKED FOR: be looked for **nandone'igaade, nandone'igaademagad** *vii;* **nandone'igaazo** *vai*

LOOM
BEAD LOOM: **mazinaabidoo'iganaatig, -oon** *ni*
BEAD ON A LOOM: bead s.t. on a loom **mazinaabidoo'an** *vti;* bead things on a loom **mazinaabidoo'ige** *vai*

LOON
LOON: **maang, -wag** *na*

LOOSE
COME LOOSE: come loose (as something string-like) **gidiskaabiigishkaa, gidiskaabiigishkaamagad** *vii*

LOOSELY
FIT LOOSELY: fit s.o. loosely **geshawishkaw** *vta;* fit s.t. loosely **geshawishkan** *vti*
PUT LOOSELY: put s.o. loosely **geshawishim** *vta;* put s.t. loosely **geshawisidoon** *vti2*

LOSE
LOSE: lose s.o. **wani'** *vta;* lose s.t. **wanitoon** *vti2*
LOSE HOPE: lose hope in s.o. **banaadenim** *vta;* lose hope in s.t. **banaadendan** *vti*

LOST
LOST: be lost **wanishin** *vai;* **wanisin** *vii*
GET LOST: **wanishin** *vai;* **wanisin** *vii*
GET LOST DRIVING: **wanibizo** *vai*

LOTION
HAND LOTION: **noomininjiiwin, -an** *ni*
PUT LOTION ON HAND: put lotion on one's hand **noomininjii** *vai*

LOUD
LOUD: be loud **ombiigizi** *vai;* be loud (in operation) **ombiigwewe** *vai;* **ombiigwewe, ombiigwewemagad** *vii*
SPEAK LOUD: **gizhiiwe** *vai*

LOUSE
LOUSE: **ikwa, -g** *na*

LOVE
LOVE: love s.o. **zaagi'** *vta;* love s.t. **zaagitoon** *vti2;* they love each other **zaagi'idiwag /zaagi'idi-/** *vai*

LOVED
LOVED: be loved **zaagichigaade, zaagichigaademagad** *vii;* **zaagichigaazo** *vai*

LOW
LOW: **dabazhish** *pc;* be low **dabasaa, dabasaamagad** *vii*
HANG LOW: **dabasagoode, dabasagoodemagad** *vii;* **dabasagoojin** *vai;* hang s.o. low **dabasagoozh /dabasagooN-/** *vta;* hang s.t. low **dabasagoodoon** *vti2*
LOW GROUND: be low ground **dabasakamigaa, dabasakamigaamagad** *vii*

LOW REGARD
HELD IN LOW REGARD: be held in low regard **dabasendaagozi** *vai;* **dabasendaagwad** *vii*
HOLD IN LOW REGARD: hold s.o. in low regard **dabasenim** *vta;* hold s.t. in low regard **dabasendan** *vti*

LUCKY
LUCKY: be lucky **debizi** *vai*

LUMBER CAMP
LUMBER CAMP: **giishka'aakwewigamig, -oon** *ni*

LUMBERJACK
LUMBERJACK: **giishka'aakwewinini, -wag** *na*

LUNCH
EAT LUNCH: eat lunch (noon meal) **naawakwe-wiisini** *vai;* eat s.t. for lunch (noon meal) **naawakwe-miijin** *vti3*
LUNCH TAKEN ALONG: **nawapwaan, -an** *ni*
MAKE A LUNCH TO TAKE ALONG: **nawapwaanike** *vai*
TAKE A LUNCH ALONG: **nawapo** *vai*
TAKE A LUNCH BREAK: **nawajii** *vai*

LUNG
LUNG: my lung **nipan, -an /-pan-/** *nid*

LYMPH NODE
LYMPH NODE: my gland (lymph node) **niniishk, -wag /-niishkw-/** *nad*

LYNX
LYNX: **bizhiw, -ag** *na*

LYNX HIDE
LYNX HIDE: **bizhiwayaan, -ag** *na*

M

MACARONI
MACARONI: macaroni *plural* **onagizhiinsan /onagizhiins-/** *ni*

MAD
MAD: be mad **nishkaadizi** *vai;* be mad at s.o. **nishkenim** *vta*
ARRIVE MAD: **bagamigidaazo** *vai*
FEEL MAD: **nishkendam** *vai2*
GO AWAY MAD: **animigidaazo** *vai*
GO HOME MAD: **giiwegidaazo** *vai*
GO OFF MAD: **maajiigidaazo** *vai*
MAKE MAD: make s.o. mad **nishki'** *vta;* speak and make s.o. mad **nishkim** *vta;* make people mad **nishkitaa** *vai;* they make each other mad **nishki'idiwag /nishki'idi-/** *vai*
MAKE MAD FOR A CERTAIN REASON: make s.o. mad for a certain reason **onjinawe'** *vta*

MADE
MADE: be made **ozhichigaade, ozhichigaademagad** *vii;* **ozhichigaazo** *vai*
MADE A CERTAIN WAY: be made a certain way **izhichigaade, izhichigaademagad** *vii;* **izhichigaazo** *vai*

MAGGOT
MAGGOT: **ookwe, -g** *na*

MAGNET
MAGNET: **manidoo-biiwaabik** *ni*

MAIL
GO GET MAIL: **naadazina'igane** *vai*

MAIL TRUCK
MAIL TRUCK: **mazina'iganiiwidaabaan, -ag** *na*

MAINTENANCE ENGINEER
MAINTENANCE ENGINEER: **boodawewinini, -wag** *na*

MAKE
MAKE: make s.o. **ozhi'** *vta;* make s.t. **ozhitoon** *vti2;* make (s.t.) for s.o. **ozhitamaw** *vta;* **ozhitaw** *vta;* make things **ozhichige** *vai*
FINISH MAKING: finish making s.t. **giizhitoon** *vti2*
HURRY MAKING: hurry making s.o. **wewiibi'** *vta;* hurry making s.t. **wewiibitoon** *vti*
KNOW HOW TO MAKE: know how to make s.o. **nitaawi'** *vta;* know how to make s.t. **nitaawitoon** *vti2;* know how to make things **nitaawichige** *vai*
MAKE A BED: **ozisijige** *vai, also* **ozhisijige**
MAKE A CERTAIN WAY: make s.t. a certain way **izhitoon** *vti2*
MAKE BADLY: make things badly **mamaazhii** *vai*
MAKE DO: make s.o. do something **izhi'** *vta*
MAKE NICE: make s.o. nice **onizhishi'** *vta;* make s.t. nice **onizhishitoon** *vti2*
MAKE OVER: make s.o. over **aanji'** *vta;* make s.t. over **aanjitoon** *vti2*
MAKE SKILFULLY: make s.o. skilfully **wawiinge'** *vta;* make s.t. skilfully **wawiingetoon** *vti2*
MAKE WELL: make s.o. well **onizhishi'** *vta;* make s.t. well **onizhishitoon** *vti2*
START TO MAKE: start to make s.o. **maaji'** *vta;* start to make s.t. **maajitoon** *vti2*

MAKE UP
MAKE UP: make s.o. up **wawezhi'** *vta;* make up oneself **wawezhi'o** *vai*

MALE
MALE: **naabe-** *pv4*

MALLARD
MALLARD: **ininishib, -ag** *na*

MAN
MAN: **inini, -wag** *na;* be a man **ininiiwi** *vai*
DRESSED-UP MAN: **zazegaa-inini, -wag** *na*
FELLOW MAN: my fellow man **niijiinini** *nad*
OLD MAN: **akiwenzii, -yag** *na*
UNMARRIED MAN: **moozhaabe, -g** *na*
YOUNG MAN: **oshki-inini, -wag** *na;* **oshkinawe, -g** *na;* be a young man **oshkinawewi** *vai*

MANAGE
MANAGE: manage s.o. **gashki'** *vta;* manage s.t. **gashkitoon** *vti2*
UNABLE TO MANAGE: be unable to manage s.o. **bwaanawi'** *vta;* be unable to manage s.t. **bwaanawitoon** *vti2*

MANITOU
MANITOU: **manidoo, -g** *na;* be a manitou **manidoowi** *vai*

MANUFACTURE
MANUFACTURE: **anokaajigan, -an** *ni*

MANY
MANY: **niibowa** *pc, also* **niibiwa***; they are many **baatayiinadoon /baatayiinad-/** *vii;* **baatayiinowag /baatayiino-/** *vai, also* **/baatayiini-/**; **niibowagadoon /niibowagad-/** *vii;* **niibowagiziwag /niibowagizi-/** *vai*
HAVE MANY: have many of s.o. **baatayiino'** *vta;* have many of s.t. **baatayiinatoon** *vti2*
HOW MANY: how many? **aaniin minik** *pc*
SO MANY: **minik** *pc*

MAP
MAP: **akii-mazina'igan, -an** *ni*

MAPLE
MAPLE: **aninaatig, -oog** *na, also* **ininaatig**

MAPLE SAP
MAPLE SAP: **wiishkobaaboo** *ni;* **ziinzibaakwadwaaboo** *ni*

MAPLE SUGAR
MAPLE SUGAR: **ziinzibaakwad** *ni;* **anishinaabe-ziinzibaakwad** *ni*
GRANULATED MAPLE SUGAR: **nase'igan** *ni*

MAPLE TAFFY
MAPLE TAFFY: **bigiwizigan** *ni*

MARBLE
MARBLE: **nemaab, -iin** *ni*

MARCH
MARCH: **onaabani-giizis** *na*

MARIAH
MARIAH: **mizay, -ag** *na*

MARK
MARK: mark s.o. **gikinawaaji'** *vta;* mark s.t. **gikinawaajitoon** *vti2;* mark things **gikinawaajichige** *vai*
LEAVE A MARK: **ezhishin** *vai;* **ezhisin** *vii*
MARK WITH A STRIPE: mark s.o. with a stripe **beshibii' /beshibii'w-/** *vta;* mark s.t. with a stripe **beshibii'an** *vti;* mark things with a stripe **beshibii'ige** *vai*

MARRIAGE LICENSE
MARRIAGE LICENSE: **aapiji-wiidige-mazina'igan, -an** *ni*

MARRIED
MARRIED: be legally married **aapiji-wiidige** *vai;* be married **wiidige** *vai;* be married to s.o. **wiidigem** *vta;* they are married to each other **wiidigendiwag /wiidigendi-/** *vai*

MARROW
EXTRACT MARROW: extract marrow from bones **zhigwaajige** *vai*
TOOL FOR EXTRACTING MARROW: tool for extracting marrow from bones **zhigwaajiganaak, -oon** *ni*

MARRY
MARRY: **wiidige** *vai;* marry s.o. **wiidigem** *vta;* they marry each other **wiidigendiwag /wiidigendi-/** *vai*

MARTEN
MARTEN: **waabizheshi, -wag** *na*

MARTEN HIDE
MARTEN HIDE: **waabizheshiwayaan, -ag** *na*

MARTIN
MARTIN: **zhaashaawanibiisens, -ag** *na*

MASSAGE
MASSAGE: massage s.o. with something **zinigobizh /zinigobiN-/** *vta;* massage s.t. with something **zinigobidoon** *vti2*

MASTER
MASTER: be the master of s.t. **dibendan** *vti;* be the master to s.o. **dibenim** *vta;* be one's own master **dibenindizo** *vai*

MAT
CATTAIL MAT: **apakweshkway, -ag** *na*
MAT ON BOTTOM OF A CANOE: mat on bottom of canoe **apishkaamon, -an** *ni*
PROTECTIVE MAT: **apisijigan, -an** *ni*
WOVEN MAT: **anaakan, -an** *ni*

MATCH
MATCH: **ishkodens, -an** *ni*

MATTRESS
MATTRESS: **apishimon, -an** *ni*

MAY
MAY: **waabigwanii-giizis** *na;* **zaagibagaa-giizis** *na*

MAYBE
MAYBE: **ganabaj** *pc;* **iidog** *pc;* **maagizhaa** *pc, also* **maazhaa**
OR MAYBE: **gemaa** *pc, also* **gemaa gaye**

MAYFLY
MAYFLY: **omiimiisi, -wag** *na*

ME
ME: **niin** *pr first person singular person pronoun*

MEADOW
BY A MEADOW: **jiigashkosiw** *pc*
MIDDLE OF A MEADOW: in the middle of a meadow **naawashkosiw** *pc*
ON THE OTHER SIDE OF THE MEADOW: **agaamashkosiw** *pc*

MEAN
MEAN: be mean **gagwaanisagizi** *vai;* be mean to s.o. **inigaa'** *vta*

MEANS
BY ANY MEANS: **ganage** *pc*

MEASLES
HAVE MEASLES: **miskwazhe** *vai*

MEASURE
MEASURE: measure s.o. (as with something string-like) **dibaabiigin** *vta;* measure s.t. (as with something string-like) **dibaabiiginan** *vti;* measure things **diba'ige** *vai*

MEASURING STICK
MEASURING STICK FOR TIMBER: **diba'aatigwaan, -an** *ni*

MEAT
MEAT: **wiiyaas** *ni;* my meat (of the body) **niiyaas /-iiyaas-/** *nid*
CUT MEAT INTO STRIPS: cut meat into strips for preservation **baanizhaawe** *vai*
DEER MEAT: **waawaashkeshiwi-wiiyaas** *ni*
FIRE-CURED MEAT OR FISH: **abwewasigan, -an** *ni*
RAW MEAT: be raw (as meat) **ashkin** *vii;* **ashkini** *vai*

MEAT MARKET
MEAT MARKET: **wiiyaas-adaawewigamig, -oon** *ni*

MECHANIC
MECHANIC: **odaabaanikewinini, -wag** *na*

MEDICINE
MEDICINE: **mashkiki, -wan** *ni;* medicine for burning **nookwezigan, -an** *ni*
BURN AS MEDICINE: burn s.t. as medicine **nookwezan** *vti;* burn things as medicine **nookwezige** *vai*
GATHER MEDICINE: **manashkikiiwe** *vai*
LIQUID MEDICINE: **mashkikiwaaboo, -n** *ni*
MAKE MEDICINE: **mashkikiike** *vai*

MEDICINE DANCE
MEDICINE DANCE: **midewiwin** *ni*

MEEK
MEEK: be meek **nookaadizi** *vai*

MEET
MEET: meet s.o. **nakweshkaw** *vta;* meet s.o. (while going somewhere) **nagishkaw** *vta;* meet s.t. (while going somewhere) **nagishkan** *vti;* they meet each other **nagishkodaadiwag /nagishkodaadi-/** *vai;* **nakweshkodaadiwag /nakweshkodaadi-/** *vai*

MEETING
COUNCIL MEETING: they have a council meeting **zagaswe'idiwag /zagaswe'idi-/** *vai*

HAVE A MEETING: they have a meeting **maawanji'idiwag /maawanji'idi-/** *vai*

MELT

MELT: **ningide, ningidemagad** *vii;* **ningizo** *vai;* melt s.o. **ningiz /ningizw-/** *vta;* melt s.t. **ningizan** *vti*

MEMBER

MEMBER: be a member **dibendaagozi** *vai*

INITIATED MEMBER: be an initiated member **dibenjigaazo** *vai*

MENOMINEE

MENOMINEE: **omanoominii, -g** *na*

MENSES

SECLUDED AT FIRST MENSES: be secluded at first menses **bakaanige** *vai*

MENTAL HOSPITAL

MENTAL HOSPITAL: **giiwanaadiziiwigamig, -oon** *ni*

MENTION

MENTION: mention s.o. **waawiinzh /waawiinN-/** *vta;* mention s.o. come to one's mind **mikom** *vta;* mention s.t. come to one's mind **mikondan** *vti;* mention the name of s.o. **wiinzh /wiinN-/** *vta;* mention the name of s.t. **wiindan** *vti*

MERCIFUL

MERCIFUL: be merciful **zhawenjige** *vai*

MERRY

DRINK AND BE MERRY: **minobii** *vai*

MESS

MAKE A MESS: **ombwewebinige** *vai*

MESSENGER

CEREMONIAL MESSENGER: **oshkaabewis, -ag** *na*

MESSY

MESSY HAIR: have messy hair **niiskindibe** *vai*

METAL

METAL: metal **biiwaabik, -oon** *ni*

ON METAL: on something mineral (e.g., metal, glass, rock) **agidaabik** *pc, also* **ogidaabik*, wagidaabik**

PIECE OF METAL: **bookwaabik, -oon** *ni*

METIS

METIS: Metis **wiisaakodewinini, -wag** *na*

METIS WOMAN

METIS WOMAN: **wiisaakodewikwe, -g** *na*

MID-SUMMER

AFTER MID-SUMMER: be after mid-summer **giiwe-niibin** *vii*

MID-WINTER

AFTER MID-WINTER: be after mid-winter **giiwe-biboon** *vii*

MIDDLE

IN THE MIDDLE: in the middle of **naawi-** *pn;* in the middle of it **naawayi'ii** *pc*

IN THE MIDDLE OF THE FLOOR: **naawisag** *pc*

IN THE MIDDLE OF THE LAKE: **naawagaam** *pc*

IN THE MIDDLE OF THE ROAD: in the middle of the road or trail **naawikana** *pc*

IN THE MIDDLE OF THE TRAIL: in the middle of the road or trail **naawikana** *pc*

MIDDLE OF A BOAT: in the middle of a boat **naawoonag** *pc*

MIDDLE OF A MEADOW: in the middle of a meadow **naawashkosiw** *pc*

MIDDLE OF THE BACK: in the middle of the back **naawaawigan** *pc*

MIDDLE OF THE CHEST: in the middle of the chest **naawaakigan** *pc*

MIDDLE OF THE FOREHEAD: in the middle of the forehead **naawigatig** *pc*

MIDDLE OF THE WOODS: in the middle of the woods **naawaakwaa** *pc*

MIDDLE FINGER

MIDDLE FINGER: **naawininj, -iin** *ni*

MIDDLING

MIDDLING: **eniwek** *pc*

MIDDLING DEGREE: to a middling degree **gomaa** *pc*

MIDE DRUM

MIDE DRUM: **mitigwakik, -oog** *na*

MIDE LODGE

MIDE LODGE: **midewigaan, -an** *ni*

MIDE LODGE FRAME

MIDE LODGE FRAME: **midewigaanaak, -oon** *ni*

MIDE SHELL

MIDE SHELL: **miigis, -ag** *na*

MIDEWIWIN

MIDEWIWIN: **midewiwin** *ni*

JOIN THE MIDEWIWIN: **midewi** *vai*

MIDNIGHT

MIDNIGHT: be midnight **aabitaa-dibikad** *vii*

MIGHT

MIGHT: might *modal* **daa-** *pv1*

MILD

MILD: be mild **nookaadad** *vii;* **nookaadizi** *vai*

MILD WEATHER: be mild weather **aabawaa, aabawaamagad** *vii*

MILE

CERTAIN NUMBER OF MILES: a certain number of miles **daso-diba'igan** *pc*

MILK

MILK: **doodooshaaboo** *ni;* milk cows **ziininiwe** *vai;* milk s.o. **ziinin** *vta*

MILL

MILL: **biisiboojigan, -an** *ni*

SAW MILL: **daashkiboojigan, -ag** *na*

MILLE LACS

MILLE LACS: Mille Lacs Reservation **Misi-zaaga'iganiing** *place*

MIND

CHANGE MIND: change one's mind **aanizhiitam** *vai2*

COME TO MIND: **mikwendaagozi** *vai;* **mikwendaagwad** *vii;* have things come to one's mind **mikwendam** *vai2*

HAVE MIND MADE UP: have one's mind made up **giizhendam** *vai2*

HAVE ON MIND: have something on one's mind **biingeyendam** *vai2*

KEEP IN MIND: keep s.o. in one's mind **minjimenim** *vta;* keep s.t. in one's mind **minjimendan** *vti*
OF A CERTAIN MIND: be of a certain mind **inendam** *vai2*
RELEASE FROM MIND: release s.o. from one's mind **bagidenim** *vta;* release s.t. from one's mind **bagidendan** *vti;* release things from one's mind **bagidenjige** *vai*

MINE
MINE: **biiwaabikokaan, -an** *ni*

MINER
MINER: **biiwaabikokewinini, -wag** *na*

MINISTER
MINISTER: **gagiikwewinini, -wag** *na*

MINK
MINK: **zhaangweshi, -wag** *na*

MINK HIDE
MINK HIDE: **zhaangweshiwayaan, -ag** *na*

MINNEAPOLIS
MINNEAPOLIS: **Gakaabikaang** *place*

MINNOW
MINNOW: **giigoozens, -ag** *na*

MINUTE
CERTAIN NUMBER OF MINUTES: a certain number of minutes **daso-diba'igaans** *pc*

MIRROR
MIRROR: **waabamoojichaagwaan, -an** *ni;* **waabandizowin, -an** *ni*

MISBEHAVE
MISBEHAVE: **maji-izhiwebizi** *vai*

MISCOUNT
MISCOUNT: **wanagindaaso** *vai;* miscount s.o. **wanagim** *vta;* miscount s.t. **wanagindan** *vti*

MISHEAR
MISHEAR: mishear s.o. **banitaw** *vta;* mishear s.t. **banitan** *vti*

MISLEAD
MISLEAD: mislead s.o. by speech **wanim** *vta*

MISPLACE
MISPLACE: misplace s.o. **wanishim** *vta;* misplace s.t. **wanisidoon** *vti2*

MISPRONOUNCE
MISPRONOUNCE: **wanigiizhwe** *vai*

MISREAD
MISREAD: **wanagindaaso** *vai;* misread s.t. **wanagindan** *vti*

MISS
MISS: miss s.o. absent **gwiinawenim** *vta;* miss s.t. absent **gwiinawendan** *vti*
MISS OUT: **banizi** *vai*
MISS USING SOMETHING: miss s.o. using something **bana' /bana'w-/** *vta;* miss s.t. using something **bana'an** *vti*
SHOOT AND MISS: **bishkonaage** *vai;* shoot at s.o. and miss **bishkonaw** *vta;* shoot at s.t. and miss **bishkonan** *vti*

MISSED
MISSED: missed it! **hay'** *pc*

MISSISSIPPI RIVER
MISSISSIPPI RIVER: **Gichi-ziibi, -wan** *ni*

MISTAKE
BY MISTAKE: **bichi-** *pv4;* **wani-** *pv4*
MAKE A MISTAKE: **wanichige** *vai*
MAKE A MISTAKE BEADING: make a mistake beading s.t. on a loom **wanaabidoo'an** *vti;* make a mistake beading things on a loom **wanaabidoo'ige** *vai*
MAKE A MISTAKE SEWING: **wanigwaaso** *vai;* make a mistake sewing on s.o. **wanigwaazh /wanigwaaN-/** *vta;* make a mistake sewing on s.t. **wanigwaadan** *vti*
MAKE A MISTAKE SPEAKING: **wanigiizhwe** *vai*
MAKE A MISTAKE WRITING: **wanibii'ige** *vai;* make a mistake writing s.t. **wanibii'an** *vti*

MISTREAT
MISTREAT: mistreat s.o. **goopaji'** *vta;* mistreat s.t. **goopajitoon** *vti2*

MISTY
MISTY: be misty **awanibiisaa, awanibiisaamagad** *vii*

MISUNDERSTAND
MISUNDERSTAND: misunderstand (what) s.o. (says) **wanitaw** *vta;* misunderstand something heard **wanitam** *vai2*

MITTEN
MITTEN: **minjikaawan, -ag** *na*
PUT ON MITTENS: put on one's mittens **biichiminjikaawane** *vai*
TAKE OFF MITTENS: take off one's mittens **giichiminjikaawane** *vai*
WEAR MITTENS: **gigiminjikaawane** *vai*

MIX
MIX: mix s.o. **ginigawin** *vta;* mix s.t. **ginigawinan** *vti;* mix things **ginigawinige** *vai*
MIX BY SHAKING: mix s.o. by shaking **ginigawiwebin** *vta;* mix s.t. by shaking **ginigawiwebinan** *vti*
MIX IN: mix s.o. in **dagon** *vta;* mix s.t. in **dagonan** *vti;* mix things in **dagonige** *vai*

MIXED
MIXED: be mixed **ginigawinigaade, ginigawinigaademagad** *vii;* **ginigawinigaazo** *vai;* **ginigawisin** *vii*
MIXED IN: be mixed in **dagonigaade, dagonigaademagad** *vii;* **dagonigaazo** *vai*

MIXED ANCESTRY
PERSON OF MIXED ANCESTRY: **wiisaakodewinini, -wag** *na*
WOMAN OF MIXED ANCESTRY: **wiisaakodewikwe, -g** *na*

MIXER
MIXER: **waninawe'igan, -an** *ni*

MOCCASIN
MOCCASIN: **makizin, -an** *ni*
HIDE MOCCASIN: **bashkweginwakizin, -an** *ni, also* **bashkwegino-makizin**
MAKE MOCCASINS: **makizinike** *vai*

PUT ON MOCCASINS: put on one's moccasins **babiichii** *vai*
TAKE OFF MOCCASINS: take off one's moccasins **gagiichii** *vai*

MOCCASIN CUFF
MOCCASIN CUFF: **apiganegwaajigan, -an** *ni, also* **apigwanegwaason, -an**

MOCCASIN GAME
MOCCASIN GAME: **makizinataagewin** *ni*
PLAY THE MOCCASIN GAME: **makizinataage** *vai;* they play the moccasin game with each other **makizinataadiwag /makizinataadi-/** *vai*

MOCCASIN GAME SONG
MOCCASIN GAME SONG: **makizinataage-nagamon, -an** *ni*

MOCCASIN VAMP
MOCCASIN VAMP: **apiingwe'igan, -an** *ni*

MOCK
MOCK: mock s.o. **naabinootaw** *vta;* mock people **naabinootaage** *vai*
MOCK DISRESPECTFULLY: mock s.o. disrespectfully **baapinodaw** *vta*

MOLD
MOLD: mold s.o. **onadin** *vta;* mold s.t. **onadinan** *vti;* mold things **onadinige** *vai*

MOLDY
MOLDY: be moldy **agwaagoshi** *vai;* **agwaagosin** *vii*

MOLE
MOLE: **nenaapaajinikesi, -wag** *na*

MONDAY
MONDAY: be Monday **ishkwaa-anama'e-giizhigad** *vii, also* **ishkwaa-aname-giizhigad**

MONEY
MONEY: **zhooniyaa** *na*
COLLECT MONEY AS A DONATION: **asigizhooniyaawe** *vai*
EARN MONEY: **zhooniyaake** *vai*
HAVE MONEY: **ozhooniyaami** *vai*
MAKE MONEY: **zhooniyaake** *vai*
USE UP MONEY: use up all of the money **jaagizhooniyaaweshin** *vai*

MONKEY
MONKEY: **nandookomeshiinh, -yag** *na*

MONSTER
WINTER CANNIBAL MONSTER: windigo: winter cannibal monster **wiindigoo, -g** *na*

MONTH
MONTH: **giizis, -oog** *na*
CERTAIN DATE OF THE MONTH: be a certain date of the month **inaginzo** *vai*
CERTAIN NUMBER OF MONTHS: a certain number of months **daso-giizis** *pc*
EVERY MONTH: **endaso-giizis** *pc*
START A MONTH: **maadaginzo** *vai*

MOON
MOON: **dibik-giizis, -oog** *na, also* **dibiki-giizis; giizis, -oog** *na*
FULL MOON: be full (as something mineral, e.g., the moon) **michaabikizi** *vai;* **miziweyaabikizi** *vai*
HALF MOON: be half (as something mineral, e.g., the moon) **aabitawaabikizi** *vai*
NEW MOON: be new (of a moon) **oshkagoojin** *vai, also* **oshki-agoojin**

MOONLIGHT
MOONLIGHT: there is moonlight **giizhigaate, giizhigaatemagad** *vii*

MOOSE
MOOSE: **mooz, -oog** *na*

MORE
MORE: **nawaj** *pc*
MUCH MORE: **awashime** *pc*

MORE AND MORE
MORE AND MORE: **eshkam** *pc*

MORNING
MORNING: be morning **gigizhebaawagad** *vii*
EARLY IN THE MORNING: **gichi-gigizheb** *pc*
EVERY MORNING: **endaso-gigizheb** *pc*
IN THE MORNING: **gigizheb** *pc*
LATE MORNING OR EARLY AFTERNOON: be late morning or early afternoon **ishpi-giizhigad** *vii*
THIS MORNING: this morning (just past) **zhebaa** *pc*

MORTAR
MORTAR: mortar for wild rice **bootaagan, -ag** *na*
STAMP IN A MORTAR: stamp s.t. in a mortar **bootaagaadan** *vti;* stamp things in a mortar (e.g., wild rice) **bootaage** *vai*

MORTUARY
MORTUARY: **niboowigamig, -oon** *ni*

MOSQUITO
MOSQUITO: **zagime, -g** *na*
MANY MOSQUITOES: there are many mosquitoes **zagimekaa, zagimekaamagad** *vii*

MOSQUITO NET
MOSQUITO NET: **zagimewayaan, -ag** *na*

MOSS
MOSS: **aasaakamig, -oon** *ni*

MOTHER
MOTHER: my mother **nimaamaa, -yag /-maamaay-/** *nad;* my mother *old-fashioned* **inga** *nad*
HAVE A MOTHER: **omaamaayi** *vai*

MOTHER-IN-LAW
MOTHER-IN-LAW: my mother-in-law **inzigozis, -ag /-zigozis-/** *nad*

MOTION
IN MOTION: be in motion **mamaajii** *vai*

MOTOR
OUTBOARD MOTOR: **akikoons, -ag** *na*

MOTOR LAUNCH
MOTOR LAUNCH: **waasamoo-jiimaan, -an** *ni*

MOUNTAIN
MOUNTAIN: **wajiw, -an** *ni*
BEYOND THE MOUNTAIN: **awasajiw** *pc*
ON TOP OF A MOUNTAIN: **agidajiw** *pc, also* **ogidajiw*, wagidajiw**

OVER ACROSS THE MOUNTAIN: **awasajiw** *pc*

MOUNTAIN ASH

MOUNTAIN ASH: **makominagaawanzh, -iig** *na*

MOURN

MOURN: **inigaazi** *vai;* **nitaage** *vai*

COMPLETE MOURNING: complete mourning for s.o. **bagidenim** *vta*

MOUSE

MOUSE: **waawaabiganoojiinh, -yag** *na*

MOUSTACHE

MOUSTACHE: have a moustache **miishidoon** *vai*

MOUTH

MOUTH: my mouth **indoon, -an /-doon-/** *nid*

INSIDE MOUTH: inside the mouth **biinjidoon** *pc*

OPEN MOUTH: open one's mouth **daawani** *vai*

PUT IN MOUTH: put (something) in one's mouth **zhakamo** *vai*

TWISTED MOUTH: have a twisted mouth (as from a stroke) **biimidoon** *vai*

WIPE MOUTH: wipe one's mouth **gaasiidoone'o** *vai*

MOVE

MOVE: **mamaajise** *vai;* **mamaajise, mamaajisemagad** *vii;* **mamaajii** *vai;* **mamaazikaa** *vai*

MOVE A CERTAIN WAY: *with a pv4* move a certain way **ayaa** *vai;* **ayaa, ayaamagad** *vii*

MOVE ARM A CERTAIN WAY: move one's arm a certain way **izhinikeni** *vai*

MOVE FAST: **gizhiibide, gizhiibidemagad** *vii;* **gizhiibizo** *vai*

MOVE FOOT A CERTAIN WAY: move one's foot a certain way **izhizideni** *vai*

MOVE HAND A CERTAIN WAY: move one's hand a certain way **izhininjiini** *vai*

MOVE OFF: **maajise** *vai;* **maajise, maajisemagad** *vii*

MOVE RESIDENCE: move one's residence **gozi** *vai*

MOVE RESIDENCE ABOUT: move one's residence about **babaamigozi** *vai*

MOVE RESIDENCE HERE: move one's residence here **biijigozi** *vai*

MOVE SLOWLY: **bejibide, bejibidemagad** *vii;* **bejibizo** *vai;* **bezikaa** *vai*

MOVE TO A NEW RESIDENCE: **aanjigozi** *vai*

START TO MOVE: **maajiishkaa, maajiishkaamagad** *vii*

MOVIE

MOVIE: be a movie **mazinaatese, mazinaatesemagad** *vii*

CERTAIN KIND OF MOVIE: be a certain kind of movie **inaatese, inaatesemagad** *vii*

FUNNY MOVIE: be a funny movie **gagiibaadaatese, gagiibaadaatesemagad** *vii*

GOOD MOVIE: be a good movie **minwaatese, minwaatesemagad** *vii*

SCARY MOVIE: be a scary movie **zegaatese, zegaatesemagad** *vii*

MOVIE PROJECTOR

MOVIE PROJECTOR: **mazinaatewebinigan, -an** *ni*

MOVIE THEATER

MOVIE THEATER: **mazinaatesewigamig, -oon** *ni, also* **mazinaatesijigewigamig**

MUCH

MUCH: **niibowa** *pc, also* **niibiwa***; be much **baatayiinad** *vii;* **baatayiino** *vai, also* **baatayiini**; there is much of it **niibowagad** *vii;* **niibowagizi** *vai*

HAVE MUCH: have much of s.o. **baatayiino'** *vta;* have much of s.t. **baatayiinatoon** *vti2*

HOW MUCH: how much? *interrogative* **aaniin minik** *pc*

SO MUCH: **minik** *pc*

TOO MUCH: **onzaam** *pc*

MUD

MUD: **azhashki** *ni*

IN THE MUD: **megwejiishkiwag** *pc*

MUCH MUD: there is much mud **azhashkiikaa, azhashkiikaamagad** *vii*

MUD HEN

MUD HEN: **aajigade, -g** *na*

MUDDY

MUDDY: be muddy **azhashkiiwan** *vii;* there is a muddy patch **wiinijiishkiwagaa, wiinijiishkiwagaamagad** *vii*

MUDDY FEET: have muddy feet **azhashkiiwizide** *vai*

MULE

MULE: **memaangishens, -ag** *na*

MUMPS

HAVE THE MUMPS: **mamagoniishkwe** *vai*

MUSCLE

MUSCLE: **mashkawiziiwin, -an** *ni*

MUSHROOM

MUSHROOM: **wazhashkwedoons, -ag** *na*

MUSIC

PLAY MUSIC: **madwewechige** *vai;* play music for s.o. **madwewetaw** *vta, also* **madwewetamaw**

MUSICAL INSTRUMENT

MUSICAL INSTRUMENT: **madwewechigan, -an** *ni;* musical instrument (especially a wind instrument) **noondaagochigan, -an** *ni*

MUSKELLUNGE

MUSKELLUNGE: **maashkinoozhe, -g** *na*

MUSKRAT

MUSKRAT: **wazhashk, -wag** *na*

MUSKRAT HIDE

MUSKRAT HIDE: **wazhashkwayaan, -ag** *na*

MUSKRAT LODGE

MUSKRAT LODGE: **wazhashkwiish, -an** *ni*

MUST BE

MUST BE: **iidog** *pc*

MYTH

MYTH: **aadizookaan, -ag** *na*

CHARACTER OF A LEGEND OR MYTH: **aadizookaan, -ag** *na*
TELL A MYTH: **aadizooke** *vai;* tell a myth to s.o. **aadizookaw** *vta*

N

NAIL
NAIL: **zaga'igan, -an** *ni*
NAIL UP AGAINST THE WALL: nail s.t. up against the wall **agwaakwa'an** *vti*
NAIL
NAIL: my nail (fingernail, toenail) **nishkanzh, -iig /-shkanzhy-/** *nad*
CUT NAILS: cut one's own nails **giishkiganzhiikonidizo** *vai*
NAKED
NAKED: be naked **mitagwazhe** *vai*
NAME
NAME: name s.o. **waawiinzh /waawiinN-/** *vta;* **wiinzh /wiinN-/** *vta;* name s.t. **wiindan** *vti*
GIVE A NAME: give s.o. a name **wiinzh /wiinN-/** *vta*
HAVE A NAME: **wiinde, wiindemagad** *vii;* **wiinzo** *vai*
HAVE AN UGLY NAME: **maazhinikaade, maazhinikaademagad** *vii;* **maazhinikaazo** *vai*
NAME A CERTAIN WAY: name s.o. a certain way **izhinikaazh /izhinikaaN-/** *vta;* **izhi-wiinzh /izhi-wiinN-/** *vta;* name s.t. a certain way **izhinikaadan** *vti;* **izhi-wiindan** *vti*
NAMED
NAMED A CERTAIN WAY: be named a certain way **izhinikaade, izhinikaademagad** *vii;* **izhinikaazo** *vai;* **izhi-wiinde, izhi-wiindemagad** *vii;* **izhi-wiinzo** *vai*
NAMESAKE
NAMESAKE: be a namesake **owiiyawen'enyi** *vai;* my namesake (reciprocal relationship between name-giving sponsor and child) **niiyawen'enh, -ag /-iiyawen'eny-/** *nad*
NAP
TAKE A QUICK NAP: **zhiibaangwashi** *vai*
NAPKIN
NAPKIN: **giziidoone'on, -an** *ni;* **giziininjii'on, -an** *ni*
NARRATE
NARRATE: **dibaajimo** *vai;* narrate (s.t.) to s.o. **dibaajimotaw** *vta*
NARRATE A CERTAIN WAY: **inaajimo** *vai;* narrate a certain way about s.t. **inaadodan** *vti;* narrate of s.o. a certain way **inaajim** *vta;* narrate (s.t.) to s.o. a certain way **inaajimotaw** *vta*
NARRATIVE
NARRATIVE: **dibaajimowin, -an** *ni*
NARROW
NARROW: be narrow **agaasadeyaa, agaasadeyaamagad** *vii;* **agaasadezi** *vai;* be narrow (as something mineral) **agaasadeyaabikad** *vii;* **agaasadeyaabikizi** *vai;* be narrow (as something sheet-like) **agaasadeyiigad** *vii;* **agaasadeyiigizi** *vai;* be narrow (as something string-like) **agaasadeyaabiigad** *vii;* **agaasadeyaabiigizi** *vai*
BECOME NARROW: **wiibwaa, wiibwaamagad** *vii*
MAKE NARROW: make s.o. narrow **agaasade'** *vta;* make s.t. narrow **agaasadetoon** *vti2*
NARROW BOAT: be narrow (as a boat) **agaasadeyoonagad** *vii*
NARROW FACE: have a narrow face **agaasadengwe** *vai*
NARROW RIVER: be narrow (as a river) **agaasadetigweyaa, agaasadetigweyaamagad** *vii*
NARROW ROAD: be narrow (as a road or trail) **agaasademon /agaasademo-/** *vii*
NARROW TRAIL: be narrow (as a road or trail) **agaasademon /agaasademo-/** *vii*
NARROWS
NARROWS: there is a narrows **wabaashiiwan** *vii;* **wabigamaa, wabigamaamagad** *vii*
NAVEL
NAVEL: my navel **indis /-disy-/** *nid*
NEAR
NEAR: **besho** *pc;* **jiigi-** *pn;* be near **beshowad** *vii*
NEAR WOODS: near the woods **jiigaakwaa** *pc*
THOUGHT NEAR: be thought near **beshwendaagozi** *vai;* **beshwendaagwad** *vii*
NEARLY
NEARLY: **gegaa** *pc;* **ingoji** *pc, also* **ningoji***
NECESSARY
NECESSARY: it is necessary **booch** *pc*
NECK
BACK OF NECK: the back of my neck **nikwegan, -an /-kwegan-/** *nid*
STIFF NECK: have a stiff neck **jiibajigwayawe** *vai*
WEAR AROUND NECK: wear s.o. around one's neck **naabikaw** *vta;* wear s.t. around one's neck **naabikan** *vti*
WRING NECK: wring s.o.'s neck **bookogwebizh /bookogwebiN-/** *vta*
NECKLACE
NECKLACE: **naabikawaagan, -ag** *na*
NECKTIE
NECKTIE: **naabikawaagan, -ag** *na*
NEED
IN NEED: be in need of (s.t.) **manezi** *vai-o*

NEED TO: **noonde-** *pv4*

NEEDLE

NEEDLE: **zhaabonigan, -an** *ni*

BEADING NEEDLE: **naabidoo'igan, -an** *ni*

NEIGHBOR

NEIGHBOR: be a neighbor to s.o. **wiijigamigishkaw** *vta*

NEPHEW

NEPHEW: my cross-nephew (male's sister's son or female's brother's son) **niningwanis, -ag /-ningwanis-/** *nad;* my parallel nephew (male's brother's son or female's sister's son) **indoozhim, -ag /-doozhim-/** *nad*

NERVOUS

NERVOUS: be nervous **zegendam** *vai2*

NEST

BIRD NEST: **wadiswan, -an** *ni*

NESTLING

NESTLING: **banajaanh, -yag** *na*

NET

NET: **asab, -iig** *na*

CAUGHT IN A NET: be caught in a net **biinda'am** *vai2*

FISH WITH A NET: **bagida'waa** *vai*

GO GET A NET: **naadasabii** *vai*

HANG UP A NET: **agoodasabii** *vai*

MAKE NETS: **asabike** *vai*

MOSQUITO NET: **zagimewayaan, -ag** *na*

PICK UP A NET: **naadasabii** *vai*

PREPARE A NET: prepare a net for setting **oninasabii** *vai*

SET A NET: **bagida'waa** *vai*

NET CORD

NET CORD: **zhinoodaagan, -an** *ni*

NET FLOAT

NET FLOAT: **agonjoonaagan, -an** *ni*

NET SINKER

NET SINKER: **asinaab, -iig** *na*

NETT LAKE

NETT LAKE: Nett Lake Reservation **Asabikone-zaaga'iganiing** *place, also* **Asabikonaye-zaaga'iganiing**

NETTLE

NETTLE: **zesab, -iig** *na*

NEVER

NEVER: **gaa wiikaa** *pc, also* **gaawiin wiikaa**

NEVER MIND: **maanoo** *pc*

NEW

NEW: **oshki-** *pv4;* be new **oshkayi'iiwan** *vii*

LOOK NEW: **oshkiinaagozi** *vai;* **oshkiinaagwad** *vii*

SOMEONE NEW: **oshkaya'aa, -g** *na, also* **oshki-aya'aa**

SOMETHING NEW: **oshkayi'ii, -n** *ni, also* **oshki-ayi'ii**

WEAR NEW CLOTHES: **oshki'o** *vai*

NEW MOON

NEW MOON: be new (of a moon) **oshkagoojin** *vai, also* **oshki-agoojin**

NEWS

ARRIVE WITH NEWS: **bagamaajimo** *vai*

COME TELLING NEWS: **biidaajimo** *vai*

SPREAD THE NEWS ABOUT: **babaamaajimo**

TELL GOOD NEWS: **minwaajimo** *vai;* tell good news of s.o. **minwaajim** *vta;* tell good news of s.t. **minwaadodan** *vti*

NEWSPAPER

NEWSPAPER: **babaamaajimoo-mazina'igan, -an** *ni*

NEXT

NEXT: they are next to each other **aanikeshkodaadiwag /aanikeshkodaadi-/** *vai*

NEXT ROOM: in the next room **aajisag** *pc*

NEXT TO: be next to s.o. **aanikeshkaw** *vta*

SOMEONE NEXT IN SUCCESSION TO THE LEADER: someone next in succession to the leader (e.g., a vice president) **aanike-ogimaa, -g** *na*

NICE

NICE: **mino-** *pv4;* be nice **onizhishi** *vai;* **onizhishin** *vii*

MAKE NICE: make s.o. nice **onizhishi'** *vta;* make s.t. nice **onizhishitoon** *vti2*

NICE DAY: be a nice day **mino-giizhigad** *vii*

NICKEL

NICKEL: nickel (coin) **aabita-zhooniyaans, -ag** *na*

NIECE

NIECE: my cross-niece (female's brother's daughter or male's sister's daughter) **nishimis, -ag /-shimis-/** *nad;* my parallel niece (male's brother's daughter or female's sister's daughter) **indoozhimis, -ag /-doozhimis-/** *nad*

NIGHT

NIGHT: be night **dibikad** *vii*

ALL NIGHT: **gabe-dibik** *pc*

AT NIGHT: **niibaa-** *pv4*

CERTAIN NUMBER OF NIGHTS: a certain number of nights **daso-dibik** *pc*

DARK AS NIGHT: be dark as night **gashkii-dibik-ayaa, gashkii-dibik-ayaamagad** *vii*

DARK AT NIGHT: be very dark at night **gashkii-dibikad** *vii*

DRIVE AT NIGHT: **niibaabizo** *vai*

EARLY IN THE NIGHT: be early in the night **oshki-dibikad** *vii*

EVERY NIGHT: **endaso-dibik** *pc*

LAST NIGHT: **dibikong** *pc*

LATE AT NIGHT: **ishpi-dibik** *pc;* **niibaa-dibik** *pc;* be late at night **ishpi-dibikad** *vii*

SPEND THE WHOLE NIGHT: **gabe-dibikwe** *vai*

TRAVEL AT NIGHT: **niibaashkaa** *vai*

NIGHTMARE

NIGHTMARE: have a nightmare **giiwanaadingwaam** *vai;* **zegingwashi** *vai*

NINE

NINE: **zhaangaswi** *nm;* **zhaangaso-** *pv4;* nine (card) **zhaangasoobii'igan, -ag** *na;* they are nine **zhaangachinoon /zhaangachin-/** *vii;* **zhaangachiwag /zhaangachi-/** *vai*

AND NINE: **ashi-zhaangaswi** *nm,* **ashi-zhaangaso-** *pv4*

NINE ACRES: **zhaangaso-diba'igaans** *pc*
NINE DAYS: **zhaangaso-giizhik** *pc;* **zhaangasogon** *pc;* be nine days **zhaangasogonagad** *vii*
NINE DAYS OLD: be nine days old **zhaangasogonagizi** *vai*
NINE DOLLARS: **zhaangaswaabik** *pc*
NINE EACH: **zhezhaangaswi** *nm*
NINE FEET: **zhaangasozid** *pc*
NINE HOURS: **zhaangaso-diba'igan** *pc*
NINE HUNDRED: **zhaangaswaak** *nm*
NINE INCHES: **zhaangasoninj** *pc*
NINE MILES: **zhaangaso-diba'igan** *pc*
NINE MINUTES: **zhaangaso-diba'igaans** *pc*
NINE MONTHS: **zhaangaso-giizis** *pc*
NINE O'CLOCK: be nine o'clock **zhaangaso-diba'iganed** *vii*
NINE PAIRS: **zhaangaswewaan** *pc*
NINE SETS: **zhaangaswewaan** *pc*
NINE THOUSAND: **zhaangasosagoons** *nm*
NINE TIMES: **zhaangaching** *pc*
NINE WEEKS: **zhaangaso-anama'e-giizhik** *pc;* be nine weeks **zhaangaso-anama'e-giizhigad** *vii*
NINE YEARS: **zhaangaso-biboon** *pc;* be nine years **zhaangaso-biboonagad** *vii;* be nine years old **zhaangaso-biboonagizi** *vai*

NINETEEN
NINETEEN: **ashi-zhaangaswi** *nm;* **midaaswi ashi-zhaangaswi** *nm*

NINETY
NINETY: **zhaangasimidana** *nm*

NINTH
NINTH DAY OF THE MONTH: be the ninth day of the month **zhaangasogonagizi** *vai*

NO
NO: **gaawiin** *pc*
NO LONGER: **gaawiin geyaabi** *pc*
NO MORE: **gaawiin geyaabi** *pc*
NO PURPOSE AT ALL: for no purpose at all **biinizikaa** *pc*
NO WAY: no way! **gaawesa** *pc*

NOBODY
NOBODY: **gaawiin awiya** *pr, also* **gaawiin awiiya**

NOD
NOD HEAD: nod one's head **wewebikweni** *vai*
NOD HEAD A CERTAIN WAY: nod one's head to s.o. a certain way **inikwetaw** *vta*

NOISE
DRIVE AWAY MAKING NOISE: **animwewebide, animwewebidemagad** *vii*
HEAR A CERTAIN NOISE: **initam** *vai2*
MAKE A CERTAIN NOISE: **inwewe, inwewemagad** *vii*
MAKE NOISE: **madwewe, madwewemagad** *vii;* **noondaagozi** *vai;* **noondaagwad** *vii;* make noise on s.t. **madwewetoon** *vti2*
MAKE NOISE BOILING: **madwegamide, madwegamidemagad** *vii;* **madwegamizo** *vai*
MAKE NOISE HITTING: **madweshin** *vai;* **madwesin** *vii;* make noise hitting s.t. **madwesidoon** *vti2;* make noise hitting things **madwesijige** *vai*
MAKING NOISE: **madwe-** *pv4*
NOISE IN A CERTAIN PLACE: there is noise in a certain place **danwewe, danwewemagad** *vii*
STOP MAKING VOCAL NOISE: **giishkowe** *vai*
WAKE BY VOCAL NOISE: wake s.o. by vocal noise **amajim** *vta*
WALK AWAY MAKING NOISE: **animwewetoo** *vai*

NOISY
NOISY: **ojaanimi-** *pv4;* be noisy **ombiigizi** *vai*

NOON
NOON: be noon **naawakwe, naawakwemagad** *vii*

NORTH
NORTH: **giiwedin** *ni*
NORTH WIND: **giiwedin** *ni*

NORTHERN LIGHTS
NORTHERN LIGHTS: they are the northern lights **jiibayag niimi'idiwag /niimi'idi-/** *vai*

NORTHERN PIKE
NORTHERN PIKE: **ginoozhe, -g** *na*

NOSE
NOSE: my nose **injaanzh, -an /-jaanzh-/** *nid*
BLOODY NOSE: bloody s.o.'s nose **gibitaneganaam** *vta;* have a bloody nose **miskwiiwijaane** *vai*
BLOODY NOSE FALLING: bloody one's nose falling **gibitaneshin** *vai*
BLOW NOSE: blow one's nose **ziinikiigome** *vai*
FLAT NOSE: have a flat nose **nabagijaane** *vai*
HAVE A BROKEN NOSE: **bookojaane** *vai*
HAVE A STUFFED-UP NOSE: **gibijaane** *vai, also* **gagiibijaane**
INSIDE NOSE: inside the nose **biinjijaanzh** *pc*
RED NOSE: have a red nose **miskojaane** *vai*
SWOLLEN NOSE: have a swollen nose **baagijaane** *vai*

NOSEBLEED
NOSEBLEED: have a nosebleed **gibitan** *vai, also* **gibitane***

NOSTRIL
NOSTRIL: my nostril **indenigom, -ag /-denigom-/** *nad*

NOT
NOT: not *negative* **gaawiin** *pc*
NOT ABLE: **gwiinawi-** *pv4*
NOT AT ALL: **gaawesa** *pc*
NOT BEFORE: **bwaa-** *pv1*
NOT IN THE LEAST: **gaawiin ganage** *pc*
NOT KNOW WHAT TO DO: **gwiinawi-doodam** *vai2*
NOT KNOW WHAT TO THINK: **gwiinawi-inendam** *vai2*
NOT KNOWING: **gwiinawi-** *pv4*
NOT NECESSARY: it's not necessary **gaawiin memwech** *pc*
NOT REALLY: **anishaa** *pc*

NOT TOO HARD: not too hard! **na'egaaj** *pc*
NOT YET: **gaa mashi** *pc, also* **gaawiin mashi**

NOTCHED
NOTCHED: be notched **aajikode, aajikodemagad** *vii*

NOTHING
NOTHING: **gaawiin gegoo** *pr*

NOTICE
NOTICE: **agwaakwa'igan, -an** *ni*

NOVEMBER
NOVEMBER: **gashkadino-giizis** *na*

NOW
NOW: **azhigwa** *pc, also* **zhigwa, zhigo; noongom** *pc;* **zhayiigwa** *pc*
JUST NOW: **bijiinag** *pc*

NOWADAYS
NOWADAYS: **noongom** *pc*

NUMB
FEEL NUMB: **giikimanizi** *vai*
NUMB ARM: have a numb arm **niboowinike** *vai*
NUMB FOOT: have a numb foot **niboowizide** *vai*
NUMB HAND: have a numb hand **niboowininjii** *vai*
NUMB LEG: have a numb leg **niboowigaade** *vai*

NUMBER
NUMBER: **asigibii'igan, -an** *ni*
CERTAIN NUMBER: a certain number **daso-** *pv3;* **daswi** *nm;* **minik** *pc;* they are a certain number **dashiwag /dashi-/** *vai;* **dasinoon /dasin-/** *vii*
CERTAIN NUMBER OF TIMES: a certain number of times **dasing** *pc*
WRITE NUMBERS: **asigibii'ige** *vai*

NUN
NUN: **anama'ewikwe, -g** *na;* **mekadewikonayewikwe, -g** *na, also* **mekadewikonayekwe**

NURSE
NURSE: nurse s.o. (e.g., a baby) **noozh /nooN-/** *vta*
NURSE A CHILD: **noonaawaso** *vai*

NURSE
NURSE: nurse (female) **mashkikiiwikwe, -g** *na*

NUT
NUT: **bagaan, -ag** *na*

O

OAK
OAK: **mitigomizh, -iig** *na*

OAR
OAR: **azheboyaanaak, -oon** *ni*

OATMEAL
OATMEAL: **daataagwa'igan, -an** *ni*

OBSERVATION
LEARN BY OBSERVATION: **gikinawaabi** *vai;* learn by observation of s.o. **gikinawaabam** *vta*

OBSERVE
OBSERVE: observe s.o. **naagadawaabam** *vta;* **naanaagadawaabam** *vta;* observe s.t. **naagadawaabandan** *vti;* **naanaagadawaabandan** *vti;* observe people **waabange** *vai*

OBSTRUCT
OBSTRUCT: obstruct s.o. **gibaakwa' /gibaakwa'w-/** *vta;* obstruct s.t. **gibaakwa'an** *vti*

OBTAIN
OBTAIN FROM A CERTAIN PLACE: obtain s.o. from a certain place **ondin** *vta;* obtain s.t. from a certain place **ondinan** *vti;* obtain (s.t.) for s.o. from a certain place **ondinamaw** *vta;* obtain things from a certain place **ondinige** *vai*

OBTAINED
OBTAINED FROM A CERTAIN PLACE: be obtained from a certain place **ondinigaade, ondinigaademagad** *vii;* **ondinigaazo** *vai*

OCCASIONALLY
OCCASIONALLY: **ayaangodinong** *pc, also* **aangodinong**

OCCUPIED
OCCUPIED: be occupied **abiichigaade, abiichigaademagad** *vii*

OCCUPY
OCCUPY: occupy s.t. **abiitan** *vti*

OCTOBER
OCTOBER: **binaakwii-giizis** *na, also* **binaakwe-giizis; waatebagaa-giizis** *na, also* **waatebago-giizis**

ODAWA
ODAWA: Odawa (Ottawa) **odaawaa, -g** *na*
SPEAK ODAWA: speak Odawa (Ottawa) **odaawaamo** *vai*

ODD
MAKE ODD: make s.o. odd **maanaaji'** *vta;* make s.t. odd **maanaajitoon** *vti2*

OF COURSE
OF COURSE: **memindage** *pc*

OFF
COME OFF: **gidiskise** *vai;* **gidiskise, gidiskisemagad** *vii*

OFFER
OFFER: offer s.o. **bagidin** *vta;* offer s.t. **bagidinan** *vti;* offer (s.t.) to s.o. **bagidinamaw** *vta;* offer things **bagidinige** *vai*

OFFERED
OFFERED: be offered **bagidinigaade, bagidinigaademagad** *vii;* **bagidinigaazo** *vai*

OFFERING
OFFERING: **bagijigan, -an** *ni*

MAKE AN OFFERING: **bagijige** *vai*
MAKE AN OFFERING OF TOBACCO: **biindaakoojige** *vai;* make an offering of tobacco to s.o. **biindaakoozh /biindaakooN-/** *vta*

OFFICE
OFFICE: **ozhibii'igewigamig, -oon** *ni*
ADMINISTRATION OFFICE: **ogimaawigamig, -oon** *ni*

OFFICER
MILITARY OFFICER: **zhimaaganishiiogimaa, -g** *na*

OFFICIAL
GOVERNMENT OFFICIAL: **wegimaawabid** *na-pt*

OFTEN
OFTEN: **moozhag** *pc;* **naaningim** *pc*

OH
OH: oh! **oo** *pc;* **oonh** *pc*

OIL
OIL: **bimide** *ni*

OJIBWE
OJIBWE: **anishinaabe, -g** *na;* **ojibwe, -g** *na;* **ojibwewanishinaabe, -g** *na, also* **ojibweanishinaabe**; be Ojibwe **anishinaabewi** *vai;* **ojibwewi** *vai*
CALL IN OJIBWE: call s.o. in Indian (Ojibwe) **anishinaabewinikaazh /anishinaabewinikaaN-/** *vta;* call s.t. in Indian (Ojibwe) **anishinaabewinikaadan** *vti*
CALLED IN OJIBWE: be called in Indian (Ojibwe) **anishinaabewinikaade, anishinaabewinikaademagad** *vii;* **anishinaabewinikaazo** *vai*
OJIBWE WRITING: Indian (Ojibwe) writing **anishinaabewibii'igan, -an** *ni*
PUT INTO OJIBWE: put s.t. into Ojibwe **ojibwewisidoon** *vti2*
SPEAK OJIBWE: **ojibwemo** *vai;* speak Ojibwe to s.o. **ojibwemotaw** *vta;* speak an Indian language (especially Ojibwe) to s.o. **anishinaabemotaw** *vta;* speak an Indian language (especially Ojibwe) **anishinaabemo** *vai*
WRITE IN OJIBWE: write in Indian (Ojibwe) **anishinaabewibii'ige** *vai;* write s.t. in Indian (Ojibwe) **anishinaabewibii'an** *vti;* write s.t. in Indian (Ojibwe) (e.g., a book) **anishinaabewisidoon** *vti2;* write s.t. in Ojibwe **ojibwewibii'an** *vti;* write (s.t.) in Indian (Ojibwe) to s.o. **anishinaabewibii'amaw** *vta;* write things in Ojibwe **ojibwewibii'ige** *vai*
WRITTEN IN OJIBWE: be written in Indian (Ojibwe) **anishinaabewibii'igaade, anishinaabewibii'igaademagad** *vii;* be written in Indian (Ojibwe) (e.g., a book or document) **anishinaabewisin** *vii;* be written in Ojibwe **ojibwewibii'igaade, ojibwewibii'igaademagad** *vii;* be written in Ojibwe (e.g., a book) **ojibwewisin** *vii*

OJIBWE LANGUAGE
OJIBWE LANGUAGE: **ojibwemowin** *ni;* Indian language (especially Ojibwe) **anishinaabemowin, -an** *ni*

OJIBWE WOMAN
OJIBWE WOMAN: **ojibwekwe, -g** *na*

OLD
OLD: **gete-** *pv4*
CERTAIN NUMBER OF DAYS OLD: be a certain number of days old **dasogonagizi** *vai*
CERTAIN NUMBER OF YEARS OLD: be a certain number of years old **dasobiboonagizi** *vai*
LOOK OLD: **gichi-aya'aawinaagozi** *vai*
SO MANY YEARS OLD: be so many years old **daso-biboonagizi** *vai*
SOMEONE OLD: **gete-aya'aa, -g** *na*
SOMETHING OLD: **gete-ayi'ii, -n** *ni*

OLD LADY
OLD LADY: **mindimooyenh, -yag** *na;* be an old lady **mindimooyenyiwi** *vai*

OLD MAN
OLD MAN: **akiwenzii, -yag** *na;* be an old man **akiwenziiyiwi** *vai*

OLD WOMAN
OLD WOMAN: **mindimooyenh, -yag** *na;* be an old woman **mindimooyenyiwi** *vai*

OLD-TIME
OLD-TIME: **gete-** *pv4*

OLDER
OLDER: be older **gitizi** *vai*

ON
ON METAL: on something mineral (e.g., metal, glass, rock) **agidaabik** *pc, also* **ogidaabik*, wagidaabik**
ON ROCK: on something mineral (e.g., metal, glass, rock) **agidaabik** *pc, also* **ogidaabik*, wagidaabik**
ON THE SHORE: **agamiing** *pc*
ON TOP: on top of **agiji-** *pn, also* **ogiji-*, wagiji-**; on top of it **agijayi'ii** *pc, also* **ogijayi'ii*, wagijayi'ii**
ON TOP OF A HILL: **agidaaki** *pc, also* **ogidaaki*, wagidaaki**
ON TOP OF A MOUNTAIN: **agidajiw** *pc, also* **ogidajiw*, wagidajiw**
ON TOP OF A ROCK: **agidasin** *pc, also* **ogidasin*, wagidasin**
ON TOP OF THE GROUND: **agidakamig** *pc, also* **ogidakamig*, wagidakamig**
ON TOP OF THE HOUSE: **agidigamig** *pc, also* **ogidigamig*, wagidigamig**
ON TOP OF THE ICE: **agidiskwam** *pc, also* **ogidiskwam*, wagidiskwam**
ON TOP OF THE WATER: **agidibiig** *pc, also* **ogidibiig*, wagidibiig**

ON PURPOSE
ON PURPOSE: **onjida** *pc*

ONCE
ONCE: **aabiding** *pc*

ONE

ONE: **bezhig** *nm;* **bezhigo-** *pv4;* **ingo- /ningo-/** *pv4, also* **ningo-***; be one **bezhigwan** *vii*

AND ONE: **ashi-bezhig** *nm;* **ashi-bezhigo-** *pv4*

AT ONE TIME: **aabiding** *pc;* **ingoding** *pc, also* **ningoding***

GONE A CERTAIN LENGTH OF TIME: be gone a certain length of time **apiitendi** *vai*

IN ONE PLACE: **bezhigwanong** *pc*

ONE ACRE: **ingo-diba'igaans** *pc, also* **ningo-diba'igaans***

ONE DAY: **ingo-giizhik** *pc, also* **ningo-giizhik***

ONE DOLLAR: **bezhigwaabik** *na*

ONE FOOT: **ingodozid** *pc, also* **ningodozid***

ONE HOUR: **ingo-diba'igan** *pc, also* **ningo-diba'igan***

ONE HUNDRED: **ingodwaak** *nm, also* **ningodwaak***

ONE INCH: **ingodoninj** *pc, also* **ningodoninj***

ONE MILE: **ingo-diba'igan** *pc, also* **ningo-diba'igan***

ONE MINUTE: **ingo-diba'igaans** *pc, also* **ningo-diba'igaans***

ONE MONTH: **ingo-giizis** *pc, also* **ningo-giizis***

ONE NIGHT: **ingo-dibik** *pc, also* **ningo-dibik***

ONE O'CLOCK: be one o'clock **ingo-diba'iganed /ningo-diba'iganed-/** *vii, also* **ningo-diba'iganed***

ONE PLACE: **bezhigwanong** *pc*

ONE THOUSAND: **ingodosagoons** *nm, also* **ningodosagoons***

ONE WEEK: **ingo-anama'e-giizhik** *pc, also* **ningo-anama'e-giizhik***

ONE YEAR: **ingo-biboon** *pc, also* **ningo-biboon***; be one year **ingo-biboonagad /ningo-biboonagad-/** *vii, also* **ningo-biboonagad***

ONE YEAR OLD: be one year old **ingo-biboonagizi /ningo-biboonagizi-/** *vai, also* **ningo-biboonagizi***

ONE-BY-ONE

ONE-BY-ONE: **bebezhig** *nm*

ONION

ONION: **zhigaagawanzh, -iig** *na*

ONLY

ONLY: **eta** *pc*

ONLY HER: only her *third person singular personal pronoun* **wiineta** *pr*

ONLY HIM: only him *third person singular personal pronoun* **wiineta** *pr*

ONLY ME: only me *first person singular personal pronoun* **niineta** *pr*

ONLY THEM: only them *third person plural personal pronoun* **wiinetawaa** *pr*

ONLY US: only us *first person exclusive plural personal pronoun* **niinetawind** *pr;* only us *first person inclusive personal pronoun* **giinetawind** *pr*

ONLY YOU: only you *second person singular personal pronoun* **giineta** *pr;* only you *second personal plural personal pronoun* **giinetawaa** *pr*

THE ONLY ONE: be the only one **bezhigo** *vai;* **bezhigwan** *vii*

OPEN

OPEN: be open **baakishin** *vai;* **baakisin** *vii;* be open (as something stick- or wood-like, e.g., a door) **baakaakosin** *vii;* open s.t. (as something stick- or wood-like, e.g., a door) **baakaakonan** *vti;* open (s.t.) for s.o. (as something stick- or wood-like, e.g., a door) **baakaakonamaw** *vta*

COME OPEN: **baakise, baakisemagad** *vii*

FLING OPEN: fling s.t. open (as something stick- or wood-like, e.g., a door) **baakaakowebinan** *vti*

FLY OPEN: **baakise, baakisemagad** *vii;* fly open (as something stick- or wood-like, e.g., a door) **baakaakose, baakaakosemagad** *vii*

OPEN EYES: open one's eyes **dooskaabi** *vai*

OPEN MOUTH: open one's mouth **daawani** *vai*

OPEN UP: open s.o. up **baakin** *vta;* open s.t. up **baakinan** *vti;* open things up **baakinige** *vai*

RIP OPEN: rip s.o.open **aabibizh /aabibiN-/** *vta;* rip s.t. open **aabibidoon** *vti2*

OPENED

OPENED: be opened (as something stick- or wood-like, e.g., a door) **baakaakonigaade, baakaakonigaademagad** *vii*

OPENER

CAN OPENER: **baakaakozhigan, -an** *ni*

OPERATE

OPERATE POORLY: **maazhibide, maazhibidemagad** *vii;* **maazhibizo** *vai*

OPPOSITE

OPPOSITE: **dibishkookamig** *pc*

OPTOMETRIST

OPTOMETRIST: **oshkiinzhigokewinini, -wag** *na*

OR

OR: **gemaa** *pc, also* **gemaa gaye**

ORANGE

ORANGE: orange (fruit) **wezaawiminagazid** *na-pt*

ORDER

ORDER: order (s.t.) for s.o. **naajinizha'amaw** *vta;* order things **naajinizha'ige** *vai*

GIVE AN ORDER: **anookii** *vai;* give an order to s.o. **anoozh /anooN-/** *vta*

PUT IN ORDER: put s.o. in order **onin** *vta;* put s.t. in order **oninan** *vti;* put things in order **oninige** *vai*

ORGAN

ORGAN: **madwewechigan, -an** *ni*

ORIENTAL

ORIENTAL: **aniibiishaabookewinini, -wag** *na;* be Oriental **aniibiishaabookewininiiwi** *vai*

ORIGINATE
ORIGINATE IN A CERTAIN PLACE: **ondaadad** *vii*
ORPHANED
ORPHANED: be orphaned **giiwizi** *vai*
OSIER
RED OSIER: **miskwaabiimizh, -iig** *na*
OTHER SIDE
ON THE OTHER SIDE: on the other side of it **agaamayi'ii** *pc;* **aazhawayi'ii** *pc*
ON THE OTHER SIDE OF: **agaami-** *pn*
ON THE OTHER SIDE OF THE CLEARING: **agaamaakwaa** *pc*
ON THE OTHER SIDE OF THE FIRE: **agaamishkode** *pc*
ON THE OTHER SIDE OF THE LAKE: **agaaming** *pc*
ON THE OTHER SIDE OF THE MEADOW: **agaamashkosiw** *pc*
ON THE OTHER SIDE OF THE ROAD: on the other side of the road or trail **agaamikana** *pc*
ON THE OTHER SIDE OF THE TRAIL: on the other side of the road or trail **agaamikana** *pc*
OTHER SIDE OF THE LODGE: **agaamindesi** *pc;* on the other side of the lodge **agaamindesing** *pc*
OTTER
OTTER: **nigig, -wag** *na*
OTTER HIDE
OTTER HIDE: **nigigwayaan, -ag** *na*
OUT
CRAWL OUT: **zaagidoode** *vai*
FLOW OUT: **zaagijiwan** *vii*
GO OUT IN A GROUP: they go out in a group **zaagidaawanidiwag /zaagidaawanidi-/** *vai*
GROW OUT: **zaagigi** *vai;* **zaagigin** *vii*
MAKE GO OUT: make s.o. go out **zaagizi'** *vta*
PUT OUT: put s.o. out **zaagidin** *vta;* put s.t. out **zaagidinan** *vti*
RUN OUT: **zaagizibatoo** *vai;* run out with s.o. **zaagiziba'** *vta;* **zaagizibatwaazh /zaagizibatwaaN-/** *vta;* run out with s.t. **zaagizibatwaadan** *vti;* they run out together **zaagiziba'idiwag /zaagiziba'idi-/** *vai*
STICK OUT HEAD: stick out one's head **zaagikweni** *vai*
TAKE OUT: take s.o. out **zaagizi'** *vta;* take s.t. out **zaagizitoon** *vti2;* take (s.t.) out for s.o. **zaagizitaw** *vta*
OUT FROM SHORE
GO OUT FROM SHORE ON THE ICE: **niminaaweyaadagaako** *vai*
PADDLE OUT FROM SHORE: **niminaawe'o** *vai*
OUT OF
OUT OF: be out of s.o. **jaagin** *vta;* be out of s.t. **jaaginan** *vti*
OUT OF SIGHT
GO OUT OF SIGHT: **ani-naagozi** *vai;* **ani-naagwad** *vii;* go out of sight (as around a corner) **aagawe** *vai*
OUT OF SORTS
FEEL OUT OF SORTS: **maazhendam** *vai2*
OUT OF THE WAY
STAND OUT OF THE WAY: **ikogaabawi** *vai*
OUTBOARD MOTOR
OUTBOARD MOTOR: **akikoons, -ag** *na*
OUTDOORS
OUTDOORS: **agwajiing** *pc*
OUTHOUSE
OUTHOUSE: **zaaga'amoowigamig, -oon** *ni*
OUTLET
OUTLET: be an outlet **biinjidawaa** *vii*
OUTSIDE
OUTSIDE: **agwajiing** *pc*
CHASE OUTSIDE: chase s.o. outside **zaagijinizhikaw** *vta*
TELL TO GO OUTSIDE: tell s.o. to go outside **zaagijinaazha' /zaagijinaazha'w-/** *vta*
THROW OUTSIDE: throw s.o. outside **zaagijiwebin** *vta;* throw s.t. outside **zaagijiwebinan** *vti;* throw things outside **zaagijiwebinige** *vai*
THROWN OUTSIDE: be thrown outside **zaagijiwebinigaade, zaagijiwebinigaademagad** *vii*
OVEN
ROAST IN THE OVEN: roast s.o. in the oven **giboz /gibozw-/** *vta;* roast s.t. in the oven **gibozan** *vti;* roast things in the oven **gibozige** *vai*
OVER
OVER: be over (of an event) **ishkwaakamigad** *vii;* over it **ishpayi'ii** *pc*
CLIMB OVER: **baazhidaandawe** *vai*
JUMP OVER: **baazhijigwaashkwani** *vai*
STEP OVER: step over s.o. **baazhida' /baazhida'w-/** *vta;* step over s.t. **baazhida'an** *vti*
THROW OVER: throw s.o. over **baazhijiwebin** *vta;* throw s.t. over **baazhijiwebinan** *vti*
OVERCOME
OVERCOME: overcome s.o. **zhaagooji'** *vta;* overcome s.o. with speech **zhaagoozom** *vta;* overcome s.t. **zhaagoojitoon** *vti2;* overcome people **zhaagooji'iwe** *vai*
OVERCOOK
OVERCOOK: overcook s.o. **onzaamiz /onzaamizw-/** *vta;* overcook s.t. **onzaamizan** *vti*
OVERCOOKED
OVERCOOKED: be overcooked **onzaamide, onzaamidemagad** *vii;* **onzaamizo** *vai*
OVERDO
OVERDO: overdo things **onzaamichige** *vai*

OVEREXCITED
OVEREXCITED: be overexcited **onzaamenimo** *vai*

OVERFILL
OVERFILL: overfill s.o. with solids **onzaamashkina'** *vta;* overfill s.t. (with a liquid) **onzaamibadoon** *vti2;* overfill s.t. with solids **onzaamashkinadoon** *vti2*

OVERFLOW
OVERFLOW: overflow (as a liquid) **bazhidebii, bazhidebiimagad** *vii*
FILL TO OVERFLOWING: fill s.o. to overflowing with solids **ziigashkina'** *vta;* fill s.t. to overflowing with a liquid **ziigibadoon** *vti2;* fill s.t. to overflowing with solids **ziigashkinadoon** *vti2*

OVERHEAT
OVERHEAT: overheat s.o. **onzaamiz /onzaamizw-/** *vta;* overheat s.t. **onzaamizan** *vti*

OVERNIGHT
GONE OVERNIGHT: be gone overnight **nikanendi** *vai*
STAY OVERNIGHT: stay overnight with s.o. **nibendaw** *vta;* stay overnight with people **nibendaage** *vai*

OVERSEAS
OVERSEAS: **agaamakiing** *pc*

OVERSHOE
OVERSHOE: **biitookizinaan, -an** *ni, also* **biitookizin**
WEAR OVERSHOES: **biitookizine** *vai*

OVERSLEEP
OVERSLEEP: **onzaamingwaam** *vai*

OVERTAKE
OVERTAKE: overtake s.o. **adim** *vta;* overtake s.t. **adindan** *vti*
OVERTAKE IN A BOAT: overtake s.o. in a boat **adima' /adima'w-/** *vta*

OVERWORK
COLLAPSE FROM OVERWORK: **gawanokii** *vai*

OWE
OWE: **mazina'ige** *vai;* owe (s.t.) to s.o. **mazina'amaw** *vta*

OWL
OWL: **gookooko'oo, -g** *na*
SCREECH OWL: **gaakaabishiinh, -yag** *na*

OWN
OWN: own s.o. **ayaaw** *vta;* **dibenim** *vta;* own s.t. **ayaan /ayaam-/** *vti3;* **dibendan** *vti;* own for oneself **dibendaaso** *vai*

OWNED
OWNED: be owned **dibendaagozi** *vai;* **dibendaagwad** *vii;* **dibenjigaade, dibenjigaademagad** *vii;* **dibenjigaazo** *vai*

P

PACK
PACK: **bimiwanaan, -an** *ni*
CARRY A BIG PACK: **mangiwane** *vai*
CARRY A LIGHT PACK: **naangiwane** *vai*
CARRY A PACK ALONG: **bimiwane** *vai*
HARDLY BE ABLE TO CARRY THE PACK: hardly be able to carry a pack **bwaawane** *vai*
LIFT A PACK: lift a pack to one's back **ombiwane** *vai*
MAKE A PACK: make a pack of s.t. **ozhiwanikaadan** *vti*
PACK TOO MUCH OF A LOAD: **onzaamiwane** *vai*
PACK UP: **ozhiwanike** *vai*
SET DOWN PACK: set down one's pack **bagijiwane** *vai*

PACK FRAME
PACK FRAME: **bimoonjigan, -an** *ni*

PACKAGE
PACKAGE: **gashkibijigan, -an** *ni*
WRAPPED PACKAGE: **wiiweginigan, -an** *ni*

PACKET
PACKET: **gashkibijigan, -an** *ni*

PADDING
LIE AS PADDING: **apishin** *vai;* **apisin** *vii*

PADDLE
PADDLE: **abwi, -in** *ni;* **jiime** *vai*
ARRIVE PADDLING: **bagamishkaa** *vai*
PADDLE A CERTAIN WAY: **inakwazhiwe** *vai*
PADDLE ABOUT: **babaamishkaa** *vai*
PADDLE AGAINST THE WIND: **onjishkawa'o** *vai, also* **onjishkawa'am**
PADDLE ALONG: **bimakwazhiwe** *vai;* **bimishkaa** *vai*
PADDLE ALONG THE SHORE: **jiigewe'am** *vai2;* **jiigewe'o** *vai;* **jiigewekwazhiwe** *vai*
PADDLE AWAY: **animishkaa** *vai*
PADDLE BACKWARDS: **azhe'o** *vai*
PADDLE FAST: **gizhiikaakwazhiwe** *vai*
PADDLE FOR STIRRING BOILING MAPLE SAP: **gaashkakokwe'igan, -an** *ni*
PADDLE FROM A CERTAIN PLACE: **ondakwazhiwe** *vai*
PADDLE HERE: **biidakwazhiwe** *vai;* **biidaasamishkaa** *vai*
PADDLE OFF: **maajiikwazhiwe** *vai*
PADDLE OUT FROM SHORE: **niminaawe'o** *vai*
PADDLE SUDDENLY INTO VIEW: **zaagewe'o** *vai;* **zaagewekwazhiwe** *vai*
PADDLE TO A CERTAIN PLACE: **ina'o** *vai;* **inakwazhiwe** *vai*

PAIL
PAIL: **akik, -oog** *na*
WASH PAIL: **giziibiiginakokwe** *vai*
WATER PAIL: **nibiiwakik, -oog** *na*

PAIN
PAIN: be in pain **wiisagine** *vai*
CHEST PAINS: have chest pains while breathing **jakanaamo** *vai*
SUFFER PAIN: **wiisagendam** *vai*
WAKE FROM PAIN: **amajine** *vai*

PAINT
PAINT: **zhizhoobii'igan, -an** *ni;* paint s.o. **zhizhoobii' /zhizhoobii'w-/** *vta;* paint s.t. **zhizhoobii'an** *vti;* paint (s.t.) for s.o. **zhizhoobii'amaw** *vta;* paint things **zhizhoobii'ige** *vai*

PAINT BRUSH
PAINT BRUSH: **zhizhoobii'iganaatig, -oon** *ni*

PAINTED TURTLE
PAINTED TURTLE: **miskwaadesi, -wag** *na*

PAINTER
PAINTER: **zhizhoobii'igewinini, -wag** *na*

PAIR
CERTAIN NUMBER OF PAIRS: a certain number of pairs **daswewaan** *pc*

PALATE
PALATE: my palate **ninagaskway /-nagaskway-/** *nid*

PALE
PALE FACED: be pale faced **waabiingwe** *vai*

PALM
PALM: my palm **ninagaakininj, -iin /-nagaakininjy-/** *nid*

PAN
PAN: **akik, -oog** *na;* **jiibaakwewakik, -oog** *na*
FRYING PAN: **abwewin, -an** *ni*
LARGE PAN: **gichi-onaagan** *ni*
ROASTING PAN: **giboziganaabik, -oon** *ni*

PANCAKE
PANCAKE: **gwekiwebinigan, -ag** *na*

PANT
PANT: **nesezo** *vai*

PANTHER
PANTHER: **mishibizhii, -g** *na*

PANTS
PANTS: **giboodiyegwaazon, -ag** *na*
PUT ON PANTS: put on one's pants **biichigiboodiyegwaazone** *vai*
TAKE OFF PANTS: take off one's pants **giichigiboodiyegwaazone** *vai*
WEAR PANTS: **gigigiboodiyegwaazone** *vai*

PAPER
PAPER: **mazina'igan, -an** *ni*

PAPER BAG
PAPER BAG: **mazina'igani-mashkimodens, -an** *ni*

PARALYZED
PARALYZED: be paralyzed **niboowi** *vai*
BECOME PARALYZED: **niboowise** *vai*

PARCH
PARCH: parch s.t. **gaapizan** *vti;* parch s.t. (e.g., wild rice) **gidasan** *vti;* parch things **gaapizige** *vai;* parch things (e.g., wild rice) **gidasige** *vai*

PARENT
PARENT: my parent **ingitiziim, -ag /-gitiziim-/** *nad*
PARENTS: my parents *plural* **niniigi'igoog /-niigi'igw-/** *nad*

PARENT-IN-LAW
PARENT-IN-LAW: my fellow parent-in-law **indindawaa, -g /-dindawaa-/** *nad*

PAROLE
ON PAROLE: be on parole **ganawaabanjigaazo** *vai;* **ganawenjigaazo** *vai*

PARROT
PARROT: **gaagiigidoo-bineshiinh, -yag** *na*

PART
PART: **bakise** *vai;* **bakise, bakisemagad** *vii*

PARTICLES
IN PARTICLES: be in particles **biisaa, biisaamagad** *vii;* **biisizi** *vai*
PULL INTO PARTICLES: pull s.o. into particles **biisibizh /biisibiN-/** *vta;* pull s.t. into particles **biisibidoon** *vti2*

PARTITION
CLOTH PARTITION: **gibagoojigan, -an** *ni*

PARTNER
PARTNER: **wiijiiwaagan, -ag** *na*

PARTRIDGE
PARTRIDGE: **bine, -wag** *na*

PASS
PASS: pass (as time) **izhise, izhisemagad** *vii;* **ojijise, ojijisemagad** *vii*
COME TO PASS: **bagami-ayaa, bagami-ayaamagad** *vii*
PASS BY: pass s.o. by **gabikaw** *vta;* pass s.t. by **gabikan** *vti*
PASS THROUGH: **zhaabose, zhaabosemagad** *vii;* **zhaabwii** *vai*

PAST
GOING PAST: **bimi-** *pv2*

PAST TENSE
PAST TENSE: *past verb prefix* **gii-** *pv1*

PASTE
PASTE: **agokiwasigan, -an** *ni;* paste something on s.o. **agokiwas /agokiwasw-/** *vta;* paste something on s.t. **agokiwasan** *vti*

PASTED
PASTED: be pasted on **agokiwaso** *vai;* **agokiwate, agokiwatemagad** *vii*

PASTRY
PASTRY: **waashkobizid bakwezhigan** *na-pt;* **wiishkobi-bakwezhigan, -ag** *na*

PATCH
PATCH: **bagwa'igan, -an** *ni;* patch s.o. **bagwa' /bagwa'w-/** *vta;* patch s.t. **bagwa'an** *vti;* patch (s.t.) for s.o. **bagwa'amaw** *vta;* patch things **bagwa'ige** *vai*
WEAR PATCHES: **bagwa'igaazo** *vai*

PATCHED
PATCHED: be patched **bagwa'igaade, bagwa'igaademagad** *vii;* **bagwa'igaazo** *vai*

PATTERN
PATTERN: pattern (in sewing) **naabizhigan, -an** *ni*
HAVE A SQUARE PATTERN: **gakakishin** *vai;* **gakakisin** *vii*
PAY
PAY: pay for s.o. **diba' /diba'w-/** *vta;* pay for s.t. **diba'an** *vti;* pay (s.t.) to s.o. **diba'amaw** *vta;* pay s.o. for (s.t.) **diba'amaw** *vta;* pay things **diba'ige** *vai;* pay people for (s.t.) **diba'amaage** *vai;* they pay each other for (s.t.) **diba'amaadiwag /diba'amaadi-/** *vai*
PAY OFF: **diba'igese, diba'igesemagad** *vii*
PAY ATTENTION
PAY ATTENTION: **babaamendam** *vai2;* pay attention to s.o. **babaamenim** *vta;* pay attention to s.t. **babaamendan** *vti*
PEA
PEAS: peas *plural* **anijiiminan /anijiimin-/** *ni*
PEA SOUP
PEA SOUP: **anijiiminaaboo** *ni*
PEACEFUL
PEACEFUL: be peaceful **bangan** *vii*
PEACH
PEACH: **miishiijiimin, -ag** *na*
PEANUT
PEANUT: **bagaan, -ag** *na*
PEANUT BUTTER
PEANUT BUTTER: **bagaani-bimide** *ni, also* **bagaanensi-bimide**
PEARL
PEARL: **miigis, -ag** *na*
PEDAL
PEDAL: **ditibiwebishkige** *vai*
PEDDLER
PEDDLER: **babaamadaawewinini, -wag** *na, also* **babaamadaawaagewinini**; be a peddlar **babaamadaawe** *vai*
PEEK
PEEK: **giimaabi** *vai;* **giimoozaabi** *vai;* **inaabi** *vai;* peek at s.o. **giimaabam** *vta*
PEEK THROUGH AN OPENING: **dapaabi** *vai;* peek through an opening at s.o. **dapaabam** *vta;* peek through an opening at s.t. **dapaabandan** *vti*
PEEL
PEEL FROM SUNBURN: **bishagaaso** *vai*
PEEL OFF: **bishagishkaa** *vai;* **bishagishkaa, bishagishkaamagad** *vii*
PEEL TIMBER USING SOMETHING: **bishagaakwa'ige** *vai*
PEEL WIGOB: peel wigob (inner bark of basswood) **bisha'igobii** *vai*
PEEL WITH A KNIFE: peel s.o. with a knife **bishagikozh /bishagikoN-/** *vta;* peel s.t. with a knife **bishagikodan** *vti*
PEEL WITH HANDS: peel s.o. with hands **bishagibizh /bishagibiN-/** *vta;* peel s.t. with hands **bishagibidoon** *vti2;* peel things with hands **bishagibijige** *vai*
PELICAN
PELICAN: **zhede, -g** *na*
PEN
PEN: **ozhibii'iganaak, -oon** *ni*
PENCIL
PENCIL: **ozhibii'iganaak, -oon** *ni*
PENINSULA
PENINSULA: **neyaashi, -wan** *ni;* there is a peninsula **neyaashiiwan** *vii*
PENIS
PENIS: my penis **niinag /-iinag-/** *nid*
PENNY
PENNY: **miskwaabikoons, -ag** *na;* **ozaawaabikoons, -ag** *na*
PEOPLE
MANY PEOPLE: there are many people **anishinaabekaa** *vii*
PEPPER
PEPPER: **gaa-wiisagang** *ni-pt*
PERCEIVE
PERCEIVE A CERTAIN WAY: perceive s.o. a certain way **izhinaw** *vta;* perceive s.t. a certain way **izhinan** *vti*
PERCH
PERCH: **asaawe, -g** *na*
PERCHED
PERCHED UP: be perched up on something **agoozi** *vai*
PERFORM
PERFORM TRICKS: **mamaandaagochige** *vai*
PERFUME
PERFUME: **minomaagochigan, -an** *ni*
USE PERFUME: **minomaagochige** *vai*
PERHAPS
PERHAPS: **ganabaj** *pc;* **maagizhaa** *pc, also* **maazhaa**
PERSISTENTLY
PERSISTENTLY: **awanjish** *pc*
PERSON
PERSON: **anishinaabe, -g** *na;* **bemaadizid** *na-pt*
PERSUADE
PERSUADE: persuade s.o. **gagaanzom** *vta*
PESTLE
PESTLE: **bootaaganaak, -oon** *ni*
PET
PET: **bami'aagaans, -ag** *na*
PHARMACIST
PHARMACIST: **mashkikii-adaawewinini, -wag** *na, also* **mashkikiiwi-adaawewinini**
PHARMACY
PHARMACY: **mashkikii-adaawewigamig, -oon** *ni, also* **mashkikiiwi-adaawewigamig**
PHEASANT
PHEASANT: **mayagi-bine, -wag** *na*
PHLEGM
PHLEGM: **agig** *na*
PHONE
CALL ON THE PHONE: call s.o. on the phone **ganoozh /ganooN-/** *vta*
PHONOGRAPH
PHONOGRAPH: **gaagiigidoo-makakoons, -an** *ni;* **nagamoo-makak, -oon** *ni*

PHOTOGRAPH
PHOTOGRAPH: **mazinaakizon, -an** *ni;* photograph s.o. **mazinaakiz /mazinaakizw-/** *vta;* photograph s.t. **mazinaakizan** *vti;* photograph things **mazinaakizige** *vai*
PHOTOGRAPHED
PHOTOGRAPHED: be photographed **mazinaakide, mazinaakidemagad** *vii;* **mazinaakizo** *vai*
PIANO
PIANO: **madwewechigan, -an** *ni*
PICK
PICK: pick s.o. **onaabam** *vta;* pick s.t. **onaabandan** *vti;* pick things **onaabanjige** *vai*
PICK BERRIES: **mawinzo** *vai*
PICK FROM: pick from s.o. **gagiigin** *vta;* pick from s.t. **gagiiginan** *vti*
PICK TEETH: pick one's teeth **zesegwaabide'o** *vai*
PICK UP
PICK UP: pick s.o. up **mami /mam-/** *vta;* **maamigin** *vta;* **odaapin** *vta;* pick s.t. up **mamoon** *vti2;* **maamiginan** *vti;* **odaapinan** *vti;* pick (s.t.) up from s.o. **mamaw** *vta;* **odaapinamaw** *vta;* pick up things **mamige** *vai;* **odaapinige** *vai*
PICK UP A NET: **naadasabii** *vai*
PICK UP IN MOUTH: pick s.o. up in mouth **niimam** *vta;* pick s.t. up in mouth **niimandan** *vti*
PICK UP USING SOMETHING: pick s.o. up (as or as with something stick- or wood-like) **niimaakwa' /niimaakwa'w-/** *vta;* pick s.o. up using something **niima' /niima'w-/** *vta;* pick s.t. up (as or as with something stick- or wood-like) **niimaakwa'an** *vti;* pick s.t. up using something **niima'an** *vti*
PICKED
PICKED: be picked **onaabanjigaade, onaabanjigaademagad** *vii;* **onaabanjigaazo** *vai*
PICKED UP
PICKED UP: be picked up **mamigaade, mamigaademagad** *vii;* **mamigaazo** *vai;* **naajigaade, naajigaademagad** *vii;* **naajigaazo** *vai*
PICKEREL
PICKEREL: **ogaa, -wag** *na*
PICKLE
PICKLE: **zhaawaabookaadeg bipakoombens** *ni;* **zhiiwi-bipakoombens, -an** *ni*
PICKLED
PICKLED: be pickled **zhiiwaabookaade, zhiiwaabookaademagad** *vii*
PICTURE
PICTURE: **mazinaakizon, -an** *ni*
TAKE PICTURES: **mazinaakizige** *vai;* take pictures of s.o. **mazinaakiz /mazinaakizw-/** *vta;* take pictures of s.t. **mazinaakizan** *vti*
PICTURED
PICTURED: be pictured **mazinaakide, mazinaakidemagad** *vii;* **mazinaakizo** *vai*
PIE
PIE: **biitoosijigan, -ag** *na;* **biitoosijigani-bakwezhigan, -ag** *na*
PIECE
BITE A PIECE OFF: bite a piece off s.o. **bakwem** *vta;* bite a piece off s.t. **bakwendan** *vti*
CHOP A PIECE OFF: chop a piece off s.o. (as something of wood) **bakwega' /bakwega'w-/** *vta;* chop a piece off s.t. (as something of wood) **bakwega'an** *vti*
CUT A PIECE OFF: cut a piece off s.o. **bakwezh /bakwezhw-/** *vta;* cut a piece off s.t. **bakwezhan** *vti*
TAKE A PIECE OFF BY HAND: take a piece off s.o. by hand **bakwen** *vta;* take a piece off s.t. by hand **bakwenan** *vti*
TAKE A PIECE OFF USING SOMETHING: take a piece off s.o. using something **bakwe'** *vta;* take a piece off s.t. using something **bakwe'an** *vti*
TEAR A PIECE OFF: tear a piece off of s.o. **bakwebizh /bakwebiN-/** *vta;* tear a piece off of s.t. **bakwebidoon** *vti2*
PIECES
CUT TO PIECES: cut s.o. to pieces **bigishkizh /bigishkizhw-/** *vta;* cut s.t. to pieces **bigishkizhan** *vti*
FALL TO PIECES: **bigishkanad** *vii;* **bigishkanani** *vai*
GO TO PIECES: **bigishkise** *vai;* **bigishkise, bigishkisemagad** *vii*
TEAR TO PIECES: tear s.o. to pieces **bigishkibizh /bigishkibiN-/** *vta;* tear s.t. to pieces **bigishkibidoon** *vti2*
PIG
PIG: **gookoosh, -ag** *na*
PIGEON
PIGEON: **omiimii, -g** *na*
PIKE
NORTHERN PIKE: **ginoozhe, -g** *na*
PILE
PILE: pile s.o. **okoshim** *vta;* pile s.t. **okosidoon** *vti2*
LIE IN A PILE: **okoshin** *vai;* **okosin** *vii*
PILL
PILL: **bebiikominagak** *ni-pt;* **mashkikiins, -an** *ni*
PILLOW
PILLOW: **apikweshimon, -an** *ni*
PILLOWCASE
PILLOWCASE: **apikweshimoniigin, -oon** *ni*
PIN
PIN: **zagaakwa'igan, -an** *ni;* **zagaakwa'on, -ag** *na;* pin s.o. **zagaakwa' /zagaakwa'w-/** *vta;* pin s.t. **zagaakwa'an** *vti;* pin things **zagaakwa'ige** *vai*
COMMON PIN: **oshtigwaanzhaabonigan, -an** *ni*

HAIRPIN: **wiinizisimaani-zagaakwa'igan, -an** *ni*

PINCH

PINCH: pinch s.o. **jiisibizh /jiisibiN-/** *vta*

PINCHERRY

PINCHERRY: **bawa'iminaan, -an** *ni*

PINCHERRY BUSH

PINCHERRY BUSH: **bawa'iminagaawanzh, -iig** *na*

PINE

JACK PINE: **okikaandag, -oog** *na, also* **wakikaandag**

WHITE PINE: **zhingwaak, -wag** *na*

PINE BOUGH

PINE BOUGH: **zhingwaakwaandag, -oog** *na*

PINNED

PINNED: be pinned **zagaakwa'igaade, zagaakwa'igaademagad** *vii;* **zagaakwa'igaazo** *vai*

PINNED DOWN: be pinned down **dasoozo** *vai*

PIPE

PIPE: pipe (for smoking) **opwaagan, -ag** *na*

LIGHT A PIPE: **zaka'ipwaagane** *vai*

STONE PIPE: **asinii-opwaagan** *na*

PIPE BAG

PIPE BAG: **gashkibidaagan, -ag** *na*

PIPE STEM

PIPE STEM: **okij, -iin** *ni*

PIPESTONE

PIPESTONE: **opwaaganasin, -iig** *na*

PITCH

PITCH: **bigiw** *ni*

APPLY PITCH: **bigiike** *vai;* apply pitch to s.t. (e.g., a canoe) **bigiikaadan** *vti*

PITCHER

PITCHER: pitcher (in baseball) **apagijigewinini, -wag** *na*

PITIABLE

PITIABLE: be pitiable **inigaazi** *vai*

PITIED

PITIED: be pitied **zhawendaagozi** *vai*

PITY

PITY: pity s.o. **gidimaagenim** *vta;* **zhawenim** *vta*

HAVE PITY: **zhawenjige** *vai*

PLACE

PLACE A BET: **achige** *vai*

PLAIN

PLAIN: **mashkode, -n** *ni*

PLAIN VIEW

IN PLAIN VIEW: **mizhisha** *pc*

PLAN

PLAN: plan s.t. **onaakonan** *vti*

CHANGE PLANS: **aandaakonige** *vai*

PLANE

PLANE: airplane **bemisemagak, -in** *ni-pt*

PLANE

PLANE: plane (tool) **mookojigan, -an** *ni*

PLANT

PLANT: **gitige** *vai;* plant s.o. **gitigaazh /gitigaaN-/** *vta;* plant s.t. **gitigaadan** *vti*

PLANT IN: plant s.o. in **badakizh /badakiN-/** *vta;* plant s.t. **badakidoon** *vti2;* plant things in **bagidinige** *vai*

PLANTED

PLANTED: be planted **gitigaade, gitigaademagad** *vii;* **gitigaazo** *vai*

PLANTED IN: be planted in **badakide, badakidemagad** *vii;* **badakizo** *vai*

PLATE

PLATE: **onaagan, -an** *ni*

DINNER PLATE: **desinaagan, -an** *ni*

SMALL PLATE: **onaagaans, -an** *ni*

PLATFORM

PLATFORM: **desa'on, -an** *ni*

PLAY

PLAY: **odamino** *vai*

PLAY A GUITAR: **madweyaabiigibijige** *vai*

PLAY A WIND INSTRUMENT: **noondaagochige** *vai;* play s.t. as a wind instrument **noondaagotoon** *vti2*

PLAY BASEBALL: **bakitejii'ige** *vai*

PLAY IN A CERTAIN PLACE: **danakamigizi** *vai;* **dazhitaa** *vai*

PLAY LACROSSE: **baaga'adowe** *vai*

PLAY MUSIC: **madwewechige** *vai;* play music for s.o. **madwewetaw** *vta, also* **madwewetamaw**

PLAY POOL: **nemaabii** *vai*

PLAY SHINNY: **bapasikawe** *vai*

PLAY THE DISH GAME: **bagese** *vai*

PLAY THE FLUTE: **bibigwe** *vai*

PLAY THE MOCCASIN GAME: **makizinataage** *vai;* they play the moccasin game with each other **makizinataadiwag /makizinataadi-/** *vai*

PLAY WITH: play with s.o. **wiiji'** *vta*

PLAYING CARD

PLAYING CARD: **ataadiwin, -ag** *na*

PLAYTHING

PLAYTHING: **odaminwaagan, -an** *ni*

PLEASE

PLEASE: please s.o. **zhoobi'** *vta;* please! **daga** *pc*

PLIERS

PLIERS: **dakwanjigan, -an** *ni*

PLOW

PLOW: **biigwakamigibijigan, -ag** *na;* **biigwakamigibijige** *vai;* plow s.t. **biigwakamigibidoon** *vti2*

PLUCK

PLUCK: pluck s.o. (e.g., a bird) **bashkobizh /bashkobiN-/** *vta;* pluck s.t. **bakwajibidoon** *vti2;* pluck s.t. (as a plant) **bashkwashkibidoon** *vti2*

PLUG

PLUG: **gibaakwa'igan, -an** *ni;* plug s.o. **giba' /giba'w-/** *vta;* plug s.t. **giba'an** *vti;* plug things **giba'ige** *vai;* **gibaakwa'ige** *vai*

PLUGGED

PLUGGED: be plugged **giba'igaade, giba'igaademagad** *vii;* **giba'igaazo** *vai*

PLUM

PLUM: **bagesaan, -ag** *na*

PLUM BUSH
PLUM BUSH: **bagesaaniminagaawanzh, -iig** *na*
PLUM TREE
PLUM TREE: **bagesaanaatig, -oog** *na*
PNEUMONIA
HAVE PNEUMONIA: **gichi-gizhizo** *vai*
POCKET
POCKET: **mashkimodegwaajigan, -an** *ni*
POINT
POINT A CERTAIN WAY: point to s.o. a certain way **izhinoo'** *vta;* point to s.t. a certain way **izhinoo'an** *vti;* point to (s.t.) for s.o. **izhinoo'amaw** *vta*
POINT WITH LIPS: point a certain way with lips **izhidooneni** *vai;* point s.o. out with lips **izhidoonem** *vta;* point (s.t.) out to s.o. with lips **izhidoonetaw** *vta*
POINT
POINT: point of land **neyaashi, -wan** *ni;* there is a point of land **neyaashiiwan** *vii*
GO OVER A POINT: **gakiiwe** *vai*
POINTED
POINTED: be pointed **bajiishkaa, bajiishkaamagad** *vii;* **bajiishkizi** *vai*
CHOP POINTED: chop s.o. pointed **bajiishkiga' /bajiishkiga'w-/** *vta;* chop s.t. pointed **bajiishkiga'an** *vti*
POISON
POISON: **maji-mashkiki, -wan** *ni*
POKER
POKER: fire poker **jiichiishkinzhe'igan, -an** *ni*
POLE
POLE: pole s.t. **gaandakii'an** *vti*
LIGHT POLE: **waazakonenjiganaatig, -oon** *ni*
POLE A BOAT: **gaandakii'ige** *vai;* **gaandakii'o** *vai*
POLE A BOAT ALONG: **bima'oodoo** *vai;* **bima'ookii** *vai*
POLE A BOAT TO A CERTAIN PLACE: **ina'oodoo** *vai*
POLE IN A BOAT: pole s.t. along in a boat **bima'oodoon** *vti2;* pole s.o. along in a boat **bima'oozh /bima'ooN-/** *vta*
POLE LOGS: **gaanjweba'ige** *vai*
POLICE CAR
POLICE CAR: **dakoniwewidaabaan, -ag** *na*
POLICE STATION
POLICE STATION: **dakoniwewigamig, -oon** *ni*
POLICEMAN
POLICEMAN: **dakoniwewinini, -wag** *na*
POLISH
POLISH: polish s.o. **waasikwa'** *vta;* polish s.t. **waasikwa'an** *vti*
POLITICS
IN POLITICS: be in politics **dibaakonige** *vai*
POND
POND: be a pond **waanzhibiiyaa, waanzhibiiyaamagad** *vii*
PONDER
PONDER: **maaminonendam** *vai2*
POOL
PLAY POOL: **nemaabii** *vai*
POOL HALL
POOL HALL: **nemaabiiwigamig, -oon** *ni*
POOR
POOR: be poor **gidimaagizi** *vai;* **inigaazi** *vai*
LOOK POOR: **gidimaaginaagozi** *vai;* **gidimaaginaagwad** *vii*
POOR HEALTH
IN POOR HEALTH: be in poor health **maanamanji'o** *vai;* **maazhi-ayaa** *vai*
POOR JOB
POOR JOB: do a poor job **mamaazhii** *vai*
POORLY
RUN POORLY: run poorly (e.g., a car) **maazhibizo** *vai;* run poorly (e.g., a machine) **maazhibide, maazhibidemagad** *vii*
POPLAR
POPLAR: **azaadi, -wag** *na*
BALSAM POPLAR: **maanazaadi, -wag** *na*
PORCUPINE
PORCUPINE: **gaag, -wag** *na*
PORK
PORK: **gookoosh, -ag** *na;* **gookooshi-wiiyaas** *ni*
SALT PORK: **zhiiwitaagani-gookoosh** *na*
PORTAGE
PORTAGE: **gakiiwe** *vai*
CARRY OVER A PORTAGE: carry things over a portage **gakiiwenige** *vai*
POSSESSED
POSSESSED: be possessed by an evil spirit **maji-manidoowaadizi** *vai*
POST
POST: post s.t. up **agwaakwa'an** *vti*
POST OFFICE
POST OFFICE: **mazina'iganiiwigamig, -oon** *ni*
POSTAGE STAMP
POSTAGE STAMP: **oshtigwaanens, -an** *ni*
POSTER
POSTER: **agwaakwa'igan, -an** *ni*
POSTMAN
POSTMAN: **mazina'iganiiwinini, -wag** *na*
POSTURE
HAVE GOOD POSTURE: **gwayakogaabawi** *vai*
POT
POT: **akik, -oog** *na*
COOKING POT: **jiibaakwewakik, -oog** *na*
POT LID
POT LID: **gibaabowe'igan, -an** *ni*
POT SCRUBBER
POT SCRUBBER: **mimigwaabika'igan, -an** *ni*
POTATO
POTATO: **opin, -iig** *na*
WILD POTATO: **bagwajipin, -iig** *na, also* **bagwaji-opin**
POTAWATOMI
POTAWATOMI: **boodewaadamii, -g** *na*

POTBELLY
POTBELLY: have a potbelly **bikonagizhii** *vai*
POTHOLDER
POTHOLDER: **apaabikinigan, -an** *ni*
POTHOLE
POTHOLE: be a pothole of water **waanzhibiiyaa, waanzhibiiyaamagad** *vii*
POUND
POUND IN: pound s.o. in **ginjida' /ginjida'w-/** *vta;* pound s.t. in **ginjida'an** *vti*
POUND ON DRUM: **baaga'akokwe** *vai*
POUND
CERTAIN NUMBER OF POUNDS: a certain number of pounds **daso-dibaabiishkoojigan** *pc*
POUR
POUR: pour s.t. **ziiginan** *vti;* pour things **ziiginige** *vai*
POUR ON: pour liquid on s.o. **ziiga'andaw** *vta;* pour liquid on s.t. **ziiga'andan** *vti*
POUR OUT: **ziigise, ziigisemagad** *vii*
POUT
POUT: **mindawe** *vai*
POWDER
FACE POWDER: **waabishkiingwechigan** *ni*
POWER
HAVE POWER: **gashki'ewizi** *vai*
POWERED
POWERED: **waasamoo-** *pv4*
PRACTICE
PRACTICE RIDING: practice riding on horseback **gagwedoomigo** *vai*
PRACTICE SHOOTING: **gagweda'aakwe** *vai*
PRACTICE SINGING: **goji-nagamo** *vai*
PRAIRIE
PRAIRIE: **mashkode, -n** *ni*
PRAIRIE CHICKEN
PRAIRIE CHICKEN: **aagask, -wag** *na*
PRAY
PRAY: **anami'aa** *vai;* pray for s.o. **anama'etaw** *vta*
PRAYER BOOK
PRAYER BOOK: **anama'e-mazina'igan, -an** *ni*
PREACH
PREACH: **gagiikwe** *vai;* preach to s.o. **gagiikim** *vta*
PREACHER
PREACHER: **gagiikwewinini, -wag** *na*
PREACHING
EDUCATION BY PREACHING AND EXHORTATION: **gagiikimaawasowin** *ni*
PREGNANT
PREGNANT: be pregnant **anjiko** *vai;* **bimiwijige** *vai;* **gigishkawaawaso** *vai;* **gigishkaajige** *vai;* be pregnant with s.o. **gigishkaw** *vta*
PREOCCUPIED
PREOCCUPIED: be preoccupied **ondamendam** *vai2;* be preoccupied with s.o. **ondamenim** *vta;* be preoccupied with s.t. **ondamendan** *vti*
PREPARE
PREPARE: **ozhiitaa** *vai*
PRESERVES
PRESERVES: **baashkiminasigan, -an** *ni*
PRESS
PRESS: press on s.o. **maagon** *vta;* press on s.t. **maagonan** *vti*
PRETTY
PRETTY: be pretty **onizhishi** *vai;* **onizhishin** *vii*
MADE PRETTY: be made pretty **wawezhichigaade, wawezhichigaademagad** *vii*
PREVAIL
PREVAIL: prevail over s.o. **gashki'** *vta;* **mamaazhi'** *vta;* prevail over s.t. **mamaazhitoon** *vti2*
PREVENT
PREVENT: prevent s.o. (from doing something) **nanagin** *vta*
PREVIOUSLY
PREVIOUSLY: **gayat** *pc*
PRICE
CHARGE A HIGH PRICE: **ishpagindaaso** *vai;* charge a high price for s.t. **ishpagindan** *vti*
HAVE A CERTAIN PRICE: **inaginde, inagindemagad** *vii;* **inaginzo** *vai*
HAVE A PRICE OF A CERTAIN HEIGHT: **apiitaginde, apiitagindemagad** *vii;* **apiitaginzo** *vai*
SET A CERTAIN PRICE: set a certain price on s.o. **inagim** *vta;* set a certain price on s.t. **inagindan** *vti;* set a certain price on (s.t.) for s.o. **inagindamaw** *vta*
SET A PRICE: **onagindaaso** *vai;* set a price on s.o. **onagim** *vta;* set a price on s.t. **onagindan** *vti*
SET A PRICE OF A CERTAIN HEIGHT: set a price of a certain height on s.o. **apiitagim** *vta;* set a price of a certain height on s.t. **apiitagindan** *vti*
PRICK
PRICK: prick s.o. **badaka' /badaka'w-/** *vta;* prick s.t. **badaka'an** *vti;* prick things **badaka'ige** *vai*
PRICKED
GET PRICKED: **badakijin** *vai*
PRIEST
PRIEST: **mekadewikonayed** *na-pt;* **mekadewikonayewinini, -wag** *na*
PRINCESS
PRINCESS: **ogimaakwens, -ag** *na*
PRINTED
PRINTED A CERTAIN WAY: be printed a certain way **izhisin** *vii*
PRISON
PRISON: **gibaakwa'odiiwigamig, -oon** *ni*
PRISONER
PRISONER: **gebaakwa'ond** *na-pt*

PRIVY
PRIVY: **zaaga'amoowigamig, -oon** *ni*
PROGRESS
IN PROGRESS: **ani-** *pv2, also* **ni-**
PROHIBITION
PROHIBITION: there is a prohibition **gina'amaadim** *vii*
PROJECT
PROJECT: **anokaajigan, -an** *ni*
PROJECTOR
MOVIE PROJECTOR: **mazinaatewebinigan, -an** *ni*
PROMISE
PROMISE: promise (s.t.) to s.o. **waawiindamaw** *vta;* promise (s.t.) to people **waawiindamaage** *vai*
PROP
PROP UP TO BE A LEVEL SURFACE: prop s.t. up to be a level surface **desa'an** *vti*
PROPER
LIVE A PROPER LIFE: **gwayako-bimaadizi** *vai*
PROPERLY
PROPERLY: **wawiinge** *pc;* **weweni** *pc*
PROPERTY
PROPERTY: **daniwin, -an** *ni*
PROTECT
PROTECT YOUNG: protect one's young **gizhaawaso** *vai*
PROTECTION
LAY SOMETHING FOR PROTECTION: lay something on or under s.t. for protection **apisidoon** *vti2*
PROUD
PROUD: be proud **ishpenimo** *vai;* be proud of oneself **apiitenimo** *vai*
PROUD THOUGHTS: have proud thoughts **maminaadendam** *vai2*
PROUD TO A CERTAIN EXTENT: be proud of s.o. to a certain extent **apiitenim** *vta;* be proud of s.t. to a certain extent **apiitendan** *vti*
PUBIC HAIR
PUBIC HAIR: my pubic hair **nimiishigwaan, -an /-miishigwaan-/** *nid*
PUDDLE
PUDDLE: be a puddle **waanzhibiiyaa, waanzhibiiyaamagad** *vii*
PULL
PULL: pull s.o. **wiikobizh /wiikobiN-/** *vta;* pull s.o. (as with something string-like) **wiikwaabiigin** *vta;* pull s.t. **wiikobidoon** *vti2;* pull s.t. (as with something string-like) **wiikwaabiiginan** *vti;* pull (s.t.) for s.o. **wiikobidaw** *vta;* pull things **wiikobijige** *vai*
PULL APART TO FORM A GAP: pull s.o. apart to form a gap **dawibizh /dawibiN-/** *vta;* pull s.t. apart to form a gap **dawibidoon** *vti2;* pull things apart to form a gap **dawibijige** *vai*
PULL ASHORE: pull s.o. ashore **agwaabizh /agwaabiN-/** *vta;* pull s.t. ashore **agwaabidoon** *vti2*
PULL BACK: pull s.o. back **azhebizh /azhebiN-/** *vta;* pull s.t. back **azhebidoon** *vti2*
PULL DOWN: pull s.o. down **niisibizh /niisibiN-/** *vta;* pull s.t. down **niisibidoon** *vti2*
PULL DOWN WITH HANDS: pull s.o. down with hands **gawiwebin** *vta;* pull s.t. down with hands **gawiwebinan** *vti*
PULL FREE: pull s.o. free **gidiskibizh /gidiskibiN-/** *vta;* pull s.t. free **gidiskibidoon** *vti2*
PULL FROM THE WATER: pull s.o. from the water **agwaabizh /agwaabiN-/** *vta;* pull s.t. from the water **agwaabidoon** *vti2*
PULL IN TWO: pull s.o. in two **bookobizh /bookobiN-/** *vta;* pull s.t. in two **bookobidoon** *vti2*
PULL INTO PARTICLES: pull s.o. into particles **biisibizh /biisibiN-/** *vta;* pull s.t. into particles **biisibidoon** *vti2*
PULL OFF: pull s.o. off **gijibizh /gijibiN-/** *vta;* pull s.t. off **gijibidoon** *vti;* **giichigobidoon** *vti2;* **giichigobizh /giichigobiN-/** *vta*
PULL OFF WITH TEETH: pull s.o. off with teeth **giichigwam** *vta;* pull s.t. off with teeth **giichigwandan** *vti*
PULL SHUT: pull s.t. shut (as something stick- or wood-like) **gibaakobidoon** *vti2*
PULL STRAIGHT: pull s.o. straight **gwayakobizh /gwayakobiN-/** *vta;* pull s.t. straight **gwayakobidoon** *vti2*
PULL UP: pull s.t. up **bakwajibidoon** *vti2*
PULLED
PULLED: be pulled **wiikobijigaade, wiikobijigaademagad** *vii;* **wiikobijigaazo** *vai*
PUMP
PUMP: **wiikwa'ibaan, -an** *ni*
PUMP WATER: **wiikwa'ibii** *vai*
TIRE PUMP: **boodaajii'igan, -an** *ni*
PUMPKIN
PUMPKIN: **okosimaan, -an** *ni;* **ozaawikosimaan, -an** *ni*
PUNK
PUNK: **zagataagan, -ag** *na*
PUPPY
PUPPY: **animoons, -ag** *na*
PURSE
PURSE: **zhooniyaa-mashkimod, -an** *ni, also* **zhooniyaa-mashkimodens**
PUS
PUS: **mini /miny-/** *ni*
PUSH
PUSH: push s.o. **gaandin** *vta;* push s.t. **gaandinan** *vti;* push (s.t.) for s.o. **gaandinamaw** *vta;* push things **gaandinige** *vai*
PUSH WITH A STICK: push s.o. with a stick **gaanjida' /gaanjida'w-/** *vta;* push s.t. with a stick **gaanjida'an** *vti;* push things with a stick **gaanjida'ige** *vai*

PUSH WITH FOOT OR BODY: push s.o. with foot or body **gaanzikaw** *vta;* push s.t. with foot or body **gaanzikan** *vti*

PUSH POLE

PUSH POLE: **gaandakii'iganaak, -oon** *ni, also* **gaandakii'iganaatig**

PUT

PUT ALONG: put s.o. along (as something stick- or wood-like) **bimaakoshim** *vta;* put s.t. along (as something stick- or wood-like) **bimaakosidoon** *vti2*

PUT AWAY: be put away **zagakinigaade, zagakinigaademagad** *vii;* **zagakinigaazo** *vai;* put s.o. away **nanaa'in** *vta;* **zagakin** *vta;* put s.t. away **nanaa'inan** *vti;* **zagakinan** *vti;* put things away **zagakinige** *vai*

PUT HEAD A CERTAIN WAY: put one's head a certain way **inikweni** *vai*

PUT IN: be put in **biina'igaade, biina'igaademagad** *vii;* **biina'igaazo** *vai;* put s.o. in **biina' /biina'w-/** *vta;* put s.t. in **biina'an** *vti*

PUT IN A CERTAIN PLACE: be put in a certain place **achigaade, achigaademagad** *vii;* **achigaazo** *vai;* put s.o. in a certain place **ashi /aS-/** *vta;* put s.t. in a certain place **atoon** *vti2;* put (s.t.) in a certain place for s.o. **ataw** *vta;* put things in a certain place **achige** *vai*

PUT IN A TIGHT PLACE: put s.o. in a tight place **zhegoshim** *vta;* put s.t. in a tight place **zhegosidoon** *vti2*

PUT IN MOUTH: put (something) in one's mouth **zhakamo** *vai;* put s.o. in one's mouth **agwanem** *vta;* put s.t. in one's mouth **agwanendan** *vti;* put things in one's mouth **agwanenjige** *vai*

PUT IN ORDER: put s.o. in order **nanaa'in** *vta;* **onin** *vta;* **zagakishim** *vta;* put s.t. in order **nanaa'inan** *vti;* **oninan** *vti;* **zagakisidoon** *vti2;* put things in order **zagakisijige** *vti;* **na'isijige** *vai;* **oninige** *vai*

PUT IN THE KETTLE: put (s.t.) in the kettle **boodaakwe** *vai+o*

PUT IN THE RIGHT POSITION: put s.o. in the right position **minoshim** *vta;* put s.t. in the right position **minosidoon** *vti2*

PUT IN TO SOAK: be put in to soak **agonjijigaade, agonjijigaademagad** *vii;* **agonjijigaazo** *vai;* put s.o. in to soak **agonjim** *vta;* put s.t. in to soak **agonjidoon** *vti2*

PUT IN WATER: put s.o. in water **gondaabiigin** *vta;* put s.t. in water **gondaabiiginan** *vti*

PUT LOOSELY: put s.o. loosely **geshawishim** *vta;* put s.t. loosely **geshawisidoon** *vti2*

PUT ON A ROOF: **apakwe** *vai*

PUT OUT: put s.o. out **zaagidin** *vta;* put s.t. out **zaagidinan** *vti*

PUT OUT OF THE WAY: put s.o. out of the way **ikoshim** *vta;* put s.t. out of the way **ikosidoon** *vti2*

PUT THROUGH: put s.o. through **zhaabon** *vta;* put s.t. through **zhaabonan** *vti*

PUT TOUCHING: put s.o. touching **daangishim** *vta;* put s.t. touching **daangisidoon** *vti2*

PUT TURNED: put s.o. turned **gwekishim** *vta;* put s.t. turned **gwekisidoon** *vti2*

PUT UNDER THE GROUND: put s.o. under the ground **ningwakamigin** *vta*

PUT WOOD ON THE FIRE: **bagidinise** *vai*

PUT ON

PUT ON: put s.t. on (e.g., clothes) **biizikan** *vti;* put s.o. on (e.g., clothes) **biizikaw** *vta*

PUT ON CLOTHES: put on one's clothes **biizikonaye** *vai*

PUT ON COAT: put on one's coat **biichibabiinzikawaagane** *vai*

PUT ON DRESS: put on one's dress **biitagoode** *vai*

PUT ON HAT: put on one's hat **biichiwakwaane** *vai*

PUT ON MITTENS: put on one's mittens **biichiminjikaawane** *vai*

PUT ON MOCCASINS: put on one's moccasins **babiichii** *vai*

PUT ON PANTS: put on one's pants **biichigiboodiyegwaazone** *vai*

PUT ON SHIRT: put on one's shirt **biichibabagiwayaane** *vai*

PUT ON SHOES: put on one's shoes **babiichii** *vai*

PUT ON SOCKS: put on one's socks **biitazhigane** *vai*

PUT OUT

PUT OUT: put s.t. out (e.g., fire or light) **aate'an** *vti*

PUT OUT A FIRE: put out a fire on s.o. with hands **aatebizh /aatebiN-/** *vta*

PUT OUT QUICKLY: put s.t. out quickly (e.g., fire or light) **aatewebinan** *vti*

PUTTY

PUTTY: **bigiike** *vai;* putty s.t. **bigiikaadan** *vti*

Q

QUARREL

QUARREL: quarrel with s.o. **giikaam** *vta;* they quarrel with each other **giikaandiwag /giikaandi-/** *vai*

QUEEN

QUEEN: **ogimaakwe, -g** *na;* queen (card) **ikwe, -wag** *na*

QUESTION

YES-NO QUESTION: *yes-no question word* **ina** *pc, also* **na**

QUICK

QUICK: be quick **dadaatabii** *vai*

QUICKLY
QUICKLY: **wewiib** *pc*
QUIET
QUIET: **bizaan** *pc;* be quiet **bangan** *vii;* **bekaadizi** *vai;* **bizaan-ayaa** *vai, also* **bizaani-ayaa**; **goshkwaawaadizi** *vai*
QUIET HOUSE: be a quiet house **bangate, bangatemagad** *vii*
QUIETLY
SIT QUIETLY: **goshkwaawaadabi** *vai*
STAND QUIETLY: **bizaanigaabawi** *vai*
QUILT
QUILT: **maawandoogwaason, -an** *ni*
QUIT
QUIT: quit s.o. **booni'** *vta;* quit s.t. **boonitoon** *vti2*
QUIT WORKING: **aanizhiitam** *vai2*
QUITE
QUITE: **aapiji** *pc*
QUIVER
QUIVER: **jiichiibishkaa** *vai*
QUOTE
QUOTE: quote s.o. a certain way **inootaw** *vta;* quote people **inootaage** *vai*

R

RABBIT
RABBIT: **waabooz, -oog** *na*
COTTONTAIL RABBIT: **manidoo-waabooz, -oog** *na*
HUNT FOR RABBITS: **nandawaaboozwe** *vai*
JACK RABBIT: **misaabooz, -oog** *na*
RABBIT SKIN
RABBIT SKIN: **waaboozwayaan, -ag** *na*
RABBIT SOUP
RABBIT SOUP: **waaboozwaaboo** *ni*
RACCOON
RACCOON: **esiban, -ag** *na*
RACE
RACE: race s.o. **gagwejikazh /gagwejikaN-/** *vta;* race people **gagwejikazhiwe** *vai;* they race each other **gagwejikanidiwag /gagwejikanidi-/** *vai*
RACE IN BOATS: race s.o. in boats **gagwejikada' /gagwejikada'w-/** *vta;* they race each other in boats **gagwejikada'odiwag /gagwejikada'odi-/** *vai*
RACE CAR
RACE CAR: **gagwejikazhiwewidaabaan, -ag** *na*
RACK
HANGING RACK FOR FOOD DRYING: **agoojiwanaanaak, -oon** *ni*
RADIO
RADIO: **bizindamowin, -an** *ni;* **bizindamoo-makak, -oon** *ni*
RADISH
RADISH: **wiisagi-jiisens, -an** *ni*
RAFTER
RAFTER: **abanzh, -iin** *ni*
RAIN
RAIN: **gimiwan** *vii*
COLD RAIN: be cold rain **dakibiisaa, dakibiisaamagad** *vii*
RAIN COMES: **biijibiisaa, biijibiisaamagad** *vii*
RAIN GOES ALONG: **bimibiisaa, bimibiisaamagad** *vii*
RAIN GOES AWAY: **animibiisaa, animibiisaamagad** *vii*
RAIN IS HEARD: **madwebiisaa, madwebiisaamagad** *vii*
RAIN IS ON THE WAY: **bagamibiisaa, bagamibiisaamagad** *vii*
SPRINKLING RAIN: be sprinkling rain **awanibiisaa, awanibiisaamagad** *vii*
START TO RAIN: **maajibiisaa, maajibiisaamagad** *vii*
STOP RAINING: **ishkwaabiisaa, ishkwaabiisaamagad** *vii*
RAINBOW
RAINBOW: **nagweyaab, -iin** *ni*
RAINCOAT
RAINCOAT: **gimiwanoowayaan, -an** *ni*
RAISE
RAISE: raise s.o. (e.g., a child) **nitaawigi'** *vta;* raise s.t. **nitaawigitoon** (e.g., a crop) *vti2*
RAISE USING SOMETHING: raise s.o. (as or as with something stick- or wood-like) **ombaakwa' /ombaakwa'w-/** *vta;* raise s.t. (as or as with something stick- or wood-like) **ombaakwa'an** *vti*
RAISIN
RAISIN: **zhoominens, -an** *ni*
RAKE
RAKE: **binaakwe'igan, -an** *ni;* **jiishakamiga'igan, -an** *ni;* rake things **binaakwe'ige** *vai*
RANCID
SMELL RANCID: **zaatemaagozi** *vai;* **zaatemaagwad** *vii*
TASTE RANCID: **zaatepogozi** *vai;* **zaatepogwad** *vii*
TURN RANCID: **zaateshin** *vai;* **zaatesin** *vii*
RANK
AT A CERTAIN RANK: be at a certain rank **apiitendaagozi** *vai;* **apiitendaagwad** *vii*
RASP
RASP: **zisiboojigan, -an** *ni*
RASPBERRY
RASPBERRY: **miskomin, -ag** *na*
RATHER
RATHER: **indawaaj** *pc*
RATIONS
RATIONS: **ashandiwin, -an** *ni*

RATTLE
RATTLE: **zhiishiigwan, -ag** *na*
RATTLESNAKE
RATTLESNAKE: **zhiishiigwe, -g** *na*
RAVEN
RAVEN: **gaagaagiw, -ag** *na, also* **gaagaagi***
RAW
RAW: **ashki-** *pv4*
RAW MEAT: be raw (as meat) **ashkin** *vii;* **ashkini** *vai*
RAZOR
RAZOR: **gaashkibaajigan, -an** *ni*
REACH
REACH: reach s.o. **odish /odiS-/** *vta;* reach s.t. **oditan** *vti*
READ
READ: **agindaaso** *vai;* be read **aginjigaade, aginjigaademagad** *vii;* read s.t. **agindan** *vti;* read (s.t.) for s.o. **agindamaw** *vta;* read (s.t.) for people **agindamaage** *vai*
READY
GET READY: **ozhiitaa** *vai*
REAL
REAL: **enda-** *pv4*
REALIZE
REALIZE: realize of s.o. that **maaminonenim** *vta;* realize of s.t. that **maaminonendan** *vti*
REALLY
REALLY: **geget** *pc;* **enda-** *pv4*
REAR END
REAR END: my rear end **indiy /-diy-/** *nid, also* **indiyaash**
LIE WITH REAR END STICKING OUT: lie with one's rear end sticking out **jaangidiyeshin** *vai*
REASON
FOR A CERTAIN REASON: **onji-** *pv3*
RECENTLY
RECENTLY: **bijiinag** *pc;* **noomaya** *pc*
RECOGNIZE
RECOGNIZE: recognize s.o. **aawekaazh /aawekaaN-/** *vta;* **aawenim** *vta;* recognize s.t. **aawendan** *vti;* they recognize each other **nisidawinaadiwag /nisidawinaadi-/** *vai*
RECOGNIZE BY SIGHT: recognize s.o. by sight **aawenaw** *vta;* **nisidawinaw** *vta;* recognize s.t. by sight **aawenan** *vti;* **nisidawinan** *vti*
RECOGNIZE BY SMELL: recognize s.o. by smell **nisidomaam** *vta;* recognize s.t. by smell **nisidomaandan** *vti*
RECOGNIZE BY SOUND: recognize s.o. by sound **aawetaw** *vta;* **nisidotaw** *vta;* recognize s.t. by sound **aawetan** *vti;* **nisidotan** *vti*
RECOLLECT
RECOLLECT: **mikwendam** *vai2;* recollect s.o. **mikwenim** *vta;* recollect s.t. **mikwendan** *vti*
RECOLLECTED
RECOLLECTED: be recollected **mikwendaagozi** *vai;* **mikwendaagwad** *vii*
RECORD PLAYER
RECORD PLAYER: **gaagiigidoo-makakoons, -an** *ni;* **nagamoo-makak, -oon** *ni*
RECOVER
RECOVER FROM AN ILLNESS: **noojimo** *vai*
RECREATION BUILDING
RECREATION BUILDING: **odaminoowigamig, -oon** *ni*
RECTUM
RECTUM: my rectum **injiid, -iin /-jiidy-/** *nid, also* **injiidiish**
RED
RED: **misko-** *pv4;* be red **miskozi** *vai;* **miskwaa, miskwaamagad** *vii;* be red (as something mineral) **miskwaabikad** *vii;* **miskwaabikizi** *vai;* be red (as something sheet-like) **miskwegad** *vii;* **miskwegizi** *vai;* be red (as something stick- or wood-like) **miskwaakozi** *vai;* **miskwaakwad** *vii;* be red (as something string-like) **miskwaabiigad** *vii;* **miskwaabiigizi** *vai*
COLORED RED: be colored red **miskwaande, miskwaandemagad** *vii;* **miskwaanzo** *vai*
DRESS IN RED: **miskwaakonaye** *vai*
RED CHEEK: have a red cheek **miskwanowe** *vai*
RED CLOUDS: be red clouds **miskwaanakwad** *vii*
RED LEAVES: have red leaves **miskobagizi** *vai;* there are red leaves on the trees **miskobagaa, miskobagaamagad** *vii*
RED NOSE: have a red nose **miskojaane** *vai*
WEAR RED: **misko'o** *vai*
RED CEDAR
RED CEDAR: **miskwaawaak, -oog** *na*
RED LAKE
RED LAKE: Red Lake Reservation **Miskwaagamiiwi-zaaga'iganiing** *place*
RED OSIER
RED OSIER: red osier (locally known as dogwood) **miskwaabiimizh, -iig** *na*
RED SQUIRREL
RED SQUIRREL: **ajidamoo, -g** *na*
RED-HEADED
RED-HEADED: be red-headed **miskondibe** *vai*
RED-HEADED WOODPECKER
RED-HEADED WOODPECKER: **meme, -g** *na*
RED-HOT
RED-HOT: be red-hot (as something mineral) **miskwaabikide, miskwaabikidemagad** *vii;* **miskwaabikizo** *vai*
REDHORSE
REDHORSE: redhorse (fish) **meskwaazhigwaneshi, -wag** *na*
REDUCE
REDUCE TO NOTHING: reduce s.o. to nothing **ango'** *vta;* reduce s.t. to nothing **angotoon** *vti2*

REED
REED: **anaakanashk, -oon** *ni;* **gichigamiiwashk, -oon** *ni*
REFLECT
REFLECT: reflect (as something mineral) **waasaabikide, waasaabikidemagad** *vii;* **waasaabikizo** *vai*
REFLECT IN WATER: **ojichaagobiishin** *vii;* **ojichaagobiisin** *vii*
REFRIGERATOR
REFRIGERATOR: **dakisijigan, -an** *ni;* **mikwamii-makak, -oon** *ni*
REGARD
REGARD TO A CERTAIN DEGREE: regard s.t. to a certain degree **apiitendan** *vti*
REGRETS
REGRETS: have regrets **minjinawezi** *vai*
REINDEER
REINDEER: **adik, -wag** *na*
REJECT
REJECT: reject s.o. **aanawenim** *vta;* reject s.t. **aanawendan** *vti;* reject things **aanawenjige** *vai*
REJECTED
REJECTED: be rejected **aanawendaagozi** *vai;* **aanawendaagwad** *vii*
RELATED
RELATED: be related to s.o. **inawem** *vta;* they are related to each other **inawendiwag /inawendi-/** *vai*
RELAXED
RELAXED: be relaxed **neshangishin** *vai*
RELEASE
RELEASE: release s.o. **bagidin** *vta;* release s.t. **bagidinan** *vti;* release (s.t.) to s.o. **bagidinamaw** *vta;* release things **bagidinige** *vai*
RELEASE FROM MIND: release s.o. from one's mind **bagidenim** *vta;* release s.t. from one's mind **bagidendan** *vti;* release things from one's mind **bagidenjige** *vai*
RELEASE QUICKLY: release s.o. quickly **bagijwebin** *vta;* release s.t. quickly **bagijwebinan** *vti*
RELEASED
RELEASED: be released **bagidinigaade, bagidinigaademagad** *vii;* **bagidinigaazo** *vai*
RELIGION
PRACTICE A CERTAIN RELIGION: **izhitwaa** *vai*
RELY
RELY ON: rely on (s.t.) **apenimo** *vai+o*
REMAIN
REMAIN TRANQUILLY IN PLACE: **goshkwaawaadabi** *vai*
REMEMBER
REMEMBER: **mikwendam** *vai2;* remember s.o. **mikwenim** *vta;* **minjimenim** *vta;* remember s.t. **mikwendan** *vti;* **minjimendan** *vti*
TRY TO REMEMBER: try to remember s.o. **nanda-mikwenim** *vta;* try to remember s.t. **nanda-mikwendan** *vti*
VAGUELY REMEMBER: **gezikwendam** *vai2;* vaguely remember s.o. **gezikwenim** *vta;* vaguely remember s.t. **gezikwendan** *vti*
REMEMBERED
REMEMBERED: be remembered **mikwendaagozi** *vai;* **mikwendaagwad** *vii*
REMOVE
REMOVE USING SOMETHING: remove s.o. using something **gida' /gida'w-/** *vta;* remove s.t. using something **gida'an** *vti*
REMOVE WITH HANDS: remove s.o. with hands **gijibizh /gijibiN-/** *vta;* remove s.t. with hands **gijibidoon** *vti*
REMOVE WITH SOMETHING SHARP: remove s.o. with something sharp **gijigwaazh /gijigwaaN-/** *vta;* remove s.t. with something sharp **gijigwaadan** *vti*
RENT
RENT: rent (s.t.) from people **adaawange** *vai+o;* rent (s.t.) from s.o. **adaawam** *vta;* rent (s.t.) to people **awi'iwe** *vai*
REPAIR
REPAIR: repair s.t. **nanaa'itoon** *vti2;* repair (s.t.) for s.o. **nanaa'itaw** *vta, also* **nanaa'itamaw**; repair things **nanaa'ichige** *vai*
REPAIR A CAR: **nanaa'idaabaane** *vai*
REPAIR GARAGE
REPAIR GARAGE: **odaabaanikewigamig, -oon** *ni*
REPEAT
REPEAT: repeat what s.o. says **naabinootaw** *vta;* repeat what people say **naabinootaage** *vai*
REPLY
REPLY: reply to s.o. **nakom** *vta;* they reply to each other **nakondiwag /nakondi-/** *vai*
REPORT
REPORT: **dadibaajimo** *vai;* report what people say **inootaage** *vai*
REPRESENTATIVE
REPRESENTATIVE: **giigidoowinini, -wag** *na*
REPRIMAND
REPRIMAND: reprimand s.o. **aanimim** *vta*
RESERVATION
RESERVATION: **ishkonigan, -an** *ni*
RESERVE
RESERVE: reserve s.o. **ishkon** *vta;* reserve s.t. **ishkonan** *vti;* reserve (s.t.) for s.o. **ishkonamaw** *vta*
RESERVED
RESERVED: be reserved **ishkonigaade, ishkonigaademagad** *vii;* **ishkonigaazo** *vai*
RESIDENCE
MOVE RESIDENCE: move one's residence **gozi** *vai*
MOVE RESIDENCE ABOUT: move one's residence about **babaamigozi** *vai*

MOVE TO A NEW RESIDENCE: **aanji-gozi** *vai*

RESORT

RESORT: **niibinishiiwigamig, -oon** *ni*

RESOUND

RESOUND: **baswewe** *vai;* **baswewe, baswewemagad** *vii*

RESPECTED

RESPECTED: be respected **minwaabamewizi** *vai*

RESPIRATION

HAVE FAST RESPIRATION: **dadaatabanaamo** *vai*

RESPIRATORY

HAVE A RESPIRATORY ILLNESS: **ozosodamwaapine** *vai*

REST

REST: **anwebi** *vai*

REST LYING DOWN: **anweshin** *vai*

RESTAURANT

RESTAURANT: **wiisiniiwigamig, -oon** *ni*

RETURN

RETURN: **azhegiiwe** *vai;* **giiwe** *vai;* return s.o. **azhen** *vta;* return s.t. **azhenan** *vti;* return (s.t.) to s.o. **azhenamaw** *vta;* return (s.t.) to people **azhenamaage** *vai*

RETURN TO OWN COUNTRY: return to one's own country **giiwekii** *vai*

THINK ABOUT RETURNING: **giiweyendam** *vai2*

REVEAL

REVEAL: reveal s.o. **naago'** *vta;* reveal s.t. **naagotoon** *vti2*

REVIVE

REVIVE: **aabaakawad** *vii;* **aabaakawizi** *vai;* **aabijiibaa** *vai;* revive s.o. **aabaakawi'** *vta*

REVOLVE

REVOLVE: **gizhibaabide, gizhibaabidemagad** *vii;* **gizhibaabise** *vai;* **gizhibaabise, gizhibaabisemagad** *vii;* **gizhibaabizo** *vai*

RHEUMATISM

RHEUMATISM: have rheumatism **okanaapine** *vai*

RHUBARB

RHUBARB: **zhiiwibag, -oon** *ni*

RIB

RIB: my rib **nipigemag, -oon /-pigemagw-/** *nid*

CANOE RIB: **waaginaa, -g** *na*

RIBBON

RIBBON: **zenibaanh, -yag** *na*

RICE

MAKE RICE: **manoominike** *vai*

WHITE RICE: **waabi-manoomin** *ni*

WILD RICE: **manoomin** *ni, also* **anishinaabe-manoomin**

RICE BAG

RICE BAG: **manoomini-mashkimod, -an** *ni;* **manoominiwazh, -an** *ni*

RICE BIRD

RICE BIRD: **manoominikeshiinh, -yag** *na*

RICE KNOCKER

RICE KNOCKER: rice knocker (stick for wild rice harvesting) **bawa'iganaak, -oog** *na*

RICH

RICH: be rich **dani** *vai*

RICHES

RICHES: **daniwin, -an** *ni*

RICING LICENSE

RICING LICENSE: **manoominike-mazina'igaans, -an** *ni*

RIDE

CATCH A RIDE: catch a ride with s.o. **boozinodaw** *vta*

GIVE A RIDE: give a ride to s.o. **boozi'** *vta*

PRACTICE RIDING: practice riding on horseback **gagwedoomigo** *vai*

RIDE ABOUT ON HORSEBACK: **babaamoomigo** *vai*

RIDE ALONG DRAWN BY HORSES: **bimiba'igo** *vai*

RIDE ALONG ON HORSEBACK: **bimoomigo** *vai*

RIDE AWAY ON HORSEBACK: **animoomigo** *vai*

RIDE FROM A CERTAIN PLACE ON HORSEBACK: **ondoomigo** *vai*

RIDE HERE ON HORSEBACK: **biidoomigo** *vai*

RIDE TO A CERTAIN PLACE ON HORSEBACK: ride to a certain place on horseback **inoomigo** *vai*

RIDE TO A CERTAIN PLACE WITH HORSES: **apa'igo** *vai*

RIDGE

RIDGE: there is a ridge **oshedinaa, oshedinaamagad** *vii*

RIGHT

RIGHT: **gwayak** *pc;* right? **naayanh** *pc*

CONSIDER RIGHT: consider s.t. right **gwayakwendan** *vti*

CONSIDERED RIGHT: be considered right **gwayakwendaagozi** *vai;* **gwayakwendaagwad** *vii*

DO RIGHT: do things right **gwayakochige** *vai*

HEAR RIGHT: hear the right thing **gwayakotam** *vai2*

MAKE RIGHT: make things right **gwayakochige** *vai*

RIGHT ACROSS

RIGHT ACROSS: **dibishkookamig** *pc*

RIGHT AT THE TIME

RIGHT AT THE TIME: **na'idaa** *pc*

RIGHT

RIGHT HAND: right hand *usually possessed* **gichinik** *ni*

RING

RING: **madweshin** *vai;* **madwesin** *vii;* ring s.t. **madwesidoon** *vti2*

RING

RING: **didibininjiibizon, -ag** *na*

RINK

RINK: **zhooshkwaada'ewigamig, -oon** *ni*

RIP
RIP: **giishkikaa** *vai;* **giishkikaa, giishkikaamagad** *vii;* rip s.o. **biigobizh /biigobiN-/** *vta;* rip s.t. **biigobidoon** *vti2;* rip things **biigobijige** *vai*
RIP OPEN: rip s.o. open **aabibizh /aabibiN-/** *vta;* rip s.t. open **aabibidoon** *vti2*

RIPE
RIPE: be ripe **atiso** *vai, also* **adiso; atite, atitemagad** *vii, also* **adite; giizhigi** *vai;* **giizhigin** *vii*
FULLY RIPE: be fully ripe **giizhaande, giizhaandemagad** *vii;* **giizhaanzo** *vai*

RIPPED
RIPPED: be ripped **biigobijigaade, biigobijigaademagad** *vii;* **biigobijigaazo** *vai*

RIPPLE
FLOW WITH A RIPPLE: **zaasijiwan** *vii*

RIPSAW
RIPSAW: **daashkiboojigan, -ag** *na*

RISE
RISE: rise (as the sun) **mooka'am** *vai2*

RIVER
RIVER: **ziibi, -wan** *ni*
BIG RIVER: **gichi-ziibi, -wan** *ni*
NARROW RIVER: be narrow (as a river) **agaasadetigweyaa, agaasadetigweyaamagad** *vii*
RIVER BRANCHES: branch (as a river) **baketigweyaa, baketigweyaamagad** *vii*
RIVER DIVIDES: divide (as a river) **baketigweyaa, baketigweyaamagad** *vii*
RIVER FLOWS ALONG: flow along (as a river) **bimitigweyaa, bimitigweyaamagad** *vii*
RIVER FLOWS AROUND A BEND: flow around a bend (as a river) **washkitigweyaa, washkitigweyaamagad** *vii*
RIVER FLOWS TO A CERTAIN PLACE: flow to a certain place (as a river) **izhitigweyaa, izhitigweyaamagad** *vii*
RIVER FORKS: fork (as a river) **niingidawitigweyaa, niingidawitigweyaamagad** *vii*
WIDE RIVER: be wide (as a river) **mangitigweyaa, mangitigweyaamagad** *vii*

ROACH HEADDRESS
ROACH HEADDRESS: **miskwaanzigan, -an** *ni*

ROAD
ROAD: **miikana, -n** *ni;* be a road **miikanaawan** *vii*
ACROSS THE ROAD: across the road or trail **agaamikana** *pc*
ALONG THE SIDE OF THE ROAD: **opimekana** *pc*
ALONGSIDE THE ROAD: **zhishwajikana** *pc*
ASPHALT ROAD: **bigii-miikana, -n** *ni*
AT THE END OF THE ROAD: at the end of the road or trail **gabekana** *pc*
BAD ROAD: be bad (as a road or trail) **maanadamon /maanadamo-/** *vii*
BY A ROAD: by a road or trail **jiigikana** *pc*
CONCRETE ROAD: **asinii-miikana, -n** *ni*
GRAVEL ROAD: **bingwii-miikana, -n** *ni*
ICY ROAD: be icy (as a road or trail) **mikwamiiwadamon /mikwamiiwadamo-/** *vii*
IN THE MIDDLE OF THE ROAD: in the middle of the road or trail **naawikana** *pc*
MAKE A ROAD: make a road or trail **miikanaake** *vai*
NARROW ROAD: be narrow (as a road or trail) **agaasademon /agaasademo-/** *vii*
ON THE OTHER SIDE OF THE ROAD: on the other side of the road or trail **agaamikana** *pc*
ON THIS SIDE OF THE ROAD: **ondaasikana** *pc*
ROAD FORKS: fork (as a road or trail) **niingidawadamon /niingidawadamo-/** *vii*
ROAD GOES ACROSS: go across (as a road or trail) **aazhoodamon /aazhoodamo-/** *vii*
ROAD GOES OFF TO THE SIDE: go off to the side (as a road or trail) **bakemon /bakemo-/** *vii*
ROAD LEADS ALONG: lead along (as a road or trail) **bimamon /bimamo-/, bimamoomagad** *vii*
ROAD LEADS FROM A CERTAIN PLACE: lead from a certain place (as a road or trail) **ondadamon /ondadamo-/** *vii*
ROAD LEADS TO A CERTAIN PLACE: lead to a certain place (as a road or trail) **inamon /inamo-/** *vii*
SLIPPERY ROAD: be slippery (as a road or trail) **ozhaashadamon /ozhaashadamo-/** *vii;* **zhooshkwadamon /zhooshkwadamo-/** *vii;* be slippery with ice (as a road or trail) **ozhaashikwadamon /ozhaashikwadamo-/** *vii*
WET ROAD: be wet (as a road or trail) **nibiiwadamon /nibiiwadamo-/** *vii*
WIDE ROAD: be wide (as a road or trail) **mangademon /mangademo-/** *vii, also* **mangadademon**

ROAD WORKER
ROAD WORKER: **miikanaakewinini, -wag** *na*

ROAR
ROAR: roar (as waves) **mamadweyaashkaa, mamadweyaashkaamagad** *vii*

ROAST
ROAST: roast (s.t.) **abwe** *vai+o;* roast s.o. **abwaazh /abwaaN-/** *vta;* roast s.t. **abwaadan** *vti;* roast things **abwaajige** *vai*
ROAST IN THE OVEN: roast s.o. in the oven **giboz /gibozw-/** *vta;* roast s.t. in the oven **gibozan** *vti;* roast things in the oven **gibozige** *vai*

ROASTED FISH
ROASTED FISH: **abwaajigan, -an** *ni*

ROASTED MEAT
ROASTED MEAT: **abwaajigan, -an** *ni*

ROASTING PAN
ROASTING PAN: **giboziganaabik, -oon** *ni*
ROB
ROB: rob s.o. of (s.t.) **makam** *vta;* rob people **makandwe** *vai*
ROBBER
ROBBER: **gimoodishkiiwinini, -wag** *na*
ROBIN
ROBIN: **opichi, -wag** *na*
ROCK
ROCK: **asin, -iig** *na;* be of rock **asiniiwan** *vii*
MANY ROCKS: there are many rocks **asiniikaa, asiniikaamagad** *vii*
ON ROCK: on something mineral (e.g., metal, glass, rock) **agidaabik** *pc, also* **ogidaabik*, wagidaabik**
ON TOP OF A ROCK: **agidasin** *pc, also* **ogidasin*, wagidasin**
ROCK CLIFF: **aazhibik, -oon** *ni;* there is a rock cliff **giishkaazhibikaa, giishkaazhibikaamagad** *vii*
ROCK FOR SWEAT LODGE: **madoodoowasin, -iig** *na*
STEEP ROCK FACE: be a steep rock face **giishkaabikaa, giishkaabikaamagad** *vii*
ROCKING CHAIR
ROCKING CHAIR: **didibise-apabiwin, -an** *ni;* **wewebizoo-apabiwin, -an** *ni*
ROLL
ROLL: **didibibide, didibibidemagad** *vii;* **didibibizo** *vai;* **ditibise** *vai;* **ditibise, ditibisemagad** *vii;* roll s.o. **didibin** *vta;* roll s.t. **didibinan** *vti*
ROLL ALONG: **ditibibide, ditibibidemagad** *vii*
ROLL ALONG KICKING: roll things along by kicking **ditibiwebishkige** *vai*
ROLL OVER: **gotigobide, gotigobidemagad** *vii;* **gotigobizo** *vai;* roll s.o. over **gotigobizh /gotigobiN-/** *vta;* roll s.t. over **gotigobidoon** *vti2*
ROLL UP SLEEVE: roll up one's sleeve **ikwanagweni** *vai*
ROLL
ROLL: **bakwezhigaans, -ag** *na*
ROLLED OATS
ROLLED OATS: **daataagwa'igan, -an** *ni*
ROOF
PUT ON A ROOF: **apakwe** *vai*
ROOFING
ROOFING: **apakwaan, -an** *ni*
ROOM
ROOM: **abiwin, -an** *ni;* be room **dawaa, dawaamagad** *vii*
COLD ROOM: be cold (as a house or room) **dakate, dakatemagad** *vii*
DARK ROOM: be dark (as in a room or house) **dibikate, dibikatemagad** *vii*
NEXT ROOM: in the next room **aajisag** *pc*
SMALL ROOM: be small (as a room or house) **agaasate, agaasatemagad** *vii*
ROOMY
ROOMY: be roomy **mangate, mangatemagad** *vii*
ROOSTER
ROOSTER: **naabese, -g** *na*
ROOT
ROOT: **ojiibik, -an** *ni*
HAVE ROOTS: **ojiibikaawan** *vii;* **ojiibikaawi** *vai*
ROOT HOUSE
ROOT HOUSE: **akiiwigamig, -oon** *ni*
ROPE
ROPE: **biiminakwaan, -an** *ni*
MAKE ROPE: **biiminakwe** *vai*
ROSARY
ROSARY: rosary *plural* **anama'eminensag** *na*
ROSE
ROSE: **oginii-waabigwan, -iin** *ni*
ROSE HIP
ROSE HIP: **ogin, -iig** *na*
ROTARY FAN
ROTARY FAN: **gizhibaayaasijigan, -an** *ni*
ROTTEN
ROTTEN: be rotten **bigishkanad** *vii;* **bigishkanani** *vai*
ROUGE
ROUGE: **miskwanowechigan, -an** *ni*
USE ROUGE: **miskwanowechige** *vai*
ROUGH
ROUGH: be rough **gaawaa, gaawaamagad** *vii;* **gaawizi** *vai;* be rough (as something mineral) **gaawaabikad** *vii;* **gaawaabikizi** *vai;* be rough (as something sheet-like) **gaawegad** *vii;* **gaawegizi** *vai*
ROUND
ROUND: be round **waawiyeyaa, waawiyeyaamagad** *vii;* **waawiyezi** *vai;* be round (as something ball-like) **waawiyeminagad** *vii;* **waawiyeminagizi** *vai;* be round (as something mineral) **waawiyeyaabikad** *vii;* **waawiyeyaabikizi** *vai;* be round (as something stick- or wood-like) **waawiyeyaakozi** *vai;* **waawiyeyaakwad** *vii*
MAKE ROUND: make s.o. round **waawiye'** *vta;* make s.t. round **waawiyetoon** *vti2*
ROUND TRIP
MAKE A ROUND TRIP: make a round trip in one day **biskaabii** *vai*
ROW
LIE SIDE BY SIDE IN A ROW: they lie side by side in a row **niibidesinoon /niibidesin-/** *vii;* they lie side by side in a row **niibideshinoog /niibideshin-/** *vai*
SIT SIDE BY SIDE IN A ROW: they sit side by side in a row **niibidebiwag /niibidebi-/** *vai*
ROW
ROW: row (a boat) **azheboye** *vai*
RUB
RUB: rub s.o. with something **zinigon** *vta;* rub s.t. with something **zinigonan** *vti*

RUBBING ALCOHOL
RUBBING ALCOHOL: **giziibiigazhewaaboo** *ni*
RUG
RUG: **anaakan, -an** *ni*
BRAIDED RUG: **okaadenigan, -an** *ni*
RUIN
RUIN: ruin s.o. **goopaaji'** *vta;* ruin s.t. **gopajitoon** *vti2*
RULE
RULE: rule s.o. **dibenim** *vta;* **ogimaakandaw** *vta;* rule s.t. **ogimaakandan** *vti*
RUMBLE
RUMBLE: **jiingwe, jiingwemagad** *vii;* **zegwewe, zegwewemagad** *vii*
RUMP
RUMP: my rump **indiy /-diy-/** *nid, also* **indiyaash**
RUN
ARRIVE ON THE RUN: **bagamibatoo** *vai;* they arrive on the run together **bagamiba'idiwag /bagamiba'idi-/** *vai*
HEARD RUNNING HERE: be heard running here **biidwewebatoo** *vai*
HEARD RUNNING HERE ON THE GROUND: be heard running here on the ground **biidwewekamigibatoo** *vai*
RUN ABOUT: **babaamibatoo** *vai;* they run about together **babaamiba'idiwag /babaamiba'idi-/** *vai*
RUN ACROSS: **aazhoobatoo** *vai, also* **aazhawibatoo**; they run across together **aazhogeba'idiwag /aazhogeba'idi-/** *vai;* **aazhooba'idiwag /aazhooba'idi-/** *vai*
RUN ACROSS WADING: **aazhawagaaziibatoo** *vai*
RUN ALONG: **bimibatoo** *vai;* they run along together **bimiba'idiwag /bimiba'idi-/** *vai*
RUN ALONG IN FLIGHT: **biminizhimo** *vai;* run along in flight from someone **bimiba'iwe** *vai*
RUN ALONG THE SHORE: **jiigewebatoo** *vai;* **jiigeweyaazhagaamebatoo** *vai*
RUN AROUND: run around s.t. **giiwitaabatwaadan** *vti;* run around something **giiwitaabatoo** *vai*
RUN ASHORE: **agwaabatoo** *vai*
RUN AT: run at s.o. **mawinazh /mawinaN-/** *vta*
RUN AT A CERTAIN SPEED: **apiichibatoo** *vai;* run at a certain speed (e.g., a machine) **apiichibide, apiichibidemagad** *vii;* **apiichibizo** *vai*
RUN AWAY: **animibatoo** *vai;* run away (in the other direction) with s.o. **animibatwaazh /animibatwaaN-/** *vta;* run away (in the other direction) with s.t. **animibatwaadan** *vti;* they run away (in the other direction) together **animiba'idiwag /animiba'idi-/** *vai*
RUN AWAY FOR GOOD: **aapijibatoo** *vai*
RUN AWAY MAKING NOISE: **animwewebatoo** *vai*
RUN AWAY SCARED: **animinizhimo** *vai*
RUN BACK: **giiwebatoo** *vai*
RUN DOWN: **niisaandawebatoo** *vai*
RUN DOWNHILL: **niisaakiiwebatoo** *vai*
RUN FAST: **gizhiibatoo** *vai;* **gizhiikaabatoo** *vai*
RUN FROM CERTAIN PLACE IN FLIGHT: run from a certain place in flight **onjinizhimo** *vai*
RUN FROM A CERTAIN PLACE: **onjibatoo** *vai*
RUN HERE: **biijibatoo** *vai;* they run here together **biijiba'idiwag /biijiba'idi-/** *vai*
RUN HOME: **giiwebatoo** *vai*
RUN IN A CERTAIN WAY: **apatoo** *vai*
RUN INLAND: **gopibatoo** *vai*
RUN INSIDE: **biindigebatoo** *vai;* they run inside together **biindigeba'idiwag /biindigeba'idi-/** *vai;* run inside with s.o. **biindigebatwaazh /biindigebatwaaN-/** *vta;* run inside with s.t. **biindigebatwaadan** *vti;* run inside from people **biindigeba'iwe** *vai*
RUN INTO THE WATER: **bakobiibatoo** *vai*
RUN OFF: **maajiibatoo** *vai;* they run off together **maajiiba'idiwag /maajiiba'idi-/** *vai*
RUN OFF TO THE SIDE: **bakebatoo** *vai*
RUN OUT: **zaagizibatoo** *vai;* run out with s.o. **zaagiziba'** *vta;* **zaagizibatwaazh /zaagizibatwaaN-/** *vta;* run out with s.t. **zaagizibatwaadan** *vti;* they run out together **zaagiziba'idiwag /zaagiziba'idi-/** *vai*
RUN POORLY: run poorly (e.g., a car) **maazhibizo** *vai;* run poorly (e.g., a machine) **maazhibide, maazhibidemagad** *vii*
RUN SLOWLY: **bejibatoo** *vai;* **bezikaabatoo** *vai*
RUN SUDDENLY INTO VIEW: **zaagewebatoo** *vai*
RUN THE WRONG WAY: **wanibatoo** *vai*
RUN THROUGH: **zhaabobatoo** *vai*
RUN TO A CERTAIN PLACE: **apatoo** *vai;* run with s.o. to a certain place **apa'** *vta*
RUN TO A CERTAIN PLACE IN FLIGHT: **izhinizhimo** *vai*
RUN TO A CERTAIN PLACE TOGETHER: they run to a certain place together **apa'idiwag /apa'idi-/** *vai*
RUN TO GET: run to get s.o. **naajibatwaazh /naajibatwaaN-/** *vta;* run to get s.t. **naajibatwaadan** *vti*
RUN TO THE SHORE: **madaabiibatoo** *vai*
RUN UPHILL: **agidaakiiwebatoo** *vai*
RUN WELL: run well (e.g., a machine) **minobide, minobidemagad** *vii;* **minobizo** *vai*
RUN WITH SAP: **onjigaa, onjigaamagad** *vii*
START TO RUN: **maajiibatoo** *vai;* start to run (e.g., a machine) **maajiibide, maajiibidemagad** *vii;* **maajiibizo** *vai*
START TO RUN WITH SAP: **maajigaa, maajigaamagad** *vii*
STOP RUNNING: **noogibatoo** *vai*

TURN RUNNING: **gwekibatoo** *vai*

RUN AWAY

RUN AWAY: run away from s.o. **ginjiba'** *vta;* run away from people **ginjiba'iwe** *vai*

RUN AWAY TO A CERTAIN PLACE: run away from people to a certain place **apa'iwe** *vai*

RUN OUT

RUN OUT: **jaagise** *vai+o;* **jaagise, jaagisemagad** *vii*

RUN OUT OF FUEL: **iskaakizige** *vai*

RUN SHORT

RUN SHORT: **noondese** *vai;* run short of s.o. **noondesa'** *vta;* run short of s.t. **noondesatoon** *vti2;* run short of things **noondesachige** *vai*

RUSH

RUSH: rush s.o. **ojaanimi'** *vta*

RUSH

RUSH: **anaakanashk, -oon** *ni*

RUSTLESS

RUSTLESS: be rustless **zhooshkwaabikad** *vii;* **zhooshkwaabikizi** *vai*

RUSTY

RUSTY: be rusty **agwaagwaabikad** *vii;* **agwaagwaabikizi** *vai*

TURN RUSTY: **agwaagwaabikishin** *vai;* **agwaagwaabikisin** *vii*

RUTABAGA

RUTABAGA: **jiis, -an** *ni*

S

SACK

SACK: **mashkimod, -an** *ni*

GUNNYSACK: **mandaaminiwazh, -an** *ni*

SAD

SAD: be sad **gashkendam** *vai2;* **osidaawendam** *vai2*

SADDLE

SADDLE: **bimoomigoo-apabiwin, -an** *ni*

SAFETY PIN

SAFETY PIN: **zagaakwa'igan, -an** *ni*

SAIL

SAIL: **ningaasimoonowin** *ni;* sail (in a boat) **ningaasimoono** *vai*

SAIL ABOUT: **babaamaashi** *vai;* **babaamaasin** *vii*

SAIL ALONG: **bimaashi** *vai;* **bimaasin** *vii*

SAIL ASHORE: **agwaayaashi** *vai*

SAIL AWAY: **animaashi** *vai;* **animaasin** *vii*

SAIL FROM A CERTAIN PLACE: **ondaashi** *vai;* **ondaasin** *vii*

SAIL HERE: **biidaashi** *vai;* **biidaasin** *vii*

SAIL IN: **bagamaashi** *vai;* **bagamaasin** *vii*

SAIL TO A CERTAIN PLACE: **inaashi** *vai;* **inaasin** *vii*

SAILBOAT

SAILBOAT: **ningaasimoo-jiimaan, -an** *ni*

SAILOR

SAILOR: **ningaasimoowinini, -wag** *na*

SALIVA

SALIVA: **zikowin** *ni*

SALT

SALT: **zhiiwitaagan** *ni;* salt s.o. **zhiiwitaagana' /zhiiwitaagana'w-/** *vta;* salt s.t. **zhiiwitaagana'an** *vti;* salt things **zhiiwitaagana'ige** *vai*

SALT PORK

SALT PORK: **zhiiwitaagani-gookoosh** *na*

SALTY

SALTY: be salty (as a liquid) **zhiiwitaaganaagamin /zhiiwitaaganaagami-/** *vii*

TASTE SALTY: **zhiiwitaaganipogozi** *vai;* **zhiiwitaaganipogwad** *vii*

SAME

SAME: be the same **bezhigwan** *vii;* the same **naasaab** *pc*

AT THE SAME TIME: **bekish** *pc*

SAME AGE: they are the same age **wiijigindiwag /wiijigindi-/** *vai*

STEP IN THE SAME TRACKS: **naaba'anidizo** *vai*

THE SAME AGE: be the same age as s.o. **wiijigim** *vta*

SAND

SAND: **bingwi** *ni*

MUCH SAND: be much sand **bingwiikaa, bingwiikaamagad** *vii*

SANDHILL CRANE

SANDHILL CRANE: **ajijaak, -wag** *na*

SANDY

SANDY BEACH: be a sandy beach **mitaawangaa, mitaawangaamagad** *vii*

SAP

FINISH BOILING SAP: **ishkwaagamizige** *vai*

GATHER SAP: **naadoobii** *vai*

MAPLE SAP: **wiishkobaaboo** *ni;* **ziinzibaakwadwaaboo** *ni*

START TO RUN WITH SAP: **maajigaa, maajigaamagad** *vii*

THE LAST RUN OF SAP: be the last run of sap **ishkwaagaa, ishkwaagaamagad** *vii*

SAP BUCKET

SAP BUCKET OF FOLDED BIRCH BARK: **biskitenaagan, -an** *ni*

SAP-BOILING FRAME

SAP-BOILING FRAME: frame for holding sap-boiling kettles **iskigamiziganaak, -oon** *ni*

SAP-BOILING LODGE

SAP-BOILING LODGE: **iskigamizigewigamig, -oon** *ni*

SAP-BOILING POLE

SAP-BOILING POLE: **iskigamiziganaatig, -oon** *ni*

SATIN
SATIN: **zenibaawegin, -oon** *ni*
SATISFIED
SATISFIED: be satisfied **debizi** *vai*
FEEL SATISFIED: **debisewendam** *vai2*
SATISFY
SATISFY: satisfy s.o. **debi'** *vta*
SATURATED
SATURATED: be saturated **zhaabobii, zhaabobiimagad** *vii*
SATURDAY
SATURDAY: be Saturday **giziibiigisaginige-giizhigad** *vii;* **ishwaajanokii-giizhigad** *vii*
SAUCER
SAUCER: **desinaagaans, -an** *ni*
SAUSAGE
SAUSAGE: **onagizh, -iin** *ni, also* **onagizhiins**
SAVE
SAVE BACK: save s.o. back **ishkon** *vta;* save s.t. back **ishkonan** *vti;* save (s.t.) back for s.o. **ishkonamaw** *vta*
SAVE LIFE: save the life of s.o. **bimaaji'** *vta*
SAVED
SAVED BACK: be saved back **ishkonigaade, ishkonigaademagad** *vii;* **ishkonigaazo** *vai*
SAW
CROSSCUT SAW: **giishkiboojigan, -an** *ni*
SAW APART LENGTHWISE: saw s.o. apart lengthwise **daashkiboozh /daashkibooN-/** *vta;* saw s.t. apart lengthwise **daashkiboodoon** *vti2;* saw things apart lengthwise **daashkiboojige** *vai*
SAW OFF: saw s.o. off **giishkiboozh /giishkibooN-/** *vta;* saw s.t. off **giishkiboodoon** *vti2;* saw things off **giishkiboojige** *vai*
SAW STRAIGHT: saw s.o. straight **gwayakoboozh /gwayakobooN-/** *vta;* saw s.t. straight **gwayakoboodoon** *vti2*
SAW MILL
SAW MILL: **daashkiboojigan, -ag** *na*
SAY
SAY: **ikido** *vai;* say so to s.t. **idan** *vti;* say to s.o. **izhi /iN-/** *vta;* they say to each other **idiwag /idi-/** *vai*
SAY AFTER: say something after s.o. **gikinootaw** *vta*
SCAB
SCABS: have scabs **omigii** *vai*
SCABS ON FACE: have scabs on one's face **omigiingwe** *vai*
SCALE
SCALE: scale s.o. **jiiga'azh /jiiga'aN-/** *vta*
SCALE FISH: **jiiga'e** *vai*
SCALES: my scales *plural* **ninaga'ayag /-naga'ay-/** *nad*
SCALE
SCALE: **dibaabiishkoojigan, -an** *ni*
SCALE TIMBER
SCALE TIMBER: **diba'aatigwe** *vai*
SCALP
DIRTY SCALP: have a dirty scalp **wiinishagaandibe** *vai*
SCANDINAVIAN
SCANDINAVIAN: **agongos, -ag** *na*
SCANDINAVIAN LANGUAGE
SPEAK A SCANDINAVIAN LANGUAGE: **agongosimo** *vai*
SCAR
HAVE A SCAR: **ojiishigi** *vai*
HAVE SCAR ON ARM: have scar on one's arm **ojiishinike** *vai*
HAVE SCAR ON FACE: have scar on one's face **ojiishiingwe** *vai*
HAVE SCAR ON HAND: have scar on one's hand **ojiishininjii** *vai*
SCARE
SCARE: scare s.o. **zegi'** *vta*
SCARE AWAY: scare s.o. away (e.g., game) **oshaakaw** *vta*
SCARED
SCARED: be scared **zegizi** *vai*
RUN AWAY SCARED: **animinizhimo** *vai*
SCARF
SCARF: **giizhoopizon, -ag** *na*
SCARY
CONSIDERED SCARY: be considered scary **zegendaagozi** *vai;* **zegendaagwad** *vii*
LOOK SCARY: **zeginaagozi** *vai;* **zeginaagwad** *vii*
SCARY DREAM: have a scary dream **zegaabandam** *vai2*
SCARY MOVIE: be a scary movie **zegaatese, zegaatesemagad** *vii*
SCATTER
SCATTER: **biiwise** *vai;* **biiwise, biiwisemagad** *vii;* scatter s.o. **biiwiwebin** *vta;* scatter s.t. **biiwiwebinan** *vti*
SCATTER USING SOMETHING: scatter s.t. using something **zaswe'an** *vti*
SCATTER WITH FOOT OR BODY: scatter s.o. with foot or body **zasweshkaw** *vta;* scatter s.t. with foot or body **zasweshkan** *vti*
SCATTER WITH HANDS: scatter s.o. with hands **zaswebizh /zaswebiN-/** *vta;* scatter s.t. with hands **zaswebidoon** *vti2*
SCHOOL
SCHOOL: **gikinoo'amaadiiwigamig, -oon** *ni*
GO TO SCHOOL: **gikinoo'amaagozi** *vai*
SCHOOL CUSTODIAN
SCHOOL CUSTODIAN: **boodawewinini, -wag** *na*
SCHOOLBOOK
SCHOOLBOOK: **gikinoo'amaadii-mazina'igan** *ni*
SCISSORS
SCISSORS: **moozhwaagan, -an** *ni*
SCOLD
SCOLD: scold s.o. **naniibikim** *vta*
SCOOP
SCOOP UP: scoop s.o. up **gwaaba'** *vta;* scoop s.t. up **gwaaba'an** *vti;* scoop (s.t.) up for s.o. **gwaaba'amaw** *vta;* scoop up things **gwaaba'ige** *vai*
SCOOP UP WATER: **gwaaba'ibii** *vai*

SCORE
SCORE IN A GAME: **gabenaage** *vai*
SCOUT
SCOUT: **nandawaatoo** *vai*
SCRAPE
SCRAPE HIDES: **jiishaakwa'ige** *vai;* scrape s.o. to remove hair (e.g., a hide) **jiishaakwa' /jiishaakwa'w-/** *vta*
SCRAPE USING SOMETHING: scrape s.o. using something **gaaskaaska' /gaaskaaska'w-/** *vta;* scrape s.t. using something **gaaskaaska'an** *vti*
SCRAPER
HIDE SCRAPER: **jiishaakwa'igan, -an** *ni*
SCRATCH
SCRATCH: scratch (leaving a visible mark) **jiichiigii** *vai;* scratch s.o. **baazagobizh /baazagobiN-/** *vta;* scratch s.o. (leaving a visible mark) **jiichiigibizh /jiichiigibiN-/** *vta;* scratch s.t. (leaving a visible mark) **jiichiigibidoon** *vti2*
SCRATCH BACK: scratch s.o.'s back **jiichiigaawiganebizh /jiichiigaawiganebiN-/** *vta*
SCREAM
SCREAM: **aazhikwe** *vai*
SCREECH OWL
SCREECH OWL: **gaakaabishiinh, -yag** *na*
SCREW
SCREW: **biimiskonigan, -an** *ni;* **biimiskwa'igaans, -an** *ni;* screw s.t. **biimiskwa'an** *vti*
SCREWDRIVER
SCREWDRIVER: **biimiskwa'igan, -an** *ni*
SCRUB BRUSH
SCRUB BRUSH: **mimigosaga'igan, -an** *ni*
SCULPT
SCULPT: sculpt s.o. **onadin** *vta;* sculpt s.t. **onadinan** *vti*
SCYTHE
SCYTHE: **giishkizhigan, -an** *ni*
SEA
SEA: **gichigami, -in** *ni*
SEAGULL
SEAGULL: **gayaashk, -wag** *na*
SEARCH
SEARCH: search for s.o. **nandawaabam** *vta;* search for s.t. **nandawaabandan** *vti;* search for things **nandawaabanjige** *vai*
SEASICK
SEASICK: be seasick **giiwashkwe'ogo** *vai*
SEASON
SEASON: season (s.t.) **apaabowe** *vai+o*
SEAT
SEAT: seat s.o. **onabi'** *vta;* seat people **onabi'iwe** *vai*
CHANGE SEAT: **aandabi** *vai*
TAKE A SEAT: **onabi** *vai*
SEATED
SEATED: be seated **wawenabi** *vai*
SECOND
SECOND: the second **eko-niizhing** *pc*
THE SECOND DAY OF THE MONTH: be the second day of the month **niizhogonagizi** *vai*
SECOND PERSON
SECOND PERSON: *second person prefix before consonants in nouns and verbs* **gi=** *pre;second person prefix before vowels in verbs and non-dependent nouns* **gid=** *pre; second person prefix before vowels in dependent nouns* **g=** *pre*
SECOND PERSON PLURAL: you *second person plural personal pronoun* **giinawaa** *pr;* only you *second personal plural personal pronoun* **giinetawaa** *pr;* your turn *second person plural personal pronoun* **giinitamawaa** *pr*
SECOND PERSON SINGULAR: you *second person singular personal pronoun* **giin** *pr;* only you *second person singular personal pronoun* **giineta** *pr;* your turn *second person singular personal pronoun* **giinitam** *pr*
SECONDHAND CLOTHING STORE
SECONDHAND CLOTHING STORE: **zhiigoshkigani-adaawewigamig, -oon** *ni*
SECRET
SECRET: be secret **giimoodad** *vii*
SECRETARY
SECRETARY: secretary (female) **ozhibii'igewikwe, -g** *na*
SECRETLY
SECRETLY: **giimooj** *pc*
EAT SECRETLY: eat things secretly **giimoodanjige** *vai*
LAUGH SECRETLY: **giimoodaapi** *vai*
SEE
SEE: **waabi** *vai;* see s.o. **waabam** *vta;* see s.t. **waabandan** *vti;* see oneself **waabandizo** *vai;* they see each other **waabandiwag /waabandi-/** *vai*
FAIL TO SEE: fail to see s.o. **gwiinawaabam** *vta;* fail to see s.t. **gwiinawaabandan** *vti*
SEE A CERTAIN WAY: see s.o. a certain way **izhinaw** *vta;* see s.t. a certain way **izhinan** *vti*
SEE A CERTAIN WAY AS IN A DREAM: see s.o. a certain way as in a dream **inaabam** *vta;* see s.t. a certain way as in a dream **inaabandan** *vti*
SEE AT A DISTANCE: see s.o. at a distance **debaabam** *vta;* see s.t. at a distance **debaabandan** *vti*
SEE CLEARLY: **bagakaabi** *vai;* see s.o. clearly **bagakaabam** *vta;* see s.t. clearly **bagakaabandan** *vti*
SEE THROUGH: see through s.o. **zhaabwaabam** *vta;* see through s.t. **zhaabwaabandan** *vti*
SEE WELL: **minwaabi** *vai*
SEED
SEED: **miinikaan, -an** *ni*
SEEK
SEEK: **nanda-** *pv4;* seek s.o. **nooji'** *vta;* seek s.t. **noojitoon** *vti2;* seek people **nooji'iwe** *vai*

SEEK TO KNOW: seek to know s.o. **nandagikenim** *vta;* seek to know s.t. **nandagikendan** *vti*
SEEK TO LEARN: seek to learn s.t. **nandagikendan** *vti*

SEEM
SEEM TO BE A CERTAIN WAY: **inendaagozi** *vai;* **inendaagwad** *vii*

SEEN
SEEN: be seen **waabanjigaade, waabanjigaademagad** *vii;* **waabanjigaazo** *vai*

SEIZE
SEIZE: seize s.o. **nawadin** *vta;* seize s.t. **nawadinan** *vti;* seize (s.t.) of s.o.'s **nawadinamaw** *vta;* seize people **nawadiniwe** *vai*

SELDOM
SELDOM: **wiikaa** *pc*

SELECT
SELECT FROM: select from s.o. **gagiigin** *vta;* select from s.t. **gagiiginan** *vti*

SELF-CONFIDENCE
LACK SELF-CONFIDENCE: **zhaagwenimo** *vai*

SELL
SELL: sell (s.t.) **adaawaage** *vai+o*
SELL OUT: sell out (of s.t.) **jaagadaawaage** *vai+o*

SEND
SEND: send for s.o. **naajinizha' /naajinizha'w-/** *vta;* send for s.t. **naajinizha'an** *vti;* send (s.t.) to s.o. **niindaa'** *vta;* send (s.t.) to people **niindaa'iwe** *vai*
SEND A LETTER HERE: **biijibii'ige** *vai*
SEND ALONG: send s.o. along **biminizhikaw** *vta;* send people along **biminaazhikaage** *vai*
SEND OFF: send s.o. off **maajinaazha' /maajinaazha'w-/** *vta;* **maajinizha' /maajinizha'w-/** *vta;* send s.t. off **maajinizha'an** *vti;* send (s.t.) off to s.o. **maajinizha'amaw** *vta*
SEND TO A CERTAIN PLACE: send s.o. to a certain place **izhinaazhikaw** *vta;* **izhinizha' /izhinizha'w-/** *vta;* send s.t. to a certain place **izhinizha'an** *vti;* send (s.t.) to s.o. to a certain place **izhinizha'amaw** *vta*

SENSELESS
KNOCK SENSELESS: knock s.o. senseless **giiwashkweganaam** *vta*
KNOCKED SENSELESS IN IMPACT: be knocked senseless in impact **giiwashkweshin** *vai*

SENT
SENT TO A CERTAIN PLACE: be sent to a certain place **izhinizha'igaade, izhinizha'igaademagad** *vii;* **izhinizha'igaazo** *vai*

SENTENCE
SENTENCE A CERTAIN WAY: sentence s.o. a certain way **inaakon** *vta*

SENTENCED
SENTENCED: be sentenced **dibaakonigaazo** *vai*
SENTENCED A CERTAIN WAY: be sentenced a certain way **inaakonigaazo** *vai*

SEPARATE
SEPARATE: they separate from each other **webinidiwag /webinidi-/** *vai*

SEPTEMBER
SEPTEMBER: **waatebagaa-giizis** *na, also* **waatebago-giizis; manoominike-giizis** *na*

SERVE
SERVE FOOD: serve food to people **ashange** *vai*

SET
SET A CERTAIN PRICE: set a certain price on s.o. **inagim** *vta;* set a certain price on s.t. **inagindan** *vti;* set a certain price on (s.t.) for s.o. **inagindamaw** *vta*
SET A CERTAIN WAY: put s.o. a certain way **izhishim** *vta;* set s.t. a certain way **izhisidoon** *vti2*
SET A NET: **bagida'waa** *vai;* set a net under the ice **ziibaaskobijige** *vai*
SET A PRICE: **onagindaaso** *vai;* set a price on s.o. **onagim** *vta;* set a price on s.t. **onagindan** *vti*
SET A PRICE OF A CERTAIN HEIGHT: set a price of a certain height on s.o. **apiitagim** *vta;* set a price of a certain height on s.t. **apiitagindan** *vti*
SET A SNARE: **agoodoo** *vai;* set a snare for s.o. **agoodaw** *vta*
SET DOWN: be set down **bagidinigaade, bagidinigaademagad** *vii;* **bagidinigaazo** *vai;* set s.o. down **bagidin** *vta;* set s.t. down **bagidinan** *vti;* set (s.t.) down for s.o. **bagidinamaw** *vta;* set things down **bagidinige** *vai*
SET DOWN OFF BACK: set s.o. down off one's back **bagidoom** *vta;* set s.t. down off one's back **bagidoondan** *vti*
SET DOWN PACK: set down one's pack **bagijiwane** *vai*
SET IN THE GROUND: set s.o. in the ground **badakishim** *vta;* set s.t. in the ground **badakisidoon** *vti2;* set things in the ground **badakisijige** *vai*
SET OUT OF THE WAY: be set out of the way **ikonigaade, ikonigaademagad** *vii;* **ikonigaazo** *vai;* set s.o. out of the way **ikon** *vta;* set s.t. out of the way **ikonan** *vti*
SET THE TABLE: **ozisinaagane** *vai*
SET TO COOL: set s.o. to cool **dakishim** *vta;* set s.t. to cool **dakisidoon** *vti2*
SUN SETS: set as the sun; *conjunct* **bangishimog** in the west **bangishimon /bangishimo-/** *vii*

SET
CERTAIN NUMBER OF SETS: a certain number of sets **daswewaan** *pc*

SET LINE
FISH WITH SET LINES: **bagidaabii** *vai*

SET UP
SET UP: set s.t. up **onakidoon** *vti2;* set s.o. up **onakizh /onakiN-/** *vta*
FINISH SETTING UP: finish setting s.o. up **giizhakizh /giizhakiN-/** *vta;* finish setting s.t. up **giizhakidoon** *vti2*
SET UP AS A FRAME: set s.t. up as a frame **onaakosidoon** *vti2*
SET UP CAMP: **gabeshi** *vai*

SETTLE DOWN
TELL TO SETTLE DOWN: tell s.o. to settle down **zagakim** *vta*

SEVEN
SEVEN: **niizhwaaswi** *nm;* **niizhwaaso-** *pv4;* seven (card) **niizhwaasoobii'igan, -ag** *na;* they are seven **niizhwaachinoon /niizhwaachin-/** *vii;* **niizhwaachiwag /niizhwaachi-/** *vai*
AND SEVEN: **ashi-niizhwaaswi** *nm;* **ashi-niizhwaaso-** *pv4*
SEVEN ACRES: **niizhwaaso-diba'igaans** *pc*
SEVEN DAYS: **niizhwaaso-giizhik** *pc;* **niizhwaasogon** *pc;* be seven days **niizhwaasogonagad** *vii*
SEVEN DAYS OLD: be seven days old **niizhwaasogonagizi** *vai*
SEVEN DOLLARS: **niizhwaaswaabik** *pc*
SEVEN EACH: **neniizhwaaswi** *nm*
SEVEN FEET: **niizhwaasozid** *pc*
SEVEN HOURS: **niizhwaaso-diba'igan** *pc*
SEVEN HUNDRED: **niizhwaaswaak** *nm*
SEVEN INCHES: **niizhwaasoninj** *pc*
SEVEN MILES: **niizhwaaso-diba'igan** *pc*
SEVEN MINUTES: **niizhwaaso-diba'igaans** *pc*
SEVEN MONTHS: **niizhwaaso-giizis** *pc*
SEVEN NIGHTS: **niizhwaaso-dibik** *pc*
SEVEN O'CLOCK: be seven o'clock **niizhwaaso-diba'iganed** *vii*
SEVEN PAIRS: **niizhwaaswewaan** *pc*
SEVEN SETS: **niizhwaaswewaan** *pc*
SEVEN THOUSAND: **niizhwaasosagoons** *nm*
SEVEN TIMES: **niizhwaaching** *pc*
SEVEN WEEKS: **niizhwaaso-anama'e-giizhik** *pc;* be seven weeks **niizhwaaso-anama'e-giizhigad** *pc*
SEVEN YEARS: **niizhwaaso-biboon** *pc;* be seven years **niizhwaaso-biboonagad** *vii*
SEVEN YEARS OLD: be seven years old **niizhwaaso-biboonagizi** *vai*

SEVENTEEN
SEVENTEEN: **ashi-niizhwaaswi** *nm;* **midaaswi ashi-niizhwaaswi** *nm*

SEVENTH
THE SEVENTH DAY OF THE MONTH: be the seventh day of the month **niizhwaasogonagizi** *vai*

SEVENTY
SEVENTY: **niizhwaasimidana** *nm*

SEW
SEW: **gashkigwaaso** *vai;* sew s.o. (e.g., a pair of pants) **gashkigwaazh /gashkigwaaN-/** *vta;* sew s.t. **gashkigwaadan** *vti*
MAKE A MISTAKE SEWING: **wanigwaaso** *vai;* make a mistake sewing on s.o. **wanigwaazh /wanigwaaN-/** *vta;* make a mistake sewing on s.t. **wanigwaadan** *vti*
SEW ON: sew s.o. on **agogwaazh /agogwaaN-/** *vta;* sew s.t. on **agogwaadan** *vti;* sew something on **agogwaaso** *vai*
SEW SHUT: sew s.o. shut **giboogwaazh /giboogwaaN-/** *vta;* sew s.t. shut **giboogwaadan** *vti*
SEW TOGETHER: **maawandoogwaaso** *vai;* sew s.o. together **maawandoogwaazh /maawandoogwaaN-/** *vta;* sew s.t. together (e.g., pieces for a quilt) **maawandoogwaadan** *vti*

SEWING MACHINE
SEWING MACHINE: **gashkigwaason, -ag** *na*

SEWING THREAD
SEWING THREAD: **gashkigwaasoneyaab, -iin** *ni*

SEWN
SEWN: be sewn **gashkigwaade, gashkigwaademagad** *vii;* **gashkigwaazo** *vai*

SHADE
SHADE: shade s.o. **agawaateshkaw** *vta;* shade s.t. **agawaateshkan** *vti;* there is shade **agawaateyaa, agawaateyaamagad** *vii*
IN SHADE: be in shade **agawaateshin** *vai;* **agawaatesin** *vii*
WINDOW SHADE: **gibiiga'iganiigin, -oon** *ni*

SHADOW
SHADOW: there is shadow **agawaateyaa, agawaateyaamagad** *vii*
CAST A SHADOW: cast a shadow on s.o. **agawaateshkaw** *vta;* cast a shadow on s.t. **agawaateshkan** *vti*
CAST A SHADOW FLYING: **agawaatese** *vai;* **agawaatese, agawaatesemagad** *vii*
IN SHADOW: be in shadow **agawaateshin** *vai;* **agawaatesin** *vii*

SHAKE
SHAKE: **baapagishkaa** *vai;* **baapagishkaa, baapagishkaamagad** *vii;* shake s.o. **bawin** *vta;* shake s.t. **bawinan** *vti*
SHAKE AWAKE: shake s.o. awake **amajwebin** *vta*
SHAKE HANDS: shake hands with s.o. **zaginiinjiin** *vta;* they shake hands with each other **zaginiinjiinidiwag /zaginiinjiinidi-/** *vai*
SHAKE HEAD: shake one's head at s.o. **wewebikwetaw** *vta*
SHAKE OUT: hold and shake s.o. out **baapaawin** *vta;* hold and shake s.t. out **baapaawinan** *vti;* shake s.o. out (as something sheet-like) **bawegin** *vta;* shake s.t. out (as something sheet-like) **baweginan** *vti*
SHAKE WINGS: shake one's wings **bapawaangeni** *vai*

SHAKING TENT
SHAKING TENT: **jiisakaan, -an** *ni*

PRACTICE DIVINATION IN A SHAKING TENT: **jiisakii** *vai*
SEER WHO USES A SHAKING TENT: **jiisakiiwinini, -wag** *na*

SHALLOW
SHALLOW: be shallow **baagwaa, baagwaamagad** *vii*

SHAME
FOR SHAME: for shame! **ise** *pc*

SHAMEFUL
SHAMEFUL: be shameful **agadendaagwad** *vii*

SHARE
SHARE: **maada'ookii** *vai;* share (s.t.) out to s.o. **maada'oozh /maada'ooN-/** *vta;* they share (s.t.) **maada'oonidiwag /maada'oonidi-/** *vai*

SHARP
SHARP: be sharp **giinaa, giinaamagad** *vii;* **giinizi** *vai*
FILE SHARP: file s.o. sharp **giiniboozh /giiniboo N-/** *vta;* file s.t. sharp **giiniboodoon** *vti2*

SHATTER
SHATTER: shatter (e.g., glass or china) **baasikaa, baasikaamagad** *vii;* shatter on impact **baasishin** *vai;* **baasisin** *vii;* shatter s.o. **baasishim** *vta;* shatter s.t. **baasisidoon** *vti2*
SHATTER BY HEAT: shatter s.o. by heat **baasiz /baasizw-/** *vta;* shatter s.t. by heat **baasizan** *vti*
SHATTER FROM HEAT: **baaside, baasidemagad** *vii;* **baasizo** *vai*
SHATTER USING SOMETHING: shatter s.o. using something **baasa' /baasa'w-/** *vta;* shatter s.t. using something **baasa'an** *vti;* shatter things using something **baasa'ige** *vai*
SHATTER WITH FOOT OR BODY: shatter s.o. with foot or body **baasikaw** *vta;* shatter s.t. with foot or body **baasikan** *vti*

SHAVE
SHAVE: **gaashkibaazo** *vai;* shave s.o. **gaashkibaazh /gaashkibaaN-/** *vta*

SHAWL
SHAWL: **moshwe, -g** *na*

SHE
SHE: she *third person singular personal pronoun* **wiin** *pr*

SHEATH
KNIFE SHEATH: **biinjikomaan, -an** *ni*

SHED
SHED: **ataasoowigamig, -oon** *ni*

SHEEP
SHEEP: **maanishtaanish, -ag** *na, also* **maanitaanish**

SHEEPSHEAD
SHEEPSHEAD: sheepshead (fish) **maanashigan, -ag** *na*

SHEEPSKIN
SHEEPSKIN: **maanishtaanishiwayaan** *ni*

SHEET
SHEET: **apishimoniigin, -oon** *ni;* **waabishkiigin, -oon** *ni*

SHELF
SHELF: **desaabaan, -an** *ni*

SHELL
SHELL: **es, -ag** *na*
MIDE SHELL: **miigis, -ag** *na*

SHELTER
SHELTER: **dabinoo'igan, -an** *ni*

SHERIFF
SHERIFF: **dakoniwewinini, -wag** *na*

SHIFT
SHIFT: shift s.o. (e.g., a car) **biindaabikibizh /biindaabikibiN-/** *vta*
GEAR SHIFT: **aandaabikinigan, -an** *ni*
SHIFT GEARS: **aandaabikinige** *vai;* **biindaabikibijige** *vai*

SHIFTLESS
SHIFTLESS: be shiftless **bagandizi** *vai*

SHIN
SHIN: my shin **nikakwan, -an /-kakwan-/** *nid*

SHINE
SHINE: shine (as something mineral) **waasaabikide, waasaabikidemagad** *vii;* **waasaabikizo** *vai;* shine s.o. **waasikwa'** *vta;* shine s.t. **waasikwa'an** *vti*
SHINE FOR GAME OR FISH: **waaswaa** *vai*

SHINNY
PLAY SHINNY: **bapasikawe** *vai*

SHINY
SHINY: be shiny (as something sheet-like) **waaseyiigad** *vii;* **waaseyiigizi** *vai*
MAKE SHINY: make s.o. shiny **waasiko'** *vta;* make s.t. shiny **waasikotoon** *vti2*

SHIP
SHIP: **ishkode-jiimaan, -an** *ni;* **naabikwaan, -an** *ni*

SHIRT
SHIRT: **babagiwayaan, -an** *ni, also* **bagiwayaan**
PUT ON SHIRT: put on one's shirt **biichibabagiwayaane** *vai*
TAKE OFF SHIRT: take off one's shirt **giichibabagiwayaane** *vai*
WEAR A SHIRT: **gigibabagiwayaane** *vai*

SHOE
SHOE: **makizin, -an** *ni*
MAKE SHOES: **makizinike** *vai*
PUT ON SHOES: put on one's shoes **babiichii** *vai*
TAKE OFF SHOES: take off one's shoes **gagiichii** *vai*
TENNIS SHOE: **babagiwayaanekizin, -an** *ni, also* **bagiwayaanekizin**

SHOELACE
SHOELACE: **makizineyaab, -iin** *ni*

SHOOT
SHOOT: shoot s.o. **baashkiz /baashkizw-/** *vta;* shoot s.t. **baashkizan** *vti;* shoot oneself **baashkizodizo** *vai;* shoot things **baashkizige** *vai*

HEARD SHOOTING: be heard shooting **madwezige** *vai*
PRACTICE SHOOTING: **gagweda'aakwe** *vai*
SHOOT ACCIDENTALLY: shoot s.o. accidentally **bichinaw** *vta;* shoot s.t. accidentally **bichinan** *vti;* shoot oneself accidentally **bichinaadizo** *vai;* shoot things accidentally **bichinaage** *vai*
SHOOT AND HIT: shoot and hit s.o. **miikonaw** *vta;* shoot and hit s.t. **miikonan** *vti*
SHOOT AND MISS: **bishkonaage** *vai;* shoot at s.o. and miss **bishkonaw** *vta;* shoot at s.t. and miss **bishkonan** *vti*
SHOOT AND WOUND: shoot and wound s.o. **maakinaw** *vta*
SHOOT IN A CERTAIN WAY OR PLACE: **ina'e** *vai*
SHOOT WITH AN ARROW: shoot s.o. with an arrow or other missile **bimo /bimw-/** *vta;* shoot s.t. with an arrow or other missile **bimodan** *vti;* shoot things with an arrow or other missile **bimojige** *vai*
SIGNAL BY SHOOTING: **nandwewezige** *vai*

SHOP
SHOP: **maa'ishkam** *vai2*

SHORE
ALONG THE SHORE: **jiigew** *pc;* **jiigibiig** *pc*
CARRY TO THE SHORE: carry s.o. to the shore **madaabiiwizh /madaabiiwiN-/** *vta;* carry s.t. to the shore **madaabiiwidoon** *vti2*
DRIVE ALONG THE SHORE: **jiigewebizo** *vai;* **jiigewedaabii'iwe** *vai*
GO ALONG THE SHORE: **bimaazhagaame** *vai;* **jiigewe** *vai*
GO TO THE SHORE: **madaabii** *vai*
ON THE SHORE: **agamiing** *pc*
PADDLE ALONG THE SHORE: **jiigewe'am** *vai2;* **jiigewe'o** *vai;* **jiigewekwazhiwe** *vai*
RUN ALONG THE SHORE: **jiigewebatoo** *vai;* **jiigeweyaazhagaamebatoo** *vai*
RUN TO THE SHORE: **madaabiibatoo** *vai*
SPEED ALONG THE SHORE: **jiigewebizo** *vai*
TAKE TO THE SHORE: take s.o. to the shore **madaabiiwizh /madaabiiwiN-/** *vta;* take s.t. to the shore **madaabiiwidoon** *vti2*
WALK ALONG SHORE TO A CERTAIN PLACE: **inaazhagaame** *vai*
WALK ALONG THE SHORE: **jiigeweyaazhagaame** *vai*

SHORT
SHORT: be short **dakoozi** *vai;* **dakwaa, dakwaamagad** *vii;* be short (as something mineral) **dakwaabikad** *vii;* **dakwaabikizi** *vai;* be short (as something sheet-like) **dakwegad** *vii;* **dakwegizi** *vai;* be short (as something stick- or wood-like) **dakwaakozi** *vai;* **dakwaakwad** *vii;* be short (as something string-like) **dakwaabiigad** *vii;* **dakwaabiigizi** *vai*
CUT SHORT: cut s.o. short (as something string-like) **dakwaabiigizh /dakwaabiigizhw-/** *vta;* cut s.t. short (as something string-like) **dakwaabiigizhan** *vti*
SHORT BOAT: be short (as a boat) **dakoonagad** *vii*
SHORT HAIR: have short hair **dadaakwaanikwe** *vai*
SHORT SLEEVES: have short sleeves **dadaakwanagweyaa, dadaakwanagweyaamagad** *vii*

SHORT
SHORT: be short of (s.t.) **manezi** *vai-o*
RUN SHORT: run short **noondese** *vai;* run short of s.o. **noondesa'** *vta;* run short of s.t. **noondesatoon** *vti2;* run short of things **noondesachige** *vai*
SHORT OF BREATH: be short of breath **akwanaamo** *vai*
SHORT OF TOBACCO: be short of tobacco **manepwaa** *vai*

SHORT WHILE
A SHORT WHILE: **noomag** *pc*

SHOT
TAKE A BAD SHOT: **maana'e** *vai*

SHOTGUN
SHOTGUN: **zhiishiibanwii-baashkizigan, -an** *ni*

SHOTGUN SHELL
SHOTGUN SHELL: **anwi, -in** *ni*

SHOULD
SHOULD: should *modal* **daa-** *pv1;* it should have been done **naanabem** *pc*

SHOULDER
SHOULDER: my shoulder **indinimaangan, -an /-dinimaangan-/** *nid*
HAUL ON SHOULDER: haul s.o. on one's shoulder **aawajinigaazh /aawajinigaaN-/** *vta;* haul s.t. on one's shoulder **aawajinigaadan** *vti;* haul things on one's shoulder **aawajinige** *vai*
WEAR ACROSS THE SHOULDER: wear s.t. across the shoulder **aazhooningwa'an** *vti*

SHOULDER BLADE
SHOULDER BLADE: my shoulder blade **indiniigan, -ag /-diniigan-/** *nad*

SHOUT
SHOUT: **biibaagi** *vai;* shout at s.o. **biibaagim** *vta;* shout at s.t. **biibaagindan** *vti*

SHOVE
SHOVE: shove s.o. **gaanjwebin** *vta;* shove s.t. **gaanjwebinan** *vti*
SHOVE ASIDE: shove aside s.o. **ikowebin** *vta;* shove aside s.t. **ikowebinan** *vti*
SHOVE AWAY USING SOMETHING: shove s.o. away using something **weba' /weba'w-/** *vta;* shove s.t. away using something **weba'an** *vti*
SHOVE OUT OF THE WAY WITH SOMETHING: shove s.o. out of the way with something **ikoweba' /ikoweba'w-/**

vta; shove s.t. out of the way with something **ikoweba'an** *vti*

SHOVE USING SOMETHING: shove s.o. using something **gaanjweba' /gaanjweba'w-/** *vta;* shove s.t. using something **gaanjweba'an** *vti;* shove things using something **gaanjweba'ige** *vai*

SHOVE WITH FOOT OR BODY: shove s.o. with foot or body **gaanjwebishkaw** *vta;* shove s.t. with foot or body **gaanjwebishkan** *vti*

SHOVEL

SHOVEL: **mangaanibaajigan, -an** *ni;* **mangaanibii** *vai;* shovel (for dirt) **gwaaba'waawangwaan, -an** *ni;* shovel s.o. (e.g., snow) **mangaanibaazh /mangaanibaaN-/** *vta;* shovel s.t. **mangaanibaadan** *vti;* shovel things **mangaanibaajige** *vai*

SHOW

SHOW: **waabanda'iwewin, -an** *ni;* show (s.t.) to s.o. **waabanda'** *vta;* show (s.t.) to people **waabanda'iwe** *vai*

MAKE SHOW: make s.o. show **naago'** *vta;* make s.t. show **naagotoon** *vti2*

SHRINK

SHRINK: **odaapishkaa, odaapishkaamagad** *vii;* **odaapishkaa** *vai*

SHRIVELLED

SHRIVELLED: be shrivelled **gaaskide, gaaskidemagad** *vii;* **gaaskizo** *vai*

SHUT

SHUT: be shut (as or as with something stick- or wood-like) **gibaakwa'igaade, gibaakwa'igaademagad** *vii;* shut s.o. (as or as with something stick- or wood-like) **gibaakwa' /gibaakwa'w-/** *vta;* shut s.t. (as or as with something stick- or wood-like) **gibaakwa'an** *vti*

FROZEN SHUT: be frozen shut **gibaakwadin** *vii;* **gibaakwaji** *vai*

GLUE SHUT: glue s.o. shut **gibokiwas** *vta;* glue s.t. shut **gibokiwasan** *vti*

GLUED SHUT: be glued shut **gibokiwasigaade, gibokiwasigaademagad** *vii;* **gibokiwasigaazo** *vai*

PULL SHUT: pull s.t. shut (as something stick- or wood-like) **gibaakobidoon** *vti2*

SEW SHUT: sew s.o. shut **giboogwaazh /giboogwaaN-/** *vta;* sew s.t. shut **giboogwaadan** *vti*

SHUT EYES: shut one's eyes **basangwaabi** *vai*

SLAM SHUT: slam s.t. shut (as something stick- or wood-like, e.g., a door) **gibaakowebinan** *vti*

TIE SHUT: tie s.o. shut **gashkapizh /gashkapiN-/** *vta;* tie s.t. shut **gashkapidoon** *vti2*

SHY

SHY: be a shy person **agajishki** *vai;* be shy **agaji** *vai;* be shy in front of s.o. **agajiitaw** *vta*

FEEL SHY: **agadendam** *vai2*

SHYPOKE

SHYPOKE: American bittern (locally called shypoke) **mooshka'osi, -wag** *na*

SIBLING

SIBLING: my sibling of the opposite sex (brother or sister) **indawemaa, -g /-dawemaaw-/** *nad*

YOUNGER SIBLING: my younger sibling (brother or sister) **nishiime, -yag /-shiimey-/** *nad*

SIBLING-IN-LAW

SIBLING-IN-LAW: my sibling-in-law of the opposite sex **niinim, -oog /-iinimw-/** *nad*

SICK

SICK: be sick **aakozi** *vai+o*

LOOK SICK: **aakoziiwinaagozi** *vai*

MAKE SICK: make s.o. sick (especially of a substance consumed); *inverse forms of:* **aakoziishkaw-** *vta*

PRETEND TO SICK: pretend to be sick **aakoziikaazo** *vai*

SICK IN A BODY PART: be sick (in s.t.) **aakozi** *vai+o*

SICK IN A CERTAIN WAY: be sick in a certain way **inaapine** *vai*

START TO GET SICK: **mizizi** *vai*

VERY SICK: be very sick **aanimizi** *vai;* **onzaamine** *vai*

SICKLY

CONSIDERED SICKLY: be considered sickly **aakoziiwendaagozi** *vai*

SICKNESS

SICKNESS: **aakoziwin, -an** *ni*

MUCH SICKNESS: there is much sickness **aakoziwinikaa, aakoziwinikaamagad** *vii*

SIDE

ALONG THE SIDE OF THE ROAD: **opimekana** *pc*

ALONG THE SIDE OF THE TRAIL: **opimekana** *pc*

DRIVE OFF TO THE SIDE: **bakebide, bakebidemagad** *vii;* **bakebizo** *vai*

FALL ON THE SIDE: **opimese** *vai*

GO OFF TO THE SIDE: **bake** *vai*

LAY ON SIDE: lay s.o. on side **opimeshim** *vai;* lay s.t. on side **opimesidoon** *vti2*

LIE ON SIDE: **opimesin** *vii;* lie on one's side **opimeshin** *vai*

ON THE SIDE: on the side of it **opime-ayi'ii** *pc, also* **opimeya'ii**

ON THIS SIDE: **ondaas** *pc;* on this side of it **ondaasayi'ii** *pc*

ON THIS SIDE OF THE FIRE: **ondaasishkode** *pc*

ON THIS SIDE OF THE ROAD: **ondaasikana** *pc*

ON THIS SIDE OF THE TRAIL: **ondaasikana** *pc*

ON THIS SIDE OF THE WATER: **ondaasagaam** *pc*

ROAD GOES OFF TO THE SIDE: go off to the side (as a road or trail) **bakemon /bakemo-/** *vii*

RUN OFF TO THE SIDE: **bakebatoo** *vai*

SPEED OFF TO THE SIDE: **bakebide, bakebidemagad** *vii;* **bakebizo** *vai*
TRAIL GOES OFF TO THE SIDE: go off to the side (as a road or trail) **bakemon /bakemo-/** *vii*

SIFT
SIFT: sift s.o. **zhaaboshkaas /zhaaboshkaasw-/** *vta;* sift s.t. **zhaaboshkaatoon** *vti2;* sift things **zhaaboshkaachige** *vai*

SIFTER
SIFTER: **zhaaboshkaachigan, -an** *ni*

SIGHT
DISTANT SIGHT: be a distant sight **naawinaagozi** *vai;* **naawinaagwad** *vii*
HAVE IN SIGHT: have s.o. in sight **debaabam** *vta;* have s.t. in sight **debaabandan** *vti*
IN SIGHT: be in sight **debaabaminaagozi** *vai;* **debaabaminaagwad** *vii*

SIGN
SIGN: sign s.t. **daangigwanenan** *vti;* sign things **daangigwanenige** *vai*

SIGN
SIGN: **agwaakwa'igan, -an** *ni*

SIGNAL
SIGNAL BY SHOOTING: **nandwewezige** *vai*

SIGNS
FIND SIGNS: find signs of s.o.'s presence **name'** *vta*
LEAVE SIGNS: leave signs of its presence **namesin** *vii;* leave signs of one's presence **nameshin** *vai;* **nametoo** *vai*

SILK
SILK: **zenibaanh, -yag** *na;* **zenibaawegin, -oon** *ni*

SILVER
SILVER: **zhooniyaawaabik, -oon** *ni*

SINCE
SINCE: **ako-** *pv3*

SINEW
SINEW: my sinew **injiitad, -an /-jiitad-/** *nid*

SING
SING: **nagamo** *vai;* sing for s.o. **nagamotaw** *vta*
GO ALONG SINGING: **bima'amaazo** *vai*
GO AWAY SINGING: **anima'amaazo** *vai*
PRACTICE SINGING: **goji-nagamo** *vai*
SING A CERTAIN WAY: **ina'am** *vai2*
SING AN ACCOMPANIMENT: sing an accompaniment (of women) **zhaabowe** *vai*
SING WAR SONGS: **bwaanzhii-nagamo** *vai*
START TO SING: **maajii'am** *vai2*

SINGE
SINGE: singe s.o. **banzo /banzw-/** *vta;* singe s.t. **banzan** *vti*

SINGED
SINGED: be singed **bande, bandemagad** *vii;* **banzo** *vai*

SINGING
SINGING: **nagamowin** *ni*

SINK
SINK: sink in water **gonzaabii, gonzaabiimagad** *vii*

SINKER
SINKER: net sinker **asinaab, -iig** *na;* sinker (fishing tackle) **gonzaabiishkoojigan, -an** *ni*

SISTER
OLDER SISTER: my older sister **nimisenh, -yag /-miseny-/** *nad*
YOUNGER SISTER: my younger sister **nishiime, -yag /-shiimey-/** *nad*

SISTER-IN-LAW
SISTER-IN-LAW: my (female's) sister-in-law **indaangwe, -g /-daangwew-/** *nad;* my (male's) sister-in-law **niinim, -oog /-iinimw-/** *nad*

SIT
SIT: **namadabi** *vai*
SIT A CERTAIN WAY: **inabi** *vai*
SIT ALONE: **nazhikewaakwadabi** *vai*
SIT ASIDE: **ikwabi** *vai*
SIT ASTRIDE: **desabi** *vai*
SIT AT THE END: **ishkwebi** *vai*
SIT COMFORTABLY: **minwabi** *vai*
SIT DOWN: **namadabi** *vai;* **wawenabi** *vai*
SIT FACING BACKWARDS: **animikwabi** *vai*
SIT FACING IN A CERTAIN WAY: **inaasamabi** *vai*
SIT FACING THIS WAY: **biidaasamabi** *vai*
SIT IN A CERTAIN PLACE: **abi** *vai*
SIT IN FRONT: **niigaanabi** *vai*
SIT ON THE BARE GROUND: **mitabi** *vai*
SIT OUT OF THE WAY: move out of the way sitting **ikwabi** *vai*
SIT QUIETLY: **goshkwaawaadabi** *vai*
SIT SIDE BY SIDE IN A ROW: they sit side by side in a row **niibidebiwag /niibidebi-/** *vai*
SIT STIFFLY: **jiibadabi** *vai*
SIT STILL: **bizaanaakwadabi** *vai*
SIT TOGETHER: they sit together **maawandoobiwag /maawandoobi-/** *vai*
SIT UNCOMFORTABLY: **maanabi** *vai*
SIT UP WITH AT A WAKE: sit up with s.o. (e.g., the deceased at a wake) **abiitaw** *vta*
SIT WITH: sit with s.o. **wiidabim** *vta*
SIT WITH BACK TO: sit with back to s.o. **animikwabiitaw** *vta*
SIT WITH LEGS CROSSED: **aazhoogaadebi** *vai*
TURN AROUND WHILE SITTING: **gwekabi** *vai*

SITUATED
SITUATED IN A CERTAIN PLACE: be situated in a certain place **dagon /dago-/** *vii*

SIX
SIX: **ingodwaaswi** *nm, also* **ningodwaaswi***; **ingodwaaso- /ningodwaaso-/** *pv4, also* **ningodwaaso***; six (card) **ingodwaasoobii'igan, -ag** *na, also* **ningodwaasoobii'igan***; **ningodwaasoobii'igan*, -ag** *na;* they are

six **ingodwaachinoon /ningodwaachin-/** *vii, also* **ningodwaachinoon***; **ingodwaachiwag /ningodwaachi-/** *vai, also* **ningodwaachiwag***

AND SIX: **ashi-ingodwaaso-** *pv4, also* **ashi-ningodwaaso-***; **ashi-ingodwaaswi** *nm, also* **ashi-ningodwaaswi***

SIX ACRES: **ingodwaaso-diba'igaans** *pc, also* **ningodwaaso-diba'igaans***

SIX DAYS: **ingodwaaso-giizhik** *pc, also* **ningodwaaso-giizhik***; **ingodwaasogon** *pc, also* **ningodwaasogon***; be six days **ingodwaasogonagad /ningodwaasogonagad-/** *vii, also* **ningodwaasogonagad***

SIX DAYS OLD: be six days old **ingodwaasogonagizi /ningodwaasogonagizi-/** *vai, also* **ningodwaasogonagizi***

SIX DOLLARS: **ingodwaaswaabik** *pc, also* **ningodwaaswaabik***

SIX EACH: **neningodwaaswi** *nm*

SIX HOURS: **ingodwaaso-diba'igan** *pc, also* **ningodwaaso-diba'igan***

SIX HUNDRED: **ingodwaaswaak** *nm, also* **ningodwaaswaak***

SIX INCHES: **ingodwaasoninj** *pc, also* **ningodwaasoninj***

SIX MILES: **ingodwaaso-diba'igan** *pc, also* **ningodwaaso-diba'igan***

SIX MINUTES: **ingodwaaso-diba'igaans** *pc, also* **ningodwaaso-diba'igaans***

SIX MONTHS: **ingodwaaso-giizis** *pc, also* **ningodwaaso-giizis***

SIX NIGHTS: **ingodwaaso-dibik** *pc, also* **ningodwaaso-dibik***

SIX O'CLOCK: be six o'clock **ingodwaaso-diba'iganed /ningodwaaso-diba'iganed-/** *vii, also* **ningodwaaso-diba'iganed***

SIX PAIRS: **ingodwaaswewaan** *pc, also* **ningodwaaswewaan***

SIX SETS: **ingodwaaswewaan** *pc, also* **ningodwaaswewaan***

SIX THOUSAND: **ingodwaasosagoons /ningodwaasosagoons-/** *pc, also* **ningodwaasosagoons***

SIX TIMES: **ingodwaaching** *pc, also* **ningodwaaching***

SIX WEEKS: **ingodwaaso-anama'e-giizhik** *pc, also* **ningodwaaso-anama'e-giizhik***; be six weeks **ingodwaaso-anama'e-giizhigad /ningodwaaso-anama'e-giizhigad-/** *vii, also* **ningodwaaso-anama'e-giizhigad***

SIX YEARS: **ingodwaaso-biboon** *pc, also* **ningodwaaso-biboon***; be six years **ingodwaaso-biboonagad /ningodwaaso-biboonagad-/** *vii, also* **ningodwaaso-biboonagad***

SIX YEARS OLD: be six years old **ingodwaaso-biboonagizi /ningodwaaso-biboonagizi-/** *vai, also* **ningodwaaso-biboonagaizi***

SIXTEEN

SIXTEEN: **ashi-ingodwaaswi** *nm, also* **ashi-ningodwaaswi***; **midaaswi ashi-ingodwaaswi** *nm, also* **midaaswi ashi-ningodwaaswi***

SIXTH

THE SIXTH DAY OF THE MONTH: be the sixth day of the month **ingodwaasogonagizi /ningodwaasogonagizi-/** *vai, also* **ningodwaasogonagizi***

SIXTY

SIXTY: **ingodwaasimidana** *nm, also* **ningodwaasimidana***

SIZE

CERTAIN SIZE: be a certain size **inigini** *vai;* **inigokwaa, inigokwaamagad** *vii;* be a certain size (as something mineral) **inigokwaabikad** *vii;* **inigokwaabikizi** *vai;* be a certain size (as something sheet-like) **inigokwegad** *vii;* **inigokwegizi** *vai;* be a certain size (as something stick- or wood-like) **inigokwaakozi** *vai;* **inigokwaakwad** *vii;* be a certain size (as something string-like) **inigokwaabiigad** *vii;* **inigokwaabiigizi** *vai*

SKATE

SKATE: **zhooshkwaada'aagan, -an** *ni;* **zhooshkwaada'e** *vai*

SKATE ABOUT: **babaamaada'e** *vai*

SKATE ALONG: **bimaada'e** *vai*

SKATE AWAY: **animaada'e** *vai*

SKATE FROM A CERTAIN PLACE: **ondaada'e** *vai*

SKATE HERE: **biidaada'e** *vai*

SKATE TO A CERTAIN PLACE: **inaada'e** *vai*

SKI

SKI: **zhooshkoshimaan, -ag** *na;* **zhooshkwaagim, -ag** *na;* **zhooshkwaagime** *vai*

SKILFUL

SKILFUL: be skilful **wawiingezi** *vai*

SKILFULLY

DO SKILFULLY: **wawiingechige** *vai*

MAKE SKILFULLY: make s.o. skilfully **wawiinge'** *vta;* make s.t. skilfully **wawiingetoon** *vti2*

SKILLED

SKILLED: being skilled at **nitaa-** *pv4;* be skilled at things **nitaawichige** *vai*

SKILLED IN SPEAKING OR SINGING: be skilled in speaking or singing **nitaawe** *vai*

SKIM

SKIM: skim s.t. **bima'an** *vti;* skim things **bima'ige** *vai*

SKIN

SKIN: my skin **inzhaga'ay /-zhaga'ay-/** *nid;* **nishkatay /-shkatay-/** *nid*

ITCHY SKIN: have itchy skin **gizhiibazhe** *vai*

SKIN

SKIN: skin s.o. **bakon** *vta;* skin things **bakonige** *vai*

SKIN KNEE: skin one's knee **bishagigidigweshin** *vai*

SKINNY

SKINNY: be skinny **bakaakadozo** *vai*

SKIRT

SKIRT: **giishkijiiwagooday, -an** *ni*

SKULL

SKULL: my skull **nishtigwaanigegan, -an /-shtigwaanigegan-/** *nid*

SKUNK

SKUNK: **zhigaag, -wag** *na*

SKY

SKY: **giizhig** *ni*

CLEAR SKY: be clear sky **mizhakwad** *vii*

IN THE SKY: **ishpiming** *pc;* be in the sky (e.g., a star, the sun, or the moon) **agoojin** *vai*

SLACK

SLACK: be slack **neshangaa, neshangaamagad** *vii;* **neshangizi** *vai;* be slack (as something string-like) **neshangaabiigad** *vii;* **neshangaabiigizi** *vai*

LIE SLACK: **neshangisin** *vii*

SLAM

SLAM SHUT: slam s.t. shut (as something stick- or wood-like, e.g., a door) **gibaakowebinan** *vti*

SLAP

SLAP ON FACE: slap s.o. on the face **basiingwe' /basiingwe'w-/** *vta*

SLAP ON HEAD: slap s.o. on the head **basindibe' /basindibe'w-/** *vta*

SLAP ON REAR: slap s.o. on the rear **basidiye' /basidiye'w-/** *vta*

SLAUGHTER

SLAUGHTER: slaughter s.o. **niiwana' /niiwana'w-/** *vta*

SLAVE

SLAVE: **awakaan, -ag** *na*

SLED

SLED: **biboonodaabaanens, -ag** *na;* **odaabaan, -ag** *na*

SLEEP

SLEEP: **nibaa** *vai*

DISTURB SLEEP: disturb s.o.'s sleep **wapaa'** *vta*

MAKE NOISE IN SLEEP: make noise in one's sleep **madwengwaam** *vai*

MAKE SLEEP: make s.o. sleep **nibe'** *vta;* make s.o. sleep *inverse forms of:* **nibeshkaw-** *vta*

PRETEND TO SLEEP: **nibekaazo** *vai*

SLEEP DEEPLY: **zoongingwashi** *vai*

SLEEP UNCOMFORTABLY: **maazhingwaam** *vai*

SLEEP WITH: sleep with s.o. **wiipem** *vta;* sleep with s.t. **wiipendan** *vti;* they sleep with each other **wiipendiwag /wiipendi-/** *vai*

SLEEP WITH CHILDREN PROTECTIVELY: **wiipemaawaso** *vai*

SLEEPY

SLEEPY: be sleepy **giikiibingwashi** *vai*

SLEEVE

SLEEVE: my sleeve **ninagway, -an /-nagway-/** *nid*

HAVE LONG SLEEVES: **gagaanonagweyaa, gagaanonagweyaamagad** *vii*

ROLL UP SLEEVE: roll up one's sleeve **ikwanagweni** *vai*

SHORT SLEEVES: have short sleeves **dadaakwanagweyaa, dadaakwanagweyaamagad** *vii*

SLEIGH

SLEIGH: **biboonodaabaan, -ag** *na;* **odaabaan, -ag** *na*

DRIVE ALONG IN A WAGON OR SLEIGH: drive along quickly in a wagon or sleigh **bimidaabiiba'igo** *vai*

SLEIGH BELL

SLEIGH BELL: **zhinawa'oojigan, -an** *ni*

SLICE

SLICE A CERTAIN WAY: slice s.o. a certain way **inikozh /inikoN-/** *vta;* slice s.t. a certain way **inikodan** *vti*

SLICE THICK: slice s.o. thick **gipagikozh /gipagikoN-/** *vta;* slice s.t. thick **gipagikodan** *vti*

SLICE THIN: slice s.o. thin **bibagikozh /bibagikoN-/** *vta;* slice s.t. thin **bibagikodan** *vti*

SLICK

SLICK: be slick **ozhaashaa, ozhaashaamagad** *vii;* **ozhaashizi** *vai;* **zhooshkozi** *vai;* **zhooshkwaa, zhooshkwaamagad** *vii*

SLIDE

SLIDE: slide s.o. with hand **zhooshkon** *vta;* slide s.t. with hand **zhooshkonan** *vti;* slide things **zhooshkonige** *vai*

GO SLIDING: **zhooshkwajiwe** *vai*

SLIDE OVER SITTING: **zhooshkwabi** *vai*

SLIDE WITH HAND: slide s.o. with hand **zhooshkon** *vta;* slide s.t. with hand **zhooshkonan** *vti*

SLINGSHOT

SLINGSHOT: **bimojigan, -an** *ni*

SLIP

SLIP AND FALL: **ozhaashishin** *vai*

SLIP AND FALL ON THE ICE: **ozhaashikoshin** *vai*

SLIP

SLIP: **biitawagoodaan, -an** *ni*

SLIPPERY

SLIPPERY: be slippery **ozhaashaa, ozhaashaamagad** *vii;* **ozhaashizi** *vai;* be slippery (as something mineral) **ozhaashaabikad** *vii;* **ozhaashaabikizi** *vai;* be slippery (as something stick- or wood-like) **ozhaashaakozi** *vai;* **ozhaashaakwad** *vii*

SLIPPERY ICE: there is slippery ice **ozhaashikwaa, ozhaashikwaamagad** *vii*

SLIPPERY ROAD: be slippery (as a road or trail) **ozhaashadamon /ozhaashadamo-/** *vii;* **zhooshkwadamon /zhooshkwadamo-/** *vii;* be slippery with

ice (as a road or trail) **ozhaashikwadamon /ozhaashikwadamo-/** *vii*
SLIPPERY TRAIL: be slippery (as a road or trail) **ozhaashadamon /ozhaashadamo-/** *vii;* **zhooshkwadamon /zhooshkwadamo-/** *vii;* be slippery with ice (as a road or trail) **ozhaashikwadamon /ozhaashikwadamo-/** *vii*

SLIPPERY ELM
SLIPPERY ELM: **ozhaashigob, -iig** *na*

SLIVER
SLIVER: sliver (in one's body) **gigaatigwaan, -an** *ni*
HAVE A SLIVER: **gigaatigwe** *vai*

SLOP PAIL
SLOP PAIL: **ziigwebinigewakik, -oog** *na*

SLOW
SLOW DOWN: slow down! **bekaa** *pc*

SLOWLY
DRIVE SLOWLY: **bejibide, bejibidemagad** *vii;* **bejibizo** *vai*
MOVE SLOWLY: **bejibide, bejibidemagad** *vii;* **bejibizo** *vai;* **bezikaa** *vai*
RUN SLOWLY: **bejibatoo** *vai;* **bezikaabatoo** *vai*
WALK SLOWLY: **bedose** *vai*

SMALL
SMALL: be small **agaasaa, agaasaamagad** *vii;* **agaashiinyi** *vai;* be small (as something ball-like) **agaasiminagad** *vii;* **agaasiminagizi** *vai;* be small (as something mineral) **agaasaabikad** *vii;* **agaasaabikizi** *vai;* be small (as something sheet-like) **agaasiigad** *vii;* **agaasiigizi** *vai;* be small (as something stick- or wood-like) **agaasaakozi** *vai;* **agaasaakwad** *vii;* be small (as something string-like) **agaasaabiigad** *vii;* **agaasaabiigizi** *vai*
APPEAR SMALL: **agaasaabaminaagozi** *vai;* **agaasaabaminaagwad** *vii*
LOOK SMALL: **agaasaabaminaagozi** *vai;* **agaasaabaminaagwad** *vii*
MAKE SMALL: make s.o. small **agaasi'** *vta;* make s.t. small **agaasaatoon** *vti2*
SMALL HILL: there is a small hill **agaasadinaa, agaasadinaamagad** *vii*
SMALL HOUSE: be small (as a room or house) **agaasate, agaasatemagad** *vii*
SMALL ROOM: be small (as a room or house) **agaasate, agaasatemagad** *vii*

SMALL OF BACK
SMALL OF BACK: the small of my back **inzhiigan /-zhiigan-/** *nid*

SMALLPOX
SMALLPOX: **mamakiziwin** *ni*

SMART
SMART: be smart **gikendaaso** *vai*

SMASH
SMASH: smash s.o. **biigoshim** *vta;* smash s.t. **biigosidoon** *vti2*

SMELL
SMELL: smell s.o. **biijimaam** *vta;* smell s.t. **biijimaandan** *vti*
GIVE OFF A SMELL: **biijimaagozi** *vai;* **biijimaagwad** *vii*
GIVE OFF A SMELL IN COOKING OR BURNING: **biijimaaso** *vai;* **biijimaate, biijimaatemagad** *vii*
GOOD SMELL: have a good smell **minomaagozi** *vai;* **minomaagwad** *vii*
HAVE SMELL A CERTAIN WAY: have s.o. smell a certain way to one **izhimaam** *vta;* have s.t. smell a certain way to one **izhimaandan** *vti*
LIKE THE SMELL: like the smell of s.o. **minomaam** *vta;* like the smell of s.t. **minomaandan** *vti*
RECOGNIZE BY SMELL: recognize s.o. by smell **nisidomaam** *vta;* recognize s.t. by smell **nisidomaandan** *vti*
SMELL A CERTAIN WAY: **izhimaagozi** *vai;* **izhimaagwad** *vii*
SMELL A CERTAIN WAY COOKING OR BURNING: **izhimaaso** *vai;* **izhimaate, izhimaatemagad** *vii*
SMELL BAD: **maazhimaagozi** *vai;* **maazhimaagwad** *vii*
SMELL BAD BURNING OR COOKING: **maazhimaaso** *vai;* **maazhimaate** *vii*
SMELL FOR: smell for s.o. **nandomaam** *vta;* smell for s.t. **nandomaandan** *vti*
SMELL GOOD: have a good smell **minomaagozi** *vai;* **minomaagwad** *vii*
SMELL GOOD BURNING OR COOKING: **minomaaso** *vai;* **minomaate, minomaatemagad** *vii*
SMELL RANCID: **zaatemaagozi** *vai;* **zaatemaagwad** *vii*
SMELL STRONG BURNING OR COOKING: **mashkawimaaso** *vai;* **mashkawimaate, mashkawimaatemagad** *vii*
TAKE A SMELL: take a smell of s.o. **gojimaam** *vta;* take a smell of s.t. **gojimaandan** *vti*

SMILE
SMILE: **zhoomiingweni** *vai;* smile at s.o. **zhoomiingwetaw** *vta*

SMOKE
SMOKE: **bakwene, bakwenemagad** *vii*
FILLED WITH SMOKE: be filled with smoke **mooshkineyaabate, mooshkineyaabatemagad** *vii*
FULL OF SMOKE: be full of smoke **gibwanaamode, gibwanaamodemagad** *vii*
GO UPWARDS AS SMOKE: **ombaabate** *vii*
SEND SMOKE TO A CERTAIN PLACE: **inaabasige** *vai*
SMOKE OUT: smoke s.o. out **gibwanaamoz /gibwanaamozw-/** *vta*
SUFFOCATE FROM SMOKE: **gibwanaamozo** *vai*

SMOKE
SMOKE: smoke (tobacco) **zagaswaa** *vai;* smoke s.o. (e.g., tobacco) **zagaswaazh**

/zagaswaaN-/ *vta;* smoke s.t. (e.g., kinnic-kinnick) **zagaswaadan** *vti*
GIVE A SMOKE: give a smoke to s.o. **zagaswe'** *vta*
NEED TO SMOKE: **manepwaa** *vai*
SHARE A SMOKE: share a smoke with s.o. (especially a pipe in a ceremony) **zagaswe'** *vta*

SMOKY
SMOKY: be smoky **bakwene, bakwenemagad** *vii*
SMOKY INSIDE: be smoky inside **giikanaamode, giikanaamodemagad** *vii*

SMOOTH
SMOOTH: be smooth **zhooshkozi** *vai;* **zhooshkwaa, zhooshkwaamagad** *vii;* be smooth (as something mineral) **zhooshkwaabikad** *vii;* **zhooshkwaabikizi** *vai;* be smooth (as something sheet-like) **zhooshkwegad** *vii;* **zhooshkwegizi** *vai;* be smooth (as something stick- or wood-like) **zhooshkwaakozi** *vai;* **zhooshkwaakwad** *vii*

SNAGGED
SNAGGED: get snagged on a limb **zagaakwajin** *vai*

SNAIL
SNAIL: **biimiskodisii, -g** *na;* **obiimiskodisii, -g** *na*

SNAKE
SNAKE: **ginebig, -oog** *na*

SNAKESKIN
SNAKESKIN: **ginebigwayaan, -ag** *na*

SNAP
SNAP OFF: snap s.o. off (e.g., something string-like) **bakibizh /bakibiN-/** *vta;* snap s.t. off (e.g., something string-like) **bakibidoon** *vti2*
SNAP OFF WITH FOOT OR BODY: snap s.o. off with foot or body (e.g., something string-like) **bakishkaw** *vta;* snap s.t. off with foot or body (e.g., something string-like) **bakishkan** *vti*

SNAPPING TURTLE
SNAPPING TURTLE: **mikinaak, -wag** *na;* **mishiikenh, -yag** *na*

SNARE
SNARE: **agoodwaagan, -an** *ni;* **nagwaagan, -an** *ni;* snare s.o. **nagwaazh /nagwaaN-/** *vta*
CHECK SNARES: check one's snares **naadagoodoo** *vai*
SET A SNARE: **agoodoo** *vai;* set a snare for s.o. **agoodaw** *vta*

SNARE WIRE
SNARE WIRE: **agoodwaaganeyaab, -iin** *ni;* **nagwaaganeyaab, -iin** *ni*

SNEAK
SNEAK UP: sneak up on s.o. **giimoozikaw** *vta*

SNEEZE
SNEEZE: **jaachaamo** *vai*

SNIFF
SNIFF: sniff s.o. **nandomaam** *vta;* sniff s.t. **nandomaandan** *vti*

SNIP
SNIP OFF: snip s.o. off (e.g., something string-like) **bakizh /bakizhw-/** *vta;* snip s.t. off (e.g., something string-like) **bakizhan** *vti*

SNOT
SNOT: **ziinikiigomaan** *na*

SNOUT
SNOUT: my snout **nishkoonzh** *nid*

SNOW
SNOW: **goon** *na;* **zoogipon /zoogipo-/** *vii*
BRUSH SNOW: brush snow off s.o. by hand **bawaagonen** *vta;* brush snow off s.o. using something **bawaagone' /bawaagone'w-/** *vta;* brush snow off s.t. by hand **bawaagonenan** *vti;* brush snow off s.t. using something **bawaagone'an** *vti*
CRUST ON THE SNOW: there is a crust on the snow **onaabanad** *vii*
DEEP SNOW: be deep snow **ishpaagonagaa, ishpaagonagaamagad** *vii*
HEAVY WET SNOW: there is heavy wet snow falling **zhakipon /zhakipo-/** *vii*
MUCH SNOW: be much snow **goonikaa, goonikaamagad** *vii*
SNOW GOES ALONG: **bimipon /bimipo-/** *vii*
SNOW IN LARGE FLAKES: **mamaangadepon /mamaangadepo-/** *vii*
SOFT SNOW: there is soft snow **zhakaagonagaa, zhakaagonagaamagad** *vii*
START TO SNOW: **maajipon /maajipo-/** *vii*
STOP SNOWING: **ishkwaapon /ishkwaapo-/** *vii*
UNDER THE SNOW: **anaamaagon** *pc, also* **anaamaagonag**

SNOWSHOE
SNOWSHOE: **aagim, -ag** *na;* **aagimose** *vai*
BEAR PAW SNOWSHOE: **makwasaagim, -ag** *na*

SNOWSHOE HARE
SNOWSHOE HARE: **waabooz, -oog** *na*

SNUFF
SNUFF: **biindaakwaan** *na*
CHEW SNUFF OR TOBACCO: **biindaakwe** *vai*

SO
SO: **izhi-** *pv3;* so... **oonh** *pc*
JUST SO: **eniwek** *pc*
SO IT IS SAID: **giiwenh** *pc*
SO THAT: **ji-** *pv1*
SO THE STORY GOES: **giiwenh** *pc*

SO MANY
SO MANY: **daso-** *pv3;* **daswi** *nm;* they are so many **dashiwag /dashi-/** *vai;* **dasinoon /dasin-/** *vii*
SO MANY ACRES: **daso-diba'igaans** *pc*
SO MANY BAGS: **dasooshkin** *pc*
SO MANY BUSHELS: so many bushels **daso-diba'iminaan** *pc*

SO MANY CUPFULS: **dasonaagaans** *pc*
SO MANY DAYS: **daso-giizhik** *pc;* **dasogon** *pc;* be so many days **dasogonagad** *vii*
SO MANY DOLLARS: **daswaabik** *pc*
SO MANY FEET: **dasozid** *pc*
SO MANY HOURS: **daso-diba'igan** *pc*
SO MANY INCHES: **dasoninj** *pc*
SO MANY MILES: **daso-diba'igan** *pc*
SO MANY MINUTES: **daso-diba'igaans** *pc*
SO MANY MONTHS: **daso-giizis** *pc*
SO MANY NIGHTS: **daso-dibik** *pc*
SO MANY PAIRS: **daswewaan** *pc*
SO MANY POUNDS: **daso-dibaabiishkoojigan** *pc*
SO MANY SETS: so many sets **daswewaan** *pc*
SO MANY THOUSAND: **dasosagoons** *nm*
SO MANY TIMES: **dasing** *pc*
SO MANY WEEKS: **daso-anama'e-giizhik** *pc;* be so many weeks **daso-anama'e-giizhikwagad** *vii, also* **daswanama'e-giizhikwagad**
SO MANY YEARS: **daso-biboon** *pc;* **daso-gikinoonowin** *pc;* be so many years **daso-biboonagad** *vii*
SO MANY YEARS OLD: be so many years old **daso-biboonagizi** *vai*

SOAK
SOAK: soak s.o. **agonjim** *vta;* soak s.t. **agonjidoon** *vti2*
PUT IN TO SOAK: be put in to soak **agonjijigaade, agonjijigaademagad** *vii;* **agonjijigaazo** *vai;* put s.o. in to soak **agonjim** *vta;* put s.t. in to soak **agonjidoon** *vti2*

SOAP
SOAP: **giziibiiga'igan, -an** *ni*

SOBER
SOBER UP: **aatebii** *vai*

SOCIAL WORKER
SOCIAL WORKER: **ashangewinini, -wag** *na;* social worker (female) **ashangewikwe, -g** *na*

SOCK
SOCK: **azhigan, -an** *ni*
PUT ON SOCKS: put on one's socks **biitazhigane** *vai*
TAKE OFF SOCKS: take off one's socks **giitazhigane** *vai*
WEAR SOCKS: **gigazhigane** *vai*

SOD HOUSE
SOD HOUSE: **akiiwigamig, -oon** *ni*

SODA
BAKING SODA: **ombizigan** *ni*

SOFT
SOFT: be soft **nookaa, nookaamagad** *vii;* **nookizi** *vai;* be soft (as something sheet-like) **nookiigad** *vii;* **nookiigizi** *vai*
HAVE A SOFT VOICE: **bedowe** *vai*
SOFT SNOW: there is soft snow **zhakaagonagaa, zhakaagonagaamagad** *vii*

SOFT DRINK
SOFT DRINK: **menwaagamig, -in** *ni-pt;* **waashkobaagamig, -in** *ni-pt*

SOFTENED
SOFTENED: be softened in water **nookaabaawe** *vai;* **nookaabaawe, nookaabaawemagad** *vii*

SOLDIER
SOLDIER: **zhimaaganish, -ag** *na*

SOLE
SOLE: my sole **ninagaakizid, -an /-nagaakizid-/** *nid*

SOLID
SOLID: be solid **zoongan** *vii;* **zoongizi** *vai*
MAKE SOLID: make s.o. solid **zoongi'** *vta;* make s.t. solid **zoongitoon** *vti2*

SOME
SOME: **aanind** *pc*
FOR SOME TIME: **gomaapii** *pc*
SOME AMOUNT: **gomaa** *pc*
SOME DISTANCE: **gomaapii** *pc*

SOMEBODY
SOMEBODY: somebody *animate indefinite* **awiya, -g** *pr, also* **awiiya**

SOMEONE
SOMEONE: **aya'aa, -g** *pr*

SOMETHING
SOMETHING: **ayi'ii, -n** *pr;* something *inanimate indefinite* **gegoo** *pr*

SOMETIME
SOMETIME: **ingoding** *pc, also* **ningoding***

SOMETIMES
SOMETIMES: **ayaangodinong** *pc, also* **aangodinong**

SOMEWHAT
SOMEWHAT: **eniwek** *pc*

SOMEWHERE
SOMEWHERE: **ingoji** *pc, also* **ningoji***

SON
SON: my son **ingozis, -ag /-gozis-/** *nad, also* **ingos, ingwizis***

SON-IN-LAW
SON-IN-LAW: **na'aangish, -iig** *na;* my son-in-law **niningwan, -ag** *nad*

SONG
SONG: **nagamon, -an** *ni;* **nagamowin** *ni*
DANCE SONG: **niimi'idii-nagamon, -an** *ni*
MOCCASIN GAME SONG: **makizinataage-nagamon, -an** *ni*
SPIRITUAL SONG: **manidoo-nagamon, -an** *ni*

SOON
SOON: **wayiiba** *pc; also* **wiiba***

SORE
SORE: be sore **gaagiidizi** *vai*
SORE ARM: have a sore arm **gaagiijinike** *vai*
SORE BACK: have a sore back **gaagiidaawigan** *vai*
SORE ELBOW: have a sore elbow **gaagiijidooskwan** *vai*
SORE FINGER: have a sore finger **gaagiijininjii** *vai*
SORE FOOT: have a sore foot **gaagiijizide** *vai*
SORE HAND: have a sore hand **gaagiijininjii** *vai*
SORE LEG: have a sore leg **gaagiijigaade** *vai*

SORE THROAT: have a sore throat **wiisagigonewe** *vai*

SORES

SORES: have sores **omigii** *vai*

SORROWFUL

SORROWFUL: be sorrowful **osidaawendam** *vai2*

SORT

SORT: sort *animate* **dino, -wag** *pr, also* **dinowa**; sort *inanimate* **dino, -wan** *pr, also* **dinowa**

SOUL

SOUL: my soul **injichaag, -wag /-jichaagw-/** *nad*

SOUND

LIKE THE SOUND: **minotam** *vai2*

MAKE SOUNDS: make sounds on s.t. **madwewetoon** *vti2;* make sounds on things **madwewechige** *vai*

SOUND FOREIGN: **mayagitaagozi** *vai*

SOUND GOOD: **minotaagozi** *vai;* **minotaagwad** *vii*

SOUND STRANGE: **mayagitaagozi** *vai*

SOUNDING GOOD: hear s.o. sounding good **minotaw** *vta;* hear s.t. sounding good **minotan** *vti*

SOUP

SOUP: **naboob, -iin** *ni*

BEAN SOUP: **mashkodesiminaaboo** *ni*

CHICKEN SOUP: **baaka'aakwenhwaaboo** *ni*

CORN SOUP: **mandaaminaaboo** *ni*

DUMPLING SOUP: **bisigadanaaboo** *ni*

FISH SOUP: **giigoonhwaaboo** *ni*

MAKE SOUP: **naboobiike** *vai*

PEA SOUP: **anijiiminaaboo** *ni*

RABBIT SOUP: **waaboozwaaboo** *ni*

SOUR

SOUR: be sour **zhiiwan** *vii;* **zhiiwizi** *vai;* be sour (as a liquid) **zhiiwaagamin /zhiiwaagami-/** *vii*

SOURDOUGH

SOURDOUGH: **zhiiwisijigan, -ag** *na*

SOUTH

SOUTH: **zhaawan** *pc*

IN THE SOUTH: **zhaawanong** *pc*

SOUTH WIND: **zhaawani-noodin** *ni*

TO THE SOUTH: **zhaawanong** *pc*

SPACE

SPACE: be space **dawaa, dawaamagad** *vii*

SPADE

SPADE SUITE CARD: **biig, -wag** *na*

SPANK

SPANK: spank s.o. **bapasidiye' /bapasidiye'w-/** *vta*

SPARE

SPARE: spare s.o. **manaaji'** *vta;* spare s.t. **manaajitoon** *vti2*

SPAWN

SPAWN: they spawn **aamiwag /aami-/** *vai*

SPEAK

SPEAK: **gaagiigido** *vai;* **giigido** *vai;* speak to s.o. **ganoozh /ganooN-/** *vta;* speak to s.t. **ganoodan** *vti;* **idan** *vti;* they speak to each other **ganoonidiwag /ganoonidi-/** *vai*

COME SPEAKING: **biidwewidam** *vai2*

GO AWAY SPEAKING: **animwewidam** *vai2*

HAVE DIFFICULTY SPEAKING: **maazhigiizhwe** *vai*

HEARD SPEAKING AT A DISTANCE: be heard speaking at a distance **debwewidam** *vai2*

HEARD SPEAKING GOING TO A CERTAIN PLACE: be heard speaking going to a certain place **inwewidam** *vai*

HEARD SPEAKING IN A CERTAIN PLACE: be heard speaking in a certain place **danwewidam** *vai2*

MAKE A MISTAKE SPEAKING: **wanigiizhwe** *vai*

SPEAK A CERTAIN LANGUAGE: **inwe** *vai*

SPEAK A SCANDINAVIAN LANGUAGE: **agongosimo** *vai*

SPEAK A STRANGE LANGUAGE: **mayagwe** *vai*

SPEAK AN INDIAN LANGUAGE: speak an Indian language (especially Ojibwe) to s.o. **anishinaabemotaw** *vta;* speak an Indian language (especially Ojibwe) **anishinaabemo** *vai*

SPEAK CORRECTLY: **gwayakowe** *vai*

SPEAK CREE: **omashkiigoomo** *vai*

SPEAK DAKOTA: **bwaanimo** *vai;* speak Dakota to s.o. **bwaanimotaw** *vta*

SPEAK ENGLISH: **zhaaganaashiimo** *vai;* speak English to s.o. **zhaaganaashiimotaw** *vta*

SPEAK FRENCH: **wemitigoozhiimo** *vai*

SPEAK IN A CERTAIN WAY: they speak to each other in a certain way **idiwag /idi-/** *vai*

SPEAK IN AN INDIAN LANGUAGE: speak in an Indian language (especially in Ojibwe) **anishinaabe-gaagiigido** *vai*

SPEAK LOUD: **gizhiiwe** *vai*

SPEAK NASTILY: **wiinigiizhwe** *vai*

SPEAK ODAWA: speak Odawa (Ottawa) **odaawaamo** *vai*

SPEAK OJIBWE: **ojibwemo** *vai;* speak Ojibwe to s.o. **ojibwemotaw** *vta;* speak an Indian language (especially Ojibwe) to s.o. **anishinaabemotaw** *vta;* speak an Indian language (especially Ojibwe) **anishinaabemo** *vai*

SPEAK SO: **ikido** *vai;* speak so to s.o. **izhi /iN-/** *vta*

SPEAK WELL: **minowe** *vai*

SPEAKER

SPEAKER: speaker (for others) **aanikanootaagewinini, -wag** *na*

SPEAR

SPEAR: **zhimaagan, -an** *ni;* spear s.t. **badaka'an** *vti;* spear things **badaka'ige** *vai*

FISH SPEAR: **anit, -iin** *ni*

FISH THROUGH THE ICE WITH SPEAR: **akwa'waa** *vai*

SPECTATOR

SPECTATOR: be a spectator **waabange** *vai*

SPEECH
SPEECH: **giigidowin, -an** *ni*
HAVE ABNORMAL SPEECH: **maazhigiizhwe** *vai*
SPEED
ARRIVE SPEEDING: **bagamibide, bagamibidemagad** *vii;* **bagamibizo** *vai*
DRIVE AT A CERTAIN SPEED: **apiichibide, apiichibidemagad** *vii;* **apiichibizo** *vai*
FLY AT A CERTAIN SPEED: **apiichibide, apiichibidemagad** *vii;* **apiichibizo** *vai*
GO A CERTAIN SPEED: **apiizikaa** *vai*
GROW AT A CERTAIN SPEED: **apiichigi** *vai;* **apiichigin** *vii*
HEARD SPEEDING ALONG: be heard speeding along **bimwewebide, bimwewebidemagad** *vii;* **bimwewebizo** *vai*
HEARD SPEEDING HERE: be heard speeding here **biidwewebide, biidwewebidemagad** *vii;* **biidwewebizo** *vai*
RUN AT A CERTAIN SPEED: **apiichibatoo** *vai;* run at a certain speed (e.g., a machine) **apiichibide, apiichibidemagad** *vii;* **apiichibizo** *vai*
SPEED ABOUT: **babaamibide, babaamibidemagad** *vii;* **babaamibizo** *vai*
SPEED ALONG: **bimibide, bimibidemagad** *vii;* **bimibizo** *vai*
SPEED ALONG THE SHORE: **jiigewebizo** *vai*
SPEED AWAY: **animibide, animibidemagad** *vii;* **animibizo** *vai*
SPEED AWAY MAKING NOISE: **animwewebide, animwewebidemagad** *vii;* **animwewebizo** *vai*
SPEED FAST: **gizhiibide, gizhiibidemagad** *vii;* **gizhiibizo** *vai*
SPEED FROM A CERTAIN PLACE: **onjibide, onjibidemagad** *vii;* **onjibizo** *vai*
SPEED HERE: **biijibide, biijibidemagad** *vii;* **biijibizo** *vai*
SPEED IN: drive in **biinjibide, biinjibidemagad** *vii;* **biinjibizo** *vai*
SPEED INSIDE: **biindigebide, biindigebidemagad** *vii;* **biindigebizo** *vai*
SPEED OFF: **maajiibide, maajiibidemagad** *vii;* **maajiibizo** *vai*
SPEED OFF TO THE SIDE: **bakebide, bakebidemagad** *vii;* **bakebizo** *vai*
SPEED SUDDENLY INTO VIEW: **zaagewebide, zaagewebidemagad** *vii;* **zaagewebizo** *vai*
SPEED TO A CERTAIN PLACE: **ipide, ipidemagad** *vii;* **ipizo** *vai*
SPEED UPWARDS: **ombibide, ombibidemagad** *vii;* **ombibizo** *vai*
STOP SPEEDING: **noogibide, noogibidemagad** *vii;* **noogibizo** *vai*
WIND HAS A CERTAIN SPEED: the wind has a certain speed **apiitaanimad** *vii*

SPEND
SPEND EVERYTHING: **jaaginige** *vai*
SPEND TIME
SPEND TIME IN A CERTAIN PLACE: **dazhitaa** *vai;* **dazhiike** *vai*
SPIDER
SPIDER: **asabikeshiinh, -yag** *na*
SPILE
SPILE: spile (for sugaring) **negwaakwaan, -an** *ni*
SPILL
SPILL: spill s.t. **ziiginan** *vti;* **ziigwebinan** *vti;* spill things **ziiginige** *vai*
SPILL OUT: **ziigise, ziigisemagad** *vii*
SPIN
SPIN: **gizhibaabide, gizhibaabidemagad** *vii;* **gizhibaabise** *vai;* **gizhibaabise, gizhibaabisemagad** *vii;* **gizhibaabizo** *vai*
SPIRIT
SPIRIT: **jiibay, -ag** *na;* **manidoo, -g** *na;* be a spirit **manidoowi** *vai;* my spirit **injichaag, -wag /-jichaagw-/** *nad*
GREAT SPIRIT: **gichi-manidoo, -g** *na*
SPIRITUAL
SPIRITUAL NATURE: have a spiritual nature **manidoowaadizi** *vai*
SPIRITUAL POWER
SPIRITUAL POWER: have spiritual power **manidooke** *vai;* take on spiritual power by one's own authority **manidookaazo** *vai*
SPIRITUAL SONG
SPIRITUAL SONG: **manidoo-nagamon, -an** *ni*
SPIT
SPIT: **ziko** *vai;* **zikowin** *ni;* spit on s.o. **zikwaazh /zikwaaN-/** *vta;* spit on s.t. **zikwaadan** *vti;* spit on things **zikwaajige** *vai*
SPLASH
SPLASH: splash s.o. **zaswebiiga'andaw** *vta*
SPLIT
SPLIT: be split **daashkaa, daashkaamagad** *vii;* split (as something of wood) **daashkigishkaa** *vai;* **daashkigishkaa, daashkigishkaamagad** *vii*
SPLIT APART: **daashkikaa, daashkikaamagad** *vii*
SPLIT BY CHOPPING: split s.o. by chopping (as something of wood) **daashkiga' /daashkiga'w-/** *vta;* split s.t. by chopping (as something of wood) **daashkiga'an** *vti*
SPLIT BY CUTTING: split s.o. by cutting **daashkizh /daashkizhw-/** *vta;* split s.t. by cutting **daashkizhan** *vti*
SPLIT FIREWOOD: **daashkiga'ise** *vai*
SPLIT LENGTHWISE WITH HANDS: split s.o. lengthwise with hands **daashkibizh /daashkibiN-/** *vta;* split s.t. lengthwise with hands **daashkibidoon** *vti2*
SPLIT WOOD: **daashkiga'ige** *vai*
SPOIL
SPOIL: **banaajishin** *vai;* **banaajisin** *vii;* spoil s.o. **banaaji'** *vta;* **nishwanaaji'** *vta;* spoil

s.t. **banaajitoon** *vti2;* **nishwanaajitoon** *vti2;* spoil things **nishwanaajichige** *vai*

SPOILED
SPOILED: be spoiled **banaadad** *vii;* **banaadizi** *vai*

SPONTANEOUSLY
SPONTANEOUSLY: **biinizikaa** *pc*

SPOOL
SPOOL: spool (for thread) **asabaabiiwaatig, -oon** *ni*

SPOON
SPOON: **emikwaanens, -an** *ni;* ladle **emikwaan, -an** *ni*
WOODEN SPOON: **mitigwemikwaan, -an** *ni*

SPOON FEED
SPOON FEED: spoon feed s.o. **zhakamodaw** *vta*
SPOON FEED A LIQUID: spoon feed s.o. a liquid **ziigana' /ziigana'w-/** *vta*

SPOTTED
SPOTTED: be spotted **gidagaa, gidagaamagad** *vii;* **gidagizi** *vai;* be spotted (as something sheet-like) **gidagiigad** *vii;* **gidagiigizi** *vai*

SPOUSE
SPOUSE: my spouse **niwiidigemaagan, -ag /-wiidigemaagan-/** *na*

SPRAIN
SPRAIN ARM: sprain one's arm **zeginikeshin** *vai*
SPRAIN FOOT: sprain one's foot **zegizideshin** *vai*
SPRAIN LEG: sprain one's leg **zegigaadeshin** *vai*

SPREAD
SPREAD ALL OVER: **miziweshkaa, miziweshkaamagad** *vii*
SPREAD THE NEWS ABOUT: **babaamaajimo** *vai*
SPREAD USING SOMETHING: spread s.o. using something **zhizhoo' /zhizhoo'w-/** *vta;* spread s.t. using something **zhizhoo'an** *vti;* spread things using something **zhizhoo'ige** *vai*

SPREAD OUT
SPREAD OUT: spread s.o. out **zhingaden** *vta;* spread s.t. out **zhingadenan** *vti*
LAY SPREAD OUT: lay s.o. spread out **zhingadeshim** *vta;* lay s.t. spread out **zhingadesidoon** *vti2*
LIE SPREAD OUT: **zhingadeshin** *vai;* **zhingadesin** *vii*

SPRING
SPRING: be spring **ziigwan** *vii*
LAST SPRING: **ziigwanong** *pc*
SPEND THE SPRING: spend the spring somewhere **ziigwanishi** *vai*
SPRING BEFORE LAST: **awas-ziigwanong** *pc*

SPRING
SPRING: spring (water source) **mookijiwanibiig** *ni*

SPRINGY
SPRINGY GROUND: be springy ground **dootooban** *vii*

SPRINKLING
SPRINKLING RAIN: be sprinkling rain **awanibiisaa, awanibiisaamagad** *vii*

SPROUT
SPROUT: **zaagakii** *vai;* **zaagakii, zaagakiimagad** *vii;* **zaagigi** *vai;* **zaagigin** *vii*

SPRUCE
WHITE SPRUCE: **gaawaandag, -oog** *na*

SPRUCE ROOT
SPRUCE ROOT: **wadab, -iig** *na*
BASKET OF SPRUCE ROOT: **wadabiimakak, -oon** *ni*

SPY
SPY: **giimaabi** *vai;* spy on s.o. **giimaabam** *vta*

SQUARE
SQUARE: be square **gakakaa, gakakaamagad** *vii;* **gakakizi** *vai;* be square (as something mineral) **gakakaabikad** *vii;* **gakakaabikizi** *vai;* be square (as something sheet-like) **gakakiigad** *vii;* **gakakiigizi** *vai;* be square (as something stick- or wood-like) **gakakaakozi** *vai;* **gakakaakwad** *vii*
HAVE A SQUARE PATTERN: **gakakishin** *vai;* **gakakisin** *vii*
MAKE SQUARE: make s.o. square **gakaki'** *vta;* make s.t. square **gakakitoon** *vti2*

SQUASH
SQUASH: **okanakosimaan, -an** *ni;* **okosimaan, -an** *ni*

SQUEAK
SQUEAK: **giziibwewe** *vai;* **giziibwewe, giziibwewemagad** *vii;* squeak in motion **giziibweweshkaa** *vai;* **giziibweweshkaa, giziibweweshkaamagad** *vii*

SQUEEZE
SQUEEZE: squeeze s.o. **maagobizh /maagobiN-/** *vta;* **ziinibizh /ziinibiN-/** *vta;* squeeze s.t. **maagobidoon** *vti2;* **ziinibidoon** *vti2*

SQUIRREL
SQUIRREL: red squirrel **ajidamoo, -g** *na*
FLYING SQUIRREL: **zhagashkaandawe, -g** *na*
GREY SQUIRREL: **misajidamoo, -g** *na*

STAB
STAB: stab s.o. **bazhiba' /bazhiba'w-/** *vta;* stab s.t. **bazhiba'an** *vti*

STACK
STACK: stack s.o. **okoshim** *vta;* stack s.o. (as something stick- or wood-like) **okwaakoshim** *vta;* stack s.t. **okosidoon** *vti2*

STAGE FRIGHT
STAGE FRIGHT: have stage fright **wanaanimizi** *vai*

STAIRWAY
STAIRWAY: **akwaandawaagan, -an** *ni*

STALLION
STALLION: **naabesim, -oog** *na*

STAMP
POSTAGE STAMP: **oshtigwaanens, -an** *ni*
STAND
STAND: **niibawi** *vai*
STAND AT THE END: **ishkwegaabawi** *vai*
STAND BACK: **azhegaabawi** *vai*
STAND FACING A CERTAIN WAY: **inaasamigaabawi** *vai*
STAND IN FRONT: **niigaanigaabawi** *vai*
STAND IN PLACE OF: stand in place of s.o. **aanikeshkaw** *vta*
STAND LEANING AGAINST: stand leaning against something **aatwaakogaabawi** *vai*
STAND OUT OF THE WAY: **ikogaabawi** *vai*
STAND QUIETLY: **bizaanigaabawi** *vai*
STAND STIFFLY: **jiibadaakogaabawi** *vai*
STAND STRAIGHT: **gwayakogaabawi** *vai*
STAND UP: **bazigwii** *vai;* make s.o. stand up **niibawi'** *vta;* make s.t. stand up **niibawitoon** *vti2*
STAND UP FROM A SURFACE: **badakide, badakidemagad** *vii;* **badakizo** *vai*
STAND UP SUDDENLY: **bazigonjise** *vai*
STAND WITH THE BACK OUT: **animikogaabawi** *vai*
STOP AND STAND IN PLACE: stop and stand in place **noogigaabawi** *vai*
TURN STANDING: turn while standing **gwekigaabawi** *vai;* **washkigaabawi** *vai*
STAR
STAR: **anang, -oog** *na*
START
START: **maajise** *vai;* **maajise, maajisemagad** *vii;* **maajii-** *pv4;* start (as an event) **maadakamigad** *vii;* start (in some event) **maadakamigizi** *vai;* start s.o. (e.g., a car) **maadwewebizoni'** *vta;* start s.o. (e.g., a car, a clock) **maajiishkaa'** *vta*
START A JOURNEY: **maadaadizi** *vai*
START A MONTH: **maadaginzo** *vai*
START AN ACTIVITY: **maajitaa** *vai*
START EATING: **maadanjige** *vai*
START OFF: **maajaa** *vai, also* **ani-maajaa; maajii-** *pv4;* they start off in a group **maadaawanidiwag /maadaawanidi-/** *vai*
START OFF ON THE ICE: **maajiiyaadagaako** *vai*
START TO DRIP: **maajigaa, maajigaamagad** *vii*
START TO FLEE: **maajiiba'iwe** *vai*
START TO FLOW: **maajijiwan** *vii*
START TO GET SICK: **mizizi** *vai*
START TO GROW: **maajiigi** *vai;* **maajiigin** *vii*
START TO LEAK: **maajigaa, maajigaamagad** *vii*
START TO MAKE: start to make s.o. **maaji'** *vta;* start to make s.t. **maajitoon** *vti2*
START TO MOVE: **maajiishkaa, maajiishkaamagad** *vii*
START TO RAIN: **maajibiisaa, maajibiisaamagad** *vii*
START TO RUN: **maajiibatoo** *vai;* start to run (as a machine) **maajiibide, maajiibidemagad** *vii;* **maajiibizo** *vai*
START TO SING: **maajii'am** *vai2*
START TO SNOW: **maajipon /maajipo-/** *vii*
START TO TELL: **maadaajimo** *vai;* start to tell of s.o. **maadaajim** *vta;* start to tell of s.t. **maadodan** *vti;* start to tell (s.t.) to s.o. **maadaajimotaw** *vta*
START TO WORK: **maadanoki** *vai;* start to work on s.o. **maadanokaazh /maadanokaaN-/** *vta;* **maajiikaw** *vta;* start to work on s.t. **maadanokaadan** *vti;* **maajiikan** *vti*
STARTLED
STARTLED: be startled **goshkokaa** *vai*
STARVE
STARVE: **gawanaandam** *vai2*
STATUE
STATUE: **mazinichigan, -ag** *na*
STAY
STAY BEHIND: **ishkwii** *vai*
STAY IN A CERTAIN PLACE: **dazhiike** *vai*
STAY OVERNIGHT: stay overnight with s.o. **nibendaw** *vta;* stay overnight with people **nibendaage** *vai*
STAY WITH: stay with s.o. **wiij'ayaaw** *vta, also* **wiiji-ayaaw**
STEADY
STEADY: steady s.o. **minjimin** *vta;* steady s.o. with foot or body **minjimishkaw** *vta;* steady s.t. **minjiminan** *vti;* steady s.t. with foot or body **minjimishkan** *vti;* steady (s.t.) for s.o. **minjiminamaw** *vta*
STEAL
STEAL: steal (s.t.) **gimoodi** *vai+o;* steal from s.o. **gimoodim** *vta;* they steal from each other **gimoodindiwag /gimoodindi-/** *vai*
STEAM
STEAM: **baashkinede, baashkinedemagad** *vii;* **baashkinezo** *vai*
STEAMBOAT
STEAMBOAT: **ishkode-jiimaan, -an** *ni*
STEEL
STEEL: **manidoo-biiwaabik** *ni*
STEEP
STEEP BANK: be a steep bank **giishkadinaa, giishkadinaamagad** *vii*
STEER
STEER: **odaake** *vai*
STEER A CERTAIN WAY: steer s.o. a certain way **inikwe' /inikwe'w-/** *vta;* steer s.t. a certain way **inikwe'an** *vti*
STEM
PIPE STEM: **okij, -iin** *ni*
STEP
STEP: **dakokii** *vai;* step on s.o. **dakokaazh /dakokaaN-/** *vta;* step on s.t. **dakokaadan** *vti*
STEP IN THE SAME TRACKS: **naaba'anidizo** *vai*

STEP OVER: step over s.o. **baazhida' /baazhida'w-/** *vta;* step over s.t. **baazhida'an** *vti*

STEPDAUGHTER

STEPDAUGHTER: my stepdaughter **indoozhimikwem, -ag /-doozhimikwem-/** *nad*

STEW

STEW: **wiiyaasi-naboob** *ni*

STICK

STICK IN: stick s.o. in **badakishim** *vta;* **badakizh /badakiN-/** *vta;* stick s.t. in **badakidoon** *vti2;* **badakisidoon** *vti2;* stick something in s.o. **badaka' /badaka'w-/** *vta;* stick something in s.t. **badaka'an** *vti;* stick something in things **badaka'ige** *vai;* stick things in **badakisijige** *vai*

STICK IN A FEATHER: stick a feather in one's hair or hat **badakibine'o** *vai*

STICK IN A SURFACE: **badakise** *vai;* **badakise, badakisemagad** *vii*

STICK IN A TIGHT PLACE: stick s.o. in a tight place **zhegon** *vta;* stick s.t. in a tight place **zhegonan** *vti*

STICK OUT HEAD: stick out one's head **zaagikweni** *vai*

STICK OUT TONGUE: stick out one's tongue **zaagidenaniweni** *vai;* stick out one's tongue at s.o. **zaagidenaniwetaw** *vta*

STICK

STICK: **mitig, -oon** *ni;* **mitigoons, -an** *ni*

STICK

STICK: **bazagoke** *vai;* **bazagoke, bazagokemagad** *vii;* stick on **agoke** *vai;* **agoke, agokemagad** *vii;* stick s.o. on **agokazh /agokaN-/** *vta;* stick s.t. on **agokadoon** *vti2*

STICKY

STICKY: be sticky **bazagozi** *vai;* **bazagwaa, bazagwaamagad** *vii*

STIFF

FREEZE STIFF: freeze s.o. stiff **mashkawaakwajim** *vta;* freeze s.t. stiff **mashkawaakwajidoon** *vti2*

FROZEN STIFF: be frozen stiff **mashkawaakwadin** *vii;* **mashkawaakwaji** *vai*

STIFF ARM: have a stiff arm **jiibadaakonike** *vai;* **jiibajinike** *vai*

STIFF HAND: have a hand stiff from cold **mashkawajininjiiwaji** *vai*

STIFF LEG: have a stiff leg **jiibadaakogaade** *vai;* **jiibajigaade** *vai*

STIFF NECK: have a stiff neck **jiibajigwayawe** *vai*

STIFFLY

SIT STIFFLY: **jiibadabi** *vai*

STAND STIFFLY: **jiibadaakogaabawi** *vai*

STILL

STILL: **bizaan** *pc;* be still **goshkwaawaadizi** *vai*

LIE STILL: **bizaanishin** *vai*

SIT STILL: **bizaanaakwadabi** *vai*

STILL

STILL: **geyaabi** *pc*

STINGILY

HELD STINGILY: be held stingily **zaagichigaade, zaagichigaademagad** *vii;* **zaagichigaazo** *vai*

STINGY

STINGY: be stingy **zazaagizi** *vai*

STIR

STIR: stir s.t. **waninawe'an** *vti*

STIR THE FIRE: **jiichiishkinzhe'ige** *vai*

STIR TO FORM SUGAR: **nase'ige** *vai;* stir s.t. to form sugar **nase'an** *vti*

STIR UP: stir s.o. up **ombi'** *vta*

STOMACH

STOMACH: my stomach **nimisad, -an /-misad-/** *nid*

SWOLLEN STOMACH: have a swollen stomach **ombijiishkaa** *vai*

STOMACHACHE

GIVE A STOMACHACHE: give s.o. a stomachache; *inverse forms of:* **aakoshkadekaw-** *vta*

HAVE A STOMACHACHE: **aakoshkade** *vai*

STONE

STONE: **asin, -iig** *na;* be of stone **asiniiwan** *vii*

MANY STONES: there are many stones **asiniikaa, asiniikaamagad** *vii*

STOP

STOP: stop (moving) **noogishkaa** *vai;* **noogishkaa, noogishkaamagad** *vii*

COME TO A STOP: **noogise** *vai*

MAKE STOP: make s.o. stop (e.g., a car) **nagaashkaa'** *vta;* make s.t. stop **nagaashkaatoon** *vti2*

STOP AN ACTIVITY: **ishkwaataa** *vai*

STOP AND STAND IN PLACE: stop and stand in places **noogigaabawi** *vai*

STOP BREATHING: **ishkwaanaamo** *vai*

STOP BY HAND: stop s.o. by hand **noogin** *vta;* stop s.t. by hand **nooginan** *vti*

STOP CRYING: **giishkowe** *vai*

STOP DRIVING: **noogibide, noogibidemagad** *vii;* **noogibizo** *vai*

STOP MAKING VOCAL NOISE: **giishkowe** *vai*

STOP MOVING: **nagaashkaa** *vai;* **nagaashkaa, nagaashkaamagad** *vii*

STOP RAINING: **ishkwaabiisaa, ishkwaabiisaamagad** *vii*

STOP RUNNING: **noogibatoo** *vai*

STOP SNOWING: **ishkwaapon /ishkwaapo-/** *vii*

STOP SPEEDING: **noogibide, noogibidemagad** *vii;* **noogibizo** *vai*

STOP TALKING: stop talking to s.o. **boonim** *vta*

STOP UP: stop s.o. up **giba' /giba'w-/** *vta;* stop s.t. up **giba'an** *vti;* stop things up **giba'ige** *vai*

STOPPED

STOPPED UP: be stopped up **giba'igaade, giba'igaademagad** *vii;* **giba'igaazo** *vai*

STOPPER
STOPPER: **gibaakwa'igan, -an** *ni*
STORAGE LODGE
STORAGE LODGE: **asanjigoowigamig, -oon** *ni;* **ataasoowigamig, -oon** *ni*
STORE
STORE: store something, store (s.t.) **ataaso** *vai+o*
STORE AWAY: store things away **na'enimo** *vai*
STORE
STORE: **adaawewigamig, -oon** *ni*
GROCERY STORE: **wiisinii-adaawewigamig, -oon** *ni*
SECOND-HAND CLOTHING STORE: second-hand clothing store **zhiigoshkigani-adaawewigamig, -oon** *ni*
STORE CLERK
STORE CLERK: **adaawewinini, -wag** *na;* store clerk (female) **adaawewininiikwe** *na*
STORM
STORM: be a storm **gichi-noodin** *vii;* there is a severe storm **nichiiwad** *vii*
STORM CLOUD
STORM CLOUDS: there are storm clouds **zegaanakwad** *vii*
STORMY
STORMY: be stormy **gichi-izhiwebad** *vii*
STORY
STORY: **dibaajimowin, -an** *ni*
TELL A GOOD STORY: **minwaajimo** *vai*
TELL A STORY: tell a story of s.o. **aajim** *vta;* tell a story of s.t. **aadodan** *vti*
TELL A TRADITIONAL STORY: **aadizooke** *vai*
TELL STORIES: **dadibaajimo** *vai;* tell stories to s.o. **dadibaajimotaw** *vta*
TRADITIONAL STORY: **aadizookaan, -ag** *na*
STORYTELLER
STORYTELLER: **aadizookewinini, -wag** *na;* **dadibaajimoowinini, -wag** *na*
STOVE
STOVE: **gizhaabikizigan, -an** *ni*
COOK STOVE: **jiibaakwe-gizhaabikizigan, -an** *ni*
STOVEPIPE
STOVEPIPE: **okijaabik, -oon** *ni*
STRAIGHT
STRAIGHT: **gwayak** *pc;* be straight **gwayakozi** *vai;* **gwayakwaa, gwayakwaamagad** *vii;* be straight (as something mineral) **gwayakwaabikad** *vii;* **gwayakwaabikizi** *vai;* be straight (as something stick- or wood-like) **gwayakwaakozi** *vai;* **gwayakwaakwad** *vii;* be straight (as something string-like) **gwayakwaabiigad** *vii;* **gwayakwaabiigizi** *vai*
CUT STRAIGHT: cut s.o. straight **gwayakozh /gwayakozhw-/** *vta;* cut s.t. straight **gwayakozhan** *vti*
GO STRAIGHT: **gwayakoshkaa** *vai*
GROW STRAIGHT: **gwayakogi** *vai;* **gwayakogin** *vii*
HOLD HEAD STRAIGHT: hold one's head straight **gwayakokweni** *vai*
LAY STRAIGHT: lay s.o. straight **gwayakoshim** *vta;* lay s.t. straight **gwayakosidoon** *vti2*
LIE STRAIGHT: **gwayakoshin** *vai;* **gwayakosin** *vii*
PULL STRAIGHT: pull s.o. straight **gwayakobizh /gwayakobiN-/** *vta;* pull s.t. straight **gwayakobidoon** *vti2*
SAW STRAIGHT: saw s.o. straight **gwayakoboozh /gwayakobooN-/** *vta;* saw s.t. straight **gwayakoboodoon** *vti2*
STAND STRAIGHT: **gwayakogaabawi** *vai*
TEAR STRAIGHT: tear s.o. straight **gwayakobizh /gwayakobiN-/** *vta;* tear s.t. straight **gwayakobidoon** *vti2*
STRAIN
STRAIN: strain s.t. **zhaabobiiginan** *vti;* **ziikoobiiginan** *vti*
STRAIN
STRAIN IN LIFTING: strain self in lifting **jakiiwii** *vai*
STRAINER
STRAINER: **zhaabobiiginigan, -an** *ni*
STRANGE
STRANGE: **mayagi-** *pv4;* be strange **mayagizi** *vai*
CONSIDER STRANGE: consider s.o. strange **mayagenim** *vta*
CONSIDERED STRANGE: be considered strange **mayagendaagwad** *vii*
FEEL STRANGE: **mayagendam** *vai2*
LOOK STRANGE: **mayaginaagozi** *vai;* **mayaginaagwad** *vii*
SOUND STRANGE: **mayagitaagozi** *vai;* **mayagitaagwad** *vii*
SPEAK A STRANGE LANGUAGE: **mayagwe** *vai*
SPEAKER OF A STRANGE LANGUAGE: **mayagwewinini, -wag** *na*
STRANGER
STRANGER: **biiwide, -g** *na*
STRAP
STRAP: **apikan, -an** *ni*
STRAWBERRY
STRAWBERRY: **ode'imin, -an** *ni*
STRENGTH
TEST STRENGTH: test one's strength **gagwejii** *vai*
STRETCH
STRETCH: stretch (as something sheet-like) **zhiibiigishkaa, zhiibiigishkaamagad** *vii;* stretch s.o. on a hide stretcher **zhiibaakwa' /zhiibaakwa'w-/** *vta*
STRETCH A HIDE: **naazhiiga'ige** *vai*
STRETCH BODY: stretch one's body **zhiibii** *vai*
STRETCH BY PULLING: stretch s.o. by pulling (as something sheet-like) **zhiibiigibizh /zhiibiigibiN-/** *vta;* stretch s.t.

by pulling (as something sheet-like) **zhiibiigibidoon** *vti2*

STRETCH USING SOMETHING: stretch s.o. using something (as something sheet-like) **zhiibiiga' /zhiibiiga'w-/** *vta;* stretch s.t. using something (as something sheet-like) **zhiibiiga'an** *vti*

STRETCHER

HIDE STRETCHER: flat hide stretcher (especially for muskrats) **zhiibaakwa'ataan, -an** *ni*

STRIKE

STRIKE: strike s.o. **bakite' /bakite'w-/** *vta;* strike s.t. **bakite'an** *vti;* strike things **bakite'ige** *vai;* they strike each other **bakite'odiwag /bakite'odi-/** *vai*

STRING

STRING: string s.o. (e.g., beads) **naabidoo' /naabidoo'w-/** *vta;* string s.t. **naabidoo'an** *vti;* string things **naabidoo'ige** *vai*

STRING A CERTAIN WAY: string s.o. a certain way **inaabiigin** *vta;* string s.t. a certain way **inaabiiginan** *vti*

STRING ALONG: string s.o. along **bimaabiigin** *vta;* string s.t. along **bimaabiiginan** *vti*

STRING

STRING: **biiminakwaanens, -an** *ni*

MAKE STRING: **biiminakwe** *vai*

STRIPE

HAVE A STRIPE: **beshaa, beshaamagad** *vii;* **beshizi** *vai*

MARK WITH A STRIPE: mark s.o. with a stripe **beshibii' /beshibii'w-/** *vta;* mark s.t. with a stripe **beshibii'an** *vti;* mark things with a stripe **beshibii'ige** *vai*

STRIPS

CUT INTO STRIPS: cut s.t. into strips **baanizhan** *vti*

STROKE

HAVE A STROKE: **niboowise** *vai*

STROLL

TAKE A STROLL: **babimose** *vai*

STRONG

STRONG: be strong **mashkawaa, mashkawaamagad** *vii;* **mashkawizi** *vai;* **zoongan** *vii;* **zoongizi** *vai;* be strong (as a liquid) **mashkawaagamin /mashkawaagami-/** *vii;* be strong (of a person) **mashkawizii** *vai*

MAKE STRONG: make s.o. strong **zoongi'** *vta;* make s.t. strong **zoongitoon** *vti2*

SMELL STRONG BURNING OR COOKING: **mashkawimaaso** *vai;* **mashkawimaate, mashkawimaatemagad** *vii*

STRONG ARM: have a strong arm **zoonginike** *vai*

STRONG BONES: have strong bones **zoongigane** *vai*

STRONG HAND: have a strong hand **zoongininjii** *vai*

STRUCK

STRUCK: be struck **bakite'igaade, bakite'igaademagad** *vii;* **bakite'igaazo** *vai*

STRUCK BY LIGHTNING: be struck by lightning **baagijigaade, baagijigaademagad** *vii;* **baagijigaazo** *vai*

STUB

STUB TOE: stub one's toe **bizozideshin** *vai*

STUBBORN

STUBBORN: be stubborn **zhazhiibitam** *vai2*

STUBBORNLY

STUBBORNLY: **awanjish** *pc*

STUCK

STUCK: be stuck **baataashin** *vai;* **baataasin** *vii;* **bwaanawi'o** *vai*

GET STUCK: **baataase** *vai;* **baataase, baataasemagad** *vii*

STUDENT

STUDENT: **gekinoo'amawind** *na-pt;* **gikinoo'amaagan, -ag** *na*

STUFF

STUFF: stuff s.o. **biindashkwaazh /biindashkwaaN-/** *vta;* stuff s.t. **biindashkwaadan** *vti*

STUFFED-UP

HAVE A STUFFED-UP NOSE: **gibijaane** *vai, also* **gagiibijaane**

STUMBLE

STUMBLE: **bizogeshin** *vai;* stumble on s.o. **bizokaw** *vta;* stumble on s.t. **bizokan** *vti*

STUMP

STUMP: **giishkanakad, -oon** *ni*

STURGEON

STURGEON: **name, -wag** *na*

STUTTER

STUTTER: **gagiibanagaskwe** *vai*

SUCCEED

SUCCEED: **gashki'ewizi** *vai;* succeed at s.t. **gashkitoon** *vti2*

SUCCESSION

SOMEONE NEXT IN SUCCESSION TO THE LEADER: someone next in succession to the leader (e.g., a vice president) **aanike-ogimaa, -g** *na*

SUCK

SUCK: **wiikwamo** *vai;* suck on s.o. **wiikwam** *vta;* suck on s.t. **wiikwandan** *vti;* suck on things **wiikwanjige** *vai*

SUCK OUT: suck out of s.o. **zoobam** *vta;* suck out of s.t. **zoobandan** *vti*

SUCKER

SUCKER: sucker (fish) **namebin, -ag** *na*

SUCKLE

SUCKLE: suckle (of child or offspring) **nooni** *vai*

SUDDENLY

SUDDENLY: **gezika** *pc*

SUFFER

SUFFER: **aanimizi** *vai;* **gagwaadagitoo** *vai*

MAKE SUFFER: make s.o. suffer **aanimi'** *vta*

SUFFER EMOTIONALLY: **aanimendam** *vai2*

SUFFER IN A CERTAIN PLACE: suffer in a certain place **dapine** *vai*
SUFFER IN MIND: suffer in one's mind **gagwaanisagendam** *vai2*
SUFFER MENTALLY: **aanimendam** *vai2*
SUFFER PAIN: **wiisagendam** *vai*

SUFFICIENT
SUFFICIENT: **de-** *pv4;* **gwech** *pc;* be sufficient **debise** *vai;* **debise, debisemagad** *vii*

SUFFOCATE
SUFFOCATE FROM SMOKE: **gibwanaamozo** *vai*

SUGAR
SUGAR: **ziinzibaakwad** *ni*
BOIL TO SUGAR: **ombigamizige** *vai;* boil s.t. to sugar **ombigamizan** *vti*
BOILING SUGAR: **ombigamizigan, -an** *ni*
GRANULATE SUGAR: **naseyaawangwe** *vai*
GRANULATED SUGAR: **bibine-ziinzibaakwad** *ni*
MAPLE SUGAR: **anishinaabe-ziinzibaakwad** *ni;* **ziinzibaakwad** *ni*
STIR TO FORM SUGAR: stir s.t. to form sugar **nase'an** *vti*
SUGAR OFF: **ombigamizige** *vai*

SUGAR BEET
SUGAR BEET: **wiishkobi-jiis, -an** *ni*

SUGAR BOWL
SUGAR BOWL: **ziinzibaakwad-onaagaans, -an** *ni*

SUGAR BUSH
SUGAR BUSH: **iskigamizigan, -an** *ni*

SUGAR CAKE
SUGAR CAKE: **ziiga'igan, -an** *ni*

SUGAR CAMP
SUGAR CAMP: **iskigamizigan, -an** *ni*

SUGAR CONE
SUGAR CONE: **zhiishiigwaans, -ag** *na;* **ziiga'igan, -an** *ni*
CAST SUGAR CONES: **ziiga'ige** *vai*
MAKE A SUGAR CONE: **ziiga'iganike** *vai*

SUICIDE
COMMIT SUICIDE: **nisidizo** *vai*

SUITABLE
SUITABLE: **de-** *pv4;* be suitable **nandawendaagozi** *vai;* **nandawendaagwad** *vii*

SUITCASE
SUITCASE: **babaamaadizii-makak, -oon** *ni*

SUMMER
SUMMER: be summer **niibin** *vii*
LAST SUMMER: **niibinong** *pc*
LATE SUMMER: **giiwe-niibin** *vii*
SPEND THE SUMMER: spend the summer somewhere **niibinishi** *vai*
SUMMER BEFORE LAST: **awas-niibinong** *pc*

SUMMON
SUMMON: summon s.o. **nandom** *vta*

SUN
SUN: **giizis, -oog** *na*
SUN SETS: set as the sun **bangishimon /bangishimo-/** *vii*

SUNBURN
PEEL FROM SUNBURN: **bishagaaso** *vai*

SUNBURNED
SUNBURNED: be sunburned **gashkaaso** *vai*

SUNDAY
SUNDAY: be Sunday **anama'e-giizhigad** *vii, also* **aname-giizhigad**

SUNFISH
SUNFISH: **agwadaashi, -wag** *na*

SUNNY
SUNNY: be sunny **waaseyaa, waaseyaamagad** *vii*

SUNRISE
SUNRISE: be sunrise **mooka'am** *vai2*

SUPPER
EAT SUPPER: **onaagoshi-wiisini** *vai;* eat s.t. for supper **onaagoshi-miijin** *vti3*

SUPPORT
SUPPORT: support s.o. **bami'** *vta*

SUPPORTED
SUPPORTED ONE: **bami'aagan, -ag** *na*

SURE
SURE: **geget** *pc;* sure! **enange** *pc*
FOR SURE: **mii nange** *pc*

SURPRISE
SURPRISE: surprise s.o. **goshko'** *vta*
SURPRISE VERBALLY: surprise s.o. verbally **goshkom** *vta*

SURPRISED
SURPRISED: be surprised **goshkokaa** *vai*

SURVEY
SURVEY LAND: **diba'akii** *vai*

SURVEYOR
SURVEYOR: **diba'akiiwinini, -wag** *na*

SURVIVE
SURVIVE: **zhaabwii** *vai*

SUSPECT
SUSPECT: suspect s.o. **anaamenim** *vta;* **moonenim** *vta;* suspect s.t. **anaamendan** *vti*

SUSPENDED
SUSPENDED IN WATER: be suspended in water **agomo** *vai;* **agonde** *vii*

SUSPENDERS
SUSPENDERS: suspenders *plural* **anikamaanan /anikamaan-/** *ni*

SWALLOW
SWALLOW: swallow s.o. **gonzhi /gonN-/** *vta;* swallow s.t. **gondan** *vti*

SWAMP
SWAMP: **waabashkiki, -in** *ni*

SWAMPY
SWAMPY: be swampy **waabashkikiiwan** *vii*

SWAN
SWAN: **waabizii, -g** *na*

SWEAR
SWEAR: **majigiizhwe** *vai*

SWEAT
SWEAT: **abwezo** *vai*

SWEAT BATH
TAKE A SWEAT BATH: **madoodoo** *vai*
SWEAT LODGE
SWEAT LODGE: **madoodiswan, -an** *ni*
ROCK FOR SWEAT LODGE: **madoodoowasin, -iig** *na*
SWEATY
SWEATY FOOT: have a sweaty foot **abwezide** *vai*
SWEATY HAND: have a sweaty hand **abweninjii** *vai*
SWEEP
SWEEP: **jiishada'ige** *vai*
SWEET
SWEET: **wiishkobi-** *pv4;* be sweet **wiishkoban** *vii;* **wiishkobizi** *vai;* be sweet (as a liquid) **wiishkobaagamin /wiishkobaagami-/** *vii*
TASTE SWEET: **wiishkobipogozi** *vai;* **wiishkobipogwad** *vii*
SWEET FLAG
SWEET FLAG: **wiikenh, -yag** *na*
SWEET GRASS
SWEET GRASS: **wiingashk, -oon** *ni*
SWEET ROLL
SWEET ROLL: **waashkobizid bakwezhigan, -ag** *na-pt;* **wiishkobi-bakwezhigan, -ag** *na*
SWEETHEART
SWEETHEART: my sweetheart **niinimoshenh, -yag /-iinimosheny-/** *nad*
SWIM
ARRIVE SWIMMING: **bagamaadagaa** *vai*
GO SWIMMING: **bagizo** *vai*
HEARD SWIMMING HERE: be heard swimming here **biidweweyaadagaa** *vai*
SWIM ABOUT: **babaamaadagaa** *vai*
SWIM ACROSS: **aazhawaadagaa** *vai*
SWIM ALONG: **bimaadagaa** *vai;* swim along (as a fish) **bimakwazhiwe** *vai*
SWIM ASHORE: **agwaayaadagaa** *vai*
SWIM AWAY: **animaadagaa** *vai*
SWIM FROM A CERTAIN PLACE: **ondaadagaa** *vai;* swim from a certain place (as a fish) **ondakwazhiwe** *vai*
SWIM HERE: **biidaadagaa** *vai;* swim here (as a fish) **biidakwazhiwe** *vai*
SWIM OFF: swim off (as a fish) **maajiikwazhiwe** *vai*
SWIM SUDDENLY INTO VIEW: swim as a fish suddenly into view **zaagewekwazhiwe** *vai*
SWIM TO A CERTAIN PLACE: **inaadagaa** *vai;* swim to a certain place (as a fish) **inakwazhiwe** *vai*
SWING
SWING: **wewebizo** *vai;* **wewebizon, -an** *ni*
SWITCH
SWITCH: **biskaakonebijigan, -an** *ni*
SWITCH ON: switch s.t. on **biskanebidoon** *vti2*
SWOLLEN
SWOLLEN: be swollen **baagishi** *vai;* **baagisin** *vii*
SWOLLEN EYES: have swollen eyes **baagishkiinzhigwe** *vai*
SWOLLEN FACE: have a swollen face **baagiingwe** *vai*
SWOLLEN FOOT: have a swollen foot **baagizide** *vai*
SWOLLEN GLAND: have a swollen gland (lymph node) **baaginiishkwe** *vai*
SWOLLEN HAND: have a swollen hand **baagininjii** *vai*
SWOLLEN NOSE: have a swollen nose **baagijaane** *vai*
SWOLLEN STOMACH: have a swollen stomach **ombijiishkaa** *vai*
SWORD
SWORD: **ashaweshk, -oon** *ni*
SYRUP
SYRUP: **zhiiwaagamizigan** *ni*
MAKE SYRUP: **zhiiwaagamiziganike** *vai;* **zhiiwaagamizige** *vai*
THICKEN INTO SYRUP: **zhiiwaagamide, zhiiwaagamidemagad** *vii*

T

TAB
TAB AT HEEL OF MOCCASIN: **odoondanegwaajigan, -an** *ni*
TABLE
TABLE: **adoopowin, -an** *ni*
SET THE TABLE: **ozisinaagane** *vai*
TABLE CLOTH
TABLE CLOTH: **adoopowiniigin, -oon** *ni*
TADPOLE
TADPOLE: **boodoonh, -yag** *na*
TAFFY
MAKE TAFFY: **bigiwizige** *vai*
MAPLE TAFFY: **bigiwizigan** *ni*
TAIL
ANIMAL TAIL: my tail (of an animal) **inzow, -an /-zow-/** *nid*
BIRD TAIL: my tail (of a bird) **ninashkid, -iin /-nashkidy-/** *nid*
FISH TAIL: my tail (of a fish) **inzhigwan /-zhigwan-/** *nid*
WAG TAIL: wag one's tail **wewebaanoweni** *vai*
TAILPIPE
TAILPIPE: **okijaabik, -oon** *ni*
TAKE
TAKE: take s.o. **mami /mam-/** *vta;* take s.o. offered **odaapin** *vta;* take s.t. **mamoon** *vti2;* take s.t. offered **odaapinan** *vti;* take (s.t.) from s.o. **mamaw** *vta;* take (s.t.) offered by s.o. **odaapinamaw** *vta;* take things **mamige** *vai;* take things offered **odaapinige** *vai*

ABLE TO TAKE: be able to take s.o. **gashkiwizh /gashkiwiN-/** *vta;* be able to take s.t. **gashkiwidoon** *vti2*

TAKE A HANDFUL: take a handful of s.o. **ganakin** *vta;* take a handful of s.t. **ganakinan** *vti*

TAKE A PIECE OFF BY HAND: take a piece off s.o. by hand **bakwen** *vta;* take a piece off s.t. by hand **bakwenan** *vti*

TAKE A PIECE OFF USING SOMETHING: take a piece off s.o. using something **bakwe'** *vta;* take a piece off s.t. using something **bakwe'an** *vti*

TAKE A TASTE: take a taste of s.o. **godandan** *vti;* take a taste of s.t. **godam** *vta;* **gojipidan** *vti*

TAKE ABOUT: take s.o. about **babaamiwizh /babaamiwiN-/** *vta;* take s.t. about **babaamiwidoon** *vti2*

TAKE ACROSS: take s.o. across **aazhogewizh /aazhogewiN-/** *vta;* take s.t. across **aazhogewidoon** *vti2*

TAKE ACROSS BY BOAT: take s.o. across by boat **aazhawa'oozh /aazhawa'ooN-/** *vta;* take s.t. across by boat **aazhawa'oodoon** *vti2*

TAKE ALONG: take s.o. along **bimiwizh /bimiwiN-/** *vta;* **maajiizh /maajiiN-/** *vta;* take s.t. along **bimiwidoon** *vti2;* **maajiidoon** *vti2;* take (s.t.) along for s.o. **maajiidaw** *vta;* take people along **bimiwizhiwe** *vai*

TAKE ALONG A GUN: **niimibaashkizigane** *vai*

TAKE ALONG FOR A RIDE: take s.o. along for a ride **bimibizoni'** *vta*

TAKE ALONG IN A BOAT: take s.o. along in a boat **bima'oozh /bima'ooN-/** *vta;* take s.t. along in a boat **bima'oodoon** *vti2*

TAKE ASHORE: take s.o. ashore **agwaashim** *vta;* take s.t. ashore **agwaasidoon** *vti2*

TAKE ASHORE BY BOAT: take s.t. ashore by boat **agwaa'oodoon** *vti2*

TAKE AWAY: take s.o. away **animiwizh /animiwiN-/** *vta;* **maajiizh /maajiiN-/** *vta;* take s.t. away **animiwidoon** *vti2;* **maajiidoon** *vti2;* take people away **maajiizhiwe** *vai*

TAKE AWAY BY BOAT: take s.o. away by boat **anima'oozh /anima'ooN-/** *vta;* take s.t. away by boat **anima'oodoon** *vti2*

TAKE BACK: take s.o. back **azhen** *vta;* take s.t. back **azhenan** *vti;* take (s.t.) back to s.o. **azhenamaw** *vta*

TAKE DOWN: take s.o. down **bina' /bina'w-/** *vta;* take s.t. down **bina'an** *vti*

TAKE EVERYTHING: **jaaginige** *vai*

TAKE FORCIBLY: take (s.t.) from s.o. forcibly **makam** *vta*

TAKE FROM A CERTAIN PLACE: take s.o. from a certain place **onjiwizh /onjiwiN-/** *vta;* take s.t. from a certain place **onjiwidoon** *vti2*

TAKE HOME: take s.o. home **giiwewizh /giiwewiN-/** *vta;* take s.t. home **giiwewidoon** *vti2;* take (s.t.) home for s.o. **giiwewidaw** *vta*

TAKE INLAND: take s.o. inland **gopiwizh /gopiwiN-/** *vta;* take s.t. inland **gopiwidoon** *vti2*

TAKE INSIDE: take s.o. inside **biindigazh /biindigaN-/** *vta;* take s.t. inside **biindigadoon** *vti2*

TAKE OFF INTO THE AIR: **bazikwa'o** *vai*

TAKE OFF THE FIRE: take s.o. off the fire **agwaabiigin** *vta;* **agwaashim** *vta;* take s.t. off the fire **agwaabiiginan** *vti;* **agwaasidoon** *vti2*

TAKE OFF THE WATER: take s.o. off the water **agwaabiigin** *vta;* take s.t. off the water **agwaabiiginan** *vti*

TAKE OFF THE WATER USING SOMETHING: take s.o. off the water using something **agwaabiiga' /agwaabiiga'w-/** *vta;* take s.t. off the water using something **agwaabiiga'an** *vti*

TAKE OUT: take s.o. out **zaagizi'** *vta;* take s.t. out **zaagizitoon** *vti2;* take (s.t.) out for s.o. **zaagizitaw** *vta*

TAKE PICTURES: **mazinaakizige** *vai;* take pictures of s.o. **mazinaakiz /mazinaakizw-/** *vta;* take pictures of s.t. **mazinaakizan** *vti*

TAKE PLACE: take s.o.'s place **naabishkaw** *vta;* take someone's place **naabishkaage** *vai*

TAKE TO A CERTAIN PLACE: take s.o. to a certain place **izhiwizh /izhiwiN-/** *vta;* take s.t. to a certain place **izhiwidoon** *vti2;* take (s.t.) to s.o. at a certain place **izhiwidaw** *vta*

TAKE TO A CERTAIN PLACE BY BOAT: take s.o. to a certain place by boat **ina'oozh /ina'ooN-/** *vta;* take s.t. to a certain place by boat **ina'oodoon** *vti2*

TAKE TO THE SHORE: take s.o. to the shore **madaabiiwizh /madaabiiwiN-/** *vta;* take s.t. to the shore **madaabiiwidoon** *vti2*

TAKE WILD RICE INLAND: **gopimine** *vai*

TAKE WRONG ONE: take s.o. who/that is the wrong one **wanin** *vta;* take s.t. that is the wrong one **waninan** *vti*

TAKE CARE

TAKE CARE: take care of s.o. **ganawenim** *vta;* take care of s.t. **ganawendan** *vti;* take care of (s.t.) for s.o. **ganawendamaw** *vta;* take care of things **ganawenjige** *vai;* they take care of each other **ganawenindiwag /ganawenindi-/** *vai*

TAKE CARE OF A CHILD: **bamoozhe** *vai;* **ganawendaawaso** *vai*

TAKE OFF

TAKE OFF: take s.o. off **gidiskin** *vta;* **giichigon** *vta;* take s.t. off **gidiskinan** *vti;* **giichigonan** *vti*

TAKE OFF CLOTHES: take off one's clothes **giizikonaye** *vai;* take s.o. off the body (e.g., clothes) **giizikaw** *vta;* take s.t. off the body (e.g., clothes) **giizikan** *vti*

TAKE OFF COAT: take off one's coat **giichibabiinzikawaagane** *vai*
TAKE OFF DRESS: take off one's dress **giitagoode** *vai*
TAKE OFF HAT: take off one's hat **giichiwakwaane** *vai*
TAKE OFF MITTENS: take off one's mittens **giichiminjikaawane** *vai*
TAKE OFF MOCCASINS: take off one's moccasins **gagiichii** *vai*
TAKE OFF PANTS: take off one's pants **giichigiboodiyegwaazone** *vai*
TAKE OFF SHIRT: take off one's shirt **giichibabagiwayaane** *vai*
TAKE OFF SHOES: take off one's shoes **gagiichii** *vai*
TAKE OFF SOCKS: take off one's socks **giitazhigane** *vai*

TAKE PLACE
TAKE PLACE IN A CERTAIN PLACE: **danakamigad** *vii*

TAKEN
TAKEN: be taken **mamigaade, mamigaademagad** *vii;* **mamigaazo** *vai;* **odaapinigaade, odaapinigaademagad** *vii;* **odaapinigaazo** *vai*
TAKEN ALONG: be taken along **maajiijigaade, maajiijigaademagad** *vii;* **maajiijigaazo** *vai*
TAKEN ASHORE: be taken ashore **agwaasijigaade, agwaasijigaademagad** *vii;* **agwaasijigaazo** *vai*
TAKEN OFF THE FIRE: be taken off the fire **agwaasijigaade, agwaasijigaademagad** *vii;* **agwaasijigaazo** *vai*
TAKEN TO A CERTAIN PLACE: be taken to a certain place **izhiwijigaade, izhiwijigaademagad** *vii;* **izhiwijigaazo** *vai*

TAKEN CARE
TAKEN CARE: be taken care of **ganawendaagwad** *vii;* **ganawenjigaade, ganawenjigaademagad** *vii;* **ganawenjigaazo** *vai*

TALK
TALK: **gaagiigido** *vai;* talk to s.o. **gaganoozh /gaganooN-/** *vta;* they talk to each other **gaganoonidiwag /gaganoonidi-/** *vai*
AVOID TALKING: avoid talking to s.o. **boonim** *vta*
STOP TALKING: stop talking to s.o. **boonim** *vta*
TALK A CERTAIN WAY: **izhigiizhwe** *vai*
TALK ABOUT: talk about s.o. **dazhim** *vta;* talk about s.t. **dazhindan** *vti;* talk about people **dazhinge** *vai*
TALK BACK: talk back to s.o. **aazhidem** *vta*
TALK QUICKLY: **dadaatabaanagidoon** *vai*
TALK TOO MUCH: **onzaamidoon** *vai*
TALK WITHOUT STOPPING: **aabidaanagidoon** *vai;* **aapidaanagidoon** *vai*

TALKED
TALKED ABOUT: be talked about all the time **waawiinjigaade, waawiinjigaademagad** *vii;* **waawiinjigaazo** *vai*

TALL
TALL: be tall **ginoozi** *vai;* be tall (of a person) **ginwaakozi** *vai*
SO TALL: be so tall **akoozi** *vai;* **akwaa, akwaamagad** *vii*

TALLOW
TALLOW: **mashkawaji-bimide** *ni*

TAMARACK
TAMARACK: **mashkiigwaatig, -oog** *na*

TAME
TAME: be tame **waangawizi** *vai;* tame s.o. **waangawi'** *vta*

TAN
TAN: tan hides **aseke** *vai;* tan s.o. (e.g., a hide) **asekaazh /asekaaN-/** *vta*

TANGLED
TANGLED: be tangled **gashka'oode, gashka'oodemagad** *vii;* **gashka'oozo** *vai*

TANK
TANK: **atoobaan, -an** *ni*

TANNED HIDE
TANNED HIDE: **asekaan, -ag** *na*

TANNING
TANNING: **asekewin** *ni*

TAP
TAP: **negwaakwaan, -an** *ni*
TAP FOOT: tap one's foot **jiichiibizideni** *vai*
TAP IN: tap s.o. in **ginjida' /ginjida'w-/** *vta;* tap s.t. in **ginjida'an** *vti*
TAP TREES: **ozhiga'ige** *vai*

TAPE RECORDER
TAPE RECORDER: **naabinootaage-makak, -oon** *ni*

TAR
TAR: **bigiw** *ni;* **bigiike** *vai;* **makade-bigiw** *na;* tar s.t. **bigiikaadan** *vti*

TARGET
HIT THE TARGET: **mizhodam** *vai2*

TASTE
TASTE: taste things **gojipijige** *vai*
FIND A GOOD TASTE: find a good taste in s.o. **minopozh /minopw-/** *vta;* find a good taste in s.t. **minopidan** *vti*
HAVE A CERTAIN TASTE: **ipogozi** *vai;* **ipogwad** *vii*
LIKE THE TASTE: like the taste of things **minopijige** *vai*
TAKE A TASTE: take a taste of s.o. **godandan** *vti;* **gojipozh /gojipw-/** *vta;* take a taste of s.t. **godam** *vta;* **gojipidan** *vti*
TASTE A SAMPLE: taste a sample of s.o. **daangam** *vta;* taste a sample of s.t. **daangandan** *vti*
TASTE BAD: **maazhipogozi** *vai;* **maazhipogwad** *vii;* taste bad (as a liquid) **maanaagamin /maanaagami-/** *vii*
TASTE BITTER: **wiisagipogozi** *vai;* **wiisagipogwad** *vii*
TASTE GOOD: **minopogozi** *vai;* **minopogwad** *vii;* taste good (as a liquid) **minwaagamin /minwaagami-/** *vii*

TASTE RANCID: **zaatepogozi** *vai;* **zaatepogwad** *vii*
TASTE SALTY: **zhiiwitaaganipogozi** *vai;* **zhiiwitaaganipogwad** *vii*
TASTE SWEET: **wiishkobipogozi** *vai;* **wiishkobipogwad** *vii*

TAUGHT
TAUGHT: be taught **gikinoo'amaagozi** *vai*

TAVERN
TAVERN: **minikwewigamig, -oon** *ni;* **ziiginigewigamig, -oon** *ni*

TAXI
TAXI: **bimiwizhiwewidaabaan, -ag** *na*

TAXI DRIVER
TAXI DRIVER: **bimiwizhiwewinini, -wag** *na*

TEA
TEA: **aniibiish, -an** *ni;* **aniibiishaaboo** *ni*
BLACK TEA: **makade-aniibiish** *ni*
GREEN TEA: **ozhaawashko-aniibiish** *ni*
MAKE TEA: **aniibiishaabooke** *vai;* **aniibiishike** *vai*

TEACH
TEACH: **gikinoo'amaage** *vai;* teach (s.t.) to s.o. **gikinoo'amaw** *vta;* teach oneself **gikinoo'amaadizo** *vai*

TEACHER
TEACHER: **gekinoo'amaaged** *na-pt;* **gikinoo'amaagewinini, -wag** *na;* teacher (female) **gikinoo'amaagewikwe, -g** *na*

TEAKETTLE
TEAKETTLE: **aniibiishakik, -oog** *na*

TEAL
TEAL: **wewiibingwaange, -g** *na*

TEAR
TEAR: **giishkikaa** *vai;* **giishkikaa, giishkikaamagad** *vii;* tear s.o. **biigobizh /biigobiN-/** *vta;* tear s.t. **biigobidoon** *vti2;* tear things **biigobijige** *vai*
TEAR A PIECE OFF: tear a piece off of s.o. **bakwebizh /bakwebiN-/** *vta;* tear a piece off of s.t. **bakwebidoon** *vti2*
TEAR APART: tear s.o. apart **daashkibizh /daashkibiN-/** *vta;* tear s.t. apart **daashkibidoon** *vti2*
TEAR DOWN: tear s.o. down **niisibizh /niisibiN-/** *vta;* tear s.t. down **niisibidoon** *vti2*
TEAR OFF: tear s.o. off **giishkibizh /giishkibiN-/** *vta;* tear s.t. off **giishkibidoon** *vti2;* tear things off **giishkibijige** *vai*
TEAR STRAIGHT: tear s.o. straight **gwayakobizh /gwayakobiN-/** *vta;* tear s.t. straight **gwayakobidoon** *vti2*
TEAR TO PIECES: tear s.o. to pieces **bigishkibizh /bigishkibiN-/** *vta;* tear s.t. to pieces **bigishkibidoon** *vti2*

TEASE
TEASE: **miikindizi** *vai;* tease s.o. **miikinji'** *vta*

TEASPOON
TEASPOON: **emikwaanens, -an** *ni*

TELEPHONE
TELEPHONE: **gaagiigidoo-makakoons, -an** *ni;* **giigidowin, -an** *ni;* **giigidoo-biiwaabikoons, -an** *ni*

TELEPHONE WIRE
TELEPHONE WIRE: **giigidoo-biiwaabikoons, -an** *ni*

TELESCOPE
TELESCOPE: **zhiibaayaabanjigan, -an** *ni*

TELEVISION
TELEVISION SET: **mazinaatesijigan, -an** *ni*

TELL
TELL: **dibaajimo** *vai;* tell of s.o. **dibaajim** *vta;* tell of s.t. **dibaadodan** *vti;* tell (s.t.) to s.o. **dibaajimotaw** *vta*
COME TELLING NEWS: **biidaajimo** *vai*
START TO TELL: **maadaajimo** *vai;* start to tell of s.o. **maadaajim** *vta;* start to tell of s.t. **maadodan** *vti;* start to tell (s.t.) to s.o. **maadaajimotaw** *vta*
TELL A CERTAIN WAY: **inaajimo** *vai;* tell a certain way about s.t. **inaadodan** *vti;* tell of s.o. a certain way **inaajim** *vta;* tell s.o. of (s.t.) a certain way **inaajimotaw** *vta*
TELL A LEGEND: **aadizooke** *vai;* tell a legend to s.o. **aadizookaw** *vta*
TELL A MYTH: **aadizooke** *vai;* tell a myth to s.o. **aadizookaw** *vta*
TELL A STORY: tell a story of s.o. **aajim** *vta;* tell a story of s.t. **aadodan** *vti*
TELL A TRADITIONAL STORY: **aadizooke** *vai*
TELL ABOUT: tell s.o. about (s.t.) **wiindamaw** *vta;* tell about (s.t.) to people **wiindamaage** *vai*
TELL ALL: **giizhaajimo** *vai*
TELL GOOD NEWS: **minwaajimo** *vai;* tell good news of s.o. **minwaajim** *vta;* tell good news of s.t. **minwaadodan** *vti*
TELL IN A CERTAIN PLACE: tell of s.o. in a certain place **danaajim** *vta;* tell of s.t. in a certain place **danaadodan** *vti*
TELL ON: tell on s.o. **baataam** *vta*
TELL STORIES: **dadibaajimo** *vai;* tell stories to s.o. **dadibaajimotaw** *vta*
TELL THE TRUTH: **debwe** *vai*
TELL TO GET IN: tell s.o. to get in (a vehicle or boat) **boozinaazha' /boozinaazha'w-/** *vta*
TELL TO GO ABOARD: tell s.o. to go aboard **boozinaazha' /boozinaazha'w-/** *vta*
TELL TO HURRY: tell s.o. to hurry **wewiibim** *vta*
TELL TO SETTLE DOWN: tell s.o. to settle down **zagakim** *vta*

TEMPTED
TEMPTED: be tempted **zhoobizi** *vai*

TEN
TEN: **midaaswi** *nm;* **midaaso-** *pv4;* they are ten **midaachinoon /midaachin-/** *vii;* **midaachiwag /midaachi-/** *vai;* ten (card) **midaasoobii'igan, -ag** *na*

TEN DAYS: **midaaso-giizhik** *pc;* **midaasogon** *pc;* be ten days **midaasogonagad** *vii*
TEN DAYS OLD: be ten days old **midaasogonagizi** *vai*
TEN DOLLARS: **midaaswaabik** *pc*
TEN EACH: **memidaaswi** *nm*
TEN HOURS: **midaaso-diba'igan** *pc*
TEN INCHES: **midaasoninj** *pc*
TEN MILES: **midaaso-diba'igan** *pc*
TEN MINUTES: **midaaso-diba'igaans** *pc*
TEN MONTHS: **midaaso-giizis** *pc*
TEN NIGHTS: **midaaso-dibik** *pc*
TEN O'CLOCK: be ten o'clock **midaaso-diba'iganed** *vii*
TEN PAIRS: **midaaswewaan** *pc*
TEN SETS: **midaaswewaan** *pc*
TEN THOUSAND: **midaasosagoons** *nm*
TEN TIMES: **midaaching** *pc*
TEN WEEKS: **midaaso-anama'e-giizhik** *pc;* **midaaso-anama'e-giizhigad** *pc*
TEN YEARS: **midaaso-biboon** *pc;* be ten years **midaaso-biboonagad** *vii*
TEN YEARS OLD: be ten years old **midaaso-biboonagizi** *vai*

TENDER
TENDER: be tender **nookaa, nookaamagad** *vii;* **nookizi** *vai*
COOK TENDER: cook s.o. tender **nookiz /nookizw-/** *vta;* cook s.t. tender **nookizan** *vti*
COOKED TENDER: be cooked tender **nookide, nookidemagad** *vii;* **nookizo** *vai*

TENNIS SHOE
TENNIS SHOE: **babagiwayaanekizin, -an** *ni, also* **bagiwayaanekizin**

TENT
TENT: **babagiwayaanegamig, -oon** *ni, also* **bagiwayaanegamig**

TENTH
THE TENTH DAY OF THE MONTH: be the tenth day of the month **midaasogonagizi** *vai*

TERRIBLE
TERRIBLE: **gagwaanisagakamig** *pc;* be terrible **gagwaanisagad** *vii;* **gagwaanisagizi** *vai*
CONSIDER TERRIBLE: consider s.o. to be terrible **gagwaanisagenim** *vta;* consider s.t. terrible **gagwaanisagendan** *vti;* consider things to be terrible **gagwaanisagendam** *vai2*
CONSIDERED TERRIBLE: be considered terrible **gagwaanisagendaagozi** *vai;* **gagwaanisagendaagwad** *vii*

TEST
TEST: test s.t. **gagwejitoon** *vti2*
TEST BY TOUCH: test s.o. by touch **gagwedin** *vta;* test s.t. by touch **gagwedinan** *vti*
TEST STRENGTH: test one's strength **gagwejii** *vai*
TEST WITH FOOT OR BODY: test s.o. with foot or body **gagwezikaw** *vta;* **gozikaw** *vta;* test s.t. with foot or body **gagwezikan** *vti;* **gozikan** *vti*
TEST WITH HAND: test s.o. with hand **godin** *vta;* test s.t. with hand **godinan** *vti*

TESTICLE
TESTICLES: my testicles *plural* **ninishiwag /-nishiw-/** *nad*

TESTIFY
TESTIFY AGAINST: testify against s.o. **baataam** *vta*

THANK
THANK: thank s.o. **miigwechiwi'** *vta*
THANKS: thanks! **miigwech** *pc*

THANKFUL
THANKFUL: be thankful **miigwechiwendam** *vai2;* be thankful for s.o. **miigwechiwenim** *vta;* be thankful for s.t. **miigwechiwendan** *vti*

THANKSGIVING DAY
THANKSGIVING DAY: be Thanksgiving Day **miigwechiwi-giizhigad** *vii*

THAT
THAT: that *animate singular demonstrative* **a'aw** *pr, also* **aw, 'aw, 'a**; that *inanimate singular demonstrative* **i'iw** *pr, also* **iw, 'iw, i'i, 'i**; that *obviative demonstrative* **iniw** *pr, also* **niw, ini, ni, aniw***
THAT OVER THERE: that over there *animate singular demonstrative* **a'awedi** *pr, also* **awedi**; that over there *inanimate singular demonstrative* **iwedi** *pr, also* **i'iwedi**; that/those over there *obviative demonstrative* **iniwedin** *pr, also* **niwedin**

THAT
THAT: **ji-** *pv1*

THAW
THAW: **ningide, ningidemagad** *vii;* **ningizo** *vai*

THEATER
MOVIE THEATER: **mazinaatesewigamig, -oon** *ni, also* **mazinaatesijigewigamig**

THEN
THEN: **apii** *pc;* **azhigwa** *pc, also* **zhigwa, zhigo**
AND THEN: **mii dash** *pc, also* **miish**
JUST THEN: **na'idaa** *pc*

THERE
THERE: **imaa** *pc, also* **maa, i'imaa**; **izhi-** pv3; **dazhi-** *pv3*
OVER THERE: **iwidi** *pc*

THEREFORE
THEREFORE: **indawaaj** *pc*

THESE
THESE: these *animate plural demonstrative* **ongow** *pr, also* **ongo, ogow*, ogo***; these *inanimate plural demonstrative,* **onow** *pr; also* **ono**; this/these *obviative demonstrative* **onow** *pr, also* **ono**
THESE OVER HERE: these over here *animate plural demonstrative* **ongowedig** *pr, also* **ogowedig***; these over here *inanimate plural demonstrative* **onowedin** *pr;* this/these over here *obviative demonstrative* **onowedin** *pr*

THEY
THEY: they *third person plural personal pronoun* **wiinawaa** *pr*
THICK
THICK: be thick **gipagaa, gipagaamagad** *vii;* **gipagizi** *vai;* be thick (as something mineral) **gipagaabikad** *vii;* **gipagaabikizi** *vai;* be thick (as something sheet-like) **gipagiigad** *vii;* **gipagiigizi** *vai;* be thick (as something string-like) **gipagaabiigad** *vii;* **gipagaabiigizi** *vai*
FROZEN THICK: be frozen thick **gipagaakwadin** *vii;* **gipagaakwaji** *vai*
LIE IN A THICK LAYER: **gipagishin** *vai;* **gipagisin** *vii*
SLICE THICK: slice s.o. thick **gipagikozh /gipagikoN-/** *vta;* slice s.t. thick **gipagikodan** *vti*
THICK FUR: have thick fur **gipagawe** *vai*
THICKEN
THICKEN INTO SYRUP: **zhiiwaagamide, zhiiwaagamidemagad** *vii*
THICKNESS
CERTAIN THICKNESS: be a certain thickness **apiitaa, apiitaamagad** *vii*
HAVE A CERTAIN THICKNESS: **apiitizi** *vai*
THIEF
THIEF: **gimoodishkiiwinini, -wag** *na;* be a thief **gimoodishki** *vai*
THIGH
THIGH: my thigh (back of thigh) **imbwaam, -an /-bwaam-/** *nid;* my thigh (front of thigh) **injiingwan, -ag /-jiingwan-/** *nad*
THIMBLE
THIMBLE: **gaanda'igwaason, -an** *ni*
THIN
THIN: be thin **bibagaa, bibagaamagad** *vii;* **bibagizi** *vai;* be thin (as something mineral) **bibagaabikaad** *vii;* **bibagaabikizi** *vai;* be thin (as something sheet-like) **bibagiigad** *vii;* **bibagiigizi** *vai;* be thin (of a person) **bakaakadozo** *vai*
FROZEN THIN: be frozen thin **bibagaakwadin** *vii;* **bibagaakwaji** *vai*
LIE IN A THIN LAYER: **bibagishin** *vai;* **bibagisin** *vii*
SLICE THIN: slice s.o. thin **bibagikozh /bibagikoN-/** *vta;* slice s.t. thin **bibagikodan** *vti*
THING
THING: **ayi'ii, -n** *pr*
VARIETY OF THINGS: a variety of things **anooj gegoo** *pr, also* **anooji-gegoo**
THINK
THINK: **maaminonendam** *vai2;* **naagadawendam** *vai2;* **naanaagadawendam** *vai2;* think on s.o. **maaminonenim** *vta;* think on s.t. **maaminonendan** *vti*
COME TO THINK OF: come to think of s.o. **mikwenim** *vta;* come to think of s.t. **mikwendan** *vti*
NOT KNOW WHAT TO THINK: **gwiinawi-inendam** *vai2*
THINK A CERTAIN WAY: **inendam** *vai2;* think a certain way of s.t. **inendan** *vti;* think of s.o. a certain way **inenim** *vta*
THINK ABOUT: think about s.o. **naagadawenim** *vta;* **naanaagadawenim** *vta;* think about s.t. **naagadawendan** *vti;* **naanaagadawendan** *vti*
THINK ABOUT GOING HOME: think about going home again **giiweyendam** *vai2*
THINK ABOUT RETURNING: **giiweyendam** *vai2*
THINK CORRECTLY: **gwayakwendam** *vai2*
TRY TO THINK: try to think of s.o. **nanda-mikwenim** *vta;* try to think of s.t. **nanda-mikwendan** *vti*
THIRD
THIRD: the third **eko-nising** *pc*
THE THIRD DAY OF THE MONTH: be the third day of the month **nisogonagizi** *vai*
THIRD PERSON
THIRD PERSON: *third person prefix before consonants in verbs and nouns* **o=** *pre; third person prefix before vowels in verbs and non-dependent nouns* **od=** *pre; third person prefix before initial* **ii** *dependent noun stems* **w=** *pre*
THIRD PERSON PLURAL: they *third person plural personal pronoun* **wiinawaa** *pr;* their turn *third person plural personal pronoun* **wiinitamawaa** *pr;* only them *third person plural personal pronoun* **wiinetawaa** *pr*
THIRD PERSON SINGULAR: she/he *third person singular personal pronoun* **wiin** *pr;* his/her turn *third person singular personal pronoun* **wiinitam** *pr;* only her/him *third person singular pronoun* **wiineta** *pr*
THIRST
SUFFER FROM THIRST: **gawaabaagwe** *vai*
THIRSTY
THIRSTY: be thirsty **giishkaabaagwe** *vai*
THIRTEEN
THIRTEEN: **ashi-niswi** *nm;* **midaaswi ashi-niswi** *nm*
THIRTY
THIRTY: **nisimidana** *nm*
THIS
THIS: this *animate singular demonstrative* **wa'aw** *pr;* this *inanimate singular demonstrative* **o'o** *pr, also* **o'ow, 'ow, 'o, o'o;** this/these *obviative demonstrative* **onow,** *also* **ono** *pr*
THIS OVER HERE: this over here *animate singular demonstrative* **wa'awedi** *pr;* this over here *inanimate singular demonstrative* **o'owedi,** *also* **owedi** *pr;* this/these over here *obviative demonstrative* **onowedin** *pr*
THISTLE
THISTLE: **mazaanaatig, -oog** *na*

THOSE

THOSE: those *animate plural demonstrative* **ingiw** *pr, also* **ingi, igiw*, igi*, agiw***; those *inanimate plural demonstrative* **iniw** *pr, also* **niw, ini, ni, aniw***; those *obviative* **iniw** *pr, also* **niw, ini, ni, aniw***

THOSE OVER THERE: those over there *animate plural demonstrative* **ingiwedig** *pr, also* **igiwedig***; those over there *inanimate plural* **iniwedin** *pr, also* **niwedin**; those over there *obviative demonstrative* **iniwedin** *pr, also* **niwedin**

THOUGHT

THOUGHT OF A CERTAIN WAY: be thought of a certain way **inendaagozi** *vai;* **inendaagwad** *vii*

THOUSAND

THOUSAND: **midaaswaak** *nm*

CERTAIN NUMBER OF THOUSANDS: a certain number of thousands **dasosagoons** *nm*

EIGHT THOUSAND: **ishwaasosagoons** *nm, also* **nishwaasosagoons***

FIVE THOUSAND: **naanosagoons** *nm*

FOUR THOUSAND: **niiwosagoons** *nm, also* **niiyosagoons**

NINE THOUSAND: **zhaangasosagoons** *nm*

ONE THOUSAND: **ingodosagoons** *nm, also* **ningodosagoons***

SEVEN THOUSAND: **niizhwaasosagoons** *nm*

SIX THOUSAND: **ingodwaasosagoons /ningodwaasosagoons-/** *nm, also* **ningodwaasosagoons***

TEN THOUSAND: **midaasosagoons** *nm*

THREE THOUSAND: **nisosagoons** *nm*

TWO THOUSAND: **niizhosagoons** *nm*

THREAD

THREAD: **asabaab, -iin** *ni;* thread s.o. **naabidoo' /naabidoo'w-/** *vta;* thread s.t. **naabidoo'an** *vti;* thread things **naabidoo'ige** *vai*

SEWING THREAD: **gashkigwaasoneyaab, -iin** *ni*

THREAD CORRECTLY: thread s.t. correctly **gwayakwaabidoo'an** *vti*

THREE

THREE: **niswi** *nm;* **niso-** *pv4;* they are three **nisinoon /nisin-/** *vii;* **nisiwag /nisi-/** *vai;* three (card) **nisoobii'igan, -ag** *na*

AND THREE: **ashi-niso-** *pv4;* **ashi-niswi** *nm*

THREE ACRES: **niso-diba'igaans** *pc*

THREE DAYS: **niso-giizhik** *pc;* **nisogon** *pc;* be three days **nisogonagad** *vii*

THREE DAYS OLD: be three days old **nisogonagizi** *vai*

THREE DOLLARS: **niswaabik** *pc*

THREE EACH: **neniswi** *nm*

THREE FEET: **nisozid** *pc*

THREE HOURS: **niso-diba'igan** *pc*

THREE HUNDRED: **niswaak** *nm*

THREE INCHES: **nisoninj** *pc*

THREE MILES: **niso-diba'igan** *pc*

THREE MINUTES: **niso-diba'igaans** *pc*

THREE MONTHS: **niso-giizis** *pc*

THREE NIGHTS: **niso-dibik** *pc*

THREE O'CLOCK: be three o'clock **niso-diba'iganed** *vii*

THREE PAIRS: **niswewaan** *pc*

THREE SETS: **niswewaan** *pc*

THREE THOUSAND: **nisosagoons** *nm*

THREE TIMES: **nising** *pc*

THREE WEEKS: **niso-anama'e-giizhik** *pc;* be three weeks **niso-anama'e-giizhigad** *vii*

THREE YEARS: **niso-biboon** *pc;* be three years **niso-biboonagad** *vii*

THREE YEARS OLD: be three years old **niso-biboonagizi** *vai*

THRESH

THRESH: thresh field crops **bakiteshka'ige** *vai;* thresh s.t. (e.g., wild rice) **mimigoshkan** *vti*

BARREL OR TUB USED IN THRESHING WILD RICE: **mimigoshkamwaagan, -an** *ni*

THRESH WILD RICE: thresh something **mimigoshkam** *vai2*

THRICE

THRICE: **nising** *pc*

THROAT

THROAT: my throat **ingondashkway /-gondashkway-/** *nid*

SORE THROAT: have a sore throat **wiisagigonewe** *vai*

THROUGH

THROUGH: through it **zhaabwayi'ii** *pc*

BITE THROUGH: bite s.o. through (e.g., something string-like) **bakam** *vta;* bite s.t. through (e.g., something string-like) **bakandan** *vti*

GO THROUGH: **zhaabose, zhaabosemagad** *vii;* **zhaabwii** *vai*

PASS THROUGH: **zhaabose, zhaabosemagad** *vii;* **zhaabwii** *vai*

PUT THROUGH: put s.o. through **zhaabon** *vta;* put s.t. through **zhaabonan** *vti*

RUN THROUGH: **zhaabobatoo** *vai*

SEE THROUGH: see through s.o. **zhaabwaabam** *vta;* see through s.t. **zhaabwaabandan** *vti*

THROUGHOUT

THROUGHOUT: **gabe-** *pv4;* throughout it **gabe-ayi'ii** *pc, also* **gabeyi'ii**

THROW

THROW: throw s.o. **apagizh /apagiN-/** *vta;* throw s.t. **apagidan** *vti, also* **apagidoon**; throw (s.t.) at s.o. **apagidaw** *vta;* throw things **apagijige** *vai;* they throw (s.t.) at each other **apagidaadiwag /apagidaadi-/** *vai*

THROW AROUND: throw things around **ombwewebinige** *vai*

THROW AWAY: throw s.o. away **webin** *vta;* throw s.t. away **webinan** *vti;* throw things away **webinige** *vai*

THROW DOWN: throw s.o. down **gawiwebin** *vta;* throw s.t. down **gawiwebinan** *vti*

THROW DOWN QUICKLY: throw s.o. down quickly **bagijwebin** *vta;* throw s.t. down quickly **bagijwebinan** *vti*
THROW HERE: throw s.o. here **biijwebin** *vta;* throw s.t. here **biijwebinan** *vti;* throw (s.t.) here to s.o. **biijwebinamaw** *vta*
THROW IN: throw s.o. in **biinjwebin** *vta;* throw s.t. in **biinjwebinan** *vti;* throw things in **biinjwebinige** *vai*
THROW INSIDE: throw s.o. inside **biindigewebin** *vta;* throw s.t. inside **biindigewebinan** *vti;* throw things inside **biindigewebinige** *vai*
THROW INTO THE WATER: throw s.o. into the water **bakobiiwebin** *vta;* throw s.t. into the water **bakobiiwebinan** *vti*
THROW OUT OF THE WATER: throw s.o. out of the water **agwaawebin** *vta;* throw s.t. out of the water **agwaawebinan** *vti;* throw (s.t.) out of the water for s.o. **agwaawebinamaw** *vta*
THROW OUTSIDE: throw s.o. outside **zaagijiwebin** *vta;* throw s.t. outside **zaagijiwebinan** *vti;* throw things outside **zaagijiwebinige** *vai*
THROW OVER: throw s.o. over **baazhijiwebin** *vta;* throw s.t. over **baazhijiwebinan** *vti*
THROW OVER BACKWARDS: throw s.o. over backwards **aazhigidwebin** *vta;* throw s.t. over backwards **aazhigidwebinan** *vti*
THROW SELF DOWN AGAINST SOMETHING: **apagizo** *vai*
THROW UP AGAINST: throw s.o. up against (as something stick- or wood-like) **aatwaakowebin** *vta;* throw s.t. up against (as something stick- or wood-like) **aatwaakowebinan** *vti*
THROW UPWARDS: throw s.o. upwards **ombiwebin** *vta;* throw s.t. upwards **ombiwebinan** *vti*

THROWN
THROWN AWAY: be thrown away **webinigaade, webinigaademagad** *vii;* **webinigaazo** *vai*
THROWN OUTSIDE: be thrown outside **zaagijiwebinigaade, zaagijiwebinigaademagad** *vii*

THUMB
THUMB: **midechininj, -iin** *ni*

THUNDER
THUNDER: come making noise (e.g., thunder) **biidwewidam** *vai2;* there is thunder **animikiikaa, animikiikaamagad** *vii*

THUNDERBIRD
THUNDERBIRD: **animikii, -g** *na;* **binesi, -wag** *na*

THUNDERCLAP
MAKE A THUNDERCLAP: make a thunderclap (of the thunderers) **baashkakwa'am** *vai2*

THUNDERER
THUNDERER: **animikii, -g** *na*

THURSDAY
THURSDAY: be Thursday **niiwo-giizhigad** *vii, also* **niiyo-giizhigad**

THUS
THUS: **izhi-** *pv3*

THWART
THWART: **bimidasaa, -g** *na, also* **bimidasaagan, -an**

TICK
WOOD TICK: **ezigaa, -g** *na*

TICKET
TICKET: **mazina'igaans, -an** *ni*

TICKLE
TICKLE: tickle s.o. (at the mid-section) **ginagijiin** *vta*

TIDIED
TIDIED: be tidied **zagakinigaade, zagakinigaademagad** *vii;* **zagakinigaazo** *vai*

TIDY
TIDY: tidy s.o. **zagakin** *vta;* tidy s.t. **zagakinan** *vti;* tidy things **zagakinige** *vai*

TIE
TIE: tie s.o. **dakobizh /dakobiN-/** *vta;* tie s.t. **dakobidoon** *vti2;* tie things **dakobijige** *vai*
TIE IN A BUNCH: tie s.o. in a bunch **okwapizh /okwapiN-/** *vta;* tie s.t. in a bunch **okwapidoon** *vti2*
TIE IN A BUNDLE: tie s.o. in a bundle **gashkapizh /gashkapiN-/** *vta;* tie s.t. in a bundle **gashkapidoon** *vti2*
TIE IN PLACE: tie s.o. in place **onapizh /onapiN-/** *vta;* tie s.t. in place **onapidoon** *vti2*
TIE ON: tie s.o. on **zagapizh /zagapiN-/** *vta;* tie s.o. on something **agwapizh /agwapiN-/** *vta;* tie s.t. on **zagapidoon** *vti2;* tie s.t. on something **agwapidoon** *vti2*
TIE SHUT: tie s.o. shut **gashkapizh /gashkapiN-/** *vta;* tie s.t. shut **gashkapidoon** *vti2*
TIE TIGHT: tie s.o. tight **mashkawapizh /mashkawapiN-/** *vta;* tie s.t. tight **mashkawapidoon** *vti2*
TIE WILD RICE: **dakobidoo** *vai*
TIE WITH A KNOT: tie s.o. with a knot **gashka'oozh /gashka'ooN-/** *vta;* tie s.t. with a knot **gashka'oodoon** *vti2*

TIED
TIED: be tied **dakobide, dakobidemagad** *vii;* **dakobizo** *vai*
TIED IN A BUNCH: be tied in a bunch **okwapide, okwapidemagad** *vii;* **okwapizo** *vai*
TIED IN PLACE: be tied in place **onapide, onapidemagad** *vii*
TIED ON: be tied on **agwapijigaade, agwapijigaademagad** *vii;* **agwapijigaazo** *vai;* **zagapide, zagapidemagad** *vii;* **zagapizo** *vai*
TIED TIGHT: be tied tight **mashkawapide, mashkawapidemagad** *vii;* **mashkawapizo** *vai*
TIED WILD RICE: **dakobijigan, -an** *ni*

TIGHT PLACE
CRAWL IN A TIGHT PLACE: **zhegoode** *vai*
LIE IN A TIGHT PLACE: **zhegoshin** *vai;* **zhegosin** *vii*
PUT IN A TIGHT PLACE: put s.o. in a tight place **zhegoshim** *vta;* put s.t. in a tight place **zhegosidoon** *vti2*
STICK IN A TIGHT PLACE: stick s.o. in a tight place **zhegon** *vta;* stick s.t. in a tight place **zhegonan** *vti*

TIMBER
CUT TIMBER: **giishka'aakwe** *vai*
PEEL TIMBER USING SOMETHING: **bishagaakwa'ige** *vai*

TIME
AT ONE TIME: **aabiding** *pc;* **ingoding** *pc, also* **ningoding***
AT THAT TIME: **iw apii** *pr, also* **i'iw apii**
AT THE TIME: **apii** *pc*
AT THIS TIME: **azhigwa** *pc, also* **zhigwa, zhigo**
CERTAIN TIME IN HOURS: be a certain time in hours **daso-diba'iganed** *vii*
COMING UP TO IN TIME: **ani-** *pv2, also* **ni-**
FOR SOME TIME: **gomaapii** *pc*

TIMES
CERTAIN NUMBER OF TIMES: a certain number of times **dasing** *pc*
SO MANY TIMES: **dasing** *pc*

TIMID
TIMID: be timid **gotaajishki** *vai*

TINDER
TINDER: **zagataagan, -ag** *na*

TINGLE
TINGLE: **giikimanizi** *vai*

TINY
TINY: they are tiny **babiiwaawan /babiiwaa-/** *vii;* **babiiwizhiinyiwag /babiiwizhiinyi-/** *vai;* they are tiny (as something ball-like) **babiiwiminagadoon /babiiwiminagad-/** *vii;* **babiiwiminagiziwag /babiiwiminagizi-/** *vai*

TIP
TIP: **gwanabishkaa** *vai;* tip s.o. **gotigobizh /gotigobiN-/** *vta;* tip s.t. **gotigobidoon** *vti2*
TIP OVER BY HAND: tip s.o. over by hand **gawin** *vta;* tip s.t. over by hand **gawinan** *vti*
TIP WITH FOOT OR BODY: tip s.t. with foot or body **gwanabishkan** *vti*

TIP
ON THE TIP: **wanakong** *pc*

TIPI
TIPI: **bajiishka'ogaan, -an** *ni*

TIRE
FLAT TIRE: have a flat tire **nabagijiishin** *vai*

TIRE PUMP
TIRE PUMP: **boodaajii'igan, -an** *ni*

TIRED
TIRED: be tired **ayekozi** *vai;* **zhigajii** *vai*
FEEL TIRED: **ayekwamanji'o** *vai*
MAKE TIRED: make s.o. tired **ayeko'** *vta*
TIRED OF WAITING: be tired of waiting **zhigajibii'o** *vai;* be tired of waiting for s.o. **zhigajibii'** *vta;* be tired of waiting for s.t. **zhigajibiitoon** *vti2*

TO
TO: to a certain place **izhi-** *pv3*
CARRIED TO A CERTAIN PLACE: be carried to a certain place **izhiwijigaade, izhiwijigaademagad** *vii;* **izhiwijigaazo** *vai*
CARRY A BABY TO A CERTAIN PLACE ON BACK: carry a baby to a certain place on one's back **inoomaawaso** *vai*
CARRY TO A CERTAIN PLACE: carry s.o. to a certain place **izhiwizh /izhiwiN-/** *vta;* carry s.t. to a certain place **izhiwidoon** *vti2*
CARRY TO A CERTAIN PLACE ON BACK: carry s.o. to a certain place on one's back **inoom** *vta;* carry s.t. to a certain place on one's back **inoondan** *vti*
CHASE TO A CERTAIN PLACE: chase s.o. to a certain place **izhinaazhikaw** *vta;* **izhinizhikaw** *vta*
CLIMB TO CERTAIN PLACE: climb to a certain place **inaandawe** *vai*
CRAWL TO A CERTAIN PLACE: **inoode** *vai*
DRAG TO A CERTAIN PLACE: drag s.o. to a certain place **izhidaabaazh /izhidaabaaN-/** *vta;* drag s.t. to a certain place **izhidaabaadan** *vti*
DRIVE TO A CERTAIN PLACE: **ipide, ipidemagad** *vii;* **ipizo** *vai;* **izhidaabii'iwe** *vai;* drive s.o. to a certain place **ipizoni'** *vta;* drive s.t. to a certain place **ipizonitoon** *vti2*
FLOW TO A CERTAIN PLACE: **izhijiwan** *vii*
FLY TO A CERTAIN PLACE: **ipide, ipidemagad** *vii;* **ipizo** *vai;* **izhise** *vai;* **izhise, izhisemagad** *vii*
FOLLOW A TRAIL TO A CERTAIN PLACE: follow s.o.'s trail to a certain place **ina'azh /ina'aN-/** *vta;* follow s.t. as a trail to a certain place **ina'adoon** *vti2*
GO TO A CERTAIN PLACE: **izhaa** *vai;* **izhaamagad** *vii*
GO TO A CERTAIN PLACE CRYING: **inademo** *vai*
GO TO A CERTAIN PLACE ON THE ICE: **inaadagaako** *vai*
GO TO A CERTAIN PLACE WITH LIGHT: **inaazakonenjige** *vai*
HAUL TO A CERTAIN PLACE: haul s.o. to a certain place **inaawazh /inaawaN-/** *vta;* haul s.t. to a certain place **inaawadoon** *vti2;* haul something to a certain place **inaawadaaso** *vai*
LEAVE TRACKS GOING TO A CERTAIN PLACE: **izhikawe** *vai*
LOOK TO A CERTAIN PLACE: **inaabi** *vai*
PADDLE TO A CERTAIN PLACE: **ina'o** *vai;* **inakwazhiwe** *vai*
POLE A BOAT TO A CERTAIN PLACE: **ina'oodoo** *vai*

RIDE TO A CERTAIN PLACE ON HORSEBACK: ride to a certain place on horseback **inoomigo** *vai*
RIDE TO A CERTAIN PLACE WITH HORSES: **apa'igo** *vai*
RIVER FLOWS TO A CERTAIN PLACE: flow to a certain place (as a river) **izhitigweyaa, izhitigweyaamagad** *vii*
ROAD LEADS TO A CERTAIN PLACE: lead to a certain place (as a road or trail) **inamon /inamo-/** *vii*
RUN AWAY TO A CERTAIN PLACE: run away from people to a certain place **apa'iwe** *vai*
RUN TO A CERTAIN PLACE: **apatoo** *vai;* run with s.o. to a certain place **apa'** *vta*
RUN TO A CERTAIN PLACE IN FLIGHT: **izhinizhimo** *vai*
RUN TO A CERTAIN PLACE TOGETHER: they run to a certain place together **apa'idiwag /apa'idi-/** *vai*
SAIL TO A CERTAIN PLACE: **inaashi** *vai;* **inaasin** *vii*
SEND SMOKE TO A CERTAIN PLACE: **inaabasige** *vai*
SEND TO A CERTAIN PLACE: send s.o. to a certain place **izhinaazhikaw** *vta;* **izhinizha' /izhinizha'w-/** *vta;* send s.t. to a certain place **izhinizha'an** *vti;* send (s.t.) to s.o. to a certain place **izhinizha'amaw** *vta*
SENT TO A CERTAIN PLACE: be sent to a certain place **izhinizha'igaade, izhinizha'igaademagad** *vii;* **izhinizha'igaazo** *vai*
SKATE TO A CERTAIN PLACE: **inaada'e** *vai*
SPEED TO A CERTAIN PLACE: **ipide, ipidemagad** *vii;* **ipizo** *vai*
SWIM TO A CERTAIN PLACE: **inaadagaa** *vai;* swim to a certain place (as a fish) **inakwazhiwe** *vai*
TAKE TO A CERTAIN PLACE: take s.o. to a certain place **izhiwizh /izhiwiN-/** *vta;* take s.t. to a certain place **izhiwidoon** *vti2;* take (s.t.) to s.o. at a certain place **izhiwidaw** *vta*
TAKE TO A CERTAIN PLACE BY BOAT: take s.o. to a certain place by boat **ina'oozh /ina'ooN-/** *vta;* take s.t. to a certain place by boat **ina'oodoon** *vti2*
TAKEN TO A CERTAIN PLACE: be taken to a certain place **izhiwijigaade, izhiwijigaademagad** *vii;* **izhiwijigaazo** *vai*
TO A CERTAIN PLACE: **izhi-** *pv3*
TRAIL LEADS TO A CERTAIN PLACE: lead to a certain place (as a road or trail) **inamon /inamo-/** *vii*
TRAVEL TO A CERTAIN PLACE: travel in a group to a certain place **inaawanidiwag /inaawanidi-/** *vai*
WADE TO A CERTAIN PLACE: **inaadagaazii** *vai*
WALK ALONG SHORE TO A CERTAIN PLACE: **inaazhagaame** *vai*
WALK TO CERTAIN PLACE: walk to a certain place **inose** *vai*

TOAD
TOAD: **babiigomakakii, -g** *na;* **obiigomakakii, -g** *na*

TOAST
TOAST BROWN: toast s.t. brown **ozaawaakizan** *vti*

TOBACCO
TOBACCO: **asemaa** *na*
CHEW SNUFF OR TOBACCO: **biindaakwe** *vai*
CHEW TOBACCO: **agwanenjige** *vai*
MAKE AN OFFERING OF TOBACCO: **biindaakoojige** *vai;* make an offering of tobacco to s.o. **biindaakoozh /biindaakooN-/** *vta*
SHORT OF TOBACCO: be short of tobacco **manepwaa** *vai*

TOBACCO BAG
TOBACCO BAG: **gashkibidaagan, -ag** *na*

TOBOGGAN
TOBOGGAN: **nabagidaabaan, -ag** *na;* **zhooshkodaabaan, -ag** *na*

TODAY
TODAY: **noongom** *pc*

TOE
TOE: **niibinaakwaanizidaan, -an** *ni*
BIG TOE: **midechizid, -an** *ni*

TOGETHER
TOGETHER: **maamawi** *pc;* **maamawoo-** *pv4*
ADD TOGETHER: **asigagindaaso** *vai;* add s.o. together (e.g., money) **asigagim** *vta;* add s.t. together **asigagindan** *vti*
BRING TOGETHER: bring s.t. together **maawandoonan** *vti*
COME TOGETHER: they come together **maawanji'idiwag /maawanji'idi-/** *vai*
SEW TOGETHER: **maawandoogwaaso** *vai;* sew s.o. together **maawandoogwaazh /maawandoogwaaN-/** *vta;* sew s.t. together (e.g., pieces for a quilt) **maawandoogwaadan** *vti*
SIT TOGETHER: they sit together **maawandoobiwag /maawandoobi-/** *vai*

TOILET
TOILET: **miiziiwigamig, -oon** *ni;* **zaaga'amoowigamig, -oon** *ni*
GO TO THE TOILET: **zaaga'am** *vai2*

TOILET TISSUE
TOILET TISSUE: **giziindime'on, -an** *ni*

TOMATO
TOMATO: **gichi-ogin, -iig** *na;* **ogin, -iig** *na*

TOMORROW
TOMORROW: be tomorrow **waaban** *vii*
DAY AFTER TOMORROW: **awas-waabang** *pc*

TONGUE
TONGUE: my tongue **indenaniw, -an /-denaniw-/** *nid*
STICK OUT TONGUE: stick out one's tongue **zaagidenaniweni** *vai;* stick out one's tongue at s.o. **zaagidenaniwetaw** *vta*

TOO
TOO: **gaye** *pc, also* **ge**
DRINK TOO MUCH: **onzaamibii** *vai*
GIVE TOO MUCH TO DRINK: give s.o. too much to drink **onzaamibazh /onzaamibaN-/** *vta*
PACK TOO MUCH OF A LOAD: **onzaamiwane** *vai*
TALK TOO MUCH: **onzaamidoon** *vai*
TOO LATE: **naanabem** *pc*
TOO MANY: be too many **onzaamiinad** *vii;* **onzaamiino** *vai*
TOO MUCH: **onzaam** *pc;* be too much **onzaamiinad** *vii;* **onzaamiino** *vai*

TOOL
TOOL: **aabajichigan, -an** *ni*

TOOTH
TOOTH: my tooth **niibid, -an /-iibid-/** *nid*
ABSCESSED TOOTH: have an abscessed tooth **miniiwaabide** *vai*
BRUSH TEETH: brush one's teeth **giziiyaabide'o** *vai;* **giziiyaabide'odizo** *vai*
FALSE TEETH: false teeth *plural* **wiibidaakaajiganan** *ni, also* **wiibidaakaanan**
PICK TEETH: pick one's teeth **zesegwaabide'o** *vai*

TOOTHACHE
TOOTHACHE: have a toothache **dewaabide** *vai*

TOOTHBRUSH
TOOTHBRUSH: **giziiyaabide'on, -an** *ni*

TOOTHLESS
TOOTHLESS: be toothless **bashkwanige** *vai*

TOOTHPICK
TOOTHPICK: **zesegwaabide'on, -an** *ni*

TOP
ON TOP: on top of **agiji-** *pn, also* **ogiji-*, wagiji-**; on top of it **agijayi'ii** *pc, also* **ogijayi'ii*, wagijayi'ii**
ON TOP OF A HILL: **agidaaki** *pc, also* **ogidaaki*, wagidaaki**
ON TOP OF A MOUNTAIN: **agidajiw** *pc, also* **ogidajiw*, wagidajiw**
ON TOP OF A ROCK: **agidasin** *pc, also* **ogidasin*, wagidasin**
ON TOP OF THE GROUND: **agidakamig** *pc, also* **ogidakamig*, wagidakamig**
ON TOP OF THE HOUSE: **agidigamig** *pc, also* **ogidigamig*, wagidigamig**
ON TOP OF THE ICE: **agidiskwam** *pc, also* **ogidiskwam*, wagidiskwam**
ON TOP OF THE WATER: **agidibiig** *pc, also* **ogidibiig*, wagidibiig**

TOP
TOY TOP: **ishkwesa'igan, -ag** *na*

TORCH
TORCH: **waaswaagan, -an** *ni*
BARK TORCH: **biimashkwemaginigan, -an** *ni*

TORN
TORN: be torn **biigobijigaade, biigobijigaademagad** *vii;* **biigobijigaazo** *vai*
TORN APART: be torn apart **daashkaa, daashkaamagad** *vii*
TORN OFF: be torn off **giishkibijigaade, giishkibijigaademagad** *vii;* **giishkibijigaazo** *vai*

TORNADO
TORNADO: be a tornado **wese'an** *vii*

TOSS
TOSS ASIDE: toss s.o. aside **ikowebin** *vta;* toss s.t. aside **ikowebinan** *vti*

TOTAL
TOTAL UP: **asigagindaaso** *vai;* total up (as an account) **maawandoogindaaso** *vai;* total up s.t. (as an account) **maawandoogindan** *vti*

TOTEM
TOTEM: my totem **indoodem, -ag /-doodem-/** *nad*
HAVE A TOTEM: have a totem (clan) **odoodemi** *vai;* they have a mutual totem (clan) **odoodemindiwag /odoodemindi-/** *vai*

TOUCH
TOUCH: touch s.o. with hand **daangin** *vta;* touch s.t. with hand **daanginan** *vti*
LIE TOUCHING: **daangishin** *vai;* **daangisin** *vii*
PUT TOUCHING: put s.o. touching **daangishim** *vta;* put s.t. touching **daangisidoon** *vti2*
TEST BY TOUCH: test s.o. by touch **gagwedin** *vta;* test s.t. by touch **gagwedinan** *vti*
TOUCH WRONG ONE: touch s.o. who/that is the wrong one **wanin** *vta;* touch s.t. that is the wrong one **waninan** *vti*

TOURIST
TOURIST: **bebaamaadizid** *na-pt*

TOW
TOW: tow s.o. **zagapizh /zagapiN-/** *vta;* tow s.t. **zagapidoon** *vti2*

TOWARD
TOWARD THE SPEAKER: **bi-** *pv2*

TOWED
TOWED: be towed **zagapide, zagapidemagad** *vii;* **zagapizo** *vai*

TOWEL
TOWEL: **giziingwe'on, -an** *ni*
DISH TOWEL: **giziiyaabika'igan, -an** *ni*

TOWN
TOWN: **oodena, -wan** *ni*
LIVE ON THE END OF TOWN: live at the end of town **ishkwege** *vai*

TOY
TOY: **odaminwaagan, -an** *ni*
USE AS A TOY: use (s.t.) as a toy **odaminwaage** *vai+o*

TRACK
TRACK: **bimikawaan, -an** *ni*
COME LEAVING TRACKS: **biijikawe** *vai*
FIND TRACKS: find s.o.'s tracks **okawi'** *vta;* find the tracks of s.t. **okawitoon** *vti2*

LEAVE TRACKS GOING ALONG: **bimikawe** *vai*
LEAVE TRACKS GOING AWAY: **animikawe** *vai*
LEAVE TRACKS GOING TO A CERTAIN PLACE: **izhikawe** *vai*
LOOK FOR TRACKS: **nandokawechige** *vai;* look for s.o.'s tracks **nandokawe'** *vta*

TRADE
TRADE: trade s.o. **meshkwadoon** *vta;* trade s.t. **meshkwadoonan** *vti;* trade (s.t.) with s.o. **meshkwadoonamaw** *vta;* trade for things **meshkwadoonige** *vai;* trade things with people **meshkwadoonamaage** *vai*
GO ABOUT TRADING: **babaamadaawe** *vai*

TRADER
TRADER: **adaawewinini, -wag** *na;* trader (female) **adaawewiniiikwe** *na*

TRAIL
TRAIL: **miikana, -n** *ni;* be a trail **miikanaawan** *vii*
ALONG THE SIDE OF THE TRAIL: **opimekana** *pc*
AT THE END OF THE TRAIL: at the end of the road or trail **gabekana** *pc*
BAD TRAIL: be bad (as a road or trail) **maanadamon /maanadamo-/** *vii*
BY A TRAIL: by a road or trail **jiigikana** *pc*
FOLLOW A TRAIL: go off following a trail **maada'adoo** *vai;* go off following s.o.'s trail **maada'azh /maada'aN-/** *vta*
FOLLOW A TRAIL ALONG: **bima'adoo** *vai;* follow s.o.'s trail along **bima'azh /bima'aN-/** *vta;* follow s.t. along as a trail **bima'adoon** *vti2*
FOLLOW A TRAIL AWAY: **anima'adoo** *vai;* follow s.o.'s trail away **anima'azh /anima'aN-/** *vta;* follow s.t. away as a trail **anima'adoon** *vti2*
FOLLOW A TRAIL HERE: **biida'adoo** *vai;* follow s.o.'s trail here **biida'azh /biida'aN-/** *vta;* follow s.t. as a trail here **biida'adoon** *vti2*
FOLLOW A TRAIL TO A CERTAIN PLACE: follow s.o.'s trail to a certain place **ina'azh /ina'aN-/** *vta;* follow s.t. as a trail to a certain place **ina'adoon** *vti2*
ICY TRAIL: be icy (as a road or trail) **mikwamiiwadamon /mikwamiiwadamo-/** *vii*
IN THE MIDDLE OF THE TRAIL: in the middle of the road or trail **naawikana** *pc*
MAKE A TRAIL: make a road or trail **miikanaake** *vai*
NARROW TRAIL: be narrow (as a road or trail) **agaasademon /agaasademo-/** *vii*
ON THE OTHER SIDE OF THE TRAIL: on the other side of the road or trail **agaamikana** *pc*
ON THIS SIDE OF THE TRAIL: **ondaasikana** *pc*
SLIPPERY TRAIL: be slippery (as a road or trail) **ozhaashadamon /ozhaashadamo-/** *vii;* **zhooshkwadamon /zhooshkwadamo-/** *vii;* be slippery with ice (as a road or trail) **ozhaashikwadamon /ozhaashikwadamo-/** *vii*
TRAIL FORKS: fork (as a road or trail) **niingidawadamon /niingidawadamo-/** *vii*
TRAIL GOES ACROSS: go across (as a road or trail) **aazhoodamon /aazhoodamo-/** *vii*
TRAIL GOES OFF TO THE SIDE: go off to the side (as a road or trail) **bakemon /bakemo-/** *vii*
TRAIL LEADS ALONG: lead along (as a road or trail) **bimamon /bimamo-/, bimamoomagad** *vii*
TRAIL LEADS FROM A CERTAIN PLACE: lead from a certain place (as a road or trail) **ondadamon /ondadamo-/** *vii*
TRAIL LEADS TO A CERTAIN PLACE: lead to a certain place (as a road or trail) **inamon /inamo-/** *vii*
WET TRAIL: be wet (as a road or trail) **nibiiwadamon /nibiiwadamo-/** *vii*
WIDE TRAIL: be wide (as a road or trail) **mangademon /mangademo-/** *vii, also* **mangadademon**

TRAILER
TRAILER: **zagapijigan, -an** *ni*

TRAIN
TRAIN: **ishkodewidaabaan, -ag** *na, also* **mashkodewidaabaan***

TRAIN TRACK
TRAIN TRACK: **ishkodewidaabaanikana, -n** *ni*

TRANQUILLY
REMAIN TRANQUILLY IN PLACE: **goshkwaawaadabi** *vai*

TRANSFORM
TRANSFORM: transform oneself in appearance **izhinaago'idizo** *vai;* transform s.o. **aanzinaago'** *vta;* transform s.t. **aanzinaagotoon** *vti2;* transform oneself **aanzinaago'idizo** *vai*

TRANSLATE
TRANSLATE: translate s.o. **aanikanootaw** *vta;* translate s.t. **aanikanootan** *vti;* translate for people **aanikanootaage** *vai*

TRANSLATOR
TRANSLATOR: **aanikanootaagewinini, -wag** *na*

TRANSPARENT
TRANSPARENT: be transparent **zhiibawaaseyaa, zhiibawaaseyaamagad** *vii;* **zhiibawaasezi** *vai*

TRAP
TRAP: **dasoonaagan, -an** *ni;* **wanii'igan, -an** *ni;* **wanii'ige** *vai;* trap for s.o. **wanii'amaw** *vta;* trap s.o. **dasoozh /dasooN-/** *vta*
CHECK TRAPS: check one's traps **naadasoonaagane** *vai*
GO AFTER TRAPS: **naajiwanii'ige** *vai*
GO GET TRAPS: go get one's traps **naadasoonaagane** *vai*
TRAP BEAVER: **noodamikwe** *vai*

TRAPPED
TRAPPED: be trapped **dasoozo** *vai*

TRAPPER
TRAPPER: **wanii'igewinini, -wag** *na*
TRASH
TRASH: **ziigwebinigan, -an** *ni*
TRAVEL
TRAVEL ABOUT: **babaamaadizi** *vai*
TRAVEL ALONG: **bimi-ayaa** *vai;* travel along in a group (as a school of fish) **bimaawadaaso** *vai*
TRAVEL AT NIGHT: **niibaashkaa** *vai*
TRAVEL TO A CERTAIN PLACE: they travel in a group to a certain place **inaawanidiwag /inaawanidi-/** *vai*
TRAVELLER
TRAVELLER: **bebaamaadizid** *na-pt*
TRAVOIS
TRAVOIS: **niswaakodaabaan, -an** *ni*
TREASURE
TREASURE: treasure s.o. **zaagi'** *vta;* treasure s.t. **zaagitoon** *vti2*
TREASURED
TREASURED: be treasured **zaagichigaade, zaagichigaademagad** *vii;* **zaagichigaazo** *vai*
TREAT
TREAT WELL: treat s.o. well **mino-doodaw** *vta*
TREATY KETTLE
TREATY KETTLE: **okaadakik, -oog** *na*
TREE
TREE: **mitig, -oog** *na*
BY A TREE: **jiigaatig** *pc*
MANY TREES: there are many trees **mitigokaa** *vii*
TREETOP
ON THE TREETOP: **wanakong** *pc*
TREMBLE
TREMBLE: **baapagishkaa** *vai;* **baapagishkaa, baapagishkaamagad** *vii*
TREY
TREY: **nisoobii'igan, -ag** *na*
TRICK
PERFORM TRICKS: **mamaandaagochige** *vai*
TRICKSTER
TRICKSTER: name of **aadizookaan** character viewed as culture hero and trickster **Wenabozho** *na, also* **Nenabozho***
TRIM
TRIM: **agogwaajigan, -an** *ni*
TRIP
TRIP: **bizozideshin** *vai*
TROUBLE
CAUSE TROUBLE: cause s.o. trouble **aanimi'** *vta*
TROUBLED
TROUBLED: be troubled in one's mind **mamiidaawendam** *vai2*
TROUGH
TROUGH: **atoobaan, -an** *ni*
SUGARING TROUGH: **naseyaawangwaan, -an** *ni*

TRUCK
TRUCK: **aawadaasoowidaabaan, -ag** *na;* **ditibidaabaan, -ag** *na*
FIRE TRUCK: **aate'ishkodawewidaabaan** *na*
MAIL TRUCK: **mazina'iganiiwidaabaan, -ag** *na*
TRUTH
FIND OUT THE TRUTH: **gwayakotam** *vai2*
TELL THE TRUTH: **debwe** *vai*
TRY
TRY: **gagwe-** *pv4;* **goji-** *pv4;* **goji'ewizi** *vai;* try s.t. **gagwejitoon** *vti2;* try things **gagwejichige** *vai;* **gojichige** *vai*
TRY ON: try on s.o. (e.g., clothes) **gozikaw** *vta;* try on s.t. (e.g., clothes) **gozikan** *vti*
TRY TO DO: try to do s.t. **wiikwajitoon** *vti2*
TRY TO GET: try to get s.o. to... **gagweji'** *vta*
TRY TO GET FREE: **wiikwaji'o** *vai;* try to get free of s.t. **wiikwajitoon** *vti2*
TUB
TUB: **makakosag, -oon** *ni*
TUBERCULOSIS
TUBERCULOSIS: **ozosodamwaapinewin** *ni*
HAVE TUBERCULOSIS: **ozosodamwaapine** *vai*
TUESDAY
TUESDAY: be Tuesday **niizho-giizhigad** *vii*
TULLIBEE
TULLIBEE: **odoonibii, -g** *na, also* **odoonibiins, -ag**
TURBULENT
TURBULENT WATER: be turbulent water **madaagamin /madaagami-/** *vii*
TURKEY
TURKEY: **mizise, -g** *na*
TURN
HER TURN: her turn *third person singular personal pronoun* **wiinitam** *pr*
HIS TURN: his turn *third person singular personal pronoun* **wiinitam** *pr*
MY TURN: my turn *first person singular personal pronoun* **niinitam** *pr*
OUR TURN: our turn *first person exclusive plural personal pronoun* **niinitamawind** *pr;* our turn *first person inclusive personal pronoun* **giinitamawind** *pr*
THEIR TURN: their turn *third person plural personal pronoun* **wiinitamawaa** *pr*
YOUR TURN: your turn *second person plural personal pronoun* **giinitamawaa** *pr;* your turn *second person singular personal pronoun* **giinitam** *pr*
TURN
TURN: turn (one's body) **gwekitaa** *vai;* turn s.o. **biimiskon** *vta;* turn s.t. **biimiskonan** *vti*
TURN AND GO BACK: **washki-giiwe** *vai*
TURN AND LOOK BACK: **aabanaabi** *vai;* turn and look back at s.o. **aabanaabam** *vta;* turn and look back at s.t. **aabanaabandan** *vti*

TURN AROUND WHILE SITTING: **gwekabi** *vai*
TURN BY HAND: turn s.o. by hand **gwekin** *vta;* turn s.t. by hand **gwekinan** *vti;* turn things by hand **gwekinige** *vai*
TURN DRIVING: **gwekibizo** *vai*
TURN FACE DOWN: turn s.o. face down **animikon** *vta;* turn s.t. face down **animikonan** *vti*
TURN FACE UP: **aazhigijise** *vai;* **aazhigijise, aazhigijisemagad** *vii*
TURN HEAD AROUND: turn one's head around **gwekikweni** *vai*
TURN IN PLACE: **washkibagizo** *vai*
TURN INSIDE OUT: **aaboozikaa** *vai;* **aaboozikaa, aaboozikaamagad** *vii;* turn s.o. inside out **aaboodin** *vta;* turn s.t. inside out **aaboodinan** *vti*
TURN LYING IN PLACE: **gwekishin** *vai;* **gwekisin** *vii*
TURN OVER: turn s.o. over (as something sheet-like) **gwekiigin** *vta;* turn s.t. over (as something sheet-like) **gwekiiginan** *vti*
TURN OVER BACKWARDS: **aazhigijise** *vai;* **aazhigijise, aazhigijisemagad** *vii*
TURN QUICKLY: turn quickly, right self **gwekibagizo** *vai*
TURN RUNNING: **gwekibatoo** *vai*
TURN STANDING: turn while standing **gwekigaabawi** *vai;* **washkigaabawi** *vai*
TURN TO FACE BACKWARDS: turn s.o. to face backwards **animikon** *vta;* turn s.t. to face backwards **animikonan** *vti*
TURN WITH HANDS: turn s.o. with hands **gwekibizh /gwekibiN-/** *vta;* turn s.t. with hands **gwekibidoon** *vti2*

TURN ON
TURN ON A LIGHT: turn s.t. on for a light **waazakonebidoon** *vti2*

TURN OUT
TURN OUT: turn s.t. out (e.g., stove or lamp) **aatebidoon** *vti2*

TURN OUT THAT
TURN OUT THAT: it turns out that **nangwana** *pc, also* **ngwana, ingwana**

TURNED
PUT TURNED: put s.o. turned **gwekishim** *vta;* put s.t. turned **gwekisidoon** *vti2*
TURNED FACE DOWN: be turned face down **animikonigaade, animikonigaademagad** *vii;* **animikonigaazo** *vai*
TURNED TO FACE BACKWARDS: be turned to face backwards **animikonigaade, animikonigaademagad** *vii;* **animikonigaazo** *vai*

TURTLE
PAINTED TURTLE: **miskwaadesi, -wag** *na*
SNAPPING TURTLE: **mikinaak, -wag** *na;* **mishiikenh, -yag** *na*

TWELVE
TWELVE: **ashi-niizh** *nm;* **midaaswi ashi-niizh** *nm*
TWELVE O'CLOCK: be twelve o'clock **ashi-niizho-diba'iganed** *vii*

TWENTY
TWENTY: **niishtana** *nm*

TWENTY-TWO
TWENTY-TWO: twenty-two (gun) **niishtana-ashi-niizh** *ni*
TWENTY-TWO BULLET: **anwiins, -an** *ni*

TWICE
TWICE: **niizhing** *pc*

TWILIGHT
TWILIGHT: be twilight **dibikaabaminaagwad** *vii*

TWIN
TWIN: **niizhoodenh, -yag** *na*

TWINE
BALL OF TWINE OR YARN: **bikoojaan, -an** *ni*

TWIST
TWIST: twist s.o. **biimiskon** *vta;* twist s.t. **biimiskonan** *vti*
FALL AND TWIST ARM: fall and twist one's arm **biimiskonikeshin** *vai*

TWISTED
TWISTED MOUTH: have a twisted mouth (as from a stroke) **biimidoon** *vai*

TWO
TWO: **niizh** *nm;* **niizho-** *pv4;* they are two **niizhinoon /niizhin-/** *vii;* **niizhiwag /niizhi-/** *vai;* two (card) **niizhoobii'igan, -ag** *na*
AND TWO: **ashi-niizh** *nm;* **ashi-niizho-** *pv4*
TWO ACRES: **niizho-diba'igaans** *pc*
TWO DAYS: **niizho-giizhik** *pc;* **niizhogon** *pc;* be two days **niizhogonagad** *vii*
TWO DAYS OLD: be two days old **niizhogonagizi** *vai*
TWO DOLLARS: **niizhwaabik** *pc*
TWO EACH: **neniizh** *nm*
TWO FEET: **niizhozid** *pc*
TWO HOURS: **niizho-diba'igan** *pc*
TWO HUNDRED: **niizhwaak** *nm*
TWO INCHES: **niizhoninj** *pc*
TWO MILES: **niizho-diba'igan** *pc*
TWO MINUTES: **niizho-diba'igaans** *pc*
TWO MONTHS: **niizho-giizis** *pc*
TWO NIGHTS: **niizho-dibik** *pc*
TWO O'CLOCK: be two o'clock **niizho-diba'iganed** *vii*
TWO PAIRS: **niizhwewaan** *pc*
TWO SETS: **niizhwewaan** *pc*
TWO THOUSAND: **niizhosagoons** *nm*
TWO TIMES: **niizhing** *pc*
TWO WEEKS: **niizho-anama'e-giizhik** *pc;* be two weeks **niizho-anama'e-giizhigad** *pc*
TWO YEARS: **niizho-biboon** *pc;* be two years **niizho-biboonagad** *vii*
TWO YEARS OLD: be two years old **niizho-biboonagizi** *vai*

TYPE
TYPE: **mazinaabikiwebinige** *vai*

TYPEWRITER
TYPEWRITER: **bakite'ibii'igan, -an** *ni;* **mazinaabikiwebinigan, -an** *ni*

U

UGLY
UGLY: be ugly **maanaadad** *vii;* **maanaadizi** *vai*
UMBILICAL CORD
UMBILICAL CORD: my umbilical cord **indis /-disy-/** *nid*
UMBRELLA
UMBRELLA: **agawaate'on, -an** *ni*
UNABLE
UNABLE TO DO: be unable to do s.t. **bwaanawitoon** *vti2;* be unable to do something **bwaanawi'o** *vai;* be unable to do something to s.o. **bwaanawi'** *vta;* be unable (to do something) **bwaanawichige** *vai*
UNABLE TO FIND A DRINK: be unable to find a drink **gwiinobii** *vai*
UNABLE TO MANAGE: be unable to manage s.o. **bwaanawi'** *vta;* be unable to manage s.t. **bwaanawitoon** *vti2*
UNCLE
UNCLE: my cross-uncle (mother's brother) **inzhishenh, -yag /-zhisheny-/** *nad;* my parallel uncle (father's brother) **nimishoome, -yag /-mishoomey-/** *nad*
UNCOMFORTABLY
LIE UNCOMFORTABLY: **maazhishin** *vai*
SIT UNCOMFORTABLY: **maanabi** *vai*
SLEEP UNCOMFORTABLY: **maazhingwaam** *vai*
UNCONNECTED
COME UNCONNECTED: come unconnected (as something string-like) **gidiskaabiigishkaa, gidiskaabiigishkaamagad** *vii*
UNCOVER
UNCOVER: uncover s.o. **baakin** *vta;* uncover s.t. **baakinan** *vti;* uncover (s.t.) for s.o. **baakinamaw** *vta;* uncover things **baakinige** *vai*
UNCOVERED
COME UNCOVERED: **baakise, baakisemagad** *vii*
LEAVE UNCOVERED: leave s.o. uncovered **baakoshim** *vta;* leave s.t. uncovered **baakosidoon** *vti2*
LIE UNCOVERED: **baakishin** *vai;* **baakisin** *vii;* **michishin** *vai;* **michisin** *vii*
UNDER
UNDER: **anaami-** *pn;* under it **anaamayi'ii** *pc*
UNDER A BOAT: **anaamoonag** *pc*
UNDER THE FLOOR: **anaamisag** *pc*
UNDER THE GROUND: **anaamakamig** *pc*
UNDER THE ICE: **anaamiskwam** *pc*
UNDER THE SNOW: **anaamaagon** *pc, also* **anaamaagonag**
UNDER WOOD: under wood (e.g., a tree or stick) **anaamaatig** *pc*
UNDERBRUSH
DENSE UNDERBRUSH: there is dense underbrush **zazagaa, zazagaamagad** *vii*
UNDERGROUND
UNDERGROUND: **anaamaki** *pc*
UNDERPANTS
UNDERPANTS: **biitoo-giboodiyegwaazon, -ag** *na*
UNDERSHIRT
UNDERSHIRT: **biitoo-babagiwayaan, -an** *ni*
UNDERSTAND
UNDERSTAND: **nisidotam** *vai2;* understand s.o. **nisidotaw** *vta;* understand s.t. **nisidotan** *vti;* they understand each other **nisidotaadiwag /nisidotaadi-/** *vai*
UNDERSTAND A CERTAIN WAY: **initam** *vai2;* understand s.o. a certain way **initaw** *vta;* understand s.t. a certain way **initan** *vti*
UNDERSTOOD
UNDERSTOOD: be understood **nisidotaagozi** *vai;* **nisidotaagwad** *vii*
UNDERSTOOD A CERTAIN WAY: be understood a certain way **initaagozi** *vai;* **initaagwad** *vii*
UNDERWATER
UNDERWATER: **anaamibiig** *pc*
UNDERWATER PANTHER
UNDERWATER PANTHER: **mishibizhii, -g** *na*
UNDERWEAR
UNDERWEAR: men's underwear **biitooshkigan, -an** *ni*
UNDO
UNDO: undo s.o. **aaba' /aaba'w-/** *vta;* undo s.t. **aaba'an** *vti;* undo (s.t.) for s.o. **aaba'amaw** *vta*
UNDO BY HAND: undo s.o. by hand **aabiskon** *vta;* undo s.t. by hand **aabiskonan** *vti*
UNDONE
UNDONE: be undone **aaba'igaade, aaba'igaademagad** *vii;* **aaba'igaazo** *vai*
COME UNDONE: **aabiskose** *vai;* **aabiskose, aabiskosemagad** *vii*
UNDRESS
UNDRESS: **giizikonaye** *vai;* undress s.o. **giizikonaye'** *vta*
UNFOLD
UNFOLD: unfold s.o. (as something sheet-like) **aabiskwegin** *vta;* unfold s.t. (as something sheet-like) **aabiskweginan** *vti*
UNITED STATES
UNITED STATES: **Gichi-mookomaan-aki** *ni*
UNIVERSITY
UNIVERSITY: **gabe-gikendaasoowigamig, -oon** *ni*
UNLOAD
UNLOAD A BOAT: **agwaanaaso** *vai*
UNLOCK
UNLOCK: unlock s.o. **aabaabika' /aabaabika'w-/** *vta;* unlock s.t.

aabaabika'an *vti;* unlock (s.t.) for s.o. **aabaabika'amaw** *vta*

UNLOCKED
UNLOCKED: be unlocked **aabaabika'igaade, aabaabika'igaademagad** *vii*

UNMARRIED
UNMARRIED MAN: **moozhaabe, -g** *na*
UNMARRIED WOMAN: **moozhikwe, -g** *na*

UNRAVEL
UNRAVEL: **aabiskose** *vai;* **aabiskose, aabiskosemagad** *vii;* unravel s.o. (as something string-like) **aabaabiigin** *vta;* unravel s.t. (as something string-like) **aabaabiiginan** *vti*

UNSATISFACTORY
FIND UNSATISFACTORY: find s.o. unsatisfactory **aanawenim** *vta;* find s.t. unsatisfactory **aanawendan** *vti;* find things unsatisfactory **aanawenjige** *vai*
FOUND UNSATISFACTORY: be found unsatisfactory **aanawendaagozi** *vai;* **aanawendaagwad** *vii*

UNSTEADY
FEEL UNSTEADY: **giiwashkweyaabandam** *vai2*

UNTIE
UNTIE: untie s.o. **aaba' /aaba'w-/** *vta;* untie s.t. **aaba'an** *vti;* **aaba'oodoon** *vti2;* untie (s.t.) for s.o. **aaba'amaw** *vta*
UNTIE WILD RICE: **aaba'oodoo** *vai*

UNTIED
UNTIED: be untied **aaba'igaade, aaba'igaademagad** *vii;* **aaba'igaazo** *vai*

UNTIL
UNTIL: **biinish** *pc*

UNWIND
UNWIND: unwind s.o. (as something string-like) **aabaabiigin** *vta;* unwind s.t. (as something string-like) **aabaabiiginan** *vti*

UP TO
UP TO: **biinish** *pc*

UP TO YOU
IT'S UP TO YOU: **booshke** *pc, also* **booshke giniin**

UPHILL
GO UPHILL: **agidaakiiwe** *vai*
RUN UPHILL: **agidaakiiwebatoo** *vai*

UPPER STORY
HAVE AN UPPER STORY: **ishpimisagokaade, ishpimisagokaademagad** *vii*

UPSET
UPSET BY HAND: upset s.o. by hand **gawin** *vta;* upset s.t. by hand **gawinan** *vti*

UPSIDE DOWN
HANG UPSIDE DOWN: **ajidagoode, ajidagoodemagad** *vii;* **ajidagoojin** *vai;* hang s.o. upside down **ajidagoozh /ajidagooN-/** *vta;* hang s.t. upside down **ajidagoodoon** *vti2*
HOLD UPSIDE DOWN: hold s.o. upside down **ajidin** *vta;* hold s.t. upside down **ajidinan** *vti*

UPSTAIRS
GO UPSTAIRS: **akwaandawe** *vai*

UPSTREAM
UPSTREAM: **agidaajiwan** *pc, also* **ogidaajiwan*, wagidaajiwan**

UPWARDS
BLOWN UPWARDS: be blown upwards **ombaashi** *vai;* **ombaasin** *vii*
FLY UPWARDS: **ombibide, ombibidemagad** *vii;* **ombibizo** *vai*
GO UPWARDS: **ombishkaa** *vai;* **ombishkaa, ombishkaamagad** *vii*
GO UPWARDS AS SMOKE: **ombaabate** *vii*
JUMP UPWARDS: **ombigwaashkwani** *vai*
SPEED UPWARDS: **ombibide, ombibidemagad** *vii;* **ombibizo** *vai*
THROW UPWARDS: throw s.o. upwards **ombiwebin** *vta;* throw s.t. upwards **ombiwebinan** *vti*

URGE
URGE: urge s.o. **gagaanzom** *vta*
URGE TO COME: urge s.o. to come **wiizhaam** *vta*

URINATE
URINATE: **zhiishiigi** *vai;* urinate on s.o. **zhigizh /zhigiN-/** *vta;* urinate on s.t. **zhigidan** *vti;* urinate on oneself **zhiginidizo** *vai*

US
US: us *first person exclusive plural pronoun* **niinawind** *pr;* us *first person inclusive personal pronoun* **giinawind** *pr*

USE
USE: use s.o. **aabaji'** *vta;* use s.t. **aabajitoon** *vti2*
GET GOOD USE: get good use of s.o. **minwaabaji'** *vta;* get good use of s.t. **minwaabajitoon** *vti2*
OF GOOD USE: be of good use **minwaabadad** *vii;* **minwaabadizi** *vai*
USE A CERTAIN WAY: use s.o. a certain way **inaabaji'** *vta;* use s.t. a certain way **inaabajitoon** *vti2;* use things a certain way **inaabajichige** *vai*

USE UP
USE UP: use s.o. up **jaagaabaji'** *vta;* use s.t. up **jaagaabajitoon** *vti2;* use things up **jaaginige** *vai*
USE UP AMMUNITION: use up all of the ammunition **jaaga'e** *vai;* **jaagizige** *vai*
USE UP MONEY: use up all of the money **jaagizhooniyaaweshin** *vai*

USED
USED: be used **aabadad** *vii;* **aabadizi** *vai*

USED TO
USED TO: be used to making s.o. **nagaji'** *vta;* be used to making s.t. **nagajitoon** *vti2;* be used to s.o. **nagadenim** *vta;* be used to s.t. **nagadendan** *vti*

USED TO
USED TO: **iko** *pc, also* **ko**
USED UP
USED UP: be used up **jaaginigaade, jaaginigaademagad** *vii*
USEFUL
USEFUL: be useful **aabadad** *vii;* **aabadizi** *vai;* be very useful **minwaabadad** *vii;* **minwaabadizi** *vai*
USEFUL IN A CERTAIN WAY: be useful in a certain way **inaabadad** *vii;* **inaabadizi** *vai*

V

VAIN
IN VAIN: **aano-** *pv1*
VALLEY
VALLEY: be a valley **basadinaa, basadinaamagad** *vii*
VALUED
VALUED TO A CERTAIN EXTENT: be valued to a certain extent **apiitendaagozi** *vai;* **apiitendaagwad** *vii*
VAMP
MOCCASIN VAMP: moccasin vamp **apiingwe'igan, -an** *ni*
VAN
VAN: **aawazhiwewidaabaan, -ag** *na*
VARIEGATED
VARIEGATED: be variegated **gidagaa, gidagaamagad** *vii;* **gidagizi** *vai;* be variegated (as something sheet-like) **gidagiigad** *vii;* **gidagiigizi** *vai*
VARIETY
VARIETY OF THINGS: a variety of things **anooj gegoo** *pr, also* **anooji-gegoo**
VARIOUS
VARIOUS: **anooj** *pc*
VARIOUS THINGS: **anooj gegoo** *pr, also* **anooji-gegoo**
VEGETABLE
VEGETABLE: **gitigaanens, -an** *ni*
VEIN
VEIN: my vein **indiskweyaab, -iin** *nid*
VELVET
VELVET: **miishiigin, -oon** *ni*
VERY
VERY: **aapiji** *pc;* **gichi-** *pv4, also* **chi-; enda-** *pv4*
VESSEL
VESSEL: **naabikwaan, -an** *ni*
VEST
VEST: **gibide'ebizon, -an** *ni*
VETERAN'S HOME
VETERAN'S HOME: **zhimaaganishiiwigamig, -oon** *ni*
VETERAN'S HOSPITAL
VETERAN'S HOSPITAL: **zhimaaganishii-aakoziiwigamig, -oon** *ni*
VIEW
COME INTO VIEW: **bi-naagozi** *vai;* **bi-naagwad** *vii*
COME SUDDENLY INTO VIEW: come suddenly into view as from around a corner **zaagewe** *vai*
DRIVE SUDDENLY INTO VIEW: **zaagewebide, zaagewebidemagad** *vii;* **zaagewebizo** *vai*
PADDLE SUDDENLY INTO VIEW: **zaagewe'o** *vai;* **zaagewekwazhiwe** *vai*
RUN SUDDENLY INTO VIEW: **zaagewebatoo** *vai*
SPEED SUDDENLY INTO VIEW: **zaagewebide, zaagewebidemagad** *vii;* **zaagewebizo** *vai*
SWIM SUDDENLY INTO VIEW: swim as a fish suddenly into view **zaagewekwazhiwe** *vai*
VINE
VINE: **biimaakwad, -oon** *ni*
VINEGAR
VINEGAR: **zhiiwaaboo** *ni*
VIOLIN
VIOLIN: **naazhaabii'igan, -an** *ni*
VISIBLE
VISIBLE: be visible **naagozi** *vai;* **naagwad** *vii*
BARELY VISIBLE: be barely visible **naawinaagozi** *vai;* **naawinaagwad** *vii*
VISIBLE AT A DISTANCE: be visible at a distance **debaabaminaagozi** *vai;* **debaabaminaagwad** *vii*
VISION
VISION: have vision **waabi** *vai*
FAST FOR A VISION: **gii'igoshimo** *vai*
VISIT
VISIT: visit s.o. **mawadish /mawadiS-/** *vta;* **odish /odiS-/** *vta;* visit people **mawadishiwe** *vai;* **odishiwe** *vai;* they visit each other **mawadisidiwag /mawadisidi-/** *vai*
VISITOR
VISITOR: **biiwide, -g** *na*
VOICE
BAD VOICE: have a bad voice **maanowe** *vai*
GOOD VOICE: have a good voice **minogondaagan** *vai;* **minowe** *vai*
HAVE A SOFT VOICE: **bedowe** *vai*
HAVE DIFFICULTY WITH VOICE: have difficulty with one's voice **maazhigondaagan** *vai*
VOMIT
VOMIT: **zhigagowe** *vai;* keep vomiting **zhishigagowe** *vai*
VOTE
VOTE: **biinjwebinige** *vai;* vote for s.o. **biinjwebinigetamaw** *vta*
VULVA
VULVA: my vulva **nikidin /-kidin-/** *nad*

W

WADE
RUN ACROSS WADING: **aazhawagaaziibatoo** *vai*
WADE ABOUT: **babaamaadagaazii** *vai*
WADE ACROSS: **aazhawagaazii** *vai*
WADE ALONG: **bimaadagaazii** *vai*
WADE AWAY: **animaadagaazii** *vai*
WADE FROM A CERTAIN PLACE: **ondaadagaazii** *vai*
WADE HERE: **biidaadagaazii** *vai*
WADE TO A CERTAIN PLACE: **inaadagaazii** *vai*

WAG
WAG TAIL: wag one's tail **wewebaanoweni** *vai*

WAGON
WAGON: **ditibidaabaan, -ag** *na;* **odaabaan, -ag** *na*
DRIVE ALONG IN A WAGON OR SLEIGH: drive along quickly in a wagon or sleigh **bimidaabiiba'igo** *vai*

WAIT
WAIT: **bii'o** *vai;* wait for s.o. **bii'** *vta;* wait for s.t. **biitoon** *vti2;* wait! **bekaa** *pc*
KEEP WAITING: **baabii'o** *vai;* keep waiting for s.o. **baabii'** *vta;* keep waiting for s.t. **baabiitoon** *vti2*
TIRED OF WAITING: be tired of waiting **zhigajibii'o** *vai;* be tired of waiting for s.o. **zhigajibii'** *vta;* be tired of waiting for s.t. **zhigajibiitoon** *vti2*
WAIT IN WATCH: **akawaabi** *vai;* wait in watch for s.o. **akawaabam** *vta;* wait in watch for s.t. **akawaabandan** *vti*

WAKE
WAKE: wake s.o. **amadin** *vta*
WAKE BY VOCAL NOISE: wake s.o. by vocal noise **amajim** *vta*
WAKE FROM BEING COLD: **amadaji** *vai*
WAKE FROM PAIN: **amajine** *vai*
WAKE UP: **goshkozi** *vai*

WAKE
SIT UP WITH AT A WAKE: sit up with s.o. (e.g., the deceased at a wake) **abiitaw** *vta*

WALK
ARRIVE WALKING: **bagamose** *vai*
HEARD WALKING: be heard walking on the floor **madwesagishin** *vai*
HEARD WALKING ALONG: be heard walking along **bimweweshin** *vai*
HEARD WALKING HERE: be heard walking here **biidweweshin** *vai*
WALK A CERTAIN WAY: **inose** *vai*
WALK ABOUT: **babaamose** *vai;* **babimose** *vai*
WALK ALONG: **bimose** *vai*
WALK ALONG ON THE ICE: **bimaadagaako** *vai*
WALK ALONG SHORE TO A CERTAIN PLACE: **inaazhagaame** *vai*
WALK ALONG THE SHORE: **jiigeweyaazhagaame** *vai*
WALK AROUND: walk around s.o. **giiwitaashkaw** *vta;* walk around s.t. **giiwitaashkan** *vti;* walk around something **giiwitaawose** *vai, also* **giiwitaa'ose**
WALK AROUND A LAKE: **giiwitaayaazhagaame** *vai*
WALK AROUND THE EDGE: **giiwitaayaazhagaame** *vai*
WALK AWAY: **animose** *vai*
WALK AWAY MAKING NOISE: **animwewetoo** *vai*
WALK FROM A CERTAIN PLACE: **ondose** *vai*
WALK HERE: **biidaasamose** *vai*
WALK SLOWLY: **bedose** *vai*
WALK TO CERTAIN PLACE: walk to a certain place **inose** *vai*
WALK WITH: walk with s.o. **wiidosem** *vta*
WALK WITH DISCOMFORT: **maanose** *vai*

WALL
WALL: **aasamisag, -oon** *ni*
BY A WALL: **jiigaatig** *pc*

WALLEYE
WALLEYE: **ogaa, -wag** *na*

WANDER
WANDER ABOUT: **babaa-ayaa** *vai*

WANT
WANT: **misawendam** *vai2;* **nandawendam** *vai2;* want s.o. **misawenim** *vta;* want s.o. (to do...) **nandawenim** *vta;* want s.t. **misawendan** *vti;* **nandawendan** *vti;* want things **misawenjige** *vai*
WANT TO: **wii-** *pv1*

WAR
WAR: **miigaadiwin, -an** *ni*
GO TO WAR: go to war *archaic* **nandobani** *vai*
SING WAR SONGS: **bwaanzhii-nagamo** *vai*

WAR CLUB
WAR CLUB: **bagamaagan, -an** *ni*

WAR DANCE
WAR DANCE: **bwaanzhii-niimi'idiwin, -an** *ni;* dance a war dance **bwaanzhii-niimi** *vai;* they dance a war dance **bwaanzhii-niimi'idiwag /bwaanzhii-niimi'idi-/** *vai*

WAR WHOOP
GIVE WAR WHOOPS: **zaasaakwe** *vai*

WARM
WARM: be warm (as a liquid) **abaagamide, abaagamidemagad** *vii;* warm s.t. (as a liquid) **abaagamizan** *vti*
WARM AT THE FIRE: warm s.o. at the fire **abiz /abizw-/** *vta;* warm s.t. at the fire **abizan** *vti;* warm (s.t.) for s.o. at the fire **abizamaw** *vta*
WARM BACK: warm one's back **abaawiganezo** *vai*
WARM BY THE FIRE: warm oneself by the fire **awazo** *vai*
WARM FEET: warm one's feet **abizidezo** *vai*

WARM HANDS: warm one's hands **abininjiizo** *vai*
WARM UP: warm up in the sun **abaaso** *vai*
WARM WEATHER: be warm weather **aabawaa, aabawaamagad** *vii*
WEATHER WARMS UP: warm up (of the weather) **abaate, abaatemagad** *vii*
WRAPPED UP WARM: be wrapped up warm **giizhoopizo** *vai*

WARMLY
DRESS WARMLY: **giizhoo'o** *vai*

WARMTH
LIE IN WARMTH: **giizhooshin** *vai*

WARN
WARN: warn s.o. **ayaangwaamim** *vta*
WARN AGAINST: warn s.o. against (s.t.) **gina'amaw** *vta*

WARRIOR
WARRIOR: **ogichidaa, -g** *na*

WART
WART: **jiichiigom, -ag** *na*

WASH
WASH: **giziibiigii** *vai;* wash s.o. by hand **giziibiigin** *vta;* wash s.o. using something **giziibiiga' /giziibiiga'w-/** *vta;* wash s.t. using something **giziibiiga'an** *vti;* wash s.t. by hand **giziibiiginan** *vti;* wash things **giziibiiga'ige** *vai*
WASH CLOTHES: **giziibiiga'ige** *vai*
WASH DISHES: **giziibiiginaagane** *vai*
WASH FACE: wash one's face **giziibiigiingwe** *vai*
WASH FLOORS: **giziibiigisaginige** *vai*
WASH HAIR: wash one's hair **giziibiigindibe** *vai*
WASH HANDS: wash one's hands **giziibiigininjii** *vai*
WASH KETTLE: **giziibiiginakokwe** *vai*
WASH PAIL: **giziibiiginakokwe** *vai*

WASH BASIN
WASH BASIN: **giziibiigiingwewinaagan** *ni*

WASH UP
WASH UP: **giziibiigazhe** *vai*

WASHBOARD
WASHBOARD: **mimigwaakosijigan, -an** *ni*

WASHED
WASHED: be washed **giziibiiginigaade, giziibiiginigaademagad** *vii*

WASHING MACHINE
WASHING MACHINE: **giziibiiga'ige-makak, -oon** *ni*

WASHINGTON
WASHINGTON: Washington, D.C. **Waashtanong** *place*

WASHTUB
WASHTUB: **giziibiiga'ige-makak, -oon** *ni*

WASP
WASP: **aamoo, -g** *na*

WASP NEST
WASP NEST: **aamoo-wadiswan, -an** *ni*

WASTE
WASTE: waste s.o. **nishwanaaji'** *vta;* waste s.t. **nishwanaajitoon** *vti2;* waste things **nishwanaajichige** *vai*

WATCH
WATCH: **ganawaabi** *vai;* watch s.o. **ganawaabam** *vta;* watch s.t. **ganawaabandan** *vti;* watch things **ganawaabanjige** *vai;* they watch each other **ganawaabandiwag /ganawaabandi-/** *vai*
WATCH CAREFULLY: watch s.o. carefully **naanaagadawaabam** *vta;* watch s.t. carefully **naanaagadawaabandan** *vti*
WATCH OVER: watch over s.o. **gizhaazh /gizhaaN-/** *vta;* watch over s.t. **gizhaadan** *vti;* watch over things **gizhaadige** *vai*

WATCH
WATCH: **diba'igiiziswaanens, -ag** *na*

WATCHED
WATCHED: be watched **ganawaabanjigaade, ganawaabanjigaademagad** *vii;* **ganawaabanjigaazo** *vai*

WATER
WATER: **nibi** *ni;* water s.t. **ziiga'andan** *vti*
AT THE WATER: **agamiing** *pc*
BLOWN INTO THE WATER: be blown into the water **bakobiiyaashi** *vai;* **bakobiiyaasin** *vii*
BY THE WATER: **jiigibiig** *pc*
COLD WATER: **dakib** *ni*
DRAG INTO THE WATER: drag s.o. into the water **bakobiidaabaazh /bakobiidaabaaN-/** *vta;* drag s.t. into the water **bakobiidaabaadan** *vti*
EMERGE FROM THE WATER: **mookibii** *vai*
FALL INTO THE WATER: **bakobiise** *vai;* **bakobiise, bakobiisemagad** *vii*
GET WATER: **nibinaadi** *vai;* get water for s.o. **gwaaba'amaw** *vta*
GET WATER FROM A CERTAIN PLACE: **onda'ibii** *vai*
GO AWAY FROM THE WATER: **gopii** *vai*
GO DOWN INTO THE WATER: **bakobii** *vai*
GO GET WATER: go get water or other liquid **naadoobii** *vai*
IN THE DEPTHS OF A BODY OF WATER: **anaamiindim** *pc*
JUMP INTO THE WATER: **bakobiigwaashkwani** *vai*
MUCH WATER: be much water **nibiikaa, nibiikaamagad** *vii*
ON THIS SIDE OF THE WATER: **ondaasagaam** *pc*
ON TOP OF THE WATER: **agidibiig** *pc, also* **ogidibiig*, wagidibiig**
OVER ACROSS THE WATER: **awasagaam** *pc*
RUN INTO THE WATER: **bakobiibatoo** *vai*
SUSPENDED IN WATER: be suspended in water **agomo** *vai;* **agonde** *vii*

THROW INTO THE WATER: throw s.o. into the water **bakobiiwebin** *vta;* throw s.t. into the water **bakobiiwebinan** *vti*
THROW OUT OF THE WATER: throw s.t. out of the water **agwaawebinan** *vti;* throw (s.t.) out of the water for s.o. **agwaawebinamaw** *vta*
WATER SOURCE: **onda'ibaan, -an** *ni*

WATER PAIL
WATER PAIL: **nibiiwakik, -oog** *na*

WATERFALL
WATERFALL: be a waterfall **gakaamikijiwan** *vii;* **gakijiwan** *vii*

WATERMELON
WATERMELON: **eshkandaming, -in** *ni-pt*

WATERY
WATERY: be watery **nibiiwan** *vii*

WAVE
WAVE: **digow, -ag** *na, also* **digo**
BIG WAVES: be big waves **mamaangaashkaa, mamaangaashkaamagad** *vii*
WAVES COME IN TO SHORE: **biidaashkaa, biidaashkaamagad** *vii*

WAY
CERTAIN WAY: be a certain way **izhi-ayaa** *vai*
IN A CERTAIN WAY: **izhi-** *pv3*
ON THE WAY: **ani-** *pv2, also* **ni-**; **bimi-** *pv2*
THIS WAY: **bi-** *pv2*

WAY OF LIFE
WAY OF LIFE: **inaadiziwin, -an** *ni*
CERTAIN WAY OF LIFE: have a certain way of life **inaadizi** *vai*

WE
WE: we *first person exclusive plural pronoun* **niinawind** *pr;* we *first person inclusive personal pronoun* **giinawind** *pr*

WEAK
WEAK: be weak **niinamad** *vii;* **niinamizi** *vai;* be weak (as a liquid) **zhaagwaagamin /zhaagwaagami-/** *vii;* be weak in muscular strength **zhaagwiiwii** *vai;* be weak in power **zhaagwaadad** *vii;* **zhaagwaadizi** *vai*
CONSIDER WEAK: consider s.o. weak **zhaagwenim** *vta;* consider s.t. weak **zhaagwendan** *vti*
LOOK WEAK: **niinaminaagozi** *vai;* **niinaminaagwad** *vii*

WEALTH
WEALTH: **daniwin** *ni*

WEAR
WEAR: wear s.o. **biizikaw** *vta;* wear s.t. **biizikan** *vti*
WEAR A BRACELET: **jiiskinikebizo** *vai*
WEAR A COAT: **gigibabiinzikawaagane** *vai*
WEAR A SHIRT: **gigibabagiwayaane** *vai*
WEAR ACROSS THE SHOULDER: wear s.t. across the shoulder **aazhooningwa'an** *vti*
WEAR ARM GARTERS: **jiiskinikebizo** *vai*
WEAR AROUND NECK: wear s.o. around one's neck **naabikaw** *vta;* wear s.t. around one's neck **naabikan** *vti*
WEAR BLACK: **makadewi'o** *vai*
WEAR BLUE: **ozhaawashko'o** *vai*
WEAR BROWN: **ozaawi'o** *vai*
WEAR EARMUFFS: **giizhootawage'o** *vai*
WEAR GREEN: **ozhaawashko'o** *vai*
WEAR INSIDE OUT: wear s.o. inside out **aaboozikaw** *vta;* wear s.t. inside out **aaboozikan** *vti*
WEAR LAYERS: wear layers (as underwear) **biitookonaye** *vai*
WEAR LEG GARTERS: **gashkidaasebizo** *vai*
WEAR MITTENS: **gigiminjikaawane** *vai*
WEAR NEW CLOTHES: **oshki'o** *vai*
WEAR OVERSHOES: **biitookizine** *vai*
WEAR PANTS: **gigigiboodiyegwaazone** *vai*
WEAR PATCHES: **bagwa'igaazo** *vai*
WEAR RED: **misko'o** *vai*
WEAR SOCKS: **gigazhigane** *vai*
WEAR THE WRONG WAY: wear s.o. the wrong way **napaazikaw** *vta;* wear s.t. the wrong way **napaazikan** *vti*
WEAR WHITE: **waabishki'o** *vai*
WEAR YELLOW: **ozaawi'o** *vai*

WEAR OUT
WEAR OUT IN OPERATION: **angobide, angobidemagad** *vii;* **angobizo** *vai*
WEAR OUT WITH FOOT OR BODY: wear s.o. out with foot or body (e.g., pants) **angoshkaw** *vta;* wear s.t. out with foot or body **angoshkan** *vti*

WEASEL
WEASEL: **zhingos, -ag** *na*

WEASEL SKIN
WEASEL SKIN: **zhingosiwayaan, -ag** *na*

WEATHER
BAD WEATHER: be bad weather **niiskaadad** *vii*
CALM WEATHER: be calm weather **anwaatin** *vii*
CERTAIN WEATHER CONDITION: be a certain weather condition **izhiwebad** *vii*
COLD WEATHER: be cold (weather) **gisinaa, gisinaamagad** *vii*
COOL WEATHER: be cool (weather) **dakaayaa, dakaayaamagad** *vii, also* **dakiayaa**
GOOD WEATHER: be good weather **mizhakwad** *vii*
HAVE GOOD TRAVELLING WEATHER: **mino-giizhiganishi** *vai*
HOT WEATHER: be hot (weather) **gizhaate, gizhaatemagad** *vii*
MILD WEATHER: be mild weather **aabawaa, aabawaamagad** *vii*
WARM WEATHER: be warm weather **aabawaa, aabawaamagad** *vii*
WEATHER WARMS UP: warm up (of the weather) **abaate, abaatemagad** *vii*

WEAVE
WEAVE: weave s.t. **niibidoon** *vti2*

WEDGED
WEDGED IN TIGHTLY: be wedged in tightly (as something stick- or wood-like) **ziindaakoshin** *vai;* **ziindaakosin** *vii*
WEDNESDAY
WEDNESDAY: be Wednesday **aabitoose, aabitoosemagad** *vii*
WEED
WEED: weed s.t. **bashkwashkibidoon** *vti2;* weed things **bashkwashkibijige** *vai*
WEEK
CERTAIN DAY OF THE WEEK: be a certain day of the week **izhi-giizhigad** *vii*
CERTAIN NUMBER OF WEEKS: a certain number of weeks **daso-anama'e-giizhik** *pc;* be a certain number of weeks **daso-anama'e-giizhikwagad** *vii, also* **daswanama'e-giizhikwagad**
WEEP
WEEP: **mawi** *vai*
WEIGH
WEIGH: weigh s.o. **dibaabiishkoozh /dibaabiishkooN-/** *vta;* weigh s.t. **dibaabiishkoodoon** *vti2;* weigh things **dibaabiishkoojige** *vai*
WEIGH A CERTAIN AMOUNT: **apiitinigozi** *vai;* **apiitinigwad** *vii*
WELFARE OFFICE
WELFARE OFFICE: **ashangewigamig, -oon** *ni*
WELFARE WORKER
WELFARE WORKER: **ashangewinini, -wag** *na;* welfare worker (female) **ashangewikwe, -g** *na*
WELL
WELL: **mino-** *pv4;* **wawiinge** *pc;* be well **mino-ayaa** *vai*
BEHAVE WELL: **mino-izhiwebizi** *vai*
COOK WELL: **minozekwe** *vai;* cook s.o. well **minoz /minozw-/** *vta;* cook s.t. well **minozan** *vti*
DO WELL: do things well **minochige** *vai*
DRESS WELL: **mino'o** *vai*
EAT WELL: **minwanjige** *vai*
FIT WELL: **minwashkine** *vai;* **minwashkine, minwashkinemagad** *vii;* fit s.o. well (e.g., pants) **minokaw** *vta;* fit s.t. well **minokan** *vti*
GET ALONG WELL: **minose** *vai*
GO WELL: **minose, minosemagad** *vii;* have things go well for one **minose** *vai*
GROW WELL: **minogi** *vai;* **minogin** *vii*
LIVE WELL: **mino-bimaadizi** *vai*
MAKE WELL: make s.o. well **onizhishi'** *vta;* make s.t. well **onizhishitoon** *vti2*
RUN WELL: run well (as a machine) **minobide, minobidemagad** *vii;* **minobizo** *vai*
SEE WELL: **minwaabi** *vai*
SPEAK WELL: **minowe** *vai*
TREAT WELL: treat s.o. well **mino-doodaw** *vta*
WELL COOKED: be well cooked **minode, minodemagad** *vii;* **minozo** *vai*
WELL FILLED: be well filled **minwashkine** *vai;* **minwashkine, minwashkinemagad** *vii*
WELL
WELL: **aanish** *pc*
WELL HOW: well how? **aaniin danaa** *pc*
WELL NOW: **aaniish** *pc;* **aaniish naa** *pc*
WELL THEN: **aanish** *pc*
WELL WHY: well why? **aaniin danaa** *pc*
WELL
WATER WELL: **onda'ibaan, -an** *ni*
WEST
WEST: **ningaabii'an** *ni*
IN THE WEST: **bangishimog** in the west; *conjunct of:* **bangishimon /bangishimo-/** *vii* set as the sun
WET
WET: be wet **nibiiwan** *vii;* **nibiiwi** *vai*
GET WET: **nisaabaawe** *vai;* **nisaabaawe, nisaabaawemagad** *vii*
HEAVY WET SNOW: there is heavy wet snow falling **zhakipon /zhakipo-/** *vii*
WET GROUND: be wet ground **nibiiwakamigaa, nibiiwakamigaamagad** *vii*
WET ROAD: be wet (as a road or trail) **nibiiwadamon /nibiiwadamo-/** *vii*
WET THE BED: **zhigingwaam** *vai*
WET TRAIL: be wet (as a road or trail) **nibiiwadamon /nibiiwadamo-/** *vii*
WHAT
WHAT: what *inanimate interrogative* **wegonen, -an** *pr;* **awegonen, -an** *pr;* **wegonesh**
I DON'T KNOW WHAT: I don't know what *inanimate dubitative* **wegodogwen, -an** *pr*
I DON'T REMEMBER WHAT: **ayi'ii, -n** *pr*
I WONDER WHAT: I wonder what *inanimate dubitative* **wegodogwen, -an** *pr*
WHATEVER
WHATEVER: whatever *inanimate dubitative* **wegodogwen igo** *pr*
WHEEL
WHEEL: **detibised** *na-pt*
WHEEZE
WHEEZE: **gaaskanaamo** *vai*
WHEN
WHEN: **apii** *pc;* when? *interrogative* **aanapii** *pc, also* **aanapiish, aaniin apii, aaniin iw apii**
I DON'T KNOW WHEN: *dubitative* **amanj apii** *pc*
I WONDER WHEN: I wonder when *dubitative* **amanj apii** *pc*
WHENEVER
WHENEVER: *dubitative* **amanj igo apii** *pc*
WHERE
WHERE: where? *interrogative* **aandi** *pc, also* **aandish, aaniindi**
I DON'T KNOW WHERE: *dubitative* **dibi** *pc*
I WONDER WHERE: I wonder where *dubitative* **dibi** *pc*
WHEREVER
WHEREVER: *dubitative* **dibi go** *pc*

WHILE
WHILE: **eshkwaa** *pc;* **megwaa** *pc*
A LITTLE WHILE: **ajina** *pc*
EVERY LITTLE WHILE: **wewayiiba** *pc*
WHIP
WHIP: **bashanzhe'igan, -an** *ni;* **bashanzhe'ige** *vai;* whip s.o. **bashanzhe' /bashanzhe'w-/** *vta*
WHIRL
WHIRL: **gizhibaabide, gizhibaabidemagad** *vii;* **gizhibaabise** *vai;* **gizhibaabise, gizhibaabisemagad** *vii;* **gizhibaabizo** *vai*
WHIRLPOOL
WHIRLPOOL: be a whirlpool **maajijiwan** *vii*
WHIRLWIND
WHIRLWIND: be a whirlwind **gizhibaayaanimad** *vii*
WHISKERS
WHITE WHISKERS: have white whiskers **waabishkawedoon** *vai*
WHISPER
WHISPER: **gaaskanazo** *vai;* whisper to s.o. **gaaskanazootaw** *vta*
WHISTLE
WHISTLE: **gwiishkoshi** *vai;* **noondaagochigan, -an** *ni;* whistle to s.o. **gwiishkoshim** *vta*
WHISTLE FROM BOILING: **gwiishkoshwewegamide, gwiishkoshwewegamidemagad** *vii;* **gwiishkoshwewegamizo** *vai*
WHITE
WHITE: **waabishki-** *pv4;* be white **waabishkaa, waabishkaamagad** *vii;* **waabishkizi** *vai;* be white (as something mineral) **waabishkaabikad** *vii;* **waabishkaabikizi** *vai;* be white (as something sheet-like) **waabishkiigad** *vii;* **waabishkiigizi** *vai;* be white (as something stick- or wood-like) **waabishkaakozi** *vai;* **waabishkaakwad** *vii;* be white (as something string-like) **waabishkaabiigad** *vii;* **waabishkaabiigizi** *vai*
COLORED WHITE: be colored white **waabishkaande, waabishkaandemagad** *vii;* **waabishkaanzo** *vai*
WEAR WHITE: **waabishki'o** *vai*
WHITE CLOUDS: there are white clouds **waabishkaanakwad** *vii*
WHITE ASH
WHITE ASH: white ash (tree) **baapaagimaak, -wag** *na*
WHITE CEDAR
WHITE CEDAR: **giizhik, -ag** *na*
WHITE CLAY
WHITE CLAY: **waabaabigan** *na*
WHITE EARTH
WHITE EARTH: White Earth Reservation **Gaa-waabaabiganikaag** *place*
WHITE HAIR
WHITE HAIR: have white hair **waabishkindibe** *vai*
WHITE PERSON
WHITE PERSON: **gichi-mookomaan, -ag** *na;* **wayaabishkiiwed** *na-pt;* be a white person **waabishkiiwe** *vai*
WHITE PINE
WHITE PINE: **zhingwaak, -wag** *na*
WHITE SPOTS
WHITE SPOTS ON FINGERNAILS: have white spots on fingernails **mindaweganzhii** *vai*
WHITE SPRUCE
WHITE SPRUCE: **gaawaandag, -oog** *na*
WHITE WOMAN
WHITE WOMAN: **gichi-mookomaanikwe, -g** *na*
WHITEFISH
WHITEFISH: **adikameg, -wag** *na*
WHITTLE
WHITTLE: **mookodaaso** *vai*
WHO
WHO: who? *animate interrogative* **awenen, -ag** *pr;* **awenesh** *pr*
I DON'T KNOW WHO: I don't know who *animate dubitative* **awegwen, -ag** *pr*
I DON'T REMEMBER WHO: **aya'aa, -g** *pr*
I WONDER WHO: I wonder who *animate dubitative* **awegwen, -ag** *pr*
WHO THEN: who then *animate interrogative* **awenesh** *pr*
WHOEVER
WHOEVER: whoever *animate dubitative* **awegwen igo** *pr*
WHOLE
WHOLE: be whole **miziweyaa, miziweyaamagad** *vii;* **miziwezi** *vai*
MAKE OF A WHOLE PIECE: make s.o. of a whole piece **miziwe'** *vta;* make s.t. of a whole piece **miziwetoon** *vti2*
WHOLE LOT
A WHOLE LOT: **neniibowa** *pc*
WHOOP
WHOOP: **zaasaakwe** *vai*
WHY
WHY: why? **aaniin** *pc;* **aaniish** *pc;* **aaniin dash** *pc*
WHY NOT: why not? **aaniin danaa** *pc*
WIDE
WIDE: be wide **mangadeyaa, mangadeyaamagad** *vii;* **mangadezi** *vai*
MAKE WIDE: make s.o. wide **mangade'** *vta;* make s.t. wide **mangadetoon** *vti2*
SO WIDE: be so wide **inigokwadeyaa, inigokwadeyaamagad** *vii;* **inigokwadezi** *vai;* be so wide (as something mineral) **inigokwadeyaabikad** *vii;* **inigokwadeyaabikizi** *vai;* be so wide (as something sheet-like) **inigokwadeyiigad** *vii;* **inigokwadeyiigizi** *vai;* be so wide (as something stick- or wood-like) **inigokwadeyaakozi** *vai;* **inigokwadeyaakwad** *vii;* be so wide (as something string-like)

inigokwadeyaabiigad *vii;* **inigokwadeyaabiigizi** *vai*
WIDE BOAT: be wide (as a boat) **mangadeyoonagad** *vii*
WIDE RIVER: be wide (as a river) **mangitigweyaa, mangitigweyaamagad** *vii*
WIDE ROAD: be wide (as a road or trail) **mangademon /mangademo-/** *vii, also* **mangadademon**
WIDE TRAIL: be wide (as a road or trail) **mangademon /mangademo-/** *vii, also* **mangadademon**

WIDEN
WIDEN: widen s.o. **mangade'** *vta;* widen s.t. **mangadetoon** *vti2*

WIDOW
WIDOW: **zhiigaa, -g** *na;* be a widow **zhiigaawi** *vai*

WIDOWER
WIDOWER: **zhiigaa, -g** *na;* be a widower **zhiigaawi** *vai*

WIDTH
CERTAIN WIDTH: be a certain width **inigokwadeyaa, inigokwadeyaamagad** *vii;* **inigokwadezi** *vai;* be a certain width (as something mineral) **inigokwadeyaabikad** *vii;* **inigokwadeyaabikizi** *vai;* be a certain width (as something sheet-like) **inigokwadeyiigad** *vii;* **inigokwadeyiigizi** *vai;* be a certain width (as something stick- or wood-like) **inigokwadeyaakozi** *vai;* **inigokwadeyaakwad** *vii;* be a certain width (as something string-like) **inigokwadeyaabiigad** *vii;* **inigokwadeyaabiigizi** *vai*

WIFE
WIFE: my wife **niwiidigemaagan, -ag /-wiidigemaagan-/** *na;* **niwiiw, -ag /-wiiw-/** *nad*

WIGOB
PEEL WIGOB: peel wigob (inner bark of basswood) **bisha'igobii** *vai*

WIGWAM
WIGWAM: **waaginogaan, -an** *ni;* **wiigiwaam, -an** *ni*
LIVE IN A WIGWAM: **wiigiwaamige** *vai*
MAKE A WIGWAM: **wiigiwaamike** *vai*

WIGWAM FRAME
WIGWAM FRAME: **wiigiwaamaak, -oon** *ni*

WIGWAM POLE
WIGWAM POLE: **wiigiwaamaatig, -oon** *ni*

WILD
WILD: **bagwaji-** *pv4*

WILD ANIMAL
WILD ANIMAL: **awesiinh, -yag** *na*

WILD POTATO
WILD POTATO: **bagwajipin, -iig** *na, also* **bagwaji-opin**

WILD RICE
WILD RICE: **manoomin** *ni, also* **anishinaabe-manoomin**
BARREL OR TUB USED IN THRESHING WILD RICE: **mimigoshkamwaagan, -an** *ni*
GREEN WILD RICE: **ozhaawashko-manoomin** *ni*
HARVEST WILD RICE: **bawa'am** *vai2;* **manoominike** *vai*
HAUL WILD RICE: **aawajimine** *vai*
KNOCK WILD RICE: **bawa'am** *vai2*
MUCH WILD RICE: there is much wild rice **manoominikaa, manoominikaamagad** *vii*
POPPED WILD RICE: **gaapizigan, -an** *ni*
TAKE WILD RICE INLAND: **gopimine** *vai*
THRESH WILD RICE: thresh something **mimigoshkam** *vai2*
TIE WILD RICE: **dakobidoo** *vai*
TIED WILD RICE: **dakobijigan, -an** *ni*
UNTIE WILD RICE: **aaba'oodoo** *vai*

WILD RICE BROTH
WILD RICE BROTH: **manoominaaboo** *ni*

WILD RICE STALK
WILD RICE STALK: **manoominaganzh, -iin** *ni*

WILDERNESS
IN THE WILDERNESS: **bagwaj** *pc*

WILL
WILL: will *future/desiderative verb prefix* **wii-** *pv1*

WILLOW
WILLOW: **oziisigobimizh, -iig** *na*

WILLOW BASKET
WILLOW BASKET: **oziisigobimizhii-makak, -oon** *ni*

WIN
WIN: **gabenaage** *vai;* **mizhodam** *vai2*
WIN IN A GAME: win from s.o. in a game **gabenaw** *vta*
WIN OVER: win over s.o. **bakinaw** *vta;* win over people **bakinaage** *vai*

WIND
WIND: there is a wind **noodin** *vii*
COLD WIND: be a cold wind **dakaanimad** *vii*
COME AS WIND FROM A CERTAIN PLACE: come as wind from a certain direction **ondaanimad** *vii*
COOLED BY THE WIND: be cooled by the wind **dakaashi** *vai;* **dakaasin** *vii*
CREAK IN THE WIND: **giziibweweyaashi** *vai;* **giziibweweyaasin** *vii*
EAST WIND: **waabani-noodin** *ni*
FAVORABLE WIND: there is a favorable wind **minwaanimad** *vii*
HOT WIND: be a hot wind **gizhaanimad** *vii*
NORTH WIND: **giiwedin** *ni*
SOUTH WIND: **zhaawani-noodin** *ni*
WIND BLOWS FAST: **gizhiiyaanimad** *vii*
WIND BLOWS WILDLY: **aanimad** *vii*
WIND COMES FROM A CERTAIN DIRECTION: **ondin** *vii*
WIND COMES IN HARD: **bagamaanimad** *vii*
WIND DIES DOWN: **boonaanimad** *vii;* **ishkwaayaanimad** *vii*

WIND HAS A CERTAIN SPEED: the wind has a certain speed **apiitaanimad** *vii*
WIND LETS UP: **boonaanimad** *vii*
WIND PICKS UP: **maadaanimad** *vii*
WIND SHIFTS: **gwekaanimad** *vii*

WINDIGO
WINDIGO: be a windigo **wiindigoowi** *vai;* windigo: winter cannibal monster **wiindigoo, -g** *na*

WINDLESS
WINDLESS: be windless **awibaa, awibaamagad** *vii*

WINDOW
WINDOW: **waasechigan, -an** *ni*
LOOK THROUGH A WINDOW: **dapaabi** *vai;* look through a window at s.o. **dapaabam** *vta;* look through a window at s.t. **dapaabandan** *vti*

WINDOW GLASS
WINDOW GLASS: **waasechiganaabik, -oon** *ni*

WINDOW PANE
WINDOW PANE: **waasechiganaabik, -oon** *ni*

WINDOW SHADE
WINDOW SHADE: **gibiiga'iganiigin, -oon** *ni*

WINDY
WINDY: be windy **noodin** *vii*
VERY WINDY: be very windy **gichi-noodin** *vii*

WINE
WINE: **zhoominaaboo** *ni, also* **zhawiminaaboo**

WING
WING: my wing **niningwiigan, -an /-ningwiigan-/** *nid*
SHAKE WINGS: shake one's wings **bapawaangeni** *vai*

WINK
WINK: **jiibiingweni** *vai;* wink at s.o. **jiibiingwetaw** *vta;* **jiichiibiingwetaw** *vta*

WINNEBAGO
WINNEBAGO: **wiinibiigoo, -g** *na*

WINNOW
WINNOW: winnow s.t. (e.g., wild rice) **nooshkaatoon** *vti2;* winnow things (e.g., wild rice) **nooshkaachige** *vai*

WINNOWED
WINNOWED: be winnowed **nooshkaachigaade, nooshkaachigaademagad** *vii*

WINNOWING TRAY
WINNOWING TRAY: **nooshkaachinaagan, -an** *ni*

WINTER
WINTER: be a winter (year) **biboonagad** *vii;* be winter **biboon** *vii*
LAST WINTER: **biboonong** *pc*
LATE WINTER: be late winter **giiwe-biboon** *vii*
SPEND THE WINTER: spend the winter somewhere **biboonishi** *vai*
WINTER BEFORE LAST: **awas-biboonong** *pc*

WIPE
WIPE: wipe s.o. by hand **giziin** *vta;* wipe s.t. by hand **giziinan** *vti*
WIPE AFTER DEFECATING: wipe oneself after defecating **giziindime'o** *vai*
WIPE DISHES: **gaasiinaagane** *vai*
WIPE FACE: wipe one's face with something **giziingwe'o** *vai*
WIPE HANDS: wipe one's hands **gaasiininjii** *vai*
WIPE MOUTH: wipe one's mouth **gaasiidoone'o** *vai*
WIPE USING SOMETHING: wipe s.o. using something **gaasii' /gaasii'w-/** *vta;* wipe s.t. using something **gaasii'an** *vti;* wipe things using something **gaasii'ige** *vai*

WIRE
WIRE: **biiwaabikoons, -an** *ni*
SNARE WIRE: **agoodwaaganeyaab, -iin** *ni;* **nagwaaganeyaab, -iin** *ni*

WISE
WISE: be wise **nibwaakaa** *vai*

WISH
WISH: **bagosendam** *vai2;* wish for s.o. **agaawaazh /agaawaaN-/** *vta;* wish for s.t. **agaawaadan** *vti;* **bagosendan** *vti;* wish of s.o. **bagosenim** *vta*
I WISH THAT: I wish that ... **apegish** *pc, also* **ambegish*, ambesh***

WITH
WITH: **wiiji-** *pv4;* be with s.o. **wiij'ayaaw** *vta, also* **wiiji-ayaaw**
DANCE WITH: dance with s.o. **wiijishimotaw** *vta*
EAT WITH: eat with s.o. **wiidoopam** *vta;* eat with people **wiidoopange** *vai*
GO WITH: go with s.o. **wiijiiw** *vta;* go with people **wiijii'iwe** *vai;* they go with each other **wiijiindiwag /wiijiindi-/** *vai*
IN A PLACE WITH: **dago-** *pv4*
PLAY WITH: play with s.o. **wiiji'** *vta*
SHARE COVER WITH: share a cover with s.o. **wiidagwazhem** *vta*
SIT WITH: sit with s.o. **wiidabim** *vta*
SLEEP WITH: sleep with s.o. **wiipem** *vta;* sleep with s.t. **wiipendan** *vti;* they sleep with each other **wiipendiwag /wiipendi-/** *vai*
SLEEP WITH CHILDREN PROTECTIVELY: **wiipemaawaso** *vai*
STAY WITH: stay with s.o. **wiij'ayaaw** *vta, also* **wiiji-ayaaw**
WALK WITH: walk with s.o. **wiidosem** *vta*
WORK WITH: work with s.o. **wiidanokiim** *vta;* **wiij'anokiim** *vta, also* **wiiji-anokiim**

WITHOUT
WITHOUT A DOUBT: **aapideg** *pc*
WITHOUT PURPOSE: **anishaa** *pc*
WITHOUT RESULT: **aano-** *pv1*

WITNESS
WITNESS: be a witness **waabange** *vai*

WOLF
WOLF: **ma'iingan, -ag** *na*

WOLF HIDE
WOLF HIDE: **ma'iinganiwayaan, -ag** *na*
WOLVERINE
WOLVERINE: **gwiingwa'aage, -g** *na*
WOMAN
WOMAN: **ikwe, -wag** *na;* be a woman **ikwewi** *vai*
DAKOTA WOMAN: **bwaanikwe, -g** *na*
DRESSED-UP WOMAN: **zazegaa-ikwe, -wag** *na*
INDIAN WOMAN: **anishinaabekwe, -g** *na;* be an Indian woman **anishinaabekwewi** *vai*
OJIBWE WOMAN: **ojibwekwe, -g** *na*
OLD WOMAN: **mindimooyenh, -yag** *na;* be an old woman **mindimooyenyiwi** *vai*
UNMARRIED WOMAN: **moozhikwe, -g** *na*
YOUNG WOMAN: **oshkiniigikwe, -g** *na;* be a young woman **oshkiniigikwewi** *vai*
WOMEN'S DANCE
WOMEN'S DANCE: **ikwe-niimi'idiwin, -an** *ni*
DANCE THE WOMEN'S DANCE: **ikwe-niimi** *vai;* they dance the women's dance **ikwe-niimi'idiwag /ikwe-niimi'idi-/** *vai*
WONDER
WONDER: wonder at s.o. **maamakaadenim** *vta;* wonder at s.t. **maamakaadendan** *vti*
I WONDER HOW: I wonder how *dubitative* **amanj** *pc, also* **amanj iidog, namanj*, namanj iidog***
I WONDER WHAT: I wonder what *inanimate dubitative* **wegodogwen, -an** *pr*
I WONDER WHEN: I wonder when *dubitative* **amanj apii** *pc*
I WONDER WHERE: I wonder where *dubitative* **dibi** *pc*
I WONDER WHO: I wonder who *animate dubitative* **awegwen, -ag** *pr*
WOOD
DRY WOOD: **mishiiwaatig, -oon** *ni*
PIECE OF WOOD: **mitig, -oon** *ni*
PUT WOOD ON THE FIRE: **bagidinise** *vai*
UNDER WOOD: under wood (e.g., a tree or stick) **anaamaatig** *pc*
WOOD TICK
WOOD TICK: **ezigaa, -g** *na*
WOODCHUCK
WOODCHUCK: **akakojiish, -ag** *na*
WOODPECKER
WOODPECKER: **baapaase, -g** *na*
RED-HEADED WOODPECKER: **meme, -g** *na*
WOODS
BEYOND THE WOODS: **awasaakwaa** *pc*
COME OUT OF THE WOODS: **bapaakwa'am** *vai2*
DENSE WOODS: be dense woods **zagaakwaa, zagaakwaamagad** *vii*
GO INTO THE WOODS: **jekaakwa'am** *vai2*
IN THE WOODS: **megwaayaak** *pc;* **noopiming** *pc*
MIDDLE OF THE WOODS: in the middle of the woods **naawaakwaa** *pc*
NEAR WOODS: near the woods **jiigaakwaa** *pc*
OVER ACROSS THE WOODS: **awasaakwaa** *pc*
WOODS GO A CERTAIN DISTANCE: **akwaakwaa, akwaakwaamagad** *vii*
WORD
WORD: **ikidowin, -an** *ni*
WORK
WORK: **anokii** *vai;* **anokiiwin, -an** *ni;* work at s.o. **anokaazh /anokaaN-/** *vta;* work at s.t. **anokaadan** *vti;* work for s.o. **anokiitaw** *vta;* work for oneself **anokiitaazo** *vai;* work for people **anokiitaage** *vai*
ABLE TO WORK: be able to work **gashkanokii** *vai*
FINISH WORK: **giizhiitaa** *vai*
KEPT BUSY IN WORK: be kept busy in work **ondamanokii** *vai*
LOOK FOR WORK: **nanda-anokii** *vai*
MAKE WORK: make s.o. work **anokii'** *vta*
PRETEND TO WORK: **anokiikaazo** *vai*
START TO WORK: **maadanoki** *vai;* start to work on s.o. **maadanokaazh /maadanokaaN-/** *vta;* **maajiikaw** *vta;* start to work on s.t. **maadanokaadan** *vti;* **maajiikan** *vti*
WORK A CERTAIN WAY: **inanokii** *vai*
WORK IN A CERTAIN PLACE: **dananokii** *vai*
WORK ON: work on s.o. **dazhiikaw** *vta;* work on s.t. **dazhiikan** *vti*
WORK UNTIL DAWN: **waabananokii** *vai*
WORK WITH: work with s.o. **wiidanokiim** *vta;* **wiij'anokiim** *vta, also* **wiiji-anokiim**
WORK WITHOUT STOPPING: **aabidanokii** *vai*
WORKED
SOMETHING WORKED ON: **anokaajigan, -an** *ni*
WORKED ON: be worked on **dazhiikigaade, dazhiikigaademagad** *vii*
WORKER
WORKER: **anokiiwinini, -wag** *na;* worker (female) **anokiiwikwe, -g** *na*
GOOD WORKER: be a good worker **gotaamigozi** *vai*
WORKSHOP
WORKSHOP: **anokiiwigamig, -oon** *ni*
WORLD
ALL OVER THE WORLD: **miziwekamig** *pc*
WORM
WORM: **moose, -g** *na*
WORRIED
WORRIED: be worried **ondamendam** *vai2*
WORRY
WORRY: **babaamendam** *vai2;* **biingeyendam** *vai2;* worry about s.o. **babaamenim** *vta;* **ondamenim** *vta;* worry about s.t. **babaamendan** *vti;* **ondamendan** *vti*
WORTHLESS
WORTHLESS: be worthless **goopadizi** *vai*

CONSIDER WORTHLESS: consider s.o. worthless **goopadenim** *vta;* consider s.t. worthless **goopadendan** *vti*

WOULD

WOULD: would *modal* **daa-** *pv1*

WOUND

SHOOT AND WOUND: shoot and wound s.o. **maakinaw** *vta*

WRAP

WRAP: wrap s.o. (as or as with something sheet-like) **wiiwegin** *vta;* wrap s.t. (as or as with something sheet-like) **wiiweginan** *vti*

WRAP AND TIE IN A BUNDLE: wrap and tie s.o. in a bundle **gashkibizh /gashkibiN-/** *vta;* wrap and tie s.t. in a bundle **gashkibidoon** *vti2;* wrap and tie things in bundle **gashkibijige** *vai*

WRAPPED

WRAPPED AND TIED IN A BUNDLE: be wrapped and tied in a bundle **gashkibide, gashkibidemagad** *vii;* **gashkibijigaade, gashkibijigaademagad** *vii;* **gashkibijigaazo** *vai*

WRAPPED UP WARM: be wrapped up warm **giizhoopizo** *vai*

WREN

WREN: **anaamisagadaweshiinh, -yag** *na*

WRENCH

WRENCH: **biimiskwa'igan, -an** *ni*

WRESTLE

WRESTLE: they wrestle each other **gagwejiiwaanidiwag /gagwejiiwaanidi-/** *vai;* wrestle s.o. **gagwejiiwaazh /gagwejiiwaaN-/** *vta*

WRESTLER

WRESTLER: **gagwejiiwaazoowinini, -wag** *na*

WRING

WRING: wring s.o. **ziinibizh /ziinibiN-/** *vta;* wring s.t. **ziinibidoon** *vti2*

WRING NECK: wring s.o.'s neck **bookogwebizh /bookogwebiN-/** *vta*

WRINKLE

WRINKLE: wrinkle up **oziigishkaa** *vai;* **oziigishkaa, oziigishkaamagad** *vii*

WRINKLED

WRINKLED: be wrinkled **oziigaa, oziigaamagad** *vii;* **oziigizi** *vai*

WRINKLED FACE: have a wrinkled face **oziigiingwe** *vai*

WRITE

WRITE: **ozhibii'ige** *vai;* write s.t. **ozhibii'an** *vti;* write (s.t.) for s.o. **ozhibii'amaw** *vta*

MAKE A MISTAKE WRITING: **wanibii'ige** *vai;* make a mistake writing s.t. **wanibii'an** *vti*

WRITE A CERTAIN WAY: write s.t. a certain way **izhibii'an** *vti;* write things a certain way **izhibii'ige** *vai*

WRITE A LETTER: **maajiibii'ige** *vai;* write a letter to s.o. **maajiibii'amaw** *vta*

WRITE ALL OVER: **miziwebii'ige** *vai;* write s.t. all over **miziwebii'an** *vti*

WRITE BACK: write (s.t.) back to s.o. **nakwebii'amaw** *vta;* they write back to each other **nakwebii'amaadiwag /nakwebii'amaadi-/** *vai*

WRITE CORRECTLY: **gwayakobii'ige** *vai;* write s.t. correctly **gwayakobii'an** *vti*

WRITE DOWN: write s.o. down **ozhibii' /ozhibii'w-/** *vta;* write s.t. down **ozhibii'an** *vti*

WRITE HERE: **biijibii'ige** *vai;* write (s.t.) here to s.o. *inverse forms of:* **biijibii'amaw-** *vta*

WRITE IN ENGLISH: **zhaaganaashiiwibii'ige** *vai;* write in English to s.o. **zhaaganaashiiwibii'amaw** *vta;* write s.t. in English **zhaaganaashiiwibii'an** *vti*

WRITE IN INDIAN: write in Indian (Ojibwe) **anishinaabewibii'ige** *vai;* write s.t. in Indian (Ojibwe) **anishinaabewibii'an** *vti;* write s.t. in Indian (Ojibwe) (e.g., a book) **anishinaabewisidoon** *vti2;* write (s.t.) in Indian (Ojibwe) to s.o. **anishinaabewibii'amaw** *vta*

WRITE IN OJIBWE: write in Indian (Ojibwe) **anishinaabewibii'ige** *vai;* write s.t. in Indian (Ojibwe) **anishinaabewibii'an** *vti;* write s.t. in Indian (Ojibwe) (e.g., a book) **anishinaabewisidoon** *vti2;* write s.t. in Ojibwe **ojibwewibii'an** *vti;* write (s.t.) in Indian (Ojibwe) to s.o. **anishinaabewibii'amaw** *vta;* write things in Ojibwe **ojibwewibii'ige** *vai*

WRITE NUMBERS: **asigibii'ige** *vai*

WRITE ON: write on something **apibii'ige** *vai*

WRITE OVER: write s.t. over **aanjibii'an** *vti*

WRITING

INDIAN WRITING: Indian (Ojibwe) writing **anishinaabewibii'igan, -an** *ni*

OJIBWE WRITING: Indian (Ojibwe) writing **anishinaabewibii'igan, -an** *ni*

WRITING SURFACE: **apibii'igan, -an** *ni*

WRITTEN

WRITTEN: be written **ozhibii'igaade, ozhibii'igaademagad** *vii*

SOMETHING WRITTEN: **ozhibii'igan, -an** *ni*

SOMETHING WRITTEN IN INDIAN: something written in Indian (Ojibwe) **anishinaabewibii'igan, -an** *ni*

WRITTEN A CERTAIN WAY: be written a certain way **izhibii'igaade, izhibii'igaademagad** *vii;* **izhisin** *vii*

WRITTEN IN INDIAN: be written in Indian (Ojibwe) **anishinaabewibii'igaade, anishinaabewibii'igaademagad** *vii;* be written in Indian (Ojibwe) (e.g., a book or document) **anishinaabewisin** *vii*

WRITTEN IN OJIBWE: be written in Indian (Ojibwe) **anishinaabewibii'igaade, anishinaabewibii'igaademagad** *vii;* be written in Indian (Ojibwe) (e.g., a book or document) **anishinaabewisin** *vii;* be written in Ojibwe **ojibwewibii'igaade, ojibwewibii'igaademagad** *vii;* be written in Ojibwe (e.g., a book) **ojibwewisin** *vii*

WRITTEN ON ALL OVER: be written on all over **miziwebii'igaade, miziwebii'igaademagad** *vii*

WRONG

GO WRONG: have things go wrong **maazhise** *vai*

MAKE WRONG: make s.o. wrong **maanaaji'** *vta;* make s.t. wrong **maanaajitoon** *vti2*

TAKE WRONG ONE: take s.o. who/that is the wrong one **wanin** *vta;* take s.t. that is the wrong one **waninan** *vti*

TOUCH WRONG ONE: touch s.o. who/that is the wrong one **wanin** *vta;* touch s.t. that is the wrong one **waninan** *vti*

X

X-RAY

GET X-RAY: get an x-ray **zhaabwaakizo** *vai*

X-RAY PLATE

X-RAY PLATE: **zhaabwaakizigan, -an** *ni*

Y

YARDSTICK

YARDSTICK: **diba'aatigwaan, -an** *ni*

YARN

YARN: **miskogaadeyaab, -iin** *ni*

BALL OF TWINE OR YARN: **bikoojaan, -an** *ni*

YAWN

YAWN: **naanibaayawe** *vai*

YEAR

YEAR: **gikinoonowin** *ni*

CERTAIN NUMBER OF YEARS: a certain number of years **daso-biboon** *pc;* **daso-gikinoonowin** *pc;* be a certain number of years **daso-biboonagad** *vii*

CERTAIN NUMBER OF YEARS OLD: be a certain number of years old **daso-biboonagizi** *vai*

YEAR PASSES: a year passes **biboonagad** *vii;* **gikinoonowagad** *vii*

YELLOW

YELLOW: **ozaawi-** *pv4;* be yellow **ozaawaa, ozaawaamagad** *vii;* **ozaawizi** *vai;* be yellow (as something mineral) **ozaawaabikad** *vii;* **ozaawaabikizi** *vai;* be yellow (as something sheet-like) **ozaawegad** *vii;* **ozaawegizi** *vai;* be yellow (as something stick- or wood-like) **ozaawaakozi** *vai;* **ozaawaakwad** *vii;* be yellow (as something string-like) **ozaawaabiigad** *vii;* **ozaawaabiigizi** *vai*

COLORED YELLOW: be colored yellow **ozaawaande, ozaawaandemagad** *vii;* **ozaawaanzo** *vai*

WEAR YELLOW: **ozaawi'o** *vai*

YELLOW BIRCH

YELLOW BIRCH: **wiinizik, -oog** *na*

YELLOW-SHAFTED FLICKER

YELLOW-SHAFTED FLICKER: **mooningwane, -g** *na*

YES

YES: **en'** *pc;* **enyan'** *pc, also* **en', eya'**; **mii nange** *pc*

YES-NO QUESTION

YES-NO QUESTION: *yes-no question word* **ina** *pc, also* **na**

YESTERDAY

YESTERDAY: **bijiinaago** *pc*

DAY BEFORE YESTERDAY: **awasonaago** *pc*

YET

YET: **geyaabi** *pc*

NOT YET: **gaa mashi** *pc, also* **gaawiin mashi**

YOU

YOU: you *second person singular personal pronoun* **giin** *pr;* you *second person plural personal pronoun* **giinawaa** *pr*

YOU BET

YOU BET: sure! you bet! **enange** *pc*

YOU SEE

YOU SEE: **aaniish naa** *pc*

YOUNG

YOUNG: **oshki-** *pv4;* be young **oshkaya'aawi** *vai, also* **oshki-aya'aawi; oshkayi'iiwan** *vii;* **oshki-bimaadizi** *vai;* **oshkiniigi** *vai*

LOOK YOUNG: **oshkiinaagozi** *vai*

PROTECT YOUNG: protect one's young **gizhaawaso** *vai*

SOMEONE YOUNG: **oshkaya'aa, -g** *na, also* **oshki-aya'aa**

SOMETHING YOUNG: **oshkayi'ii, -n** *ni, also* **oshki-ayi'ii**

YOUNG MAN

YOUNG MAN: **oshki-inini, -wag** *na;* **oshkinawe, -g** *na;* be a young man **oshkinawewi** *vai*

YOUNG WOMAN

YOUNG WOMAN: **oshkiniigikwe, -g** *na;* be a young woman **oshkiniigikwewi** *vai*

YOUNGEST

YOUNGEST CHILD: **ishkwejaagan, -ag** *na*

Z

ZIP

ZIP UP: zip oneself up **giboobinidizo** *vai*